D0819163

Berlitz

CRUISING
& CRUISE SHIPS

2014

BY DOUGLAS WARD

THE WORLD'S FOREMOST AUTHORITY ON CRUISING

Introduction

Welcome to the 2014 edition of Berlitz Cruising & Cruise Ships.

The cruise industry is a fiercely competitive business, and one within which any marketing opportunity is seized upon and hyped to the nth degree. Travel industry awards – often in the form of magazine readers' polls – provide a perfect such opportunity and are extremely valuable to the cruise lines.

Yet these polls are only ever as good as the number of people who vote in them, the number of ships and the criteria established for measuring quality. For example, if a magazine in the United States initiates a readers' poll and no readers have cruised aboard a Spanish-speaking cruise ship, that ship will receive no votes. It stands to reason that the votes will go to the most traveled ships, which are not necessarily the best. The magazines never state the criteria for their decisions, and the polls results are therefore unreliable.

At Berlitz, we always state our criteria, clearly and honestly. That's why the Berlitz Guide to Cruising and Cruise Ships 2014 is the most authoritative and dependable guide on the market. What's more, this book is totally independent and in no way subsidized or influenced by advertising or sponsorship.

My 5,900 days at sea

In welcoming new readers to this edition, I should mention my qualifications for assessing cruise ships on your behalf. I first fell in love with ships when, in 1965, I worked Cunard Line's 83,673-ton ocean liner RMS *Queen Elizabeth* – then the world's largest passenger ship. Over the next 17 years, I worked for eight companies in various roles.

To date, I have completed over 5,900 days at sea, participating in more than 1,000 cruises, 158 transatlantic crossings, and countless Panama Canal transits, plus shipyard visits, ship-naming ceremonies, and maiden voyages.

The first edition of this book, reviewing, testing, and evaluating 120 ships, appeared in 1985, when cruising seemed to most people an expensive, rarefied experience. Today, the book is the most highly regarded source of comparative information not only for cruise purchasers, but also for cruise industry executives, crew members, and travel agents.

This book is a tribute to everyone who has made my seafaring experiences possible, and I thank the cruise lines for their assistance during the complex scheduling, sailing, inspection, evaluation, and rating processes.

Legend of the Seas sails past St. Mark's Square, Venice.

How to Use This Book

This book is divided into two main parts, followed by a short section of practical information and useful addresses. The first part helps you define what you are looking for in a cruise vacation and advises you on how to find it. It provides a wealth of information, including a look at life aboard ship and how to get the best from it. Specialist cruises are discussed, too, culminating with that ultimate travel experience: the around-the-world cruise.

The book's main section profiles 285 ocean-going cruise vessels. From large to small, from unabashed luxury and exclusivity to ships for the budget-minded, new and old, they are all here.

The ratings and evaluations in this book are a painstaking documentation of my personal work. I travel throughout the world, and am at sea for up to 200 days each year. All evaluations have been made objectively, without bias, partiality, or prejudice. In almost all instances, the ships have been visited recently by me or one of my team in order to assess the current status. Passenger comments are taken into account, so please don't hesitate to contact me at *shipratings@hotmail.com*.

Please note that, although price indicators are supplied for some things such as alternative restaurants, spa treatments, and other items, prices and price categories may have changed since this book went to press. Check all prices with your cruise line.

Most of the statistical information contained in the ship profiles was supplied and checked by the cruise lines and ship owners. Any errors or updated information should be sent to me at *shipratings@hotmail.com*.

Please note that my constant ship inspection schedule means I am frequently at sea, and I am no longer able to answer letters. However, every comment received will be reviewed and taken into account when updating the next edition of the book. Your contributions are gratefully appreciated.

Table of Contents

Star Clipper under sail.

Beginners Please

Are you all at sea about cruise vacations, when it seems like everyone around you has taken a cruise? Here are the basics you'll need to know before casting off for the first time.

Actually, there are thousands of others like you. It's a bit of an obstacle course, like trying to choose between different models of automobiles and deciding on all the optional extras before actually getting the car you want. About 75 cruise companies operate around 350 ocean-going cruise ships (not to mention over 1,000 river ships) in the business of cruise vacations.

Nothing has the potential to offer more variety, a better value, or a more unforgettable vacation experience than a cruise, and with a little planning it'll all go smoothly. Look at it as a prepaid vacation – with extras you choose yourself. But, after your first cruise, be prepared for the feeling of addiction because it happens often.

You'll need to do a little planning in order to find the right ship and cruise to suit your needs – whether you are a lively young couple, a family with children, sophisticated and well-traveled seniors, or you want unabashed luxury and total relaxation.

What exactly is a cruise?

A cruise is a vacation – an escape from the stresses and strains of life on land. It is virtually a pre-paid, hassle-free, and more importantly, a crime-free vacation where you only have to pack and unpack once. You seldom have to make blind choices, you sleep in the same bed each night, and the ship moves the scenery for you.

Everything's close at hand, and there are always polite people to help you. A cruise provides a chance to explore new places, meet new people, and make new friends and, above all, the ingredients for a delightful vacation. It can facilitate multi-generational togetherness, solo adventuring, or escapism for couples. And, some of the world's most beautiful places are seen best from the deck of a cruise ship.

What a cruise is not

Some cruises simply aren't relaxing despite cruise brochure claims that 'you can do as much or as little as you want to.' For example, large resort ships carrying between 1,750 and 6,400 passengers pack lots of people into small cabins and provide almost nonstop activities and entertainment.

Reasons to take a cruise

Value. A cruise represents the best vacation value for your money. Period! A cruise is a well-packaged vaca-

Europa 2, by Hapag-Lloyd Cruises.

tion that includes so many things, and you don't have to constantly make decisions.

Convenience. You can probably drive to your port of embarkation. If not, the cruise line can make all the arrangements, including flights, baggage handling, and transfers to and from the ship. And you only have to unpack once!

Choice. There are over 30,000 cruises to choose from! You can cruise the Caribbean, Alaska, South America, Europe, the Greek Isles, the Middle East, Southeast Asia, the South Pacific, the Arctic, and Antarctica. And that's just the beginning!

See new places. A cruise provides you with a chance to see new places. You simply board, and the ship will change the destination for you – almost daily. Organized excursions can add to the sense of discovery.

Comfort. A cruise ship suite or cabin is your home away from home. It can be as small as a tent (at about 60 square feet) or as large as a villa (at 3,000 square feet), or anything in between.

Good Food. Dining is one of the greatest pleasures of ship life, and all your meals are included from breakfast through to late-night snacks.

Family Togetherness. Cruising is great for families with children. Many ships have well-supervised activities for kids – and it's a safe, friendly environment. Cruising is also an excellent way for groups of friends to vacation together for lifelong memories.

Learning Experience. Most cruise ships have guest speakers/lecturers, so you can learn while you cruise.

Make new friends. A cruise ship provides a relaxed environment in which to make new friends – some you may keep for life.

Adventure. A cruise can be an adventure. It can take you places that are impossible to reach by almost any other means, such as the Antarctic Peninsula, the Arctic, or to remote islands. A cruise can inspire the explorer in you.

Staying Healthy. A cruise allows you to pamper yourself in a spa, although body-pampering treatments are at extra cost. And, with all the available food, learn to pace yourself, and you'll stay healthy.

Entertainment. Cruise ships provide a wide range of professional entertainment, from spectacular Vegas-style production shows to intimate piano, guitar, and jazz bars. And during the day, there are activities, fun, and games galore – enough to keep even the active occupied.

How long does a cruise last?

The popular standard length is seven days, although cruises can vary from two-day party outings to exotic voyages around the world of three or more months. For your first cruise, consider trying a short cruise to 'get your feet wet.' After that, the world awaits.

About the price

Price is, of course, a consideration for most people. The amount you are prepared to spend will determine the

Royal Court Theatre aboard *Queen Elizabeth II*.

size, location, and style of accommodation you get. Be wary of huge discounts – it either means that the product was unrealistically priced at source or that quality is reduced somewhere.

Will I need a passport?

Yes. You'll need to ensure that any appropriate authorizations and visas are obtained ahead of your cruise. If you already have a valid passport, make sure you have at least six months left on your passport at the *end* of the cruise. If you don't have a passport, allow plenty of time to apply for one. Also, some ports (such as Venice, Italy, and all ports in Russia) require you to carry your passport when ashore.

10 Steps to a good first cruise experience

1. Find a Cruise Specialist. Although the Internet is a popular research tool, it pays to find a specialist cruise agent as soon as possible (note that some Internet-only

10 Question to Ask Your Booking Agent

1. What size ship would you recommend?
2. What should I budget for the cruise?
3. What kind of accommodation would suit my tastes and budget?
4. What is included in the cruise price?
5. What is not included?
6. What is the ship's onboard ambience like?
7. What facilities does the ship have?
8. What kind of food and service is provided?
9. What kind of entertainment should I expect?
10. What are the Internet or Wi-Fi charges?

'agencies' with slick websites have been known to disappear without trace – with your money).

Describe your preferences (relaxation, visiting destinations, adventure, activities, or fun), so that the specialist can suggest what's appropriate. A good cruise specialist agent will then find a cruise that is right for you, for the right reasons, and find the best fares available.

They can guide you through all the important details, such as choice of cabin, dining seating, ships, and cruise lines best suited to your needs. Their advice and help costs nothing; they also have insider tips, as well as knowledge about upgrades, pre- and post-cruise programs, and hotel and other travel arrangements.

2. Where To? Choose where you want to cruise (Bahamas, Bermuda, Caribbean, Alaska, Hawaii, USA east coast, Baltic, Northern Europe, Mediterranean, Indian Ocean, Southeast Asia, Australia/New Zealand, South Africa, South America, South Pacific). And when you want to cruise (Alaska is only in the summertime, when the Caribbean may be too hot for you; Northern Europe is best in the summer, although South America and Southeast Asia are best in the winter). If you are interested in a special theme, choose accordingly (example: Carnival in Rio, Formula One racing in Monte Carlo).

3. How Long? Decide on the length of cruise vacation you can afford to take. Allow traveling time to get to and from your ship, particularly if it is in a region far from home, or during winter. The standard length of cruise in the Caribbean, for example, is seven days (although short-break Bahamas or Mexican Riviera cruises for three or four days are popular, too), but in Northern Europe it is more like 12–14 days, while for an around-South America cruise, you'll need to plan for 30 days or more. For visiting the Antarctic Peninsula, allow 21 days. Finally, a complete around-the-world cruise will take 90–120 memorable days.

4. Choose the Right Ship. Size matters! Choose the right size ship for your needs. Do you want to be with 100, 200, 500, 1,000, or 5,000-plus others on your vacation? As a rule of thumb, the larger the ship, the more the cruise itinerary focuses on the ship as the destination.

Or perhaps you would like to experience cruising under sail; or with specialist lecturers; or an adventure/expedition cruise; or a coastal and inland waterways cruise; or with a large spa and choice of body-pampering treatments; or aboard a ship with non-stop entertainment and fun activities.

5. Choose the Right Cabin, For a first cruise, choose an outside-view cabin. In an interior (no-view) cabin you won't know how to dress when you wake up because you can't see what the weather is like outside (although interior no-view cabins are good if you like to sleep in a really dark room). If you are concerned about motion sickness (it's not common, but it can happen), choose a cabin in the mid-section of the ship.

The average cabin size aboard a large resort ship is 180–200 sq ft (16.5–18.5 sq m); anything less and you will feel cramped. With limited closet space, you'll need fewer clothes than you might think. The more space you want, the more it will cost. Today, many passengers like to have a private balcony.

Visiting the Norwegian fjords aboard *Balmoral* (Fred. Olsen Cruise Lines).

6. Dining. If the ship still has two seatings for dinner – as many large resort ships do – it could be wise to choose the later seating (typically 8:30pm), so that you have enough time ashore on the days the ship is in port without having to rush back to shower and change for the first seating, which is typically at 6:30pm.

Some ships have several dining venues, and you go where and when and with whom you like.

7. Health and Fitness. If you are interested in wellness or spa treatments, ask your agent to make sure that your chosen ship has adequate facilities, space, and equipment. Note that aboard some of the largest ships, you'll need to sign up for many exercise classes, and there may be a 30-minute time limit to use the treadmill or video bike.

It's best to book early for spa treatments, because the appointment times go quickly. Some cruise lines with large resort ships allow you to book online, although this means planning your time in advance.

8. Families. If you have a family, choose a family-friendly ship. While most large resort ships have good facilities, mid-size and small ships have more limited facilities. Some have none at all. Children love cruising – it's an educational, fun, learning, entertaining and social experience for them.

Conversely, if you don't want to cruise with lots of children, avoid the main school vacation periods. For those who don't want children around them, there are several child-free ships to choose from.

9. Dress Codes. Dress codes today are informal, if not downright casual, particularly aboard the large resort ships. So, no tux needed (exception: a transatlantic crossing aboard Cunard Line's *Queen Mary 2*, when dressing more formally is part of the crossing tradition). Do remember that ships move, however; so flat (or low heel) shoes are strongly recommended for women.

10. Extra Expenses. Finally, you'll need to budget for extra-cost items such as shore excursions, drinks (unless they are included), meals in any 'specialty' dining venue, spa treatments, gaming, and other personal items. Also, allow some additional money to cover sou-

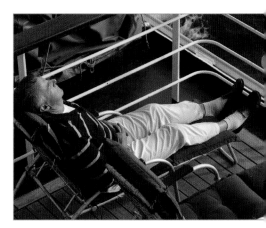

Relaxing on a deckchair on a transatlantic crossing.

venirs and other purchases. Last, but not least, make sure you have full insurance cover for your vacation.

Digital details

Today, many passengers use smartphones and tablet computers, and expect to be able to use these devices during their cruise. But you should know the details before you travel, so you can make the best decision on how to use your digital devices.

You can't use your smartphone or tablet for embarkation check-in yet (unlike some airlines), but you can use your device aboard ship – in port. However, once you leave port, your mobile/smartphone will automatically lock into the ship's digital network, and this will incur a charge. Once at sea, your mobile/smartphone is out of range with your land-based carrier and locks into a 'mini-cell' aboard a ship (Cellular at Sea), controlled by the MTN (Marine Telephone Network).

The ship's digital shipboard system will ask you to establish a user name and password before allowing you to access websites or your e-mail. Computer and tablet users should note that each ship-received e-mail arrives separately and takes longer to load. This is because ships use different software from home-based systems, and you will share the space with marine requirements. Wi-Fi is available aboard many ships – at extra cost.

Some mobile phone carriers (example: Verizon in the USA) have a Preferred Carrier List built into every phone that pre-selects preferred carriers throughout the world with whom they have roaming agreements – at optimum rates to the carrier.

Also, be aware that some ships have notices outside restaurants prohibiting the use of mobile phones. The best advice is to leave your smartphone in 'Airplane Mode' – which turns of all wireless services, but allows you to use your device as a camera, music player, and e-book reader without being charged.

How to get the best deal

Find out what's available by reading newspaper advertising and checking the Internet. Then identify a travel agency that *specializes* in cruises. In some countries, such as the UK, they'll be bonded if they belong to a shipping association. A good agent will get you the best price, as well as upgrades and other benefits you won't be able to get elsewhere.

Big travel agency groups and consortiums often reserve large blocks of cabins, and smaller independent agencies can access extensive discounts, upgrades, and other benefits not available on the Internet. Because the cruise lines consider travel agents as their principal distribution system, they can provide special discounts and value-added amenities that aren't provided to Internet sites.

What's Coming in 2014

More than 22 million people took a cruise in 2013, and all the new ships offer attractions aimed at expanding the market despite tough economic conditions.

By the end of 2014, more than 50 ships measuring over 100,000 gross tons will be in service, with more on their way. As this book went to press, 18 new ships (including options) of various sizes were scheduled for delivery between January 2014 and the end of 2017, including a third Oasis-class ship for Royal Caribbean International – this time built in a French shipyard, plus an option for a fourth.

Financing the building of new ships always takes priority as cruise lines plan for future ships and marketing plans. Insurance costs also rose following the loss of the 114,147-ton, 3,000-passenger *Costa Concordia* off the coast of Tuscany in January 2012. In addition, there's the higher price of steel, the higher cost of labor, and the higher fees demanded by banks and private finance groups lending money for construction and shipbuilding guarantees.

Phoenix Reisen's *Artania* (seen here in her former colors) leaving Stockholm.

In 2014, of the five new ships scheduled for delivery the smallest in capacity is TUI Cruises' 2,500-passenger *Mein Schiff 3*, while the largest is Royal Caribbean International's 4,100-passenger *Quantum of the Seas*. Perhaps the most notable newcomer in 2014 is the first new ship for Germany's fast-growing, family-friendly TUI Cruises. Given the economics of scale and shipbuilding costs, the new 'optimum' size for the large resort ships appears to be about 140,000 tons, with a capacity of 3,500-4,000 passengers.

Some of the new ships are clones of a similar series in terms of size, layout, and configuration, helping to reduce costs. With the exception of two AIDA Cruises ships being built by Mitsubishi Heavy Industries, Japan, for introduction is 2015 and 2016, all are being built by specialist shipyards in France, Finland, Germany, and Italy.

Costa Cruises

Costa Diadema, the first in a new class of ships for Costa Cruises, arrives in 2014. The 132,500-ton, 3,700-passenger ship will be the largest in the Italian company's fleet and promises more of the Italian family-friendly facilities enjoyed by its multi-national passengers. Although Costa Cruises' fortunes declined in the aftermath of the *Costa Concordia* tragedy, they have since rebounded, and it is good to see the effort that the company has put into its newbuild program, in dispensing with its two smaller, older ships *Costa Allegra* and *Costa Marina*, and in rebuilding its name and brand.

Norwegian Cruise Line

NCL's *Norwegian Breakaway* arrived in 2013, and sister ship *Norwegian Getaway follows in* 2014. Both ships are marginally smaller than *Norwegian Epic*, on which they are based.

Much effort has gone into the design of cabin layouts, and the separated bathroom facilities of *Norwegian Epic* have gone. NCL has pushed the choice of dining venues to the limit. The new ship caters to families with children, but it also features a number of the popular (capsule-like) 'studio' cabins for solo-occupancy.

Applying the 'pay more, get more' principle, the ship also features 'The Haven' exclusive suite accommodation area located forward and above the ship's navigation bridge – as aboard *Norwegian Breakaway and Norwegian Epic,* though trendier.

Princess Cruises

Princess Cruises' *Regal Princess* arrives in 2014 (the first of the new pair, sister ship *Royal Princess* arrived in 2013 and was named by the Duchess of Cambridge). The previous *Regal Princess* was named by the late Margaret Thatcher in 1991.

One major feature aboard *Regal Princess* is its Sea-Walk – a half-moon-shaped walkway that is cantilevered over both sides of the ship. One side is a walkway, while the other includes a bar. In both, you can look straight down through the glass bottom of the walkway, which extends about 28ft (8.5m) from the side of the ship, to the ocean 128ft (39m) beneath your feet.

The Horizon Food Court casual eatery has been expanded and includes a pastry shop, a crab shack, and a fondue eatery. Other eateries include a seafood bar and a larger version of the always-popular Alfredo's Pizzeria – this one has 121 seats. In the Piazza (atrium) stands a Tea Tower, and there's a sommelier to guide you through a huge variety of teas and tisanes.

Royal Caribbean International

At a cost of over $1 billion each, the first of a pair of 158,000-ton 'Project Sunshine' ships, *Quantum of the Seas,* arrives in the latter part of 2014. This ship will be more akin to the *Voyager*-class ships rather than the larger (spread-superstructure) *Oasis*-class ships. This size means that the ships will be able to operate a much greater range of itineraries than the *Oasis*-class ships can. The passenger capacity is 4,100 (based on two per cabin).

RCI was keeping quiet about the facilities to be included aboard the new ship, but I feel sure that a Royal Promenade will be included, as will many of the popular dining venues, but I think we'll see some new things that will provide lots of 'Wow factor for RCI's regular passengers – particularly for families with children. A

The colorful hull of *Norwegian Getaway*.

second ship, *Anthem of the Seas* is scheduled for spring 2015.

TUI Cruises

TUI Cruises is now really well entrenched in the family-friendly market for its German-speaking clientele, and the company's two new ships – *Mein Schiff 3* arrives in 2014, and a second, *Mein Schiff 4,* will be delivered in 2015 – promise to be exceptional, and packed with trendy facilities and outstanding eateries, including a 'Blue Balcony,' a 118.4 sq ft (11 sq m), glass-floored platform some 121.3ft (37 m) above the sea, which gives the sensation of floating over the ocean.

Mein Schiff 3 features multi-option dining venues, with the sit-down food service and child-friendly facilities that today's families seek. Two specialty restaurants – Richard's Fine Essen and a Surf and Turf Steakhouse – will be housed in a futuristic-looking 'glass diamond' wall at the ship's stern.

Mein Schiff 3 and *Mein Schiff 4* will be slightly larger than the company's first two ships (*Mein Schiff 1* and *Mein Schiff 2*), with a range of public rooms and general passenger flow designed by the company from the ground up, including a concert hall – designed to high acoustic specifications.

Looking ahead to 2015

Looking ahead, the widening of the Panama Canal and the opening of two sets of additional locks (each with three chambers and nine water-saving basins per chamber) – one on the Atlantic and one on the Pacific side of the canal in 2015 will mean that most of the Large Resort Ships, including the ocean liner *Queen Mary 2* (but not *Allure of the Seas* and *Oasis of the Seas*) will be able to move easily between the US east and west coasts, presenting more opportunities for the major cruise companies.

Choppy economic waters

Although more than 22 million people took a cruise in 2013, cruise companies found the economic waters

---

At a glance: The latest trends

Long multi-deck water slides and power drenchers in Aqua Park pool deck facilities.

More multi-generational cruising can be found aboard the large resort ships.

More adults-only ships, for those who have matured beyond noise and games and want peace and quiet.

Small ship cruising, for those seeking to avoid large resort ships and noisy crowds.

More specialty dining, wine and drinks packages.

More 'pay as you eat' venues.

More sophisticated spas and well-being treatment options for the health-conscious.

More 'healthy eating' and 'spa' menu choices.

Greater variety of active adventures ashore.

More demand for smoking-free ships.

More demand for longer cruises.

More demand for short 'getaway' cruises.

More demand for well-packaged river cruises.

Water slides aboard *Norwegian Epic.*

somewhat choppy. Enacting cost-efficiencies was the order of the day. Head offices reduced management and staff, squeezed suppliers and port costs, and tried to make their ships more efficient.

As a result of the looming low-sulphur fuel regulations, ships have slowed down and itineraries have been changed accordingly. The new sulfur cap in Emission Control Areas (ECAs) is scheduled to drop to 0.1 percent in 2015. For cruise lines, it's coming fast. It means that ships will be required to use distillate – a lighter fuel. Whether there'll be enough distillate available is still an unanswered question. It could become more difficult for ECA cruise regions such as Alaska and Northern Europe to attract cruise ships in future, given the additional fuel and operating costs.

The truth about low fares

Although bargains still exist, it's important to read the small print. A highly discounted fare may apply only to certain dates and itineraries – for example, the eastern Caribbean instead of the more popular western Caribbean. It may be subject to a booking deadline or, typically, is 'cruise-only,' which means you must arrange your own air transportation separately. This can prove expensive. If air transportation is included, deviations may not be possible.

Your cabin choice, grade, and location may not be available. You could be limited to first seating at dinner aboard a ship that operates two seatings, and some highly discounted fares may not apply to children. Port charges, handling fees, fuel surcharges, or other taxes may cost extra.

Is cruising still good value?

Yes, it is. In fact, it's never been better, thanks in part to the economic downturn that forced cruise lines to offer more incentives – such as onboard credit, cabin upgrades, and other perks – in an effort to keep their companies afloat and their ships full.

The price of your vacation is protected by advance pricing, so you know before you go that your major outgoings have already been set. A fuel surcharge is the only additional cost that may change at the last minute.

Cruise lines offer their best prices to those booking early. It's worth taking the bait to get the best choice of cabin and location, and the best chance of any upgrades, in case any are offered closer to your sailing date. Booking late may sometimes get you cheaper prices, too, but you *won't* get a choice of cabins and locations, so you could end up with a tiny cupboard above the galley.

Choose an older ship – the newest, much publicized ships command a premium.

If you're on a tight budget, book an interior (no view) cabin on one of the best ships, instead of an outside cabin on a less fancy ship. This buys you better food and entertainment for the same money.

A number of ships offer drinks-inclusive pricing, saving you a bundle in extra onboard costs.

Savvy passengers join frequent passenger clubs to get maximum benefits. These offer additional perks (onboard credit, free Wi-Fi service, private cocktail parties), and further discounts for booking your next cruise while on board (at prices not available on the Internet).

Check to make sure that all port charges, government fees, and any fuel surcharges are included in an advertised price quote.

If you find a highly discounted cruise rate on the Internet, fine. But, if a cruise line suddenly offers special discounts for your sailing, or cabin upgrades, or things go wrong with your booking, your Internet booking service may prove quite unfriendly – many are not licensed or bonded. Your specialist travel agent, however, can probably work magic in making those special discounts and upgrades benefit you. And there's a bonus: travel agents don't charge for their service.

Getting on the brandwagon

Image-conscious cruise lines are constantly jockeying to become the 'greenest' brand – or have the largest ship – or the ship with the longest waterslide! Size is a major factor, and so each line touts the benefits of its particular size of ship. For that reason, choosing the right-size ship for your vacation is now more important than ever.

More shopping

Onboard 'enhancement' items – such as luggage and tote bags, bed linen, personal amenities, wooden deck lounge (steamer) chairs, coffee tables and chairs, ship posters, cruise line memorabilia and collectibles, wine glasses, chocolate, flowers, and even mattresses – can now be purchased online from the major cruise lines. However, such online shopping usually only works if you have a US address and credit card.

The floating playgrounds

The world's 'largest ever' cruise ships, Royal Caribbean International's *Allure of the Seas* and *Oasis of the Seas* (a third sister ship will join the fleet in 2016), redefined large resort ship cruising. With a capacity of 6,000-plus passengers, they are innovative and exciting – outstanding for families with children, which means they are neither quiet nor relaxing.

Midsize ships benefit from the introduction of so many large resort ships because more and more experienced cruisers are downsizing to avoid the big ships' sanitized cruise experience and long lines.

Dining and service

'Specialty' pay-extra restaurants are fashionable, particularly aboard the large resort ships, and are ideal for escaping from huge dining halls full of noise and singing, table-dancing waiters. These are typically à la carte restaurants serving superior food. But a couple each having two glasses of palatable wine could, with the cover charge, easily end up paying $100 for dinner. Some companies (such as Celebrity Cruises and Royal Caribbean International) with multiple restaurants aboard some ships offer specialty-dining packages.

Cruise lines stuck with traditional two-seating dining are looking for ways to be more flexible. An open-seating option is now available aboard most of the major lines, including Carnival Cruise Lines, Celebrity Cruises, Holland America Line, Norwegian Cruise Line, Princess Cruises, and Royal Caribbean International – but not Costa Cruises, Cunard Line, or MSC Cruises.

More ships offer flexible dining and almost round-the-clock casual (get-your-own-food) eateries, so you can eat or snack when you want. Although the concept is good, the delivery often is not; it is typically rather soulless, self-service eating.

Security hassles

Most destinations throughout the world strive to welcome cruise ships and passengers, valuing their visits and business and helping create jobs for local communities. However, I have been hearing a large number of complaints from passengers concerning arrivals in the United States.

Homeland Security officials in the US have never been noted for warmly welcoming visitors at America's airports, and their elaborate red tape has been increasingly wrapped around cruise ships. Although they seldom have a problem with ships operated locally in or from the US, they often carry out a 'face check' when a foreign cruise ship arrives – that is, they want to see each passenger individually.

The resulting delays, can shorten passengers' time in port by as much as eight hours. In one case, the first passengers from P&O's *Arcadia* were allowed off the ship in Los Angeles before 11am, but the last passengers weren't cleared until 4:30pm. Even though all passengers had completed applications for multiple-entry ESTA visas and the ship had just come from Alaska, another US state, the officials insisted on carrying out detailed passport checks, extensive background interviews, and full biometric checks, including fingerprints of both hands and retina scans. All of this clearly costs the US both revenue and visitors because some 'foreign' cruise lines such as Fred. Olsen Cruise Lines, responding to passenger complaints, have decided it is no longer worth calling at American ports, and other lines are thinking of following suit.

Twin titans: *Allure of the Seas* and *Oasis of the Seas* can each carry 6,360 passengers plus 2,162 crew.

Cruising's Continuing Growth

When the first jet aircraft made many former passenger
liners redundant, some were scrapped, but others gave
birth to the modern cruise industry.

Cunard linked up with BOAC in the early 1960s.

Who goes cruising	
The Maritime Evaluations Group has analyzed by nationality the breakdown of cruise passengers (approx.):	
United States	13,500,000
Europe (excluding UK)	4,000,000
UK	1,780,000
Brazil	762,000
Canada	770,000
Asia (excluding Japan)	600,000
Australia/New Zealand	694,000
Scandinavia	200,000
Japan	180,000
Cyprus *	30,000
Cargo ship passengers	3,000
Total	22,619,000

* Local Cyprus market only.

Note: The above numbers include the approximately 1 million passengers who took a river/inland waterway cruise, but not the 300,000 passengers who took a coastal voyage aboard the Hurtigruten (Norwegian Coastal Voyages) ships. All figures are for 2013.

Although Bahamas/Caribbean cruises from Miami had resurfaced in the 1950s with a ship named *Nuevo Dominicano* (ex-*New Northland*), it was not until the 1960s that cruising had been updated and re-packaged for a society that found an increasing amount of leisure time on its hands.

Twenty-nine years ago, the first edition of this book listed 120 ships, some of which are still operating in one form or another. Today, that number has grown to more than 280 (around 350 ships operating coastal cruises). Throughout the period, the cruise industry has maintained a global growth rate of over 7 percent each year. But many well-known cruise lines have also gone to the deep blue seabed in the past 25 years. Indeed, since 1990 more than 65 cruise companies have either merged, or been taken over, or simply gone out of business, including such well-liked companies as Chandris Cruises, Epirotiki, Renaissance Cruises, Royal Cruise Lines, Royal Viking Line, and Sun Line Cruises.

Some start-up lines, using older ships and aimed at specific markets, also came and went – operations such as American Family Cruises, Festival Cruises, Fiesta Marina Cruises, Premier Cruise Lines, and Regency Cruises. In came new shiny tonnage, complete with vanity logos and adornments painted on all-white hulls – the attributes of the industry's emerging giants. Fresh thinking transformed the design of accommodation, the use of public spaces, and more food and entertainment venues.

Yield management, a term purloined from the airline industry, was introduced. These days company executives think of little else, because running a cruise company is all about economics.

Modern cruising is born

In the early 1960s, passenger-shipping directories listed over 100 passenger lines. Until the mid-1960s, it was cheaper to cross the Atlantic by ship than by plane, but the appearance of the jet aircraft changed that rapidly, particularly with the introduction of the Boeing 747 in the early 1970s. In 1962, more than 1 million people crossed the North Atlantic by ship; in 1970, that number was down to 250,000.

The success of the jumbo jets created a fleet of unprofitable and out-of-work passenger liners that appeared doomed for the scrap heap. Even the famous big 'Queens,' noted for their regular weekly transatlantic service, were at risk. Cunard White Star Line's *Queen*

Mary (81,237 gross tonnage) was withdrawn in September 1967. Cunard tried to fight back with Cunard-Eagle Airways but then formed a short-lived BOAC-Cunard joint venture with the British Overseas Aircraft Corporation, flying 707s and Super VC10s.

Cunard Line's *Queen Elizabeth,* at 83,673 gross tonnage the largest-ever passenger liner (until 1996), made its final crossing in November 1968.

Ships were sold for a fraction of their value. Many lines went out of business and ships were scrapped. Those that survived attempted to mix transatlantic crossings with voyages south to the sun. The Caribbean (including the Bahamas) became appealing, cruising became an alternative, and an entire new industry was born, with new lines being formed exclusively for cruising.

Then smaller, more specialized ships arrived, capable of getting into the tiny ports of developing Caribbean islands; there were no commercial airlines taking vacationers to the Caribbean then, and few hotels. Instead of cruising long distances south from more northerly ports such as New York, companies established their headquarters in Florida. This avoided the cold weather, choppy seas, and expense of the northern ports and saved fuel costs with shorter runs to the Caribbean.

Cruising was reborn. California became the base for cruises to the Mexican Riviera, and Vancouver

---

Berlitz rates North America's best and worst homeland ports

Berlitz constantly receives complaints about the forceful tactics of baggage handlers (porters) at the Port of Miami, and Port Everglades (Fort Lauderdale). As passengers alight from buses from the airport (which often have a sign stating: 'Tips Not Included'), the baggage handlers ask passengers to identify their baggage, which they then place into luggage cages. For this 'service,' passengers are asked to tip generously – for what is a simple 'lift and move three feet' job.

So, do the math. If each baggage handler receives the requested $1–$2 per bag tip, and the ship carries 5,000 passengers, that's a lot of moolah. Be smart: *don't* let them bully you into thinking your luggage won't get to your ship in time for your cruise – a threat often used. They are responsible for making sure that all bags *do* go to the ship on time – yours included.

Pier pressure

Bigger ships can mean overcrowded ports. The most crowded in the world – where several ships carrying thousands of passengers may be in port at the same time – include the following:

Caribbean/Bahamas: Antigua, Barbados, Grand Cayman, Nassau, St Maarten, St Thomas.

Europe/Mediterranean: Barcelona, Civitavecchia (the port for Rome), Kuşadasi, Venice.

Other ports: Cabo San Lucas, Juneau, Ketchikan, Mazatlan, Sydney.

Some large-city ports, such as Barcelona and St Petersburg, can handle the influx of large resort ships during the busy summer months, helped by the number of shore excursion choices available. However, stretching the cruising season in these areas also helps lessen overcrowding.

Coping with the giants

There's no reason why ports should be any more immune from terrorist attacks than airports, but the need for sensible safety measures has been taken to extremes by overenthusiastic security personnel at some United States and Canadian ports. After many complaints, the Maritime Evaluations Group has built a picture of ports based on their user-friendliness and sense of hospitality. Maximum score is 100.

As a benchmark, the terminal facilities, luggage handling, user-friendliness, and hospitality factor of personnel at the Port of Yokohama in Japan score an impressive 94 out of 100. The comparison with the typical experience in US homeland ports is telling.

What the berth marks mean

In allocating points, we took account of the following factors: terminals and appearance and cleanliness, security personnel, attitude, check-in, security control, luggage handling by porters (often seeking tips), ease of disembarkation, immigration and customs, security personnel, luggage storage and identification system, porters, and ease of access to transportation and car parks.

Facilities rated out of 100

Port	Total
Baltimore	75
Boston	62
Cape Liberty (Bayonne, New Jersey)	56
Charleston	53
Ft Lauderdale (Port Everglades)	45
Galveston	45
Gulfport	44
Honolulu	54
Houston	52
Jacksonville	44
Los Angeles (Long Beach)	48
Los Angeles (San Pedro)	52
Miami	42
Montreal	53
New Orleans	50
New York (Brooklyn)	81
New York (Manhattan)	72
Norfolk	52
Philadelphia	48
Port Canaveral	54
St Thomas	51
San Diego	55
San Francisco	49
San Juan	46
Seattle	59
Tampa	53
Vancouver	73

Oasis of the Seas and *Allure of the Seas* are true floating resorts, with parks and boulevards.

on Canada's west coast was the focus for summer cruises to Alaska.

Flying passengers to embarkation ports was the next logical step, and soon a working relationship emerged between the cruise lines and the airlines. Air/sea and 'sail and stay' packages thrived – joint cruise and hotel vacations with inclusive pricing. Some of the old liners came out of mothballs, purchased by emerging cruise lines and refurbished for warm-weather cruising operations, often with their interiors redesigned and refitted. During the late 1970s, the modern cruise industry grew at a rapid rate.

Cruising today

Today's cruise concept hasn't changed much from that of earlier days, although it has been improved, refined, expanded, and packaged for ease of consumption. No longer the domain of affluent retirees, cruising today attracts people of all ages, socio-economic background, and dress sense. It's no longer the shipping business, but the hospitality industry – although it has to be said that some cruise ship personnel appear to be in the hostility industry.

New ships are generally larger than their predecessors, yet cabin size is 'standardized' to provide more space for entertainment and other public facilities. To-day's ships boast air conditioning to keep out heat and humidity; stabilizers to keep the ship on an even keel; a high level of maintenance, safety, and hygiene; and more emphasis on health and fitness facilities.

Although ships have long been devoted to eating and relaxation in comfort, ships today offer more activities, and more learning and life-enriching experiences than before. For the same prices as a quarter of a century ago, you can cruise aboard the latest large resort ships that offer ice-skating, rock climbing, golfing, roller-blading, wave surfing, bowling, and so on, while dining at fine restaurants that offer varied cuisines, being pampered in luxurious spas, and being entertained by high-quality production shows. And there are many more places you can visit on a cruise: from Antarctica to Acapulco, Bermuda to Bergen, Dakar to Dominica, Shanghai to St Thomas.

Cruising tomorrow

Current ship design follows two quite distinct paths: large resort ships or smaller niche-market ships.

Large resort ships, where 'economy of scale' helps the operator to keep down the cost per passenger. The first, *Carnival Destiny* (re-named *Carnival Sunshine* in 2013), debuted in 1996, and today nine companies have ships measuring over 100,000 gross tons. Some accom-

Disney Magic alongside Terminal 8 in Port Canaveral, Florida.

modate more than 6,000 passengers, with the 'bigger is better' principle being pursued for all it's worth. Many are, however, too big to transit the Panama Canal (until it is widened by 2014).

Small ships, where the 'small is beautiful' concept has taken hold, particularly in the exclusive and luxury categories. Cruise lines offer high-quality ships of low capacity, which can provide a highly personalized range of quality services. This means better-trained, more-experienced staff (and more of them to serve fewer passengers), higher-quality food, and more meals cooked to order. Small ships can also visit the less crowded ports.

Some cruise lines have expanded by 'stretching' their ships. This is accomplished by cutting a ship in half and inserting a newly constructed midsection, thus instantly adding more accommodation and public rooms, while maintaining the same draft.

Ships that have been 'stretched' (with year of construction and length of stretch) include: *Albatros* (1983, 91ft/27.7m), *Balmoral* (2007, 98.4ft/30m), *Black Watch* (1981, 91ft/27.7m), *Boudicca* (1982, 91ft/ 27.7m), *Braemar* (2008, 102.4ft/31.2m), *Enchantment of the Seas* (2005, 72.8ft/22.2m), *FTI Berlin* (1986, 65.6ft/20m), *SuperStar Aquarius* (1998, 131.2ft/40m), *SuperStar Gemini* (1998, 131.2ft/40m), *Thomson Dream* (1990, 131.2ft/40m), and *Thomson Majesty* (1999, 98.4ft/30m).

Caribbean cruising as depicted in a 1947 advertisement.

Exclusivity

Exclusive communities at sea are likely to proliferate. These 'gated' areas are for those willing to pay extra to live in a larger suite and gain access to 'private' facilities, concierge lounges, and private sunbathing areas. Ships that have them: *MSC Divina, MSC Fantasia, MSC Preziosa, MSC Splendida, Norwegian Breakaway, Norwegian Epic, Norwegian Getaway, Norwegian Gem, Norwegian Jade,* and *Norwegian Pearl.* So two-class cruising (in some cases, three-class cruising) is back in vogue.

What's new in the modern cruise industry (but not always an improvement)

The onboard experience
Cashless cruising ('just sign here!')
Lack of dress code
Better facilities for the frail and physically challenged
Passengers with tattoos and tracksuits
A crew that can't speak your language
Security personnel aboard ship who don't understand hospitality (but they're worse in the cruise terminals)
Gratuities charged automatically to your onboard account or online pre-pay
Pay-extra spa and wellness facilities
Pay-extra tours to view the 'Back of House'
Adults-only ships
Deluge of sales flyers under cabin door
Digital photographs and personal videos
Sunbed hoggers
Roll-over lifeboats
'Art' auctions, jewelry shops
Headline-making attacks of norovirus
Overboards (whether for crime, accident, 'assisted' suicide, or insurance money)
High-tech production shows, click-tracks
Internet-connect centers, Wi-Fi, and e-mail facilities
Large casinos, themed lounges and bars

Cuisine and dining
Wider choice of dining venues, eateries, and food

Pay-extra dining venues
Huge self-serve stuff-your-face buffets (camping at sea)
Online check-in for some of the major cruise lines

Accommodation
Balcony and French-balcony, loft and lobby cabins
Satellite-linked telephones in cabins
Interactive touch- and flat-screen cabin television sets
Electronic cabin key cards
Pay-extra adults-only sanctuaries
Personal safes
Exclusive private accommodation areas (effectively gated communities)
Multi-room suites for multi-generational families or friends
Vacuum (barking-dog) toilets

Innovations
Vibration-less 'pod' propulsion systems
Cruise-only travel agents
Child-only playrooms and teen clubs
More sports facilities (rock-climbing walls, ice-skating rinks, golf simulators, bowling alleys, boxing rings, race-car simulators, surf-riders)
'Private island' beach days
Cruises for gays, singles, and special interest groups
More active and adventurous shore excursions
Medivac helicopter lift for medical treatment

What the Brochures Don't Say

Most cruise brochures are hype over reality. We answer the questions about ocean cruising most frequently asked by those new to this type of vacation and by experienced passengers.

Cruises are, in effect, packaged vacations – and offer good value for money – with your accommodation, meals, and entertainment included. But it's the little hidden extras that are not made clear in the brochures. Some ships have 'drinks-inclusive' fares, while others let you choose from one of several 'beverage packages' on offer. Here are some of the most commonly asked questions, covering those items that the brochures gloss over.

Isn't cruising just for old people?

Not at all. The average age of passengers gets younger each year, with the average age of first-timers now well under 40. But retirees do find that cruising is a safe, comfortable way to travel and many have plenty of get-up-and-go. On a typical cruise you're likely to meet singles, couples, families with children of all ages, honeymooners, groups of friends, and college buddies.

Won't I get bored?

There are more things to do aboard today's ships than there are on almost any Caribbean island. So, whether you want to lie back and be pampered, or be active non-

Hanseatic passengers explore a new destination.

stop, you can do it on a cruise. Just being at sea provides an intoxicating sense of freedom that few places on dry land can offer. And, in case you think you may feel cut off without contact, almost all large resort ships (those carrying over 1,750 passengers) have ship-wide Wi-Fi access, Internet-connectivity, access, movies, and digital music libraries.

Isn't it all very regimented?

Some cruises simply aren't relaxing, despite brochure claims that 'you can do as much or as little as you want to.' For example, the large resort ships carrying more than 1,600 passengers, and particularly those with 5,000-plus, cram lots of people into small cabins and provide nonstop activities. The purpose of this book is to help you identify the cruise that's right for you.

Are there facilities for solo travelers?

A cruise is good for those traveling alone, because it is easy to meet other people in a non-competitive environment. Many ships have dedicated cabins for singles and special add-on rates for single occupancy of double cabins. Some cruise lines will even find a cabin mate for you to share with, if you so desire. However, in cabins with three or four berths (two beds plus upper berths), personal privacy doesn't exist. Some companies sell two-bed cabins at a special single rate.

How about holiday season cruises?

Celebrating the festive lifestyle is even more special aboard ship, where decorations add to the sense of occasion at this special time of year. However, the large resort ships can be very busy during the main holiday periods. These periods would be good to ignore if you want to have the facilities of a large resort ship, but want to be able to relax.

What about 'Spring Break' cruises?

If you take a cruise aboard one of the large resort ships (the most popular brands for Spring Break cruises are Carnival Cruise Lines, Norwegian Cruise Line, and Royal Caribbean International) during the annual Spring Break (usually in March, but dependent on the decisions of the school-curriculum), you should expect to find hoards of students causing mayhem.

Do cruise lines have loyalty programs?

All of the major cruise lines, and several of the smaller ones, have loyalty clubs. You can earn credits and onboard

Freedom of the Seas passes the Statue of Liberty in New York City.

benefits by belonging to a cruise line's loyalty club. Like airline clubs, these provide you with a number of benefits unavailable to non-members, although some of the benefits would also be available to passengers booking certain suite-grade accommodation. The programs are based either on the number of cruises taken, or, probably more fairly, on the number of days sailed. There's no charge to join, but a whole lot of benefits to gain if you keep cruising with the same line.

Some companies, such as Celebrity Cruises, allow you to transfer point levels to sister a company, Azamara Club Cruises or Royal Caribbean International. Other multi-cruise line companies, such as Carnival, may also allow this across the company's various brands. There are usually several levels, such as Silver, Gold, Platinum, and Diamond, depending on the cruise line, the number of voyages, or cruises, or cruise days.

Why is it so expensive for singles?

Because throughout most of the travel industry it's a couples' world, almost all cruise lines base their rates on double occupancy. Thus, when you travel alone, the cabin portion of your fare reflects an additional supplement. Although almost all new ships are built with cabins for double occupancy, older ships have more single-occupancy cabins (examples include: *Aegean Odyssey, Hebridean Princess, Saga Sapphire*). Cruise line special offers are nearly always aimed at double-occupancy passengers.

Can I pay in cash for purchases on board?

Not all cruise lines accept cash for purchases on board, and may ask for a cash deposit when you check-in (typically $500). Many older passengers (particularly from countries like Germany and Japan) do not possess credit cards, and always pay in cash. Cruise lines need to be more flexible.

How do I get my tickets?

E-Cruising is in! Most cruise lines have changed to on-line bookings and check-in. You'll need to print your own boarding passes, travel documents, and luggage tags. Make sure you have a functioning printer or know someone who does. If you go through a cruise-travel agent, they can print these for you. The reliance on e-technology means a reduction in the number of paper tickets issued by the cruise lines – but you'll have to spend more money to print out your tickets, boarding passes, paper luggage tags, and other documents.

Your printed documents will allow you to pass through the port's security station to get to your ship. Only the more exclusive, upscale cruise lines, expedition companies, and tall ship lines now provide boxes or wallets packed with documents, cruise tickets, leather (or faux-leather) luggage tags, and colorful destination booklets – cruise lines operating large resort ships have all but abandoned such niceties.

Is there enough to keep kids busy?

Most cruises provide families with more quality time than any other type of vacation, and family cruising is the industry's largest growth segment, with activities tailored to various age groups. Responding to this trend, Disney Cruise Line doubled its fleet, from two to four ships, with the introduction of *Disney Dream* in 2011 and *Disney Fantasy* in 2012.

If you cruise aboard one of the major cruise lines, you may find gratuities for your children automatically

Kids have fun aboard *Carnival Magic*.

added to your onboard account – or you may be able to pre-pay online. NCL, for example, requests $6 per day from each child of 3–12 years, while those over 13 pay the adult rate of $10 or more per day.

Do youth programs operate on port days?
Most cruise lines also operate programs on port days, although they may not be as extensive as on days at sea.

Are there adults-only ships?
Companies that operate small and mid-size adults-only ships include Cruise & Maritime Voyages (*Discovery, Marco Polo*), P&O Cruises (*Adonia, Arcadia, Oriana*) and Saga Cruises (*Saga Pearl II, Saga Sapphire*). The minimum age may be different depending on the company, so do check for the latest information.

How can I celebrate a birthday or anniversary?
If you have a birthday or anniversary or other special occasion to celebrate during your cruise, let the cruise line know in advance. You should be able to arrange a special cake for you, or a special 'champagne breakfast' in bed. Some cruise lines offer special anniversary packages – for a fee – or a meal in an alternative restaurant, where available.

Can I bring my pet?
Pets are not allowed aboard cruise ships, with one exception: the regular transatlantic crossings aboard Cunard Line's ocean liner *Queen Mary 2*, which has carried more than 500 pet animals since its debut in 2004. It provides air-conditioned kennels, plus a New York fire hydrant for dogs' convenience, and cat containers.

Do cruises suit honeymooners?
Absolutely. A cruise is the ideal setting for romance, for shipboard weddings aboard ships with the right registry (they can also be arranged in some ports, depending on local regulations), receptions, and honeymoons. And for those on a second honeymoon, many ships can perform a 'renewal of vows' ceremony; some will make a charge for this service.

Do some people really live on board?
Absolutely! There are several 'live aboard' passengers who simply love traveling the world continuously – and why not? They sell their house, put possessions into storage, step on board, and disembark only when the ship has to go into dry dock for refits.

Isn't cruising expensive?
Compare what it would cost on land to have all your meals and entertainment provided, as well as transportation, fitness and sports facilities, social activities, educational talks, parties, and other functions, and you can see the remarkable value of a cruise.

What you pay determines the size, location, and style of accommodation. Be wary of huge discounts – it either means that the product was unrealistically priced or that quality will be reduced somewhere. Most discounting is done by cruise agencies competing for business. Ships are as individual as fingerprints: each can change its 'personality' from cruise to cruise, depending on the mix of passengers (and crew). The choice ranges from basic to luxury, so give yourself a budget, and ask your professional travel supplier how to make the best use of it.

Will a repositioning cruise be cheaper?
When ships move from one cruise region to another, it is termed repositioning. When ships move between the

---

10 Money-Saving Tips

1. Research online, but book through a specialist cruise-travel agency.
2. Cut through the sales hype and get to the bottom line.
3. Make sure that all taxes are included.
4. Book early – the most desirable itineraries go soonest. If air travel is involved, remember that air fares tend to rise in peak seasons.
5. Book early – the best cabins and locations go sooner rather than later.
6. Book a cabin on a lower deck – the higher the deck, the more expensive will it be.
7. An interior (no view) cabin is cheaper, if you can live without natural light.
8. Be flexible with your dates – go off-season, when fares will be lower.
9. Book an older (pre-1980) ship – the newest ships are more expensive.
10. Purchase travel cancellation insurance – your cruise is an investment, after all.

Caribbean and Europe, typically in April/May, or between Europe and the Caribbean (typically in October/November), for example, the cruise fares are usually discounted. The ships rarely sail full, and offer excellent value for money.

I've found a seven-day cruise advertised at a very cheap price. Is there a catch?

If the price is a fraction of what you might pay for a decent hotel room in London or New York without meals or entertainment, something is not quite as it seems. Look at all the extra costs such as tips to cabin and dining room stewards, shore excursions, drinks, plus getting to and from the ship. The price per person advertised could well be for a non-desirable location.

Is the brochure price firm?

Cruise brochure prices are set by the sales and marketing departments of cruise lines. It's the price they would like to achieve to cover themselves against currency fluctuations, international bonding schemes, and the like. But discounts attract business, and so there is always some leeway. Also, travel agents receive a commission (typically 10 percent). So, as a consumer, always ask for the 'best price,' watch for special offers in newspapers and magazines, and talk to your travel agent.

Why do European cruises cost more than in the Caribbean?

There are several reasons. Almost all aspects of operations, including fuel costs, port charges, air transportation, and supplying food to the ships, are higher. Companies can make more money than in the cut-price Caribbean. Many services cost more in Europe than in the US, so the price of shore excursions in Europe is higher.

How inclusive is all-inclusive?

It usually means that transportation, accommodation, food, and entertainment are wrapped up in one neat package. Today on land, however, 'super clubs' offer everything 'all-in,' including drinks, although mostly low-quality brands are provided, with a much smaller selection than aboard most cruise ships. While that concept works better aboard small ships (those carrying fewer than 750 passengers), large cruise ships (those carrying more than 1,750 passengers) provide more facilities and more reasons for you to spend money on board. So 'mostly inclusive' might be a better term to use.

Should I take a back-to-back cruise?

If you're considering two seven-day back-to-back cruises (for example: eastern Caribbean/western Caribbean), bear in mind that many aspects of the cruise – the seven-day menu cycle, one or more ports, all shows and cabaret entertainment, even the cruise director's jokes and spiel – may be duplicated.

Do cruise lines have their own credit cards?

Most don't. Among those that do: Carnival Cruise Lines, Celebrity Cruises, Disney Cruise Line, Holland America Line, Princess Cruises, Saga Cruises, and Seabourn. You'll earn credits for any spending charged to the card. If you accrue enough points, you can exchange them for cruises or onboard credit.

Passengers enjoying the water on *Carnival Ecstasy's* Lido Deck.

Breakfast Veranda Deck aboard *Seven Seas Voyager*.

Do ships have different classes?

Gone are the class distinctions and the pretensions of formality of the past. Differences are now found mainly in the type of accommodation chosen, in the price you pay for a larger cabin (or suite), the location of your cabin (or suite), and whether or not you have butler service.

Some cruise lines, including Celebrity Cruises (not all ships), Holland America Line, MSC Cruises (*MSC Divina, MSC Fantasia, MSC Preziosa,* and *MSC Splendida* only) and Royal Caribbean International (except *Sovereign-* and *Vision-*class ships), have a 'concierge lounge' that can be used only by occupants of accommodation designated as suites (thus reviving a two-class system).

Private areas have been created by Cunard Line, MSC Cruises (Yacht Club), and Norwegian Cruise Line (The Haven) for occupants of the top suites, in an effort to insulate their occupants from the masses. The result is like a 'ship within a ship.'

Celebrity Cruises has, in essence, created four classes: (1) Reflection Suites; (2) Concierge Class (middle-level) mini-suites/cabins; (3) Aqua-class; and (4) Standard cabins (either exterior view or interior – no view). Perhaps it's less complicated to think in general terms of 'Balcony Class' and 'Non-Balcony Class.'

Cunard Line has always had several classes for transatlantic travel (just like the airlines), but today's ships (*Queen Elizabeth, Queen Mary 2, Queen Victoria*) are classed according to the restaurant and accommodation grade chosen.

What does a category guarantee mean?

It means you have purchased a specific grade of accommodation (just as in a hotel), although the actual cabin may not have been assigned to your booking yet. Your cabin may be assigned before you go, or when you arrive for embarkation.

What are port charges?

These are levied by various ports visited, rather like city taxes imposed on hotel guests. They help pay for the infrastructure required to provide facilities including docks, linesmen, security and operations personnel, and porters at embarkation and disembarkation ports.

Can I eat when I want to?

Most major cruise lines now offer 'flexible dining' which allows you to choose (with some limitations) when you want to eat, and with whom you dine, during your cruise. As with restaurants ashore, reservations may be required, you may also have to wait in line at busy periods, and occupants of the most expensive suites get priority.

Aboard large resort ships (1,750-plus passengers) the big evening entertainment shows typically are staged twice each evening, so you end up with the equivalent of two-seating dining anyway.

What is specialty dining?

Mass-market dining isn't to everyone's taste, so some ships now have alternative dining spots other than the main restaurant. These à la carte restaurants usually cost extra – typically between $15 and $75 a person – but the food quality, preparation, and presentation are decidedly better, as is service and ambience. You may need to make a reservation.

What's the minimum age for drinking alcohol?

Aboard most ships based in the US and Canada, the minimum drinking age is 21. However, for ships based throughout the rest of the world, it is generally 18. But you should always check with your chosen cruise line.

15 things not included in 'all-inclusive'
1. Dining in extra-cost restaurants
2. Premium (vintage) wines
3. Specialty ice creams
4. Specialty teas and coffees
5. Wine tastings/seminars
6. Internet and Wi-Fi access
7. Spa treatments
8. Some fitness classes
9. Personal training instruction
10. Use of steam room/saunas
11. Laundry, pressing, and dry-cleaning
12. Personal shopping
13. Professional souvenir photographs
14. Casino gaming
15. Medical services

How expensive are drinks?

Most US-based cruise lines see drinks, both alcoholic and non-alcoholic, as a huge source of revenue. As an example, drinks aboard Royal Caribbean International-al's *Independence of the Seas* when it is based in the UK during the summer are at least twice the cost of those aboard the UK-based ships of Fred. Olsen Cruise Lines, P&O Cruises, and Saga Cruises.

Do ships have room service?

While most cruise ships provide free 24-hour room service, some ships charge a delivery fee for things like food and beverages, including tea and coffee. A menu of room service items can be found in your cabin. However, aboard sail-cruise ships such as those of Sea Cloud Cruises or Star Clippers, there's no room service, nor do riverships have room service.

Most ships have free 24-hour room service, but if you occupy suite-grade accommodation, you may get things like afternoon tea trolley service and evening canapés – at no extra cost. Some ships may offer room service specialties like a Champagne breakfast, at an extra cost (Louis Cruises, Princess Cruises, for example).

Can I bring my own booze on board?

No, at least not aboard the major cruise lines, who will confiscate it. But some smaller lines turn a blind eye if you want to bring your favorite wine or spirit on board for in-cabin consumption.

Do ships still serve bouillon on sea days?

Some ships carry on the tradition of serving or making bouillon available at 11am each sea day. Examples include the ships of Cunard Line, Discovery Cruises, Fred. Olsen Cruise Lines, Hapag-Lloyd Cruises, Hebridean Island Cruises, P&O Cruises, Phoenix Reisen, and Saga Cruises.

Do all ships have proper dance floors?

For social dancing, a properly 'sprung' wood floor is the best for social (ballroom) dancing. However, most of the newest cruise ships have marble floors – if there is any dance space at all (except for a disco). Ships with really good, large wooden dance floors: *Aurora, Oriana, Queen Elizabeth, Queen Mary 2, Queen Victoria, Saga Sapphire.*

Do all ships have swimming pools?

There's no standard size, but all large resorts ships have swimming pools (none are Olympic-size – most are a maximum of just over 56 ft (17m) long and 19.6 ft (6m) wide), because they are usually located on one of the uppermost decks of a ship. – for stability – and ocean crossings, often in poor weather conditions.

Some ships have multi-pool complexes that include water slides (examples: *Allure of the Seas, Norwegian Breakaway, Norwegian Epic,* and *Oasis of the Seas*). Some ships have 'infinity' pools on an aft deck, so when you swim or take a dip it looks like you're one with the sea (*MSC Divina* and*MSC*

Carnival Freedom sailing away from Venice, Italy.

Poolside movie screens adorn large resort ships, like *Carnival Destiny* (now *Carnival Sunshine*).

Preziosa), and some have rentable poolside cabanas for more exclusivity.

Some ships have completely separate adult-only, family pools and toddler pools (*Disney Dream, Disney Magic, Disney Fantasy,* and *Disney Wonder*). The family-friendly large resort ships usually have separate pools and tubs for children in different age groups located within a children-only zone, or a water park with great water-slide and flume-like experiences.

Some ships have pools that can be covered by a retractable glass dome (useful in case of inclement weather); some ships have only open-air pools, yet trade in cold weather areas in winter. A few ships have heated pools (examples include *Freedom of the Seas, Independence of the Seas, Liberty of the Seas,* and *Saga Sapphire*).

While most pools are outside, some ships also have indoor pools set low down in the ship, so the water doesn't move about when the sea conditions are unkind (examples include *Astor, Deutschland,* and *Saga Sapphire*).

Some of the smaller ships have only a 'dip' pool – just big enough to cool off in on hot days, while others may have hot tubs and no pool.

Note that when there is inclement weather, swimming pools are emptied to avoid the water sloshing around.

Do all ships have fresh water pools?

All the ships of Disney Cruise Line and most of the large resort ships (such as *Allure of the Seas* and *Oasis of the Seas*) have freshwater pools. Some ships, however, do have saltwater pools (the water for the pools being drawn from the sea, and filtered.

How are swimming pools kept clean?

All shipboard swimming pools have chlorine (a member of the residual halogen group) added (a minimum of 1.0-3.0 ppm in recirculated swimming pools), while some have chemically treated saltwater pools. Pools are regularly checked for water flow rates, pH balance, alkalinity, and clarity – all of which are entered into a daily log.

Do any ships have walk-in pools (instead of steps)?

Not many, because of space considerations, although they can often be useful for older passengers. Some examples: *Aurora, Crystal Serenity, Crystal Symphony,* and *Oriana*.

What's the difference between an outside and an interior cabin?

An 'outside' (or 'exterior') cabin has a window (or porthole) with a view of the outside, or there is a private balcony for you physically to be – or look – outside. An 'interior' (or 'inside') cabin means that it doesn't have a view of the outside, but it will have artwork or curtains on one wall instead of a window or patio-like (balcony) door.

Should I tip for room service?

No. It's part of the normal onboard duties that the hotel staff are paid to carry out. Watch out for staff aboard the large resort ships saying that they don't always get the tips that are 'automatically added' to onboard accounts – it's a ploy to get you to tip them more in cash.

Do cruise ships vibrate?

Ships built before 1990 sometimes suffer from vibration, usually at the stern; it is usually during slow-speed maneuvering. Anyone occupying a cabin on the lowest decks at the stern is likely to be affected most. Vibration-free cruising is almost guaranteed aboard ships that have the latest 'pod' propulsion system fitted.

Can I visit the bridge?
Usually not – for insurance and security reasons – and never when the ship is maneuvering into and out of port. But some companies, such as Celebrity Cruises, Cunard Line, NCL, and Princess Cruises, run extra-cost 'Behind the Scenes' tours. The cost varies between $120 and $150 per person.

Can I bring golf clubs?
Yes, you can. However, although cruise lines do not charge for carrying them, some airlines do – worth checking if you have to fly to join your cruise because the 'budget' airlines charge a fortune. Some ships cater for golfers with mini-golf courses on deck and electronically monitored practice areas.

Golf-themed cruises are popular, with 'all-in' packages allowing participants to play on some of the world's most desirable courses. Hapag-Lloyd Cruises and Silversea Cruises, for example, operate a number of golf-themed sailings each year, and if you take your own clubs, they will provide storage space and arrange everything.

Do mobile phones work on board?
Most cruise lines have contracts with maritime phone service companies. Mobile phone signals piggyback off systems that transmit Internet data via satellite. When your ship is in port, the ship's network may be switched off and you will pay the going local (country-specific) rate for mobile calls if you can manage to access a local network.

Keeping in touch with children's whereabouts on a big resort ship can be expensive using mobile phones. Instead, use two-way radio transceivers (walkie-talkies); at sea they won't interfere with any public-service radio frequency.

Can I send and receive emails?
Aboard most ships, e-mail facilities have now been added to some degree. Many ships have Wi-Fi, for a fee, allowing you to connect your own laptop. Several ships have an Internet café or Internet-connect center. Note that connections and downloads are often very slow compared to land-based services (shipboard e-mails link through satellite systems, and are therefore more expensive than land-based connections). Attachments are not generally allowed. For many cruise companies, e-mail has now become an important revenue generator.

Where can I watch movies?
Some – but not many – ships have a dedicated movie theater. The movies are provided by a licensed film distribution or leasing service. Many newer ships have replaced or supplemented the movie theater with TV sets and DVD players in cabins, or with giant poolside screens for 24-hour viewing.

Do all cabins have flat-screen TV sets?
No. some older cruise ships still have bulky CRT sets, but these are replaced when a ship goes for refurbishment. The latest ships have flat-screen TVs, which take up much less space.

Can I take an iron to use in my cabin?
No. However, some ships have self-service launderettes, which include an ironing area. Check with your cruise line.

What is expedition cruising?
Expedition cruises are operated by specialists such as Quark Expeditions, using small ships that have ice-strengthened hulls or with specially constructed ice-breakers that enable them to reach areas totally inaccessible to 'normal' cruise ships. The ships are usually converted to carry passengers in some degree of basic comfort, with comfortable accommodation and a relaxed, informal atmosphere, with expert lecturers and expedition leaders accompanying every cruise.

What is a Panamax ship?
This is one that conforms to the maximum dimensions possible for passage through the Panama Canal – useful particularly for around-the-world voyages. These dimensions are: 965ft (294m) long, with a beam of 106ft (32m); or below approximately 90,000 gross tonnage. Because of the locks, the 50-mile (80-km) journey takes from eight to nine hours. Most large resort cruise ships (examples: *Carnival Dream, Celebrity Reflection, MSC Preziosa, Queen Mary 2, Royal*

Crystal Symphony passes through the Panama Canal.

Princess) are too big to go through the Panama Canal, and are classed as 'post-Panamax' ships – at least until 2015, when a new, large lock is scheduled to open.

Can I shop in ports of call?
Many passengers embrace retail therapy when visiting ports of call such as Dubai, Hong Kong, Singapore, St Maarten, and St Thomas, among many others. However, it's prudent to exercise self-control. Remember that you'll have to carry all those purchases home at the end of your cruise.

Do I have to go ashore in each port?
Absolutely not. In fact, many passengers enjoy being aboard 'their' ships when there are virtually no other passengers aboard. Also, if you have a spa treatment, it could be less expensive during this period than when the ship is at sea; some ships, such as *Queen Mary 2*, have price differentials for sea days and port days.

Do I need to bring my own beach towels?
No. Cruise ships have plenty of towels for both shipboard and shore use – but you'll be charged if you don't return them.

Can I fly in the day before or stay an extra day after the cruise?
Cruise lines often offer pre- and post-cruise stay packages at an additional cost. The advantage is that you

Europa provides free bicycles for passengers.

don't have to do anything else – all will be taken care of, as they say. If you book a hotel on your own, however, you may have to pay an 'air deviation' fee if you don't take the cruise line's air arrangements or you want to change them.

Should I book early?
The farther ahead you book, the better the discount. You'll get the cabin you want, in the location you want, and you may even be upgraded. When you book close to the sailing date, you may get a low price, but you probably won't get the cabin or location you'd like, or – worse still – in ships with two seatings for dinner, you won't be able to choose early or late seating.

What legal rights do I have?
Almost none! After reading a cruise line's Passenger Ticket Contract, you'll see why. A 189-word sentence in one contract begins 'The Carrier shall not be liable for …' and goes on to cover the legal waterfront.

What are the downsides to cruising?
Much-anticipated ports of call can be aborted or changed due to poor weather or other conditions. Some popular ports (particularly in the Caribbean) can become extremely crowded – there can be up to 12 ships in St Thomas, or six in St Maarten at the same time, disgorging 20,000 people.

Many frequent irritations could be fixed if the cruise lines really tried. Entertainment, for instance, whether production shows or cabaret acts, is always linked to dinner times. Also, many aggressive, young, so-called 'cruise directors' insist on interposing themselves into every part of your cruise, day and night, through the public address system.

Where did all the money go?
Apart from the cruise fare itself, incidentals could include government taxes, port charges, air ticket tax, and fuel surcharges. On board, extra costs may include drinks, mini-bar items, cappuccino and espresso coffees, shore excursions (especially those involving flightseeing tours), Internet access, sending or receiving e-mail, beauty treatments, casino gaming, photographs, laundry and dry-cleaning, babysitting services, wine tasting, bottled water placed in your cabin, and medical services.

A cruise aboard a ship belonging to a major cruise line could be compared to buying a car, whereby motor manufacturers offer a basic model at a set price, and then tempt you with optional extras to inflate the cost. Cruise lines say income generated on board helps to keep the basic cost of a cruise reasonable. In the end, it's up to your self-restraint to keep those little extras from mounting up to a very large sum.

Does a ship's registry (flag state) matter?
Not really. Some years ago, cruise ships used to be registered in their country of operation. For example,

Italian Line ships (with all-Italian crews) would be registered only in Italy, and Greek ships (with all-Greek crews) would be registered only in Greece.

To avoid prohibition, some American-owned ships were re-registered to Panama. Thus was born the flag of convenience (now called the 'Flag State').

Today's ships no longer have single-nationality crews, so where a ship is registered is not of such great importance. Cunard Line and P&O Cruises ships, for example, are now registered in Bermuda so that weddings can be performed on board.

Today, the most popular flag registries are (in alphabetical order) the Bahamas, Bermuda, Italy, Japan, Malta, Marshall Islands, Panama, and The Netherlands. This fragmented authority means that all cruise ships come under the IMO (International Maritime Organization, within the United Nations) when operating in international waters – 12 nautical miles from shore. A country (such as the United States, for example) only has authority over the ship when it is either in a US port or within 12 nautical miles offshore.

How are ships weighed?

They aren't. They are measured. Gross tonnage is a measurement of the enclosed space within a ship's hull and superstructure (1 gross ton = 100 cubic ft).

Is anyone building a cruise ship powered by liquefied natural gas?

Not yet, but the possibility of powering a cruise ship using LNG has been under consideration for several years. One or two companies, however, are getting close. There's already one nuclear-powered cruise vessel: the Russian Arctic expedition ship *50 Years of Victory,* which debuted in 2008.

How long do cruise ships last?

In general, a very long time. For example, during the *QE2*'s almost-40-year service for Cunard Line, the ship sailed more than 5½ million nautical miles, carried 2½ million passengers, completed 25 full world cruises, and crossed the Atlantic more than 800 times. But *QE2* was built with a very thick hull, whereas today's thin-hulled cruise ships probably won't last so long. Even so, the life expectancy is typically a healthy 30 years.

Where do old cruise ships go when they're scrapped?

They go to the beach. Actually, they are driven at speed onto a not very nice beach at Alang in India, or to Chittagong in Bangladesh, or to Pan Yo in China – the main shipbreaking places. Greenpeace has claimed that workers, including children, at some sites have to work under primitive conditions without adequate equipment to protect them against the toxic materials that can be released into the environment. In 2009, a new IMO guideline – 'International Convention for the Safe and Environmentally Sound Recycling of Ships' – was adopted.

Ships with a shallow draft, such as *Hanseatic*, can get surprisingly close to shore.

Will I get seasick?

Today's ships have stabilizers – large underwater 'fins' on each side of the hull – to counteract any rolling motion, and most cruises are in warm, calm waters. As a result, fewer than 3 percent of passengers become seasick. Yet it's possible to develop some symptoms – anything from slight nausea to vomiting.

Both old-time sailors and modern physicians have their own remedies, and you can take your choice or try them all (just not all at the same time). When you notice the first movement of a ship, walk back and forth on the deck. You will find that your knees will start getting their feel of balance and counteraction.

Get the sea breeze into your face (arguably the best antidote) and, if nauseous, suck an orange or a lemon.

Eat lightly. Don't make the mistake of thinking a heavy meal will keep your stomach anchored. It won't.

When on deck, focus on a steady point, such as the horizon.

Dramamine (dimenhydrinate, an antihistamine and sedative introduced just after World War II) will be available aboard in tablet (chewable) form. A stronger version (Meclazine) is available on prescription (brand names: Antivert, Antrizine, Bonine, Meni-D). Ciba-Geigy's Scopoderm (or Transderm Scop), known as 'The Patch,' contains scopolamine and has proven effective. Possible side effects are dry mouth, blurred vision, drowsiness, and problems with urinating.

If you are really distressed, the ship's doctor can give you, at extra cost, an injection to alleviate discomfort. It may make you drowsy, but the last thing on your mind will be staying awake during the movie.

A natural preventive is ginger in powder form. Mix half a teaspoon in a glass of warm water or milk, and drink it before sailing. This is said to settle any stomach for up to eight hours.

'Sea Bands' are a drug-free method of controlling motion sickness. These are slim bands (in varying colors) that are wrapped around the wrist, with a circular 'button' that presses against the acupressure point

Pericardium 6 (nei kuan) on the lower arm. Attach them a few minutes before you step aboard and wear on both wrists throughout the cruise.

Another drug-free remedy can be found in Reletex, a watch-like device worn on the wrist. First used for patients undergoing chemotherapy, it emits a small neuromodulating current that stops peristaltic waves in the stomach causing nausea and vomiting.

Is having hay fever a problem?

People who suffer from hay fever and pollen allergies benefit greatly from a cruise. Almost all sufferers I have met say that their problems simply disappear on a ship – particularly when it is at sea.

Are hygiene standards high enough?

News reports often focus on hygiene and sanitation aboard cruise ships. In the 1980s, the North American cruise industry agreed with the Centers for Disease Control (CDC) that hygiene and sanitation inspections should be carried out once or twice yearly aboard all cruise ships carrying American passengers, and the Vessel Sanitation Program (VSP) was born. The original intention of the VSP was to achieve and maintain a level of sanitation that would lower the risk of gastro-intestinal disease outbreaks and assist the cruise industry to provide a healthy environment for passengers and crew.

It is a voluntary inspection, and cruise lines pay handsomely for each one. For a ship the size of *Queen Mary 2*, for example, the cost would be about $15,000; for a ship the size of *Azamara Journey*, it would be about $7,800. However, the inspection points are accepted by the international cruise industry as a good system. Inspections cover two main areas: 1) Water sanitation, including free chlorine residuals in the potable water system, swimming pool, and hot tub filters; and 2) Food sanitation: food storage, preparation, and serving areas, including bars and passenger service pantries.

The ships score extremely well – the ones that undergo inspections, that is. Some ships that don't call on US ports would possibly not pass the inspections every time. Older ships with outdated galley equipment and poor food storage facilities would have a harder time complying with the United States Public Health (USPH) inspection standards. Some other countries also have strict health inspection standards. However, if the same USPH inspection standards were applied to restaurants and hotels ashore (in the USA), it is estimated that at least 95 percent or more would fail, *consistently*.

What about the norovirus?

This temporary but highly contagious condition occurs worldwide. Humans are the only known hosts, and only the common cold is reported more frequently than viral gastroenteritis as a cause of illness in the USA. About 23 million Americans each year are diagnosed with the effects of the Norwalk-like virus (NLV gastroenteritis, sometimes known as winter vomiting virus or norovirus). It is more prevalent in adults and older children than in the very young.

Water can also be a common source of outbreaks – water aboard cruise ships stored in tanks, etc. A mild and brief illness typically occurs 24 to 48 hours after contaminated food or water has been consumed, and lasts for 24 to 72 hours. If you board a large resort ship after norovirus has struck, bread and bread rolls, butter, and salt and pepper shakers may not be placed on tables, but will be available on request during meals.

When an outbreak occurs, a cruise line will immediately sanitize the entire ship and will usually confine

Bars and restaurants are smoke-free, as aboard MSC *Fantasia*.

affected passengers to their cabins to stop the condition spreading. Hand gel dispensers are provided at the entrance to all eateries. Crew members and their livelihoods can also be affected, so they will want to get any outbreak under control as quickly as possible.

Are incidents on the rise? Yes, but so is the number of cruise ships and riverships. Should cruise lines pay compensation? I don't think so. In my experience, almost all outbreaks have occurred because someone has brought the condition with them from ashore.

What do ships do about garbage?
The newest ships are models of recycling. Items such as used cooking oil, for example, is turned into biodiesel. Garbage is sorted into dry and wet garbage, and the dry garbage is burned on board or compacted for offloading in selected ports. Aluminum cans, for instance, are offloaded for recycling. As for sewage, ships must be three nautical miles from land before they can dump treated sewage and 12 miles for untreated sewage and food waste.

Where is smoking allowed?
Some cruise lines allow smoking in cabins, while others permit it only in cabins with balconies. Some, such as P&O Cruises (Australia), place a notice in each cabin advising passengers: 'A $300 cleaning fee will be added to your onboard account if we find evidence of smoking in your cabin.' But it does allow smoking on balconies.

Almost all cruise lines prohibit smoking in restaurants and food service areas; almost no ships have smoking sections in dining rooms. Most ships now allow smoking only on the open decks. But that means when non-smokers are sunbathing on an open deck the person next to them can light up.

What about cigars?
Cigar-smoking lounges are found aboard *Adventure of the Seas, Amadea, Artania, Asuka II, Brilliance of the Seas, Crystal Serenity, Crystal Symphony, Europa, Europa 2, Explorer of the Seas, Freedom of the Seas, Grand Mistral, Independence of the Seas, Liberty of the Seas, Mariner of the Seas, MSC Armonia, MSC Divina, MSC Fantasia, MSC Lirica, MSC Magnifica, MSC Musica, MSC Opera, MSC Orchestra, MSC Poesia, MSC Preziosa, MSC Sinfonia, MSC Splendida, Navigator of the*

10 ways to manage onboard spending
1. Plan spa treatments for days when the ship is in port.
2. Buy a soda package only if you drink a lot of sodasy.
3. Check anything you sign for on board.
4. Say no to souvenir glasses that come with your cocktail.
5. Say no to extra-cost name-brand ice creams at the pool.
6. Don't use your cell phone except for emergencies.
7. Don't pay extra to access the Internet.
8. Don't use the ship's (extra-charge) laundry service.
9. Be selective about hiring water-sports gear.
10. Use a debit card for payment of your onboard account.

Gaming table chips.

Seas, Norwegian Breakaway, Norwegian Dawn, Norwegian Epic, Norwegian Gem, Norwegian Jewel, Norwegian Pearl, Norwegian Star, Norwegian Sun, Queen Elizabeth, Queen Mary 2, Queen Victoria, Radiance of the Seas, Seabourn Odyssey, Seabourn Quest, Seabourn Sojourn, Serenade of the Seas, Seven Seas Mariner, Seven Seas Voyager, Silver Shadow, Silver Spirit, Silver Whisper, SuperStar Virgo, and *Voyager of the Seas.*

Ships starting or ending their cruises in a United States port are not permitted to carry genuine Cuban cigars. Instead, most cigars will be made in the Dominican Republic. Remember that, if you smoke a cigar in a ship's dedicated cigar lounge, the air purification system will often not be effective enough if someone comes in to smoke a cigarette, and you may suffer the consequences of inhaling second-hand cigarette smoke.

Do accidents happen aboard ship?
Broken bones seem to be the most common, the result of passengers stumbling on stairways. In 2012, a 47-year-old woman died aboard Royal Caribbean International's *Liberty of the Seas* when she fell down a short flight of stairs. Also in 2012, a 26-year-old man died aboard Carnival Cruise Lines' *Carnival Fantasy*. He fell from an upper level in the ship's nine-deck-high atrium to the lobby floor below while the ship was docked in Nassau late one evening. It was thought he had been trying to jump from one deck to another. Both of these were highly unusual occurrences.

Have there been murders during a cruise?
Generally, violent crime is much less common on a cruise than during land-based vacations, but there have been a few suspicious deaths, and a number of passengers have gone missing, mainly in the Caribbean and on Mexican Riviera cruises. A small number have been thrown over a balcony by another passenger, typically after an alcohol-fueled argument.

One problem with violence on board is that if the alleged crime happens at sea, the jurisdiction responsible for investigating will depend on the ship's registry, so a policeman may need to be whistled up from some distant place.

Choosing Your Destination

Cruise lines visit around 2,000 destinations, from the Caribbean to Antarctica, from the Mediterranean to the Baltic, and from Northern Europe to the South Pacific.

Where can I go on a cruise? As the saying goes: the world is your oyster! There are more than 30,000 different cruises to choose from each year, and about 2,000 cruise destinations in the world. A cruise can also take you to places inaccessible by almost any other means, such as Antarctica, the North Cape, or the South Sea islands.

Itineraries vary widely, so it is wise to make as many comparisons as you can by reading the cruise brochures for descriptions of the ports of call. Several ships may offer the same or similar itineraries simply because these have been tried and tested. Narrow the choice by noting the time spent at each port (few ships stay overnight in port) and whether the ship docks in port or lies at anchor – it can take time to get ashore by the tender.

Caribbean cruises

There are more than 7,000 islands in the Caribbean Sea, although many are small or uninhabited. Caribbean cruises are usually destination-intensive, cramming between four and eight ports into one week, depend-

Castaway Cay, Disney's private island in the Bahamas.

ing on whether you sail from a Florida port or from a port already in the Caribbean, such as Barbados or San Juan. This means you could be visiting at least one port a day, with little time at sea for relaxation. Although you may see several places in a week, by the end of the cruise you might need another week to unwind.

June 10 to November 30 is the official Atlantic hurricane season in the Caribbean (including Bermuda and the Bahamas) and Florida. Cruise ships can change course quickly to avoid weather problems, which can also mean a change of ports or itinerary. When that happens, cruise lines will generally not offer compensation, nor will travel insurance providers.

Geographically, the Caribbean region is large enough to be split into sections: eastern, western, and southern.

Eastern Caribbean. Cruises sail to the Leeward and Windward Islands, and might include calls at Antigua, Barbados, Dominica, Martinique, Puerto Rico, St Croix, St Kitts, St Maarten, St Lucia, and St Thomas.

Western Caribbean. Cruises sail to the Cayman Islands, Mexico, and Jamaica, and might call at Calica, Cozumel, Grand Cayman, Grand Turk, Playa del Carmen, Ocho Rios, and Roatan Island.

Southern Caribbean. Cruises might call at Antigua, the Netherlands Antilles (Aruba, Bonaire, Curaçao), Barbados, La Guaira (Venezuela), Tortola, and San Juan.

Private islands

Several cruise lines with Bahamas/Caribbean itineraries feature a 'private island' (also called an 'outisland'). NCL pioneered the trend when it bought a former military outpost in 1977, and it is currently spending $22 million to upgrade its facilities. Disney Cruise Line recently spent $13 million on upgrading and expanding its facilities – Disney's Castaway Cay has separate areas for adults and families with children, and is the only private island which permits its ships can berth alongside, so passengers do not have to take a tender to go ashore. Disney's private island is the only one which permits its ships can berth alongside, so passengers do not have to take a tender to go ashore.

These islands, usually leased from the owning governments, have all that's needed for an all-day beach party – water sports, scuba, snorkeling, crystal-clear waters, warm sands, even a hammock or two, and, possibly, massage in a beach cabana. There are no reservations to make, no tickets to buy, no hassles with taxis. But you may be sharing your private island with more than 5,000 others from a single large resort ship anchored for a 'beach day.'

Such beach days are not all-inclusive, however, and command premium prices for things like snorkel gear and mandatory swim vest, rental pleasure craft, 'banana' boat fun rides, floating beach mats, private waterfront cabanas for the day, sunfish sailboat rental, floating foam mattresses, and hammock rental. Rent a cabana (example; Cabanas on the Cay at NCL's Great Stirrup Cay beach day) with deck and sunbeds for the day (around $300), and you even get 'butler' service, with lunch and drinks.

One bonus is that such an island will not be cluttered with hawkers and hustlers, as are so many Caribbean beaches. And, because they are private, there is security, and no fear of being mugged, as occurs in some islands. Reality can intrude, however, as it did in Royal Caribbean International's private resort of Labadee in Haiti when it narrowly escaped the devastating 2010 earthquake.

Alaska cruises

These are especially popular because Alaska is a vast, relatively unexplored region. Cruise ships offer the best way to see the state's magnificent shoreline and glaciers. There is a wide range of shore excursions, including many floatplane and helicopter tours, some going to glaciers and salmon fisheries. There are many excursions, including 'dome car' rail journeys to Denali National Park to see North America's highest peak, Mt McKinley.

Pre- and post-cruise journeys to Banff and Jasper National Parks can be made from Vancouver.

There are two popular cruise routes: **The Inside Passage Route,** a 1,000-mile (1,600-km) stretch of protected waterways carved by Ice Age glaciers. This usually includes visits to tidewater glaciers, such as those in Glacier Bay's Hubbard Glacier or Tracy Arm (just two of the 15 active glaciers along the bay's 60-mile/100-km coastline). Glacier Bay was established in 1986 as a biosphere reserve, and in 1992 the 3.3-million-acre (1.3-million-hectare) park became a World Heritage Site. Typical ports of call might include Juneau, Ketchikan, Skagway, and Haines. **The Glacier Route** usually includes the Gulf of Alaska during a one-way cruise between Vancouver and Anchorage. Typical ports of call might include Seward, Sitka, and Valdez.

Holland America Line and Princess Cruises own many facilities in Alaska (hotels, tour buses, even trains), and between them have invested more than $300 million in the state. Indeed, Holland America Line-Westours is Alaska's largest private employer. Both companies take in excess of 250,000 passengers to Alaska each year. Other lines depend on what's left of the local transportation for their land tours.

In ports where docking space is limited, some ships anchor rather than dock. Many cruise brochures do not indicate which ports are known to be anchor (tender) ports.

With around 930,000 cruise passengers a year visiting Alaska and several large resort ships likely to be in port on any given day, there's so much congestion in many of the small ports that avoiding crowded streets can be difficult. Even nature is retreating; with more people around, wildlife is harder to spot. And many of the same shops are now found in Alaska as well as in the Caribbean.

The more adventurous might consider one of the more unusual Alaska cruises to the far north, around the Pribilof Islands (superb for bird-watching) and into the Bering Sea.

Alaska isn't always good-weather cruising – it can be wet and windy and excursions may be canceled or changed. Even if it's sunny in port, glaciers have their own weather systems and helicopter flightseeing excursions are vulnerable. Take an Alaska cruise in May or August, when it gets darker earlier, for the best chance of seeing the Northern Lights.

Greenland cruises

The world's largest island, the inappropriately named Greenland, in the Arctic Circle, is 82 percent covered with ice – actually compressed snow – up to 11,000ft (3,350m) thick. Its rocks are among the world's oldest, yet its ecosystem is one of the newest.

The glacier at Jacobshavn, also known as Ilulissat, is the world's fastest moving and creates a new iceberg every five minutes. Greenland, which was granted home rule by Denmark in 1978, makes its living from fishing. It is said to have more dogs than people – its population is 68,400 – and dogs are an important means of transport.

Iceland cruises

Iceland is located just south of the Arctic Circle. Cruising around Iceland and her fjords is akin to tracing Viking legends across the land of fire and ice. Towns are built on lava fields, and it is not uncommon to witness some volcanic eruption somewhere.

Geysers, lava fields, ice sheets, hot springs, fjords, inlets, remote coastal stretches, waterfalls, snow-clad peaks, and the towering icebergs of Jokulsarlon can all be part of an Icelandic adventure cruise.

Canada/New England cruises

These 10–14 day cruises travel between New York or Boston and Montreal (northbound and southbound). Ports of call may include Boston; Québec City, Québec; Charlottetown, Prince Edward Island; Sydney and Halifax, Nova Scotia; Bar Harbor, Maine; and Saguenay, Québec.

The ideal time to sail is during the fall, when the leaves dramatically change color. Shorter five-to-seven day cruises – usually from New York or Boston – go north to take in the fall foliage.

European and Mediterranean cruises

Traveling within Europe (including the Aegean, Baltic, Black Sea, Mediterranean, and Norwegian fjord areas) by cruise ship makes economic sense. Although no single cruise covers every port, cruise ships do offer a comfortable way of exploring a rich mix of destinations, cultures, history, architecture, lifestyles, and cuisines – and without having to pack and unpack each day.

European cruises have become increasingly popular because so many of Europe's major cities – Amsterdam, Athens, Barcelona, Copenhagen, Dubrovnik, Genoa, Helsinki, Lisbon, London, Monte Carlo, Nice, Oslo, St Petersburg, Stockholm, and Venice – are on the water. It is far less expensive to take a cruise than to fly and stay in decent hotels, paying extra for food and transport. You will not have to try to speak or understand different languages when you are aboard ship as you would ashore – if you choose the right ship. Aboard ship you use a single currency – typically US dollars, British pounds, or euros. A wide variety of shore excursions are offered. Lecture programs provide insights into a culture before you step ashore.

Who goes where

This is a selection of just some of the cruise companies that operate cruises regularly in the world's most popular cruise regions. These are not recommendations but rather suggestions to help you research what's right for you.

Caribbean
Carnival Cruise Lines, Celebrity Cruises, Disney Cruise Line, Holland America Line, Norwegian Cruise Line, Oceania Cruises, Princess Cruises, Regent Seven Seas Cruises, Royal Caribbean International, SeaDream Yacht Club, Star Clippers, Windstar Cruises

Alaska
American Safari Cruises, Celebrity Cruises, Crystal Cruises, Holland America Line, Lindblad Expeditions, InnerSea Discoveries, Norwegian Cruise Line, Oceania Cruises, Princess Cruises, Regent Seven Seas Cruises, Royal Caribbean International, Silversea Cruises

Polar Expeditions (Arctic/Antarctic)
Aurora Expeditions, Gap Adventures, Hapag-Lloyd Expedition Cruises, Heritage Expeditions, Lindblad Expeditions, Oceanwide Expeditions, Quark Expeditions, Orion Expedition Cruises, Poseidon Arctic Adventures, Silversea Cruises, Zegrahm Expeditions

Baltic/Northern Europe
Azamara Cruises, Crystal Cruises, Cunard Line, Fred. Olsen Cruise Lines, Hapag-Lloyd Cruises, Oceania Cruises, P&O Cruises, Phoenix Reisen, Saga Cruises, Swan Hellenic Cruises, Voyages of Discovery

Greenland/Iceland
Fred. Olsen Cruise Lines, Hurtigruten, Lindblad Expeditions, Saga Cruises

Mediterranean
AIDA Cruises, Azamara Club Cruises, Celebrity Cruises, Costa Cruises, Cunard Line, MSC Cruises, Oceania Cruises, P&O Cruises, Princess Cruises, Pullmantur Cruises, Regent Seven Seas Cruises, Saga Cruises, SeaDream Yacht Club, Seabourn, Silversea Cruises, Star Clippers, Swan Hellenic Cruises, Thomson Cruises, TUI Cruises, Voyages of Discovery, Windstar Cruises

Greek Islands
Louis Cruises, Noble Caledonia, Oceania Cruises, Swan Hellenic Cruises, Voyages of Discovery, Voyages to Antiquity

Around Britain
Cunard Line, Fred. Olsen Cruise Lines, P&O Cruises, Saga Cruises, Seabourn, Silversea Cruises, Voyages of Discovery

Canary Islands
Fred. Olsen Cruise Lines, P&O Cruises, TUI Cruises

Middle East
AIDA Cruises, Costa Cruises, Hapag-Lloyd Cruises, Noble Caledonia, Phoenix Reisen, Swan Hellenic Cruises, TUI Cruises

Indian Ocean
Hapag-Lloyd Cruises, Phoenix Reisen, Ponant Cruises

South America
Celebrity Cruises, Costa Cruises, Crystal Cruises, Holland America Line, MSC Cruises, Oceania Cruises, Princess Cruises, Regent Seven Seas Cruises, Silversea Cruises

Great Lakes (USA)
Noble Caledonia, Ponant Cruises, Travel Dynamics International

New England/Canada
Celebrity Cruises, Crystal Cruises, Holland America Line, Oceania Cruises, Princess Cruises, Regent Seven Seas Cruises

Australia/New Zealand
Celebrity Cruises, Cunard Line, Orion Expedition Cruises, P&O Cruises (Australia), Orion Expedition Cruises, Princess Cruises, Royal Caribbean International

Southeast Asia
Crystal Cruises, Asuka Cruise, Oceania Cruises, Seabourn, Silversea Cruises, Star Cruises/Genting Hong Kong

South Pacific
Paul Gauguin Cruises, P&O Cruises (Australia), Oceania Cruises, Princess Cruises

South Africa
MSC Cruises, plus several cruise lines operating around-the-world cruises

Transatlantic Crossings
Cunard Line

Small ships are arguably better than large resort ships, as they can obtain berthing space – the large resort ships may have to anchor in more of the smaller ports, so it can take time to get to and from shore, and you'll probably have to wait for shore tender tickets. Many Greek islands are accessible only by shore tender. Some companies allow more time ashore than others, so compare itineraries in the brochures; it's probably best to choose a regional cruise line (such as Louis Cruises) for these destination-intensive cruises, for example.

The Baltic and Northern capitals cruises

A Baltic and Northern capitals cruise is an excellent way to see several countries in a week or so, and enjoy different architecture, cultures, cuisines, history, and stunning scenery. The season for most cruises to this region runs from May to September, when the weather really is at its best.

Copenhagen, Stockholm (the entry through the archipelago is awash with islands and country cottages), Helsinki, Tallinn, and an overnight stay in the treasure chest city of St Petersburg – for many the highlight of the cruise – with its sumptuous architecture, palaces, and, of course, the Hermitage Museum. Most ships include at least one overnight stay so you can also take in a ballet or circus performance.

Norwegian fjords cruises

These cruises usually include a visit to Bergen, and perhaps a tram ride to the peak of Mount Floyen, and the stunning views over the city and harbor. A highlight could be a visit to Troldhaugen in Bergen – the stunning home (and now a museum) of Edvard Grieg, Norway's most famous composer.

However, it's the sheer scenic beauty of cruising through fjords like Eidfjord, Geiranger, Hardangerfjord, and Sognefjord that inspires the traveller. Typical stops will be made at Bergen, Flam, Olden, Alesund, and Oslo.

Around Britain cruises

Traveling around the British Isles by cruise ship provides a unique perspective. The major sights – and some unexpected gems – of England, Scotland, Wales, the Republic of Ireland, and Northern Ireland can be covered in a single cruise that typically lasts 10–14 days. Because the British Isles are compact – Great Britain actually consists of over 1,000 islands – the actual time at sea is quite short. But the range of experiences is vast: the turquoise waters off the Scilly Isles and the coast of Cornwall in England's southwest; the northern highlights in Scotland's more remote, nature-rich islands; the laid-back lifestyle of Ireland and the charm and distinctive voices of Wales, not to mention towering castles, incredible gardens, the England of Shakespeare, and, of course, the coastline itself.

Canary Islands cruises

The sun-kissed Islas Canarias, a Spanish archipelago and the outermost region of the European Union, are located just off the northwest coast of mainland Africa – they are actually closer to Africa than Europe. With a year-round temperature of 70 degrees Fahrenheit (21 degrees Celsius) provide a fine setting for a winter escape.

The islands of Gran Canaria, Tenerife, Lanzarote, Fuerteventura, and Hierro make up the itinerary of most cruises to the region.

A Canary Islands cruise usually includes a call at Funchal on the Portuguese island of Madeira. You should head to Ponta de São Lourenço for some of the island's most stunning views. Some cruises may also include a stop at Agadir in Morocco.

Middle East cruises

The Middle East cruise region includes the Arab countries bordering the Arabian and Red seas, and the southeastern Mediterranean. Countries with cruise facilities and places of historic interest are: Bahrain, Egypt, Iran (one of the author's favorite shore excursions was to the ancient site of Persepolis, near Shiraz), Jordan, Oman, Qatar, Yemen, and the seven sheikdoms – the governing bodies of the United Arab Emirates (UAE). You will need to carry your passport with you in almost all these countries – it will be available at the ship's reception desk.

Queen Mary 2 in Sydney harbor.

Cruise lines: private islands						
Cruise line	Name of island	Location	Size (acres)	Size (hectares)	First used	Rating (out of 10)
Celebrity Cruises	Catalina Island	Dominican Republic	3,840	1,554	1995	5.7
Costa Cruises	Serena Cay	Dominican Republic	3,840	1,554	1996	5.7
Disney Cruise Line	Castaway Cay	Bahamas	1,000	400	1998	8.5
Holland America Line	Half Moon Cay	Bahamas	1,700	688	1997	8.7
MSC Cruises	Cayo Lecantado	Dominican Republic	*	*	2005	6.8
Norwegian Cruise Line	Great Stirrup Cay	Bahamas	250	101	1977	7.5
Princess Cruises	Princess Cays	Eleuthera, Bahamas	40	16	1992	7.8
Royal Caribbean Int.	Coco Cay	Bahamas	54	22	1990	6.4
Royal Caribbean Int.	Labadee	Haiti	260	105	1986	7.2

* Not exactly private, but a fine leased beach/palm tree island.

Abu Dhabi and Dubai are fast becoming cruise bases, although cruise terminal and handling facilities are still quite limited. If you visit Dubai, note that displays of affection such as hand-holding or kissing are not permitted in public, and you can't drink alcohol in a public place. If you fly into Dubai with prescription medicines, make sure you have the appropriate, signed prescription.

South Africa and Indian Ocean
Attractions include cosmopolitan cities, wine tours, wildlife safaris, unspoiled landscapes, and uninhabited beaches. Itineraries (usually 10–14 days) include sailings starting and finishing in Cape Town, or from Cape Town to East African ports such as Port Elizabeth, Richards Bay, Durban, Zanzibar, and Mombasa (Kenya).

The Mexican Riviera
These typically sail from Los Angeles or San Diego, along Mexico's west coast, calling at ports such as Cabo San Lucas, Mazatlán, Puerto Vallarta, Ixtapa/Zihuatanejo, Manzanillo, and Acapulco. They usually include a call in the Baja Peninsula, Mexico's northernmost state. Be aware that there has been a considerable amount of crime even in the most visited ports such as Puerto Vallarta and Manzanillo in the past few years. Also, a number of cruise tourists have been caught out by rip tides and rogue waves when swimming in Cabo San Lucas.

Route Canal (Transcanal cruises)
Between the Caribbean and the Pacific, a ship is lifted 85ft (26m) in a continuous flight of three steps at Gatun

Locks to Gatun Lake through which it travels to Gaillard Cut where the Canal slices through the Continental Divide. It is lowered at Pedro Miguel Locks 31ft (9.4m) in one step to Miraflores Lake, then the remaining two steps to sea level at Miraflores Locks before passing into the Pacific.

Ships move through the locks under their own power, guided by towing locomotives. The 50-mile (80-km) trip takes eight to nine hours. All this effort isn't cheap; *Disney Magic* paid a record $331,200 for one transit of the canal in 2008.

Most Panama Canal cruises depart from Fort Lauderdale or San Juan, calling at islands such as Aruba or Curaçao before entering the canal and ending in Acapulco, Los Angeles, or San Francisco. In 2008, the Inter-American Development Bank's (IDB) board of directors approved a $400 million loan to help finance the historic Panama Canal Expansion Program. Two new sets of locks – each with three chambers – with rolling instead of mitre gates, will allow non-Panamax ships such as *Queen Mary 2* (but not *Allure of the Seas* or *Oasis of the Seas*) to use the waterway, accommodating ships of up to 1,400.9ft (427m) by 180ft (55m) wide. It is scheduled to open in 2015.

The Hawaiian islands
The islands of Hawaii, America's 50th state, are a tropical feast. Although relatively close together, they have many differences. For example, the lush, Garden-of-Eden-like Kauai is a world away from Oahu, with its urban metropolis of always busy Honolulu. The two parts of the Big Island, Kona and Hilo, are really opposites.

Although several cruise lines feature Hawaii once or twice a year, usually on Circle Pacific or special Hawaii sailings, only one ship is allowed to cruise in the state year-round: NCL's US-flagged *Pride of America*. Note that anything purchased aboard, including drinks, is subject to Hawaii sales tax (which doesn't apply to ships registered outside the US).

South America cruises

Cruises around Cape Horn between Santiago or Valparaíso in Chile and Buenos Aires in Argentina are increasingly popular. The optimum season is November to March and most cruises last 14 days. However, operating costs are high because several countries are involved. Pilotage charges, for example, are among the highest in the world. Chile and Peru require compulsory tugs. Steep charges for provisioning and supplies, visa complexities, and infrastructure issues all push up the cost.

Sailing southbound, ports of call might include Puerto Montt (Chile), the magnificent Chilean fjords, Punta Arenas (Chile), and Ushuaia (Argentina), the world's southernmost city (pop. 64,000) and the starting point for many cruises to the Antarctic Peninsula.

Coming up the continent's east coast, ports of call might include Puerto Madryn (Argentina) and Montevideo (Uruguay). Slightly longer itineraries may include a call at Port Stanley in the Falkland Islands.

A number of cruise lines also operate seven-day cruises from Rio de Janeiro, Brazil, mainly for Brazilians (who love to dance the night away and don't arise until nearly afternoon). Called 'eat late, sleep late' cruises, these are typically aboard large resort ships chartered to local companies such as CVC.

Australia and New Zealand

Australia and New Zealand offer a wealth of cruising possibilities, with more port cities attracting cruise ships. Apart from the major destinations, such as Sydney, Melbourne, Brisbane and Perth (Australia), and Auckland, Christchurch, and Wellington (New Zealand), there are numerous smaller ports, such as Adelaide, Cairns, and the Great Barrier Reef.

Then there's Tasmania's Hobart and the now stunning former penal colony, and its beautiful green park-like grounds, of Port Arthur – Tasmania's official top tourist attraction. Scenic cruising along Tasmania's coastline is stunning, particularly in the area such as Wineglass Bay and Great Oyster Bay. The best time to go is November to March, which, in Australasia, is the summer.

The extraordinarily beautiful Kimberley region, in Australia's Northwest Territories, essentially in the area between Broome and Darwin, is an absolute must. Perhaps the best

time to go is in April or May, after the rainy season, so that you get to see the best waterfall action. Landings are done aboard Zodiac inflatable rubber craft (and by helicopter for a visit to the sandstone formation of the 350-million years old Bungle Bungle Ranges).

Asia cruises

With such a rich tapestry of different countries, cultures, traditions, food, and sights to see, Asia is a must for the inquisitive traveler, and what better way to do this than by cruise ship. Hong Kong, China, Japan, Indonesia, Malaysia, Singapore, Thailand, and Vietnam can all be visited by cruise ship. Indeed, 'marquee' ports such as Singapore, Hong Kong, Yokohama, and Bangkok are all good points from which to join your cruise. The region has so much to offer that it's worth taking a cruise of 14 days or longer to discover many of the fascinating destinations that await you.

South Pacific cruises

The region is large, and so are the distances between island groups. Still, the region has inspired many people to travel to them to discover the unique lifestyle of its indigenous peoples. The region encompasses French Polynesia, the Marquesas, Trobriand, Pitcairn, and Cook island groups, among others – like string of pearls. Some magical names come to mind – Bora Bora, Moorea, Easter Island, Fiji, and Tonga.

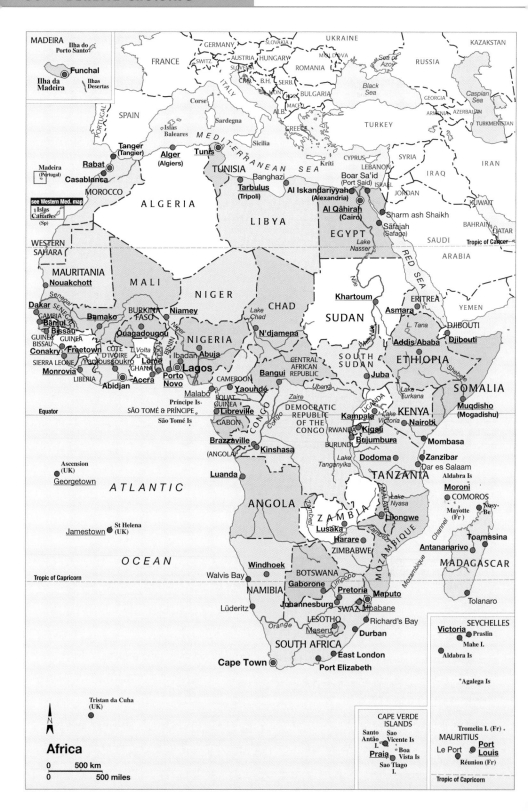

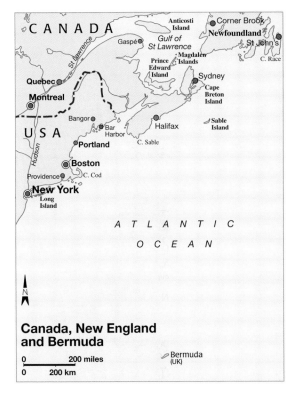

Canada, New England and Bermuda

United Kingdom

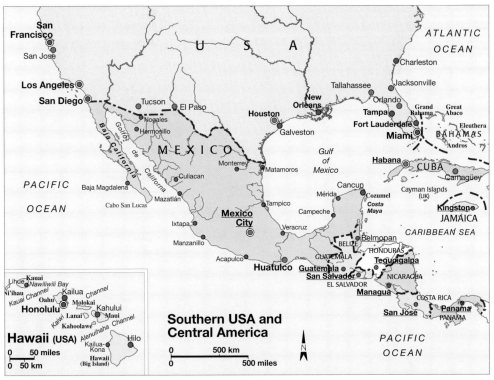

Southern USA and Central America

Hawaii (USA)

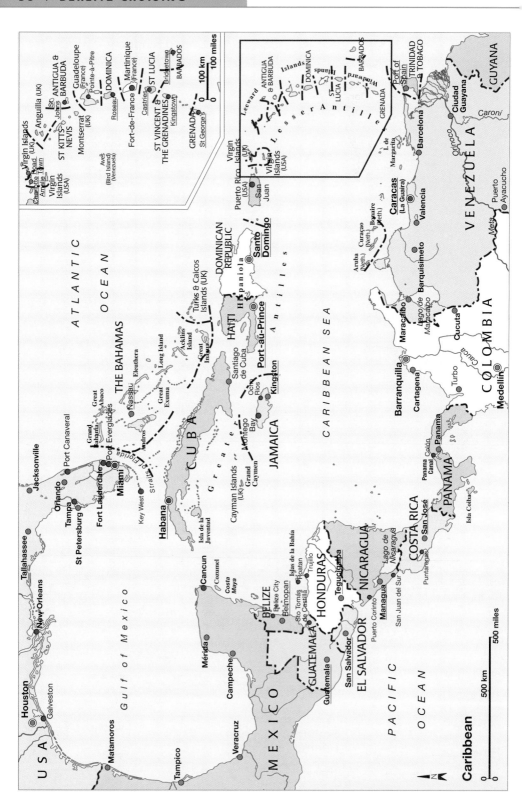

Caribbean

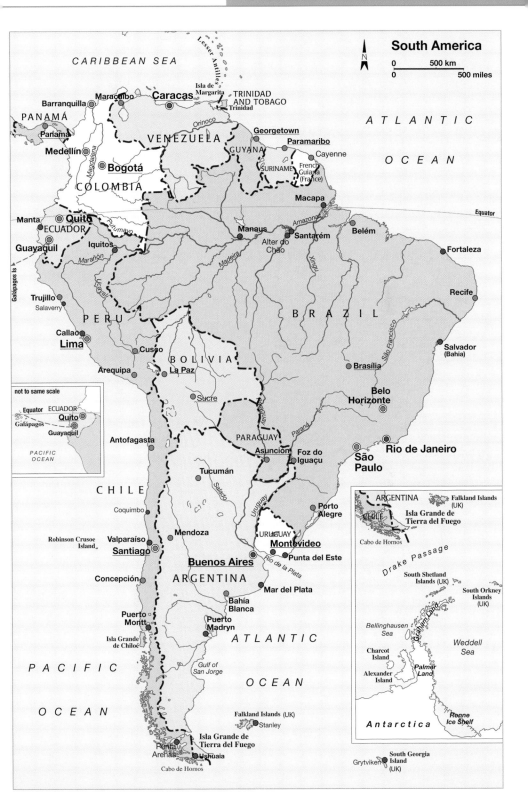

South America

0 — 500 km
0 — 500 miles

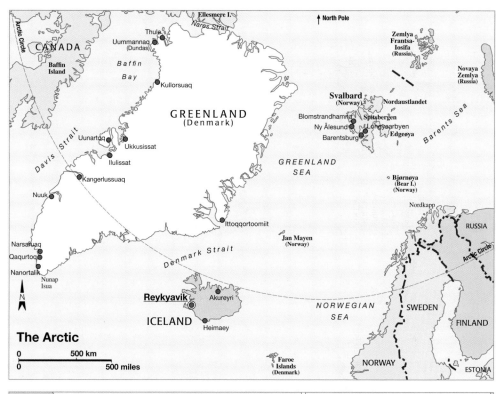

The Arctic

0   500 km
0   500 miles

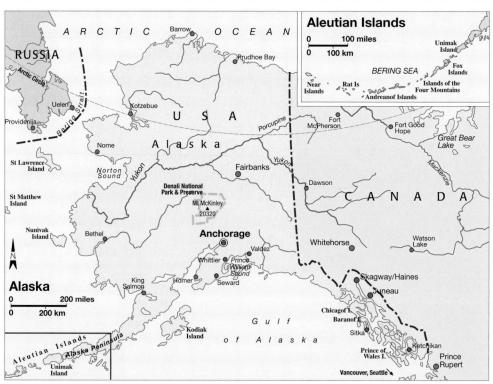

Alaska

0   200 miles
0   200 km

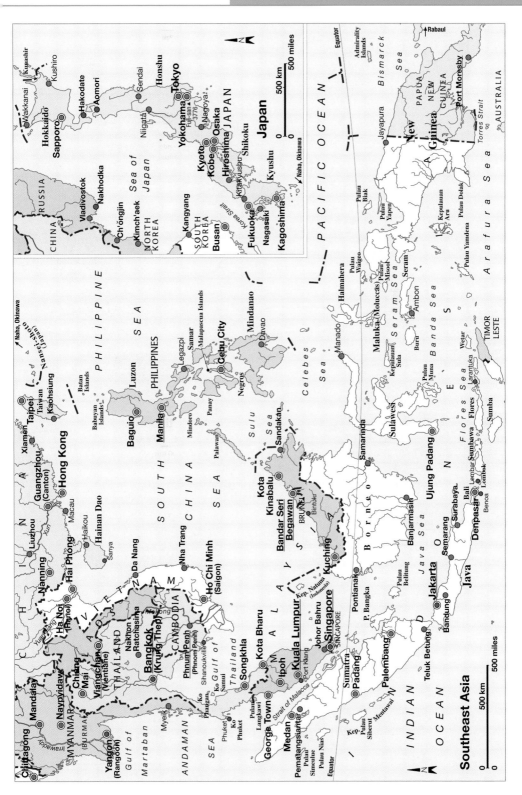

Japan

Southeast Asia

Australasia

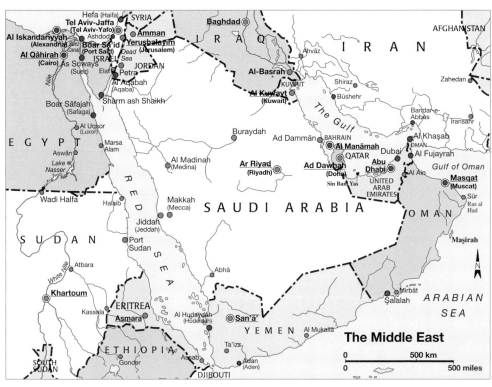

The Middle East

Western Mediterranean

ATLANTIC OCEAN

Bay of Biscay

FRANCE

Genève • SWITZERLAND
Lyon • • Milano (Milan)
Bordeaux • Torino (Turin) • Venézia (Venice) • Trieste • SLOVENIA
Rovinj • Rijeka • CROATIA • B.H.
• Genova (Genoa) • Po • Ravenna • Pula • Split
Nîmes • Monte Carlo • Portofino • SAN MARINO
Monte Carlo • Portovenere • Firenze • Ancona • ADRIATIC SEA
Cannes • Nice • LIGURIAN SEA • Livorno
Marseille • St-Tropez • Calvi • Basfía • Tevere
• Ajaccio • Corse • Roma (Rome) • Nápoli (Naples) • Salerno
Bonifacio • ITALY • Sorrento • Capri
Alghero • Sardegna • TYRRHENIAN SEA
• Isole Lípari
Menorca • Mahon • Cágliari • Lípari
Palma • Mallorca • Palermo
Eivissa (Ibiza) • Sicilia
Formentera • Islas Baleares (Balearic Islands)
MEDITERRANEAN SEA

A Coruña • Vigo
Santander • Bilbao • Toulouse
Porto (Oporto) • Douro • ANDORRA
PORTUGAL • Zaragoza
SPAIN • Barcelona
Tajo • Madrid • Valencia
Lisboa (Lisbon)
Portimao • Córdoba • Cartagena
Sevilla • Almería • Oran
Cádiz • Puerto Banus • Málaga • Alger (Algiers) • Annaba
Gibraltar (UK) • Marbella
Tanger (Tangier) • Ceuta (Spain) • Tunis • Sousse • Gozo • MALTA
Rabat
MOROCCO • ALGERIA • TUNISIA
Ebro • Garonne • Rhône

0 — 200 km
0 — 200 miles

N

ISLAS CANARIAS (Canary Islands) (SP)
La Palma • Santa Cruz de Tenerife • Lanzarote • Arrecife
Santa Cruz de la Palma • Tenerife • Puerto del Rosario
La Gomera • Puerto de la Cruz • Las Palmas de Gran Canaria • Fuerteventura
El Hierro • Gran Canaria

Eastern Mediterranean

Firenze • CROATIA • Split • BOSNIA-HERZEGOVINA • Beograd (Belgrade) • ROMANIA • UKRAINE
Ancona • Sarajevo • SERBIA • Danube • Bucuresti (Bucharest) • Constanţa
ADRIATIC SEA • Hvar • Korčula • Dubrovnik • MONTENEGRO • Priština • BULGARIA • Varna • BLACK SEA
ITALY • Kotor • Podgorica • KOSOVO • Sofiya (Sofia)
Roma (Rome) • Bari • Tiranë • Skopje • Thessaloniki • Istanbul
Nápoli (Naples) • ALBANIA • MACEDONIA
Sorrento • Capri • Salerno • Kerkyra (Corfu) • Ankara
TYRRHENIAN SEA • Kerkyra (Corfu) • GREECE • TURKEY
Isole Lípari • Lípari • IONIAN SEA • AEGEAN SEA • Izmir • Konya • Kizilmak
Palermo • Messina • Athina (Athens) • Kuşadası • Adana
Sicilia • Catania • Patra • Katakolon • Mýkonos • Antalya
Gozo • Valletta • Santorini (Thíra) • Ródos • Nicosia • SYRIA
MALTA • Iráklio (Heráklion) • CYPRUS • Lemesos • LEBANON • Beirut
Kríti • Dimashq (Damascus)
MEDITERRANEAN SEA • Hefa (Haifa)
Tel Aviv-Jaffa (Tel Aviv-Yafo) • Amman
Tarbulus (Tripoli) • Yerushalayim (Jerusalem) • Dead Sea
Al Iskandariyyah (Alexandria) • Boar Sa'id (Port Said) • ISRAEL • JORDAN
LIBYA • EGYPT • Al Qâhirah (Cairo)

Ionian Islands

0 — 200 km
0 — 200 miles

N

The Baltic and Northern Europe

Theme and Special Cruises

A whole world of hobby, special interest, and lifestyle theme cruises awaits your participation.

Think of your favorite interest or theme and you'll probably find a special cruise dedicated to it. These are the special theme cruises that don't really fit into the normal range of offerings, although they usually follow the same itinerary.

Theme cruises are primarily 'regular' cruises, but with additional programs, linked to personalities and theme subject specialists. With special seminars and hands-on learning sessions, dances or concerts, sports, and leisure on the menu, the possibilities are endless. On a theme cruise, you'll be traveling with people who have the same hobbies, interests, passions, or obsessions, or to increase your knowledge of a particular subject.

Music on the high seas

Music has always been a popular feature of shipboard entertainment, and special interest music festivals, celebrations, and even competitions at sea have been part of the modern-day cruise scene since the 1960s. It's like having a special backstage pass to be up-close-and-personal with world-class musical talent.

Solo instruments are an unusual item for a theme cruise, but in 1986 the first Accordion Festival at Sea – with over 600 accordionists on board competing for financial and other prizes – took place aboard Chandris Fantasy Cruises' *Galileo*. Although not a full ship charter, the other passengers were fascinated in the richness of performances of this much misunderstood, but versatile instrument.

Even before that, however, starting in 1976 a Classical Music Festival At Sea took place annually aboard the Paquet French Cruises' 650-passenger *Mermoz* until the early 1990s (and wine, all drinks, and shore excursions were included in the fare). The artistic director Borocz Andre organized the whole event, including booking about 70 musicians who sailed on each of these very special musical cruises (either in the Mediterranean or Caribbean). Illustrious world-class artists like James Galway, Barbara Hendricks, Jean-Pierre Rampal, Maurice Andre, Mstislav Rostropovich, Yo-Yo Ma, Emmanuel Ax, Schlomo Mintz, Bobby McFerrin, and the English Chamber Orchestra sailed aboard

A dancing competition aboard P&O Cruises' *Oriana*.

the ship, with music concerts performed ashore – usually in the evening – in Caribbean venues such as Papa Doc's Citadel in Haiti, La Popa Monastery in Cartagena, or, in Europe, the ancient Greek theatre at Epidaurus, the Theater Mercandante in Naples, or the ancient open-air theatre at Xanthos, Turkey.

What was unusual, and fun, was to watch these world-famous artistes doing rehearsals in the daytime – often in their bathrobes – with passengers (also in bathrobes or casual clothing) attending, until 6pm, when everyone donned tuxedos for the evening. The close contact and interaction between performers and the music-loving passengers were wonderful. Suffice it to say that this was indeed a very special theme cruise, unlike any other. In 1993 Paquet French Cruises was purchased by Costa Cruises, which was itself purchased by the Carnival Corporation in 1996. In 1999 Paquet Cruises was dismantled and the *Mermoz* was sold to Louis Cruise Lines (the ship was scrapped in 2008).

Today, several cruise lines have taken up the Classical Music Festival at Sea theme, with Hapag-Lloyd's annual Ocean Sun Festival the most prestigious event. It has seen great success each year. The company also hosts the annual Stella Maris International Vocal Competition in cooperation with renowned opera houses throughout the world. It is organized under the direction of Canadian tenor Michael Schade aboard *Europa,* with up-and-coming opera singers from around the world competing to win a recording contract with Deutsche Grammophon.

Cool jazz

Staying on the music theme, Big Band theme cruises have also always been popular, with bands such as the Glenn Miller Orchestra, Tommy Dorsey Orchestra, Count Basie Orchestra, and the Duke Ellington Orchestra – all have been part of the music on the high seas theme.

Jazz greats such as Dizzy Gillespie and Clark Terry (trumpet), Woody Herman (clarinet), Benny Carter, Buddy Tate, Gerry Mulligan (saxophone), Junior Mance, Mel Powell, and Paul Broadnax (piano), Howard Alden (guitar), Keter Betts, Major Holley, Milt Hinton, and Kiyoshi Kitagawa (double bass), Chuck Riggs and Louis Bellson (drums), Mel Tormé (voice), the Harlem Blues and Jazz Band, Joe Williams and the Festival Jazzers have all sailed and played on Norwegian Cruise Line's Floating Jazz Festival cruises aboard the now-scrapped *Norway* and other NCL ships of the time (organized by Hank O'Neal).

Today, the Smooth Jazz Cruise (also known as 'The Greatest Party At Sea') has been attracting well-known names like the jazz violinist Ken Ford, guitarist-vocalist George Benson, bassist Marcus Miller, guitarist Earl Klugh, saxophonists David Sanborn, Mindy Abair, Paul Taylor, and Richard Elliott, and jazz fans – principally aboard the Holland America Line ships *Eurodam* and *Westerdam*.

Off your rocker

Today, even rock 'n' roll stars (well, a booking is a booking, isn't it?) and fans have taken to cruising, with music-themed charters of ships becoming more prevalent. In 2013, Weezer – the LA rockers – took more than 2,500 fans aboard *Carnival Destiny* (now renamed *Carnival Sunshine,* though not because fans rocked and rolled with the band with the most make-up (www.thekisscruise.com).

In 2013, the '70,000 Tons of Metal' theme cruise had almost two dozen heavy metal bands from around the world taking over Royal Caribbean International's *Majesty of the Seas.*

Not to be left out, 'boy bands,' including the Backstreet Boys and New Kids on the Block, have also gone cruising.

You can expect more of the same as rock 'n' roll and blues bands take to the high seas to replace the loss of land-based venues, and revenue (merchandising aboard a cruise ship with a captive audience is a massive incentive).

Although classical music and jazz cruises tend to be 7–14 days, other music themes, such as rock 'n' roll, or heavy metal, tend to be shorter.

Soul Train

Usually a full-ship charter, a re-creation of the popular music show Soul Train includes artists like Gladys Knight and Earth, Wind and Fire, together with numerous artists that have been part of the television show, created and hosted by Don Cornelius. The artists, dancers, and fans have a blast, and enjoy the close interaction with each other (www.soultraincruise.com).

Going up country

Country and Western and Gospel music theme cruises also pop up occasionally. In fact, in 2013, the country and western band Alabama sailed with a flotilla of some of their biggest fans on a country music festival at sea to celebrate the band's 40th Anniversary of their first show at The Bowery.

In 2014, The 'Best Country Cruise Ever' takes place aboard *Norwegian Pearl.* Among the featured artists are: Trace Adkins, Montgomery Gentry, Wynonna, Neal McCoy, Love and Theft, Craig Morgan, and Lonestar, as well as up-and-coming hopefuls. There will also be songwriter workshops and, of course, karaoke (judged by the professionals) and late night dance parties, plus a little unscheduled jammin' along the way.

Meanwhile, in January 2014, Kenny Rogers, Vince Gill, and Larry Gatlin and the Gatlin Brothers will be among the star performers aboard Holland America Line's *Eurodam.* Expect a few line dances along the way, too!

Family themes

Although it could be said that, for families with children, every cruise is a theme cruise, some themes are

Making music aboard *Crystal Serenity*.

more prominent than others. Aboard the ships of Disney Cruise Line, *everything* is Disney – every song heard, every game played, every participation event, race, or party – it's the complete Disney at sea package.

Norwegian Cruise Line and Royal Caribbean International have their own star themes at sea. Norwegian Cruise Line teamed up with TV's Nickelodeon to provide cruises with characters SpongeBob, Patrick, Dora the Explorer and Diego, among others (not all ships).

Aboard some of the ships of Royal Caribbean International, the Premium Barbie Experience holds sway; so do characters from the DreamWorks Experience such as Madagascar's Alex and the Penguins, Shrek's Fiona and Puss in Boots, and Po of Kung Fu Panda.

Culinary theme cruises

Culinary themes (food and wine) have attracted enormous interest recently, probably due to the rise of television's celebrity chefs (some are real chefs who become celebrities, while others are television personalities who become [sort-of] chefs).

Many ships now have culinary classes and demonstration kitchens (those aboard Holland America Line ships are set up in the theatre and are among the best). However, Oceania Cruises' *Marina* and *Riviera* have gone one better, and each has 24 individual cooking workstations for classes on days at sea at the Bon Apétit Culinary Center.

One example of a television chef's popularity is that of Paula Deen (www.pauladeencruise.com), whose Party-At-Sea cruises have become popular with the show's fans.

Food and wine cruises have always attracted interest although some are better than others. Most have tended to be more like presentation lectures at cooking stations set on a large stage – more show than go – and always seem to leave audiences wanting to ask questions one-on-one rather than as part of a general audience.

Wine themed cruises are especially popular with oenophiles (wine lovers) who get to meet owners and specialists from various world-famous vineyards with wine talks and wine tasting as part of the pleasure of these special voyages.

Finally, cruises for 'chocaholics' have been a big draw in the past, but how many chocolates can you really taste in a week?

An astronomical event

Total Solar Eclipse at Sea. For anyone who is an eclipse chaser (www.eclipse-chasers.com), a cruise ship can represent the ideal place to be. Ships can position themselves – using the latest in weather technologies to avoid cloud banks – in the best location for the best viewing opportunities.

The author remembers over 600 astronomers aboard one 1,200-passenger ship – you couldn't move on deck because of the tripods, huge telescopes, and long camera lenses. The ship, however, had a deep draft and so it was very stable – good for the photo-snappers!

The next total solar eclipse, said to be the eclipse of the decade, will take place on March 20, 2015 and the best location will be in the Arctic, off the coast of the Faroe Islands – north of Scotland – where the longest duration of totality will be two minutes 47 seconds.

Not your regular theme cruise

Other unusual theme cruises include naturist vacations, nudity – or 'clothing-free vacations.' Bare

The *Titanic* Memorial Cruise sailed in 2012 (without incident).

Necessities has been doing it since 1990; www. cruisenude.com, although participants do dress to go to the dining room. Then there's Dream Pleasure Tours, founded in 2007 (www.dreampleasuretours. com) for sensual pleasure indulgence at sea. This company usually charters boutique-size ships (such as *SeaDream I* or *SeaDream II*) for hedonistic lifestyle cruises, such as those for the gay, lesbian, and swinger community.

The Harley-Davidson Motorcycle Rally At Sea has been happening for almost 10 years aboard Celebrity Cruises. Dress code: biker attire. Naturally, there's a belly smacker contest; a treasured chest (women); best beard (men); and, of course, a contest for the best tattoo.

Some cruises are just magical adventures in themselves. But, in 2013, everyone's favorite wizard, the venerable Harry Potter took to the seas with his own theme cruise. It's the latest movie-themed voyage to hit the high seas, and follows in the footsteps of recent additions such as the *Saw* film franchise cruise.

Shipboard fans morphed into students of wizardry and probably left spellbound ... so to speak (www. whimsicalley.com) on a recent Harry Potter cruise. If the wizard could just whisk me to the ship without having to board an aircraft – wouldn't that be magical?

Other theme cruises

Wellness, Fitness, 'Mind, Body and Spirit' and 'Life Modification' cruises (the first Holistic Health Cruise at sea was aboard Cunard Countess in 1976, with the well-known Ida Rolf – creator of the extreme massage technique known as Rolfing – on board. Quilting and Girlfriends cruise – for women

who cruise to quilt, without their husbands (www. stitchinheaven.com).

Strictly Come Dancing (ballroom dancing, P&O Cruises; www.pocruises.com).

Castles and gardens cruises (www.hebridean.co.uk).

Scrapbooking cruises (www.cruiseandcrop.com) Horror theme cruise, with all the thrills of the 'Saw' franchise but none of the morbid consequences (www. scare-zone.com).

Photography and marine biology theme cruises (American Safari Cruises; www.un-cruise.com)

Star Trek cruise – with actors who have appeared in the cult television show (www.startrekcruise.com).

Baseball giants cruise (MSC Cruises; www.msc cruises.com).

Golf. Several cruise lines have golf-themed cruises, but perhaps the best packages are put together by companies like Crystal Cruises, Hapag-Lloyd Cruises, Regent Seven Seas Cruises, and SeaDream Yacht Club – all of whom operate smaller-size ships for a more personal experience.

Meanwhile, in 2012 a 'Titanic 100th-Anniversary Memorial Cruise' took place, with two ships chartered for the somber celebration (*Azamara Journey, Balmoral*), following the path of the ill-fated ship on her maiden voyage 100 years previously.

River cruise themes

Festive Christmas Markets cruises are always popular in November/December on the Danube, Main, and Rhine rivers. The most celebrated Christmas markets can be found in Bamberg, Cochem, Nuremberg, Rothenburg, Wurtzburg, and Wertheim, where merrymaking at stalls on cobblestone streets – and *glühwein* – means festive spirits for all. (www.amawaterways.com; www.

avaloncruises.com; www.uniworld.com; www.viking rivercruises.com).

Another popular theme is the annual 'Celebration of Wine' cruise (www.amawaterways.com). This cruise includes excursions to historic vineyards and cellars along Europe's Rhone, Danube, and Rhine rivers, as well as wine talks by celebrated wine hosts, and, of course, much wine tasting.

In the USA, Mark Twain is always a popular theme aboard a Mississippi River cruise (www.american cruiselines.com). Become reacquainted with one of the world's best-loved authors. Visit Hannibal, Missouri, to explore Injun Joe's cave and visit Mark Twain's home – now a museum.

Corporate cruising

Corporate incentive organizations and seagoing conferences need to have such things as accommodation, food, or entertainment for their delegates organized as one contract, and cruise companies have specialized departments to deal with all the details. Helpfully, many larger ships have almost identical cabin sizes and configurations.

Once a corporate contract is signed, no refund is possible, so insurance is essential. Although you may need to charter only 70 percent of a ship's capacity for your purposes, you will have to pay for the whole ship if you want an *exclusive* charter.

Although you can contact cruise lines directly, I strongly recommend contacting the professionals at www.seasite.com, which contains all cruise brands designed for event planners by the Miami-based ship charter specialists Landry & Kling (who can also arrange whole-ship charters for theme cruises). You can download a Meeting Planner Guide for ships from the website.

Maiden and inaugural voyages

It can be fun to take part in the maiden voyage of a new cruise ship. Or you could join an inaugural voyage aboard a refurbished, reconstructed, or stretched ship. However, you'll need a degree of tolerance – and be prepared for some inconveniences such as slow or non-existent service in dining venues.

One thing is certain: any maiden voyage is a collector's item, but Murphy's Law – 'If anything can go wrong, it will' – can prevail. For example:

Service aboard new or recently refurbished ships (or a new cruise line) is likely to be uncertain and could be a disaster. An existing cruise line may use experienced crew from its other vessels to help 'bring out' a new ship, but they may be unfamiliar with the ship's layout and may have problems training other staff.

Plumbing and electrical items tend to cause the most problems, particularly aboard reconstructed and refurbished vessels. Examples: toilets that don't flush or don't stop flushing; faucets incorrectly marked, where 'hot' really means 'cold'; and 'automatic' telephones that refuse to function.

In the entertainment department, items such as spare spotlight bulbs may not be in stock. Or what if the pianos arrive damaged, or audio-visual materials for the lecturers didn't show up? Manuals for high-tech sound and lighting equipment may be in a foreign language.

Items such as menus, postcards, writing paper, or TV remote control units, door keys, towels, pillowcases, glassware, and even toilet paper may be lost in the bowels of the ship, or simply not ordered.

The galley (kitchen) of a new ship is in trouble if the right supplies don't turn up on time.

If you feel any of these mishaps might spoil your cruise, it would probably be better to wait until the ship has been in service for at least three months.

Taking a river cruise during the holidays can be an excellent way to visit the European Christmas markets.

Life Aboard

This A to Z survey covers the astonishing range
of facilities that modern cruise ships offer and
tells you how to make the most of them.

Air conditioning
Cabin temperature can be regulated by an individually controlled thermostat, so you can adjust it to suit
yourself. Public room temperatures are controlled automatically. Air temperatures are often kept cooler than
you may be used to. In some cases, the air conditioning
can't be turned off.

Art auctions
Aboard most large resort ships, intrusive art auctions
form part of the 'entertainment' program. They may be
fun participation events – though the 'free Champagne'
given to entice you is mostly sparkling wine and not
Champagne – but most of the art is rubbish.

Art 'appraisal prices' are done by the art provider,
a company that pays a cruise line to be onboard.
Watch out for the words: 'retail replacement value.'
Also, listen for phrases such as 'signed in the stone'
– it means that the artists did not sign the work –
or 'pochoire' (a stencil print less valuable than an
original etching or lithograph). If the auctioneer tries

An art auction aboard P&O Cruises' *Arcadia*.

to sell a piece of art (particularly a 'block' print or
woodcut/engraving) with an 'authenticated signature,' don't buy it – when it's delivered to your home
and you have it appraised, you'll probably find it's
not genuine.

Babysitting
In some ships, stewards, stewardesses, and other staff
may be available as babysitters for an hourly fee.
Make arrangements at the reception desk. Aboard
some ships, evening babysitting services may not
start until late; check times and availability before
you book a cruise.

Beauty salon/barber shop
Make appointments as soon after boarding as possible,
particularly on short cruises. Appointment times fill up
rapidly, especially before social events such as a 'Welcome Aboard' cocktail party. Charges are comparable
to city prices ashore.

Cashless cruising
You simply settle your account with one payment (by
cash or credit card) before disembarking on the last
day. An imprint of your credit card is taken at embarkation or when you register online, permitting you to sign
for everything. Before the end of the cruise, a detailed
statement is delivered to your cabin.

Some cruise lines, irritatingly, discontinue their
'cashless' system for the last day of the cruise. Some
may add a 'currency conversion service charge' to your
credit card account if it is not in the currency of the
cruise line.

Casino gaming
Many cruise ships have casinos, where the range of
table games includes blackjack or 21, Caribbean stud
poker, roulette, craps, and baccarat. Under-18s are not
allowed in casinos, and photography is usually banned
inside them. Customs regulations mean that casinos
generally don't open when the ship is in port.

Gaming casino operations aboard cruise ships are
unregulated. However, some companies, such as Celebrity Cruises and Royal Caribbean International,
abide by Nevada Gaming Control Board regulations.
Most table games have a $5 minimum and $200 maximum – but, for serious players, Carnival Cruise Lines'
casinos have blackjack tables with a $25 minimum and
$500 maximum.

Some cruise lines have 'private gaming club' memberships, with regular newsletters, rebates, and special offers (example: Star Cruises/Genting Hong Kong). Slot machines are also in evidence and bring in more than half of a casino's profits.

Comment cards

On the last day of the cruise you will be asked to fill out a company 'comment card.' Some lines offer 'incentives' such as a bottle of Champagne. Be truthful, as the form serves as a means of communication between you and the cruise line. Pressure from staff to write 'excellent' for everything is rampant but, unless you highlight problems you have encountered, things are unlikely to improve.

Disembarkation

This can be the most trying end to any cruise. The cruise director gives an informal talk on customs, immigration, and disembarkation procedures. The night before the ship reaches its destination, you will be given a customs form. Include any duty-free items, whether purchased aboard or ashore. Save the receipts in case a customs officer asks for them after you disembark.

The night before arrival, place your main baggage outside your cabin on retiring, or before 2am. It will be collected and offloaded on arrival. Leave out fragile items *and the clothes you intend to wear* for disembarkation and onward travel – it is amazing just how many people pack absolutely everything. Anything left in your cabin will be considered hand luggage.

Before leaving the ship, remember to claim any items placed in your in-cabin safe. Passengers can-

Disembarking from large resort ships can be tedious.

not go ashore until all baggage has been offloaded and customs and/or immigration inspections or pre-inspections have been carried out. In most ports, this takes two to three hours after arrival.

On disembarkation day, breakfast will probably be early. It might be better to miss breakfast and sleep later. Even worse than early breakfast is the fact that aboard many ships you will be commanded to leave your cabin early, only to wait in crowded public rooms, sometimes for hours.

Some companies, such as Princess Cruises, offer a more relaxed system that allows you to stay in your cabin as long as you wish, or until your tag color is called, instead of waiting in public areas.

Once off the ship, you identify your baggage on the pier before going through customs inspection. Porters may be there to assist you.

Relax upstairs, gamble downstairs aboard NCL's *Norwegian Epic.*

Duty-free liquor

If you buy any 'duty-free' liquor along the way, it will be taken from you at the gangway as you reboard and given back to you the day before you disembark. (Cruise lines want you to buy your alcohol on board.)

Engine room

For insurance and security reasons, visits to the engine room are seldom allowed. Some ships may have a technical information leaflet. Aboard others, a behind-the-scenes video may be shown on the cabin TV system.

Gratuities (tips to staff)

Aboard many large resort ships, tipping seems to be mandatory rather than voluntary. Gratuities, typically of around $12 per person (slightly more for occupants of suite-grade accommodation or for butler-service accommodation), per day, are added automatically to your shipboard account by almost all the major cruise lines, and may need to be converted to your local credit card currency at the prevailing rate, whether you have received extra service or not.

Be aware that cabin stewards have been known to scroll through their passengers' on-board account on the television, so they can see whether you have opted out of the automatic gratuity charge!

Gratuities are included in the cruise fare aboard a small number of ships, mainly those at the luxury ('all-inclusive') end of the market, where no extra tipping is permitted – at least in theory. Even when cruise brochures state 'tipping is not required,' they will be expected by the staff. Aboard some ships, subtle suggestions are made regarding tips; in others, cruise directors get carried away and dictate rules.

Here are the accepted industry guidelines: dining room waiter, $3–$4 per person, per day; assistant waiter (busboy), $1.50–$2 per day; cabin steward or stewardess, $3–$3.50 per person, per day; Butler: $5 per person, per day. Tips are normally given on the last evening of a cruise of up to 14 days' duration. For longer cruises, hand over half the tip halfway through and the rest on your last evening.

Aboard many ships, a gratuity of 15 percent is automatically added to your bar check, whether you get good service or not, and a gratuity (of 15–18 percent) is also added for spa treatments.

Internet access, email, and cell phones

Smartphone/cell phone use aboard ships is certainly growing, and most cruise ships built after 2000 are wired for Internet access and cell phone use, but at a price. You can use your own device, but it must be set for roaming – and extra charges will apply. All calls (at sea) are handled by a marine satellite provider, which will pass on the international roaming charges to your phone operator. Before you cruise, check with your phone operator for the international roaming rates applicable to your tariff.

As for Internet use, most new ships have a room – often part of the library – with Internet-connect computers. The best-wired ships also have strong signals to cabins and public areas, so you can use your own laptop in the privacy of your cabin or on deck (extra charges apply).

Tenders transport passengers when a ship can't dock, as seen here aboard *Regatta*.

The lido deck aboard *Carnival Magic* is devoted to swimming pools and hot tubs.

The signal strength can vary substantially from hour to hour, minute to minute. The farther north you get, the closer the telecommunications satellite is to the horizon, so signals tend to fade in and out, and waiting for Web pages to appear on your computer screen can be frustrating.

The cost of Internet time ranges from about 50¢ to 75¢ a minute. If you think you will use the Internet a lot, perhaps for emails, it makes sense to buy a package of minutes. Typical charges are around $50 for 100 online minutes and $100 for 250 minutes.

Digital shipboard systems will ask you to establish a user name and password before you can access websites or your email. Each ship-received email arrives separately (unlike on your home computer) and takes longer to load. This is because ships use different software from home-based systems, and you will be sharing the space with marine requirements. Attachments usually cannot be downloaded.

Launch (shore tender) services

Enclosed or open motor launches ('tenders') are used when your cruise ship is unable to berth at a port or island. In such cases, a regular launch service is operated between ship and shore for the duration of the port call. Aboard the large resort ships, you'll need to obtain a tender ticket, usually given out in one of the lounges, unless you are on an organized excursion (these take priority). The procedure can take a long time.

When stepping on or off a tender, extend 'forearm to forearm' to the person who is assisting you. Do not grip their hands because this has the unintentional effect of immobilizing the helper.

Laundry and drycleaning

Most ships offer a full laundry and pressing service. Some ships may also offer dry-cleaning facilities. A detailed list of services, and prices, will be in your cab-in. Your steward will collect and deliver your clothes. Some ships have self-service launderettes, well equipped with washers, dryers, and ironing facilities. There may be a charge for washing powder and for the use of the machines.

Library

Some cruise ships have a library offering a good selection of books, reference material, and periodicals. A small, refundable deposit may be required when you borrow a book. Aboard small luxury ships, the library is open 24 hours a day, and no deposit is required. Aboard the large resort ships, the library may be open only a couple of hours a day. *QM2, Queen Elizabeth,* and *Queen Victoria* have full-time, qualified librarians provided by the dedicated specialist company Ocean Books, which also sells a superb range of specialist maritime books and memorabilia aboard the three Queens.

Aboard the small expedition ships, the library is one of the most important – and most used – facilities, and high-quality reference books on all aspects of nature, marine life, and polar exploration are usually provided.

Lido

This is a deck devoted to swimming pools, hot tubs, showers, and general recreation, often with intrusive 'background' music. Aboard most cruise ships, it also includes a self-serve buffet.

Lost property

Contact the reception desk immediately if you lose or find something aboard the ship.

Mail

You can buy stamps and mail letters aboard most ships, at the reception desk. Some ships use the postal privileges and stamps of their flag of registration, while others buy local stamps at ports of call. Mail is usually taken ashore by the ship's port agent just before the ship sails.

Medical care

Doctors aboard most cruise ships are required to have current medical licensing, three years of post-medical school clinical practice, certification in emergency medicine, family practice, or internal medicine or experience as a GP or Emergency ward doctor. So, if you have a serious health issue that predates your cruise, or a permanent disability, you need to be upfront about it with your travel agent or the cruise line's reservationist. They may be able to advise you on a ship that best meets your needs.

If you have long-term health issues, get your prescriptions made up for the whole period of the cruise because many places will not process prescriptions from other countries. Take out a travel insurance policy that reimburses you for visits to the onboard medical service, but check the small print. These policies often refuse to pay out if you had a condition you didn't mention when you bought the policy. Most medical care on cruise ships is perfectly adequate. Just in case it isn't, the cruise lines have a clause that says they aren't responsible for the malpractice of a ship's doctors.

News/sports bulletins

Most ships have satellite TV for world news and sports coverage. Others print world news and sports results in

The reception desk is the ship's information hub.

A Seabourn ship disgorges watersports fans.

the ship's newspaper or place details on a bulletin board near the reception desk or in the library. For sports results not listed, ask at the reception desk. A few ships can even print a version of your favorite newspaper.

Photographs

Professional photographers on board take digital pictures of passengers during embarkation and throughout the cruise. They cover all the main events and social functions, such as the captain's cocktail party. The pictures can be viewed without any obligation to buy, but the prices may surprise. The cost is likely to exceed $10 for a postcard-size photograph, and a 10 x 8–inch embarkation photo aboard *Queen Mary 2* will set you back a whopping $27.50.

Postcards/stationery

These are typically available from the writing room, the library, or the reception desk. Some cruise lines now charge for them, although if you are in suite-grade accommodation, you may get stationery personalized with your name and suite number when you embark.

Pre-paid drinks

Most large resort ships offer drinks packages in an effort to 'add value.' However, although these booze-cruise packages mean you don't need to sign each time you order a drink, they really are a temptation to drink more (example: $29–$49 per person, per day aboard the ships of Royal Caribbean International, depending on what you want included). Some packages include wine, although the choice is the cruise line's – not yours.

Reception desk

This is also known as the purser's office, guest relations, or information desk. Centrally located, it is the nerve center of the ship for general passenger information and problems. Opening hours – in some ships, 24 hours a day – are posted outside the office and given in the Daily Program.

Religious services

Interdenominational services are conducted on board many ships – usually by the captain or staff captain. Costa Cruises' ships have a small private chapel. Denominational services may also be held by clergy traveling as passengers.

Room service

Beverages and snacks are available at most times. Liquor is normally limited to the opening hours of the ship's bars. Some ships charge for room service.

Sailing time

In each port of call, sailing and all-aboard times are posted at the gangway. The all-aboard time is usually half an hour before sailing. If you miss the ship, it's entirely your responsibility to get to the next port of call to rejoin the vessel.

Shipboard etiquette

Two points that are sometimes overlooked: 1) If you take a video camera with you, be aware that international copyright laws prohibit you from recording the professional entertainment shows. 2) It is all right to be casual but not to enter a ship's dining room in just a bathing suit, or with bare feet.

Swimming pools

Most ships have swimming pools outdoors; some have pools that can be covered by a glass dome in case of inclement weather, while a handful of ships have indoor pools located on the lowest deck. All pools may be closed in port owing to local health regulations or cleaning requirements. Diving is not allowed – pools are shallow.

Parents should note that most ship pools are unsupervised. Some ships use excessive chlorine or bleaching agents; these could cause bathing suit colors to run.

Telephone calls

Most ships have a direct-dial satellite link, so you can call from your cabin to anywhere in the world. All ships have an internationally recognized call sign, a combination of letters and digits (example: C6SE7). Satellite calls can also be made when the ship is in port. Satellite telephone calls cost between US$5 and $12 a minute, depending on the type of equipment the ship carries.

To reach any ship, dial the International Direct Dial (IDD) code for the country you are calling from, followed by the ship's telephone number.

Anyone without a direct-dial telephone should call the High Seas Operator (in the United States, dial 1-800-SEA-CALL). The operator will need the name of the ship, together with the ocean code (Atlantic East is 871; Pacific is 872; Indian Ocean is 873; Atlantic West/Caribbean/US is 874).

A wine tower aboard *Celebrity Eclipse*.

Television

Programming is obtained from a mixture of satellite feeds and onboard videos. Some ships lock on to live international news programs such as CNN or BBC World, or to text-only news services. Satellite TV reception can be poor because ships constantly move out of the narrow beam transmitted from the satellite.

Valuables

Most ships have a small personal safe in each cabin, but items of special value should be kept in a safety deposit box in the purser's office. This is accessible during the cruise.

Water sports

Some small ships have a water sports platform that lowers from the ship's stern or side. These ships usually carry windsurfers, waterski boats, jet skis, water skis, and scuba and snorkel equipment, usually at no extra charge (except for scuba equipment).

Such facilities look good in brochures, but ships are often reluctant to use them. This is because many itineraries have too few useful anchor ports. Also, the sea must be in an almost flat calm condition – seldom the case. Insurance regulations can be restrictive, too.

Wine and liquor

The cost of drinks on board is generally lower than on land, since ships have access to duty-free liquor. Drinks may be ordered in the dining room, at any of the ship's bars, or from room service. Dining rooms have extensive and reasonably priced wine lists.

Some ships sell duty-free wine and liquor to drink in your cabin. You can't normally bring these into the dining room or public rooms, nor any duty-free wine or liquor bought in port. These rules protect bar sales, a substantial source of onboard revenue.

Cuisine

Anyone determined to eat around the clock could do so aboard many ships, but the health-conscious should exercise restraint, especially at self-service buffets

The dining rooms and restaurants aboard any cruise ship are the collective lifeblood of the entire ship, cruise, and hospitality experience. Except for the destinations, it's the food that most people remember and talk about.

Cruise lines love to boast about their food, but the reality is that most meals aboard most ships are not gourmet affairs. How could they be when a kitchen has to turn out hundreds of meals at the same time? I've never actually met a passenger able to recite the menu of their most memorable meal (including appetizer, main course, and dessert) aboard a cruise ship. Why? It's just that most ships simply can't deliver the Wow factor the brochure promises, and so the hype about the "gourmet" food is mostly overstated puffery.

The message to remember is this: generally speaking, as in most restaurants on land, you get what you pay for. High-quality food ingredients cost money, so it's pointless expecting low-cost cruises to offer anything other than low-cost food. Most cruise ship cuisine compares favorably with 'banquet' food in a family restaurant. Mass catering is a fine art, and there will be moments when meals are tasty and well presented, although these are increasingly rare.

The major cruise lines sometimes bulk-purchase lower-cost food, which means lower quality ingredients, cheaper cuts of meat, and fish which would, in yesteryear, be considered only for use as bait. But many of the food items ordered today by large central purchasing departments are 'enhanced' with preservatives. But cruise lines do sometimes upgrade food items. Carnival and RCI, for example, introduced free-range eggs aboard their ships in 2011.

Fresh versus frozen

Aboard low-priced cruises, you will typically be served portion-controlled frozen food that has been reheated. Fresh fish and the best cuts of meats cost the cruise lines more, and that cost is reflected in the cruise price. Aboard some ships, the 'fresh' fish – often described as 'Catch of the Day' – has clearly had no contact with the sea for quite some time.

Crystal Cruises' celebrity chef Nobu Matsuhisa (right).

Hebridean Princess provides the antithesis to mass catering.

Sushi bars are a recent fad but, in 90 percent of cases, fish used in sushi (with rice) is steamed, and raw (sashimi-style, without rice) fish is not available, as storage and preparation facilities are inadequate. The only ships with authentic sushi bars and authentic sushi/sashimi are *Asuka II, Crystal Serenity, MSC Musica,* and *MSC Poesia*. Note also that many items of 'fresh' fruit may have been treated with 1-MCP (methylcyclopropene) to make them last longer – apples, for example, may be up to a year old.

Bread and pastry items
While there are exceptions, much of the bread baked aboard cruise ships is unappealing because, with little time for fermentation of natural yeast, it is made instead with instant dough that contains dried yeast from packets. Many baked goods and pastry items are made mostly from refined flours and sugars.

Specialty restaurants
Most new cruise ships have a number of specialty restaurants and dining venues that provide alternatives to the large main dining rooms.

These specialist restaurants are typically smaller, à la carte venues where you must make a reservation, and pay an extra charge of between $6 and $75 a person. In return, you get better food, wines, service, and ambience. Celebrity chefs add to the mix and are asked to establish their own 'at sea' dining venues, or collaborate on menus for shipboard eateries, although they seldom appear on board.

Barbecues and hot rock grills
Although some ships – usually the smaller ones – offer barbecues on deck, the latest trend is the Hot Rocks Grill. This consists of steaks, grilled meats, and seafood presented on a platter that includes a scorchingly-hot rock base – so you can cook it yourself however little or well you want it done. It makes for a pleasant, refreshing change, all in a casual pool deck environment. Seabourn and Silversea Cruises have pioneered this option, and more lines are likely to follow.

Molecular gastronomy
The term, invented in 1992 by the physicist Nicholas Kurti, signals food's collision with science to create molecularly synthesized food. The cuisine was first introduced to the cruising industry by Italy's Emilio Bocchia in the extra-cost restaurants aboard some Costa

---

Celebrity chefs

Several cruise lines have signed up well-known chefs to devise menus for their alternative dining venues. Celebrity Cruises, for example, worked with three-star Michelin chef Michel Roux from 1989 until 2007.

Celebrated chefs have included Georges Blanc (Carnival Cruise Lines), Elizabeth Blau (Celebrity Cruises), Geoffrey Zakarian (Norwegian Cruise Line), Jacques Pépin (Oceania Cruises), Nobu Matsuhisa (Crystal Cruises), Todd English (Cunard Line), Mauro Uliassi (MSC Cruises), Marco Pierre White (P&O Cruises), and Aldo Zilli (Thomson Cruises).

Most celebrity chefs sail only one or two cruises a year, but Germany's three-star Michelin chef Dieter Müller has set a new benchmark by sailing for up to half a year in order to run his eponymous restaurant aboard Hapag-Lloyd Cruises' *Europa*.

Cruises ships. To provide it, kitchens need blast chillers, atomizers, vacuum sealers, a Pacojet (a machine that can turn everyday ingredients into ice cream), liquid nitrogen, thickening gums (such as algin and xantham), malic acid, and flame retardants such as gellan. It also requires a serious qualification in molecular engineering and pharmaceutical know-how, and access to mountains of gelatin.

The end result is rather like a plate of colorful toy portions of 'foam food.' It can look pretty, and is reassuringly expensive. In the world of molecular gastronomy, bacon can be made to taste like melon. This type of cooking is, in the most literal sense, a matter of taste.

Special needs

Cruise lines tend to cater to general tastes. If you are allergic to ingredients such as nuts or shellfish, want lactose-free or gluten-free food, or have any other dietary restrictions, let the cruise line know in writing well ahead of time and, once on board, check with the restaurant manager.

If you are vegetarian, vegan, macrobiotic, or counting calories or want a salt-free, sugar-restricted, low-fat, low-cholesterol, or any other diet, advise your travel agent when you book, and get the cruise line to confirm that the ship can meet your needs. Cruise ship food tends to be liberally sprinkled with salt, and vegetables are often cooked with sauces containing dairy products, salt, and sugar.

Most cruise ships don't cope well with those on vegan or macrobiotic diets who regularly need fresh-squeezed juices; most large resort ships use commercial canned or bottled juices containing preservatives and aren't able to provide really fresh juices in their bars.

Self-serve buffets

Most ships have self-serve buffets for breakfast and luncheon (some also for dinner), one of the effects of discounted fares and dumbing down – and fewer staff are needed.

Strangely, passengers don't seem to mind lining up for self-service food in scandalously overcrowded venues. But while buffets look fine when they're fresh, they don't after a few minutes of passengers helping themselves. Self-serve buffets have become more user-friendly by increasing the number of 'active cooking' stations and food islands, which help to break up lines created by typical straight-line buffet counters.

Healthy eating

It's easy to gain weight when cruising – but not inevitable. In fact, taking a cruise could well be a good reason to get serious about your well-being. Weight-conscious passengers should exercise self-restraint, particularly at self-service buffets.

Many ships' menus include 'heart-healthy' or 'lean and light' options, with calorie-filled sauces replaced by so-called 'spa' cuisine. It may also be wise to choose grilled or poached fish (salmon or sea bass, for example), rather than heavy meat dishes, chicken, or fried food items.

Quality and variety are directly linked to the per-passenger budget set by each cruise line and are dictated by suppliers, regions, and seasons. Companies operating large resort ships buy fruit at the lowest price, which can translate to unripe bananas, tasteless grapes, and hard-as-nails plums. The smaller, more upscale ships usually carry better-quality ripe fruits as well as the more expensive varieties such as dragon fruit,

Afternoon tea in *Crystal Symphony*'s Palm Court.

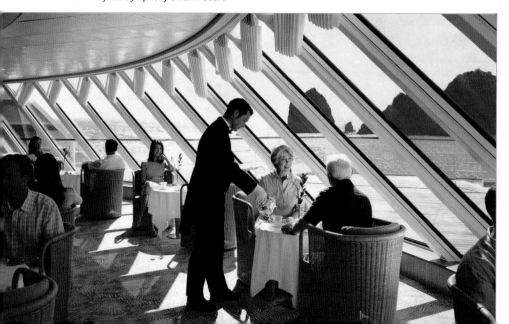

carambola (star fruit), cherimoya, cactus pear, guava, kumquat, loquat, passion fruit, persimmon, *physalis* (Cape gooseberry), rambutan, and sharon fruit.

Even some of the large resort ships, such as *Allure of the Seas* and *Oasis of the Seas,* have calorie-control food items at the Solarum Bistro, where no dish is more than 500 calories. Carnival Cruise Lines have a Mongolian barbecue on their buffets where tofu is a regular feature. Crystal Cruises features more grains and fresh fruits on its buffet lines, and you'll find Ayervedic breakfast items in *Europa 2*'s Yacht Club.

Raw food

In 2011, SeaDream Yacht Club introduced raw food dishes. The cruise line has tapped into the Hippocrates Health Institute's Life Transformation Program and introduced a complete additional menu of raw food items. 'Raw' means that ingredients are raw, organic, enzyme-rich, and vegan: no meat, fish, eggs, or dairy items, and nothing heated above 118° in order to retain as many micronutrients as possible.

Items include fresh sprout and vegetable juices, plant-based protein foods, and items like pasta made from spinach leaves and coconut meat. Even desserts are created from raw foods such as cashews, almond milk, and coconut butter. It's a growing trend that will help you achieve more balance in their dietary intake.

General Service

Aboard many ships today, passengers are often in a hurry (to get to a show or shore excursion) and simply want service to be as fast as possible. They also don't like seeing empty plates in front of them, and so service speeds up because waiters need to clear the empty plates away as soon as someone has finished eating a particular course. In what is correctly termed European Service, however, there should *always* be a pause between courses, not only for conversation, but to let the appetite recover, and also to anticipate the arrival of the next course.

Plate service versus silver service

Plate service. When the food is presented as a complete dish, as the chef wants it to look. In most cruise ships, 'plate service' is now the norm. It works well and

An iPad menu and wine list makes selection easy at *Celebrity Reflection*'s QSine.

means that most people seated at a table will be served at the same time and can eat together, rather than letting their food become cold.

Silver service. When the component parts are brought to the table separately, so that the diner, not the chef, can choose what goes on the plate and in what proportion. Silver service is best when there is plenty of time, and is rare aboard today's ships. What some cruise lines class as silver service is actually silver service of vegetables only, with the main item, whether it is fish, fowl, or meat, already on the plate.

National differences

Different nationalities tend to eat at different times. North Americans and Japanese, for example, tend to dine early (6pm–7pm), while many Europeans and South Americans prefer to eat much later (at least 8pm–11pm). Brazilians like dinner at midnight. During Ramadan, Muslims cannot eat during the daytime, but often order room-service meals during the night.

Beef, lamb, and pork cuts are different on both sides of the Atlantic, so what you ordered may not be the cut, shape, or size you expected. For example, there are 15 British cuts of beef, 17 American cuts, and 24 French cuts. There are six American cuts of lamb, eight British cuts, and nine French cuts. There are eight American cuts of pork, 10 British cuts, and 17 French cuts.

While American passengers typically like iced water or a jug of iced tea at lunch, most European passengers don't want ice in their water, and few drink iced tea.

If you care about cutlery, note that few large resort ships provide correctly shaped fish knives or the correct soup spoons (oval for thin bouillon-style soups and round for creamy soups).

In the Arctic, *Hanseatic* lays on a shoreside buffet.

Seating

Depending on the size of the ship, it may have single, two, or open seatings:

Open seating. You can be seated with whomever you wish at any available table, at any time when the restaurant is open.

Single seating. Doesn't mean seating for single passengers. It means you can choose when you wish to eat (within dining room hours) but have the same table assigned for the cruise.

Two seatings. You are assigned (or choose) one of two seatings, early or late. Typical meal times for two-seating ships are: breakfast, 6.30am–8.30am; lunch, 12 noon–1.30pm; dinner, 6.30pm–8.30pm.

Some ships operate two seatings for all meals and some just for dinner. Some ships operate a mix of open seating (dine when you want) or fixed dining times, for greater flexibility. Dinner hours may vary when the ship is in port to allow for the timing of shore excursions. Ships that operate in Europe and the Mediterranean or in South America may have later meal times to suit their clientele.

The captain's and senior tables

The captain usually occupies a large table in or near the center of the dining room on 'formal' nights (with senior officers such as the chief engineer and hotel manager hosting adjacent tables), although this tradition is fast disappearing as ship dress codes become more casual. The table usually seats between eight and 12 people picked from the passenger or 'commend' list by the hotel manager. If you are invited to the captain's table (or any senior officer's table), it is gracious to accept, and you will have the chance to ask questions about shipboard life.

Dining room and kitchen staff

Although celebrity chefs make the headlines, it's the ship's executive chef who plans the menus, orders the food, organizes and supervises staff, and arranges all the meals.

The restaurant manager – also known as the maître d'hôtel – not to be confused with the ship's hotel manager – is an experienced host, with shrewd perceptions about compatibility. It is his or her responsibility to seat you with suitable companions.

The best waiters are those trained in hotels or catering schools. They provide fine service and quickly learn your likes and dislikes. They normally work aboard the best ships, where dignified professionalism is expected and living conditions are good.

Many lines contract the running and staffing of dining rooms to a specialist maritime catering organization. Ships that cruise far from their home country find that professional caterers, such as Hamburg-based Sea Chefs, do an outstanding job. However, ships that control their own catering staff and food often try very hard for good quality.

Hygiene standards

Galley equipment is in almost constant use, and regular inspections and maintenance help detect potential problems. There is continual cleaning of equipment, utensils, bulkheads, floors, and hands.

Cruise ships sailing from or visiting US ports are subject to in-port sanitation inspections. These are voluntary, not mandatory inspections, carried out by the United States Public Health (USPH) Department of Health and Human Services, under the auspices of the Centers for Disease Control (CDC). Cruise lines pay for each inspection.

A tour of the galley proves to be a highlight for some passengers, when a ship's insurance company permits.

In accordance with international standards, all potable water brought on board, or produced by distillation aboard cruise ships, should contain a free chlorine or bromine residual greater than or equal to 0.2ppm (parts per million). This is why drinking water served in dining rooms often tastes of chlorine.

Smoking and no-smoking areas

Most ships now have totally no-smoking dining rooms, although a handful still provide smoking (cigarettes only, not cigars or pipes) and no-smoking sections. Those wishing to sit in a no-smoking area should tell the restaurant manager when reserving a table.

Douglas Ward's top restaurants

If asked to pick a baker's dozen, I would choose: Dieter Müller aboard *Europa,* Tarragon aboard *Europa 2,* Kaito aboard *MSC Musica* and *MSC Poesia,* Le Champagne aboard *Silver Spirit,* Le Cordon Bleu aboard *Seven Seas Voyager,* Olympic Restaurant aboard *Celebrity Millennium,* Prime 7 aboard Regent Seven Seas Cruises, Red Ginger aboard *Marina,* Remy aboard *Disney Dream,* The Sushi Bar aboard *Crystal Serenity* and *Crystal Symphony,* Teppanyaki Grill aboard *Norwegian Epic,* Umihiko aboard *Asuka II,* and Veranda Grill aboard *Queen Elizabeth.*

Major cruise lines: cuisine/service scores

	Carnival Cruise Lines	Celebrity Cruises	Costa Cruises	Cunard Line	Holland America Line	MSC Cruises	Norwegian Cruise Line	P&O Cruises	Princess Cruises	Royal Caribbean Intl.	Star Cruises
Food											
Dining Room/Cuisine	5.7	7.3	5.9	7.6	7.1	7	6	6.5	7.3	5.0	6
Buffets/Informal Dining	5.8	7	5.6	7.0	6.2	6.4	6.2	6	6.7	5.8	5.7
Quality of Ingredients	6	7.1	6	7.5	6.6	7.5	6.1	6.6	6.8	6.0	6.4
Afternoon Tea/Snacks	4	6.6	4.2	7.4	5.6	6.6	4.5	6.5	6.3	4	5.2
Wine List	5.7	7.5	5.6	8	6.1	7.3	6.2	6.7	6.6	5.4	5.5
Overall Food Score	**5.44**	**7.1**	**5.46**	**7.5**	**6.32**	**6.96**	**5.8**	**6.46**	**6.74**	**5.24**	**5.76**
Service											
Dining Rooms	6	7.6	6	7.6	7.4	7.3	6.6	6.8	7.5	5.7	6.3
Bars	5.8	7.4	6.2	7.6	7.1	7.5	6.4	7.1	7.5	5.6	6
Cabins	6	7.6	6.8	7.7	7.5	7.5	6.2	7.6	7.3	6.2	6.1
Open Decks	5.5	7.2	5.6	7.4	6.6	7.2	6	6.2	6.8	5.6	6
Wines	5	7.5	5.2	8	6.1	7.4	6	6	6.2	5.2	5.2
Overall Service Score	**5.66**	**7.46**	**5.96**	**7.66**	**6.94**	**7.38**	**6.24**	**6.74**	**7.06**	**5.66**	**5.92**
Combined food/service	**5.55**	**7.28**	**5.71**	**7.58**	**6.63**	**7.17**	**6.02**	**6.6**	**6.9-**	**5.45**	**5.84**

Note: scores out of a maximum of 10. These ratings do not reflect extra-cost "alternative" restaurants.

Entertainment

The bigger the ship, the bigger the show, but the tired old song-and-dance routines are now being replaced by well-known Broadway musicals.

Cruise lines with large resort ships have been upping the ante lately, competing to attract attention by staging lavish, high-tech-reliant productions that are licensed versions of Broadway shows. Examples include *Chicago* and *Hairspray* aboard Royal Caribbean International's Oasis-class ships, with impressively large casts. These big theater shows are abridged versions specially adapted to the cruise ships' showroom stage, typically by trimming and fine-tuning them so that the performance fits in with the ship's operational schedule – not to mention dinner.

Also, on an Aqua (outdoor) combination water and stage aboard Royal Caribbean International's *Allure of the Seas* and *Oasis of the Seas,* aquabatics and comedy provide a nighttime entertainment spectacular on the outside deck at the aft of the ships.

Aboard Norwegian Cruise Line's *Norwegian Breakaway, Norwegian Epic,* and Norwegian Getaway, the *Blue Man Group,* a mime and multi-sensory effects show that involves passengers, is a hit with families, as is *Cirque Dreams & Dinner*; each show is in a dedicated venue as there's no main show-lounge as such.

Then there's Disney Cruise Line with its own superb stage shows taken from the vast choices available in the Disney stable, plus *Believe,* developed specifically for *Disney Dream.* There's a proven family favorite, *Toy Story – The Musical. Disney Fantasy* lets *Aladdin* out of his lamp. Disney has separate entertainment shows for adults, too. Winningly, children are invited to meet and greet Disney characters in designated places and during special surprise appearances aboard its four ships.

The good news is you don't pay extra to see the show; there are few bad seats in the house; you don't have to find a parking place; you don't even have to carry tickets, or find a restaurant to eat in before or after the show. And there's always a handy bar nearby.

Onboard productions

Colorful Las Vegas–style production shows have evolved enormously aboard the large resort ships, as have the stages, technical equipment, and facilities.

Old-style cabaret aboard *Celebrity Millennium*.

Allure of the Seas mounts an abridged version of *Chicago*.

Although they still can't match the budgets of Las Vegas, they can certainly beat many shore-side venues. Most shipboard production shows have two things in common: no audience contact (well, almost none), and intense volume. With few exceptions, the equation 'volume = ambience' is thoroughly entrenched in the minds of the young, musically challenged audio-visual technicians.

With few exceptions, there's little elegance in most production shows, and all are too long. The after-dinner attention span of most cruise passengers – who are generally not unlike a television studio audience – is about 35 minutes. Most production shows run for about 45 to 50 minutes, and follow the 'more is better' theory. The classic show business dictum, of course, is that it's better to 'leave 'em wanting more.'

Most production show 'dancing' today consists of stepping in place, while pre-recorded backing tracks are often synthetic and grossly imbalanced. Synthetic string sections, for example, are acceptable only to the aurally impaired.

Some cruise lines have a live showband that backs the large-scale production shows. This band plays along with a pre-recorded backing track to create an 'enhanced' or larger sound. Some companies, such as Disney Cruise Line, use only a prerecorded track. This has little 'feel' to it, unlike a live showband that can generate empathy and variation – as well as create work for musicians. Although live music may contain minor imperfections (which some might regard as 'character'), most passengers would prefer it to canned music – a term invented by John Philip Sousa, composer of many military marches and author, in 1906, of *The Menace of Mechanical Music*.

Great expectations

Many passengers, despite having paid comparatively little for their cruise, expect to see top-notch entertainment, headline cabaret artists, the world's most popular singers, and the most dazzling shows with slick special effects, just as one would find in the best venues in Las Vegas, London, or Paris. There are many reasons why the reality is different. Cruise line brochures tend to over-hype entertainment – just like food – to the hilt. International star acts invariably have an entourage that accompanies them to any venue: their personal manager, their musical director (often a pianist or conductor), a rhythm section with bass player and drummer, even their hairdresser.

On land, one-night shows are possible, but with a ship, an artist cannot always disembark after just one night, especially when it involves moving equipment, costumes, stage props, and baggage. This makes the deal logistically and financially unattractive for all but the very largest ships on fixed itineraries, where a marquee-name act might be a marketing plus.

For their part, most entertainers don't like to be away from their 'home base' for long periods, as they rely on reliable telephone contact for managing their careers. Nor do they like the long contracts that most ships must offer in order to amortize the high costs.

The cost of staging a show

Staging a lavish 50-minute production show can easily cost between $500,000 and $1 million, plus performers' pay, costume cleaning and repair, royalties, and so on. To justify that cost, shows must remain aboard for 18 to 24 months.

Some smaller operators see entertainment as an area for cost-cutting, so you could find yourself entertained by cheaper singers and bands that can't read musical arrangements.

A certain sameness

So many acts working aboard cruise ships are interchangeable with so many other acts also working aboard cruise ships. Ever wonder why? It relates to the limited appeal of a cruise ship gig. Entertainers aboard ships have to live with their audiences for several days and perhaps weeks – something unheard of on land – as well as work on stages aboard older ships that weren't designed for live performances. Nevertheless, there is no question that cruise ships have become the new location for vaudeville acts, where a guaranteed audience is a bonus for many former club-date acts, as well as fresh acts trying to break into the big time on land.

As for the 'sameness' of so many shows, entertainment aboard large resort ships is market-driven. In other words, it is directed toward that segment of the industry that marketing departments are specifically targeting. This is predominantly a family audience, so the fare must appeal to a broad age range. That partly accounts for the frequency of formulaic Cirque du Soleil–style acrobatic routines and rope climbing.

A cruise line with several ships will normally employ an entertainment director and several assistants, and most cruise lines use entertainment agencies that

Movies under the stars aboard a Princess cruise.

specialize in entertainment for cruise ships. As a result, regular passengers are likely to see the same acts time after time on various ships.

Mistakes do happen. It is no use, for example, booking a juggler who needs a floor-to-ceiling height of 12ft but finds that the ship has a showlounge with a height of just 7ft (although I did overhear one cruise director ask if the act 'couldn't juggle sideways'); or an acrobatic knife-throwing act (in a moving ship?); or a concert pianist when the ship only has an upright honky-tonk piano; or a singer who sings only in English when the passengers are German-speaking.

Trying to please everyone

The toughest audience is one of mixed nationalities (each of whom will expect entertainers to cater exclusively to their particular linguistic group). Given that cruise lines are now marketing to more international audiences in order to fill ever-larger ships, the problem of finding the right entertainment is far more acute – which is why *Queen Mary 2* is to be envied for the visual appeal of its Illuminations Planetarium.

The 'luxury' cruise lines (typically those operating small ships) offer more classical music, even some light opera, more guest lecturers and top authors than the seven-day package cruises heading for the sun.

These performers, and ship entertainers generally, need to enjoy socializing. Successful shipboard acts tend to be good mixers, are presentable when in public, do not do drugs or take excess alcohol, are not late for rehearsals, and must cooperate with the cruise director.

Part of the entertainment experience aboard large resort ships is the glamorous 'production show,' the kind of show you would expect to see in any good Las Vegas show palace – think flesh and feathers – with male and female lead singers and Madonna or Marilyn Monroe look-alike dancers, a production manager, lavish backdrops, extravagant sets, grand lighting, special effects, and stunning custom-designed costumes. Unfortunately, most cruise line executives, who know little or nothing about entertainment, still favor plumes and huge feather boas paraded by showgirls who *step*, but don't *dance*. Some cruise ships have coarse shows, and topless performances can be found aboard the ships of Star Cruises/Genting Hong Kong.

Book back-to-back seven-day cruises (on alternating eastern and western Caribbean itineraries, for example), and you'll probably find the same two or three production shows and the same acts on the second week of your cruise. The way to avoid seeing everything twice is to pace yourself.

Other entertainment

Most ships organize acts that, while not nationally known 'names,' can provide two or three different shows during a seven-day cruise. These will be singers, illusionists, puppeteers, reality TV show wannabes, hypnotists, and even circus acts, with wide age-range appeal. Also, comedians who perform 'clean' material can find employment year-round on the cruise ship circuit. These popular comics enjoy good accommodation, are mini-stars while on board, and may go from ship to ship on a standard rotation every few days. There are raunchy, late-night 'adults only' comedy acts in some of the ships with younger, clued-in audiences, but few have enough material for several shows. In general, the larger a ship, the broader the entertainment program will be.

Movies on deck

Showing movies on the open deck has been part of the cruise scene since the 1970s, when they were often classic black and white films shown at midnight. In those days, the screens were small, roll-down affairs, and the projectors were set up on makeshift pedestals. The result was often images that vibrated and sound that quivered.

Speed forward into the 21st century. Many large resort ships now have huge outdoor poolside LED (light emitting diode) movie screens 300 sq ft (approximately 28 sq m) that cost around $1 million each. The screens are complemented by 50,000- to 80,000-watt sound systems for a complete 'surround the deck' experience.

Princess Cruises started the trend in 2004 aboard *Grand Princess* with its Movies Under the Stars program – not that you could always see the stars – but now all companies with large resort ships have them. The experience is reminiscent of the old drive-in movies, the difference being that cruise lines often supply blankets and even popcorn free of charge.

Blue Man Group performs aboard *Norwegian Epic*.

Movies are shown throughout the day and evening. Aboard the family-friendly ships, they may include special films for junior cruisers. Big sports events such as the Super Bowl or World Cup soccer are also presented.

Smaller cruise ships, expedition cruise ships, and sail-cruise ships may have little or no entertainment. Aboard those ships, after-dinner conversation, reading, and relaxation become the entertainment of choice.

What's on

You can keep up with entertainment on offer by reading the daily program – a mini-newspaper that appears in your suite/cabin each night when your bed is turned down. It describes the next evening's shows and lists performance times. Any changes – due to bad weather, for example – are announced over the PA system.

Who's who in shipboard entertainment

Although production companies differ in their approach, the following gives an idea of the people involved behind the scenes:

Executive Producer. Transfers the show's concept from design to reality. First, the brief from the cruise line's director of entertainment might be for a new production show (the average being two major shows per seven-day cruise). After deciding on an initial concept, they then call in the choreographer, vocal coach, and musical arranger.

Choreographer. Responsible for auditioning the dancers and for creating, selecting, and teaching the routines.

Musical Director. Coordinates all musical scores and arrangements; trains the singers in voice and microphone techniques, projection, accenting, phrasing, memory, and general presentation; and oversees session singers and musicians for the recording sessions.

Musical Arranger. After the music has been selected, the musical arrangements must be made. This is a time-consuming task. Just one song can cost more than $2,000 for a single arrangement for a 12-piece orchestra.

Costume Designer. Provides creative original designs for a minimum of seven costume changes in one show lasting 45 minutes. The costumes must also be practical, as they will be used repeatedly.

Costume Maker. Buys all materials, and must be able to produce all required costumes in time for a show.

Graphic Designer. Provides all the set designs, whether they are physical two- or three-dimensional sets for the stage, or photographic images created on slide film, video, laser disk, or other electronic media.

Lighting Designer. Creates lighting patterns and effects for a production show. Sequences and action on stage must be carefully lit to the best advantage. The completed lighting plot is computerized.

Bands/Musicians. Before the big production shows and artists can be booked, bands and musicians must be hired, often for long contracts. Naturally, live musicians are favored for a ship's showband, as they are excellent music readers (necessary for all visiting cabaret artists and for big production shows). Big bands are often placed in some of the larger ships for special sailings, or for world cruises, on which ballroom dancing plays a large part. Most musicians work to contracts of about six months.

Spas and Wellness Facilities

The 'feel good factor' is alive and well aboard the latest cruise ships, which offer a growing array of beauty salons and body-pampering treatments.

Pampering in *Disney Dream*'s Senses spa.

Land-based health spas have long provided a range of body treatments and services for those who wanted to hide away at a health farm in the countryside. Responding to the rise in popularity of 'wellness' breaks, today's cruise ships have elaborate spas to rival those on land, where, for an extra fee, whole days of almost continuous treatments are on offer.

Once the domain of adult women, spas now cater almost as equally for men. Interestingly, passengers of different nationalities behave differently – for example, Europeans will walk all over a ship in their bathrobes to reach its spa, but most Asians and North Americans will wear day clothes en route to the spa and change when they get there.

A ship's spa will help you to relax and feel pampered. Many people not used to spas may find some of the terminology daunting: aromatherapy, hydrotherapy, ionithermie, rasul, thalassotherapy. The spa staff are used to first-time clients, however, and will help you choose the massage or other treatment that best suits you and your needs. It's a good idea to visit the spa on embarkation day, when staff will be on hand to show you around, and answer your questions. Some cruise lines let you pre-book spa treatments online before your cruise. But take note of prices, which can quickly add up.

It's best to avoid booking massage treatments at a time when the ship is about to leave port (usually in the late afternoon/early evening), because there may be interruptive announcements, and noise and vibration from the propulsion machinery, particularly if the spa is located in the aft section of the ship.

The best spas

My choice of excellent spas would be those aboard *AIDAbella, AIDAluna, AIDAmar, AIDAsol, AIDAstella, Crystal Serenity, Europa, Europa 2, Mein Schiff 1, Mein Schiff 2, Mein Schiff 3, MSC Divina, MSC Fantasia, MSC Preziosa, MSC Splendida, Pacific Pearl, Queen Mary 2, Seabourn Odyssey, Seabourn Quest, Seabourn Sojourn,* and *Silver Spirit.*

Facilities

Large resort ships will have a large gymnasium with ocean views, saunas, steam rooms, rasul chamber, several body treatment rooms, thalassotherapy pool, relaxation area, changing/locker rooms, and a beauty salon. Some ships even have acupuncture treatment clinics, and some have a built-in juice bar. Some onboard spas offer a 'couples' experience, and some have 'spa suites' for rent by the day or half-day.

Thermal suites

Thermal suites (no, they're not specially insulated cabins) are private areas that provide a combination of various warm scented rain showers, saunas, steam rooms, and thalassotherapy (saltwater) pools, and relaxation zones offer the promise of ultimate relaxation. Although most ships don't charge for use of the sauna or steam room, some make a per-day charge, typically about $30–$35. Some ships even add a gratuity to a spa Day Pass, although it's supposed to be included, and some ships limited the number of people that can get a Day Pass (for example, aboard *Queen Elizabeth* and *Queen Victoria* the limit is 40 persons per day); consequently, day passes may not be available if 40 people have booked ahead (i.e., online).

Spa suites

Many ships now have 'spa suites,' which include spa access and special amenities, and even a treatment or two, whereas regular cabin occupants pay extra to use the sauna/steam room and relaxation rooms; examples include *Celebrity Reflection, Costa Deliziosa, Costa Fascinosa, Costa Favolosa, Costa Luminosa, Costa Pacifica, Costa Serena, Europa, Europa 2, MSC Divina, MSC Fantasia, MSC Preziosa,* and *MSC Splendida.* Some even have a special spa-food-menu-only restaurant; examples include *Celebrity Eclipse, Celebrity Equinox, Celebrity Reflection, Celebrity Silhouette, Celebrity Solstice, Costa Deliziosa, Costa Fascinosa, Costa Favolosa,* and *Costa Serena.*

Personal spa suites

Each consists of a large room with floor-to-ceiling windows (one-way glass, of course), a heated floor, lots of space (about the size of three or four standard cabins), and plenty of towels. It has a two-person sauna, steam room, shower enclosure, two hot tile relaxation loungers, plus two hydraulic massage tables. When you want massage, the therapist comes, but a choice of oils is already in one of the room's storage cupboards. You can also book therapists for treatments such as manicure, pedicure, or facial – all in complete privacy.

A personal spa suite has herbal tea-making facilities and is bookable for a couple of hours, a half-day, or a full day – all at extra cost. AIDA Cruises and TUI Cruises already have such facilities, and other companies are expected to follow soon.

Spa design

Many ship spas have Asian-themed decor, with warm woods and gently flowing water to provide a soothing atmosphere, with therapy staff dressed in the appropriate attire. But interior designers often forget to include dimmers and mood lighting, particularly in reception areas, where lighting is often too bright.

Pampering treatments

Stress-reducing and relaxation treatments are offered, combined with the use of seawater, which contains minerals, micronutrients, and vitamins. Massages might include Swedish remedial massage, shiatsu, and aromatherapy oils. You can even get a massage on your private balcony aboard some ships.

Having body-pampering treatments aboard a cruise ship can be wonderful, as the ship can provide a serene environment in itself; so, when enhanced by something like a massage or facial, the benefits can be more therapeutic. Ship interior designers do, however, need to pay more attention not only to lighting dimmers but also to soundproofing (so that facilities can be used at all hours). Examples of poor soundproofing include the treatment rooms aboard *Golden Princess* and *Grand Princess,* where they are located directly underneath a sports court. So, before you actually book your relaxing massage, find out whether the treatment rooms are quiet enough.

Unfortunately, treatments are usually available only until about 8pm, whereas some passengers would welcome being able to have a massage late at night before retiring to bed – the problem is that most shipboard spas are run by concessions, with well-being treated as a daytime-only event.

Also, be aware that the latest rip-off in the revenue game is to charge more for treatments on days at sea, and lower on port days. Check the daily program for 'port day specials' and packages that make prices more palatable.

A hot stone massage aboard an AIDA cruise offers complete body relaxation.

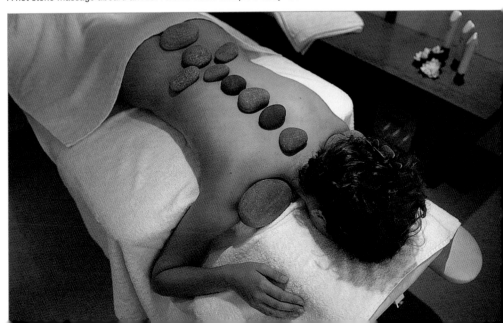

A gym with a view on a Celebrity cruise.

Some of the smaller, more upscale ships now offer 'Spa Days' with a whole day of body-pampering treatments (often termed 'wellness packages'). Expect to pay up to $500 a day *in addition to* the basic cruise fare.

Fitness centers

A typical large resort ship spa will include a gymnasium, probably with ocean-view windows. Virtual-reality exercise machines are found in the techno-gyms aboard most large resort ships, with state-of-the-art muscle-pumping and body-strengthening equipment, universal stations, treadmills, bicycles, rowing machines, and free weights.

Most fitness centers are open only until early evening (one exception: NCL ships, whose gyms are open 24 hours a day). And if you've forgotten your workout clothes, you can probably purchase new items on board.

Typical exercise classes include aerobics (for beginners, intermediate, and advanced), high-intensity/low-impact aerobics, step aerobics, interval training, stretch and relax, super body sculpting, fab abdominals, sit and be fit, and walk-a-mile.

Group exercycling, kick-boxing, Pilates and yoga classes, body composition analysis, and sessions with a personal trainer will cost extra.

Massage

Getting a massage aboard ship is a treat that more people are discovering. Today, many ships have suites and cabins with a 'private' balcony, although you'll need a balcony with plenty of space in order to set up a proper portable massage table and allow the masseur/masseuse room to walk around it and work from all sides.

It can be a real stress-busting experience, but if it's not right it can prove frustrating, and expensive.

Here are some favorite massage moments (always taken in the late afternoon or early evening, preferably just before sundown):

Aboard *Celebrity Constellation, Celebrity Infinity, Celebrity Millennium, Celebrity Summit* (on the balcony of a Sky Suite).

Aboard *Royal Clipper* (in a private massage hut on an outside deck).

Aboard *SuperStar Virgo* (on the floor of a junior suite bedroom).

Inside a beach cabana ashore on Castaway Cay or Half Moon Cay in the Bahamas, or as part of the beach, caviar, and champagne experience of ships such as *SeaDream I* and *II* in the British Virgin Islands.

Make appointments for a massage as soon after embarkation as possible, so you can obtain the time and day of your choice. Large resort ships have more staff and offer more flexibility in appointment times,

5 tips on spa etiquette

1. Do not shave in the sauna (this applies to both men and women); it's unhygienic and uncool.
2. Arrive at least 10 minutes before your appointment.
3. Take a shower before entering a sauna or steam room.
4. It's better not to talk during a massage – simply close your eyes, relax, and enjoy.
5. You can cancel an appointment up to 24 hours before your treatment time without charge. If you cancel within the 24 hours before your appointment time, you will be charged for the treatment you booked.

although cruises tend to be shorter than those aboard smaller, more upscale ships. The cost averages $2 a minute. In some ships, a massage service may be available in your cabin (or on your private balcony), if it's large enough to accommodate a portable massage table.

Although it's easy to telephone and make an appointment for a massage or facial or two (some cruise lines let you do this online), do watch the cost. When you charge treatments to your onboard account, remember that gratuities are often added automatically (typically 10–15 percent). Elixirs of youth, lotions and potions, creams and scrubs – all are sold by therapists, typically at the end of your treatment, for you to use when you get home. But be warned, these are expensive items; beware of falling for subtle and flattering sales talk.

A whole range of treatments and styles has evolved from the standard Swedish Remedial Massage. The most popular are:

Swedish Massage. Developed by Swedish physiologist Per Hendrik Ling in the 1830s, there are two main effects of massage – a reflex effect and a mechanical effect. There are four basic movements in this general massage: effleurage (the stroking movements that benefit the circulation of lymphatic fluids and drainage), petrissage (the picking, kneading, rolling, and wringing movements), friction (the application of circular pressure), and tapotement (percussive tapping, flicking, and hacking movements that stimulate circulation). Long strokes are employed over your well-oiled body to reduce stress and to provide a feeling of relaxation for sore joints and muscles. A Swedish Massage is the most common form of massage today.

Ayurvedic Head Massage. Using warmed herbal oils, the therapist will apply the oil to the scalp, neck, and shoulders to stimulate circulation and nourish the hair (you'll need to wash your hair afterward, as it will be extremely oily). Shirodhara is the form of Ayurvedic medicine that involves gently pouring warm oil (made from tulsi, or holy basil) over the forehead. Ayurveda is a compound word meaning life and knowledge.

Chinese Tui Na. This is a therapeutic massage based on a diagnostic evaluation, manipulation of the joints and muscle fibers, and identification and prevention of wrong body postures, habits, and degenerative conditions.

Couples Massage. Sometimes known as a 'duet massage,' this is typically a 90-minute session for a couple that includes a hands-on lesson from a massage specialist on the art of massaging each other.

Hot Stones Massage. The therapist typically places 24 to 36 smooth basalt volcanic stones of varying sizes in a special oven. These are heated, and then applied to various key energy points of your oiled body, using the stones to gently massage specific areas and muscles. The heated volcanic stones are then left in place while the therapist works on other parts of the body. The heat from the stones promotes a sense of deep relaxation. Cold stones may be used on the face, due to their firming action.

Lomi-Lomi Massage. This is a more rhythmic massage inspired by Hawaiian healing traditions that restore the free flow of 'mana' or life force; it is typically given using warm aromatherapy oils, and may be a two-hand or four-hand massage.

Lymphatic Massage. This detox massage – developed in France in the 1930s by Emil and Estrid Vodder – is designed to improve circulation by releasing body toxins and nodes that build up in key lymphatic points. It is usually recommended for those who have poor circulation and can help deliver cellular waste.

Some RCI ships have a full-size boxing ring.

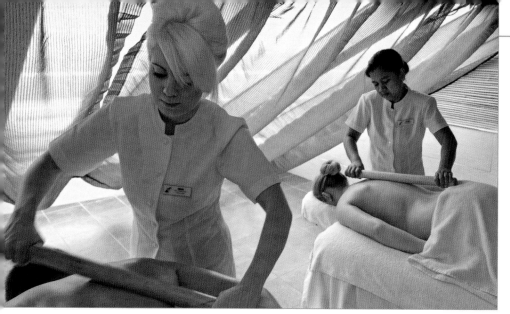

Bamboo massage for two in *Carnival Magic*'s Cloud 9 spa.

Shiatsu Massage. Originating in Japan, this means 'finger pressure,' applied to the pressure points of the body as a preventative measure. It typically promotes a peaceful awareness of both body and mind, and is administered in a calm environment, without oil.

Sports Massage. Typically provided by a male therapist, sports massage is a deep-tissue massage designed to unlock the kinks and knots.

Thai Massage. Uses pressure points and stretching techniques employed by the therapist, using both hands and feet, to stretch and relax muscles, improve circulation, and reduce stress. It is usually carried out on a mat or thin mattress, which is laid out on the floor.

Underwater Massage. You soak in a large tub of warm water, possibly with rose petals floating around you, while the therapist massages joints and muscles.

Ultimate Massage. Two therapists provide a synchronized full body massage, using Swedish massage movements to provide the ultimate in stress-busting relief. But it can be less than good if the two therapists are even slightly out of sync.

Well-being Massage. This puts more emphasis on effleurage movements, the use of complementary, warmed aromatic (aromatherapy) oils, and four-hand massage (two therapists working rhythmically in unison).

Recent variations of massage include a warm candle massage and a bamboo tamping treatment. Aboard some ships (MSC Cruises, for example), combinations of Balinese massage and reflexology are popular, an Asian massage that is part Thai massage and part deep-tissue massage.

Other treatments

Although massage is the most popular shipboard spa treatment, some ships offer other body-pampering treatments such as facials, manicures, pedicures, teeth whitening, and acupuncture. Most are based on holistic Asian therapies. Some examples: *mandi lulur,* a scrub made from herbs, essential oils, and rice to soften the skin); *boreh,* a warm Balinese herb, rice, spice, galangal water, and oil body wrap for detoxification;

The spa will provide towels, robes, and slippers, but it's best to store valuables safely in your cabin prior to your appointment. Some spas offer disposable panties for body treatments such as a Body Salt Glow or Seaweed Wrap.

One of the latest body detox treatments is Halotherapy, which uses a Himalayan crystal salt bed for deep relaxation and body detoxing. It involves lying on a bed of 290 lbs (130kg) of Himalayan salt crystals heated from 90 to 104 degrees Fahrenheit (32–40 degrees Celsius), and breathing the salt-infused air. The salt contains 84 essential minerals as fine particles.Acupuncture

This can be used to prevent and remedy many maladies. Moxibustion(heat is a treatment that involves the insertion of hair-thin needles, dipped into mugwort (*Artemisa capillaris*) into one of the body's 1,100-plus acupuncture points.

Body scrub

The aim of this treatment is to cleanse and soften the skin, and to draw out impurities from within, using aromatic oils, creams, lotions, and perhaps sea salt, together with exfoliation (removal of dead skin cells) using skin-brushing techniques.

Body wrap

Often called a body mask, this treatment typically includes the use of algae and seaweeds applied to the whole body. The body is then covered in aluminum foil and blankets. There are many variations on this theme, using mud from the Dead Sea or the Mediterranean, or sea salt and ginger, or cooling cucumber and aloe, or combinations of herbs and oils that leave you with a warm glow. The aim is to detoxify, firm, and tone the skin, and reduce cellulite.

Dry flotation

This gives you the sensation of floating without getting wet; you lie on a plush rubberized warm blanket between your body and the water. A therapist then gently massages your head and neck.

Facials

Aromatherapy facial: This treatment typically uses aromatic oils such as lavender, sandalwood, and geranium, plus a rejuvenating mask and accompanying creams and essences to 'lift' the skin and facial muscles.

Rejuvenation facial. This is typically a classic French facial, which utilizes the latest skin care products that may include essential plant and vitamin-rich oils. This facial aims to reduce lines and wrinkles.

Other popular treatments include eye lifting, volcanic mud mask, and manicure with back and neck massage.

Rasul chamber

This is a steam chamber (Hammam) that is typically fully tiled, with a domed roof and Moorish decor. You paste yourself or your partner – it's a much better experience with a partner – with three types of mud, and sit down while gentle steam surrounds you. The various types of mud become heated and then you're in a mud bath, after which you rub yourself (and each other) with large crystals of rock salt.

Reflexology

The body's energy meridians exist as reflex points on the soles of the feet. The therapist uses thumb pressure to stimulate these points to improve circulation and restore energy flow throughout the body.

Teeth whitening

This treatment is done using one of several methods, including bleaching strips, pen, gel, and laser bleaching. Carbomine peroxide, when mixed with water, forms hydrogen peroxide – the substance most used in teeth whitening procedures. Power bleaching uses light energy to accelerate the process. Expect to pay about $200.

Thalassotherapy

The use of seawater to promote well-being and healing dates back to ancient Greece. Today, shipboard spas have whole bath rituals involving water and flower petals, herbs, or mineral salts.

Sample prices

Prices of body-pampering treatments have escalated recently and are now equal to the prices you would find at land-based spas in the United States. You can expect to pay up to:
$200 for a 75-minute Hot Stones Massage
$125 for a 50-minute Well-being Massage
$200 for a 75-minute Seaweed Wrap
$125 for a 50-minute Reflexology Session

Spa cuisine

Originally designed as low-fat, low-calorie (almost tasteless) meals for weight loss using grains, greens, and sprouts, spa cuisine now includes whole grains, seasonal fruits and vegetables, and lean proteins – ingredients low in saturated fats and cholesterol, low-fat dairy products, and reduced salt. They provide the basis for balanced nutrition and portion sizes while maintaining some flavor, texture, and taste, and foods are grilled rather than baked or fried.

Sports facilities

Sports facilities might include basketball, paddle tennis (a sort of downsized tennis court), and electronic golf simulators. Some boutique/small 'luxury' ships offer kayaking, water-skiing, jet skiing, and wake boarding for no extra charge. In reality, however, the water sports equipment is typically only used on one or two days (or part days) during a seven-day cruise.

Who runs the spas

Aboard most ships, the spa and fitness areas are operated by a specialist concession, although each cruise line may have a separate name for the spa, such as AquaSpa (Celebrity Cruises), The Greenhouse Spa (Holland America Line), Lotus Spas (Princess Cruises), etc.

Aboard the large resort ships, spa staff tends to be young, enthusiastic 'therapists' who will try hard to sell you own-brand beauty products, for a commission. Steiner Leisure is by far the largest concession, operating spas aboard more than 100 ships.

This company, founded in London in 1901 by Henry Steiner, began its ambitious growth in 1926 when Herman Steiner got involved in the family beauty salon on his father's death. He opened salons throughout England, became official cosmetician to Queen Elizabeth the Queen Mother, and won his first cruise ship contract in 1956.

The company closed its land-based salons in the 1990s as its cruise ship business burgeoned. It bought Elemis, a lifestyle range of plant-based beauty products, and acquired Mandara Spas, which it has developed in the US alongside its Elemis Spas. In 2010 it bought The Onboard Spa Company. It runs 14 training schools. Steiner's corporate headquarters is now in the Bahamas.

Other shipboard concessions include Blue Ocean (MSC Cruises), Canyon Ranch At Sea (Cunard, Oceania Cruises, Regent Seven Seas Cruises), Carita, Espace Elegance, Flair (Louis), and Ocean Spa (Hapag-Lloyd).

Excursions Ashore

Escorted tours in ports of call cost extra, but they are often the best way to get a nutshell view of a destination and make the most efficient use of your limited time ashore.

Shore excursions used to be limited to city tours and venues that offered folkloric dances by local troupes. Today's excursions are almost limitless, and some are really active, encompassing crocodile hunting in the Amazon, kayaking in Alaska, elephant riding in Thailand, or flying over Moscow in a MiG jet Most offer good value, but it's easy to spend more on shore excursions on than on buying the cruise.

Shore excursions are offered by cruise lines in order to enhance a destination visit. Booking with a cruise line avoids the hassle of arranging your own excursions, and you'll be covered by the cruise line's insurance (yes, things can go wrong). General city tours are designed to give you an overview and show you the highlights in a limited time period – typically about 3 hours. Other excursions provide a mind-boggling array of possibilities, including some that may be exclusive to a particular cruise line – even overland tours are part of the excursions available on longer cruises.

Not all tours are by bus. Some may be by bicycle, boat, car, or mini-van. Some cruise lines also offer pri-

Playing with the stingrays in Nassau.

vate, tailor-made excursions to suit you, a family, or small group. A private car, with a tour guide who speaks your language, for example, may be a good way for a family to get to know a foreign destination.

To get the most out of your shore visits, doing a little research – particularly if you are visiting foreign countries – will pay dividends. Once on board, attend the shore excursion lectures, or watch destination and shore excursion videos on your cabin tv system.

Once your ship reaches a destination, it must be cleared by local officials before you are free to go ashore. In most ports, this is accomplished speedily. Meanwhile, you may be asked to assemble for your organized tours in one of the ship's public rooms. You'll need to carry the ship's identification card with you (remember to take the ship's telephone number with you, in case of emergencies), to be checked at the gangway, and when you re-board.

How tiring are excursions?

Most tours will involve some walking, and some extensive walking. Most cruise lines grade their excursions with visual symbols to indicate the degree of fitness required.

How expensive are they?

For an average three-hour city sightseeing tour, expect to pay $40–$100, and for whole-day excursions with lunch, $100–$250. Flightseeing or seaplane sightseeing tours will cost $250–$350, depending on the location, what is included, and how long they last – the flightseeing itself usually lasts about 30–45 minutes.

What if my first choice is sold out?

Some excursions do sell out, owing to limited space or transport, but there can be last-minute cancellations. Check with the shore excursion manager on board.

What should I take with me?

Only what's necessary; leave any valuables aboard ship, together with any money and credit cards you do not plan to use. Groups of people are often targets for pickpockets in popular sightseeing destinations. Also, beware of excursion guides who give you a colored disk to wear for 'identification' – they may be marking you as a 'rich' tourist for local shopkeepers. It's always prudent to wear comfortable rubber-soled shoes, particularly in older ports when there may be cobblestones or other uneven surfaces.

How can I make a booking?

Several cruise lines allow you to book shore excursions online *before* you cruise. But this means some popular excursions may sell out before you even get to your ship. So book early. Payment aboard ship is normally made via a ship's central billing system.

If you need to cancel a shore excursion, you usually need to do so at least 24 hours before its advertised departure time. Otherwise, refunds are at the discretion of the cruise line, and refunds of pre-paid tickets booked over the Internet can take a long time to make and can incur currency losses. You may be able to sell your ticket to another passenger – tickets don't normally have names or cabin numbers on them, except those involving flights or overland arrangements – but check first with the shore excursion manager.

How can I know which are good?

If it's your first cruise, try to attend the shore excursion briefing. Read the excursion literature and circle tours that appeal to you. Then go to the shore excursion office and ask any other questions you may have before you book.

Shore excursions are put together for general interest. If you want to see something that isn't described in the excursion literature, skip the excursion. Go on your own or with friends.

Brochure descriptions of shore excursions, often written by personnel who haven't visited the ports of call, can be imprecise. All cruise lines should adopt the following definitions in their descriptive literature and for their lectures and presentations: The term 'visit' should mean actually entering the place or building concerned. The term 'see' should mean viewing from the outside – as from a bus, for example.

Shopping on a shore excursion with Norwegian Cruise Line.

City excursions are basically superficial. To get to know a city intimately, go alone or with a small group. Go by taxi or bus, or explore on foot.

If you don't want to miss the major sightseeing attractions in each port, organized shore excursions provide a good solution. They also allow you to meet fellow passengers with similar interests.

In the Caribbean, many sightseeing tours cover the same ground, regardless of the cruise line you sail with. Choose one and then do something different in the next port. The same is true of the history and archaeology excursions in the Greek islands, where the same ancient gods will put in frequent appearances.

What if I lose my ticket?

Report lost or misplaced tickets to the shore excursion manager. Aboard most ships, excursion tickets, once sold, become the sole responsibility of the buyer, and the cruise line isn't generally able to issue replacements.

Are there private excursions?

Most cruise line-organized excursions work on the 'one-size-fits-all' principle. However, a more personalized alternative exists for anyone looking for privately guided tours and land experiences. Tailor-made 'build-your-own' excursions provide private tours of a destination and its environs, all arranged by a 'travel concierge.' These could include lunch or dinner in a hard-to-book top-class restaurant, a visit to a private museum, or other bespoke requirements for small groups.

The right transportation and private guide will be arranged, and all arrangements taken care of – at a cost, of course. A cruise line destination 'expert' will plan an

---

10 Destination Disappointments

1. Cagliari, Italy. Poor beaches and staggeringly overpriced shops.
2. Grenada. Hawkers on Grand Anse and other beaches.
3. Gibraltar. The rock's fine, but that's it – there's nothing else other than duty-free liquor.
4. Naples, Italy. Trying to cross the road from the cruise terminals to town can be frightening.
5. Cannes/Nice, France. There's dog poop all over the sidewalks!
6. Portofino, Italy. On a summer's day when several ships disgorge passengers onto a strip of land 6 inches wide.
7. St Maarten. When six large resort ships are docked at the same time.
8. Ensenada, Mexico. Poor area surrounding the cruise ship docking area.
9. Ocho Rios, Jamaica. Constant hustling to get you to buy something, and the general unsafe feeling.
10. Juneau, Alaska. The tacky souvenir shops are overwhelming.

Rafting in Costa Rica with Sea Dream Yacht Club.

excursion, arrange the right transportation, and attend to all the other details that make the experience more personal. It's all about exclusivity – at a price.

Examples of some of the more upscale ships such as those of Hebridean Island Cruises, Hapag-Lloyd, Regent Seven Seas Cruises, SeaDream Yacht Club, Seabourn and Silversea Cruises, shore excursions can be tailored to your specific needs. But even large resort ship lines like Norwegian Cruise Line (NCL) can book something special under its Freestyle Private Touring program.

Shopping ashore

Aboard ship, a 'shopping lecturer' will give a presentation about shopping in the various ports of call. Many cruise lines operating in Alaska, the Bahamas, the Caribbean, and the Mexican Riviera engage an outside company that provides the services of a 'shopping lecturer.' Most of the talk will be about designer jewelry and watches – high ticket items that boost commissions to cruise lines. The 'shopping lecturer' heavily promotes 'selected' shops, goods, and services, fully authorized by the cruise line, which receives a commission. Shopping maps, with 'selected' stores highlighted, are usually placed in your cabin, and sometimes include a guarantee of satisfaction valid for 30 days. By all means take any maps, but don't tie yourself into the 'approved' or 'selected' shops listed.

During organized shore excursions, be wary of stores recommended by tour guides – they may be receiving commissions from the merchants. Shop around before you purchase. When buying local handicrafts, make sure they have indeed been made locally. Be wary of 'bargain-priced' name brands, as they may be counterfeit. For watches, check the guarantee.

Some of the world's shopping havens put serious temptation in the way of cruise passengers. Top of the list are Hong Kong, Singapore, and Dubai (especially in the Mall of the Emirates – a shopping resort rather than a mall – and the Dubai Mall, with over 1,200 shops, including the only Bloomingdale's outside the USA).

A few shopping tips

Know in advance just what you are looking for, especially if your time is limited. If time is no problem, browsing can be fun.

When shopping time is included in shore excursions, be careful of stores repeatedly recommended by tour guides; the guides are likely to be receiving commissions from the merchants.

Shop around and compare prices before you buy. Good shopping hints and recommendations are often given in the cruise director's port lecture at the start of your cruise. If you notice cruise directors 'pushing' certain stores, it is likely that they, too, are on commission.

When shopping for local handicrafts, make sure they have indeed been made locally. It can happen that a so-called local product has in fact been made in Taiwan, Hong Kong, or another Far Eastern country. It pays to check.

Be wary of 'bargain priced' name brands such as Gucci bags and Rolex or Omega watches, as they may well be counterfeit. For watches, check the guarantee. If you have specific questions, ask the cruise director or shore excursion manager.

Remember that the ship's shops are also duty-free, and, for the most part, competitive in price. The shops on board are closed while in port, however, due to international customs regulations. Worthwhile discounts are often offered on the last day of the cruise.

Cruising for Families

Cruising can be a great vacation for families, but be sure to choose the right ship for your needs.

Cruising is child's play! More than 2 *million* under-18s went on a cruise in 2013; Carnival Cruise Lines alone carried over 725,000. Active parents can have the best of all worlds: family togetherness, social contact, and privacy. Cruise ships provide a virtually crime-free, encapsulated environment, and give young passengers a lot of freedom without parents having to be concerned about where their children are at all times. In other words, parents feel like they're on vacation, too – not just looking after the children. Mom can go and be pampered in the spa, while Dad can go to the sports bar.

Before you book a cruise, be sure that the ship really is family-friendly. Generally speaking, the new resort ships have dedicated spaces for children of all ages, while older ships offer only limited facilities. From the viewpoint of a cruise line, young children don't bring much revenue (they don't drink alcohol, play in the casino, or patronize the shop – except, perhaps, for diapers), and they can annoy older passengers, so some operators don't go out of their way to help. Facilities range from token family programs, with limited activities and only a couple of general staff allocated to look after children, to cruise lines that employ whole teams of counselors who run special programs off-limits to adults.

Some ships provide children's programs and youth counselors only during the summer holidays, Christmas, New Year, and Easter. Check whether the cruise line offers the right facilities for your needs at other times. Although many ships have full programs for children during days at sea, these may be limited when the ship is in port. If the ship has a playroom, find out if it is open and supervised on all days of the cruise.

Cruise companies like Carnival Cruise Lines, Disney Cruise Line, Norwegian Cruise Line, Princess Cruises, and Royal Caribbean International provide pagers for parents, while others provide them only for special needs children. In-cabin telephones aboard some ships can be set to 'in-cabin listening,' allowing parents to call their cabin from any of the ships' telephones and eavesdrop.

Most cruise lines give out colored bracelets to children; these must be worn at all times. These identify which muster station they belong to in the event of an emergency, as well as showing which children are enrolled in which activity programs.

Some youth programs allow older children (usually 10 and older, but it varies by cruise line) to sign themselves out of youth centers if authorized to do so by a parent. This makes it easy for children to meet family members somewhere else – by the pool or casual restaurant, for example – or go back to the cabin. If authorization isn't granted, only designated adults can sign them out of programs, typically by showing some ID or by providing a password created at the beginning of the cruise.

Bear in mind that a ship's medical department isn't set up for pediatric services: cruise ship doctors are generalists.

Disney goes cruising

In 1998, Disney Cruise Line introduced the first of two large resort ships to cater for families with children, with cruises of three, four, and seven days. *Disney Magic* and *Disney Wonder* were joined by *Disney Dream* in 2011 and by *Disney Fantasy* in 2012. The casino-free ships have ambitious entertainment pro-

Teaching kids how to draw Disney characters.

Architectural ambitions aboard *Enchantment of the Seas*.

grams, with everything centered around Disney and its superb stable of famous characters. Disney has its own Art Deco passenger terminal at Port Canaveral, Florida, plus a fleet of motorcoaches.

Each ship carries over 40 children's and youth counselors, and families preparing to sail with children under three years of age have access to an online service that allows them to order baby supplies in advance of their cruise and have them delivered to their cabin. The service, exclusive to Disney Cruise Line passengers, is provided by Babies Travel Lite, an online retailer offering more than 1,000 brand-name baby products including diapers, baby food, infant formula, and specialty travel items. On disneycruise.com, you can access a section of the Babies Travel Lite website where you can create orders for familiar brands in quantities customized to the length of your cruise.

One ship sails in the Mediterranean in summer from Barcelona, and another sails in Alaska in summer. Disney calls at its own 1,000-acre (400-hectare) private island on three-, four-, and seven-day Bahamas and Caribbean cruises. About 50 miles (80km) north of Nassau in the Bahamas it's called Castaway Cay – Disney's own private country, with its own ship docking pier. (Locals say it had a military landing strip that was once used by drug runners.) Beaches are divided into family-friendly and adults-only 'quiet' sections.

Barbie steps aboard

Mattel and Royal Caribbean International now offer free Barbie-related activities (ages four to 11 are the main consumers) in the Adventure Ocean youth club. There's also a Barbie Premium Experience, complete with special pink cabin decor and a free Barbie doll blanket, tote bag and toothbrush, a special tea with pink cupcakes and dainty dishes, and a mermaid dance class featuring dances from the movie 'Barbie in a Mermaid Tale 2'; plus other perks. Price: $349 per child.

Before you embark

You should remember to pack a child's favorite toys and any medications for your journey to the ship. If flying to an embarkation port, pack games, books, a bathing suit, and a change of clothes for your child in your carry-on, plus any important medication – just in case any checked-in luggage gets lost.

On embarkation day, it's wise to take essentials in a carry-on or tote bag, because your luggage may not be delivered to your cabin until several hours after you embark. This is especially so aboard the large resort ships.

Children's fares

Children under two travel free on most cruise lines and airlines (aboard MSC Cruises, kids under 12 sail free, paying only port taxes). If they're older, however, you have to pay. Most cruise lines offer special rates for children sharing their parents' cabin. The cost is often lower than third and fourth person share rates. For best rates, book early.

Although many adult cruise rates include airfare, most children's rates don't. Also, although some lines say children sail 'free,' they must pay port taxes as well as airfare. The cruise line should be able to get the airfare at the best rate.

Dining with children

Flexibility is the key. Coaxing children out of a pool, getting them dressed and ready to sit quietly through a four-course dinner every night can be tough. Work out a compromise by eating dinner together occasionally at the buffet. Most ships offer a tempting menu of children's favorites, and some ships have special mealtimes for children.

Children with special needs

If a child has special needs, you'll need to advise the cruise line when you book. Children needing one-to-one care or assistance must be accompanied by a parent or guardian when in the children's play center.

Choosing a cabin

Ship designers now take into account the notion that 'families who play together want to stay together.' Although connecting cabins and Pullman beds are nothing new on family-friendly ships, brands like Norwegian Cruise Lines and Royal Caribbean International have taken group-friendly accommodations to new levels.

Families cruising together often find that sharing a confined space causes most distress. So, before booking, check the size of the cabin and pace it out at home, remembering that the size quoted on ship deck plans includes the bathroom. There's no doubt that certain ships work best for certain age groups. For example, multigenerational groups might consider gigantic re-

sort ships such as Royal Caribbean International's *Allure of the Seas* or *Oasis of the Seas*.

If you are a large family, some ships (such as NCL's) have three-bedroom suites that can accommodate as many as 14. Larger cabins or suites have much more space, and may include sofa beds. Several cruise lines have special family cabins that can accommodate two adults and several junior cruisers – 14 family cabins, 39 junior suites, and 12 suites aboard *Mein Schiff 2* include an Xbox games console.

It's best to choose the largest cabin you can afford, because, if there's not enough storage space, you can expect to use your suitcase a lot for young children's dolls, games or toys, and for toddlers' diapers and baby food. If you have a large or extended family, cabins with interconnecting doors may be more practical.

If you are travelling with teens, consider booking them an adjoining cabinet or one across the hallway from yours. You'll get your own space, and your teens will have their bathroom and some privacy. You give them freedom, but at arm's length. If your children are younger, perhaps a cabin with an interconnecting door would make more sense. Many ships have with two lower beds and one or two upper berths. But in some cabins, the two lower beds can't be pushed together to form a queen-size bed for parents. This means mom and dad and one or two children all have separate beds.

Some ships, such as *Disney Dream, Disney Fantasy, Disney Magic, Disney Wonder,* and *Norwegian Epic,* have cabins with two bathrooms.

If possible, opt for a cabin with a balcony for yourselves. An interior (no-view) cabin may be adequate for a short cruise, but could be claustrophobic on a 10-day

---

Why teens love cruising

After talking to many teenagers and younger children aboard various cruise ships, I decided it was time to include a couple of quotes about how they enjoy cruising and their experiences.

Jens S., from Copenhagen, Denmark, (in his early teens, Jens has sailed for more than 200 cruise days aboard some very nice ships), says: "I really like cruise vacations, because they are a lot more fun than staying at a hotel. You get to see several places and nice beaches, and the staff is always kind and smiling."

"It's exciting to sail, especially when you see dolphins and whales. And in the restaurants you can get all your favorite meals – and desserts, and even extra portions if you want (my favorite dessert is Chocolate Fondant). If you want popcorn or a hamburger – or almost anything – you just order it from room service and it comes free!"

"I have been lucky enough to be invited to the bridge several times – some captains let me sound the horn. Now I have started a collection of plaques from the ships I sail with. My favorite ship is *Silver Wind,* because it sails to so many nice areas of the world, and the captain and I have become good

friends. But I also like *SeaDream I.* But my favorite trip of all is a transatlantic crossing aboard *Queen Mary 2.* My ultimate Christmas present, however, is going to be a cruise aboard *Europa 2.* Please, dad..."

Alexandra T.C., from Brighton, Colorado, USA, who was sailing aboard *Celebrity Reflection* (on her third cruise), says: "I like this ship because the crew is so accommodating, the fact that the ship has so many different aspects and interesting rooms, and the fresh new experiences I get every day, whether on my own or with other teenagers."

"The ship is big, with lots of people, but I never feel it's crowded, because there are so many different areas, and I like the cabanas on the lawn. I also like all the different shore excursions available – there's so much choice I absolutely never feel bored."

"I also like the many different choices and types of food, the service (you can't get this kind of service on land today), and the social interaction with other teenagers in such a comfortable environment. Also, we teenagers really appreciate having our own 'get away-from-parents' chill-out room with nobody to keep bothering us."

Even upscale ships such as *Europa* cater for kids.

Mediterranean vacation. To get access to fresh air without a balcony, you'd have to keep trudging up to the open deck, carrying towels and other . If you have a baby, having a balcony gives you somewhere to escape to in the evening while keeping an eye on a (hopefully) sleeping infant. On the other hand, if you don't anticipate spending much time in your cabin, an interior (no-view) cabin is cheaper.

Try to book an *assigned* cabin rather than a *guaranteed* cabin; the latter means that only the space within a specific category is *guaranteed* for you – the room and bed configuration may not be the same as the one you wanted.

Age groups

Cruise lines divide young cruisers into distinct age groups: Toddlers (ages two to four), Juniors (five to seven), Intermediate (ages eight to 10), Tweens (11–13), and Teens (14–17). It often seems to be children under 12 who get the most from a cruise. However, you might, for example, have an 11-year-old who is 'old' for his age; he may want to join the 12-to-14 group, but the line may not allow him to do so. Perhaps there could be more flexibility in future, to judge children on their individual merits – in fact, Disney has started thinking about it.

Note that some cruise lines with ships that only call in U.S. ports infrequently question whether it's worth going through the expense of putting peepholes in all doors as required under the 2010 Cruise Vessel Security and Safety Act (USA).

When you check-in online, note that if you don't register a credit card for your children, you may not be able to print out their boarding passes.

Children's passports

Note that separate passports are required for all children traveling internationally. If you have an *adopted* child, you may need not only a passport, but Adoption Placement Papers, as well as the child's Birth Certificate.

Confirming a guardian's identity

A Parent and Guardian Consent Form (PGCSA) will be needed at or before embarkation if you are a grandparent, parent, or guardian with a passport surname different from that of any child traveling with you. Without this form, which includes passport information of the child's legal parent, you will be denied boarding.

Single parents

Only a few cruise lines have introduced their versions of the 'Single Parent Plan' (e.g., Disney Cruise Line, P&O Cruises). This offers an economical way for single parents to take their children on a cruise, with parent and child sharing a two-berth cabin, or parent and children sharing a three-berth cabin. Reduced rates may apply to children of single parents in the same cabin.

As a single parent, you should expect to pay about one-third the normal single-person rate for your children. However, as a single parent with just one child, you may have to pay for two adults (double occupancy), so it's important to check the pricing policy of each cruise line you're interested in. It may also be better to take an adult friend and share the cost (in some cases, your child could travel free).

Babysitting

If you do take baby (or babies) along, and you want some time to yourself, you'll need the services of a babysitter, so choose your ship carefully. Some, but not all, ships have babysitting services; some have restricted hours (meaning you'll need to be back by midnight like a grown-up Cinderella); and some have only group babysitting and not in-cabin care. In some ships, stewards, stewardesses, and other staff may be available as private babysitters for an hourly charge. For example, *Queen Mary 2* has children's nurses and English nannies trained in arm-to-arm combat. *Aurora, Azura, Oceana,* and *Ventura* have a 'night nursery' for two- to five-year-olds.

Family reunions and birthdays

A cruise can provide the ideal place for a family get-together, with or without children. Let your travel agent make the arrangements, and ask for a group discount if there are more than 15 of you.

With pricing that includes accommodations, meals, entertainment, use of most of the ship's recreational facilities, and travel from destination to destination, any cruise represents excellent value for money. Cruise lines also make special offers to groups.

Family groups may have the option to ensure even greater value by purchasing everything in advance, from cruise fares to shore excursions, drinks packages, spa packages, and even pre-paid gratuities. Additional savings can be realized through reduced fares for third and fourth passengers in each cabin, and some cruise lines offer 'kids sail free' programs.

Formal nights

Some ships have nights when traditional 'formal attire' is the required dress code. If you don't want your children to dress formally (although some children really enjoy getting dressed up – it's a bit like going to a prom night), you can opt out of the festivities, and simply head for one of the casual dining options. Or your kids may prefer to opt out and go to the children's clubs or teen rooms and hang out while you go to the captain's cocktail party.

Tips for happy family cruising

Take wet wipes for those inevitable clothes stains, and anti-bacterial hand wipes and face wipes to keep you cool when it's hot outside.

Take a highlighter pen – good for marking the daily program and shore excursion literature, so you can focus on what's important to you and the children.

Take an extension cord or power strip (not all cruise lines allow them), because there will be plenty of things to plug in (chargers for games consoles, mobile phone , and iPod/iPad, etc.). Most cabins provide only one electrical outlet.

Use plastic compression bags for packing clothes (squeezing or vacuuming the air out); use one each for parents, and each child. They help keep clothes fresh, and makes it easier to sort out when you return home

Take around-the-neck lanyards for security. Your child(ren) can pop their cabin/sign card into it and not

On the look-out for icebergs.

have to think about misplacing it. Lanyards are also good for beach days, so you have somewhere to put things when wearing only a bathing suit.

Wide-mouth water bottles (empty until you are on board ship) are useful for shore excursions, beach days, and other outings.

A pop-up laundry basket could prove useful for keeping everyone's dirty laundry separate from clean items (really useful in small cabins).

Take lots of sunscreen (including SPF45 or above face cream).

A set of walkie-talkie radios can prove useful for keeping track of everyone's whereabouts, but only if everyone remembers to turn them on!

Glow sticks – kids love them – for use as night lights (they are cheap and come in different colors – one for each night).

If you have very young children, take lots of plastic bags – they are always useful.

Post-it notes are great for leaving messages in the cabin – for your children – or the cabin attendant.

The ships that cater well for children

These ships have been selected for the quality of their children's programs:

Aida Cruises: *AIDAbella, AIDAblu, AIDAluna, AIDAmar, AIDAsol, AIDAstella*

Carnival Cruise Lines: *Carnival Breeze, Carnival Conquest, Carnival Dream, Carnival Freedom, Carnival Glory, Carnival Legend, Carnival Liberty, Carnival Pride, Carnival Spirit, Carnival Splendor, Carnival Sunshine, Carnival Triumph, Carnival Valor, Carnival Victory*

Celebrity Cruises: *Celebrity Constellation, Celebrity Eclipse, Celebrity Equinox, Celebrity Infinity, Celebrity Millennium, Celebrity Reflection, Celebrity Solstice, Celebrity Summit*

Costa Cruises: *Costa Atlantica, Costa Deliziosa, Costa Fascinosa, Costa Favolosa, Costa Fortuna, Costa Luminosa, Costa Magica, Costa Mediterranea, Costa Pacifica, Costa Serena*

Cunard Line: *Queen Elizabeth, Queen Mary 2, Queen Victoria*

Disney Cruise Line: *Disney Dream, Disney Fantasy, Disney Magic, Disney Wonder*

MSC Cruises: *MSC Divina, MSC Fantasia, MSC Preziosa, MSC Splendida*

Norwegian Cruise Line: *Norwegian Breakaway, Norwegian Epic, Norwegian Getaway, Norwegian Star*

P&O Cruises: *Aurora, Azura, Oceana, Ventura*

Princess Cruises: *Crown Princess, Diamond Princess, Emerald Princess, Golden Princess, Grand Princess, Royal Princess, Ruby Princess, Sapphire Princess, Star Princess*

Royal Caribbean International: *Adventure of the Seas, Allure of the Seas, Explorer of the Seas, Freedom of the Seas, Independence of the Seas, Liberty of the Seas, Mariner of the Seas, Navigator of the Seas, Oasis of the Seas, Voyager of the Seas*

Star Cruises: *SuperStar Virgo*

Thomson Cruises: *Thomson Dream, Thomson Majesty*

TUI Cruises: *Mein Schiff I, Mein Schiff 2, Mein Schiff 3*

Cruising with children under three

Many new or recent parents want to take their babies with them when they cruise. Perhaps the most attractive consideration is that they need to pack and unpack the baby things only once, they'll get to see new destinations, and experience life on the ocean wave.

First, check with your travel agent or cruise line whether your new baby is old enough. Some companies, such as Carnival Cruise Lines, don't accept babies under six months old because of concerns over specialist medical attention that they might require.

It's important to check the ship's itinerary. Why? Because it's easier if a ship docks alongside in each port, rather than being at anchor, when shore tenders must be used (these may require you to go down a rigged ladder to a small boat waiting to take you ashore – not easy with an infant in tow).

Remember that you'll need to look after your child the whole time, unless you choose one of the few ships that have a proper nursery and qualified staff to look after toddlers. Ships with a nursery for ages six months to 36 months: *Allure of the Seas, Disney Dream, Disney Fantasy, Disney Magic, Disney Wonder,* and *Oasis of the Seas.*

Children under three years old need to be potty-trained to take part in any group activities that are available. Check whether babies and toddlers are allowed in paddling and swimming pools, and whether they must wear swim diapers.

Check with the cruise line or your travel agent *before* you book, what equipment is available, and whether it must be pre-booked. Some cruise ships will lend you bouncy seats, cribs, strollers, books, toys, cots, and bed guards. Bear in mind that you may have to bathe small children in a small shower enclosure with a fixed-head shower.

Disposable diapers (nappies), wipes, and sterilizing fluid can be purchased aboard most child-friendly ships, but they are expensive so it's wise to bring your own supplies. You may be able to pre-order diapers – they'll be in your cabin when you embark.

Feeding children under three

Selected baby foods are stocked by ships catering to children, but ask your travel agent to get confirmation in writing that they'll be provided. If you need a special brand of baby food, let your travel agent know well in advance, or bring your own. Parents using organic baby foods, such as those obtained from health food stores, should be aware that cruise lines buy their supplies from major general food suppliers and not from the smaller specialized food houses.

Shore excursions

When going ashore, remember that if you want to take your children swimming or to the beach, it is wise to telephone ahead to a local hotel with a beach or pool. Many hotels will be happy to show off their property to you, hoping to gain your future business.

Some cruise ships in the Caribbean have the use of a 'private' island for a day, including waterpark areas for children and adults. A lifeguard will be on duty, and there will be water-sports and snorkeling equipment you can rent. But remember that the beaches on some 'private' islands are fine for 200 passengers, but with 2,000 they quickly become crowded, forcing you to stand in line for beach barbecues and toilet facilities. Also, since operators take advantage of the captive

A family goes scuba diving in the Caribbean.

Junior chefs of Princess Cruises.

market, rental of beach and water-sports items can be very expensive.

Activities for pre-teens
Supervised group activities and activity/play centers mean that you won't have to be concerned, and will be able to enjoy yourself, knowing that your children are in good hands. Some cruise lines issue beepers in case of problems. Activities typically include make-up and cookery classes, arts and crafts projects, group games, interactive computer programs, character parades and scavenger hunts, and watching movies and video wall programming. Then there are the outdoor activities like water slides, miniature golf, and swimming.

Activities for teens
Many large resort ships have dedicated 'no adults allowed' zones. Teens-only activities include deck parties, pool parties, sports tournaments, poolside games, karaoke, discos, dances, computer games, video arcades, activity clubs, and talent shows. Some Royal Caribbean International ships provide musical instruments for jam sessions. Sports include rock-climbing, rollerblading, basketball, and riding the wave surfer. With some cruise lines, the fun even extends ashore, with beach barbecues and excursions aimed at younger passengers. There's usually almost unlimited food, too, although some of it may not be very nutritious.

How grandparents can bridge the generation gap
Many children love to go cruising with grandparents, perhaps because they anticipate fewer restrictions than they have at home. And busy parents like the idea, too, particularly if the grandparents make a contribution to the cost.

Having enrolled their grandchildren in age-related groups for daytime activities aboard ship (note the limitations on activities for children under three, as mentioned above), grandparents will be able to enjoy the adults-only facilities, such as the wellness and spa treatments. Not surprisingly, it's the large resort ships that provide the widest choice of facilities for both age groups. For those not averse to ubiquitous cartoon characters, Disney Cruise Line provides some facilities for adults and children in separate areas, but also allows them to mix in others.

On board
Most cruise lines offer scheduled activities from 9am to noon, 2–5pm, and 7–10pm. This means you can drop your grandchild off after breakfast, relax by the pool, go to a lecture, or take part in other activities, and pick them up for lunch. After a couple of hours together, they can rejoin their friends while you enjoy an afternoon movie or siesta.

Shore excursions
Consider your grandchild's interests before booking expensive shore excursions (example: flightseeing in Alaska). It's also best to avoid long bus rides, shopping trips, and scenic tours, and better to choose excursions that feature water and/or animals. Examples include snorkeling, aquariums, or nature walks. Remember to pack snacks. In some ports, it may be better to explore on your own. If your grandchildren are really young, full-day shore excursions are a bad idea.

Cruising for Seniors

Many people are living longer and healthier lives, and cruise lines are keen to cater to their particular needs.

Although cruise lines have been striving, with some success, to embrace all age groups, the over-60s remain an important segment of the market. Group cruising for seniors, in fact, is growing in popularity and is a good way for like-minded people to vacation together. Nowhere is this more evident than in Japan's 'Golden Week,' a collection of four national holidays within seven days in late April/early May, when seniors clamor for available cabins.

One trend for seniors is toward longer cruises – even round-the-world cruises if they can afford them. Some opt for an adults-only ship such as *Adonia, Arcadia,* or *Oriana* (P&O Cruises) or *Saga Sapphire* (Saga Cruises). There are bargains to be had, too. Organizations for seniors such as AARP (American Association of Retired Persons) in the United States and Saga in the UK often offer discount fares and upgrades.

Some seniors who may have had major surgery or have mobility problems cannot fly, or don't wish to, are helped by the 'Homeland Cruising' trend, which enables them to embark at and disembark from a nearby port in their home country. In the United States, the number of homeland ports increased dramatically following the terrorist attacks of September 2001. In the UK, some cruise ships sail from ports in both the north and south of the country. The same is true elsewhere, as language-specific cruise lines and ships proliferate.

But all is far from perfect. Some cruise lines have yet to recognize that, with seniors as with other groups, one size does *not* fit all. Only a few, for example, take the trouble to provide the kind of items that millions of seniors need, such as large-print editions of daily programs, menus, and other printed matter.

Special diets

While the wide range of cuisine aboard many ships is a big attraction, cruise lines understand that many passengers are on special diets. Lighter menu options are available aboard most ships, as well as vegetarian and vegan choices. Options can include low sodium, low fat, low cholesterol, and sugar-free entrées and

---

Why seniors like cruising – but can often find it frustrating

Thumbs Up

A cruise is an excellent choice for those who like to be independent while having the chance to meet other like-minded people.

Cruising is stress-free and relaxing. You don't have to keep packing and unpacking as you do on a land-based tour.

It's safe. You travel and dine in comfort and safety, while your floating hotel takes you to a choice of around 2,000 destinations all over the world.

Lecturers and lessons in everything from golf to computing provide a chance to learn something new.

There's plenty of entertainment – shows, cinema, casinos, games, dances.

All main and self-serve buffet meals are included in the fare, and those on special diets can be easily accommodated.

Senior singles, in particular, find it easy to meet others in a non-threatening environment. Some ships provide male dance hosts, screened and subject to a strict code of ethics, who can also act as escorts on shore excursions.

Most ships have 24-hour room service and a 24-hour reception desk.

The disabled can find ships that cater to their needs.

Ships carry a medical doctor and one or more trained nurses. In an emergency, treatment can be arranged.

Thumbs Down

Online check-in procedures, and unreadable Passenger Ticket Conditions and Contracts that are provided only online.

Credit card-size electronic key cards to cabins that often don't make it clear which end to insert and penalize those passengers with poor eyesight.

Booking events and meals via the in-cabin 'interactive' television/keypad system; it is user-unfriendly for many seniors (all services should be readily accessible via telephone).

Poor, difficult-to-read signage such as 'You are here' deck plans unreadable from farther away than an inch.

Menus with small, hard-to-read typefaces, and daily programs that require a magnifying glass.

Buffets with plates only, requiring several visits, and cutlery too heavy to hold comfortably.

Anything that requires a signature – for example: bar, shore excursions, spa bills with small print.

Libraries with few books, if any, in large-print format – notably recent novels.

The absence of a 'concierge' for seniors.

Public toilets not clearly marked.

The lack of music-free lounges and bars for conversation and drinks.

Making new friends aboard *Oasis of the Seas*.

desserts. A booking agent will ensure that special dietary needs are recorded.

Healthier eating

You don't have to put on weight during a cruise. Many health-conscious seniors prefer smaller portions of food with taste and nutritional value rather than the overflowing plates.

Heart-healthy diets are in demand, as are low-fat, low-carbohydrate, salt-free, or low-salt foods. Denture wearers often request food that includes softer items.

Those seeking lighter fare should be aware that most cruise lines have an 'always available' section of heart-healthy items that can be cooked plainly, such as grilled or steamed salmon, skinless chicken breast, lean sirloin steak, or baked potatoes.

Gentlemen hosts

Because more female than male seniors cruise, cruise lines have developed 'gentlemen host' programs. These are gentlemen, typically over 55 years of age, selected for their social skills and competence as dance partners, for dining table conversation, and for accompanying passengers on shore excursions.

Cruise lines with gentlemen hosts include: Celebrity Cruises, Crystal Cruises, Cunard Line, Holland America Line, P&O Cruises, Princess Cruises, Regent Seven Seas Cruises, Seabourn, Silversea Cruises, Swan Hellenic Cruises, Voyages of Discovery Cruises and Voyages to Antiquity.

Enrichment programs

Many seniors want to learn about a destination's history and culture rather than be told which shops to visit ashore. Lecturers of academic quality are found aboard some smaller ships such as *Aegean Odyssey* (Voyages to Antiquity), *Minerva* (Swan Hellenic Cruises), and *Saga Sapphire* (Saga Cruises). Some lines, such as Crystal Cruises, have special interest lecturers on topics such as archaeology, food and wine, ornithology, and military history.

Tips for seniors

If you're traveling solo, it's important to check the price of any single supplements.

If you take medication, make sure you have enough with you. Some ships are dressy, some are casual. Choose a ship according to your own lifestyle and tastes.

If you have mobility difficulties, choose one of the newer ships that have public rooms with an 'open-flow' style of interior design. Examples include *Arcadia, Balmoral, Eurodam, Nieuw Amsterdam, Oosterdam, Queen Elizabeth, Queen Mary 2, Queen Victoria, Westerdam,* and *Zuiderdam.* Older ships, such as *Marco Polo,* have 'lips' or doors between public rooms.

Best facilities

Among the cruise lines that provide the facilities and onboard environment that seniors tend to enjoy most are: American Cruise Lines, Azamara Club Cruises, Blount Small Ship Adventures, Classic International Cruises, Crystal Cruises, Delphin Cruises, Fred Olsen Cruise Lines, Hebridean Island Cruises, Holland America Line, Noble Caledonia, Oceania Cruises, P&O Cruises, Pearl Seas Cruises, Regent Seven Seas Cruises, Saga Cruises, Sea Cloud Cruises, Seabourn, Silversea Cruises, Swan Hellenic Cruises, Voyages of Discovery, and Voyages to Antiquity.

Cruising for Romantics

No need to worry about getting to the church on time; you can be married at sea, get engaged, renew your vows, or enjoy a second honeymoon.

Two classic TV shows, *The Love Boat* (US) and *Traumschiff* (Germany), boosted the concept of cruising as a romantic vacation, the natural culmination of which would be getting married at sea. Such ceremonies have become such big money-earners that, after 171 years, Cunard Line changed the registry of its three ships in 2011 from its traditional home port of Southampton to Hamilton, Bermuda, partly because its British registry didn't allow it to perform weddings. As a result, couples can now say 'I do' aboard *Queen Mary 2* in the middle of the North Atlantic.

Tying the knot at sea

This popular option includes a honeymoon and a wedding planner who can sort out all the details such as arranging flights, hotels, transportation, and packages. For the bride, spa and beauty services are on hand, and you can sail into the sunset after the reception.

You first need to inquire in your country of domicile whether such a marriage is legal, and ascertain what paperwork and blood tests are required. It is up to you to prove the validity of such a marriage. The captain could be held legally responsible if he or she married a couple not entitled to be wed.

It's relatively easy to get wed aboard almost any cruise ship when it's in port. Carnival Cruise Lines, Celebrity Cruises, Costa Cruises, Holland America Line, Princess Cruises, and Royal Caribbean International, among others, offer special wedding packages. These include the services of a minister to marry you, wedding cake, Champagne, bouquet and boutonnière, a band to perform at the ceremony, and an album of wedding pictures. Note that US citizens and legal residents may need to pay sales tax on wedding packages.

Asuka Cruise, Azamara Club Cruises, Celebrity Cruises, Cunard Line, P&O Cruises, Princess Cruises, and Royal Caribbean International offer weddings aboard their ships. The ceremonies can be performed by the captain, who is certified as a notary, when the ships' registry – Bermuda, Japan, or Malta, for example – recognizes such unions. Japanese citizens can also be married at sea aboard one of the Japan-registered cruise ships.

Expect to pay about $3,000, plus about $500 for licensing fees. Harbor-side or shore-side packages vary according to the port.

Even if you don't get married aboard ship, you could have your wedding reception aboard one. Contact the director of hotel services at the cruise line. The cruise

Afternoon tea aboard a Cunard ship can be a romantic experience.

A honeymoon couple enjoy being pampered on an MSC Cruises ship.

line should go out of its way to help, especially if you follow the reception with a honeymoon cruise.

UK-based passengers should know that P&O Cruises hosts a series of cruises called the 'Red-Letter Anniversary Collection' for those celebrating 10, 15, 20, 25, 30, 35, 40, 45, 50, 55, or 60 years of marriage. The cruise comes with a complimentary gift, such as a brass carriage clock, leather photograph album, or free car parking at Southampton.

Getting married ashore
An alternative is to have a marriage ceremony in an exotic destination with your reception and honeymoon aboard ship afterwards. For example, you could get married on the beach in Barbados or Hawaii; on a glacier in Juneau, Alaska; in a villa in Rome or Venice; in an authentic Tahitian village; in Central Park, New York; or on Disney's Castaway Cay in the Bahamas, with Mickey and Minnie at hand. Note that your marriage license must be from the jurisdiction in which you will be married. If you set your heart on a Bermuda beach wedding, for example, the license must be obtained in Bermuda, no matter what your nationality is.

Getting engaged aboard ship
For those who aren't quite ready to tie the knot, Princess Cruises has a special 'Engagement Under the Stars' package that allows you to propose to your loved one in a personal video that is then screened just before an evening movie at a large outdoor screen aboard some of the company's ships. Current cost: $695.

Renewal of vows
Many cruise lines perform 'renewal of vows' ceremonies. A cruise is a wonderful setting for reaffirming to one's partner the strength of commitment. A handful of ships have a small chapel where this ceremony can take place; otherwise, it can be anywhere aboard ship – a most romantic time is at sunrise or sunset on the open deck. The renewal of vows ceremony is conducted by the ship's captain, using a non-denominational text.

Although some companies, such as Carnival Cruise Lines, Celebrity Cruises, Cunard Line, Holland America Line, P&O Cruises, and Princess Cruises, have complete packages for purchase, which include music, champagne, hors d'oeuvres, certificate, corsages for the women, and so on, most other companies do not charge – yet.

Cruising for honeymooners
There are many advantages in honeymooning at sea: you pack and unpack only once; it is a hassle-free and safe environment; and you get special attention, if you want it. It is easy to budget in advance, as one price often includes airfare, cruise, food, entertainment, several destinations, shore excursions, and pre- and post-cruise hotel stays. Also, some cruise lines offer discounts if you book a future cruise to celebrate an anniversary.

Although no ship as yet provides real bridal suites, many ships have suites with king- or queen-size beds. Some also provide tables for two in the dining room, should you wish to dine together without having to make friends with others. A variety of honeymoon packages is available; these might include champagne and caviar for breakfast, flowers in the suite or cabin, a complimentary cake, and a private captain's cocktail party.

Some cruise ships have Sunday departures, so couples can plan a Saturday wedding and reception before traveling to their ship. Pre- and post-cruise hotel accommodation can also be arranged.

Most large resort ships accommodate honeymoon couples well. However, couples averse to crowds might try one of the smaller cruise ships such as those of Regent Seven Seas Cruises, Seabourn, Silversea Cruises, or Windstar Cruises.

And for quiet moments? The deck to the forward part of a ship, near the bridge, is the most dimly lit part and the quietest – except perhaps for some wind noise.

Cruising for Solo Travelers

Cruise prices are geared toward couples, yet about
one in four cruise passengers travels alone or as
a single parent. How do they fare?

Cruising, in general, is designed for couples. Many solo passengers (including GLBT – gay, lesbian, bisexual, and transgender) are prejudiced against cruising because most lines charge them a single-occupancy supplement. The reason is that the most precious commodity aboard any ship is space. Since a solo-occupancy cabin is often as large as a double and is just as expensive to build, cruise lines feel the premium price is justified. What's more, because solo-occupancy cabins are at a premium, they are less likely to be discounted.

Single supplements

If you are not sharing a cabin, you'll be asked to pay either a flat rate or a single 'supplement' to occupy a double-occupancy cabin by yourself. Some lines charge a fixed amount – $250, for instance – as a supplement, no matter what the cabin category, ship, itinerary, or length of cruise. Such rates vary between lines, and sometimes between a particular line's ships. Because there are so few single-occupancy cabins, it's best to book as far ahead as you can.

Cruise lines that charge low single supplements –

Cunard Line provides dance hosts as partners.

on selected voyages – include Azamara Club Cruises, Crystal Cruises, Fred Olsen Cruise Lines, Peter Deilmann Ocean Cruises, Orion Expedition Cruises, Saga Cruises, Seabourn, Silversea Cruises, and Voyages of Discovery. Note that Saga Cruises has no additional supplements for solo travelers on any cruise, but has special fares built-in. Do watch out for sneaky cruise lines that may try to charge you *twice* for port charges and government taxes (by including that non-existent second person in the cabin you occupy as a single), so check your cruise fare invoice carefully.

Other cruise lines, such as MSC Cruises and Norwegian Cruise Line (and some of the river cruise companies such as Viking River Cruises), often have special promotions for solo occupancy of what are normally priced as double-person cabins.

Guaranteed singles rates

Some lines offer singles a set price for a double cabin but reserve the right to choose the cabin. So you could end up with a rotten cabin in a poor location or a wonderful cabin that happened to be unallocated.

Guaranteed share programs

These allow you to pay what it would cost each half of a couple for a double-occupancy cabin, but the cruise line will find another passenger of the same sex (and preferences such as smoking or non-smoking) to share it with you. If the line doesn't find a cabin-mate, the single passenger may get the cabin to himself or herself at no extra charge. Some cruise lines don't advertise a guaranteed-share program in their brochures but will often try to accommodate such bookings at times when demand for space is comparatively light.

Solo dining

A common irritation concerns dining arrangements. Before you take your cruise, make sure that you request a table assignment based on your personal preferences; table sizes are typically for two, four, six, or eight people. Do you want to sit with other singles? Or do you like to sit with couples? Or perhaps with a mixture of both? Or with passengers who may not speak your language?

When you are on board, make sure that you are comfortable with the dining arrangements, particularly in ships with fixed table assignments, or ask the maître d' to move you to a different table. Aboard ships with open seating or with several different dining venues, you can choose which venue you want to eat in, and when; Norwegian Cruise Line (NCL) is an example of this arrangement, with its Freestyle Dining, as is Star Cruises.

Cruising for single women

A cruise ship is at least as safe for single women as any major vacation destination, but of course that doesn't mean it is entirely hassle-free. It's easy to strike up conversations with other passengers, and cruising is not a 'meat market' that keeps you under constant observation. The easiest way to meet other singles is to participate in scheduled activities. Single black women may find there is often a dearth of single black men for dancing or socializing with.

Beware of embarking on an easy affair with a ship's officer or crew member. They meet new people on every cruise and could transmit sexual diseases. Crew members have few romantic illusions – indeed, they have been known to award an imaginary Golden Mattress to whoever can bed the most passengers.

Gentlemen cruise hosts

The female-to-male passenger ratio is typically high, especially among older people, so some cruise lines provide male social hosts. They may host a table in the dining room, appear as dance partners at cocktail parties and dance classes, join bridge games, and accompany women on shore excursions.

These men, usually over 55 and retired, are outgoing, mingle easily, and are well groomed. First intro-

A DJ keeps the music going at a late-night disco.

duced aboard Cunard Line's *QE2* in the mid-1970s, gentlemen hosts are now employed by a number of cruise lines, including Crystal Cruises, Cunard Line, Holland America Line, Regent Seven Seas Cruises, Silversea Cruises, and Voyages to Antiquity.

If you think you'd like such a job, do remember that you'll have to dance for several hours most nights, and be proficient in just about every kind of dance.

Options for gays, lesbians, and others

Several US companies specialize in ship charters or large group bookings for gay and lesbian passengers. These include the California-based Atlantis (www.atlantisevents.com), San Francisco's lesbian specialist Olivia (www.olivia.com), or New York's Pied Piper Travel (piedpipertravel.com/gaygroupcruises).

One drawback of gay charters is that they're as much as 20 percent more expensive than the equivalent general cruise. Another is that they have been greeted with hostility by church groups on some Caribbean islands such as Grand Cayman, Jamaica, and Bermuda. One Atlantis cruise was even denied the right to dock. But their great advantage is that they provide an accepting environment and gay-oriented entertainment, with some big-name comedians and singers.

Another idea is to join a gay affinity group on a regular cruise at normal prices; these groups may be offered amenities such as private dining rooms and separate shore excursions.

Many gays, of course, have no wish to travel exclusively with other gays but may worry that, on a mainstream cruise, they might be seated for dinner with unsympathetic companions. They would prefer to sit where they want, when they want, and such open seating is now offered by most of the major operators such as Carnival Cruise Lines, Celebrity Cruises, Holland America Line, Norwegian Cruise Line, Princess Cruises, and Royal Caribbean International (request this option when you book) and by upscale lines such as Crystal Cruises, Oceania

Cruises, Regent Seven Seas Cruises, Seabourn, and Silversea Cruises. Open-seating dining is not currently offered by Costa Cruises, Cunard Line, or MSC Cruises.

That doesn't mean that any of the major cruise companies are not gay-friendly – many hold regular 'Friends of Dorothy' gatherings, sometimes scheduled and sometimes on request – though it would be prudent to realize that Disney Cruise Line, for example, will not really offer the ideal entertainment and ambience. Among the smaller companies, Windstar's sail-powered cruise yachts have a reputation for being gay-friendly.

Gay families are catered to by R Family Vacations (www.rfamilyvacations.com), although it's not essential to bring children. Events may include seminars on adoption and discussion groups for teenagers in gay families. One of the company's founders was the former TV talk show host Rosie O'Donnell.

Bisexual and transgender travelers also like to cruise, and are in general welcomed by most cruise lines as regular passengers (whether traveling solo or as couples). Transgender passengers, however, may encounter some problems, such as the passport name being of one gender (the birth gender), while appearance and dress suggest another. Ships sometimes encounter problems in some ports when passenger ID cards do not match the gender on the ship's manifest.

Cruising to Suit Special Needs

Cruising offers one of the most hassle-free vacations
possible for the physically challenged, but it's important
to choose the right ship and prepare in advance.

If you are mobility-limited or otherwise physically challenged (this includes sight or hearing impairments), make sure you tell the cruise line (or your travel agent) at the time you book; otherwise, you may legally be denied boarding by the cruise line.

Anyone in a wheelchair but considering a cruise may be nervous at the thought of getting around. However, you'll find that crew members aboard most ships are extremely helpful. Indeed, cruise ships have become much more accessible for people with most types of disabilities. Ships built in the past five to 10 years will have the most up-to-date suites, cabins, and accessible shipboard facilities for those with special needs. Many new ships also have text telephones and listening device kits for the hearing-impaired (including show-lounges aboard some ships). Special dietary needs can often be met, and many cabins have refrigerators – useful for those with diabetes who need to keep supplies of insulin cool.

Wheelchair users should check in advance
whether help is available.

Special cruises cater for dialysis patients (check out www.dialysisatsea.com and www.dialysis-cruises. com) and for those who need oxygen regularly. Some cruise lines publish a special needs brochure.

If you use a wheelchair, take it with you, as ships carry only a limited number for emergency hospital use only. An alternative is to rent an electric wheelchair, which can be delivered to the ship on your sailing date.

Arguably the weakest point of cruising for the mobility-limited is any shore tender operation. Ship tenders simply aren't designed properly for the wheelchair-bound.

Little problems to consider

It is appropriate to begin with the disadvantages of a cruise for the physically challenged. Unless cabins and bathrooms are specifically designed, problem areas include the entrance, furniture configuration, closet hanging rails, beds, grab bars, height of toiletries cabinet, and wheel-in shower stall. The elevators may present the biggest obstacle, and you may get frustrated at the waiting time involved. In older ships, controls often can't be reached from a wheelchair.

Few ships have access-help hoists installed at swimming pools. Exceptions include Celebrity Cruises' *Celebrity Reflection* and *Celebrity Silhouette*, the pool in 'The Haven' aboard Norwegian Cruise Line's *Norwegian Breakaway*, *Norwegian Epic*, *Norwegian Getaway*, and P&O Cruises' *Oriana* and *Aurora*.

It can be hard to access areas like self-serve buffets, and many large resort ships provide only oval plates (no trays) in their casual eateries. So you may need to ask for help.

Some insurance companies may prohibit smaller ships from accepting passengers with severe disabilities. Some cruise lines will send you a form requesting the dimensions and weight of the wheelchair, stating that it had to fold to take inside the cabin.

Note that wheelchairs, mobility scooters, and walking aids must be stored in your cabin – they *cannot* be left in the corridor outside your cabin.

Only five cruise ships have direct access ramps to lifeboats: *Amadea*, *Asuka II*, *Crystal Serenity*, *Crystal Symphony*, and *Europa*.

Tips to avoid pitfalls

Start by planning an itinerary and date, and find a travel agent who knows your needs. But follow up on all aspects of the booking yourself to avoid slip-ups; many cruise lines have a department or person to handle requests from disabled passengers.

Choose a cruise line that lets you select a specific cabin, not just a price category.

If the ship doesn't have any specially equipped cabins, book the best outside cabin in your price range, or choose another ship.

Check whether your wheelchair will fit through your cabin's bathroom door or into the shower area and whether there is a 'lip' at the door. Don't accept 'I think so' as an answer. Get specific measurements.

Choose a cabin close to an elevator. Not all elevators go to all decks, so check the deck plan. Smaller and older vessels may not even have elevators, making access to even the dining room difficult.

Avoid, at all costs, a cabin down a little alleyway shared by several other cabins, even if the price is attractive. It's hard to access a cabin in a wheelchair from such an alleyway. Cabins located amidships are less affected by vessel motion, so choose something in the middle of the ship if you are concerned about possible rough seas. The larger – and therefore more expensive – the cabin, the more room you will have to maneuver in.

The hanging rails in the closets on most ships are positioned too high for someone in a wheelchair to reach – even the latest ships seem to repeat this basic error. Many cruise ships, however, have cabins to suit the mobility-limited. They are typically fitted with roll-in closets and have a pull-down facility to bring your clothes down to any height you want.

Meals in some ships may be served in your cabin, on special request, but few ships have enough space in the cabin for dining tables. If you opt for a dining room with two fixed-time seatings for meals, choose the second – it's more leisurely. Alert the restaurant manager in advance that you would like a table that leaves plenty of room for your wheelchair.

Hand-carry your medical information. Once on board, tell the reception desk help may be needed in an emergency.

Douglas Ward tests accessibility around a ship.

Make sure that the contract specifically states that if, for any reason, the cabin is not available, that you will get a full refund and transportation back home as well as a refund on any hotel bills incurred.

Advise the cruise line of the need for proper transfer facilities such as buses or vans with wheelchair ramps or hydraulic lifts.

If you live near the port of embarkation, arrange to visit the ship to check its suitability – most cruise lines will be accommodating.

Coping with embarkation

The boarding process can pose problems. If you embark at ground level, the gangway may be level or inclined. It will depend on the embarkation deck of the ship and/or the tide in the port.

Alternatively, you may be required to embark from an upper level of a terminal, in which case the gangway could well be of the floating loading-bridge type, like those used at major airports. Some have flat floors; others may have raised lips at regular intervals.

Why doors can present a problem for wheelchair users

The design of cruise ships has traditionally worked against the mobility-limited. To keep water out or to prevent water escaping from a flooded area, raised edges (lips) – unfriendly to wheelchairs – are often placed in doorways and across exit pathways. Also, cabin doorways, at a standard 24ins (60cm) wide, are often not wide enough for wheelchairs – about 30ins (76cm) is needed.

Bathroom doors, whether they open outward or inward, similarly hinder maneuverability. An electrically operated sliding door would be better. Bathrooms in many older ships are small and full of plumbing fixtures, often at odd angles, awkward when moving about in a wheelchair. Those aboard new ships are more accessible, but the plumbing may be located beneath the complete prefabricated module, making the floor higher than that in the cabin, which means a ramp is needed. Some cruise lines will, if given advance notice, remove a bathroom door and hang a fabric curtain in its place. Many lines will provide ramps for the bathroom doorway if needed.

Access to outside decks is usually through doors that must be opened manually rather than via automatic electric-eye doors.

It's not cheap to provide facilities for wheelchair-bound passengers. Trained crew members are needed to assist them, which translates to two crew members per eight-hour shift. Thus, six crew members would be required according to the latest safety and evacuation regulations solely to provide the necessary support for one wheelchair-bound passenger – a big drain on the cruise ship's labor resources.

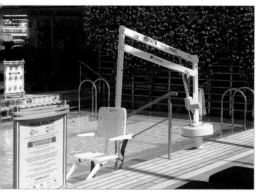

A pool access hoist installed at one of the swimming pools on *Celebrity Reflection*.

Ship-to-shore launches

Cruise lines should – but don't always – provide an anchor emblem in brochures for those ports of call where a ship will be at anchor instead of alongside. If the ship is at anchor, the crew will lower you and your wheelchair into a waiting tender and then, after a short boat ride, lift you out again onto a rigged gangway or integral platform. If the sea is calm, this maneuver proceeds uneventfully; if the sea is choppy, it could vary from exciting to somewhat harrowing.

This type of embarkation is rare except in a busy port with several ships sailing the same day. Holland America Line is one of the few companies to make shore tenders accessible to the disabled, with a special boarding ramp and scissor lift so that wheelchair passengers can see out of the shore tender's windows.

Help for the hearing-impaired

Difficulties for such passengers include hearing announcements on the public address system, using the telephone, and poor acoustics in key areas such as boarding shore tenders.

Some cruise lines have special 'alert kits.' These include 'visual-tactile' devices for those unable to hear a knock on the door, a telephone ringing, or the sound of an alarm clock. Crystal Cruises' *Crystal Serenity* and *Crystal Symphony*, Celebrity Cruises' *Celebrity Century* and TUI Cruises' *Mein Schiff* and *Mein Schiff 2* have movie theaters fitted with special headsets for those with hearing difficulties.

Finally, when going ashore, particularly on organized excursions, be aware that some destinations are simply not equipped to handle people with hearing impairment.

Cruising for the blind and sight-impaired

Any totally or almost blind persons must be accompanied by a fully able-bodied person, occupying the same cabin. A few lines will allow seeing-eye dogs. Taking an around-the-world cruise or long voyage aboard a cruise ship is one way for them to enjoy the sea, the aromas of the world, and to feel things that they are unable to at home.

All elevators and cabins have Braille text. Some large resort ships (examples include *Celebrity Reflection*, *Celebrity Silhouette*, *MSC Divina*, *MSC Fantasia*, *MSC Preziosa*, and *MSC Splendida*) have Braille pads subtly hidden under each lower section of handrail in the main foyers – very user-friendly, and most welcome.

Recent improvements

Many new ships now provide mobility-limited cabin bathrooms with collapsible shower stools mounted on shower walls, and bathroom toilets have collapsible arm guards and lower washbasin. Other cabin equipment may include a vibrating alarm clock, door beacon (light flashes when someone knock on the door), television with closed-caption decoders, and a flashing light as fire alarm. Look out, too, for:

Hearing-impaired kits on request.
Dedicated wheelchair positions in the showlounge.
Induction systems for the hearing impaired.
Electrical hoist to access pool and hot tubs.

Although public rooms do not have special seating areas, most showlounges do – almost always at the back, adjacent to the elevators – for wheelchair passengers. But these are sometimes occupied by inconsiderate non-disabled passengers.

Wheelchair accessibility

Each cruise ship reviewed in this book is rated in its data listing for wheelchair accessibility.

Questions to ask before you book
Are any public rooms or public decks inaccessible to wheelchairs?
Will you be guaranteed a good viewing place in the main showlounge if seated in a wheelchair?
Can the ship supply a raised toilet seat?
Will crew be on hand to help?
Will special transportation be provided to transfer you from airport to ship?
If you need a collapsible wheelchair, can this be provided by the cruise line?
Do passengers have to sign a medical release?
Are the ship's tenders accessible to wheelchairs?
How do you get from your cabin to lifeboats in an emergency if the elevators are out of action?
Do passengers need a doctor's note to qualify for a cabin for the physically challenged?
Does the cruise line's travel insurance (with a cancellation or trip interruption) cover you for any injuries while you are aboard ship?
Most disabled cabins have twin beds or one queen-size bed.
Anyone with a disabled child should ask whether a suitable portable bed can be moved in.

Expedition Cruises

Like sport utility vehicles, some ships have become crossovers, operating as expedition cruise ships but offering a quite plush and comfortable lifestyle.

Expedition cruising is poles apart from all other types of cruising. It is total immersion in nature, wildlife, and discovery, with a sense of pioneering thrown in. Passengers joining cruise expeditions become 'participants' and need to be more self-reliant and more interested in doing or learning than in being entertained. They become 'participants' and take very active roles in almost every aspect of a voyage.

Naturalists, historians, and lecturers (rather than entertainers) are aboard each ship to provide background information and observations about wildlife. Each participant receives a personal logbook, illustrated and written by the wildlife artists and writers who accompany each cruise – a fine souvenir.

My top expeditions

You can venture to the North Pole, walk on pack ice in the islands and land masses in the Arctic Ocean and Arctic Circle, explore a huge penguin rookery on an island in the Antarctic Peninsula, the Falkland Islands, or South Georgia, or search for 'lost' peoples in Melanesia. Or you can cruise close to the source of the Amazon, gaze at species of flora and fauna in the Galápagos Islands (Darwin's laboratory), or watch a genuine dragon on the island of Komodo – from a comfortable distance, of course.

My 10 favorite destinations are: Aleutian-Pribiloff Islands, Amazon (Manaus-Iquitos), Antarctic Peninsula, Arctic (North Pole), Galápagos Islands, Islands of Micronesia, Northwest Passage, Northeast Passage, Papua New Guinea, and Ross Ice Shelf (Antarctica).

Explore in comfort

Briefings and lectures bring cultural and intellectual elements to expedition cruise vessels. There is no formal entertainment as such; participants enjoy this type of cruise more for the camaraderie and learning experience, and being close to nature. There is no cruise director, but an experienced expedition leader who works closely with the ship's captain and marine operations department. The ships are designed and equipped to sail in ice-laden waters, yet they have a shallow enough draft to glide over coral reefs.

Despite being rugged, expedition cruise vessels can provide comfortable and even elegant surroundings for up to 200 participants, and offer good food and service. Without traditional cruise ports at which to stop, a ship must be self-sufficient, be capable of long-range cruis-

ing, and be totally environmentally friendly. Although there's no professional entertainment, recaps of the day's experiences usually take place each evening, and, if you're not too tired (this expedition cruising can be exhausting), board games and library books are always available.

However, the expedition experience itself really comes alive by the use 'Zodiacs' – inflatable but rigid craft that can seat up to a dozen participants. The feel of sea spray and wind on your face gives you a thrill, and the feeling that this really is something different from any cruising you may have done previously.

Wildlife migrations

Lars-Eric Lindblad pioneered expedition cruising in 1966. A Swedish-American, he turned travel into adventure by going to parts of the world tourists had not visited. After chartering several vessels for voyages to Antarctica, he organized the design and construction

Kayakers in Antarctica.

As global warming melts the ice, polar bears are increasingly threatened.

of a small ship capable of going almost anywhere in comfort and safety. In 1969, *Lindblad Explorer* was launched; it soon earned an enviable reputation in adventure travel. Others followed.

To put together cruise expeditions, companies turn to knowledgeable sources and advisers. Scientific institutions are consulted; experienced world explorers and naturalists provide up-to-date reports on wildlife sightings, migrations, and other natural phenomena. Sea days are usually spent preparing, and participants are kept physically and mentally active. Avoid such an adventure cruise if you are not completely ambulatory, because getting into and out of Zodiacs (inflatable shore landing craft) can be very tricky.

Adventure cruise companies provide expedition parkas and waterproof boots, but you will need to take waterproof trousers for Antarctica and the Arctic.

Antarctica

See the 'Frozen Planet' for yourself. While Arctic ice is only a few feet thick, the ice of Antarctica is thousands of feet thick. The continent was first sighted in 1820 by the American sealer Nathaniel Palmer, British naval officer Edward Bransfield, and Russian captain Fabian Bellingshausen.

For most, it is just a windswept frozen wasteland – it has been calculated that the ice mass contains almost 90 percent of the world's snow and ice, while its treeless land mass is twice the size of Australia. For others, it represents the last pristine place on earth, offering an abundance of marine and bird life.

As many as 36,000 people a year visit Antarctica, which has 24-hour sunshine during the austral summer but not a single native inhabitant. Its ice is as much as 2 miles (3km) thick, and its total land mass equals more than all the rivers and lakes on earth and exceeds that of China and India combined. Icebergs

can easily be the size of Belgium. The region has a raw beauty.

Although visited by 'soft' expedition cruise ships and even normal-size cruise ships with ice-hardened hulls, the more remote 'far side' – the Oates and Scott coasts, McMurdo Sound, and the famous Ross Ice Shelf – can be visited only by genuine icebreakers, as the katabatic winds can easily reach more than 100mph (160km/h). The first ship carrying participants on a circumnavigation of Antarctica was the 114-passenger *Kapitan Khlebnikov,* operated by Quark Expeditions, in 1996–97.

Only 100 participants *per ship* are now allowed ashore at any given time, so if you sail aboard one of the larger ships that claim to include Antarctica on their itineraries, it will probably be to view it – but only from the ship. Indeed, since 2011 cruise ships with more than 500 participants have not been allowed to sail in Antarctic waters unless they use lighter-grade distillate fuel. Moreover, the chances of rescue in the event of pack ice crushing a normal cruise ship hull are virtually nil. For real expedition cruising, choose a ship that includes a flotilla of Zodiacs, proper boot washing stations, expedition equipment, experienced expedition leaders, and ice captains. Two companies that stand out from the crowd are Hapag-Lloyd Expedition Cruises and Quark Expeditions.

There are no docks in Antarctica, so venturing 'ashore' is done by Zodiacs – an integral part of the experience.

Be aware that you can still get stuck even aboard these specialized expedition ships, as did *Nordkapp,* which ran aground near Deception Island in 2007. In the same year, Canadian company GAP Expeditions' (now renamed G Adventures) *Explorer* hit an iceberg in Bransfield Strait off King George Island and sank; all 91 participants, nine expedition staff, and 54 crew members were rescued thanks to the coordination efforts of the British Coast Guard and the Hurtigruten cruise ship *Nordnorge.* In 2008 Antarply Expeditions' *Ushuaia* was grounded; all 89 participants were rescued by the Chilean navy vessel *Achilles.* In 2009, Quark Expeditions' *Ocean Nova* was grounded, and in 2011 *Polar Star* grounded on an uncharted rock; fortunately there were no injuries to participants or crew.

Tip: Wear an ID bracelet or belt at all times while on an Antarctic expedition cruise, and take thermal underwear. Anyone on a special diet should advise the cruise operator as early as possible so that any needed items can be obtained.

Wildlife you may see or come into contact with include orcas, dolphins, the six species of Antarctic seals, penguins, birds, and various species of lichen and flora, depending on the area visited.

Take plastic bags to cover your camera, so that condensation forms inside the bag and not on your camera when changing from the cold of the outside Antarctic air to the warmth of your expedition cruise vessel. Make sure you know how to operate your camera with gloves on – frostbite is a real danger.

The High Arctic

This is an ocean surrounded by continents, whereas Antarctica is an ice-covered continent surrounded by ocean. The Arctic Circle is located at 66 degrees, 33 minutes, 3 seconds North, although this really designates where 24-hour days and nights begin. The High Arctic is best defined as that region north of which no trees grow, and where water is the primary feature of the landscape.

Quark Expeditions, the Arctic expedition cruise specialist, operates under the strict guidelines of Arctic Expedition Cruise Operators (AECO), the body committed to minimizing the impact of visit to the Far North. These expeditions to the North Pole (90 degrees North) are undertaken only at the height of the Arctic summer, in June and July, usually aboard the world's most powerful icebreaker – the Russian nuclear-powered *50 Years of Victory*. It can crush ice up to 10ft (3m) thick. An onboard helicopter whisks participants between the ship and the North Pole.

This really is a once-in-a-lifetime adventure. Only 250 participants visited the North Pole in 2013, and some took the optional excursion in a tethered hot-air balloon.

Northwest Passage

Passenger ships that have navigated the often dangerous Northwest Passage linking the Atlantic and Pacific Oceans include *Lindblad Explorer* (1984), *World Discoverer* (1985), *Society Explorer* (1988), *Frontier Spirit* (1992), *Kapitan Khlebnikov* (1994, 1995, 1998, 2006, 2007, 2008), *Hanseatic* (1995, 1996, 1997, 1999, 2007), *Bremen* (2009), both *Bremen* and *Hanseatic* (2010), and Hanseatic (2012). In 2013, an unusual double crossing took place; Hanseatic went east to west, while Bremen went west to east.

The Amazon

The River Amazon is huge – 4,080 miles (6,466km) from close to its source in the Peruvian Andes, to Belem on South America's Atlantic coast – and contains one fifth of the earth's water supply. Home to a tenth of the planet's animal species and plant life, it has thousands of tributaries, and often is so wide you cannot see the riverbank on the opposite side.

Cruises usually start in the Caribbean from ports such as Barbados and end up in Manaus (or vice versa). Starting in Manaus, with its muddy red-brown water, and ending up in the clear blue waters of the Caribbean may be the more appealing option. Calls along the way may be made in Parintins, Alter do Chão, Santarém, and Belém. Few ships venture farther upriver from Manaus to Iquitos; Hapag-Lloyd Expedition Cruises' *Hanseatic* is one that does.

The city of Manaus, 1,000 miles (1,600km) from the ocean, was built by barons of the rubber industry. Today, it really is a gaudy metropolis, but its Opera House, built at the end of the 19th century, remains a much visited icon and still stages concerts.

The nuclear-powered *50 Years of Victory* at the North Pole.

Exploring the Amazon by Zodiac.

One must-do shore excursion is a rainforest walk with a knowledgeable Brazilian guide, which will give you an insight into the richest variety of life on the planet. But make sure you have plenty of insect repellent – more than 200 varieties of mosquito inhabit the Amazon Basin.

The Galápagos Islands

These islands, 600 miles (960km) off the coast of Ecuador in the Pacific Ocean, are a microcosm of our planet. More than 100 islands, plus mineral-rich and lava outcroppings, make up the Galápagos, which are fed by the nutrient-rich Cromwell and Humboldt currents. The fertile waters can be cold, even on the equator.

The Ecuadorians jealously guard their islands and prohibit the movement of almost all non-Ecuador-registered cruise vessels within its boundaries. The best way to follow in the footsteps of Charles Darwin, who visited the islands in 1835 aboard the *Beagle*, is to fly to Quito and cruise aboard an Ecuadorian-registered vessel. Ecological fact: cruising leaves a smaller carbon footprint because it does not contribute to the building of hotels, restaurants, roads, and cars.

The government of Ecuador set aside most of the islands as a wildlife sanctuary in 1934, while uninhabited areas were declared national parks in 1959. The national park includes approximately 97 percent of the islands' landmass, together with 20,000 sq miles (50,000 sq km) of ocean. The Charles Darwin Research Station was established in 1964, and the government created the Galápagos Marine Resources Reserve in 1986.

The Galápagos National Park tax is now $200. Smoking is prohibited on the islands, and no more than 50,000 visitors a year are admitted. In 2012 new rules stopped ships from visiting most islands more than once in a 14-day period. Some cruise lines require vaccinations for cruises that include Ecuador, although the World Health Organization does not.

The ships

It's important to explain that few cruise operators, such as Hapag-Lloyd Cruises and Silversea Cruises, actually own their specialist expedition ships. Most of these vessels are owned by companies formed of investors who charter the ships to cruise operators. Also, ship management and operations may be unrelated to the catering company, the marketing company, or the expedition tour operator, making it difficult to guarantee consistency.

Protecting sensitive environments

In the future, only ships capable of meeting new 'zero discharge' standards will be allowed to cross environmentally sensitive areas. Expedition cruise companies are concerned about the environment, and they spend much time and money in educating their crews and participants about safe procedures.

They observe the 'Antarctic Traveler's Code,' based on 1978's Antarctic Conservation Act, designed to protect the region's ecosystem, flora, and fauna.

The Antarctic Treaty Meeting in Kyoto in 1994 made it unlawful, unless authorized by permit, to take native animals, birds, and certain native plants, introduce species, enter certain special protected areas (SPAs), or discharge or dispose of pollutants. The original Antarctic Treaty, signed in 1959 by 12 nations active in the region, defined Antarctica as all of the land and ice shelves south of 60 degrees South latitude. The signatories were Argentina, Australia, Belgium, Chile, France, Japan, New Zealand, Norway, South Africa, the Soviet Union, the UK, and the US.

There are now 28 countries comprising the Antarctic Treaty Consultative committee, and 39 research stations across the continent.

To 'take' means to remove, harass, molest, harm, pursue, hunt, shoot, kill, trap, capture, restrain, or tag any native mammal or bird, or to attempt to do so. Violators face civil penalties, including a fine of up to $10,000 and one-year imprisonment for each violation. A copy of the Act can be found in the library of each adventure or expedition ship that visits the continent.

Ships carrying over 500 participants are not allowed to land and are restricted to 'scenic' cruising, so the likelihood of a single-hulled mega-ship zooming in on the penguins with 3,000-plus participants is unlikely. Nor would it be possible to rescue so many participants and crew in the event of an emergency. Also, the large resort ships burn heavy oil rather than the lighter oil used by the specialist expedition ships, which also have ice-strengthened hulls – so the danger of pollution arising from an accident is far greater.

Comparing expedition ships

Ship Name	Rating (out of 100)	Company/Operator (1)	Built	Pass. Cabins	Max. No. of Passengers	Tonnage	Length (m)
Akademik Ioffe (3)	55	One Ocean Expeditions	1988	55	138	6,460	117.10
Akademik Sergey Vavilov (3)	53	One Ocean Expeditions	1988	40	110	6,231	117.80
Akademik Sholaskiy (3)	46	Aurora Expeditions	1982	22	44	2,140	71.56
Aleksey Maryshev	48	Oceanwide Expeditions	1990	23	46	2,000	70.00
Antarctic Dream	35	Oceanwide Expeditions	1959	39	78	2,180	83.00
Bremen	83	Hapag-Lloyd Cruises	1990	82	184	6,752	111.51
Clipper Adventurer	57	Quark Expeditions	1976	61	122	5,750	100.01
Expedition	50	G Adventures	1972	58	120	6,336	105.00
50 Years of Victory (1) (2)	95	Quark Expeditions	2007	66	128	23,439	159.00
Hanseatic	88	Hapag-Lloyd Cruises	1993	92	194	8,378	122.80
Kapitan Dranitsyn (1)	58	Quark Expeditions	1980	53	113	10,471	131.00
Marco Polo	54	Cruise and Maritime Voyages	1965	425	915	22,080	176.28
Minerva	62	Swan Hellenic Cruises	1996	178	474	12,500	133.00
National Geographic Endeavour	58	Lindblad Expeditions	1966	62	110	3,132	89.20
National Geographic Explorer	46	Lindblad Expeditions	1982	81	148	6,200	108.60
Ocean Diamond	57	Quark Expeditions	1986	112	189	8,282	124.00
Ortelius (3)	51	Oceanwide Expeditions	1989	45	100	4,575	89.98
Polar Pioneer (3)	47	Aurora Expeditions	1985	26	54	2,140	71.60
Professor Molchanov (3)	44	Southern Explorations	1983	29	52	1,753	71.60
Professor Multanovskiy (3)	44	Southern Explorations	1983	29	49	1,753	71.60
Ocean Nova	47	Quark Expeditions	1992	45	96	2,118	73.00
Orion	82	Orion Expedition Cruises	2003	53	139	4,050	102.70
Plancius (3)	68	Oceanwide Expeditions	1976	53	114	3,434	89.00
Quest	48	Noble Caledonia	1992	26	52	1,268	49.65
Sea Spirit	62	Quark Expeditions	1991	60	127	4,200	89.70
Serenissima	56	Serenissima Cruises	1960	59	118	2,362	84.7
Silver Explorer	83	Silversea Cruises	1989	66	158	6,072	108.20
Spirit of Enderby (3)	44	Heritage Expeditions	1984	29	48	6,231	72.00
Ushuaia (3)	40	Ushuaia Adventure Corp/ Antarpply Expeditions	1970	41	84	2,963	84.73

NOTES:
(1) = true expedition (ice-breaker) vessel
(2) = nuclear powered
(3) = built originally as a research vessel

Coastal Cruises

**Being all at sea doesn't appeal? You can stay close
to dry land by journeying along the coasts of Australia,
Europe, and North and South America.**

The marine wonderland of the Great Barrier Reef, a World Heritage Site off the northeast coast of Australia, is the earth's largest living coral reef – it actually consists of more than 2,800 individual coral reefs. It is visited by around 70 local Australian boutique ship operators, who mostly offer one- to four-night cruises to the reefs and Whitsunday Islands. The area is excellent for scuba diving and snorkeling.

June through September is humpback whale-watching season; the Reef shelters the young whales while the adults nurture them in the shallow waters. Note that the Australian government levies an environmental charge of A$5 on everyone over four years of age visiting the Great Barrier Reef and its environs.

Norway

An alternative to traditional cruise ships can be found in the year-round coastal cruising along the shores of Norway to the Land of the Midnight Sun aboard the ships of the Hurtigruten Group, formerly known as Norwegian Coastal Voyages. The fleet consists of small, comfortable, working express coastal packet steamers and contemporary cruise vessels that deliver mail, small packaged goods, and foodstuffs, and take passengers to the communities spread on the shoreline.

Invariably dubbed 'the world's most beautiful voyage,' this is a 1,250-mile (2,000-km) journey from Bergen in Norway to Kirkenes, close to the Russian border (half of which is north of the Arctic Circle) and takes 12 days. The service started in 1893 to provide connection to communities when there were no roads, and the name Hurtigruten – meaning 'fast route' – reflects the fact that this coastal express was once the most reliable communication link between southern Norway and its remote north. Today the company carries more than 300,000 passengers a year. It's a good way to meet Norwegians, who treat the service like a bus.

You can join it at any of the 34 ports of call and stay as long as you wish because the vessels, being working ships, sail every day of the year (some port calls are of only one hour or so – enough to get off and on and unload freight). Most ports are repeated on the return journey, but stop at different times (so you get a different feeling).

Note that double beds are available only in suite-grade accommodation; many of the beds are fixed in an L-shape, or in a bed and sofa/bed combination. Note that most of the ships do not have stabilizers, and there is no doctor on board, nor indeed any medical facilities.

At the height of summer, north of the Arctic Circle, there are almost 24 hours of daylight (there is no sunset

Glass-bottomed boat over the Great Barrier Reef.

Hurtigruten ships			
Ship	Tonnage	Built	Berths
Finnmarken	15,000	2002	638
Fram *	12,700	2007	328
Kong Harald	11,200	1993	490
Lofoten	2,621	1964	147
Midnatsol	16,053	2003	652
Nordkapp	11,386	1996	464
Nordlys	11,200	1994	482
Nordnorge	11,386	1997	455
Nordstjernen **	2,621	1956	114
Polar Star **	4,998	1969	100
Polarlys	12,000	1996	479
Richard With	11,205	1993	483
Trollfjord	15,000	2002	648
Vesteralen	6,261	1983	316

* for expedition voyages only
** for 'soft' expedition-style cruises

Getting up close to feeding humpback whales.

between April 19 and August 23). Between November and February the northern lights – if the atmospheric conditions are right – create spectacular arcs across the sky. Some specialist voyages are aimed at wildlife, birdwatchers, astronomy, and others, while onboard concerts and lectures celebrate the work of Norwegian composer Edvard Grieg.

The ships can accommodate between 144 and 652 passengers. The newest ships have an elevator that can accommodate a wheelchair passenger, but otherwise, they are fairly plain and basic, practical vessels, with food that is more bistro than restaurant. A 24-hour restaurant provides items at extra cost. Note that the price of alcoholic drinks is extremely high (you can take your own on board), as they are throughout Norway, and that the currency is the Norwegian krone.

Archipelago hopping can be done along Sweden's eastern coast, too, by sailing in the daytime and staying overnight in one of the many small hotels. One vessel sails from Norrtalje, north of Stockholm, to Oskarshamn, near the Baltic island of Öland, right through the spectacular Swedish archipelago.

The Hurtigruten Group also operates utilitarian ships for expeditions to the Arctic, Antarctic, and Greenland.

Scotland
The fishing town of Oban, two hours west of Glasgow by road, is the base for one of the world's finest cruise experiences. *Hebridean Princess* is a little gem, with Laura Ashley–style interiors – friendly enough to have been chartered by Queen Elizabeth II for a family-only celebration of her 80th birthday in 2006. The food is

excellent, and includes Scottish beef, local seafood, and seasonal vegetables. There's fine personal service.

This ship, owned by Hebridean Island Cruises, carries up to 50 passengers around some of Scotland's most magnificent coastline and islands. If you cruise from Oban, you can be met at Glasgow airport or rail station and taken to the ship by motor coach. Take lots of warm clothing, however (layers are best), as the weather can be flexible and often unkind.

As an alternative, there's the 54-passenger *Lord of the Glens*, operated by the Magna Carta Steamship Company. It cruises in style through Scotland's lakes and canals, although it's not a steamship but a modern deluxe vessel. Some seven- and 10-night high-season sailings are accompanied by historians and guest lecturers.

North America
Coastal cruise ships flying the American flag offer a complete change of style from the large resort cruise ships. They are American-owned and American-crewed, and very informal. Being US-registered, they can start from and return to a US port without being required to call at a foreign port along the way – which a foreign-flagged cruise ship must do.

Accommodating up to 150 passengers, the ships are more like private family affairs, and are rarely out of sight of land. These cruises are low-key, low-pace, and not for active, adventurous types. Their operators seek out lesser-known areas, offering in-depth visits to destinations inaccessible to larger ships, along both the eastern and western seaboards of the USA, including Alaska.

Most passengers are of senior years. Many prefer not to fly, and wherever possible drive or take a train to join their ship. During the summer, you might see a couple of children on board, but in general small kids are not allowed. There are no facilities for them, and no staff to look after them.

Destinations: Eastern US and Canadian seaboard cruises include the St Lawrence River, Atlantic Coastal Waterways, New England (good for fall cruises), Cape Cod and the Islands – and Cape Cod Canal, the Great

Lakes – and Welland Canal, the Colonial Deep South, and Florida waterways.

Western seaboard cruises cover Alaska, the Pacific Northwest, California Wine Country, and Baja California/Sea of Cortés. Cruises focus on historically relevant destinations, nature and wildlife spotting, and coastal viewing. On some cruises, these boutique ships can dock adjacent to a town, allowing easy access on foot.

The ships. These 'D-class' vessels are less than 2,500 gross tonnage, and are subject neither to bureaucratic regulations nor to union rules. They are restricted to cruising no more than 20 miles (32km) offshore, at a comfortable 12 knots (13.8mph). Public room facilities are limited. Because the vessels are USA-registered, there is no casino. They really are ultra-casual, no-frills ships with the most basic of facilities, no swimming pools, little artwork, and no glitz in interior decor. They usually have three or four decks and, except for the ships of American Cruise Lines, no elevator. Stairs can be steep and are not recommended for people with walking difficulties. Because of this, some ships have an electric chair-lift on indoor or outdoor stairways.

Cabins. Accommodation is in outside-view cabins, some of which open directly onto a walking deck – inconvenient when it rains. Each has a picture window and small bathroom. They are small and basic, with very

Balmoral cruises in the Norwegian fjords.

limited closet space – perhaps just a curtain across a space with a hanging rod for clothes. Many don't have a TV set or telephone. There's no room service, and you may have to turn your own bed down. Cabins are closer to the engines and generators than aboard the large resort ships, so generator humming noises can be disturbing at night. The quietest cabins are at the bows – although there could be noise if the ship is equipped with a bow thruster – and most cruising is done in the early morning so that passengers can sleep better at night.

Tall passengers should note that the overall length of beds rarely exceeds 6ft (1.8m). Although soap is provided, it's best to bring your own shampoo, conditioner, and other toiletries. The ships of Blount Small Ship Adventures do not have cabin keys.

Although some of the older ships are really basic, the latest, particularly those of American Cruise Lines, are very comfortable. Because they are not classified for open-water cruising, though, they don't have to conform to the same rigorous shipbuilding standards that larger ocean-going cruise ships do. You may find that hot and cold water lines run close to each other in your bathroom, thus delivering neither really hot nor really cold water. Sound insulation could be almost non-existent.

Activities. The main evening event is dinner in the dining room, with one seating. This can be a family-style affair, with passengers at long tables, and the food passed around.

The cuisine is decidedly American, with fresh local specialties. Menus aboard the ships of Alaskan Dream Cruises and Blount Small Ship Adventures are very limited, while those aboard the ships of American Cruise Lines offer slightly more variety, including seasonal items. You'll probably be asked in the morning to choose which of the two main courses you'd like for dinner.

Evening entertainment consists mainly of after-dinner conversation. Most vessels are in port during the time, so you can easily go ashore for the local nightlife, although most passengers simply go to bed early.

The cost. These cruises are expensive, with an average daily rate of $400–$800 a person. Suggested gratuities are high – typically about $125 per person, per seven-day cruise – but they are shared by all personnel.

Coastal cruise lines in North America

There are several small ship cruise companies: Alaskan Dream Cruises, American Cruise Lines, Blount Small Ship Adventures, Lindblad Expeditions, and Un-Cruise Adventures.

What differentiates them? American Cruise Lines and American Safari Cruises provide better food and service than the others. American Cruise Lines' ships have larger cabins, and more public rooms. Drinks are included aboard the ships of American Cruise Lines only.

American Cruise Lines and Blount Small Ship Adventures operate on the USA's East Coast; Lindblad Expeditions and Un-Cruise Adventures operate on the USA's West Coast and Alaska.

Comparing coastal ships

Ship Name	Cruise Line	Passengers	Region	Length (m)
Admiralty Dream	Alaskan Dream Cruises	78	Alaska	50.5
Alaskan Dream	Alaskan Dream Cruises	42	Alaska	31.6
American Glory	American Cruise Lines	54	USA Coastal Cruises	53
American Spirit	American Cruise Lines	100	USA Coastal Cruises	67
American Star	American Cruise Lines	104	USA Coastal Cruises	67
Baranof Dream	Alaskan Dream Cruises	78	Alaska	47.5
Celebrity Xpedition	Celebrity Cruises	96	Galapagos Islands	88.5
Coral Princess	Captain Cook Cruises	50	Australia (Great Barrier Reef)	35
Coral Princess II	Captain Cook Cruises	50	Australia (Great Barrier Reef)	35
Discovery	Panama Marine Adventures	24	Panama	33
Emeraude	Emeraude Classic Cruises	76	Halong Bay (Vietnam)	56
Fiji Princess	Blue Lagoon Cruises	68	Yasawa Islands (Fiji)	60
Grande Caribe	Blount Small Ship Adventures	96	USA Coastal Cruises	55.7
Grande Mariner	Blount Small Ship Adventures	100	USA Coastal Cruises	55.7
Independence	American Cruise Lines	104	USA Coastal Cruises	67.9
Isabela II	Metropolitan Touring	42	Galapagos Islands	50.5
Mystique Princess	Blue Lagoon Cruises	72	Yasawa Islands (Fiji)	56
National Geographic Endeavour	Lindblad Expeditions	96	Various Regions	89.2
National Geographic Explorer	Lindblad Expeditions	162	Various Regions	112
National Geographic Sea Bird	Lindblad Expeditions	70	Alaska, Baja	46.3
National Geographic Sea Lion	Lindblad Expeditions	70	Alaska, Baja	46.3
Oceanic Discoverer	Coral Princess Cruises	72	Australia	63
Reef Endeavour	Captain Cook Cruises	140	Yasawa Islands (Fiji)	73
Reef Escape	Captain Cook Cruises	120	Yasawa Islands (Fiji)	68
Safari Endeavour	Un-Cruise Adventures	86	Alaska	70.7
Safari Explorer	Un-Cruise Adventures	36	Alaska/Mexican Coast	44.1
Safari Legacy	Un-Cruise Adventures	96	Alaska/Pacific Northwest	58.2
Safari Quest	Un-Cruise Adventures	22	Alaska/Mexican Coast	36.5
Santa Cruz	Metropolitan Touring	86	Galapagos Islands	72.3
Sarfaq Ittuk	Arctic Umiaq Line	52	Greenland	73
Sea Voyager	Sea Voyager Expeditions	60	Central America	53
Stella Australis	Cruceros Australis	200	Chilean Fjords	89
Tu Moana	Bora Bora Cruises	40	Tahitian Islands	69.1
True North	North Star Cruises	36	Australia (west coast)	50
Via Australis	Cruceros Australis	136	Chilean Fjords (Patagonia)	72.3
Wilderness Adventurer	Un-Cruise Adventures	60	Alaska	47.7
Wilderness Discoverer	Un-Cruise Adventures	76	Alaska	51.5
Wilderness Explorer	Un-Cruise Adventures	76	Alaska	56.5
Yorktown	Travel Dynamics International	138	Great Lakes	78.3

Transatlantic Crossings

You may be facing some unpredictable – or shall we say flexible – weather, but there's something romantic and adventurous about this classic ocean voyage.

Crossing the 3,000 miles (4,800km) of the North Atlantic by passenger vessel is a great way to avoid the hassles of airports. I have done it 158 times and always enjoy it immensely – and unlike flying, there's no jet lag. Yet the days when ships were built specifically for crossings are almost gone. The only one offering a regularly scheduled service is Cunard Line's *Queen Mary 2,* built with a thick hull designed to survive the worst weather the North Atlantic has to offer.

It's a leisurely seven-day voyage, on five of which the clocks will be advanced (eastbound) or put back (westbound) by one hour. You can take as many bags as you want, and even your pets – *QM2*'s 12 kennels are overseen by a full-time kennel master, and there is an outdoor walking area.

The 2,620 passenger *QM2* is the largest ocean liner ever built, and a destination on its own. New in 2004, it measures 148,528 gross tons. By comparison, *QM2*'s smaller half-sisters *Queen Elizabeth* and *Queen Victoria* both measure about 90,000 gross tons. The *QE2,* which was retired in 2008, measured 70,327 gross tons – the ill-fated *Titanic* a mere 46,328 gross tons. The difference is that *QM2* is a real, thick-hulled ocean liner, designed to withstand the pressures of the North Atlantic and its unpredictable weather.

The North Atlantic can be as smooth as glass or as rough as old boots, although in my experience it's rare

for the weather to be bad for an entire crossing. But when it *is* a bit choppy, its heavy beauty really is mesmerizing – never, ever boring. However, make sure you always use the handrails when you move around, and use the elevators rather than the stairs.

When the ship is under way at high speed (above 25 knots – about 30 land miles per hour) on a windy day, a cabin balcony is pretty useless, and the promenade deck is a challenging place to be – if you can even get outside, that is! Sometimes, visibility is low (think pea soup fog), and you'll hear the ship's horn – a powerful, haunting sound – bellowing every two minutes.

If the weather is kind and the sun is shining, and you book a balcony cabin on the port side on westbound crossings, or on the starboard side on eastbound crossings, you'll get the sunshine.

Queen Mary 2 has a wide walk-around promenade deck outdoors, and its forward section is under cover from the weather or wind (three times around is 6,102 ft/1,860 m, or 1.1 miles/1.6km.

During the crossing

Once *Queen Mary 2* has left port, and settled down at sea on the second day, the natural rhythm of life slows down, and you begin to understand that time spent at sea, with few distractions, is special indeed, and completely different from any 'normal' cruise. It allows

Queen Mary 2 leaving New York City.

you some well-earned 'me' time – to pamper yourself in the Canyon Ranch Spa (it's the only one at sea), to attend a lecture by a well-known author or other personality, or simply to relax and read a book from the superb library on board. Indeed, taking a nap certainly counts as an activity on an ocean crossing! Indeed, Cunard has a list of '101 Things To Do On A Queen Mary 2 Transatlantic Crossing' – just in case you really do want to be active. A 'crossing' also provides a great backdrop for observing people.

There are now usually three formal (tuxedo) and four informal nights during a 7-night crossing, when elegance prevails – this is pleasingly different from the usual disheveled world on land. The formal nights are an integral part of a 'proper' crossing.

Apart from distinguished guest speakers, QM2 has a wide variety of leisure facilities, including a superb planetarium (several different shows, for which you'll need to make a reservation) and a 1,094-seat theater. There are acting classes, bridge (the card-playing kind) groups, big-band-style dance sessions, movies, exercise, cooking, and computer classes, so you'll never be bored in mid-ocean. And the gentlemen dance hosts are always kept busy by the number of solo female passengers who love to go dancing.

One of its most used facilities is the ship's outstanding library and bookshop – it offers over 8,000 books in 132 cabinets that have to be locked by hand – central locking was never part of the ocean liner setup – in several languages and staffed by full-time librarians from maritime library specialists Ocean Books. The bookstore not only sells books, but also Cunard memorabilia and souvenirs.

There's always a cozy chair to curl up on to read, or just admire the sea, and if the weather's decent, you can even swim outside (this, however, tends to be rare except in the height of summer, because of the ship's speed and wind speed).

One of the classic things to do is enjoy the typically British afternoon teatime, complete with cakes, scones, pastries, and finger sandwiches – all served by a rather hurried white-gloved staff – together with tea, and accompanied by live, light classical music.

The problem is that there simply isn't enough time to do everything, and there's no way you'll ever get bored aboard this ship – a *real* ocean liner.

You can also get married in mid-Atlantic during a crossing. Cunard Line started its now immensely popular Weddings At Sea program in 2012. The first couple to be married by the ship's captain was Dr. William De-Luca (from the USA) and Kelly Lewis (from the UK). They couldn't decide whether to marry in the UK or the USA, so they chose halfway between the two (it was their first crossing, and, indeed, their first-ever vacation at sea). The couple chose Cunard Line because of the company's 'distinguished history of transatlantic crossings.' Note that only one wedding per day can be arranged, with a time of 11am or 3:30pm (ceremo-

nies take place only on days at sea, and every detail is planned by an onboard wedding coordinator – and the cost starts at $2,500).

A memorable arrival

The day before you arrive in New York, Southampton, or (occasionally) in Hamburg, Germany, the disembarkation procedures will arrive in your suite or cabin. If you are in a hurry to disembark, you can opt to carry your own bags by registering for 'Express Disembarkation.'

Arriving in New York is one of cruising's iconic experiences, but you'll need to be up early. You'll see the lights of Long Island on your starboard side at about 4:30am, while the Verrazzano Narrows suspension bridge, at the entrance to New York harbor, will be dead ahead. QM2 usually passes the State of Liberty at about 6am (when a cabin with a balcony on the port side is useful), and then makes a right turn opposite the statue towards the Brooklyn Cruise Terminal. On the occasions when the ship berths at Pier 90 in Manhattan at the Passenger Terminal, it will turn left towards the Hudson River (in which case you'll get the best views of the Manhattan skyline from a cabin with balcony on the starboard side). Arrival always creates a sense of anticipation of what lies ahead, and the feeling that, after a week of being cosseted, you will be thrust back into the fast lane with full force.

Leaving New York/arrival in Southampton

If you sail from Red Hook Point in Brooklyn, the last thing you'll notice before entering the ship is the overhead banner which declares: "Leaving Brooklyn? Fuh-geddaboudit!" And that, dear reader, is *precisely* what a transatlantic crossing will have you do.

For arrival in Southampton, QM2 will usually round the Isle of Wight at about 4:30am, and be berthed alongside in Southampton by about 6:30am. Immigration is upon arrival in either New York or Southampton.

Repositioning crossings

Other cruise ships crossing the Atlantic are really little more than repositioning cruises – a way of moving ships that cruise the Mediterranean in summer to the Caribbean in winter, and vice versa, usually in spring and fall. Most of these ships cross the Atlantic using the sunny southern route, departing from southern ports such as Fort Lauderdale, San Juan, or Barbados, and ending the journey in Lisbon, Genoa, or Copenhagen via the Azores or the Canary Islands off the coast of northern Africa.

In this way, they avoid the more difficult weather often encountered in the North Atlantic. Such crossings take longer – between eight and 12 days – but they do offer an alternative way of experiencing the romance and adventure of a crossing – with a number of sea days for total relaxation. However, on these repositioning crossings, when the weather is not so friendly, the outdoor swimming pools will probably be out of use.

Sail-Cruise Ships

Want to be free as the wind? Think about cruising under sail, with towering masts, the creak of the deck, and gleaming white sails to speed the boat along.

There's simply nothing that beats the thrill of being aboard a multi-mast tall ship, sailing under thousands of square feet of canvas through waters that mariners have sailed for centuries. This is cruising in the traditional manner of seafaring, aboard authentic sailing ships, contemporary copies of clipper ships, or high-tech cruise-sail ships. But it gives you a genuine sailing experience while keeping creature comforts.

There are no rigid schedules, and life aboard equates to an unstructured lifestyle, apart from meal times. Weather conditions may often dictate whether a scheduled port visit will be made or not, but passengers sailing on these vessels are usually unconcerned. They would rather savor the feeling of being at one with nature, albeit in a comfortable, civilized setting, and without having to do the work themselves. The more luxurious sailing ships are the closest most people will get to owning their own mega-yacht.

Wind Surf offers extensive water-sports facilities.

Real tall ships

While we have all been dreaming of adventure, a pocketful of designers and yachtsmen committed pen to paper, hand in pocket and rigging to mast, and came up with a potpourri of stunning vessels to delight the eye and refresh the spirit. Examples are *Royal Clipper, Sea Cloud, Sea Cloud II, Star Clipper,* and *Star Flyer* – all of which have beautiful retro decor to convey the feeling of yesteryear and a slower pace of life.

Of these, *Sea Cloud,* built in 1931, restored in 1979, and adapted to satisfy the latest international safety of Life at Sea (SOLAS) regulations in 2011, is the most romantic sailing ship afloat. It operates under charter for part of the year, and sails in both the Caribbean and the Mediterranean. A kind of stately home afloat, *Sea Cloud* remains one of the finest and most exhilarating travel experiences in the world.

How to measure wind speeds

Understanding wind patterns is important to sailing ships, but the numbering system for wind velocity can confuse. There are 12 velocities, known as 'force' on the Beaufort scale, devised in 1805 by Sir Francis Beaufort, an Irish-born hydrographer and officer in Britain's Royal Navy. It was adopted internationally in 1874 as the official means of recording wind velocity. They are as follows, with descriptions of the ocean surface:

Force 0 (0–1mph): Calm; glassy (like a mirror).
Force 1 (1–3mph): Light wind; rippled surface.
Force 2 (4–7mph): Light breeze; small wavelets.
Force 3 (8–12mph): Gentle breeze; large wavelets, scattered whitecaps.
Force 4 (13–18mph): Moderate breeze; small waves, frequent whitecaps.
Force 5 (19–24mph): Fresh breeze; moderate waves, numerous whitecaps.
Force 6 (25–31mph): Strong breeze; large waves, white foam crests.
Force 7 (32–38mph): Moderate gale; streaky white foam.
Force 8 (39–46mph): Fresh gale; moderate waves.
Force 9 (47–54mph): Strong gale; high waves.
Force 10 (55–63mph): Whole gale; very high waves, curling crests.
Force 11 (64–73mph): Violent storm; extremely high waves, froth and foam, poor visibility.
Force 12 (73+mph): Hurricane; huge waves, thundering white spray, visibility nil.

Sails are rigged as *Sea Cloud* leaves Hamburg Harbour.

The activities are few, so relaxation is the key, in a stylish but unpretentious setting. The food and service are good, as is the interaction between the 69 passengers and 60 crew members, many of whom have worked aboard the ship for many years. One bonus is the fact that a doctor is available on board at no charge for emergencies or seasickness medication.

Although passengers may be able to participate occasionally in the furling and unfurling of the sails, they are not permitted to climb the rigging, as may be possible aboard some of the other, more modern tall ships. A modern interpretation of the original *Sea Cloud* – named *Sea Cloud II,* was built and introduced in 2001.

Contemporary sail-cruise ships

To combine sailing with push-button automation, try *Club Med 2* (Club Méditerranée) or *Wind Surf* (Windstar Cruises) – with five tall aluminum masts, they are the world's largest sail-cruise ships – and *Wind Spirit* and *Wind Star* (Windstar Cruises), with four masts. Not a hand touches the sails; they are computer-controlled from the navigation bridge.

The traditional sense of sailing is almost absent in these ocean-going robots, because the computer keeps the ship on an even keel. Also, some people find it hard to get used to the whine of the vessels' generators, which run the lighting and air-conditioning systems 24 hours a day.

From a yachtsman's viewpoint, the sail-to-power ratio is poor. That's why these cruise ships with sails have engine power to get them into and out of port. The *Sea Cloud* and *Star Clipper* ships do it by sail alone, except when there is no wind, which doesn't happen all that often.

On some itineraries, when there's little wind, you could be motor-powered for most of the cruise, with only a few hours under sail. The three Windstar Cruises vessels and one Club Med ship are typically under sail for about 40 percent of the time.

The Windstar ships carry mainly North Americans and the Club Med vessel mainly French speakers.

Another slightly smaller but chic vessel is *Le Ponant*. This three-mast ship caters to just 64 French-speaking passengers in elegant, yet casual, high-tech surroundings, advancing the technology of the original Windstar concept. The ship made news in 2008 when its crew was held to ransom by pirates off the Somali coast; no passengers were on board at the time.

When the engine cuts in

So, do you get to cruise under sail most of the time? Not really. Aboard the ships of Sea Cloud Cruises and Star Clippers, because they are real tall ships, you could be under sail for most of the night when the ships are under way, as long as there is wind, of course, and on the days or part days at sea.

The ship's small engine is used for maneuvering in and out of port. In the Caribbean, for example, the trade winds are good for most of the year, although in the Mediterranean the winds are not so potent. But many passengers enjoy helping to furl and unfurl the sails, and being able to climb the rigging. Lying in the netting under the ship's bows is a memorable experience.

Aboard the ships of Windstar Cruises, however, the itineraries are so port-intensive that the computer-controlled sails are hardly ever used today – so the experience can be disappointing.

Cargo Ship Cruising

These slow freighter voyages appeal to independent travelers who don't require constant entertainment, but do want comfortable accommodation and the joy of days at sea.

More than 3,000 passengers a year travel on about 300 cargo ships (freighters) and the number is growing as passengers become further disenchanted with the large resort ships that dominate the cruise industry. Traveling by freighter is also the ultimate way to travel for anyone seeking a totally unstructured voyage – far from the world of mass tourism – without entertainment or other diversions. It is a very flexible way to travel independently – to experience complete relaxation and tranquility.

Freighters are either: containerships (the most common and modern passenger-carrying freighters at sea today); general cargo ships; or refrigerated cargo ships, plus a variety of mail and coastal freighters. Fares range from about $90 to $180 per day. While schedules do exist, dates of departure and arrival are always given as 'on or about.'

The experience has particular appeal for retirees, relocating executives, those with far-flung family connections, graduates returning home from an overseas college, or professors on sabbatical leave. Freighters travel the busiest trade routes; you can even take one around the world aboard the vessels of Bank Line – a complete circumnavigation takes about four months.

About 300 freighters and cargo ships offer berths, with German operators accounting for more than half of them. True freighters – the general breakbulk carrier ships and feeder container vessels – carry up to 12 passengers; the only exception is the Royal Mail Ship RMS *St Helena*, which carries up to 128 passengers, together with animals such as goats and sheep, and goods from the UK to the Ascension Island. While RMS *St Helena* carries a doctor, freighters do not, and remember that they are working vessels, not cruise ships.

Freighter schedules change constantly, depending on the whim of the owner and the cargo to be carried, whereas container ships travel on regular schedules. For the sake of simplicity, they are all termed freighters. But cargo ships have changed dramatically as cost management and efficiency have become vital. Container ships are operated as passenger liners used to be: running line voyages on set schedules. You can also make a one-way voyage.

Most freighter companies don't allow children or pregnant women to travel, and won't accept anyone younger than five or older than 80. You'll need to be fully mobile – there are no elevators to connect the various decks. Because there are no medical facilities (unless the ship carries over 12 passengers), anyone over 65 is usually required to produce a medical certificate of good health – by any doctor; it doesn't have to be your own GP. Note that if your ship visits a US port at any point, non-Americans will need a full US visa, because freighters aren't part of the visa-waiver program.

Passenger-carrying cargo ships

You can travel as a passenger aboard the three largest passenger-carrying ships in the world, *Alexander von Humboldt*, *Jacques Cartier*, and *Marco Polo*. The ships are 395 meters long; by comparison, *Allure of the Seas* is 360 meters, and *Queen Mary 2* is 345 meters. The ships operated by France's CMA CGM have space for 16,020 TEUs (container-carrying capacity) and there are five double-bed cabins measuring 215 sq ft (20 sq m) for passengers on the ship's Europe–Asia route.

Also, the following lines, among others, offer regular passenger voyages year-round: Christian F. Ahrenkiel, Alpha Ship, Bank Line, H Buss, CMA CGM The French Line, Compagnie Polynésienne de Transport Maritime (CPTM), Coopérative de Transport Maritime & Aérien (CTMA), Deutsche-Afrika Line, French Asia Line, French West Indies Line, Grimaldi Lines, Hamburg-Süd, Hansa Shipmanagement, Horn Line, Independent Container Line, Interorient Navigation, Reederei F Laeisz, Leonhardt & Blumberg, Mare Schifffahrtsgesellschaft, Martime Gesellschaft, Maruba Lines, MCC Passage, Mediterranean Club Express, Melfi Lines, MSC Mediterranean Shipping Company, NSB Freighter Cruises, NSB Niederelbe Schifffahrtsgesellschaft, Reederei Nord, OPDR, Oldendorff Carriers, Oltmann Shipping, PZM Polish Steamship Company, Pearl String Service, Peter Doehle, Rickmers Reederei, St Helena Line, Reederei Heinrich Schepers, Reederei Karl Schlüter, H Schuldt, Swire Shipping, Transeste Shipping, Andrew Weir Shipping, Tom Wörden, Reederei Hermann Wulff, Zim Integrated Shipping, Kapitän Peter Zylmann Freighter Cruises. Remember that, due to the changing economic climate, ships may be cancelled or laid up at short notice.

Booking and Information
www.cruisepeople.co.uk/freighters.htm
www.freightertravel.co.nz
www.freightervoyages.eu
www.travltips.com

Cabins on most cargo ships are surprisingly comfortable.

Cargo ship facilities

What do you get when you book a cargo ship voyage? You get a cabin with double or twin beds, a small writing table, and a private bathroom. You also get good company, cocktails with conversation, hearty food (you'll eat in one seating with the ship's officers), an interesting voyage, a lot of water (and great stargazing opportunities), and the allure of days at sea.

What don't you get? Organized entertainment. You will certainly have time to relax and read books (some freighters have a small library), play cards, spend time on the navigation bridge, as well as observe the crew as they help with loading, unloading, and constant up-keep, rust control, and maintenance.

Accommodation consists of a spacious, well-equipped outside-view cabin high above the water line, with a large window rather than a porthole, comfortable lounge/sitting area, and private facilities – far larger than most standard cruise ship cabins are.

How much does it cost?

On a per day basis, cargo ship travel costs between $90 and $180. The fares are mostly estimated, with final fares provided prior to sailing. If you book with a US specialist and the cargo ship line is based in euros, there may be an additional cost depending on the rate of conversion when final payment is due.

A 28-day round-trip sailing aboard one of four CMA-CGM container vessels (Le Havre, France, to Guadeloupe and Martinique), for example, costs just over $120 (€83) per person, per day in a twin-bedded cabin, and slightly more in a single-occupancy cabin, plus any expenses incurred in getting to/from the em-barkation and disembarkation ports.

Remember that voyages last much longer – typically 30 days or more – so the cost can be considerable. Many are sold out more than a year ahead – two years for some routes – and the cargo-carrying fleet has been reduced as a result of the credit crunch, so plan wisely, and remember to purchase trip cancellation insurance.

What to bring

What to take with you? Casual clothing (check with the shipping line, as some require a jacket and tie for dinner), all medications, cosmetics, and toiletry items, hairdryer, multi-voltage converter plug, washing powder, and other sundry items such as soap, sun protection, insect repellent, and small flashlight. There may be a small 'shop' on board (for the crew) carrying bare essentials like toothpaste.

Bring along your medical certificate, travel insurance details, money in cash, and some extra photos of yourself in case the ship makes unannounced port stops and visas are required. The only gratuities needed are for the waiter and cabin steward, which are generally set at about $1–$2 per day, per person.

New international security regulations mean that if you book a one-way voyage, you *must* have all onward travel documents with you. Check with embassies and consulates of the countries you will visit. Note that freighters visit cargo ports, so private transportation such as taxis will need to be arranged in advance.

Cargo ships sometimes have to cancel port calls for commercial reasons at short notice. Bear this in mind if you're attracted by a particular itinerary or port.

River Cruising

Almost 1 million people a year take a river or inland waterway cruise, making this one of the industry's fastest-growing sectors.

Whether you want to cruise down the Nile, along the mighty Amazon, the stately Volga, the magnificent Rhine, or the 'blue' Danube, along the mystical Ayeyarwady (formerly the Irrawaddy) or the 'yellow' Yangtze – to say nothing of the Don and the Dnieper, the Elbe, or Australia's Murray – there are more than 1,000 riverships to choose from.

River cruises are like a crossover between ocean-going ships and a land tour. What sort of person enjoys cruising aboard these vessels? Well, anyone who survives well without formal dinners, bingo, casinos, discos, or lavish entertainment, and those who want an unstructured lifestyle, enhanced with a little culture.

The plus points

You need to pack and unpack only once.

Riverships enable you to enjoy the ever-changing scenery (the 'riverscape'), all at eye level.

You'll wake up in a different place each day, often in the very heart of a city or town.

Cruising along the Seine in Paris.

You never have to take a tender ashore – you simply step off the vessel when it ties up.

There are never any crowds.

The atmosphere on board is friendly and informal, never stuffy or pretentious.

Cruising along one of the world's rivers is a delightful way to unwind at a slow pace.

The ride is typically silky smooth – there's no rolling like aboard many of the ocean-going cruise ships, so you won't suffer from seasickness.

Good food and service are essential elements of a successful rivercruise operation.

All meals are provided, typically in a self-serve buffet arrangement for breakfast and lunch, with sit-down service for dinner. On European river cruises, basic table wines may also be included with lunch and dinner.

Almost all cabins have outside views; there are virtually no interior (no-view) cabins, as aboard most of the ocean-going cruise ships.

A whole range of optional, extra-cost excursions is available, while some excursions may be included.

You will typically sail by day, and dock at night (exceptions: Danube and Russian river cruises, where most vessels sail at night), so you can get a restful sleep without engine noise. However, bear in mind that, if your cabin is toward the aft, there may well be the soft humming of a generator, which supplies power for air-conditioning, heating, water supply, lighting, and cooking.

You can, if you wish, leave the vessel in the evening to go out to dinner, or to the cinema, theater, or a concert (exceptions: Danube and Russian river cruises).

Rivers provide a sense of continuity – difficult to achieve from a coach tour, where you may change lodgings each night, and encounter border crossings. Also, while on board, you deal in a single currency.

The dress code is completely casual.

The minus points

The flow of water in almost all rivers can't always be controlled, so there will be times when the water level is so low that even a specially constructed rivercruise vessel, with its shallow draft, cannot travel.

If you are tall, note that the beds aboard most riverships are less than 6ft (1.8m) long.

Don't wear white. Riverships are long and low, which means that their funnels are also low. Soot, created by the emissions from diesel engines and genera-

A Viking River Cruises 'longship' in Passau, Germany.

tors, can be a problem, particularly at the stern of a vessel, and on the upper (open) deck.

Aboard some of the vessels that have an aft, open but sheltered deck area, or an open upper deck – almost all riverships have one – smokers may be seated next to you. Few vessels distinguish between smoking and non-smoking areas outdoors, though almost none allow smoking in the public rooms.

The best time to cruise

There are advantages and disadvantages to every season in Europe. Early spring and late summer will be less crowded and can have beautiful weather. In July and August the weather is often more reliable, though it can be too hot for some and there are more crowds.

It's possible to time a river cruise to coincide with, say, the Rhine in Flames festival in high summer, or the paprika harvest in Hungary, or the beautiful autumnal colors along the Danube's Wachau Valley. Special winter cruises operate on the Rhine and Danube to take in the Christmas markets – if you're lucky you'll get crisp, cool weather and snow on the ground, but rain and slush are just as likely.

Russia tends to be hot and humid in summer. Take insect repellent for travel in August and September, when midges can be a problem, and something warm to wear in the evening in spring and fall.

Nile cruises operate year-round, the peak months being January to March when it's cooler. August is really too hot for anybody except the most dedicated sun-worshipper. September is tolerable if you take things slowly, and there'll be hardly any crowds at the temples. Wearing shorts and a tank top might keep you cool, but they'll indicate a lack of respect if you wear them when visiting tombs and you may be hassled.

Depending on the vessel, river, the operating company, and tour operators that send passengers to the vessels, there could be passengers of several nationalities. Communication could be a problem if you don't speak the same language.

European river cruising

Cruising down one of Europe's great waterways is a soothing experience – different from sailing on an open sea, where wave motion is a factor. These cruises provide a constant change of scenery, often passing through several countries, each with its own history and architecture, in a week-long journey.

Imagine, on the Danube you could actually have breakfast in Bratislava, lunch in Esztergom, and dinner in Budapest – and all on the same day. Or, on a River Rhine cruise, you could have breakfast in Rudesheim, lunch in Cologne, and dinner in Dusseldorf.

River vessels are always close to land and provide a chance to visit cities and areas inaccessible to the large resort ships. A cruise along the Danube, for example, will take you through nine countries: Germany, Austria, Slovakia, Hungary, Croatia, Serbia, Romania, Bulgaria, and Ukraine.

The Rhine–Main–Danube waterway, at 2,175 miles (3,500km), is the longest waterway in Europe. It connects 14 countries, from Rotterdam on the North Sea to Sulina and Izmail on the Black Sea, and offers travelers varied and fascinating sights.

River vessels are long and low in the water, and their masts fold down in order to negotiate low bridges. Although small when compared to oceangoing cruise ships, they have a unique and friendly international atmosphere. The most modern are air-conditioned and offer the discreet luxury of a small floating hotel, with

Cruising on the river Neva, St. Petersburg, Russia.

several public rooms including a dining room, observation lounge, bar, heated swimming 'dip' pool (some even have a small heated indoor pool), sauna, solarium, whirlpool, gymnasium, massage, hairdresser, and shop kiosk.

Although the cabins may be small, with limited closet space (take casual clothing, as informality is the order of the day), they are functional. Almost all have an outside view (facing the river), with a private bathroom, and will prove very comfortable for a one-week journey. Romantics may lament the fact that twin beds are the norm on the older vessels, but many cabins in the latest vessels have twin beds that can be converted to a queen-size bed. They also have a safe, a mini-bar, flat-screen TV, and an alarm clock/radio.

Viking River Cruises' fleet of new, trend-setting 'Viking Longships' have a unique design with an off-center hallway on two of the three accommodation decks. This arrangement provides two balconies: one full balcony and one 'French' balcony (room only to stick your toes outside), in two-room suites with separate sleeping and living rooms, plus a bathroom. Sixteen 'Viking Longships' were delivered in 2012 and 2013, with another 12 coming in 2014.

River cruising in Europe has thus reached quite a sophisticated level, and you can be assured of good service and meals of a consistently good local standard. Dining is a pleasant if not a gourmet experience, although some companies (such as AMA Waterways) are making strenuous efforts to provide fine cuisine. The best food is typically catered by Austrian, German, or Swiss companies. Breakfast and lunch are generally a buffet affair; dinners offer a set menu.

Typical fares for river cruises are from $800 to over $3,000 per person for a one-week cruise, including meals, cabin with private facilities, side trips, and airport/railway transfers. If you are already in Europe, many cruises can be purchased 'cruise-only.'

Theme cruises are gaining in popularity. For example, greenery lovers might enjoy the 'Gardens of the Rhine,' with visits to famous botanical gardens, arboretums, and herbariums. There are cruises for classical and jazz music fans, gourmets (including a meal at top restaurants in France, for example), and wine lovers. Christmas Markets cruises in Germany are popular, particularly along the Rhine – the best can be found in Cologne and Cochem.

Although just a few years ago riverships were little more than floating buses, today they have become like sophisticated, floating boutique hotels. While most are of the single-hull type (propulsion machinery, accommodation areas, and public rooms are all in one hull), new 'twin-cruisers' have been introduced. These vessels have their power unit and navigation bridge located aft in a separate unit attached to the longer body that contains the accommodation areas and public rooms. Although this guarantees that every cabin will be ultra-quiet for sleeping, captains find that the vessels are not easy to maneuver.

To ensure a degree of peace and quiet, it is best to go for a cabin on a deck that doesn't have a promenade deck walkway outside it. Normally, cabins on the lowest deck have a four-berth configuration. It doesn't matter which side of the rivership you are on, as you will see a riverbank and scenery on either side.

Recommended river cruise companies: AMA Waterways, APT Touring, Uniworld, and Viking River Cruises.

Russia's rivers

The 'Waterways of the Tsars' are a well-developed network of rivers, lakes, and canals. Geographically, river routes for tourists are divided into three main areas: Central European Russia, Northwestern European Russia, and Asian Russia. There are more than 80 riverships carrying international tourists.

In the Central Basin, Moscow is the hub of river tourism, and the newly opened waterways between Moscow and St Petersburg allow a seven-day cruise link between the present and former capitals, including the transit of the Volga-Baltic Canal System and its many locks. The best-known Russian rivers are the Don, Moskva, Neva, and Volga, but the lesser-known Belaya, Dvina (and North Dvina), Irtysh, Kama, Ob (longest river in Siberia), Oka, Svir, Tura, and Vyatka connect Russia's vast system of rivers and lakes.

Many Russian vessels are chartered to foreign cruise wholesalers and tour packagers, and are dedicated to a specific onboard language. The vessels vary in quality and facilities. Some are air-conditioned and most are clean. Cruises include the services of a cruise manager and lecturers. In Russia, all river cruise passengers who are non-Russian citizens must carry their passports at all times.

Recommended riverships: *AMAKatarina*, *Viking Helgi*, *Viking Ingvar*, *Viking Rurik*, *Viking Truvor*, *Aiking Lomonosov*, and *Volga Dream*.

The Nile

The scenery has changed remarkably little in more than 2,000 years, and the best way to see it, of course, is from a river vessel. However, political turmoil in Egypt over the past couple of years sharply reduced the number of tourists, leaving the 300 or so Nile riverships with seri-

Tranquility on the Burgundy Canal in France.

ous overcapacity, which translates to bargain prices for the intrepid traveler until the situation stabilizes.

In normal times, the vessels offer standards of comfort, food, and service that vary between very good and extremely poor. Most have a small, shallow 'plunge' pool, lounge, piano bar, and disco. It's prudent to subtract two stars from any rating provided in brochures or on cruise company and tour operator websites.

A lecturer in ancient Egyptian history accompanies almost all sailings, which cruise the 140 miles (220km) downstream between Aswan and Luxor in three or four days. Extended cruises, of seven or eight days, cover about 295 miles (475km) and visit Dendera and Abydos. The longest cruises, of 10 to 12 days, cover 590 miles (950km) and may include visits to Sohag, El Amarna, Tuna El Gabal, and Ashmunein, ending in Cairo. Most Nile cruises include sightseeing excursions, accompanied by experienced guides who may reside on

River cruising: who to contact

This is a complicated sector, with product details changing frequently and rivercruise operators chartering their vessels to many different tour operators. The websites below will help you find what's available in your preferred destination.

EUROPE
AMA Waterways: www.amawaterways.com
APT Waterways: www.aptouring.co.uk
A'Rosa Cruises: www.a-rosa.de
Avalon Waterways: www.avalonwaterways.com
CroisiEurope: www.croisieurope.com
Grand Circle Travel: www.gct.com
Lüftner Cruises: www.lueftner-cruises.com
Phoenix Reisen: www.poenixreisen.com
Scenic Tours: www.scenictours.com
Scylla Tours: www.scylla.ch/Home-130
Sea Cloud Cruises: www.seacloud.com
Tauck Tours: www.tauck.com
Uniworld: www.uniworld.com
Viking River Cruises: www.vikingrivercruises.com

RUSSIA and UKRAINE
AMA Waterways: www.amawaterways.com
Noble Caledonia: www.noblecaledonia.com
Uniworld: www.uniworld.com
Viking River Cruises: www.vikingrivercruises.com

YANGTZE
Noble Caledonia: www.noblecaledonia.com
Uniworld: www.uniworld.com
Victoria Cruises: www.victoriacruises.com
Viking River Cruises: www.vikingrivercruises.com

THE NILE
Hilton Hotels: www.hiltonhotels.com
Movenpick: www.movenpick-nilecruises.com
Nabila Tours: www.nabilatours.com
Noble Caledonia: www.noblecaledonia.com
Oberoi Hotels: www.oberoihotels.com/cruises.asp
Sonesta Cruise Collection: www.sonesta.com/nilecruises
Viking River Cruises: www.vikingrivercruises.com

board, or who may meet the vessel at each call.

Perhaps it was Agatha Christie who made cruising along the Nile popular when she wrote *Death on the Nile*, first published in the UK in 1937. She wrote it while staying in the Old Cataract Hotel, located on Elephantine Island.

The best peak time to take a River Nile cruise is between December and February when the weather is hot but not quite so humid. The water level can be low between October and May to conserve water at the Aswan Dam, so getting through the locks at Esna can take a long time as riverships compete with cargo vessels and feluccas to get through.

Gratuities are usually not included in the cruise fare, but any tips you give will be divided among all crew members. Some vessels accept credit cards for payment of your onboard account, but others accept only cash.

A few useful tips

When you visit the major historic sites and temples, note that there are few public toilet facilities. Toilet paper is not normally provided, so take tissues with you.

Most Nile riverships provide 220-volt outlets in cabins. If you have 110-volt appliances, take adapters (plugs have European-style two round pins).

If you take a camera with you to any of the 62 tombs in the Valley of the Kings (only a few are open at any one time), you will need to buy a ticket for your camera, too. Museums and other major tourist sites also charge for the use of video and still cameras.

China's rivers

More than 50 vessels offer cruises along the Yangtze, the world's third-longest river. The most popular include the area known as the Three River Gorges, a 100-mile (160-km) stretch between Nanjin Pass in the east and White King City in the west.

The Yangtze stretches 3,900 miles (6,300km) from

Riverships triple-park on the Nile at Aswan, Egypt.

Shanghai through the very heartland of China. The Three Gorges include the 47-mile (76-km) Xiling Gorge, the 25-mile (40-km) Wu Gorge, and the 28-mile (45-km) Qutang Gorge, known locally as 'Wind Box Gorge.' The Lesser Three Gorges (or Three Small Gorges) are also an impressive sight, often part of the main cruise but also reached by small vessels from Wushan. If possible, take a cabin with a balcony. It is worth the extra money, and the view is better.

Standards of hygiene are generally far lower than you may be used to at home. In China, rats and rivers often go together, and rat poison may well be found under your bed. Some vessels, such as those of Viking River Cruises, have Chinese- and Western-style restaurants, a beauty salon, a small health club with sauna, and private mahjong and karaoke rooms. Fine Asian hospitality and service prevail, and cabins are kept supplied with fresh towels and hot tea.

There are several operators, but do check on the facilities, meet-and-greet service, and the newness of the vessels before booking. The best time of the year to go is May–June, and late August–October (July and early August are extremely hot and humid). However, in the Yangtze Valley, temperatures between April and September can reach 97°F (36°C), and summer rains can be torrential. Monsoons – seasonally changing winds – dominate the region's weather conditions.

The Mekong: This has become a popular rivercruise destination, although there are sometimes some security concerns. At 2,700 miles (4,350km), it is Southeast Asia's longest river and the world's 12th longest, although much of it is unnavigable. Its name (known locally as Mae Nam Khong) means 'the mother of all water' as it births and feeds many of China's life-giving waters. Stretching from the Plateau of Tibet to the South China Sea, it has two main sections: the Upper Mekong, and the Lower Mekong.

The Lower Mekong forms part of the international border between Myanmar (Burma) and Laos, as well as between Laos and Thailand (often referred to as the Golden Triangle). It also flows through Laos, Cambodia (Kampuchea), and Vietnam before draining into the South China Sea to the south of Ho Chi Minh City (Saigon). Vientiane, capital of Laos, and Phnom Penh, Cambodia's capital, are located on the river's banks. I recommend traveling with reliable, seasoned operators such as AMA Waterways, Pandaw Cruises, or Viking River Cruises.

River Murray, Australia

The fifth-largest river in the world, the Murray was the lifeblood of the pioneers who lived on the driest continent on earth. Today, the river flows for more than 1,250 miles (2,760km) across a third of Australia, its banks forming protected lagoons for an astonishing variety of bird and animal life. A paddlewheel boat such as *Murray Princess* even has six cabins for the physically disabled.

Murray Princess paddles along Australia's Murray River.

Barge cruising in France

Smaller and more intimate than river vessels and more accurately called boats, 'cruise barges' ply the inland waterways and canals of France from spring to fall, when the weather is best. Barge cruises (usually lasting three to 13 days) offer a completely informal atmosphere, and a slow pace of life, for up to a dozen passengers. They chug along slowly in the daytime, and moor early each evening, giving you time to pay a visit to a local village and get a restful night's sleep.

Most cruise barges are comfortable and beautifully fitted out with rich wood paneling, full carpeting, custom-built furniture, and tastefully chosen fabrics. Each has a dining room or lounge-bar. Captains take pride in their vessel, often displaying rare memorabilia.

Locally grown fresh foods are usually purchased and prepared each day, allowing you to live well and feel like a houseguest. Dining ranges from home-style cooking to some outstanding nouvelle cuisine, with all the trimmings. Often, the barge's owner, or spouse, cooks. Most cruise barges can be chartered exclusively so you can just take your family and friends. The waterways of France especially offer beauty, tranquility, and a diversity of interests, and barge cruising is an excellent way of exploring an unfamiliar area. Most cruises include a visit to a famous vineyard and wine cellar, as well as side trips to places of historic, architectural, or scenic interest. Shopping opportunities are limited; evening entertainment is impromptu.

Barging on the canals often means going through a constant succession of locks. Nowhere is this more enjoyable and entertaining than in the Burgundy region of France where, between Dijon and Mâcon, for example, a barge can negotiate as many as 54 locks during a six-day cruise. Interestingly, all lockkeepers in France are women.

Rates range from $600 to more than $3,000 per person for a six-day cruise. I don't recommend taking children. Rates include a cabin with private facilities, all meals, good wine with lunch and dinner, all other beverages, use of bicycles, side trips, and airport or railway transfers. Some operators provide a hotel the night before or after the cruise. Clothing is totally casual – but, at the beginning and end of the season, it's a good idea to take sweaters and rain gear.

The best views

With a bit of cunning, you can secure a better view on a Nile cruise. As vessels head north from Aswan to Luxor, they almost always tie up on the river's left bank – except in Aswan, where they tie up on the right bank. Also, they tend to moor two or three deep. But if you ask for a starboard cabin and your vessel gets the outside position, your view across the Nile while you are in port – particularly in Luxor, where you will spend a couple of nights – will be uninterrupted. In a port cabin, all you would see would be the riverbank or the vessel tied up next to you. Reverse this logic for southbound cruises.

United States

Although the former Delta Queen Steamboat Company no longer exists and the steamboats stopped operating in 2008, a small American company, American Cruise Lines, bought the *Columbia Queen, Empress of the North,* and *Queen of the West* steamboats and started operations in 2010 on the Columbia and Snake rivers in the Pacific Northwest. In 2012 steamboats returned to the Mississippi with the introduction of the company's brand new riverboat, *Queen of the Mississippi,* and the Great American Steamboat Company's refitted classic steamboat *American Queen.*

Around-the-World Cruises

They are a great way to roam the world without having to constantly pack and unpack. But choose carefully: some cruises spend very little time in ports.

Since Cunard operated its first world cruise aboard the *Laconia* in 1922, this has become the ultimate classic journey – more a voyage of discovery than a cruise. It is defined as the complete circumnavigation of the earth in a continuous one-way voyage, typically including both the Panama and the Suez Canals. Ports of call are carefully planned for their interest and diversity, and the entire voyage can last six months or longer.

Galas, themed balls (for example, Cunard's Black & White Ball, Royal Ascot Ball), special social events, top entertainers, and, typically, well-known lecturers are all part of the package. It's a great way of exchanging the northern winter for the southern sun in a grand voyage that is over 32,000 nautical miles long, following in the wake of Ferdinand Magellan, who led his round-the-world voyage in 1519–22, although he himself was killed en route.

Around-the-world cruises generally pursue the sun in a westbound direction, which gives an added bonus: that of gaining an hour each time a ship goes into the

Aurora transiting the Panama Canal.

next time zone. Travel in an eastbound direction – between, for example, Europe and Australia – and you lose an hour each time. A few ships that include an around-South America voyage will generally travel in a southbound, then westbound, direction.

A world cruise aboard a modern ship means enjoying stabilized, air-conditioned comfort in luxury cabins, combined with extraordinary sightseeing and excursions on shore and overland. Such a cruise is all about exchanging familiar environments with new ones, glamorous evening soirées, special social parties, black-and-white-themed balls, and entertainment that ranges from intimate recitals to large-scale shows and headline cabaret specialty acts. Best of all: you need pack and unpack just once during a three-month circumnavigation.

It appeals to retirees, the widowed, those who simply want to escape the winter, and those who delight in roaming the world in search of new experiences, sights, sounds, cultures, and aromas. There'll be lots of sea days, during which your suite or cabin can be a private refuge, so it's worth choosing the best you can afford.

There are four aspects to a good world cruise: itinerary, ship, price, and the cruise line's experience. Some of the most ambitious itineraries are those operated by the German cruise lines such as Hapag-Lloyd Cruises and Phoenix Reisen (whose itineraries usually feature more than 60 ports of call, compared to the average 35). Spending overnight in several ports of call means you can plan to meet friends, go out for dinner, and enjoy nights out on the town. But check cruise line websites and brochures and itineraries carefully, because some ships spend surprisingly little time in port.

World cruise segments

If you want to experience all the extra things that around-the-world cruises provide but don't have the three months needed, remember that most lines offer the cruise in several 'segments.' This also allows you to 'test' the ship and service levels before investing the time and money needed for a full circumnavigation. *Queen Mary 2*, for example, offer 16 segments on its 2012 around-the-world cruise, from 16 nights to 73 nights. The most popular length for a segment is around 30 days.

'Segmenters,' as they are called, typically add on a stay pre- or post-cruise in a destination combining a cruise 'n' stay vacation. In this way they can visit

Table Mountain provides a backdrop to Cape Town's harbor for *Crystal Symphony*.

exotic destinations such as China, the South Pacific, the Indian Ocean, or South America while enjoying elegance, comfort, splendid food, and good company.

Bear in mind that you get what you pay for. Ships rated at four stars or more will probably include shuttle buses from your ship to town centers; ships rated three stars or less will not.

Ships that roam worldwide during the year offer the most experienced world cruises or segments. Most operate at about 75 percent capacity, providing much more space per person than they could normally expect.

Calculating the cost

Prices for a full world cruise vary depending on the cruise line, ship, and accommodation chosen. The fol-lowing examples are taken from 2014 world cruise brochures (per person rates are quoted, based on dou-ble occupancy for an interior cabin. Single-occupancy rates are available on request:

Amsterdam (113 nights: from $19,999 per person).
Black Watch (104 nights: from £9,799 per person).
Queen Mary 2 (119 nights, from $21,995 per person).
Seabourn Sojourn ($52,214 per person).

Naturally, substantial discounts (up to 50 percent) and special incentives are offered by many cruise lines, particularly if you book early. In today's difficult eco-nomic times, the lowest-grade cabins tend to sell out fastest. Some cruise lines quote only a 'from' price as a lead-in rate, and provide the price for the large suites only upon application.

Passengers who book a full world cruise will prob-ably enjoy a pre-cruise five-star hotel stay and extrava-gant dinner with the cruise line's top executives, on-board credit, plus other special events during the cruise (not available to 'segmenters'). Note that some cruise lines reserve the right to add a surcharge if the NYNEX oil price exceeds $70 a barrel – read the fine print in the brochure. Also, the lowest prices may not include the airfare, if any is required.

Some ships include alcoholic drinks and wine in their cruise fares (examples include *Crystal Serenity, Seabourn Quest, Seven Seas Voyager, Silver Spirit*), but most do not. There will inevitably be the ques-tion of gratuities to staff, which are included for the 2014 world cruises aboard *Albatros, Amadea, Asuka II, Crystal Serenity, Seabourn Quest, Seven Seas Voyager,* and *Silver Spirit*. You'll need to factor in about $10 per person, per day to your budget for these. On a 90-day world cruise, that's $1,800. If you are in one of the larg-est suites, it would be considerably more – allow about $3,000 per couple.

Planning

For passengers, one of the most important decisions to make will be about what clothes to pack for different climates and conditions. What's really good is that once you have boarded the ship, you need unpack only once. Also, you can take as much luggage as you wish; if you need to fly to join the cruise, you can send your luggage on ahead with a courier service. Although all ships have laundries, some also have self-service launderettes (the place to go for all the inside gossip), so you can clean small items that you need to reuse quickly.

For an operator, planning a world cruise involves daunting organization. For example, more than 700,000 main meals will be prepared during a typical world cruise aboard *Queen Mary 2*. A ship of its size needs two major crew changes during a three-month-long voyage. Hundreds of professional entertainers, lecturers, bands, and musicians must be booked a year in advance.

Queen Mary 2 leaving Sydney, Australia.

Shore excursions

Part of the excitement of an around-the-world voyage is the anticipation of seeing new destinations, and planning how best to use your time. This is where the expertise of cruise line shore excursion departments and concierges can prove worthwhile.

Cruise lines provide an extensive array of shore excursions in the many ports of call. On the 2012 around-the-world of Cunard Line's *Queen Elizabeth*, for example, the cheapest excursion was $27 (for an iPod Discovery Walk in Athens) and the most expensive was $1,700 per person (for a private mini-bus tour in Rome).

Aboard some more 'upscale' ships, tailor-made excursions are always available, as are things like arranging private cars with driver and guide for a few hours or a whole day.

Overland tours lasting from one to five days are sometimes featured. Here, you leave the ship in one port and rejoin in another a few days later – for example, leave the ship in Mumbai, fly to Agra to see the Taj Mahal, and perhaps ride aboard the Maharaja Express train, then fly to another port to rejoin the ship. The cost for a three-day overland excursion on the *Queen Elizabeth* 2012 world cruise was $3,250 per person. Depending on the 'overland' country, you may need to apply for a visa before your voyage.

Always popular are helicopter or seaplane flightseeing tours, typically costing around $300.

One problem is the lack of port information for independent passengers not wishing to join organized excursions. The answer is to do the research yourself. Books in the ship's library should help if you haven't done your homework before embarking.

Extra baggage

One of the nice things about an around-the-world cruise is that if you buy big or heavy items along the way (in Hong Kong or in Singapore, for example), the ship can store the item on board for you. If you only do a segment (Southampton to Sydney, say), you may be able to collect the items when the ship completes its voyage at your home port. Not all cruise lines offer this service.

Celebrations at sea

On around-the-world cruises, special dates for English-speaking passengers are usually observed with decorations, dinners, dances, teas, and menus that reflect the occasion. Examples include: Burns Night, Valentine's Day, Australia Day, April Fool's Day, May Day, etc.

Two special ceremonies form part of the passenger participation events on a traditional around-the-world cruise:

Crossing the Equator, when King Neptune (Neptunus Rex, the old man of the sea), his wife Amphitrite, and the Royal Court initiate those crossing the line for the first time (called Pollywogs). An old naval tradition, it is usually conducted at the poolside – with inevitable results.

Crossing the International Date Line, where you gain or lose a day, depending on whether you're traveling eastbound or westbound. The imaginary line, at approximately 180° longitude, isn't straight but zigzags to avoid splitting countries apart. Although it was established with international agreement, there are no formal treaties or conventions. It has confused explorers, navigators, and travelers ever since humans began circumnavigating the globe 500 years ago. In Jules Verne's *Around the World in 80 Days* Phileas Fogg and his crew returned to London one day late (or so they thought), but it was the extra day gained by crossing the International Date Line that enabled them to win their wager.

10 typical excursions
1. 4WD Desert Safari (Dubai) – about five hours
2. Night Safari (Singapore Zoo) – about four hours
3. James Bond Island (Phang Nga Bay, Phuket, Thailand) – about 3.5 to four hours
4. Luxor, Karnak, and the Valley of the Kings (Cairo, Egypt) – about 13 hours
5. The Lost City of Petra (from Aqaba, Jordan) – about 10 hours
6. The Acropolis – Crown Jewel of Athens (from Piraeus, Greece) – about four hours
7. A Night at the Opera (Sydney, Australia) – about four hours
8. America's Cup Experience (Auckland, New Zealand) – about four hours
9. Pearl Harbor and Honolulu (Hawaii) – about six hours
10. Alcatraz and Sausalito (San Francisco, USA) – about four hours

Around-the-world cruises in 2014						
Ship Name	Type of cruise	Company	Nights	Date (Start)	From	Date (Finish)	To
Amadea	Full Circumnavigation	Phoenix Reisen	133	December 20, 2014	Nice	May 7, 2015	Hamburg
Amsterdam	Full Circumnavigation	Holland America Line	113	January 4, 2014	Ft. Lauderdale	April 28, 2014	Ft Lauderdale
Arcadia	Full Circumnavigation	P&O Cruises	92	January 10, 2014	Southampton	April 13, 2014	Southampton
Asuka II	Full Circumnavigation	NYK Cruises	104	March 12, 2014	Yokohama	July 2, 2014	Kobe
Aurora	Full Circumnavigation	P&O Cruises	109	January 4, 2014	Southampton	April 24, 2014	Southampton
Balmoral	Full Circumnavigation	Fred. Olsen Cruise Lines	104	January 5, 2014	Southampton	April 19, 2014	Southampton
Black Watch	Full Circumnavigation	Fred. Olsen Cruise Lines	113	January 14, 2014	Southampton	March 31, 2014	Southampton
Costa Atlantica	Full Circumnavigation	Costa Cruises	100	March 22, 2014	Savona	June 13, 2014	Shanghai
Costa Deliziosa	Full Circumnavigation	Costa Cruises	100	January 6, 2014	Savona	April 16, 2014	Savona
Crystal Serenity	Around South America/Amazon Cruise	Crystal Cruises	88	January 18, 2014	Miami	April 18, 2014	Southampton
Dawn Princess	Circle Pacific Cruise	Princess Cruises	104	May 18, 2014	Sydney	August 31, 2014	Sydney
Europa	Full Circumnavigation	Hapag-Lloyd Cruises	100	January 4, 2014	Progresso	April 15, 2014	Dubai
Queen Elizabeth	Full Circumnavigation	Cunard Line	118	January 10, 2014	Southampton	May 9, 2014	Southampton
Queen Mary 2	Full Circumnavigation	Cunard Line	119	January 10, 2014	Southampton	May 9, 2014	Southampton
Queen Victoria	Southern Hemisphere	Cunard Line	116	January 2, 2014	Southampton	April 28, 2014	Southampton
Seabourn Sojourn	Part-Circumnavigation	Seabourn	116	January 4, 2014	Los Angeles	May 1, 2014	Venice
Seven Seas Mariner	Around South America Cruise	Regent Seven Seas Cruises	62	January 25, 2014	Miami	March 28, 2014	Barcelona
Silver Whisper	Full Circumnavigation	Silversea Cruises	113	January 6, 2014	Los Angeles	April 30, 2014	Ft Lauderdale

Choosing the Right Ship

What's the difference between large and small ships?
Are new ships better than older ones? Here is the latest
to make sure you select the right ship to sail away.

Which ship? There's something to suit virtually all tastes, so take into account your own personality and tastes. Ships are measured (not weighed) in gross tonnage (gt) and come in four principal size categories:

Large resort ships: for 1,750–6,500 passengers (typically measure 50,000–220,000 gross tonnage). *Think:* double-decker bus (with some seats that are better than others).

Mid-size ships: for 750–1,750 passengers (typically 25,000–50,000 gross tonnage). *Think:* long-distance coach (comfortable seats).

Small ships: for 250–750 passengers (typically 5,000–25,000 gross tonnage). *Think:* mini-van (some are executive types; some are more mainstream).

Boutique ships: for up to 250 passengers (typically 1,000–5,000 gross tonnage). *Think:* private car (luxury, mid-range, or compact).

Space

For an idea of the amount of the space around you (I call it the 'crowd factor'), check the Passenger Space Ratio given for each ship in the listings section (gross tonnage divided by number of passengers).

Passenger space ratio:
50 and above is outstanding
30 to 50 is very spacious
20 to 30 is not very spacious
10 to 20 is high density
10 or below is extremely cramped

Large resort ships
(1,750–6,500 passengers)

Choose a large resort ship if you like being with lots of other people in a bustling big-city environment, you enjoy being sociable, and you want to have plenty of entertainment and dining (well, eating) options. These balcony-rich ships provide a well-packaged standard or premium vacation, usually in a seven-day cruise. It is the interaction between passengers and crew that determines the quality of the onboard experience.

Large resort ships have extensive facilities and programs for families with children of all ages. But if you meet someone on the first day and want to see them again, make sure you appoint a very specific

Costa Classica in Norway's Gierangerfjord, Norway.

place and time (apart from the size of the ship, they may be at a different meal seating). These ships have a highly structured array of activities and passenger participation events each day, together with large entertainment venues, and the most lavish production shows at sea.

It is the standard of service, entertainment, lecture programs, level of communication, and finesse in dining services that really can move these ships into high rating categories, but they must be exceptional to do so. Choose higher-priced suite accommodation and the service improves. In other words: pay more, get more.

Large resort ships are highly programmed. It is difficult, for example, to go swimming in the late evening – the decks are cleaned and pools are often netted over by 6pm. Having champagne delivered to

Snacking at sea aboard *Celebrity Constellation*.

more entertainment, and more dining options. There is some entertainment and more structured activities than aboard small ships, but less than aboard large resort ships.

Smll ships (250–750 passengers) and Boutique ships (50–250 passengers)

Choose a small or boutique ship for an intimate cruise experience and a small number of passengers. Some of the world's most exclusive cruise ships belong in this group – but so do most of the coastal vessels with basic, unpretentious amenities, sail-cruise ships, and the expedition-style cruise vessels that take passengers to see nature.

Select this size of ship if you don't need much entertainment, large resort ship facilities, gambling casinos, several restaurants, and if you don't like to wait in lines for anything. If you want to swim in the late evening, or have champagne in the hot tub at midnight, it's easier aboard boutique or small ships than aboard larger ships, where more rigid programs lead to inflexible, passenger-unfriendly thinking.

What about age?

A ship built before 1990 is considered old. However, its quality depends on the level of maintenance it has received, and whether it has operated on short or longer cruises – short cruises get more passenger throughput and wear and tear. Many passengers like older ships, as they tend to have fewer synthetic materials in their interior decor. It's inevitable that most of the older tonnage won't match the latest high-tech hardware, but today's ships aren't built with the same loving care as in the past.

Most cruise advertising you'll see revolves around the newer, larger ships, but some older ships have much to offer if you don't want the latest trendy facilities and city high street feel. Indeed, some of the older, smaller ships have adequate facilities, tend to have more character, and provide a more relaxing vacation experience than the go-go-go contemporary ships, where you're just one of a large crowd.

The crew

You can estimate the standard of service by looking at the crew-to-passenger ratio (provided in the ship profiles in this book). The best service levels are aboard ships that have a ratio of one crew member to every two passengers, or higher. The best ships in the world, from the point of view of crew living and working conditions, also tend to be the most expensive ones – the adage 'you get what you pay for' tends to be all too true.

Most ships, with one or two exceptions, have multinational crews. Indeed, the crew mixture can resemble a miniature United Nations. However, if the crew is happy, the ship will be happy, too; this will communicate itself to passengers.

Some P&O ships retain traditional games such as shuffleboard.

outdoor hot tubs late at night is virtually impossible. They have lost the flexibility for which cruise ships were once known, becoming victims of company 'policy' and insurance regulations. There can be a feeling of 'conveyor-belt' cruising, with cultural offerings scarcely extending beyond rap, rock, alcohol, and gambling.

Mid-size ships (750–1,750 passengers)

These suit the smaller ports of the Aegean and Mediterranean, and are more maneuverable than larger ships. Several operate around-the-world cruises and other long-distance itineraries to exotic destinations not really feasible aboard many small ships or large resort ships.

There is a big difference in the amount of space available. Accommodation varies from large 'penthouse suites' complete with butler service to tiny interior (no-view) cabins. These ships will generally be more stable at sea than 'small ships,' due to their increased size and draft. They provide more facilities,

Newer ships (post-1990): Advantages

Newer ships typically incorporate the latest in high-tech electronic equipment and in advanced ship design and construction; they also meet the latest safety and operating standards.

Typically, newer ships have been built with 'pod' propulsion systems, which have replaced conventional propeller shafts, propellers, and rudders, with the result that there is little or no vibration. This type of propulsion system is also more fuel efficient.

Although the trade-off is debatable, more recent ships have been built with more interior public rooms, and less exterior promenade deck. This is great for traveling to destinations where the weather is less predictable, but not so great for sunbathing.

More standardized cabin layouts, with fewer categories to cause confusion when booking. These cabins also have better plumbing and air-conditioning systems.

Newer ships have design advantages as well, including: a shallower draft, which makes it easier for them to enter and leave ports; bow and stern thrusters, so they seldom require tug assistance in many ports,

An illustrated nature talk aboard *National Geographic Explorer.*

Advantages and disadvantages of large resort ships

Advantages	Disadvantages
The newest ships have state-of-the-art electronic interactive entertainment facilities – good if you like computers and high-tech gadgetry.	The itineraries may be limited by ship size, and there may be tender ports where you need to take a number, sit in a lounge, and wait … and wait.
Often have a walk-around promenade deck outdoors.	Room-service breakfast is not generally available on the day of disembarkation.
Have the widest range of public rooms and facilities.	They are floating hotels (but with many announcements), and many items cost extra. They are like retail parks surrounded by cabins.
Have a greater amount of space, although this does mean more passengers.	Finding your way around the ship can be frustrating, and signage is often confusing.
Generally have more dining options.	There will be a lack of available elevators at peak times.
There are more facilities and activities for people of all ages, particularly for families with children.	You may have to use a sign-up sheet to use gym equipment such as treadmills or exercise bikes.
Generally sail well in open seas in bad weather.	Announcements could be in several languages.
	The restaurant service staff is trained to provide fast service, so it's almost impossible to dine in leisurely fashion.
	Food may well be bland – cooking for 5,000 is not quite the same as cooking for a dinner party of eight.
	Telephoning room service can be frustrating, particularly in ships with automatic telephone answering systems.
	Lines to wait in: for embarkation, reception, elevators, buffet meals, shore excursions, security checkpoint, and disembarkation.
	In early evening, the deckchairs are taken away, or strapped up so they can't be used.
	The in-cabin music aboard the latest ships is supplied through the television set; it may be impossible to turn off the picture while listening.
	Some large resort ships have only two main passenger stairways, which can cause congestion in passenger flow.

Advantages and disadvantages of mid-size ships	
Advantages	Disadvantages
They are neither too large, nor too small; their size and facilities often strike a happy balance.	Few have large showlounges for large-scale production shows, so entertainment tends to be more of the cabaret variety.
It is easy to find one's way around.	They don't offer as wide a range of public rooms and facilities as the large resort ships.
They generally sail well in bad weather, being neither high-sided like the large resort ships, nor too shallow draft like some of the small ships.	
Lines seldom form, except for ships approaching 1,600 passengers.	
They appear more like traditional ships than most of the larger vessels, which tend to be more 'boxy' in shape and profile.	

which reduces operating costs; and many have the latest submersible lifeboats, creating a safer operating environment.

Newer ships (post-1990): Disadvantages

Unfortunately, these newer ships don't 'take the weather' as well as older ships – sailing across the North Atlantic in November on one of the new large resort ships can be unforgettable. Because of their shallow draft, these ships roll, even when there's the

Formal dining aboard Cunard's *Queen Victoria*.

slightest puff of wind. Recent design changes also mean that newer ships have thin hulls and do not withstand the bangs and dents as well as older, more heavily plated vessels.

Newer ships tend to have smaller (although more standardized) cabins, which can mean narrow, short beds. The interior decor is made mostly from synthetic materials, due to stringent regulations, and could cause problems for passengers sensitive to such materials. The cabin windows are usually completely sealed, instead of portholes that can be opened. Most egregiously, newer ships almost always have toilets of the powerful vacuum suction, which I like to call the 'barking dog' type.

Pre-1990 ships: Advantages

Older ships have strong, plated hulls that can withstand tremendously hard wear and tear; they 'take the weather' well. They have deep drafts that help them to achieve a smooth ride in the open seas.

The interiors of older ships are usually built from traditional materials such as wood and brass, with less use of synthetic fibers, so are less likely to affect anyone with allergies. The cabins tend to be larger, with long, wide beds/berths, because passengers needed more space in the days when voyages were much longer. Also, toilets of an older generation are of the 'gentle flush' variety instead of today's vacuum toilets.

Pre-1990 ships: Disadvantages

Older ships are not very fuel-efficient and are, therefore, more expensive to operate than new ships. Because of their construction, they might have a tough time complying with current international fire, safety, and environmental regulations. Older ships need a larger crew, because of the more awkward, labor-intensive layouts. As well, ships built before 1990 typically have a deep draft, which makes for a smooth ride, but means they may need tugs to negotiate ports and tight berths.

Casual lunch aboard *Carnival Magic*.

Advantages and disadvantages of small and boutique ships	
Advantages	**Disadvantages**
Most provide 'open seating' in the dining room; this means that you can sit with whomever you wish, whenever you wish, for all meals.	They don't have the bulk, length, or beam to sail well in open seas in inclement weather conditions.
Provide a totally unstructured lifestyle, offering a level of service not found aboard most of the larger ships, and no – or almost no – announcements.	They don't have the range of public rooms that the large resort ships can provide.
At their best in warm-weather areas.	Options for entertainment are limited.
Capable of true culinary excellence, with fresh foods cooked to order.	They don't have the range of open spaces that the large resort ships can provide.
They're more like small inns than mega-resorts.	
It's easy to find your way around, and signage is usually clear and concise.	
Provide an 'open bridge' policy, allowing passengers to visit the navigation bridge when safe to do so.	
Some small ships have a hydraulic marina water-sports platform at the stern and carry equipment such as jet skis and scuba/ snorkeling gear.	
They can visit the more off-beat ports of call that larger ships can't.	
When the ship is at anchor, going ashore is easy and speedy, with a continuous tender service and no lines.	
Less crowded ports mean more exclusivity.	

Choosing the Right Cabin

Does cabin size count? Are suites sweeter than cabins?
How desirable is a balcony? What about location?

Ideally, you should feel at home when at sea, so it is important to choose the right accommodation, even if most of your time in it is spent with your eyes shut. Accommodation sizes range from a whopping 4,390 sq ft (407 sq m) to a minuscule 60 sq ft (5.5 sq m). Choose wisely, for if you find your cabin (incorrectly called a 'stateroom' by some companies) is too small when you get to the ship, it may be impossible to change it, as the ship could be full.

Cruise lines designate cabins only when deposits have been received – they may, however, guarantee the grade and rate requested. If this isn't done, or if you find a disclaimer such as 'All cabin assignments are confirmed upon embarkation of the vessel,' get a guarantee in writing that your cabin will *not* be changed on embarkation.

There are three main types of accommodation: suites, outside-view cabins, and interior cabins. But many variations on each type, detailed below.

The suite life

Suites are the most luxurious and spacious of all shipboard accommodation, and typically come with butler service. A suite (in the sense of a 'suite of rooms') should comprise a lounge or sitting room separated from a bedroom by a solid door (not just a curtain), a bedroom with a large bed, one or more bathrooms, and an abundance of closet, drawer, and other storage space. The best suites have the most desirable position, privacy, good views, and bed linen. Many cruise lines inaccurately describe some accommodation as suites, when they are nothing more than a large cabin with a curtain that divides sitting and sleeping areas.

Suites are best on long voyages with several days at sea (aboard some ships, this might include an extended room service breakfast). Be aware that, although the large resort ships may devote a whole deck or two to penthouses and suites, you will have to share the rest of the ship with those in lower-priced accommodation.

That means there is no preferential seating in the showroom, dining rooms, or on sunbathing decks. You may get separate check-in facilities and preferential treatment upon disembarkation, but your luggage will be lumped with everyone else's.

Balconies, like this one aboard *Celebrity Solstice*, provide a refuge from the bustle of big ships.

'Spa Suite' accommodation

Spa suites – not to be confused with 'thermal spa suites' (comprising sauna, steam room, and herbal showers) found in the on-board spa – are usually located adjacent to or near the ship's spa. They often have 'spa-added' features such as a bathroom with window into the sleeping area, bathtub and mood lighting, and perhaps special health teas or herbal infusions. Some cruise lines may even include a spa treatment such as a massage or facial, in the 'spa suite' package, plus unlimited access to the actual spa.

Are balconies worth it?

Romeo and Juliet thought so. And they're addictive, too. A private balcony (or veranda, terrace, or lanai), for which you pay a premium, is just that. It is a mini-terrace adjoining your cabin where you can sit, enjoy the private view, smell the sea, dine, or even have a massage. It's a desirable space.

Some private balconies aren't so private, though. Balconies not separated by full floor-to-ceiling partitions don't quite cut it (examples: *Carnival Sunshine, Carnival Triumph, Carnival Victory, Maasdam, Oriana, Queen Mary 2, Ryndam, Seven Seas Mariner, Seven Seas Voyager, Statendam,* and *Veendam*). You could get noise or smoke from your neighbor. Some ships have balconies with full floor-to-ceiling privacy partitions and an outside light (example: *Celebrity Century,* some of whose partitions are full and others partial).

Many large resort ships have balconies too small to accommodate even two reclining chairs, and may have plastic or plain painted steel decking instead of traditional, more expensive teakwood decking. The average size of a cabin balcony aboard the large resort ships is about 9ft x 6ft (2.7m by 1.8m) or about 55 sq ft (5.2 sq m). But they can measure as much as 30 times that.

Some suites with forward-facing private balconies may not be so good, as the wind speed can make them all but unusable (examples: *Seabourn Legend, Seabourn Pride, Seabourn Spirit, Silver Cloud, Silver Shadow, Silver Spirit, Silver Whisper, Silver Wind*). And when the ship drops anchor in ports of call, the noise pollution can be irritating (examples: *Silver Cloud, Silver Wind*).

Allure of the Seas' Royal Loft Suite.

For the best in privacy, a balcony suite at a ship's stern is hard to beat, and some of the largest afloat can be found there – sheltered from the wind, such as aboard *Marina* and *Riviera* (Oceania Cruises).

Installing a balcony means that space is often taken away from either the cabin or the bathroom – which is why today's bathrooms are smaller and almost none have full-size tubs.

All private balconies have railings to lean on, but some have solid steel plates between railing and deck, so you can't look out to sea when seated *(Costa Classica, Costa neoRomantica, Dawn Princess, Oceana, Sea Princess,* and *Sun Princess).* Better are ships whose balconies have clear glass *(Aurora, Brilliance of the Seas, Celebrity Century, Empress, Mein Schiff, Mein Schiff 2, Radiance of the Seas,* and *Serenade of the Seas)* or horizontal bars.

French balconies

A French balcony (sometimes known as a Juliet balcony) is neither French nor a balcony as such. But it does have a full floor-to-ceiling sliding door and a ledge (not really a balcony) that allows you to stick out your toes and smell the fresh air.

Interior-view balconies

Aboard the largest cruise ships, Royal Caribbean International's *Allure of the Seas* and *Oasis of the Seas,* 'interior' balcony cabins are novel. They overlook one of two neighborhoods: Central Park, with its trees and plants (hopefully, there are no muggers), or The Boardwalk at the stern of the ship, although these really are classed as outside balcony cabins – if it rains, your balcony *can* get wet, but it's unlikely. However, people scream as they career along the Zipline above the Boardwalk balconies, so they can be really noisy by day. And, when no one is zipping, you may have a view of the sea (and perhaps the excellent acrobatic AquaShow) at the ship's stern.

Balcony doors can be quite heavy and difficult to open. Many ships have doors that slide open (examples:

10 things a butler can do
1. Assist with unpacking your suitcase
2. Bring you DVDs, CDs, board games, a pack of cards
3. Bring you menus for all dining venues and serve course-by-course meals in your suite
4. Arrange a private cocktail party
5. Arrange for laundry/cleaning items
6. Make dining venue reservations
7. Provide afternoon tea or canapés
8. Book shore excursions
9. Make your spa reservations
10. Make your shoes shine

Seabourn Legend's French balconies.

Celebrity Century, Crystal Serenity, Grand Princess, Norwegian Gem); a few have doors that open inward (examples: *Seabourn Legend, Seabourn Pride, Seabourn Spirit, Silver Cloud, Silver Wind*); some have doors that open outward (examples: *Eurodam, Legend of the Seas, Queen Elizabeth, Queen Victoria*).

Balconies that lack privacy

If you choose a Riviera Deck (Deck 14) balcony cabin aboard *Azura* or *Ventura*, for example, you can oversee many balconies on the decks below yours – particularly those on C Deck and D Deck – because they are built right out to the sides of the ship. If you have such a cabin, it would be unwise to sunbathe or sit naked on your balcony. Not only that, but almost *all* balcony cabins can be seen from the navigation bridge, where the staff are equipped with binoculars.

Balconies to covet

Some of my favorite large balcony suites and cabins include Celebrity Cruises' *Celebrity Constellation, Celebrity Infinity, Celebrity Millennium,* and *Celebrity Summit* (6147, 6148, 9096, 9098, 9156, 9197); Cunard Line's *Queen Mary 2* (9069, 9078, the Balmoral and Sandringham duplexes at the stern); Oceania Cruises' *Nautica* and *Regatta* (6088, 6091, 7114, 7119, 8064, 8067*), Marina and Riviera* (8143, 9147, 10111 – these suites each measure 1,991 sq ft/185 sq m and span the ship's entire width, although the balcony is actually split into two); Regent Seven Seas Cruises' *Seven Seas Mariner* (780, 781, 8100, 8101, 988, 989, 1080, 1081) and *Seven Seas Voyager* (673, 674, 781, 782, 970, 971).

Upstairs and downstairs

With the introduction of *Oasis of the Seas* and sister ship *Allure of the Seas*, 'loft' accommodation – living room downstairs and sleeping quarters upstairs – is a 'must have' for regulars not on a budget.

How much?

The cost of accommodation is directly related to the size of the cabin, its location, and the facilities and services. Each line implements its own system according to ship size, age, construction, and profit potential. Many cruise lines still do not give accurate cabin sizes in their brochures. It may be better to book a low-grade cabin on a good ship than a high-grade cabin on a poor ship. If you are in a party of three or more and don't mind sharing a cabin, you'll save a lot per person, so you may be able to afford a higher-grade cabin.

Cabin sizes

Cabins provide more or less the same facilities as hotel rooms, except space. Most owners favor large public rooms over cabins. In some smaller interior (no-view) and outside cabins, changing clothes is a challenge.

The latest ships have more standardized cabin sizes, because they are made in modular form. I consider 180 sq ft (16.7 sq m) to be the *minimum* acceptable size for a standard cabin today.

Cabin location

An 'outside-view' cabin is recommended for first-time passengers: an 'interior' cabin has no portholes or windows, making it more difficult to get oriented or to gauge the weather or time.

Cabins in the center of a ship are more stable and tend to be noise- and vibration- free. Ships powered by diesel engines (i.e., most modern vessels) create and transmit some vibration, especially at the stern.

Take into account personal habits when choosing the cabin location. If you like to go to bed early, avoid a cabin close to the disco. If you have trouble walking, choose a cabin close to the elevator.

Generally, the higher the deck, the higher the cabin price, and the better the service. This is an inheritance from transoceanic times, when upper-deck cabins and suites were sunnier and warmer.

Cabins at the front of a ship are slightly crescent-shaped, given that the outer wall follows the curvature of the ship's hull. But they can be exposed to early-morning noises, such as the anchor being dropped at ports where the ship is too big to dock.

Cabins with interconnecting doors are fine for families or close friends, but the dividing wall is usually so thin you can hear the conversation next door.

Many brochures indicate cabins with 'obstructed views.' Cabins on lower decks are closer to engine noise and heat, especially at the stern of the vessel and around the engine casing. In many older ships, elevators may not operate to the lowermost decks.

And so to bed

Aboard ship, the bedframes are usually made of steel or tubular aluminum for fire protection purposes, although some older ships may have (flame retardant) wood frames. Some have rounded edges while some have square edges (tell your legs to watch out), particularly when the mattress is contained within the bedframe.

Some beds have space underneath for your luggage, while some have drawers fitted for additional storage space, so your luggage has to be stored elsewhere in the cabin.

Mattresses

Mattresses can be hard, semi-hard, or soft. If your mattress is not to your liking, ask your cabin steward if it can be changed – most ships have spare mattresses, and bed boards – in case you have back problems and want a really hard bed.

Some cruise lines provide simple foam mattresses while others place more emphasis on provide extra comfort. Regent Seven Seas Cruises, for example, provides a custom-designed Suite Slumber Bed (a plush euro-top mattress capped with a double layer of memory foam and dressed in the finest linens to assure a refreshing sleep.

There are differences between mattress sizes in the UK, USA, and Europe, depending on which supplier a cruise line specifies when a ship is outfitted or when bed frames and mattresses are replaced.

Duvets

Down duvets, fine bed linens, and plush mattresses are what fine sleeping environments are all about. Also, a bed 'runner' is often used to add a color splash across the bed during daytime.

Duvets are usually goose down or cotton filled, and range from 3.5 togs (thin) to 13.5 togs (thick), the tog rating being the warmth rating. Anyone with allergies should try a spundown duvet, which is filled with non-allergenic polyester microfiber.

Duvet covers can be for single, double, queen-, or king-size mattresses. If you request a queen-size bed configuration when you book, request an overlay, otherwise there will be a crack between the beds. Not all ships have them but the luxury/premium grade ships, and ships with suite-grade accommodation, should.

Duvet covers and sheets of 100% cotton (up to 400 thread count) are best, but may be more difficult for a ship's laundry to handle. But they do provide those wonderful 'pampership' moments when you slip into bed.

Sleep tight

Many ships have a 'pillow menu' in suite-grade accommodation. This gives you a choice of several different pillow types, including hop-filled or hypoallergenic, goose down, Hungarian goose down (considered the best), silk-filled, body pillow (as long as an adult body, providing full support at to the head and neck at the top and, lower down, to legs and knees), Tempur-Pedic, isotonic or copycat memory foam.

Ultra-expensive Tempur-Pedic memory foam mattresses can be found aboard the tiny coastal boutique-size cruise ships of un-Cruise Adventures (*Safari Endeavor*, *Safari Explorer*, *Safari Legacy*, and *Safari Quest*).

Facilities

Private bathroom (generally small) with shower, washbasin, and toilet. Higher-grade cabins and suites may have full-size bathtubs. Some have a whirlpool bath and/or bidet, a hairdryer, and more space. Most cabins come with the following: multi-channel radio, TV (regular satellite channels or closed circuit), and DVD player; two beds or a lower and upper berth (possibly, another one or two upper berths) or a double, queen- or king-size bed. Some twin beds can be pushed together to form a double; depending on cabin size, a chair, or chair and table, or sofa and table, or, in higher grades, even a separate lounge/sitting area; telephone, for inter-cabin or ship-to-shore calls; refrigerator/wet bar (higher grades); electrical outlets for personal appliances, usually 110 and/or 220 volts, vanity/desk unit with chair or stool, personal safe; closet space, some drawer space, plus storage room under beds for suitcases; bedside night stand/table unit; towels, soap, shampoo, and conditioner (Upscale ships provide a greater selection).

Some ships have upper and lower berths. A 'berth' is a nautical term for a bed held in a wooden or metal frame. A 'Pullman berth' tucks away out of sight during the day, usually into the bulkhead or ceiling. You climb up a short ladder at night to get into an upper berth.

International mattress size comparisons		
United Kingdom	**Inches**	**Centimeters**
Single	36 x 75	99 x 180
Double	54 x 75	140 x 190
Queen	60 x 78	150 x 200
King	72 x 78	180 x 200
Europe		
Single	35 x 79	90 x 200
Double	55 x 79	140 x 200
Queen	63 x 79	160 x 200
King	72 x 78	80 x 200
USA/Canada		
Single or Twin	39 x 75	99 x 180
Double or Full	54 x 75	137 x 191
Queen	60 x 80	150 x 203
King	76 x 80	193 x 203

Typical Cabin Layouts

The following rates are typical of those you can expect to pay for ⓐ a seven-day and ⓑ a 10-day Caribbean cruise aboard a modern cruise ship. The rates are per person and include free round-trip airfare or low-cost air add-ons from principal North American gateways.

Large outside-view double with bed and convertible daytime sofabed, bathroom with shower, and good closet and drawer space. Typical size: 270 sq.ft (23 sq. meters).
ⓐ $1,000 ⓑ $2,000

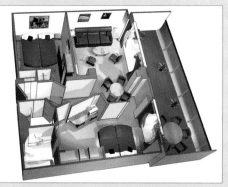

Luxury outside-view suite with private veranda, separate lounge area, vanity area, extra-large double or queen-size bed, bathroom with tub, shower, and extensive closet and storage space.
ⓐ $1,750 ⓑ $3,000

Junior suite with lounge, double or queen-size beds, bathroom with tub, shower, and ample closet and storage space. Typical size: 375 sq.ft (35 sq.meters).
ⓐ $1,500 ⓑ $2,000

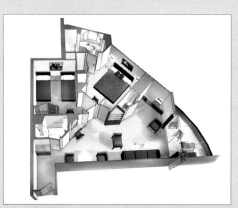

Luxury outside-view suite with private veranda, separate lounge, vanity area, king- or queen-size bed, bathroom with full-sized tub and separate shower, and extensive walk-in closet and storage space (plus a guest bathroom). Typical size: 550 sq. ft (50 sq. meters).
ⓐ $2,000 ⓑ $3,000

Note that in some ships, third- and fourth-person upper berths are available for families or friends wishing to share. The upper Pullman berths, not shown on these cabin layouts, are recessed into the wall or ceiling above the lower beds.

Junior suite with lounge, double or queen-size beds, bathroom with tub, shower, and ample closet and storage space. Typical size: 375 sq.ft (35 sq.meters).
ⓐ $1,500 ⓑ $2,000

Comparing the biggest of the big

Ship Name	Cruise Line	Gross Tonnage	No. of Passengers	Space Ratio	Year Built
Allure of the Seas	Royal Caribbean Int.	225,282	5,400	41.2	2010
Oasis of the Seas	Royal Caribbean Int.	225,282	5,400	41.2	2009
Quantum of the Seas	Royal Caribbean Int.	158,000	4,100	38.5	2013
Freedom of the Seas	Royal Caribbean Int.	154,407	3,634	42	2006
Independence of the Seas	Royal Caribbean Int.	154,407	3,634	42	2008
Liberty of the Seas	Royal Caribbean Int.	154,407	3,634	42	2007
Norwegian Epic	Norwegian Cruise Line	153,000	4,200	36.4	2010
Queen Mary 2	Cunard Line	148,528	2,620	56.6	2004
Norwegian Breakaway	Norwegian Cruise Line	145,655	3,998	36.4	2013
Norwegian Getaway	Norwegian Cruise Line	145,655	3,998	36.4	2014
Royal Princess	Princess Cruises	141,000	3,600	39.1	2013
Regal Princess	Princess Cruises	141,000	3,600		2014
MSC Preziosa	MSC Cruises	140,000	3,502	40.2	2013
MSC Divina	MSC Cruises	139,400	3,502	39.6	2012
MSC Fantasia	MSC Cruises	137,936	3,274	41.2	2008
MSC Splendida	MSC Cruises	137,936	3,274	41.2	2009
Explorer of the Seas	Royal Caribbean Int.	137,308	3,634	42	2000
Voyager of the Seas	Royal Caribbean Int.	137,280	3,634	42	1999
Adventure of the Seas	Royal Caribbean Int.	137,276	3,634	42	2001
Mariner of the Seas	Royal Caribbean Int.	137,276	3,634	42	2004
Navigator of the Seas	Royal Caribbean Int.	137,276	3,634	42	2003
Costa Diadema	Costa Cruises	132,500	3,700	35.8	2014
Disney Dream	Disney Cruise Line	129,690	2,500	51.2	2011
Disney Fantasy	Disney Cruise Line	129,690	2,500	51.2	2012
Carnival Breeze	Carnival Cruise Lines	128,251	3,646	35.6	2012
Carnival Dream	Carnival Cruise Lines	128,251	3,646	35.6	2009
Carnival Magic	Carnival Cruise Lines	128,251	3,646	35.6	2011
Celebrity Reflection	Celebrity Cruises	122,210	2,852	42.7	2012
Celebrity Silhouette	Celebrity Cruises	122,210	2,852	42.7	2011
Celebrity Eclipse	Celebrity Cruises	121,878	2,852	42.7	2010
Celebrity Equinox	Celebrity Cruises	121,878	2,852	42.7	2009
Celebrity Solstice	Celebrity Cruises	121,878	2,852	42.7	2008
Ventura	P&O Cruises	116,017	3,092	37.5	2008
Diamond Princess	Princess Cruises	115,875	2,674	43.3	2004
Sapphire Princess	Princess Cruises	115,875	2,674	43.3	2004
Azura	P&O Cruises	115,055	3,092	37.5	2010
Costa Fascinosa	Costa Cruises	114,500	3,012	38	2012
Costa Favolosa	Costa Cruises	114,500	3,012	38	2011
Costa Serena	Costa Cruises	114,147	3,000	38	2007

Compare the Major Cruise Lines

We compare what the world's 10 largest, best-known cruise companies, reviewed in alphabetical order, have to offer when it comes to facilities, cuisine, service, and ambience.

White star service aboard *Queen Mary 2*.

The major cruise lines today are global in scale. Although the industry may appear diverse, it is dominated by just a few conglomerates, principally Carnival Corporation and Royal Caribbean Cruises. Dig deeper and you'll find, for example, that two Carnival subsidiaries, Holland America Line and Princess Cruises, virtually control large resort ship cruising in Alaska, where they own hotels, lodges, tour companies, and much land-based transportation (other operators have to buy their services). This came about in 2002–3 when Princess Cruises' parent company, P&O Group, sold its cruising division to the Carnival Corporation.

What makes them different

Today's major cruise lines are global in scale. Ships belonging to the big companies may look the same, but they differ not only in their layout, decor, and passenger flow but also in such small details. Even the size of towels varies widely.

What they have in common

All offer one thing: a well-packaged cruise vacation, generally of seven days, typically with a mix of days at sea and days in port, plenty of food, reasonable service, large-scale production shows, and trendy cabaret acts, plus large casinos, shopping malls, and extensive, busy spa and fitness facilities. Nine offer a variety of 'drive to' embarkation ports within the US ('homeland cruising').

Their ships have a lot in common, too. Except for MSC Cruises, all have art auctions, bingo, horse racing, shopping talks for ports of call, programs for children and teens, wedding vows/renewal programs, and Wi-Fi or Internet connect centers.

Standing in line for embarkation, disembarkation (and shore tenders, shore excursion and shuttle buses in ports of call), and for self-serve buffet meals is inevitable aboard all large resort ships. But the ships differ in their characters, facilities, maintenance, space, crew-to-passenger ratio, food and service, and crew training. You'll be escorted to your cabin aboard the ships of Cunard Line (Queen Grill-grade accommodation only), and MSC Cruises (Yacht Club-grade only). Aboard other lines, the minimal duty staff at the ship-side gangway, simply point you in the right direction – even if you have heavy carry-on luggage – and gangway staff may even try to give you a daily program, or spa details, or shop specials – in other words, too much paper, even before you've reached the cabin.

Carnival Cruise Lines

Ships

Fantasy-class ships: *Carnival Ecstasy* (1991), *Carnival Elation* (1998), *Carnival Fantasy* (1990), *Carnival Fascination* (1994), *Carnival Imagination* (1995), *Carnival Inspiration* (1996), *Carnival Paradise* (1998), *Carnival Sensation* (1993)

Sunshine-class ships: *Carnival Conquest* (2002), *Carnival Freedom* (2007), *Carnival Glory* (2003), *Carnival Liberty* (2005), *Carnival Splendor* (2008), *Carnival Sunshine* (1996), *Carnival Triumph* (1999), *Carnival Valor* (2004), *Carnival Victory* (2000)

Dream-class ships: *Carnival Breeze* (2012), *Carnival Dream* (2009), *Carnival Magic* (2011)

Spirit-class ships: *Carnival Legend* (2002), *Carnival Miracle* (2004), *Carnival Pride* (2002), *Carnival Spirit* (2001)

About the company

Israel-born Ted Arison (born Theodore Arisohn), whose ambition was to be a concert pianist, founded Carnival Cruise Lines, now the world's largest and most successful single cruise line, in 1972 with one ship, *Mardi Gras* (formerly *Empress of Canada*). Carnival wanted to be different, youthful, and fun, and developed the 'fun ship' concept. It worked, appealing to people of all ages and backgrounds.

The company's first new ship, *Tropicale,* debuted in 1982. In 1984 Carnival started advertising on television, introducing a wider public to the idea of cruising. It introduced the first cruise ship measuring over 100,000 gross tons – *Carnival Destiny,* (now named *Carnival Sunshine*) in 1996.

Today, the Carnival Corporation, parent company of Carnival Cruise Lines, is run by Ted Arison's son, Micky Arison, who is chairman of the board – as well

Which cruise line does what best

 Carnival Cruise Lines is known for all-round fun, activities, and casinos for the lively, no-sleep-needed youth market – although many passengers are over 45. Carnival doesn't sell itself as a 'luxury' or 'premium' cruise line, which it certainly isn't. It consistently delivers exactly the well-packaged cruise vacation its brochures promise, for which there is a huge first-time cruise market. Its smart ships have high-tech entertainment facilities and features, and some include extra-cost alternative dining spots for the more discerning. Carnival is all about 'participatory fun.'

 Celebrity Cruises has the best food, the most elegant ships and spas, and its cruises are under-priced. Although it advertises itself as a 'premium' line, some aspects are no longer premium – for example, recorded 'music' blaring over pool decks 24 hours a day is not relaxing. But the term still sums up Celebrity reasonably well.

 Costa Cruises has the edge on (quasi-Italian) European style and lively ambience, with a mix of passengers of many nationalities, but the swimming pools are full of noisy children, especially in peak holiday periods. Costa provides first-time cruise passengers with a packaged holiday that is a mix of sophistication and basic fare, accompanied by loud music. Most passengers are Italian.

 Cunard Line has one real ocean liner *(Queen Mary 2)* that provides a regular transatlantic service, while its other two ships are more about regular cruising. All three are best suited to a wide range of seasoned and well-traveled couples and single passengers who enjoy the cosmopolitan setting of an ocean liner. Dressing formally for dinner is encouraged, though except in the grill rooms the cuisine is largely of mass-market quality, with many traditional British favorites and extensive French dishes.

 Holland America Line has all the right touches for seniors and retirees: smiling service staff, lots of flowers, traditions of the past, good cooking demonstrations, and specialty grill rooms. The ships are best suited to older couples and singles who like to mingle in a large ship, in an unhurried setting with fine-quality surroundings. There's plenty of eclectic antique artwork, decent – though not gourmet – food, and service from a smiling Indonesian/Filipino crew who don't have the finesse many passengers expect from a 'premium' product.

 MSC Cruises tailors its onboard product to pan-European passengers of all ages (its name, after all, is Mediterranean Shipping Company) and displays fine Italian flair, with a high level of service and hospitality from a friendly, multilingual crew. It has evolved quickly as the 'new kid on the block.' Of all the major cruise lines, it's also the cleanest. It changes bed linen and towels the most; typically, bed linen is changed every second day, towels daily, and bathrobes in suites daily, unlike most other large cruise lines.

 Norwegian Cruise Line is good for a first cruise for families with children, with a great choice of eateries, good entertainment, and friendly service staff. NCL ships are best suited to first-time young and young-at-heart couples, single passengers, children, and teenagers who want upbeat, color-rich surroundings, plenty of entertainment lounges and bars, and high-tech sophistication – all in one programmed but well-packaged vacation.

 P&O Cruises operates mainly ex-UK cruises for its predominantly UK-based passengers, with very good facilities for families with children, as well as adults-only ships (minimum age 18). The company specializes in providing all the little things that British passengers have come to expect, including tea/coffee-making sets in all cabins, and a choice of Indian food.

Princess Cruises has consistent product delivery, although the ships have decor that is rather bland, and passengers tend to be somewhat older. Choose Princess Cruises if you enjoy being with families and fellow passengers of mid-50s and upwards, who want a well-organized cruise experience with unpretentious middle-of-the-road cuisine, a good range of entertainment, and an excellent shore excursion program – arguably the best-run of any of the major cruise lines.

 Royal Caribbean International is a good bet for the Caribbean (naturally), especially for first-time cruisers and families. It has a good variety of entertainment, and interesting programs, including many for children. RCI ships are liked by active, young-minded couples and solo cruisers of all ages, and families with toddlers, children, and teenagers who enjoy mingling in a large ship setting with plenty of life, high-energy entertainment, and bright lighting everywhere. The food is more notable for quantity than quality – unless you pay extra for dining in a 'specialty' restaurant (not all RCI ships have them). There's background music everywhere.

as owning the NBA's Miami Heat basketball team. More than 20 new ships have been introduced since the line was founded in 1972.

The line has upgraded some aspects of its operation and product. It needed to. The *Fantasy*-class ships are receiving an overdue multi-million-dollar makeover, including an adults-only sunbathing area, pool decks (a thatched roof over one of two hot tubs and the addition of palm trees and new mid-deck stairways), a new lobby bar, expanded children's and teens' areas, and more interconnecting cabins. Balconies have been retrofitted to 98 cabins; the *Fantasy*-class ships have few balcony cabins and no walk-around open promenade deck. Meanwhile, giant poolside movie screens have been fitted to most non-*Fantasy*-class ships.

Frequent passengers' club: Carnival Concierge Club.

What is it really like?

Carnival's 'fun' cruising is good for families with children and teens (anyone under 21 must be accompanied by a parent, relative, or guardian) and youthful adults. Carnival ships are also good for whole-ship charters and incentive groups, for multi-generational passengers, and for family reunions. Typically, about half of Carnival's passengers are taking their first cruise. About 30 percent are under the age of 35, 30 percent are over 55, the other 40 percent are between 35 and 55.

The dress code is ultra-casual – indeed, the waiters are better dressed than most passengers – particularly

Slide at WaterWorks, part of the aqua park aboard *Carnival Ecstasy*.

during youth-heavy holiday seasons and spring breaks. Carnival is all about 'happy' and 'fun' – cruise directors actually tell passengers to 'make some noise,' so Camp Carnival is for adults as well as children. But it's a very impersonal cruise experience. Solo cruise goers can get lost in the crowds of doubles. It's all about towels shaped like animals, programmed participation activities, yelling and screaming, and having fun.

Perhaps the tone doesn't matter so much because this will be a first cruise for most passengers. Repeat customers, however, have a distinct sense of déjà vu, but carry a Gold Card for better recognition from hotel staff (Platinum for those who have cruised with Carnival more than 10 times).

The ships are clean and well maintained – if you don't peer too closely. Open deck space may look adequate when you board, but on days at sea you can expect your plastic deck chair, if you can find one that's free, to be kissing its neighbor – it's probably tied to it. There are no cushioned pads for the deck lounge chairs, which are hard to sit on, if you use just a towel, for any length of time.

The decibel level is high: it is difficult to escape from noise and loud music, and 'background' music is played even in cabin hallways and elevators 24 hours a day. Huge poolside movie screens have been fitted aboard the ships. Also, new 'Serenity' sunbathing areas are being retrofitted across the fleet to provide extra-cost peaceful 'away from it all' areas.

Expect to be subjected to lots of advertising daily art auctions, 'designer' watches, gold and silver chains, and other promotions, while 'artworks' for auction are strewn throughout the ships. Also, expect intrusive announcements (particularly for activities that bring revenue), and waiters hustling you to have drinks.

Carnival Capers, the ship's daily program, is among the industry's poorest information sheets, in terms of layout and print quality, and most of it is devoted to persuading you to spend money.

There are libraries but few books, and bookshelves are always locked by 6pm, because you are expected to be out in the (revenue-earning) public areas each evening. If you enjoy casino gaming at sea, you could join Carnival's Ocean Players Club, which brings benefits to frequent players, depending on your level of skill.

Between 2008 and 2010, a multimillion-dollar renovation added 98 small balconies to existing cabins aboard the *Fantasy*-class ships. Also included: Circle 'C' facilities for 12- to 14-year-olds, a waterpark with water-spray area, and oversize umbrellas. An adults-only Serenity retreat was added to the aft area of the Promenade Deck. The main pool now has more of a resort-style ambience.

Accommodation: In 2008 Carnival reorganized some cabin categories, and, following the European way of doing things, cabins in the best locations now cost more. Note that balconies in many of the cabins with 'private' balconies aren't so private – most can be overlooked from other cabins located on the deck above and from various public locations. You may have to carry a credit card to operate the personal safes – inconvenient. High-quality mattresses and bed linen, also available for sale, have been fitted to all beds.

Passenger niggles: The most consistent complaints are that most activities are geared around trying to sell you something. Free-to-enter onboard games have pint-size 'prizes,' while the cost of playing bingo keeps rising. The intrusive photographers are almost impossible to escape. There's no listing of the free in-cabin TV movies – only those that are pay-per-view. The non-stop recorded poolside music is intrusive. There's little finesse and not enough attention to individuals. Carnival operates from many 'drive to' embarkation ports in the US.

Decor

The decor is very creative, although you probably wouldn't want to let the ships' interior designer loose in your home. If you love color, you'll be fine. If you prefer monochrome, take sunglasses. Public toilets, however, are not colorful and could do with a lot of cheering up.

Cuisine/Dining

Carnival ships have one or two main dining rooms, and its 'Your Choice Dining' program offers three dinner seating options, including 'Your Time' open seating. Dining assignments are confirmed at time of booking. Menus are standardized across the fleet, and all the dining venues are non-smoking.

Don't even think about a quiet table for two, or a candlelight dinner on deck – it's not Carnival's style – unless you pay extra at a 'specialty' restaurant. Dining aboard a Carnival ship is all about table mates, social chat, lively meals, fast eating.

Tables are, however, nicely set with white tablecloths, plenty of silverware, and iced water/iced tea whenever you want it.

The main dining rooms marry food and show business. Waiters sing and dance, and there are constant waiter parades with flashing lights in an attempt to create some excitement.

Taste-filled food is not the company's strong point, but quantity, not quality, is – although consultant chef Georges Blanc has created daily 'Georges Blanc Signature' menu items. The company has been striving to improve its cuisine and the menu choices often look good, but the actual food delivered is simply banquet-style catering, with its attendant standardization and production cooking.

Although meats are of a decent quality, poultry, fish, seafood, and desserts can be disappointing. Sauces and gravies are used well as disguises, and there are few garnishes. The selection of fresh green vegetables, breads, rolls, cheese, and ripe fruit could be better, and there is much use of canned fruit and jellied desserts, not to mention packets of jam, marmalade, butter, sugar – the same stuff you'd find in a diner or family eatery in the USA.

Carnival Liberty calls at Roatán in Honduras Bay.

Bakery items are thawed and heated from frozen. It is virtually impossible to obtain anything remotely unusual or off-menu, and the 'always available' items seem to have disappeared from the menus.

Vegetarian and children's menus are available for all meals, but they wouldn't get a generous score for their nutritional content. Spa Carnival Fare was introduced to provide a more healthy dining option.

The wine list is adequate, but there are no wine waiters or decent-size wine glasses. Carnival also has a 'wines by the glass' program, with good storage and presentation facilities that enable wines to be served properly in several locations and not just in the restaurants aboard each ship.

Specialty dining venues: *Carnival Breeze, Carnival Conquest, Carnival Dream, Carnival Freedom, Carnival Glory, Carnival Liberty, Carnival Miracle, Carnival Splendor, Carnival Sunshine, Carnival Triumph, Carnival Valor*

These extra-cost steak houses have better table settings, china and silverware, and leather-bound menus. Menu favorites include prime American steaks such as filet mignon (9oz), porterhouse steak (24oz), and New York strip loin (be prepared for huge cuts of meat – shown to you at your table before you order), broiled lobster tail, and stone crab claws from Joe's Stone Crabs of South Miami Beach.

Reservations are necessary, and a cover charge for service/gratuity applies. The food is good, and the ambience is reasonably quiet. But if you are a couple and you have just two glasses of wine each (Grgich Hills Chardonnay or Merlot, for example, at $12.50 a glass), and pay the cover charge, that's over $100 for dinner.

Casual eateries: All ships also have large food court-style spaces for casual food, fast-food items, grilled meats, pizzas (each ship serves over 800 pizzas in a typical day), stir-fry, deli, and salad items. There are also self-help beverage stands, coffee that looks like rusty water, and tea provided in paper cups with a teabag (tea dust, as far as I'm concerned), plastic or wooden stirrers (no teaspoons and no saucers), and packets of chemical 'milk' or creamer. Guy Fieri's Burger Joints have appeared aboard Carnival's ships for good reason – the Food Network audience is typical of Carnival's clientele. So you can get a Plain Jane, Straight Up, Pig Patty, Chilius Maximus, or The Ringer burger, all served with hand cut fries and Guy's signature seasoning.

But some people are happy to have it that way, and it's actually better than what's offered aboard the ships of its competitor, Royal Caribbean International. Late-night 'snacks' consist of greasy fast-food items instead of healthy alternatives such as light fruit bites, and are usually the same every night. Breakfast buffets are as repetitive as canned laughter on television.

The coffee/tea factor: Regular coffee is weak and poor, scoring 1 out of 10 (paper/foam cups in buffet areas). Extra-cost Java Blue coffee corners – including 'comfort' snacks – have started appearing recently and should help to improve the coffee image.

For children

Carnival is a fine family-friendly cruise line, carrying more than 575,000 children a year, and 'Camp Carnival,' the line's extensive child/youth program, is well organized and extensive. There are five age groups: Toddlers (ages two to five), Juniors (six to eight), Intermediate (nine to 11), Tweens (12–14, Circle C), and Late Teens (15–17, with Club 02). Even the under-twos are now being catered to, with special programs aboard each ship. Meanwhile, Family Fun Nights are all about reconnecting parents to their children – something many can do only while on vacation.

Soft-drinks packages can be bought for children (adults, too). Note that a babysitting service is not generally available after 10pm.

Best ships for children: *Carnival Breeze, Carnival Conquest, Carnival Dream, Carnival Freedom, Carnival Glory, Carnival Legend, Carnival Liberty, Carnival Miracle, Carnival Pride, Carnival Spirit, Carnival Splendor, Carnival Sunshine, Carnival Triumph, Carnival Valor, and Carnival Victory.*

Ships with fewer facilities: *Carnival Ecstasy, Carnival Elation, Carnival Fantasy, Carnival Fascination, Carnival Imagination, Carnival Inspiration, Carnival Paradise, and Carnival Sensation.*

Entertainment

The ships have big showlounges, and feature large-scale flesh-and-feather production shows. On a typical cruise, there will be one or two large-scale shows, with male and female lead singers and a clutch of dancers backed by a live showband and supported by pre-recorded backing tracks.

These are loud, Las Vegas-style revues. The skimpy costumes are very colorful, as is the lighting, with extensive use of 'color mover' lights. Stage 'smoke' is much overused – to the irritation of anyone unfortunate enough to be seated in the front few rows.

Carnival often rotates entertainers aboard its ships, so that passengers see different acts each night, and specialty acts take center stage on nights when there's no production show. There's also live music in just about every bar and lounge – although there appears to be a trend to replace live music with more DJs – and there's also a strong trend toward late-night adults-only comedy.

Cabaret acts include vocalists, magic acts, ventriloquists, and comedy jugglers. Each cruise has karaoke nights, a passenger talent show, and a discotheque with ear-splitting volumes and megaphones to enable you to converse with your partner.

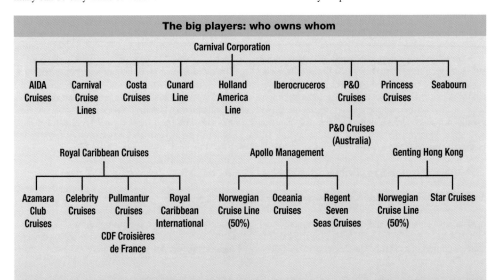

The big players: who owns whom

Getting to know the ropes aboard *Carnival Magic.*

Celebrity Cruises

Ships
Century-class ships: *Celebrity Century* (1995)
Millennium-class ships: *Celebrity Constellation* (2002), *Celebrity Infinity* (2001), *Celebrity Millennium* (2000), *Celebrity Summit* (2001)
Solstice-class ships: *Celebrity Eclipse (2010), Celebrity Equinox* (2009), *Celebrity Reflection* (2012), *Celebrity Silhouette* (2011), *Celebrity Solstice* (2008)
Other ships: *Celebrity Xpedition* (2001)

About the company
Celebrity Cruises was the brainchild of Harry H. Haralambopoulos, and the brothers John and Michael Chandris, London-based Greek cargo ship owners and operators of the former Chandris Lines and Chandris Cruises. In 1989, as the cruise industry was gaining momentum, they were determined to create a newer, better cruise line, with new ships, larger, more standard cabins, and focusing more on food and service in the European tradition.

Its image as a 'premium' line is justified because the product delivery on board is superior to that of its parent company, Royal Caribbean International, which bought it in 1997 for $1.3 billion. The ships are recognizable, thanks to the 'X' on the funnel denoting the third letter from the end of the Greek alphabet, the Greek 'chi' or 'Ch' in English, for Chandris, the founding family.

In 2007 Celebrity Cruises created a new company, Azamara Cruises (now Azamara Club Cruises, with small ships, including *Azamara Journey* (2000) and *Azamara Quest* (2000). The idea is to focus on lesser-visited destinations, and offer a more personal cruise experience. All hotel services and cruise operations are, however, operated by Celebrity Cruises.
Frequent passengers' club: Captain's Club.

What is it really like?
The ships are usually very clean and well maintained. There are always lots of flowers and flower displays –
some ships have flower shops, where you can buy fresh blooms for special occasions.

There's a lot of fine artwork aboard Celebrity's ships; it may not be to everybody's taste, but it is probably the cruise industry's most remarkable collection of contemporary art. The company provides a lot of the niceties that other lines have long forgotten, although some are now playing 'catch up': waiters who carry your trays when you obtain food from buffets or casual eateries; water spritzes on the pool deck. On days at sea in warm-weather areas, if you are sunbathing on deck, someone will bring you a cold towel, and a sorbet, iced water, or iced tea.

Regardless of the accommodation grade, Celebrity Cruises delivers a well-defined North American cruise experience at a modest price. Book a suite-category cabin for the extra benefits it brings – it's worth it. Strong points include the many European staff and the higher standard of service, good spas with a wide range of facilities and treatments, taste-filled food served in the European dining tradition, and a 'zero announcement policy.' Such touches differentiate Celebrity Cruises from its competitors.

The ships have more staff than other ships of comparable size and capacity, especially in the housekeeping and food and beverage departments. This helps to create a better product. However, the company has seen fit to take away some items, such as personalized stationary (from some accommodation grades), has substituted paper napkins for what used to be cloth napkins, and reduced the amount and quality of fresh flower displays.

Even so, such things as topless sunbathing spaces are now available aboard the ships (except, *Celebrity Xpedition*). Some cruises aboard some ships are designated adults-only.

Unfortunately, background music is played almost everywhere, and any lounge designated as 'music-free' is typically full of activities and participation events, so it's hard to find a quiet corner to sit and read.

So, what are the differences between Celebrity Cruises and its parent, Royal Caribbean International?

Celebrity Equinox leaves Istanbul, Turkey.

Here are a few food-related examples:

RCI *(Brilliance of the Seas):*
Café: Seattle Coffee Company coffee, in paper cups.
Dining Room: no tables for two.
In the Windjammer Café, waiters don't help passengers to tables with trays; plastic plates are used; cutlery is wrapped in paper napkins; melamine mugs are used for coffee/tea; tea selection poor – impossible to get hot water.

Celebrity Cruises *(Celebrity Century):*
Café el Bacio: Coffees/teas served in china cups and saucers, with doily and chocolate.
Dining Room food: Good quality and presentation.
Dining Room: Tables for two are available.
Lido Café: Staff line up to help passengers with trays to tables. Real china, white cloth napkins, polished cutlery, and a decent selection of teas are provided.

Decor

All ships: there are no glitzy atrium lobbies, rock-climbing walls, ice-skating rinks, or other puffery – just good European style in the elegant interiors. The exception is in the casinos, which are simply coin boxes wrapped in garish, unfriendly lighting – like pachinko parlors. You can book spa, salon, and personal fitness appointments, make main (Celebrity Select) and specialty dining reservations, and shore excursions online before you cruise – so planning ahead will pay off (exception: *Celebrity Xpedition*).

Solstice-class ships: The layout is sensible, and the decor and colors are pleasing and elegant. There's also an abundance of designer chairs and sunloungers, including two-person clam-shell deck loungers.

Other ships: The decor is elegant – Greek, classical, minimalist, although some might find it a little antiseptic and cool in places. *Celebrity Constellation, Celebrity Infinity, Celebrity Millennium,* and *Celebrity Summit*

were 'Solsticized' in 2011-2012 to make them more consistent with the latest design and culinary trends in the newer ships.

Celebrity Cruises has some of the most eclectic sculptures and original artwork, from Picasso to Warhol, found at sea. The colors don't jar the senses, and cannot be said to be glitzy – except for the casinos, which are mostly vulgar.

The ships absorb people well, and the flow is, for the most part, good, except for entrances to showlounges and in photo galleries. Each public room subtly invites you to move on to the next.

For children

Junior passengers are divided into Shipmates (three to six years), Cadets (seven to nine), Ensigns (10–12), Teens (13–17).
Best ships for children: *Celebrity Eclipse, Celebrity Equinox, Celebrity Reflection, Celebrity Silhouette, Celebrity Solstice.*

Cuisine/Dining

Table settings are excellent, with fine-quality linen, china, and glassware. Tables for two are available – far more than by most other major lines. What sets Celebrity apart is the superior training and supervision of dining room waiters, and the service.

The food represents a range of culinary influences; it is based loosely on classic French cuisine, modified to appeal to North Americans and Europeans alike, and menus are standardized across the fleet and have been dumbed down since a new regime took over from Michel Roux – meatloaf, spaghetti, and striploin for dinner are pathetic for what is supposed to be a 'premium' product. Items that can be made at home cannot be considered as acceptable. For better quality, Celebrity Cruises wants you to pay extra to eat in the specialty venues. Full service in-cabin dining is also available for all meals, including dinner.

The food is made from good-quality ingredients. Take croissants, for example. Those found aboard Celebrity ships are made fresh each morning, while aboard most competitors' ships they are purchased ashore.

Celebrity Cruises also has well-trained wine waiters. *Celebrity Eclipse, Celebrity Equinox, Celebrity Reflection, Celebrity Silhouette,* and *Celebrity Solstice* have a special wine room for tastings. *Celebrity Constellation, Celebrity Infinity, Celebrity Millennium,* and *Celebrity Summit* have special wine rooms in one of the 'specialty' restaurants that you can dine in, and fine wines that can cost thousands of dollars a bottle. But there are also wines that start at about $20.

Casual eateries: There are casual self-serve buffets aboard all Celebrity Cruises' ships. Except for *Celebrity Eclipse, Celebrity Equinox, Celebrity Reflection, Celebrity Silhouette,* and *Celebrity Solstice,* most are laid out in continuous straight lines, which cause congestion at peak times. Celebrity tries to be more creative with these buffets, and, like other cruise lines, has stations for pasta, faux sushi, salads, grill/rotisserie items, and hot food items. A waiter will – or should – take your tray to a table. A bar trolley service for drinks and wines is provided at lunchtime, and wine waiters are always on hand to discuss and take wine orders for dinner. All the ships make great martinis.

The coffee/tea factor: Regular (free) coffee is weak and poor. Score: 2 out of 10. If you order espresso/cappuccino coffees in the dining room, there is a charge, because they are treated like a bar item.

Café el Bacio: The cafés are in prominent locations and provide an agreeable setting for those who like decent Italian coffees, pastries, and cakes.

Entertainment

The company's big production shows have been improving, particularly aboard *Celebrity Eclipse, Celebrity Equinox, Celebrity Reflection, Celebrity Silhouette,* and *Celebrity Solstice.* Some shows are quite decent, with good costuming and lighting, but others look dated and lack storyline, flow, or connectivity. Each ship carries its own resident troupe of singers/dancers and audiovisual support staff. Bar service, available throughout shows, disrupts concentration.

Celebrity ships have a variety of bands and small musical units, although there is very little music for social dancing, other than disco and pop music. Then there are the summer camp-style audience participation events, games, and talent shows that don't sit well with Celebrity's quality of food and service. There are also the inevitable country line dances and playschool routines.

On days at sea the program is crammed with things to do, though the emphasis is on revenue-enhancing activities such as art auctions, bingo, and horse racing.

Costa Cruises

Ships

Atlantica-class ships: *Costa Atlantica* (2000), *Costa Deliziosa* (2010), *Costa Fascinosa* (2012), *Costa Favolosa* (2010), *Costa Luminosa* (2009), *Costa Mediterranea* (2003)

Fortuna-class ships: *Costa Fortuna* (2003), *Costa Magica* (2004), *Costa Pacifica* (2009), *Costa Serena* (2007)

Classica-class ships: *Costa Classica* (1992), *Costa neoRomantica* (1993)

Other ships: *Costa Victoria* (1996), and *Costa Voyager* (2000)

A Baroque parade aboard *Celebrity Eclipse.*

Celebrity's classy approach

There really are four 'classes' aboard Celebrity ships: accommodation designated as suites; those in standard (exterior-view) and interior (no-view) cabins; a third that comes between the two, known as Concierge Class; and Aqua (Spa) Class.

Concierge Class brings added value to passengers with enhanced facilities including priority embarkation, disembarkation, priority tender tickets, specialty dining, and spa reservations; European duvet; double-bed overlay (no more falling 'between the cracks' for couples); choice of four pillows (goose down pillow, isotonic pillow, body pillow, conformance pillow); eight-vial flower vase on vanity desk; throw pillows on sofa; fruit basket; binoculars; golf umbrella; leather telephone notepad; larger beach towels; hand-held hairdryer. Balconies get better furniture. In the bathrooms: plusher Frette bathrobe; larger towels in sea-green and pink (alternating days); flower in silver vase in bathroom.

Aqua Class accommodation occupants get priority access to spa treatments, and special 'uprated' spa amenities.

About the company

Costa Cruises traces its history back to 1860, when Giacomo Costa started an olive oil business. The first ship, in 1924, transported that oil. After he died in 1924, his sons, Federico, Eugenio, and Enrico, inherited the business. First they bought *Ravenna*, a cargo ship, to cut transport costs for their olive oil empire. In 1948 Costa's first passenger ship, the *Anna 'C'*, carried passengers in style from Genoa to South America. In 1997, Costa Cruises was bought by the USA's Carnival Corporation and UK's Airtours plc. Three years later Carnival took full control.

Costa specializes in cruises for Europeans or passengers with European tastes, and particularly Italians, during the summer. It has initiated an aggressive new-build policy in recent years, in order to modernize the company's aging fleet of different-size ships. The ships operate in three main markets: the Mediterranean, the Caribbean, and South America.

Most ships are well maintained, although there are inconsistencies throughout the fleet. The same is true of cleanliness – some ships are very clean, while others are a little dusty around the edges, as are its shore tenders. The company's safety procedures came under scrutiny when *Costa Concordia* struck rocks and capsized off the Italian island of Giglio in January 2012. **Frequent passengers' club:** Costa Club.

What is it really like?

Costa is noted for its lively 'Italian' ambience. There are few Italian crew members, however; although many officers are Italian. The dress code is casual, even on formal nights.

One night at the end of each cruise may be reserved for a Roman Bacchanal, when passengers dress up toga-style for dinner and beyond. This is a cruise line for those who like to party. If you want quiet, take earplugs – good ones.

On European and Mediterranean cruises, English will be the language least spoken, as most passengers will be Italian, Spanish, French, or German. On Caribbean itineraries, a high percentage of passengers will speak Spanish, as the ships carry passengers from Latin American countries in addition to passengers from North America.

Expect to cruise with a lot of children of all ages if you book for peak holiday cruises – and remember that in Europe schoolchildren at certain times such as Easter have longer vacations. On some European itineraries, passengers embark and disembark in almost every port along the way, which makes for a disjointed cruise experience since there's almost no start or end to the cruise. There is almost no information for passengers who want to be independent in ports of call, and not take the ship's organized general excursions.

There is extensive smoking on board. No-smoking zones and signs are often ignored to the frustration of non-smoking passengers, and ashtrays are moved at whim; many of the officers and crew also smoke, even when moving through public rooms, so they don't bother to enforce the no-smoking zones.

Cabins tend to be small, but the decor is fresh, and the bathrooms are very practical units. Some ships have cabin bathrooms with sliding doors – an excellent alternative to inward-openers that use up space.

Decor

Older ships: *Costa Classica, Costa neoRomantica, and Costa Victoria* have a more European feel. They

Celebrity Reflection bocce champion officers

are lively without being brash, or pastel-toned without being boring, depending on the ship you choose.

Newer, larger ships: *Costa Atlantica, Costa Deliziosa, Costa Fascinosa, Costa Favolosa, Costa Fortuna, Costa Luminosa, Costa Magica, Costa Mediterranea, Costa Pacifica,* and *Costa Serena* have an in-your-face brashness similar to Carnival's ships, with grainy and unflattering digital artwork on walls and panels, and even inside elevators.

Cuisine/Dining

If you expect to be served by jovial Italian waiters, you'll be disappointed – although the restaurant managers might be Italian. All ships have two seatings for dinner; dining times on Europe/Mediterranean and South America cruises are usually later than those in the Caribbean because Europeans and Latin passengers eat much later than North Americans. Few tables for two are available, most being for four, six, or eight. All dining rooms are smoke-free – in theory.

The cuisine is best described as Continental, with many regional Italian dishes and much emphasis on pasta: there can be as many as 50 pasta dishes per cruise. Except for pasta dishes (made fresh on board) and cream sauces, presentation and food quality are not memorable, and are the subject of many negative comments from passengers. While the quality of meat is adequate, it is too often disguised with gravies and rich sauces. Fish and seafood tend to lack taste, and are often overcooked. Green vegetables are hard to come by. Breads and bread rolls are usually good, but the desserts are of supermarket quality and lack taste.

There is a wine list but no wine waiters; table waiters are expected to serve both food and wine, which does not work well. Almost all wines are young – very young.
Specialty dining venues: If you opt for one of the specialty restaurants aboard the larger ships, note that a cover charge applies.
Casual eateries: All ships have self-serve lido buffets. In most, you have to move along with your tray, but the latest ships have more active stations and individual islands. The items available are quite basic.
The coffee/tea factor: Regular coffee is decent and quite strong. Score: 5 out of 10. Espresso/cappuccino coffees (Lavazza) are among the best served by the

Making a Celebrity-style entrance down the Grand Foyer.

major cruise lines: the main competition is from Celebrity Cruises' Café el Bacio. Star Cruises also serves Lavazza.

For children

Junior passengers are in three groups: Kids Club (ages three to six); Junior Club (seven to 12); and Teen Club (13–17). The program varies by ship, itinerary, and season. Group babysitting is available 6:30–11pm. During port days, babysitting is available generally 8:30am–12:30pm and 2:30–6:30pm.
Best ships for children: *Costa Atlantica, Costa Deliziosa, Costa Fascinosa, Costa Fortuna, Costa Fabolosa, Costa Luminosa, Costa Magica, Costa Mediterranea, Costa Pacifica, Costa Serena.* But not: *Costa Classica, Costa neoRomantica, Costa Victoria.*

Entertainment

Each ship carries its own resident troupe of singers/dancers and audiovisual support staff, but Costa Cruises is not known for the quality of its entertainment. What it does present tends to be of the 'no finesse' variety, with revue-style shows that have little storyline, poor choreography and execution, but plenty of fast-moving action – more stepping in place than dancing – and lots of volume. It's entertainment to pass the time rather than remember.

Costa Cruises

Costa ships are best suited to young couples, singles, and families with children who enjoy big-city life, multicultural fellow passengers, outdoor cafés, constant activity, eating late, loud entertainment, and food more notable for quantity than quality. All printed materials (room service folio, menus, etc.) are in six languages: Italian, English, French, German, Portuguese, and Spanish. Announcements are made in at least two languages in the Caribbean and at least four in Europe and the Mediterranean.

The Lawn Club aboard *Celebrity Silhouette.*

Cabaret acts – typically singers, magicians, comedy jugglers, ventriloquists, and so on – are entertaining but rather ho-hum. Most passenger participation activities include poolside games such as a Belly Flop competition, election of the Ideal Couple, and other juvenile games – but some families love them. There are also dance classes, and the inevitable Fine Art Auction.

Cunard Line

Ships
Queen Elizabeth (2010), *Queen Mary 2* (2004), *Queen Victoria* (2007).

About the company
Cunard Line was established in 1839, as the British and North American Royal Mail Steam Packet Company, to carry the Royal Mail and passengers from the Old World to the New.Since 1840, Cunard Line has always had ships built to sail across the North Atlantic. From 1850 until the arrival of *QE2* in 1969, all of the line's ships and those of White Star Line (with which Cunard merged in 1934) had several classes. Your luggage label, therefore, declared not only your name but also what you could afford. Today, there's no class distinction, other than by the grade of accommodation you choose.

What is it really like?
Sailing with Cunard Line is quite different from being aboard a standard cruise ship. The ships incorporate a lot of maritime history and the grand traditions of ocean liners – as opposed to the other ships, with their tendency toward tacky high-street trappings.

Assuming your sea legs can cope with sometimes less than calm waters, a transatlantic crossing is supremely civilized, particularly if you can enjoy being cosseted in accommodation that allows you to dine in the 'grill'-class restaurants with their fine cuisine and presentation. There's less pressure from staff to get you to buy drinks than with other lines, and the itineraries are well spaced and not so hectic.

Cunard Line's three vessels are best suited to a wide range of seasoned and well-traveled couples and single passengers who enjoy the cosmopolitan setting of an ocean liner, with their extensive array of facilities, public rooms, dining rooms, and lecture programs. All three ships have art-deco decor, fine wood mosaics, and many attributes of the old ocean liners, albeit in a more modern, contemporary setting.

Cunard Line is the only cruise line that lets you take your dog or cat with you (*Queen Mary 2* transatlantic crossings only). Also, one of its most successful formulas is its adherence to formal dress – in contrast to the downward spiral of most cruise lines. Distinctly un-British, however, is the onboard currency: the US dollar.

Accommodation
Cunard has four distinct accommodation classes, with the class linked to a specific restaurant: Queens Grill, Princess Grill, Britannia Club, and Britannia.

Cuisine/Dining
Cunard Line uses good-quality ingredients, sourced in Europe and the USA. The cuisine is still of a mass-market standard – some venues have butter in packets. However, in self-serve buffets, salt and pepper are usually provided on each table. Espressos and cappuccinos are -available in the dining rooms, and at extra cost in many bars. Cunard uses Italian coffee – Café Mosetti, a sub-brand of Lavazza.

All ships have 'grill rooms' as well as traditional large restaurants and casual self-service dining venues. Grill rooms are more exclusive and some have à la carte menus, while the main restaurants have fixed menus. The grill rooms have seating dining at assigned tables, when you wish, while the main Britannia restaurants in all ships have two seatings.

The cuisine includes many traditional British favorites, together with extensive French dishes as well as regional specialties from around the world, nicely presented on Wedgwood porcelain.

For children

Children's facilities are best aboard *Queen Mary 2*, although not as extensive as aboard the former *Queen Elizabeth 2*. Youngsters are supervised by real English nannies.

Entertainment

Production shows are colorful and visual, with prerecorded backing tracks supplementing the showband. Other shows consist of cabaret acts – typically singers, magicians, mimes, comedy jugglers, and, occasionally, comedians – doing the cruise ship circuit. A number of bands and small musical units provide live music for dancing and listening.

Holland America Line

Ships

Statendam-class: *Maasdam* (1993), *Ryndam* (1994), *Statendam* (1993), *Veendam* (1996)
Rotterdam-class: *Amsterdam* (2000), *Rotterdam* (1997), *Volendam* (1999), *Zaandam* (2000)

Zuiderdam-class: *Eurodam* (2008), *Nieuw Amsterdam* (2010), *Noordam* (2006), *Oosterdam* (2003), *Westerdam* (2004), *Zuiderdam* (2002)
Others: *Prinsendam* (1988)

About the company

Holland America Line was founded in 1873 as the Netherlands-America Steamship Company, shipping immigrants to the New World from Rotterdam. It moved its headquarters to New York in 1971. It bought into Alaskan hotels and transportation when it acquired Westours in 1983, and is one of the state's biggest employers. In 1989, it was acquired by Carnival Cruise Lines, but retained its Seattle-based headquarters.

HAL carries both traditional cruise passengers (senior citizens, alumni groups) and multi-generational families. It tries hard to keep its Dutch connections, with antique artifacts and traditional decor, as well as Indonesian stewards. It has a private island, Half Moon Cay, in the Bahamas.

What is it really like?

Fresh management with updated ideas, the line's Signature of Excellence program, the food variety, and creativity have improved the HAL experience. The ships benefit from lots of fresh flowers, museum-quality art pieces, and more attention to detail than all the other major lines, with the exception of Celebrity Cruises.

The brand encompasses basically two types of ship. Younger families with children and grandchildren are best suited to the newer, larger vessels such as *Euro-*

Queen Elizabeth and *Queen Mary 2* rendezvous in Sydney, Australia.

dam, Nieuw Amsterdam, Noordam, Oosterdam, Westerdam, and Zuiderdam, whereas those of senior years – HAL's traditional audience of repeat passengers from alumni groups – are best suited to ships that are smaller and less glitzy (Amsterdam, Maasdam, Prinsendam, Rotterdam, Ryndam, Statendam, Veendam, and Zaandam). All the ships are well maintained, and cleaning takes place constantly. All ships have teakwood outdoor promenade decks, whereas most rivals have artificial grass or some other form of indoor-outdoor carpeting. Explorations Cafés have been built into its ships recently.

Holland America Line has its own training school in Jakarta, Indonesia, and pre-trains crew members who have never been to sea before. Many crew members have been promoted to supervisory positions due to a host of new ships introduced, but few of those promoted have the formal training, professional, or management skills. Internal promotion is fine, but decreased professionalism is not the price that passengers should pay.

HAL is one of only three major cruise lines with cinemas built into all its ships. It also operates many theme-related cruises, and has an extensive 'University at Sea' program of life-enrichment lecturers. The cinemas also have superb full demonstration kitchens built in for a 'Culinary Arts' program that includes celebrity chefs and interactive cooking demos.

Costa Cruises covers the Greek Islands.

HAL has established smoking and no-smoking areas throughout its ships, but there are many more smokers than you might expect, depending on ship and itinerary.

Decor

Aboard Amsterdam, Maasdam, Nieuw Amsterdam, Prinsendam, Rotterdam, Ryndam, Statendam, Veendam, Volendam, and Zaandam, the decor is rather bland (restful), with eclectic artwork focused on Dutch artifacts, mainly from the 16th and 17th centuries.

As part of its Signature of Excellence refurbishment program, its ships received a 'Mix' lifestyle facility – an open area with three themed specialty bars: Champagne (serving Champagne and sparkling wines from around the world), Martinis (martinis in individual shakers), and Spirits & Ales (a sports bar with beer, baseball, and basketball). You can play checkers and chess, air hockey, and other sports games.

Aboard the newer ships (Eurodam, Nieuw Amsterdam, Noordam, Oosterdam, Westerdam, and Zuiderdam) the decor is livelier – good for families with children who like bright things such as large wall panels with digital in-your-face artwork that present an Alice in Wonderland look. You wouldn't go for it in your living room, but aboard these large resort ships it works.

Cuisine/Dining

For dinner, Holland America Line features both open seating (on one level) or assigned tables (at fixed times, on the other level) in its two-deck dining rooms; it's called As You Wish dining. For breakfast and lunch in the main dining room, an open-seating policy applies. All dining venues are non-smoking.

Some tables for two are available, but most are for four, six, eight, or 10. The larger tables are ideal for multi-generational families. Fine Rosenthal china and cutlery are used. Live music is provided for dinner. 'Lighter option' meals are always available for the nutrition-conscious and the weight-conscious.

Holland America Line food was upgraded slightly when master chef Rudi Sodamin arrived in 2005 as a

HAL's Signature of Excellence

Between 2004 and 2006, Signature of Excellence improvements were introduced at a cost of $225 million. These covered dining, service, accommodation, and activities, and included 'Premium-Plus' Euro-Top mattresses, cotton bed linens or duvets (top suites only), massage showerheads, fruit baskets, and DVD players. Elemis personal bathroom amenities are provided for all passengers (these are better than Celebrity's present bathroom amenities, for example). Suite occupants also have access to a Neptune Lounge (with concierge services), thus in effect creating a two-class system that suite occupants like. Bathrobes and a range of personal toiletries are provided for all passengers, and hot hors d'oeuvres and canapés are always part of the pre-dinner cocktail scene.

consultant; he introduced his 'Wild about Salmon' and other creative ideas, and the Culinary Arts Center (with its own dedicated live interactive demonstration kitchen and guest chef program) has been a success story. The company now includes more regional cuisine and local ingredients. The main course portions are small (better for passengers of senior years).

However, while the USDA beef is very good, poultry and most fish tend to be overcooked (except when the ships are in Alaska, where the halibut and salmon are excellent). Note that 'downmarket' packets of sugar and packets (instead of glass jars) of supermarket-brand breakfast jams, marmalade and honey, sugar, and butter are the norm. Also, coffees and teas are poor-quality, except in the extra-charge Explorations Café. Dessert and pastry items are good, but canned fruit and jellied desserts are much in evidence. Most of the 'international' cheeses are highly colored, processed cheese (cruises in Europe have access to European cheeses).

HAL also offers complimentary ice cream during certain hours of the day, as well as hot hors d'oeuvres in all bars – something other major lines seem to have dropped, or charge extra for. Cabin service breakfasts are very basic, with only Continental breakfast available and little hot food.

HAL can provide kosher meals. As the ships don't have kosher kitchens, these are prepared ashore, frozen, and brought to your table sealed in containers.

The wine list relies heavily on wines from California and Washington State, with few decent French or German wines, other than those found in a typical supermarket ashore. A Connoisseur List is available in the Pinnacle Grill.

Specialty dining venues: All HAL ships have specialty spots called Pinnacle Grill (or Pinnacle Grill at the Odyssey Restaurant), specializing in Pacific Northwest cuisine. Items include sesame-crusted halibut with ginger-miso, and an array of premium-quality steaks, presented tableside prior to cooking. These are more intimate restaurants, with tablecloths, linen napkins, and decent-size wine glasses. The food is better than in the main dining rooms. There is a cover charge, and reservations are required. Bulgari china, Frette linens, and Reidel glasses are part of this enhanced dining experience.

Casual eateries: All ships have a Lido Deck self-serve buffet. Most are lines you move along with your tray, although the latest ships have more 'active' stations (examples: omelets and pasta cooked to order) and individual islands. There are decent salad bars, dessert bars, regional specialties, and grilled fast-food items such as hamburgers, salmon burgers, hot dogs, and french fries. These venues become overcrowded during breakfast and lunch.

Regular coffee is half-decent, but weak. Score: 3 out of 10. Espresso/cappuccino coffees (Dutch) are better, served in proper china, but not quite up to the standard of Celebrity or Costa. Score: 6 out of 10.

Daily exercise beside a Costa funnel.

For children
Club HAL: Junior passengers are divided into three age-appropriate groups: three to eight, nine to 12, and teens. Programming is based on the number of children booked on any given sailing, and children's counselors are provided accordingly. HAL's children's programs are not as extensive as those of Carnival Cruise Lines, for example, although they are improving with the latest ships.

Best ships for children: *Eurodam, Nieuw Amsterdam, Noordam, Oosterdam, Westerdam, Zaandam, Zuiderdam.*

Entertainment
Holland America Line is not known for lavish entertainment (the budgets aren't high enough). The production shows, while a good attempt, fall short on storyline, choreography, and performance, while colorful costuming and lighting hide the weak spots. Each ship carries its own resident troupe of singers and dancers and audio-visual support staff. HAL also offers a consistently good, tried and tested array of cabaret acts that constantly pop up on the cruise ship circuit.

A number of bands, a string ensemble, and solo musicians present live music for dancing and listening in many of the lounges and bars. Each ship has a Crow's Nest Lounge (by day an observation lounge) for social dancing, and there is always serenading string music in the Explorer's Lounge and dining room.

MSC Cruises

Ships
Fantasia-class ships: *MSC Divina* (2012), *MSC Fantasia* (2008), *MSC Preziosa (2013), MSC Splendida* (2009)

Lirica-class ships: *MSC Armonia* (2001), *MSC Lirica* (2003), *MSC Opera* (2004), *MSC Sinfonia* (2005)

Musica-class ships: *MSC Magnifica* (2010), *MSC Musica* (2006), *MSC Orchestra* (2007), *MSC Poesia* (2008)

About the company

The HQ of the world's largest privately owned cruise line is in Geneva, Switzerland, home of parent company Mediterranean Shipping Company, the world's second-biggest container shipping company. Operations and marketing are based in Genoa, Italy. It started in the passenger shipping business by acquiring the Italian company Star Lauro in 1995, together with two older ships, *Monterey* and *Rhapsody*. It expanded with the purchase of *Melody*, followed by almost new ships bought from the bankrupt Festival Cruises.

MSC Cruises has grown incredibly fast, and has a number of large resort ships on order. Also, it is owned by a shipping-based family, not a faceless corporation.

What is it really like?

MSC Cruises' ships are really suited to adult couples and singles, and families with children. They are good for those who enjoy big-city life, multicultural and multinational fellow passengers, outdoor cafés, constant activity accompanied by plenty of live music, late nights, and food ranging from adequate to very good.

MSC Cruises uses the most environmentally friendly detergents and cleaning materials in its housekeeping department and laundries. It has drastically reduced its onboard use of plastic items and is aiming to eliminate them entirely. The larger ships *(MSC Divina, MSC Fantasia, MSC Preziosa,* and *MSC Splendida)* have

Costa ships incorporate eye-catching sculptures.

an exclusive Yacht Club lounge for suite-grade passengers. This provides exclusive open-seating dining, a private sun deck oasis area, access to the well-run Aurea Spa, priority embarkation, and butler service.

The ships typically operate in five languages, with embarkation-day announcements in English, French, German, Italian, and Spanish. Thankfully, during the cruise, there are few announcements. Given this multilingual emphasis, production shows and other major entertainment displays are more visual than verbal. For the same reason, the ships don't generally carry lecturers.

Cigar lovers will find a selection of Cuban (including Cohiba, Montecristo, Romeo e Julieta, Partagás), Dominican (Davidoff), and Italian (Toscano) smokes in the cigar lounges.

Decor

The decor is decidedly European/Mediterranean, with much understated elegance and really high-quality soft furnishings and other materials such as Italian marble, and Swarovski glass stairways. The latest ships are much brighter and more contemporary, albeit with restraint.

Cuisine/Dining

MSC Cruises provides better-quality ingredients, almost all sourced in Europe, than some other major cruise lines. The cuisine is still mainstream – you'll find butter in packets, for example. But, at the self-serve buffets, salt and pepper are typically provided on each table, not in packets as on most major cruise lines. Espresso and cappuccino (Segafredo brand Italian coffee) are available in the dining rooms, at extra cost, and in almost all bars – which also have coffees from Brazil, Costa Rica, and Peru.

Aboard the newest ships, MSC Cruises has introduced the Italian 'slow food' concept. Always available items include spaghetti, chicken breast, salmon fillet, and vegetables of the day. Refreshingly, the company spotlights regional Italian cuisine and wine, so daily dining room menus feature food from regions such as Calabria, Piedmont, Lazio, Puglia, and Sicily.

All pizza dough is made on board, and risotto is a daily signature item for MSC Cruises and something the ships do really well; each ship also makes one type of pasta almost daily. Spaghetti is always available, with a tomato sauce freshly made each day. Several varieties of Italian breads such as bruschetta, focaccia, and panettone are provided.

Specialty dining venues: The newer ships have a specialty restaurant. Aboard *MSC Divina, MSC Fantasia,* and *MSC Splendida,* it is Tex-Mex. Aboard *MSC Musica* and *MSC Poesia,* it is Kaito, an authentic Japanese restaurant and sushi bar with an extensive menu. Aboard *MSC Magnifica* and *MSC Orchestra,* it is Shanghai, a Chinese restaurant with real wok cooking, dim sum, and other Chinese and Asian specialties. The

Queen Elizabeth's decor is classic and timeless.

quality is high, and it really is worth having at least one meal in these venues; the à la carte prices are very reasonable.

Room service: Continental breakfast is complimentary from 7:30 to 10am, while room service snacks can be bought at any other time. A basket of fruit is provided to all cabins at embarkation, and replenished daily for suite-grade accommodation.

For children

Up to three children over two and under 17, cruise free when sharing a cabin with two adults (paying only port dues). Children are divided into three age groups, with facilities to match: Mini Club (ages three to nine); Junior Club (10–13); Teenagers Club (over 14, a pre-paid Teen Card is available). While the facilities and play areas aren't as extensive as those aboard some other major lines, a 'baby parking' service is useful when parents want to go ashore on excursions. MSC Cruises' mascot is Do-Re-Mi – the von Trapp family of *Sound of Music* fame would no doubt be delighted.

Best ships for children: *MSC Divina, MSC Fantasia, MSC Magnifica, MSC Musica, MSC Opera, MSC Orchestra, MSC Poesia, MSC Preziosa, MSC Splendida.*

Entertainment

Because of the multilingual passenger mix, production shows are colorful and visual, particularly aboard the newest ships. Other shows consist of unknown cabaret acts such as singers, magicians, mimes, and comedy jugglers doing the cruise ship circuit. The ship carries a number of bands and small musical units that pro-vide live music for dancing or listening, but there is no showband, and production shows use pre-recorded backing tracks.

Norwegian Cruise Line

Ships

Dawn-class: *Norwegian Dawn* (2002), *Norwegian Star* (2002)

Epic-class: *Norwegian Breakaway* (2013), *Norwegian Epic* (2010), *Norwegian Getaway* (2014)

Jewel-class: *Norwegian Gem* (2007), *Norwegian Jade* (2006), *Norwegian Jewel* (2005), *Norwegian Pearl* (2006)

Others: *Norwegian Sky* (1999), *Norwegian Spirit* (1998), *Norwegian Sun* (2001), *Pride of America* (2005)

About the company

Norwegian Cruise Line, the originator of contemporary cruising, was founded in 1966 by three Norwegian shipping companies as Klosters Sunward Ferries and was renamed Norwegian Caribbean Line in 1967. It was bought by Star Cruises in 2000, and has been replacing its older, smaller ships with brand new, larger vessels. NCL also operates one ship with mostly American crews and a base in Hawaii.

Freestyle Cruising is how NCL describes its operation – although it's hard to detect style in the onboard product (I call it American Bistro-style). Its fleet is diverse, so the cruise experience can vary, although this makes for interesting character variation between the

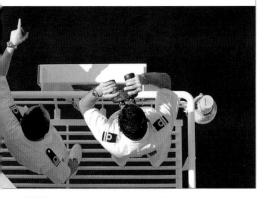

MSC crews typically operate in five languages.

various ship categories. There is more standardization aboard the larger, newer ships. The senior officers are the only thing that's Norwegian.

Most standard cabins are extremely small, though they have reasonably attractive decor and are functional. Closet and drawer space is limited.
Frequent passengers' club: Latitudes.

What is it really like?
If this is your first cruise, you should enjoy a good overall vacation in a lively, upbeat setting. The lifestyle is contemporary, fresh, creative, and sporty, with a casualness typical of youthful city dwellers, and with its 'eat when you want' philosophy, the shipboard ambience is ultra-casual – best described as US east-coast 'edgy.' So is the dress code – indeed, the waiters are probably better dressed than many passengers. The staff is generally congenial, and you'll find a high percentage of females in cabin and restaurant service departments – more than most major cruise lines.

There's plenty of lively music, constant activity, entertainment, and food that's mainstream and acceptable but nothing more – unless you pay extra to eat in the specialty dining spots. All this is delivered by a smiling, very friendly service staff who lack polish but are willing. In the latest wheeze to extract revenue, NCL has started 'Backstage Tours' costing $55 or $150 (depending on what's included).
NCL's Private Island (Great Stirrup Cay): Only coffee and iced water are free (there's no iced tea), all other drinks are charged.

Decor
The newest ships have colorful, eye-catching designs on their hulls, differentiating them from the competition.

Cuisine/Dining
NCL has recognized the increasing trend away from formal restaurants (purpose: dining) toward bistros (purpose: eating faster). For cruising, NCL has cham-

pioned more choices in dining than any other cruise line, except sister company Star Cruises, which started Freestyle Dining.

This allows you to try different types of cuisine, in different settings, when you want. In practice, however, it means that you have to make reservations, which can prove frustrating at times, and getting it just right takes a little planning and, often, waiting. Food in the main dining rooms is poor to average and marginally better in the extra-charge venues.

Freestyle Dining works best aboard the ships that have been specially designed to accommodate it: *Norwegian Breakaway, Norwegian Dawn, Norwegian Epic, Norwegian Gem, Norwegian Getaway, Norwegian Jade, Norwegian Jewel, Norwegian Pearl, Norwegian Spirit, Norwegian Star, Norwegian Sun,* and *Pride of America.*

On production show presentation nights, most people want to eat at the same time in order to see the shows, causing massive prime-time congestion, slow service, and utter and complete frustration; pagers are given out for anyone waiting for a table. The ships have plasma screens in various locations so you can make reservations when you want, and see at a glance the waiting times for a table; an updated version of its 'Silverware' reservation program was introduced in 2009. The self-serve buffets are mostly chaotic, mob-scene affairs (and very repetitive), and should be avoided.

After-dinner espresso/cappuccino coffees are available in the dining rooms without extra charge – a nice feature. Once each cruise there's a Chocoholics Buffet with paper plates and plastic cutlery. The wine list is quite good, with many excellent wines in the $20–$30 range. But the wine is typically served by table waiters, whose knowledge of wines is poor.

Cabin service breakfasts are very basic, with only Continental breakfast available and no hot food items – for those, you'll need to go to a restaurant or self-serve buffet. The non-breakfast Room Service menu has only two hot items available throughout the day: Oriental soup and pizza – the rest is cold (salads and sandwiches).
The coffee/tea factor: Regular coffee: weak and poor. Score: 2 out of 10. Iced tea: pitifully weak. Espresso/cappuccino coffees score 4 out of 10. Some bars have (extra-cost) espresso/cappuccino machines.

For children
NCL's Splash Academy and Entourage programs divide children into several groups, according to age: Guppies (ages 6 months to three years); Junior sailors (three to five); First Mates (six to eight); Navigators (nine to 12); and two Teens groups (13–14 and 15–17). NCL's revamped kids and teens programming was developed in conjunction with the King's Foundation and Camps, a UK-based organization that provides quality sports and activity programs. There's also program-

ming for babies and toddlers ages six months to three years (Guppies). Group babysitting services are also available, at an extra change. Special price packages are available for soft drinks.

Best ships for children: *Norwegian Breakaway, Norwegian Dawn, Norwegian Epic, Norwegian Gem, Norwegian Getaway, Norwegian Jade, Norwegian Jewel, Norwegian Pearl, Norwegian Spirit, Norwegian Star, Norwegian Sun.*

Entertainment
NCL has good production shows that provide color and spectacle in a predictable – though now dated – format. Each ship has a resident troupe of singers/dancers. There are two or three production shows in a typical seven-day cruise. They are all very colorful, high-energy, razzle-dazzle shows, with much use of laser and color-mover lights. They're not memorable – but, it must be said, they're very entertaining. Most activities and passenger participation events range from poor to extremely poor. Nintendo Wii interactive games are available on large screens.

P&O Cruises

Ships
Adults-only ships: *Adonia* (2001), *Arcadia* (2005), *Oriana* (1995)
Family-friendly ships: *Aurora* (2000), *Azura* (2010), *Oceana* (2000), *Ventura* (2008)

About the company
Its full name is the Peninsular and Oriental Steam Navigation Company, though none of its ships is still operated by steam turbines. Based in Southampton, England, it was founded in 1837, just before Samuel Cunard established his company, and was awarded a UK government contract in 1840 to carry the mails from Gibraltar to Alexandria.

P&O Cruises acquired Princess Cruises in 1974, Swan Hellenic in 1982, and Sitmar Cruises in 1988. In 2000 it demerged from its parent to establish itself as P&O Princess plc. It was bought by Carnival Corporation in 2003, and celebrated its 175th anniversary on July 3, 2012, when all seven ships assembled in Southampton.
Frequent passengers' club: Peninsular Club.

What is it really like?
P&O Cruises has always been a traditional British cruise company, but never quite matching the quality aboard the Cunard Line ships (whose onboard currency is, oddly, the US dollar), which usually have greater number of international passengers. With British captains and navigation officers and Indian/Goanese service staff, the British traditions of unobtrusive service are preserved and well presented. British food favorites (considered bland by some)

provide the real comfort factor in a single-language setting that provides a true home away from home on ships for families with children, or on adults-only ships.

It is targeted at British passengers who wanted to sail from a UK port – except for winter Caribbean cruises from Barbados. But now it's also known for having adults-only ships, and so the two products differ widely in their communal spaces. It also makes an effort to provide theme cruises – antiques, art appreciation, classical music, comedy, cricket, gardening and horticulture, jazz, Scottish dance, etc. The ships usually carry ballroom dance instructors. Bed linen is not changed as often (twice a week) as on some lines, such as MSC Cruises (every two days).

Decor
A mix of British 'traditional' (think: comfy, dated armchairs, wood paneling, bistro-style food, nonglitzy). British artists are featured aboard all ships – *Ventura*, for example, displays works by more than 40 of them.

Cuisine/Dining
The cuisine is straightforward, no-nonsense British food, reasonably well presented on nice Wedgwood china. But it tends to be rather bland and uninspiring. It

Holland America Line gets up-close to Alaska.

is typical of mass-banquet catering with standard fare comparable to that found in a family hotel in an English seaside town like Scarborough.

The ingredients of many meals are disguised by gravies and sauces, as in Indian curries – well liked, of course, by most British passengers. Bread, desserts, and cakes are made well, and there is a wide variety. P&O Cruises always carries a decent selection of British, and some French, cheeses.

Most of the dining room staff are from India and provide warm and friendly service. Wine service is amateurish and the lack of knowledge is lamentable.

Specialty dining venues: Extra-cost restaurants with menus designed by some of Britain's well-known television celebrity chefs such as Marco Pierre White and Atul Kochhar, have their own eateries aboard the ships. They are a mix of trendy bistro-style venues and restaurants with an Asia-Pacific theme.

Casual eateries: The self-serve buffets suffer from small, cramped facilities, and passengers complain of having to share them with the countless concession staff who take over tables and congregate in groups. In other words, the buffets are too small to accommodate the needs of most passengers today.

The coffee/tea factor: Regular coffee: weak, and poor. Score: 3 out of 10. Good-quality tea- and coffee-making setup is provided in all cabins. Self-serve beverage stations are provided at the buffets, but it's often difficult to find proper teaspoons – often only wooden stirrers are available. Espresso/cappuccino coffees in the extra-charge venues are slightly better,

but not as good as aboard the ships of Costa Cruises or MSC Cruises.

Entertainment

P&O Cruises has always been known for its traditional British-style entertainment, with lots of pub-like sing-along sessions for the masses. These have been augmented with in-house production shows that provide lots of color, costume changes, and high-tech lighting. Each ship carries its own resident troupe of singers and dancers, called Headliners.

P&O Cruises does a good job in providing guest lecturers with varying themes, as well as occasional after-dinner speakers such as well-known television personalities and book authors.

Princess Cruises

Ships

Grand-class ships (over 100,000 gross tonnage): *Caribbean Princess* (2004), *Crown Princess* (2006), *Diamond Princess* (2004), *Emerald Princess* (2007), *Golden Princess* (2001), *Grand Princess* (1998), *Royal Princess* (2013), *Ruby Princess* (2008), *Sapphire Princess* (2005), *Star Princess* (2002)

Pacific-class ships: *Ocean Princess* (1999), *Pacific Princess* (1999)

Coral-class ships: *Coral Princess* (2002), *Island Princess* (2003)

Other ships: *Dawn Princess* (1997), *Sea Princess* (1998), *Sun Princess* (1995)

MSC Poesia lights up Manhattan.

About the company

Princess Cruises was founded by Stanley McDonald in 1965 with one ship, the former passenger ferry *Princess Patricia,* for cruises along the Mexican Riviera. In 1974, the company was bought by the UK's Peninsular and Oriental Steam Navigation Company (P&O), and in 1988 P&O/Princess Cruises merged with the Italian line Sitmar Cruises. In 2000, Carnival Corporation and Royal Caribbean Cruises fought a protracted battle to buy Princess Cruises. Carnival won.

Princess Cruises provides comfortable mainstream cruising aboard a fleet of mainly large resort ships (plus two small ships), and covers the world. The ships have a higher-than-average Passenger Space Ratio than competitors Carnival or RCI, and the service is friendly without being showy. In 2010 the company converted to fully digital travel documents, so there are no more ticket document wallets and everything is online.

Frequent passengers' club: Captain's Circle.

What is it really like?

Ships in both the small and large resort categories are clean and always well maintained, and the open promenade decks of some ships have teak deck lounge chairs – others are plastic. Only *Coral Princess* and *Island Princess* have full walk-around open promenade decks; aboard all other Princess ships you can't walk completely around the open promenade decks. The line also has a nice balance of officers, staff, and crew members, and its British connections help it to achieve the feeling of calmness aboard its ships that some other lines lack.

There are proper cinemas aboard most ships, as well as outdoor poolside mega-screens for showing evening 'movies under the skies.'

Lines form at peak times for the information office, and for open-seating breakfast and lunch in the main dining rooms. Lines for shore excursions and shore tenders are a fact of life aboard large resort ships.

All passengers receive turndown service and chocolates on pillows each night, as well as bathrobes (on request) and toiletry kits – larger, naturally, for suite/mini-suite occupants – that typically include soap, shampoo, conditioner, and hand/body lotion. A hairdryer is provided in all cabins, sensibly located at a vanity desk unit in the lounge area. In 2012, smoking was prohibited in cabins and on cabin balconies.

The dress code is either formal – usually one formal night per seven-day cruise – or smart casual. The latter is interpreted by many as jeans or tracksuits and trainers.

All the Grand-class ships include an adults-only area called The Sanctuary, an extra-cost retreat at the top of the ship, forward of the mast. This provides a 'private' place to relax and unwind and includes attendants to provide chilled face towels and deliver light bites. It has thick-padded sunloungers both in the sun and in the

Perfecting a high-tech swing aboard HAL's *Prinsendam.*

shade, a swim-against-the-current pool, and there are also two outdoor cabanas for massages. I particularly recommend The Sanctuary as a retreat from the business of the rest of the ship. It's worth the extra cost.

Princess's onboard product, especially food and entertainment, is well established, and is totally geared to the North American market. But British and other European nationalities should feel at ease, as long as they realize that this is all about highly organized, packaged cruising, food, and service. There is, however, an increasing emphasis on onboard revenue, so you can expect to be subjected to a stream of flyers advertising daily art auctions, 'designer' watches, specialized classes such as the cruise line's ScholarShip@ Sea programs, and the like.

Princess Cruises' ships are best suited to couples, families with children and teenagers, and older singles who like to mingle in a large ship setting with sophisticated surroundings and lifestyle, reasonably good entertainment, and fairly decent food and service, packaged affordably.

Shipboard hospitals have live SeaMed tele-medicine link-ups with specialists at the Cedars-Sinai Medical Center in Los Angeles for emergency help – useful mainly for passengers who reside in the USA.

Princess Cays is the company's own 'private island' in the Caribbean. It's all yours (along with a couple of thousand other passengers) for a day. However, it's a tender ride away from the ship, so getting to it can take some time.

Decor

If Carnival's ships have the brightest decor imaginable, the decor aboard Princess Cruises' ships is almost the opposite – perhaps a little bland in places, with much use of neutral tones, calm colors, and pastels. This really does suit the passengers who cruise with Princess.

P&O Cruises' *Ventura's* maiden arrival in Southampton.

Cuisine/Dining

Although portions are generous, the food and its presentation are disappointing. Fish is often disguised by crumb or batter coating, the selection of fresh green vegetables is limited, and few garnishes are used. However, do remember that this is big-ship banquet catering, with all its attendant standardization and production cooking. Meats are of a decent quality, although often disguised by gravy-based sauces, and pasta dishes are acceptable (though voluminous), and are typically served by section headwaiters who may also make 'something special just for you' – in search of favorable comments and gratuities.

If you like desserts, order a sundae at dinner, as most other desserts are just so-so. Ice cream, when ordered in the dining room, is included, but costs extra elsewhere (Häagen-Dazs can be found at poolside).

Specially designed dinnerware and good-quality linens and silverware are used, such as Dudson of England dinnerware, Frette Egyptian cotton table linens, with silverware by Hepp of Germany.

An extra-cost Chef's Table Dinner is an indulgent, three-hour 'foodertainment' event (at $75 per person), in which the ship's executive chef interacts with diners; appetizers and cocktails in the galley are followed by a multi-course tasting dinner with wines paired to the meal. The wine list is fair (not good). There are no dedicated wine waiters (waiters serve it).

Passengers in balcony-grade accommodation can enjoy a full-service Balcony Dinner for two at $50 per person extra, plus wine, and a truly indulgent Balcony Champagne Breakfast – it's good value.

Casual eateries: For casual eating, each ship has a Horizon Buffet (open almost round the clock), and, at night, provides an informal dinner setting with sit-down waiter service. A small, limited bistro menu is also available. The buffet displays are mostly repetitious, but far better than in past years. There is no finesse in pres-

entation, however, as plastic plates are provided, instead of trays. The cabin service menu is quite limited, and the presentation of food items is poor.

The coffee/tea factor: Regular coffee: weak and poor. Score: 2 out of 10. Except for the beverage station at the serve-yourself buffets, coffees/teas in bars cost extra.

For children

Children are divided into three age groups: Princess Pelicans (ages two to five); Shockwaves (eight to 12); and Off-Limits or Remix (13–17). The groups are split into age-related activities, and Princess Cruises has good children's counselors and supervised activities.

Best ships for children: *Caribbean Princess, Coral Princess, Crown Princess, Dawn Princess, Diamond Princess, Emerald Princess, Golden Princess, Grand Princess, Island Princess, Ruby Princess, Sapphire Princess, Sea Princess, Star Princess, Sun Princess.* But not: *Ocean Princess, Pacific Princess.*

Entertainment

Princess Cruises' production shows have always been aimed at its slightly older, more elegant passengers. The company prides itself on its glamorous all-American shows, and they should not disappoint. For variety, there are typically two or three shows during each seven-day cruise. Each ship has a resident troupe of singers and dancers.

Passenger participation events are put on by members of the cruise staff – who might be well advised to hang on to their day jobs. Most lounges and bars have live music. Musical units range from solo pianists to string quartets, from a cappella singers to bands that can provide music for ballroom dancing. Princess Cruises also provides a number of male hosts as dance partners for women traveling alone.

Royal Caribbean International

Ships

Oasis-class ships: *Allure of the Seas* (2010), *Oasis of the Seas* (2009)

Quantum-class ships: *Quantum of the Seas* (2014)

Freedom-class ships: *Freedom of the Seas* (2006), *Independence of the Seas* (2008), *Liberty of the Seas* (2007)

Voyager-class ships: *Adventure of the Seas* (2001), *Explorer of the Seas* (2000), *Mariner of the Seas* (2004), *Navigator of the Seas* (2003), *Voyager of the Seas* (1999)

Radiance-class ships: *Brilliance of the Seas* (2002), *Jewel of the Seas* (2004), *Radiance of the Seas* (2001), *Serenade of the Seas* (2003)

Vision-class ships: *Enchantment of the Seas* (1997), *Grandeur of the Seas* (1996), *Legend of the Seas* (1995), *Rhapsody of the Seas* (1997), *Splendour of the Seas* (1996), *Vision of the Seas* (1998)

Sovereign-class ships: *Majesty of the Seas* (1992)

About the company

Royal Caribbean Cruise Line was set up by three Norwegian shipping company dynasties in 1969: Arne Wilhelmsen, I.M. Skaugen, and Gotaas-Larsen (who was more of a sleeping partner). Its first ship, *Song of Norway,* debuted in 1970, followed by *Nordic Prince* and *Sun Viking.* Royal Caribbean was different from Carnival and NCL in that it launched its cruise operations with brand new ships, whereas the others had only older, pre-owned tonnage. In 1978 the cruise industry's first 'chop-and-stretch' operation enlarged *Song of Norway,* and 1988 saw the debut of the first really large cruise ship, *Sovereign of the Seas.*

In 1997, Royal Caribbean International bought Celebrity Cruises for $1.3 billion and in 2006 acquired Pullmantur Cruises for $889.9 million. In 2007 its Celebrity Cruises division created a new cruise line, Azamara Cruises, with two ships. In 2007 RCI established CDF Croisières de France with one ship, diverted from the Pullmantur Cruises fleet.

At first the operation was excellent. But, with shareholders to please, the onboard product has slipped to equal that of Carnival Cruise Lines (whose ships, in general, have larger standard cabins). RCI's ships are shapely, with well-rounded sterns, and interesting design profiles that make them instantly recognizable. They have large, brightly lit casinos, and revenue-raising shopping galleries that passengers have to walk through to get almost anywhere else.

Frequent passengers club: Crown and Anchor Society.

What is it really like?

RCI provides a well-integrated, fine-tuned, and comfortable cruise experience, but there's nothing royal about it except the name. The product is consistent but homogeneous. This is cruising for mainstream America. The ships are all quite pleasing, and some have really comfortable public rooms, lounges, bars, and innovative gimmicks such as ice-skating rinks.

RCI's largest ships are termed *Oasis*-class, *Freedom*-class, and *Voyager*-class. They differ from other ships in the fleet, mainly in the internal layout, by having a large mall-like high street – the focal point for most passengers. Many public rooms, lounges, and bars are located as adjuncts to the mall. Indeed, it's rather like a mall with a ship built around it. Also, in placing so much emphasis on 'active' outdoors areas, space has been taken away from the pool areas, leaving little room left just to sit and relax or sunbathe.

The next group of ships *(Brilliance of the Seas, Jewel of the Seas, Radiance of the Seas, Serenade of the Seas)* has lots of balcony cabins, and large expanses of glass. *Enchantment of the Seas, Grandeur of the Seas, Legend of the Seas, Rhapsody of the Seas, Splendour of the Seas,* and *Vision of the Seas* also have lots of glass in the public areas, but not so many balcony cabins. *Freedom of the Seas* pioneered a concierge lounge available only to suite-grade occupants.

The oldest ship, *Majesty of the Seas,* innovative in the late 1980s, now looks very tired and dated. It has extremely small, barely adequate cabins, and tiny tub chairs in public rooms, for example, although the average passenger has become larger.

All ships have a rock-climbing wall with several separate climbing tracks. You'll need to plan what you want to take part in wisely, as almost everything requires you to sign up in advance.

There are few quiet places to sit and read – almost everywhere has intrusive background music, played even in elevators and all passenger hallways. Bars also have very loud music. There are many, many unwelcome announcements for activities that bring revenue, such as art auctions and bingo.

Standing in line for embarkation, the reception desk, disembarkation, for port visits, shore tenders, and for the self-serve buffet stations in the Windjammer Café is an inevitable aspect of cruising aboard large resort ships. It's often hard to escape the ship's photographers – they're everywhere. Take lots of extra pennies – you'll need them to pay for all the additional-cost items. Expect to be subjected to a stream of flyers advertising promotions, while 'artwork' for auction is strewn throughout the ship, and frosted drinks in 'souvenir' glasses are pushed to the hilt. There are no cushioned pads for the deck lounge chairs.

Balconies on *Ruby Princess* can be overlooked.

Service personnel are friendly, but not many greet you when passing in the corridors, so the hospitality factor could be improved. The elevators talk to you, though 'going up/going down' is informative but monotonous. However, the signage and illuminated picture displays of decks are good, particularly aboard the Oasis-class ships.

Occupants of the Presidential Family Suite, Royal Suite, Royal Family Suite, Owner's Suite, and Grand Suite get a dedicated security line, where available. Royal and Presidential Family Suite occupants are welcomed by a senior officer and escorted aboard. Those in Grand Suites and higher categories get gold SeaPass cards for better staff recognition. On embarkation: free bottled water and a fruit plate, slippers, spa bathrobes, Vitality bathroom amenities, and Ghirardelli chocolates or petits fours at turndown. Free 24-hour room service, coffee, and tea are provided, along with the option of ordering from the main dining room's full breakfast, lunch, and dinner menus. There's also free garment pressing on 'formal' evenings.

Other perks include a cocktail reception with the captain, reserved showlounge seating, and priority bookings for spa/salon appointments, tender tickets, and excursions. On *Voyager-* and *Freedom-*class

AquaParks are one of NCL's major attractions.

ships, suite guests get reserved seating poolside and at Studio B ice shows. During breakfast and lunch in the casual Windjammer buffet venue, there's reserved private seating in the adjacent specialty restaurants. Aboard *Radiance-*, *Voyager-*, and *Freedom-*class ships, suite occupants receive a Concierge Club key. Junior Suite occupants get silver SeaPass cards for extra benefits.

Decor

Interior decor is bright and contemporary, but not as neon-intensive and glitzy as Carnival's ships. There is much Scandinavian design influence, with some eclectic sculpture and artwork. The 'you are here' signage and deck plans are excellent. The furniture in public lounges tends to include small 'tub' chairs, often broken by large passengers.

Cuisine/Dining

Most ships have large dining halls that are two or three decks high, giving a sense of space and grandeur. Few tables for two are available, most being for four, six, or eight people. All dining rooms and eateries are non-smoking. The efficient dining operation emphasizes highly programmed, extremely hurried service that many find insensitive. There are no fish knives.

'My Time Dining' (rolled out in 2009) means you can choose either a fixed dining time or any time you want. For this option, you pre-pay gratuities and enroll either on board or in advance through www.royalcaribbean.com or by asking your travel agent to arrange it via the reservations system.

The cuisine in the main dining rooms is typical of mass banquet catering, with mediocre standard fare. The food costs per passenger are below those for sister companies Azamara Club Cruises and Celebrity Cruises, so don't expect the same food quality. Dinner menus typically include a Welcome Aboard Dinner, French Dinner, Italian Dinner, International Dinner, and Captain's Gala Dinner, and all offer plenty of choice. Menu descriptions sound tempting, but the food, although well enough prepared, is unmemorable. A decent selection of light meals is provided, and there's a vegetarian menu.

The quality of meat, particularly beef, is poor – unless you pay extra for a 'better quality' sirloin steak cooked to order. Other meats are often disguised with gravies or heavy sauces. Most fish (except salmon) and seafood items tend to be overcooked and lack taste. Green vegetables are scarce – they're provided basically for decoration – but salad items are plentiful. Rice is often used as a source of carbohydrates, potatoes being more expensive.

Breads and pastry items are generally good, although some items, such as croissants, may not be made on board. The selection of breads, rolls, and fruit could be better. Dessert items are standardized and lack flavor, and the cheese and cracker selections are poor.

Caviar, once a standard menu item, is now lumpfish caviar – poor, incredibly salty, and nothing to do with real caviar.

Specialty dining venues: All *Freedom-*, *Radiance-*, and *Voyager*-class ships have two additional dining venues: Chops Grille Steakhouse (for premium veal chops and steaks, cover charge $30 per person) and Portofino (for Italian-American cuisine; cover charge $25 per person). Both venues serve food of a much higher quality than that in the main dining room. Reservations are required in both venues. Vision-class ships have one extra-charge specialty dining venue, Portofino. Be prepared to eat Texas-sized portions, presented on large plates. Note that menus do not change throughout the cruise. *Oasis*-class ships have more extra-cost dining venues, and include reservation-only parties in Rita's Cantina and the Seafood Shack. The dress code is smart casual.

Specialty dining packages range from $50 to $120 per person, and save at least 25 percent compared to the sum of the individual restaurants' cover charges.

Casual eateries: All ships have informal venues called Windjammer Café or Windjammer Marketplace for fast food, salads, and the like. Some are of the single-line (move along with your plate) type, while the newer ships have individual islands for more variety and fewer lines. However, the actual quality of cooked food items is nutritionally poor, as are the tacky salad dressings.

Breakfast buffet items are virtually the same each day, monotonous and mostly below the standards of diner food. The same is true of lunchtime salad items. The beverage stations have only the most basic items. Hamburgers and hot dogs in self-serve buffet locations are generally left in steam tables. They are steamed rather than grilled, although you can ask for one to be grilled in front of you. Trays are not provided – only oval plates – so if you are disabled or have mobility difficulties, you may need to ask for help. Also, because the plates are plastic, it's impossible to get your food on a heated plate.

Almost all ships also have Johnny Rockets 1950s-style diners (extra charge, per person, whether you eat in or take out, and, while the food is included, shakes and drinks cost extra). These serve hamburgers, hot dogs, desserts, and sodas, although the typical waiting time is about 30 minutes – pagers are provided, allowing you to wander off in the meantime.

Drinks packages are available in bars, in the form of cards or stickers so that you can pre-pay for a selection of soft drinks and alcoholic drinks. However, the rules for using the pre-paid packages are a bit cumbersome. There is a $3.95 charge for cabin service deliveries midnight–5am.

The coffee/tea factor: Regular coffee: weak, poor quality. Score: 1 out of 10. Espresso/cappuccino coffees (Seattle's Best brand) score 4 out of 10 – but they come in paper cups.

Azura is P&O Cruises most advanced ship.

For children

RCI's new youth programs include 'My Family Time' dining and extra-cost packages such as a supervised 'Lunch and Play' option. An extra-cost in-cabin babysitting service is available.

Adventure Ocean is RCI's 'edutainment' area, while aboard Oasis- and Freedom-class ships, there's also The H2O Zone. Children and teens are divided into seven age-appropriate groups: Royal Babies (six to 18 months); Royal Tots (18–36 months); Aquanauts (three to five years); Explorers (six to eight years); Voyagers (nine to 12 years); Navigators (12–14 years); and Teens (15–17 years).

An unlimited soda and juice package for under-17s is available. There are lots of activities, and a host of children's counselors is aboard each ship.

Best ships for children: *Adventure of the Seas, Allure of the Seas, Explorer of the Seas, Freedom of the Seas, Independence of the Seas, Liberty of the Seas, Mariner of the Seas, Navigator of the Seas, Oasis of the Seas, Voyager of the Seas.* **Ships with fewer facilities:** *Brilliance of the Seas, Enchantment of the Seas, Grandeur of the Seas, Jewel of the Seas, Legend of the Seas, Radiance of the Seas, Rhapsody of the Seas, Serenade of the Seas, Splendour of the Seas, Vision of the Seas.* **Ships with poor facilities for children:** *Majesty of the Seas.*

Entertainment

RCI's entertainment is upbeat, similar to what you would find in a resort hotel in Las Vegas. Production shows are colorful, fast-paced, high-volume razzle-dazzle spectaculars, but with little or no storyline, poor linkage between themes and scenes, and basic choreography. The live band is augmented by pre-recorded backing tracks to make it sound like a big, professional orchestra. Each ship has its resident troupe of singers and dancers.

Then there are silly audience participation events (summer camp-style, but often funny) and activities – something RCI has always done well.

The Smaller Operators

While the major cruise lines dominate the mass market, dozens of smaller companies cater for more specialist tastes and can offer some exotic destinations.

These profiles, in alphabetical order, include cruise lines with boutique (very small), small or mid-size ships and small fleets, those with a small number of large resort ships, those with tall ships (with either real working sail propulsion or computer-controlled assistance), those that specialize in hardy or 'soft' expedition cruises, and those that cruise along coastal and inland waterways.

Abercrombie & Kent (A&K)

Geoffrey Kent started A&K as a safari company in 1962 – there was no Mr Abercrombie, it just sounded good – and then specialized in upscale train journeys around the globe for small groups. The company got started in the cruise business when it went into a marketing agreement with the now defunct Society Expeditions in 1990. Two years later it bought the little expedition ship *Society Explorer* (formerly *Lindblad Explorer*) when Society Expeditions ceased operations. The ship, renamed *National Geographic Explorer*, now belongs to Lindblad Expeditions. Today, A&K specializes in escorted educational and nature cruises, and charters

Germany-based AIDA Cruises is one of the Carnival brands.

various ships, such as those of Swan Hellenic Cruises, for its cruise programs, taking passengers to the more remote destinations such as the Antarctic, in relative comfort. The company is also involved in river cruises and hotel barges, for which it acts as sales agents. Gratuities are not included in the cruise fare.

AIDA Cruises

The former East German shipping company Deutsche Seerederei (DSR) and its marketing arm Seetours (Deutsche Seetouristik) were assigned the traditional cruise ship *Arkona* as part of the east–west integration in 1985, which included a contractual agreement with the Treuhandanstalt (the agency that privatized East German enterprises) to build a new ship. It did this in 1996 with the newly built *Aida*, designed to appeal to young, active German-speaking families. The concept was to create a seagoing version of the popular Robinson Clubs – a sort of German Club Med concept. When *Aida* first debuted, there were almost no passengers and the company struggled.

In 1998 the company was sold to Norwegian Cruise Line, which sold it back to its original Rostock-based owners. P&O acquired it in 1999, and it is now a very successful multi-ship brand belonging to the Carnival Corporation, under the direct control of its Costa Cruises division (which also overseas is Spanish division, called Iberocruceros). AIDA Cruises, Germany's largest cruise line, is known for its über-casual cruising, with two main self-serve buffet restaurants instead of the traditional waiter service. It's a tablecloth-less method of eating, a bit like camping at sea, with little contact with the staff.

Alaskan Dream Cruises

Allen Marine Tours is an operator of local day vessels in Alaska, operating only in Alaska and family-owned by members of the Kaagwaantaan Clans of the Tlingit people. It formed a new micro-cruise company, Alaskan Dream Cruises, in 2010 after buying two Cruise West 78-passenger vessels when Cruise West declared insolvency and ceased operations. *Spirit of Columbia* and *Spirit of Alaska* were converted into *Admiralty Dream* and *Baranhof Dream* in 2011. Gratuities are not included in the cruise fare.

American Cruise Lines

ACL was originally formed in 1974, at the beginning of American coastal passenger shipping, but it went

Queen of the West, American Cruise Lines' paddlewheel riverboat.

bankrupt in 1989, the ships were sold off, and the company lay dormant. The original owner, Charles Robertson, a renowned yachtsman who used to race 12-meter America's Cup yachts, resurrected it in 2000, and built its own ships in its own wholly owned small shipyard in Salisbury, Maryland, on the Chesapeake Bay.

ACL's ships *(American Glory, American Spirit, American Star, Independence)* ply the inter-coastal waterways and rivers of the USA's east coast between Maine and Florida, and provide an up-close, intimate experience for passengers who don't need luxury or much pampering but do like American history and culture, as well as service from an all-American college-age staff. The 'D-class' vessels are less than 2,500 gross tonnage, and are subject neither to bureaucratic regulations nor to union rules.

In 2011, the company also started operating *Queen of the West,* a 120-passenger paddlewheel (replica steamboat) on rivers in the USA's Pacific Northwest. In 2012 it introduced the brand new *Queen of the Mississippi,* a replica steamboat, for Mississippi River cruises. Gratuities are not included in the company's cruise fares.

Antarpply Expeditions

Based in Ushuaia, Argentina, this company specializes in inexpensive Antarctic expedition cruises, including the Falkland Isles, Shetland Isles, and South Georgia, during the Austral summer. It has one expedition ship, *Ushuaia,* but the quality of its voyages and operation should not be confused with the better-run, more experienced European companies. Gratuities are not included in the fare.

Aurora Expeditions

This Australian company was founded in 1993 by Australian Mount Everest veteran and geologist Greg Mortimer and adventure travel specialist Margaret Werner. The company, which specializes in small-group expeditions, uses the chartered expedition ship *Polar Pioneer* for its Antarctic expedition programs. Other destinations include Papua New Guinea, Australia's Kimberley region, and the Russian Far East, for which the ship is the chartered Russian expedition vessel *Akademik Shokalskiy*. Gratuities are not included in the fare.

Azamara Club Cruises

This company, formerly Azamara Cruises, is an offshoot of Celebrity Cruises, and was created in 2007. Having started with little direction, the company was revitalized in 2009–10 by a new president, Larry Pimentel, formerly with SeaDream Yacht Cruises. It operates two 700-passenger ships, taking people to smaller ports that some of the large resort ships can't get into.

The company specializes in providing high-quality dining, and the ships try to provide a floating 'country club' experience. They are in direct competition with the ships of Oceania Cruises – except that Oceania doesn't charge extra to dine in its specialty restaurants. But Azamara has longer port stays and more overnight port stays than Oceania – a bonus during longer itineraries.

Blount Small Ship Adventures

Founded in 1966 by the late Luther H. Blount, an engineer and inventor of the American steam trawler, who built his cruise vessels in his own shipyard in Warren, Rhode Island, the company started as a family-run venture. Today, as the oldest US-flag cruise line still operating, it is run by his daughter, Nancy Blount.

Cruises are operated like private family outings, using two unpretentious ships that were specially constructed to operate in close-in coastal areas and inland waterways of the eastern US seaboard, with forays to the Bahamas and Caribbean during the win-

Crystal Serenity in Malta.

ter. The onboard experience is strictly no-frills cruising in really basic, down-to-earth surroundings that have a 1950s feel.

Its early-to-bed passengers – average age 72 years – are typical of those who don't like glitz or trendy. Gratuities are not included in the cruise fare. Blount Small Ship Adventures introduced select beers and house wines with lunch and dinner on cruises in 2013.

CDF Croisières de France

Founded and wholly owned by Royal Caribbean Cruise Line (RCCL), CDF Croisières de France was created in 2007, with headquarters in Paris. The brand is now under the overall control of Pullmantur Cruises, also owned by RCCL. The company devotes all its resources to cruising for French-speaking passengers, with one ship, the former *Horizon*. The emphasis is on fine French cuisine and all-inclusive pricing. Gratuities are included in the fare.

Celebration Cruise Line

This company, a one-ship operation, is owned by Celebration Cruise Holdings, which also owned the now-defunct Imperial Majesty Cruise Line, whose reputation suffered from high-pressure telemarketing campaigns. Its *Bahamas Celebration* operates two-night cruises from the Port of Palm Beach to the Bahamas.

Despite the company's claims to 'international gourmet dining,' the ship provides a highly programmed but absolutely basic party getaway cruise with very standard food, and with much pressure for onboard revenue from its dining, casino, and shore excursion operations.

Club Med Cruises

Club Med became renowned for providing hassle-free vacations for the whole family. The first Club Med village was started in 1950 on the island of Majorca, but the concept became so popular that it grew to more than 100 vacation villages throughout the world.

Club Med Cruises, an offshoot of the French all-inclusive vacation clubs, introduced its first ocean-going cruise vessel in 1990, the computer-controlled sail-cruise ship *Club Med II* (extensively refurbished in 2008). Aboard the all-inclusive ship, the *gentils ordinaires* serve as both super-cruise staff and 'rah-rah' cheerleaders for the mainly French-speaking passengers. *Club Med II* has a sister ship, Windstar Cruises' *Wind Surf*, which also provides a relaxed onboard experience. Gratuities are included in the fare.

Cruceros Australis

This company, based in Santiago, Chile, operates cruise ships on 'soft' expedition cruises to the Chilean fjords, Patagonia, and Tierra del Fuego – some of the world's most fascinating but hostile environments. Catering increasingly to an international clientele, with Spanish as the official onboard language, cruising with this company is all about Chile and its truly dramatic coastline. Don't expect high standards aboard its two ships, but service is very friendly, and its organization and operations are extremely good. The onboard languages are English and Spanish.

The company introduced a brand new ship in 2010, the 210-passenger *Stella Australis,* and now operates a three-ship fleet. The other two ships are *Mare Australis* and *Via Australis*. Its cruises are 'all-inclusive,' with an open bar for all beverages, including wine, and gratuities included.

Cruise and Maritime Voyages

This UK-based company, which has existed for many years as a sales and marketing organization representing several small cruise lines, now charters two older ships owned by other companies. The company, whose owners originally worked for the now-defunct CTC Cruises, specializes in adults-only (16 and over) cruises from several UK ports, and provides traditional cruise features such as mid-morning bouillon, and captain's welcome and farewell dinners. The onboard product, particularly the food, is at the lower end of the market. *Discovery* and *Marco Polo* are the featured ships for ex-UK cruises (*Discovery* replaced *Ocean Countess* in early 2013). Gratuities are not included in the cruise fare.

Crystal Cruises

Crystal Cruises was founded in 1988 by Nippon Yusen Kaisha (NYK), the world's largest cargo ship and transportation logistics company – with a fleet of more than 700 ships. The American-managed company is based in Century City, Los Angeles. *Crystal Harmony,* the company's first ship, was built in Japan, and debuted in New York in May 1990 to great acclaim. Meanwhile, Crystal Cruises introduced two new ships, *Crystal Symphony* in 1995, and *Crystal Serenity* in 2000, one built in Finland, the other in France.

In 2006 *Crystal Harmony* was transferred to parent company NYK as *Asuka II* for its Asuka Cruise division, for Japanese speakers. Crystal Cruises continues to provide excellent food and service aboard its two spacious ships (*Crystal Serenity* and *Crystal Symphony*), including an excellent Nobu sushi/sashimi bar aboard *Crystal Serenity*.

The ships operate worldwide itineraries with flair. Both ships are superbly maintained, and passengers who seek fine food in a sophisticated setting should be delighted with their choice of ship and company. Open-seating dining was introduced in January 2011 for the first time, or passengers can opt for a choice of fixed-time dining. In spring 2012 Crystal Cruises adopted all-inclusive pricing, with drinks, wines, and gratuities included in the fare.

Disney Cruise Line
Its two large resort ships, *Disney Magic* (1998) and *Disney Wonder* (1999), the first cruise ships since the 1950s to be built with two funnels, cater to loyal Disney followers, and everything aboard the ships is Disney – every song, every piece of artwork, every movie and production show – and Mickey's ears adorn the ships' funnels. But there's no casino (hooray!), and no library (boo!). However, its 'rotation dining' concept proved to be completely Disneylogical; you move, together with your waiter, to each of three identically sized restaurants – each with different decor – in turn.

One new, larger ship, *Disney Dream,* joined the fleet in 2011, and sister ship *Disney Fantasy* arrived in 2012.

Disney is all about families with children, and the ships cater to both. You can buy a package combining a short stay at a Disney resort and a cruise. Disney has its own cruise terminal at Port Canaveral, Florida, its design being an imaginative but close copy of the Ocean Terminal in Southampton, UK, frequented by

yesteryear's ocean liners but little used today. The terminal and pier were extended in 2010 and connected to a new parking garage. Gratuities are not included in the cruise fare.

Fred. Olsen Cruise Lines
This Norwegian family-owned and family-run company was founded in Hvitstein, a town on Oslofjord, Norway, in 1848. Today, a fifth-generation Olsen, Fred Jr, runs the company from its headquarters in Suffolk, England. The group also has interests in the hotels, aviation, shipbuilding, ferries, and offshore industries. The company specializes in cruises for adults who are usually retired and of senior years – typically over 65.

The first ship dedicated exclusively to cruising debuted in 1987, and now ships cruise year-round out of UK ports such as Dover, Southampton, Liverpool, Newcastle, Greenock, Leith, Belfast, and Dublin (ideal for anyone based in the UK to join one of the ships without having to fly), with some ships operating fly-cruises from Canary Island ports, or Caribbean ports such as Barbados in winter.

Coffee- and tea-making facilities are provided in each cabin. Smoking is allowed only on the open decks, and nowhere inside the ships. Gratuities are not included in the cruise fare, but are automatically charged to your onboard account. Drink prices are extremely reasonable aboard all the company's ships, where the social scene is courteous, friendly, and warm.

FTI Cruises
This company, part of the Munich-based FTI Touristik (founded in 1983), bought its only ship from Saga Cruises in 2011 and started its cruise operations in May 2012 for the German-speaking market. The ship, *FTI*

Asuka II leaving port.

Berlin, is well-known in Germany, being the star of the TV series *Traumschiff* (Dream Ship), the long-running show that preceded Aaron Spelling's *The Love Boat* series in the USA.

Galápagos Cruises

Metropolitan Touring, Ecuador's foremost tour and travel company is based in Quito and sells its cruises through general sales agents such as the USA's Dallas-based Adventure Associates. Its pocket-size ships, the well-run *Isabella* and *Santa Cruz,* visit the Galápagos Islands with all-Ecuadorean crew and food. Go because of the nature-filled destination, not for the ships, which are old and have few facilities. Gratuities are not included in the fare.

G Adventures

This Canadian company, based in Toronto, was founded in 1990 as GAP Adventures by Bruce Poon Tip, using only his own personal credit cards. The company has a grassroots approach to travel, creating meaningful, memorable adventures on the path less traveled. It has grown into one of the world's largest adventure travel companies, with over 850 employees, and charters small ships suitable for expedition-style cruises. Its present ship is the 58-cabin MS *Expedition.*

Grand Circle Cruise Line

Ethel Andrus, a retired teacher, wanted to share her vision of helping Americans lead more vital, challenging, and politically active lives. She founded the American Association of Retired Persons (AARP) in 1958. The company has exclusive charters for its small group travel (the company's foundation has donated more than $91 million to cultural, educational, and humanitarian organizations since 1992). For many years, this Boston-based travel company (its brands are Grand Circle Travel, Overseas Adventure Travel, and Grand Circle Cruise Line) has chartered riverships and small ocean-going vessels. The company now has three of its own custom designed and built sea-going ships for in-depth coastal cruises for two groups of 25 persons each (*Arethusa, Artemis, Athena*). However, general cruise/travel agents cannot easily book into the company's cruise programs.

Hapag-Lloyd Cruises

Germany's two most famous ocean liner companies, the Bremen-based Norddeutscher Lloyd and the Hamburg-based Hamburg America Line, merged in 1970 to become Hapag-Lloyd. The company no longer operates regularly scheduled transatlantic crossings. Instead, it promotes five ships in three different market segments.

Two small ships are in the specialized expedition cruise market (the 164-passenger *Bremen* and the 184-passenger *Hanseatic* (run by Hapag-Lloyd Expedition Cruises); one is in the mid-price market (the 684-passenger *Columbus 2*), and two (the more formal 400-passenger *Europa and the more informal 516-passenger Europa 2*) are in the luxury market. All provide destination-intensive cruises aimed at the German-speaking market, with occasional dual-language cruises for English-speakers.

Sea shanty session aboard Hapag-Lloyd Cruises' *Europa.*

Aboard *Europa and Europa 2*, gratuities are not included in the fare, but *Columbus 2* operates certain cruises as 'all-inclusive.' Two ships operate an annual around-the-world cruise, which typically starts in November–December and lasts for three or four months. The *Columbus 2* charter ends in April 2014, however. After this date Hapag-Lloyd will concentrate only on its luxury and expedition cruise clientele. The staff on board makes all its own breads and soups, pâtés, jams, and preserves – all from scratch.

Hapag-Lloyd Expedition Cruises

The company operates two specialist expedition cruise ships, the 164-passenger *Bremen* and the 184-passenger *Hanseatic*. There are occasional dual-language cruises for the English-speaking market, but all the crew speak English anyway.

Both ships carry a fleet of Zodiac inflatable rubber craft for shore landings in the polar region and other destinations with no pier facilities. They have excellent cuisine, proper boot-washing and storage stations, lecture rooms, extensive libraries, and other expedition facilities to suit adventurous itineraries, plus some of the world's best expedition leaders.

Hapag-Lloyd Expedition Cruises is a member of IAATO (International Association of Antarctica Tour Operators), a body committed to the highest standards of responsible tourism to Antarctica and to operating its ships in the most environmentally friendly manner, accompanied by the very best expedition leaders in the business.

Harmony Cruises

This company, founded in 2011, is a new entrant to cruise tourism. A subsidiary of Polaris Shipping (owner of a fleet of 16 bulk ore carriers and one container ship), it is based in Seoul, South Korea, and targets the Korean-speaking market. Its single ship, *Club Harmony* (formerly *Costa Marina*) is specifically geared to Korean tastes, and operates itineraries that highlight Southeast Asia, and particularly Japan. The cruise operation began in March 2012, with the ship based on Seoul, South Korea. The ship is on a three-year charter.

Hebridean Island Cruises

The company (formerly Hebridean International Cruises) was set up in 1989 under the Thatcher government's British Enterprise Scheme, and is headquartered in Skipton, Yorkshire. It operates one all-inclusive boutique ship, *Hebridean Princess,* which conveys the atmosphere of English country-house life – think Laura Ashley fabrics and soft furnishings – and specializes in cruises for mature adults. Gratuities and all port taxes are included, as are most excursions. The ship runs cruises around the Scottish islands. There are occasional sailings to English ports, the Channel Islands, and Norway. Each cabin has coffee- and tea-making

Disney takes its brand to Alaska.

facilities. Gratuities are included in the fare. The Queen granted Hebridean Island Cruises a royal warrant in her jubilee year.

Heritage Expeditions

This youth-minded adventure travel company, based in Christchurch, New Zealand, focuses on small group expedition-style cruising – specifically to Antarctica, the Sub-Antarctic and Russian Far East. The company was founded in 1985 by biologist Rodney Russ who worked for the New Zealand Wildlife Service for many years. The company's single ship, *Spirit of Enderby* was formerly *Professor Khromov,* a small Russian oceanographic research vessel.

Henna Cruises

Henna Cruises is owned by the HNA Group (Hainan), a multi-enterprise industry group that covers air transportation (Hainan Air), airport management, hotel (this division provided the accommodation for the 16th Asian Games in 2010), logistics, real estate, tourism, and other related businesses. It has five airlines, including Grand China Express – among the largest regional airlines in China operating over 30 aircraft on 80 domestic routes. In 2012, this company purchased the former *Pacific Sun* (originally Carnival Cruise Lines' *Jubilee*) from P&O Cruises Australia and became the first mainland China-based company to own and operate a cruise ship for its domestic market. The slogan of HNA Tourism Group is 'My Travel, My Life.' *Henna* (the ship's new name) started operations in January 2013,

Hurtigruten

The company is an amalgamation of two shipping companies (OVDS and TVDS) and provides year-round service along the Norwegian coast, calling at 33 ports in 11 days. Hurtigruten, formerly known as the

Norwegian Coastal Voyage, has also recently developed expedition-style cruises, albeit aboard ships that have been converted for the purpose, rather than specifically built for expedition cruises. So, as long as you think utilitarian and modest decor, you'll get the idea of life aboard one of the Hurtigruten ships, which are practical rather than beautiful. Even aboard the newest ships, the food and service are fairly basic – there's a lack of green vegetables – but the ships provide a great way to see many, many ports along the coast of Norway in a comfortable manner.

Norway's Crown Princess Mette-Marit was the godmother of the newest ship, *Fram,* a 318-berth expedition-style vessel built for polar and Greenland cruising.

Iberocruceros

Founded originally as one of the Iberojet (tour operator) companies, this venture company is 75 percent–owned by the Carnival Corporation and 25 percent by the Orizonia Corporation. The company's ships operate well-organized, all-inclusive cruises for the Spanish-speaking market, in direct competition to Pullmantur Cruises. The onboard product has developed well and now provides a well-established style of cruise and service for the family-friendly cruise segment of Spain's growing cruise market, with three ships: *Grand Celebration, Grand Holiday,* and *Grand Mistral.* Gratuities are included in the fare.

Hapag-Lloyd's *Bremen* in the Corinth Canal, Greece.

Island Cruises

Island Cruises was founded as a joint venture between Royal Caribbean Cruises and the British low-cost tour operator First Choice Holidays. Its first ship started operations in 2002. However, in 2007, First Choice merged with Germany's largest travel company TUI, to become TUI Travel. Its two-ship fleet was reduced to one ship *(Island Escape)* in 2009, and the company is presently operated as a sub-brand of Thomson Cruises.

It provides its mainly British passengers with an 'all-inclusive' cruise experience in ultra-casual, lager lout-style surroundings. Its self-serve, self-carry buffet meals from an always-busy, congested café are the mainstay of the 'culinary' offerings, although slightly better food can be had in a smaller extra-cost dining venue. Gratuities are not included in the fare.

Kristina Cruises

This Finnish Partanen family-owned company was founded in 1985 as Rannikkolinjat to operate short cruises on Lake Saimaa. In 1987 it purchased its first ship and started to open Baltic and Russian ports on the Gulf of Finland to international cruise passengers.

Today, Kristina Cruises owns and operates one modern cruise vessel, *Kristina Katarina,* principally on cruises in the Baltic, Caribbean, and Mediterranean, and continues to preserve nautical traditions on board. Gratuities are not included in the fare, and drinks prices are very high.

Lindblad Expeditions

Lars-Eric Lindblad started the whole concept of expedition cruising with a single ship, *Lindblad Explorer,* in 1969, taking adventurous travelers to remote regions of the world. Today, his son, Sven-Olof Lindblad, runs the company, but with an array of small ships. It's all about nature, wilderness, wildlife, off-the-beaten-path adventures, and learning. Zodiac inflatable craft are used to ferry participants ashore in remote Arctic and Antarctic polar regions.

The ships carry excellent lecturers, who are more academic than entertaining. In partnership with the National Geographic Society, the company operates the wholly-owned *National Geographic Endeavour* and *National Geographic Explorer* (both with ice-strengthened hulls), together with two small ships (*National Geographic Sea Bird* and *National Geographic Sea Lion*) for coastal or 'soft' expedition-style cruising, in, for example, Alaska. National Geographic photographers take part in all cruises. Zodiac inflatable craft are often used for shore landings, and the ships have extensive libraries. Gratuities are not included in the fare. Incidentally, the National Geographic Society celebrated its 125th birth in 2013, when the company also purchased Orion Expedition Cruises, based in Sydney, Australia. *Orion* will be renamed *National Geographic Orion* when the ship is transferred in March 2014.

Louis Olympia off Santorini, Greece

Louis Cruises

In the 1930s and 1940s, Louis Loizou became the undisputed father of tourism in Cyprus. His venture into sea tourism started with the charter of ships transferring immigrants from Cyprus to other continents. His son, Costakis Loizou, who took over the running of the company after his death in 1971, started organizing short cruises from Cyprus and in 1986 Louis Cruises was officially founded with the acquisition of the company's first fully owned ship, *Princesa Marissa*.

Today, Louis Group owns almost two dozen hotels in the Greek islands and Cyprus, together with a multi-ship fleet of mainly older, small and mid-size ships which operate principally from Greece and ports in the Mediterranean. Louis Cruises charters two of its ships to TUI Travel's UK-based Thomson Cruises and has over the years chartered some of its ships to many major UK and European tour operators.

MOPAS

Osaka Shosen Kaisha was founded in 1884 in Osaka, Japan. In 1964 it merged with Mitsui Steamship, to become Mitsui OSK. It is now one of the oldest and largest shipping companies in the world.

It entered cruise shipping in 1989 with *Fuji Maru*, the first cruise ship in the Japanese-speaking domestic market (now no longer in service). The company specialized in incentive meetings and groups at sea rather than cruising for individuals. But the company (formerly known as Mitsui OSK Passenger Line) steadily changed to more cruises for individuals. The company operates a single ship, the highly comfortable *Nippon Maru* (extensively refurbished in 2010), based in Japan for Japanese-speaking passengers. Gratuities are included in the cruise fare.

Noble Caledonia

London-based Noble Caledonia, established in 1991, operates two boutique-size sister ships, *Caledonian Star* and *Island Sky*, each carrying around 100 passengers. It also sells cruises aboard a wide range of small-ship and expedition cruise companies as well as river cruises. It markets to British passengers of mature years, and operates cruises, generally in sheltered water areas, with cultural interest themes, and so is not recommended for children.

The company, whose financial partners include Norway's Salen family, who were very involved with expedition cruising in the past, has an excellent reputation for well-organized cruises and tours, accompanied by good lecturers. It specializes in itineraries impossible to operate aboard larger ships. A Commodore Club gives repeat passengers advance information about new voyages and special offers. Gratuities are not generally included in the fare, unless otherwise stated in the brochures – whether printed or on the Noble Caledonia website.

NYK Cruises

Nippon Yusen Kaisha, the world's largest shipping company, owns the well-known US-based upscale brand Crystal Cruises. It created its own NYK Cruise division – today branded as Asuka Cruise – in 1989 with one Mitsubishi-built ship, *Asuka*, for Japanese-speaking passengers. In 2006, the company sold the original *Asuka* to Germany's Phoenix Reisen, and the former *Crystal Harmony* was transferred from Crystal Cruises to become *Asuka II*. The ship, known for its excellent Japanese and western food, operates an annual around-the-world cruise, plus a wide array of both short and long cruises in the Asia-Pacific region. Coffee- and tea-making facilities are provided in each cabin, as is a large selection of personal toiletries. Gratuities are included in the cruise fare.

Oceania Cruises

The company's ships provide faux English charm in a country-club atmosphere ideal for middle-aged and older couples seeking relaxation. Cruises are usually 10–14 days. Its trademarks are comfortable cabins, warm and attentive service, and fine dining combining French culinary expertise and top-quality ingredients. Breads and baked goods, such as Poilâne-quality croissants, are outstanding.

In 2006, Oceania Cruises was bought by Apollo Management, a private equity company that owns Regent Seven Seas Cruises, and 50 percent of NCL. The brand was placed under the umbrella of Apollo's cruise brand, Prestige Cruise Holdings. With *Nautica* and *Regatta* now very well established and with two new, much larger and faster ships – the 1,250-passenger *Marina* (2011) and *Riviera* (2012) – the company is set to grow.

With multiple-choice dining at no extra cost, the 700- and 1,250-passenger ships suit those who prefer

mid-size ships to large resort vessels. Bottled mineral water, soft drinks, and beer are included in the price. Gratuities are added at $10.50 per person, per day, and butler-service suites have an additional charge of $3 per person. Bar drinks and spa treatments have 15–18 percent added.

Oceanwide Expeditions

Founded in 1961 as the Dutch 'Plancius Foundation' to operate cruises around Spitzbergen (Norway), the company changed its name in 1996 to Oceanwide Expeditions in order to offer adventures farther afield. It specializes in small group polar expedition voyages and active shore visits rather than employing experienced lecturers. It operates two expedition ships, *Ortelius* and *Plancius,* and charters others as needed.

One Ocean Expeditions

Based in Toronto, Canada, this small company was founded by Andrew Prossin. It doesn't own any expedition ships itself, but charters them from the Russian pool of specialist vessels. Environmental responsibility is a key ingredient for its staff, all of whom are personable and very customer-oriented. The company operates two sister specialist polar expedition ships, *Akademik Ioffe* and *Akademik Sergey Vavilov,* on its Arctic and Antarctic programs.

Orion Expedition Cruises

This Australia-based expedition cruise company was created in 2004 by Sarina Bratton, specifically for

The horseshoe staircase aboard Oceania's *Marina*.

'soft' expedition-style cruises to Antarctica, Australia's Kimberley region, Tasmania, and Papua New Guinea and its islands, including Melanesia and the Solomon Islands. The ship *Orion,* built in Germany, is a little gem, with handcrafted cabinetry in every cabin, together with marble bathrooms and a health spa and gymnasium. Shore excursions range from camel safaris to snorkeling over pristine coral formations. In 2008, the company was sold to the US-based KSL Capital Partners, and again was sold in 2013, to Lindblad Expeditions. Gratuities are not included in the fare. In 2014, Orion Expedition Cruises will change name and become Lindblad Expeditions.

P&O Cruises (Australia)

Founded in 1932, this Australian division of P&O Cruises provides fun entertainment for the beer-and-bikini brigade and their families, and specializes in cruises in the Pacific and to New Zealand. The line is maturing, though, becoming more of a mainstream operator – particularly so with its latest ships, three larger, more contemporary hand-me-down vessels (*Pacific Dawn, Pacific Jewel, Pacific Pearl*) from P&O Cruises and Princess Cruises – sister companies that are part of the Carnival Corporation. The ships have open-seating dining and specialty restaurants such as Australian celebrity chef, Luke Mangan's 'Salt Grill.' Gratuities are not included in the cruise fare.

Passat Cruises

This company is a sort of born-again Delfin Cruises, which was declared bankrupt in 2010 with the loss of many jobs. The new owner operates the same ship and some of the same management team. The ship, *Delfin,* has a loyal following, and the new company is trying to continue its traditions.

Paul Gauguin Cruises

Created by Boston-based tour operator Grand Circle Travel, Paul Gauguin Cruises took over the marketing and operation of *Paul Gauguin* in 2009 from Regent Seven Seas Cruises, which had operated the ship since its inception. Also in 2009, the ship was bought by the Tahiti-based investor Richard Bailey and his company Pacific Beachcomber, which owns Polynesian resort hotels (including four InterContinental Hotels). The company acquired a second ship, *Le Levant,* and renamed it *Tere Moana.* Gratuities are not included in the cruise fare.

Peter Deilmann Cruises

Peter Deilmann, a former seagoing navigator, had a dream: to create a cruise company in the best German tradition. He founded his company in 1972. For many years, it also operated a fleet of up to eight riverships and was instrumental in creating some excellent river cruises in Europe. The company got into financial difficulties after its founder died in 2003, and his two

In the Dalmatian islands with Paul Gauguin Cruises.

daughters, who took it over, were unable to keep the river cruise division afloat. The division went into administration in 2009, and the two daughters were declared bankrupt in 2011. However, the oceangoing division is healthy under a new equity investment partner, and operates a single cruise ship with opulent interiors, the 548-passenger, Germany-flagged *Deutschland,* on worldwide itineraries.

Phoenix Reisen

Based in Bonn, Germany, the company for many years operated low-budget, tour-operator-style destination-intensive cruises for German speakers. It now has a loyal, widespread audience and more contemporary ships, with better food and service, particularly aboard *Amadea* and *Artania.*

To keep costs down, Phoenix charters its ships for long periods. It is consistently praised for its extremely good itineraries, particularly on world cruises, its pre- and post-cruise programs, and its excellent value for money. The utterly comprehensive Phoenix brochure provides photographs of its captains and cruise director, as well as bar lists and drink prices – a refreshing change from the brochures provided by most cruise companies. Single-seating dining is standard, as are low drink prices, and there is no constant pushing for onboard revenue – again different from most rivals.

Phoenix acquired *Artania* (formerly P&O Cruises' *Artemis* and originally *Royal Princess,* named by Princess Diana) in 2011. Gratuities are included in the fare.

Plantours Cruises

This company, based in Bremen, Germany, provides low-budget cruises for German speakers aboard its single small, chartered cruise ship, *Hamburg,* which was formerly Hapag-Lloyd Cruises' original *Columbus.* The company also sells cruises on the rivers of Europe and Russia. Gratuities are not included in the cruise fare.

P&O is a growing force in Australia.

Polar Latitudes

Founded by Shanchen Ting, the company's president is John McKeon. The US-based company was founded to create opportunities for people to experience polar travel in a small group environment, with a specific focus on Antarctica, the Falkland Islands, and South Georgia. The company operates one chartered ship, the 112-passenger *Sea Explorer* (formerly *Corinthian II*). The charter is shared by Quark Expeditions, who also market the ship.

Ponant Cruises

The company was founded in 1988 by Philippe Videau and Jean-Emmanuel Sauvé. It started life as La Compagnie des Iles du Ponant, and is a subsidiary of the state-owned CMA CGM (Compagnie Maritime Atlantique/Compagnie Générale Transatlantique), both of which began in 1855 but merged in 1977 to become the world's third largest container shipping firm.

The cruise company, whose head office is in Marseille, France, was created in 1988, and operates one boutique-size high-tech sail ship, *Le Ponant*, for French speakers. In 2004, the company bought the Paris-based tour operator Tapis Rouge International, which specializes in upscale travel. Three new small ships – *Le Boréal*, introduced in 2010, *L'Austral*, introduced in 2011, and *Le Soleal*, introduced in 2013 – provide more space and more options for passengers. The company increasingly markets cruises in both English and French to international passengers, and onboard announcements are made in both languages. Gratuities are not included in the fare. The company was purchased in 2012 by Bridgepoint, a European private equity company.

Pullmantur Cruises

The company was set up as part of Pullmantur, the Spain-based holiday tour operator founded in 1971. Its cruising division was established in 2000 when it bought *Oceanic* (then known as the Big Red Boat) from the defunct Florida operator Premier Cruise Lines. In 2006, Pullmantur Cruises was bought by Royal Caribbean Cruises. The company, mainly serving the Spanish-speaking market, operates all-inclusive cruises for families with children to the Caribbean and Europe and, during the South American summer, serves the Brazilian market. Although most passengers are Spanish, the company now also markets heavily to US and other cruise goers. Gratuities are included in the fare.

Quark Expeditions

Cruising with Quark Expeditions is all about being close to nature, wilderness, wildlife, off-the-beaten-path adventures, and learning. The company, an associate member of IAATO (International Association of Antarctica Tour Operators), an association committed to the highest standards of responsible tourism to Antarctica, Quark Expeditions still specializes in chartering nuclear- and diesel-powered Russian icebreakers, the most powerful in the world, to provide participants with a truly memorable expedition experience. This is adventure cruising for toughies. Gratuities are not included in the cruise fare.

Regent Seven Seas Cruises

The company has a complicated history. It was born out of Seven Seas Cruises, which was originally based in San Francisco to market the cruise ship *Song of Flower* (belonging to 'K'-Line, a cargo operator based in New Jersey), as well as expedition cruises aboard the chartered *Hanseatic* (then belonging to Hanseatic Tours). The lyre, logo of that ship, became RSSC's logo.

For many years, the company was part of the Carlson group, and operated as Radisson Seven Seas Cruises. Carlson Hospitality Worldwide ventured into cruising via its Radisson Hotels International division – hence, Radisson Diamond Cruises (when Radisson Diamond joined in 1992). In 1994 Radisson Diamond Cruises and Seven Seas Cruise Line merged to become Radisson Seven Seas Cruises, and in 2007 it became Regent Seven Seas Cruises. It strives to pay close attention to detail and provide high-quality service aboard its fleet of three small cruise ships *(Seven Seas Mariner, Seven Seas Navigator,* and *Seven Seas Voyager)* operating worldwide itineraries.

In 2007 the company was bought by US-based investment group Apollo Management, and, together with Oceania Cruises, was placed under the umbrella of its Prestige Cruise Holdings. The company spent $40 million to refurbish its three ships in 2009–10.

It provides drinks-inclusive cruising, which means that drinks and gratuities are included in the fare, as are shore excursions – even delightful *illy* coffees are included. Passengers pay extra only for laundry services, beauty services, casino, and other personal items.

Saga Cruises

Saga, based in Folkestone, England, was created by Sydney de Haan as a company offering financial services and holidays to an over-60s clientele. As the company's success grew, it reduced this limitation in 1995 to the over-50s and allowed companions older than 40. Its popular travel flourished because it was good at providing personal attention and competent staff. Instead of sending passengers to ships operated by other companies, it decided to buy its own ships and market its own product under the Saga Holidays brand.

Saga Shipping (Saga Cruises), the cruising division of Saga Holidays, was set up in 1997 when it purchased *Saga Rose* (formerly *Sagafjord*), followed not long after by *Saga Ruby* (formerly *Vistafjord*) and, in 2010, *Saga Pearl II* (formerly *Astoria*). *Saga Sapphire* arrived in 2012.

Another brand, Spirit of Adventure, was added in 2006, the year that parent company Saga and Britain's Automobile Association merged. The 'Adventure' cruise brand ended in November 2013 when *Quest for Adventure* became *Saga Pearl II* again.

The cruise company emphasizes British seamanship and training, and its fleet manages to retain the feel of traditional, elegant, adults-only cruising aboard *Saga Pearl II and Saga Sapphire*. Saga Cruises offers single-seating dining, friendly, attentive service from a

mainly Filipino hotel service crew, and its ships have many single-occupancy cabins. It takes care of all the many little details other lines have long forgotten.

All gratuities are included in the fare. Coffee- and tea-making facilities are provided in each cabin (not *Saga Sapphire*).

Sea Cloud Cruises

The company was founded in 1979 by a consortium of shipowners and investors known as the Hansa Treuhand (active in commercial vessel management, engineering, and construction), headquartered in Hamburg, Germany. It owns and operates two tall ships (sailing vessels), the legendary *Sea Cloud* and *Sea Cloud II*, and European rivership, *River Cloud I*.

The company has many corporate clients who charter the two tall ships, while a number of upscale cruise and travel companies sell cruises to individuals. The onboard style and product delivery are quite upscale, with elegant retro decor and fine food and service. Gratuities are not included in the cruise fare.

Seabourn

Originally founded in 1986 as Signet Cruise Line, the company, then owned by Norwegian industrialist Atle Brynestad, had to change its name in 1988 as a result of a lawsuit brought by a Texas ferry company that had already registered the name Signet Cruise Lines (no ships were ever built for cruising, however).

In 1998, a consortium, which included the Carnival Corporation and Norwegian investors, bought Seabourn Cruise Line and merged its operations into

Seven Seas Voyager in Santorini, Greece.

Seabourn Pride is reflected in the water.

Cunard Line, which was acquired from Kvaerner. The fleet then included its three present ships plus *Seabourn Goddess I* and *Seabourn Goddess II* (bought by SeaDream Yacht Cruises in 2002 and named *SeaDream I* and *SeaDream II*) and *Seabourn Sun* (which became Holland America Line's *Prinsendam*). The Carnival Corporation acquired 100 percent of Seabourn Cruise Line in 1999.

Three new, larger ships joined the company between 2009 and 2011. All three have an aft water-sports platform, as well as more dining and spa options, more space, and more passengers. Seabourn Cruise Line was briefly rebranded as The Yachts of Seabourn in 2009–10, but then became simply Seabourn. The company is managed from within the Holland America Line headquarters in Seattle, USA. Gratuities are included in the fare.

In February 2013, the three smaller ships were sold to Xanterra Parks & Resorts, parent company of Windstar Cruises. *Seabourn Pride* will be delivered in mid-2014, while *Seabourn Legend* and *Seabourn Spirit* will be delivered in April and May 2015, respectively.

SeaDream Yacht Club

Larry Pimentel, an American, and his Norwegian business partner Atle Brynestad, founder of Seabourn Cruise Line (now called, simply, Seabourn), jointly created the company by buying the former Sea Goddess Cruises' ships. They introduced them in 2002 to an audience anxious for exclusivity, personal pampering, and cuisine prepared to order.

The two ships, *SeaDream I* and *SeaDream II*, have been refreshed several times – although *SeaDream I* is, in a better shape than *SeaDream II* – and are of-

ten chartered by companies or private individuals who appreciate the refined, elegant, but casual atmosphere on board. The 100-passenger ships operate year-round in the Caribbean and Mediterranean, and provide all-inclusive beverages and open-seating dining at all times, and a high degree of personalized service, all in a cozy, club-like atmosphere, with great attention to detail and personal idiosyncrasies. Atle Brynestad is the company's chairman and sole owner, while Larry Pimentel is now with Azamara Cruises. Gratuities are included in the fare.

Silversea Cruises

Silversea Cruises is a mostly privately owned cruise line. It was founded in 1992 by the Lefebvre D'Ovidio family from Rome (previously co-owners of Sitmar Cruises; 90 percent partners are the Lefebvre D'Ovidios, 10 percent by V-Ships) and is based in Monaco.

Antonio Lefebvre D'Ovidio was a maritime lawyer and professor of maritime law before acquiring and operating cargo ships and ferries in the Adriatic. He took the family into partnership with Boris Vlasov's Vlasov Group (V-Ships) to co-own Sitmar Cruises until that company merged with Princess Cruises in 1988.

Silversea Cruises has generated tremendous loyalty from its frequent passengers, who view the ships as their own. All seven Silversea ships have teak verandas and all-inclusive beverages. Open-seating dining prevails at all times, and the company is known for its partnership with the hospitality organization Relais & Châteaux. A new, larger, 540-passenger all-suite luxury ship, *Silver Spirit*, debuted at the end of 2009, while *Silver Whisper* and *Silver Shadow* were refurbished in 2010 and 2011. Silversea Cruises has two specialist ships for expedition cruising (*Silver Explorer* and *Silver Galapagos,* added in 2008 and 2013, respectively). Gratuities are included in the fare for all ships as part of the company's 'all-inclusive' culture.

Star Clippers
Swedish-born yachtsman Mikhail Krafft founded Star Clippers in 1991 with *Star Flyer* and then *Star Clipper,* both true tall ships. The company went on to build the largest tall ship presently sailing, the five-mast *Royal Clipper,* a truly stunning ship under sail. Friendly service in a casual, extremely laid-back setting, under the romance of sail (when there is enough wind), is what Star Clippers is all about, and the food variety, creativity, and quality are all extremely good.

These real tall (sail-cruise) ships sail in the Caribbean, Baltic, and Mediterranean. Gratuities are not included in the fare.

Star Cruises
Presently part of the world's third-largest cruise operator, the company was incorporated in 1993 as a subsidiary of Malaysia's Genting Berhad, set up in 1965 by the late Tan Sri Dr Lim Goh Tong as an Asian multinational corporation. Today, Star Cruises is formally known Star Cruises/Genting Hong Kong but still comes under the umbrella of Genting Berhad. The group's various business include palm oil production, power generation, property development, biotechnology, oil and gas production, together with leisure activities including resort hotels and casino/entertainment complexes in Malaysia, Manila, and Singapore, and cruise ships. Almost single-handedly, Star Cruises opened up the Asia-Pacific cruise region (except for Japan).

Genting Hong Kong operates ships dedicated to specific markets. Its brands include Star Cruises and Norwegian Cruise Line (jointly owned with Apollo Management).

Star Cruises also owns the pier facility in Langkawi. Its marketing base is in Hong Kong. Its ships are *MegaStar Aries* (1991), *Star Pisces* (1990), *SuperStar Aquarius* (1993), *SuperStar Libra* (1988), and *SuperStar Virgo* (1999). Gratuities are included in all fares.

Swan Hellenic Cruises
Founded in 1954 By R.K. Swan, the company chartered small cruise ships for years. The company was bought by P&O Cruises in 1982, and then it changed hands when Carnival Corporation merged with P&O in April 2004. In 2007, the Carnival Corporation disbanded Swan Hellenic, and its single ship *(Minerva II)* was transferred to the Princess Cruises fleet to become *Royal Princess* (now P&O Cruises' *Adonia*). Some months later, a semi-retired Lord Sterling purchased the brand from the Carnival Corporation and

joined forces with the UK's Voyages of Discovery to operate as a separate brand. So, the 'swanners,' as its clever passengers are called, now have their own ship *(Minerva).*

The company's strengths are its program of highly academic lecturers and speakers, in a small-ship setting that is unpretentious but comfortable, and includes gratuities, drinks (on Antarctic voyages), tailor-made shore excursions, and entrance fees to museums and places of interest. The company operates special-interest themes such as archaeology, history, nature, and wildlife. Coffee- and tea-making facilities are provided in each cabin. Gratuities are included in the fare.

Thomson Cruises
Thomson Cruises' first foray into cruising was in 1973 when it chartered two ships, *Calypso* and *Ithaca,* from the Greek-owned Ulysses Line. It was not a success, and the company withdrew from cruising two years later. Ulysses Line became known as Useless Line.

The company started again in 2002 after seeing rival tour operator Airtours operate ships successfully. Thomson Cruises charters its ships, preferring instead to leave ship operations, management, and catering to specialist maritime companies. The company operates cruises for the whole family aboard its ships – *Thomson Dream, Thomson Majesty,* and *Thomson Spirit* – catering principally to the British market, but also to the Scandinavian market. A whole range of cruises is marketed as adults-only.

Thomson Cruises operates sub-brand Island Cruises, with just one ship, *Island Escape,* for the ultra-casual market. Basic gratuities are included in the price. The company owns its own airline, Thomsonfly, part of the TUI Travel group.

Transocean Cruises
Founded in 1954, Transocean Cruises (formerly Transocean Tours) has headquarters in Bremen, Germany. The company specializes in providing low-cost but high-value cruises aboard a ship under long-term

Top of the Yacht Bar aboard *SeaDream I.*

Aegean Odyssey in Ko Samui, Thailand.

charter *(Astor)*, with traditional decor and excellent itineraries. The company also sells river cruises, operated by chartered vessels under the banner of Transocean River Cruises. The ship was sub-chartered to the UK's Cruise & Maritime Voyages for cruises in Australasia. Gratuities and all port charges are included in the fare.

Travel Dynamics International

Founded by brothers George and Vasos Papagapitos, the company specializes in providing small and boutique cruise ships to culturally minded passengers. Long a provider of vacations and cruises to university alumni, cultural associations, and museum groups, the company seeks out unusual itineraries and destinations according to a group's interest or travel theme. It is also known for its US Great Lakes cruises (with its chartered ship *Yorktown*), cruises to remote regions, and for its academically trained lecturers. Gratuities are not included in the fare.

TUI Cruises

The German-owned TUI Group has several divisions, but started its own cruise line in 2009 with *Mein Schiff*, a large resort ship (formerly *Celebrity Galaxy*) that underwent a massive reconstruction program. *Mein Schiff 2* (formerly *Celebrity Mercury*) was added in 2011. Two new ships – *Mein Schiff 3* will debut in spring 2014, with *Mein Schiff 4* arriving in 2015.

Aboard all TUI Cruises ships, all cabins have their own espresso machine, and there is a wide choice of dining venues and food styles, with an emphasis on healthy eating. Much emphasis is placed on the extensive wellness facilities aboard its ships. Gratuities are included in the fare.

Un-Cruise Adventures

This micro-cruise line was founded in 1997 as American Safari Cruises. It was bought in 2008 by InnerSea Discoveries, owned by the former chief executive officer of American Safari Cruises, Dan Blanchard. ASC It bought the website and database files of now defunct Cruise West in order to expand its reach to small-ship enthusiasts, and has a fleet of very small motor yacht-type vessels for six to 86 passengers taking expensive cruises in Alaska and the Pacific Northwest. While the vessels are decent, the onboard facilities are few and the one-seat dining experience is quite casual. However, they all have superb Tempur-Pedic mattresses. The advantage of these intimate vessels is that they really can take you up close to fascinating parts of Alaska that large resort ships can't reach. Gratuities are not included. InnerSea Discoveries changed its name to Un-Cruise Adventures in 2013.

Venus Cruise

Founded in 1988, the company's headquarters are in Osaka, Japan. Venus Cruise, which was first known as Japan Cruise Line, is owned by four ferry companies: Shin Nipponkai Ferry, Kyowa Shoji, Hankyu Ferry, and Kanko Kisen. As Japan Cruise Line, the company at first operated company and incentive charter cruises before branching out into cruises for individuals. The company, catering exclusively to Japanese speakers, has a single one ship, *Pacific Venus,* which operates an annual around-the-world cruise as well as shorter Asia-Pacific cruises. Gratuities are included in the cruise fare.

Viking Ocean Cruises

A sister company to the long-established Viking River Cruises, the company aims to provide both oceangoing and river cruises to the same market segment. Its chairman is Torstein Hagen, originally a one-third owner of the long-defunct Royal Viking Line. So the Viking connection lives on!

A sneak preview of one of a pair of 928-passenger, mid-size ships on order for this new company – a sister company to the long-established Viking River Cruises – reveals that, for their size, the ships will offer an outstanding array of public rooms and dining options. The first in a series of ships is scheduled to debut in spring 2015.

One of the company's objectives is to provide both oceangoing and river cruises to the same group of passengers – this is unique in the cruise industry at present. Watch this space.

Voyages of Discovery

UK-based Roger Allard and Dudley Smith jointly founded the company to offer low-cost cruises aboard comfortable and roomy but older small ships, to UK passengers, but with good food and service. The company's *Discovery* is one of the former 'Love Boats' of US television fame, but is now operated by Cruise & Maritime Voyages. It was replaced by *Voyager* in late 2013. Voyages of Discovery went public in 2006 and, with the help of Lord Sterling of Plaistow, purchased Swan Hellenic Cruises. It now operates both brands from its HQ in the south of England, and also owns the premium brand Hebridean Island Cruises.

Voyages to Antiquity

Founded in 2007 by Gerry Herrod, who formerly created the now defunct Ocean Cruise Lines, the company has just one ship, *Aegean Odyssey,* painstakingly converted into a comfortable cruise ship with a fairly handsome profile. It operates seven- and 14-day cruises to ancient lands, specializing in the Aegean and Mediterranean regions and Asia. The cruises are aimed at British and American passengers who seek educational experiences. Gratuities to dining and housekeeping staff are included, as are most shore excursions, and wines with lunch and dinner.

Windstar Cruises

Founded by New York-based Karl Andren in 1984 as Windstar Sail Cruises, the company built high-class sail-cruise ships with computer-controlled sails, outfitting them in a contemporary decor designed by Marc Held. The first ship, *Wind Star*, debuted in 1986 to much acclaim, and was followed by *Wind Spirit* (1988) and *Wind Surf* (1990).

Windstar Cruises was sold to Holland America Line in 1988. The company, with headquarters in Seattle, USA, was sold again in 2007 to the Ambassadors Cruise Group, wholly owned by Ambassadors International. It was purchased again in 2011 by Xanterra Parks & Resorts.

The style is casual and unregimented, but smart, with service by Indonesian and Filipino crew. The ships carry a variety of water-sports equipment, accessed from a retractable stern platform. Itineraries include off-the-beaten-track ports not frequented by large resort ships. The onboard product is decidedly American ultra-casual, with unfussy bistro-style cuisine, and service that lacks the finesse and the small details that could make it a much better experience overall. Gratuities are not included in the fare.

Between mid-2014 and mid-2015, Windstar Cruises will take delivery of three Seabourn ships – *Seabourn Legend, Seabourn Pride,* and *Seabourn Spirit.*

Zegrahm Expeditions

This small expedition cruise company, which takes inquisitive travelers to remote or unusual destinations, including the Arctic and Antarctica, was founded in 1990 and bought in 2009 by TUI Travel. Although it doesn't own any ships, it charters high-quality specialized vessels. It also sells cruises operated by other expedition companies and operates safaris and small-group adventure vacations. Two- or three-week expedition cruises are headed by experienced leaders and expert naturalists. Gratuities are not included in the fare.

Sea Lion with *Silver Galapagos* in the distance.

Living in Luxury

Of the 70-plus cruise lines operating internationally, only a handful provide the kind of stylish ships aboard which the word 'no' is virtually unheard.

Luxury cruises versus standard (large resort ship) cruises are like the difference between a Bentley automobile and a motor scooter. 'Luxury cruising' should be a flawless combination of ship, facilities, food, and service. Unfortunately, the word has been degraded by marketing people and advertising agencies – you can even buy a 'luxury' burger these days – but the accompanying panel tells you what the term ought to mean in a cruise ship.

Little and large

Size is important. Boutique and small ships can get into ports that larger ships can't. They can also get closer to the center of large cities. For example, in St. Petersburg, Russia, large and mid-size ships (such as those of Crystal Cruises and Regent Seven Seas Cruises) dock about one hour from the city center, while boutique ships such as those of Hapag-Lloyd Cruises, Silversea Cruises, or Seabourn can dock right next to the Hermitage Museum in the heart of the city.

One area where 'luxury' ships differ least from large resort ships is in shore excursions, particularly in the Caribbean and Alaska, where almost all cruise operators are obliged to use the same specialist tour operators ashore – simply because 'luxury' is virtually unknown in these regions and local tour operators consider all cruise passengers to be the same.

Large resort ships (carrying more than 1,750 passengers) simply cannot provide the kind of personal service and attention to detail that the boutique/small ships can. Although you can book one of the largest suites afloat aboard a large ship and have a really good cruise, once you leave your 'private living space' you'll have to mix with everyone else, particularly if you want to go to a show, have an informal alfresco meal or coffee in the café, disembark at ports of call (think: lines at gangway security checkpoints), or go on organized shore excursions. That's when you appreciate the fact that smaller may suit you better.

These are ships suited to those not seeking the active, family- and entertainment-driven cruise experiences that large resort ships offer, and provide facilities and service levels hard to find elsewhere. While most of them boast about being the best, or boast the awards they receive annually from various magazines (whose respondents are almost never global in scope), not all provide the same degree of luxury, and there *are* differences in the cruise product delivered.

What are the differences?

Once you know the main differences, you'll be better equipped to choose the right cruise line and ship to provide the level of food and service you're looking for. Although most of the differences are immediately noticeable when you sail aboard (and compare) them all, some of the variations in style and service are more subtle. One thing is certain: the word 'no' will be virtually unheard.

Some have more crew per passenger. Some have more public space per passenger. Some have more expensive European crew. Some have better food and service. Some have entertainment, some don't. Some have more fresh flowers in public areas than others – they're very evident aboard the ships of Hapag-Lloyd Cruises but not aboard Silversea Cruises' ships, for instance.

Crystal Cruises, for example, has an excellent program of cultural lecturers, professional bridge (card game, not the navigation bridge) instructors, together with its Yamaha 'Passport to Music' program on each cruise, whereas others (SeaDream, Regent, Seabourn, and Silversea) don't. Hapag-Lloyd has excellent lectur-

20 things to expect

1. Flawless (well, close to) personal service and attention to detail.
2. Real (not faux) Champagne at embarkation.
3. Personalized stationery.
4. Pillow choice menu.
5. A crew that anticipates your needs, responds quickly to your requests, and doesn't say 'no' or 'impossible.'
6. No announcements (except for emergencies).
7. No background music in public rooms, hallways, and elevators.
8. High Passenger Space Ratio (35 to 83 gross tonnage per passenger).
9. High Crew to Passenger Ratio (1.5 to 1.0 or better).
10. Finest-quality bed linens, duvets, towels, and bathrobes.
11. High-quality toiletries (e.g., Aveda, Bulgari, etc.).
12. Gratuities included in the fare.
13. No extra charge for on-demand movies or music.
14. No machinery vibration (engines/propulsion equipment).
15. No lines anywhere.
16. More overnight port stays.
17. Separate gangway for passengers and crew (where possible).
18. Shoeshine service.
19. No signing for drinks or other items.
20. European hotel service crew.

A moment of serenity aboard *Crystal Serenity*.

ers, and a PGA golf professional aboard every cruise.

Also, the following facilities and services are found aboard the ships of Hapag-Lloyd Cruises, SeaDream Yacht Cruises, and Seabourn, but not aboard the ships of Crystal Cruises, Regent Seven Seas Cruises, or Silversea Cruises:

Anticipation – more widely practiced by a staff that is better trained and is better at passenger recognition (remembering your name).

Waiters/waitresses escort guests to the dining table and to the dining room exit after meals.

Relaxed embarkation/disembarkation at your leisure. Cabin stewardesses leave handwritten notes.

There are no announcements, and no mindless background music plays in public rooms, accommodation hallways, or elevators.

The chef invites passengers to accompany him/her on visits to local food markets.

More space, better service

These ships have an excellent amount of open deck and lounging space, and a high Passenger/Space Ratio when compared to large resort ships (which are typically under 35), the two SeaDreams being the exception.

Almost all have a better Crew to Passenger Ratio than the large resort ships. In warm-weather areas, the ships of SeaDream Yacht Cruises and Seabourn, all of which have fold-down platforms at the stern, provide jet skis, kayaks, snorkeling gear, windsurfers, and the like at no extra cost, typically for one day each cruise (the others do not).

Hapag-Lloyd's *Europa* (space ratio: 70.4) and *Europa 2* (space ratio: 83.0) both have a fleet of Zodiac rigid inflatable craft for in-depth exploration and shore adventures, plus an ice-hardened hull and crew members who understand the *culture* of their passengers. And mattresses that are 7ft (2.1m) long.

A good night's sleep

These ships feature premium-quality mattresses and bed linen (all of 100% cotton, with a thread count of 200 or more). There's always a little brand-consciousness going on, and some may be better than others.

Crystal Cruises, for example, features Bellora, from Milan (made in India using Egyptian cotton). Silversea Cruises features Egyptian cotton sheets, pillowcases, and duvet covers by Pratesi, founded in 1860, whose custom-made linens come from Tuscany, Italy – the company is known for supplying the Italian and other European aristocracy.

Good pillows are also important for a good night's sleep. You may be able to choose one of several different shapes and fillings. Crystal Cruises' pillow menu, for example, offers a choice of seven:

Side Sleeper Pillow (down or down alternative); Back Sleeper Pillow (down or down alternative); Stomach Sleeper Pillow (down or down alternative); Body Pillow (down alternative).

Depending on the cruise line, other choices might include hypoallergenic, hop-filled, or lavender-scented pillows.

View of the Winter Palace in St. Petersburg, Russia, from the Neva river.

A good night's sleep – outside

For something quite different, SeaDream Yacht Cruises has delightfully indulgent Balinese Dream Beds for sleeping under the stars – in a secluded area at the front of the ship on the uppermost open deck – a delightful idea for honeymooners or anyone celebrating a special occasion. Custom-made pajamas are supplied, and you can take them home. Hapag-Lloyd's *Europa 2* also has 12 Balinese beds.

Creative cuisine

Fine dining is the highlight of ships in this category and is more of an entertainment feature than the ship's entertainment shows – if there are any. Good company and conversation are crucial. You can expect to find plenty of tables for two, a calm refined dining atmosphere, open or one-seating dining, by candlelight (when permitted), high-quality china and silverware, large wine glasses, fresh flowers, a connoisseur wine list, and sommeliers who can discuss fine wines. Service should be unhurried (not like the two-seating ships, where meals tend to be served as speed trials by waiters), well-paced, and unobtrusive.

It's really about non-repetitive, highly creative menus, high-quality ingredients, moderate portions, and attractive presentation, with fresh local fish and other items provided (when available) and cooked to order (not in batches), and meat of the highest grade. Caviar, foie gras, black/white truffles and other exotic foods, and fresh green vegetables (instead of frozen or canned vegetables) are provided. Caviar aboard *Europa* and *Europa 2* is usually from French farmed sturgeon, and is excellent, while caviar aboard most other ships in this category is from the American farmed hackleback variety of sturgeon, or paddlefish caviar (nowhere near as good). The caviar (from Uruguay) aboard the Seabourn ships is quite decent, however.

Most of the ships provide silver covers for main courses, creating extra wow effect. Passengers may

also be invited to visit local markets with the chef aboard the ships of Hapag-Lloyd Cruises, Seabourn, and SeaDream Yacht Cruises.

Some luxury ships provide even more special touches. *Europa* and *Europa 2*, for example, make their own breakfast preserves and ice cream, on board. Strangely, Regent Seven Seas Cruises does not have fish knives – needed if you like to debone the Dover sole yourself. *Europa* uses only loose tea (over 30 types) – all the others use teabags of varying quality.

Typically, lunch and dinner menus are provided in your suite/cabin in advance, and special orders are often possible. Room service menus are extensive, and meals can be served in your suite/cabin (either on the balcony or inside on portable tables). It is also possible to have a special dinner setup on deck – wonderful in the right location.

Drinks: included or not?

Crystal Cruises, Regent Seven Seas Cruises, Seabourn, SeaDream Yacht Cruises, and Silversea Cruises provide wine with dinner (Crystal Cruises, Seabourn, and Silversea also include wine with lunch), although the wines are typically young, and not from first-class houses. However, real premium brands and classic vintage wines cost extra.

Hapag-Lloyd Cruises charges for all alcoholic beverages (beer and soft drinks are provided in each cabin/suite). Crystal Cruises and Regent Seven Seas Cruise Line provide an all-inclusive product, including gratuities. Crystal, Regent, SeaDream, Seabourn, and Silversea include all drinks (but only standard brands). Hapag-Lloyd Cruises doesn't include alcoholic drinks, because its passengers know and want their favorite brands, many of which are well above the level of standard brands carried by those cruise lines that do include alcoholic beverages, which are normally tailored to suit North American tastes (also, its non-drinking passengers do not want to subsidize those that drink).

Other differences

Aboard the ships of Regent Seven Seas Cruises and Seabourn, white plastic deck lounge chairs are provided. Aboard the ships of SeaDream Yacht Cruises they are made of teak (or other hardwood). Aboard Hapag-Lloyd Cruises' *Europa* and *Europa 2* they are made of aluminum and wood, while aboard the ships of Silversea Cruises they are made of faux-wicker or aluminum.

Crystal Serenity, Crystal Symphony, Europa, Europa 2, Seven Seas Mariner, Seven Seas Navigator, and *Seven Seas Voyager* that include entertainment featuring multi-cast production shows and cabaret acts. To a lesser extent, so do the Seabourn and Silversea Cruises ships; the others do not have entertainment as such, but instead rely on their intimacy and friendliness, and promote after-dinner conversation or, aboard the ships of Silversea Cruises, individual specialist cabaret acts.

Comparing the luxury ships

Ship Name	Company	Size	Pod Propulsion	Passenger Space Ratio	Crew to Passenger Ratio	Cabins w/ Balcony	Largest Suite (sq.m)	Tips incl.	Watersports Toys	Hand-held Showers	Toiletries
Crystal Serenity	Crystal Cruises	Mid-Size	Yes	62.6	1.7	466	125	Yes	No	Yes	Aveda
Crystal Symphony	Crystal Cruises	Mid-Size	No	53.1	1.7	276	91.2	Yes	No	Yes	Aveda
Europa	Hapag-Lloyd Cruises	Small	Yes	69.6	1.5	168	85	Yes	No	Yes	Own Brand
Europa 2	Hapag-Lloyd Cruises	Small	Yes	83.0	1.3	258	114	Yes	No	Yes	Own Brand
Marina	Oceania Cruises	Mid-Size	No	51.6	1.5	593	185	No	No	Yes	L'Occitane
Paul Gauguin	Paul Gauguin Cruises	Small	No	57.8	1.5	89	54.6	Yes	Yes	Yes	L'Occitane
Riviera	Oceania Cruises	Mid-Size	No	51.6	1.5	593	185	No	No	Yes	L'Occitane
Seabourn Legend *	Seabourn	Boutique	No	46.9	1.3	6	53.5	Yes	Yes	Yes	Therapies (Molton Brown)
Seabourn Odyssey	Seabourn	Small	No	71.1	1.3	199	133.6	Yes	Yes	Yes	Therapies (Molton Brown)
Seabourn Pride *	Seabourn	Boutique	No	46.9	1.3	6	53.4	Yes	Yes	Yes	Therapies (Molton Brown)
Seabourn Quest	Seabourn	Small	No	71.1	1.3	199	133.6	Yes	Yes	Yes	Therapies (Molton Brown)
Seabourn Sojourn	Seabourn	Small	No	71.1	1.3	199	133.6	Yes	Yes	Yes	Therapies (Molton Brown)
Seabourn Spirit *	Seabourn	Boutique	No	46.9	1.3	6	53.4	Yes	Yes	Yes	Therapies (Molton Brown)
SeaDream I	SeaDream Yacht Cruises	Boutique	No	39.4	1.2	0	45.5	Yes	Yes	Yes	Bulgari
SeaDream II	SeaDream Yacht Cruises	Boutique	No	39.4	1.2	0	45.5	Yes	Yes	Yes	Bulgari
Seven Seas Mariner	Regent Seven Seas Cruises	Mid-Size	Yes	67.8	1.6	354	142	Yes	No	Yes	Canyon Ranch
Seven Seas Navigator	Regent Seven Seas Cruises	Mid-Size	No	58.2	1.5	196	109	Yes	No	Yes	Canyon Ranch
Seven Seas Voyager	Regent Seven Seas Cruises	Mid-Size	Yes	59	1.6	354	130	Yes	No	Yes	Canyon Ranch
Silver Cloud	Silversea Cruises	Small	No	57.1	1.4	110	122	Yes	No	No	Bulgari
Silver Shadow	Silversea Cruises	Small	No	72.8	1.3	157	133.3	Yes	No	No	Bulgari
Silver Spirit	Silversea Cruises	Small	No	66.6	1.4	258	150	Yes	No	No	Bulgari
Silver Whisper	Silversea Cruises	Small	No	72.8	1.3	157	133.3	Yes	No	No	Bulgari
Silver Wind	Silversea Cruises	Small	No	57.1	1.4	110	122	Yes	No	No	Bulgari

Booking and Budgeting

Is it better to book a cruise directly with the operator
or through a specialist cruise agency? And what hidden
extras should you look for when calculating costs?

Booking direct

In the 1960s, about 90 percent of all cruises were
booked by passengers directly with cruise lines and
about 10 percent were booked by travel agents. Then
along came some enterprising travel agents. They saw
an opportunity and started to act on behalf of the cruise
lines, which were happy to accept such bookings because they could then reduce staff and overheads in
their sales offices.

Established companies such as American Express
and Thomas Cook booked cruises, as did many others, and received a commission. Today, about 80 percent of all cruises are booked by travel agents, and
about 20 percent are booked direct (including Internet bookings).

When you see newspaper adverts for cruises, check
what's included in any heavily discounted offers. Make
sure that all port charges, government fees, and any additional fuel surcharges are included in the quote.

Accessing the internet aboard *Seven Seas Mariner*.

The Internet

The Internet may be a useful *resource* tool, but it is not
the place to book your cruise, unless you know exactly
what you want, and can plan ahead. You can't ask questions, and most of the information provided by the cruise
companies is strictly marketing hype. Most sites providing cruise ship reviews have something to sell, and the
sound-byte information can be misleading or outdated.
Also, many discounts for senior citizens, military personnel, and alumni groups, or special discounts for various regions and locales are typically not available on the
web, but only through cruise-booking agencies

If you book with an Internet-based cruise agency
or wholesaler: 1) Confirm with the cruise line that the
booking has been made. 2) Confirm that final payment
has been received. 3) Be aware that many Internet
booking agents are unlicensed and unregulated – some
add a 'booking fee' – which can be substantial.

The Internet vs travel agents

So, you've found a discounted rate for your cruise on
the net. That's fine. But, if a cruise line suddenly offers
special discounts for your sailing, or cabin upgrades,
or if things go wrong with your booking, your Internet booking service may prove unfriendly or may even
have disappeared. Your travel agent, however, can probably make special discounts work for you and perhaps
even provide upgrades. It's called personal service.

Large travel agency groups and consortiums, such
as American Express, often reserve huge blocks of
cabins, and smaller independent agencies can access
extensive discounts not available on the Internet. Fur-
thermore, the cruise lines consider travel agents as
their distribution system and provide special discounts
and value-added amenities that are not provided over
the Internet.

Travel agents

Travel agents do not charge for their services, although
they earn a commission from cruise lines. Consider a
travel agent as your business advisor, not just a ticket
agent. He/she will handle all matters relevant to your
booking and should have the latest information on
changes of itinerary, cruise fares, fuel surcharges, discounts, and any other related items, including insurance in case you have to cancel prior to sailing – perhaps for medical reasons. Travel agents are linked into
cruise line computer systems and have access to most
shipboard information.

Deck service aboard *Balmoral*.

Your travel agent should find exactly the right ship for your needs and lifestyle. Some sell only a limited number of cruises and are known as 'preferred suppliers,' because they receive 'overrides' on top of their normal commission (they probably know their limited number of ships well, however).

10 Questions to ask a travel agent

1. Is air transportation included in the cabin rate quoted? If not, what will be the extra cost? What other extra costs will be involved? These can include port charges, insurance, gratuities, shore excursions, laundry, and drinks.
2. What is the cruise line's cancellation policy?
3. If I want to make changes to my flight, routing, dates, and so on, will the insurance policy cover everything in case of missed or canceled flights?
4. Does your agency deal with only one, or several different insurance companies?
5. Does the cruise line offer advance booking discounts or other incentives?
6. Do you have preferred suppliers, or do you book any cruise on any cruise ship?
7. Have you sailed aboard the ship I want to book or that you are recommending?
8. Is your agency bonded and insured? If so, by whom?
9. If you book the shore excursions offered by the cruise line, is insurance coverage provided?
10. Can I occupy my cabin on the day of disembarkation until I am ready to disembark?

If you have chosen a ship and cruise, be firm and book exactly what you want, or change agencies. In the UK, look for a member of the Guild of Professional Cruise Agents. ACE (Association for Cruise Education), part of the UK's Passenger Shipping Association, provides in-depth agent training, as well as a full 'bonding' scheme to protect passengers from failed cruise lines. In the US, look for a CLIA (Cruise Lines International Association) affiliated agency, or one belonging to the National Association of Cruise Oriented Agencies (NACOA) or the National Association of Commissioned Travel Agents (NACTA).

Reservations
Plan ahead and book early. After choosing a ship, cruise, date, and cabin, you pay a deposit that is roughly 10 percent for long cruises, 20 percent for short cruises. The balance is normally payable 45 to 60 days before departure. For a late reservation, you pay in full when space is confirmed (when booking via the Internet, for example). Cruise lines reserve the right to change prices in the event of tax increases, fluctuating exchange rates, fuel surcharges, or other costs beyond their control.

When you make your reservation, also make special dining requests known, and any seating preferences. It's useful to keep a note of them.

After the line has received full payment, your cruise ticket will be sent by mail, or as an e-document. Check all documents. Make sure the ship, date, and cruise de-

Waterskiing in Labadee, on the coast of Haiti, in the Caribbean.

tails are correct, and verify connecting flight times that seem suspiciously short.

Extra costs

Cruise brochures boldly proclaim that 'almost everything's included,' but in most cases you will find this is not true. In fact, for some cruises 'all-exclusive' would be a more appropriate term. In the recent credit crisis, many cruise lines cut their fares dramatically in order to attract business. At the same time, the cost of many onboard items went up. So allow for extra onboard costs.

Your fare covers the ship as transportation, your cabin, meals, entertainment, activities, and service on board; it typically does not include alcoholic drinks, laundry, dry cleaning or valet services, shore excursions, meals ashore, spa treatments, wine/martini tasting seminars, gratuities, port charges, cancellation insurance, or optional onboard activities such as gambling.

Expect to spend at least $25 a day per person on extras, plus $10–$12 a day per person in gratuities (unless they are included in the price of the cruise; check with your cruise line or travel agent for details).

Calculate the total cost of your cruise (not including any extra-cost services you might decide you want once on board) with the help of your travel agent. Here are the approximate prices per person for a typical seven-day cruise aboard a well-rated mid-size or large cruise ship, based on an outside-view two-bed cabin:

Cruise fare: $1,000
Port charges: $100 (if not included)
Gratuities: $50
Total per person: $1,150

This is less than $165 per person per day. For this price, you wouldn't get a decent hotel room, without meals, in London, Miami, New York, Tokyo, or Venice.

However, your seven-day cruise can become expensive when you start adding on any extras. For example, add two flight-seeing excursions in Alaska (at about $250 each), two cappuccinos each a day ($25), a scotch and soda each a day ($35), a massage ($125), 7 mineral waters ($28), 30 minutes' access to the Internet for email ($15), three other assorted excursions ($150), and gratuities ($50). That's an extra $928 – without even one bottle of wine with dinner! So a couple will need to add an extra $1,856 for a seven-day cruise, plus the cruise fare, of course, and the cost of getting to and from your local airport, or ship port.

Discounts and incentives

Book ahead to get the best discounts (they normally decrease closer to the cruise date). You may be able to reserve a cabin grade, but not a specific cabin – 'TBA' (to be assigned). Some lines will accept this arrangement and may even upgrade you. The first cabins to be sold out are usually those at minimum and maximum rates. Note: Premium rates usually apply to Christmas/New Year cruises.

Cancellations and refunds

Do take out full cancellation insurance (if it is not included), as cruises (and air transportation to/from them) must be paid in full before your tickets are issued. Otherwise, if you cancel at the last minute – even for medical reasons – you could lose the whole fare. Insurance coverage can be obtained from your travel agent or from an independent company, and paying by credit card makes sense (you'll probably get your money back if the agency goes bust) or through the Internet.

Note that cancellation insurance offered by a cruise line is a 'one-size-fits-all' product, so personalization is impossible. It covers only the cruise itself but not any add-ons that you may have arranged on your own – such as non-refundable air tickets.

Cruise lines usually accept cancellations more than 30 days before sailing, but all charge full fare if you don't turn up on sailing day. Other cancellation fees depend on the cruise and length of trip. Many lines do not return port taxes, which are not part of the cruise fare.

If your cruise company appears to have gone out of business, some insurance policies will not cover you unless the cruise company declares bankruptcy.

Medical insurance

Whether you intend to travel overseas or cruise down a local river, and your present medical insurance does not cover you, you should look into extra coverage for your cruise. The cruise line may offer a 'passenger protection program,' the charge for which will appear on your final invoice, unless you decline. It is worth every penny, and typically covers such things as evacuation at sea by air ambulance (Medivac), high-limit baggage, baggage transfers, personal liability, and missed departure.

Port taxes/Handling charges

These are assessed by individual port authorities and are usually shown in the brochure. Port charges form part of the final payment, although they can be changed right up to the day of embarkation.

Fuel surcharges

Cruise lines publish their brochures a year ahead. If oil and other fuel costs rise in the interim, a fuel surcharge may be imposed, in addition to the quoted fare.

Air/sea packages

If your cruise fare includes air transportation (as in a one-way or round-trip air ticket), then airline arrangements usually cannot be changed without paying a premium, as cruise lines often book group space on aircraft to obtain the lowest rates. If you do make changes, remember that, if the airline cancels your flight, the cruise line is under no obligation to help you or return your cruise fare if you don't reach the ship on time. If flying to a foreign country, allow extra time (particularly in winter) for flight delays and cancellations.

Airlines often use a 'hub-and-spoke' system, which can prove frustrating. Because of changes to air schedules, cruise and air tickets may not be sent to passengers until a few days before the cruise.

In Europe, air/sea packages generally start at a major metropolitan airport; some include first-class rail travel from outlying districts. In the US, many cruise lines include connecting flights from suburban airports convenient to the traveler. If you fly and want to lock your check-in baggage, use a TSA (Transportation Security Administration)-approved security lock.

Most cruise lines allow you to fly out to join a ship in one port and fly home from another. An advantage is that you only have to check your baggage once at the departure airport and its transfer from plane to ship is handled for you. This doesn't include intercontinental fly/cruises, where you must claim your baggage at the airport on arrival to clear it through customs.

Travel insurance

Note that cruise lines and travel agents routinely sell travel cover policies that, on close inspection, appear to wriggle out of payment due to a litany of exclusion clauses, most of which are never explained. Example include: Pre-existing medical conditions (ignoring this little gem could cost you dearly) and valuables left unattended on a tour bus, even if the guide says it is safe and that the driver will lock the door.

10 tips to get the best travel insurance

1. Allow time to shop around, and don't accept the first travel insurance policy you are offered.
2. Read the contract carefully, and make sure you know exactly what you are covered for.
3. If you purchase your own air transportation, your insurance policy may not cover you if the airline fails, or if bad weather prevents you from joining your ship on time.
4. Beware of the 'box ticking' approach to travel cover, which is often done quickly at the travel agent's office in lieu of providing expert advice. Insurers should not, in reality, be allowed to apply exclusions that have not been clearly pointed out to the policyholder.
5. Ask for a detailed explanation of all exclusions, excesses, and limitations.
6. Check out the procedure you need to follow if you are the victim of a crime, such as your wallet or camera being stolen while on a shore excursion.
7. If you are the victim of a crime, always obtain a police report as soon as possible. Many insurance policies will reimburse you only for the second-hand value of any lost or stolen item, rather than the full cost of replacement, and you may have to produce the original receipt for any such items claimed.
8. Watch out for exclusions for 'hazardous sports.' These could include things typically offered as shore excursions aboard ships. Examples: horseback riding (there goes that horseback riding on the beach excursion in Jamaica), cycling (mountain biking excursions), jet skiing (most beaches), or ziplining.
9. If you purchase travel cover over the Internet, check the credentials of the company underwriting the scheme. It is best to deal with well-established names, and not to take what appears to be the cheapest deal offered.
10. Different countries have different requirements for travel insurance providers. Be sure to check the details in the country where you purchased your policy.

What to Expect

Stepping aboard for the first time? Here is what you need to know about a typical embarkation.

Taking your first cruise? Make sure you have your passport and any visas required (in some countries – such as China or Russia – you might go ashore on organized excursions under a group visa. Pack any medication you may need (in original, labeled containers) in your carry-on hand luggage.

You already have been sent your cruise tickets, documents (including immigration form to be completed before you get to your ship), and luggage tags by the cruise line or your travel agent, or e-documents via the Internet.

You've arrived at the airport closest to your ship's embarkation point, and retrieved your luggage. There will be a representative from the cruise line waiting, holding aloft the company's name. You then place your luggage in a cluster together with those of other passengers. The next time you see your luggage should be in your cabin.

You'll find check-in desks in the passenger terminal. If your accommodation is designated as a 'suite,' there should be a separate check-in facility.

Anyone cruising from a US port who is a non-US citizen or 'resident alien' will go to a separate desk to check in (*Note:* Do not buy duty-free liquor to take on board – it won't be allowed by the cruise line and will

Passengers embarking aboard *Island Escape*.

be confiscated until the last day of the cruise). You will leave your passport with the check-in personnel. Ask for a receipt – it is a valuable document – and preferably have a photocopy of the main pages to keep with you. If you are cruising from any other port in the world that is not a US port, be aware that each country has its own check-in requirements.

Getting aboard

You then proceed through a security-screening device, for both your body and hand luggage, as at airports. Then it's a few paces to get to the gangway. This may be a covered, airport-type gangway, or an open one (hopefully with a net underneath it in case you drop something over the side). The gangway could be level, or you may have to walk up (or down) an incline, depending on the location of the gangway, the tide, or other local conditions. As you approach the gangway you will probably be greeted by the ship's photographers, a snap-happy team ready to take your photograph, bedraggled as you may appear after having traveled for hours. If you don't want your photograph taken, say 'no' firmly.

At the ship end of the gangway, you will find the ship's cruise staff will welcome you aboard, but may or may not guide you to your cabin.

Things to check

The door to your cabin should be open. If it is locked, ask the steward to obtain the key to open the door. You will have received an electronically coded key card at check-in. Once inside the cabin, take a good look around. Is it clean? Is it tidy? Are the beds properly made? Make sure there is ice in the ice container. Check the bathroom, bathtub (if there is one), or shower. Make sure there are towels and soap.

If there are problems, tell your cabin steward immediately. Or call the reception desk, explain the problem, and establish how it will be resolved and by whom.

Memorize the telephone number for the ship's hospital, doctor, or for medical emergencies, just so you know how to call for help should an emergency arise.

Your luggage probably will not have arrived yet – especially if it is a large resort ship carrying more than 1,750 passengers – but don't sit in the cabin waiting for it. Put your hand luggage away somewhere, and, deck plan in hand, take a walk. If you're hungry, you may want to head to the self-serve buffet – but, be warned that aboard the large resort ships, it'll probably be a bit of a free-for-all.

The funnels on a Disney ship prominently display Mickey Mouse ears.

Familiarize yourself with the layout of the ship. Learn which way is forward, which way is aft, and how to reach your cabin from the main stairways. This is also a good time to learn how to get from your cabin to the outside decks in an emergency – these are rare, but they do happen.

Control that thirst

You're thirsty when you arrive in your cabin. You notice a bottle of water with a tab around its neck. Be sure to read the notice on the tab: 'This bottle is provided for your convenience. If you open it, your account will be charged $4.50.'

On deck, you are greeted by a smiling waiter offering you a colorful, cool drink. But, put your fingers on the glass as he hands it to you and he'll also ask for your cruise card. Bang, you've just paid $6.95 for a drink full of ice worth 5 cents. The cost of drinks soon adds up. Aboard ships operated by Europe-based companies, mixers such as tonic for gin are usually charged separately.

The safety drill

Make sure you attend, and pay attention – it could save your life. Regulations dictate that a Passenger Lifeboat Drill must take place within 24 hours after the ship sails from the embarkation port, but typically it takes place before the ship sails and this will probably become law following the *Costa Concordia* tragedy in January 2012. Directions to your assembly station will be posted on the back of the cabin door. After the drill, you can take off the lifejacket and relax. By now, your luggage probably will have arrived.

Checking in online

Most cruise lines now expect you to check in online. This helps reduce staff numbers – usually locally sourced part-time retirees – at check-in desks in embarkation cruise terminals. This could be smooth if you are computer-literate or a frustrating nightmare if you are not.

The truth is that the paper cruise tickets and other documents formerly used by most major cruise lines have become collectors' items, because paperless ticketing is now the norm (at least in their offices). You will need to print your boarding pass at your own cost. Expect more cruise lines to follow suit in an effort to cut costs. It typically takes about 10–15 minutes to complete the online check-in process, assuming that you have all your booking details at hand.

Pretty soon there'll be self-serve cruising, where you wait your own tables, and…? Wait a moment, didn't easyCruise try the no-frills style of cruising – and fail? Warning to cruise line accountants: you may soon not be needed.

Depending on the cruise line, there are usually four major steps to complete, each step requesting information, before you can actually reach the stage where you can print out your 'boarding pass.' Before you start the online check-in procedure, however, you'll need to put in your name, reservation number, and any other pertinent personal information requested.

Step 1: Passenger information.
Step 2: Your onboard expense account information (pre-register your credit card).
Step 3: Cruise ticket contract (you'll need to have 20/20 eyesight to read this, or take it to your local optician).
Step 4: Print your boarding pass and baggage tags.

Offer to do the online check-in for your whole family or group, and you could end up spending hours and hours at your computer. Note that if you don't register a credit card for your children, you may not be able to print out their boarding passes.

What To Do If ...

Twenty practical tips for a good cruise experience,
and advice on what to do if you have a problem.

1 Your luggage does not arrive at the ship

If you booked as part of the cruise line's air/sea package, the airline is responsible for locating your luggage and delivering it to the next port. If you arranged your own air transportation, it is wholly *your* problem. Always have easy-to-read name and address tags *inside* as well as *outside* your luggage. Keep track of claim documents, and give the airline a detailed itinerary and list of port agents.

2. You miss the ship

If you miss the ship's departure at the port of embarkation, and you are traveling on an air/sea package, the airline will arrange to get you to the ship, possibly at the next port of call. If you are traveling 'cruise-only,' however, then you are responsible for flights, hotel stays, and transfers. If you arrive at the port just as your ship is pulling away, see the ship's port agent immediately.

You miss the ship in a port of call. It is up to you to get back to the ship before its appointed sailing time, unless you are participating in a ship-organized shore excursion. Miss the ship and you'll need to get to its next port at your own cost. *Always* take a copy of your passport with you, just in case.

Ships have also been known to leave port early because of impending inclement weather conditions or natural disasters. However, if you do miss your ship, the ship's port agent should be close by to assist you. Always take the name and telephone contact details with you.

3. Your cabin is too small

Almost all cruise ship cabins are too small. When you book a cruise, you pay for a certain category and type of cabin but have little or no control over which one you actually get. Go to the reception desk as soon as possible and explain what is wrong with the cabin. If the ship is full, it may be difficult to change.

4. Your cabin has no air conditioning, it is noisy, or there are plumbing problems

If there is anything wrong in your cabin, or with your bathroom plumbing, tell your cabin steward immediately. If nothing gets better, complain at the reception desk. Some cabins, for example, are located above the ship's laundry, generator, or galley; others may be above the disco. If the ship is full, it may be difficult to change.

5. You have noisy cabin neighbors

First, politely tell your neighbors that you can hear them brushing their hair as the cabin walls are so thin, and would they please not bang the drawers shut at 2am! If that does not work, complain to the purser or hotel manager, and ask them to attend to the problem.

6. You have a problem with a crew member

Go to the manager or chief purser and explain the problem. No one will do anything unless you complain. Cruise ships try to hire decent staff, but, with so many crew, there are bound to be a few bad apples. Insist on a full written report of the incident, which must be entered into the ship's daily log by the staff captain (deputy captain).

7. You have small children and the brochure implied that the ship has special

Passengers wait to rejoin their ship in Fläm, Norway.

programs for them, but when on board you find out it is not a year-round program

In this instance, either the brochure was misleading, or your travel agent did not know enough about the ship. If you have genuine cause for complaint, then see your travel agent when you get home. Most ships will try to accommodate your young ones, but may not be covered by their insurance for looking after them throughout the day. Check thoroughly with your travel agent *before* you book.

8. You don't like your dining room seating

The large resort ships typically operate two seatings for dinner. When you book your cruise, you are asked whether you want the first or second seating. The line will make every attempt to please you. But if you want second seating and are given first seating, there may be little the restaurant manager can do if the ship is full.

9. You want a table for two and are put at a table for eight

Again, see the restaurant manager (maître d') and explain why you are not satisfied. A little gratuity should prove helpful.

10. You cannot communicate with your dining room waiter

Dining room waiters might be of a nationality and language completely foreign to yours, and all they can do is smile. This could prove frustrating for a whole cruise, especially if you need something out of the ordinary. See the restaurant manager, and tell him/her you want a waiter with whom you can communicate.

11. The food is definitely not gourmet cuisine as portrayed in the brochure

If the food is not as described (for example, whole lobster in the brochure, but only cold lobster salad once during the cruise, or the 'fresh squeezed' orange juice on the breakfast menu is anything but), do inform the maître d' of the problem.

12. A large group has taken over the ship

Sometimes, large groups have pre-booked several public rooms for meetings – seemingly every hour on the hour in the rooms you want to use. Make your displeasure known to the hotel manager immediately, tell your travel agent, and write a follow-up letter to the line when you get home.

13. A port of call is deleted from the itinerary

If you only took the cruise because the ship goes to the place you have wanted to go for years, then read the fine print in the brochure *before* you book. A cruise line is under no obligation to perform the stated itinerary. For whatever reason – political unrest, weather, mechanical problems, no berth space, safety, etc. – the ship's captain has the ultimate say.

14. You leave personal belongings on a tour bus

If, when you're back on board your ship, you find you've left something on a tour bus, the first thing to do is advise the shore excursion manager or the purser's office. The tour operator ashore will then be contacted to see whether any items have been handed in to their office.

15. You are unwell aboard ship

There will be a qualified doctor (who generally operates as a concession and, therefore, charges) and medical facilities, including a small pharmacy. You will be well taken care of. Although there are charges for medical services, almost all cruise lines offer insurance packages that include medical coverage for most eventualities. It is wise to take out this insurance when you book.

16. The cruise line's air arrangements have you flying from Los Angeles via Timbuktu to get to your cruise ship

Most cruise lines with low rates also use the cheapest air routing to get you to your ship. That could mean flights from a central hub. Be warned: you get what you pay for. Ask questions *before* you book.

17. You fly internationally to take a cruise

If your cruise is a long distance away from your home, then it usually makes good sense to fly to your cruise embarkation point and stay for at least a day or two before the cruise. You will be better rested and able to adjust to any time changes. You will step aboard your ship ready for a vacation. As a bonus, you will get to know the port of departure.

18. The ship's laundry ruins your clothes

If any of your clothing is ruined or discolored by the ship's laundry, first tell your cabin steward(ess), and then follow up by going to the purser's office and getting it registered as a proper complaint. Take a copy of the complaint with you, so you can follow up when you get home. Unfortunately, you will probably find a disclaimer on the laundry list saying something to the effect that liability is limited to about $1 per item.

19. You have extra charges on your bill

Check your itemized bill carefully. Then talk to the purser's office and ask them to show you the charge slips. Finally, make sure you are given a copy of your bill *after* any modifications have been made.

20. You're unhappy with your cruise experience

If your ship does not meet your specific lifestyle and interests, or the ship performs less well than the brochure promises, then let your travel agent and the cruise line know. If your grievance is valid, many cruise lines will offer a credit, good towards a future cruise.

Eco Cruising and Emissions

The good news: traveling by sea produces an
estimated 36 times less carbon dioxide than flying.
The bad news: that's still not good enough.

Although marine vessels are responsible for almost 3 percent of the world's greenhouse gases, the world's fleet of around 350 oceangoing cruise ships produces just 0.1 percent of those emissions.

Eco diligence

Cruise companies have spent millions on environmental improvements and continue to invest vast amounts of money in order to be as eco-compatible as possible. Apart from "cold-ironing" in some ports (where cruise ships switch to land power instead of using their own generators), many ships switch to low-sulphur fuel when coming into ports.

Cruise companies are trying to achieve an integrated, industry-wide approach to reduce air emissions, to provide more fuel-efficient ships, and to retrofit some older ships with more efficient replacement machinery. New ships benefit from better hydrodynamic hull design, and advanced hull coatings can also improve efficiency. Careful handling of solid and liquid waste results in lower fuel consumption, and, therefore, CO2 emissions. Further, flue gas from shipboard incinerators is recycled and wastewater treated according to the toughest legal and eco-friendly standards.

Since 2011, new diesel ship engines have had to comply with MARPOL Annex VI Tier II standards, requiring a more efficient use of current engine technologies including engine timing, engine cooling and advanced computer controls resulting in a 15 to 25 percent reduction in NOx. By 2016, new ship engines will need to comply with even stricter Tier III standards. This means using high-efficiency emissions control technology such as selective catalytic converters to reduce NOx.

All *MSC Fantasia*-class ships, for example, use only low-sulfur fuels worldwide. *Celebrity Solstice*-class ships each feature 80 solar panels that help power the elevators. Some ships have their hulls painted with "foul release" paint with fluoropolymers or glass-flake vinyl ester resins, non-toxic substances that help reduce CO2 emissions through reduced fuel use. However, cruise ships that have switched from heavy fuel oil to low-sulfur fuels when operating both outside and inside environmental zones have experienced greater fuel pump wear when switching over, thereby adding to maintenance, operational, and replacement costs.

Most large resort ship operators exited Antarctica in 2011 due to a ban on carrying or burning heavy fuel oil below 60° south latitude, leaving travel mainly in the hands of specialist expedition ship operators. Antarctic fuel (lighter-grade distillate fuel) is the highest cost fuel in the world for ship use. However, some large resort ships and mid-size ships also carry the special fuel, which allows them to continue traveling to Antarctica – although these are for cruising only, not passenger landings.

Norwegian Breakaway, which debuted in 2013, became the first cruise ship to take advantage of MARPOL rule MEPC.1/Circ.642 – permitting the recovery and re-use of the HFO fraction of waste oil as fuel for the diesel engines. The ship's waste oil separator system has only two moving parts and leaves only non-pumpable 'super-dry' solids for landing as dry waste. Waste oil volumes are reduced by 99%, with around 5–15 kg per day of solids left for disposal ashore. The separated water, with an oil content of less than 1,000 ppm, is pumped to the

---

The 146 signatories to MARPOL

Albania, Algeria, Angola, Antigua and Barbuda, Argentina, Australia, Austria, Azerbaijan, Bahamas, Bahrain, Bangladesh, Barbados, Belarus, Belgium, Belize, Benin, Bolivia, Brazil, Brunei, Bulgaria, Cambodia, Cameroon, Canada, Cape Verde, Chile, China, Colombia, Comoros, Congo, Côte d'Ivoire, Croatia, Cyprus, Czech Republic, Denmark, Djibouti, Dominica, Dominican Republic, Ecuador, Egypt, El Salvador, Equatorial Guinea, Estonia, Finland, France, Gabon, Gambia, Georgia, Germany, Ghana, Greece, Guatemala, Guinea, Guyana, Honduras, Hungary, Iceland, India, Indonesia, Iran, Ireland, Italy, Israel, Jamaica, Japan, Jordan, Kazakhstan, Kenya, Kiribati, Kuwait, Latvia, Lebanon, Liberia, Libya, Lithuania, Luxembourg, Madagascar, Malawi, Malaysia, Maldives, Malta, Marshall Islands, Mauritania, Mauritius, Moldova, Monaco, Mongolia, Montenegro, Morocco, Mozambique, Myanmar, Namibia, Netherlands, New Zealand, Nicaragua, Nigeria, Norway, Niue, Oman, Pakistan, Palau, Panama, Papua New Guinea, Peru, Philippines, Poland, Portugal, Qatar, Republic of Korea, Romania, Russian Federation, Saint Kitts and Nevis, Saint Lucia, Saint Vincent and the Grenadines, Samoa, São Tomé and Príncipe, Saudi Arabia, Senegal, Serbia, Seychelles, Sierra Leone, Singapore, Slovakia, Slovenia, Solomon Islands, Spain, Sri Lanka, Suriname, Sweden, Switzerland, Syrian Arab Republic, Thailand, Togo, Tonga, Trinidad and Tobago, Tunisia, Turkey, Turkmenistan, Tuvalu, Ukraine, United Arab Emirates, United Kingdom, United Republic of Tanzania, United States, Uruguay, Vanuatu, Venezuela, Vietnam.

bilge-water tank as part of an integrated waste oil and bilge-water handling system.

Other measures

Other eco-friendly measures include the use of LED lighting rather than fuel-guzzling halogen lighting; cabin lights and other electrical devices that function only when a cabin key card is in a card device inside the cabin; motion-activated lighting in closets; single-use plastic cups replaced by melamine and/or porcelain; plastic single-use soap/shampoo packs replaced by permanent dispensers; plastic laundry bags replaced by re-washable cotton bags; high-tech tunnel washers fitted into laundries to save water; dry-cleaning chemicals being replaced by fruit-based washing chemical; water flow reducers fitted to faucets (taps) and showers; paper towels made from recycled paper; use of darkness-activated sensors that switch on the ship's external lights at dusk; the use of chilled river rocks that retain low temperatures for buffet items, rather than ice; heat-deflecting window coatings; and the latest wastewater treatment technology.

Sorting of waste items is done by cabin attendants and other cleaning staff, with final sorting conducted in the garbage room. After all the sorting has been done, the resulting trash goes into the incinerator or is of-floaded ashore to be managed by reputable waste management companies. While all these measures help, they must be weighed against the costs of implementing them.

Emissions control areas

In 2009 the British Isles introduced the first Emissions Control Areas (ECA) around its shores and in the English Channel. They were followed by 10 countries in the Baltic and North Sea region. The International Maritime Organization (IMO) formally established a North American Emission Control Area, an area ringing the USA/Canada (including Alaska) coast with a 200-mile (320-km) exclusion zone; this came into force in August 2012. The IMO's global air emissions standards called for a progressive reduction of SOx emissions from 4.5 to 3.5 percent by January 2012, then to 0.5 percent by January 2020, subject to a review to be completed by 2018.

When the North American Emission Control Area was implemented in August 2012, it raised fuel costs 10% to 15%. When the sulfur limit drops to 0.1% in 2015, those costs will shoot up another 25% to 50%. At present, no technological solution exists.

Wastewater discharge

The IMO also introduced an International Convention on the Management of Ballast Water and Sediments (wastewater discharge) in 2010. By the end of 2010, MSC Cruises, for example, had almost eliminated the use of plastics, and no chemical detergents were being used in its shipboard laundries.

Cold ironing

This means plugging a ship into a land-based energy supply capable of running its essential functions while in port. The procedure only really makes sense in areas where electricity can be generated from renewable sources through a national grid, and allows the cruise ship to turn off its engines, thus reducing emissions. So far, cold ironing has been introduced in Juneau, Los Angeles, San Diego, Seattle, San Francisco, and Vancouver, and other ports are looking at the possibilities.

Because the power requirements of a large resort ship are high, any such hook-ups must be able to cope with demand. It's not cost-effective for ships to convert to cold ironing unless more ports build such facilities. Also, it may not be energy-efficient to use shore power if it has to be transported over great distances to the port.

The Port of San Francisco has calculated that the provision of shore-side power supply prevents 140 lbs of diesel soot emissions and 1.3 tons of airborne nitrogen oxide emissions for each 10-hour ship call. It also reduces carbon dioxide by 19.7 tons. More city ports are expected to build this option into their infrastructure, but while shore power delivers excellent local air quality benefits, it costs about $5 million to install.

LNG

In future, cruise ships will probably be built with the ability to use LNG (liquefied natural gas) fuel to avoid running the diesel generators in port. An LNG-based power barge would generate and supply electricity while in port. This would reduce CO_2 emissions considerably, and produce almost no SOx (the term for the chemical compound of sulfur dioxide), NOx (the term for a group of highly reactive gases, all of which contain nitrogen and oxygen in varying amounts), or particle emissions. This would certainly be a better solution than cold ironing, in which power is simply generated in the normal manner and made available to a ship in port.

What is MARPOL?

Short for "Marine Pollution," the International Convention for the Prevention of Pollution from Ships (MARPOL 73/78 – the dates refer to its adoption) is the convention that all member countries of the UN specialized agency the International Maritime Organization (IMO) subscribe to. It was designed to minimize pollution of the oceans and seas, including dumping, and pollution by oil and exhaust gases, whether by operational or accidental causes. The original MARPOL Convention was signed on February 17, 1973, but did not come into force then. The present Convention took effect on October 2, 1983. Presently, some 146 countries, representing 98 percent of the world's shipping tonnage, are signatories to the Convention. Ships flagged under these countries are subject to its requirements, regardless of where they sail.

Cruise Ship Safety

How likely is an accident at sea? What if there's a fire? Can you fall overboard? How good are medical facilities aboard?

When Costa Cruises' 3,800-passenger *Costa Concordia* capsized off the coast of Tuscany in January 2012 with the loss of 32 lives, questions of safety at sea inevitably arose. But this tragedy was entirely avoidable: if *Costa Concordia*'s captain hadn't deviated from his computer-set course to sail too close to the island of Giglia, it would have been just another uneventful Mediterranean cruise. The company was so fortunate in its crew, who did such a wonderful job of evacuating more than 3,000 passengers from the stricken ship, in what were rather chaotic circumstances.

Other losses over the past 25 years include Jupiter in 1988 and *Royal Pacific* in 1992, both following collisions; *Explorer*, which struck an iceberg near Antarctica in 2007; and *Sea Diamond*, which foundered on a reef off the Greek island of Santorini in 2007. Given that more than 22 million people take

A typical life jacket demonstration.

a cruise every year, it's not a bad record and, after 48 years of going to sea, during which I have experienced minor fires and groundings, I have no doubt that cruising remains one of the safest forms of transportation.

Evacuations are rare events and may become rarer still. At the time of the *Costa Concordia* calamity, the IMO (International Maritime Organization) was just bringing in new regulations requiring all new cruise ships to be designed with the capability of making the nearest port in the event of a major casualty, fire, or loss of power.

Safety measures

New safety procedures have been implemented both upon the industry's own initiative and by regulators, and further regulations will be discussed and implemented for some time due to the *Costa Concordia* incident.

All cruise ships built after 2010 having a length of 120 meters or greater, or three or more main vertical zones, must have two engine rooms, so that, in the event one is flooded or rendered unusable, a ship can safely return to port without requiring passengers to evacuate the ship – after all, a ship is its own best lifeboat. This requirement (contained in the 2009 SOLAS treaty) came about as a result of the growth in size of today's cruise ships, and the fact that several ship fires and loss of propulsion/steering have occurred during the past 20 years or so.

Following an industry-led operational safety review during 2012, some 10 new policies were introduced. These include muster drills, bridge access and procedures, life jacket availability and location, lifeboat loading drills, recording of passenger nationalities for on-shore emergency services personnel and securing of heavy objects.

Also, a mandatory passenger muster drill prior to departure from port is now part of the international SOLAS Convention. Passengers who don't attend may be disembarked prior to sailing.

International regulations require all crew to undergo basic safety training *before* they are allowed to work aboard any cruise ship. On-the-job training is no longer enough. And safety regulations are getting more stringent all the time, governed by an international convention called SOLAS (Safety of Life at Sea), introduced in 1914 in the aftermath of *Titanic*'s sinking in 1912.

The crew practice a fire drill aboard *Hanseatic*.

All cruise ships built since 1986 must have either totally or partially enclosed lifeboats with diesel engines that will operate even if the lifeboat is inverted.

Since October 1997, cruise ships have had: all stairways enclosed in self-contained fire zones; smoke detectors and smoke alarms fitted in all passenger cabins and all public spaces; low-level lighting showing routes of escape (such as in corridors and stairways); all fire doors throughout the ship controllable from the ship's navigation bridge; all fire doors that are held open by hinges capable of release from a remote location; and emergency alarms made audible in all cabins.

Since 2002, all ocean-going cruise ships on international voyages have had to carry voyage data recorders (VDRs), similar to black boxes carried by aircraft and, since October 2010, new SOLAS regulations have prohibited the use of combustible materials in all new cruise ships.

Crew members attend frequent emergency drills, the lifeboat equipment is regularly tested, and the fire-detecting devices, and alarm and fire-fighting systems are checked. Any passenger spotting fire or smoke is encouraged to use the nearest fire alarm box, alert a member of staff, or contact the bridge.

Always take a small flashlight, in case an emergency arises during a blackout or during the night. I have strongly recommended that all cruise lines fit rechargeable flashlights under each passenger bed (this recommendation was forwarded to the IMO).

Is security good enough?

Cruise lines are subject to stringent international safety and security regulations. Passengers and crew can embark or disembark only by passing through a security checkpoint. Cruise ships maintain zero tolerance for onboard crime or offenses against the person. Trained security professionals are employed aboard all cruise ships. In the case of the USA, where more than 60 percent of cruise passengers reside, you will be far more secure aboard a cruise ship than almost anywhere on land.

It is recommended that you keep your cabin locked at all times when you are not there. All new ships have encoded plastic key cards that operate a lock electronically; older ships have metal keys. Cruise lines do not accept responsibility for any money or valuables left in cabins and suggest that you store them in a safety deposit box at the purser's office, or, if one is provided, in your in-cabin personal safe.

You will be issued a personal boarding pass when you embark. This typically includes your photo, lifeboat station, restaurant seating, and other pertinent information, and serves as identification to be shown at the gangway each time you board. You may also be asked for a government-issued photo ID, such as a passport.

Passenger lifeboat drill

A passenger lifeboat drill, announced publicly by the captain, must be held for embarking passengers *before* the ship departs the port of embarkation. The rule was

A lifeboat aboard *Aegean Odyssey*.

adopted by the global cruise industry following the *Costa Concordia* accident and improved on the existing SOLAS regulations, which require a drill to be held within 24 hours of departure.

Attendance is compulsory. Learn your boat station or assembly point and how to get to it in an emergency. Note your exit and escape pathways and learn how to put on your lifejacket correctly. The drill takes no more than 20 minutes and is a good investment – the 600-passenger *Royal Pacific* took less than 20 minutes to sink after its collision in 1992.

General emergency alarm signal
In the event of a real emergency, you'll hear the ship's general emergency alarm signal. This consists of seven short blasts followed by one long blast on the ship's whistle and public address system.

On hearing the signal, go directly to your assembly station. Follow the direction signs and arrows. If you are close to your cabin, go to your cabin (if possible), put on some warm clothing, collect any essential medication, grab your lifejacket, and go quickly, but quietly, to your assembly station.

Assist anyone who needs help.

Follow the directions of crew members or those given over the public address system.

Don't return to your cabin to collect your property.

Don't search for others in your party (the assembly station is the meeting point).

Don't use the elevators.

If the nearest exit is blocked, use an alternative exit as marked in the plan (usually shown as a dotted arrow).

Low location lighting
In an emergency, a light strip in the floor will lead to an exit. If there is smoke in the corridor, keep close to the floor and crawl if necessary to avoid breathing the smoke and to be able to see more clearly (smoke typically rises).

Assembly stations
The assembly station is where passengers assemble in an emergency. They are marked by a sign on the plan on the back of your cabin door. Follow the instructions of crew members, and remain calm. You will be provided with a lifejacket (and with children's lifejackets) if do not already have one.

Can you accidentally fall overboard?
Of course, you can't always stop passengers having too much to drink and falling over balconies. But all cruise ships have railings at least 42ins (1.1m) high to protect you and your children.

Medical services
Except for ships registered in the UK or Norway, there are no mandatory international maritime requirements for cruise lines to carry a licensed physician or to have hospital facilities aboard. However, in general, all ships carrying over 50 passengers do have medical facilities and at least one doctor.

The standard of medical practice and of the doctors themselves may vary from line to line. Most shipboard doctors are generalists; there are no cardiologists or neurosurgeons. Doctors are typically employed as outside contractors and will charge for use of their services, including seasickness shots.

Regrettably, many cruise lines make medical services a low priority. Most shipboard physicians are not certified in trauma treatment or medical evacuation procedures, for example. However, some medical organizations, such as the American College of Emergency Physicians, have a special division for cruise medicine. Most ships catering to North American passengers carry doctors licensed in the United States, Canada, or Britain, but doctors aboard many other ships come from a variety of countries and disciplines.

Cunard Line's *Queen Mary 2*, with 4,344 passengers and crew, has a fully equipped hospital with one surgeon, one doctor, a staff of six nurses, and two medical orderlies; contrast this with *Carnival Paradise*, which carries up to 3,514 passengers and crew, with just one doctor and two nurses.

Ideally, a ship's medical staff should be certified in advanced cardiac life support. The equipment should include an examination room, isolation ward/bed, X-ray machine (to verify fractures), cardiac monitor (EKG) and defibrillator, oxygen-saturation monitor, external pacemaker, oxygen, suction and ventilators, hematology analyzer, culture incubator, and a mobile trolley intensive care unit.

Existing health problems requiring treatment on board must be reported when you book. Aboard some ships, you may be charged for filling a prescription as well as for the cost of prescribed drugs. There may also be a charge if you have to cancel a shore excursion and need a doctor's letter to prove that you are ill.

Shipboard injury

Slipping, tripping, and falling are the major sources of shipboard injury. Here are 6 things you can do to minimize the chance of injury.

Aboard many ships, raised thresholds separate a cabin's bathroom from its sleeping area. Mind your step to avoid a stubbed toe or banged head.

Don't hang anything from the fire sprinkler heads on the cabin ceilings.

On older ships, note how the door lock works. Some require a key on the inside in order to unlock the door. Leave the key in the lock, so that in the event of a real emergency, you don't have to hunt for the key.

Aboard older ships, take care not to trip over raised thresholds in doorways leading to the open deck.

Walk with caution when the outer decks are wet. This applies especially to solid steel decks – falling on them is really painful.

Do not throw a lighted cigarette or cigar butt, or knock out your pipe, over the ship's side. They can easily be sucked into an opening in the ship's side or onto an aft open deck area and cause a fire.

Surviving a shipboard fire

Shipboard fires can generate an incredible amount of heat, smoke, and often panic. In the unlikely event that you are in one, try to remain calm and think logically and clearly.

When you first get to your cabin, check the way to the nearest emergency exits. Count the number of cabin doorways and other distinguishing features to the exits in case you have to escape without the benefit of lighting. All ships provide 'low location' lighting systems.

Exit signs are normally located just above your head – this is virtually useless, as smoke and flames rise. Note the nearest fire alarm location and know how to use it in case of dense smoke. In future, it is likely that directional sound evacuation beacons will be mandated; these will direct passengers to exits, escape-ways, and other safe areas and may be better than the present inadequate visual aids.

If you are in your cabin and there is fire in the passageway outside, put on your lifejacket. If the cabin's door handle is hot, soak a towel in water and use it to turn the handle. If a fire is raging in the passageway, cover yourself in wet towels and go through the flames.

Check the passageway. If there are no flames, walk to the nearest emergency exit or stairway. If there is smoke in the passageway, crawl to the nearest exit. If the exit is blocked, go to an alternate one. It may take considerable effort to open a heavy fire door to the exit. Don't use the elevators.

If there's a fire in your cabin or on the balcony, report it immediately by telephone. Then get out of your cabin, close the door behind you, sound the alarm, and alert your neighbors.

Piracy in the Gulf of Aden

The UN Security Council has renewed its authorization for countries to use military force against the pirates operating off Somalia who have been sabotaging one of the world's busiest shipping lanes. There were scores of pirate attacks in Somali waters in 2010, with nearly 40 cargo ships, several fishing vessels, one yacht, and one cruise ship attacked or hijacked.

The pirates rarely harm people – their aim is to take hostages and demand a ransom from a ship's owners. Cruise ships are not immune from attack, particularly smaller ones. But *MSC Melody*, carrying 1,500 passengers, was attacked in 2009; its crew repelled the pirates by firing in the air and spraying water on them. *Oceanic*, the Maltese-flagged educational cruise ship attacked with grenades in 2010, escaped by blasting the pirates with high-pressure water hoses.

In 2008, the US Navy created a special unit, called Combined Task Force 150, to combat piracy in the Gulf of Aden.

In February 2009 the Maritime Security Patrol Area, introduced by coalition navies in 2008 as a safe passage corridor, was replaced by two separate 5-mile-wide (8-km-wide) eastbound and westbound, separated by a 2-mile buffer. Today, passengers aboard ships in areas of potential piracy are usually given a briefing before entering the area.

This Year's Star Performers

Having reviewed the following 285 cruise ships, Berlitz names the top-rated ships for 2014

Despite constant cruise company claims that their ship has been named the 'Best Cruise Line' or 'Best Cruise Ship,' there really is no such thing – there is only the ship that is right for you. Most ship owners want to be a 'luxury' cruise operator, and most passengers want to sail aboard one of the top-rated ships. But few operators can really deliver a ship, product, and crew worthy of the highest Berlitz star rating. For this 2014 edition, only two ships have achieved the score required for them to be awarded membership in the most exclusive Five-Stars-Plus club – a cruise industry first in the 29-year history of this book.

#1. *Europa 2*	Hapag-Lloyd Cruises	1,860 points	★★★★★+
#2. *Europa*	Hapag-Lloyd Cruises	1,851 points	★★★★★+

Why does *Europe 2* score the best? Because it's a beautiful ship, with an incredible amount of space per passenger, the number of public rooms, passageways with high ceilings, the choice and range of all the dining venues and types of cuisine, and the attentive, friendly, attentive, unobtrusive personal service. But, it's not just the facilities and appointments that contribute to the ship's high rating – it's also in the cruise experience itself – including the ship's entertainment shows designed for today's informal international clientele. The indoor-outdoor Sansibar, the Jazz Club, and the Herrenzimmer Cigar Lounge – all are top-notch venues for today's sophisticated travelers. It all adds up to the very best informal cruise ship available today – unless you own a private motor yacht. Also, thanks to its Rolls-Royce pod propulsion system, there is absolutely no vibration.

Top Tens of Cruising

The top 10 large resort ships
(more than 1,750 passengers)

Ship	Points	Rating
Queen Mary 2 (Grill Class)	1,673	★★★★+
Queen Elizabeth	1,585	★★★★+
Queen Victoria	1,579	★★★★+
Celebrity Reflection	1,571	★★★★+
Celebrity Silhouette	1,567	★★★★+
Celebrity Eclipse	1,560	★★★★+
Celebrity Equinox	1,559	★★★★+
MSC Preziosa	1,553	★★★★+
MSC Divina	1,552	★★★★+
Celebrity Solstice	1,551	★★★★+

The top 10 small ships
(251–750 passengers)

Ship	Points	Rating
Europa 2	1,860	★★★★★+
Europa	1,851	★★★★★+
Silver Spirit	1,762	★★★★★
Silver Whisper	1,749	★★★★★
Silver Shadow	1,747	★★★★★
Seabourn Quest	1,707	★★★★★
Seabourn Odyssey	1,706	★★★★★
Seabourn Sojourn	1,704	★★★★★
Silver Wind	1,661	★★★★+
Silver Cloud	1,658	★★★★+

The top 10 mid-size ships
(751–1,750 passengers)

Ship	Points	Rating
Crystal Serenity	1,714	★★★★★
Crystal Symphony	1,702	★★★★★
Riviera	1,682	★★★★+
Marina	1,680	★★★★+
Asuka II	1,673	★★★★+
Artania	1,540	★★★★
Prinsendam	1,483	★★★★
Rotterdam	1,457	★★★★
Amsterdam	1,456	★★★★
Zaandam	1,433	★★★★

The top 10 boutique ships
(50–250 passengers)

Ship	Points	Rating
Hanseatic	1,765	★★★★★
SeaDream I	1,761	★★★★★
SeaDream II	1,754	★★★★★
Sea Cloud	1,702	★★★★★
Sea Cloud II	1,701	★★★★★
Hebridean Princess	1,678	★★★★+
Seabourn Legend	1,654	★★★★+
Seabourn Spirit	1,642	★★★★+
Seabourn Pride	1,640	★★★★+
Silver Explorer	1,617	★★★★+

How We Evaluate the Ships

Their facilities count, but so do the factors and standards relating to food, service, staff, and hospitality. This section explains how the Berlitz points system works.

I have been evaluating and rating cruise ships and the onboard product professionally since 1980. In addition, I receive regular reports from my small team of trained assessors. The ratings are conducted with *total objectivity*, from a set of predetermined criteria and a modus operandi designed to work *globally*, not just regionally, across the entire spectrum of oceangoing cruise ships today, in all segments of the marketplace.

There really is no 'best cruise line in the world' or 'best cruise ship' – only the ship and cruise that is right for you. After all, it's the overall enjoyment of a cruise as a vacation that's really important. Therefore, different criteria are applied to ships of different sizes, styles, and market segments throughout the world (vacationers of different nationalities are looking for different things).

The evaluation and rating of cruise ships is about as contrary to soccer as you can get. In soccer, the goalposts are always in the same place. But with cruise ships, they keep changing as the industry evolves and matures.

This section includes 285 oceangoing cruise ships in service (or due to enter service) and chosen by the author for inclusion when this book was completed. Almost all except the newest ships have been carefully evaluated, taking into account around 400 separate items based on personal cruises, visits, and revisits to ships. In the scoring room, these are channeled into 20 major areas, each with a possible 100 points. The maximum possible score for any ship is 2,000 points. These scores are tabulated into five main sections: Ship, Accommodation, Food, Service, and Cruise Operation.

Cruise lines, ship owners, and operators should note that the ratings may be adjusted annually as a result of increased competition, the introduction of newer ships with better facilities, and other market- or passenger-driven factors.

The ratings more reflect the *standards* of the cruise product delivered to passengers (the software: the dining experience, the service, and the hospitality aspects of the cruise), and less the physical plant (the hardware). Thus, although a ship may be the latest, most stunning vessel in the world in terms of design and decor, if the 'software' and onboard product delivery are not so good, the scores and ratings will reflect these aspects more clearly.

The stars beside the name of the ship at the top of each page relate directly to the Overall Rating. The highest number of stars awarded is five stars (★★★★★), and the lowest is one star. This system is universally recognized throughout the global hospitality industry. A plus (+) indicates that a ship deserves just that little bit more than the number of stars attained. However, I must emphasize that it is the number of points achieved rather than the number of stars attained that is more meaningful.

Britannia Restaurant aboard *Queen Elizabeth.*

The star system

★★★★★+	1,851–2,000 points
★★★★★	1,701–1,850 points
★★★★+	1,551–1,700 points
★★★★	1,401–1,550 points
★★★+	1,251–1,400 points
★★★	1,101–1,250 points
★★+	951–1,100 points
★★	801–950 points
★+	651–800 points
★	501–650 points

Enjoying the balcony aboard *Costa Classica*.

What the ratings mean

1,851–2,000 points ★★★★★+

You can expect an outstanding, top-class cruise experience – it doesn't get any better than this. It should be truly memorable, and with the highest attention to detail, finesse, and personal service – how important you are made to feel is critical. The decor must be elegant and tasteful, measured by restraint and not flashiness, with fresh flowers and other decorative touches in abundance, and the layout of the public rooms might well follow *feng shui* principles.

Any ship with this rating must be just about unsurpassable in the cruise industry, and it has to be very, very special, with service and hospitality levels to match. There must be the very highest-quality surroundings, comfort, and service levels, the finest and freshest quality foods, including all breads and rolls baked on board. Highly creative menus, regional cuisine, and dining alternatives should provide maximum choice and variety, and special orders will be part of the dining ritual.

Dining room meals (particularly dinners) are expected to be memorable affairs, correctly served on the finest china, with a choice of wines of suitable character and vintage available, and served in the correct-sized sommelier glasses of the highest quality (Reidel or Schott).

The service staff will take pleasure in providing you with the ultimate personal, yet unobtrusive, attention with the utmost of finesse, and the word 'no' should not be in their vocabulary. This is the very best of the best in terms of refined, unstructured living at sea, but it is seriously expensive.

1,701–1,850 points ★★★★★

You can expect a truly excellent, memorable cruise experience, with the finesse and attention to detail commensurate with the amount of money paid. The service and hospitality levels will be extremely high from all levels of officers and staff, with strong emphasis on fine hospitality training – all service personnel members *must* make you feel important.

The food will be commensurate with the high level expected from what is virtually the best possible at sea, with service that should be very attentive yet unobtrusive. The cuisine should be memorable, with ample taste. Special orders should never be a problem. There must be a varied selection of wines, which should be served in glasses of the correct size.

Entertainment is expected to be of prime quality and variety. Again, the word 'no' should not be in the vocabulary of any member of staff aboard a ship with this rating. Few things will cost extra once you are on board, and brochures should be more 'truthful' than those for ships with a lower rating.

1,551–1,700 points ★★★★+

You should expect to have a high-quality cruise experience that will be quite memorable, and just a little short of being excellent in all aspects. Perhaps the personal service and attention to detail could be slightly better, but, nonetheless, this should prove to be a fine all-round cruise experience, in a setting that is extremely clean and comfortable, with few lines anywhere, a caring attitude from service personnel, and a good standard of entertainment that appeals to a mainstream market.

The cuisine and service will be carefully balanced, with mostly fresh ingredients and varied menus that should appeal to almost anyone, served on high-quality china.

This should prove to be an extremely well-rounded cruise experience, probably in a ship that is new or almost new. There will probably be fewer 'extra-cost' items than ships with a slightly lower rating.

1,401–1,550 points ★★★★

You should expect to have a very good quality all-round cruise experience, most probably aboard a modern, highly comfortable ship that will provide a good range of facilities and services. The food and service will be quite decent overall, although decidedly not as 'gourmet' and fanciful as the brochures with the always-smiling faces might have you believe.

The service on board will be well-organized, if a little robotic and impersonal at times, and only as good as the cruise line's training program allows. You may notice a lot of things cost extra once you are on board, although the typically vague brochure tells you that the things are 'available' or are an 'option.' However, you should have a good time, and your bank account will be only moderately damaged.

1,251–1,400 points ★★★+

You should expect to have a decent-quality cruise experience, aboard a ship where the service levels should be good, but perhaps without the finesse that could be expected from a more upscale environment. The crew aboard any ship achieving this score should reflect a

Douglas Ward inspects the quality of spa towels aboard *Nippon Maru*.

positive attitude with regard to hospitality, and a willingness to accommodate your needs, up to a point. Staff training will probably be in need of more attention to detail and flexibility.

Food and service levels in the dining room(s) should be reasonably good, although special or unusual orders might prove more difficult. There will probably be a number of extra-cost items you thought were included in the price of your cruise – although the brochure typically is vague and states that the things are 'available' or are an 'option.'

1,101–1,250 points ★★★

You can expect a reasonably decent, middle-of-the-road cruise experience, with a moderate amount of space and quality in furnishings, fixtures, and fittings. The cabins are likely to be a little on the small side. The food and service levels will be quite acceptable, although not at all memorable, and somewhat inflexible with regard to special orders, as almost everything is standardized.

Crew attitude could be improved, the level of hospitality and cleanliness will be moderate but little more, and the entertainment will probably be weak. This is a good option, however, for those looking for the reasonable comforts of home without pretentious attitudes, and little damage to their bank statement.

951–1,100 points ★★★+

You should expect an average cruise experience in terms of accommodation (typically with cabins that are dimensionally challenged), quality of the ship's facilities, food, wine list, service, and hospitality levels, in surroundings that are unpretentious. In particular, the food and its service will probably be disappointing.

There will be little flexibility in the levels of service, hospitality, and staff training and supervision, which will be no better than poor. Thus, the overall experience will be commensurate with the small amount of money you paid for the cruise.

801–950 points ★★

You should expect to have a cruise experience of modest quality aboard a ship that is probably in need of more attention to maintenance and service levels, not to mention hospitality. The food may be quite tasteless, homogenized, and of low quality, and service will leave much to be desired in terms of attitude, which will tend to be mediocre at best. Staff training is likely to be minimal, and turnover may be high. The 'end-of-pier' entertainment could well leave you wanting to read a good book.

651–800 points ★+

You can expect to have only the most basic cruise experience, with little or no attention to detail, from a poorly trained staff that is probably paid low wages and to whom you are just another body. The ship will, in many cases, probably be in need of much maintenance and upgrading, and will probably have few facilities.

Cleanliness and hygiene may well be questionable, and there will be absolutely no finesse in personal service levels, with poor attitude from the crew, and dismal entertainment as significant factors in the low score and rating. On the other hand, the price of a cruise is probably alluringly low.

501–650 points   ★

You can expect to have a cruise experience that is the absolute bottom of the barrel, with almost nothing in terms of hospitality or finesse. You can forget about attention to detail – there won't be any. This will be the kind of experience that would equal a stay in the most basic motel on land, with few facilities, a poorly trained, uncaring staff, and a ship that needs better maintenance.

The low cost of a cruise aboard a ship with this rating should provide a strong clue to the complete absence of any quality. This will be particularly evident in the areas of food, service, and entertainment. You might remember this cruise, but for all the wrong reasons.

Distribution of points

These are the percentage of the total points available that are allocated to each of the main areas evaluated:

The Ship: 25 percent
Accommodation: 10 percent
Cuisine: 20 percent
Service: 20 percent
Entertainment: 5 percent
The Cruise Experience: 20 percent

These last two categories may be combined for boutique ships, tall ships, and expedition ships.

Criteria

The Ship

Hardware/Maintenance/Safety. This score reflects the general profile and condition of the ship (hardware), its age and maintenance, exterior paint, decking and caulking, swimming pool and surrounds, deck furniture, shore tenders, lifeboats, and other safety items. It also reflects interior cleanliness (public restrooms, elevators, floor coverings, wall coverings, stairways, passageways, and doorways), food preparation areas, refrigerators, garbage handling, compacting, incineration, and waste disposal facilities.

Outdoor Facilities/Space. This score reflects the overall space per passenger on open decks, crowding, swimming pools/whirlpools and their surrounds, lido deck areas, number and type of deck lounge chairs (with or without cushioned pads) and other deck furniture, outdoor sports facilities, shower enclosures and

Balcony cabins, stacked on top of one another, at the aft (back) of *Costa Serena*.

changing facilities, towels, and quiet areas (those without music).

Interior Facilities/Space/Flow. This score reflects the use of common interior public spaces, including enclosed promenades; passenger flow and congestion points; ceiling height; lobby areas, stairways, and all passenger hallways; elevators; public restrooms and facilities; signage, lighting, air conditioning and ventilation; and degree of comfort and density.

Decor/Furnishings/Artwork. This score reflects the overall interior decor (decoration and colors); hard and soft furnishings, wood or veneer paneling, carpeting (color, and practicality), fit and finish, chairs (comfort, height, and support), ceilings and decor treatments, artwork (paintings, sculptures, and atrium centerpieces), and lighting.

Spa/Fitness Facilities. This score reflects any health spa, wellness center, and fitness facilities: location, accessibility, and noise levels; lighting and flooring materials; fitness and muscle-training machines and other equipment; fitness programs; sports and games facilities; indoor pools; hot tubs; grand baths; hydrotherapy pools; saunas and steam rooms; treatment rooms; range of personal body treatments; changing facilities; jogging and walking tracks; and open promenades.

Accommodation

Cabins: Suites and Deluxe Grades. This score reflects the design and layout of all suites and deluxe-grade cabins, private balconies (whether full floor-to-ceiling partition or part partitions, balcony lighting, balcony furniture). Also beds/berths and furniture (position and practicality), cabinetry, and other fittings; hanging space, drawer space, and bedside tables; vanity unit, bathroom facilities, cabinets, and toiletries storage; lighting, air conditioning, and ventilation; audio-visual facilities; artwork; bulkhead insulation, and noise and vibration levels. Suites should not be so designated unless the sleeping room is completely separated from the living area.

The Persian Garden spa aboard *Celebrity Solstice*.

Also, soft furnishings, cabin service directory, interactive TV; paper, postcards, and personalized stationery; telephone directory; laundry lists; tea- and coffee-making equipment; flowers; fruit; bathroom personal amenities kits, bathrobes, slippers, and the size and quality of towels.

Cabins: Standard Sizes. This score reflects the design and layout, beds, furniture (functionality), and other fittings; closets and other hanging space, drawer space, bedside tables, and vanity unit; bathroom facilities, washbasin, cabinets, and toiletries storage; lighting, air conditioning, and ventilation; audiovisual facilities; quality of fittings and furnishings; artwork; insulation, noise, and vibration levels.

In addition, we have taken into account the usefulness of the information directory; laundry lists; tea- and coffee-making equipment; flowers (if any); fruit (if any); and bathroom amenities, bathrobes, slippers, and the size, thickness, quality, and material content of towels.

Cuisine

Cruise lines put maximum emphasis on promising passengers how good their food will be, often to the point of being unable to deliver what is promised. Generally, the standard of food is good. The rule of thumb is: if you were to eat out in a good restaurant, what would you expect? Does the ship meet your expectations? Would you come back again for the food?

There are perhaps as many different tastes as there are passengers. The 'standard' market cruise lines cater to a wide range of tastes, while the more exclusive cruise lines can offer better-quality food, cooked individually to your taste. As in any good restaurant, you get what you pay for.

Dining Room/Cuisine. This score reflects the physical structure of dining rooms, layout and seating (alcoves and individual chairs), and waiter stations; lighting and ambience; table setups; linen, china, and cutlery quality and condition; and table centerpieces (flowers). It also reflects menus, food quality, presentation, food combinations, culinary creativity, appeal, taste, texture, freshness, color, balance; garnishes and decorations; appetizers, soups, pastas, tableside cooking (if any); fresh fruit and cakes; and the wine list (and connoisseur wine list), price range, and wine service. Specialty dining venues are also checked for menu variety, food and service quality, decor, seating, and noise levels. China, cutlery and glassware are also included.

Informal Eateries/Buffets. This score reflects the hardware (hot and cold display units, sneeze guards, 'active' stations, tongs, ice containers and ladles, and serving utensils); buffet displays (most are disappointing and institutionalized); trays, plates, and setups; correct food temperatures; food labeling; breakfast, luncheon, deck buffets, and late-night snacks; decorative elements; and staff service and communication

Quality of Ingredients. This score reflects the quality of ingredients, taste, consistency, and portion size; grades of meat, fish, and fowl; and the price paid by the cruise line for food per passenger per day. It is the quality of ingredients that most dictates the presentation of the finished product, as well as its taste.

Tea/Coffee/Bar Snacks. This score reflects the quality and variety of teas and coffees available, including afternoon teas/coffees and their presentation; whether mugs or cups and saucers are presented; whether milk is served in the correct open containers or in sealed packets; whether self-service or graciously served. The quality of such items as cakes, scones, and pastries, as well as bar/lounge snacks, hot and cold canapés, and hors d'oeuvres also forms part of this section.

Service

Dining Room. This score reflects the professionalism of the restaurant staff: the maître d'hôtel, under managers, section headwaiters, waiters and assistant waiters (busboys), and sommeliers and wine waiters; place settings, cutlery, and glasses; and proper service (serving, taking from the correct side), communication skills, attitude, flair, uniform, appearance, and finesse. Waiters should note whether passengers are right- or left-handed and, when tables are assigned, make sure that cutlery and glasses are placed on the side of preference.

Bars. This score reflects the lighting and ambience; seating, noise levels; communication skills (between bar staff and passengers); staff attitude, personality, flair, and service finesse; correct use of glasses (and correct size of glasses); and attitude when presenting the bill (aboard those ships where a charge is made).

Cabins. This score reflects the cleaning and housekeeping staff, butlers (for penthouse and suite passengers), cabin stewards/stewardesses and their supervisory staff, attention to detail and cleanliness, linen and bathrobe changes, and language and communication skills.

Open Decks. This score reflects steward/stewardess service for beverages and food items around the open decks; placement and replacement of towels on deck lounge chairs, towel supply, emptying of used towel bins; and general tidiness of all associated deck equipment.

Entertainment

Aboard specialist ships, such as those offering expedition cruises, or tall ships, where entertainment is not a feature, it is the lecture program that forms this portion of the evaluations.

The score reflects the overall entertainment program. The entertainment has to appeal to passengers of many ages and types. Included is the physical plant (stage/bandstand) of the main show lounge; technical support, lighting, set/backdrop design; all sound and light systems; pre-recorded tracks and special effects; large-scale production shows (including story, plot, content, cohesion, costumes, quality, choreography, and vocal content); variety shows; cabaret acts; and bands and solo musicians.

The cruise experience

Activities Program. This score reflects the daytime activities and events. It includes the cruise director and staff (their visibility, availability, and professionalism), sports and water sports programs, participation games, special interest programs, port and shopping lecturers, and mind-enrichment lecturers. Also the extent and quality of any water-sports equipment, instruction, staff supervision, marina or side-retractable water sports platforms, and any enclosed swimming area.

Movies/Television Programming. This score reflects movies screened in theaters and on poolside screens, picture and sound quality; videos on the in-cabin system; other programming, including a ship's own TV station programs; content, and audio channels.

Hospitality Standard. This score reflects the level of hospitality and professionalism of senior officers, middle management, supervisors, cruise staff, and all crew; social contact, personal appearance, and dress codes or uniforms; motivation; and communication skills.

Overall Product Delivery. This score reflects the quality of the overall cruise as a vacation – what the brochure states and promises (real or implied), and the onboard hospitality and services.

Notes on the rating results

Cruise ship evaluations and ratings have become ever more complex. Although a ship may be the newest, with all the latest facilities possible, it is the onboard food and service that often disappoint, as well as standing in lines and signing up for activities. It's about delivering a cohesive, consistent onboard product.

Cruise companies say that food quality is a trade-off against lower prices. However, this implies a downward spiral that affects food quality as well as service, quality of personnel, crew training, safety, and maintenance.

In the final analysis, it is the little things that add to points lost on the great scorecard.

Serenade of the Seas cruises past the Statue of Liberty in New York City.

What the Descriptions Mean

Each of the following ship reviews is preceded by a panel providing basic data on the ship's size and facilities. Below, we explain how to interpret some of the headings

Ship Size
Large resort ship: 1,751–6,500 passengers
Mid-size ship: 751–1,750 passengers
Small ship: 251–750 passengers
Boutique ship: 50–250 passengers

Lifestyle
Designated as Standard, Premium, or Luxury, according to a general classification into which segment of the market the ship falls. This should help you choose the right size ship and cruise experience to fit your lifestyle.

Standard. The least expensive, offering the basic amenities, food, and service.

Premium. More expensive than Standard, has generally better food, service, facilities, and amenities, more attention to detail, and greater differentiation of suites (with butler service) than standard accommodation.

Luxury. More expensive than Premium or Standard, provides more personal comfort, space, open or one-seating dining, much better food (no processed items, more menu creativity, and everything made as fresh as possible), and highly trained staff.

A luxury lifestyle aboard a Cunard ship.

The oatmeal factor
One factor that I have found to be quite consistent across most ships is what I call the Oatmeal Factor: how various cruise ships provide a passenger with a basic item such as a bowl of oatmeal. It's a good example to illustrate how I review each vessel.

Standard. Hot oatmeal (supermarket brand oats) mixed with water, with little or no chance of obtaining tahini to add taste to the oatmeal. You get it from a soup tureen at the buffet, and put it into a plastic or inexpensive bowl yourself (or it may be served in the dining room by a waiter/waitress); it is eaten with plastic or basic canteen cutlery.

Premium. Hot oatmeal, water, salt, and a little olive oil; served in a higher-quality bowl, by a waiter or waitress, with hotel-quality (or better) cutlery. It's possible that the ship will have tahini, to add taste and creaminess. It's also possible that the waiter/waitress will ask if you'd like hot or cold milk with your oatmeal. There may even be a doily between the oatmeal bowl and base plate.

Luxury. Hot oatmeal (medium or large flakes), water, salt, tahini, a little (extra virgin) olive oil and nutmeg, with a dash of blended Scotch (whisky); served in a high-quality brand-name bowl (Versace), with base plate and doily, and Hepp- or Robbe & Berking-quality silverware. The waiter/waitress will ask if you'd like hot or cold milk with your oatmeal.

Incomparable. Hot Scottish (large flakes, hand-ground) oatmeal, water, sea salt, tahini, and nutmeg (grated at the table), high-quality cold-pressed olive oil and a layer of rare single-malt Scotch; served in small-production hand-made china, with base plate and doily, and sterling silver cutlery. The waiter/waitress will ask if you'd like hot or cold milk (or anything else) with your oatmeal.

Cruise line
The cruise line and the operator may be different if the company that owns the vessel does not routinely market and operate it. Tour operators often charter ships for their exclusive use (e.g., Thomson Cruises).

IMO numbers
Each ocean-going ship must have an IMO (International Maritime Organization) number clearly displayed on a ship's hull. This was agreed after the terrorist attacks of September 11, 2001 in New York and Washington, DC, so that each ship can be clearly identified. This statistic is a new feature in the 2014 book.

Entered service

Where two dates are given, the first is for the ship's maiden passenger voyage, and the second is the date it began service for the current operator.

Propulsion

The type of propulsion is given (i.e., gas turbine, diesel, diesel-electric, nuclear, or steam turbine), together with the output (at 100 percent), expressed as kW (kilowatts) generated.

Propellers

This heading refers to the number of propellers or fixed or azimuthing pods.

The favored drivers are now eco-friendly diesel-electric or diesel-mechanical propulsion systems that propel ships at speeds of up to 28 knots (32mph). Only Cunard Line's *QM2*, with a top speed of more than 30 knots (34.8mph), is faster.

More than 60 cruise ships are now fitted with the pod propulsion system, first introduced to the industry in 1990. It resembles a huge outboard motor fitted below the waterline. It replaces the long-used conventional rudder, shaft, and propeller mechanisms, saves valuable machinery space, and makes stern thrusters redundant.

The pods are compact, self-contained units powered by internal electric propulsion motors. They are turned by the hydraulic motors of the steering gear, and can turn through 360 degrees (azimuthing). This allows even the largest ships to maneuver into smaller spaces without help from tugs.

Most ships have two pods, although some have three (*Allure of the Seas*, *Oasis of the Seas*) or even four units (*Queen Mary 2*). Each pod weighs about 170 tons. But the four pods attached to *Queen Mary 2* weigh 250 tons each – more than an empty Boeing 747 jumbo jet; two are fixed, two are of the azimuthing variety. Although they are at the stern, pods pull, rather than push, a ship through the water, thanks to their forward-facing propellers, and provide greater maneuverability.

Ships with pod propulsion systems should have no noticeable vibration or engine noise at the stern, unlike ships with conventional propulsion systems. Competing manufacturers have different names for their pod systems – examples: Azipod, Dolphin, Mermaid. The design of the pods has been improved, resulting in slimmer, more efficient units, including safe access for routine maintenance.

Some ships may be fitted with Becker rudders. A Becker rudder is one where its main body has a hinged, second part. This second, or aft, section can be pointed in a different direction from the main body so that more control over waterflow can be achieved.

Passenger capacity

This is based on two factors: 1) Two lower beds/berths per cabin, plus all cabins for single occupancy; and 2) All available beds/berths filled. (Note: This figure may not always be accurate, as cruise lines often make changes by adding or taking away third/fourth berths according to demand.)

Passenger space ratio (Gross Tonnage per Passenger)

Achieved by dividing the gross tonnage by the number of passengers.

Crew to passenger ratio

Achieved by dividing the number of passengers by the number of crew (lower beds/all possible beds and berths filled).

Cabin size range

From the smallest cabin to the largest suite (including 'private' balconies/verandas), these are provided in square feet and square meters, rounded up to the nearest whole number.

Wheelchair-accessible ratings

Cabins designed to accommodate passengers with limited mobility.

There are four wheelchair accessibility ratings:

Best. The ship is recommended as being most suitable for wheelchair passengers.

Good. Reasonably accessible.

Fair. Moderately accessible.

None. The ship is not suitable.

Dedicated cinema/seats

A 'yes' means that there is a separate cinema dedicated solely to showing large-screen movies throughout the day and during the evening. This is distinct from a showlounge that may be used to screen movies during the day (afternoon) and for live shows in the evening, or poolside screens. The number of seats is provided where known.

A note about prices

Some price examples are given throughout the ship reviews (for massage, the cover price for 'specialty' restaurants, Internet access, or gratuities added to your onboard account, for example), but please note that these are provided *only* as a guideline and may have changed since publication. Always check with the cruise line, the onboard concession, or your travel provider for the latest prices.

Footnote to the silhouettes

You may wonder why we do not use color photos of ships (as we do in the app version of this book), so I thought you might like to know that when the book was first published, I asked a charming lady named Susan Alpert to draw the ship silhouettes. She did a great job. However, she died of ovarian cancer at the age of 33. Ever since then, I have decided to honor her memory by using hand-drawn silhouettes.

How A New Cruise Ship Is Created

Ships used to be constructed from the keel up. Today they are built in as many as 100 huge sections that are joined together in a shipyard.

One of 55 prefabricated ship blocks is moved into position in Meyer Werft's shipyard in Papenburg, Germany.

The prefabricated bridge section is moved into position. The yard's massive cranes can carry 600 tons.

It is the job of the shipyard, its marine architects, consultants, interior designers, and a mass of specialist suppliers to turn those dreams and concepts into a ship without unduly straining the laws of naval architecture, safety regulations, or – crucially – budgets. Computers have simplified this complex process, although shipboard management and operations personnel often become frustrated with designers who are more idealistic than they are practical.

Today's ships begin life as huge sections – as many as 100 sections, each weighing up to 450 tons, for a large resort ship such as *Carnival Freedom* or *Celebrity Solstice*. Most are extensively pre-outfitted and may not even be constructed in the shipyard – simply assembled there.

Formerly, passenger spaces were slotted in wherever there was space within a given hull. Today, a new ship to be built in two years instead of four or five.

Maximum noise and vibration levels allowable in the accommodation spaces and recreation areas are stipulated in any owner's contract. Vibration tests, focusing on propellers and main engines, are carried out once a ship is built and launched.

An engine unit is added. The ship looks like a stack of containers bolted together – which is pretty close to reality.

Prefabricated cabin modules, including in situ bathrooms complete with toilets and plumbing, are used. When the steel structure of the relevant deck is ready, with main lines and insulation installed, cabin modules are then affixed to the deck, and power lines and sanitary plumbing connected.

Cloning a design

With the costs of developing new designs prohibitively expensive, some companies go into 'clone' mode, using the same basic platform, space, and machinery configuration for the hull, but varying the upper structure and layout of public spaces.

Gradually the 122,000-ton *Celebrity Solstice*, with its 14 passenger decks, assumes its final shape.

The best example of this is in the 'Vista'-class ships, with the same basic platform shared by cruise lines belonging to the Carnival Corporation. Examples include *Carnival Legend, Carnival Miracle, Carnival Pride, Carnival Spirit, Costa Atlantica, Costa Luminosa, Costa Mediterranea, Eurodam, Nieuw Amsterdam, Oosterdam, Westerdam, Zuiderdam*. More modified versions can be found in Cunard Line's *Queen Elizabeth* and *Queen Victoria*.

Today's ships are a compromise between a designer's ideal, maximizing use of interior space, and financial constraints.

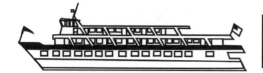

Admiralty Dream
★★

Size:.......................................Boutique Ship	Cabins (total):...43
Tonnage:..514	Size range (sq ft/m):..................64–126.0/5.9–11.7
Lifestyle:.......................................Standard	Cabins (outside view):....................................43
Cruise line:........................ Alaskan Dream Cruises	Cabins (interior/no view):..................................0
Former names:...... Spirit of Columbia, Independence, Columbia	Cabins (for one person):...................................2
IMO number:....................................8963727	Cabins (with private balcony):..............................0
Builder:............................ Eastern Shipping (USA)	Cabins (wheelchair accessible):.............................0
Original cost:......................................n/a	Wheelchair accessibility:...............................None
Entered service:........................... 1982/May 2011	Cabin voltage:...................................110 volts
Registry:..USA	Elevators:...0
Length (ft/m):................................ 166.0/50.5	Casino (gaming tables):..................................No
Beam (ft/m):................................... 37.0/11.2	Slot machines:...No
Draft (ft/m):.................................... 7.5/2.2	Swimming pools:..0
Propulsion/Propellers:......................... diesel/2	Hot tubs (on deck):.......................................0
Passenger decks:.....................................3	Self-service launderette:................................No
Total crew:...20	Dedicated cinema/seats:..................................No
Passengers (lower beds/alll berths):................. 84/84	Library:..Yes
Passenger Space Ratio (lower beds/all berths):......... 6.1/6.1	Onboard currency:......................................US$
Crew/Passenger Ratio (lower beds/all berths):......... 4.2/4.2	

A small Alaska coastal cruising ship with limited facilities

OVERVIEW. This little ship, once part of the Cruise West fleet, is all about eco-tourism, and can take you close to nature and wildlife for an up-close experience. *Admiralty Dream* suits couples and single travelers, mostly over 60, who enjoy nature and wildlife at close quarters, and has an all-American crew.

THE SHIP. Public rooms consist of a lounge that is a multi-functional space for meetings (plus a couple of bookcases with books about nature and wildlife), and a dining room. Naturalists and other specialists give talks and act as leaders on shore excursions.

The young, cheerful staff is multi-flexible, doing a little of this and a little of that. Service comes with a smile, but rarely with finesse – homely but not perfect. The captain is able to deviate to take in particular areas of interest. The dress code is utterly casual – not even a jacket for men, and no ties, please. However, do take comfortable walking shoes, as well as photographic materials for wildlife spotting. Smoking is permitted only on the outside decks. All tips are pooled by all staff, using the amounts recommended in the cruise line's brochure. Alaska cruises start and end in Sitka. A sister ship, *Baranof Dream*, also with 39 cabins, is available for groups and charters.

Note that, because the ship is small, there is an almost constant throbbing from the diesel engines/generator.

ACCOMMODATION. There are seven price categories – a lot for such a small ship. All cabins are small

Berlitz's Ratings

	Possible	Achieved
Ship	500	156
Accommodation	200	74
Food	400	174
Service	400	203
Entertainment	100	30
Cruise	500	165

OVERALL SCORE
802 points out of 2000

when compared to most cruise ships, but they are basically comfortable, and each has a large picture window – a few cabins have portholes – and a very small clothes closet. Some cabins have double beds, but most have singles that can't be moved together. Some may also have upper/lower berths instead of beds. Each has its own little bathroom, with a wall-mounted shower, and there's a small washbasin. There is no room service for food or snack items.

Cool-weather clothing for the outdoors is necessary in Alaska, but there's almost no storage space for it in the tiny, utilitarian cabins aboard this small ship.

DINING. All meals are taken in the dining room at a set time, except for Continental breakfast, which is typically provided in the lounge. This tends to be early, so it's regimented and not at all flexible. Don't expect outstanding cuisine – the galley is small, and the range of food items limited, except for fresh local fish and seafood, which can be very good, as well as organic dairy products. It's really simple American fare.

ENTERTAINMENT. Dinner and after-dinner conversation with fellow passengers in the ship's lounge/bar constitutes the entertainment each evening.

SPA/FITNESS. There are no spa or fitness facilities.

Adonia
★★★★

Size:	Small Ship	Cabins (total):	355
Tonnage:	30,277	Size range (sq ft/m):	145.3–968.7/13.5–90.0
Lifestyle:	Standard	Cabins (outside view):	332
Cruise line:	P&O Cruises	Cabins (interior/no view):	23
Former names:	Royal Princess, Minerva II, R8	Cabins (for one person):	0
IMO number:	9210220	Cabins (with private balcony):	258
Builder:	Chantiers de l'Atlantique (France)	Cabins (wheelchair accessible):	4
Original cost:	$150 million	Wheelchair accessibility:	Good
Entered service:	Feb 2001/May 2011	Cabin voltage:	110 and 220 volts
Registry:	Bermuda	Elevators:	4
Length (ft/m):	592.0/180.4	Casino (gaming tables):	Yes
Beam (ft/m):	83.5/25.4	Slot machines:	Yes
Draft (ft/m):	19.5/6.0	Swimming pools:	1
Propulsion/Propellers:	diesel (18,600 kW)/2	Hot tubs (on deck):	3
Passenger decks:	9	Self-service launderette:	Yes
Total crew:	300	Dedicated cinema/seats:	No
Passengers (lower beds/alll berths):	710/838	Library:	Yes
Passenger Space Ratio (lower beds/all berths):	42.6/36.1	Onboard currency:	UK£
Crew/Passenger Ratio (lower beds/all berths):	1.8/2.2		

An adults-only, friendly ship, ideal for British tastes

OVERVIEW. There may not be marble bathroom fittings or other expensive niceties, but this adults-only ship provides a value-for-money cruise and tour programs geared specifically to more mature British passengers, in a hassle-free environment with expert speakers.

THE SHIP. *Adonia*, the last of eight almost identical ships originally built for the defunct Renaissance Cruises, has the feel of an informal old-world British country hotel – warm, comfortable, cosseting, and friendly. P&O's trademark buff-colored funnel balances the ship's all-white hull and superstructure. An outside lido deck has a swimming pool and good sunbathing space.

Although there is no walk-around promenade deck outdoors, there is a small jogging track above the perimeter of the swimming pool, and you can stroll on open decks on the port and starboard sides. There are no wooden decks outdoors; they are covered by Bolidt, a sand-colored rubberized material.

The interior decor, designed by a Scotsman, John McNeece, is quite elegant, a throwback to the dark woods style of the ocean liners of the 1920s and '30s. It includes detailed ceiling cornices, both real and faux wrought-iron staircase railings, wood- and leather-paneled walls, trompe l'oeil ceilings, rich carpeting in hallways, and many other interesting and expensive-looking decorative touches.

Public rooms. These are basically spread over three decks. The reception hall has a staircase with

Berlitz's Ratings

	Possible	Achieved
Ship	500	398
Accommodation	200	154
Food	400	275
Service	400	285
Entertainment	100	71
Cruise	400	293

OVERALL SCORE
1476 points out of 2000

intricate, real wrought-iron railings, but these are cleverly painted on plexiglas panels on the stairways on other decks – a copy of the staircase aboard *SS Titanic*.

The Library is a beautiful, restful room – perhaps the nicest public room – designed in the Regency style. It has a fireplace, a high, indented, trompe l'oeil ceiling, and a collection of about 2,000 books, plus comfortable wingback chairs with footstools, and sofas to fall asleep on.

A Crow's Nest Lounge is high atop the ship, with great views from its floor-to-ceiling windows. The room has a long bar which faces forward – the barmen actually have the best view – and very comfortable seating. There is a small central bandstand and wooden dance floor forward of the bar.

Anderson's Lounge, a P&O Cruises favorite also found aboard *Aurora* and *Oriana*, is a delightful wood-paneled lounge with a fireplace, a long bar with sit-up bar stools, and it has the feel of a proper traditional gentleman's club.

The Cabaret Lounge is used mainly for evening theatrical shows and musical performances. There are several bars, including one in each of the restaurant entrances.

Adonia is already a successful ship for P&O Cruises and for passengers who simply don't like the larger resort-style ships – or cruising with children. And it allows P&O regulars to sail into some of the smaller ports the larger ships in the fleet can't get into. Drink prices are quite reasonable.

ACCOMMODATION. There are six basic cabin size categories, in 20 price categories (14 for double occupancy and six for single occupancy). Some cabins have interconnecting doors, and 18 cabins on Deck 6 have lifeboat-obstructed views. All grades have tea/coffee-making facilities. There are two interior accommodation passageways.

Standard Outside-View and Interior Cabins. These are compact units, and tight for two persons, particularly for cruises longer than five days. They have twin beds or a queen-size bed, with good under-bed storage, personal safe, vanity desk with large mirror, reasonable closet and drawer space in rich, dark woods, TV, and cotton bathrobe. TV sets carry major news channels, where obtainable, plus sport and several movie channels.

Cabins with Private Balcony. Cabins with private balconies – about 66 percent of all cabins – have partial, and not full, balcony partitions, sliding glass doors and, thanks to good design and layout, only 14 cabins on Deck 6 have lifeboat-obstructed views. The tiled-floor, plain wall bathrooms are compact units, and include a shower stall with a removable hand-held shower unit, wall-mounted hairdryer, 100 percent cotton towels, toiletries storage shelves, and retractable clothesline.

Owner's Suites/Master Suites. The six Owner's Suites and four Master Suites provide abundant space and are worth the extra cost. They are large living spaces located in the forward-most and aft-most sections of the ship. Particularly nice are those that overlook the stern, on decks 6, 7, and 8. They have more extensive private balconies that really are private and cannot be overlooked by anyone on the decks above. There is an entrance foyer, living room, bedroom (the bed faces the sea), audio unit, bathroom with Jacuzzi tub, and small guest bathroom.

DINING. There are three proper restaurants, plus a casual self-serve buffet-style venue and an outdoor grill: The Pacific Restaurant, in the aft section, is the most formal, with 338 seats and a raised central section. It has large ocean-view windows on three sides, and several prime tables overlook the stern. Dining is at assigned tables, in two seatings. The menu changes daily for lunch and dinner. The noise level can be high, the result of a single-deck-height ceiling and noisy waiter stations. Adjacent to the restaurant entrance (it actually forms part of it) there's a Club Bar – a cozy, open lounge and bar, with an attractive fireplace. The food is rather bland, and quite standardized, more suited to those of a certain age.

Other dining options. Ocean Grill, by Marco Pierre White, has ocean-view windows along one side and aft. The menu is small, and concentrates on steak (there's a nice Casterbridge 28-day dry-aged filet steak) and seafood dishes. There is a cover charge to eat here, and reservations are needed. A second reservations-only venue, the Sorrento Restaurant, offers rather pleasant Italian cuisine; it also has a cover charge. Both of these L-shaped venues are the same size, and have ocean-view windows along two sides and at the stern. Tables are mostly for four or six.

The Conservatory, with both indoor and outdoor seating, is the ship's casual dining spot, in a self-serve style. It is open for breakfast, lunch, and casual theme-night dinners. The selection is and quality of items presented is average, so don't expect haute cuisine – P&O's casual eateries are not known for this.

Additionally, there is a Poolside Grill, providing casual fast food and grilled food fare.

ENTERTAINMENT. The Curzon Lounge is the venue for all main entertainment events, and occasional social functions. It is a single level room, with a large bar set at the back – the bartender probably has the best views of the stage and acts. The entertainment consists mainly of cabaret and small group shows.

There's also a Crow's Nest Lounge; it sits atop the ship at the front, has good forward views; it includes a dance floor and live music, and lots of seating alcoves to the port and starboard sides of the room. However, from most of these seats you don't have a view of the live band or dance floor.

SPA/FITNESS. The Oasis Spa has a gymnasium with some muscle-toning equipment, a large hot tub, steam rooms for men and women (there are no saunas), several treatment rooms, and a beauty salon. A spa concession provides beauty and wellness treatments, as well as exercise classes – some of which may cost extra. Out on deck, there are a small swimming pool, two hot tubs, a jogging track, a golf practice net, and shuffleboard courts.

Adventure of the Seas
★★★+

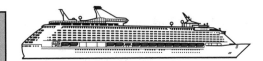

Size:................................Large Resort Ship	Crew/Passenger Ratio (lower beds/all berths):.......... 2.6/3.2
Tonnage:....................................... 137,276	Cabins (total):................................... 1,557
Lifestyle: ....Standard	Size range (sq ft/m): 151.0–1,358.0/14.0–126.1
Cruise line:.................. Royal Caribbean International	Cabins (outside view):.................................939
Former names: ....none	Cabins (interior/no view):..............................618
IMO number: 9167227	Cabins (for one person):..................................0
Builder: .... Kvaerner Masa-Yards (Finland)	Cabins (with private balcony): 765
Original cost:................................ $500 million	Cabins (wheelchair accessible): 26
Entered service:.............................. Nov 2001	Wheelchair accessibility:..............................Best
Registry:...................................... Bahamas	Cabin voltage: .... 110 volts
Length (ft/m):..........................1,020.6/311.1	Elevators:...14
Beam (ft/m):............................... 155.5/47.4	Casino (gaming tables):...............................Yes
Draft (ft/m):................................. 28.8/8.8	Slot machines:.......................................Yes
Propulsion/Propellers:......diesel-electric (75,600kW)/3 pods (2	Swimming pools:.......................................3
azimuthing, 1 fixed)	Hot tubs (on deck):....................................6
Passenger decks:.....................................14	Self-service launderette:...............................No
Total crew:..................................... 1,185	Dedicated cinema/seats:................................No
Passengers (lower beds/alll berths):............. 3,114/3,838	Library: ....Yes
Passenger Space Ratio (lower beds/all berths): 44.0/35.7	Onboard currency: ....US$

A large ship that's big on things to do for the whole family

OVERVIEW. *Adventure of the Seas* is a large, floating leisure resort. It provides a host of facilities, rather like a small town, yet offers a healthy amount of space per passenger. Too large to go through the Panama Canal, it limits its itineraries almost exclusively to the Caribbean, where only a few islands can accept it.

THE SHIP. Embarkation and disembarkation typically take place through two access points, designed to minimize lines – that's over 1,500 people for each access point. Once inside the ship, you'll need good walking shoes – it really is quite a long way from one end to the other. Spend the first few hours exploring all the facilities and public spaces and it will be time well spent.

A four-deck-high Royal Promenade is the main interior focal point; it's a good place to hang out, or to arrange to meet someone. The length of two American football fields, it has two internal lobbies rising through 11 decks. Cafés, shops, and entertainment locations front this winding street and interior 'with-view' cabins look into it from above. It is an imaginative piece of design work, and fans of shopping malls enjoy it immensely.

The long super-atrium houses a 'traditional' pub. There's also a Champagne Bar, a Sidewalk Café (for Continental breakfast, all-day pizzas, specialty coffees, and desserts), Sprinkles (for round-the-clock ice cream and yoghurt), and a sports bar. There are also several shops – for jewelry, gifts, liquor, perfumes, and souve-

Berlitz's Ratings

	Possible	Achieved
Ship	500	392
Accommodation	200	141
Food	400	222
Service	400	268
Entertainment	100	76
Cruise	400	264
OVERALL SCORE		
1363 points out of 2000		

nirs. Comedy art has its place here, too, for example in the trompe l'oeil painter climbing up the walls.

The cabin hallways are warm and attractive, with artwork cabinets and wavy lines to lead you along and break up the monotony. In fact, there are plenty of colorful, even whimsical, decorative touches to avoid what could be a very clinical environment.

The Guest Reception and Shore Excursion counters are located at the aft end of the promenade, as is an ATM machine. Things to watch for: look up to see the large moving, asteroid-like sculpture (constantly growing and contracting). At times, street entertainers appear, and parades are staged, while at other (carefully orchestrated) times it's difficult to walk through the area as it's filled to the brim with tacky shopping items – like a cheap bazaar.

Arched across the promenade is a captain's balcony, and in the center of the promenade a stairway connects you to the deck below, where you'll find the Schooner Bar (a piano lounge common to all RCI ships) and the flashy Casino Royale. Gaming includes blackjack, Caribbean stud poker, roulette, and craps, plus 300 slot machines.

Aft of the casino is the neat Aquarium Bar, with 50 tons of glass and water in four large aquariums, while close by are some neat displays of oceanographic interest. RCI has teamed up with the University of Miami's Rosenstiel School of Marine and Atmospheric Science to study the ocean and the atmosphere. A small onboard laboratory is part of the project.

There's a regulation-size ice-skating rink (Studio B), with real ice, with 'bleacher' seating for up to 900, and the latest in broadcast facilities. Superb Ice Follies shows are presented here. A stunning two-deck library, open 24 hours a day, includes $12 million worth of artwork.

Other drinking places include the small and intimate Champagne Bar, Crown & Anchor Pub, and Connoisseur Club – for cigars and cognacs. Lovers of jazz might appreciate Blue Moon, an intimate room for cool music atop the ship in the Viking Crown Lounge. Golfers might enjoy the 19th Hole, a golf bar, as they play the Adventure Links.

There is a TV studio with high-tech broadcast facilities, located adjacent to rooms that can be used for trade show exhibit space, with a conference center seating 400 and a multi-media screening room that seats 60.

High atop the ship, you can tie the knot in a wedding chapel in the sky, the Skylight Chapel; located on the upper level of the Viking Crown Lounge, it has wheelchair access via an electric stairlift. Outdoors, the pool and open deck areas provide a resort-like environment.

If possible, visit the Helicopter deck at the front of the ship for great starry-sky views at night.

Passenger niggles include having to negotiate the 'sale' bazaar tables along the Royal Promenade; the lunchtime chaos in the Windjammer Café on embarkation day (before you have access to your cabin); and the problem of getting a table in the extra-cost dining venues.

The ship has four sisters: *Explorer of the Seas*, *Mariner of the Seas*, *Navigator of the Seas* and *Voyager of the Seas*.

FAMILIES. Facilities for children and teenagers are quite extensive. Aquanauts is for three- to five-year-olds; Explorers is for six- to eight-year-olds; Voyagers is for nine- to 12-year-olds. Optix is a dedicated area for teenagers, including a daytime club with several computers, a soda bar, and a dance floor. Challenger's Arcade has an array of video games. Paint and Clay is an arts and crafts center for younger children. Adjacent is Adventure Beach, an area for all the family to enjoy; it includes swimming pools, a water slide, and outdoor game areas.

ACCOMMODATION. There is a wide range of 22 cabin price grades, in four major groupings: Premium ocean-view suites and cabins, Interior (atrium-view) cabins, Ocean-view cabins, and Interior cabins. Many cabins are of a similar size – good for incentives and large groups – and 300 have interconnecting doors (good for families).

Some 138 interior cabins have bay windows that look into an interior horizontal atrium – a cruise industry first when the ship debuted. Regardless of what cabin grade you choose, all except for the Royal Suite and Owner's Suite have twin beds that convert to a queen-size unit, TV set, radio and telephone, personal safe, vanity unit, hairdryer, and private bathroom. However, you'll need to keep the curtains closed in the bay windows if you wear little clothing, because you can be seen easily from adjacent bay windows.

Royal Suite (Deck 10). At around 1,146 sq ft (107 sq m), the Royal Suite is the largest private living space, located almost at the top of the Centrum lobby on the port side. It is a nicely appointed penthouse suite, whose occupants, sadly, must share the rest of the ship with everyone else, except for access to their own exclusive concierge club. It has a king-size circular bed in a separate large bedroom that can be fully closed off; a living room with an additional queen-size sofa bed, baby grand piano, refrigerator/wet bar, dining table and four chairs, expansive entertainment center, and a reasonably large bathroom.

Royal Family Suite. The four Royal Family suites (two aft on Deck 9, two aft on Deck 8, each measuring around 574 sq ft/53 sq m) have two separate bedrooms. The main bedroom has a large vanity desk; the second, smaller bedroom also includes two beds and third/fourth upper Pullman berths. There's a lounge with dining table and four chairs, wet bar, walk-in closet; and large bathroom with Jacuzzi tub, washbasin, and separate shower enclosure. The suites, at the stern, have large balconies with views out over the ship's wash.

Owner's Suites. Ten slightly smaller but desirable Owner's Suites (around 468 sq ft/43 sq m) are in the center of the ship, on both port and starboard sides, adjacent to the Centrum lobby on Deck 10. Each has a bedroom with queen-size bed or twin beds; lounge with large sofa; wet bar; bathroom with Jacuzzi tub, washbasin and separate shower enclosure. There's also a private balcony, although it's not very large.

Standard Outside-View and Interior Cabins. All cabins have a private bathroom, as well as interactive TV and pay-per-view movies, including an X-rated channel. Cabin bathrooms really are compact, but at least they have a proper shower enclosure instead of a shower curtain.

Some accommodation grades have a refrigerator/mini-bar, although there is no space left because it is crammed with 'take-and-pay' items. If you take anything from the mini-bar/refrigerator on the day of embarkation in Miami, Florida, sales tax will be added to your bill.

Cabins with 'private balconies' aren't so private. The balcony decking is made of Bolidt – a sort of rubberized sand – and not wood, though the balcony rail is of wood. If you have a cabin with a connecting door to another cabin, be aware that you'll probably be able to hear everything your next-door neighbors say and do. Bathroom toilets are explosively noisy, based on the vacuum system. Cabin bath towels are small and skimpy. Note that room service food menus are very basic.

DINING. The main dining room has a total capacity of 1,919. It is close to being massive, and consists of three levels, each of which is named after a famous composer: Mozart, Strauss, and Vivaldi. The menu is the same on all three levels. A dramatic staircase connects all three levels, and huge, fat support pillars obstruct sight lines from a number of seats. However, the ambiance is good and there's always a good buzz when the ship is full dinner is in progress.

Two small private wings serve private groups: La Cetra and La Notte, each with 58 seats. When you book, choose one of two seatings, or 'My Time Dining' (eat when you want during dining room hours). Tables are for four, six, eight, 10, or 12. The place settings, china, and cutlery are of good quality.

Other dining options. Portofino, the ship's upscale Euro-Italian restaurant. It's open for dinner only, reservations are required, and there's a cover charge. The food and its presentation are better than the food in the dining room, although the restaurant isn't large enough for all passengers to try even once during a cruise. Choices include antipasti, soup, salad, pasta, main dish, dessert, cheese, and coffee.

Casual and informal meals at all hours can be taken at:

Windjammer Café: this is a really large, sprawling venue for casual buffet-style, self-help breakfast (this tends to be the busiest time of the day), lunch, and light dinners (but not on the last night of the cruise); it's often difficult to find a table and by the time you do your food could be cold.

The Island Grill (it's actually a section inside the Windjammer Café), for casual dinner (no reservations needed), with a grill and open kitchen.

Johnny Rockets, a retro 1950s all-day, all-night diner-style eatery, has hamburgers, malt shakes (at extra cost), and jukebox hits, with both indoor and outdoor seating.

Promenade Café: for Continental breakfast, all-day pizzas, and speciality coffees – which are provided in paper cups.

Sprinkles, located on the Royal promenade is for round-the-clock ice cream and yogurt, pastries and coffee.

ENTERTAINMENT. The 1,350-seat Lyric Theater, the principal showlounge, is a stunning room located at the forward end of the ship. It has Art Nouveau themed décor, spans the height of five decks, with only a few slim pillars and almost no disruption of sight lines. Production shows are presented here by a large cast and a live band. There's also an array of up-and-coming cabaret acts and late-night adults-only comedy.

In addition, the ship has an array of cabaret acts. Although many are not what you'd call headliners, they regularly travel the cruise ship circuit. The strongest cabaret acts are presented in the main showlounge, while others appear in the Imperial Lounge (it's on the deck above), which is also the venue for adult-only late-night comedy. The best shows of all, for many, are, however, the Ice Spectaculars.

There is also a TV studio that can be used, for example, for trade show exhibit space – good for conventions at sea.

Entertainment is always upbeat. There is even background music in all corridors and elevators, and constant music outdoors on the pool deck. If you want a quiet relaxing vacation, this is not the right ship for you.

SPA/FITNESS. The ShipShape health spa is reasonably large, and measures 15,000 sq ft (1,400 sq m). It includes an aerobics room, fitness center (with the usual stairmasters, treadmills, stationary bikes, weight machines, and free weights), treatment rooms, and men's and women's sauna/steam rooms. Another 10,000 sq ft (930 sq m) of space is devoted to a Solarium (with sliding glass-dome roof) to relax in after you've exercised.

On the back of the funnel is a 32.8-ft (10-m) rock-climbing wall, with five climbing tracks. It's a great buzz being 200ft (60m) above the ocean while the ship is moving. Other sports facilities include a roller-blading track, a dive-and-snorkel shop, a full-size basketball court, and a nine-hole, par 26 golf 'course.' A dive-and-snorkel shop provides equipment for rental, and diving classes.

Nautical Expressions

If you've ever wondered where some terms or phrases came from, you have only to look to the sea, ships, and seamen.

Square meal. This derives from the meals served on square wooden platters used on board ship. The platters could be easily stowed in racks between meals. Any substantial meal is now described as a 'square meal.'

Three sheets to the wind. A term said of a man who is clearly behaving under the influence of drink. A ship with three sheets in the wind would 'stagger to and fro like a drunken man.' Conversely, a drunken man behaves like a ship with three sheets in the wind.

To know the ropes. There were miles and miles of cordage in the rigging of a square rigged ship. The only way of keeping track of and knowing the function of all of these lines was to know their locations. It took an experienced seaman to know the ropes.

Under the weather. Refers to a sailor being in the uncomfortable position of having his station at the weather bow, subject to the pitching of the boat with spray constantly blown in his face. It is used today to mean feeling unwell.

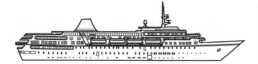

Aegean Odyssey
★★★ +

Size:..................................... Small Ship	Cabins (total):.....................................198
Tonnage:.. 12,094	Size range (sq ft/m): 130.0–550.0/12.0–51.0
Lifestyle:......................................Standard	Cabins (outside view):..............................175
Cruise line:..........................Voyages to Antiquity	Cabins (interior/no view):............................41
Former names: Aegean I, Aegean Dolphin, Dolphin, Alkyon, Narcis	Cabins (for one person):.............................26
IMO number: 7225910	Cabins (with private balcony):........................42
Builder: .... Santierul N. Galatz (Romania)	Cabins (wheelchair accessible): 2
Original cost:..................................... n/a	Wheelchair accessibility:............................Fair
Entered service:......................... 1974/May 2010	Cabin voltage: .... 220 volts
Registry:.. Malta	Elevators:..2
Length (ft/m):............................. 460.9/140.5	Casino (gaming tables):..............................No
Beam (ft/m):............................... 67.2/20.5	Slot machines:......................................No
Draft (ft/m):.................................. 20.3/6.2	Swimming pools:.....................................1
Propulsion/Propellers:..................diesel (10,296kW)/2	Hot tubs (on deck):..................................0
Passenger decks:...................................8	Self-service launderette:.............................No
Total crew:......................................200	Dedicated cinema/seats:..............................No
Passengers (lower beds/alll berths):................ 378/410	Library: ....Yes
Passenger Space Ratio (lower beds/all berths): 30.5/29.8	Onboard currency: ....US$
Crew/Passenger Ratio (lower beds/all berths):.......... 1.8/1.9	

OVERVIEW. *Aegean Odyssey* will appeal to couples and single travelers looking for a life enrichment experience in a smart, yet somewhat traditional classic ship environment. The credo is based on history, ancient civilizations, and learning and the main appeal is the quality of the excursions and lecturers.

THE SHIP. Although this isn't a new ship by any stretch of the imagination, it has been tastefully and skillfully converted to provide an extremely comfortable environment. Its profile is quite smart, with a well-shaped funnel that balances a rather angular stern – the result of a $26 million 'chop and stretch' operation some years ago. The present operator, Voyages to Antiquity, bought the ship in December 2007, then set about a painstaking refit and refurbishment program that ended up more like a complete rebuild, because the ship now looks much nicer, and has a pleasing profile.

Originally built to carry munitions, the ship's hull is really strong. The passenger capacity was significantly reduced – from 650 to 378, with a subsequent increase in the passenger space ratio – in a well thought-out conversion. As a result, the open deck space, covered in teak, is extremely good, and measures 37,674 sq ft (3,500 sq m) – a lot for a small ship.

The Promenade Deck houses most of the public rooms. There is a forward observation lounge, with many windows providing plenty of natural light. The Charleston Lounge – actually a large lounge with a

Berlitz's Ratings		
	Possible	Achieved
Ship	500	350
Accommodation	200	141
Food	400	269
Service	400	291
Entertainment	100	68
Cruise	400	279
OVERALL SCORE		
1398 points out of 2000		

large dance floor and bar – is quite stunning, and sports a classy black and red decor.

Some materials in public rooms are held together by the 'patch and fix' method, but subtle, pleasing, warm color combinations – most with earth tones – help to create a spacious, light, and open feel.

Excellent academic-style lecturers are an intrinsic part of the cruises, which are typically 14 days long, and a good-size library is an important facility. Itineraries include several port overnights.

Gratuities to dining and cabin staff are included in the fare, together with selected wines with dinner (or beer/soft drinks) otherwise, 12½ percent is added to bar accounts. Most shore excursions are also included (together with bottled mineral water for the included excursions).

Despite the shakes and rattles of the ship's interior fittings when going at maximum speed, it's the character of the ship, its generous open deck space (and gorgeous thick, highly polished handrails), and an excellent lecture and enrichment program that all help to nudge the final score higher than one might normally expect for a 1970s-built ship.

ACCOMMODATION. There are now 20 cabin price grades (6 of which are for single-occupancy cabins), with half designated as Balcony Class. The accommodation numbering system is nautically incorrect, however, with even numbered cabins on the starboard side instead of on the port, or left, side of the ship. Most cabins do have an outside view, with similar sizes and configuration. All have a small refrigerator.

They are reasonably spacious, considering the ship's size, and pleasantly decorated, although closet, drawer, and luggage storage space for two is limited in the lower-grade cabins, particularly for longer cruises. Most bathrooms are partly tiled, with decent storage space for toiletries.

Single travelers have a choice of 36 single-occupancy cabins (in 6 different grades), most of which are quite spacious.

Two owner's suites are located forward on Sun Deck. These are rather nice and have forward ocean views over the bow, and include a narrow balcony on either port or starboard side. They have a separate bedroom, a walk-in closet, and a bathroom with a tub-shower combination.

DINING. The Marco Polo Restaurant is the ship's main dining room. It is located on the lowest passenger deck (so it's very stable when the ship is at sea). It has a restful color scheme, and a high ceiling. Seating is mostly at large tables – there are no tables for two – in an open-seating arrangement that allows you to dine when you want and with whom you want. The amount of space around each table is good. Portholes on both sides, rather than windows, are set high up, and allow some natural light during the day.

The cuisine is a mixture of Continental and Asian, but the selection of breads, cheeses, and fruit is limited. Meats, fish, and poultry items are not of a high quality, although they are decent enough for most passengers. For casual meals, self-serve breakfast and lunch buffets are available at the Terrace Café, aft on Promenade Deck, with indoor-outdoor seating that includes a Tapas Bar each evening ('Tapas on the Terrace'), and daily grilled specialties.

ENTERTAINMENT. The Ambassador Lounge is a single-level showlounge that has a bar at one end, and seating that is mainly in tub-style chairs or old-style banquette seating. The sight lines to the 'stage' from many seats are obstructed, however, because of several support pillars. This room principally serves as a presentation room for the specialist lecturers, and for classical concerts.

SPA/FITNESS. A new indoor wellness centre was built in 2012. It is an attractive facility, and includes a separate male sauna, female wet sauna (steam 'pods'), and a changing area for males and females, two body treatment rooms, plus a beauty salon, and a good-size fitness area.

Rules of the road

Ships, the largest moving objects made by man, are subject to stringent international regulations. They must keep to the right in shipping lanes, and pass on the right (with certain exceptions). When circumstances raise some doubt, or shipping lanes are crowded, ships use their whistles in the same way an automobile driver uses directional signals to show which way he will turn. When one ship passes another and gives a single blast on its whistle, this means it is turning to starboard (right). Two blasts mean a turn to port (left).

The other ship acknowledges by repeating the same signal. Ships switch on navigational running lights at night – green for starboard, red for port, plus two white lights on the masts, the forward one lower than the aft one.

Flags and pennants form another part of a ship's communication facilities and are displayed for identification purposes. Each time a country is visited, its national flag is shown. While entering and leaving a port, the ship flies a blue-and-white vertically striped flag to request a pilot, while a half-red, half-white flag (divided vertically) indicates that a pilot is on board. Cruise lines also display their own 'house' flag from the mast.

A ship's funnel (smokestack) is one other means of identification, each line having its own design and color scheme. The size, height, and number of funnels were all points worth advertising at the turn of the 20th century. Most ocean liners of the time had four funnels and were called 'four-stackers.'

There are numerous customs at sea, many of them older than any maritime law. Superstition has always been an important element, as in the following example quoted from the British Admiralty Manual of Seamanship: 'The custom of breaking a bottle of wine over the stem of a ship when it is being launched originates from the old practice of toasting prosperity to a ship with a silver goblet of wine, which was then cast into the sea in order to prevent a toast of ill intent being drunk from the same cup. This was a practice that proved too expensive, and it was replaced in 1690 by the breaking of a bottle of wine over the stem.

Aegean Paradise
★★★

Size:.. Small Ship	Cabins (total):.......................................325
Tonnage: 21,884	Size range (sq ft/m): 182.9-595.0/17.0-55.0
Lifestyle: ....Standard	Cabins (outside view):.................................269
Cruise line:.....................................EstTur	Cabins (interior/no view):..............................56
Former names: .... Delphin Voyager, Orient Venus	Cabins (for one person):..............................0
IMO number: 8902333	Cabins (with private balcony):.......................177
Builder: ....Ishikawajima Heavy Indistries (Japan)	Cabins (wheelchair accessible): 2
Original cost: .... $150 million	Wheelchair accessibility:...............................Fair
Entered service:....................... Jul 1990/May 2012	Cabin voltage: .... 110 volts
Registry:.. Bahamas	Elevators:...4
Length (ft/m):............................. 570.8/174.0	Casino (gaming tables):.................................No
Beam (ft/m):............................... 78.7/24.0	Slot machines:.......................................No
Draft (ft/m): 21.3/6.5	Swimming pools:....................................1
Propulsion/Propellers:..................diesel (13,830kW)/2	Hot tubs (on deck):....................................0
Passenger decks:..................................8	Self-service launderette:.............................Yes
Total crew:..250	Dedicated cinema/seats:.................................No
Passengers (lower beds/alll berths):.............. 650/650	Library:...Yes
Passenger Space Ratio (lower beds/all berths): 33.6/33.6	Onboard currency: ....Lira
Crew/Passenger Ratio (lower beds/all berths):......... 2.6/2.6	

Small, casual, comfortable ship for Turkish-speakers

OVERVIEW. Aegean Paradise is a ship suited to couples and families with children, for short cruises, at a moderate cost.

THE SHIP. Aegean Paradise is a conventional-shaped ship, originally built for Venus Cruise. The ship has a pleasant profile (there's no mistaking 'EtsTur' painted in big red letters on the ship's hull). There is a good amount of open deck and sunbathing space, aft of funnel. Great views can be had from a Panorama observation lounge, which is wrapped around the funnel housing; there is no elevator access, but stairs include a chairlift. The pool deck is nicely laid out, and has a wood surround, including a raised section that houses two hot tubs.

There is a good array of public rooms with tasteful light-color décor including a three-deck-high entrance lobby (with glass chandelier and a nice bronze statue of Venus); the reception desk and shore excursion desk are located on the lower level. Most public rooms are set on one deck, and these include a casino with gaming tables, and a small array of slot machines. Close by is a small library and card room, and internet-connect workstations.

ACCOMMODATION. There are several cabin price grades. Standard cabins have decor that is best described as plain, with a reasonable amount of closet space; the drawer space is quite limited. All accommodation grades have a flat-screen television set,

Berlitz's Ratings		
	Possible	Achieved
Ship	500	305
Accommodation	200	122
Food	400	230
Service	400	242
Entertainment	100	63
Cruise	400	235
OVERALL SCORE		
1197 points out of 2000		

telephone, refrigerator and hairdryer. All cabins have a shower, with the exception of the three suites. Some 36 cabins have lifeboat obstructed views, while 177 have a balcony (these cabins were added in a 2007 refit).

Three suites are the largest accommodation and these feature an expansive lounge area with plush armchairs, coffee table, and window-side chairs and drinks table, large windows, and a larger private balcony. There is a separate sleeping room (curtained off from the living room) with twin- or queen-sized bed, vanity/office desk, and larger bathroom with bathtub and separate shower.

CUISINE. The main dining room operates in a single seating at assigned tables. It is an attractive restaurant, and there is plenty of space around the dining tables. The aft section is the most desirable, because of views over the stern. Breakfast and lunch are of the self-serve buffet-style. An alternative (extra-cost) Romanesque Grill has classic period Roman decor and a high ceiling.

ENTERTAINMENT. The Main Lounge is a single deck height, horseshoe-shaped room, and there are good sightlines to the platform stage. Cabaret acts are featured, and there is plenty of live music.

SPA/FITNESS. There is a small spa which consists of a gym, saunas, and treatment rooms.

AIDAaura
★★★ +

Size:....................................... Mid-size Ship	Cabins (total):..................................633
Tonnage:................................. 42,289	Size range (sq ft/m):................ 145.3–344.4/13.5–32.0
Lifestyle:.................................Standard	Cabins (outside view):............................422
Cruise line:..............................AIDA Cruises	Cabins (interior/no view):..........................211
Former names:..............................none	Cabins (for one person):............................0
IMO number:...............................9221566	Cabins (with private balcony):........................60
Builder:..........................Aker MTW (Germany)	Cabins (wheelchair accessible):.......................4
Original cost:.............................$350 million	Wheelchair accessibility:.........................Good
Entered service:..........................Apr 2003	Cabin voltage:........................110 and 220 volts
Registry:................................. Italy	Elevators:....................................6
Length (ft/m):......................... 665.5/202.8	Casino (gaming tables):............................No
Beam (ft/m):.......................... 92.2/28.1	Slot machines:.................................No
Draft (ft/m):.......................... 20.3/6.2	Swimming pools:................................2
Propulsion/Propellers:.......... diesel-electric (27,150kW)/2	Hot tubs (on deck):..............................5
Passenger decks:...............................10	Self-service launderette:..........................Yes
Total crew:..................................389	Dedicated cinema/seats:...........................No
Passengers (lower beds/all berths):.............. 1,266/1,582	Library:.....................................Yes
Passenger Space Ratio (lower beds/all berths):....... 33.4/26.7	Onboard currency:.............................Euros
Crew/Passenger Ratio (lower beds/all berths):.......... 3.0/3.7	

Upbeat, family-friendly ship for casual no-frills cruising

OVERVIEW. An AIDA Cruise is for youthful German-speaking couples, singles, and particularly families seeking good value for money in a party-like environment, with excellent entertainment. This is all about über-casual cruising, with two main self-serve buffet restaurants instead of the traditional waiter service. It's tablecloth-less eating, and there is little contact with the relatively few staff.

Berlitz's Ratings		
	Possible	Achieved
Ship	500	361
Accommodation	200	131
Food	400	259
Service	400	269
Entertainment	100	75
Cruise	400	277
OVERALL SCORE		
1372 points out of 2000		

THE SHIP. The ship has a smart, contemporary profile, with a swept-back funnel and wedge-shaped stern. The bows display the red lips, as well as the blue eyes, of Aïda (from Verdi's opera, written to commemorate the opening of the Suez Canal in 1871). AIDA Cruises, Germany's largest cruise line, is part of Costa Cruises, which is itself part of Carnival Corporation. Its expanding fleet allows it to offer a wide choice of itineraries, including the Middle East and Asia.

Overall, this really is cruising for urban dwellers, and for those that don't mind busy places and lines. An AIDA cruise isn't cheap, but you get a lot of high-tech entertainment, and there's always plenty of food. Some frustration occurs when shore excursions sell out, when lines form after shore excursion buses return to the ship and you have to go through the slow security check – and at peak times in the self-serve restaurants, and for shore tenders.

The AIDA-class ships (known as AIDA Clubships) evolved from the first and smallest ship, AIDA (over 15 years old and now named AIDA cara), in which the

central idea was to get passengers to participate in public-area activities together, as in the Robinson Club concept on land. This led to 'open plan' interiors and the feeling that the ship is one large space, but cleverly split into intimate rooms – although, in reality, rooms 'flow' into each other at each fire zone section (a length of 157ft/48m).

The use of bright tropical colors throughout the interiors is really noticeable. Most of the chairs, counter stools, and bar seats are quite small, designed for thin, youthful passengers.

There is, however, constant high-street music everywhere, so these ships are not for those wanting a 'quiet escape' vacation, even though volume levels are well controlled.

AIDA Cruises has really grown up over the past few years, and no longer focuses on summer-camp style participation events. The ships have become more sophisticated, entertaining venues, and the old *animateurs* – somewhat like the *gentils ordinaires* of Club Med, but better – have grown up and morphed into what is now known as Club Teams. They, along with other staff, interact with passengers throughout the ship.

About 20 nationalities are represented among the crew, who are upbeat and cheerful. Staff hospitality training is now at a high level in all departments, and AIDA Cruises has its own training schools in several countries, plus a recognized training academy in Rostock.

Sport biking is part of its youthful image, with three different levels of cycling to suit differing fitness levels. The line has also successfully appealed to golfers, with golf-theme packages, cruises, and excursions ashore in many ports of call.

The open deck space is tight, but sunbathing space includes some rather pleasant, reasonably quiet space above the navigation bridge. Dip pools and hot tubs, plus seating areas, are provided in a cascading, tiered setting atop the ship on the pool deck, providing a decent amount of sunbathing space. It's all designed to be in a 'beach-like' environment, with splash and play areas.

Other facilities include a shore excursion counter, library, seminar rooms, duty-free shop, several bars and lounges, a small casino with blackjack, roulette and poker gaming tables, and slot machines.

There is a separate aft sports deck, a 'no music' observation lounge, and an art gallery. The embarkation entryway is really innovative, has a bar and a lookout balcony, and is cheerfully painted to look like a city street scene. It is different from the utilitarian gangway entry areas found aboard most cruise ships. A welcoming environment, it helps to calm tempers after waiting in a line to go through the security process for embarkation or in ports of call.

There are three pricing levels – Aida Premium, Aida Vario, and Just Aida – depending on what you want to be included, plus differences in price according to accommodation size and grade, and the itinerary. Opt for the basic, price-driven Just Aida package and the cruise line chooses the ship, itinerary, and accommodation for you – sort of a pot-luck cruise, based on or close to the dates you choose.

The dress code is simple: casual (no ties) at all times – there are no formal nights on board. All port taxes and gratuities are included in all packages, and, with very attractive rates, a cruise provides much better value than almost any land-based vacation.

Several decks of public rooms and facilities are positioned above the accommodation decks, and AIDAaura shares public room names that are common aboard all the ships in the fleet: Aida Bar, the main social gathering place, whose principal feature is a star-shaped bar (whose combined length makes it among the longest at sea), with many tables for standing drinkers.

Overall, this really is cruising for youthful German-speaking families, and for anyone who doesn't mind busy places and lines. An AIDA cruise isn't cheap, but you do get lots of trendy high-tech entertainment, and there's always plenty of food (although there's no room service). Some frustration occurs when shore excursions sell out, when lines form after shore excursion buses return to the ship and you have to go through the slow security check – and at peak times in the self-serve restaurants, and for shore tenders.

FAMILIES. This is a family-friendly ship. Children are split into four age groups: Seepferdchen (4–6 years), Delfin (7–9), Orcas (10–12), and Teens (14–17). Each has its own play area. There is a diverse selection of children's and youth programs, and special Club Team members dedicated to making sure that everyone has a good time.

ACCOMMODATION. There are eight or nine grades, from deluxe suites to interior (no view) cabins, depending on the ship, which keeps your cabin choice simple.

Contrary to maritime traditions (even-numbered cabins on the port side, odd-numbered cabins on the starboard side), cabin numbers progress numerically (example: 8201–8276 on the port side; 8101–8176 on the starboard side). All suites and cabins have two beds (convertible to queen-size bed). Some cabins also have two extra beds/berths for children, and some cabins have interconnecting doors – useful for families.

The decor in all accommodation grades is bright, youthful, rather minimalist, and slightly whimsical. All are accented with multi-patterned fabrics, wood-trimmed cabinetry (with nicely rounded edges), and rattan or wood-look furniture. Beds have duvets and a colorful Arabian-style fabric canopy that goes from the headboard to the ceiling. The windows have full pull-down blackout blinds (useful in destinations with long daylight hours). Lifeboats may obstruct views in some cabins in the ship's center.

The bathrooms are compact, practical units; they have a shower enclosure, small washbasin, and small toilet. As in the most basic hotels and motels, only a wall-mounted body wash/shampoo dispenser is provided, so take your own conditioner, hand lotion, and other toiletries you may need.

Thick, 100 percent cotton bathrobes are provided for suite-grade accommodation, although non-suite grade passengers can obtain one from the spa. Two towels are provided – a face towel and a 'bath' towel, in two different colors. The 'bath' towels are not very large, at 54 by 27 inches – compared to 72 by 36 inches aboard the P&O Cruises' Ventura, for example. Although the bathrooms do not have a hairdryer, one is located in the vanity unit in the cabin. Unusually, night-time turn-down service is not provided (there is no cabin service after 3pm).

Cabins with balconies have a sliding door that's easy to open and doesn't impinge on balcony space; a small drinks table and two small, light chairs are provided. Note that balconies on the lowest deck can be overlooked by anyone on a balcony on the decks above. Some cabins (forward on Deck 5 – Nos 5103, 5104, 5105, 5106, 5203, 5204, 5206) aboard these ships have cabins with an outside view (well, outside light), but they are totally obstructed by steel bulkheads that form the front section of the ship.

Suite-grade accommodation offers more space, including more drawer and storage space, better quality furniture and furnishings, a larger lounge area and a slightly larger bathroom with a tub – and, of course, a larger balcony (those at the front and stern of the ship have the best).

DINING. Two eateries are included in the cruise fare; these are the Markt and Karibik self-serve buffet-style restaurants. The opening times for lunch and dinner are 12:30-14:00 and 18:30-21:00 respectively.

The meal concept is simple: main meals are taken when you want them in one of the large self-serve buffet-style restaurants, with open seating at tables of four, six, or eight. Cutlery hangs in a rack (rather unhygienic because it can be touched by many fingers); there are no soup spoons, only dessert spoons. It's very casual and easy-going mass catering, so think food court eating, not dining.

Also, the tables are almost all large (for six or eight persons), and, when the ship is full, it can prove challenging to find a seat, not to mention any service personnel to clean the tables. Because it's a buffet venue, you'll probably sit with different people for each meal – which could be a good way to make new friends.

The standard of food at the self-serve buffet islands ranges from adequate to quite good, with creative displays and presentation, and table-clearing service that is sometimes efficient, but mostly not.

The many food islands and active stations cut down on the waiting time for food. There is always a big selection of breads, cheeses, cold cuts, fruits, and make-your-own coffee and teas – with a choice of more than 30 types of loose-leaf regular and herbal teas, and over 1,200 items of food are offered.

You can sit where you want, when you want, and with whom you want, so eating is a socially interactive occasion. In fact, it's hard to be an unsociable couple and have a table for only two. At peak times, the venues may remind you of noisy roadside cafés. Because of the large buffet rooms and self-serve dining concept, the crew to passenger ratio looks poor; but this is because there are no waiters as such (except in à la carte venues), only staff for clearing tables.

Beer is available at the push of a button or a pull of the tap, and table wine – of the sort that would make a good drain cleaner – is usually provided in carafes on each table for lunch and dinner. Note that the beverage stations open only during restaurant opening hours, unless you go to the extra-cost coffee bar (Café Mare). Vending machines dispense out-of-hours snacks.

Other dining options. The Rossini Restaurant (à la carte) has a quieter, more intimate atmosphere. It is open for dinner only, and has a set five- or six-course menu (plus daily specials). There is no cover charge, but an extra charge applies to everything on the à la carte menu (such as caviar, chateaubriand, ribeye steak), wine or any other drinks. Reservations are needed, tablecloths are provided, the food is good, and the waiter and sommelier service are friendly.

Vinotheque. The wine bar, located in front of the Weide Welt (Wide World) Restaurant, has a good list of premium wines, and Davidoff cigars (although you can't smoke them at the bar – or anywhere inside the ship). Pizzeria Mare. Ever popular – but overcooked – pizzas.

ENTERTAINMENT. The Theater (Das Theater) is the main venue for all shows and most cabaret, and is two decks high. It has a raised stage, and amphitheater-style bench seating on all levels. The benches have back rests, and are quite comfortable, and sight lines are good from most seats, with the exception of port and starboard balcony sections, where sight lines are interrupted by thick safety railings.

The shows are produced by AIDA Cruises' in-house department in a joint venture with SeeLive (Hamburg's Schmidt's Tivoli Theater), and typically consist of 12 performers. All vocals in the shows are performed live, to pre-recorded backing tracks that provide a mix of recorded live music and synthesized sound. The shows are trendy, upbeat, fun, and very entertaining. The whole entertainment experience is lively and fun – in fact, it's a little like going to the circus.

In addition, there is a live band in the Aida Bar, the only room with a large dance floor (except for the disco).

SPA/FITNESS. The Body and Soul Spa, is located forward on Deck 11. It measures 11,840 sq ft (1,100 sq m), and contains two saunas (one dry, one wet, both with seats for more than 20 persons, and glass walls that look onto the deck), massage and other treatment rooms, and a large lounging area. There are also showers, and two whole 'ice walls' to use when you come out of the saunas (simply lean into the ice wall for maximum effect). Forward and outside the wellness center, is an FKK (FreiKoerperKultur) nude sunbathing deck, on two levels.

'Sport bikes' (mountain bikes with tough front and rear suspension units) are provided for conducted biking excursions in each port of call by a concession run by of Austrian downhill champion skier Erwin Resch. You can also book biking, diving, and golfing excursions.

Sporting types can also play golf in the electronic golf simulator, or billiards, volleyball or squash – or go jogging.

AIDAbella
★★★★

Size:. . . . . .Large Resort Ship		Cabins (total):. 1,025		
Tonnage: 69,203		Size range (sq ft/m): 145.3–473.2/13.5–44		
Lifestyle: . . . . .Standard		Cabins (outside view): 666		
Cruise line:. . . . . .AIDA Cruises		Cabins (interior/no view):. 359		
Former names: . . . .*none*		Cabins (for one person):. 0		
IMO number: 9362542		Cabins (with private balcony): 480		
Builder: . . . . Meyer Werft (Germany)		Cabins (wheelchair accessible): 11		
Original cost: . . . .$390 million		Wheelchair accessibility:. . . . . .Good		
Entered service:. . . . . .Apr 2008		Cabin voltage: . . . . .110 and 220 volts		
Registry:. . . . . .Italy		Elevators:. 10		
Length (ft/m):. 826.7/252.0		Casino (gaming tables):. . . . . Yes		
Beam (ft/m):. 105.6/32.2		Slot machines:. . . . . .No		
Draft (ft/m): 24.6/7.5		Swimming pools:. 3		
Propulsion/Propellers:. . . . . .diesel-electric (36,000 kW)/2		Hot tubs (on deck):. 0		
Passenger decks:. 13		Self-service launderette:. . . . . Yes		
Total crew:. 646		Dedicated cinema/seats:. . . . . .No		
Passengers (lower beds/alll berths):. 2,050/2,500		Library: . . . . Yes		
Passenger Space Ratio (lower beds/all berths): 33.7/27.6		Onboard currency: . . . . Euros		
Crew/Passenger Ratio (lower beds/all berths):. 3.1/3.8				

Upbeat, family-friendly ship for no-frills cruising

OVERVIEW. An AIDA Cruise is for youthful German-speaking couples, singles, and particularly families seeking good value for money in a party-like environment, with excellent entertainment. This is all about über-casual cruising, with two main self-serve buffet restaurants instead of the traditional waiter service. It's tablecloth-less eating, and there is little contact with staff.

THE SHIP. The ship has a smart, contemporary profile, with a swept-back funnel and wedge-shaped stern. The bows display the red lips, as well as the blue eyes, of *Aïda* (from Verdi's opera, written to commemorate the opening of the Suez Canal in 1871). AIDA Cruises, Germany's largest cruise line, is part of Costa Cruises, which is itself part of Carnival Corporation. Its expanding fleet allows it to offer a wide choice of itineraries, including the Middle East and Asia.

The AIDA-class ships – known as AIDA Clubships – evolved from the first and smallest ship, AIDA (now named *AIDAcara*), in which the central idea was to get passengers to participate in public-area activities together, as in the Robinson Club concept on land. This led to 'open plan' interiors and the feeling that the ship is one large space, but cleverly split into intimate rooms – although, in reality, rooms 'flow' into each other at each fire zone section (a length of 157ft/48m).

The use of bright colors throughout is noticeable. Most of the chairs, counter stools, and bar seats are quite small, designed for thin, youthful passengers.

Berlitz's Ratings		
	Possible	Achieved
Ship	500	401
Accommodation	200	146
Food	400	264
Service	400	284
Entertainment	100	71
Cruise	400	296
OVERALL SCORE		
1462 points out of 2000		

Throughout the ship there is constant music, so this ship is not for anyone seeking a 'quiet escape.'

AIDA Cruises has really grown up over the past few years, and no longer focuses on summer-camp style participation events. The ships have become more sophisticated, entertaining venues, and the old *animateurs* – somewhat like the *gentils ordinaires* of Club Med, but better – have grown up and morphed into what is now known as Club Teams. They, along with other staff, interact with passengers throughout the ship.

About 20 nationalities are represented among the crew, who are upbeat and cheerful. Staff hospitality training is good. AIDA Cruises has its own training schools in several countries, plus a recognized training academy in Rostock.

Sport biking is part of its youthful image, with three different levels of cycling to suit differing fitness levels. AIDA Cruises has also successfully appealed to golfers, with several golf-theme packages that include playing at notable courses ashore in many ports of call.

The open deck space is rather limited, but sunbathing space includes some reasonably quiet space above the navigation bridge. Dip pools and hot tubs, plus seating areas, are provided in a cascading, tiered setting atop the ship on the pool deck, providing a decent amount of sunbathing space. It's all designed to be in a 'beach-like' environment, with splash and play areas.

Several decks of public rooms and facilities are positioned above the accommodation decks, and *AIDAbella* shares public room names that are common aboard all the ships in the fleet: Aida Bar, the main social gathering place, whose principal feature is a star-shaped bar (whose combined length makes it among the longest at sea), with many tables for standing drinkers.

A small casino features blackjack, roulette and poker gaming tables, and there are also a number of slot machines. There are many more balcony cabins, a separate aft sports deck, a 'no music' observation lounge, and an art gallery. The embarkation entryway is innovative, has a bar and a lookout 'balcony,' and is cheerfully painted to look like a street scene in a city such as Copenhagen. It is quite different from the utilitarian gangway entry areas found aboard most cruise ships; a welcoming environment, it helps to calm tempers after waiting in a line to go through the security process for embarkation or in ports of call.

There are three pricing levels – Aida Premium, Aida Vario, and Just Aida – depending on what you want to be included, plus differences in price according to accommodation size and grade, and the itinerary. Opt for the basic, price-driven Just Aida package and the cruise line chooses the ship, itinerary, and accommodation for you – sort of a pot-luck cruise, based on or close to the dates you choose.

The dress code is simple: casual (no ties) at all times, and there are no 'formal' dress-up nights on board.

An AIDA cruise isn't cheap, but you do get lots of high-tech entertainment, and there's always plenty of food (although there's no room service). Some frustration occurs when shore excursions sell out, when lines form after shore excursion buses return to the ship and you have to go through the slow security check, and for shore tenders.

FAMILIES. *AIDAbella* really is a family-friendly ship. Children are split into four age groups: Seepferdchen (4–6 years), Delfin (7–9), Orcas (10–12), and Teens (14–17). Each has its own play area. There is a diverse selection of children's and youth programs in a holiday camp atmosphere, and special Club Team members dedicated to making it all happen. Supervised by a chef, children can make their own menus for the week, and visit the galley to make cookies and other items – a novel idea more cruise lines could adopt.

ACCOMMODATION. There are eight or nine grades, from deluxe suites to interior (no view) cabins, depending on the ship, which keeps your cabin choice simple.

Contrary to maritime traditions (even-numbered cabins on the port side, odd-numbered cabins on the starboard side), cabin numbers progress numerically (example: 8201–8276 on the port side; 8101–8176 on the starboard side). All suites and cabins have two beds (convertible to queen-size bed). Some cabins also have two extra beds/berths for children, and some cabins have interconnecting doors – useful for families.

The decor in all accommodation grades is bright, youthful, rather minimalist, and slightly whimsical. All are accented with multi-patterned fabrics, wood-trimmed cabinetry (with nicely rounded edges), and rattan or wood-look furniture. Beds have duvets and a colorful Arabian-style fabric canopy that goes from the headboard to the ceiling. The windows have full pull-down blackout blinds (useful in destinations with long daylight hours).

The bathrooms are compact, practical units; they have a shower enclosure, small washbasin, and small toilet. As in the most basic hotels and motels, only a wall-mounted body wash/shampoo dispenser is provided, so take your own conditioner, hand lotion, and other toiletries you may need.

Thick cotton bathrobes are provided for all grades of accommodation, as are two towels – a face towel and a 'bath' towel, in two different colors. The 'bath' towels are not large, at 54 by 27 inches – compared to 72 by 36 inches aboard P&O Cruises' Ventura, for example. The bathroom does not have a hairdryer, but one is located in the vanity unit in the cabin. Note that the usual nighttime turndown service provided aboard most ships is not provided, and there is no cabin service after 3pm.

Cabins with balconies have a sliding door that's easy to open and doesn't impinge on balcony space; a small drinks table and two small, light chairs are provided. Note that balconies on the lowest deck can be overlooked by anyone on a balcony on the decks above. Balcony cabins have a hammock as standard, although it only accommodates one (thin) person. Some cabins – forward on Deck 5 – Nos 5103, 5104, 5105, 5106, 5203, 5204, 5206) have cabins with an outside view (well, outside light), but they are obstructed by steel bulkheads.

Suite-grade accommodation offers more space, including more drawer and storage space, better quality furniture and furnishings, a larger lounge area and a slightly larger bathroom with a tub – and a larger balcony – those at the front and stern of the ship are the best and most desirable.

DINING. There are three self-serve eateries: Markt (Market), Bella Vista (for Italian cuisine), and Weite Welt (Wide World) restaurants. The opening times for lunch and dinner are 12:30-14:00 and 18:30-21:00 respectively. Additionally, there's a Buffalo Steakhouse (which serves excellent steaks), an à la carte Rossini Restaurant with waiter and sommelier service, a Sushi Bar, a Pizzeria Mare, and a Café Mare. These venues are open at set times (there are no 24-hour-a-day outlets, because there is little demand for them), although the Pizzeria stays open until midnight.

In the three self-serve restaurants, the meal concept is simple: main meals are taken when you want them in one of the large self-serve buffet-style restaurants, with open seating at tables of four, six, or eight. Cutlery can be found hanging in a rack (but this is rather unhygienic because many fingers can touch it); there are no soup spoons, only dessert spoons.

Also, the tables are almost all large, and, when the ship is full, it can prove challenging to find a seat, not to mention any service personnel to clean the tables. Because it's a buffet venue, you'll probably sit with different people for each meal – which could be a good way to make new friends.

The many food islands and active stations cut down on the waiting time for food. There is always a big selection of breads, cheeses, cold cuts, fruits, and coffee and teas – with a choice of more than 30 types of loose-leaf regular and herbal teas. More than 1,200 items of food are offered. The fish section has its own fish smoking unit.

You can sit where you want, when you want, and with whom you want, so eating is a socially interactive occasion. At peak times, the venues may remind you of noisy roadside cafés. Because of the large buffet rooms and self-serve dining concept, the crew to passenger ratio looks poor; but this is because there are no waiters as such (except in à la carte venues), only staff for clearing tables.

Beer is available at the push of a button or a pull of the tap, and table wine is usually provided in carafes on each table for lunch and dinner. Note that the beverage stations open only during restaurant opening hours, unless you go to the extra-cost coffee bar (Café Mare). Vending machines dispense out-of-hours snacks.

Other dining options. The à la carte Rossini Restaurant, with mostly high-back seats, has an intimate atmosphere. It is open for dinner only, and has a set five- or six-course menu, plus daily 'specials.' There is no cover charge, but an extra charge applies to everything on the à la carte menu, and for wines. Reservations are needed. Tablecloths are provided, the food is very good, and service is sound.

The Buffalo Steakhouse has an open 'display' kitchen, and offers various steak cuts and sizes – Delmonico, New York Strip Loin, Porterhouse, and Filét, plus bison steaks – and roast lamb rack. There's a daily special – a prix-fixe meal (example: a 180g fillet steak, house salad, and dessert). It's like going out to eat in a decent restaurant ashore – but there are no tablecloths. Wine and any other drinks are extra.

A 12-seater sushi counter is for Japanese-style sushi and sashimi dishes. While the counter provides stools for seating, two low-slung tables with well-type seating are difficult to sit at and get up from (notice to women: avoid wearing short skirts). The sushi is uninspiring, but typical of what you'd expect in a sushi bar not run by Japanese sushi masters. While the presentation is appetizing, you can be subjected to intense noise level from the adjacent 'open-plan' showlounge.

A wine bar, called Vinoteque, located in front of the Weide Welt (Wide World) Restaurant, has a list of premium wines, and Davidoff cigars (although you can't smoke them at the bar – or anywhere inside the ship).

The Pizzeria Mare provides a small selection of ever popular pizzas.

ENTERTAINMENT. The Theatrium (theatre) is in the center of the ship. It is open to the main foyer and other public areas, on three levels (Decks 9, 10, 11), and topped by a glass dome. Amphitheater-style seating is on three decks (the bench seating on the two upper levels has back supports, but not on the lower level), plus standing tables, although sight lines to the raised thrust stage area are less than good from many of the seats.

The layout also means that people walk through the area constantly, distracting you from what's on the stage. For the performers, it's a bit like being in a TV studio, and trying to perform in front of the cameras, but with the audience in a different location. You can also watch the rehearsals, because this is really all about an active/interactive lifestyle.

The shows (each is just 30 minutes long, with four different shows scheduled each evening (usually between 8pm and 11pm), so there's plenty to see and experience. They are produced by AIDA Cruises' in-house department in a joint venture with SeeLive (Hamburg's Schmidt's Tivoli Theater), and consist of around 12 performers. All vocals in the shows are performed live (because there's no live band on stage), to pre-recorded backing tracks that provide a mix of recorded live music and synthesized sound. The shows are upbeat, fun, and very entertaining.

In addition, there is a live band in the Aida Bar, the only room with a large dance floor (except for the disco).

SPA/FITNESS. The spa, fitness and sports programming are extensive.

The Body and Soul wellness/oasis area is located on two decks (connected by a stairway) and encompasses some 24,750 sq ft (2,300 sq m). There is an open-air wellness deck for FKK relaxation/nude sunbathing in an area atop the ship forward of the ship's mast. In keeping with the times, all the treatments are featured in an appealing contemporary setting.

In addition to a large fitness room (with an abundance of weight-training exercycle and Nordic-Trak machines, there are also saunas and steam rooms, and 14 rooms for massage and other treatments (most named after places associated with the design theme), neat showers, funky changing rooms, and a tropical garden with real (waxed) palm trees and relaxation loungers. Sport enthusiasts can also play billiards, volleyball or squash – or go jogging.

The ship has a bike excursion counter. 'Sport bikes' (mountain bikes with tough front and rear suspension units) are provided for conducted biking excursions in each port of call, a concession run by of Austrian downhill champion skier Erwin Resch. You can also book diving, and golfing excursions.

AIDAblu
★★★★

Size:...................................Large Resort Ship		Cabins (total):.....................................1,096		
Tonnage:..71,100		Size range (sq ft/m):.................145.3–473.2/13.5–44		
Lifestyle:...Standard		Cabins (outside view):.................................715		
Cruise line:................................AIDA Cruises		Cabins (interior/no view):.............................381		
Former names:..................................*none*		Cabins (for one person):................................0		
IMO number:...................................9398888		Cabins (with private balcony):.........................491		
Builder:..........................Meyer Werft (Germany)		Cabins (wheelchair accessible):.........................11		
Original cost:................................€350 million		Wheelchair accessibility:............................Good		
Entered service:..............................Apr 2010		Cabin voltage:........................110 and 220 volts		
Registry:..Italy		Elevators:..10		
Length (ft/m):..............................831.1/253.3		Casino (gaming tables):...............................Yes		
Beam (ft/m):...............................105.6/32.2		Slot machines:..No		
Draft (ft/m):..................................24.6/7.5		Swimming pools:.......................................3		
Propulsion/Propellers:...........diesel-electric (36,000 kW)/2		Hot tubs (on deck):....................................0		
Passenger decks:....................................14		Self-service launderette:.............................Yes		
Total crew:...646		Dedicated cinema/seats:...............................No		
Passengers (lower beds/alll berths):..............2,194/2,500		Library:..Yes		
Passenger Space Ratio (lower beds/all berths):.......34.6/28.4		Onboard currency:..................................Euros		
Crew/Passenger Ratio (lower beds/all berths):..........3.1/3.8				

Upbeat, family-friendly ship for no-frills cruising

OVERVIEW. AIDA Cruises is for youthful German-speaking couples, singles, and particularly families seeking good value for money in a party-like environment, with excellent entertainment. This is all about über-casual cruising, with two main self-serve buffet restaurants instead of the traditional waiter service. It's tablecloth-less eating, and there is little contact with the relatively few staff.

Berlitz's Ratings

	Possible	Achieved
Ship	500	403
Accommodation	200	146
Food	400	265
Service	400	284
Entertainment	100	71
Cruise	400	296
OVERALL SCORE		
1465 points out of 2000		

THE SHIP. The ship has a smart, contemporary profile, with a swept-back funnel and wedge-shaped stern. The bows display the red lips, as well as the blue eyes, of *Aïda* (from Verdi's opera, written to commemorate the opening of the Suez Canal in 1871). AIDA Cruises, Germany's largest cruise line, is part of Costa Cruises, which is itself part of Carnival Corporation. Its expanding fleet allows it to offer a wide choice of itineraries, including the Middle East and Asia.

The AIDA-class ships – known as AIDA Clubships – evolved from the first and smallest ship, AIDA (now named *AIDAcara*), in which the central idea was to get passengers to participate in public-area activities together, as in the Robinson Club concept on land. This led to 'open plan' interiors and the feeling that the ship is one large space, but cleverly split into intimate rooms – although, in reality, rooms 'flow' into each other at each fire zone section (a length of 157ft/48m).

The use of bright tropical colors throughout the interiors is really noticeable. Most of the chairs, counter stools, and bar seats are quite small, designed for thin, youthful passengers.

Throughout the ship there is constant high-street music everywhere, so this ship is not for anyone seeking a 'quiet escape' vacation, even though volume levels are well controlled.

AIDA Cruises has really grown up over the past few years, and no longer focuses on summer-camp style participation events. The ships have become more sophisticated, entertaining venues, and the old *animateurs* – somewhat like the *gentils ordinaires* of Club Med, but better – have grown up and morphed into what is now known as Club Teams. They, along with other staff, interact with passengers throughout the ship.

About 20 nationalities are represented among the crew, who are upbeat and cheerful. Staff hospitality training is good. AIDA Cruises has its own training schools in several countries, plus a recognized training academy in Rostock.

Sport biking is part of its youthful image, with three different levels of cycling to suit differing fitness levels. AIDA Cruises has also successfully appealed to golfers, with several golf-theme packages that include playing at notable courses ashore in many ports of call.

The open deck space is rather limited, but sunbathing space includes some reasonably quiet space above the navigation bridge. Dip pools and hot tubs, plus seating areas, are provided in a cascading, tiered setting atop the ship on the pool deck, providing a decent amount of sunbathing space. It's all designed to be in a 'beach-like' environment, with splash and play areas.

Several decks of public rooms and facilities are positioned above the accommodation decks, and *AIDAblu* shares public room names that are common aboard all the ships in the fleet: Aida Bar, the main social gathering place, whose principal feature is a star-shaped bar (whose combined length makes it among the longest at sea), with many tables for standing drinkers.

A small casino features blackjack, roulette and poker gaming tables, and there are also a number of slot machines. There are many more balcony cabins, a separate aft sports deck, a 'no music' observation lounge, and an art gallery. The embarkation entryway is innovative, has a bar and a lookout 'balcony,' and is cheerfully painted to look like a street scene in a city such as Copenhagen. It is quite different from the utilitarian gangway entry areas found aboard most cruise ships; a welcoming environment, it helps to calm tempers after waiting in a line to go through the security process for embarkation or in ports of call.

There are three pricing levels – Aida Premium, Aida Vario, and Just Aida – depending on what you want to be included, plus differences in price according to accommodation size and grade, and the itinerary. Opt for the basic, price-driven Just Aida package and the cruise line chooses the ship, itinerary, and accommodation for you – sort of a pot-luck cruise, based on or close to the dates you choose.

The dress code is simple: casual (no ties) at all times, and there are no 'formal' dress-up nights on board. All port taxes and gratuities are included in all cruises.

An AIDA cruise isn't cheap, but you do get lots of high-tech entertainment, and there's always plenty of food (but there is no room service). Some frustration occurs when shore excursions sell out, when lines form after shore excursion buses return to the ship and you have to go through the slow security check – and at peak times in the self-serve restaurants, and for shore tenders.

FAMILIES. *AIDAblu* really is a family-friendly ship. Children are split into four age groups: Seepferdchen (4–6 years), Delfin (7–9), Orcas (10–12), and Teens (14–17). Each has its own play area. There is a diverse selection of children's and youth programs in a holiday camp atmosphere, and special Club Team members dedicated to making at all happen. Supervised by a chef, children can make their own menus for the week, and visit the galley to make cookies and other items – a novel idea more cruise lines could adopt.

ACCOMMODATION. There are eight or nine grades, from deluxe suites to interior (no view) cabins, depending on the ship, which keeps your cabin choice simple.

Contrary to maritime traditions (even-numbered cabins on the port side, odd-numbered cabins on the starboard side), cabin numbers progress numerically (example: 8201–8276 on the port side; 8101–8176 on the starboard side). All suites and cabins have two beds (convertible to queen-size bed). Some cabins also have two extra beds/berths for children, and some cabins have interconnecting doors.

The decor in all accommodation grades is bright, youthful, rather minimalist, and slightly whimsical. All are accented with multi-patterned fabrics, wood-trimmed cabinetry, and rattan or wood-look furniture. Beds have duvets and a colorful canopy that goes from the headboard to the ceiling. The windows have full pull-down blackout blinds (useful in destinations with long daylight hours).

The bathrooms are compact, practical units; they have a shower enclosure, small washbasin, and small toilet. As in the most basic hotels and motels, only a wall-mounted body wash/shampoo dispenser is provided, so take your own conditioner, hand lotion, and other toiletries you may need.

Thick cotton bathrobes are provided for all grades of accommodation, as are two towels – a face towel and a 'bath' towel, in two different colors. The 'bath' towels are not large, at 54 by 27 inches – compared to 72 by 36 inches aboard P&O Cruises' Ventura, for example. The bathroom does not have a hairdryer, but one is located in the vanity unit in the cabin. Note that the usual night-time turndown service provided aboard most ships is not provided, and there is no cabin service after 3pm.

Cabins with balconies have a sliding door that's easy to open and doesn't impinge on balcony space; a small drinks table and two small, light chairs are provided. Note that balconies on the lowest deck can be overlooked by anyone on a balcony on the decks above. Balcony cabins have a hammock as standard, although it only accommodates one (thin) person. Some cabins (forward on Deck 5 – Nos 5103, 5104, 5105, 5106, 5203, 5204, 5206) have cabins with an outside view (well, outside light), but they are obstructed by steel bulkheads.

Naturally, suite-grade accommodation offers more space, including more drawer and storage space, better quality furniture and furnishings, a larger lounge area and a bathroom with a tub – and a larger balcony – those at the front and stern of the ship are the most desirable.

DINING. There are three self-serve eateries: Markt (Market), Bella Vista (for Italian cuisine), and Weite Welt (Wide World) restaurants. The opening times for lunch and dinner are 12:30-14:00 and 18:30-21:00 respectively. Additionally, there's a Buffalo Steakhouse (which serves excellent steaks), an à la carte Rossini Restaurant with waiter and sommelier service, a Sushi Bar, a Pizzeria Mare, and a Café Mare. These venues are open at set times (there are no 24-hour-a-day outlets, because there is little demand for them), although the Pizzeria typically is open until midnight.

In the three self-serve restaurants, the meal concept is simple: main meals are taken when you want them in one of the large self-serve buffet-style restaurants, with open seating at tables of four, six, or eight. Cutlery hangs in a rack (a rather unhygienic arrangement), and there are no soup spoons, only dessert spoons.

The tables are almost all large, and, when the ship is full, it can prove challenging to find a seat, not to mention any service personnel to clean the tables. Because it's a buffet venue, you'll probably sit with different people for each meal – which could be a good way to make new friends.

The many food islands and active stations cut down on the waiting time for food. There is always a big selection of breads, cheeses, cold cuts, fruits, and make-your-own coffee and teas – with a choice of more than 30 types of loose-leaf regular and herbal teas. More than 1,200 items of food are offered. The fish section has its own fish smoking unit.

You can sit where you want, when you want, and with whom you want, so eating is a socially interactive occasion. At peak times, the venues may remind you of noisy roadside cafés. Because of the large buffet rooms and self-serve dining concept, the crew to passenger ratio looks poor; but this is because there are no waiters as such (except in à la carte venues), only staff for clearing tables.

Beer is available at the push of a button or a pull of the tap, and table wine is usually provided in carafes on each table for lunch and dinner. Note that the beverage stations open only during restaurant opening hours, unless you go to the extra-cost coffee bar (Café Mare). In case you want something to nibble on, vending machines dispense out-of-hours snacks.

Other dining options. The à la carte Rossini Restaurant, with mostly high-back seats, has an intimate atmosphere. It is open for dinner only, and has a set five- or six-course menu, plus daily 'specials.' There is no cover charge, but an extra charge applies to everything on the à la carte menu (such as caviar, chateaubriand, rib-eye steak), and for wines. Reservations are needed. Tablecloths are provided, the food is very good, and service is sound.

The Buffalo Steakhouse has an open 'display' kitchen, and offers various steak cuts and sizes – Delmonico, New York Strip Loin, Porterhouse, and Filét, plus bison steaks – and roast lamb rack. There's a daily special – a prix-fixe meal (example: a 180g fillet steak, house salad, and dessert). It's like going out to eat in a decent restaurant ashore – but there are no tablecloths. Wine or any other drinks cost extra.

A 12-seater sushi counter is for Japanese-style sushi and sashimi dishes. While the counter provides stools for seating, two low-slung tables with well-type seating are difficult to sit at and get up from (notice to women: avoid wearing short skirts). The sushi is uninspiring, but typical of what you'd expect in a sushi bar not run by Japanese sushi masters.

While the presentation is appetizing, the actual fare is somewhat light on taste – and you can be subjected to intense noise level from the adjacent 'open-plan' showlounge.

A wine bar, Vinotheque, located in front of the Weide Welt (Wide World) Restaurant, has a list of premium wines, and Davidoff cigars (although you can't smoke them at the bar – or anywhere inside the ship).

ENTERTAINMENT. The Theatrium (theatre) is in the center of the ship. It is open to the main foyer and other public areas, on three levels (Decks 9, 10, 11), and topped by a glass dome. Amphitheater-style seating is on three decks (the bench seating on the two upper levels has back supports, but not on the lower level), plus standing tables, although sight lines to the raised thrust stage area are less than good from many of the seats.

The layout also means that people walk through the area constantly, distracting you from what's on the stage. For the performers, it's a bit like being in a TV studio, and trying to perform in front of the cameras, but with the audience in a different location. You can also watch the rehearsals, because this is really all about an active/interactive lifestyle.

The shows (each is just 30 minutes long, with four different shows scheduled each evening (usually between 8pm and 11pm), so there's plenty to see and experience. They are produced by AIDA Cruises' in-house department in a joint venture with SeeLive (Hamburg's Schmidt's Tivoli Theater), and consist of around 12 performers. All vocals in the shows are performed live (because there's no live band on stage), to pre-recorded backing tracks that provide a mix of recorded live music and synthesized sound.

There is a live band in the Aida Bar, the only room with a large dance floor (except for the disco).

SPA/FITNESS. The spa, fitness and sports programming are extensive. The Body and Soul wellness/oasis area is located on two decks (connected by a stairway) and encompasses some 24,750 sq ft (2,300 sq m). There is also an open-air wellness deck for FKK relaxation/nude sunbathing in an area atop the ship forward of the ship's mast.

In addition to a large fitness room (with an abundance of weight-training, exercycle, and Nordic-Trak machines, there are also saunas and steam rooms, and 14 rooms for massage and other treatments, showers, changing rooms, and a tropical garden with real (waxed) palm trees and relaxation loungers.

There is also a bike excursion counter for bike rentals, at which you can also book diving, and golfing excursions. 'Sport bikes' (mountain bikes with tough front and rear suspension units) are provided for conducted biking excursions in each port of call, a concession run by of Austrian downhill champion skier Erwin Resch.

AIDAcara
★★★ +

Size:.	Mid-size Ship	Cabins (total):.	.590
Tonnage:.	38,557	Size range (sq ft/m):.	145.3–376.7/13.5–35.0
Lifestyle:.	Standard	Cabins (outside view):.	.390
Cruise line:.	AIDA Cruises	Cabins (interior/no view):.	.200
Former names:.	Aida, Das Clubschiff	Cabins (for one person):.	.0
IMO number:.	.9112789	Cabins (with private balcony):.	.48
Builder:.	Kvaerner Masa-Yards (Finland)	Cabins (wheelchair accessible):.	.6
Original cost:.	DM300 million	Wheelchair accessibility:.	Good
Entered service:.	Jun 1996	Cabin voltage:.	.110 and 220 volts
Registry:.	Italy	Elevators:.	.5
Length (ft/m):.	634.1/193.3	Casino (gaming tables):.	.No
Beam (ft/m):.	90.5/27.6	Slot machines:.	.No
Draft (ft/m):.	19.6/6.0	Swimming pools:.	.1
Propulsion/Propellers:.	diesel(21,720kw)/2	Hot tubs (on deck):.	.2
Passenger decks:.	.9	Self-service launderette:.	Yes
Total crew:.	.370	Dedicated cinema/seats:.	.No
Passengers (lower beds/alll berths):.	1,180/1,339	Library:.	Yes
Passenger Space Ratio (lower beds/all berths):.	32.6/27.5	Onboard currency:.	Euros
Crew/Passenger Ratio (lower beds/all berths):.	3.1/3.7		

A busy, family-friendly ship for a frugal cruise

OVERVIEW. *AIDAcara* is for youthful and young at heart German-speaking couples, singles, and particularly families seeking good value for money in a party-like environment, with good entertainment. This is über-casual cruising, with two main self-serve buffet restaurants instead of traditional waiter service. It's tablecloth-less eating, a bit like camping at sea, with little contact with the relatively few staff.

THE SHIP. The ship has a reasonably contemporary profile, with a swept-back funnel and wedge-shaped stern. The bows display the red lips, as well as the blue eyes, of *Aïda* (from Verdi's opera, written to commemorate the opening of the Suez Canal in 1871). AIDA Cruises, Germany's largest cruise line, is part of Costa Cruises, which is itself part of the giant Carnival Corporation. Its expanding fleet allows it to offer a wide choice of itineraries, including the Middle East and Asia.

AIDAcara (formerly known as AIDA) evolved from the central idea which was to get passengers to participate in public-area activities together, as in the Robinson Club concept on land. This led to 'open plan' interiors and the feeling that the ship is one large space, but cleverly split into intimate rooms – although, in reality, rooms 'flow' into each other at each fire zone section (a length of 157ft/48m).

The use of bright tropical colors throughout the interiors is really noticeable, but appropriate. Most of the chairs, counter stools, and bar seats are quite small, designed for thin young passengers, typically under 40.

Berlitz's Ratings

	Possible	Achieved
Ship	500	346
Accommodation	200	131
Food	400	249
Service	400	268
Entertainment	100	70
Cruise	400	270

OVERALL SCORE
1334 points out of 2000

There is, however, constant high-street music everywhere, so these ships are not for those wanting a 'quiet escape' vacation, even though volume levels are well controlled.

AIDA Cruises has really grown up over the past few years, and no longer focuses on summer-camp style participation events. The ship's original *animateurs* – somewhat like the *gentils ordinaires* of Club Med, but better – have now grown up and morphed into what is now known as Club Teams. They, along with other staff, interact with passengers throughout the ship.

About 20 nationalities are represented among the crew, who are upbeat and cheerful. Staff hospitality training is at a high level, and AIDA Cruises has its own training schools in several countries, plus a recognized training academy in Rostock.

Sport biking is part of its youthful image, with three different levels of cycling to suit differing fitness levels. The line has also successfully appealed to golfers, with golf-theme packages, cruises, and excursions ashore in many ports of call.

The open deck space is pretty tight, but sunbathing space includes some rather pleasant, reasonably quiet space above the navigation bridge. Dip pools and hot tubs, plus seating areas, are provided in a cascading, tiered setting atop the ship on the pool deck, providing a decent amount of sunbathing space. It's all designed to be in a 'beach-like' environment, with splash and play areas.

Several decks of public rooms and facilities are positioned above the accommodation decks. Public rooms that have become common aboard all the ships are: Aida Bar, the main social gathering place, whose principal feature is a star-shaped bar (whose combined length per ship probably makes them the longest at sea), with many tables for standing drinkers.

Other facilities include a 'shore excursion counter, library, seminar rooms, duty-free shop, Nordic Walking machines, several bars and lounges, and eateries.

There are three pricing levels – Aida Premium, Aida Vario, and Just Aida – depending on what you want to be included, plus differences in price according to accommodation size and grade, and the itinerary. Opt for the basic, price-driven Just Aida package and the cruise line chooses the ship, itinerary, and accommodation for you – sort of a pot-luck cruise, based on or close to the dates you choose.

The dress code is simple: casual (no ties) at all times – there are no formal nights on board. All port taxes and gratuities are included in all packages, and, with very attractive rates, a cruise provides much better value than almost any land-based vacation.

An AIDA cruise isn't cheap, but you get a lot of fun entertainment, and there's always plenty of food. Some frustration occurs when shore excursions sell out, when lines form after shore excursion buses return to the ship and you have to go through the slow security check – and at peak times in the self-serve restaurants, and for shore tenders.

Niggles include the fact that the open deck space is tight; there's not enough seating in the two self-serve buffet eateries at peak times, and there is room service. A cruise aboard this ship is a comfortable, but slightly cramped, experience.

FAMILIES. *AIDAcara* is a family-friendly ship. Children are split into four age groups: Seepferdchen (4–6 years), Delfin (7–9), Orcas (10–12), and Teens (14–17). Each has its own play area. There is a selection of children's and youth programs in a holiday camp atmosphere, and special Club Team members dedicated to making at all happen. Supervised by a chef, children can make their own menus for the week, and visit the galley to make cookies and other items.

ACCOMMODATION. There are eight or nine grades, from deluxe suites to interior (no view) cabins, depending on the ship, which keeps your cabin choice simple.

Contrary to maritime traditions (even-numbered cabins on the port side, odd-numbered cabins on the starboard side), cabin numbers progress numerically (example: 8201–8276 on the port side; 8101–8176 on the starboard side). All suites and cabins have two beds (convertible to queen-size bed). Some cabins also have two extra beds/berths for children, and some cabins have interconnecting doors – useful for families.

The decor in all accommodation grades is bright, youthful, rather minimalist, and slightly whimsical. All are accented with multi-patterned fabrics, wood-trimmed cabinetry (with nicely rounded edges), and rattan or wood-look furniture. Beds have duvets and a colorful Arabian-style fabric canopy that goes from the headboard to the ceiling. The windows have full pull-down blackout blinds (useful in destinations with long daylight hours). Lifeboats may obstruct views in some cabins in the ship's center.

The bathrooms are compact, practical units; they have a shower enclosure, small washbasin, and small toilet. As in the most basic hotels and motels, only a wall-mounted body wash/shampoo dispenser is provided, so take your own conditioner, hand lotion, and other toiletries you may need.

Thick cotton bathrobes are provided for suite-grade accommodation only, although non-suite grade passengers can obtain one from the spa. Two towels are provided – a face towel and a 'bath' towel, in two different colors. The 'bath' towels are not very large, at 54 by 27 inches – compared to 72 by 36 inches aboard the P&O Cruises' Azura, for example. Although the bathrooms do not have a hairdryer, one is located in the vanity unit in the cabin. Night-time turndown service is not provided, and there is no cabin service after 3pm.

Cabins with balconies have a sliding door that's easy to open and doesn't impinge on balcony space; a small drinks table and two small, light chairs are provided. Note that balconies on the lowest deck can be overlooked by anyone on a balcony on the decks above. Naturally, suite-grade accommodation offers more space, including more drawer and storage space, better quality furniture and furnishings, a larger lounge area and a slightly larger bathroom with a tub – and a larger balcony (those at the front and stern of the ship have the best).

DINING. Two eateries are included in the cruise fare: the self-serve Markt and Karibik restaurants. The opening times for lunch and dinner are 12:30-14:00 and 18:30-21:00 respectively. There's also Rossini, a decent enough à la carte (extra-charge) tablecloth dining spot that serves good-quality meals cooked à la minute, and has friendly waiter service.

The meal concept is simple: main meals are taken when you want them in one of the large self-serve buffet-style restaurants, with open seating at tables of four, six, or eight. Cutlery is hung in a rack, but there are no soup spoons, only dessert spoons.

The tables are almost all large, and, when the ship is full, it can prove challenging to find a seat, not to mention any service personnel to clean the tables. Because it's a buffet venue, you'll probably sit with different people for each meal – which could be a good way to make new friends.

The standard of food at the self-serve buffet islands ranges from adequate to quite good, with creative displays and presentation, and table-clearing service that is sometimes efficient, but mostly not.

The many food islands and active stations cut down on the waiting time for food. There is always a big selection of breads, cheeses, cold cuts, fruits, and make-your-own coffee and teas – with a choice of more than 30 types of loose-leaf regular and herbal teas. In all, over 1,200 items of food are offered.

You can sit where you want, when you want, and with whom you want, so eating is a socially interactive occasion. In fact, it's hard to be an unsociable couple and have a table for only two. At peak times, the venues may remind you of noisy roadside cafés. Because of the large buffet rooms and self-serve dining concept, the crew to passenger ratio looks poor; but this is because there are no waiters as such (except in à la carte venues), only staff for clearing tables.

Beer is available at the push of a button or a pull of the tap, and table wine – of the sort that would make a good drain cleaner – is usually provided in carafes on each table for lunch and dinner. Note that the beverage stations open only during restaurant opening hours, unless you go to the extra-cost coffee bar (Café Mare). Vending machines dispense out-of-hours snacks.

Other dining options. The Rossini Restaurant (à la carte), with mostly high-back seats, has an intimate atmosphere. It is open for dinner only, and has a set five- or six-course menu (plus daily specials). There is no cover charge, but an extra charge applies to everything on the à la carte menu (such as caviar, chateaubriand, rib-eye steak), and for wines. Reservations are needed. Tablecloths are provided, the food is good, and waiter and sommelier service are quite friendly.

ENTERTAINMENT. The Theater, the main venue for all shows and most cabaret, is two decks high. It has a raised stage, and amphitheater-style bench seating on all levels. The benches have back rests, and are quite comfortable, and sight lines are good from most seats, with the exception of port and starboard balcony sections, where sight lines are interrupted by thick safety railings.

The shows (each is just 30 minutes long, with four different shows scheduled each evening (usually between 8pm and 11pm), so there's plenty to see and experience. They are produced by AIDA Cruises' in-house department in a joint venture with SeeLive (Hamburg's Schmidt's Tivoli Theater), and consist of around 12 performers. All vocals in the shows are performed live (because there's no live band on stage) to pre-recorded backing tracks that provide a mix of recorded live music and synthesized sound. The shows are trendy, upbeat, fun, and entertaining. The whole entertainment experience is lively and fun – in fact, it's a little like the informal atmosphere one would find at the circus.

In addition, there is a live band in the Aida Bar, the only room with a large dance floor (except for the disco).

SPA/FITNESS. The Body and Soul Spa, is located forward on Deck 11. It measures 11,840 sq ft (1,100 sq m), and contains two saunas (one dry, one wet, both with seats for more than 20 persons, and glass walls that look onto the deck), massage and other treatment rooms, and a large lounging area. There are also showers, and two whole 'ice walls' to use when you come out of the saunas (simply lean into the ice wall for maximum effect). Forward and outside the wellness center, is an FKK (FreiKoerperKultur) nude sunbathing deck, on two levels. A beauty and hair salon is located just behind the balcony level of the showlounge.

'Sport bikes' (mountain bikes with tough front and rear suspension units) are available for conducted biking excursions in each port of call, a concession run by of Austrian downhill champion skier Erwin Resch. You can also book biking, diving, and golfing excursions.

Nautical Expressions

If you've ever wondered where some terms or phrases came from, you have only to look to the sea, ships, and seamen.

Scuttlebutt. A small drinking ladle with scuttles or holes in it to discourage sailors from idle chit chat (scuttlebutt) around the water barrel while their water ration dribbled back into the barrel. Today it usually refers to gossip or the latest news concerning a given situation or person.

Shape up. A helmsman working off a lee shore would point up and 'shape up' to his course in order to avoid danger. In modern-day usage it is used similar sense to mean 'smarten up' or 'pull yourself together.'

Showing your true colors. The early warships often carried flags from many nations on board in order to elude or deceive the enemy. The rules of civilized warfare called for all ships to hoist their true national ensigns before firing a shot. Someone who finally 'shows his true colors' is acting like a warship, which hails another ship flying one flag, but then hoisted its own flag when the vessel got within firing range.

Skyscraper. A small, triangular shaped sail that was set above the mains on the old square-riggers to try to scrape (catch) more wind in areas of calm air. The term came ashore to represent anything that was tall enough to 'scrape' the sky.

Slush fund. The fat obtained by 'scraping the bottom of the barrel' by the ship's cook and secreted away in his 'slush fund' for selling ashore to candle makers, tanneries, etc. Today the words describe a rainy-day fund or cash reserve. Another version of the term's derivation is that the grease (slush) from frying the salt pork on a voyage was kept and sold when the ship returned to port. The money raised was put into a 'fund' for the crew.

AIDAdiva
★★★★

Size:.................................Large Resort Ship	Cabins (total):.. 1,025
Tonnage: 69,203	Size range (sq ft/m): 145.3–473.2/13.5–44
Lifestyle: ....Standard	Cabins (outside view):................................ 666
Cruise line:...............................AIDA Cruises	Cabins (interior/no view):............................ 359
Former names: ....none	Cabins (for one person):................................0
IMO number:................................9334856	Cabins (with private balcony):........................ 480
Builder: .... Meyer Werft (Germany)	Cabins (wheelchair accessible): 11
Original cost:............................$390 million	Wheelchair accessibility:............................Good
Entered service:..............................Apr 2007	Cabin voltage: ....110 and 220 volts
Registry:... Italy	Elevators:..10
Length (ft/m):............................. 830.0/253.3	Casino (gaming tables):.............................. Yes
Beam (ft/m):............................. 105.6/32.2	Slot machines:..No
Draft (ft/m):................................ 24.6/7.5	Swimming pools:.......................................3
Propulsion/Propellers:...........diesel-electric (36,000 kW)/2	Hot tubs (on deck):....................................0
Passenger decks:..................................13	Self-service launderette:............................ Yes
Total crew:.......................................646	Dedicated cinema/seats:..............................No
Passengers (lower beds/all berths):............. 2,050/2,500	Library: .... Yes
Passenger Space Ratio (lower beds/all berths): 33.7/27.6	Onboard currency: .... Euros
Crew/Passenger Ratio (lower beds/all berths):..........3.1/3.8	

A large family-friendly ship for a good-time experience

OVERVIEW. An AIDA Cruise is for youthful German-speaking couples, singles, and particularly families seeking good value for money in a party-like environment, with excellent entertainment. This is all about über-casual cruising, with two main self-serve buffet restaurants instead of the traditional waiter service. It's tablecloth-less eating, and there is little contact with staff.

THE SHIP. The ship has a smart, contemporary profile, with a swept-back funnel and wedge-shaped stern. The bows display the red lips, as well as the blue eyes, of *Aïda* (from Verdi's opera, written to commemorate the opening of the Suez Canal in 1871). AIDA Cruises, Germany's largest cruise line, is part of Costa Cruises, which is itself part of Carnival Corporation. Its expanding fleet allows it to offer a wide choice of itineraries, including the Middle East and Asia.

The AIDA-class ships – known as AIDA Clubships – evolved from the first and smallest ship, AIDA (now named *AIDAcara*), in which the central idea was to get passengers to participate in public-area activities together, as in the Robinson Club concept on land. This led to 'open plan' interiors and the feeling that the ship is one large space, but cleverly split into intimate rooms – although, in reality, rooms 'flow' into each other at each fire zone section (a length of 157ft/48m).

The use of bright tropical colors throughout the interiors is really noticeable. Most of the chairs, counter stools, and bar seats are quite small, designed for thin, youthful passengers.

Berlitz's Ratings

	Possible	Achieved
Ship	500	385
Accommodation	200	146
Food	400	255
Service	400	284,
Entertainment	100	71
Cruise	400	289

OVERALL SCORE
1430 points out of 2000

Throughout the ship there is constant music, so this ship is not for anyone seeking a 'quiet escape' vacation.

AIDA Cruises has really grown up over the past few years, and no longer focuses on summer-camp style participation events. The ships have become more sophisticated, entertaining venues, and the old *animateurs* – somewhat like the *gentils ordinaires* of Club Med, but better – have grown up and morphed into what is now known as Club Teams.

Sport biking is part of its youthful image, with three different levels of cycling to suit differing fitness levels. AIDA Cruises has also successfully appealed to golfers, with several golf-theme packages that include playing at notable courses ashore in many ports of call.

The open deck space is rather limited, but sunbathing space includes some reasonably quiet space above the navigation bridge. Dip pools and hot tubs, plus seating areas, are provided in a cascading, tiered setting atop the ship on the pool deck, providing a decent amount of sunbathing space. It's all designed to be in a 'beach-like' environment, with splash and play areas.

Several decks of public rooms and facilities are positioned above the accommodation decks, and *AIDAdiva* shares public room names that are common aboard all the ships in the fleet: Aida Bar, the main social gathering place, whose principal feature is a star-shaped bar (whose combined length makes it among the longest at sea), with many tables for standing drinkers.

A small casino features blackjack, roulette and poker gaming tables, and there are also a number of slot machines. There are many more balcony cabins, a separate aft sports deck, a 'no music' observation lounge, and an art gallery. The embarkation entryway is innovative, has a bar and a lookout 'balcony,' and is cheerfully painted to look like a street scene in a city such as Copenhagen. It is quite different from the utilitarian gangway entry areas found aboard most cruise ships; a welcoming environment, it helps to calm tempers after waiting in a line to go through the security process for embarkation or in ports of call.

There are three pricing levels – Aida Premium, Aida Vario, and Just Aida – depending on what you want to be included, plus differences in price according to accommodation size and grade, and the itinerary. Opt for the basic, price-driven Just Aida package and the cruise line chooses the ship, itinerary, and accommodation for you – sort of a pot-luck cruise, based on or close to the dates you choose.

The dress code is simple: casual (no ties) at all times, and there are no 'formal' dress-up nights on board. All port taxes and gratuities are included in all cruises.

An AIDA cruise isn't cheap, but you do get lots of high-tech entertainment, and there's always plenty of food (but there's no room service at all). Some frustration occurs when shore excursions sell out, when lines form after shore excursion buses return to the ship and you have to go through the slow security check – and at peak times in the self-serve restaurants, and for shore tenders.

FAMILIES. *AIDAdiva* really is a family-friendly ship. Children are split into four age groups: Seepferdchen (4–6 years), Delfin (7–9), Orcas (10–12), and Teens (14–17). Each has its own play area. There is a diverse selection of children's and youth programs in a holiday camp atmosphere, and special Club Team members dedicated to making it all happen. Supervised by a chef, children can make their own menus for the week, and visit the galley to make cookies and other items – a novel idea more cruise lines could adopt.

ACCOMMODATION. There are eight or nine grades, from deluxe suites to interior (no view) cabins, depending on the ship, which keeps your cabin choice simple.

Contrary to maritime traditions (even-numbered cabins on the port side, odd-numbered cabins on the starboard side), cabin numbers progress numerically (example: 8201–8276 on the port side; 8101–8176 on the starboard side). All suites and cabins have two beds (convertible to queen-size bed). Some cabins also have two extra beds/berths for children, and some cabins have interconnecting doors – useful for families.

The decor in all accommodation grades is bright, youthful, rather minimalist, and slightly whimsical. All are accented with multi-patterned fabrics, wood-trimmed cabinetry, and rattan or wood-look furniture.

Beds have duvets and a colourful canopy that goes from the headboard to the ceiling. The windows have full pull-down blackout blinds (useful in destinations with long daylight hours).

The bathrooms are compact, practical units; they have a shower enclosure, small washbasin, and small toilet. As in the most basic hotels and motels, only a wall-mounted body wash/shampoo dispenser is provided, so take your own conditioner, hand lotion, and other toiletries you may need.

Thick cotton bathrobes are provided for all grades of accommodation, as are two towels – a face towel and a 'bath' towel, in two different colors. The 'bath' towels are not large, at 54 by 27 inches – compared to 72 by 36 inches aboard P&O Cruises' Ventura, for example. The bathroom does not have a hairdryer, but one is located in the vanity unit in the cabin. Note that the usual night-time turndown service provided aboard most ships is not provided, and there is no cabin service after 3pm.

Cabins with balconies have a sliding door that's easy to open and doesn't impinge on balcony space; a small drinks table and two small, light chairs are provided. Note that balconies on the lowest deck can be overlooked by anyone on a balcony on the decks above. Balcony cabins have a hammock as standard, although it only accommodates one (thin) person. Some cabins (forward on Deck 5 – Nos 5103, 5104, 5105, 5106, 5203, 5204, 5206) have cabins with an outside view (well, outside light), but they are obstructed by steel bulkheads that form the front section of the ship.

Naturally, suite-grade accommodation offers more space, including more drawer and storage space, better quality furniture and furnishings, a larger lounge area and a slightly larger bathroom with a tub – and a larger balcony – those at the front and stern of the ship are the best and most desirable.

DINING. There are three self-serve eateries: Markt (Market), Bella Vista (for Italian cuisine), and Weite Welt (Wide World) restaurants. The opening times for lunch and dinner are 12:30-14:00 and 18:30-21:00 respectively. Additionally, there's a Buffalo Steakhouse (which serves excellent steaks), an à la carte Rossini Restaurant with waiter and sommelier service, a Sushi Bar, a Pizzeria Mare, and a Café Mare. These venues are open at set times (there are no 24-hour-a-day outlets, because there is little demand for them), although the Pizzeria typically stays open until midnight.

In the three self-serve restaurants, the meal concept is simple: main meals are taken when you want them in one of the large self-serve buffet-style restaurants, with open seating at tables of four, six, or eight. Cutlery can be found hanging in a rack (this is thought to be somewhat unhygienic), but there are no soup spoons, only dessert spoons.

The tables are almost all large, and, when the ship is full, it can prove quite challenging to find a seat, not to mention any service personnel to clean the tables. Because it's a buffet venue, you'll probably sit with different people for each meal – which could be a good way to make new friends.

The many food islands and active stations cut down on the waiting time for food. There is always a big selection of breads, cheeses, cold cuts, fruits, and make-your-own coffee and teas – with a choice of more than 30 types of loose-leaf regular and herbal teas. More than 1,200 items of food are offered. The fish section has its own fish smoking unit (which resembles a wine cabinet).

You can sit where you want, when you want, and with whom you want, so eating is a socially interactive occasion. In fact, it's hard to be an unsociable couple and have a table for only two. At peak times, the venues may remind you of noisy roadside cafés. Because of the large buffet rooms and self-serve dining concept, the crew to passenger ratio looks poor; but this is because there are no waiters as such (except in à la carte venues), only staff for clearing tables.

Beer is available at the push of a button or a pull of the tap, and table wine – of the sort that would make a good drain cleaner – is usually provided in carafes on each table for lunch and dinner. Note that the beverage stations open only during restaurant opening hours, unless you go to the extra-cost coffee bar (Café Mare). Vending machines dispense out-of-hours snacks.

Other dining options. The à la carte Rossini Restaurant, with mostly high-back seats, has an intimate atmosphere. It is open for dinner only, and has a set five- or six-course menu, plus daily 'specials.' There is no cover charge, but an extra charge applies to everything on the à la carte menu (such as caviar, chateaubriand, rib-eye steak), wine or any other drinks. Reservations are needed. Tablecloths are provided, the food is very good, and service is sound.

The Buffalo Steakhouse has an open 'display' kitchen, and offers various steak cuts and sizes – Delmonico, New York Strip Loin, Porterhouse, and Filét, plus bison steaks – and roast lamb rack. There's a daily special – a prix-fixe meal (example: a 180g fillet steak, house salad, and dessert). It's like going out to eat in a decent restaurant ashore – but there are no tablecloths. Wine or any other drinks cost extra.

A 12-seater sushi counter is for Japanese-style sushi and sashimi dishes. While the counter provides stools for seating, two low-slung tables with well-type seating are difficult to sit at and get up from (notice to women: avoid wearing short skirts). The sushi is uninspiring, but typical of what you'd expect in a sushi bar not run by Japanese sushi masters. While the presentation is appetizing, the actual fare is somewhat light on taste – and you can be subjected to intense noise level from the adjacent 'open-plan' showlounge.

A wine bar, Vinotheque, is located in front of the Weide Welt (Wide World) Restaurant, has a list of premium wines, and Davidoff cigars (although you can't smoke them at the bar – or anywhere inside the ship).

The Pizzeria Mare provides a small selection of ever popular pizzas.

ENTERTAINMENT. The Theatrium (theatre) is in the center of the ship. It is open to the main foyer and other public areas, on three levels (Decks 9, 10, 11), and topped by a glass dome. Amphitheater-style seating is on three decks (the bench seating on the two upper levels has back supports, but not on the lower level), plus standing tables, although sight lines to the raised thrust stage area are less than good from many of the seats.

The layout also means that people walk through the area constantly, distracting you from what's on the stage. For the performers, it's a bit like being in a TV studio, and trying to perform in front of the cameras, but with the audience in a different location. You can also watch the rehearsals, because this is really all about an active/interactive lifestyle.

The shows (each is just 30 minutes long, with four different shows scheduled each evening (usually between 8pm and 11pm), so there's plenty to see and experience. They are produced by AIDA Cruises' in-house department in a joint venture with SeeLive (Hamburg's Schmidt's Tivoli Theater), and consist of around 12 performers. All vocals in the shows are performed live (because there's no live band on stage), to pre-recorded backing tracks that provide a mix of recorded live music and synthesized sound. The shows are trendy, upbeat, fun, and very entertaining.

SPA/FITNESS. The spa, fitness and sports programming are extensive. The Body and Soul wellness/oasis area is located on two decks (connected by a stairway) and encompasses some 24,750 sq ft (2,300 sq m). There is also an open-air wellness deck for FKK relaxation/nude sunbathing in an area atop the ship forward of the ship's mast. In keeping with the times, all the treatments are featured in an appealing contemporary setting.

In addition to a large fitness room (with an abundance of weight-training exercycle and Nordic-Trak machines, there are also saunas and steam rooms, and 14 rooms for massage and other treatments, showers, changing rooms, and a tropical garden with real (waxed) palm trees and relaxation loungers. Sport enthusiasts can also play billiards, volleyball or squash – or go jogging.

The ship has a bike excursion counter. 'Sport bikes' (mountain bikes with tough front and rear suspension units) are provided for conducted biking excursions in each port of call, a concession run by of Austrian downhill champion skier Erwin Resch. You can also book diving, and golfing excursions.

AIDAluna
★★★★

Size:....................................Large Resort Ship				

Size:....................................Large Resort Ship
Tonnage: 69,203
Lifestyle: ....Standard
Cruise line:.................................AIDA Cruises
Former names: ....*none*
IMO number: 9334868
Builder: .... Meyer Werft (Germany)
Original cost: .... $390 million
Entered service:................................Apr 2009
Registry:... Italy
Length (ft/m):.............................. 831.1/253.3
Beam (ft/m):............................... 105.6/32.2
Draft (ft/m):.................................. 24.6/7.5
Propulsion/Propellers:...........diesel-electric (36,000 kW)/2
Passenger decks:...................................13
Total crew:.......................................646
Passengers (lower beds/alll berths):.............. 2,050/2,500
Passenger Space Ratio (lower beds/all berths): 33.7/27.6
Crew/Passenger Ratio (lower beds/all berths):.......... 3.1/3.8

Cabins (total):.................................... 1,025
Size range (sq ft/m): .... 145.3 –473.2/13.5–44
Cabins (outside view):...............................666
Cabins (interior/no view):...........................359
Cabins (for one person):.............................0
Cabins (with private balcony):......................480
Cabins (wheelchair accessible): 11
Wheelchair accessibility:..........................Good
Cabin voltage: ....110 and 220 volts
Elevators:...10
Casino (gaming tables):.............................Yes
Slot machines:.....................................No
Swimming pools:....................................3
Hot tubs (on deck):.................................0
Self-service launderette:...........................Yes
Dedicated cinema/seats:............................No
Library: ....Yes
Onboard currency: ....Euros

Upbeat, family-friendly, and cheerful, but no finesse

OVERVIEW. An AIDA Cruise is for youthful German-speaking couples, singles, and particularly families seeking good value for money in a party-like environment, with excellent entertainment. This is all about über-casual cruising, with two main self-serve buffet restaurants instead of the traditional waiter service. It's tablecloth-less eating, and there is little contact with staff.

Berlitz's Ratings		
	Possible	Achieved
Ship	500	386
Accommodation	200	146
Food	400	264
Service	400	284
Entertainment	100	71
Cruise	400	290
OVERALL SCORE		
1441 points out of 2000		

THE SHIP. The ship has a smart, contemporary profile, with a swept-back funnel and wedge-shaped stern. The bows display the red lips, as well as the blue eyes, of *Aïda* (from Verdi's opera, written to commemorate the opening of the Suez Canal in 1871). AIDA Cruises, Germany's largest cruise line, is part of Costa Cruises, which is itself part of Carnival Corporation. Its expanding fleet allows it to offer a wide choice of itineraries, including the Middle East and Asia.

The AIDA-class ships – known as AIDA Clubships – evolved from the first and smallest ship, AIDA (now named *AIDAcara*), in which the central idea was to get passengers to participate in public-area activities together, as in the Robinson Club concept on land. This led to 'open plan' interiors and the feeling that the ship is one large space, but cleverly split into intimate rooms – although, in reality, rooms 'flow' into each other at each fire zone section (a length of 157ft/48m).

The use of bright colors is really noticeable. Most of the chairs, counter stools, and bar seats are quite small.

Throughout the ship there is constant music, so this ship is not for anyone seeking a 'quiet escape' vacation.

AIDA Cruises has really grown up over the past few years, and no longer focuses on summer-camp style participation events. The ships have become more sophisticated, entertaining venues, and the old *animateurs* – somewhat like the *gentils ordinaires* of Club Med, but better – have grown up and morphed into what is now known as Club Teams. They, along with other staff, interact with passengers throughout the ship.

Sport biking is part of its youthful image, with three different levels of cycling to suit differing fitness levels. AIDA Cruises has also successfully appealed to golfers, with several golf-theme packages that include playing at notable courses ashore in many ports of call.

The open deck space is rather limited, but sunbathing space includes some reasonably quiet space above the navigation bridge. Dip pools and hot tubs, plus seating areas, are provided in a cascading, tiered setting atop the ship on the pool deck, providing a decent amount of sunbathing space. It's all designed to be in a 'beach-like' environment, with splash and play areas.

Several decks of public rooms and facilities are positioned above the accommodation decks, and *AIDAluna* shares public room names that are common aboard all the ships in the fleet: Aida Bar, the main social gathering place, whose principal feature is a star-shaped bar (whose combined length makes it among the longest at sea), with many tables for standing drinkers.

A small casino features blackjack, roulette and poker gaming tables, and there are also a number of slot machines. There are many more balcony cabins, a separate aft sports deck, a 'no music' observation lounge, and an art gallery. The embarkation entryway is innovative, has a bar and a lookout 'balcony,' and is cheerfully painted to look like a street scene in a city such as Copenhagen. It is quite different from the utilitarian gangway entry areas found aboard most cruise ships; a welcoming environment, it helps to calm tempers after waiting in a line to go through the security process for embarkation or in ports of call.

There are three pricing levels – Aida Premium, Aida Vario, and Just Aida – depending on what you want to be included, plus differences in price according to accommodation size and grade, and the itinerary. Opt for the basic, price-driven Just Aida package and the cruise line chooses the ship, itinerary, and accommodation for you – sort of a pot-luck cruise, based on or close to the dates you choose.

The dress code is simple: casual (no ties) at all times, and there are no 'formal' dress-up nights on board. All port taxes and gratuities are included in all cruises.

An AIDA cruise isn't cheap, but you do get lots of high-tech entertainment, and there's always plenty of food (although there is no room service). Some frustration occurs when shore excursions sell out, when lines form after shore excursion buses return to the ship and you have to go through the slow security check – and at peak times in the self-serve restaurants, and for shore tenders.

FAMILIES. AIDAluna really is a family-friendly ship. Children are split into four age groups: Seepferdchen (4–6 years), Delfin (7–9), Orcas (10–12), and Teens (14–17). Each has its own play area. There is a wide selection of children's and youth programs in a holiday camp atmosphere, and special Club Team members dedicated to making at all happen. Supervised by a chef, children can make their own menus for the week, and visit the galley to make cookies and other items – a novel idea more cruise lines could adopt.

ACCOMMODATION. There are eight or nine grades, from deluxe suites to interior (no view) cabins, depending on the ship, which keeps your cabin choice simple.

Contrary to maritime traditions (even-numbered cabins on the port side, odd-numbered cabins on the starboard side), cabin numbers progress numerically (example: 8201–8276 on the port side; 8101–8176 on the starboard side). All suites and cabins have two beds (convertible to queen-size bed). Some cabins also have two extra beds/berths for children, and some cabins have interconnecting doors – useful for families.

The decor in all accommodation grades is bright, youthful, rather minimalist, and slightly whimsical. All are accented with multi-patterned fabrics, wood-trimmed cabinetry (with nicely rounded edges), and rattan or wood-look furniture. Beds have duvets and

a colorful Arabian-style fabric canopy that goes from the headboard to the ceiling. The windows have full pull-down blackout blinds (useful in destinations with long daylight hours).

The bathrooms are compact, practical units; they have a shower enclosure, small washbasin, and small toilet. As in the most basic hotels and motels, only a wall-mounted body wash/shampoo dispenser is provided, so take your own conditioner, hand lotion, and other toiletries you may need.

Thick cotton bathrobes are provided for all grades of accommodation, as are two towels – a face towel and a 'bath' towel, in two different colors. The 'bath' towels are not large, at 54 by 27 inches – compared to 72 by 36 inches aboard P&O Cruises' Ventura, for example. The bathroom does not have a hairdryer, but one is located in the vanity unit in the cabin. Note that the usual night-time turndown service provided aboard most ships is not provided, and there is no cabin service after 3pm.

Cabins with balconies have a sliding door that's easy to open and doesn't impinge on balcony space; a small drinks table and two small, light chairs are provided. Note that balconies on the lowest deck can be overlooked by anyone on a balcony on the decks above. Balcony cabins have a hammock as standard, although it only accommodates one (thin) person. Some cabins (forward on Deck 5 – Nos 5103, 5104, 5105, 5106, 5203, 5204, 5206) have cabins with an outside view (well, outside light), but they are obstructed by steel bulkheads that form the front section of the ship.

Naturally, suite-grade accommodation offers more space, including more drawer and storage space, better quality furniture and furnishings, a larger lounge area and a slightly larger bathroom with a tub – and a larger balcony – those at the front and stern of the ship are the best and most desirable.

DINING. There are three self-serve eateries: Markt (Market), Bella Vista (for Italian cuisine), and Weite Welt (Wide World) restaurants. Additionally, there's a Buffalo Steakhouse (which serves excellent steaks), an à la carte Rossini Restaurant with waiter and sommelier service, a Sushi Bar, a Pizzeria Mare, and a Café Mare. These venues are open at set times (there are no 24-hour-a-day outlets, because there is little demand for them), although the Pizzeria typically stays open until midnight.

In the three self-serve restaurants, the meal concept is simple: main meals are taken when you want them in one of the large self-serve buffet-style restaurants, with open seating at tables of four, six, or eight. Cutlery can be found hanging in a rack (this is thought to be somewhat unhygienic), but there are no soup spoons, only dessert spoons.

The tables are almost all large, and, when the ship is full, it can prove challenging to find a seat, not to mention any service personnel to clean the tables. Because it's a buffet venue, you'll probably sit with different people for each meal – which could be a good way to make new friends.

The standard of food at the self-serve buffet islands ranges from adequate to quite good, with creative displays and presentation, and table-clearing service that is sometimes efficient, but mostly not.

The many food islands and active stations cut down on the waiting time for food. There is always a big selection of breads, cheeses, cold cuts, fruits, and make-your-own coffee and teas – with a choice of more than 30 types of loose-leaf regular and herbal teas. More than 1,200 items of food are offered. The fish section has its own fish smoking unit (it resembles a wine cabinet).

You can sit where you want, when you want, and with whom you want, so eating is a socially interactive occasion. In fact, it's hard to be an unsociable couple and have a table for only two. At peak times, the venues may remind you of noisy roadside cafés. Because of the large buffet rooms and self-serve dining concept, the crew to passenger ratio looks poor; but this is because there are no waiters as such (except in à la carte venues), only staff for clearing tables.

Beer is available at the push of a button or a pull of the tap, and table wine – of the sort that would make a good drain cleaner – is usually provided in carafes on each table for lunch and dinner. It's simply casual and easy-going mass catering, so think food court eating – it certainly can't be called dining, but is more like camping at sea. The beverage stations open only during restaurant opening hours, unless you go to the extra-cost coffee bar. Vending machines dispense out-of-hours snacks.

Other dining options. The à la carte Rossini Restaurant, with mostly high-back seats, has an intimate atmosphere. It is open for dinner only, and has a set five- or six-course menu, plus daily 'specials.' There is no cover charge, but an extra charge applies to everything on the à la carte menu (such as caviar, chateaubriand, rib-eye steak), and for wines. Reservations are needed. Tablecloths are provided, the food is very good, and service is sound.

The Buffalo Steakhouse has an open 'display' kitchen, and offers various steak cuts and sizes – Delmonico, New York Strip Loin, Porterhouse, and Filét, plus bison steaks – and roast lamb rack. There's a daily special – a prix-fixe meal (example: a 180g fillet steak, house salad, and dessert). It's like going out to eat in a decent restaurant ashore – but there are no tablecloths. Wine or any other drinks cost extra.

A 12-seater sushi counter is for Japanese-style sushi and sashimi dishes. While the counter provides stools for seating, two low-slung tables with well-type seating are difficult to sit at and get up from (notice to women: avoid wearing short skirts). The sushi is uninspiring, but typical of what you'd expect in a sushi bar not run by Japanese sushi masters. While the presentation is appetizing, the actual fare is

somewhat light on taste – and you can be subjected to intense noise level from the adjacent 'open-plan' showlounge.

A wine bar, Vinotheque, is located in front of the Weide Welt (Wide World) Restaurant, has a list of premium wines, and Davidoff cigars (although you can't smoke them at the bar – or anywhere inside the ship).

The Pizzeria Mare provides a small selection of ever popular pizzas.

ENTERTAINMENT. The Theatrium (theatre) is in the center of the ship. It is open to the main foyer and other public areas, on three levels (Decks 9, 10, 11), and topped by a glass dome. Amphitheater-style seating is on three decks (the bench seating on the two upper levels has back supports, but not on the lower level), plus standing tables, although sight lines to the raised thrust stage area are less than good from many of the seats.

The layout also means that people walk through the area constantly, distracting you from what's on the stage. For the performers, it's a bit like being in a TV studio, and trying to perform in front of the cameras, but with the audience in a different location. You can also watch the rehearsals, because this is really all about an active/interactive lifestyle.

The shows are produced by AIDA Cruises' in-house department in a joint venture with SeeLive (Hamburg's Schmidt's Tivoli Theater), and typically consist of 12 performers. All vocals in the shows are performed live, to pre-recorded backing tracks that provide a mix of recorded live music and synthesized sound. The shows are trendy, upbeat, fun, and very entertaining.

SPA/FITNESS. The spa, fitness and sports programming are extensive. The Body and Soul wellness/oasis area is located on two decks (connected by a stairway) and encompasses some 24,750 sq ft (2,300 sq m). There is also an open-air wellness deck for FKK relaxation/nude sunbathing in an area atop the ship forward of the ship's mast. In keeping with the times, all the trendy treatments are featured in an appealing contemporary setting.

In addition to a large fitness room (with an abundance of weight-training exercycle and Nordic-Trak machines, there are also saunas and steam rooms, and 14 rooms for massage and other treatments (most named after places associated with the design theme), neat showers, funky changing rooms, and a tropical garden with real (waxed) palm trees and relaxation loungers. Sport enthusiasts can also play billiards, volleyball or squash – or go jogging.

The ship has a bike excursion counter. 'Sport bikes' (mountain bikes with tough front and rear suspension units) are provided for conducted biking excursions in each port of call, a concession run by of Austrian downhill champion skier Erwin Resch. You can also book diving, and golfing excursions.

AIDAmar
★★★★

Size:..............................Large Resort Ship		Cabins (total):.........................1,097		
Tonnage:................................71,304		Size range (sq ft/m):............145.3–473.2/13.5–44		
Lifestyle:...............................Standard		Cabins (outside view):.....................715		
Cruise line:............................AIDA Cruises		Cabins (interior/no view):..................381		
Former names:............................none		Cabins (for one person):.......................0		
IMO number:............................9490052		Cabins (with private balcony):.................491		
Builder:.......................Meyer Werft (Germany)		Cabins (wheelchair accessible):.................11		
Original cost:..........................€350 million		Wheelchair accessibility:.......................Good		
Entered service:.......................Apr 2011		Cabin voltage:....................110 and 220 volts		
Registry:.................................Italy		Elevators:...............................10		
Length (ft/m):........................831.1/253.3		Casino (gaming tables):......................Yes		
Beam (ft/m):.........................105.6/32.2		Slot machines:.............................No		
Draft (ft/m):............................24.6/7.5		Swimming pools:.............................3		
Propulsion/Propellers:..........diesel-electric (36,000 kW)/2		Hot tubs (on deck):...........................0		
Passenger decks:...........................14		Self-service launderette:.....................Yes		
Total crew:................................646		Dedicated cinema/seats:......................No		
Passengers (lower beds/alll berths):............2,194/2,500		Library:...................................Yes		
Passenger Space Ratio (lower beds/all berths):.......34.6/28.4		Onboard currency:...........................Euros		
Crew/Passenger Ratio (lower beds/all berths):..........3.1/3.8				

A family-friendly large ship for casual, lively cruises

OVERVIEW. *AIDAmar* is for youthful German-speaking couples, singles, and particularly families seeking good value for money in a party-like environment, with excellent entertainment. This is all about über-casual cruising, with two main self-serve buffet restaurants instead of the traditional waiter service. It's tablecloth-less eating, and there is little contact with staff.

THE SHIP. The ship has a smart, contemporary profile that is quite well proportioned, with a swept-back funnel and wedge-shaped stern. The bows display the bright red lips, as well as the blue eyes, of *Aïda* (from Verdi's opera, written to commemorate the opening of the Suez Canal in 1871). AIDA Cruises, Germany's largest cruise line, is part of Costa Cruises, which is itself part of Carnival Corporation. Its expanding fleet allows it to offer a wide choice of itineraries, including the Middle East and Asia.

An AIDA cruise isn't cheap, but you do get lots of high-tech entertainment, and there's always plenty of food. Some frustration occurs when shore excursions sell out, when lines form after shore excursion buses return to the ship and you have to go through the slow security check, and for shore tenders.

The AIDA-class ships (known as AIDA Clubships) evolved from the first and smallest ship, AIDA (now named *AIDAcara*), in which the central idea was to get passengers to participate in public-area activities together, as in the Robinson Club concept on land. This led to 'open plan' interiors and the feeling that

Berlitz's Ratings		
	Possible	Achieved
Ship	500	402
Accommodation	200	146
Food	400	262
Service	400	284
Entertainment	100	71
Cruise	400	293
OVERALL SCORE		
1458 points out of 2000		

the ship is one large space, but cleverly split into intimate rooms – although, in reality, rooms 'flow' into each other at each fire zone section (a length of 157ft/48m).

The use of bright colors throughout is noticeable. Most of the chairs, counter stools, and bar seats are quite small. Also, one thing that differentiates AIDA's ships from most others is the cheerful welcoming embarkation/tender loading zone. There is, however, constant music, so this ship is not for anyone seeking a 'quiet escape' vacation.

AIDA Cruises has really grown up over the past few years, and no longer focuses on summer-camp style participation events. The ships have become more sophisticated, entertaining venues, and the old *animateurs* – somewhat like the *gentils ordinaires* of Club Med, but better – have grown up and morphed into what is now known as Club Teams.

Sport biking is part of its youthful image, with three different levels of cycling to suit differing fitness levels. AIDA Cruises has also successfully appealed to golfers, with several golf-theme packages that include playing at notable courses ashore in many ports of call.

The open deck space is rather limited, but sunbathing space includes some reasonably quiet space above the navigation bridge. Dip pools and hot tubs, plus seating areas, are provided in a cascading, tiered setting atop the ship on the pool deck, providing a decent amount of sunbathing space. It's all designed to be in a 'beach-like' environment, with splash and play areas.

There are three pricing levels – Aida Premium, Aida Vario, and Just Aida – depending on what you want to be included, plus differences in price according to accommodation size and grade, and the itinerary. Opt for the basic, price-driven Just Aida package and the cruise line chooses the ship, itinerary, and accommodation for you – sort of a pot-luck cruise, based on or close to the dates you choose.

The dress code is simple: casual (no ties) at all times, and there are no 'formal' dress-up nights on board. All port taxes and gratuities are included in all cruises.

Several decks of public rooms and facilities are positioned above the accommodation decks, and AIDAmar shares public room names that are common aboard all the ships in the fleet: Aida Bar, the main social gathering place, whose principal feature is a star-shaped bar (whose combined length makes it among the longest at sea), with many tables for standing drinkers.

A small casino features blackjack, roulette and poker gaming tables, and slot machines. There are many more balcony cabins, a separate aft sports deck, a 'no music' observation lounge, and an art gallery. The embarkation entryway is really innovative, has a bar and a lookout balcony, and is cheerfully painted to look like a city waterfront street scene. It is quite different from the utilitarian gangway entry areas found aboard most cruise ships; a welcoming environment, it helps to calm tempers after waiting in a line to go through the security process for embarkation or in ports of call. Note that there is room service.

FAMILIES. *AIDAmar* really is a family-friendly ship. Children are split into four age groups: Seepferdchen (4–6 years), Delfin (7–9), Orcas (10–12), and Teens (14–17). Each has its own play area. There is a diverse selection of children's and youth programs in a holiday camp atmosphere, and special Club Team members dedicated to making it all happen. Supervised by a chef, children can make their own menus for the week, and visit the galley to make cookies and other items – a novel idea more cruise lines could adopt.

ACCOMMODATION. There are eight or nine grades, from deluxe suites to interior (no view) cabins, depending on the ship, which keeps your cabin choice simple.

Contrary to maritime traditions (even-numbered cabins on the port side, odd-numbered cabins on the starboard side), cabin numbers progress numerically (example: 8201–8276 on the port side; 8101–8176 on the starboard side). All suites and cabins have two beds (convertible to queen-size bed). Some cabins also have two extra beds/berths for children, and some cabins have interconnecting doors – useful for families.

The decor in all accommodation grades is bright, youthful, rather minimalist, and slightly whimsical. All are accented with multi-patterned fabrics, wood-trimmed cabinetry (with nicely rounded edges), and rattan or wood-look furniture. Beds have duvets and a colorful Arabian-style fabric canopy that goes from the headboard to the ceiling. The windows have full pull-down blackout blinds (useful in destinations with long daylight hours).

The bathrooms are compact, practical units; they have a shower enclosure, small washbasin, and small toilet. As in the most basic hotels and motels, only a wall-mounted body wash/shampoo dispenser is provided, so take your own conditioner, hand lotion, and other toiletries you may need.

Thick cotton bathrobes are provided for all grades of accommodation, as are two towels – a face towel and a 'bath' towel, in two different colors. The 'bath' towels are not large, at 54 by 27 inches – compared to 72 by 36 inches aboard P&O Cruises' Ventura, for example. The bathroom does not have a hairdryer, but one is located in the vanity unit in the cabin. Note that the usual night-time turndown service provided aboard most ships is not provided, and there is no cabin service after 3pm.

Cabins with balconies have a sliding door that's easy to open and doesn't impinge on balcony space; a small drinks table and two small, light chairs are provided. Note that balconies on the lowest deck can be overlooked by anyone on a balcony on the decks above. Balcony cabins have a hammock as standard, although it only accommodates one (thin) person. Some cabins (forward on Deck 5 – Nos 5103, 5104, 5105, 5106, 5203, 5204, 5206) have cabins with an outside view (well, outside light), but they are obstructed by steel bulkheads that form the front section of the ship.

Naturally, suite-grade accommodation offers more space, including more drawer and storage space, better quality furniture and furnishings, a larger lounge area and a slightly larger bathroom with a tub – and a larger balcony – those at the front and stern of the ship are the best and most desirable.

DINING. There are three self-serve eateries: Markt (Market), Bella Vista (for Italian cuisine), and Weite Welt (Wide World) restaurants. The opening times for lunch and dinner are 12:30-14:00 and 18:30-21:00 respectively. Additionally, there's a Buffalo Steakhouse (which serves excellent steaks), an à la carte Rossini Restaurant with waiter and sommelier service, a Sushi Bar, a Pizzeria Mare, and a Café Mare. These venues are open at set times, although the Pizzeria typically stays open until midnight.

In the three self-serve restaurants, the meal concept is simple: main meals are taken when you want them in one of the large self-serve buffet-style restaurants, with open seating at tables of four, six, or eight. Cutlery can be found hanging in a rack, but there are no soup spoons, only dessert spoons.

The tables are almost all large, and, when the ship is full, it can prove challenging to find a seat, not to mention any service personnel to clean the tables. Because it's a buffet venue, you'll probably sit with different people for each meal – which could be a good way to make new friends.

The standard of food at the self-serve buffet islands ranges from adequate to quite good, with creative displays and presentation, and table-clearing service that is sometimes efficient, but mostly not.

The many food islands and active stations cut down on the waiting time for food. There is always a big selection of breads, cheeses, cold cuts, fruits, and make-your-own coffee and teas – with a choice of more than 30 types of loose-leaf regular and herbal teas. More than 1,200 items of food are offered. The fish section has its own fish smoking unit (which resembles a wine cabinet).

You can sit where you want, when you want, and with whom you want, so eating is a socially interactive occasion. In fact, it's hard to be an unsociable couple and have a table for only two. At peak times, the venues may remind you of noisy roadside cafés. Because of the large buffet rooms and self-serve dining concept, the crew to passenger ratio looks poor; but this is because there are no waiters as such (except in à la carte venues), only staff for clearing tables.

Beer is available at the push of a button or a pull of the tap, and table wine – of the sort that would make a good drain cleaner – is usually provided in carafes on each table for lunch and dinner. Note that the beverage stations open only during restaurant opening hours, unless you go to the extra-cost coffee bar (Café Mare). Vending machines dispense out-of-hours snacks.

Other dining options. The à la carte Rossini Restaurant, with mostly high-back seats, has an intimate atmosphere. It is open for dinner only, and has a set five- or six-course menu, plus daily 'specials.' There is no cover charge, but an extra charge applies to everything on the à la carte menu (such as caviar, chateaubriand, rib-eye steak), and for wines. Reservations are needed. Tablecloths are provided, the food is very good, and service is sound.

The Buffalo Steakhouse has an open 'display' kitchen, and offers various steak cuts and sizes – Delmonico, New York Strip Loin, Porterhouse, and Filét, plus bison steaks – and roast lamb rack. There's a daily special – a prix-fixe meal (example: a 180g fillet steak, house salad, and dessert). It's like going out to eat in a decent restaurant ashore – but there are no tablecloths. Wine or any other drinks cost extra.

A 12-seater sushi counter is for Japanese-style sushi and sashimi dishes. While the counter provides stools for seating, two low-slung tables with well-type seating are difficult to sit at and get up from (notice to women: avoid wearing short skirts). The sushi is uninspiring, but typical of what you'd expect in a sushi bar not run by Japanese sushi masters. While the presentation is appetizing, the actual fare is somewhat light on taste – and you can be subjected to intense noise level from the adjacent 'open-plan' showlounge.

A wine bar, Vinotheque, is located in front of the Weide Welt (Wide World) Restaurant, has a list of premium wines, and Davidoff cigars (although you can't smoke them at the bar – or anywhere inside the ship). **The Pizzeria Mare provides a small selection of** ever popular pizzas.

ENTERTAINMENT. The Theatrium (theatre) is in the center of the ship. It is open to the main foyer and other public areas, on three levels (Decks 9, 10, 11), and topped by a glass dome. Amphitheater-style seating is on three decks (the bench seating on the two upper levels has back supports, but not on the lower level), plus standing tables, although sight lines to the raised thrust stage area are less than good from many of the seats.

The layout also means that people walk through the area constantly, distracting you from what's on the stage. For the performers, it's a bit like being in a TV studio, and trying to perform in front of the cameras, but with the audience in a different location. You can also watch the rehearsals, because this is really all about an active/interactive lifestyle.

The shows (each is just 30 minutes long, with four different shows scheduled each evening (usually between 8pm and 11pm), so there's plenty to see and experience. They are produced by AIDA Cruises' in-house department in a joint venture with SeeLive (Hamburg's Schmidt's Tivoli Theater), and consist of around 12 performers. All vocals in the shows are performed live to pre-recorded tracks. The shows are trendy, upbeat, fun, and very entertaining. The whole entertainment experience is lively and fun – in fact, it's a little like going to the circus.

SPA/FITNESS. The spa, fitness and sports programming are extensive.

The Body and Soul wellness/oasis area is located on two decks (connected by a stairway) and encompasses some 24,750 sq ft (2,300 sq m). There is also an open-air wellness deck for FKK relaxation/nude sunbathing in an area atop the ship forward of the ship's mast. In keeping with the times, all the trendy treatments are featured in an appealing contemporary setting.

In addition to a large fitness room (with an abundance of weight-training exercycle and Nordic-Trak machines, there are also saunas and steam rooms, and 14 rooms for massage and other treatments (most named after places associated with the design theme), neat showers, funky changing rooms, and a tropical garden with real (waxed) palm trees and relaxation loungers. Sport enthusiasts can also play billiards, volleyball or squash – or go jogging.

There is a bike excursion counter, at which you can also book diving, and golfing excursions. 'Sport bikes' (mountain bikes with tough front and rear suspension units) are provided for conducted biking excursions in each port of call, a concession run by of Austrian downhill champion skier Erwin Resch.

AIDAsol
★★★★

Size:................................Large Resort Ship	Cabins (total):..................................1,097
Tonnage:...71,304	Size range (sq ft/m):.................145.3–473.2/13.5–44
Lifestyle:.......................................Standard	Cabins (outside view):..............................715
Cruise line:................................AIDA Cruises	Cabins (interior/no view):...........................381
Former names:....................................none	Cabins (for one person):..............................0
IMO number:..................................9490040	Cabins (with private balcony):.......................491
Builder:.......................... Meyer Werft (Germany)	Cabins (wheelchair accessible):.......................11
Original cost:.............................€350 million	Wheelchair accessibility:..........................Good
Entered service:.............................Apr 2-11	Cabin voltage:..........................110 and 220 volts
Registry:...Italy	Elevators:...10
Length (ft/m):............................. 831.1/253.3	Casino (gaming tables):.............................Yes
Beam (ft/m):............................. 105.6/32.2	Slot machines:......................................No
Draft (ft/m):.................................. 24.6/7.5	Swimming pools:.....................................3
Propulsion/Propellers:...........diesel-electric (36,000 kW)/2	Hot tubs (on deck):..................................0
Passenger decks:.....................................14	Self-service launderette:...........................Yes
Total crew:......................................646	Dedicated cinema/seats:.............................No
Passengers (lower beds/alll berths):.............2,194/2,500	Library:..Yes
Passenger Space Ratio (lower beds/all berths):.......34.6/28.4	Onboard currency:................................Euros
Crew/Passenger Ratio (lower beds/all berths):..........3.1/3.8	

Contemporary, casual no-frills cruising for families

OVERVIEW. *AIDAsol* is for youthful German-speaking couples, singles, and particularly families seeking good value for money in a party-like environment, with excellent entertainment. This is all about über-casual cruising, with two main self-serve buffet restaurants instead of waiter service. It's tablecloth-less eating, and there is little contact with staff.

THE SHIP. The ship has a smart, contemporary profile that is quite well proportioned, with a swept-back funnel and wedge-shaped stern. The bows display the bright red lips, as well as the blue eyes, of *Aïda* (from Verdi's opera, written to commemorate the opening of the Suez Canal in 1871). AIDA Cruises, Germany's largest cruise line, is part of Costa Cruises, which is itself part of Carnival Corporation. Its expanding fleet allows it to offer a wide choice of itineraries, including the Middle East and Asia.

Overall, this really is cruising for youthful German-speaking families, and for anyone who doesn't mind busy places and lines. An AIDA cruise isn't cheap, but you do get lots of high-tech entertainment, and there's always plenty of food. Some frustration occurs when shore excursions sell out, when lines form after shore excursion buses return to the ship and you have to go through the slow security check, and for shore tenders.

The AIDA-class ships (known as AIDA Clubships) evolved from the first and smallest ship, AIDA (now named *AIDAcara*), in which the central idea was to

Berlitz's Ratings	Possible	Achieved
Ship	500	402
Accommodation	200	146
Food	400	262
Service	400	284
Entertainment	100	71
Cruise	400	294
OVERALL SCORE		
1459 points out of 2000		

get passengers to participate in public-area activities together, as in the Robinson Club concept on land. This led to 'open plan' interiors and the feeling that the ship is one large space, but cleverly split into intimate rooms – although, in reality, rooms 'flow' into each other at each fire zone section (a length of 157ft/48m).

The use of bright colors is really noticeable, and designed to excite the senses. Most of the chairs, counter stools, and bar seats are quite small, designed for the thinner passenger, typically under 40. Also, one thing that differentiates AIDA's ships from most others is the cheerful welcoming embarkation/tender loading zone, which has an integral café and bar for you to wait in comfort for shore tenders, and before and after going ashore, etc.

There is, however, constant music, so this ship is not for anyone seeking a 'quiet escape' vacation.

AIDA Cruises has really grown up over the past few years, and no longer focuses on summer-camp style participation events. The ships have become more sophisticated, entertaining venues, and the old *animateurs* – somewhat like the *gentils ordinaires* of Club Med, but better – have grown up and morphed into what is now known as Club Teams. They, along with other staff, interact with passengers throughout the ship.

Sport biking is part of its youthful image, with three different levels of cycling to suit differing fitness levels. AIDA Cruises has also successfully appealed to golfers, with several golf-theme packages that include playing at notable courses ashore in many ports of call.

The open deck space is rather limited, but sunbathing space includes some reasonably quiet space above the navigation bridge. Dip pools and hot tubs, plus seating areas, are provided in a cascading, tiered setting atop the ship on the pool deck, providing a decent amount of sunbathing space. It's all designed to be in a 'beach-like' environment, with splash and play areas.

There are three pricing levels – Aida Premium, Aida Vario, and Just Aida – depending on what you want to be included, plus differences in price according to accommodation size and grade, and the itinerary. Opt for the basic, price-driven Just Aida package and the cruise line chooses the ship, itinerary, and accommodation for you – sort of a pot-luck cruise, based on or close to the dates you choose.

The dress code is simple: casual (no ties) at all times, and there are no 'formal' dress-up nights on board. All port taxes and gratuities are included in all cruises.

Several decks of public rooms and facilities are positioned above the accommodation decks, and AIDAsol shares public room names that are common aboard all the ships in the fleet: Aida Bar, the main social gathering place, whose principal feature is a star-shaped bar (whose combined length makes it among the longest at sea), with many tables for standing drinkers.

A small casino features blackjack, roulette and poker gaming tables, and slot machines. There are many more balcony cabins, a separate aft sports deck, a 'no music' observation lounge, and an art gallery. The embarkation entryway is really innovative, has a bar and a lookout balcony, and is cheerfully painted to look like a city waterfront street scene. It is quite different from the utilitarian gangway entry areas found aboard most cruise ships; a welcoming environment, it helps to calm tempers after waiting in a line to go through the security process for embarkation or in ports of call.

Note that there is no room service.

FAMILIES. *AIDAsol* really is a family-friendly ship. Children are split into four age groups: Seepferdchen (4–6 years), Delfin (7–9), Orcas (10–12), and Teens (14–17). Each has its own play area. There is a diverse selection of children's and youth programs in a holiday camp atmosphere, and special Club Team members dedicated to making at all happen. Supervised by a chef, children can make their own menus for the week, and visit the galley to make cookies and other items.

ACCOMMODATION. There are eight or nine grades, from deluxe suites to interior (no view) cabins, depending on the ship, which keeps your cabin choice simple.

Contrary to maritime traditions (even-numbered cabins on the port side, odd-numbered cabins on the starboard side), cabin numbers progress numerically (example: 8201–8276 on the port side; 8101–8176 on

the starboard side). All suites and cabins have two beds (convertible to queen-size bed). Some cabins also have two extra beds/berths for children, and some cabins have interconnecting doors – useful for families.

The decor in all accommodation grades is bright, youthful, rather minimalist, and slightly whimsical. All are accented with multi-patterned fabrics, wood-trimmed cabinetry (with nicely rounded edges), and rattan or wood-look furniture. Beds have duvets and a colorful Arabian-style fabric canopy that goes from the headboard to the ceiling. The windows have full pull-down blackout blinds (useful in destinations with long daylight hours).

The bathrooms are compact, practical units; they have a shower enclosure, small washbasin, and small toilet. As in the most basic hotels and motels, only a wall-mounted body wash/shampoo dispenser is provided, so take your own conditioner, hand lotion, and other toiletries you may need.

Thick cotton bathrobes are provided for all grades of accommodation, as are two towels – a face towel and a 'bath' towel, in two different colors. The 'bath' towels are not large, at 54 by 27 inches – compared to 72 by 36 inches aboard P&O Cruises' Ventura, for example. The bathroom does not have a hairdryer, but one is located in the vanity unit in the cabin. Note that the usual nighttime turndown service provided aboard most ships is not provided, and there is no cabin service after 3pm.

Cabins with balconies have a sliding door that's easy to open and doesn't impinge on balcony space; a small drinks table and two small, light chairs are provided. Note that balconies on the lowest deck can be overlooked by anyone on a balcony on the decks above. Balcony cabins have a hammock as standard, although it only accommodates one (thin) person. Some cabins (forward on Deck 5 – Nos 5103, 5104, 5105, 5106, 5203, 5204, 5206) have cabins with an outside view (well, outside light), but they are obstructed by steel bulkheads that form the front section of the ship.

Naturally, suite-grade accommodation offers more space, including more drawer and storage space, better quality furniture and furnishings, a larger lounge area and a slightly larger bathroom with a tub – and a larger balcony – those at the front and stern of the ship are the best and most desirable.

DINING. There are three self-serve eateries: Markt (Market), Bella Vista (for Italian cuisine), and Weite Welt (Wide World) restaurants. The opening times for lunch and dinner are 12:30-14:00 and 18:30-21:00 respectively. Additionally, there's a Buffalo Steakhouse (which serves excellent steaks), an à la carte Rossini Restaurant with waiter and sommelier service, a Sushi Bar, a Pizzeria Mare, and a Café Mare. These venues are open at set times (there are no 24-hour-a-day outlets, because there is little demand for them), although the Pizzeria stays open until midnight.

In the three self-serve restaurants, the meal concept is simple: main meals are taken when you want them in one of the large self-serve buffet-style restaurants, with open seating at tables of four, six, or eight. Cutlery can be found hanging in a rack (a bit unhygienic), but there are no soup spoons, only dessert spoons.

The tables are almost all large, and, when the ship is full, it can prove challenging to find a seat, not to mention any service personnel to clean the tables.

The standard of food at the buffet islands ranges from adequate to quite good, with creative displays and presentation, and table-clearing service that is sometimes efficient, but mostly not.

The many food islands and active stations cut down on the waiting time for food. There is always a big selection of breads, cheeses, cold cuts, fruits, and make-your-own coffee and teas – with a choice of more than 30 types of loose-leaf regular and herbal teas. More than 1,200 items of food are offered. The fish section has its own fish smoking unit (which resembles a wine cabinet).

You can sit where you want, when you want, and with whom you want, so eating is a socially interactive occasion. In fact, it's hard to be an unsociable couple and have a table for only two. At peak times, the venues may remind you of noisy roadside cafés. Because of the large buffet rooms and self-serve dining concept, the crew to passenger ratio looks poor; but this is because there are no waiters as such (except in à la carte venues), only staff for clearing tables.

Beer is available at the push of a button or a pull of the tap, and table wine – of the sort that would make a good drain cleaner – is usually provided in carafes on each table for lunch and dinner. Note that the beverage stations open only during restaurant opening hours, unless you go to the extra-cost coffee bar (Café Mare). Vending machines dispense out-of-hours snacks.

Other dining options. The à la carte Rossini Restaurant, with mostly high-back seats, has an intimate atmosphere. It is open for dinner only, and has a set five- or six-course menu, plus daily 'specials.' There is no cover charge, but an extra charge applies to everything on the à la carte menu (such as caviar, chateaubriand, rib-eye steak), and for wines. Reservations are needed. Tablecloths are provided, the food is very good, and service is sound.

The Buffalo Steakhouse has an open 'display' kitchen, and offers various steak cuts and sizes – Delmonico, New York Strip Loin, Porterhouse, and Filét, plus bison steaks – and roast lamb rack. There's a daily special – a prix-fixe meal (example: a 180g fillet steak, house salad, and dessert). It's like going out to eat in a decent restaurant ashore – but there are no tablecloths. Wine or any other drinks cost extra.

A 12-seater sushi counter is for Japanese-style sushi and sashimi dishes. While the counter provides stools for seating, two low-slung tables with well-type seating are difficult to sit at and get up from (notice to women:

avoid wearing short skirts). The sushi is uninspiring, but typical of what you'd expect in a sushi bar not run by Japanese sushi masters. While the presentation is appetizing, the actual fare is somewhat light on taste – and you can be subjected to some noise level from the adjacent 'open-plan' showlounge.

A wine bar, Vinotheque, is located in front of the Weide Welt (Wide World) Restaurant, has a list of premium wines, and Davidoff cigars (although you can't smoke them at the bar – or anywhere inside the ship).

The Pizzeria Mare provides a small selection of ever popular pizzas.

ENTERTAINMENT. The Theatrium (theatre) is in the center of the ship. It is open to the main foyer and other public areas, on three levels (Decks 9, 10, 11), and topped by a glass dome. Amphitheater-style seating is on three decks (the bench seating on the two upper levels has back supports, but not on the lower level), plus standing tables, although sight lines to the raised thrust stage area are less than good from many of the seats.

The layout also means that people walk through the area constantly, distracting you from what's on the stage. For the performers, it's a bit like being in a TV studio, and trying to perform in front of the cameras, but with the audience in a different location. You can also watch the rehearsals, because this is really all about an active/interactive lifestyle.

The shows (each is just 30 minutes long, with four different shows scheduled each evening (usually between 8pm and 11pm), so there's plenty to see and experience. They are produced by AIDA Cruises' in-house department in a joint venture with SeeLive (Hamburg's Schmidt's Tivoli Theater), and consist of around 12 performers. All vocals in the shows are performed live (because there's no live band on stage), to pre-recorded backing tracks.

SPA/FITNESS. The spa, fitness and sports programming are extensive. The Body and Soul wellness/oasis area is located on two decks (connected by a stairway) and encompasses some 24,750 sq ft (2,300 sq m). There is also an open-air wellness deck for FKK relaxation/nude sunbathing in an area atop the ship forward of the ship's mast.

In addition to a large fitness room there are also saunas and steam rooms, and 14 rooms for massage and other treatments, neat showers, funky changing rooms, and a tropical garden with real (waxed) palm trees and relaxation loungers. Sport enthusiasts can also play billiards, volleyball or squash – or go jogging.

There is a bike excursion counter, at which you can also book diving, and golfing excursions. 'Sport bikes' (mountain bikes with tough front and rear suspension units) are provided for conducted biking excursions in each port of call, a concession run by of Austrian downhill champion skier Erwin Resch.

AIDAstella
★★★★

Size:................................Large Resort Ship	Cabins (total):.................................. 1,096
Tonnage:... 71,304	Size range (sq ft/m):..................145.3–473.2/13.5–44
Lifestyle: ....Standard	Cabins (outside view):............................715
Cruise line:.............................AIDA Cruises	Cabins (interior/no view):.........................381
Former names: ....none	Cabins (for one person):............................0
IMO number: 9601132	Cabins (with private balcony): 722
Builder: ....Meyer Werft (Germany)	Cabins (wheelchair accessible): 11
Original cost: ....€350 million	Wheelchair accessibility:.........................Good
Entered service:...............................Mar 2013	Cabin voltage: ....110 and 220 volts
Registry:... Italy	Elevators:..10
Length (ft/m):............................... 831.1/253.3	Casino (gaming tables):...........................Yes
Beam (ft/m):................................ 105.6/32.2	Slot machines:......................................No
Draft (ft/m):.................................. 24.6/7.5	Swimming pools:.....................................3
Propulsion/Propellers:..........diesel-electric (36,000 kW)/2	Hot tubs (on deck):..................................0
Passenger decks:....................................14	Self-service launderette:..........................Yes
Total crew:.......................................646	Dedicated cinema/seats:.............................No
Passengers (lower beds/all berths):.............2,194/2,500	Library: ....Yes
Passenger Space Ratio (lower beds/all berths):.......34.6/28.4	Onboard currency: ....Euros
Crew/Passenger Ratio (lower beds/all berths):..........3.1/3.8	

Large family-friendly resort ship for no-frills cruising

OVERVIEW. *AIDAstella* is for youthful German-speaking couples, singles, and particularly families seeking good value for money in an urban party-like environment, with excellent entertainment. This is all about über-casual cruising, with two main self-serve buffet restaurants instead of waiter service. It's table-cloth-less eating, and there is little contact with staff.

Berlitz's Ratings		
	Possible	Achieved
Ship	500	402
Accommodation	200	146
Food	400	262
Service	400	284
Entertainment	100	71
Cruise	400	294
OVERALL SCORE		
1459 points out of 2000		

THE SHIP. The ship has a smart, contemporary profile that is quite well proportioned, with a swept-back funnel and wedge-shaped stern. The bows display the bright red lips, as well as the blue eyes, of *Aïda* (from Verdi's opera, which was written to commemorate the opening of the Suez Canal in 1871). AIDA Cruises, Germany's largest cruise line, comes under the wing of Costa Cruises, which is itself part of Carnival Corporation. Its expanding fleet allows it to offer a wide choice of itineraries, including the Middle East and Asia.

Overall, this really is cruising for youthful German-speaking families, and for anyone who doesn't mind busy places and lines. An AIDA cruise isn't cheap, but you do get lots of high-tech entertainment, and there's always plenty of food. Some frustration occurs when shore excursions sell out, when lines form after shore excursion buses return to the ship and you have to go through the slow security check, and for shore tenders.

The AIDA-class ships (known as AIDA Clubships) evolved from the first and smallest ship, AIDA (now named *AIDAcara*), in which the central idea was to get passengers to participate in public-area activities together, as in the Robinson Club concept on land. This led to 'open plan' interiors and the feeling that the ship is one large space, but cleverly split into intimate rooms – although, in reality, rooms 'flow' into each other at each fire zone section (a length of 157ft/48m).

The use of bright colors is really noticeable, and designed to excite the senses. Most of the chairs, counter stools, and bar seats are quite small, designed for the thinner passenger, typically under 40. Also, one thing that differentiates AIDA's ships from most others is the cheerful welcoming embarkation/tender loading zone, which has an integral café and bar for you to wait in comfort for shore tenders, and before and after going ashore, etc.

There is, however, constant music, so this ship is not for anyone seeking a 'quiet escape' vacation.

AIDA Cruises has really grown up over the past few years, and no longer focuses on summer-camp style participation events. The ships have become more sophisticated, entertaining venues, and the old *animateurs* – somewhat like the *gentils ordinaires* of Club Med, but better – have grown up and morphed into what is now known as Club Teams.

Sport biking is part of its youthful image, with three different levels of cycling to suit differing fitness levels. AIDA Cruises has also successfully appealed to golfers, with several golf-theme packages that include playing at notable courses ashore in many ports of call.

The open deck space is rather limited, but sunbathing space includes some reasonably quiet space above the navigation bridge. Dip pools and hot tubs, plus seating areas, are provided in a cascading, tiered setting atop the ship on the pool deck, providing a decent amount of sunbathing space. It's all designed to be in a 'beach-like' environment, with splash and play areas.

There are three pricing levels – Aida Premium, Aida Vario, and Just Aida – depending on what you want to be included, plus differences in price according to accommodation size and grade, and the itinerary. Opt for the basic, price-driven Just Aida package and the cruise line chooses the ship, itinerary, and accommodation for you – sort of a pot-luck cruise, based on or close to the dates you choose.

The dress code is simple: casual (no ties) at all times, and there are no 'formal' dress-up nights on board. All port taxes and gratuities are included in all cruises.

Several decks of public rooms and facilities are positioned above the accommodation decks, and AIDAstella shares public room names that are common aboard all the ships in the fleet: Aida Bar, the main social gathering place,for example, whose principal feature is a star-shaped bar (whose combined length makes it one of the longest at sea), with many tables for standing drinkers.

A small casino features blackjack, roulette and poker gaming tables, as well as slot machines. There are many more balcony cabins, a separate aft sports deck, a 'no music' observation lounge, and an art gallery. The embarkation entryway is really innovative, has a bar and a lookout balcony, and is cheerfully painted to look like a city waterfront street scene. It is quite different from the utilitarian gangway entry areas found aboard most cruise ships.

FAMILIES. *AIDAstella* really is a family-friendly ship. Children are split into four age groups: Seeperfdchen (4–6 years), Delfin (7–9), Orcas (10–12), and Teens (14–17). Each has its own play area. There is a diverse selection of children's and youth programs in a holiday camp atmosphere, and special Club Team members dedicated to making at all happen. Supervised by a chef, children can make their own menus for the week, and visit the galley to make cookies and other items.

ACCOMMODATION. There are eight or nine grades, from deluxe suites to interior (no view) cabins, depending on the ship, which keeps your cabin choice simple.

Contrary to maritime traditions (even-numbered cabins on the port side, odd-numbered cabins on the starboard side), cabin numbers progress numerically (example: 8201–8276 on the port side; 8101–8176 on the starboard side). All suites and cabins have two beds (convertible to queen-size bed). Some cabins also have

two extra beds/berths for children, and some cabins have interconnecting doors – useful for families.

The decor in all accommodation grades is bright, youthful, rather minimalist, and slightly whimsical. All are accented with multi-patterned fabrics, wood-trimmed cabinetry (with nicely rounded edges), and rattan or wood-look furniture. Beds have duvets and a colorful Arabian-style fabric canopy that goes from the headboard to the ceiling. The windows have full pull-down blackout blinds (useful in destinations with long daylight hours).

The bathrooms are compact, practical units; they have a shower enclosure, small washbasin, and small toilet. As in the most basic hotels and motels, only a wall-mounted body wash/shampoo dispenser is provided, so take your own conditioner, hand lotion, and other toiletries you may need.

Thick cotton bathrobes are provided for all grades of accommodation, as are two towels – a face towel and a 'bath' towel, in two different colors. The 'bath' towels are not large, at 54 by 27 inches – compared to 72 by 36 inches aboard P&O Cruises' Ventura, for example. The bathroom does not have a hairdryer, but one is located in the vanity unit in the cabin. Note that the usual nighttime turndown service provided aboard most ships is not provided, and there is no cabin service after 3pm.

Cabins with balconies have a sliding door that's easy to open and doesn't impinge on balcony space; a small drinks table and two small, light chairs are provided. Note that balconies on the lowest deck can be overlooked by anyone on a balcony on the decks above. Balcony cabins have a hammock as standard, although it only accommodates one (thin) person. Some cabins (forward on Deck 5 – Nos 5103, 5104, 5105, 5106, 5203, 5204, 5206) have cabins with an outside view (well, outside light), but they are obstructed by steel bulkheads that form the front section of the ship.

Naturally, suite-grade accommodation offers more space, including more drawer and storage space, better quality furniture and furnishings, a larger lounge area and a slightly larger bathroom with a tub – and a larger balcony – those at the front and stern of the ship are best and most desirable.

DINING. There are three self-serve eateries: Markt (Market), Bella Vista (for Italian cuisine), and Weite Welt (Wide World) restaurants. The opening times for lunch and dinner are 12:30-14:00 and 18:30-21:00 respectively. Additionally, there's a Buffalo Steakhouse (which serves excellent steaks), an à la carte Rossini Restaurant with waiter and sommelier service, a Sushi Bar, a Pizzeria Mare, and a Café Mare. These venues are open at set times (there are no 24-hour-a-day outlets, because there is little demand for them), although the Pizzeria typically stays open until midnight.

In the three self-serve restaurants, the meal concept is simple: main meals are taken when you want them in one of the large self-serve buffet-style restaurants, with open seating at tables of four, six, or eight. Cutlery hangs in a rack (this is unhygienic), but there are no soup spoons, only dessert spoons.

The tables are almost all large, and, when the ship is full, it can prove challenging to find a seat, not to mention any service personnel to clean the tables. Because it's a buffet venue, you'll probably sit with different people for each meal – which could be a good way to make new friends.

The standard of food at the self-serve buffet islands ranges from adequate to quite good, with creative displays and presentation, and table-clearing service that is sometimes efficient, but mostly not.

The many food islands and active stations cut down on the waiting time for food. There is always a big selection of breads, cheeses, cold cuts, fruits, and make-your-own coffee and teas – with a choice of more than 30 types of loose-leaf regular and herbal teas. More than 1,200 items of food are offered. The fish section has its own fish smoking unit (which resembles a wine cabinet).

You can sit where you want, when you want, and with whom you want, so eating is a socially interactive occasion. In fact, it's hard to be an unsociable couple and have a table for only two. At peak times, the venues may remind you of noisy roadside cafés. Because of the large buffet rooms and self-serve dining concept, the crew to passenger ratio looks poor; but this is because there are no waiters as such (except in à la carte venues), only staff for clearing tables.

Beer is available at the push of a button or a pull of the tap, and table wine – of the sort that would make a good drain cleaner – is usually provided in carafes on each table for lunch and dinner. Note that the beverage stations open only during restaurant opening hours, unless you go to the extra-cost coffee bar (Café Mare). Vending machines dispense out-of-hours snacks.

Other dining options. The à la carte Rossini Restaurant, with mostly high-back seats, has an intimate atmosphere. It is open for dinner only, and has a set five- or six-course menu, plus daily 'specials.' There is no cover charge, but an extra charge applies to everything on the à la carte menu (such as caviar, chateaubriand, rib-eye steak), and for wines. Reservations are needed. Tablecloths are provided, the food is very good, and service is sound.

The Buffalo Steakhouse has an open 'display' kitchen, and offers various steak cuts and sizes – Delmonico, New York Strip Loin, Porterhouse, and Filét, plus bison steaks – and roast lamb rack. There's a daily special – a prix-fixe meal (example: a 180g fillet steak, house salad, and dessert). It's like going out to eat in a decent restaurant ashore – but there are no tablecloths. Wine or any other drinks cost extra.

A 12-seater sushi counter is for Japanese-style sushi and sashimi dishes. While the counter provides stools for seating, two low-slung tables with well-type seating are difficult to sit at and get up from (notice to women:

avoid wearing short skirts). The sushi is uninspiring, but typical of what you'd expect in a sushi bar not run by Japanese sushi masters. While the presentation is appetizing, you can be subjected to intense noise level from the adjacent 'open-plan' showlounge.

A wine bar, Vinotheque, is located in front of the Weide Welt (Wide World) Restaurant, has a list of premium wines, and Davidoff cigars (although you can't smoke them at the bar – or anywhere inside the ship).

The Pizzeria Mare provides a small selection of ever popular pizzas.

ENTERTAINMENT. The Theatrium (theatre) is in the center of the ship. It is open to the main foyer and other public areas, on three levels (Decks 9, 10, 11), and topped by a glass dome. Amphitheater-style seating is on three decks (the bench seating on the two upper levels has back supports, but not on the lower level), plus standing tables, although sight lines to the raised thrust stage area are less than good from many of the seats.

The layout also means that people walk through the area constantly, distracting you from what's on the stage. For the performers, it's a bit like being in a TV studio, and trying to perform in front of the cameras, but with the audience in a different location. You can also watch the rehearsals, because this is really all about an active/interactive lifestyle.

The shows (each is just 30 minutes long, with four different shows scheduled each evening (usually between 8pm and 11pm), so there's plenty to see and experience. They are produced by AIDA Cruises' in-house department in a joint venture with SeeLive (Hamburg's Schmidt's Tivoli Theater), and consist of around 12 performers. All vocals in the shows are performed live (because there's no live band on stage), to pre-recorded backing tracks.

SPA/FITNESS. The spa, fitness and sports programming are extensive.

The Body and Soul wellness/oasis area is located on two decks (connected by a stairway) and encompasses some 24,750 sq ft (2,300 sq m). There is also an open-air wellness deck for FKK relaxation/nude sunbathing in an area atop the ship forward of the ship's mast.

In addition to a large fitness room, there are also saunas and steam rooms, and 14 rooms for massage and other treatments, showers, changing rooms, and a tropical garden with real (waxed) palm trees and relaxation loungers. Sport enthusiasts can also play billiards, volleyball or squash – or go jogging.

There is a bike excursion counter, at which you can also book diving, and golfing excursions. 'Sport bikes' (mountain bikes with tough front and rear suspension units) are provided for conducted biking excursions in each port of call, a concession run by of Austrian downhill champion skier Erwin Resch.

AIDAvita
★★★+

Size:.	Mid-size Ship	Cabins (total):.	633
Tonnage:	42,289	Size range (sq ft/m):	145.3–344.4/13.5–32.0
Lifestyle:	Standard	Cabins (outside view):	422
Cruise line:.	AIDA Cruises	Cabins (interior/no view):	211
Former names:	none	Cabins (for one person):.	0
IMO number:	9221554	Cabins (with private balcony):	60
Builder:	Aker MTW (Germany)	Cabins (wheelchair accessible):	4
Original cost:	$350 million	Wheelchair accessibility:	Good
Entered service:.	Apr 2002	Cabin voltage:	110 and 220 volts
Registry:.	Italy	Elevators:	6
Length (ft/m):	666.5/202.8	Casino (gaming tables):	No
Beam (ft/m):	92.2/28.1	Slot machines:	No
Draft (ft/m):	20.7/6.3	Swimming pools:	3
Propulsion/Propellers:	diesel-electric/2	Hot tubs (on deck):	5
Passenger decks:	10	Self-service launderette:	Yes
Total crew:	389	Dedicated cinema/seats:	No
Passenger (lower beds/alll berths):	1,266/1,582	Library:	Yes
Passenger Space Ratio (lower beds/all berths):	33.4/26.7	Onboard currency:	Euros
Crew/Passenger Ratio (lower beds/all berths):	3.0/3.7		

Upbeat, family-friendly ship for busy, basic cruising

OVERVIEW. An AIDA Cruise is for youthful German-speaking couples, singles, and particularly families seeking good value for money in a party-like environment, with excellent entertainment. This is all about über-casual cruising, with two main self-serve buffet restaurants instead of the traditional waiter service. It's tablecloth-less eating, and there is little contact with the relatively few staff.

THE SHIP. The ship has a smart, contemporary profile, with a swept-back funnel and wedge-shaped stern. The bows display the red lips, as well as the blue eyes, of *Aïda* (from Verdi's opera, written to commemorate the opening of the Suez Canal in 1871). AIDA Cruises, Germany's largest cruise line, is part of Costa Cruises, which is itself part of Carnival Corporation. Its expanding fleet allows it to offer a wide choice of itineraries, including the Middle East and Asia.

Overall, this really is cruising for urban dwellers, and for those that don't mind busy places and lines. An AIDA cruise isn't cheap, but you get a lot of high-tech entertainment, and there's always plenty of food. Some frustration occurs when shore excursions sell out, when lines form after shore excursion buses return to the ship and you have to go through the slow security check – and at peak times in the self-serve restaurants, and for shore tenders.

The AIDA-class ships (known as AIDA Clubships) evolved from the first and smallest ship, AIDA (over 15 years old and now named *AIDA cara*), in which the

Berlitz's Ratings

	Possible	Achieved
Ship	500	361
Accommodation	200	131
Food	400	251
Service	400	268
Entertainment	100	75
Cruise	400	277

OVERALL SCORE
1363 points out of 2000

central idea was to get passengers to participate in public-area activities together, as in the Robinson Club concept on land. This led to 'open plan' interiors and the feeling that the ship is one large space, but cleverly split into intimate rooms – although, in reality, rooms 'flow' into each other at each fire zone section (a length of 157ft/48m).

The use of bright tropical colors throughout the interiors is really noticeable. Most of the chairs, counter stools, and bar seats are quite small, designed for thin, youthful passengers.

There is, however, constant high-street music everywhere, so these ships are not for those wanting a 'quiet escape' vacation, even though volume levels are well controlled.

AIDA Cruises has really grown up over the past few years, and no longer focuses on summer-camp style participation events. The ships have become more sophisticated, entertaining venues, and the old *animateurs* – somewhat like the *gentils ordinaires* of Club Med, but better – have grown up and morphed into what is now known as Club Teams. They, along with other staff, interact with passengers throughout the ship.

About 20 nationalities are represented among the crew, who are upbeat and cheerful. Staff hospitality training is now at a high level in all departments, and AIDA Cruises has its own training schools in several countries, plus a recognized training academy in Rostock.

Sport biking is part of its youthful image, with three different levels of cycling to suit differing fitness levels. The line has also successfully appealed to golfers, with golf-theme packages, cruises, and excursions ashore in many ports of call.

The open deck space is tight, but sunbathing space includes some rather pleasant, reasonably quiet space above the navigation bridge. Dip pools and hot tubs, plus seating areas, are provided in a cascading, tiered setting atop the ship on the pool deck, providing a decent amount of sunbathing space. It's all designed to be in a 'beach-like' environment, with splash and play areas.

Other facilities include a shore excursion counter, library, seminar rooms, duty-free shop, several bars and lounges, a small casino with blackjack, roulette and poker gaming tables, and slot machines.

There is a separate aft sports deck, a 'no music' observation lounge, and an art gallery. The embarkation entryway is really innovative, has a bar and a lookout balcony, and is cheerfully painted to look like a city street scene. It is different from the utilitarian gangway entry areas found aboard most cruise ships. A welcoming environment, it helps to calm tempers after waiting in a line to go through the security process for embarkation or in ports of call.

There are three pricing levels – Aida Premium, Aida Vario, and Just Aida – depending on what you want to be included, plus differences in price according to accommodation size and grade, and the itinerary. Opt for the basic, price-driven Just Aida package and the cruise line chooses the ship, itinerary, and accommodation for you – sort of a pot-luck cruise, based on or close to the dates you choose.

The dress code is simple: casual (no ties) at all times – there are no formal nights on board. All port taxes and gratuities are included in all packages, and, with very attractive rates, a cruise provides much better value than almost any land-based vacation.

Several decks of public rooms and facilities are positioned above the accommodation decks, and *AIDAvita* shares public room names that are common aboard all the ships in the fleet: Aida Bar, the main social gathering place, whose principal feature is a star-shaped bar (whose combined length makes it among the longest at sea), with many tables for standing drinkers.

Overall, this really is cruising for youthful German-speaking families, and for anyone who doesn't mind busy places and lines. An AIDA cruise isn't cheap, but you do get lots of high-tech entertainment, and there's always plenty of food (however, there is no room service). Some frustration occurs when shore excursions sell out, when lines form after shore excursion buses return to the ship and you have to go through the slow security check – and at peak times in the self-serve restaurants, and for shore tenders.

FAMILIES. This is a family-friendly ship. Children are split into four age groups: Seepferdchen (4–6 years), Delfin (7–9), Orcas (10–12), and Teens (14–17). Each

has its own play area. There is a diverse selection of children's and youth programs, and special Club Team members dedicated to making sure that everyone has a good time.

ACCOMMODATION. There are eight or nine grades, from deluxe suites to interior (no view) cabins, depending on the ship, which keeps your cabin choice simple.

Contrary to maritime traditions (even-numbered cabins on the port side, odd-numbered cabins on the starboard side), cabin numbers progress numerically (example: 8201–8276 on the port side; 8101–8176 on the starboard side). All suites and cabins have two beds (convertible to queen-size bed). Some cabins also have two extra beds/berths for children, and some cabins have interconnecting doors – useful for families.

The decor in all accommodation grades is bright, youthful, rather minimalist, and slightly whimsical. All are accented with multi-patterned fabrics, wood-trimmed cabinetry (with nicely rounded edges), and rattan or wood-look furniture. Beds have duvets and a colorful Arabian-style fabric canopy that goes from the headboard to the ceiling. The windows have full pull-down blackout blinds (useful in destinations with long daylight hours). Lifeboats may obstruct views in some cabins in the ship's center.

The bathrooms are compact, practical units; they have a shower enclosure, small washbasin, and small toilet. As in the most basic hotels and motels, only a wall-mounted body wash/shampoo dispenser is provided, so take your own conditioner, hand lotion, and other toiletries you may need.

Thick, 100 percent cotton bathrobes are provided for suite-grade accommodation, although non-suite grade passengers can obtain one from the spa. Two towels are provided – a face towel and a 'bath' towel, in two different colors. The 'bath' towels are not very large, at 54 by 27 inches – compared to 72 by 36 inches aboard the P&O Cruises' Ventura, for example. Although the bathrooms do not have a hairdryer, one is located in the vanity unit in the cabin. Unusually, night-time turn-down service is not provided (there is no cabin service after 3pm).

Cabins with balconies have a sliding door that's easy to open and doesn't impinge on balcony space; a small drinks table and two small, light chairs are provided. Note that balconies on the lowest deck can be overlooked by anyone on a balcony on the decks above. Some cabins (forward on Deck 5 – Nos 5103, 5104, 5105, 5106, 5203, 5204, 5206) aboard these ships have cabins with an outside view (well, outside light), but they are totally obstructed by steel bulkheads that form the front section of the ship.

Naturally, suite-grade accommodation offers more space, including more drawer and storage space, better quality furniture and furnishings, a larger lounge area and a slightly larger bathroom with a tub – and, of course, a larger balcony (those at the front and stern of the ship have the best).

DINING. Two eateries are included in the cruise fare; these are the Markt and Karibik self-serve buffet-style restaurants. The opening times for lunch and dinner are 12:30–14:00 and 18:30–21:00 respectively.

The meal concept is simple: main meals are taken when you want them in one of the large self-serve buffet-style restaurants, with open seating at tables of four, six, or eight. Cutlery hangs in a rack (considered unhygienic), but there are no soup spoons, only dessert spoons. It's very casual and easy-going mass catering, so think food court eating, not dining.

The tables are almost all large, and, when the ship is full, it can prove challenging to find a seat, not to mention any service personnel to clean the tables. Because it's a buffet venue, you'll probably sit with different people for each meal – which could be a good way to make new friends.

The standard of food at the buffet islands ranges from adequate to quite good, with creative displays and presentation, and table-clearing service that is sometimes efficient, but mostly not.

The many food islands and active stations cut down on the waiting time for food. There is always a big selection of breads, cheeses, cold cuts, fruits, and make-your-own coffee and teas – with a choice of more than 30 types of loose-leaf regular and herbal teas, and over 1,200 items of food are offered.

You can sit where you want, when you want, and with whom you want, so eating is a socially interactive occasion. In fact, it's hard to be an unsociable couple and have a table for only two. At peak times, the venues may remind you of noisy roadside cafés. Because of the large buffet rooms and self-serve dining concept, the crew to passenger ratio looks poor; but this is because there are no waiters as such (except in à la carte venues), only staff for clearing tables.

Beer is available at the push of a button or a pull of the tap, and table wine – of the sort that would make a good drain cleaner – is usually provided in carafes on each table for lunch and dinner. Note that the beverage stations open only during restaurant opening hours, unless you go to the extra-cost coffee bar (Café Mare). Vending machines dispense out-of-hours snacks.

Other dining options. The Rossini Restaurant (à la carte) has a quieter, more intimate atmosphere. It is open for dinner only, and has a set five- or six-course menu (plus daily specials). There is no cover charge, but an extra charge applies to everything on the à la carte menu (such as caviar, chateaubriand, rib-eye steak), and for wines. Reservations are needed, tablecloths are provided, the food is good, and the waiter and sommelier service are friendly.

The wine bar, Vinotheque, is located in front of the Weide Welt (Wide World) Restaurant, has a good list of premium wines, and Davidoff cigars (although you can't smoke them at the bar – or anywhere inside the ship).

ENTERTAINMENT. The Theater (Das Theater) is the main venue for all shows and most cabaret, and is two decks high. It has a raised stage, and amphitheater-style bench seating on all levels. The benches have back rests, and are quite comfortable, and sight lines are good from most seats, with the exception of port and starboard balcony sections, where sight lines are interrupted by thick safety railings.

The shows (each is just 30 minutes long, with four different shows scheduled each evening (usually between 8pm and 11pm), so there's plenty to see and experience. They are produced by AIDA Cruises' in-house department in a joint venture with SeeLive (Hamburg's Schmidt's Tivoli Theater), and consist of around 12 performers. Any vocals in the shows are performed live (because there's no live band on stage) to pre-recorded backing tracks that provide a mix of recorded live music and synthesized sound. The shows are trendy, upbeat, fun, and very entertaining. The whole entertainment experience is lively and fun – in fact, it's a little like going to the circus – and it's the informality of it all that passengers like.

In addition, there is a live band in the Aida Bar, the only room with a large dance floor (except for the disco).

SPA/FITNESS. The Body and Soul Spa, is located forward on Deck 11. It measures 11,840 sq ft (1,100 sq m), and contains two saunas (one dry, one wet, both with seats for more than 20 persons, and glass walls that look onto the deck), massage and other treatment rooms, and a large lounging area. There are also showers, and two whole 'ice walls' to use when you come out of the saunas (simply lean into the ice wall for maximum effect). Forward and outside the wellness center, is an FKK (FreiKoerperKultur) nude sunbathing deck, on two levels.

'Sport bikes' (mountain bikes with tough front and rear suspension units) are provided for conducted biking excursions in each port of call by a concession run by of Austrian downhill champion skier Erwin Resch. You can also book biking, diving, and golfing excursions.

Sporting types can also play golf in the electronic golf simulator, or billiards, volleyball or squash – or go jogging.

Akademik Ioffe
★★ +

Size:.	Boutique ship	Cabins (total):.	46
Tonnage:.	6,450 tons	Size range (sq ft/m):.	n/a
Lifestyle:.	Standard	Cabins (outside view):.	46
Cruise line:.	One Ocean Expeditions	Cabins (interior/no view):.	0
Former names:.	none	Cabins (for one person):.	0
IMO number:.	8507731	Cabins (with private balcony):.	0
Builder:.	Rauma Shipyard (Finland)	Cabins (wheelchair accessible):.	0
Original cost:.	n/a	Wheelchair accessibility:.	none
Entered service:.	1989/2011	Cabin voltage:.	110 and 220 volts
Registry:.	Russia	Elevators:.	1
Length (ft/m):.	383.9/117.0	Casino (gaming tables):.	No
Beam (ft/m):.	59.9/18.2	Slot machines:.	No
Draft (ft/m):.	19.9/6.0	Swimming pools:.	1
Propulsion/Propellers:.	diesel (10,000kW)/2	Hot tubs (on deck):.	1
Passenger decks:.	4	Self-service launderette:.	No
Total crew:.	63	Dedicated cinema/seats:.	No
Passengers (lower beds/alll berths):.	92/96	Library:.	Yes
Passenger Space Ratio (lower beds/all berths):.	70.1/67.1	Onboard currency:.	US$
Crew/Passenger Ratio (lower beds/all berths):.	1.4/1.5		

A tough little ship for adventurous polar travelers

OVERVIEW. This very small ship is for hardy couples and single travelers who enjoy nature and exploring. The ship is purely a means of transportation and accommodation to reach the polar region in comfort. Unusually for an expedition ship, the funnel is located quite far aft, and there is an elevator.

THE SHIP. Originally built for the former Soviet Union as a high-tech 'spy' ship, *Akademik Ioffe* was instead used as a polar and oceanographic research vessel, its ultra-quiet engines being ideal for hydroacoustic research programs. It was converted in the early 1990s to carry passengers, and then refurbished in 1996 specifically for expedition cruising. It is a sister ship to *Akademik Sergey Vavilov*, also operated under charter to Canada-based One Ocean Expeditions (whose sales partners are Active Travel, in Australia) in conjunction with the owner of the vessel, the Shirsov Oceanological Institute.

The all-white vessel has an ice-strengthened steel hull, which makes it suitable for slicing its way through pack-ice. Passengers are welcome to visit the navigation bridge. The ship has nine Zodiacs for close-in shore landings and nature observation trips, and there is a seawater 'plunge' pool outdoors.

Inside, the public rooms consist of a library, a multimedia room (with battery recharging stations), dining room, lounge/bar with 24-hour tea/coffee facility (this is usually the main social contact point), and a little gift shop. The dining room acts as the lecture room.

Berlitz's Ratings

	Possible	Achieved
Ship	500	226
Accommodation	200	103
Food	400	215
Service	400	236
Entertainment	100	52
Cruise	400	224

OVERALL SCORE
1056 points out of 2000

The medical facilities are good, and there's a mud room for boot washing, boot storage and for storage of your outerwear items.

One Ocean Expeditions is a small, highly personal company, and the expedition staff offer participants a choice of activities such as guided hikes and sea-kayaking. Note that the elevator services Decks 1 to 5, but does not go to Deck 6 (bridge and passenger cabins).

ACCOMMODATION. This is arranged over three decks. Except for a single 'suite,' quite large for the size of the ship, almost all other cabins are extremely small and utilitarian, although all have a small desk and a reasonable amount of closet space. There are two-berth cabins with shower and toilet, and two-bed cabins on the lowest deck, whose occupants must share an adjacent bathroom and toilet.

DINING. The dining room accommodates all passengers in a single seating. It is basic, but comfortable. The meals consist of international fare with no frills.

ENTERTAINMENT. Recaps, forward planning, and general after-dinner conversation with fellow participants takes place in the ship's lounge/bar.

SPA/FITNESS. The compact area includes a sauna, changing room, and hot tub, and there's a registered massage therapist and fitness trainer, plus a small fitness room with exercise mats, weights, and machines.

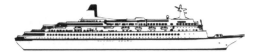

Albatros
★★★

Size:	Mid-Size Ship	Crew/Passenger Ratio (lower beds/all berths):	2.5/3.2
Tonnage:	28,078	Cabins (total):	449
Lifestyle:	Standard	Size range (sq ft/m):	123.7– 679.2/11.8–63.1
Cruise line:	Phoenix Reisen	Cabins (outside view):	375
Former names:	...Crown, Norwegian Star I, Royal Odyssey, Royal Viking Sea	Cabins (interior/no view):	62
		Cabins (for one person):	12
IMO number:	5347245	Cabins (with private balcony):	15
Builder:	Wartsila (Finland)	Cabins (wheelchair accessible):	0
Original cost:	$22.5 million	Wheelchair accessibility:	Fair
Entered service:	Nov 1973/Apr 2004	Cabin voltage:	110 and 220 volts
Registry:	The Bahamas	Elevators:	5
Length (ft/m):	674.2/205.5	Casino (gaming tables):	No
Beam (ft/m):	82.0/25.0	Slot machines:	No
Draft (ft/m):	23.9/7.3	Swimming pools:	1
Propulsion/Propellers:	diesel (15,840 kW)/2	Hot tubs (on deck):	1
Passenger decks:	8	Self-service launderette:	Yes
Total crew:	340	Dedicated cinema/seats:	Yes/156
Passengers (lower beds/alll berths):	862/1,110	Library:	Yes
Passenger Space Ratio (lower beds/all berths):	32.5/25.2	Onboard currency:	Euros

Contemporary setting for low-price, no-frills cruising

OVERVIEW. *Albatros* appeals to mature German-speaking adults and families seeking a low-budget, good-value vacation in a comfortable (but not new) ship.

THE SHIP. *Albatros*, built for long-distance cruising for the long-defunct Royal Viking Line, was refurbished in 2004 prior to replacing Phoenix Reisen's much loved but outdated *Albatros*. There is plenty of open deck and sunbathing space, although the popular aft pool area can become crowded.

The ship has a good array of public rooms, including several lounges and bars, most of which are sort of old-world elegant, and have high, indented ceilings. The Observation Lounge is a particularly pleasant place to spend time. Wide stairways and foyers give a sense of space, even when the ship is full. The atmosphere is very casual, as is the dress code. A low 7 percent gratuity is added to bar accounts, and drink prices are very reasonable.

The Phoenix cruise staff is always bright, bubby and friendly, and the shore excursion team is knowledge-able and helpful.

ACCOMMODATION. There are more than 20 price grades, from expansive suites with private balcony to standard outside-view cabins and small interior cabins. A Captain's Suite is located at the front, directly under the navigation bridge, with fine forward-facing views. Nine other Penthouse Suites include a private balcony

Berlitz's Ratings

	Possible	Achieved
Ship	500	310
Accommodation	200	128
Food	400	211
Service	400	237
Entertainment	100	60
Cruise	400	251
OVERALL SCORE		
1197 points out of 2000		

(with separate bedroom and living area). Most other cabins have an outside view and are quite well appointed, and there is a good amount of storage space; however, some bathrooms in the lower categories have awkward access. All cabins have a TV, bathrobe, and personal safe. Suites and 'comfort cabins' also have a minibar. Occupants of eight (mostly suite) accommodation grades receive 'Phoenix VIP' service.

DINING. There are two dining rooms (Mowe and Pelikan); both have high ceilings, and are spacious. Dining is in one seating at assigned tables for two, four, six, or eight. Breakfast and lunch can be taken in the dining room or outdoors in a self-service buffet. Mid-morning bouillon is a Phoenix seagoing tradition, as is a Captain's Dinner (formal night), and a Buffet Magnifique.

The service is friendly and attentive, although there is little finesse. Table wines are included for lunch and dinner, although the quality is not good. Slightly better quality wines can be purchased.

ENTERTAINMENT. The Pacific Lounge is the ship's showlounge. It seats about 500, but several pillars obstruct the sightlines for some. Small-scale production shows are presented by a small team of resident singers/dancers.

SPA/FITNESS. There are a gymnasium and sauna, two steam rooms, body treatment rooms, and a beauty salon.

Allure of the Seas
★★★★

Size:................................Large Resort Ship	Crew/Passenger Ratio (lower beds/all berths):.........2.4/2.9
Tonnage:......................................225,062	Cabins (total):.....................................2,704
Lifestyle:.....................................Standard	Size range (sq ft/m):............150.6–1,523.1/14.0–141.5
Cruise line:..................Royal Caribbean International	Cabins (outside view):...........................2,208
Former names:.....................................none	Cabins (interior/no view):...........................496
IMO number:.................................9383948	Cabins (for one person):..............................0
Builder:.............................Aker Yards (Finland)	Cabins (with private balcony):....................1,956
Original cost:...............................$1.5 billion	Cabins (wheelchair accessible):.......................46
Entered service:............................Dec 2010	Wheelchair accessibility:..........................Good
Registry:...................................The Bahamas	Cabin voltage:..............................110 volts
Length (ft/m):...........................1181.1/360.0	Elevators:...24
Beam (ft/m):..............................216.5 /66.0	Casino (gaming tables):..............................Yes
Draft (ft/m):...............................30.0/9.1	Slot machines:......................................Yes
Propulsion/Propellers:..diesel-electric (97,200 kW)/2 azimuthing	Swimming pools:......................................3
pods, 1 fixed	Hot tubs (on deck):...................................10
Passenger decks:....................................16	Self-service launderette:............................No
Total crew:.....................................2,164	Dedicated cinema/seats:.............................No
Passengers (lower beds/alll berths):.............5,408 /6,360	Library:...Yes
Passenger Space Ratio (lower beds/all berths):.......41.6 /35.4	Onboard currency:..................................US$

The world's largest, family-friendly, multi-choice ship

OVERVIEW. This stunning ship (whose size is five times larger than the ill-fated *Titanic*) provides a fine cruise experience and wide range of choices for young adults and families with children. It's packed with innovative design elements such as the dramatic Central Park, taking urban greenery to sea. The ship is a benchmark for self-contained resorts with propellers.

THE SHIP. *Allure of the Seas* qualifies at present as the world's largest cruise ship by less than 2ins (5cm) – that's how much longer it is than its twin sister, *Oasis of the Seas*, the first cruise ship in the world measuring over 200,000 tons, which debuted in 2009. In almost every other way, however, the ships are just about identical.

Built as a 'Moveable Resort Vacation' for families with children, it is a stunning ship and a massive credit to Royal Caribbean International's design team. There is a lot of outdoor and indoor/outdoor space for aqua-bathing and sports, although there's not much actual space for sunbathing. There are several swimming pools, three of which – 'main,' 'beach,' and 'sports' – are positioned high on Deck 15 (Pool and Sports Zone) of the 16 passenger decks, as is an H2O Zone. Two large hot tubs are cantilevered over the ship's side. The water for the swimming pools alone weighs 2,300 tons.

While the design of Allure of the Seas from the front aspect is quite handsome, if rather bulky, the aft end looks as if it's been chopped off and unfinished when viewed from the side. Perhaps a more rounded

Berlitz's Ratings

	Possible	Achieved
Ship	500	409
Accommodation	200	148
Food	400	234
Service	400	291
Entertainment	100	83
Cruise	400	293

OVERALL SCORE
1458 points out of 2000

stern would have improved the profile – although, when you're on board, it looks fine. The open stern makes it look like a ship with a huge aft aircraft hangar. Overall, though, it's an amazing ship that has lots of 'wow' factor.

The design is a continuum of the *Freedom*-class ships, themselves an extension of the *Voyager*-class ships. But the increase in size has meant that RCI has been able to incorporate more of the facilities that young families seek for action-packed cruise vacations, including 37 bars and more than 20 places to eat or snack. And the latest technology means that *Allure* and *Oasis* are 30 percent more energy-efficient than even the *Freedom*-class ships.

The ship has been designed remarkably well, with large public spaces made possible by the split aft superstructure – the idea of Harri Kulovaara, who first achieved this with Silja Serenade in 1986. This gives the ship the interior space needed to provide The Boardwalk, Central Park, and the Royal Promenade (all parts of the 'seven neighborhoods' concept). Large touch-screen ship information screens provide electronic maps at each stairway, and elevators are color-coordinated in either pink or blue for the fore and aft sections of the ship. There are no elevators in the center of the ship; all are in forward and aft locations, but there are enough of them, and they are speedy.

The public spaces are arranged as seven 'neighborhoods': Central Park, the Boardwalk, the Royal Promenade, the Pool and Sports Zone, Vitality at Sea

Spa/Fitness Center, Entertainment Place, and Youth Zone. The most popular are the Boardwalk and Central Park, both open to the air, and the indoor Royal Promenade.

The Boardwalk. An echo of Coney Island, the Boardwalk – which is open to the skies – contains shops (naturally) and an art gallery for those peculiar people who go on a cruise to peruse or buy 'artwork.' Art is displayed in Central Park's Art Actually, where artists who contributed to the ship's multi-million dollar collection can sell items to passengers.

Eateries include the Boardwalk Donut Shop; Johnny Rockets, a burger/milk shake diner; and a covered Seafood Shack for fish and seafood. If you are in a Central Park cabin, you'll need to take the elevator to get to the closest pool – it's like going to the top of your building to take a dip. Let's hope the pool volleyball game doesn't end up with the ball being tossed into the park – or onto someone's balcony while they're having coffee.

Central Park. This space is 328ft (100m) long. The vegetation is real, with 27 trees and almost 12,000 plants, including a vertical 'living' plant wall. But, unlike its New York inspiration, it includes, at its lower level, a 'town center.' At night, it's just about the only quiet and serene area, and is best for couples. Vintages wine bar is a great place to chill-out, and there are several reservations-required, extra-charge dining venues; arguably the best is 150 Central Park, while Chops Grille and Giovanni's Table are favorites for South Beach types. But Vintages wine and tapas bar is a nice place to relax in the late afternoon.

The Royal Promenade really is the equivalent of a floating shopping mall, with casual food eateries (including a Starbucks coffee store, located at the forward end and open 7am–11pm daily), shops with all kinds of merchandise, video screens, and changing color lights at every step. It's all a bit surreal – like being in a circus at sea, with something going on every minute. But one thing not to be missed is the 'Move On! Move On!' parade, a 15-minute circus-like extravaganza that includes characters from DreamWorks Animation's Madagascar. Interior-view promenade cabins have balconies that look down onto the action in Central Park. A hydraulic, oval-shaped Rising Tide Bar moves slowly through three floors and links the double-width Royal Promenade with Central Park.

The ship is so large that it doesn't feel so crowded in most areas, except for the pool deck and in the Windjammer Café (particularly on days when the ship is in port and everyone is scrambling to get breakfast at the same time). As far as facilities go, this ship really has it all for trendy waterside (or parkside) living. Don't be concerned about long lines at check-in – there aren't any, because RCI has a custom-built terminal in Fort Lauderdale (Port Everglades) designed to get you on board in about 15 minutes.

The Passenger Space Ratio is good for such a large vessel, so there's not generally the hugely crowded feeling you might expect. The design concept is a continuum of the Freedom-class ships (*Allure* of the Seas is, however, 30 percent more energy-efficient), themselves an extension of the Voyager-class ships – and then some. The increase in size has meant that RCI has been able to incorporate more of the facilities that young families seek for action-packed cruise vacations, including 37 bars and more than 20 places to eat or snack.

The ship has been designed remarkably well, with large public spaces made possible by the split superstructure design – the idea of Harri Kulovaara, who first achieved this with Silja Serenade in 1986. This gives the ship the interior space needed to provide The Boardwalk, Central Park, and the Royal Promenade (all parts of the 'seven neighborhoods' concept). Excellent, large touch-screen ship information screens provide electronic maps at each stairway, and elevators are color-coordinated in either pink or blue for the fore and aft sections of the ship. There are no elevators in the center of the ship; all are in forward and aft locations, but there are enough of them, and they are speedy.

It's all rather novel, and should appeal to families with children. The only reminder that you're aboard a ship is the presence of the other 5,400 or so passengers – in a ship that could swallow 6,295. Because Central Park and the Boardwalk are open to the elements – so you could hide under a tree – but better take an umbrella just in case it rains in the sunny Caribbean.

Although not quite as stunning as the Aquaventure experience at Dubai's Atlantis Resort Hotel, where you can slide 27m down a ziggurat through shark-infested waters or sleep underwater, the Pool and Sports Zone forward of the twin funnels is a real adventurous fun place for families. An adults-only open-air solarium and rentable cabanas are part of the outdoor scene today, and Oasis provides several. Two Flow-Riders are part of the sports line-up; these are located atop the ship around the aft exhaust mast, together with basketball courts and golf. The ship also has the largest jogging track at sea.

The Solarium is the most welcoming large, light-filled and restful (despite the background music) space. High atop ship, it is frequented by few children – so adults can 'escape' the Las Vegas–like atmosphere of most other parts of the ship. On the subject of casinos, the roulette tables are stunning – all electronic and touch-buttony (no need to place chips on the table – simply touch a screen with your finger). There are also blackjack, craps, Caribbean Stud Poker, and 450 slot machines, plus a player's club and poker room – but this really can be a smoke-filled place, even in the 'no-smoking' area. The casino entrance is dedicated to the history of gaming.

The Caribbean itinerary for this ship includes a 'private' beach day at Labadee, the company's leased island, whose facilities were upgraded in 2009. RCI has built its own 800-ft (244-m) pier, making it a logistically simple matter for anyone to access the ship and beach several times during the day-long stay. Do try the zipline – it's one of the world's longest, and a real blast. Other new additions: an alpine coaster, a beach club with 20 private cabanas, updated dining facilities, a larger artisans' market, and a Haitian Cultural Center.

A cruise aboard *Allure of the Seas* provides a fine family cruise experience, with a wide range of choices (many at extra cost). This means you'll need to plan how you will spend your time, and where you would like to eat, well in advance of your cruise. Overall, if you are in suite-grade accommodation, you'll be treated well, while those in anything else receive second-class service, and will hear the word 'no' a lot. But that's part and parcel of a large resort ship with its 'metropolitan' style cruise experience.

If all 5,400 passengers want a sunlounger at the same time, forget it! Anyone able to secure one will find them so tightly packed together that there's little space to put any belongings. It's sad to see that exterior wooden railings have mostly been replaced by fibreglass railings – this is particularly noticeable on the balconies.

Standing in line to make reservations for the main shows can be time-consuming and frustrating (the reservation booth is in the middle of the Royal Promenade). You could make them online before your cruise – good for families that like to plan their vacations together – but who knows in advance what you may want to do when?

The sense of being aboard a cruise ship is somewhat lost in all the large spaces to play in, but what this ship offers is a moveable resort full of facilities. There are few quiet nooks and crannies – except for a small, cramped library, with oversize leather chairs, and perhaps the Solarium.

Ordering room service is complicated – you can't do it by phone, only by using the interactive touch-screen television in your suite/cabin. Getting reservations in one of the specialty restaurants takes a bit of effort, unless you are occupying suite-grade accommodation. Smoking is permitted in several bars and lounges aboard this ship and the smell of stale smoke permeates several areas. Cigar smokers will probably be underwhelmed by the cigar lounge.

While RCI has programming and passenger flow down to a fine art, a few bottlenecks occur – but then, they do also at baseball stadiums and airports, both of which are as impersonal as this ship.

You'll need to plan how you will spend your time, and where you would like to eat, well in advance of your cruise. Overall, if you are in suite-grade accommodation, you'll be treated well, while those in anything else receive second-class service, and will hear the word 'no' a lot. But that's part and parcel of a large resort ship with its 'metropolitan' style cruise experience.

Allure of the Seas operates from the purpose-built $75 million Terminal 18 in Port Everglades (Fort Lauderdale), whose restroom facilities are minimal.

Disembarkation. If the two 'flybridge' gangways are working, disembarkation is relatively speedy. However, when only one is working, a line forms in the Royal Promenade, in which case it's better to sit somewhere until the line gets shorter. Disembarkation for non-US citizens can be appallingly slow.

Passenger Niggles include: Live or recorded music is everywhere, 24 hours a day, whether inside or outside the ship, including elevators and accommodation hallways. Waiting for elevators; that the ship is simply too large to meet friends unless you are very specific about place and time; that the Windjammer Café is always busy; the fact that wine packages for purchase can be served only in certain venues; and the fact that bars do not have any snacks such as nuts. While RCI has programming and passenger flow down to a fine art, a few bottlenecks occur – but then, they do also at baseball stadiums and airports, both of which are as impersonal as this ship.

ACCOMMODATION. There are a mind-boggling number of accommodation price grades, reflecting the choice of location and size. Suite occupants get access to a concierge lounge and associated services. There are many family-friendly cabins, good for family reunions, but there are no single-occupancy cabins. The cabin numbering system is a bit awkward to get used to. In a first for RCI, cabin doors open outwards (towards you), as in most European and Scandinavian hotels. In many of the lower grade accommodation, access to the closet is awkward – often with small sofas in the way. Most cabins feel extremely small, given the size of the ship. All cabins have an iPod dock.

Some 395 interior balcony cabins have either Central Park or Royal Promenade views from their curved interior balconies, four of which are wheelchair-accessible, plus 80 cabins with windows (no balconies) and views of Central Park. But you'll need to keep your curtains closed for privacy, which rather defeats the object. Noise could be generated along the inner promenades, particularly late at night with street parades and non-stop music.

Loft suites. Although a few ships such as the now withdrawn Saga Rose and Saga Ruby had upstairs/downstairs suites, RCI has introduced 'loft' suites to the Oasis-class ships. These offer fine ocean views from floor-to-ceiling, double-height windows. Each has a lower living area plus a private balcony with sun chairs, and a stairway that connects to the sleeping area which overlooks the living area and has extended ocean views. Modern designs are dotted with abstract, modern art pieces.

There are 28 Loft Suites, with 25 Crown Loft suites measuring 545 sq ft (51 sq m). Three more spacious Loft Suites (called Royal Loft Suites) measure 1,524 sq ft (141 sq m). Each sleeps up to six, and each a baby grand piano, indoor and outdoor dining areas, a private wet bar, a library, and an extended 843-sq-ft (78.3-sq-m) balcony with flat-screen TV set, entertainment area, and Jacuzzi. Two large Sky Loft Suites measure 722 sq ft (67 sq m) and 770 sq ft (71 sq m), and a 737-sq-ft (68-sq-m) Crown Accessible Loft Suite includes an elevator to aid disabled passengers.

Standard Cabins (balcony and non-balcony class). Electrical sockets are located below the vanity desk unit in a user-unfriendly position. This is particularly poor for anyone trying to use the hairdryer in the 50 percent of cabins where the sockets are positioned on the right side. Also, it's difficult to watch television from the bed.

The washbasins in non-suite grade cabins are very small and low, at just 30½ins (77.5cm) above the floor level. Be careful – it's easy to hit your head on the mirror above. Small soap bars are provided, while shampoo is provided in a dispenser in the shower enclosure. Unfortunately, the shower head is fixed, making it difficult to wash yourself thoroughly. Although there is no soap dish or indentation in the washbasin surround for soap, useful touches include a blue ceiling bathroom nightlight.

Cabins are exposed to noise and whatever is happening on the Boardwalk itself, including rehearsals and sports activities in the Aqua Theater aft, bells from the carousel (its 18 sculptured wooden animal figures took six weeks to carve), rowdy revelers on the Boardwalk late at night, plus screaming ziplining participants high above during the day, not to mention loud music from bands playing at one of the pools, and exceedingly loud announcements by the cruise director repeating what's already printed in the daily program.

If you have a Boardwalk-view balcony cabin, you'll need to close your curtains for privacy at times. However, the curved balconies – good for storing luggage to free up space inside the cabin – connect you with the open air and provide a community feeling, as you look across at balconies on the opposite side. Almost all have a sea view aft (just); those close to the aft Aqua Theater can use their balconies for a great view of any shows or events. The lowest deck of Boardwalk-view cabins has windows but no balcony – and actually the view is mainly of the top of things such as the carousel or beach hut-like structures. The best Boardwalk balcony cabins are, in my view, located on decks 8–12. For more privacy, however, it might be best to book a sea-facing balcony cabin, not one that overlooks the Boardwalk.

Many suite-grade cabins have bathrooms with granite-look washbasin counter tops, and two washbasins. Some have bidets, Jacuzzi tubs, and a separate shower enclosure. Some Family Suite grades have a separate, small room with bunk beds; some, not all, have curtains to separate them.

DINING. Because *Allure of the Seas* is a large resort ship, meals in the main dining room – there are over 500 tables spread over three decks – are all about well-timed production cooking and fast delivery. It is essentially a banquet catering operation. Almost inevitably, the food is mostly underwhelming. When you book, choose one of two seatings, or 'My Time Dining' (eat when you want, during dining room hours).

Other dining options. 150 Central Park, the most exclusive restaurant aboard the ship, combines haute-cuisine with interesting design. A kitchen observation window allows passers-by to watch the chefs. KeriAnn Van Raesfeld offers a multi-course tasting menu. It's open for dinner only, reservations are required and there's an extra charge.

Chops Grille, RCI's popular 'signature' steakhouse is open for dinner only, and features large premium-cut steaks and grilled seafood. There's a cover charge, and reservation are required.

Chef's Table, on the upper level of the Concierge lounge, is available to all, and features a six-course meal with wine. It is hosted by the executive chef, but, with just 14 seats, getting a reservation could prove challenging (a high cover charge applies).

Giovanni's Table (cover charge for dinner and reservations are required): This casual Italian dining spot has a rustic feel, yet modern flair. It offers toasted herb breads, pizzas, salads, pastas, sandwiches, braised meat dishes, and stews – and the food is good (worth the price if you're hungry).

Central Park Café, a casual dining spot with a high level of variety and flexibility, is an indoor/outdoor food market with line-up counters and limited waiter service. Items include freshly prepared salads, made-to-order sandwiches, panini, crêpes, and hearty soups. You order directly from the chefs behind the food stations.

Rita's Cantina, on the Boardwalk, is a noisy canteen offering quasi-Mexican fare. The cover charge is high for what it is and you'll need to a wait to get a table-cloth-less table. But then it is a bit of a cantina – so it lives up to its name.

Vintages, is a wine bar with a robust selection of decent wines, accompanied by cheese and tapas (with an à la carte item charge).

Other Boardwalk snacking spots: Donut Shop (for hot dogs, wieners, bratwurst, and sausages), and Ice Cream Parlor.

Elsewhere, dining venues/eateries include Izumi, offering Japanese-style cuisine, at an à la carte price; Sorrento's Pizzeria; Park Café (for salads and light bites); and Wipe Out Café. For those with a sweet tooth, there's a 1940s-style Cupcake Shop. Naturally, if you're thinking of getting married, you could have a cupcake wedding cake. For lighter, more health-conscious fare, there's a self-serve section in the Solarium Bistro for breakfast and lunch – it's usually the quietest place, too.

Windjammer Café is a (free) casual, self-serve buffet-style eatery common to all RCI ships. Note that no trays are provided – only oval plates – so if you are disabled or have mobility difficulties you may need to ask for help. Also, because they're plastic, it's not possible to get a hot plate. The venue is simply too small to handle the invasion of passengers at peak times – my advice is to try some of the other venues to avoid the overcrowding. The food varies from acceptable to less than acceptable – fresh fruit tends to be hard and unripe. It's best to arrive early, when things have just been cooked and displayed. Although there's a decent enough variety, the quality of some of the meat is poor and overcooked.

Regular (weak) coffee is available free in many venues, but espresso and cappuccino (in paper cups) costs extra – in the first Starbucks at sea.

Johnny Rockets and Rita's Cantina usually have the longest lines and wait times. Note that the cover charges quoted above are subject to change – check with RCI's website or your travel provider for the latest prices.

Reservation-only evening 'parties' in Rita's Cantina and the Seafood Shack include popular food items and drinks. Also, three dining packages (Central Park, Chef's, and Choice) for several of the specialty restaurants are available. But the packaged pricing is a little confusing.

ENTERTAINMENT. The 1,380-seat main showlounge, spread over three decks, stages the popular musical Chicago – an excellent, 90-minute-long production, just like a Broadway show, and is performed four times during each cruise. Frozen in Time is a stunning, must-see ice show at the ice-skating rink.

There's no charge for any of the shows, and bookings can be made at www.royalcaribbean.com up to three months before your cruise, although reservations are not required. It is, however, quite difficult to change any reservations.

The 750-seat AquaTheater, located outside at the ship's stern with a 6,000-sq-ft (560-sq-m) stage, is a stunning combination show theatre, sound stage, and events space (some great viewing places can be found high in the aft wings of the ship on both sides). The stern has some 'overhang,' to accommodate the venue. A DreamWorks Animation aquatic acrobatic and dive show is also presented.

DreamWorks Animation Studios also provides interactive shows featuring characters from popular animation such as *Shrek*, *King Fu Panda*, *Madagascar*, and *How to Train Your Dragon*.

SPA/FITNESS. The Vitality at Sea Spa includes a Vitality Café for extra-cost health drinks and snacks. The fitness center includes 158 cardio and resistance machines. An extra-cost thermal suite includes saunas, steam rooms, and heated tiled loungers. You can't just take a sauna for 10 minutes without paying for a one-day pass, at $30 per person. Steiner Leisure provides the staff and treatments, and gratuities are at your discretion.

The facility really is not that large, given the number of passengers carried. It's best not to book a massage when the ship is due to arrive or leave an anchor port because some treatment rooms experience immense vibration when the anchor chain is in use. Sports facilities include two surfboard pools, golf putting course, ziplining (screaming is mandatory), and an ice-skating rink – it's amazing just how popular this is with children.

The truth about tonnage

The International Convention of Tonnage Measurement of Ships, was introduced in 1969, implemented in 1982, and actually came into force on July 18, 1994. It required ship owners to re-measure the (former) gross register tonnage of their vessels (1 grt = 100 cubic ft of enclosed space/2.8 cubic meters).

The Convention states: 'The gross tonnage (GT) of a ship shall be determined by the following formula: GT-K1V where V = Total volume of all enclosed spaces of the ship in cubic meters; and K1 = 0.2+0.02 log 10 V...' Actually, measurements of gross and net tonnage are really dimensionless numbers. So the word 'ton' is no longer used in maritime terminology.

Tonnage (gt) was originally a key measure of the carrying capacity of a ship was not how much it weighed, but how much space it had available for cargo. A common cargo was wine, which was shipped in large casks called 'tuns.' A tun held eight barrels of wine or about 242 gallons. Soon they started measuring the cargo area based on how many of these boxes or tuns could be fit in. Thus, a ship that could transport 8,000 barrels of wine was known as a 1,000-tun ship. 'Tun' evolved into 'ton' and then into 'Gross Registered Ton.' The clipper (tall)

ships in the mid-1800s ranged in size from 400 grt to 4,000 grt.

The advent of steel hulled ships and steam engines allowed the building of larger vessels, with, for example, the Titanic measuring what was then a large 48,000 gt.

What is 'displacement tonnage?'

Displacement tonnage is a measurement of the weight of a merchant vessel's structure to the nearest 100 long tons or metric tons (they are not quite the same); or volumetric tonnage (measured by volume).

How does a giant ship stay afloat?

As the Greek scientist Archimedes (c.287–212BC) discovered, an object will float provided its weight is equal to or less than the amount of water it displaces.

Large resort ships such as *Oasis of the Seas*, which has a tonnage of 222,900, displace a lot of water, although they are essentially hollow, because most of the internal weight, such as engines and propulsion machinery, is placed at the bottom of the hull. This allows the ship to remain upright, even though many decks tower above the waterline.

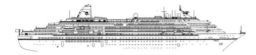

Amadea
★★★★

Size:.	Small Ship
Tonnage:.	28,856
Lifestyle:	Standard
Cruise line:.	Phoenix Reisen
Former names:.	Asuka
IMO number:.	8913162
Builder:.	Mitsubishi Heavy Industries (Japan)
Original cost:.	$150 million
Entered service:.	Dec 1991/Mar 2006
Registry:.	The Bahamas
Length (ft/m):.	632.5/192.8
Beam (ft/m):.	81.0/24.7
Draft (ft/m):.	21.6/6.6
Propulsion/Propellers:.	diesel (17,300kW)/2
Passenger decks:.	8
Total crew:.	292
Passengers (lower beds/alll berths):.	594/46.6
Passenger Space Ratio (lower beds/all berths):.	48.5/46.6
Crew/Passenger Ratio (lower beds/all berths):.	2.0/2.1

Cabins (total):.	297
Size range (sq ft/m):.	182.9–649.0/17.0–60.3
Cabins (outside view):.	297
Cabins (interior/no view):.	0
Cabins (for one person):.	0
Cabins (with private balcony):.	122
Cabins (wheelchair accessible):.	2
Wheelchair accessibility:.	Fair
Cabin voltage:.	110 volts
Elevators:.	5
Casino (gaming tables):.	No
Slot machines:.	No
Swimming pools:.	1
Hot tubs (on deck):.	1
Self-service launderette:.	Yes
Dedicated cinema/seats:.	Yes/97
Library:.	Yes
Onboard currency:.	Euros

A stylish, spacious ship with fine food and service

OVERVIEW. *Amadea* is best suited to German-speaking couples, single travelers, and families with children, who enjoy cruising in very comfortable surroundings aboard a contemporary ship. Because it absorbs people well, there is never any feeling of crowding.

THE SHIP. When introduced in 1991 as *Asuka*, this was the first all-new large ship specially designed and built in Japan for the domestic market. It was sold to Phoenix Reisen and, as *Amadea*, started cruising for German-speaking passengers in 2006.

The ship, a more upscale vessel than other ships in the Phoenix Reisen fleet, has pleasing exterior styling and a contemporary profile, with a large, rounded, but squat funnel. There is a generous amount of open deck and sunbathing space, plus a wide walk-around teakwood promenade deck outdoors, good for strolling.

The 'cake-layer' stacking of the public rooms hampers passenger flow and makes it a little disjointed, although passengers will like the separation of public rooms from accommodation areas. There are many intimate public rooms, plenty of space, and lots of light.

The interior decor is understated but elegant, with pleasing color combinations, quality fabrics, and fine soft furnishings. There's some fascinating Japanese artwork, including Noriko Tamura's *Song of the Seasons*, a four-deck-high mural on the wall of the main foyer staircase – in many shades of pink and red.

Berlitz's Ratings

	Possible	Achieved
Ship	500	395
Accommodation	200	156
Food	400	319
Service	400	310
Entertainment	100	76
Cruise	400	291

OVERALL SCORE
1547 points out of 2000

Public rooms and lounges include the delightfully relaxing Vista Lounge, the ship's observation lounge and bar – it is also used for afternoon tea service.

Harry's Bar is a bar and lounge is decorated in the style of a contemporary gentleman's club, complete with wood-paneled walls and burgundy leather chairs. This popular drinking spot has a light, airy feel. Located in a quiet area is the ship's library, with deeply comfortable armchairs, and a fireplace with electric fire. Cigar smokers will find the Havanna Bar a cosy little hideaway.

As for the dress code, there is a mix of formal and informal nights, while during the day attire is very casual. There is a self-service launderette with eight washing machines – useful for long voyages. Overall, the ship provides an extremely comfortable and serene cruising environment. All gratuities are included.

ACCOMMODATION. There are several price categories, although in reality there are just five types of suites and cabins. Three decks (8, 9, and 10) have suites and cabins with a private balcony. (The balcony floors are laid with green simulated turf, and there is no outside light.)

Suites and cabins in all grades have ocean views, although some are slightly obstructed by the ship's gangway when it is in the raised (stowed) position.

In all grades, cherry wood cabinetry, which is in beautiful condition, has nicely rounded edges. Cabin soundproofing is excellent, and there is a good amount of closet and drawer space (including lockable drawers), refrigerator, and personal safe.

Most grades have bathrooms with bathtubs (and cabins available with shower0, and all have a tiled floor and bath/shower area. While the suite bathrooms are generously proportioned, the 'standard' bathrooms are practical but small.

Two suites provide the largest accommodation; these are larger versions of the 'A' grade cabins. Each has a separate bedroom, with walk-in closet that includes a luggage deck, and twin beds that convert to a queen-size bed, sofa, two chairs and coffee table, large vanity desk, plenty of drawer space, and large color TV set. The marble-clad bathroom is large and has a whirlpool tub set alongside large ocean-view windows overlooking the private balcony, and twin washbasins set in a marble surround; a living room, and separate guest bathroom. The private balcony is quite large and features a tropical plant set in a glass display enclosure.

In 2009, the company added two Spa Junior Suites; each has a private balcony with whirlpool tub.

The top grade cabins are excellent living spaces and have twice the size and space of the standard cabins. They are very nicely decorated and outfitted, and have twin beds (convertible to a queen-size bed), sofa, two chairs and coffee table, large vanity desk, plenty of drawer space, and large color TV set. However, when in its twin-bed configuration, the room's feng shui is poor, as one of the beds is facing a large mirror at the writing/vanity desk – a negative for some people.

Many cabins have a private balcony with full floor-to-ceiling partition and a green synthetic turf floor (but no outside light) with floor-to-ceiling sliding door – the door handles are awkward.

There's also an illuminated walk-in closet with long hanging rail and plenty of drawer space. The bathrooms, partly tiled and generously proportioned, include a plastic, glass-fronted toiletries cabinet, and two washbasins set in a thick marble surround.

DINING. There are two main restaurants, both with open-seating for all meals. The Four Seasons has two sections; there are ocean-view windows along one side of the aft section, and along two sides of the forward section. The Amadea Restaurant is located on a higher deck, with ocean view windows on two sides. The cuisine is the same in both venues. For casual breakfasts and lunches, there's an informal self-serve Lido Café with plenty of outdoor seating, adjacent to a small pool and hot tub.

With this ship, Phoenix Reisen has taken its cuisine and service to a much higher level than that aboard its other ships (except *Artania*), by spending more money per passenger per day (this is also reflected in the cruise fare).

ENTERTAINMENT. The Atlantic Lounge is the venue for most entertainment events, including shows, social functions, and lectures. The room spans two decks, with seating on both main and balcony levels, and an extra-large wooden dance floor is provided for social dancing.

SPA/FITNESS. There is a spacious wellness center. It has large ocean-view windows, two baths, one hot tub, two saunas, steam room with wooden floor; several shower enclosures, plus a changing area with vanity counter, and a gymnasium. There are also five body treatment rooms, plus a relaxation area. Sports facilities include a golf court, driving cage, putting green.

Satellite Navigator

Using this high-tech piece of equipment, ship's officers can read, on a small television screen, the ship's position in the open ocean anywhere in the world, any time, and in any weather with pinpoint accuracy.

Satellite navigation systems use the information transmitted by a constellation of orbiting satellites. Each is in a normal circular polar orbit at an altitude of 450 to 700 nautical miles, and orbits the Earth in about 108 minutes.

Data from each gives the current orbital position every two minutes. Apart from telling the ship where it is, it continuously provides the distance from any given point, calculates the drift caused by currents and so on, and tells the ship when the next satellite will pass.

The basis of the satellite navigation is the US Navy Navigation Satellite System (NNSS). This first became operational in January 1964 as the precision guidance system for the Polaris submarine fleet and was made available for commercial use in 1967.

The latest (and more accurate) system is the GPS (Global Positioning System), which is now fitted to an increasing number of ships. This uses 24 satellites (18 of which are online at any given time) that provide accuracy in estimating a ship's position to plus or minus 6ft. Another variation is the NACOS (Navigational Command System), which collects information from a variety of sources: satellites, radar, gyroscopic compass, speed log, and surface navigational systems as well as engines, thrusters, rudders, and human input. It then displays relevant computations and information on one screen, controlled by a single keyboard.

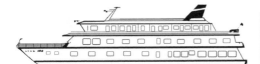

American Glory
★★

Size:..Boutique Ship		Cabins (total):.....................................27		
Tonnage:..1,287		Size range (sq ft/m):.............. 176.0–382.0/16.3–35.4		
Lifestyle:......................................Standard		Cabins (outside view):.............................27		
Cruise line:........................American Cruise Lines		Cabins (interior/no view):..........................0		
Former names:.....................................none		Cabins (for one person):............................5		
IMO number:..................................8972338		Cabins (with private balcony):......................14		
Builder:....................Chesapeake Shipbuilding (USA)		Cabins (wheelchair accessible):......................3		
Original cost:......................................n/a		Wheelchair accessibility:........................None		
Entered service:.................................Jul 2002		Cabin voltage:...............................110 volts		
Registry:...USA		Elevators:..1		
Length (ft/m):...............................174.0/53.0		Casino (gaming tables):............................No		
Beam (ft/m):.................................40.5/12.3		Slot machines:....................................No		
Draft (ft/m):...................................6.5/1.9		Swimming pools:...................................0		
Propulsion/Propellers:......................... diesel/2		Hot tubs (on deck):................................0		
Passenger decks:....................................4		Self-service launderette:...........................No		
Total crew:..22		Dedicated cinema/seats:...........................No		
Passengers (lower beds/alll berths):.................. 49/49		Library:...No		
Passenger Space Ratio (lower beds/all berths):....... 26.2/26.2		Onboard currency:...............................US$		
Crew/Passenger Ratio (lower beds/all berths):.......... 2.2/2.2				

A US coastal ship with limited facilities for retirees

OVERVIEW. *American Glory* is best suited to mature couples and single travelers sharing a cabin who want to cruise in an all-American environment where the itineraries and destinations are more important than food, service, or entertainment.

THE SHIP. American Cruise Lines is the resurrection of a company with the same name that existed between 1974 and 1989. It features intracoastal waterway cruising, as well as sailings in New England and the Hudson River Valley. *American Glory* was built specifically for coastal cruising and cannot venture far from the coastline. The ship's uppermost deck is open (good for views), and there are tables and chairs, a few sunloungers, and a small putting green.

There are two public lounges. The observation lounge, is located forward, with windows on three sides, and an open bar is set up each afternoon. A second, smaller lounge is sandwiched between cabins on the same deck.

The point is to get close to the inland areas, cities, and towns of America's intra-coastal waterways and coastline. There's no waiting in line – you can board whenever you want. The ship docks in town centers, or within walking distance of most towns on the itineraries. The dress code is 'no ties casual.' But it really is extremely expensive for what you get, compared even to similar ships, although this is a new ship and the cabins are of a better size and are better equipped. There is an elevator, which goes to all decks.

Berlitz's Ratings

	Possible	Achieved
Ship	500	253
Accommodation	200	110
Food	400	228
Service	400	170
Entertainment	100	0
Cruise	500	123

OVERALL SCORE
884 points out of 2000

ACCOMMODATION. There are cabins for couples and singles, seven suites, and five wheelchair-accessible cabins. All cabins have twin beds that convert to a king-size bed, color TV, a small desk with chair, and clothes hanging space. The seven most expensive cabins also have a VCR and CD player. Accommodation designated as suites also have a private balcony; although narrow, it does have two chairs and a small drinks table.

DINING. The dining salon, located in the latter third of the vessel, has large, panoramic picture windows on three of its sides. There's open seating (no assigned tables). There are no tables for two, and the chairs do not have armrests.

There is little choice of entrées, appetizers, or soups, although there have been recent improvements. There is no wine list, although basic white and red table wines are included. On the last morning of each cruise, only Continental breakfast is available.

ENTERTAINMENT. There is no formal entertainment, although dinner and after-dinner conversation with fellow passengers in the ship's lounge/bar really becomes the entertainment each evening. Otherwise, take a good book.

SPA/FITNESS. There are no health spa facilities or medical facilities – but then the vessel is always close to land.

American Spirit
★★

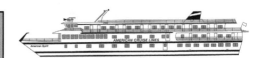

Size:	Boutique Ship	Cabins (total):	47
Tonnage:	2,000	Size range (sq ft/m):	204.0–240.0/18.9–22.2
Lifestyle:	Standard	Cabins (outside view):	47
Cruise line:	American Cruise Lines	Cabins (interior/no view):	0
Former names:	none	Cabins (for one person):	2
IMO number:	9283124	Cabins (with private balcony):	26
Builder:	Chesapeake Shipbuilding (USA)	Cabins (wheelchair accessible):	1
Original cost:	n/a	Wheelchair accessibility:	None
Entered service:	Jun 2005	Cabin voltage:	110 volts
Registry:	USA	Elevators:	1
Length (ft/m):	220.0/67.0	Casino (gaming tables):	No
Beam (ft/m):	46.0/14.0	Slot machines:	No
Draft (ft/m):	8.2/2.5	Swimming pools:	0
Propulsion/Propellers:	diesel/2	Hot tubs (on deck):	0
Passenger decks:	4	Self-service launderette:	No
Total crew:	27	Dedicated cinema/seats:	No
Passengers (lower beds/all berths):	92/92	Library:	Yes
Passenger Space Ratio (lower beds/all berths):	21.7/21.7	Onboard currency:	US$
Crew/Passenger Ratio (lower beds/all berths):	3.4/3.4		

A small, expensive US coastal cruising ship for retirees

OVERVIEW. *American Spirit* is best suited to mature couples and single travelers sharing a cabin who want to cruise where the itineraries are more important than food, service, or entertainment.

THE SHIP. American Cruise Lines builds its vessels in its own shipyard in Chesapeake, Maryland. *American Spirit* is built specifically for coastal cruising and cannot venture far from the coastline. Its uppermost deck is open (good for views) behind the forward windbreaker, and the expansive open deck has many sunloungers, and a small putting green.

Inside, the public rooms include an observation lounge, with views forward and to port and starboard side (complimentary cocktails and hors d'oeuvres are offered before dinner); a library/lounge; a small midships lounge; and an elevator that goes to all decks.

Cruises are typically of seven days' duration. Given the small number of passengers, there's no waiting in line – you can board whenever you want. The ship docks in town centers, or within walking distance of most towns on the itineraries. The dress code is 'no ties casual.'

It really is extremely expensive for what you get, but at least the cabins are of a better size and are slightly better equipped than those of smaller half-sister *American Glory*, but not as nice as those aboard *American Star*.

ACCOMMODATION. There are five cabin price grades (four are doubles, one is for singles). All cabins

Berlitz's Ratings

	Possible	Achieved
Ship	500	284
Accommodation	200	125
Food	400	210
Service	400	175
Entertainment	100	10
Cruise	500	115

OVERALL SCORE
919 points out of 2000

have twin beds that convert to king-size, a small desk with chair, color TV, and clothes hanging space. The seven most expensive cabins also have a DVD and CD player. Accommodation designated as suites also have a private balcony; although narrow, it has two chairs and a small drinks table. Some 23 cabins have a French balcony – you can open the door for fresh air, but it's too narrow to place chairs on.

DINING. The dining salon has large, panoramic picture windows on three sides. There's open seating (no assigned tables) and everyone dines at a single seating, at large tables, allowing you to get to know your fellow passengers.

The food is American fare. There is a limited choice of entrées, appetizers, and soups. There is no wine list, although basic white and red table wines are included. Note that on the last morning of each cruise, only Continental breakfast is available – quite poor really, when you consider the high cost of a cruise.

ENTERTAINMENT. There is no formal entertainment, conversation with fellow passengers in the ship's lounge/bar becomes the entertainment.

SPA/FITNESS. There is a small fitness room with a bicycles and other machines.

American Star
★★

Size:.....................................Boutique Ship	Cabins (total):.......................................48
Tonnage:... 2,000	Size range (sq ft/m):................. 204.0–240.0/18.9–22.2
Lifestyle:.......................................Standard	Cabins (outside view):................................48
Cruise line:........................American Cruise Lines	Cabins (interior/no view):..............................0
Former names:.....................................none	Cabins (for one person):..............................2
IMO number:....................................9427615	Cabins (with private balcony):.........................27
Builder:.....................Chesapeake Shipbuilding (USA)	Cabins (wheelchair accessible):........................1
Original cost:.. n/a	Wheelchair accessibility:...........................None
Entered service:...............................Jun 2007	Cabin voltage:................................ 110 volts
Registry:.. USA	Elevators:..1
Length (ft/m):............................... 220.0/67.0	Casino (gaming tables):.............................No
Beam (ft/m):................................. 46.0/14.0	Slot machines:....................................No
Draft (ft/m):................................. 8.2/2.5	Swimming pools:...................................0
Propulsion/Propellers:.......................... diesel/2	Hot tubs (on deck):................................0
Passenger decks:....................................4	Self-service launderette:...........................No
Total crew:.......................................27	Dedicated cinema/seats:............................No
Passengers (lower beds/alll berths):................. 94/100	Library:..Yes
Passenger Space Ratio (lower beds/all berths):....... 21.2/20.0	Onboard currency:................................US$
Crew/Passenger Ratio (lower beds/all berths):.......... 3.4/3.4	

A small US coastal cruising ship with limited facilities

OVERVIEW. *American Star* suits mature couples and single travelers sharing a cabin and wishing to cruise in an all-American environment where the destinations are more important than food, service, or entertainment.

THE SHIP. This is one of three coastal cruise ships in the fleet of American Cruise Lines, which has its own shipyard in Chesapeake, Maryland. It is the company's nicest ship by far. *American Star* is built specifically for coastal and inland cruising to destinations unreachable by large cruise ships. The uppermost deck is open (good for views) behind a forward windbreaker; many sunloungers are provided, as is a small golf putting green.

Inside the ship, the public rooms include an observation lounge, with views forward and to port and starboard side (complimentary cocktails and hors d'oeuvres are offered before dinner); a library/lounge; a small midships lounge, and an elevator that goes to all decks, including the outdoor sun deck.

Cruises are typically of seven to 14 days' duration. The ship docks in town centers, or within walking distance of most towns and ports. The dress code is 'no ties casual.' It is extremely expensive for what you get. There are no additional costs, except for gratuities and port charges, because it's all included.

ACCOMMODATION. There are five cabin price grades (four are doubles, one is for singles). All cabins have twin beds, convertible to a king-size bed, a

Berlitz's Ratings

	Possible	Achieved
Ship	500	285
Accommodation	200	125
Food	400	210
Service	400	178
Entertainment	100	10
Cruise	500	117
OVERALL SCORE		
925 points out of 2000		

small desk with chair, satellite-feed flat-screen TV set, DVD player and Internet access, clothes hanging space, and a modular bathroom with separate shower, washbasin, and toilet (no cabin has a bathtub), and windows that open. Accommodation incorrectly designated as suites (23) also have a private balcony; although narrow, it does have two chairs and a small drinks table.

DINING. The dining salon, in the latter third of the vessel, has large, panoramic picture windows on three sides. Everyone dines at a single, open seating. The cuisine is American. The choice of entrées, appetizers, and soups is limited. There is no wine list, although basic white and red table wines are included.

Note that on the last morning of each cruise, only Continental breakfast is available (no hot food).

ENTERTAINMENT. There is no formal entertainment, although dinner and after-dinner conversation with fellow passengers in the ship's lounge/bar really becomes the entertainment each evening. Otherwise, take a good book.

SPA/FITNESS. There is a tiny fitness room with a few bicycles and other exercise machines.

Amsterdam
★★★★

Size:. . . . . Mid-size Ship	Crew/Passenger Ratio (lower beds/all berths): 2.3/2.7
Tonnage: 62,735	Cabins (total):. 690
Lifestyle: . . . . .Premium	Size range (sq ft/m): 184.0–1,124.8/17.1–104.5
Cruise line:. . . . . Holland America Line	Cabins (outside view):. 557
Former names:. . . . . none	Cabins (interior/no view):. 133
IMO number:. 9188037	Cabins (for one person):. 0
Builder: . . . . Fincantieri (Italy)	Cabins (with private balcony):. 172
Original cost:. . . . . $400 million	Cabins (wheelchair accessible): 20
Entered service:. . . . . .Oct 2000	Wheelchair accessibility:. . . . . .Good
Registry:. . . . . .The Netherlands	Cabin voltage: . . . . .110 and 220 volts
Length (ft/m):. 780.8/238.0	Elevators:. 12
Beam (ft/m):. 105.8/32.2	Casino (gaming tables):. . . . . .Yes
Draft (ft/m):. 25.5/7.8	Slot machines:. . . . . .Yes
Propulsion/Propellers: . . .diesel-electric (37,500kW)/2 azimuthing	Swimming pools:. . . . . .1 (1 w/sliding glass dome)
pods	Hot tubs (on deck):. 2
Passenger decks:. 12	Self-service launderette:. . . . . .Yes
Total crew:. 600	Dedicated cinema/seats:. Yes/235
Passengers (lower beds/alll berths):. 1,380/1,653	Library: . . . . .Yes
Passenger Space Ratio (lower beds/all berths): 45.4/37.9	Onboard currency: . . . . .US$

Dutch-style decor and friendly service for mature cruisers

OVERVIEW. *Amsterdam* is extremely comfortable, with fine, elegant, and luxurious decorative features. On the negative side, the quality of food and service is poor and there's a lack of understanding of what it really takes to make a 'luxury' cruise experience, despite what is touted in Holland America Line's brochures.

THE SHIP. *Amsterdam*, a close sister ship to Rotterdam, has a nicely raked bow, as well as the familiar interior flow and design style. It was the first ship in the HAL fleet to feature an azimuthing pod propulsion system. The pods are powered by a diesel-electric system.

The decor retains much of the traditional ocean liner detailing so loved by frequent Holland America Line passengers, with some use of medium and dark wood paneling. However, some color combinations – particularly for the chairs and soft furnishings – are rather wacky. Much of the artwork reflects HAL's glorious past, as well as items depicting the city of Amsterdam's history.

The interior focal point is a three-deck high atrium, in an oval, instead of circular, shape. A whimsical 'Astrolobe' is the featured centerpiece in this atrium. Also clustered in the atrium lobby are the reception desk, shore excursion desk, photo shop, and photo gallery.

The ship has three principal passenger stairways – so much better than two from the viewpoint of safety, flow, and accessibility. There is a glass-covered pool

Berlitz's Ratings	Possible	Achieved
Ship	500	402
Accommodation	200	156
Food	400	267
Service	400	268
Entertainment	100	73
Cruise	400	290

OVERALL SCORE
1456 points out of 2000

on the Lido Deck between the mast and the twin funnels, watched over by a sculpture of a brown bear catching salmon.

The casino, in the middle of a major passenger flow on one of the entertainment decks, has blackjack, roulette, poker, and dice tables alongside the requisite rows of slot machines.

HAL provides cappuccino and espresso coffees and free ice cream at certain times, as well as hot hors d'oeuvres in all bars – something other major lines have dropped, or charge extra for.

With one whole deck of suites (and a dedicated, private concierge lounge, with preferential passenger treatment), the company has in effect created a two-class ship. The charge to use the washing machines and dryers in the self-service launderette is irritating.

Perhaps the ship's best asset is its friendly and personable Filipino and Indonesian crew, although communication (in English) can prove frustrating at times, particularly in the dining room and informal buffet areas. The room service menu is limited, and room service is very basic.

FAMILIES. There are children's and teens' play areas – token gestures by a company that traditionally does not cater well to children. Popcorn is available at the Wajang Theater for moviegoers, while adjacent is the popular Java Café.

ACCOMMODATION. This is spread over five decks (some cabins have full or partially obstructed views) and is in 16 grades: 11 with outside views, and five interior grades (no view). There are four penthouse suites, and 50 suites – 14 more than aboard sister ship *Rotterdam*. No cabin is more than 130ft (40m) from a stairway, which makes it very easy to find your way from your cabin to the public rooms. Although 81 percent of cabins have outside views, only 25 percent of those have balconies.

All of the 'standard' interior and outside-view cabins are tastefully furnished, and have twin beds that convert to a queen-size bed – but the space is a little tight for walking between beds and the vanity unit. There is a decent amount of closet and drawer space, although this will be tight for longer voyages. The fully tiled bathrooms are disappointingly small, particularly on long cruises, the shower tubs are very small, and the storage for toiletries is quite basic. There is little detailing to distinguish the bathrooms from those aboard the Statendam-class ships. All cabin TV sets carry CNN and TNT, as well as movies, and ship information and shopping channels.

There are 50 Verandah Suites and four Penthouse Suites on Navigation Deck. The suites all share a private Concierge Lounge, with a concierge to handle such things as special dining arrangements, shore excursions, and special requests. Strangely there are no butlers for these suites, as aboard ships with similar facilities. The lounge, with its wood detailing and private library, is accessible only by private key-card.

Four Penthouse Suites are extremely civilized. Each has a separate steward's entrance, as well as a separate bedroom with king-size bed, vanity desk, large walk-in closet with excellent drawer and hanging space, living room, dining room (seating up to eight), wet bar, and pantry. The bathroom is large, and has a big oval Jacuzzi tub, separate shower enclosure, two washbasins, and separate toilet and bidet. A guest bathroom has a toilet and washbasin. There is a good-size private balcony. Suite occupants get personal stationery, complimentary laundry and ironing, cocktail-hour hors d'oeuvres and other goodies, as well as priority embarkation and disembarkation.

DINING. The La Fontaine Dining Room seats 747, spans two decks, and has a huge stained-glass ceiling measuring almost 1,500 sq ft (140 sq m), with a floral motif and fiber-optic lighting. There are tables for two, four, six, or eight, but few tables for two. Both open seating and fixed (assigned tables and times) seating are available, while breakfast and lunch are open-seating (you'll be seated by restaurant staff when you enter). Rosenthal china and fine cutlery are provided.

Other dining options. The 88-seat Pinnacle Grill is available to all passengers on a reservation-only basis, with priority reservations given to those in suite grades. There is a cover charge, but there's bet-ter food and presentation than in the main dining room (it's open for lunch and dinner, reservations required). The whimsically surreal artwork features scenic landscapes. The cuisine is California-Italian in style, with small portions and few vegetables. The wine list is good, and wines are served in the correct stemware.

Another venue, the Lido Buffet Restaurant, is open for casual dinners on all except the last night of each cruise, in an open-seating arrangement. Tables are set with crisp linens, flatware, and standard stemware. A set menu includes a choice of four entrées.

For casual breakfasts and lunches, the Lido Buffet Restaurant provides old-style, stand-in-line serve-yourself canteen food – adequate for anyone used to TV dinner food, but most definitely not as lavish as the brochures claim. Although the salad items appear adequate when displayed, they are too cold and quite devoid of taste. The constant supply of iceberg lettuce doesn't seem to go away, but there is little choice of other, more suitable, lettuces and greens.

ENTERTAINMENT. The 577-seat Queen's Lounge is the venue for all production shows, strong cabaret, and other entertainment. It is two decks high, with main and balcony level seating. The stage has hydraulic lifts and three video screens, and closed-loop system for the hearing-impaired.

While Holland America Line is not known for its fine entertainment (the budgets aren't high enough), what the line does offer is a consistently good, tried and tested array of cabaret acts. The production shows, while a good attempt, fall short on storyline, choreography, and performance, with colorful costuming and lighting hiding the weak spots.

A number of bands, a string ensemble, and solo musicians present live music for dancing and listening in many of the lounges and bars. There's dancing in the Crows Nest (atop the navigation bridge) and serenading string music in the Explorer's Lounge, among other venues.

SPA/FITNESS. The Ocean Spa is located one deck above the navigation bridge at the very forward part of the ship. It includes a gymnasium with all the latest muscle-pumping exercise machines, including an abundance of treadmills. It has forward views over the ship's bows. There's an aerobics exercise area, large beauty salon with ocean-view windows to the port side, several treatment rooms, and men's and women's saunas, steam rooms, and changing areas.

The spa is operated by Steiner, a specialist concession, whose young staff will try to sell you Steiner's own-brand Elemis beauty products. Some fitness classes are free. Massage facials, pedicures, and beauty salon treatments cost extra.

For the sports-minded, two paddle-tennis courts are located at the aft of the Sports Deck.

Arcadia
★★★★

Size:.......................Large Resort Ship		Crew/Passenger Ratio (lower beds/all berths):.........2.3/2.9	
Tonnage:........................82,972		Cabins (total):....................1,032	
Lifestyle:.......................Standard		Size range (sq ft/m):...............170–516.6/15.7–48	
Cruise line:......................P&O Cruises		Cabins (outside view):................690	
Former names:.....................none		Cabins (interior/no view):................342	
IMO number:.....................9226906		Cabins (for one person):....................0	
Builder:.......................Fincantieri (Italy)		Cabins (with private balcony):................677	
Original cost:....................$400 million		Cabins (wheelchair accessible):................30	
Entered service:...................Apr 2005		Wheelchair accessibility:................Good	
Registry:.......................Bermuda		Cabin voltage:...............110 and 220 volts	
Length (ft/m):...................936.0/285.3		Elevators:........................14	
Beam (ft/m):....................105.0/32.0		Casino (gaming tables):................Yes	
Draft (ft/m):....................25.5/7.8		Slot machines:......................Yes	
Propulsion/Propellers:...........diesel-electric (34,000kW)/		Swimming pools:......................2	
2 azimuthing pods		Hot tubs (on deck):....................5	
Passenger decks:..................10		Self-service launderette:................Yes	
Total crew:......................886		Dedicated cinema/seats:................Yes	
Passengers (lower beds/alll berths):..........2,064/2,628		Library:........................Yes	
Passenger Space Ratio (lower beds/all berths):.......41.5/32.4		Onboard currency:....................UK£	

A contemporary, adults-only ship for trendy Brits

OVERVIEW. *Arcadia* is a trendy, modern cruise ship based in Southampton, England – so UK passengers can avoid airports. It is best suited to couples and singles looking for a large, adults-only ship, with entertainment geared to British tastes, an informal setting, and plenty of public rooms.

THE SHIP. P&O's *Arcadia*, intended to be Cunard Line's *Queen Victoria*, was transferred to the P&O Cruises brand (both companies are owned by the giant Carnival Corporation).

Outdoors facilities include a walk-around promenade deck (covered in the ship's forward section), with plenty of sunloungers (and cushioned pads). A large Lido Deck pool has a moveable glass domed cover – useful in poor weather. Panoramic exterior glass-wall elevators grace the central foyer to port and starboard and travel between all 10 passenger decks. Pod propulsion is provided.

The layout provides a horizontal flow, with most public rooms, shops, bars, and lounges set open-plan style on two principal decks, so finding your way around is relatively easy. However, the layout of upper public room decks is not so good. The interior decor is geared towards those with youthful, contemporary tastes. It is, however, restrained (if a bit bland), and has many warm, earthy pastel colors, assisted by 3,000 works of art by British artists, at a cost of $4 million. Although *Arcadia* is one of the Carnival Corporation's Vista-class ships, the decor is perhaps the most refined

Berlitz's Ratings

	Possible	Achieved
Ship	500	398
Accommodation	200	144
Food	400	250
Service	400	287
Entertainment	100	73
Cruise	400	274

OVERALL SCORE
1426 points out of 2000

of them all, and both passenger flow and signage are generally good.

Facilities include a forward-facing Crow's Nest observation lounge high atop the ship (in a contemporary setting); a florist, a gift shop arcade, a Monte Carlo casino, a library (with leather armchairs and a Waterstone's section for paperback sales), a 30-seat boutique screening room which replaced the cyberstudy in a 2008 refit, and The Retreat (a good place to meet and chill out).

The 14 bars include the Spinnaker Bar (good for ship buffs, with its fine display of ship models), a 'traditional' English pub (The Rising Sun, with Boddington's draught beer), plus a bar overlooking a very modest three-deck-high atrium lobby. The ship really lacks a 'soul', because there is no central meeting point – no atrium lobby as such to act as a social centre – quite different to *Oceana*, for example.

Arcadia blends time-honored British cruising with contemporary facilities, but it is completely different from the more traditional *Aurora*, *Oceana*, or *Oriana*. It is registered in Bermuda, so UK and US passport holders can be legally married by the ship's captain (check with P&O Cruises for the latest requirements). You can also renew your vows in a special ceremony.

The New Horizons lecture program provides an array of lectures on a range of subjects (introductory sessions at no charge; more in-depth subject matter study in smaller groups, at an additional cost).

Many extra onboard revenue centers have appeared aboard P&O Cruises' ships, including *Arcadia* – such as paying for lectures and thalassotherapy pool use. Also, smoking is permitted only on cabin balconies and in designated spots on the open decks.

Passenger niggles: There is no room for card games such as bridge; the ship's dance floor space is pitiful; and the embarkation system keeps people waiting in a lounge after lines at the check-in desks and security until boarding card letters are called. The small public toilets lack touches like flowers and hand towels; there are no poolside towels (you must take them from your cabin); poolside gala receptions lack atmosphere; and pre-dinner announcements are robotic. The often noisy air conditioning cannot be turned off in cabins or bathrooms.

ACCOMMODATION. There are 26 price grades of accommodation in seven types of suites/cabins; the choice includes 23 suites, 24 mini-suites, and 685 outside-view cabins with a private balcony. While there are plenty of price grades, there are really only five types of accommodation: suites, mini-suites, cabins with private balcony, and twin-bedded cabins with or without a window. All cabin doors and elevators have numbers in Braille.

There are 67 suites and mini-suites. All accommodation has duvets as standard (blankets and pillows if you prefer), flat-screen TV sets (the audio channels are also on the television, but you can't turn the picture off), tea/coffee-making sets with Tetley teabags and long-life milk, small refrigerator, vanity/writing desk, personal safe, hairdryer; bathrooms have half-size tubs/shower/washbasin, and toilet. Personal toiletries are by Temple Spa, with larger bottles and more selection choice provided for suite occupants.

Also standard are stylish bed runners, Slumberland eight-inch sprung mattresses, 10.5 tog duvets (blankets and pillows if you prefer), Egyptian cotton towels and robes, improved tea/coffee-making facilities with speciality teas (long-life is provided), and a Nick Munro-designed bespoke tray, as well as in-cabin toning and fitness facilities for passengers who would prefer to exercise in private.

In twin-bedded cabin grades (approximately 170 sq ft/16 sq m), when the beds are pushed together, there's little room to maneuver.

Accommodation designated as suites (approximately 516 sq ft/48 sq m, including balcony) and mini-suites (approximately 384 sq ft/36 sq m, including balcony) benefit from more space (some are really just the size of two cabins), king-size bed, trouser press, ironing board and iron, three-seat sofa (suites) or two-seat sofa (mini-suites), wall clock, and binoculars. The bathrooms are larger, and include an aquajet tub, two washbasins, toilet, and separate shower (suites only).

So-called 'butler' service is provided, but, unlike most lines with these kinds of grades, bottled water costs extra, as do soft drinks.

Passenger niggles include the space-hogging tea/coffee-making set on the small vanity desk in the standard cabin grades, although the set itself is comprehensive. Other gripes about standard cabins include: closets with hanging space too narrow for the width of a jacket; little drawer space; poor-quality plastic hangars, and no hooks for belts.

DINING. The Meridian Restaurant, located aft, is two decks high (the two decks are connected by a spiral staircase); it has 11 superb glass-fiber optic ceiling chandeliers created by Neil Wilkin, and a podium with grand piano graces the upper level. There are two seatings in both restaurants, and tables are for two, four, six, or eight. Note that the glasses for both red and white wines are small.

Other dining options. Ocean Grill, by Marco Pierre White, specializes in prime steaks and seafood – with lots of taste. The Orchid Restaurant (on Deck 11) has fine panoramic views, Asian-fusion (heavy on the spices) cuisine, and is its own bar for pre-meal drinks. Reservations are required in both venues, and a cover charge applies.

For casual meals and snacks, there's a self-serve 24-hour eatery (Belvedere), a section of which becomes another dining venue at night, serving Indian cuisine. There's also an open-deck Neptune Grill and Caffe Vivo.

ENTERTAINMENT. The Palladium show lounge is an entertainment palace with three seating tiers and excellent high-tech staging, lighting, and sound systems. Seating is in both banquette-style and individual tub chairs, and the sightlines to the stage are generally good. There are several major production shows – some have a Cirque du Soleil feel – complete with major bungee-diving acrobatics and fine adagio dancers. Classical concerts are scheduled for many cruises.

P&O Cruises' ships usually carry professional dance hosts and teachers. But ballroom dance aficionados should note that there are few wooden dance floors.

SPA/FITNESS. The Ocean Spa includes a gymnasium with good forward ocean views, 10 body-pampering treatment rooms, a thermal suite that incorporates a hydrotherapy pool, sauna and steam room, and two small unisex saunas at no charge, but in a location that discourages their use (the thermal suite is better). While the tiny sauna is free, there's a charge to use the Aqua Pool. To get from the changing room to the sauna you need to walk across a carpeted foyer.

Additionally, The Retreat is a cool space for relaxation, and for calming classes like tai chi and yoga. The spa is operated by the UK-based Harding Brothers. Sports facilities include a sports court for racquet or football games, a golf driving range, and the traditional shuffleboard and ringtoss.

Artania
★★★★

Size:. . . . . Mid-size Ship		Cabins (total):. 588	
Tonnage: 44,348		Size range (sq ft/m): 186.0–1,126.0/17.2–104.5	
Lifestyle: . . . . .Standard		Cabins (outside view): 588	
Cruise line:. . . . . .Phoenix Reisen		Cabins (interior/no view):. 0	
Former names: . . . . Royal Princess		Cabins (for one person):. 0	
IMO number: 8201480		Cabins (with private balcony): 273	
Builder: . . . . Wartsila (Finland)		Cabins (wheelchair accessible): 4	
Original cost:. . . . . $165 million		Wheelchair accessibility:. . . . . .Good	
Entered service:. . . . . Nov 1984/Apr 2011		Cabin voltage: . . . . .110 and 220 volts	
Registry:. . . . . The Bahamas		Elevators:. 6	
Length (ft/m):. 754.5/230.0		Casino (gaming tables):. . . . . Yes	
Beam (ft/m):. 95.8/29.2		Slot machines:. . . . . Yes	
Draft (ft/m):. 25.5/7.8		Swimming pools:. 2	
Propulsion/Propellers:. . . . . .diesel (29,160kW)/2		Hot tubs (on deck):. 2	
Passenger decks:. 9		Self-service launderette:. . . . . Yes	
Total crew:. 520		Dedicated cinema/seats:. Yes/150	
Passengers (lower beds/alll berths):. 1,176/1,260		Library:. . . . . Yes	
Passenger Space Ratio (lower beds/all berths): 37.7/35.1		Onboard currency: . . . . Euros	
Crew/Passenger Ratio (lower beds/all berths):. 2.2/2.4			

A comfortable, spacious ship for mature-age cruisers

OVERVIEW. *Artania* should provide a fine experience in spacious, reserved contemporary surroundings, at a decent price. It is best suited to couples and singles seeking to cruise in a modern mid-size ship.

THE SHIP. There's a traditional walk-around teak deck, and the ship has extensive outdoor deck and sunbathing space, plus a wave-action swimming pool.

The interior decor reflects the feeling of space, openness, and light; the passenger flow is good. There are several nicely appointed public rooms, bars, and lounges, plus wide passageways and three spacious stairways (with slightly different carpet colors).

A Pacific Lounge, set around the funnel base, has fine views and a peaceful environment during the day; each evening it becomes a lively nightclub. Around the centra stairway foyer, is the popular Harry's Bar; there's also a Bodega (tavern) for food and drinks. A 7 percent gratuity is added to bar accounts.

ACCOMMODATION. The all-outside view cabins (270 with private balcony) represent just four accommodation types (including suites), although there are 21 price categories. All of the cabins (most of which have twin beds convertible into a queen-size bed) are comfortable and well appointed.

All have a large shower enclosure, color TV set, hairdryer, personal safe, and European two-pin sockets. Also standard are stylish bed runners, high-quality

Berlitz's Ratings		
	Possible	Achieved
Ship	500	384
Accommodation	200	153
Food	400	321
Service	400	313
Entertainment	100	76
Cruise	400	293
OVERALL SCORE		
1540 points out of 2000		

sprung mattresses, European duvets, and cotton towels. L'Occitane personal toiletries are provided, as are chocolates on your pillow each night. Prompt, attentive room service is provided 24 hours a day.

Some cabins on both Apollo Deck and Orion Deck have full or partial lifeboat and safety equipment-obstructed views, and some cabins have extra sofa beds fitted (good for families during the busy summer and school months).

The 12 largest suites are attractive, but, with the exception of the Royal Suite, are not large, and the balconies are small, although all have teak decking. Suite occupants get an expanded range of toiletries and complimentary mineral water.

DINING. The Vier Jahreszeiten (Four Seasons) restaurant is set low down in the ship, conveniently adjacent to the lobby. One deck above is the Artania Restaurant, with adjacent bar. Casual meals can be taken in the indoor-outdoor Lido Restaurant.

ENTERTAINMENT. The Atlantik Showlounge hosts shows, drama, and cabaret acts. Volume is normally kept to an acceptable level.

SPA/FITNESS. The Artania Spa contains a gym with muscle-toning equipment, saunas and changing rooms. There's also a steam bath, ice-fountain, and salon. For the sports-minded, there's table tennis, tables-soccer, shuffleboard, and darts.

Artemis
★★★ +

Size:.....Boutique Ship		Cabins (total):.....26	
Tonnage:.....1206		Size range (sq ft/m):.....140.0-210.0/13.0-19.5	
Lifestyle:.....Premium		Cabins (outside view):.....26	
Cruise line:.....Grand Circle Cruise Line		Cabins (interior/no view):.....0	
Former names:.....none		Cabins (for one person):.....2	
IMO number:.....9398010		Cabins (with private balcony):.....18	
Builder:.....Brodogaliste Shipyard (Croatia)		Cabins (wheelchair accessible):.....0	
Original cost:.....n/a		Wheelchair accessibility:.....None	
Entered service:.....2007		Cabin voltage:.....110 volts	
Registry:.....Malta		Elevators:.....1	
Length (ft/m):.....196.8/60.0		Casino (gaming tables):.....No	
Beam (ft/m):.....36.0/11.0		Slot machines:.....No	
Draft (ft/m):.....9.8/3.0		Swimming pools:.....1	
Propulsion/Propellers:.....diesel/2		Hot tubs (on deck):.....0	
Passenger decks:.....4		Self-service launderette:.....No	
Total crew:.....		Dedicated cinema/seats:.....No	
Passengers (lower beds/alll berths):.....50		Library:.....No	
Passenger Space Ratio (lower beds/all berths):.....50		Onboard currency:.....US$	
Crew/Passenger Ratio (lower beds/all berths):.....2.3/2.3			

A cute pocket-sized ship for in-depth cultural voyages

OVERVIEW. Artemis is one of three fully-owned sister ships (the others are Arethusa and Athena) for Grand Circle Cruise Line.

THE SHIP. Artemis is a cute little ship, with a dark blue hull, and built specifically for in-depth coastal cruising. The lobby is reminiscent of those found aboard the company's riverships.

Outdoor aft deck area has bar, and canopy cover (can be removed for warm climate cruising) inboard from two lifeboats that also act as shore tenders.

ACCOMMODATION. The cabins, though small, each have a bed that can be used as a sofa during the day, flat-screen TV with CNN, telephone, personal safe, mini-fridge, indivually controlled air-conditioning, hair dryer, and dual electrical outlets.

The 18 cabins on Upper Deck have en-suite bathrooms with showers (no cabins have bathtubs), and large sliding-glass doors that open onto a private bal-

Berlitz's Ratings		
	Possible	Achieved
Ship	500	377
Accommodation	200	144
Food	400	269
Service	400	270
Entertainment	100	62
Cruise	400	275
OVERALL SCORE		
1397 points out of 2000		

cony. The six cabins on Main Deck have portholes that can be opened, while the two single-occupancy cabins have a porthole, but it cannot be opened.

DINING. No information was available at press time.

ENTERTAINMENT. The entertainment is strictly limited to conversation with fellow travellers.

SPA/FITNESS. It's such a small ship, there are no facilities.

Did You Know?

...that the first à la carte restaurant aboard a passenger ship was in the German ship Amerika of 1905?

...that TUI Cruises' Mein Schiff is the only ship with an espresso coffee machine in every cabin?

...that a whole county in Iowa raises all its beef cattle for sale to Carnival Cruise Lines?

...that the first single-berth cabins built as such were also aboard the Campania?

...that the whole disc of the sun is visible for 24 hours a day at some points north of the Arctic Circle? North Cape (May 14–July 29); Hammerfest (May 16–July 27); Tromso (May 20–July 22); Harstad (May 26–July 19); Bodo (June 4–July 8).

Astor
★★★ +

Size:	Small Ship	Cabins (total):	.295
Tonnage:	20,606	Size range (sq ft/m):	140.0–280.0/13.0–26.0
Lifestyle:	Standard	Cabins (outside view):	.199
Cruise line:	Transocean Cruises	Cabins (interior/no view):	.96
Former names:	Fedor Dostoyevskiy, Astor (II)	Cabins (for one person):	.0
IMO number:	8506373	Cabins (with private balcony):	.0
Builder:	Howaldtswerke Deutsche Werft (Germany)	Cabins (wheelchair accessible):	.0
Original cost:	$65 million	Wheelchair accessibility:	Fair
Entered service:	Feb 1987/Apr 1997	Cabin voltage:	220 volts
Registry:	The Bahamas	Elevators:	.3
Length (ft/m):	579.0/176.5	Casino (gaming tables):	Yes
Beam (ft/m):	74.1/22.6	Slot machines:	Yes
Draft (ft/m):	20.0/6.1	Swimming pools:	.2
Propulsion/Propellers:	diesel (15,400kW)/2	Hot tubs (on deck):	.1
Passenger decks:	.7	Self-service launderette:	No (ironing room only)
Total crew:	.300	Dedicated cinema/seats:	No
Passengers (lower beds/all berths):	590/650	Library:	Yes
Passenger Space Ratio (lower beds/all berths):	34.9/31.7	Onboard currency:	Euros
Crew/Passenger Ratio (lower beds/all berths):	1.9/2.1		

Traditional style and restful decor for German cruisers

OVERVIEW. *Astor* caters exclusively to German-speaking couples and single travelers of mature years and provides a degree of style, comfort and elegance in a relaxed, spacious setting that is less formal than a ship such as *Europa*. It offers a good-value-for-money vacation in a traditional cruise ship setting, with appealing itineraries and destinations, good food, and friendly service.

Berlitz's Ratings		
	Possible	Achieved
Ship	500	355
Accommodation	200	141
Food	400	258
Service	400	286
Entertainment	100	62
Cruise	400	274
OVERALL SCORE		
1376 points out of 2000		

THE SHIP. This is an attractive modern ship with a raked bow, a large square funnel and a nicely balanced almost contemporary profile. It is slightly larger than the first *Astor*, and has been well maintained and refurbished over the years. Introduced by Transocean Tours (as it then was called) in 1997, this ship was placed under a long-term charter agreement from its present owner, Premicon (which also owns a number of fine riverships).

Astor was the original name for this ship, the larger of two vessels bearing the same name in the 1980s (the other being the former Transocean Cruises ship *Astoria*), originally built for the now-defunct Astor Cruises. Its previous owners, the also defunct AquaMarin Cruises, brought back the ship's name to *Astor* from its previous identity as *Fedor Dostoyevskiy*.

This ship represents a good mix of traditional and modern styling, with restful decor that doesn't jar the senses in any way – though some say it's a little too dark. Its high standard of German construction can be seen in the fine teakwood decking, polished wood railings and interior fittings, much of it refurbished in 2010.

There is an excellent amount of open deck and sunbathing space, plus cushioned pads for the sun-loungers. There is a basketball court for active passengers, as well as a large deck-chess game on an aft deck, and shuffleboard courts.

The public rooms and conference facilities are supremely comfortable and varied, most with high ceilings. Apart from a showlounge, there's a Captain's Club lounge, a library and card room, and two large boutiques. The wood-paneled Hanse Bar, with good German lager on draft, is a fine retreat; it has an outdoor area, too, and is popular as a late-night hangout. There is no crowding anywhere and no annoying background music in hallways or elevators.

Transocean Cruises has interesting and well-designed destination-intensive worldwide itineraries, and cruises are provided at a very attractive price. The mainly European hotel staff members are friendly without being obtrusive.

Transocean Cruises staff can be found aboard every cruise, some of which are designated as special-theme cruises. Port taxes, insurance, and gratuities to staff are all included in the fare. The drinks prices are inexpensive, particularly when compared to land-based prices.

A service provided by ABX Logistics can collect your luggage from your house, and transport it to the ship for you; when you return, the service will collect it from the ship and bring it to your house – all for a nominal fee.

Note that for the 2013, 2014, and 15 winter seasons, Astor will be operated under charter to the UK's Cruise & Maritime Voyages, and sent to Australasian waters for a series of summer cruises from Australia. The ship will also continue to be marketed Transocean Tours.

ACCOMMODATION. The accommodation, spanning 20 price categories, is spread over three decks, and comprises 32 suites and 263 outside-view and interior cabins. No matter what grade of accommodation is chosen, rosewood cabinetry and plain beige walls is the norm – a restful environment. All suites and cabins with outside-view windows have blackout blinds – good for cruises to the land of the midnight sun.

Astor Suite. This new suite measures approximately 635 sq ft (59 sq m) and includes a private balcony, with a separate bedroom and living room. The large bathroom has a tub, separate shower enclosure, dual washbasins, and a separate toilet with washbasin.

Senator Suites. These two suites (516.6 sq ft/48 sq m), also added in the 2010 refit, are tastefully decorated in pastel colors, and have wood cabinetry and accents. Each has a separate bedroom, lounge/living room, private balcony, and a French balcony. The bathroom has decent-size storage cabinets for toiletries, as well as a tub, separate shower enclosure, toilet, and dual washbasins. A wide variety of bathroom amenities is provided.

Outside-view and Interior Cabins. These cabins (139.9 sq ft/13 sq m) are well appointed and tastefully decorated in fresh pastel colors, and have dark wood accents and cabinetry, making them very restful. There is plenty of closet and drawer space, as well as some under-bed storage space for luggage. The bathrooms are very practical, and each has a decent-size cabinet for toiletries, as well as all the necessary fittings, including a white enamel washbasin.

Suite 105, facing the piano in the conference room opposite, is subject to the sounds of practice and musical rehearsals. In standard cabins, many day sofas convert to beds. Twin beds cannot be pushed together.

Outside-view Family Cabins. These large, four-berth cabins (258.3 sq ft/24 sq m) have two lower beds, one upper berth and one sofa bed – good for families with children. The tiled bathroom has a shower enclosure, white enamel washbasin and toilet.

All grades have a mini-bar and personal safe, European duvets, 100 percent cotton towels and bathrobe, soap, shampoo, shower cap, sewing kit, and a basket of fruit. The bathroom towels, however, are small.

The cabin service menu is limited, although German-speaking passengers in general seldom use room service for food items. There is an extra charge for sandwiches, and little else is available. However, there is plenty of food elsewhere around the ship. There is an extra charge for freshly squeezed orange juice, as aboard all ships in the German-speaking market.

DINING. The Waldorf Dining Room is reasonably elegant, well laid-out, and operates two seatings. It also has one small wing – good for groups of up to 30. The service throughout is friendly and unpretentious, and the food quality and presentation has received some attention from the food caterer, although remember that you get what you pay for, and food is not a particularly high priority for Transocean Cruises.

The menus are reasonably attractive, and both quality and presentation are acceptable standard fare, but nothing special – there's certainly no 'wow' factor. In addition to the regular entrées (typically three entrées for dinner), there may also be a pasta dish and a vegetarian specialty dish. The wine list contains a decent selection of wines from many regions, and all at inexpensive to moderate price levels, but wine glasses are small.

Other dining options. Two small specialty dining venues (one serving Italian cuisine, the other a 'romantic dinner') are reservations-only, extra-cost dining spots for those wanting something a little more special and as an alternative to the main dining room. Larger wine glasses are provided.

Casual breakfast and lunch buffets (both in the restaurant and another lounge) are reasonably well presented, and constantly refreshed, although they tend to be somewhat repetitive; the choice of foods is limited and there is room for improvement. In typical German style, a Frühschoppen with the appropriate music, Bavarian sausages, and complimentary beer, is presented on the open lido deck once each cruise and is not to be missed.

ENTERTAINMENT. The Showlounge is a single-level room with 14 pillars obstructing the sight lines. It is better suited to cabaret and mini-concerts than large-scale staged production shows. The stage itself is also the dance floor, and cannot be raised for shows. The entertainment possibilities, therefore, are limited, with singers, magicians, and other visual acts providing the bulk of the shows.

SPA/FITNESS. The Wellness Oasis, located on the lowest passenger deck, contains a sauna, steam room, solarium, indoor swimming pool, beauty salon, treatment rooms, and changing areas. Massage, facials, manicures, and pedicures are some of the services offered. A separate fitness center, equipped with techno-machinery and exercycles, is located on an upper deck (Bridge Deck), complete with ocean views.

Asuka II
★★★★ +

Size:	Mid-size Ship	Cabins (total):	462
Tonnage:	50,142	Size range (sq ft/m):	198.1–949.4/18.4–88.2
Lifestyle:	Luxury/Premium	Cabins (outside view):	462
Cruise line:	NYK Cruises	Cabins (interior/no view):	0
Former names:	Crystal Harmony	Cabins (for one person):	0
IMO number:	8806204	Cabins (with private balcony):	260
Builder:	Mitsubishi Heavy Industries, Japan	Cabins (wheelchair accessible):	4
Original cost:	$240 million	Wheelchair accessibility:	Best
Entered service:	Jul 1990/May 2006	Cabin voltage:	115 and 220 volts
Registry:	Japan	Elevators:	8
Length (ft/m):	790.5/240.96	Casino (gaming tables):	Yes
Beam (ft/m):	97.1/29.60	Slot machines:	Yes
Draft (ft/m):	24.6/7.50	Swimming pools:	1
Propulsion/Propellers:	diesel-electric (32,800kW)/2	Hot tubs (on deck):	1
Passenger decks:	8	Self-service launderette:	Yes
Total crew:	470	Dedicated cinema/seats:	Yes/263
Passengers (lower beds/alll berths):	800/1,010	Library:	Yes
Passenger Space Ratio (lower beds/all berths):	52.0/45.2	Onboard currency:	Japanese yen
Crew/Passenger Ratio (lower beds/all berths):	1.7/1.8		

An elegant, spacious ship with fine food, for Japanese cruisers

OVERVIEW. *Asuka II* is best suited to Japanese-speaking travelers, typically over 60, seeking a sophisticated ship with fine-quality fittings and furnishings, a wide range of public rooms and facilities, and excellent food and service from a well-trained staff. It is the attention to detail that makes this ship so pleasant, such as almost no announcements and little background music.

Berlitz's Ratings		
	Possible	Achieved
Ship	500	418
Accommodation	200	160
Food	400	339
Service	400	336
Entertainment	100	83
Cruise	400	337
OVERALL SCORE		
1673 points out of 2000		

THE SHIP. Although now 20 years old, *Asuka II*, formerly *Crystal Harmony*, underwent a four-month long drydocking and refit in 2005–06, and further refurbishment in 2009. It is a handsome, well-balanced contemporary ship with raked clipper bow, sleek lines, and NYK's double red band on the funnel. There is almost no sense of crowding anywhere, and the fact that form follows function means that comfort is built-in. There is a wrap-around teakwood deck for walking, and an abundance of open deck and sunbathing space.

Inside, the layout is completely different from the previous *Asuka* in that there is a horizontal flow through the public rooms, as opposed to the previous vertical arrangement, and this better suits the age range of NYK's typical passengers. The design combines some large ship facilities with the intimacy of rooms found aboard many smaller ships. There is a wide assortment of public entertainment lounges and small intimate rooms, and passenger flow is excellent. Fine-quality fabrics and soft furnishings, china, flatware, and silver are used throughout.

Outstanding are the Vista (observation) Lounge and the tranquil, elegant Palm Court, one of the nicest rooms afloat, while adjacent are an Internet room and a Chashitsu (Japanese 12-tatami mat room). Other public spaces and facilities include the Mariner's Club Lounge (piano bar/lounge), Cigar Bar, Bistro Café, Casino Corner, Mahjong Room with eight tables, Compass Room (meeting and activities room), a book/video library, and the Stars karaoke bar. The theater is a dedicated room with high-definition video projection. There is a self-service launderette on each deck – practical for long voyages.

Asuka II is a hotel afloat – approximately the equivalent of Tokyo's Imperial Hotel – and provides abundant choices and flexibility. It has just about everything for the discerning traveler prepared to pay for high style, space, and the comfort and the facilities of a mid-size vessel capable of long voyages. The company pays attention to its repeat passengers, particularly those in Deck 10 penthouses and suites.

Unfortunately, dining is in two seatings, which makes its timing highly structured – there are two shows, because the showlounge can't seat everyone at once. This works well in the Japanese market, and you can always choose to eat in a specialty dining venue, but the arrangement detracts from the otherwise fine setting of the ship and the professionalism of its staff. All gratuities are included.

ACCOMMODATION. There are five categories of suites and cabins (including four Royal Suites with private balcony; 26 Asuka Suites with balcony; 32 Suites with balcony; 202 Cabins with balcony; 172 Cabins without balcony). Regardless of the category, duvets and down pillows are provided, as are lots of other niceties. All cabins have a color TV set, DVD player, mini-refrigerator, personal safe, small couch and coffee table, excellent soundproofing, a refrigerator and mini-bar, full tea-making set, satellite-linked telephone, hairdryer, and slippers. A full range of toiletries (including Shiseido shampoo, hair rinse, shower cap, soap, cotton pads, razor set, hairbrush, and more) is provided, and cotton towels are plentiful.

Deck 10 Penthouses. Four Royal Suites, whose entrance doorway has a door phone and camera, measure 949.4 sq ft (88.2 sq m) and have a large private balcony and lounge with elegant walnut furniture, new soft furnishings, and audio-visual entertainment center (Bose audio system, Blu-Ray player); separate master bedroom with twin beds (flat-screen TV); and large walk-in closets. The excellent ocean-view Japanese-style bathrooms, with German quality fittings that include a large overhead shower, come with jet bathtub, two washbasins, and plenty of storage space for toiletries (a range of L'Occitane toiletries is provided). These fine, private, pampered living spaces at sea were totally refurbished in 2010, and include perks such as priority service, free laundry service, a wide variety of alcoholic beverages and many other goodies.

Other Deck 10 Suites. These are worth the asking price. All have a private balcony, with outside light, and plenty of space including a lounge with large couch, coffee table and chairs, large TV set, and a separate sleeping area that can be curtained off with thick drapes that allow you to sleep totally in the dark. The bathrooms are quite large and extremely well appointed. All deck 10 suites/cabins are attended by social officers, and complimentary in-room dining service is offered.

Deck 9/8/7/5 Cabins. Many of the cabins have a private balcony (in fact, half of all cabins have private balconies, with outside lights) and are extremely comfortable. But they are a little tight for space, with one-way traffic past the bed. There is a reasonable amount of drawer and storage space, although the drawers are small and the closet hanging space and the storage space for shoes are very limited for long voyages. Some cabins have lifeboat-obstructed views, so it's best to check the deck plan carefully.

Although well appointed, the bathrooms (except for those in Deck 10 accommodation) are of the 'you first, me next' variety – and size. But they do come with generously sized toiletries and amenities, and all bathrooms are fitted with electric 'washlet' high-cleanse toilets.

DINING. There are several choices. The non-smoking Four Seasons Dining Room is quite elegant, and has a raised central section. There is plenty of space around each table, well-placed waiter service stations and a number of tables for two, as well as tables for four, six, or eight.

Dinner in the main dining room is in two seatings, with no set table assignments. Afternoon tea and coffee can be taken in the Vista Lounge, a restful venue.

Other dining options. Umihiko is a Japanese extra-charge restaurant, complete with a wholly authentic sushi bar and live fish tanks for absolutely fresh sashimi. It specializes in sushi and authentic sashimi dishes, and provides a refined, intimate dining experience with fine ocean views. Reservations are required.

Prego, which has 40 seats with ocean views to starboard and aft, is for occupants of the Royal Suites and Asuka Suites. The menu is the same as the main dining room, but with more intensive waiter service.

For casual meals, beverages, and ice cream, the Lido Café, which was completely reconstructed in the refit, has an extensive self-serve buffet area; it is located high up in the ship and has ocean views from large picture windows. For casual meals, there is also a Lido Garden Grill, a large area with wooden tables and chairs, and bar.

Additionally, The Bistro, located on the upper level of the two-deck-high lobby, is a casual spot for coffees and pastries, served in the style and atmosphere of a European street café.

ENTERTAINMENT. The Grand Hall, the ship's showlounge, is a large room on one level, with a tiered floor. The sight lines are good from most seats, although a few pillars obstruct the view from some seats. Both banquette and individual seating is available.

In addition, there are often good-caliber cabaret acts that change constantly. The bands and musical units are also, for the most part, of a high standard, and there is plenty of music for social dancing.

SPA/FITNESS. The Grand Spa includes a large Grand Bath/cleansing center (one for men, one for women), with integral sauna and steam room. Other facilities include five treatment rooms (longevity, water, wind, prosperity, harmony) including one for couples. There's a separate sauna, steam rooms, changing rooms for men and women, a beauty salon, and a relaxation area. Another part of the spa houses the gymnasium, with ocean-view windows on one side.

The Asuka Aveda Salon and Spa offers a wide range of body pampering treatments using Aveda brand products. The spa also offers a kimono dressing service, which costs ¥12,600 (about $110).

There is an excellent amount of open deck space, including a swimming pool that's one of the longest aboard any cruise ship. Sports facilities include a full-size paddle tennis court, putting green, and golf driving range.

Aurora
★★★★

Size:.....................................Large Resort Ship	Cabins (total):...934
Tonnage: 76,152	Size range (sq ft/m): 150.6–953.0/14.0–88.5
Lifestyle: ....Standard	Cabins (outside view):.....................................655
Cruise line:.................................P&O Cruises	Cabins (interior/no view):.................................279
Former names: ....none	Cabins (for one person):....................................0
IMO number: 9169524	Cabins (with private balcony):.............................406
Builder: ....Meyer Werft (Germany)	Cabins (wheelchair accessible): 22
Original cost:.............................$375 million	Wheelchair accessibility:................................Good
Entered service:..............................May 2000	Cabin voltage: ....110 and 220 volts
Registry:.....................................Great Britain	Elevators:...10
Length (ft/m):...............................885.8/270.0	Casino (gaming tables):..................................Yes
Beam (ft/m):.................................105.6/32.2	Slot machines:...Yes
Draft (ft/m):....................................25.9/7.9	Swimming pools:....................3 (1 w/sliding glass dome)
Propulsion/Propellers:...........diesel-electric (40,000kW)/2	Hot tubs (on deck):..5
Passenger decks:............................10	Self-service launderette:...............................Yes
Total crew:...................................816	Dedicated cinema/seats:...........................Yes/200
Passengers (lower beds/all berths):.............1,868/1,975	Library:...Yes
Passenger Space Ratio (lower beds/all berths):.......40.7/38.5	Onboard currency:...UK£
Crew/Passenger Ratio (lower beds/all berths):..........2.2/2.4	

A traditional British-style ship for the whole family

OVERVIEW. *Aurora* is best for adults of all ages (although most cruises attract the over-50s) and families with children, who want a cruise that starts and ends in the UK, aboard a large ship with all the facilities of a small resort, with food and service that come with a sense of British-ness.

THE SHIP. *Aurora* is named after the goddess of the dawn in Greek, Melanesian, and Slavonic mythologies, or perhaps the carnation Dianthus Aurora. Or it could be the famous Northern and Southern Lights, Aurora Borealis and Aurora Australis. Anyway, it was built specifically for Britain's traditional cruise market. P&O Cruises has improved on the facilities of its older *Oriana*, with larger cabins and suites and more dining options and choice of public areas.

As cruise ships evolve, slight differences in layout occur, as is the case with Aurora compared to *Oriana*. One difference can be found in the addition of a large, glass-domed indoor/outdoor swimming pool – good in all weathers. The stern superstructure is nicely rounded and has several tiers that overlook the aft decks, pool, and children's outdoor facilities. There is a good sunbathing space, an important plus for the outdoors-loving mainly British passengers, and an extra-wide walk-around outdoor promenade deck, with plenty of white plastic sunloungers (cushioned pads are available).

The interiors are gentle, welcoming and restrained. The public rooms and areas were designed so that each room is individual, yet contributes to an open, cohesive

Berlitz's Ratings		
	Possible	Achieved
Ship	500	386
Accommodation	200	158
Food	400	254
Service	400	299
Entertainment	100	76
Cruise	400	287
OVERALL SCORE		
1460 points out of 2000		

flow. There is good horizontal passenger flow, and wide passageways help to avoid congestion.

As it is a ship for all types of people, specific areas have been designed to attract different age groups and life-styles. The focal point is a four-decks-high atrium lobby and a dramatic, calming, 35-ft (10.6-m) high, Lalique-style fiberglass sculpture of two mythical figures behind a veil of water. At the top of the atrium is the ship's library.

Much of the carpeting was custom designed and made of long-lasting 100 percent wool, and original artworks by British artists include several tapestries and sculptures. For a weird experience, try standing on the mid-ships staircase – look at the oil on the curved canvas paintings by Nicholas Hely Hutchinson; it has a dramatic effect on one's ability not to feel motion sickness while cruising through the Bay of Biscay.

Other features include a virtual reality games room, 12 lounges/bars (among the nicest are Anderson's – similar to Anderson's aboard *Oriana*, with a fireplace and mahogany paneling), and the Crow's Nest – complete with a lovely one-sided model of a former P&O liner: *Strathnaver* of 1931, scrapped in Hong Kong in 1962. There is also a cinema that doubles as a concert and lecture hall.

The library has several writing desks, large leather audio listening chairs, a good range of hardbacks (and a librarian), and skillfully crafted inlaid wood tables. By the second day of almost any cruise, however, it will have been almost stripped of books by word-hungry passengers. The library also sells some nautical books. An Internet-connect center is located on the port side, aft of the popular Crow's Nest observation lounge, but sending emails can be expensive.

The ship's layout is a little disjointed in certain places, and there are several dead-ends and some poor signage. The reception desk's opening hours (7am–8pm) are too short. Standing in line for embarkation, disembarkation, shore tenders, and for self-serve buffet meals is inevitable. Other passenger niggles include noisy air-conditioning in cabins, and the proliferation of extra-charge activities.

In the quest for more onboard revenue, even birthday cakes now cost extra, as do espressos and cappuccinos. Also at extra cost are ice creams and bottled water. Otherwise, it's a very comfortable ship, although you'd probably find the self-serve buffet offerings quite repetitive.

A small British brass band send-off accompanies all sailings. Other touches include church bells that sound throughout the ship for the interdenominational Sunday church service. A coach service for passengers embarking or disembarking in Southampton covers much of the UK. Gratuities are automatically charged to your onboard account.

FAMILIES. Toybox is a playroom for two- to five-year-olds, Jumpin' Jack's for six to nines, Quarterdeck for 10–13s, and Decibels for 14–17s. An entire deck includes swimming pools and whirlpools just for youngsters. Children and teens have 'Club Aurora' programs with their own rooms and their own outdoor pool. Children can be entertained until 10pm, which gives parents time to have dinner and go dancing. All cabins also have a baby-listening device. A night nursery for children aged two to five is available (6pm–midnight, no charge; from midnight to 2am a fee applies), as well as slumber parties for 6-9 year-olds. Sixteen passenger cabins have interconnecting doors – good for families. At peak holiday times (summer, Christmas, Easter) there could be 400 or more children on board. However, the ship absorbs them well, and there's a lot to keep them occupied.

ACCOMMODATION. There are five main grades of cabins, in numerous price categories. Included are two two-level penthouses, 10 suites with balconies, 18 mini-suites with balconies, 368 cabins with balconies, 225 standard outside-view cabins, 16 interconnecting family cabins, and 279 interior cabins.

All grades, from the largest to the smallest, provide the following common features: polished cherry wood laminate cabinetry, full-length mirror, personal safe, refrigerator, television, individually controlled air conditioning; twin beds that convert to a queen-size double bed, sofa, and coffee table. Also standard are stylish bed runners, Slumberland eight-inch sprung mattresses, 10.5 tog duvets, Egyptian cotton towels and robes,

improved tea/coffee-making facilities with specialty teas (long-life milk is provided).

There are four whole decks of cabins with private balconies (about 40 percent of all cabins); these have easy-to-open sliding glass floor-to-ceiling doors; the partitions are of the almost full floor-to-ceiling type – so they really are quite private and cannot be overlooked from above.

Cabin insulation could better, and the magnetic catches in drawers and on the closet doors are noisy. Although most doorways are 26ins (66cm) wide, the actual access is 2ins (5cm) less because of the doorframe; however, some doorways are only 21.5ins (55cm) wide.

A range of Molton Brown products is provided in penthouse suites, suites, and mini-suites. For all other cabins, only soap is provided, plus a 'sport wash' combination soap and shampoo in a dispenser in the shower (so take your favorite shampoo and conditioner), and a small pouch of assorted personal-care items. All grades get cotton bathrobes and towels. Except for the suites, no cabins have illuminated closets, and cabin ceilings are very plain.

Penthouse Suites. The largest cabins consist of two penthouse suites (Library Suite and Piano Suite), each 953 sq ft (88.5 sq m). They have forward-facing views, being located directly underneath the navigation bridge (the blinds must be drawn at night so as not to affect navigation). Each is spread over two decks in height, and connected by a beautiful curved wooden staircase. One suite has a baby grand piano which can be played manually or electronically, while the other has a private library. The living area is on the lower deck (Deck 10), and incorporates a dining suite (a first in a P&O ship) and a small private balcony. In the bedroom, upstairs, there is a walk-in closet, with a bathroom decked out in porcelain and polished granite, with twin washbasins, tub, and separate shower enclosure. There is also a small private balcony.

Suites. The 10 suites measure about 445 sq ft (41.3 sq m). They have a separate bedroom with two lower beds that convert to a queen-size bed. There is a walk-in dressing area and closet, with plenty of drawer space, a trouser press and ironing board. The lounge has a sofa, armchairs, dining table and chairs, writing desk, television, and audio system. The marble-clad bathroom has a whirlpool bath, shower and toilet. The private balcony has space for two sunloungers, plus two chairs and two tables. 'Butler' service is standard.

Mini-Suites. These measure 325 sq ft (30.1 sq m) and have a separate bedroom area with two lower beds that convert to a queen-size bed. There are one double and two single closets, a good amount of drawer space, binoculars, a trouser press, and an ironing board. Each private balcony has a blue plastic deck covering, one deck lounge chair, one chair and table, and exterior light.

Standard Outside-view/Interior Cabins. Any cabin designated as a double with private balcony measures about 175 sq ft (16.2 sq m). They have two lower beds that convert to a queen-size bed. The sitting area has a sofa and table. There's also a vanity table/writing desk, and a private balcony with blue deck covering, two chairs (with only a small recline), and a small table. Note that a 110-volt (American) socket is located underneath the vanity desk drawer – a difficult-to-access position.

Outside-view or Interior Cabins. These have two lower beds that convert to a queen-size bed, closet (but few drawers), and are 150 sq ft (14 sq m). The bathroom has a mini-bath/shower and toilet, or shower and toilet.

All bathrooms in all grades (except those designated as suites) are compact, modular units, and have mirror-fronted cabinets, and, in cabins with bathtubs, the retractable clothesline is located too high for most people to reach.

There are 22 wheelchair-accessible cabins, well outfitted for the physically challenged passenger and almost all within easy access to lifts. However, one cabin (D165 on Deck 8) is located between forward and mid-ships stairways, and it is difficult to access the public rooms on Deck 8 without first going to the deck below, due to several steps and tight corners. All other wheelchair-accessible cabins are well positioned, and eight have a private balcony.

DINING. The two main dining rooms (each seats about 525) have tables for two, four, six, eight, and 10, in two seatings. The midships Medina has a vaguely Moorish theme, while Alexandria, with windows on three sides, has Egyptian decor. Both have more tables for two than in the equivalent restaurants aboard close sister ship *Oriana*. The china is Wedgwood, and the silverware is by Elkington.

The typical menu cycle is 14 days; anyone on a long voyage may find it repetitive. Don't expect exquisite dining, though. What it does present is attractive and tasty, with some rich gravies and sauces to accompany all dining room meals.

Other dining options. You can also have dinner in the 24-hour, 120-seat French bistro-style restaurant, Café Bordeaux, for which a cover charge applied (for dinner only), with menus designed by Marco Pierre-White. Breakfasts and lunches are also served here, as are several (extra-cost) coffees: espresso, cappuccino, latte, ristretto, as well as flavored coffees. So, if you want a croque-monsieur (a toasted ham and Gruyère

cheese sandwich) at 5am, you can have it. A 'Tasting Menu' is available, containing a selection of small cosmopolitan dishes.

Casual, self-serve breakfasts and lunches can be taken from the buffet in a colorful eatery named The Orangery, which has fine ocean views. Other casual dining spots include the Sidewalk Café (for fast-food items poolside), Champagne bar, and, in a first for a P&O cruise ship, Raffles coffee and chocolate bar (but without the ceiling fans).

ENTERTAINMENT. There is a wide variety of mainly British entertainment, from production shows to top British 'name' and lesser name cabaret artists. The ship has its own group of resident actors, singers, and dancers.

Ballroom dance fans will appreciate the four good-sized wood dance floors aboard his ship, and a professional dance couple acts as hosts and teachers (plenty of dancing time is included in the programming).

SPA/FITNESS. The Oasis Spa is amidships on Lido Deck – almost at the top of the ship, just forward of the Crystal swimming pool. It is moderately large, and facilities include a gymnasium with the latest high-tech muscle-pumping and body toning equipment. There is also a sauna and steam room (both unisex, so you'll need a bathing suit). There's a beauty salon, a spiral staircase, and a relaxation area overlooking the forward Riviera swimming pool.

The spa is operated by a specialist spa concession that provides the staff and a wide range of beauty and wellness treatments. Examples of treatments include: Body Toning (detox for the body), Seaweed Wrap, Collagen Velvet Facial Mask, and a range of aromatherapy treatments. Book spa treatments as soon after you embark as possible, as time slots fill up quickly aboard large ships such as this.

A sports court incorporates a golf practice cage and a golf simulator, for which there is an extra charge.

Did you know...

...that Holland America Line passengers consume around 1.3 million pounds (589,680kg) of Alaska fish and seafood during the Alaska summer cruise season? These include wild salmon, halibut, crab, and scallops.

...that Cunard Line used to be the world's largest single buyer of Russian caviar – spending about $500,000 a year – after the Russian and Ukrainian governments? (Today the line buys American caviar from the lower-grade hackleback sturgeon.)

...that *Legend of the Seas* was named in 1995 with the world's largest bottle of Champagne? It had to be specially made, and was a "Sovereign-size" bottle (the equivalent of 34 bottles) of Moët & Chandon Champagne.

Azamara Journey
★★★★

Size:. . . . . Small Ship	Cabins (total):. 338
Tonnage: 30,277	Size range (sq ft/m): 151.0–818.0/14.0–76.0
Lifestyle: . . . . .Premium	Cabins (outside view):. 312
Cruise line:. . . . . Azamara Club Cruises	Cabins (interior/no view):. 26
Former names: . . . . Blue Star, Blue Dream, R6	Cabins (for one person):. 0
IMO number: 9200940	Cabins (with private balcony):. .249
Builder: . . . . Chantiers de l'Atlantique (France)	Cabins (wheelchair accessible): 6
Original cost: . . . . $150 million	Wheelchair accessibility:. . . . . .Fair
Entered service:. . . . . Feb 2000/May 2007	Cabin voltage: . . . . .110 and 220 volts
Registry:. . . . . Malta	Elevators:. 4
Length (ft/m):. 593.7/181.4	Casino (gaming tables):. . . . . Yes
Beam (ft/m):. 95.1/29.0	Slot machines:. . . . . Yes
Draft (ft/m): 19.8/6.0	Swimming pools:. 1
Propulsion/Propellers: . . . . diesel (18,600kW)/2	Hot tubs (on deck):. 3
Passenger decks:. 9	Self-service launderette:. . . . . Yes
Total crew:. 407	Dedicated cinema/seats:. . . . . .No
Passengers (lower beds/alll berths):. 676/777	Library: . . . . Yes
Passenger Space Ratio (lower beds/all berths): 42.7/38.9	Onboard currency: . . . . .US$
Crew/Passenger Ratio (lower beds/all berths):. 1.6/1.9	

An informal ship with country-house decor and fine food

OVERVIEW. The *Azamara Journey*, virtually identical to *Azamara Quest* in features and fittings, suits mature couples seeking to get away from the crowds aboard a contemporary, mid-size ship with a wide range of bars and lounges, at a slightly lower cost than the luxury lines.

THE SHIP. The ship's exterior has a deep blue hull, and white superstructure topped by a large, square blue funnel. A lido deck has a tiny swimming pool, and good sunbathing space. There is no outdoor walk-around promenade deck, although a short jogging track encircles the pool deck (one deck above it). The uppermost outdoors deck includes a golf driving net and shuffleboard court. There are no wooden decks outdoors, but are covered by a sand-colored rubberized material.

The interior decor is in good taste, and is a throwback to ship decor of the ocean liners of the 1920s and '30s. The public rooms are spread over three decks. The reception hall has a staircase with intricate wrought-iron railings. A large observation lounge (The Looking Glass) is high atop the ship. This has a long bar with forward views – for the barmen, that is, as passengers sitting at the bar face aft. There's a bar in each of the restaurant entrances, as well as a Martini Bar. There's also a Mosaic Café, a Luxe Casino, and a shop (Boutique C).

The Drawing Room (the ship's library) is a beautiful, restful room, designed in the Regency style. It has a fireplace, a high, indented, trompe l'oeil ceiling, and a

Berlitz's Ratings

	Possible	Achieved
Ship	500	408
Accommodation	200	156
Food	400	292
Service	400	320
Entertainment	100	78
Cruise	400	294
OVERALL SCORE		
1548 points out of 2000		

good selection of books, comfortable wingback chairs with footstools, and sofas. Smoking is permitted only in designated spots on the open decks.

Gratuities to housekeeping and dining staff are included in the fare. Shuttle buses are provided free when needed in ports of call. Note that a 15 percent gratuity applies to all wines and drinks.

ACCOMMODATION. There are several suite and cabin price grades. The price you pay reflects the size and location of your chosen accommodation. All have so-called butler service (merely better-dressed cabin stewards). All of the standard interior and outside-view cabins (the lowest four grades) are extremely compact units. *Azamara Journey* calls them staterooms, but they are simply cabins – and rather tight for two persons, particularly during cruises longer than seven days. The bathrooms are postage-stamp-sized and you'll be fighting with the shower curtain, as well as storage space for toiletries. The standard cabins cannot, in any sense, be considered luxury, and even premium is stretching it a bit. But all suites and cabins receive 'butler' service.

For the extra cost, it's wise to choose a suite or cabin with a balcony. Some cabins have interconnecting doors while 18 cabins on Deck 6 have lifeboat-obstructed views.

Standard Interior/Standard Outside-view Cabins. These have twin beds (convertible to a queen-size bed), with good under-bed storage areas, safe, vanity desk with large mirror, and good closet and drawer space.

Ocean-view Cabins. These have two lower beds convertible to queen size (some have an extra sofa bed); flat-screen TV; refrigerator with mini-bar; thermostat-controlled air conditioning; direct-dial telephone and voicemail; desk; in-room safe; hairdryer. Approximate size: 161 sq ft (15 sq m).

Deluxe Ocean-view Cabins with Balcony. Features: two lower beds convertible to queen-size; floor-to-ceiling sliding glass doors; sitting area with sofa bed; private veranda; flat-screen TV; refrigerator with mini-bar; thermostat--controlled air conditioning; direct-dial telephone and voicemail; desk; in-room safe; hand-held hairdryer. Approximate size: 215 sq ft (20 sq m); balcony 38 sq ft (3.5 sq m).

Sunset Verandah Cabins. Features: two lower beds convertible to queen size; floor-to-ceiling sliding glass doors; sitting area with sofa bed; private veranda; flat-screen television; refrigerator with mini-bar; thermostat-controlled air conditioning; direct-dial telephone and voicemail; desk; in-room safe; hand-held hairdryer. Approximate size: 215 sq ft (20 sq m); balcony 154 sq ft (14 sq m).

Sky Suites. Superior Exterior View Cabins with Balcony: The cabins with private balconies have partial balcony partitions and sliding glass doors. The bathrooms, with tiled floors and plain walls, are compact units and include either a tub/shower or a shower stall with a strong, removable hand-held shower unit, hairdryer, 100 percent cotton towels, toiletries storage shelves, and retractable clothesline. Approximate size: 323 sq ft (30 sq m); balcony 57 sq ft (3.3 sq m).

Royal Suites (Decks 6, 7). In reality these are large cabins, as the sleeping and lounge areas are not divided. The bathrooms have a good-size tub and ample space for toiletries. The living area has a refrigerated mini-bar, lounge area with breakfast table, and a balcony with two plastic chairs and a table. Approximate size: 538 sq ft (50 sq m); balcony 173 sq ft (16 sq m).

Penthouse Deluxe Suite with Balcony. Providing the most spacious accommodation, these are fine, large living spaces located in the forward-most and aft-most sections of the accommodation decks (particularly nice are those that overlook the stern, on decks 6, 7, and 8). An entrance foyer leads to a living room, bedroom (the bed faces the sea, which can be seen through the floor-to-ceiling windows and sliding glass door), CD player with selection of audio discs, bathroom with Jacuzzi tub, and a small guest bathroom. They have more extensive private balconies that really are private. Approximate size: 603 sq ft (56 sq m); balcony 215 sq ft (20 sq m).

Suite occupants get priority boarding, tender service, specialty dining venue reservations, and light bites at 4pm, in-suite spa treatments, in-suite portrait sitting, free espressos/cappuccinos, bottled water, and silk-wrapped hangers. All suites/cabins located at the stern can suffer from vibration and noise, particularly when the ship is proceeding at or close to full speed, or maneuvering in port.

DINING. Discoveries, the main dining room, has around 340 seats, a raised central section (conversation at these tables may be difficult, due to its low ceiling height), and open-seating dining. There are large ocean-view windows on three sides, several prime tables overlooking the stern, and a small bandstand for live dinner music. The menu changes daily for lunch and dinner, and wine is included. Adjacent to the restaurant is a Martini Bar, with a cozy fireplace.

Other dining options. Aqualina Restaurant (service charge $5) is at the aft of the ship on the port side of Deck 10; it has 96 seats, windows along two sides, and serves Mediterranean cuisine. A $70 per person Tasting Menu includes wine.

Prime C (cover charge $25), is located at the aft of the ship on the starboard side of Deck 10, and features premium-quality steaks and grilled seafood items. It has 98 seats, windows along two sides, and a set menu.

The Windows Café has indoor seating for just over 150 (not really enough when cruising in cold areas or in the winter months), and 186 seats outdoors. Many tables do, however, have ocean views. It is open for breakfast, lunch and casual dinners, and incorporates a small Sushi Café.

All dining venues have open-seating dining, although reservations are needed in the Aqualina Restaurant and Prime C, where there are mostly tables for four or six (there are few tables for two). Suite-grade occupants get two nights free, while other accommodation categories get one night free in one of the two specialty dining venues. All cappuccino and espresso coffees cost extra.

The Mosaic Café serves Italian coffees, as well as teas and pastries (no extra cost). Additionally, a Poolside Grill provides fast-food items (some items are grilled to order). A self-serve soft ice cream machine is located adjacent to its beverage station. Coffee and tea are free 24 hours a day.

ENTERTAINMENT. Celebrity Cabaret, located forward, is the venue for all main entertainment events. In the evenings, the entertainment consists of a mix of classical concerts, revues, as well as comedy and drama.

SPA/FITNESS. The Astral Spa has a gymnasium with some high-tech muscle toning equipment, an extra-cost thalassotherapy pool, and several treatment rooms. The spa is staffed and operated by Steiner Leisure. An 'Acupuncture at Sea' clinic provides treatments that are operated independently of the spa (but also as a concession). Outside on the Lido Deck, there are a small swimming pool, two hot tubs, and a jogging track (one deck above the pool).

Azamara Quest
★★★★

Size:. . . . . Small Ship		Cabins (total):. 358	
Tonnage: 30,277		Size range (sq ft/m): 156.0–484.3/14.5–45.0	
Lifestyle: . . . . .Premium		Cabins (outside view): 332	
Cruise line:. . . . . Azamara Club Cruises		Cabins (interior/no view):. 26	
Former names: . . . . .Blue Moon, Delphin Renaissance, R7		Cabins (for one person):. 0	
IMO number: 9210218		Cabins (with private balcony):. 232	
Builder: . . . . Chantiers de l'Atlantique (France)		Cabins (wheelchair accessible): 4	
Original cost:. . . . . $150 million		Wheelchair accessibility:. . . . . .Fair	
Entered service:. . . . . .Oct 2000/Oct 2007		Cabin voltage: . . . . .110 and 220 volts	
Registry:. . . . . Malta		Elevators:. 4	
Length (ft/m):. 591.8/180.4		Casino (gaming tables):. . . . . .No	
Beam (ft/m):. 83.3/25.4		Slot machines:. . . . . .No	
Draft (ft/m): 19.0/5.8		Swimming pools:. 1	
Propulsion/Propellers: . . . . diesel (18,600kW)/2		Hot tubs (on deck):. 3	
Passenger decks:. 9		Self-service launderette: . . . . .Yes	
Total crew:. 306		Dedicated cinema/seats:. . . . . .No	
Passengers (lower beds/alll berths):. 716/777		Library: . . . . .Yes	
Passenger Space Ratio (lower beds/all berths): 42.2/38.9		Onboard currency: . . . . .US$	
Crew/Passenger Ratio (lower beds/all berths):. 2.3/2.5			

It reminds you of an elegant country club

OVERVIEW. Like its sister, *Azamara Journey*, this ship has the ambience of an old-world country club. Passengers should be pleased with its tasteful, traditional-style interiors.

THE SHIP. *Azamara Quest* was originally R7, one of a series of eight almost identical ships in the long defunct Renaissance Cruises fleet (when it was in operation, between 1998 and 2001, it was the cruise industry's only totally no-smoking cruise line). It was purchased by Pullmantur in 2006, but transferred in 2007 to Celebrity Cruises' then new small ship brand, Azamara Cruises (renamed Azamara Club Cruises in 2009). Before entering service, the ship underwent an almost $20 million make-over. The hull is deep blue, while the superstructure is white.

An outdoors lido deck has a swimming pool and good sunbathing space, while one of the aft decks has a thalassaotherapy pool. The exterior decks are covered by a rubber and sand-like surface. The uppermost outdoors deck includes a golf driving net and shuffleboard court. The interior decor is elegant, in the style of the ocean liner decor of the 1920s.

Note that a 15 percent gratuity applies to all wines and drinks.

ACCOMMODATION. There are several suite and cabin price grades. The price you pay reflects the size and location of your chosen accommodation. All have so-called butler service (merely better-dressed cabin

Berlitz's Ratings

	Possible	Achieved
Ship	500	408
Accommodation	200	156
Food	400	292
Service	400	320
Entertainment	100	78
Cruise	400	295
OVERALL SCORE		
1549 points out of 2000		

stewards). All of the standard interior and outside-view cabins (the lowest four grades) are extremely compact units. The company calls them staterooms (a real misnomer), but they are simply cabins – and rather tight for two persons, particularly during cruises longer than seven days. The bathrooms are postage-stamp-sized and you'll be fighting with the shower curtain, as well as storage space for toiletries. The standard cabins cannot, in any sense, be considered luxury, and even premium is stretching it a bit. But all suites and cabins receive 'butler' service.

For the extra cost, it's wise to choose a suite or cabin with a balcony. Some cabins have interconnecting doors while 18 cabins on Deck 6 have lifeboat-obstructed views. All grades of accommodation have TV sets that carry European news, a sports channel (where obtainable), and several movie channels.

Standard Interior/Standard Outside-view Cabins. These have twin beds (convertible to a queen-size bed), with good under-bed storage areas, safe, vanity desk with large mirror, and good closet and drawer space.

Ocean-view Cabins. These have two lower beds convertible to queen size (some have an extra sofa bed); flat-screen TV; refrigerator with mini-bar; thermostat-controlled air conditioning; direct-dial telephone and voicemail; desk; in-room safe; hand-held hairdryer. Approximate size: 161 sq ft (15 sq m).

Some cabins have a panorama window with an obstructed view. Those on the lowest deck have just a porthole.

Deluxe Ocean-view Cabins with Balcony. Features: two lower beds convertible to queen-size; floor-to-ceiling sliding glass doors; sitting area with sofa bed; private veranda; flat-screen TV; refrigerator with mini-bar; thermostat-controlled air conditioning; direct-dial telephone and voicemail; desk; in-room safe; hand-held hairdryer. Approximate size: 215 sq ft (20 sq m); balcony 38 sq ft (3.5 sq m).

Sunset Verandah Cabins. Features: two lower beds convertible to queen size; floor-to-ceiling sliding glass doors; sitting area with sofa bed; private veranda; flat-screen television; refrigerator with mini-bar; thermostat-controlled air conditioning; direct-dial telephone and voicemail; desk; in-room safe; hand-held hairdryer. Approximate size: 215 sq ft (20 sq m); balcony 154 sq ft (14 sq m).

Sky Suites. Superior Exterior View Cabins with Balcony: The cabins with private balconies have partial balcony partitions and sliding glass doors. The bathrooms, with tiled floors and plain walls, are compact units and include either a tub/shower or a shower stall with a strong, removable hand-held shower unit, hairdryer, 100 percent cotton towels, toiletries storage shelves and retractable clothesline. Approximate size: 323 sq ft (30 sq m); balcony 57 sq ft (3.3 sq m).

Royal Suites (Decks 6, 7). In reality these are large cabins, as the sleeping and lounge areas are not divided. The bathrooms have a good-size tub and ample space for toiletries. The living area has a refrigerated mini-bar, lounge area with breakfast table, and a balcony with two plastic chairs and a table. Approximate size: 538 sq ft (50 sq m); balcony 173 sq ft (16 sq m).

Penthouse Deluxe Suite with Balcony. Providing the most spacious accommodation, these are fine, large living spaces located in the forward-most and aft-most sections of the accommodation decks (particularly nice are those that overlook the stern, on decks 6, 7, and 8). An entrance foyer leads to a living room, bedroom (the bed faces the sea, which can be seen through the floor-to-ceiling windows and sliding glass door), CD player with selection of audio discs, bathroom with Jacuzzi tub, and a small guest bathroom. They have more extensive private balconies that really are private. Approximate size: 603 sq ft (56 sq m); balcony 215 sq ft (20 sq m).

Suite occupants get priority boarding, tender service, specialty dining venue reservations, and light bites at 4pm, in-suite spa treatments, in-suite portrait sitting, free espressos/cappuccinos, bottled water, and silk-wrapped hangers. All suites/cabins located at the stern can suffer from vibration and noise, particularly when the ship is proceeding at or close to full speed, or maneuvering in port.

DINING. Discoveries, the main dining room, has around 340 seats, a raised central section (conversation at these tables may be difficult, due to its low ceiling height), and open-seating dining. There are large ocean-view windows on three sides, several prime tables overlooking the stern, and a small bandstand for live dinner music. Some tables for two are so close to adjacent tables for four that privacy is non-existent. The menu changes daily for lunch and dinner, and wine is included. Adjacent to the restaurant is a Martini Bar, with a cozy fireplace.

Other dining options. Aqualina Restaurant (service charge $5) is at the aft of the ship on the port side of Deck 10; it has 96 seats, windows along two sides, and serves Mediterranean cuisine. A $70 per person Tasting Menu includes wine.

Prime C (cover charge $25), is located at the aft of the ship on the starboard side of Deck 10, and features premium-quality steaks and grilled seafood items. It has 98 seats, windows along two sides, and a set menu.

The Windows Café has indoor seating for just over 150 (not really enough when cruising in cold areas or in the winter months), and 186 seats outdoors. Many tables do, however, have ocean views. It is open for breakfast, lunch and casual dinners, and incorporates a small Sushi Café.

All dining venues have open-seating dining, although reservations are needed in the Aqualina Restaurant and Prime C, where there are mostly tables for four or six (there are few tables for two). Suite-grade occupants get two nights free, while other accommodation categories get one night free in one of the two specialty dining venues. All cappuccino and espresso coffees cost extra, even in the restaurants.

The Mosaic Café serves Italian coffees, as well as teas and pastries (no extra cost). And a Wine Bar with an extensive cellar has wine-and-food pairings, wine tasting sessions, and wines by the glass or bottle. Additionally, a Poolside Grill provides fast-food items (some items are grilled to order). A self-serve soft ice cream machine is located adjacent to its beverage station. Coffee and tea are free 24 hours a day.

ENTERTAINMENT. Celebrity Cabaret, located forward, is the venue for all main entertainment events. In the evenings, the entertainment consists of a mix of classical concerts, revues, as well as comedy and drama.

SPA/FITNESS. The Astral Spa has a gymnasium with some high-tech muscle toning equipment, an extra-cost thalassotherapy pool (outside, forward on deck), and several treatment rooms. The spa is staffed and operated by Steiner Leisure. An 'Acupuncture at Sea' clinic provides treatments that are operated independently of the spa (but also as a concession). Spa treatments are possible in your suite, too. Outside on the Lido Deck, there are a small swimming pool, two hot tubs, and a jogging track (one deck above the pool).

Azura
★★★★

Size:.	.Large Resort Ship	Cabins (total):.	1,557
Tonnage:	115,055	Size range (sq ft/m):	134.5–534.0/12.5–49.6
Lifestyle:	.Standard	Cabins (outside view):	1,117
Cruise line:	P&O Cruises	Cabins (interior/no view):	440
Former names:	none	Cabins (for one person):	18
IMO number:	9424883	Cabins (with private balcony):	910
Builder:	Fincantieri (Italy)	Cabins (wheelchair accessible):	25
Original cost:	€535 million	Wheelchair accessibility:	Good
Entered service:	.Apr 2010	Cabin voltage:	110 and 220 volts
Registry:	Bermuda	Elevators:	12
Length (ft/m):	951.4/290.0	Casino (gaming tables):	Yes
Beam (ft/m):	118.1/36.0	Slot machines:	Yes
Draft (ft/m):	27.8/8.5	Swimming pools:	3
Propulsion/Propellers:	diesel-electric (42,000kW)/2	Hot tubs (on deck):	6
Passenger decks:	14	Self-service launderette:	Yes
Total crew:	1,239	Dedicated cinema/seats:	No
Passengers (lower beds/alll berths):	3,096/3,574	Library:	Yes
Passenger Space Ratio (lower beds/all berths):	37.2/32.1	Onboard currency:	UK£
Crew/Passenger Ratio (lower beds/all berths):	2.4/2.8		

A large ship with sedate decor to suit British tastes

OVERVIEW. *Azura* is P&O Cruises' most advanced cruise ship. It is best suited to families with children and adult couples who are seeking a big-ship environment with comfortable, unstuffy surroundings, lots of options, and a British flavor.

THE SHIP. *Azura* and sister ship *Ventura*, which debuted in 2008, are the largest cruise ships yet built specifically for British passengers (until a new 141,000-gross ton ship debuts in 2015) and are P&O's version of Princess Cruises' Grand-class ships. With its rather flat, upright stern, *Azura* looks a bit like a giant hatchback, although the ship's side profile is softer and more balanced. Promenade walking decks are to port and starboard sides, underneath the lifeboats. You can't walk completely around; it's narrow in some places, with deck lounge chairs in your way.

There are three main pools: two on the pool deck, one at the stern. Considering the number of passengers carried, there's not a lot of outdoor deck space – unless you pay extra to go into a covered, adults-only zone called The Retreat, with its faux-grass floor, private cabanas, and personal waiter service. What's new is a huge open-air movie screen, the aptly-named SeaScreen, forward of the funnel by the Aqua Pool.

Inside, a three-deck atrium, with integral dance floor, is the focal point for social interaction. It's a bit like a town center at sea. Four large, three-deck-high black granite archways provide 'gateways' to the center. It's the place to see and be seen – as are the specialty dining venues – and a good location to arrange to meet friends.

Berlitz's Ratings

	Possible	Achieved
Ship	500	399
Accommodation	200	155
Food	400	249
Service	400	287
Entertainment	100	77
Cruise	400	304

OVERALL SCORE
1471 points out of 2000

Also in the atrium are a smallish open-plan library that isn't at all intimate or good for reading in, particularly when noisy events are staged in the atrium; the library includes computers for Internet access; and Java Café for extra-cost coffees, teas, cakes, pastries, and snacks.

Other rooms, bars and lounges include the casino, The Exchange, an urban 'warehouse' bar; the Blue Bar, the ship's social hub; Brodies, a 'traditional' British pub (named after Brodie McGhie Wilcox, P&O's co-founder); and the Planet Bar, set high in the ship, featuring a video wall.

The upper-deck public room layout means you can't easily go from one end of the ship to the other without first going down, along, and up. Those with mobility problems will need to plan their journey and use the most appropriate of three elevator banks. Overall, the ship attracts more traditional P&O repeaters and fewer families than sister ship *Ventura*, depending on the itinerary and cruise date.

Gratuities are optional, unless you choose Freedom Dining, when they are automatically applied to your onboard account. Smoking is permitted only on cabin balconies and in designated spots on the open decks.

FAMILIES. *Azura* is really child-friendly. There are clubs for the under-twos up to 17 years, plus a rock 'n' roll school. Children between two and four will find Noddy, the popular Enid Blyton character, on board. There's a Night Nursery for under-fives. Youngsters can also enjoy a dedicated Wii room; Scalextric at sea with Grand Prix-style track; 3-D cinema; and interactive classes. Family shore programs include aqua and 'theme parks.'

ACCOMMODATION. There are 27 price grades, but really just five types of accommodation: suite with balcony; family suite with balcony; outside-view twin/queen with balcony; outside-view twin/queen; interior cabin. Although there are more balconies than aboard *Ventura*, more than a third of all cabins have no outside view. Some have extra third/fourth berths that fold down from the ceiling.

Most welcome are 18 single-occupancy cabins, a first for P&O Cruises. They are located in a small section on the port side. Also new are spa cabins, with added amenities and direct access to the ship's spa, and two large suites for large groups.

While the suites are small when compared to those of lines such as Celebrity Cruises or Norwegian Cruise Line, whose top suites are four or five times the size, they are intelligently laid out, and feel spacious.

Standard in all cabins: bed runners, 10.5 tog duvets, Slumberland eight-inch sprung mattresses, and Egyptian cotton towels. Tea/coffee-making facilities are adequate, with UHT, rather than fresh milk. Bathrobes are available only for passengers occupying grades A, B and D accommodation. There are UK three-pin sockets plus US-style 110-volt sockets for electrical devices.

Open closets provide easy access, but the 'no trust' attached hangars can bang against the wall when the ship is 'moving'. Balcony cabins have wooden railings atop glass dividers, green plastic floors, a couple of small chairs and drinks table, and an outside light. Most cabin bathrooms are small, as are the shower enclosures.

Wheelchair-accessible cabins, which have a large, user-friendly shower enclosure, are mostly located in the front section of the ship, but one of the main restaurants is aft. So be prepared for lots of wheeling time, and waiting time at the elevators.

There is no room service breakfast on disembarkation day, when you must vacate your cabin by 8am.

DINING. P&O's marketing blurb claims that there are 10 restaurants. There aren't. There are five genuine restaurants (Peninsular, Oriental, Meridian, Sindhu, and Seventeen), the rest are bistro-style eateries or fast food joints.

The three main dining rooms, Peninsular, Oriental, and Meridian, all have the same menus. Peninsular and Oriental offer fixed seating dining with assigned tables (typical seating times: 6:30pm or 8:45pm). In the Meridian restaurant, you can dine when you want, with whomever you want, between 6pm and 10pm – P&O calls it 'Freedom Dining,' although at peak times there can be a bit of a wait, and it's not open for breakfast or lunch. Occasionally, special dinners are served in the main dining rooms, one of which is a Chaîne des Rôtisseurs event.

Wheelchair users should note that breakfast in the fixed dining restaurants typically ends at 9:30am on sea days and 9am on port days. To take breakfast in the self-serve casual eatery, you may need to wheel across the decks containing the forward and mid-ship pools and lots of deck chairs – not easy. Alternatively, you can order room service breakfast – typically cold items only.

Other dining options. Sindhu is an Indian restaurant (reservation-only, extra-charge). It is overseen by Michelin-star chef Atul Kochhar, whose specialty is British and Indian fusion cuisine. The food is cooked to order, unlike in the three main dining rooms. Table seating includes several alcove-style areas that make it impossible for waiters to serve food correctly without reaching across others at the same table.

For the Glass House, TV wine expert Olly Smith has helped create a 'Select Dining' restaurant and wine bar. The venue offers seafood and grilled items, paired with wines chosen by Smith. You can, of course, have a glass of wine, without food.

The cuisine is very good in Seventeen, a reservations-only, extra-charge, à la carte restaurant in a quiet setting, with plenty of space around tables for waiters to serve correctly. The venue also features an outdoor terrace for warm-weather areas.

Venezia is the ship's large, casual, self-serve buffet eatery/food court, open almost around the clock, with a large indoor-outdoor seating area. The buffet layout is confined, and can get congested. On the same deck, adjacent to the forward pool, are a poolside grill and pizzeria. Verona is a family-friendly self-service eatery.

In addition, 24-hour room service is available in cabins.

ENTERTAINMENT. The 800-seat Playhouse Theatre, which spans two decks and is located at the front of the ship, is an excellent venue for shows and, with two large video screens on either side of the stage; the sightlines are very good from all seats.

The Manhattan Lounge, a multi-function social/entertainment venue, hosts family shows and cabaret acts, and is a late-night disco. Malabar, another night venue, has decor based on the hotels on Marine Drive, Mumbai. Cabaret, live bands, and dancing are featured here. Meanwhile, the Planet Bar, a nightclub and entertainment venue, is an activities room by day and a club by night.

SPA/FITNESS. The Oasis Spa – located forward, almost atop the ship – has a gymnasium, aerobics room, beauty salon, separate male and female sauna and steam rooms (no charge), and 11 treatment rooms. An internal stairway connects to the deck below, which contains an extra-charge Thermal Suite (£15 per person, per day, or a composite price per cruise). Treatments include special packages for couples, and the SilverSpa Generation.

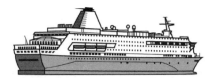

Bahamas Celebration
★★ +

Size:................................Mid-Size Ship	Cabins (total):..515
Tonnage:...35,855	Size range (sq ft/m):..................86–239/7.9–22.2
Lifestyle:...Standard	Cabins (outside view):............................331
Cruise line:..................... Celebration Cruise Line	Cabins (interior/no view):.........................184
Former names: .... Prinsesse Ragnhild	Cabins (for one person):..............................0
IMO number: 7904891	Cabins (with private balcony):........................0
Builder: .... HDW (Germany)	Cabins (wheelchair accessible):.......................0
Original cost:...n/a	Wheelchair accessibility:.........................None
Entered service:..........................1981/Mar 2009	Cabin voltage: .... 220 volts
Registry:... Bahamas	Elevators:..4
Length (ft/m):........................... 673.2/202.2	Casino (gaming tables):............................. Yes
Beam (ft/m):................................ 87.4/26.6	Slot machines:...................................... Yes
Draft (ft/m):................................. 20.0/6.1	Swimming pools:.......................................1
Propulsion/Propellers:..................diesel (36,356kW)/2	Hot tubs (on deck):...................................2
Passenger decks:......................................7	Self-service launderette:............................No
Total crew:..360	Dedicated cinema/seats:.............................No
Passengers (lower beds/alll berths):..............1,030/1875	Library:..No
Passenger Space Ratio (lower beds/all berths): 34.8/19.1	Onboard currency: ....US$
Crew/Passenger Ratio (lower beds/all berths):......... 4.1/5.2	

Good for a short getaway, but lacks any finesse

OVERVIEW. This ship operates cheap and cheerful two- and three-night get-away 'party' cruises from Florida's Port of Palm Beach that masquerade as real cruises. It appeals to adult couples and singles who enjoy gambling, and fellow passengers will typically walk around with a bottle or a glass in their hands.

THE SHIP. This ship, now with a bright blue hull and sponson ducktail stern, was originally constructed as a ferry and operated in Scandinavia by Jahre Line until 1990, and then Color Line until 2008 (some Color Line signage can still be found). In 1992, it was extensively reconstructed and lengthened by the addition of a 116-ft (35-m) section. Celebration Cruise Line – which isn't really a cruise 'line' but a one-ship company – is owned by Celebration Cruise Holdings, once the parent company of the now defunct Imperial Majesty Cruise Line.

The ship underwent a further extensive refit and refurbishment before starting its new life as a short-cruise ship, based in the Port of Palm Beach. The ship also provides a cargo service to the Bahamas (passengers upstairs/cargo downstairs) via two stern ro-ro ramps.

Bahamas Celebration retains its bow and stern loading doors and has an extremely unsightly exterior ducktail (sponson) skirt – the aft part is large enough to hold a small party on. Because it was built as a ferry, it has a rather boxy, slab-sided look, and the open deck space is extremely limited, with plastic chairs everywhere. Consequently, the Passenger Space Ratio is a very poor 23.6 (and that's with two per cabin), while

Berlitz's Ratings		
	Possible	Achieved
Ship	500	266
Accommodation	200	110
Food	400	184
Service	400	206
Entertainment	100	52
Cruise	400	191
OVERALL SCORE		
1009 points out of 2000		

passenger to crew ratio is the worst in the cruise industry, at 4.1.

The pool deck, with port and starboard hot tubs and twin Tiki bars, is pleasant, but there is simply not enough outdoor seating for the aft-positioned self-serve buffet. However, it's good to find shuffleboard courts on deck.

Inside, a glass-walled atrium spans six decks. Public rooms include a rather large casino, cutely named Wynmore, with a double-height ceiling. A small library and card room exist, but there's almost no time to use them on such short party cruises. Many of the chairs in the lounges and bars are of the small, Scandinavian tub chair type – too cramped for many people today and with little back support. There are many support pillars in odd locations throughout the public rooms – a throwback to the ship's days as a ferry.

One neat feature is a cut-away model of the ship, adjacent to elevators on the main deck (Deck 4). Overall, the interiors have the same kind of Scandinavian feel as the Royal Caribbean Cruise Line ships from the early 1970s. You can even see the transport decks of the original design in the model, so you can compare the old with the new. Indeed, throughout the ship, there is evidence of its original life, with signs to the trailer deck, Color Line emblems, and other items remaining as a tribute to the ship's days as *Prinsesse Ragnhild*.

Perhaps the most popular room is the warm, inviting Pub 437, with its rather comfortable leather chairs and Victorian English decor and feel.

FAMILIES. As for cruising with kids, the ship has reasonably decent facilities for its size. It features Island Club Coconuts, a club for ages four to 10, while Club Wave is for 11–14s. A number of counselors keep the children busy, and a waterpark-style aft deck outside has a 180-ft (55-m) waterslide in an area called 'Kids of the Caribbean.'

ACCOMMODATION. There are nine cabin price grades, the price depending on location and size. When the ship was built as a cold-water Baltic ferry, it contained tiny cabins built for truckers doing an overnight sailing. These still exist, and are called Oceanview Couch cabins. Upper berths have a posted weight limit of 200lbs (90kg). Note that all cabins have European-style round-pin electrical sockets, so you may need a converter plug for anything electrical such as phone chargers, adapters, etc.

Most cabins are small, with plain, minimalist decor that is practical. There's room under beds to store luggage, however. Bedside reading lights in most cabins are poor. The bathrooms are of the extremely compact 'you first, me next' variety, with a shower, washbasin, and toilet.

Six 'suites' face forward and have views over the bow (there's no balcony), while four others face aft. These have more space, although there's no separation of sleeping and lounge areas, so they are not real suites – though they have larger bathrooms (with tiny bath), and more storage space.

DINING. There are several dining venues. The Crystal Dining Room is the main dining room, with reserved tables; the restaurant entrance has nicely polished parquet wood flooring. It's a pleasant venue, although the chairs have 'sit-up-and-beg' backs without armrests. Wine is served by the waiters. The cuisine is strictly American family eatery fare, quite bland, and shows little creativity and even less presentation.

Other dining options. For better cuisine and slightly better service, The Cove, located between the Crystal Dining Room and the Wynmore Casino, is an intimate, extra-charge, reservations-only venue open for dinner only, with a $25 per person cover charge. Make your reservations as soon as possible – there are so few tables.

Rio's is a self-serve, all-you-can-eat Brazilian-style buffet venue, open for breakfast, lunch and dinner, and serves meat carved by Brazilian staff moving from table to table. Other items are provided in a self-serve buffet.

The Trattoria Di Gerry is a casual Italian-style eatery, with plain, uninspiring, bland decor, with wooden, school classroom-style chairs that don't have armrests. However, it is lively, extremely popular, and is included in the basic cruise fare, although some items cost extra.

ENTERTAINMENT. The 'View' is the ship's 630-seat showlounge/nightclub and disco. Entertainment is of the ear-splitting, in-your-face variety.

SPA/FITNESS. The Fountain of Youth 'spa' – it's not much of a spa – includes a 'Mussel Beach' fitness room with muscle-pumping equipment.

Watertight passenger ticket contracts

Cruise lines are masters of small print when it comes to contracts. They were drafted by the cruise line's lawyers to protect the cruise lines at the consumer's expense, and so is a one-sided document.

The ticket contract addresses everything from what the cruise line owes you when something goes wrong (not much), when it's responsible for your well-being (hardly ever), to where and when you can sue them (in a faraway court).

A typical cruise line ticket contract states that XYZ Cruises can change arrival or departure times without notice, for any reason whatsoever, including weather. The company shall have no liability for any compensation or other damages in such circumstances. Cruise contracts are filled with clauses and supported by laws that the average passenger is unaware of. There will be a cap on damages you can collect from a cruise line and time limits on any lawsuit. So, read the fine print.

A clause in the ticket typically reads: 'The Carrier's legal responsibility for death, injury, illness, damage, delay, or other loss or detriment of person or property of whatever kind suffered by the Passenger will, in the first instance, be governed by the Athens Convention relating to the Carriage of Passengers and their Luggage by Sea, 1974, with protocols and amendments, together with the further provisions of the International Convention on Limitation of Liability for Maritime Claims, 1976, with revisions and amendments (hereinafter collectively referred to as the "Convention"). The Carrier shall not be liable for any such death, injury, illness, damage, delay, loss, or detriment caused by Act of God, war or warlike operations, civil commotions, labor trouble, interference by Authorities, perils of the sea, or any other cause beyond the control of the Carrier, fire, thefts or any other crime, errors in the navigation or management of the Vessel, or defect in, or un-seaworthiness of hull, machinery, appurtenances, equipment, furnishings, or supplies of the Vessel, fault or neglect of pilot, tugs, agents, independent contractors, such as ship's Physician, Passengers or other persons on board not in the Carrier's employ or for any other cause of whatsoever nature except and unless it is proven that such death, injury, illness, damage, delay, loss resulting from Carrier's act or omission was committed with the intent to cause such loss or with knowledge that such loss would probably result therefrom and in that event the Carrier's liability therefore shall not exceed the specified limitations per Passenger in Special Drawing Rights (SDR) as defined in the applicable conventions or in any further revision and/or amendment thereto as shall become applicable.'

Balmoral
★★★+

Size:................................... Mid-size Ship	Cabins (total):....................................828
Tonnage: 43,537	Size range (sq ft/m): 153.9–613.5/14.3–57.0
Lifestyle:.....................................Standard	Cabins (outside view):...............................737
Cruise line:..................... Fred. Olsen Cruise Lines	Cabins (interior/no view):...........................182
Former names: .... Norwegian Crown, Crown Odyssey	Cabins (for one person):..............................91
IMO number: 5034927	Cabins (with private balcony):.......................121
Builder: .... Meyer Werft (Germany)	Cabins (wheelchair accessible): 9
Original cost:............................... $178 million	Wheelchair accessibility:...........................Good
Entered service:..................... Jun 1988/Jan 2008	Cabin voltage: ....110 and 220 volts
Registry:................................The Bahamas	Elevators:...4
Length (ft/m):............................. 715.2/218.1	Casino (gaming tables):..............................Yes
Beam (ft/m):............................... 92.5/28.2	Slot machines:.......................................No
Draft (ft/m):............................... 23.8/7.26	Swimming pools:......................................2
Propulsion/Propellers: .... diesel (21,330kW)/2	Hot tubs (on deck):..................................4
Passenger decks:....................................10	Self-service launderette:............................Yes
Total crew:...471	Dedicated cinema/seats:..............................No
Passengers (lower beds/alll berths):............. 1,747/1,930	Library:...Yes
Passenger Space Ratio (lower beds/all berths): 24.9	Onboard currency: ....UK£
Crew/Passenger Ratio (lower beds/all berths):......... 3.0/3.0	

A well-designed ship with a homely British ambience

OVERVIEW. *Balmoral* is best suited to British couples and single travelers wanting destination-intensive cruising in a ship that has European quality, style, and character, a sense of space, comfortable surroundings, decent facilities, and realistic pricing, and that provides good value for money.

THE SHIP. *Balmoral*, formerly *Norwegian Crown*, is a well-designed and built ship, originally constructed for the long defunct Royal Cruise Line. Norwegian Cruise Line then operated the ship for many years, before it was transferred to Orient Lines in 2000, and then back to Norwegian Cruise Line in September 2003.

Fred Olsen Cruise Lines bought the ship in 2007 and gave it a major refurbishment, including a 'chop and stretch' operation involving the addition of a 99-ft (30.2-m) midsection. Although the company's logo includes the Norwegian flag, the ship is registered in the Bahamas.

The all-white ship has a relatively handsome, nicely balanced exterior profile, and one of its plus features is its full, walk-around teak promenade deck outdoors, although it becomes a little narrow in the forward section of the vessel. There are many nicely polished wood railings on balconies and open decks, and there is a jogging track on the uppermost deck outdoors. Atop the ship is the Observatory Lounge, with fine ocean views, central dance floor, and bar. Out on deck, there is a heated salt-water pool, but little shade (no glass dome for inclement weather).

Berlitz's Ratings

	Possible	Achieved
Ship	500	369
Accommodation	200	149
Food	400	253
Service	400	264
Entertainment	100	64
Cruise	400	271

OVERALL SCORE
1370 points out of 2000

The main public room spaces are on Lounge Deck. At the front of the ship is the Neptune Lounge, the main showlounge, with an integral bar at the back of the room; the raised stage and wood dance floor are surrounded by amphitheater-style seating in banquettes with small drinks tables. To its aft are the shops – a curved staircase connects this deck with the reception lobby on the deck below.

Next is the Braemar Lounge, alongside a lifestyle area that includes an Internet center with good separation for privacy; there are also a library and a separate card room. Aft of the Braemar Lounge is the Morning Light Pub (named after the very first Fred Olsen ship, *Morning Light*). This venue is more like a lounge than a real pub, although it does have draft beers. Aft is the Palms Café, the ship's casual self-service buffet-style café.

The high lobby has a large gold sculpture in the shape of a globe of the world by the famous sculpture artist Arnaldo Pomodoro (called Microcosm, Macrocosm); it used to revolve.

Balmoral offers a wide range of itineraries, which keeps people coming back to this very comfortable ship; passengers also receive a log of each cruise to take home. Niggles include an inflexible bed layout in some cabins, and the dated decor in some older cabins.

Port taxes are included for UK passengers. Gratuities of £4 ($6) per passenger, per day, are suggested. The drinks prices are very reasonable, but laundry/dry-cleaning prices are quite high. The mostly Filipino/Thai crew are warm and friendly, and should help make your cruise enjoyable.

ACCOMMODATION. There are 21 price categories; typically, the higher the deck, the higher the price. Most cabins are of the same size and layout, have blond wood cabinetry and accents, an abundance of mirrors, and closet and drawer space, and are very well equipped. All accommodation grades have a color TV set, a hairdryer, music console (plus a button that can be used to turn announcements on or off), personal safe, and private bathroom with shower (many upper-grade cabins have a good-size tub).

All towels are 100 percent cotton, and quite large; soap, shampoo, conditioner, body lotion, shower cap, and sewing kit are provided. Duvets (single) are standard, blankets and bed linen are available on request, as are double-bed-size duvets. On-demand movies are £2.95 from the in-cabin Infotainment System.

The cabin soundproofing is generally good. Some cabins have interconnecting doors, so that they can make a two-room suite – good for families with children.

The largest accommodations are the suites on Highland Deck 10. They are quite spacious units, and provide a sleeping area and separate living room, including some nicely finished wood cabinetry and a large amount of closet and drawer space, together with a large, white marble-clad bathroom with a full-size tub and integral shower. There is a large private balcony, although some balconies can be overlooked from the deck above.

There are nine wheelchair-accessible cabins; these provide plenty of space to maneuver, and all include a bathroom with roll-in shower. But wheelchair accessibility in some ports on the many itineraries operated by this ship – particularly in Europe – may prove quite frustrating and wheelchair-accessible transportation may be limited.

Cabins in the new midsection have attractive, contemporary decor that is light and airy. Some of those on the upper decks (Decks 8, 9) have bathrooms with a vertical window with a direct view from the large shower enclosure through the sleeping space to the outside, providing an enhanced feeling of spaciousness. Bathrooms have shower enclosures rather than tub/shower combinations (some have two washbasins), and enough storage space for toiletries.

DINING. The Ballindalloch Restaurant, in the aft third section of the ship, is the main dining room. It has ocean-view windows on port and starboard sides, and operates two seatings. It has comfortable seating at tables for two, four, six, or eight. However, the waiter stations are exposed and can be extremely noisy; indeed, the noise level in this main restaurant is high, so trying to hold a conversation can be frustrating.

Other dining options. The Avon Restaurant and Spey Restaurant, both named after rivers, are located aft on Highland Deck 10 – the deck that contains the higher-priced suites. The floor-to-ceiling windows provide lots of light. The decor is contemporary and minimalist, and the noise level is low, which makes for comfortable conversation. However, these venues also operate two seatings.

The 70-seat Palms Café is an alternative, more intimate venue for informal self-serve buffet meals.

All venues have open seating for breakfast and lunch.

ENTERTAINMENT. The Neptune Lounge is the setting for all entertainment shows, cabaret acts, lectures, and some social functions. It is a single level room with tiered seating levels. Sight lines are generally good, but could be better.

Revue-style production shows are staged by a resident troupe of singers and dancers, and there are cabaret acts. The quality of the shows, however, is average. Cabaret acts – typically singers, magicians, ventriloquists, comedy jugglers, and comedians – perform individually or as part of the revues.

A piece of trivia for ship buffs: a bar at the back of the showlounge was originally named Theo's bar after one of the former Royal Cruise Line's most popular bartenders.

SPA/FITNESS. There is a reasonably decent – but not large enough – indoor wellness center, which includes a fitness room with great forward ocean views, plenty of muscle-pumping equipment, and several body treatment rooms. The wellness facilities and treatment staff are provided by Asian staff.

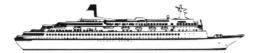

Black Watch
★★★ +

Size:.....................................Mid-size Ship	Cabins (total):.......................................421
Tonnage: 28,613	Size range (sq ft/m): 135.6–819.1/12.6–76.1
Lifestyle:...Standard	Cabins (outside view):................................383
Cruise line:.....................Fred. Olsen Cruise Lines	Cabins (interior/no view):..............................48
Former names: ......Star Odyssey, Westward, Royal Viking Star	Cabins (for one person):...............................38
IMO number: 7108930	Cabins (with private balcony):..........................43
Builder: ....Wartsila (Finland)	Cabins (wheelchair accessible): 4
Original cost: ....$22.5 million	Wheelchair accessibility:.............................Fair
Entered service:.........................Jun 1972/Nov 1996	Cabin voltage: ....110 and 220 volts
Registry:.....................................The Bahamas	Elevators:...4
Length (ft/m):................................674.1/205.4	Casino (gaming tables):...............................Yes
Beam (ft/m):..................................82.6/25.2	Slot machines:.......................................No
Draft (ft/m): 24.7/7.5	Swimming pools:......................................2
Propulsion/Propellers:..................diesel (13,400kW)/2	Hot tubs (on deck):..................................3
Passenger decks:....................................8	Self-service launderette:.............................Yes
Total crew:..350	Dedicated cinema/seats:..........................Yes/156
Passengers (lower beds/alll berths):................804/868	Library: ....Yes
Passenger Space Ratio (lower beds/all berths): 35.5/32.9	Onboard currency: ....UK£
Crew/Passenger Ratio (lower beds/all berths):..........2.2/2.4	

This older ship provides good value for mature-age cruisers

OVERVIEW. *Black Watch* is a comfortable but not luxurious ship best suited to the older traveler who wants a British cruise environment, wearing relatively formal attire. Cruises are well organized, with interesting itineraries and free shuttle buses in many ports of call.

THE SHIP. The name is taken from the famous Scottish Black Watch regiment. There is a good amount of open deck and sunbathing space, and a decent health and fitness area high atop the ship, as well as a wide wrap-around teakwood promenade deck with wind-breaker on the aft part of the deck.

The interior decor is quiet and restful, with wide stairways and foyers, soft lighting and no glitz anywhere, though many passengers find the artwork a little drab. In general, good materials, fabrics (including the use of the Black Watch tartan), and soft furnishings give a pleasant ambience and comfortable feeling to the public rooms. Most of these are quite spacious, with high ceilings, and located on one deck in a user-friendly horizontal layout.

An observation lounge, The Observatory displays nautical memorabilia and has commanding views. Draft beers are available in all bars. The whole ship indoors is a smoke-free zone.

There is a good cinema (few ships today have a dedicated cinema) with a steeply tiered floor.

A popular meeting place is the Braemar Room, a large lounge close to the restaurant; it has a self-help beverage corner for coffees and teas (open 24 hours

Berlitz's Ratings		
	Possible	Achieved
Ship	500	323
Accommodation	200	130
Food	400	241
Service	400	255
Entertainment	100	62
Cruise	400	251
OVERALL SCORE		
1262 points out of 2000		

a day, although it becomes overly busy during afternoon tea time), comfortable chairs, and large ocean-view windows along one side. The Library and Card Room is a very pleasant facility with an adjacent room containing two computer terminals for Internet access. There is a self-serve launderette, useful on the longer cruises, with washing machines, dryers, and irons.

Although it is being well maintained, do remember that this ship is now 40 years old, which means that little problems such as gurgling plumbing, creaking joints, and other idiosyncrasies can occur, and air conditioning may not be all that it should be in some cabins. But the ship still looks good, and is very comfortable. The company suggests gratuities of £4 per passenger per day.

Black Watch offers a moderate standard of service from a friendly, mostly Filipino staff that provides decent, though not faultless, service. There is ample space per passenger, even when the ship is full. Port taxes are included for UK passengers.

The National Express bus operator works in conjunction with Fred Olsen Cruise Lines to provide a dedicated Cruiselink service via London's Victoria Coach Station to the UK departure ports of Dover or Southampton.

Passenger niggles include: noticeable cutbacks in food variety and quality; packets of butter, margarine, and preserves; very poor coffee; long lines at the cramped buffet; poor wine service; and too few staff for the increased passenger numbers following the addition of more cabins.

ACCOMMODATION. There are 18 price categories of cabins (plus one for the owner's suite, whose price is not listed in the brochure). These include four grades of cabin, spread around most of the decks, for solo travelers. The wide range of cabins provides something for everyone, from spacious suites with separate bedrooms, to small, no-view cabins. While most cabins are for two, some can sleep up to five people.

In all grades, duvets are provided, and the decently sized bathroom towels are 100 percent cotton. A hairdryer and a package of Gilchrist & Soames toiletries are supplied to all passengers. Occupants of suite grades also get a cotton bathrobe and cold canapés each evening, plus priority seating in the dining rooms.

The suites and cabins on decks 7, 8, and 9 are quiet units. A number of cabins in the aft section of decks 3, 4, and 5 can be uncomfortable, with noise from throbbing engines and generator units a major distraction, particularly in the cabins adjacent to the engine casing. The room service menu is quite limited and could be improved.

Outside-view and Interior Cabins. Spread across decks 3, 4, 5, 7, and 8, all cabins are quite well equipped, and there is plenty of good (illuminated) closet, drawer, and storage space. Some bathrooms have awkward access, and insulation between some of the lower grade cabins could be better. The bathrooms are of a decent size. Some cabins have a small bathtub; others have only a shower.

Deluxe/Bridge/Junior Suites. These suites, on decks 7 and 8, have a large sleeping area and lounge area with ocean-view picture windows and refrigerator, plenty of hooks for hanging bathrobes, outerwear, and luggage; and a bathroom with tub and shower (cabin 8019 is the exception, with a shower only).

Marquee Suites. These suites have a large sleeping area and lounge area with bigger ocean-view picture windows and a refrigerator, more hooks for hanging bathrobes, outerwear, and luggage; and a bathroom with tub and shower.

Premier Suites. Each of these nine suites is named after a place: Amalfi (9006), Lindos (9002), Nice (9004), each measuring 547.7 sq ft/50.8 sq m; Seville (9001), Singapore (9003), Carmel (9005), Bergen (9007), Waterford (9009), each measuring 341.7 sq ft/31.7 sq m; and Windsor (9008), measuring 574.8 sq ft/53.4 sq m. They have a separate bedroom with ample closet and other storage space, a lounge with large windows (with large television and video player, refrigerator, and mini-bar), and bathroom with full-size tub and shower, and separate toilet.

Owner's Suite. This measures 819.1 sq ft/76.1 sq m, including a large balcony. It consists of a foyer leading into a lounge, with sofa, table and chairs, audio center (TV set, DVD player), refrigerator and mini-bar.

A separate bedroom has a double bed, and ample closet and drawer space. A second bedroom has two bunk beds – good for families with children. The bathroom is large and has a full-size tub, separate shower, toilet, and two washbasins. The balcony has space enough for a table and six chairs, plus a couple of sunloungers. It is located just aft of the navigation bridge on the starboard side of the ship.

DINING. The Glentanar Dining Room has a high ceiling, a white sail-like focal point at its center, and ample space at each table. The chairs have armrests, and are quite comfortable. The Orchid Room is a smaller offshoot of the dining room, which can be reserved for more intimate, quieter dining. While breakfast and lunch are typically in an open-seating arrangement, there are two seatings for dinner. Passengers help themselves from two cold food display counters during breakfast and lunch.

The Garden Café is a small, more casual dining spot with a light, breezy decor. It sometimes has themed dinners, such as French, Indian, or Thai. There is a self-help salad bar and hot food display. This is also the place for late-night snacks.

Fred. Olsen Cruise Lines has above-average cuisine that is attractively presented, with a good range of fish, seafood, meat, and chicken dishes, and has a good selection of cheeses as well as vegetarian options. There is a decent range of wines, at really moderate prices, but few of the stewards have much knowledge of wines. Coffee and tea are always available in the Braemar Room, next to the Glentanar Restaurant.

ENTERTAINMENT. The Neptune Lounge, the ship's showlounge, seats about 400, although some sightlines are obstructed by pillars. The entertainment mainly consists of small-scale production shows presented by a small team of resident singers/dancers, and cabaret acts. Standards are quite poor though, to be fair, passengers who cruise aboard this ship are not especially looking for first-rate entertainment, but rather something to fill the time after dinner. There is plenty of live music in several lounges, and there are good British singalongs.

SPA/FITNESS. The spa/fitness facilities are located at the top and front of the ship – inaccessible for wheelchair users. There is a combined gymnasium/aerobics room, while a door provides access to steam rooms, saunas, and changing rooms. Sample treatment prices: Elemis Aromapure facial: £29; Well-being massage (50 minutes): £35; Personal Training Session (60 minutes): £20. Steiner's staff will try to sell their own-brand Elemis beauty products. Some fitness classes are free, while some, such as yoga and kick-boxing, cost extra. It's prudent to make appointments as early as possible. Sports facilities include a large paddle tennis court, golf practice nets, shuffleboard, and ringtoss.

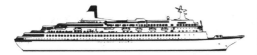

Boudicca
★★★ +

Size:.....................................Mid-size Ship		Passenger Space Ratio (lower beds/all berths): 33.8/31.5
Tonnage: 28,388		Crew/Passenger Ratio (lower beds/all berths):..........2.3/2.5
Lifestyle: ....Standard		Cabins (total):...437
Cruise line:...................... Fred. Olsen Cruise Lines		Size range (sq ft/m): 135.6–579.1/12.6–53.8
Former names: .... Grand Latino, SuperStar Capricorn,		Cabins (outside view):...................................363
Hyundai Keumgang, SuperStar Capricorn,		Cabins (interior/no view):..................................39
Golden Princess, Sunward, Birka Queen, Sunward,		Cabins (for one person):..................................35
Royal Viking Sky		Cabins (with private balcony):.............................64
IMO number: 7218395		Cabins (wheelchair accessible): 4
Builder: ....Wartsila (Finland)		Wheelchair accessibility:..............................Fair
Original cost: .... $22.5 million		Cabin voltage: ....110 and 220 volts
Entered service:......................Jun 1973/Feb 2006		Elevators:...5
Registry:...................................The Bahamas		Casino (gaming tables):.................................Yes
Length (ft/m):..............................674.1/205.47		Slot machines:...Yes
Beam (ft/m):.................................82.6/25.20		Swimming pools:...2
Draft (ft/m):..................................24.7/7.55		Hot tubs (on deck):..2
Propulsion/Propellers:..............diesel (13,400kW)/2 (CP)		Self-service launderette:...............................Yes
Passenger decks:..8		Dedicated cinema/seats:.................................No
Total crew:..320		Library: ....Yes
Passengers (lower beds/alll berths):................839/900		Onboard currency: ....UK£

OVERVIEW. The ship appeals to British couples and single travelers seeking a sense of space, comfortable surroundings, decent facilities, realistic pricing, and good value for money, with British food and entertainment.

THE SHIP. Acquired by Fred. Olsen Cruise Lines in 2005, this well-proportioned ship, originally built for long-distance cruising for the now-defunct Royal Viking Line (it was built for one of the three original shipping partners who formed the line – Bergenske Dampskibsselskab), has a sharply raked bow and a sleek appearance. The ship was 'stretched' in 1982 with the addition of a 91-ft (28-m) midsection.

The outer styling is quite handsome for an early 1970s-built vessel. The single funnel bears the company's starfish logo and balances the profile of this attractive (now contemporary-classic) ship. The name *Boudicca* comes from the Queen of the Iceni tribe that occupied England's East Anglia; she led a dramatic revolt against the Romans in AD61, and her body is supposedly buried under Platform 10 of King's Cross Station in London.

The ship has a good amount of open deck and sunbathing space; in fact, there is plenty of space everywhere and little sense of crowding because the ship absorbs passengers well. There are port and starboard teak walking promenade decks outdoors.

The interior decor is restful, with a mix of English and Norwegian styles (particularly the artwork) with wide

Berlitz's Ratings

	Possible	Achieved
Ship	500	323
Accommodation	200	130
Food	400	241
Service	400	255
Entertainment	100	62
Cruise	400	250

**OVERALL SCORE
1261 points out of 2000**

stairways and foyers, good passenger flow, soft lighting, and no glitz. In general, good materials, fabrics, and soft furnishings add to a pleasant ambience and comfortable feeling experienced throughout the public rooms, most of which are quite spacious and have high, indented ceilings.

There are lots of (small) public rooms, bars, and lounges, unlike the newer (larger) ships built today, including a delightful observation lounge, a small casino, card room, large library, and the Secret Garden Lounge.

Boudicca is an extremely comfortable ship in which to cruise, with a moderate standard of food and service from a friendly, mostly Filipino staff, featuring extremely good value for money cruises in a relaxed environment that provides passengers with many of the comforts of home.

Although the ship has benefited from an extensive refit and refurbishment, do remember that it'll soon be 40 years old, which means that little problems such as gurgling plumbing, creaking joints, and other idiosyncrasies can occur, and air conditioning may not be all that it should be. Port taxes are included for UK passengers. Gratuities of £4 ($6) per passenger, per day, are suggested.

Passenger niggles include: noticeable cutbacks in food variety and quality, an increased use of packets of butter, margarine, and preserves, the lack of choice of sugar, very poor coffee, long lines at the cramped buffet, and too few wine waiters.

For the ship's mainly British passengers, the National Express bus operator works in conjunction with Fred Olsen Cruise Lines to provide a dedicated Cruiselink service via London's Victoria Coach Station to the UK departure ports of Dover or Southampton.

ACCOMMODATION. There is something for every taste and wallet, from spacious family suites to small interior cabins. While most cabins are for two persons, some can accommodate a third, fourth, or even a fifth person. There are 20 price categories of cabins (plus one for the owner's suite, whose price isn't listed in the brochure), including four grades of cabin for those traveling solo (these are spread across most of the cabin decks, and not just the lower decks, as is the case with some cruise lines), and three of these have a private balcony. While most cabins have bathtubs, some lower grades have only a shower enclosure.

Some of the quietest cabins are those located just under the navigation bridge, on Lido Deck, as well as those suites and cabins on Bridge Deck. In the refit, a vacuum toilet system was fitted.

In all grades, duvets are provided, the bathroom towels are 100 percent cotton and are quite large, and a hairdryer is provided. A package of Gilchrist & Soames personal toiletry items (bath gel, shampoo/conditioner, sewing kit, shower cap) is supplied to all passengers. Occupants of suite grades also get a cotton bathrobe and cold canapés each evening, as well as priority seating in the dining rooms.

The room service menu is quite limited and could be improved, although there is an abundance of food available at most times of the day. All cabins have had a facelift. Only a few suites have private balconies.

Outside-view/Inside Cabins. These are quite well equipped, and there is plenty of good (illuminated) closet, drawer and storage space, but insulation between some of the lower grade cabins could be better. While most cabin bathrooms are of a decent size, some have awkward access. Some have a small tub, although many have only a shower enclosure.

Deluxe/Bridge/Junior Suites. These suites, on decks 7 and 8, have a large sleeping area and lounge area with ocean-view picture windows and refrigerator, plenty of hooks for hanging bathrobes, outerwear, and luggage; and a bathroom with bathtub and shower.

Marquee Suites. These suites have a large sleeping area and lounge area with bigger ocean view picture windows and a refrigerator, more hooks for hanging bathrobes, outerwear, and luggage; and a bathroom with tub and shower.

Premier Suites. Anyone wanting the most space should consider one of these suites (each is named after a place). These have a separate bedroom with ample closet and other storage space, a lounge with large windows (with large television/video player, refrigerator/ mini-bar), and bathroom with full-size tub and shower, and a separate toilet.

DINING. The main dining room is divided into three venues: Heligan, Tintagel, and Four Seasons; each has a high ceiling, and ample space at each table. Although the decor is reserved, the chairs, which have armrests, are comfortable. Window-side tables for two are the most sought after, naturally.

Breakfast is typically in an open-seating arrangement, while there are two seatings for lunch and dinner. Cold food display counters are provided for passengers to help themselves to breakfast and lunch items.

Fred Olsen Cruise Lines has above-average cuisine that is attractively presented and includes a good range of fish, seafood, meat, and chicken dishes, as well as vegetarian options, and a wide selection of cheeses to suit most British tastes. You'll also find a number of popular British pub standards such as bangers and mash, toad in the hole, and spotted dick. Breakfast buffets tend to be a little repetitious, although they appear to satisfy most passengers. There is a reasonably decent range of wines, at unpretentious prices.

Coffee and tea are available in the Secret Garden Café (part of the Secret Garden Lounge), just aft of the main dining venues – but, sadly, not around-the-clock.

Casual self-serve deck buffets are provided outdoors at the Poolside Café, while fast-food items can be obtained from the Marquee Bar (also outdoors).

ENTERTAINMENT. The Neptune Lounge is the venue for shows, cabaret acts, and lectures. It is a large room that seats about 400, although some pillars obstruct sight lines from some seats. The entertainment consists of small-scale production shows presented by a small team of resident singers/dancers, and cabaret acts (these typically rotate around many cruise ships of the same standard).

There is plenty of live music for social dancing (many of the musicians are Filipino) and listening in several lounges, and good British singalongs are a feature on each cruise.

SPA/FITNESS. A decent amount of (windowless) space is given to providing health and fitness facilities on Atlantic Deck. However, they are split in three separate areas. Forward are the sauna/steam rooms; the center section contains a gymnasium/aerobics room and changing rooms; while the aft section houses a beauty salon.

Some fitness classes are free, while some, such as yoga and kick-boxing, cost extra.

It's best to make appointments as early as possible as treatment time slots go quickly. Sports facilities include a large paddle tennis court, golf practice nets, shuffleboard, and ringtoss.

Braemar
★★★ +

Size:. . . . . Mid-size Ship	Crew/Passenger Ratio (lower beds/all berths):. 2.3/2.3
Tonnage: 24,344	Cabins (total):. 484
Lifestyle: . . . . .Standard	Size range (sq ft/m): 139.9–349.8/13.0–32.5
Cruise line:. . . . . Fred. Olsen Cruise Lines	Cabins (outside view): 373
Former names: . . . . . Crown Dynasty, Norwegian Dynasty, Crown	Cabins (interior/no view):. 110
Majesty, Cunard Dynasty	Cabins (for one person):. 38
IMO number: 9000699	Cabins (with private balcony):. 79
Builder: . . . . Union Navale de Levante (Spain)	Cabins (wheelchair accessible): 4
Original cost:. . . . . $100 million	Wheelchair accessibility:. . . . . .Fair
Entered service:. . . . . .Jul 1993/Aug 2001	Cabin voltage: . . . . .110 and 220 volts
Registry:. . . . . The Bahamas	Elevators:. 5
Length (ft/m):. 639.7/195.0	Casino (gaming tables):. . . . . .Yes
Beam (ft/m):. 73.8/22.5	Slot machines:. . . . . .No
Draft (ft/m): 17.7/5.4	Swimming pools:. 2
Propulsion/Propellers:. . . . . diesel (13,200kW)/2	Hot tubs (on deck):. 2
Passenger decks:. 7	Self-service launderette:. . . . . .Yes
Total crew:. 371	Dedicated cinema/seats:. . . . . .No
Passengers (lower beds/alll berths):. 930/930	Library: . . . . .Yes
Passenger Space Ratio (lower beds/all berths): 25.9/25.9	Onboard currency: . . . . .UK£

A smart ship with decor suited to casual cruisers

OVERVIEW. This handsome-looking mid-size ship suits middle-aged and older UK and Scandinavian passengers who want to cruise in a casual, unstuffy environment, in a ship with British food and entertainment. It's a refreshing change for those who don't enjoy larger, warehouse-size ships. But it does roll somewhat, probably because of its shallow draft design, meant for warm-weather cruise areas.

THE SHIP. *Braemar* has attractive exterior styling, and a lot of glass space. There is a good amount of open deck and sunbathing space for its size, and this includes two outdoor bars – one aft and one midships adjacent to the two swimming pools and paddling pool – that have Boddington's and Stella Artois keg beers. Four open decks, located aft of the funnel, provide good, quiet places to sit and read.

The teak promenade deck is a complete walk-around deck, wrapping around Lounge Deck. Passengers can go right to the ship's bow – good for photographs. Faux teak floor covering is used on the pool deck, which has two pools; it looks tacky, but works well in the heat of the Caribbean, where the ship was meant to spend much of its time.

Inside, there is a pleasant five-deck-high, glass-walled atrium on the starboard side. Off-center stairways add a sense of spaciousness to a clever interior design that surrounds passengers with light. The interior decor in public spaces is warm and inviting, with contemporary, but not brash, art-deco color combinations. The artwork is quite colorful and pleasant, in the Nordic manner.

Berlitz's Ratings

	Possible	Achieved
Ship	500	323
Accommodation	200	128
Food	400	230
Service	400	252
Entertainment	100	61
Cruise	400	262

**OVERALL SCORE
1256 points out of 2000**

The Morning Light Club is an open-plan lounge, with its own bar, split by a walkway that leads to the showlounge (forward), the library/card room/Internet center, and the boutique (midships). Despite being open, it has cozy seating areas and is very comfortable, with a tartan carpet. A model of the first Fred Olsen ship named Braemar (4,775 gross tonnage) is displayed in the center of the room, as is a large carved wood plaque bearing the name Braemar Castle in Scotland.

The mostly Filipino staff are friendly and attentive, and the hospitality factor is good. This is noticeable in the restaurant and other food service areas. The company has come a long way from its humble beginnings, and now offers extremely good value for money cruises in a relaxed, welcoming environment that provides passengers with many of the comforts of home. The dress code is casual.

In 2008, a 102-ft (31-m) midsection extension was added, providing additional cabins and balcony 'suites.' Facilities added or changed include a second swimming pool and more sunbathing space, an observatory lounge, a new restaurant, and a pub-style bar.

There can be a bit of a wait for shore tenders and for the few elevators aboard this ship. British passengers should note that no suites or cabins have bathtubs.

Passenger niggles include: lines at the cramped self-service buffet; poor wine service (not enough wine waiters); an increase in the use of packets of butter, margarine, and preserves; the lack of choice of sugar;

weak coffee; and badly worn bathroom fittings. There is a self-service launderette (£2 for wash and dry) – and the company may charge for shuttle buses in some ports of call.

ACCOMMODATION. There are 16 cabin-price categories; the higher the deck, the higher the price. All grades have a small television and hairdryer (some are awkward to retract from their wall-mount holders), plus European-style duvets. The large bathroom towels are 100 percent cotton (bathrobes are available upon request in suite-grade cabins). Gilchrist & Soames toiletry items are provided. There is no separate audio system in the cabin, but music can be obtained from one of the TV channels, although you'll have to leave the picture on. Suites, however, do have a CD music system.

Standard (Outside-view)/Inside Cabins. Almost all are the same size – which is really quite small – although they are nicely furnished. Most have broad picture windows, but some deluxe cabins on decks 6 and 7 have lifeboat-obstructed views. They are practical and comfortable, with blond wood-trimmed accents and multi-colored soft furnishings, but there is very little drawer space, and hanging space is extremely limited (the ship was purpose-built originally for seven-day cruises). So take only the clothing you think necessary. Each outside-view cabin on Deck 4 has a large picture window, while those on the lower decks 2 and 3 have a porthole. They are quite well-equipped, with a small vanity desk unit, minimal drawer space, curtained windows, and personal safe (hard to reach).

Each cabin has a private bathroom (of the 'me first, you next' variety) with a tiled floor, small shower enclosure, toiletries cupboard, washbasin, and low-height toilet of the barking dog vacuum variety. There is some under-basin storage space, and an electrical socket for shavers.

When Fred Olsen Cruise Lines bought the ship, it converted a number of cabins from double-occupancy units to cabins for the single traveler.

Some cabins do suffer from inadequate soundproofing; passengers in cabins on Deck 4 in particular are disturbed by anyone running or jogging on the promenade deck above. Cabins on the lowest deck (Deck 2) in the ship's center are subject to noise from the adjacent engine room.

Suites. On Deck 7, suites have city names such as Rio de Janeiro and Toronto. While they are not large, the suites do have a sleeping area that can be curtained off from the living area. All suites are decorated in individual styles befitting their name, and each has its own small CD player/music system.

DINING. The Thistle Restaurant is a pleasing and attractive venue, with large ocean-view windows on three sides. The focal point is a large oil painting on a wall behind the buffet food display counter. However,

space is tight, and tables are extremely close together, making proper service difficult. There are tables for two, four, six, or eight; the Porsgrund china has the familiar Venus pattern. The ambience, however, is warm, and service is attentive.

There are two seatings for dinner, and an open seating for breakfast and lunch. The menu is varied. Salad items are quite poor and very basic, with little variety, although there is a decent choice of dessert items. For breakfast and lunch the dual food counters are functional, but the layout is not ideal and at peak times they create much congestion. The Grampian Restaurant is an additional dining venue, located aft at the top of the ship, with some fine aft views.

Other dining options. Casual breakfasts and luncheons can also be taken in the self-service buffet located in the Palms Café, although these tend to be repetitive and poorly supervised, with dishes not replaced or refreshed properly. There is indoor and outdoor seating. Although it is the casual dining spot, tablecloths are provided. The indoor flooring is wood, which makes it rather a noisy room, and some tables adjacent to the galley entrance are to be avoided at all costs.

Out on the pool deck, there is a barbecue grill for casual eating – welcome when the ship is in warm-weather areas.

ENTERTAINMENT. The Neptune Showlounge sits longitudinally along one side of the ship, with amphitheater-style seating in several tiers, but its layout is less than ideal for either shows or cocktail parties. There is often congestion between first- and second-seating passengers at the entrance.

Unfortunately, 15 pillars obstruct sight lines to the stage, and the banquet and individual tub chair seating arrangement is quite poor.

The entertainment mainly consists of small-scale production shows and mini-musicals presented by a small troupe of resident singers/dancers, and cabaret acts. They are rather amateurish, but enjoyable. Apart from the production shows, there are the typical cabaret acts often found on the cruise ship circuit.

SPA/FITNESS. The health spa facilities are limited. It includes a combined gymnasium/aerobics room, and a separate room for women and men, with sauna, steam room, and small changing area. Spa Rituals treatments are provided by Steiner. Some fitness classes are free; others, such as yoga and kick-boxing, cost extra.

Bremen
★★★★ +

Size:. . . . . .Boutique Ship			
Tonnage:. 6,752			
Lifestyle:. . . . . .Premium			
Cruise line:. . . . . Hapag-Lloyd Expedition Cruises			
Former names:. . . . . Frontier Spirit			
IMO number:. 8907424			
Builder:. . . . . Mitsubishi Heavy Industries (Japan)			
Original cost:. . . . .$42 million			
Entered service:. . . . . Nov 1990/Nov 1993			
Registry:. . . . . .The Bahamas			
Length (ft/m):. 365.8/111.5			
Beam (ft/m):. 55.7/17.0			
Draft (ft/m):. 15.7/4.8			
Propulsion/Propellers:. . . . . .diesel (4,855kW)/2			
Passenger decks:. 6			
Total crew:. 94			
Passengers (lower beds/alll berths):. 164/184			
Passenger Space Ratio (lower beds/all berths):. 41.1/36.6			
Crew/Passenger Ratio (lower beds/all berths):. 1.7/1.9			

Cabins (total):. 82	
Size range (sq ft/m):. 174.3–322.9/16.2–30.0	
Cabins (outside view):. 82	
Cabins (interior/no view):. 0	
Cabins (for one person):. 0	
Cabins (with private balcony):. 18	
Cabins (wheelchair accessible):. 2	
Wheelchair accessibility:. . . . . .None	
Cabin voltage:. . . . . .110 and 220 volts	
Elevators:. 2	
Casino (gaming tables):. . . . . .No	
Slot machines:. . . . . .No	
Swimming pools:. 1	
Hot tubs (on deck):. 0	
Self-service launderette:. . . . . .No	
Dedicated cinema/seats:. Yes/164	
Library:. . . . . Yes	
Onboard currency:. . . . . Euros	

A fine, strong expedition ship for in-depth discovery

OVERVIEW. This ship will suit anyone who enjoys the natural world, and traveling in remote, unspoiled areas. Venturing on the wild side of cruising, *Bremen* has some superb destination-intensive itineraries, with a good degree of comfort and useful documentation, including port information and maps. It's a charming, very friendly ship with a homely, welcoming ambience that's hard to beat.

Berlitz's Ratings		
	Possible	Achieved
Ship	500	365
Accommodation	200	155
Food	400	312
Service	400	320
Entertainment	100	81
Cruise	400	322
OVERALL SCORE		
1555 points out of 2000		

THE SHIP. This purpose-built all-white expedition cruise vessel, equipped with 12 Zodiacs and a helicopter pad, has a handsome, wide, squat, contemporary profile and good equipment. Its wide beam provides good stability and the vessel's long cruising range and ice-hardened hull allows it access to remote destinations. The ship carries the highest ice classification for passenger vessels.

Sutainable tourism is the norm. Zero-discharge of waste matter is fiercely practiced; this means that absolutely nothing is discharged into the ocean that does not meet with the international conventions on ocean pollution (MARPOL). Equipment for in-depth marine and shore excursions is provided, including a boot-washing station with three water hoses and boot cleaning brushes.

There is almost a walk-around deck – you have to go up and down steps at the front of the deck to complete the 'walk.' A large open deck aft of the mast provides a good viewing platform that's also useful for sunbathing on warm-weather cruises.

The ship has a good number of public rooms for its size, including a forward-facing observation lounge/ lecture room, and a main lounge (the Club) with a high ceiling, bandstand, dance floor and large bar, and an adjacent library with 12 bookcases (most books are in German).

Bremen is a practical expedition cruise vessel, nicely refurbished in 2009 when flat-screen TV sets were placed in all cabins, and the number of Internet-connect computers was increased to four. Arguably, it is a better expedition vessel than *Hanseatic*, and, although not quite as luxurious in its interiors and appointments, the ship has a loyal following. Its cruises will provide you with a fine learning and expedition experience, particularly its Antarctic cruises. All shore landings and tours are included, as is seasickness medication. There's a fine array of expert lecturers, and a friendly crew. The ship has two microscopes, and a plankton-collection net for in-depth studies.

The onboard ambience is completely casual, comfortable, unstuffy (no dressy clothes needed), and very accommodating. Passengers appreciate the fact that there is no music in hallways or on open decks. The reception desk is open 24 hours a day, and there's an 'invitation to the bridge' policy.

Arctic/Antarctic Cruises. Parkas (waterproof outdoor jackets) and tough 'snow-grip' boots are supplied, but you should take strong waterproof trousers and thick socks, plus thermal underwear. Each of the fleet of 12 Zodiacs (rubber-inflatable landing craft) is named after a place or region: Amazon, Antarctic, Asmat, Bora Bora, Cape Horn, Deception, Jan Mayen,

Luzon, Pitcairn, San Blas, Spitzbergen, and Ushuaia. On Arctic and Antarctic cruises, it is particularly pleasing to go to the bridge wings late at night to stargaze under pollution-free skies – the watch officers will be pleased to explain star formations.

Special sailings may be under the auspices of various tour operators, although the ship is operated by Hapag-Lloyd Expedition Cruises. Thus, your fellow expedition voyagers may well be from many different countries. Insurance, port taxes, and all staff gratuities are typically included in the cruise fare, and a logbook is provided at the end of each expedition cruise for all participants – a reminder of what's been seen and done during the course of the adventure.

There's no 'bulbous bow' and so the ship can pitch in some sea conditions; but it does have stabilizers. The swimming pool is small, as is the open deck space around it, although there are both shaded and open areas. In-cabin announcements cannot be turned off (on cruises in the Arctic and Antarctic regions, announcements are often made at or before 7am on days when shore landings are permitted). Sadly, the ship was not built with good cabin soundproofing.

Hapag-Lloyd publishes its own excellent handbooks, in both English and German, on expedition regions such as the Arctic, Antarctica, Amazonia, and the South Sea Islands, as well as exclusive maps.

ACCOMMODATION. There are just four different configurations. All cabins have an outside view – those on the lowest deck have portholes, and the others have good-size picture windows. All are well-equipped for the size of the vessel. Each has wood accenting, a color TV and DVD player, telephone, refrigerator (soft drinks are provided free and replenished daily), vanity desk with 220-volt European-style electrical sockets, sitting area with small drinks table, and wireless access.

Cabins have either twin beds (convertible to a queen-size bed, but with individual European cotton duvets) or double bed, according to location, plus bedside reading lights and alarm clock. There is a small indented area for outerwear and rubber boots, while a small drawer above the refrigerator unit provides warmth when needed for such things as wet socks and gloves.

Each cabin has a private bathroom (totally replaced in 2010) with a tiled floor, shower enclosure with curtain, toiletries shelf, washbasin and low-height toilet (vacuum type), a decent amount of under-basin storage space, and an electrical socket for shavers. Large towels and 100 percent cotton bathrobes are provided, as is a range of Crabtree & Evelyn toiletries (shampoo, body lotion, shower gel, soap, and shower cap).

Each cabin has a moderate amount of illuminated closet space (large enough for two weeks for two persons, but tight for longer cruises), although the drawer space is limited – suitcases can be stored under the beds. Some Sun Deck and Bridge Deck cabins also have a small balcony (*Bremen* was the first expedition cruise vessel to have these) with blue plastic, easily cleanable decking and wooden handrail, but no exterior light. The balconies have two teak chairs and a small drinks table, but are small and narrow, with partial partitions and doors that open outwards onto the balcony, taking up space.

Two Sun Deck suites have a separate lounge area with sofa and coffee table, bedroom with wall clock, large walk-in closet, and marble bathroom with tub and basin.

DINING. The dining room has open seating when operating for mixed German and international passenger cruises, and open seating for breakfast and lunch, with one seating for dinner (assigned seats) when operated solely as a German-speaking cruise. It is fairly attractive, with pleasing decor and pastel colors; it has big picture windows and 12 pillars placed in inconvenient positions – the result of old shipbuilding techniques.

The food, made with high-quality ingredients, is extremely good. Although the portions are small, the presentation is appealing to the eye – and you can always ask for more. There is an excellent choice of freshly made breads and pastries, and a good selection of cheeses and fruits.

Dinner typically includes a choice of two appetizers, two soups, an in-between course, two entrées, and two or three desserts, plus a cheese board (note that Europeans typically have cheese before dessert). There is always a vegetarian specialty, as well as a healthy eating option. The service is good, with smartly dressed, bilingual (German- and English-speaking) waiters and waitresses.

As an alternative to the dining room, breakfast and luncheon buffets are available in The Club, or outside on the Lido Deck (weather permitting), where the Starboard Bar/Grill provides grilled food.

ENTERTAINMENT. The Club is the main lounge, used as a gathering place after meals and before expedition landings ashore. There is no formal entertainment as such. At the end of each cruise, the ship's chart is auctioned off one evening to the highest bidder, with profits donated to charity.

SPA/FITNESS. There is a small fitness room, a large sauna, and beauty salon with integral massage table. Out on the open deck is a small swimming pool, which is heated when the ship is sailing in cold-weather regions such as the Arctic or Antarctica.

Brilliance of the Seas
★★★+

Size:.................................Large Resort Ship	Cabins (total):.................................... 1,056
Tonnage: 90,090	Size range (sq ft/m): 165.8–1,216.3/15.4–113.0
Lifestyle: ....Standard	Cabins (outside view):...............................818
Cruise line:.................. Royal Caribbean International	Cabins (interior/no view):..........................238
Former names: ....none	Cabins (for one person):..............................0
IMO number: 9195200	Cabins (with private balcony):.......................577
Builder: .... Meyer Werft (Germany)	Cabins (wheelchair accessible): 24
Original cost: .... $350 million	Wheelchair accessibility:...........................Good
Entered service:.................................Jul 2002	Cabin voltage: ....110 and 220 volts
Registry:.....................................The Bahamas	Elevators:..9
Length (ft/m):............................... 961.9/293.2	Casino (gaming tables):............................. Yes
Beam (ft/m):............................... 105.6/32.2	Slot machines:..................................... Yes
Draft (ft/m):...................................27.8/8.5	Swimming pools:.....................................3
Propulsion/Propellers:.......... gas turbine/2 azimuthing pods	Hot tubs (on deck):....................................
Passenger decks:.....................................12	Self-service launderette:...........................No
Total crew:..869	Dedicated cinema/seats:....................... Yes/40
Passengers (lower beds/alll berths):............. 2,112/2,500	Library: .... Yes
Passenger Space Ratio (lower beds/all berths): 42.6/36.0	Onboard currency: ....US$
Crew/Passenger Ratio (lower beds/all berths):.......... 2.5/2.8	

Contemporary decor and style for the young at heart

OVERVIEW. This ship was constructed for longer itineraries, with more space and comfortable public areas, larger cabins and more dining options. For the more sporting, youthful passengers, there is activity galore – including a 30-ft (9-m) rock-climbing wall with five separate climbing tracks.

THE SHIP. *Brilliance of the Seas* is a streamlined contemporary ship, built in 66 blocks, and has a two-deck-high wrap-around structure in the forward section of the funnel. Along the port side, a central glass wall protrudes, giving great views (cabins with balconies occupy the space directly opposite on the starboard side). The gently rounded stern has nicely tiered decks, which gives the ship an extremely well-balanced look. As is common aboard all Royal Caribbean International ships, the navigation bridge is of the fully enclosed type – good for cold-weather areas. One of two swimming pools can be covered by a large glass dome for use as an all-weather indoor/outdoor pool.

The interior decor is contemporary, yet elegant and cheerful, designed for active, young and trendy types. The artwork is abundant and truly eclectic. A nine-deck high atrium lobby has glass-walled elevators (on the port side) that travel through 12 decks, face the sea, and provide a link with nature and the ocean. The Centrum (as the atrium is called) has several public rooms connected to it: the guest relations and shore excursions desks, an atrium bar, Champagne Bar, a

Berlitz's Ratings		
	Possible	Achieved
Ship	500	381
Accommodation	200	143
Food	400	242
Service	400	279
Entertainment	100	73
Cruise	400	270
OVERALL SCORE		
1388 points out of 2000		

Library, Royal Caribbean Online, the Concierge Club, and a Crown & Anchor Lounge. A great view can be had of the atrium by looking down through the flat glass dome high above it.

There's also a large Schooner Bar, which houses maritime art in an integral art gallery, not to mention Casino Royale. There's a small, deeply tiered, movie screening room (with space for two wheelchairs), as well as a 194-seat conference center, a business center, and several conference rooms.

A Viking Crown Lounge is set around the ship's funnel. This functions as an observation lounge during the day; in the evening, the space hosts Starquest, a futuristic, high-energy dance club, and Hollywood Odyssey, a more intimate and relaxed entertainment venue for softer mood music and 'black-box' theater. A computer business center has 12 PCs with high-speed Internet access. Gratuities are automatically charged to your onboard account.

FAMILIES. Youth facilities include Adventure Ocean, an 'edutainment' area with four separate age-appropriate sections for junior passengers: Aquanaut Center (for ages three to five); Explorer Center (six to eight); Voyager Center (nine to 12); and the Optix Teen Center (13–17). Adventure Beach includes a splash pool with waterslide. Surfside has computer stations with entertaining software. Ocean Arcade is a video games hangout.

The largest family-friendly cabins consist of a suite

with two bedrooms. One bedroom has twin beds (convertible to queen-size bed), while a second has two lower beds and two upper Pullman berths, a combination that can sleep up to eight persons – good for large families.

ACCOMMODATION. A wide range of suites and standard outside-view and interior cabins comes in 10 categories and 19 price groups. Apart from the six largest suites (called owner's suites), which have king-size beds, almost all other cabins have twin beds that convert to a queen-size bed. There are 14 wheelchair-accessible cabins, 8 of which have a private balcony.

All cabins have rich (faux) wood cabinetry, including a vanity desk (with hairdryer), faux wood drawers that close silently (hooray), television, personal safe, and three-sided mirrors. Some cabins have ceiling recessed, pull-down berths for third and fourth persons, although closet and drawer space would be extremely tight for four persons (even if two are children), and some have interconnecting doors. Audio channels are available through the TV set, so if you want to go to sleep with soft music playing you'll need to put a towel over the television screen.

Most bathrooms have tiled accenting and a terrazzo-style tiled floor, and a rather small half-moon shower enclosure, 100 percent Egyptian cotton towels, a small cabinet for toiletries and a shelf.

Occupants of cabins designated as suites get the use of a private Concierge Lounge where priority dining room reservations, shore excursion bookings, and beauty salon/spa appointments can be made.

Many 'private' balcony cabins are not very private, as they can be overlooked from the port and starboard wings of the Solarium, and from other locations.

DINING. Minstrel, the main dining room, spans two decks (the upper deck level has floor-to-ceiling windows, while the lower deck level has windows). It seats 1,104, and has Middle Ages music as its themed decor. There are tables for two, four, six, eight, or 10 in two seatings for dinner. Two small private dining rooms (Zephyr, with 94 seats, and Lute, with 30 seats) are located off the main dining room.

Choose one of two seatings, or 'My Time Dining' (eat when you want during dining room hours) when you book. Minstrel is closed for lunch on most days, which leaves passengers scrambling for food and seating in the Windjammer Café – an awful prospect after passengers return from morning excursions.

The cuisine in the main dining room is typical of mass banquet catering that offers standard fare comparable to that found in American family-style restaurants ashore – mostly disappointing and without much taste. However, a decent selection of light meals is provided, and a vegetarian menu is available. Caviar, once a standard menu item, incurs a hefty extra charge.

Other dining options. There are two specialty alternative dining spots: Portofino, with 112 seats, has Italian-American cuisine (choices include antipasti, soup, salad, pasta, main dish, dessert, cheese, and coffee); and Chops Grille Steakhouse, with 95 seats and an open kitchen, has premium veal chops and steaks (New York Striploin Steak, Filet Mignon, Prime Rib of Beef). Both venues have food that is of a much higher quality than in the main dining room. There is an additional per-person cover charge for both, and reservations are required. Newly added in 2013 are Giovanni's Table (an Italian trattoria), Izumi (for Asian cuisine), Rita's Cantina, a Chef's Table, and a Park Cafe (deli-style).

Also, casual meals can be taken (for breakfast, lunch, and dinner) in the self-serve, buffet-style Windjammer Café, which can be accessed directly from the pool deck. It has a peculiar layout, and has several islands – so you may have to hunt for the items you like. It is impossible to get a hot plate for hot food because the plates are plastic, so things go cold quickly. The selection of cold cuts of meat is poor, cheeses have absolutely no taste, and salad items almost always look unappetizing.

Additionally, the Seaview Café is open for lunch and dinner. Choose from the self-serve buffet, or from the menu for fast-food seafood items, hamburgers, and hot dogs. The decor, naturally, is marine-, and ocean-related.

ENTERTAINMENT. The Pacifica Theatre, the main showlounge, is three decks high, has 874 seats, including 24 stations for wheelchairs, and good sight lines from most seats.

The entertainment aboard all Royal Caribbean International ships is always lively and upbeat. There is even background music in all corridors and elevators, and constant music outdoors on the pool deck. If you want a quiet, relaxing holiday, choose another ship.

SPA/FITNESS. The ShipShape Spa's health, fitness, and spa facilities have themed decor, and include a 10,176-sq-ft (945-sq-m) solarium with whirlpool and counter current swimming under a retractable glass roof, a gymnasium with 44 cardiovascular machines, a 50-person aerobics room, sauna and steam rooms, and therapy treatment rooms. All of these located are on two of the uppermost decks.

Sports facilities include a 30-ft (9-m) rock-climbing wall, golf course, exterior jogging track, basketball court, nine-hole miniature golf course with novel decorative ornaments, and an indoor/outdoor country club with golf simulator. There is also an exterior jogging track.

Caledonian Sky
★★★★ +

Size:	Boutique Ship	Crew/Passenger Ratio (lower beds/all berths):	1.5/1.7
Tonnage:	4,200	Cabins (total):	57
Lifestyle:	Premium	Size range (sq ft/m):	215.0–365.9/20.0–34.0
Cruise line:	Noble Caledonia	Cabins (outside view):	57
Former names:	Hebridean Spirit, Sun Viva II, MegaStar Capricorn, Renaissance VI	Cabins (interior/no view):	0
		Cabins (for one person):	0
IMO number:	8802870	Cabins (with private balcony):	8
Builder:	Nuovi Cantieri Apuania (Italy)	Cabins (wheelchair accessible):	0
Original cost:	$25 million	Wheelchair accessibility:	none
Entered service:	Mar 1991/Jul 2012	Cabin voltage:	110 and 220 volts
Registry:	Great Britain	Elevators:	1
Length (ft/m):	297.2/90.6	Casino (gaming tables):	No
Beam (ft/m):	50.1/15.3	Slot machines:	No
Draft (ft/m):	13.7/4.2	Swimming pools:	1
Propulsion/Propellers:	diesel (5,000kW)/2	Hot tubs (on deck):	0
Passenger decks:	5	Self-service launderette:	No
Total crew:	74	Dedicated cinema/seats:	No
Passengers (lower beds/alll berths):	114/114	Library:	Yes
Passenger Space Ratio (lower beds/all berths):	36.8/36.8	Onboard currency:	UK£

Delightful country inn afloat for educated, seasoned travelers

OVERVIEW. The delightful pocket-sized *Caledonian Sky* is best suited to couples and singles that enjoy learning about the natural sciences, geography, history, gardening, art, architecture, and want to be aboard a very small ship with little or no entertainment. This is ideal for those who abhor big ship cruising, and the crew is extremely personable.

Berlitz's Ratings		
	Possible	Achieved
Ship	500	402
Accommodation	200	163
Food	400	318
Service	400	313
Entertainment	100	70
Cruise	400	325
OVERALL SCORE		
1591 points out of 2000		

THE SHIP. This ship has a neat, modern look, coupled with a traditional single funnel and a navigation bridge in a well-rounded half-moon design. It was one of a series of eight similar vessels originally built for the long-defunct Renaissance Cruises, and acquired by Noble Caledonia in 2011, after being in the possession of a private Dubai-based individual for use as his private yacht.

The exterior design has been altered somewhat with the addition of an enclosed lounge deck forward of the funnel. There is a walk-around teakwood promenade deck outdoors, and a very reasonable amount of open deck space. All of the deck furniture – the tables and chairs – are made of teak and sunloungers have thick cushioned pads. All exterior handrails are of beautifully polished wood. There is also a teakwood water sports platform at the stern of the ship, where two water-jet driven shore tenders are located (these have high central rails inside for passengers to hold when standing up).

You'll find elegant interior design and the touches reminiscent of a small, lavish country house hotel.

The lounge has the unmistakable feel of a British traditional drawing room; it includes a large, white Bath stone fireplace with an imitation log fire (safety regulations prohibit a real one) and is the focal point for all social activities and cocktail parties. There is also a good travel library/reading room. Inspector Hercule Poirot would be very much at home here, as it is rather like a small, exclusive club. The fact that the ship doesn't have photographers and other trappings found aboard larger ships doesn't matter one bit.

Although the dress code is casual and comfortable, most passengers tend to dress nicely well for dinner. The service is friendly but unobtrusive; the atmosphere is quiet (no music in passageways or elevator) and refined, and the ship is well run by a crew proud to provide the kind of personal service expected by intelligent, well-traveled passengers. In fact, unobtrusive service from a Filipino and East European crew are hallmarks of a cruise aboard this ship. Ship-wide Wi-Fi is provided, and the fare includes gratuities, transfers, and shore excursions, plus house wine, beer, and soft drinks during lunch and dinner.

Although several pillars, needed for structural support, are obstructions in some public rooms and hallways, and the interior decor consists of wood laminates instead of real wood, the ambience is warm.

The ship's itineraries take participants mostly to quiet, off-the-beaten-track ports not often visited by larger cruise ships. Destination lecturers are provided.

ACCOMMODATION. There are several grades of double or twin-bedded cabins and four grades of cabins for single travelers, priced by grade, size, and location. The cabins are quite spacious, measuring 215–365 sq ft (20–34 sq m), including bathrooms and balconies – generous for such a small ship. All have outside views, and most feature wallpapered walls, lighted closets, full-length mirror, dressing table with three-sided vanity mirrors, tea/coffee-making equipment, combination large-screen TV and DVD player, refrigerator/mini-bar (always stocked with fresh milk and mineral water), direct-dial satellite telephone, personal safe, ironing board, and electric trouser press. However, there is no switch to turn announcements off in your cabin. There are two suites that provide lots of extra space, and several other cabins have an additional sofa bed.

The bathrooms are of a decent size, and marble-clad; towels and thick, plush bathrobe are 100 percent cotton, as is the bed linen, but note that there is a small step between bedroom and bathroom.

DINING. The Restaurant has ocean-view portholes, and operates with table assignments for dinner, in a single seating, and an open-seating arrangement for breakfast and lunch. It is a very elegant and pleasant room, with wood paneling, fine furnishings, subtle lighting, and plenty of space around each table. A mix of chairs with and without armrests is provided. There are many tables for two, but also for four, six, and eight. Breakfast is buffet-style, while lunch and dinner are served.

Fresh ingredients are often bought locally when possible – a welcome change from the mass catering of many ships today, and the desserts are worth saving space for.

Breakfasts and lunches can also be taken outdoors at the alfresco café, particularly when the ship is operating in warm-weather areas. Morning coffee and afternoon tea can be taken in the lounge areas or, weather permitting, on the open decks.

ENTERTAINMENT. The Club Lounge is the room for social gatherings and talks. Passengers really like the fact that there is no formal entertainment or mindless parlor games – just good company and easy conversation.

SPA/FITNESS. The Asian-style spa, at the aft end of Promenade Deck, is a peaceful place. It contains a hairdressing salon, gymnasium, steam room shower, and a relaxation area.

Safety measures

Fire Control. If anyone sounds the fire alarm, an alarm is automatically set off on the bridge. A red panel light will be illuminated on a large plan, indicating the section of the ship that has to be checked so that the crew can take immediate action. Ships are sectioned into several zones, each of which can be tightly closed off. In addition, almost all ships have a water-fed sprinkler system that can be activated at the touch of a button, or automatically activated when sprinkler vials are broken by fire-generated heat. New electronic fire-detection systems are being installed aboard ships in order to increase safety further.

Emergency Ventilation Control. This automatic fire damper system also has a manual switch that is activated to stop or control the flow of air to all areas of the ship, in this way reducing the fanning effect on flame and smoke via air-conditioning and fan systems.

Watertight Doors Control. Watertight doors throughout the ship can be closed off, in order to contain the movement of water flooding the ship. A master switch activates all the doors in a matter of seconds. All watertight doors can be operated electrically and manually, which means that nobody can be trapped in a watertight compartment.

Stabilizers Control. The ship's two stabilizing fins can be extended, housed, or controlled. They normally operate automatically under the command of a gyroscope located in the engine control room.

Caribbean Princess
★★★★

Size:...............................Large Resort Ship	Cabins (total):...................................1,557
Tonnage: 112,894	Size range (sq ft/m): 163–1,279/15.1–118.8
Lifestyle:......................................Standard	Cabins (outside view):............................1,105
Cruise line:...........................Princess Cruises	Cabins (interior/no view):...........................452
Former names: ....None	Cabins (for one person):.............................0
IMO number:................................9215490	Cabins (with private balcony):......................881
Builder: ....Fincantieri (Italy)	Cabins (wheelchair accessible): 25
Original cost: ....$500 million	Wheelchair accessibility:..........................Good
Entered service:..............................Apr 2004	Cabin voltage: ....110 volts
Registry:.....................................Bermuda	Elevators:..14
Length (ft/m):...........................951.4/290.0	Casino (gaming tables):............................Yes
Beam (ft/m):.............................118.1/36.0	Slot machines:....................................Yes
Draft (ft/m): 28.3/8.6	Swimming pools:....................................3
Propulsion/Propellers:...........diesel-electric (42,000kW)/2	Hot tubs (on deck):.................................9
Passenger decks:..................................15	Self-service launderette:...........................Yes
Total crew:....................................1,163	Dedicated cinema/seats:............................No
Passengers (lower beds/alll berths):............3,114/3,622	Library: ....Yes
Passenger Space Ratio (lower beds/all berths): 36.2/31.1	Onboard currency: ....US$
Crew/Passenger Ratio (lower beds/all berths):.........2.6/3.1	

A multi-choice large ship for informal family cruising

OVERVIEW. The ship is a grand resort. Princess Cruises delivers a consistent, well-packaged vacation at an attractive price. If you're not used to large ships, it'll take you some time to find your way around this one, despite the company's claim that it offers a 'small ship feel, big ship choice.'

THE SHIP. *Caribbean Princess* has the same profile as its half-sisters *Golden Princess*, *Grand Princess*, and *Star Princess*. However, it takes 500 more passengers, thanks to an extra accommodation deck (Riviera Deck). Despite its greater capacity, the outdoor deck space remains the same, as do the number of elevators – so there's a longer wait during peak usage.

There is a good sheltered faux-teak promenade deck – it's actually painted steel – which almost wraps around the ship (three times around equals one mile). The outdoor pools have various beach-like surroundings. 'Movies Under the Skies' and major sporting events are shown on a 300-sq-ft (28-sq-m) poolside movie screen.

Unlike the outside decks, there is plenty of space inside, and a wide array of public rooms, with many intimate spaces. The passenger flow is good, and there is little congestion, except the wait for elevators at peak times.

High atop the stern is a ship-wide glass-walled disco pod with spectacular views from the extreme port and starboard side windows.

Berlitz's Ratings

	Possible	Achieved
Ship	500	373
Accommodation	200	145
Food	400	254
Service	400	290
Entertainment	100	78
Cruise	400	293

OVERALL SCORE
1433 points out of 2000

The interior decor is attractive, with mainly earth tones. An extensive collection of artworks complements the interior design and colors well. *Caribbean Princess* also has a Wedding Chapel. The captain can legally marry American couples, thanks to the ship's Bermuda registry. The 'Hearts & Minds' chapel is also useful for renewal of vows ceremonies.

The ship has a large casino (Grand Casino), with more than 260 slot machines, and blackjack, craps, and roulette tables, plus games such as Let It Ride Bonus, Spanish 21, and Caribbean Draw Progressive. But the highlight could be the specially linked slot machines that provide a combined payout.

Other facilities include a small library and Internet-connect room. A wood-paneled Wheelhouse Bar is finely decorated with memorabilia and ship models tracing part of parent company P&O's history. Churchill's cigar/sports bar has several TV screens. A high-tech hospital has SeaMed tele-medicine link-ups to specialists at the Cedars-Sinai Medical Center in Los Angeles.

FAMILIES. Children's facilities include a large playroom, a teens-only room, and a host of youth counselors. Children have their own pools, hot tubs, and open deck area at the stern of the ship. There are good netted-in areas; one section has a dip pool, while another has a mini-basketball court. Two family suites consist of two suites with an interconnecting door, plus a large balcony.

ACCOMMODATION. There are six principal types of cabins and configurations: (a) grand suite, (b) suite, (c) mini-suite, (d) outside-view double cabins with balcony, (e) outside-view double cabins, and (f) interior double cabins. These come in 35 different brochure price categories. The choice is quite bewildering for both travel agents and passengers; pricing depends on two things, size and location.

Note that the cabin bath towels are small, and drawer space is limited. Even the top-grade suites are not really large in comparison to similar suites aboard some other ships. Cabin attendants have too many cabins to look after (typically 20), which does not translate to fine personal service.

Occupants of suite-grade accommodation receive more attention, including priority embarkation and disembarkation privileges.

(a) The largest, most lavish suite is the Grand Suite, at the stern. It has a large bedroom with queen-size bed, large walk-in (illuminated) closets, two bathrooms, a lounge with fireplace and sofa bed with wet bar and refrigerator, and a large private balcony on the port side – with a hot tub that can be accessed from both balcony and bedroom.

(b/c) Suites (with a semi-private balcony) have a separate living room (with sofa bed) and bedroom, both with a TV set. The bathroom is quite large and has both a tub and shower stall. Mini-suites also have a private balcony, and separate living and sleeping area, with a TV set in each.

(d/e/f) Both interior and outside-view cabins – 80 percent of the latter have a private balcony – are functional, although almost no drawers are provided. They are quite attractive, with warm, pleasing decor and fine soft furnishing fabrics. Interior cabins measure 163 sq ft (15.1 sq m).

The 28 wheelchair-accessible cabins, surprisingly, have no mirror for dressing, and no full-length hanging space for long dresses – yes, many passengers in wheelchairs like to mirrors and the females often wear long dresses.

All cabins receive turndown service and chocolates on pillows each night, bathrobes (on request), and toiletry kits. A hairdryer is provided in all cabins. All bathrooms have tiled floors, and there is a decent amount of open shelf storage space for toiletries, although the plain beige decor is very basic and unappealing.

Most outside-view cabins on Emerald Deck have views obstructed by lifeboats. There are no cabins for singles.

Some cabins can accommodate a third and fourth person in upper berths. However, in such cabins, the lower beds cannot then be pushed together to make queen-size bed.

Almost all balcony suites and cabins can be overlooked both from the navigation bridge wing and from sections of the discotheque. Passengers in some the most expensive suites with balconies at the stern may experience some vibration during certain ship manoeuvers.

DINING. The three principal dining rooms for formal dining are Coral, Island, and Palm. The Palm Dining Room has traditional two seating dining, while Coral and Island have 'anytime dining'. All are split into multi-tier sections in a non-symmetrical design that breaks what are quite large spaces into smaller sections for better ambience. Each dining room has its own galley. While four elevators go to Fiesta Deck, where the Coral and Island restaurants are located, only two go to Plaza Deck 5, where the Palm Restaurant is located. Note that 15 percent is added to all beverage bills, including wines.

Other dining options. Sabatini's Trattoria serves Italian-style pizzas and pastas, with a variety of sauces, as well as Italian entrées including tiger prawns and lobster tail (reservation only; cover charge).

Sterling Steakhouse is located in a somewhat open area, to tempt you as you pass by, with people walking through as you eat – not a particularly comfortable arrangement. There is a cover charge.

Casual eateries include a poolside hamburger grill and pizza bar (no additional charge), while extra charges do apply if you order items to eat at the coffee bar/patisserie, or the caviar/Champagne bar. Other casual meals can be taken in the Horizon Court, open 24 hours a day.

For something different, you could try an 'Ultimate Balcony Dinner or Breakfast' – an all-inclusive evening, featuring cocktails, fresh flowers, Champagne, and a deluxe four-course meal including Caribbean lobster tail. There's 24-hour room service – but some room service menu items are unavailable during early morning hours.

ENTERTAINMENT. The Princess Theater, the main entertainment venue, spans two decks and has comfortable seating on both main and balcony levels. It has $3 million worth of sound and light equipment, plus a nine-piece orchestra, and a scenery loading bay that connects directly from stage to a hull door for direct transfer to the dockside. The ship carries a resident troupe of singers and dancers.

Club Fusion, located aft, has cabaret spots at night, and lectures, bingo, and horse racing during the day. Explorers can also host cabaret acts and dance bands. Other lounges and bars have live music, and Princess Cruises employs dance hosts.

SPA/FITNESS. The Lotus Spa is located forward on Sun Deck – one of the uppermost decks. Facilities include a sauna, steam room, and changing rooms; common facilities include a relaxation/waiting zone, body-pampering treatment rooms, and a gymnasium with packed with high-tech muscle-pumping, cardiovascular equipment, and great ocean views.

Carnival Breeze
★★★ +

Size:.................................Large Resort Ship	Cabins (total):....................................1,845
Tonnage: 128,251	Size range (sq ft/m): 185.0–430.5/17.1–40.0
Lifestyle: ....Standard	Cabins (outside view): 1,182
Cruise line:........................ Carnival Cruise Lines	Cabins (interior/no view):..........................663
Former names: ....none	Cabins (for one person):..............................0
IMO number: 9555723	Cabins (with private balcony):......................905
Builder: .... Fincantieri (Italy)	Cabins (wheelchair accessible): 35
Original cost: .... $740 million	Wheelchair accessibility:..........................Good
Entered service:........................... Jun 2012	Cabin voltage: .... 110 volts
Registry:.................................... Panama	Elevators:...20
Length (ft/m):...........................1,004.0/306.0	Casino (gaming tables):............................Yes
Beam (ft/m):............................... 158.0/48.0	Slot machines:....................................Yes
Draft (ft/m): 26.2/8.0	Swimming pools:.....................................2
Propulsion/Propellers:.............diesel-electric (75.6MW)/2	Hot tubs (on deck):.................................7
Passenger decks:.....................................13	Self-service launderette:...........................Yes
Total crew:...................................... 1,386	Dedicated cinema/seats:.............................No
Passengers (lower beds/alll berths):....... 3,690/4,891	Library: ....Yes
Passenger Space Ratio (lower beds/all berths): 34.7/26.2	Onboard currency: ....US$
Crew/Passenger Ratio (lower beds/all berths):......... 2.6/3.5	

A fun ship for family cruising, with a great water park

OVERVIEW. *Carnival Breeze* is a big floating playground, carrying almost 5,000 passengers when full. It has lots of facilities for young families with children, who will love the outdoor pool deck and its facilities. Serenity is an adults-only, extra-charge retreat, with two large hot tubs on deck.

THE SHIP. This ship and its sisters, *Carnival Dream and Carnival Magic*, are the largest 'fun ships' yet for this cruise line. Although its bows (front part) are short, the ship's profile is quite well balanced, with a rakish front and more rounded stern than most other Carnival ships.

A Waterworks pool deck has lots of water and sports amusements – not to mention a really long orange multi-deck 'Twister Water Slide' and popular 'Power Drencher.' There's also a large Seaside Theatre LED screen for poolside movies and a laser light show at night. The general open deck space is not large enough for the number of passengers. The ship has a full walk-around open promenade deck lined with deck chairs. Also along the outdoor promenade, four 'scenic whirlpools' are cantilevered over the water, and provide fine sea views.

On a lower deck, The Ocean Plaza, with around 190 seats, is a comfortable place by day and a trendy entertainment venue by night. Its indoor/outdoor café and live music venue has a bandstand and a large circular dance floor.

The Caribbean-themed interior decor is bright, but well executed. Many of the public rooms, lounges,

Berlitz's Ratings		
	Possible	Achieved
Ship	500	380
Accommodation	200	144
Food	400	220
Service	400	260
Entertainment	100	77
Cruise	400	265
OVERALL SCORE		
1346 points out of 2000		

bars, and nightspots are located on two main public room/entertainment decks. These can be accessed via an 11-deck-high atrium lobby, whose ground level has a cantilevered bandstand atop a massive dance floor.

Jackpot is the colorful, large, and always lively casino. Other rooms include The Song (Jazz Bar), and Ocean Plaza, a sort of quiet area during the day, but lively at night with live entertainment. Three dozen Internet terminals are scattered around the ship, although most have no privacy. There's a 232-capacity conference room. The Library has a bar, board games, and even a few books.

Although passenger flow is generally sound, the ship's layout is a bit disjointed; the Reception Desk and Shore Excursion Desk are simply too small and crowded for the number of passengers. Passenger niggles highlight the barely warm food in the two main dining rooms, lines for self-serve buffet food items, and congestion in the public areas just before the second seating for dinner. Gratuities are automatically charged to your onboard account.

FAMILIES. Children's facilities are purpose-built for the line's three age-related programs: Camp Carnival for kids aged two to 11, Circle C for 12–14s, and Club O2 for 15–17s, together with a full schedule of morning-to-night activities catering to each age group. About 5,000 sq ft (465 sq m) of space has been devoted to junior cruisers, and they get their own restaurant towards the top of the atrium. Carnival WaterWorks, the expansive aqua park offering exhilarating multi-deck tunnel water slides and various water spray apparatus, is a big hit with the active kids.

ACCOMMODATION. There are numerous cabin-price categories, priced by size, grade and location. Whether you go for high end or low end, all accommodation includes plush mattresses, good-quality duvets, linens, and pillows. The suites aren't very large, although they are laid out in a practical manner, while some of the standard cabins are fine for two but become crowded for three or more.

The decor is a mix of light browns and nautical blues, but the accommodation deck hallways are bright, even at night.

There are a lot of interior cabins. All in all, the cabins to go for are those right at the stern of the ship, with great rearward ocean views, on decks 6, 7, 8, and 9.

'Deluxe' ocean-view cabins, with two bathrooms, provide comfort and convenience for families. In addition to twin beds that convert to a king, decent closet space and elegant decor, the two-bathroom configuration includes one full bathroom and a second bathroom containing a small tub with shower and sink.

Some cabins can sleep five persons – useful for families. There's a wide selection of balcony cabins and suites (not really suites because they don't have separate sleeping and living quarters).

Adjacent to the Cloud 9 Spa are 50 spa cabins, designated as no-smoking; these come with a number of 'exclusive' amenities and privileges. All have direct access to the spa. Note that cabins on Deck 12 are subject to lots of noise from kids having fun on the deck above – so forget the afternoon nap.

DINING. There are two main dining rooms: the Sapphire (mid-ships) and the smaller Blush (aft). Each has a main and balcony level (stairways connect them). There are also two small restaurant annexes, which can be reserved by small groups as a private dining room. Choose either fixed time dining (6pm or 8:15pm) or flexible dining (any time between 5:45pm and 9:30pm). Although the menu choice looks good, the cuisine delivered is simply adequate, but unmemorable. Note that the two main dining rooms are not open for lunch on port days.

Other dining options. Fahrenheit 555 Steakhouse (and bar) features an à la carte menu. It has good table settings, china and silverware, and leather-bound menus. The specialties are premium-quality steaks and grilled seafood items. It's worth paying the cover charge for food that is cooked to order.

The Lido Marketplace – a direct copy of the name used aboard the AIDA Cruises ships – is a large, self-serve buffet facility, with indoor/outdoor seating areas on a lower (main) level and indoor-only seating on an upper level. A number of designated areas serve different types of ethnic cuisine (including 'Comfort Kitchen' – for Americana favorites), although it does become very congested at peak times – the worst is during breakfast – especially around the beverage stands. Go off-peak and it's much better. The venue includes a Mongolian Wok and Pasta Bar on the upper level, open 6–9pm for tablecloth-free, candle-less buffet dinners. Outside and aft you'll find the Deli and Tandoor.

Forward of the Lido Marketplace, adjacent to the 'beach pool' you'll find Guy's Burger Joint. There's also BlueIguana Cantina for Tex-Mex fast food items like burritos, tacos and enchiladas.

Down on Promenade Deck on the starboard (right) side is Fat Jimmy's C-Side BBQ. Reminiscent of a backyard barbeque, it features grilled items like kielbasa, grilled chicken breast, and the venue's signature item – pulled pork sandwiches.

Inside on Promenade Deck is Bonsai Sushi – Carnival's first full-service sushi restaurant, with décor by graffiti artist Erni Vales, and sushi, sashimi and bento boxes by Carnival.

Cucina del Capitano is an Italian extra-charge eatery, located on the upper level of the Lido Marketplace, with pasta served at lunchtime, and 'authentic' Italian specialties at night (now you know where the ship's navigation officers go).

ENTERTAINMENT. The 1,964-seat Ovation Showlounge spans three decks at the front of the ship, with seating set in a horseshoe shape around a large proscenium arched stage; the sight lines are generally good, except from some of the seats at the back of the lowest level. Large-scale production shows, with lots of feathers and skimpy costumes, are staged, together with snappy cabaret acts, all accompanied by a live showband.

The Limelight, at the aft of the ship (the showlounge is at the front), seats 425, has a stage, dance floor, and large bar. For late-night raunchy adult comedy, it becomes the Punchline Comedy Club.

For an active movie experience, check out the Thrill 5D Theater, where the seats really move you.

SPA/FITNESS. The expansive 23,750-sq-ft (2,206-sq-m) Cloud 9 Spa is large, positioned over three decks in the front section of the ship. The uppermost deck includes indoor/outdoor private spa relaxation areas, at extra cost. A spiral staircase connects the two decks.

The spa offers a wide range of treatments. There are 10 treatment rooms, including a VIP room, a large massage room for couples, and a Rasul mud treatment room, plus two dry flotation rooms. An extra-charge Thermal Suite features the sensory-enhanced soothing heated chambers: Laconium, Tepidarium, Aroma, and Oriental steam baths.

There are male and female steam rooms, and a small unisex sauna with a floor-to-ceiling window on its starboard side.

Carnival Conquest
★★★ +

Size:	Large Resort Ship
Tonnage:	110,239
Lifestyle:	Standard
Cruise line:	Carnival Cruise Lines
Former names:	none
IMO number:	9198355
Builder:	Fincantieri (Italy)
Original cost:	$500 million
Entered service:	Dec 2002
Registry:	Panama
Length (ft/m):	951.4/290.0
Beam (ft/m):	116.4/35.5
Draft (ft/m):	27.0/8.2
Propulsion/Propellers:	diesel-electric (63,400kW)/2
Passenger decks:	13
Total crew:	1,160
Passengers (lower beds/alll berths):	2,974/3,700
Passenger Space Ratio (lower beds/all berths):	37.0/29.7
Crew/Passenger Ratio (lower beds/all berths):	2.5/3.1

Cabins (total):	1,487
Size range (sq ft/m):	179.7–482.2/16.7–44.8
Cabins (outside view):	917
Cabins (interior/no view):	570
Cabins (for one person):	0
Cabins (with private balcony):	574
Cabins (wheelchair accessible):	25
Wheelchair accessibility:	Good
Cabin voltage:	110 volts
Elevators:	18
Casino (gaming tables):	Yes
Slot machines:	Yes
Swimming pools:	2 (1 w/sliding glass dome)
Hot tubs (on deck):	7
Self-service launderette:	Yes
Dedicated cinema/seats:	No
Library:	Yes
Onboard currency:	US$

A vivid, fun-filled ship for ultra-casual cruising

OVERVIEW. This is quite a stunning ship, built to impress at every turn. The layout is quite logical, so finding your way around is easy. The decor features great Impressionist painters, such as Degas, Monet, and Van Gogh. Murano glass flowers on antiqued brass stems are displayed in several public areas.

THE SHIP. *Carnival Conquest* has the same well-balanced profile as its sisters: *Carnival Sunshine, Carnival Freedom, Carnival Glory, Carnival Liberty, Carnival Triumph,* and *Carnival Victory.* Because of its size, it can't transit the Panama Canal and is dedicated to the Caribbean area.

Amidships on the open deck is a long water slide (200ft/60m long), as well as tiered sunbathing decks positioned between two swimming pools, several hot tubs, and a giant poolside (Seaside Theater) movie screen. It's all about imagination and sensorial fantasy and is more reserved than Carnival's *Fantasy*-class ships.

There are three decks full of lounges, 10 bars, and lots of rooms to play in. There are two atriums: the largest, the forward, glass-domed Artists Atrium spans nine decks, while the aft atrium goes through three decks.

The ship's interior décor is all about the Impressionist painters such as Degas, Toulouse Lautrec, Gauguin, Cezanne, and others.

The Tahiti casino is large and action-packed, with over 320 slot machines alongside all the popular gaming tables. There are several other nightspots for just

Berlitz's Ratings

	Possible	Achieved
Ship	500	366
Accommodation	200	144
Food	400	218
Service	400	259
Entertainment	100	77
Cruise	400	259

OVERALL SCORE
1323 points out of 2000

about every musical taste (except for opera, ballet, and classical music lovers), such as the Degas Lounge, Vincent's Piano Bar, Henri's Dance Club, and Gauguin's Bar.

Carnival Conquest is a floating playground for the young and young-at-heart, and anyone who enjoys constant stimulation and lots of participation events, together with the three 'Gs' – glitz, glamour, and gambling. This really is cruising Splash Vegas style – and an all-American fun experience. Because it's a large resort ship, there will be lines for things like shore excursions, security control when re-boarding,

Forget fashion – the sine qua non – of a Carnival cruise is all about having fun. While the cuisine is just so-so, the real fun begins at sundown when Carnival really excels in sound, lights, razzle-dazzle shows, and late-night high volume sounds.

Niggles include: many pillars in the dining room make it difficult for proper food service by the waiters; public toilets that are somewhat utilitarian and could do with some cheering up. It is impossible to escape from noise and loud music (it's even played in cabin hallways and lifts), not to mention smokers, and people walking around in unsuitable clothing, clutching plastic sport drinks bottles, at any time of the day or night. You have to carry a credit card to operate the personal safes, which is inconvenient.

The ship underwent an extensive refurbishment program in 2012 to modernize it and give it a facelift. This included the addition of Guy's Burger Joint (in partnership with Guy Fieri of Food Network) for burgers, hand-cut fries (chips) and assorted toppings, a poolside RedFrog rum bar (including Thirsty-RedFrog – Carnival's private label draft-brew) and BlueIguana Tequila Bar (for Mexican-themed frozen cocktails as well as Tequila), and an EA Sports (this includes video games and a 24/7 sports ticker). Meanwhile, Cherry on Top is a sweet-tooth shop full of bins of – you guessed it – bulk candy, as well as novelty gift items.

FAMILIES. *Carnival Conquest* provides children with good facilities, including a two-level Children's Club with an outdoor pool, and are well cared for with 'Camp Carnival,' the line's extensive children's program. The game room and teen area resembles the back alleys of the infamous Montmartre district of 19th century Paris.

ACCOMMODATION. There are numerous cabin-price categories, in seven different grades: suites with private balcony; deluxe outside-view cabins with private balcony; outside-view cabins with private balcony; outside-view cabins with window; cabins with a porthole instead of a window; interior cabins; interior cabins with upper and lower berths. The price reflects the grade, location, and size.

Five decks of cabins have a private balcony – over 150 more than *Carnival Triumph* or *Carnival Victory*, for example. But many are not so private, and can be overlooked from various public locations.

There are 18 'fitness' cabins, located directly around and behind the SpaCarnival. This allows fitness devotees to get out of bed and go straight to the treadmill without having to go through any of the public rooms first.

The standard cabins are of good size and are equipped with all the basics, although the furniture is rather angular, with no rounded edges. Three decks of cabins (eight on each deck, each with private balcony) overlook the stern. Most cabins with twin beds can be converted to a queen-size bed format. A gift basket is provided in all grades of cabin; it includes aloe soap, shampoo, conditioner, deodorant, breath mints, candy, and pain relief tablets (all in sample sizes).

Note: If you book one of the Category 11 or 12 suites you get 'Skipper's Club' priority check-in at any US homeland port – useful for getting ahead of the crowd.

DINING. There are two principal dining rooms: the 744-seat Renoir Restaurant, and the larger 1,044-seat Monet Restaurant. Both are two decks high, and both have a balcony level for diners (the balcony level in the Monet Restaurant is larger). Cassat and Pissaro, two additional wings in the Renoir Restaurant, can accommodate large groups in a private dining setting. There's a choice of either fixed time dining (6pm or 8:15pm) or flexible dining (any time between 5:45pm and 9:30pm). Although the menu choice looks varies, the cuisine delivered is usually adequate but quite unmemorable. Note that the two main dining rooms are not open for lunch on port days, so you will need to go to the serve-yourself buffet – or order room service.

Other dining options. The Steakhouse is the reservations-only, extra-cost, specialty dining spot. The decor includes wall murals in the style of Seurat's famous Le Cirque (The Circus). There are fine table settings, china, and silverware, as well as leather-bound menus (steaks and seafood are featured).

The Cézanne Restaurant is a casual self-serve 'international' food court-style lido deck eatery, with a capacity for over 1,200. Its decor reflects the style of a 19th-century French café. It has two main serving lines, is adjacent to the aft pool, and can be covered by a glass cover in poor weather. Included are Paul's Deli, PC's Wok (Chinese cuisine, with wok preparation), a 24-hour pizzeria, and a patisserie (there's an extra charge for pastries, however). There's also Guy's Burger Joint (created in partnership with Guy Fieri), for hamburgers, hot dogs and hand-cut fries, and BlueIguana Cantina – a Mexican-themed taco and burrito joint with a self-serve salsa and toppings bar.

At night, the Cézanne Restaurant becomes the Seaview Bistro, providing a casual alternative to eating in the main restaurants. It features pasta, steaks, salads, and desserts, typically between 6pm and 9pm.

ENTERTAINMENT. The Toulouse-Lautrec Showlounge is a multi-deck showroom seating 1,400. It has a revolving stage, hydraulic orchestra pit, superb sound, and seating on three levels (the upper levels being tiered through two decks). A proscenium over the stage acts as a scenery loft.

Hasbro, The Game Show was also added in 2012; the show includes audience participation, as competitive interpretations of the larger-than-life board games.

SPA/FITNESS. SpaCarnival is a large health, fitness, and spa complex that spans two decks (the walls display hand-painted reproductions of the artist's poster work). It is directly above the navigation bridge in the forward part of the ship and is accessed from the forward stairway.

Facilities on the lower level include a solarium, eight treatment rooms, lecture rooms, sauna and steam rooms for men and women, and a beauty parlor. The upper level consists of a large gymnasium with floor-to-ceiling windows on three sides, including forward-facing ocean views, and an aerobics room with instructor-led classes, some at extra cost.

Carnival Dream
★★★ +

Size:....................................Large Resort Ship		Cabins (total):..................................... 1,823	
Tonnage: 128,251		Size range (sq ft/m):.................. 185.0–430.5/17.1–40.0	
Lifestyle: ....Standard		Cabins (outside view):................................ 1,145	
Cruise line:......................... Carnival Cruise Lines		Cabins (interior/no view):.............................678	
Former names: ....none		Cabins (for one person):.................................0	
IMO number: 9378474		Cabins (with private balcony):........................887	
Builder: .... Fincantieri (Italy)		Cabins (wheelchair accessible): 35	
Original cost:.............................. $740 million		Wheelchair accessibility:............................Good	
Entered service:............................. Sep 2009		Cabin voltage: .... 110 volts	
Registry:... Panama		Elevators:...20	
Length (ft/m):............................1,004.0/306.0		Casino (gaming tables):...............................Yes	
Beam (ft/m):............................. 158.0/48.0		Slot machines:.......................................Yes	
Draft (ft/m):............................... 26.2/8.0		Swimming pools:.......................................2	
Propulsion/Propellers: .... diesel-electric (75,600kW)/2		Hot tubs (on deck):....................................7	
Passenger decks:....................................13		Self-service launderette:............................Yes	
Total crew:..................................... 1,367		Dedicated cinema/seats:...............................No	
Passengers (lower beds/alll berths):............. 3,646/4,631		Library: ....Yes	
Passenger Space Ratio (lower beds/all berths): 35.1/27.6		Onboard currency: ....US$	
Crew/Passenger Ratio (lower beds/all berths):.......... 2.6/3.3			

Fun for a first cruise, with a great water-slide

OVERVIEW. *Carnival Dream*, whose sister ships are *Carnival Breeze* and *Carnival Magic*, operates year-round Caribbean cruises from Florida. There are ample facilities for children, who should particularly enjoy the outdoor waterpark and pool facilities. There's also a Serenity adults-only, extra-charge retreat as well as a sports activity area on deck.

THE SHIP. Although the ship's bows are short, the ship's profile is nicely balanced, with a rakish front and more rounded stern than most of the other ships in the Carnival fleet.

The Waterworks pool deck has lots of water and sports amusements – not to mention a really long orange multi-deck 'Twister Water Slide' and popular 'Power Drencher.' However, the general open deck space is really not enough for the number of passengers carried, so the sunbed loungers are packed in tightly.

There is a full walk-around open promenade deck, lined with deck chairs, though it can be difficult to navigate your way through them. Along the outdoor promenade, four 'scenic whirlpools' are cantilevered over the water and provide fine sea views. Higher up, Lido Deck 10 offers the best open-deck area of any Carnival ship with a tropical, resort-style main pool complete with a giant Seaside Theatre LED screen for outdoor movies. *Carnival Dream* was the first Carnival ship to have a laser light show outdoors.

The interior decor is bright (take sunglasses), but well executed. Most public rooms, lounges, and bars are on Dream Street or Upper Dream Street. The stun-

Berlitz's Ratings		
	Possible	Achieved
Ship	500	380
Accommodation	200	144
Food	400	218
Service	400	260
Entertainment	100	77
Cruise	400	261
OVERALL SCORE		
1340 points out of 2000		

ning Dream Lobby is the connection point for ship functions and people. Take the glass-walled elevators for a neat view. It's good to note that there are three main elevator towers: forward, amidships, and aft.

Many lounges, bars, and nightspots – including a dance club with a twist, offering indoor/outdoor access – are accessible via an 11-deck-high atrium whose ground level has a neatly cantilevered bandstand atop a large dance floor. The Page Turner (great name) is the library, while Jackpot is – you guessed it – the colorful, large, and lively casino. Other rooms include The Song (Jazz Bar), and Ocean Plaza, a sort of quiet area during the day, but lively at night with live entertainment. Three dozen Internet terminals are scattered around the ship, although most have no privacy. There's a 232-capacity conference room, The Chambers.

The indoor/outdoor Ocean Plaza, with around 190 seats, is a comfortable spot for people-watching by day and becomes a trendy entertainment venue by night, with its own dance floor and bandstand.

Although passenger flow is generally sound, the ship's layout is rather disjointed. Just before the second seating, there is much congestion on Upper and Lower Dream Streets, both located on the starboard side. Congestion also appears around the photo gallery in the atrium lobby. Passenger niggles highlight the barely warm food in the two main dining rooms, lines for self-serve food items, and congestion in the public areas just before the second seating for dinner. Gratuities are automatically charged to your onboard account.

Carnival Dream is a floating playground for the young and young-at-heart, and anyone who enjoys constant stimulation and lots of participation events, together with the three 'Gs' – glitz, glamour, and gambling. This really is cruising Splash Vegas style an all-American experience. Because it's a large resort ship, there will be lines for things like shore excursions, security control when re-boarding, and disembarkation, as well as sign-up sheets for fitness equipment.

FAMILIES. Children's facilities are purpose-built for the line's three age-related programs: 'Camp Carnival' for kids aged two to 11, 'Circle C' for 12 to 14s, and 'Club O2' for teens aged 15–17, together with a full schedule of morning-to-night activities catering to each age group. About 5,000 sq ft (460 sq m) of space has been devoted to junior cruisers. Carnival WaterWorks, an aqua park offering exhilarating multi-deck tunnel slides and various water spray apparatus, is a huge hit with the kids.

ACCOMMODATION. There are 19 cabin-price categories, but just six cabin types. The price depends on the accommodation grade and location. Whether you go for high end or low end, all accommodation includes the Carnival Comfort Bed with plush mattresses, good-quality duvets, linens and pillows. However, the straight accommodation deck hallways create rather a cell-block look – and they are bright, very bright, even at night. There are also lot of interior cabins. The cabins to go for are those at the stern: they are quieter and offer great rearward ocean views on decks 6, 7, 8, and 9.

'Deluxe' ocean-view cabins, with two bathrooms, provide comfort and convenience for families. In addition to twin beds that convert to a king, decent closet space and elegant decor, the two-bathroom configuration includes one full bathroom and a second bathroom containing a small tub with shower and washbasin.

Some cabins can accommodate five persons – useful for families. There is a wide selection of balcony cabins and suites, including 'Cove Balcony' cabins that are the closest to the waterline.

Additionally, adjacent to the Serenity Spa are 65 'Cloud 9' spa cabins, designated as no-smoking. They provide a number of 'exclusive' amenities and privileges. Twenty of these are positioned directly aft of the lower level of the spa, with direct access to it. Some cabins located directly over loud late-night venues (such as Encore), with poor soundproofing, have resulted in many restless nights. Also, cabins on Deck 12 are subject to lots of noise from kids having fun on the deck above – so afternoon naps are out.

DINING. There are two main restaurants: the 1,180-seat Crimson (midships) and the smaller 828-seat Scarlet (aft). Each has two levels: main and balcony (stairways connect both levels), with the galley set on the lower level. Forward of Crimson are two small restaurant annexes; these can be reserved by small groups

as private dining rooms. Choose either fixed-time dining (6pm or 8:15pm) or flexible dining (any time between 5:45 and 9:30pm). Note that the two main dining rooms are not open for lunch on port days.

The Gathering is the ship's Lido Deck self-serve buffet facility, with indoor/outdoor seating areas on the lower (main) level, and indoor-only seating on the upper level. A number of designated areas serve different types of ethnic cuisine, although it does become very congested at peak times – especially breakfast – especially around the beverage stands. Go off-peak and it's much better. The venue includes a Mongolian Wok and Pasta Bar on the upper level, open 6–9pm.

Outside, aft is where the Deli and Tandoor (Indian food) counters can be found, for snack food items, while forward of the self-serve buffet, and outdoors is a fast-food grille and Pizzeria.

Other dining options. The Chef's Art Supper Club (and bar) seats 139 and has great views for port and starboard from its aft location high on Spa Deck 12, and an à la carte menu. It has fine table settings, china, and silverware. The specialties are steaks and seafood items. It's worth paying the cover charge to get a taste of what Carnival can deliver. On Promenade Deck you'll find Wasabi – the ship's tribute-to-sushi venue.

ENTERTAINMENT. The 1,964-seat Encore Showlounge spans three decks at the front of the ship, with seating set in a horseshoe shape around the stage; the sight lines are generally good, except from some of the seats at the back of the lowest level. Large-scale production shows, with lots of feathers and skimpy costumes, are staged, together with snappy cabaret acts, all accompanied by a live showband.

The 425-seat Burgundy Lounge, at the aft end of the ship (opposite to the showlounge, at the front), has a stage, dance floor, and large bar, and is a comedy venue, including late-night in-your-face, smutty 'adult comedy.' Caliente, the ship's nightclub, provides loud Latin dance music.

SPA/FITNESS. The expansive 23,750-sq-ft (2,206 sq-m) Cloud 9 Spa is Carnival's largest and most elaborate health and wellness center to date. It is positioned over three decks in the front section of the ship. The uppermost deck includes indoor/outdoor private spa relaxation areas, at extra cost. A spiral staircase connects the two decks.

There are 10 body treatment rooms, including a VIP room, a large massage room for couples, and a Rasul mud treatment room, plus two dry flotation rooms. An extra-charge 'Thermal Suite' comes with the typical sensory-enhanced soothing heated chambers: Laconium, Tepidarium, Aroma, and Oriental steam baths.

There are two steam rooms, one each for men and women, and a small unisex sauna with a floor-to-ceiling window on its starboard side. There's also a two-level miniature golf course.

Carnival Ecstasy
★★★

Size:.....Large Resort Ship	Cabins (total):.....1,026 or 1,028
Tonnage:.....70,526	Size range (sq ft/m):.....173.2–409.7/16.0–38.0
Lifestyle:.....Standard	Cabins (outside view):.....618 or 620
Cruise line:.....Carnival Cruise Lines	Cabins (interior/no view):.....408
Former names:.....Ecstasy	Cabins (for one person):.....0
IMO number:.....8711344	Cabins (with private balcony):.....52
Builder:.....Kvaerner Masa-Yards (Finland)	Cabins (wheelchair accessible):.....22
Original cost:.....$225 million	Wheelchair accessibility:.....Fair
Entered service:.....Jun 1991	Cabin voltage:.....110 volts
Registry:.....Panama	Elevators:.....14
Length (ft/m):.....855.8/263.6	Casino (gaming tables):.....Yes
Beam (ft/m):.....103.0/31.4	Slot machines:.....Yes
Draft (ft/m):.....25.9/7.9	Swimming pools:.....3
Propulsion/Propellers:.....diesel-electric (42,240kW)/2	Hot tubs (on deck):.....6
Passenger decks:.....10	Self-service launderette:.....Yes
Total crew:.....920	Dedicated cinema/seats:.....No
Passengers (lower beds/alll berths):.....2,056/2,634	Library:.....Yes
Passenger Space Ratio (lower beds/all berths):.....34.4/26.7	Onboard currency:.....US$
Crew/Passenger Ratio (lower beds/all berths):.....2.2/2.8	

Floating fun palace for ultra-casual first-time cruisers

OVERVIEW. *Carnival Ecstasy* is the second in a series of eight almost identical ships in the Carnival Fantasy-class ships. Although externally angular and not at all handsome, this is nonetheless a popular ship – aimed at anyone taking their first cruise.

THE SHIP. *Carnival Ecstasy* – now over 20 years old and looking tired – has open deck space that is inadequate when the ship is full. The aft decks tend to be less noisy, whereas all the activities are focused around the main swimming pool and hot tubs (one with a thatched shade). For those who prefer European-style sunning there's also a topless sunbathing area, as well as Serenity – an adult-only 'quiet' lounging space on Deck 9 aft. There is no walk-around open promenade deck, although there is a short jogging track atop ship. The lifeboats, six of which double as shore tenders, are positioned high in the ship.

The interior spaces are well utilized and the general passenger flow is good. The interior design – the work of Miami-based creative genius Joe Farcus – is clever, functional, and extremely colorful. He calls it 'entertainment architecture.' The ship's interior design theme is Mythical Muses and Music. You'll find a rather nice Rolls-Royce car (and coffee shop) located on the indoor promenade.

The interior focal point is an 'open' atrium lobby, whose balconied shape recalls some of the world's great opera houses; dressed to impress, it spans six decks, and is topped by a large glass dome. The low-

Berlitz's Ratings	Possible	Achieved
Ship	500	309
Accommodation	200	138
Food	400	212
Service	400	256
Entertainment	100	73
Cruise	400	244
OVERALL SCORE		
1232 points out of 2000		

est level of the atrium lobby is where you'll find the Purser's Desk and Shore Excursion Desk, together with a popular atrium Bar (with live music), as well as a small sushi bar off to one side.

There are public entertainment lounges, bars, and clubs galore, with something for everyone (except quiet space). The public rooms, connected by a double-width promenade called City Highlights Boulevard, combine a colorful mix of classic and contemporary (think garish) design elements. Most public rooms and attractions lead off from this boulevard – a sort of shipboard Main Street which runs between the showlounge (forward) and the Starlight Aft Lounge/nightclub. Gamers and slot players alike will enjoy the almost non-stop action in the Crystal Palace Casino. There is also a fine looking library and reading room, but few books, and a 1,200-sq-ft (111-sq-m) conference room.

Carnival Ecstasy is a floating playground for the young and young-at-heart, and anyone who enjoys constant stimulation and lots of participation events. Because it's a large resort ship, there will be lines for things like shore excursions, security control when re-boarding, and disembarkation, as well as sign-up sheets for fitness equipment.

Forget fashion – the sine qua non – of a Carnival cruise is all about having fun. While the cuisine is just so-so, the real fun begins at sundown when Carnival really excels in sound, lights, and shows. From venues such as the Stripes Dance Club/Disco to the Society Cigar Bar, the ships' interior decor will certainly entertain you. Carnival Ecstasy, however, is not for those seeking a quiet, relaxing cruise experience. There are many annoying announcements, and the never-ending hustling to get you to spend more money.

Carnival Ecstasy is not for those who want a quiet, relaxing cruise experience. There are simply too many annoying announcements, and a great deal of hustling for drinks. Shore excursions are booked via the in-cabin "Fun Vision" television system, so obtaining advice and suggestions is not easy. The art in the Art Gallery is rather tacky, to say the least!

FAMILIES. Kids will, I am sure, enjoy Children's World (part of Camp Carnival children's programming), a 1,600-sq-ft (149-sq-m) play area with games and fun stuff for youngsters of all ages, including Apple computers loaded with educational software, and an arts and crafts area with spin- and sand-art machines. An expansive children's water park is a lot of fun as an outdoor play area. Group babysitting is available ($6 per hour for the first child; $4 per hour for each additional child of the same immediate family). Meanwhile teens have their chill-out club, as part of the line's popular Club 02 teen program.

ACCOMMODATION. There are 13 grades of accommodation, ranked by facilities, size, and location. The standard outside-view and interior cabins have decor that is rather plain and unmemorable. They are marginally comfortable, yet spacious enough and practical (most are of the same size and appointments), with good storage space and practical, well-designed no-nonsense bathrooms. However, if you have a queen-bed configuration instead of the standard twin-bed layout, note that one person has to clamber over the bed – an ungainly exercise.

Anyone booking an outside suite will find more space, whirlpool bathtubs, and some rather eclectic decor and furniture. These are mildly attractive, but so-so, and they are much smaller than those aboard ships of a similar size of competing companies. A small gift basket of toiletry samples is provided in all grades.

Book a Category 11 or 12 suite and you get Skipper's Club priority check-in at any US homeland port – useful for getting ahead of the crowd.

Room service items are available 24 hours a day, although in standard-grade cabins, only cold food is available, while occupants of suite-grade accommodation have a greater range of items (both hot and cold) to choose from.

DINING. The two large main dining rooms, Wind Star and Wind Song, are located amidships and aft. They have ocean-view windows and are noisy, but the decor is attractive, although extremely bright. Choose either fixed-time dining (6pm or 8:15pm) or flexible dining (any time between 5:45 and 9:30pm).

The food is so-so. Presentation is simple, and few garnishes are used. Many meat and fowl dishes are disguised with gravies and sauces – and few garnishes are used. The selection of fresh green vegetables, breads, rolls, cheeses, and fruits is limited, and there is much use of canned fruit and jellied desserts. There's a decent wine list, but no wine waiters. The waiters sing and dance, and there are constant waiter parades – so it's really more about 'foodertainment' than food quality. Remember, however, that this is standard catering. If you want something really simple, there's an 'always available' (when the dining rooms are open) list of 'Carnival Classics' that includes mahi mahi (fish), baby back ribs (beef), and grilled chicken. Note that the two main dining rooms are not open for lunch on port days.

Other dining options. A Lido Café, called the Panorama Bar & Grill, features the usual casual self-serve buffet eats, most of which are non-memorable. The venue includes a deli counter and pizzeria. At night, the venue morphs into the Seaview Bistro, and provides a casual alternative to the main dining rooms, for pasta, steaks, salads, and desserts – it typically operates only between 6pm and 9pm. The food selection, though limited, makes a change from the large, crowded and noisy main dining rooms. Outside on deck is a Mongolian Rotisserie Grill.

A patisserie offers specialty coffees and sweets (extra charge), and a so-called sushi bar off to one side of the atrium lobby bar on Promenade Deck is open prior to dinner; if you know anything about sushi, don't expect authenticity.

There is no specialty (extra-charge) restaurant, as aboard some of the larger ships in the Carnival fleet.

ENTERTAINMENT. The 1,010-seat Blue Sapphire Showlounge is the venue for large-scale production shows and major cabaret acts – although 20 pillars obstruct some views. During a typical cruise, there will be one or two high-energy production shows, with a cast of two lead singers and a clutch of dancers, backed by a large live band.

SPA/FITNESS. SpaCarnival is a large, glass-wrapped health, fitness, and spa complex is located on the uppermost interior deck, forward of the ship's mast, and is typically open from 6am to 8pm daily. It consists of a gymnasium with ocean-view windows that look out over the bow and the latest in muscle-pumping electronic machines, an aerobics exercise room, men's and women's changing rooms, sauna and steam rooms, beauty salon, and body treatment rooms. Some fitness classes incur an extra charge. A common complaint is that there aren't enough staff to keep the area clean and tidy.

Sporting types can play basketball or volleyball, or table tennis. There is also a banked jogging track outdoors, and a mini-golf course.

Carnival Elation
★★★

Size:.....................................Large Resort Ship		Crew/Passenger Ratio (lower beds/all berths):.......... 2.2/2.8	
Tonnage:...................................... 70,390		Cabins (total):............................. 1,026 or 1,028	
Lifestyle:.....................................Standard		Size range (sq ft/m):................. 173.2–409.7/16.0–38.0	
Cruise line:...........................Carnival Cruise Line		Cabins (outside view):......................... 618 or 620	
Former names:................................. Elation		Cabins (interior/no view):............................408	
IMO number:...............................9118721		Cabins (for one person):...............................0	
Builder:...................Kvaerner Masa-Yards (Finland)		Cabins (with private balcony):........................152	
Original cost:............................... $225 million		Cabins (wheelchair accessible):.......................22	
Entered service:............................. Mar 1998		Wheelchair accessibility:..............................Fair	
Registry:.......................................Panama		Cabin voltage:............................... 110 volts	
Length (ft/m):............................. 855.8/263.6		Elevators:..14	
Beam (ft/m):................................ 103.0/31.4		Casino (gaming tables):............................. Yes	
Draft (ft/m):................................... 25.9/7.9		Slot machines:................................... Yes	
Propulsion/Propellers:...diesel-electric (42,842kW)/2 azimuthing pods		Swimming pools:.....................................3	
Passenger decks:....................................10		Hot tubs (on deck):..................................6	
Total crew:.......................................920		Self-service launderette:............................ Yes	
Passengers (lower beds/alll berths):............. 2,056/2,634		Dedicated cinema/seats:.............................No	
Passenger Space Ratio (lower beds/all berths): 34.4/26.7		Library: .... Yes	
		Onboard currency: ....US$	

Floating fun palace for ultra-casual first-time cruisers

OVERVIEW. *Carnival Elation* is the seventh in a series of eight almost identical ships in the *Fantasy*-class (sister ships: *Carnival Ecstasy, Carnival Fantasy, Carnival Fascination, Carnival Imagination, Carnival Inspiration, Carnival Paradise*, and *Carnival Sensation* – all of which have extremely short bows. The ship has an angular exterior profile and is not very handsome, *Carnival Elation* is nonetheless a popular ship – aimed at anyone taking their first cruise.

THE SHIP. *Carnival Elation* is one of only two ships in the series of eight (the other is *Carnival Paradise*) with a 'pod' propulsion system, which gives a vibration-free ride, rather than the traditional propeller shaft and rudder system. The open deck space, however, gets really crowded when the ship is full and everyone wants to be out on deck. The aft decks tend to be less noisy, whereas all the activities are focused around the main swimming pool and hot tubs (one with a thatched shade). For those who prefer European-style sunning there's also a topless sunbathing area, as well as Serenity – an adult-only 'quiet' lounging space on Deck 9 aft. There is no walk-around open promenade deck, although there is a short jogging track atop ship. The lifeboats, six of which double as shore tenders, are positioned high in the ship.

The interior spaces are well utilized. The general passenger flow is good, and the interior design – the work of Miami-based creative genius Joe Farcus – is

Berlitz's Ratings

	Possible	Achieved
Ship	500	309
Accommodation	200	138
Food	400	212
Service	400	262
Entertainment	100	73
Cruise	400	243

OVERALL SCORE
1237 points out of 2000

clever, functional, and extremely colorful. The interior décor theme is mythical muses, and composers and their compositions.

The interior focal point is an 'open' atrium lobby, whose balconied shape recalls some of the world's great opera houses; dressed to impress, it spans six decks, and is topped by a large glass dome. The lowest level of the atrium lobby is where you'll find the Purser's Desk and Shore Excursion Desk, together with a popular Atrium Bar (with live music), as well as a small sushi bar off to one side; it's a good central meeting place.

There are public entertainment lounges, bars, and clubs galore, with something for everyone (except quiet space). The public rooms, connected by a double-width Elation's Way and Promenade, combine a colorful mix of classic and contemporary design elements. Most public rooms and attractions lead off from this boulevard – a sort of shipboard Main Street which runs between the showlounge (forward) and the Cole Porter lounge/nightclub aft. Gamers and slot players alike will enjoy the almost non-stop action in the Casablanca Casino. There is also a fine looking library and reading room, but few books, and a 1,200-sq-ft (111-sq-m) conference room.

While the cuisine is just so-so, the real fun begins at sundown when Carnival really excels in sound, lights, razzle-dazzle shows, and late-night high volume sounds. From venues such as the Jekyll & Hyde Dance Club/Disco to Gatsby's Great Cigar Bar, the ships' interior decor will certainly entertain you. Carnival Elation, however, is not for those seeking a quiet, relaxing cruise experience. There are many annoying announcements, and the never-ending hustling to get you to buy drinks and many other things.

Carnival Elation is a floating playground for the young and young-at-heart, and anyone who enjoys constant stimulation and lots of participation events, together with the three 'Gs' – glitz, glamour, and gambling. This really is cruising Splash Vegas style – and fun, all-American experience. Because it's a large resort ship, there will be lines for things like shore excursions, security control when re-boarding, and disembarkation, as well as sign-up sheets for fitness equipment.

Forget fashion – the sine qua non – of a Carnival cruise is all about having fun. *Carnival Elation* is not for those who want a quiet, relaxing cruise experience. There are simply too many annoying announcements, and a great deal of hustling for drinks. Shore excursions are booked via the in-cabin 'Fun Vision' television system, so obtaining advice and suggestions is not easy.

FAMILIES. Kids will enjoy Children's World (part of Camp Carnival children's programming), a 1,600-sq-ft (149-sq-m) play area with games and fun stuff for youngsters of all ages, including Apple computers loaded with educational software, and an arts and crafts area with spin- and sand-art machines. An expansive children's water park is a lot of fun as an outdoor play area. Group babysitting is available. Meanwhile teens have their chill-out club, as part of the line's popular Club O2 teen program.

ACCOMMODATION. There are 13 grades of accommodation, ranked by facilities, size, and location. The standard outside-view and interior cabins have decor that is rather plain and unmemorable. They are marginally comfortable, yet spacious enough and practical (most are of the same size and appointments), with good storage space and practical, well-designed nononsense bathrooms. However, if you have a queen-bed configuration instead of the standard twin-bed layout, note that one person has to clamber over the bed – an ungainly exercise.

Anyone booking an outside suite will find more space, whirlpool bathtubs, and some rather eclectic decor and furniture. These are mildly attractive, but so-so, and they are much smaller than those aboard ships of a similar size of competing companies. A small gift basket of toiletry samples is provided in all grades.

If you book a Category 11 or 12 suite and you get Skipper's Club priority check-in at any US homeland port – useful for getting ahead of the crowd.

Room service items are available 24 hours a day, although in standard-grade cabins, only cold food is available, while occupants of suite-grade accommodation have a greater range of items (both hot and cold) to choose from.

DINING. There are two large main dining rooms, Imagination and Inspiration, located amidships and aft. They have ocean-view windows and are noisy, but the decor is attractive, bright and colorful. Choose either fixed-time dining (6pm or 8:15pm) or flexible dining (any time between 5:45 and 9:30pm).

The food is so-so. Presentation is simple, and few garnishes are used. Many meat and fowl dishes are disguised with gravies and sauces – and few garnishes are used. There's a decent wine list, but no wine waiters. The waiters sing and dance, and there are constant waiter parades – so it's really more about 'foodertainment' than food quality. If you want something really simple, there's an 'always available' (when the dinng rooms are open) list of 'Carnival Classics' that includes mahi mahi (fish), baby back ribs (beef), and grilled chicken. Note that the two main dining rooms are not open for lunch on port days.

Other dining options. A Lido café, called Tiffany's Lido Restaurant, features the usual casual self-serve buffet eats, most of which are non-memorable. The venue includes a deli counter and pizzeria. At night, the venue morphs into the Seaview Bistro, and provides a casual alternative to the main dining rooms, for pasta, steaks, salads, and desserts – it typically operates only between 6pm and 9pm. The food selection, though limited, makes a change from the large, crowded and noisy main dining rooms. Outside on deck is a Mongolian Rotisserie Grill.

There is no specialty (extra-charge) restaurant, as aboard some of the larger ships in the Carnival fleet.

ENTERTAINMENT. The Mikado Showlounge is the venue for large-scale production shows and major cabaret acts – although 20 pillars obstruct some views. During a typical cruise, there will be one or two high-energy production shows, with a cast of two lead singers and a clutch of dancers, backed by a large live band.

SPA/FITNESS. SpaCarnival is a large, glass-wrapped health, fitness, and spa complex is located on the uppermost interior deck, forward of the ship's mast, and is typically open from 6am to 8pm daily. It consists of a gymnasium with ocean-view windows that look out over the bow and the latest in muscle-pumping electronic machines, an aerobics exercise room, men's and women's changing rooms, sauna and steam rooms, beauty salon, and body treatment rooms. Some fitness classes incur an extra charge. A common complaint is that there aren't enough staff to keep the area clean and tidy.

Sporting types can play basketball or volleyball, or table tennis. There is also a banked jogging track on the deck above the spa, and a mini-golf course.

Carnival Fantasy
★★★

Size:.................................Large Resort Ship	Cabins (total):............................. 1,026 or 1,028
Tonnage: 70,367	Size range (sq ft/m): 173.2–409.7/16.0–38.0
Lifestyle: ....Standard	Cabins (outside view):............................. 618 or 620
Cruise line:.......................... Carnival Cruise Lines	Cabins (interior/no view):..............................408
Former names: ....*Fantasy*	Cabins (for one person):...................................0
IMO number: 8700773	Cabins (with private balcony):..........................152
Builder: .... Kvaerner Masa-Yards (Finland)	Cabins (wheelchair accessible): 22
Original cost: .... $225 million	Wheelchair accessibility:...............................Fair
Entered service:................................ Mar 1990	Cabin voltage: .... 110 volts
Registry:.. Panama	Elevators:...14
Length (ft/m):............................... 855.8/263.6	Casino (gaming tables):.................................Yes
Beam (ft/m):................................ 103.0/31.4	Slot machines:..Yes
Draft (ft/m):.................................. 25.9/7.9	Swimming pools:..3
Propulsion/Propellers: .... diesel-electric (42,240kW)/2	Hot tubs (on deck):....................................6
Passenger decks:....................................10	Self-service launderette:..............................Yes
Total crew:...920	Dedicated cinema/seats:................................No
Passengers (lower beds/alll berths):............. 2,056/2,634	Library: ....Yes
Passenger Space Ratio (lower beds/all berths): 34.4/26.7	Onboard currency: ....US$
Crew/Passenger Ratio (lower beds/all berths):.......... 2.2/2.8	

Floating fun palace for ultra-casual first-time cruisers

OVERVIEW. *Carnival Fantasy* is the first (in a series of eight almost identical ships) in the *Fantasy*-class. *Carnival Fantasy* has always been a popular ship – aimed at anyone taking their first cruise.

THE SHIP. The ship, now well over 20 years old, sports the company's trademark red, white, and blue wing-tipped funnel. The open deck space is inadequate when the ship is full and everyone wants to be out on deck. The aft decks used to be less noisy when all the activities are focused around the main swimming pool and hot tubs, but now that a Carnival Waterworks – complete with long (about 300 feet) and short water slides and water-burst fountains – has been added, it's now the noisy, active area. If you enjoy European-style sunning there's also a topless sunbathing area, as well as Serenity – an adult-only 'quiet' lounging space on Deck 9 aft.

There is no walk-around open promenade deck, although there is a short jogging track atop ship. The lifeboats, six of which double as shore tenders are positioned high in the ship – an old design that's not acceptable today.

The interior spaces are well utilized. The general passenger flow is good, and the interior design – the work of Miami-based creative genius Joe Farcus – is clever, functional, and extremely colorful. The ship's interior design theme is inspired by the ancient city of Pompeii, and includes a colorful mix of classic and contemporary.

Berlitz's Ratings

	Possible	Achieved
Ship	500	308
Accommodation	200	138
Food	400	212
Service	400	256
Entertainment	100	73
Cruise	400	244
OVERALL SCORE		
1231 points out of 2000		

The interior focal point is an 'open' atrium lobby. It has a balconied shape, and is dressed to impress. Spanning six decks, it is topped by a large glass dome. The lowest level of the atrium lobby is where you'll find the Purser's Desk and Shore Excursion Desk, together with a popular Atrium Bar (with live music), as well as a small sushi bar off to one side; it's a good central meeting place.

There are public entertainment lounges, bars, and clubs galore, with something for everyone (except quiet space). The public rooms, connected by a double-width Via Marina Promenade, combine a colorful mix of classic and contemporary design elements. Most public rooms and attractions lead off from this boulevard – a sort of shipboard Main Street which runs between the showlounge (forward) and The Forum aft lounge. Gamers and slot players alike will enjoy the almost non-stop action in the Club 21 Casino. There is also a nice looking library and reading room, but few books.

Carnival Fantasy is a floating playground for the young and young-at-heart, and anyone who enjoys constant stimulation and lots of participation events. Because it's a large resort ship, there will be lines for things like shore excursions, security control when re-boarding, and disembarkation, as well as sign-up sheets for fitness equipment.

Forget fashion – the sine qua non – of a Carnival cruise is all about having fun. While the cuisine is just so-so, the real fun begins at sundown when Carnival really excels in sound, lights, and shows. From venues such as the Electricity Dance Club/Disco to the Majestic Cigar Bar, the ships' bars and lounges will certainly entertain you.

Carnival Fantasy, however, is not for those seeking a quiet, relaxing cruise experience. There are many annoying announcements, and the never-ending hustling to get you to buy drinks and many other things. Also, shore excursions are booked via the in-cabin 'Fun Vision' television system, so obtaining advice and suggestions is not easy.

FAMILIES. Kids will almost certainly enjoy Children's World (part of Camp Carnival children's programming), a 1,600-sq-ft (149-sq-m) play area with games and fun stuff for youngsters of all ages, including Apple computers loaded with educational software, and an arts and crafts area with spin- and sand-art machines. An expansive children's water park is a lot of fun as an outdoor play area. Group babysitting is available. Meanwhile teens have their chill-out club, as part of the line's popular Club 02 teen program.

ACCOMMODATION. There are 13 grades of accommodation, ranked by facilities, size, and location. The standard outside-view and interior cabins have decor that is rather plain and unmemorable. They are marginally comfortable, yet spacious enough and practical (most are of the same size and appointments), with good storage space and practical, well-designed no-nonsense bathrooms. However, if you have a queen-bed configuration instead of the standard twin-bed layout, note that one person has to clamber over the bed – an ungainly exercise for those of a heavier build.

Anyone booking an outside suite will find more space, whirlpool bathtubs, and some rather eclectic decor and furniture. These are mildly attractive, but so-so, and they are much smaller than those aboard ships of a similar size of competing companies. A small gift basket of toiletry samples is provided in all grades.

Book a Category 11 or 12 suite and you get Skipper's Club priority check-in at any US homeland port – useful for getting ahead of the crowd.

Some 50 cabins feature inter-connecting doors – these cabins are good for families with children who want them to be close – but not so close.

Room service items are available 24 hours a day, although in standard-grade cabins, only cold food is available, while occupants of suite-grade accommodation have a greater range of items (both hot and cold) to choose from.

DINING. The two large main dining rooms, Celebration and Jubilee, are located amidships and aft. Both have ocean-view windows and attractive, but very bright décor, but they are noisy. Choose either fixed-time dining (6pm or 8:15pm) or flexible dining (any time between 5:45 and 9:30pm).

The food is just so-so. Presentation is simple, and few garnishes are used. Many meat and fowl dishes are disguised with gravies and sauces – and few garnishes are used. The selection of fresh green vegetables, breads, rolls, cheeses, and fruits is limited, and there is much use of canned fruit and jellied desserts. There's a decent wine list, but no wine waiters. The waiters sing and dance, and there are constant waiter parades – so it's really more about 'foodertainment' than food quality. If you want something really simple, there's an 'always available' list of 'Carnival Classics' that includes mahi mahi (fish), baby back ribs (beef), and grilled chicken. Note that the two main dining rooms are not open for lunch on port days.

Other dining options. A Lido café, the Paris Lido restaurant, features the usual casual self-serve buffet eats, most of which are non-memorable. The venue includes a deli counter and pizzeria. At night, the venue morphs into the Seaview Bistro, and provides a casual alternative to the main dining rooms, for pasta, steaks, salads, and desserts – it typically operates only between 6pm and 9pm. The food selection, though limited, makes a change from the large, crowded and noisy main dining rooms. Outside on deck is a Mongolian Rotisserie Grill; it has a fancy name for wok-stir-fried food and grilled items

A patisserie offers specialty coffees and sweets (extra charge), and a so-called sushi bar off to one side of the atrium lobby bar on Promenade Deck is open prior to dinner; if you know anything about sushi, don't expect authenticity.

There is no specialty (extra-charge) restaurant, as aboard some of the larger ships in the Carnival fleet.

ENTERTAINMENT. The Universe Showlounge is the venue for large-scale production shows and major cabaret acts – although 20 pillars obstruct some views. During a typical cruise, there will be one or two high-energy production shows, with a cast of two lead singers and a clutch of dancers, backed by a large live band.

SPA/FITNESS. SpaCarnival is a large, glass-wrapped health, fitness, and spa complex is located on the uppermost interior deck, forward of the ship's mast, and is typically open from 6am to 8pm daily. It consists of a gymnasium with ocean-view windows that look out over the bow and the latest in muscle-pumping electronic machines, an aerobics exercise room, men's and women's changing rooms, sauna and steam rooms, beauty salon, and body treatment rooms. Some fitness classes may incur an extra charge. A common complaint is that there aren't enough staff to keep the area clean and tidy.

Sporting types can play basketball or volleyball, or table tennis. There is also a banked jogging track outdoors on the deck above the spa, and a mini-golf course.

Carnival Fascination
★★★

Size:.................................Large Resort Ship	Cabins (total):............................ 1,026 or 1,028
Tonnage: 70,538	Size range (sq ft/m): 173.2-409.7/16.0-38.0
Lifestyle: ....Standard	Cabins (outside view):........................ 618 or 620
Cruise line:........................ Carnival Cruise Lines	Cabins (interior/no view):...........................408
Former names: ....Fascination	Cabins (for one person):...............................0
IMO number: 9041253	Cabins (with private balcony):.......................250
Builder: .... Kvaerner Masa-Yards (Finland)	Cabins (wheelchair accessible): 22
Original cost:...............................$225 million	Wheelchair accessibility:...........................Fair
Entered service:.................................Jul 1994	Cabin voltage: .... 110 volts
Registry:....................................The Bahamas	Elevators:...14
Length (ft/m):.............................. 855.8/263.6	Casino (gaming tables):.............................Yes
Beam (ft/m):............................... 103.0/31.4	Slot machines:.....................................Yes
Draft (ft/m):.................................. 25.9/7.9	Swimming pools:.....................................3
Propulsion/Propellers:...........diesel-electric (42,240 kW)/2	Hot tubs (on deck):.................................6
Passenger decks:....................................10	Self-service launderette:...........................Yes
Total crew:.......................................920	Dedicated cinema/seats:.............................No
Passengers (lower beds/alll berths):............. 2,056/2,634	Library: ....Yes
Passenger Space Ratio (lower beds/all berths): 34.4/26.7	Onboard currency: ....US$
Crew/Passenger Ratio (lower beds/all berths):.......... 2.2/2.8	

Floating fun palace for ultra-casual first-time cruisers

OVERVIEW. *Carnival Fascination* is the fourth (in a series of eight almost identical ships) in the Carnival *Fantasy*-class. This has always been a popular ship – aimed at anyone taking their first cruise.

THE SHIP. *Carnival Fascination*'s open deck space is really inadequate when the ship is full and everyone wants to be out on deck. The aft decks, however, tend to be less noisy, because all the activities are focused around the main swimming pool and hot tubs (one with a thatched shade). For anyone who prefers European-style sunning there's also a topless sunbathing area, as well as Serenity – an adult-only 'quiet' lounging space on Deck 9 aft. While there isn't a walk-around open promenade deck, there is a short jogging track atop ship. The lifeboats, six of which double as shore tenders, are positioned high in the ship – this wouldn't be acceptable in new ships today.

The interior spaces are well utilized. The general passenger flow is good, and the interior design – the work of Miami-based creative genius Joe Farcus – is clever, functional, and extremely colorful, and includes plenty of neon and glitz. He calls it 'entertainment architecture' and considers every part of a ship as a piece of a giant jigsaw puzzle. The ship's interior design theme is all about Hollywood and the movies. There are great photo opportunities with some 24 life-like figures from the movies.

The interior focal point is an 'open' atrium lobby, with its balconied shape, and is dressed to impress, it

Berlitz's Ratings		
	Possible	Achieved
Ship	500	309
Accommodation	200	138
Food	400	212
Service	400	262
Entertainment	100	73
Cruise	400	245
OVERALL SCORE		
1239 points out of 2000		

spans six decks, and is topped by a large glass dome. The lowest level of the atrium lobby is where you'll find the Purser's Desk and Shore Excursion Desk, together with a popular atrium Bar (with live music), as well as a small sushi bar off to one side; it's a good central meeting place.

There are public entertainment lounges, bars, and clubs galore, with something for everyone (except quiet space). The public rooms, connected by a double-width Via Marina Promenade, combine a colorful mix of classic and contemporary design elements. Most public rooms and attractions lead off from this boulevard – a sort of shipboard Main Street which runs between the showlounge (forward) and the Puttin' on the Ritz aft lounge. Gamers and slot players alike will enjoy the almost non-stop action in the Club 21 Casino. There is also a nice looking library and reading room, but few books, and there's also a 1,200-sq-ft (111-sq-m) conference room. As for the 'art' in the Art Gallery it's rather tacky, to say the least!

Forget fashion – the sine qua non – of a Carnival cruise is all about having fun. While the cuisine is just so-so, the real fun begins at sundown when Carnival really excels in sound, lights, and shows. From venues such as the Diamonds are Forever Dance Club/Disco to the Beverly Hills Cigar Bar, the ships' interior decor will certainly entertain you.

Carnival Fascination is a floating playground for the young and young-at-heart, and anyone who enjoys constant stimulation and lots of participation events. This really is cruising Splash Vegas style. Because it's a large resort ship, there will be lines for things like shore excursions.

Carnival Fascination, however, is not for those seeking a quiet, relaxing cruise experience. There are many annoying announcements, and the never-ending hustling to get you to buy drinks and many other things. Also, shore excursions are booked via the in-cabin 'Fun Vision' television system, so obtaining advice and suggestions is not easy.

FAMILIES. Kids will almost certainly enjoy Children's World (part of Camp Carnival children's programming), a 1,600-sq-ft (149-sq-m) play area with games and fun stuff for youngsters of all ages, including Apple computers loaded with educational software, and an arts and crafts area with spin- and sand-art machines. An expansive children's water park is a lot of fun as an outdoor play area. Group babysitting is available ($6 per hour for the first child; $4 per hour for each additional child of the same immediate family). Meanwhile teens have their chill-out club, as part of the line's popular Club O2 teen program.

ACCOMMODATION. There are 13 grades of accommodation, ranked by facilities, size, and location. The standard outside-view and interior cabins have decor that is rather plain and unmemorable. They are marginally comfortable, yet spacious enough and practical (most are of the same size and appointments), with good storage space and practical, well-designed no-nonsense bathrooms. However, if you have a queen-bed configuration instead of the standard twin-bed layout, note that one person has to clamber over the bed – an ungainly exercise for those of a heavier build.

Anyone booking an outside suite will find more space, whirlpool bathtubs, and some rather eclectic decor and furniture. These are mildly attractive, but so-so, and they are much smaller than those aboard ships of a similar size of competing companies. A small gift basket of toiletry samples is provided in all grades.

Book a Category 11 or 12 suite and you get Skipper's Club priority check-in at any US homeland port – useful for getting ahead of the crowd.

Room service items are available 24 hours a day, although in standard cabins, only cold food is available, while those in suite-grade accommodation get a greater range of items (both hot and cold) to choose from.

CUISINE. The two large main dining rooms, Sensation and Imagination, are located midships and aft. Both have ocean-view windows and attractive, but very bright décor, but they are noisy. Choose either fixed-time dining (6pm or 8:15pm) or flexible dining (any time between 5:45 and 9:30pm).

The food is so-so. Presentation is simple, and few garnishes are used. Many meat and fowl dishes are disguised with gravies and sauces – and few garnishes are used. The selection of fresh green vegetables, breads, rolls, cheeses, and fruits is limited, and there is much use of canned fruit and jellied desserts. There's a decent wine list, but no wine waiters. The waiters sing and dance, and there are constant waiter parades – so it's really more about 'foodertainment' than food quality. Remember, however, that this is bog-standard catering – with all its attendant standardization and production cooking (it is, therefore, difficult to obtain anything unusual or 'off-menu.'

A Lido café, called Coconut Grove Bar & Grill, features the usual casual self-serve buffet eats, most of which are non-memorable. The venue includes a deli counter and pizzeria. At night, the venue morphs into the Seaview Bistro, and provides a casual alternative to the main dining rooms, for pasta, steaks, salads, and desserts – it typically operates only between 6pm and 9pm. The food selection, though limited, makes a change from the large, crowded and noisy main dining rooms. Outside on deck is a Mongolian Rotisserie Grill; it has a fancy name for wok-stir-fried food and grilled items

A patisserie offers specialty coffees and sweets (extra charge), and a so-called sushi bar off to one side of the atrium lobby bar on Promenade Deck is open prior to dinner; if you know anything about sushi, don't expect authenticity.

There is no specialty (extra-charge) restaurant, as aboard some of the larger ships in the Carnival fleet.

ENTERTAINMENT. The Palace Showlounge is the venue for large-scale production shows and major cabaret acts – although 20 pillars obstruct some views. During a typical cruise, there will be one or two high-energy production shows, with a cast of two lead singers and a clutch of dancers, backed by a large live band.

SPA/FITNESS. SpaCarnival is a large, glass-wrapped health, fitness, and spa complex is located on the uppermost interior deck, forward of the ship's mast; it is typically open from 6am to 8pm daily. It consists of a gymnasium with ocean-view windows that look out over the bow and the latest in muscle-pumping electronic machines, an aerobics exercise room, men's and women's changing rooms, sauna and steam rooms, beauty salon, and body treatment rooms. Some fitness classes (such as kick-boxing or yoga) may incur an extra charge. A common complaint is that there aren't enough staff to keep the area clean and tidy, and used towels are often strewn around the changing rooms.

Sporting types can play basketball or volleyball, or table tennis. There is also a banked jogging track outdoors on the deck above the spa, and a mini-golf course.

Carnival Freedom
★★★ +

Size:................................Large Resort Ship	Cabins (total):.................................... 1,487
Tonnage: 110,320	Size range (sq ft/m): 179.7–484.2/16.7–44.8
Lifestyle: ....Standard	Cabins (outside view):................................917
Cruise line:...................... Carnival Cruise Lines	Cabins (interior/no view):.............................570
Former names: ....none	Cabins (for one person):...............................0
IMO number: 9333149	Cabins (with private balcony):........................574
Builder: .... Fincantieri (Italy)	Cabins (wheelchair accessible): 25
Original cost: .... $500 million	Wheelchair accessibility:.............................Good
Entered service:........................... Feb 2007	Cabin voltage: .... 110 volts
Registry:...................................... Panama	Elevators:...20
Length (ft/m):.............................. 951.4/290.0	Casino (gaming tables):.............................. Yes
Beam (ft/m):............................... 105.6/32.2	Slot machines:..................................... Yes
Draft (ft/m): 27.2/8.3	Swimming pools:....................2 (1 w/sliding glass dome)
Propulsion/Propellers:............ diesel-electric (63,400kW)/2	Hot tubs (on deck):..................................7
Passenger decks:...................................13	Self-service launderette:........................... Yes
Total crew:....................................... 1,150	Dedicated cinema/seats:..............................No
Passengers (lower beds/alll berths):............ 2,974/3,700	Library: .... Yes
Passenger Space Ratio (lower beds/all berths): 37.0/29.7	Onboard currency: ....US$
Crew/Passenger Ratio (lower beds/all berths):......... 2.5/3.1	

A fun-filled, alive-at-night ship with exciting decor

OVERVIEW. *Carnival Freedom* shares the same generally balanced profile as sisters *Carnival Conquest*, *Carnival Sunshine*, *Carnival Glory*, *Carnival Liberty*, *Carnival Triumph*, *Carnival Valor*, and *Carnival Victory*. It is too big to transit the Panama Canal. Immediately recognizable is the swept-back wingtip funnel, Carnival's trademark.

THE SHIP. The interior decor is a kaleidoscopic blend of colors that stimulate and excite the senses, and is dedicated to time, and the decades. The deck and public room layout is logical, and finding your way around is quite easy. Most of the public rooms are located on one deck off a main interior boulevard, above a deck which contains the two main dining rooms. The public rooms include a large casino with gaming tables and over 300 slot machines.

If you remember drive-in movie theaters, Carnival's Seaside Theatre for movies on deck recalls classic drive-in movie theaters, with seating in tiered rows and the screen facing forward. The ship has bow-to-stern Wi-Fi Internet access, including all passenger cabins.

Carnival Freedom is a large floating playground for the young and young-at-heart, and anyone who enjoys constant stimulation and lots of participation events, together with the three 'Gs' – glitz, glamour, and gambling. This really is cruising Splash Vegas style – and fun, all-American experience. Because it's a large resort ship, there will be lines for things like

Berlitz's Ratings

	Possible	Achieved
Ship	500	377
Accommodation	200	144
Food	400	218
Service	400	260
Entertainment	100	77
Cruise	400	260

OVERALL SCORE
1336 points out of 2000

shore excursions, security control when re-boarding, and disembarkation, as well as sign-up sheets for fitness equipment.

Forget fashion – the sine qua non – of a Carnival cruise is all about having fun. While the cuisine is just so-so, the real fun begins at sundown when Carnival really excels in sound, lights, razzle-dazzle shows, and late-night high volume sounds.

Minor niggles include the fact that many pillars obstruct passenger flow, particularly in the dining room, where they make it difficult for the waiters to serve food properly.

FAMILIES. Youngsters are provided with their own Camp Carnival children's club with its own small outdoor pool, and are well cared for with the line's extensive children's program. Camp Carnival is located on Sun Deck, out of the way of older passengers.

ACCOMMODATION. There are 20 cabin-price categories, in seven different suite/cabin types, sizes, and grades. These include suites with private balcony; deluxe outside-view cabins with private balcony; outside-view cabins with private balcony; outside-view cabins with window; cabins with a porthole instead of a window; interior cabins; and interior with upper and lower berths.

There are five decks of cabins with private balconies. Standard cabins are of good size and come equipped with all the basics, although the furniture is rather square and angular, with no rounded edges.

Three decks of cabins (eight on each deck, each with private balcony) overlook the stern. Most cabins with twin beds convert to a queen-size bed format.

Book a suite (Category 11 or 12 in the Carnival Cruise Lines brochure), and you'll get Skipper's Club priority check-in at any US homeland port – useful for getting ahead of the crowd.

There are even 'spa' cabins aboard this ship – a grouping of 18 cabins located directly around and behind SpaCarnival; so fitness devotees can get out of bed and go straight to the treadmill without having to go through any of the public rooms first.

A gift basket of toiletries is provided in all grades of cabins; it includes aloe soap, shampoo, conditioner, deodorant, breath mints, candy, and pain relief tablets (all in sample sizes – and most in paper packets that are difficult, sometimes frustrating, to open).

DINING. There are two principal dining rooms (Chic, located midships, seating 744; and Posh, aft, seating 1,122). Both are two decks high and have a balcony level (the balcony level in Posh is larger than the one in Chic. There's a choice of either fixed time dining (6pm or 8:15pm) or flexible dining (any time between 5:45pm and 9:30pm). Note that the two main dining rooms are not open for lunch on port days.

There are few tables for two, but among my favorites are two tables for two right at the very back of the restaurant, with ocean views astern.

Other dining options. The Sun King Supper Club has fine table settings, china, and silverware, as well as leather-bound menus. The featured specialties are steaks and seafood items. It's worth paying the cover charge to get a taste of what Carnival can really deliver in terms of food that's of better quality than what's served in the main dining rooms.

The Freedom Restaurant, a casual self-serve international food court-style lido deck eatery, has two main serving lines. Included in this eating mall are a deli, an Asian eatery with wok preparation, a 24-hour pizzeria, and a grill for fast foods such as hamburgers and hot dogs. Each night the Freedom Restaurant morphs into the Seaview Bistro and provides a dress-down alternative to eating in the main dining rooms, serving pasta, steaks, salads, and desserts (typically 6–9pm).

Other nook-and-cranny food- and drink-related places include the Nouveau Wine Bar, the Viennese Café, and the cute little Meiji Sushi Bar. All are located on Promenade Deck and cost extra.

ENTERTAINMENT. The Victoriana Theater (named after England's Queen Victoria) is the ship's multi-deck showlounge, seating up to 1,400 and staging colorful Las Vegas-style production shows and major cabaret acts. It has a revolving stage, hydraulic orchestra pit, superb sound, and seating on three levels (the upper levels being tiered through two decks). A proscenium arch acts as a scenery loft. The decor is medieval – drinks tables look like shields, and coats of armor and towers with stained-glass windows flank the stage.

An alternative entertainment venue is the aft lounge, which seats 425 and typically features live music and late-night cabaret acts including smutty adult comedy.

Body-throbbing loud music sensations can be found in the ship's discotheque; it includes a video wall with live projections from the dance floor. Meanwhile piano bar lovers should enjoy the 100-seat Lindy Hop piano bar.

SPA/FITNESS. SpaCarnival, spanning two decks with a total area of approximately 13,300 sq ft/1,235 sq m, is located above the navigation bridge, and accessed from the forward stairway. Lower-level facilities include a solarium, eight treatment rooms, lecture rooms, sauna and steam rooms for men and women, and a beauty parlor; the upper level consists of a large gymnasium with floor-to-ceiling windows including forward-facing ocean views, and an aerobics room with instructor-led classes (some at extra cost) for which you'll need to sign up.

Plimsoll mark

The safety of ships at sea and all those aboard owes much to the 19th-century social reformer Samuel Plimsoll, a member of the British Parliament concerned about the frequent loss of ships due to overloading. In those days, some ship owners would load their vessels down to the gunwales to squeeze every ounce of revenue out of them. They gambled on good weather, good fortune, and good seamanship to bring them safely into port. Consequently, many ships went to the bottom of the sea – the result of their buoyancy being seriously impaired by overloading.

Plimsoll helped to enact legislation that came to be known as the Merchant Shipping Act of 1875. This required ship owners to mark their vessels with a circular disc 12ins (30cm) long bisected by a line 18ins (46cm) long, as a measure of their maximum draft; that is, the depth to which a ship's hull could be safely immersed at sea.

The Merchant Shipping Act of 1890 went even further and required the Plimsoll mark (or line) to be positioned on the sides of vessels in accordance with tables drawn up by competent authorities.

The Plimsoll mark is now found on the ships of every nation. It indicates three different depths: the depth to which a vessel can be loaded in fresh water, which is less buoyant than salt water; the depth in summer, when seas are generally calmer; and the depth in winter, when seas are much rougher.

Carnival Glory
★★★ +

Size:....................................Large Resort Ship	Cabins (total):....................................1,487
Tonnage: 110,239	Size range (sq ft/m): 179.7–482.2/16.7–44.8
Lifestyle: ....Standard	Cabins (outside view):...............................917
Cruise line:........................Carnival Cruise Lines	Cabins (interior/no view):............................570
Former names: ....none	Cabins (for one person):................................0
IMO number: 9198367	Cabins (with private balcony):.........................590
Builder: ....Fincantieri (Italy)	Cabins (wheelchair accessible): 25
Original cost:...........................$500 million	Wheelchair accessibility:............................Good
Entered service:............................Jul 2003	Cabin voltage: ....110 volts
Registry:....................................Panama	Elevators:.....................................14
Length (ft/m):............................951.4/290.0	Casino (gaming tables):............................Yes
Beam (ft/m):..............................116.4/35.5	Slot machines:..................................Yes
Draft (ft/m):...............................27.0/8.2	Swimming pools:.................2 (1 w/sliding glass dome)
Propulsion/Propellers: ....diesel-electric (63,400kW)/2	Hot tubs (on deck):..................................7
Passenger decks:................................13	Self-service launderette:............................Yes
Total crew:...................................1,160	Dedicated cinema/seats:..............................No
Passengers (lower beds/alll berths):.............2,974/3,700	Library: ....Yes
Passenger Space Ratio (lower beds/all berths):.......37.0/29.7	Onboard currency: ....US$
Crew/Passenger Ratio (lower beds/all berths):..........2.5/3.1	

An ultra-casual fun-filled ship for first-time cruisers

OVERVIEW. Like its sisters – *Carnival Conquest*, *Carnival Sunshine*, *Carnival Freedom*, *Carnival Liberty*, *Carnival Triumph*, and *Carnival Victory* – this ship has three decks full of lounges, 10 bars, and lots of rooms to play in. Its interior decor is a fantasyland of colors, with every hue of the rainbow represented. The layout is logical, so finding your way around is easy. It has extremely short bows and cannot transit the Panama Canal.

Berlitz's Ratings		
	Possible	Achieved
Ship	500	363
Accommodation	200	144
Food	400	218
Service	400	259
Entertainment	100	76
Cruise	400	256
OVERALL SCORE		
1316 points out of 2000		

THE SHIP. Most of *Carnival Glory*'s public rooms are located off the Kaleidoscope Boulevard, the main interior promenade – great for strolling and people-watching. The larger of two atriums, The Colors Lobby spans nine decks in the forward third of the ship. Check out the interpretative paintings of US flags at the Color Bar – the colors really are kaleidoscopic. The aft atrium goes through three decks.

Amidships on the open deck is a long water slide (200ft/60m long), as well as tiered sunbathing decks positioned between two swimming pools, several hot tubs, and a giant poolside (Seaside Theater) movie screen. It's all about imagination and sensorial fantasy and is more reserved than Carnival's *Fantasy*-class ships.

There are three decks full of lounges, 10 bars, and lots of rooms to play in. There are two atriums: the largest, the forward, glass-domed Artists Atrium spans nine decks, while the aft atrium goes through three decks.

The Camel Club casino is large and action-packed, with over 320 slot machines alongside all the popular gaming tables. There are several other nightspots for

just about every musical taste (except for opera, ballet, and classical music lovers), such as the Ivory Club Bar, Ebony Aft Cabaret Lounge, Cinn-a-Bar (Piano Bar), White Heat Dance Club, and Bar Blue.

Carnival Glory is a large floating playground for the young and young-at-heart, and anyone who enjoys constant stimulation and lots of participation events, together with the three 'Gs' – glitz, glamour, and gambling. This really is cruising Splash Vegas style – and fun, all-American experience. Because it's a large resort ship, there will be lines for things like shore excursions, security control when re-boarding, and disembarkation, as well as sign-up sheets for fitness equipment.

Forget fashion – the sine qua non – of a Carnival cruise is all about having fun. While the cuisine is just so-so, the real fun begins at sundown when Carnival really excels in sound, lights, razzle-dazzle shows, and late-night high volume sounds.

FAMILIES. Youngsters have good facilities, such as their own two-level Children's Club (including an outdoor pool), and are well cared for with Camp Carnival, the line's extensive children's program. Teens have their very own 'Circle C' club as a chill-out hangout. Note that soft-drinks packages can be purchased for children (and adults).

ACCOMMODATION. There are numerous cabin-price categories, in seven different grades: suites with private balcony; deluxe outside-view cabins with private balcony; outside-view cabins with private balcony; outside-view cabins with window; cabins with a porthole instead of a window; interior cabins; interior cabins with upper and lower berths. The price reflects the grade, location, and size.

Five decks of cabins have a private balcony – but many are not quite so private, and can be overlooked from various public locations.

There are 18 'fitness' cabins, located directly around and behind the SpaCarnival. This allows fitness devotees to get out of bed and go straight to the treadmill without having to go through any of the public rooms first.

The standard cabins are of good size and are equipped with all the basics, although the furniture is rather angular, with no rounded edges. Three decks of cabins (eight on each deck, each with private balcony) overlook the stern. Most cabins with twin beds can be converted to a queen-size bed format. A gift basket is provided in all grades of cabin; it includes aloe soap, shampoo, conditioner, deodorant, breath mints, candy, and pain relief tablets (all in sample sizes).

Note: If you book one of the Category 11 or 12 suites you get 'Skipper's Club' priority check-in at any US homeland port – useful for getting ahead of the crowd.

Facilities are similar to those aboard *Carnival Conquest*.

DINING. The two principal dining rooms, Golden and Platinum, are two decks high, and both have a balcony level for diners. The decor includes wall coverings featuring a pattern of Japanese bonsai trees. There is also a casual self-serve food court-style lido deck eatery, the two-level Red Sail Restaurant, which includes Paul's Deli, Mongolian Wok, a 24-hour pizzeria, and a patisserie. Choose either fixed-time dining (6pm or 8:15pm) or flexible dining (any time between 5:45 and 9:30pm). Note that the two main dining rooms are not open for lunch on port days.

Specialty dining (reservations-only, extra cost) is provided in The Steakhouse, which serves prime steaks and grilled seafood and has lighting fixtures that look like giant emeralds.

ENTERTAINMENT. The Amber Palace Showlounge is is a multi-deck showroom seating 1,400. It has a revolving stage, hydraulic orchestra pit, superb sound, and seating on three levels (the upper levels being tiered through two decks). A proscenium over the stage acts as a scenery loft.

Hasbro, The Game Show was also added in 2012; the show includes audience participation, as competitive interpretations of the larger-than-life board games.

Jazz lovers should head for the Bar Blue. The Cinn-A-Bar is a piano bar with curved aluminum walls – so 'bending' notes should be easy.

SPA/FITNESS. SpaCarnival is a large health, fitness, and spa complex that spans two decks (the walls display hand-painted reproductions of the artist's poster work). It is directly above the navigation bridge in the forward part of the ship and is accessed from the forward stairway.

Facilities on the lower level include a solarium, eight treatment rooms, lecture rooms, sauna and steam rooms for men and women, and a beauty parlor. The upper level consists of a large gymnasium with floor-to-ceiling windows on three sides, including forward-facing ocean views, and an aerobics room with instructor-led classes, some at extra cost.

The bridge

A ship's navigation bridge is manned at all times, both at sea and in port. The captain is always on call. Other senior officers take 'watch' turns for four- or eight-hour periods. In addition, junior officers are continually honing their skills as experienced navigators, waiting for the day when they will be promoted to master.

The captain is always in command at times of high risk, such as when the ship is entering or leaving a port, when the density of traffic is particularly high, or when visibility is severely restricted by poor weather.

Navigation has come a long way since the days of the ancient mariners, who used only the sun and the stars to calculate their course across the oceans. The space-age development of sophisticated navigation devices (using satellites) has enabled us to eliminate the guesswork of early navigation (the first global mobile satellite system came into being in 1979).

A ship's navigator today uses a variety of sophisticated instruments to pinpoint the ship's position at any time and establish its course.

Carnival Imagination
★★★

Size:.....Large Resort Ship	Cabins (total):.....1,028
Tonnage: 70,367	Size range (sq ft/m): 173.2–409.7/16–38
Lifestyle: .....Standard	Cabins (outside view):.....620
Cruise line:.....Carnival Cruise Lines	Cabins (interior/no view):.....408
Former names: .....*Imagination*	Cabins (for one person):.....0
IMO number: 9053878	Cabins (with private balcony):.....152
Builder: .....Kvaerner Masa-Yards (Finland)	Cabins (wheelchair accessible): 22
Original cost:.....$330 million	Wheelchair accessibility:.....Fair
Entered service:.....Jul 1995	Cabin voltage: .....110 volts
Registry:.....The Bahamas	Elevators:.....14
Length (ft/m):.....855.0/260.6	Casino (gaming tables):.....Yes
Beam (ft/m):.....103.0/31.4	Slot machines:.....Yes
Draft (ft/m):.....25.9/7.9	Swimming pools:.....3
Propulsion/Propellers: .....diesel-electric (42,240kW)/2	Hot tubs (on deck):.....6
Passenger decks:.....10	Self-service launderette:.....Yes
Total crew:.....920	Dedicated cinema/seats:.....No
Passengers (lower beds/alll berths):.....2,056/2,634	Library:.....Yes
Passenger Space Ratio (lower beds/all berths): 34.4/26.7	Onboard currency: .....US$
Crew/Passenger Ratio (lower beds/all berths):.....2.2/2.8	

It's a fun ship filled with high-energy cruisers

OVERVIEW. *Carnival Imagination* is the fifth (in a series of eight almost identical ships) in the Carnival Fantasy-class. *Carnival Imagination* has always been a popular ship – aimed at anyone taking their first cruise.

THE SHIP. While the open deck space is reasonable, it is really inadequate when the ship is full and everyone wants to be out on deck. The aft decks used to be less noisy when all the activities are focused around the main swimming pool and hot tubs, but now that a Carnival Waterworks – complete with long (about 300 feet) and short water slides and water-burst fountains – has been added, it's now the noisy, active area.

For those who prefer European-style sunning there's also a topless sunbathing area, as well as Serenity – an adult-only 'quiet' lounging space on Deck 9 aft. There is no walk-around open promenade deck, although there is a short jogging track atop ship. The lifeboats, six of which double as shore tenders are positioned high in the ship.

The interior spaces are well utilized. The general passenger flow is good and the interior design – the work of Miami-based creative genius Joe Farcus – is clever, functional, and extremely colorful. The interior design theme is all about the legendary symbols of antiquity (think winged deities and beings).

The interior focal point is an 'open' atrium lobby, with its balconied shape, dressed to impress. It spans six decks, and topped by a large glass dome. The lowest level of the atrium lobby is where you'll find the Purs-

Berlitz's Ratings		
	Possible	Achieved
Ship	500	309
Accommodation	200	138
Food	400	212
Service	400	262
Entertainment	100	73
Cruise	400	242
OVERALL SCORE		
1236 points out of 2000		

er's Desk and Shore Excursion Desk, together with a popular Atrium Bar (with live music), as well as a small sushi bar off to one side.

There are public entertainment lounges, bars, and clubs galore, with something for everyone (except quiet space). The public rooms, connected by a double-width Via Marina Promenade, combine a colorful mix of classic and contemporary design elements. Most public rooms and attractions lead off from this boulevard – a sort of shipboard Main Street which runs between the showlounge (forward) and Xanadu aft lounge. Gamers and slot players alike will enjoy the almost non-stop action in the El Dorado Casino. There is also a nice looking library and reading room, but few books, and there's also a 1,200-sq-ft (111-sq-m) conference room.

Forget fashion – the sine qua non – of a Carnival cruise is all about having fun. While the cuisine is just so-so, the real fun begins at sundown when Carnival really excels in sound, lights, and shows. From venues such as the Illusions Dance Club/Disco to the Pinnacle Cigar Bar, the ships' interior decor will certainly entertain you.

Carnival Imagination is a floating playground for the young and young-at-heart, and anyone who enjoys constant stimulation and lots of participation events. This really is cruising Splash Vegas style. Because it's a large resort ship, there will be lines for things like shore excursions, security control when re-boarding, and disembarkation.

Carnival Imagination, however, is not for those seeking a quiet, relaxing cruise experience. There are many annoying announcements, and the never-ending hustling to get you to buy drinks and many other things. Also, shore excursions are booked via the in-cabin 'Fun Vision' television system, so obtaining advice and suggestions is not easy.

FAMILIES. Kids will almost certainly enjoy Children's World (part of Camp Carnival children's programming), a 1,600-sq-ft (149-sq-m) play area with games and fun stuff for youngsters of all ages, including Apple computers loaded with educational software, and an arts and crafts area with spin- and sand-art machines. An expansive children's water park is a lot of fun as an outdoor play area. Group babysitting is available. Meanwhile teens have their chill-out club, as part of the line's popular Club 02 teen program.

ACCOMMODATION. There are 13 grades of accommodation, ranked by facilities, size, and location. The standard outside-view and interior cabins have decor that is rather plain and unmemorable. They are marginally comfortable, yet spacious enough and practical (most are of the same size and appointments), with good storage space and practical, well-designed no-nonsense bathrooms. However, if you have a queen-bed configuration instead of the standard twin-bed layout, note that one person has to clamber over the bed – an ungainly exercise.

Anyone booking an outside suite will find more space, whirlpool bathtubs, and some rather eclectic decor and furniture. These are mildly attractive, but so-so, and they are much smaller than those aboard ships of a similar size of competing companies. A small gift basket of toiletry samples is provided in all grades.

Book a Category 11 or 12 suite and you get Skipper's Club priority check-in at any US homeland port – useful for getting ahead of the crowd.

Families now have 50 connecting cabins to choose from – good if you have children and want them close by, but not that close.

Room service items are available 24 hours a day, although in standard cabins, only cold food is available, while those in suite-grade accommodation get a greater range of items (both hot and cold) to choose from a large health, fitness, and spa complex that spans two decks (the walls display hand-painted reproductions of the artist's poster work). It is directly above the navigation bridge in the forward part of the ship and is accessed from the forward stairway.

DINING. The two large main dining rooms, Pride and Spirit, are located amidships and aft. Both have ocean-view windows and attractive, but very bright décor, but they are noisy. Choose either fixed-time dining (6pm or 8:15pm) or flexible dining (any time between 5:45 and 9:30pm). Note that the two main dining rooms are not open for lunch on port days.

The food is so-so; presentation is simple, and few garnishes are used. Many meat and fowl dishes are disguised with gravies and sauces – and few garnishes are used. The selection of fresh green vegetables, breads, rolls, cheeses, and fruits is limited, and there is much use of canned fruit and jellied desserts. There's a decent wine list, but no wine waiters.

Waiters sing and dance, and there are constant waiter parades – so it's really more about 'foodertainment' than food quality. Remember, however, that this is bog-standard catering – with all its attendant standardization and production cooking; it is, therefore, difficult to obtain anything unusual or 'off-menu.' For something simple, a selection of always available (when the dining rooms are open) 'Carnival Classics' includes mahi mahi (fish), baby back ribs (beef), and grilled chicken. Note that the two main dining rooms are not open for lunch on port days.

Other dining options. The Horizon Bar & Grill acts as a lido cafe, and features casual self-serve buffet eats, most of which are non-memorable. The venue includes a deli counter and pizzeria. At night, the venue morphs into the Seaview Bistro, and provides a casual alternative to the main dining rooms, for pasta, steaks, salads, and desserts – it typically operates only between 6pm and 9pm. The food selection, though limited, makes a change from the large, crowded and noisy main dining rooms. Outside on deck is a Mongolian Rotisserie Grill.

A patisserie offers specialty coffees and sweets (extra charge), and a so-called sushi bar off to one side of the atrium lobby bar on Promenade Deck is open prior to dinner; if you know anything about sushi, don't expect authenticity.

There is no specialty (extra-charge) restaurant, as aboard some of the larger ships in the Carnival fleet.

ENTERTAINMENT. The Universe Showlounge is the venue for the large-scale production shows and major cabaret acts – although 20 pillars obstruct the views from some seats. During a typical cruise, there will be one or two shows, with a cast of two lead singers and a clutch of dancers, backed by a large live band.

SPA/FITNESS. SpaCarnival is a large, glass-wrapped health, fitness, and spa complex. It is located on the uppermost interior deck, forward of the ship's mast, and is typically open from 6am to 8pm daily. It consists of a gym with windows that look out over the bow and the latest in machines, an aerobics room, changing rooms, sauna and steam rooms, beauty salon, and body treatment rooms. A common complaint is that there is not enough staff to keep the area clean and tidy.

Sporting types can play basketball or volleyball, or table tennis. There is also a banked jogging track on the deck above the spa, and a mini-golf course.

Carnival Inspiration
★★★

Size:	.Large Resort Ship	Cabins (total):	1,028
Tonnage:	70,367	Size range (sq ft/m):	173.2–409.7/16–38
Lifestyle:	.Standard	Cabins (outside view):	.620
Cruise line:	Carnival Cruise Lines	Cabins (interior/no view):	.408
Former names:	Inspiration	Cabins (for one person):	.0
IMO number:	9047489	Cabins (with private balcony):	.152
Builder:	Kvaerner Masa-Yards (Finland)	Cabins (wheelchair accessible):	.22
Original cost:	$270 million	Wheelchair accessibility:	.Fair
Entered service:	.Apr 1996	Cabin voltage:	110 volts
Registry:	The Bahamas	Elevators:	.14
Length (ft/m):	855.0/260.6	Casino (gaming tables):	Yes
Beam (ft/m):	103.0/31.4	Slot machines:	Yes
Draft (ft/m):	25.9/7.9	Swimming pools:	.3
Propulsion/Propellers:	diesel-electric (42,240kW)/2	Hot tubs (on deck):	.6
Passenger decks:	10	Self-service launderette:	Yes
Total crew:	920	Dedicated cinema/seats:	.No
Passengers (lower beds/alll berths):	2,056/2,634	Library:	Yes
Passenger Space Ratio (lower beds/all berths):	34.4/26.7	Onboard currency:	.US$
Crew/Passenger Ratio (lower beds/all berths):	2.2/2.8		

An ultra-colorful ship for first-time casual cruising

OVERVIEW. *Carnival Inspiration* is the sixth (in a series of eight almost identical ships) in Carnival's *Fantasy*-class. *Carnival Inspiration* is a well-liked ship – and is aimed at anyone taking their first cruise.

THE SHIP. The open deck space is reasonable, but it is really inadequate when the ship is full and everyone wants to be out on deck. However, the aft decks tend to be less noisy because all the activities are focused around the main swimming pool and hot tubs (one has a thatched shade). For anyone who prefers European-style sunning there's also a topless sunbathing area, as well as Serenity – an adult-only 'quiet' (extra-cost) lounging space on Deck 9 aft – you need to be over 21 to use it. Sadly, there is no walk-around open promenade deck, although there is a short jogging track atop ship. The lifeboats, six of which double as shore tenders are positioned high in the ship.

The interior of the ship is well designed. The general passenger flow is good, and the interior design – the work of Miami-based creative genius Joe Farcus – is clever, functional, and extremely colorful. The underlying decor theme is the arts (in an art nouveau style) and literature. It includes a colorful mix of classic and contemporary design elements.

The interior focal point is an 'open' atrium lobby, with its balconied shape, and this is dressed to impress, with scrolled shapes resembling the necks and heads of violins. The lobby spans six decks, has a marble

Berlitz's Ratings

	Possible	Achieved
Ship	500	309
Accommodation	200	138
Food	400	212
Service	400	262
Entertainment	100	73
Cruise	400	244
OVERALL SCORE		
1238 points out of 2000		

staircase, and is topped by a large glass dome. The lowest level of the atrium lobby is where you'll find the Purser's Desk and Shore Excursion Desk, together with a popular atrium Bar with live music, as well as a small sushi bar off to one side; it's a good central meeting place.

There are public entertainment lounges, bars, and clubs galore, with something for everyone (except quiet space). The public rooms, connected by a double-width Inspiration Boulevard, feature many contemporary design elements. Most public rooms and attractions lead off from this boulevard – a sort of shipboard Main Street which runs between the showlounge (forward) and the Candlelight aft lounge. Gamers and slot players alike will enjoy the almost non-stop action in the Monte Carlo Casino. The Shakespeare Library is a rather stately room, and 25 of his quotations adorn the oak veneer walls, but, sadly, there are few books. One of the most dazzling rooms is the Rock and Roll Discotheque, with its guitar-shaped dance floor, video dance club, and dozens of video monitors. There's also a 1,200-sq-ft (111-sq-m) conference room for meetings and group use.

Forget fashion – the sine qua non – of a Carnival cruise is all about having fun. While the cuisine is just so-so, the real fun begins at sundown when Carnival really excels in sound, lights, and shows. From venues such as the Rock and Roll Dance Club/Disco to the Chopin Cigar Bar, the ships' interior decor will certainly entertain you.

Carnival Inspiration is a floating playground for the young and young-at-heart. Because it's a large resort ship, there will be lines for things like shore excursions, security control when re-boarding, and disembarkation, as well as sign-up sheets for fitness equipment.

The ship is not for those seeking a quiet, relaxing cruise experience. There are many annoying announcements, and the never-ending hustling to get you to buy drinks and many other things. Also, shore excursions are booked via the in-cabin 'Fun Vision' television system, so obtaining advice and suggestions is not easy.

FAMILIES. Kids will almost certainly enjoy Children's World (part of Camp Carnival children's programming), a 1,600-sq-ft (149-sq-m) play area with games and fun stuff for youngsters of all ages, including Apple computers loaded with educational software, and an arts and crafts area with spin- and sand-art machines. An expansive children's water park is a lot of fun as an outdoor play area. Group babysitting is available. Meanwhile teens have their chill-out club, as part of the line's popular Club O2 teen program.

ACCOMMODATION. There are 13 grades of accommodation, ranked by facilities, size, and location. The standard outside-view and interior cabins have decor that is rather plain and unmemorable. They are marginally comfortable, yet spacious enough and practical (most are of the same size and appointments), with good storage space and practical, well-designed no-nonsense bathrooms. However, if you have a queen-bed configuration instead of the standard twin-bed layout, note that one person has to clamber over the bed – an ungainly exercise.

Choose a suite and you get more space, whirlpool bathtubs, and some rather eclectic decor and furniture. These are mildly attractive, but so-so, and they are much smaller than those aboard ships of a similar size of competing companies. A small gift basket of toiletry samples is provided in all grades.

Book a Category 11 or 12 suite and you get Skipper's Club priority check-in at any US homeland port – useful for getting ahead of the crowd.

Room service items are available 24 hours a day, although in standard cabins, only cold food is available, while those in suite-grade accommodation get a greater range of items (both hot and cold) to choose from.

DINING. The two large main dining rooms, Mardi Gras and Carnivale (the names given to Carnival's first two ship), are located amidships and aft, respectively. Both have ocean-view windows and attractive, but very bright décor, but they are noisy. Choose either fixed-time dining (6pm or 8:15pm) or flexible dining (any time between 5:45 and 9:30pm). For something really simple, there's an 'always available' (when the dining

room is open) list of 'Carnival Classics' that includes mahi mahi (fish), baby back ribs (beef), and grilled chicken. Note that the two main dining rooms are not open for lunch on port days.

The food is best described as underwhelming. Its presentation is simple, and few garnishes are used to decorate plates. Many meat and fowl dishes are disguised with gravies and sauces – and few garnishes are used. The selection of fresh green vegetables, breads, rolls, cheeses, and fruits is limited, and there is much use of canned fruit and jellied desserts. There's a decent wine list, but no wine waiters. The waiters sing and dance, and there are constant waiter parades – so it's really more about 'foodertainment' than food quality. If you want something really simple, there's an 'always available' list of 'Carnival Classics' that includes mahi mahi (fish), baby back ribs (beef), and grilled chicken.

Other dining options. A Lido café, called the Brasserie Bar & Grill, features the usual casual self-serve buffet eats, most of which are non-memorable. The venue includes a deli counter and pizzeria. At night, the venue morphs into the Seaview Bistro, and provides a casual alternative to the main dining rooms, for pasta, steaks, salads, and desserts – it typically operates only between 6pm and 9pm. The food selection, though limited, makes a change from the large, crowded and noisy main dining rooms. Outside on deck is a Mongolian Rotisserie Grill.

A patisserie offers specialty coffees and sweets (extra charge), and a so-called sushi bar off to one side of the atrium lobby bar on Promenade Deck is open prior to dinner only; the sushi is just so-so.

There is no specialty (extra-charge) restaurant, as aboard some of the larger ships in the Carnival fleet.

ENTERTAINMENT. Paris Main Lounge is the ship's principal showlounge – the venue for large-scale production shows and major cabaret acts – although 20 pillars obstruct some views. During a typical cruise, there will be one or two shows, with a cast of two lead singers and a clutch of dancers, backed by a large live band.

SPA/FITNESS. SpaCarnival is a large, glass-wrapped health, fitness, and spa complex. It is located on the uppermost interior deck, forward of the ship's mast, and is typically open from 6am to 8pm daily. It consists of a gymnasium with ocean-view windows that look out over the bow and the latest in muscle-pumping machines, an aerobics room, changing rooms, sauna and steam rooms, beauty salon, and body treatment rooms. Some fitness classes may incur an extra charge. A common complaint is that there isn't enough staff to keep the area clean and tidy.

Sporting types can play basketball or volleyball, or table tennis. There is also a banked jogging track on the deck above the spa, and a mini-golf course.

Carnival Legend
★★★ +

Size:. . . . . .Large Resort Ship	
Tonnage:. 85,942	
Lifestyle: . . . . .Standard	
Cruise line:. . . . . Carnival Cruise Lines	
Former names: . . . . none	
IMO number: 9224726	
Builder: . . . . Kvaerner Masa-Yards (Finland)	
Original cost: . . . . $375 million	
Entered service:. . . . . Aug 2002	
Registry:. . . . . Panama	
Length (ft/m):. 959.6/292.5	
Beam (ft/m):. 105.6/32.2	
Draft (ft/m):. 25.5/7.8	
Propulsion/Propellers: . . .diesel-electric (62,370kW)/2 azimuthing pods	
Passenger decks:. 12	
Total crew:. 1,030	
Passengers (lower beds/alll berths):. 2,124/2,680	
Passenger Space Ratio (lower beds/all berths): 40.4/32.0	

Crew/Passenger Ratio (lower beds/all berths):. 2.2/2.6	
Cabins (total):. 1,062	
Size range (sq ft/m): 185–490/17.1–45.5	
Cabins (outside view):. 849	
Cabins (interior/no view):. 213	
Cabins (for one person):. 0	
Cabins (with private balcony):. .750	
Cabins (wheelchair accessible): .16	
Wheelchair accessibility:. . . . . .Good	
Cabin voltage: . . . . 110 volts	
Elevators:. 15	
Casino (gaming tables):. . . . . .Yes	
Slot machines:. . . . . Yes	
Swimming pools:. 2	
Hot tubs (on deck):. 5	
Self-service launderette:. . . . . Yes	
Dedicated cinema/seats:. . . . . .No	
Library: . . . . Yes	
Onboard currency: . . . . .US$	

For a fun-filled cruise in a contemporary setting

OVERVIEW. *Carnival Legend* is sister to *Carnival Miracle, Carnival Pride,* and *Carnival Spirit,* and shares the same layout and configuration. It was built in 100 blocks, each weighing up to 450 tons, and assembled in the shipyard.

THE SHIP. The open deck and sunbathing space is not extensive, but there are two swimming pools, one of which can be covered by a sliding glass dome in case of inclement weather. An extra-charge, adults-only area, Sanctuary has its own bar, pool, hot tub and other facilities; it was added in a 2011 refit. Located at the aft of the ship, it is a good area for anyone wanting to have a quieter space for sunbathing and relaxation.

Inside the ship, the interior decor is dedicated to the world's great legends, from the heroes of antiquity to 20th-century jazz masters and athletes – an eclectic mix that somehow works well.

There are two entertainment/public room decks, the upper with an exterior promenade deck. A walkway, named Hollywood Boulevard, connects many of the major public rooms on Atlantic Deck, one deck above Promenade Deck, which also sports a number of public rooms, including a large Club Merlin Casino (you have to walk though it to get to the main level of the showlounge from the restaurant, which is located aft).

The colorful atrium lobby, which spans eight decks, has wall decorations best seen from any of the multiple viewing balconies on any deck above the main lobby level. Take a drink from the lobby bar and look

Berlitz's Ratings	Possible	Achieved
Ship	500	363
Accommodation	200	143
Food	400	223
Service	400	252
Entertainment	100	76
Cruise	400	266
OVERALL SCORE		
1323 points out of 2000		

upwards – the surroundings are stunning, with a mural of the Colossus of Rhodes the focal point.

Perhaps the most dramatic room is the Follies Showlounge. Spanning three decks in the forward section, it recalls a 1920s movie palace.

A small wedding chapel is forward of the uppermost level of the two main entertainment decks, adjacent to the library and Internet center. Other facilities include a winding shopping street with boutique stores, photo gallery, video games room, and an observation balcony in the center of the vessel, at the top of the multi-deck atrium.

Carnival Legend is a floating playground for the young and young-at-heart, and anyone who enjoys constant stimulation and lots of participation events, together with the three 'Gs' – glitz, glamour, and gambling. This really is cruising Splash Vegas style – an all-American experience. Because it's a large resort ship, there will be lines for things like shore excursions, security control when re-boarding, and disembarkation, as well as sign-up sheets for fitness equipment.

While the cuisine is just so-so, the real fun begins at sundown when Carnival really excels in sound, lights, razzle-dazzle shows, and loud, late-night music.

Niggles include the small reception desk in the atrium lobby, which can get congested at times. It's hard to escape from noise and loud music (even in cabin hallways and lifts), and masses of people milling around day and night. Many private balconies are not so private and can be overlooked from public locations.

Many pillars obstruct passenger flow (those in the dining room, for example, make it difficult for proper food service by the waiters). Books and computers are cohabitants in the ship's Holmes library/Internet center, but anyone wanting a book has to lean over others who may be using a computer – an awkward arrangement.

FAMILIES. Youngsters have their own play areas. Carnival's children's programs are divided into five age-specific groups. Meanwhile, tweens have 'Circle C,' which is next to the Gigabyte Video arcade. Teenagers have their own 'Club O2' – a chill-out room/disco.

ACCOMMODATION. There are numerous cabin categories, priced by grade, location, and size. The range of cabins includes suites (with private balcony), outside-view cabins with private balcony, 68 ocean-view cabins with French doors (pseudo balconies that have doors which open, but no balcony to step out onto), and a healthy proportion of standard outside-view to interior cabins.

All cabins have spy-hole doors, twin beds that can be converted into a queen-size bed, individually controlled air-conditioning, TV set, and telephone. A number of cabins on the lowest deck have views that are obstructed by lifeboats. Some cabins can accommodate a third and fourth person, but have little closet space, and there's only one personal safe. You can't turn off the air conditioning in cabins or bathrooms.

Book one of the suites (Category 11 or 12 in the Carnival Cruise Lines brochure) and you automatically qualify for Skipper's Club priority check-in at any US homeland port – useful for getting ahead of the crowd.

Among the most desirable suites and cabins are those on five of the aft-facing decks; these have private balconies overlooking the stern. You might think that these units would suffer from vibration, but they don't – a bonus provided by the pod propulsion system.

For extra space, it's worthwhile booking one of the larger deluxe balcony suites on Deck 6, with private teakwood balcony. These tend to be quiet suites, with a lounge and sleeping area, a good-size bathroom with twin washbasins, toilet and bidet, and whirlpool tub. They have twin beds convertible to a queen-size bed and a huge amount of storage space. The balcony has a wide teakwood deck with smoked glass and wood railing (you could easily seat 10 people).

Even the largest suites, however, are quite small compared with suites aboard other ships of a similar size – for example, Celebrity Cruises' *Celebrity Constellation*, *Celebrity Infinity*, *Celebrity Millennium*, and *Celebrity Summit*, where penthouse suites measure up to 2,530 sq ft (235 sq m).

DINING. This ship has a single, large, two-deck-high, 1,300-seat main dining room, Truffles Restaurant, with seating on both upper and main levels. Its huge ceiling has large murals of a china pattern made famous by Roy-

al Copenhagen, and wall-mounted glass display cases contain fine china. Small rooms on both upper and lower levels can be closed off for groups of up to 60. Choose either fixed time dining (6pm or 8:15pm) or flexible dining (between 5:45pm and 9:30pm). Note that the main dining room is not open for lunch on port days.

For casual eaters, the Unicorn Café (Lido restaurant) is an extensive self-serve buffet-style eatery that forms the aft third of Deck 9 (part of it wraps around the upper section of the huge atrium). The café includes a central area with a deli sandwich corner, Asian corner, rotisserie, and International (Taste of the Nations) counter. There are salad counters, a dessert counter, and a 24-hour Pizzeria counter, all of which offer both indoor and outdoor seating. Movement around the buffet area is slow, and you have to stand in line for everything. Each night, the Unicorn Café becomes Seaview Bistro, for serve-yourself dinners (typically 6pm–9.30pm).

Other dining options. The Steakhouse is a more upscale dining spot atop the ship, with just 156 seats and a show kitchen featuring prime steaks and grilled seafood. It is located on two of the uppermost decks of the ship, above the Unicorn Café, in the lower, forward section of the funnel housing, with great atrium views. The decor is set around the Greek legend of Jason and the Argonauts. The bar includes a large sculpture of the Golden Fleece. Fine table settings, china, and silverware are provided.

ENTERTAINMENT. The glamorous Follies Showlounge is the ship's principal venue for large-scale production shows and cabaret shows. Shows are best seen from the upper three levels. Directly underneath the showlounge is the Firebird lounge and bar.

Almost every lounge/bar, including Billie's Bar (a piano lounge) and Satchmo's Club (a nightclub with bar and dance floor), has live music in the evening. Finally, for the very lively, there's the disco; and there's always karaoke as well as a Passenger Talent Show during each cruise.

SPA/FITNESS. SpaCarnival, spanning two decks, is located directly above the navigation bridge in the forward part of the ship and has 13,700 sq ft (1,272 sq m) of space. Facilities on the lower level include a solarium, eight treatment rooms, lecture rooms, sauna and steam rooms for men and women, and a beauty parlor. The upper level consists of a large gymnasium with floor-to-ceiling windows on three sides, including forward-facing ocean views, and an aerobics room with instructor-led classes.

There are two centrally located swimming pools outdoors, and one can be used in inclement weather due to its retractable glass dome. Adjacent are two whirlpool tubs. A winding water slide two decks high is located aft. Another smaller pool is available for children. An outdoor jogging track is located around the ship's mast and the forward third of the ship; it doesn't go around the whole ship, but it's long enough for some serious walking.

Carnival Liberty
★★★ +

Size:.	Large Resort Ship	Cabins (total):.	1,487
Tonnage:.	110,320	Size range (sq ft/m):.	179.7–482.2/16.7–44.8
Lifestyle:.	Standard	Cabins (outside view):.	917
Cruise line:.	Carnival Cruise Lines	Cabins (interior/no view):.	570
Former names:.	none	Cabins (for one person):.	0
IMO number:.	9278181	Cabins (with private balcony):.	574
Builder:.	Fincantieri (Italy)	Cabins (wheelchair accessible):.	25
Original cost:.	$500 million	Wheelchair accessibility:.	Good
Entered service:.	Jul 2005	Cabin voltage:.	110 volts
Registry:.	Panama	Elevators:.	18
Length (ft/m):.	951.4/290.0	Casino (gaming tables):.	Yes
Beam (ft/m):.	116.4/35.5	Slot machines:.	Yes
Draft (ft/m):.	27.0/8.2	Swimming pools:.	2 (1 w/sliding glass dome)
Propulsion/Propellers:.	diesel-electric (63,400kW)/2	Hot tubs (on deck):.	7
Passenger decks:.	13	Self-service launderette:.	Yes
Total crew:.	1,160	Dedicated cinema/seats:.	No
Passengers (lower beds/alll berths):.	2,974/3,700	Library:.	Yes
Passenger Space Ratio (lower beds/all berths):.	37.0/29.7	Onboard currency:.	US$
Crew/Passenger Ratio (lower beds/all berths):.	2.5/3.1		

An ultra-colorful ship for first-time casual cruising

OVERVIEW. *Carnival Liberty* shares the same generally well-balanced profile as sisters *Carnival Conquest*, *Carnival Sunshine*, *Carnival Freedom*, *Carnival Glory*, *Carnival Triumph*, *Carnival Valor*, and *Carnival Victory*. A giant Seaside Theater LED movie screen adorns the open pool deck, and a new Serenity area provides an adults-only escape.

THE SHIP. The decor in the public rooms, hallways, and atrium adopts a design theme saluting master trades such as ironwork, masonry, pottery, and painting. The layout is logical, so finding your way around is easy. Most public rooms are located off a main boulevard (an interior promenade that is great for strolling and people watching – particularly from the Jardin Café or Promenade Bar). Other hangouts and drinking places include The Stage (live music/ karaoke lounge), the Flower Bar (main lobby), Gloves Bar (sports Bar), Paparazzi (wine bar), and The Cabinet.

Amidships on the open deck is a long water slide (200ft/60m long), as well as tiered sunbathing decks positioned between two swimming pools, several hot tubs, and a giant poolside (Seaside Theater) movie screen. It's all about imagination and sensorial fantasy and is more reserved than Carnival's Fantasy-class ships.

There are two atriums: the largest, in the forward third of the ship spans nine decks (the Grand Villa Garden Atrium combines all four of the design themes), while a small aft atrium spans three decks. The large Czar's Palace Casino, with its Russian motifs and theme, is action-packed, with more than 320 slot machines.

Berlitz's Ratings

	Possible	Achieved
Ship	500	363
Accommodation	200	144
Food	400	218
Service	400	257
Entertainment	100	76
Cruise	400	258
OVERALL SCORE		
1316 points out of 2000		

Carnival Liberty is a veritable floating playground for the young and young-at-heart, and anyone who enjoys constant stimulation and lots of participation events, together with the three 'Gs' – glitz, glamour, and gambling. This really is cruising Splash Vegas style – and fun, all-American experience. Because it's a large resort ship, there will be lines for things like shore excursions, security control when re-boarding, and disembarkation, as well as sign-up sheets for fitness equipment.

Forget fashion – the sine qua non – of a Carnival cruise is all about having fun. While the cuisine is just so-so, the real fun begins at sundown when Carnival really does excel in terms of sound, lights, razzle-dazzle shows, and late-night high volume sounds.

Niggles include: many pillars in the dining room make it difficult for proper food service by the waiters; public toilets that are somewhat utilitarian and could do with some cheering up. It is impossible to escape from noise and loud music (it's even played in cabin hallways and lifts), not to mention smokers, and people walking around in unsuitable clothing, clutching plastic sport drinks bottles, at any time of the day or night. You have to carry a credit card to operate the personal safes, which is inconvenient.

FAMILIES. Youngsters are provided with good facilities, including their own two-level Children's Club (including an outdoor pool), and are well cared for with Camp Carnival, the line's extensive children's program. Soft-drinks packages can be purchased for children (and adults).

ACCOMMODATION. There are numerous cabin-price categories, in seven different grades: suites with private balcony; deluxe outside-view cabins with private balcony; outside-view cabins with private balcony; outside-view cabins with window; cabins with a porthole instead of a window; interior cabins; interior cabins with upper and lower berths. The price reflects the grade, location, and size.

Five decks of cabins have a private balcony – over 150 more than *Carnival Sunshine, Carnival Triumph*, or *Carnival Victory*, for example. But many are not so private, and can be overlooked from various public locations.

There are 18 'fitness' cabins, located directly around and behind the SpaCarnival. This gives fitness devotees an opportunity to get out of bed and head straight to the treadmill without having to go through any of the public rooms first.

The standard cabins are of good size and are equipped with all the basics, although the furniture is rather angular, with no rounded edges. Three decks of cabins (eight on each deck, each with private balcony) overlook the stern. Most cabins with twin beds can be converted to a queen-size bed format. A gift basket is provided in all grades of cabin; it includes aloe soap, shampoo, conditioner, deodorant, breath mints, candy, and pain relief tablets (all in sample sizes).

Note: If you book one of the Category 11 or 12 suites you get 'Skipper's Club' priority check-in at any US homeland port – useful for getting ahead of the crowd.

DINING. There are two main dining rooms, Golden Olympian Restaurant, forward, seating 744, and Silver Olympian Restaurant, aft, seating 1,122. Two additional wings (the Persian Room and Satin Room) can accommodate large groups in a private dining arrangement.

Other dining options. There is a casual self-serve international food court-style lido deck eatery, the two-level Emile's, which morphs into the Seaview Bistro in the evening to provide a casual alternative to the main dining rooms. The specialty dining venue is The Steakhouse, for prime meats and seafood.

ENTERTAINMENT. The Venetian Palace Showlounge is a 1,400-seat multi-deck showroom for large-scale Las Vegas-style production shows and major cabaret acts. The Victoria Lounge, located aft, seats 425 and typically features live music and late-night cabaret acts, including adult comedy. The Tattooed Lady Dance Club is the ship's discotheque; it includes a video wall with projections live from the dance floor. Piano bar lovers should enjoy the 100-seat Piano Man piano bar.

SPA/FITNESS. SpaCarnival is a large health, fitness, and spa complex that spans two decks (the walls display hand-painted reproductions of the artist's poster work). It is directly above the navigation bridge in the forward part of the ship and is accessed from the forward stairway.

Facilities on the lower level include a solarium, eight treatment rooms, lecture rooms, sauna and steam rooms for men and women, and a beauty parlor. The upper level consists of a large gymnasium with floor-to-ceiling windows on three sides, including forward-facing ocean views, and an aerobics room with instructor-led classes, some at extra cost.

Waste disposal

The sheer magnitude of waste materials can be highly problematic, especially on long cruises. If solid waste is not burnable, or cannot be disposed of overboard (this must be biodegradable), it must be stored for later off-loading and disposal on land.

The latest cruise ships have 'zero-discharge' facilities. These include incinerators and food waste handling systems that include vacuum transportation from feeding stations in all galleys and food preparation areas, recycling and storage systems for ash, glass, metal, and paper. But many older cruise ships have outdated garbage handling equipment.

Food waste is typically sent to a pulping machine that has been partially filled with water. Cutting mechanisms reduce the waste and allow it to pass through a special sizing ring to be pumped directly overboard or into a holding tank or an incinerator when the ship is within three-mile limits.

Carnival Magic
★★★ +

Size:. . . . . .Large Resort Ship		Cabins (total):. 1,823	
Tonnage:. 128,048		Size range (sq ft/m):. 185.0–430.5/17.1–40.0	
Lifestyle:. . . . . .Standard		Cabins (outside view):. 1,145	
Cruise line:. . . . . Carnival Cruise Lines		Cabins (interior/no view):. 678	
Former names:. . . . .*none*		Cabins (for one person):. 0	
IMO number:. 93778486		Cabins (with private balcony):. .887	
Builder:. . . . . Fincantieri (Italy)		Cabins (wheelchair accessible):. 35	
Original cost:. . . . . $740 million		Wheelchair accessibility:. . . . . .Good	
Entered service:. . . . . Jun 2011		Cabin voltage:. . . . . 110 volts	
Registry:. . . . . Panama		Elevators:. 20	
Length (ft/m):. 1,004.0/306.0		Casino (gaming tables):. . . . . Yes	
Beam (ft/m):. 158.0/48.0		Slot machines:. . . . . Yes	
Draft (ft/m):. 26.2/8.0		Swimming pools:. 2	
Propulsion/Propellers:. . . . . Diesel-electric (75.6MW)/2		Hot tubs (on deck):. 7	
Passenger decks:. 13		Self-service launderette:. . . . . Yes	
Total crew:. 1,367		Dedicated cinema/seats:. . . . . .No	
Passengers (lower beds/alll berths):. 3,646/4,631		Library:. . . . . Yes	
Passenger Space Ratio (lower beds/all berths):. 35.1/27.6		Onboard currency:. . . . . .US$	
Crew/Passenger Ratio (lower beds/all berths):. 2.6/3.3			

A family-friendly, high-energy ship for fun-filled cruising

OVERVIEW. *Carnival Magic* is a sister ship to *Carnival Dream*, introduced in 2010, and both are 13 percent larger than their close sister *Carnival Splendor*. One thing that stands out is a long Twister Water Slide, part of The Waterworks on pool deck, which is really for kids. There's an adults-only, extra-charge retreat called Serenity.

THE SHIP. Although the ship's bows are short, its profile is nicely balanced, with a rakish front and a more rounded stern. The propulsion system consists of the conventional twin rudder, with twin propellers. However, the ship is based on the original design for *Carnival Sunshine*, and includes some of the design flaws of the *Sunshine*-class, with a passenger capacity that has been increased by just over 1,000. Strangely, the cabin numbering system – even numbers, starboard side; odd numbers, port side – goes against the maritime tradition that places even-numbered cabins on the port, or left, side; and odd-numbered cabins on the starboard, or right, side.

A Waterworks pool deck has lots of water and sports amusements – not to mention a really long orange multi-deck 'Twister Water Slide' and popular 'Power Drencher.' However, there simply isn't enough open deck space for the number of passengers the ship carries, so the sunbed loungers are tightly packed together.

The ship has a full walk-around open promenade deck, lined with deck chairs. Four 'scenic hot tubs' are cantilevered over the sea and provide fine views, but they do get crowded, and rowdy. Higher up, Lido Deck 10 offers a very good open-deck area, with small pool

Berlitz's Ratings		
	Possible	Achieved
Ship	500	374
Accommodation	200	144
Food	400	218
Service	400	260
Entertainment	100	76
Cruise	400	259
OVERALL SCORE		
1331 points out of 2000		

and a large Seaside Theatre LED movie screen. *Carnival Magic* is the second Carnival ship to stage a laser light show outdoors.

The interior decor is vivid – really vivid. The main lobby is the stunning connection point for ship functions and people. Take the glass-walled elevators for a neat view, though you may need sunglasses. It's good to see three main elevator towers: forward, amidships, and aft, unlike larger ships such as *Oasis of the Seas*, which, although it carries many more passengers, has only two such towers. So, well done, Carnival, this is much better for safety.

The Ocean Plaza is a comfortable area by day and an entertainment venue by night. The indoor/outdoor café and live music venue has a bandstand where a variety of musical genres are showcased, a large circular dance floor, and around 190 seats. A floor-to-ceiling curved glass wall separates the room, dividing indoor and outdoor seating areas. An adjacent bar also offers coffee, ice creams, and pastries. The Page Turner (great name) is the ship's library, while Jackpot is – you guessed it – the colorful, large, lively, and noisy casino.

Other rooms include The Song (Jazz Bar) and Ocean Plaza (a sort of quiet area during the day, but lively at night with live entertainment); Internet-connect computer terminals are scattered through-out the ship, but few have much privacy. There's also a 232-capacity conference room called The Chambers. This was the first Carnival ship to have a pub, the Red Frog Pub, with its own-label beer, ThirstyRedFrog.

There is much congestion just before the second seating, on both Upper and Lower Dream Streets, both located on the starboard side. Further congestion appears around the photo gallery, which surrounds the atrium lobby.

Carnival Magic is a veritable floating playground for the young and young-at-heart, and anyone who enjoys constant stimulation and lots of participation events, together with the three 'Gs' – glitz, glamour, and gambling. This really is cruising Splash Vegas style – a fun, all-American experience. Because it's a large resort ship, there will be lines for things like shore excursions, security control when re-boarding, and disembarkation, as well as sign-up sheets for fitness equipment.

FAMILIES. About 5,000 sq ft (465 sq m) of space is devoted to the line's three age-related children's programs: Camp Carnival for ages two to 11, 'Circle C' for 12–14s, and 'Club O2' for 15–17s. A full schedule of morning-to-night activities caters to each age group. All kids love Carnival WaterWorks, an aqua park with exhilarating water slides.

'Deluxe' ocean-view cabins, with two bathrooms, provide comfort and convenience for families. In addition to twin beds that convert to a king, decent closet space, and elegant decor, the two-bathroom configuration includes one full bathroom and a second bathroom containing a small tub with shower and sink. Some cabins can accommodate five people.

ACCOMMODATION. There are many different cabin price categories, but just six cabin types. All accommodation includes the Carnival Comfort Bed with plush mattresses, good-quality duvets, linens and pillows. However, the straight accommodation deck hallways create rather a cell block look – and they are bright, very bright, even at night. There are also lot of interior cabins. The cabins to go for are those at the stern, with great rearward ocean views on decks 6, 7, 8 and 9.

Apart from the Deluxe cabins described above, there is a wide selection of balcony cabins and suites, including 'Cove Balcony' cabins that are the closest to the waterline. Adjacent to the Cloud 9 Spa are 65 'Cloud 9' spa cabins, designated as no-smoking. They provide a number of 'exclusive' amenities and privileges.

You should be aware that some cabins are located directly over loud late-night venues, with poor soundproofing. Also, cabins on Deck 12 are subject to lots of noise from kids having fun on the deck above – so afternoon naps are out.

DINING. There are two main restaurants: Northern Lights, a 1,180-seat amidships dining room, and a smaller 828-seat aft dining room, Southern Lights. Each has two levels: main and balcony, with the galley set on the lower level. Two small restaurant annexes can be reserved by small groups as a private dining room. Expect all-singing, all-dancing waiters to entertain while you search for the elusive green vegetables. Choose either fixed-time dining (6pm or 8:15pm) or flexible dining (any time between 5:45 and 9:30pm). Note that the two main dining rooms are not open for lunch on port days.

Other dining options. The Lido Marketplace, the ship's large (but not large enough) self-serve buffet facility, has indoor/outdoor seating areas on the lower (main) level and indoor-only seating on the upper level. A number of designated areas serve different types of ethnic cuisine. It really does get congested – particularly for breakfast – and the food is pretty basic, but it works, just. The venue includes a Mongolian Wok and Pasta Bar on the upper level, open 6–9pm for tablecloth-free buffet dinners.

Forward of the buffet venue, and adjacent to the 'beach pool' is a Pizzeria and fast-food Grille. Aft on the same deck is a Tandoor (Indian), and a Deli Counter (for sandwiches and wraps).

An extra-charge, reservations required Prime Steakhouse and bar seats 139. Located on Promenade Deck aft, it features an à la carte menu, fine table settings, and china and silverware. It's worth paying the cover charge to get a taste of what Carnival can really deliver. There's a sushi venue, too, called Sushi and More, on Promenade Deck, close to the Red Frog Pub.

ENTERTAINMENT. The 1,964-seat Showtime Theater spans three decks at the front of the ship, with seating set in a horseshoe shape around a large proscenium arched stage; the sight lines are generally good, except from some of the seats at the back of the lowest level. Large-scale production shows with lots of feathers and skimpy costumes are staged, together with snappy cabaret acts, all with a live showband.

The 425-seat Spotlight Lounge, at the aft end of the ship, has a stage, dance floor, and large bar, and is a comedy venue, including late-night 'adult comedy.' Caliente is the ship's loud, Latin nightclub.

SPA/FITNESS. The expansive 23,750-sq-ft (2,206-sq-m) Cloud 9 Spa is a large and elaborate health and wellness center. The uppermost deck includes indoor/outdoor private spa relaxation areas, at extra cost.

There are 10 treatment rooms, including a VIP room, a large massage room for couples, and a Rasul mud treatment room, plus two dry flotation rooms. An extra-charge 'Thermal Suite' comes with the typical sensory-enhanced soothing heated chambers: Laconium, Tepidarium, Aroma, and Oriental steam baths. There are two steam rooms, one each for men and women, and a small unisex sauna with a floor-to-ceiling window on its starboard side.

A large outdoor SportsSquare for adults is a fenced area for basketball, football, and volleyball. Then there's an outdoor weight-training circuit (SkyFitness), and the cutely named Turf on Surf miniature golf course. Perhaps the highlight is SkyCourse, a 230-ft (70-m) long outdoor ropes course, suspended above the uppermost deck. After all those activities, you'll need a cruise to relax.

Carnival Miracle
★★★ +

Size:.................................Large Resort Ship			
Tonnage:... 85,942			
Lifestyle:...Standard			
Cruise line:...........................Carnival Cruise Lines			
Former names:..................................... none			
IMO number:....................................9237357			
Builder:...................Kvaerner Masa-Yards (Finland)			
Original cost:...............................$375 million			
Entered service:..............................Apr 2004			
Registry:.. Panama			
Length (ft/m):............................... 959.6/292.5			
Beam (ft/m):................................ 105.6/32.2			
Draft (ft/m):.................................... 25.5/7.8			
Propulsion/Propellers:...diesel-electric (62,370kW)/2 azimuthing pods			
Passenger decks:...................................13			
Total crew:...961			
Passengers (lower beds/alll berths):............. 2,124/2,680			
Passenger Space Ratio (lower beds/all berths): 40.4/32.0			
Crew/Passenger Ratio (lower beds/all berths):.......... 2.2/2.7			
Cabins (total):.................................... 1,062			
Size range (sq ft/m):................. 185.0–490.0/17.1–45.5			
Cabins (outside view):.................................849			
Cabins (interior/no view):.............................213			
Cabins (for one person):................................0			
Cabins (with private balcony):.........................750			
Cabins (wheelchair accessible):.........................16			
Wheelchair accessibility:............................Good			
Cabin voltage:................................ 110 volts			
Elevators:...15			
Casino (gaming tables):.............................Yes			
Slot machines:......................................Yes			
Swimming pools:.................2 (1 w/sliding glass dome)			
Hot tubs (on deck):....................................5			
Self-service launderette:.............................Yes			
Dedicated cinema/seats:.............................No			
Library:...Yes			
Onboard currency:...............................US$			

A fun-filled, family-friendly ship for high-energy cruising

OVERVIEW. *Carnival Miracle* is sister to *Carnival Legend, Carnival Pride,* and *Carnival Spirit, and shares the same layout and configuration.* It was built in 100 blocks, each weighing up to 450 tons, and assembled in the shipyard.

THE SHIP. The open deck and sunbathing space is not extensive, but there are two swimming pools, one of which can be covered by a sliding glass dome in case of inclement weather. An extra-charge, adults-only area, Sanctuary has its own bar, pool, hot tub and other facilities. Located at the aft of the ship on Lido Deck, it is a good area for anyone wanting to have a quieter space for sunbathing and relaxation.

Inside the ship, the interior decor is dedicated to 'fictional icons,' including such luminaries as the Phantom of the Opera, Sherlock Holmes, Philip Marlowe, and Captain Ahab. Bronze statues of Orpheus and Ulysses adorn the swimming pools.

There are two entertainment/public room decks, the upper with an exterior promenade deck. A walkway, named the Yellow Brick Road, connects many of the major public rooms on Atlantic Deck, one deck above Promenade Deck, which also sports a number of public rooms, including a large Club Merlin Casino.

The colorful atrium lobby, which spans eight decks, has wall decorations best seen from any of the multiple viewing balconies on any deck above the main lobby level. Take a drink from the lobby bar and look upwards – the surroundings are visually stunning.

Berlitz's Ratings		
	Possible	Achieved
Ship	500	364
Accommodation	200	143
Food	400	223
Service	400	251
Entertainment	100	76
Cruise	400	270
OVERALL SCORE		
1327 points out of 2000		

Perhaps the most dramatic room is the Phantom Showlounge, which spans three decks in the forward section. Directly underneath is the Firebird Lounge, which has a bar in its starboard aft section.

A small wedding chapel is located forward of the uppermost level of the two main entertainment decks, adjacent to the Raven Library and Internet center. Other facilities include a shopping street, with boutique stores, photo gallery, video games room, and an observation balcony in the center of the vessel, at the top of the multi-deck atrium. The large Mr Lucky's Casino invites wishful gamers and slot players.

Niggles include the small reception desk in the atrium lobby, which can become really congested. Many private balconies are not so private and can be overlooked from public locations. You need a credit card to open the personal safe in your cabin – inconvenient if your credit cards and wallet are inside the safe!

Many pillars obstruct passenger flow (those in the dining room, for example, make it difficult for proper food service by the waiters). Books and computers are cohabitants in the ship's Holmes library/Internet center, but anyone wanting a book has to lean over others who may be using a computer – an awkward arrangement.

FAMILIES. Youngsters have their own play areas. Carnival's children's programs are divided into five age-specific groups. Meanwhile, tweens have 'Circle C,' which is next to the Gigabyte Video arcade. Teenagers have their own 'Club O2' – a chill-out room/disco – away from the adults – and younger children.

ACCOMMODATION. There are 20 cabin categories, priced by grade, location, and size. The range of cabins includes suites (with private balcony), outside-view cabins with private balcony, 68 ocean-view cabins with French doors (pseudo balconies that have doors which open, but no balcony to step out onto), and a healthy proportion of standard outside-view to interior cabins.

All cabins have spy-hole doors, twin beds that can be converted into a queen-size bed, individually controlled air-conditioning, TV set, and telephone. A number of cabins on the lowest deck have views that are obstructed by lifeboats. Some cabins can accommodate a third and fourth person, but have little closet space, and there's only one personal safe. There is no separate radio in each cabin – instead, audio channels are provided on the in-cabin TV system, but you can't turn the picture off. Nor can you turn off the air conditioning in cabins or bathrooms.

Book one of the suites (Category 11 or 12 in the Carnival Cruise Lines brochure) and you automatically qualify for Skipper's Club priority check-in at any US homeland port – useful for getting ahead of the crowd.

Among the most desirable suites and cabins are those on five of the aft-facing decks; these have private balconies overlooking the stern and ship's wash. You might think that these units would suffer from vibration, but they don't – a bonus provided by the pod propulsion system.

For extra space, it's worthwhile booking one of the larger deluxe balcony suites on Deck 6, with private teakwood balcony. These tend to be quiet suites, with a lounge and sleeping area, a good-size bathroom with twin washbasins, toilet and bidet, and whirlpool tub. They have twin beds convertible to a queen-size bed, three (illuminated) closets, and a huge amount of drawer space. The balcony has an outside light and a wide teakwood deck with smoked glass and wood railing (you could easily seat 10 people).

Even the largest suites, however, are quite small compared with suites aboard other ships of a similar size – for example, Celebrity Cruises' *Celebrity Constellation*, *Celebrity Infinity*, *Celebrity Millennium*, and *Celebrity Summit*, where penthouse suites measure up to 2,530 sq ft (235 sq m).

DINING. The Bacchus Dining Room is the ship's large, two-deck-high, 1,300-seat main restaurant, with seating on both upper and main levels. Its huge ceiling sports large murals. The galley is located underneath the restaurant, with escalator access. Tables are for two, four, six, or eight, and small rooms on both upper and lower levels can be closed off for groups of up to 60. Choose either fixed time dining (6pm or 8:15pm) or flexible dining (between 5:45pm and 9:30pm). Note that the dining room is not open for lunch on port days.

Other dining options. For casual eaters, Horatio's Lido restaurant (Lido restaurant) is an extensive self-serve buffet-style eatery that forms the aft third of Deck 9 (part of it wraps around the upper section of the huge atrium). Murals of unicorns are everywhere. The café includes a central area with a deli sandwich corner, Asian corner, rotisserie, salad bar, and International (Taste of the Nations) counter. There are salad counters, a dessert counter, and a 24-hour Pizzeria counter, all of which offer both indoor and outdoor seating. Movement around the buffet area is slow, and you have to stand in line for everything. Each night, the venue morphs into the Seaview Bistro, for casual, serve-your-self-style dinners (typically 6pm–9.30pm).

Nick & Nora's Steakhouse is a more upscale dining spot atop the ship, with just 156 seats and a show kitchen. It is located on two of the uppermost decks of the ship, above Horatio's Lido Restaurant, with great views over the atrium lobby.

ENTERTAINMENT. The stunning 1,170-seat Phantom Showlounge is the ship's principal venue for large-scale production shows and cabaret shows. Spiral stairways at the back of the lounge connect all three levels. Shows are best seen from the upper three levels. Directly underneath the showlounge is the Mad Hatter's Ball Lounge, which has a bar in its starboard aft section.

Almost every lounge/bar, including Sam's Piano Bar, the Jazz Lounge, and Jeeves Lounge, has live music in the evening. Finally, for the very lively, there's the disco; and there's always karaoke.

SPA/FITNESS. SpaCarnival, spanning two decks, is located directly above the navigation bridge in the forward part of the ship and has 13,700 sq ft (1,272 sq m) of space. Facilities on the lower level include a solarium, eight treatment rooms, lecture rooms, sauna and steam rooms for men and women, and a beauty parlor. The upper level consists of a large gymnasium with floor-to-ceiling windows on three sides, including forward-facing ocean views, and an aerobics room with instructor-led classes.

There are two centrally located swimming pools outdoors, and one can be used in inclement weather due to its retractable glass dome. Adjacent are two whirlpool tubs. A winding water slide two decks high is located aft. Another smaller pool is available for children. An outdoor jogging track is located around the ship's mast and the forward third of the ship; it doesn't go around the whole ship, but it's long enough for some serious walking.

Carnival Paradise
★★★

Size:..................................Large Resort Ship	Crew/Passenger Ratio (lower beds/all berths):.......... 2.2/2.8
Tonnage:... 70,390	Cabins (total):.................................... 1,026
Lifestyle:......................................Standard	Size range (sq ft/m):.................. 173.2–409.7/16–38
Cruise line:........................ Carnival Cruise Lines	Cabins (outside view):.............................618
Former names:............................... *Paradise*	Cabins (interior/no view):..........................408
IMO number:.................................9120877	Cabins (for one person):............................0
Builder:.................... Kvaerner Masa-Yards (Finland)	Cabins (with private balcony):......................152
Original cost:........................... $300 million	Cabins (wheelchair accessible):......................22
Entered service:............................ Nov 1998	Wheelchair accessibility:............................Fair
Registry:...................................... Panama	Cabin voltage:........................... 110 volts
Length (ft/m):............................. 855.0/260.6	Elevators:......................................14
Beam (ft/m):................................ 103.3/31.5	Casino (gaming tables):............................Yes
Draft (ft/m):................................ 25.9/7.9	Slot machines:....................................Yes
Propulsion/Propellers:...diesel-electric (42,842kW)/2 azimuthing pods	Swimming pools:...................................3
	Hot tubs (on deck):................................6
Passenger decks:....................................10	Self-service launderette:...........................Yes
Total crew:.......................................920	Dedicated cinema/seats:..............................No
Passengers (lower beds/alll berths):............. 2,052/2,594	Library:...Yes
Passenger Space Ratio (lower beds/all berths): 34.2/26.7	Onboard currency:................................US$

A family-friendly, high-energy ship for ultra-casual cruising

OVERVIEW. *Carnival Paradise* is the eighth (and final, in a series of eight almost identical ships) in the Carnival *Fantasy*-class. *Carnival Paradise* has always been a popular fun ship for anyone taking their first cruise.

THE SHIP. *Carnival Paradise* is one of only two ships in the series of eight (the other is *Carnival Elation*) which has a 'pod' propulsion system; this provides a vibration-free ride. While the open deck space is reasonable, it is inadequate when the ship is full and everyone wants to be out on deck. The aft decks tend to be less noisy, whereas all the activities are focused around the main swimming pool and hot tubs (one with a thatched shade). For those who prefer European-style sunning there's also a topless sunbathing area, as well as Serenity – an adult-only 'quiet' lounging space on Deck 9 aft. There is no walk-around open promenade deck, although there is a short jogging track atop ship. The lifeboats, six of which double as shore tenders are positioned high in the ship, rather than lower down, as in Carnival's newer ships.

The interior of the ship is well designed. The general passenger flow is good, and the interior design – the work of Miami-based creative genius Joe Farcus – is clever, functional, and extremely colorful. The underlying decor theme is all about the ocean liners of yesteryear.

The ship's interior focal point is an 'open' atrium lobby, with a balconied shape; it is dressed to impress, spans six decks, and is topped by a large glass dome.

Berlitz's Ratings	Possible	Achieved
Ship	500	309
Accommodation	200	138
Food	400	212
Service	400	260
Entertainment	100	76
Cruise	400	244
OVERALL SCORE		
1239 points out of 2000		

The lowest level of the atrium lobby is where you'll find the Purser's Desk and Shore Excursion Desk, together with a popular Atrium Bar with live music, as well as a small sushi bar off to one side; it's a good central meeting place.

There are many public entertainment lounges, bars, and clubs, with something for everyone (except quiet space). Most of the public rooms, connected by a double-width Carnival Boulevard Promenade and lead off from this boulevard – a sort of shipboard Main Street which runs between the showlounge (forward) and the Queen Mary Lounge aft. Gamers and slot players alike will enjoy the serious action in the Majestic Casino, with its blackjack and roulette tables, and an array of slot machines. The Blue Riband library is a pleasant room; although it has only a few books, there are several models of ocean liners. Another dazzling room is the Rock and Roll Discotheque, with its guitar-shaped dance floor, video dance club, and dozens of video monitors.

Carnival Paradise is a floating playground for the young and young-at-heart. This really is cruising Splash Vegas style. Because it's a large resort ship, there will be lines for things like shore excursions, security control when re-boarding, and disembarkation.

The sine qua non – of a Carnival cruise is all about having fun. While the cuisine is just so-so, the real fun begins at sundown when Carnival really excels in sound, lights, and shows. From venues such as the Rex Dance Club/Disco to the Rotterdam Cigar Bar, the ships' interior decor will certainly entertain you.

This ship, however, is not for those seeking a quiet, relaxing cruise experience. There are annoying announcements, and the never-ending hustling to get you to spend money. Also, shore excursions are booked via the in-cabin 'Fun Vision' television system, so obtaining advice and suggestions is not easy.

FAMILIES. Kids have their own Children's World, as part of Camp Carnival. It's a 1,600-sq-ft (149-sq-m) play area with games and fun stuff for youngsters of all ages, including Apple computers loaded with educational software and an arts and crafts area with spin- and sand-art machines. A children's water park is a lot of fun as an outdoor play area. Group babysitting is available; although it costs extra, it allows parent some 'me' time. Also, teenagers have their chill-out club, as part of the line's popular Club 02 program.

ACCOMMODATION. There are numerous price grades for accommodation, ranked by facilities, size, and location. The standard outside-view and interior cabins have decor that is rather plain and unmemorable. They are marginally comfortable, yet spacious enough and practical (most are of the same size and appointments), with good storage space and practical, well-designed no-nonsense bathrooms. However, if you have a queen-bed configuration instead of the standard twin-bed layout, note that one person has to clamber over the bed – an ungainly exercise.

Choose a suite and you get more space, whirlpool bathtubs, and some rather eclectic decor and furniture. These are mildly attractive, but so-so, and they are much smaller than those aboard ships of a similar size of competing companies. A small gift basket of toiletry samples is provided in all grades.

Book a Category 11 or 12 suite and you get Skipper's Club priority check-in at any US homeland port – useful for getting ahead of the crowd.

Room service items are available 24 hours a day, although in standard cabins, only cold food is available, while those in suite-grade accommodation get a greater range of items (both hot and cold) to choose from.

DINING. The two large main dining rooms, Elation and Destiny, are located amidships and aft. Both have ocean-view windows and attractive, but very bright décor, but they are noisy. Choose either fixed-time dining (6pm or 8:15pm) or flexible dining (any time between 5:45 and 9:30pm).

The food is best described as uneventful, with simple presentation and a lack of garnishes. Many meat and fowl dishes are disguised with gravies and sauces. The selection of fresh green vegetables, breads, rolls, cheeses, and fruits is quite unimaginative, and there is too much use of canned fruit and jellied desserts. There's a decent wine list, but no wine waiters. The waiters sing and dance, and there are constant waiter parades – so it's really more about 'foodertainment' than food quality. If you want something really simple, there's an 'always available' list of 'Carnival Classics' that includes mahi mahi (fish), baby back ribs (beef), and grilled chicken. Note that the two main dining rooms are not open for lunch on port days.

Other dining options. A Lido café, called the Brasserie Bar & Grill, features the usual casual self-serve buffet eats, most of which are non-memorable. The venue includes a deli counter and pizzeria. At night, the venue morphs into the Seaview Bistro, and provides a casual alternative to the main dining rooms, for pasta, steaks, salads, and desserts – it typically operates only between 6pm and 9pm. The food selection, though limited, makes a change from the large, crowded and noisy main dining rooms. Outside on deck is a Mongolian Rotisserie Grill.

A patisserie offers specialty coffees and sweets (extra charge), and a so-called sushi bar off to one side of the atrium lobby bar on Promenade Deck is open prior to dinner only; the sushi is just so-so.

There is no specialty (extra-charge) restaurant, as aboard some of the larger ships in the Carnival fleet.

ENTERTAINMENT. The 1,010-seat Normandie Main Lounge is the ship's showlounge, and is the venue for large-scale production shows and major cabaret acts – although 20 pillars obstruct some views. During a typical cruise, there will be one or two high-energy production shows, with a cast of two lead singers and a clutch of dancers, backed by a large live band.

SPA/FITNESS. SpaCarnival is a large, glass-wrapped health, fitness, and spa complex. It is located on the uppermost interior deck, forward of the ship's mast, and is typically open from 6am to 8pm daily. It consists of a gymnasium with windows that look out over the bow and the latest in electronic machines, an aerobics room, changing rooms, sauna and steam rooms, beauty salon, and body treatment rooms. Some fitness classes may incur an extra charge. A common complaint is about there not being enough staff to keep the area clean and tidy.

Sporting types can play basketball or volleyball, or table tennis. There is also a banked jogging track outdoors on the deck above the spa, and a mini-golf course.

Carnival Pride
★★★ +

Size:................................Large Resort Ship	Crew/Passenger Ratio (lower beds/all berths):..........2.2/2.6
Tonnage: 85,920	Cabins (total):....................................1,062
Lifestyle: ....Standard	Size range (sq ft/m): 185.0–490.0/17.1–45.5
Cruise line:.........................Carnival Cruise Lines	Cabins (outside view):...............................849
Former names: ....none	Cabins (interior/no view):............................213
IMO number: 9223954	Cabins (for one person):................................0
Builder: ....Kvaerner Masa-Yards (Finland)	Cabins (with private balcony):.........................750
Original cost: ....$375 million	Cabins (wheelchair accessible): 16
Entered service:.............................Jan 2002	Wheelchair accessibility:............................Good
Registry:...................................Panama	Cabin voltage: ....110 volts
Length (ft/m):............................959.6/292.5	Elevators:.......................................15
Beam (ft/m):..............................105.6/32.2	Casino (gaming tables):..............................Yes
Draft (ft/m): 25.5/7.8	Slot machines:....................................Yes
Propulsion/Propellers: ...diesel-electric (62,370kW)/2 azimuthing	Swimming pools:.................3 (1 w/sliding glass dome)
pods	Hot tubs (on deck):.................................6
Passenger decks:..................................12	Self-service launderette:.............................Yes
Total crew:...................................1,029	Dedicated cinema/seats:..............................No
Passengers (lower beds/alll berths):.............2,124/2,680	Library: ....Yes
Passenger Space Ratio (lower beds/all berths): 40.4/32.0	Onboard currency: ....US$

For a fun-filled cruise in a contemporary setting

OVERVIEW. *Carnival Pride* is sister to *Carnival Legend, Carnival Miracle,* and *Carnival Spirit, and shares the same layout and configuration.* It was built in 100 blocks, each weighing up to 450 tons, and assembled in the shipyard.

THE SHIP. The open deck and sunbathing space is not extensive, but there are two swimming pools, one of which can be covered by a sliding glass dome in case of inclement weather. An extra-charge, adults-only area, Sanctuary has its own bar, pool, hot tub and other facilities. Located at the aft of the ship on Lido Deck, it is a good area for anyone wanting to have a quieter space for sunbathing and relaxation.

Inside, the interior decor is very artistic – with art being the theme. Even the elevator doors and interiors contain reproductions (blown-up photographic copies that are too grainy for comfort) of some the great masters from the Renaissance period, such as Gauguin, Matisse, and Jacopo Vignali. Throughout the rest of the ship, you'll see lots of nude figures – all reproductions from the Renaissance period. It's all a bit of an eclectic mix. Somehow, it all works – well, sort of!

An interior walkway, named the Yellow Brick Road, connects many of the major public rooms on Atlantic Deck, one deck above Promenade Deck, which also sports a number of public rooms, including a large Club Merlin Casino (you have to walk though it to get to the main level of the showlounge from the restaurant, which is located aft).

Berlitz's Ratings

	Possible	Achieved
Ship	500	365
Accommodation	200	143
Food	400	223
Service	400	251
Entertainment	100	76
Cruise	400	273
OVERALL SCORE		
1331 points out of 2000		

The colorful atrium lobby, which spans eight decks, has wall decorations best seen from any of the multiple viewing balconies on any deck above the main lobby level. Take a drink from the lobby bar and look upwards – the surroundings are visually stunning. You'll see an 11-meter (37-ft) tall reproduction of Raphael's Nymph Galatea – best seen from any of the multiple viewing balconies on each deck above the main lobby deck level.

A small wedding chapel is located forward of the uppermost level of the two main entertainment decks, adjacent to the Nobel Library and Internet center. Other facilities include a shopping street, with boutique stores, photo gallery, video games room, and an observation balcony in the center of the vessel, at the top of the multi-deck atrium. The large Winners Club Casino invites hopeful gamers and slot players.

Carnival Pride is a veritable floating playground for the young and young-at-heart, and anyone who enjoys constant stimulation and lots of participation events, together with the three 'Gs' – glitz, glamour, and gambling. This really is cruising Splash Vegas style – a fun, all-American experience. Because it's a large resort ship, there will be lines for things like shore excursions, security control when re-boarding, and disembarkation, as well as sign-up sheets for fitness equipment.

This ship is definitely not for anyone seeking a quiet, relaxing cruise experience. Niggles include the many annoying announcements, and the never-ending hustling to get you to buy drinks, jewelry and trinkets. Also, shore excursions are booked via the in-cabin 'Fun Vision' television system, so obtaining advice and suggestions is not easy. The small reception desk in the atrium lobby can become congested at times. It's hard to escape from noise and loud music (even in cabin hallways and lifts), and masses of people walking around day and night. Many private balconies can be overlooked from public locations. You need a credit card to open the personal safe in your cabin – inconvenient if your credit cards and wallet are inside the safe!

Many pillars obstruct passenger flow (those in the dining room, for example, make it difficult for proper food service by the waiters). Books and computers are cohabitants in the ship's Holmes library/Internet center, but anyone wanting a book has to lean over others who may be using a computer – an awkward arrangement.

FAMILIES. Youngsters have their own play areas. Carnival's children's programs are divided into five age-specific groups. Meanwhile, tweens have 'Circle C,' which is next to the Gigabyte Video arcade. Teenagers have their own 'Club O2' – a chill-out room/disco.

ACCOMMODATION. There are 20 cabin categories, priced by grade, location, and size. The range of cabins includes suites (with private balcony), outside-view cabins with private balcony, 68 ocean-view cabins with French doors (pseudo balconies that have doors which open, but no balcony to step out onto), and a healthy proportion of standard outside-view to interior cabins.

All cabins have spy-hole doors, twin beds that can be converted into a queen-size bed, individually controlled air-conditioning, TV set, and telephone. A number of cabins on the lowest deck have views that are obstructed by lifeboats. Some cabins can accommodate a third and fourth person, but have little closet space, and there's only one personal safe.

Book one of the suites (Category 11 or 12 in the Carnival Cruise Lines brochure) and you automatically qualify for Skipper's Club priority check-in at any US homeland port – useful for getting ahead of the crowd.

Among the most desirable suites and cabins are those on five of the aft-facing decks; these have private balconies overlooking the stern and ship's wash. You might think that these units would suffer from vibration, but they don't – a bonus of the pod propulsion system.

For extra space, it's worthwhile booking one of the larger deluxe balcony suites on Deck 6, with private teakwood balcony. These tend to be quiet suites, with a lounge and sleeping area, a good-size bathroom with twin washbasins, toilet and bidet, and whirlpool tub. They have twin beds convertible to a queen-size bed and a huge amount of storage space. The balcony has a wide teakwood deck with smoked glass and wood railing (you could easily seat 10 people).

Even the largest suites, however, are quite small compared with suites aboard other ships of a similar size – for example, Celebrity Cruises' Celebrity Constellation, Celebrity Infinity, Celebrity Millennium, and Celebrity Summit, where penthouse suites measure up to 2,530 sq ft (235 sq m).

DINING. The Normandie Restaurant is the ship's 1,300-seat main restaurant, with seating on two levels. Small rooms can be closed off for groups of up to 60. Choose either fixed time dining (6pm or 8:15pm) or flexible dining (between 5:45pm and 9:30pm). Note that the dining room is not open for lunch on port days.

Other dining options. For casual eaters, there's Mermaid's Grill Lido Restaurant – it's a fancy name for a self-serve buffet-style eatery. It's located in the aft third of Deck 9. The venue includes a central area with a deli sandwich corner, Asian corner, rotisserie, salad bar, dessert counter, and a 24-hour Pizzeria, all of which offer both indoor and outdoor seating. Movement around the buffet area is slow, and lines form for everything. Each night, the venue morphs into the Seaview Bistro, for serve-yourself-style dinners (typically 6pm–9.30pm).

David's Steakhouse – a more upscale dining spot atop the ship, with just 156 seats and a show kitchen. There are great views over the atrium lobby and fine table settings, with proper china and silverware. Reservations are required and a cover charge applies.

ENTERTAINMENT. The glamorous 1,170-seat TajMahal Showlounge is the ship's principal venue for large-scale production shows and cabaret shows. Spiral stairways at the back of the lounge connect all three levels. Shows are best seen from the upper three levels. Directly underneath the showlounge is the Butterflies lounge and bar.

Almost every lounge/bar, including the Ivory Piano Bar, the Starry Night Jazz Club, and the Florentine Lounge, has live music in the evening. Finally, for the very lively, there's the Beauties Dance Club for thump music; and there's always karaoke.

SPA/FITNESS. SpaCarnival, spanning two decks, is located directly above the navigation bridge in the forward part of the ship and has 13,700 sq ft (1,272 sq m) of space. Facilities on the lower level include a solarium, eight treatment rooms, lecture rooms, sauna and steam rooms for men and women, and a beauty parlor. The upper level consists of a large gymnasium with forward-facing ocean views, and an aerobics room.

There are two centrally located pools outdoors, one with a retractable glass dome cover. A winding water slide two decks high is located aft. Another smaller pool is available for children. An outdoor jogging track is located around the ship's mast and the forward third of the ship; it doesn't go around the whole ship, but it's long enough for some serious walking.

Carnival Sensation
★★★

Size:.	.Large Resort Ship	Cabins (total):.	1,020
Tonnage:.	70,536	Size range (sq ft/m):.	173.2–409.7/16.0–38.0
Lifestyle:.	.Standard	Cabins (outside view):.	.618
Cruise line:.	Carnival Cruise Lines	Cabins (interior/no view):.	.402
Former names:.	Sensation	Cabins (for one person):.	.0
IMO number:.	.8711356	Cabins (with private balcony):.	.152
Builder:.	Kvaerner Masa-Yards (Finland)	Cabins (wheelchair accessible):.	.20
Original cost:.	.$300 million	Wheelchair accessibility:.	.Fair
Entered service:.	Nov 1993	Cabin voltage:.	110 volts
Registry:.	The Bahamas	Elevators:.	.14
Length (ft/m):.	855.0/260.6	Casino (gaming tables):.	Yes
Beam (ft/m):.	104.0/31.4	Slot machines:.	Yes
Draft (ft/m):.	25.9/7.9	Swimming pools:.	.3
Propulsion/Propellers:.	diesel-electric (42,240kW)/2	Hot tubs (on deck):.	.6
Passenger decks:.	10	Self-service launderette:.	Yes
Total crew:.	.920	Dedicated cinema/seats:.	.No
Passengers (lower beds/alll berths):.	2,040/2,594	Library:.	Yes
Passenger Space Ratio (lower beds/all berths):.	34.4/26.7	Onboard currency:.	.US$
Crew/Passenger Ratio (lower beds/all berths):.	2.2/2.8		

An ultra-colorful ship for first-time casual cruising

OVERVIEW. *Carnival Sensation* is the third (in a series of eight almost identical ships) in the Carnival *Fantasy*-class (sister ships: *Carnival Ecstasy*, *Carnival Elation*, *Carnival Fantasy*, *Carnival Fascination*, *Carnival Imagination*, and *Carnival Inspiration* – all of which have extremely short bows. Carnival Sensation is well-liked, and good for families and party types taking a first cruise.

Berlitz's Ratings		
	Possible	Achieved
Ship	500	314
Accommodation	200	138
Food	400	212
Service	400	255
Entertainment	100	73
Cruise	400	243
OVERALL SCORE		
1235 points out of 2000		

THE SHIP. While the ship's open deck space is reasonable, it is totally inadequate when the ship is full and everyone wants to be out on deck. The aft decks used to be less noisy when all the activities were focused around the main swimming pool and hot tubs, but now that a Carnival Waterworks – complete with long and short water slides and water-burst fountains – has been added, it's the noisy, active area.

For anyone who prefers European-style sunning there's also a topless sunbathing area, as well as Serenity – an adult-only 'quiet' lounging space on Deck 9 aft. There is no walk-around open promenade deck, although there is a short jogging track atop ship. The lifeboats, six of which double as shore tenders, are positioned high in the ship, whereas they are located much lower aboard Carnival's newer ships.

The interior of the ship is well designed and the general passenger flow is good. The interior design – the work of Miami-based creative genius Joe Farcus – is clever, functional, and extremely colorful, and includes plenty of glitz. He calls it 'entertainment architecture' and considers every part of a ship as a piece of a giant jigsaw puzzle. The underlying decor theme is the arts (in a sort of art nouveau style) and literature. It includes a colorful mix of classic and contemporary design elements that beg indulgence.

The interior focal point is an 'open' atrium lobby, with its balconied shape, and dressed to impress. It spans six decks, and is topped by a large glass dome. The lowest level of the atrium lobby is where you'll find the Purser's Desk and Shore Excursion Desk, together with a popular Atrium Bar with live music, as well as a small sushi bar off to one side; it's a good central meeting place.

There are public entertainment lounges, bars, and clubs galore, with something for everyone (except quiet space). Most public rooms and attractions lead off from Sensation Boulevard – a sort of shipboard Main Street which runs between the showlounge (forward) and the Plaza Aft lounge, with Joe's Café a popular spot for coffees and teas. Gamers and slot players alike will surely enjoy the almost non-stop action in the Club Vegas Casino close by.

The Oak Room Library is a rather stately reading room, but there are few books. Meanwhile, the Kaleidoscope Discotheque, with its dozens of video monitors and dance floor, hits you with a dazzling variety of stimulating, electric colors. There's also a 1,200-sq-ft (111-sq-m) conference room.

Carnival Sensation is a floating playground for the young and young-at-heart, and anyone who enjoys constant stimulation and lots of participation events, together with the three 'Gs' – glitz, glamour, and gambling. This really is cruising Splash Vegas style – a fun, all-American experience. Because it's a large resort ship, there will be lines for things like shore excursions, security control when re-boarding, and disembarkation, as well as sign-up sheets for fitness equipment.

This ship is definitely not for anyone seeking a quiet, relaxing cruise experience. Niggles include the many annoying announcements, and the never-ending hustling to get you to buy drinks, jewelry and trinkets. Also, shore excursions are booked via the in-cabin 'Fun Vision' television system, so obtaining advice and suggestions is not easy.

FAMILIES. Kids will almost certainly enjoy Children's World (part of the Camp Carnival children's programming), a 1,600-sq-ft (149-sq-m) play area with games and fun stuff for youngsters of all ages, including Apple computers loaded with educational software, and an arts and crafts area with spin- and sand-art machines. A children's water park is a lot of fun as an outdoor play area. For really young ones, group babysitting is available ($6 per hour for the first child; $4 per hour for each additional child of the same immediate family). Meanwhile teens have their chill-out club, as part of the line's popular Club 02 teen program.

ACCOMMODATION. There are several different accommodation price grades, ranked by facilities, size, and location. The standard outside-view and interior cabins have decor that is rather plain. They are fairly comfortable, yet spacious enough and practical (most are of the same size and appointments), with good storage and no-nonsense bathrooms. However, if you have a queen-bed configuration instead of the standard twin-bed layout, note that one person has to clamber over the bed – an ungainly exercise for those of a heavier build.

Choose a suite and you get more space, whirlpool bathtubs, and rather eclectic decor and furniture. These are reasonably attractive, but much smaller than those aboard ships of a similar size of competing companies.

Book a Category 11 or 12 suite and you get Skipper's Club priority check-in at any US homeland port – useful for getting ahead of the crowd.

There are 50 cabins with inter-connecting doors – good for families with children.

Room service items are available 24 hours a day, although in standard cabins, only cold food is available, while those in suite-grade accommodation get a greater range of items (both hot and cold) to choose from.

DINING. The two large main dining rooms, Fantasy and Ecstasy, are located amidships and aft. Both have ocean-view windows and attractive, but very bright décor, and they are noisy – full of anticipatory excitement. Choose either fixed-time dining (6pm or 8:15pm) or flexible dining (any time between 5:45 and 9:30pm).

The food is really not memorable, with simple presentation and few garnishes used. Meat and fowl main courses are often disguised with gravies and sauces. The selection of fresh green vegetables, breads, rolls, cheeses, and fruits is limited, and there is much use of canned fruit and jellied desserts. There's a decent wine list, but no wine waiters. The waiters sing and dance, and there are constant waiter parades – so it's more about 'foodertainment' than food quality.

Remember, however, that this is bog-standard catering – with all its attendant standardization and production cooking; it is, therefore, difficult to obtain anything unusual or 'off-menu.' For something really simple, there's an 'always available' list of 'Carnival Classics' that includes mahi mahi (fish), baby back ribs (beef), and grilled chicken (when the dining rooms are open). The two main dining rooms are not open for lunch on port days.

Other dining options. The Seaview Bar & Grill is like a lido cafe, and features casual self-serve buffet eats, most of which are non-memorable. The venue includes a deli counter and pizzeria. At night, the venue morphs into the Seaview Bistro, and provides a casual alternative to the main dining rooms, for pasta, steaks, salads, and desserts – it typically operates only between 6pm and 9pm. The food selection, though limited, makes a change from the large, crowded and noisy main dining rooms. Outside on deck is a Mongolian Rotisserie Grill.

A patisserie offers specialty coffees and sweets (extra charge), and a so-called sushi bar on Promenade Deck is open prior to dinner only.

There is no specialty (extra-charge) restaurant, as aboard some of the larger ships in the Carnival fleet.

ENTERTAINMENT. The Fantasia Lounge is the ship's principal showlounge, and the venue for large-scale production shows and major cabaret acts. However, some 20 pillars obstruct the views from several seats. During a typical cruise, there will be one or two high-energy production shows, backed by a large live band.

SPA/FITNESS. SpaCarnival is a large, glass-wrapped health, fitness, and spa complex. It is located on the uppermost interior deck, forward of the ship's mast, and is typically open from 6am to 8pm daily. It consists of a gymnasium with ocean-view windows that look out over the bow and the latest electronic machines, an aerobics exercise room, sauna and steam rooms, beauty salon, and body treatment rooms. Some fitness classes (such as kick-boxing or yoga) may incur an extra charge. A common complaint is that there are not enough staff to keep the area clean and tidy, and used towels are often strewn around the changing rooms.

Sporting types can play basketball, volleyball, or table tennis. There is a banked jogging track outdoors on the deck above the spa, and a mini-golf course.

Carnival Spirit
★★★ +

Size:.................................Large Resort Ship	Crew/Passenger Ratio (lower beds/all berths):.........2.2/2.6
Tonnage:...85,920	Cabins (total):..1,062
Lifestyle:.......................................Standard	Size range (sq ft/m):.................185.0–490.0/17.1–45.5
Cruise line:..........................Carnival Cruise Lines	Cabins (outside view):..................................849
Former names:.....................................none	Cabins (interior/no view):..............................213
IMO number:....................................9188647	Cabins (for one person):.................................0
Builder:...........................Kvaerner Masa-Yards	Cabins (with private balcony):..........................750
Original cost:................................$375 million	Cabins (wheelchair accessible):..........................16
Entered service:.................................Apr 2001	Wheelchair accessibility:...............................Good
Registry:..Panama	Cabin voltage:..................................110 volts
Length (ft/m):..............................959.6/292.5	Elevators:...15
Beam (ft/m):................................105.6/32.2	Casino (gaming tables):..................................Yes
Draft (ft/m):..................................25.5/7.8	Slot machines:.......................................Yes
Propulsion/Propellers:...diesel-electric (62,370kW)/2 azimuthing	Swimming pools:.................3 (1 w/sliding glass dome)
pods	Hot tubs (on deck):....................................5
Passenger decks:....................................12	Self-service launderette:..............................Yes
Total crew:..930	Dedicated cinema/seats:................................No
Passengers (lower beds/alll berths):..............2,124/2,680	Library:...Yes
Passenger Space Ratio (lower beds/all berths):.......40.4/32.0	Onboard currency:.................................Aus$

For a fun-filled cruise in a contemporary setting

OVERVIEW. *Carnival Spirit* is a sister ship to *Carnival Legend, Carnival Miracle,* and *Carnival Pride, and shares the same layout and configuration.* It was built in 100 blocks, each weighing up to 450 tons, and assembled in the shipyard. In October 2012, *Carnival Spirit* was moved to Sydney, Australia, for year-round fun-in-the-sun cruises – something new for Carnival Cruise Lines. Could it be rebranded as a P&O Cruises (Australia) ship soon?

Berlitz's Ratings		
	Possible	Achieved
Ship	500	364
Accommodation	200	143
Food	400	223
Service	400	252
Entertainment	100	76
Cruise	400	269
OVERALL SCORE		
1327 points out of 2000		

THE SHIP. Following a 2012 refurbishment before its deployment to Australia, much of the outdoor deck space has been designated a Water Park and Splash Zone, with water wheels, spraying jets, water blasters, pull ropes, two Mini Racer slides, and more.

Then there's the really big attraction, Green Thunder, a thrill ride that starts 100ft (30m) above sea level. The floor suddenly drops out of the platform and you plummet in a near-vertical drop at about 23ft (7m) a second. When you hit the water in the fast water-slide, you twist and turn through a transparent tube that extends over the side of the ship. Kids will love it, but need to be 42ins (1.1m) tall to be able to experience it. The open deck space is a bit tight when the ship sails full in warm-weather areas.

An extra-charge, adults-only area, Sanctuary has its own bar, pool, hot tub and other facilities. Located at the aft of the ship on Lido Deck, it is a pleasant area for anyone wanting to have a quieter space for sunbathing and relaxation – and to escape the many

children on board during the major holidays.

An interior walkway, named the Fashion Boulevard, connects many of the major public rooms on Atlantic Deck, one deck above Promenade Deck, which also sports a number of public rooms, including a large Louis XIV Casino.

The colorful atrium lobby, which spans eight decks, has wall decorations best seen from any of the multiple viewing balconies on any deck above the main lobby level. Take a drink from the lobby bar and look upwards – the surroundings and artwork are visually stunning.

Perhaps the most dramatic room is the Pharaoh's Palace Showlounge, which spans three decks in the forward section. Directly underneath is the Versailles Lounge, which has a bar in its starboard aft section.

A small wedding chapel is located forward of the uppermost level of the two main entertainment decks, adjacent to the Nobel Library and Internet center. Other facilities include a winding shopping street, with boutique stores, photo gallery, video games room, and an observation balcony in the center of the vessel, at the top of the multi-deck atrium. The large Winners Club Casino invites hopeful gamers and slot players alike.

Carnival Spirit is a floating playground for the young and young-at-heart, and anyone who enjoys constant stimulation and lots of participation events, together with the three 'Gs' – glitz, glamour, and gambling. This really is cruising Splash Vegas style – a fun, all-

American experience. Because it's a large resort ship, there will be lines for things like shore excursions, security control when re-boarding, and disembarkation, as well as sign-up sheets for fitness equipment.

Niggles include the small reception desk in the atrium lobby, which can become really congested at times. It's hard to escape from noise and loud music (even in cabin hallways and lifts), and masses of people milling around day and night. Many private balconies can be overlooked from public locations. You need a credit card to open the personal safe in your cabin – inconvenient if your credit cards and wallet are inside the safe!

FAMILIES. Youngsters have their own play areas. Carnival's children's programs are divided into five age-specific groups. Meanwhile, tweens have 'Circle C,' which is next to the Gigabyte Video arcade. Teenagers have their own 'Club O2' – a chill-out room/disco.

ACCOMMODATION. There are 20 cabin categories, priced by grade, location, and size. The range of cabins includes suites (with private balcony), outside-view cabins with private balcony, 68 ocean-view cabins with French doors (pseudo balconies that have doors which open, but no balcony to step out onto), and a healthy proportion of standard outside-view to interior cabins.

All cabins have spy-hole doors, twin beds that can be converted into a queen-size bed, individually controlled air-conditioning, TV set, and telephone. A number of cabins on the lowest deck have views that are obstructed by lifeboats. Some cabins can accommodate a third and fourth person, but have little closet space, and there's only one personal safe.

Book one of the suites (Category 11 or 12 in the Carnival Cruise Lines brochure) and you automatically qualify for Skipper's Club priority check-in at any US homeland port – useful for getting ahead of the crowd.

Among the most desirable suites and cabins are those on five of the aft-facing decks; these have private balconies overlooking the stern and ship's wash. You might think that these units would suffer from vibration, but they don't – a bonus provided by the pod propulsion system.

For extra space, it's worthwhile booking one of the larger deluxe balcony suites on Deck 6, with private teakwood balcony. These tend to be quiet suites, with a lounge and sleeping area, a good-size bathroom with twin washbasins, toilet and bidet, and whirlpool tub. They have twin beds convertible to a queen-size bed, and a huge amount of storage space. The balcony has a wide teakwood deck with smoked glass and wood railing (you could easily seat 10 people).

Even the largest suites, however, are quite small compared with suites aboard other ships of a similar size – for example, Celebrity Cruises' *Celebrity Constellation*, *Celebrity Infinity*, *Celebrity Millennium*, and *Celebrity Summit*, where penthouse suites measure up to 2,530 sq ft (235 sq m).

DINING. The Empire Restaurant is the ship's large, two-deck-high, 1,300-seat main restaurant. Small rooms on both upper and lower levels can be closed off for groups of up to 60. Choose either fixed time dining (6pm or 8:15pm) or flexible dining (between 5:45pm and 9:30pm). Note that the dining room is not open for lunch on port days.

Other dining options. For casual eaters, there's La Playa Grille Lido Restaurant – a self-serve buffet-style eatery. It's located in the aft third of Deck 9 (part of it wraps around the upper section of the huge atrium). The venue includes a central area with a deli sandwich corner, Asian corner, rotisserie, salad bar, an International (Taste of the Nations) counter, and a 24-hour Pizzeria counter, all of which offer both indoor and outdoor seating. Movement around the buffet area is slow, and lines form for everything. Each night, the venue morphs into the Seaview Bistro, for serve-yourself-style dinners (typically 6pm–9.30pm).

David's Steakhouse – an upscale (reservations required) dining spot atop the ship, with just 156 seats and a show kitchen. It is located on two of the uppermost decks of the ship, above the Mermaid's Grille Lido Restaurant, in the lower, forward section of the funnel housing, with neat views over the colourful atrium lobby. Fine table settings, china, and silverware are provided, and a cover charge applies.

ENTERTAINMENT. The glamorous 1,170-seat Pharaoh's Palace is the ship's principal venue for large-scale production shows and cabaret shows. Shows are best seen from the upper three levels. Directly underneath the showlounge is the Versailles lounge and bar.

Almost every lounge/bar, including the Shanghai Piano Bar, the Club Cool Jazz Club, and the Artists' Lobby Lounge, has live music in the evening. Finally, for the very lively, there's the Dancin' Dance Club for thump music; and there's always karaoke.

SPA/FITNESS. SpaCarnival spans two decks; it is located directly above the navigation bridge in the forward part of the ship and has 13,700 sq ft (1,272 sq m) of space. Facilities on the lower level include a solarium, eight treatment rooms, lecture rooms, sauna and steam rooms for men and women, and a beauty parlor. The upper level consists of a large gymnasium with floor-to-ceiling windows on three sides, including forward-facing ocean views, and an aerobics room with instructor-led classes.

There are two centrally located pools outdoors, one with a retractable glass dome cover. An outdoor jogging track is located around the ship's mast and the forward third of the ship; it doesn't go around the whole ship, but it's long enough for some serious walking.

Carnival Splendor
★★★ +

Size:....................................Large Resort Ship	Cabins (total):....................................1,487
Tonnage: 113,323	Size range (sq ft/m): 179.7–484.2/16.7–44.8
Lifestyle: ....Standard	Cabins (outside view):................................917
Cruise line:......................... Carnival Cruise Lines	Cabins (interior/no view):.............................570
Former names: ....none	Cabins (for one person):................................0
IMO number: 9333163	Cabins (with private balcony):........................574
Builder: .... Fincantieri (Italy)	Cabins (wheelchair accessible): 25
Original cost:.............................. $500 million	Wheelchair accessibility:............................Good
Entered service:...............................July 2008	Cabin voltage: .... 110 volts
Registry:... Panama	Elevators:...18
Length (ft/m):............................... 951.4/290.0	Casino (gaming tables):...............................Yes
Beam (ft/m):................................. 105.6/32.2	Slot machines:......................................Yes
Draft (ft/m):.................................... 27.2/8.3	Swimming pools:..................3 (1 w/sliding glass dome)
Propulsion/Propellers:........... diesel-electric (63,400kW)/2	Hot tubs (on deck):....................................7
Passenger decks:.....................................13	Self-service launderette:..............................Yes
Total crew:... 1,150	Dedicated cinema/seats:...............................No
Passengers (lower beds/alll berths):.............. 2,974/3,700	Library: ....Yes
Passenger Space Ratio (lower beds/all berths): 37.0/29.7	Onboard currency: ....US$
Crew/Passenger Ratio (lower beds/all berths):.......... 2.5/3.1	

A family-friendly, fun-filled ship with a great water-slide

OVERVIEW. *Carnival Splendor* shares the same generally balanced profile as sisters *Carnival Conquest*, *Carnival Sunshine*, *Carnival Freedom*, *Carnival Glory*, *Carnival Liberty*, *Carnival Triumph*, *Carnival Valor*, and *Carnival Victory*, although it was originally designated as a ship for the Costa Cruises brand. It cannot transit the Panama Canal at present, due to its size (this will change in 2015). The interior decor displays a vivid palette of colors that excite the senses.

THE SHIP. The deck and public room layout is logical, and finding your way around is relatively easy. Most of the public rooms are located on one deck off a main interior boulevard, above a deck which contains the two main dining rooms.

Public rooms include a large Royal Flush Casino. Gaming includes blackjack, craps, roulette, three-card poker, Caribbean Stud poker, Face Up, Let it Ride, Bonus, and Wheel of Madness, and an array of more than 300 slot machines.

Recalling the drive-in movie theaters of the 1950s, the Seaside Theater shows movies, and sports features on deck, with seating in tiered rows and the screen facing forward (popcorn obligatory, of course). The ship has bow-to-stern Wi-Fi Internet access – for a fee, and this includes all passenger cabins.

Carnival Splendor is a floating playground for the young and young-at-heart, and anyone who enjoys constant stimulation and lots of participation events,

Berlitz's Ratings

	Possible	Achieved
Ship	500	372
Accommodation	200	144
Food	400	218
Service	400	260
Entertainment	100	77
Cruise	400	261

OVERALL SCORE
1332 points out of 2000

together with the three 'Gs' – glitz, glamour, and gambling. This really is cruising Splash Vegas style – and fun, all-American experience. Because it's a large resort ship, there will be lines for things like shore excursions, security control when re-boarding, and disembarkation, as well as sign-up sheets for fitness equipment.

Forget fashion – the sine qua non – of a Carnival cruise is all about having fun. While the cuisine is just so-so, the real fun begins at sundown when Carnival really excels in sound, lights, razzle-dazzle shows, and late-night high volume sounds.

Minor niggles include the fact that many pillars obstruct passenger flow, particularly in the dining rooms, where they make it difficult for the waiters to serve properly, and the food itself (particularly the bakery items).

FAMILIES. Youngsters are provided with their own Camp Carnival children's club (with its own small outdoor pool), and are well cared for with the line's extensive children's program. Camp Carnival is located on Sun Deck, out of the way of older passengers.

ACCOMMODATION. There are 20 cabin-price categories, in seven different suite/cabin types, sizes, and grades. These include suites with private balcony; deluxe outside-view cabins with private balcony; outside-view cabins with private balcony; outside-view cabins with window; cabins with a porthole instead of a window; interior cabins; and interior cabins with upper and lower berths. There are five decks of cabins with private balconies.

The standard cabins are of good size and come equipped with all the basics, although the furniture is angular, with no rounded edges. Three decks of cabins (eight per deck, each with private balcony) overlook the stern. Most cabins with twin beds convert to a queen-size bed format. Book one of the suites (Category 11 or 12 in the Carnival Cruise Lines brochure) and you'll get Skipper's Club priority check-in at any US homeland port – useful for getting ahead of the crowd.

There are even 'spa' cabins – a grouping of 18 cabins located directly around and behind SpaCarnival; so fitness devotees can get out of bed and go straight to the treadmill without having to go through any of the public rooms first.

A basket of small sample toiletries is provided in all cabins, although it's better to take your own preferred brands.

DINING. There are two principal dining rooms, the 744-seat Black Pearl – located amidships, and the 1,122-seat Gold Pearl, located aft. Both are two decks high and include a balcony level – Gold Pearls is the larger of the two balconies. There's a choice of either fixed-time dining (6pm or 8:15pm) or flexible dining (any time between 5:45pm and 9:30pm). There are few tables for two, but my favorites are the two tables for two, right at the very back of the Gold Pearl restaurant, with ocean views astern. Note that the two main dining rooms are not open for lunch on port days.

Other dining options. The Steakhouse has fine table settings, china, and silverware, and leather-bound menus. The specialties are USDA dry-aged prime steaks and seafood items. It's worth paying the cover charge to get a taste of what Carnival can really deliver in terms of food that is of better quality than what is served in the main dining rooms Reservations are required, and a cover charge applies.

The Lido Restaurant is a casual self-serve international food court-style eatery. It has two main serving lines and several stand-alone sections. Included in this eating mall are a New York-style deli, a 24-hour pizzeria, and a grill for fast foods such as hamburgers and hot dogs; one section has a Tandoori oven for Indian-theme items.

Each night, this venue morphs into Seaview Bistro to provide a dress-down alternative the main dining rooms, serving pasta, steaks, salads, and desserts (typically between 6pm and 9pm). An upstairs Rotisserie offers chicken.

ENTERTAINMENT. The large, multi-deck Spectacular Showlounge seats 1,400, and hosts colorful large-scale entertainment including Las Vegas-style production shows (think girls, feathers and flesh) and major cabaret acts. It has a revolving stage, hydraulic orchestra pit, excellent sound, and seating on three levels, the upper levels are tiered through two decks.

An alternative entertainment venue is the El Morocco, a 425-seat lounge located aft; this typically features live music and late-night cabaret acts including smutty adult comedy. Adjacent is the Grand Piano Lounge/Bar.

SPA/FITNESS. The Cloud 9 Spa spans two decks (with a total area of around 40,000 sq ft/3,715 sq m, including the 16 spa suites – or 13,000 sq ft/1,235 sq m, excluding them). Located directly above the navigation bridge in the forward part of the ship, it is accessed from the forward stairway.

Facilities on the lower level include a gymnasium, solarium, a thermal suite (a number of saunas and steam rooms – some infused with herbal aromas), thalassotherapy pool (check out the huge Chinese dogs), and a beauty salon. The upper level houses 17 massage/body treatment rooms, including two VIP suites (one for couples, one specially configured for wheelchair access), rasul (Mediterranean mud treatment – best for couples) chamber, floatation therapy room, treatment rooms, and outdoor relaxation areas on both port and starboard sides with integrated massage cabana. If you simply want to use the thermal suite, there's an extra cost.

Latitude and longitude

Latitude signifies the distance north or south of the equator, while **longitude** signifies distance east or west of the 0 degree at Greenwich Observatory in London ('where time begins'). Both are recorded in degrees, minutes, and seconds. At the equator, one minute of longitude is equal to one nautical mile, but as the meridians converge after leaving the equator and meeting at the poles, the size of a degree becomes smaller. It was in 1714 that an Act of Parliament established a Board of Commissioners for the Discovery of Longitude at Sea. A prize of £20,000, then a huge sum, was set. The English clockmaker John Harrison (1693–1776) won it for his highly accurate chronometer. Indeed, none other than Captain Cook used a Harrison-designed chronometer on one of his voyages to the Pacific in 1775.

Carnival Sunshine
★★★ +

Size:. . . . . .Large Resort Ship	Cabins (total):. 1,503
Tonnage: 102853	Size range (sq ft/m): 179.7–482.2/16.7–44.8
Lifestyle: . . . . .Standard	Cabins (outside view): 938
Cruise line:. . . . . Carnival Cruise Lines	Cabins (interior/no view):. 565
Former names: . . . . Carnival Destiny	Cabins (for one person):. 0
IMO number: 9070058	Cabins (with private balcony): 418
Builder: . . . . Fincantieri (Italy)	Cabins (wheelchair accessible): 25
Original cost: . . . . $400 million	Wheelchair accessibility:. . . . . .Good
Entered service:. . . . . Nov 1996	Cabin voltage: . . . . 110 volts
Registry:. . . . . The Bahamas	Elevators:. 18
Length (ft/m):. 892.3/272.0	Casino (gaming tables):. . . . . Yes
Beam (ft/m):. 116.0/35.3	Slot machines:. . . . . Yes
Draft (ft/m): 27.0/8.2	Swimming pools:. . . . . .3 (1 w/sliding glass dome)
Propulsion/Propellers: . . . . diesel-electric (63,400kW)/2	Hot tubs (on deck):. 7
Passenger decks:. 12	Self-service launderette:. . . . . Yes
Total crew:. 1,150	Dedicated cinema/seats:. . . . . .No
Passengers (lower beds/alll berths):. 3,006/3,758	Library: . . . . Yes
Passenger Space Ratio (lower beds/all berths): 34.2/27.3	Onboard currency: . . . . .US$
Crew/Passenger Ratio (lower beds/all berths):. 2.6/3.2	

A vibrant ship suited to first-time casual cruisers

OVERVIEW. *Carnival Sunshine (formerly Carnival Destiny)* was the first cruise ship whose gross tonnage exceeded 100,000. After a lengthy refurbishment, the ship shouts "party, party, party!" It's a good ship for families with children.

THE SHIP. The ship has short bows and a distinctive, large, swept-back wing-tipped funnel. Tiered sunbathing decks positioned between small swimming pools, several hot tubs, and a large poolside movie screen have transformed the area into a relaxation zone, complete with a small waterfall feature.

Also, on the open deck and aft of the funnel, are dual long water slides (200ft/60m long), and a stairway that leads to a platform – the setting-off point that is close to the height of the top of the funnel. The water slides, one yellow, one blue allow you and a competitor to race down the Twister to a splashy finish.

The interior decor is a sensory wonderland. There are three decks full of lounges and bars, lots of rooms to play in, and a double-wide indoor promenade. A glass-domed rotunda Sunshine Atrium lobby – with bar, two panoramic elevators and dual stairway – is nine decks high. An action-packed Sunshine Casino has ample gaming tables for serious gamers (poker, craps, blackjack and roulette), and over 320 slot machines.

In spring 2013 the ship's much-needed $155 million refit lasted almost two months and added a half-deck, extended two other decks, added 182 cabins (but no extra elevators), a Fahrenheit 555 Steakhouse, a new Asian-

Berlitz's Ratings

	Possible	Achieved
Ship	500	382
Accommodation	200	144
Food	400	226
Service	400	260
Entertainment	100	74
Cruise	400	263
OVERALL SCORE		
1349 points out of 2000		

cuisine venue, a poolside BlueIguana Cantina Mexican-style street eatery, a car-culture-inspired Guy's Burger Joint, a Cucina del Capitano (Italian dining spot), and a Lido Marketplace. Other eateries were also revamped, and a JavaBlue Café – with 'comfort' snacks was introduced into the Fun Hub internet-connect area. A Havana Bar was also added, as was a RedFrog Pub – starring Carnival's own tasty house brew – Thirsty Red Frog, as well as a poolside RedFrog Rum Bar. Other public rooms include Piano Bar 88; Alchemy Bar; Library Bar; an EA Sports Bar; and an art gallery.

Niggles: The terraced pool deck does get rather cluttered, and there are no cushioned pads for the deck chairs. Also, the Photo Gallery, adjacent to the atrium/purser's office, becomes congested when photos are on display. There is constant hustling for drinks.

FAMILIES. Youngsters will find a good range of facilities, including their own two-level Children's Club (with an outdoor pool), and are well cared for with 'Camp Carnival,' the line's extensive children's program. Circle 'C' is for the 12-14-year olds, while Club O2 is the hot spot and chill-out room for 15-17-year olds. There are lots of sporty-exercise-type things for kids to do, too, like take the adventure course – with its tightropes, nets, and swinging planks, not to mention the real 'wow' – the two waterslides in the Waterpark.

ACCOMMODATION. There are several accommodation categories (Captain's Suite, Grand Suite, Ocean

Suite, Premium Balcony Cabin, Scenic Oceanview Cabin, Oceanview Cabin, Interior Cabin, and Small Interior, and a multitude of different price grades, depending on size and location. Over half of all cabins have an ocean view and, at 225 sq ft/21 sq m, they are a decent size. The cabins, spread over four decks, have private balconies with glass rather than steel balustrades for better, unobstructed ocean views; balconies have bright fluorescent lighting. However, there are many, many interior (no-view) cabins.

During the 2013 refit, 95 Cloud 9 Spa Cabins were added over three decks in the front of the ship, adjacent to the Cloud 9 Spa and Serenity adult-only area; these have all the usual fittings, plus special spa-like extras, and access to the Cloud 9 Spa.

The standard cabins are of an adequate size and are equipped with all the basics, although the furniture is angular (think Ikea flatpack), with no rounded edges – in other words, nothing is superfluous. Three decks of cabins (eight on each deck, each with private balcony) overlook the stern.

Eight penthouse suites each have a large private balcony. Although they are quite well-appointed, they are really modest when compared to the good-sized suites even in many smaller ships. Other suites each feature a decent-size bathroom and lounge space.

In cabins with balconies, the partition between each balcony is open at top and bottom, so you can hear noise from neighbors. Three categories of cabins, both outside and interior, have upper and lower bunk beds, useful for families with small children.

The cabins have a pastel color scheme and soft furnishings. Interactive 'Fun Vision' technology lets you choose movies on demand, for a fee (although the television screen is not very large). The bathrooms, which have good-size showers, have adequate storage space in the toiletries cabinet. A gift basket is provided in all grades; it includes aloe soap, shampoo, conditioner, deodorant, breath mints, candy, and pain relief tablets – albeit all in sample sizes.

Book one of the suite-grades and you get 'Skipper's Club' priority check-in at any US homeland port.

Note that the soundproofing between cabins is poor and the cabin doors have (non-closable) vents – so noise from the hallway filters through.

DINING. There are two principal dining rooms: the Sunrise Forward Dining Room, with windows on two sides; and the Sunrise Aft Dining Room, with windows on three sides). Each spans two decks and incorporates a dozen pyramid-shaped domes and chandeliers, and a soft, mellow peachy color scheme.

The Universe dining room has a two-deck-high wall of glass overlooking the stern. There are tables for four, six, and eight and even a few tables for two – nice for honeymooners. Choose either fixed-time dining (6pm or 8:15pm) or flexible dining (any time between 5:45 and 9:30pm). Although menu choices look good, the actual cuisine delivered is adequate, but unmemorable. Still, the waiters do try to make up with lots of show and hoopla, telling everyone they're having fun. Note that the two main dining rooms are not open for lunch on port days.

Other dining options. Farenheit 555 Steakhouse is an extra-cost, reservations-required dining spot for fine steaks and grilled seafood dishes. There are many tables for two (although they are quite close together) as well as larger tables, and the seating is comfortable.

For casual eats, there's Market Restaurant, a rather large self-serve buffet venue. It's open for breakfast and lunch, and there are plenty of food displays (it's a copy of the self-serve Market Restaurants aboard the AIDA Cruises ships). For dinner this turns into the Seaview Bistro for use as an alternative eatery for anyone not wishing to dress for the formal dining rooms (between 6pm and 9pm). The dining room entrances have comfortable drinking areas.

The Sun and Sea Restaurant, two decks high, is the ship's informal international food court-style eatery, which is adjacent to the aft pool and can be covered by a glass dome-shaped cover. There is a Cucina del Capitano (for Italian cuisine, with made-to-order pasta dishes); a Ji Ji Asian Kitchen, which features lunchtime stir-fry dishes, while (extra-cost) dinners include more exotic favorites; a 24-hour pizzeria; a patisserie (extra charge for pastries); and Guy's Burger Joint for fast foods like burgers and hot dogs.

You can also choose to eat at the Chef's Table (reserved for only 12 hungry diners, at $75 each) including a look into the galley when it's in full operation, followed by a specially-prepared multi-course dinner.

ENTERTAINMENT. The three-level Liquid Lounge – the ship's showlounge – the setting for carnival's high energy production legs and feathers shows and large-scale cabaret acts, is quite stunning. It has a revolving stage, hydraulic orchestra pit, good sound, and seating on three levels (the upper levels being tiered through two decks). A proscenium over the stage acts as a scenery loft.

SPA/FITNESS. The Cloud 9 Spa spans two decks, with a total area of 13,700 sq ft/1,272 sq m. It is located directly above the navigation bridge in the forward part of the ship (accessible via the forward stairway). Facilities on the lower level include a solarium, eight treatment rooms, lecture rooms, sauna and steam rooms for men and women, and a beauty parlor; the upper level consists of a large gymnasium with floor-to-ceiling windows on three sides, including forward-facing ocean views, and an aerobics room with instructor-led classes (some at extra cost).

Carnival Triumph
★★★ +

Size:.	Large Resort Ship	Cabins (total):.	1,379
Tonnage:	101,509	Size range (sq ft/m):	179.7–482.2/16.7–44.8
Lifestyle:	Standard	Cabins (outside view):	853
Cruise line:.	Carnival Cruise Lines	Cabins (interior/no view):.	526
Former names:	none	Cabins (for one person):.	0
IMO number:		Cabins (with private balcony):	508
Builder:	Fincantieri (Italy)	Cabins (wheelchair accessible):	25
Original cost:	$420 million	Wheelchair accessibility:	Good
Entered service:	Oct 1999	Cabin voltage:	110 volts
Registry:	The Bahamas	Elevators:	18
Length (ft/m):	893.0/272.2	Casino (gaming tables):	Yes
Beam (ft/m):	116.0/35.3	Slot machines:	Yes
Draft (ft/m):	27.0/8.2	Swimming pools:	2 (+1 with sliding glass dome)
Propulsion/Propellers:	2 azimuthing pods (17.6MW each)	Hot tubs (on deck):.	
Passenger decks:	13	Self-service launderette:	Yes
Total crew:	1,100	Dedicated cinema/seats:	No
Passengers (lower beds/alll berths):	2,758/3,473	Library:	Yes
Passenger Space Ratio (lower beds/all berths):	36.8/29.2	Onboard currency:	US$
Crew/Passenger Ratio (lower beds/all berths):	2.3/3.0		

Floating fun palace for ultra-casual first-time cruisers

OVERVIEW. *Carnival Triumph is* quite a stunning ship, built to impress at every turn, although the bows (the pointy bit at the front) are extremely short. (sister ships *Carnival Conquest, Carnival Freedom, Carnival Glory, Carnival Liberty, Carnival Splendor, Carnival Sunshine, Carnival Valor, and Carnival Victory* . It is too large to transit the Panama Canal at present.

Berlitz's Ratings		
	Possible	Achieved
Ship	500	361
Accommodation	200	144
Food	400	218
Service	400	259
Entertainment	100	76
Cruise	400	252
OVERALL SCORE		
1310 points out of 2000		

THE SHIP. The decor is quite tasteful, and is themed after great European cities like Rome and Paris. The layout is logical and quite easy to navigate.

The terraced pool deck is really cluttered, and there are no cushioned pads for the deck chairs. Getting away from people and noise is extremely difficult. The photo gallery becomes extremely congested when photographs are on display.

There are three decks full of lounges, 10 bars, and lots of rooms to play in. Like many of the Carnival ships, this one has a doublewide indoor promenade. It spans nine decks, and has a glass-domed rotunda atrium lobby. Amidships on the open deck is a long water slide; 200ft (60m) long, it travels from just aft of the ship's mast. Tiered sunbathing decks are positioned between two small swimming pools and several hot tubs.

The lowest deck of the atrium lobby features a square-shaped bar, facing forward to the glass-walled lifts; it is located under the dome at the top of the atrium. A sports bar has tables displaying sports memorabilia.

From a safety viewpoint, passengers can embark directly into the lifeboats from their secured position without having to wait for them to be lowered, which can save time in the event of a real emergency.

Carnival Triumph is a floating playground for the young and young-at-heart, and anyone who enjoys constant stimulation and participation events, together with the three 'Gs' – glitz, glamour, and gambling. This really is cruising Splash Vegas style – and fun, all-American experience. Because it's a large resort ship, there will be lines for things like shore excursions, security control when re-boarding, and disembarkation, as well as sign-up sheets for fitness equipment.

FAMILIES. Children have good facilities, including their own two-level Children's Club, including an outdoor pool, and are well cared for with Camp Carnival, the cruise line's extensive children's program.

ACCOMMODATION. There are numerous price categories, depending on grade, location and size. Over half of all cabins are outside and, at 225 sq ft/21 sq m, are among the largest in the standard market. They are spread over four decks and have private balconies extending from the ship's side; these have glass rather than steel balustrades for unobstructed ocean views, as well as bright fluorescent lighting. The standard cabins are of good size and have all the basics, although the furniture is angular, with no rounded edges. Three decks of cabins – eight per deck, each with private balcony – overlook the stern.

There are eight penthouse suites, each with a large private balcony. Although quite lavish in their appointments, at only 483 sq ft (44.8 sq m), they are really quite small when compared to the best suites even in many smaller ships. There are also 40 other suites that are nothing special, although each has a decent-size bathroom and a good amount of lounge space.

In cabins with balconies, the partition between each balcony is open at the top and bottom, so you may well hear noise from neighbors. It is disappointing to see three categories of cabins (both outside and interior) with upper and lower bunk beds – lower beds are far more preferable, but this is how the ships absorb hundreds of extra passengers over and above the lower bed capacity.

Cabins have a light color scheme. Interactive 'Fun Vision' technology lets you choose movies on demand, for a fee. The bathrooms, which have good-size showers, have good storage space for toiletries. All grades get a gift basket of toiletry samples.

Book one of the suites (Category 11 or 12 in the Carnival Cruise Lines brochure), and you get Skipper's Club priority check-in at any US homeland port.

DINING. The ship has two main dining rooms, one forward (London) with windows on two sides and 706 seats, and the other (Paris) aft with windows on three sides and 1,090 seats. Each spans two decks, and incorporates a dozen domes and chandeliers. The aft dining room has a two-deck-high wall of glass overlooking the stern. Tables are for four, six, and eight, but there are even a few tables for two. The dining room entrances have comfortable drinking areas for pre-dinner cocktails.

There's a choice of either fixed-time dining (6pm or 8:15pm), or flexible dining (any time between 5:45pm and 9:30pm). This gives you very little time to 'dine' – although it should give you some idea of what to expect from your dining experience. Although the menu choice looks good, the actual cuisine delivered is adequate, but quite unmemorable. Note that the two main dining rooms are not open for lunch on port days.

Other dining options. An informal international self-serve buffet-style eatery has seating on two levels. Included in this eatery are a New York-style deli (open 11am–11pm), a Chinese restaurant with wok preparation, and a 24-hour pizzeria which typically serves an average of more than 800 pizzas every day.

At night, the Seaview Bistro provides a casual alternative to the main dining rooms, serving pasta, steaks, salads, and desserts. In a 2013 refit, Guy Fieri's Burger Joint (for burgers and fast food items), Blue Iguana Cantina Bar, EA Sports Bar, and a Red Frog Rum Bar were added. In addition, there is a self-serve ice cream and frozen yoghurt station, at no extra charge. If you want to eat 24 hours a day, you can.

The Steakhouse is a reservations-required extra-cost dining venue (serving prime USDA steaks and grilled seafood). It has fine table settings, china, and silverware, as well as leather-bound menus, and a design theme set around Scarlett O'Hara, the heroine of Margaret Mitchell's classic novel *Gone With the Wind*.

ENTERTAINMENT. The three-level showlounges are stunning, with a revolving stage, hydraulic orchestra pit, superb sound, and seating on three levels, the upper levels being tiered through two decks. A proscenium over the stage acts as a scenery loft.

SPA/FITNESS. SpaCarnival spans two decks, with a total area of 13,700 sq ft/1,272 sq m, and is located directly above the navigation bridge in the forward part of the ship; it is accessed from the forward stairway. Facilities on the lower level include a solarium, eight massage/body treatment rooms, lecture rooms, sauna and steam rooms for men and women, and a beauty parlor; the upper level consists of a large gymnasium with floor-to-ceiling windows on three sides, including forward-facing ocean views, and an aerobics room with instructor-led classes, some at extra cost.

Steering

Two different methods can be used to steer a ship:

Electrohydraulic steering uses automatic (telemotor-type) transmission from the wheel itself to the steering gear aft. This is generally used when traffic is heavy, during maneuvers into and out of ports, or when there is poor visibility.

Automatic steering (gyropilot) is used only in the open sea. This system does not require anyone at the wheel because it is controlled by computer. However, aboard all ships, a quartermaster is always at the wheel, for extra safety, and just in case a need should arise to switch from one steering system to another.

Carnival Valor
★★★ +

Size:.....................................Large Resort Ship	Cabins (total):...................................1,487 79
Tonnage: 110,239	Size range (sq ft/m): 179.7–482.2/16.7–44.8
Lifestyle: ....Standard	Cabins (outside view):..................................917
Cruise line:.........................Carnival Cruise Lines	Cabins (interior/no view):..............................570
Former names: ....none	Cabins (for one person):..................................0
IMO number: 9236389	Cabins (with private balcony):..........................574
Builder: ....Fincantieri (Italy)	Cabins (wheelchair accessible):..........................25
Original cost: ....$500 million	Wheelchair accessibility:.............................Good
Entered service:............................. Dec 2004	Cabin voltage: ....110 volts
Registry:..Panama	Elevators:..18
Length (ft/m):..............................951.4/290.0	Casino (gaming tables):..............................Yes
Beam (ft/m):...............................116.0/35.3	Slot machines:......................................Yes
Draft (ft/m):..................................27.0/8.2	Swimming pools:.................3 (1 w/sliding glass dome)
Propulsion/Propellers:...........diesel-electric (34,000kW)/2	Hot tubs (on deck):....................................7
Passenger decks:..................................13	Self-service launderette:..............................Yes
Total crew:......................................1,160	Dedicated cinema/seats:................................No
Passengers (lower beds/alll berths):.............2,974/3,700	Library: ....Yes
Passenger Space Ratio (lower beds/all berths): 37.0/29.7	Onboard currency: ....US$
Crew/Passenger Ratio (lower beds/all berths):..........2.3/2.9	

Floating fun palace for a casual first-time family cruise

OVERVIEW. *Carnival Valor* is one of a series of look-alike ships; the other are *Carnival Conquest, Carnival Freedom, Carnival Glory, Carnival Liberty, Carnival Splendor, Carnival Sunshine, Carnival Triumph, Carnival Valor, and Carnival Victory*. It is a stunning ship, built to impress at every turn, but with extremely short bows.

THE SHIPS. The public rooms are given a visual theme. On *Carnival Valor* it's famous personalities like Josephine Baker and Charles Lindbergh. The layout is fairly logical and easy to navigate.

There are three decks full of lounges, 10 bars, and lots of rooms to play in. There is a doublewide indoor promenade, and an atrium lobby that spans nine decks, topped by a glass-dome. Amidships on the open deck is a long water slide. At 200ft (60m) long, it travels from just aft of the ship's mast. Tiered sunbathing decks are positioned between two small swimming pools and several hot tubs.

The terraced pool deck is cluttered, particularly when the ship is full and at sea, and there are no cushioned pads for the deck chairs. Getting away from people and noise is extremely difficult. The photo gallery becomes extremely congested when photographs are on display.

A square-shaped bar sits on the lowest deck of the atrium, and faces forward towards panoramic glass-walled elevators. A sports bar has tables displaying sports memorabilia.

Berlitz's Ratings

	Possible	Achieved
Ship	500	360
Accommodation	200	144
Food	400	218
Service	400	259
Entertainment	100	76
Cruise	400	253

OVERALL SCORE
1310 points out of 2000

From a safety viewpoint, passengers can embark directly into the lifeboats from their secured position without having to wait for them to be lowered, thus saving time in the event of a real emergency.

Carnival Valor is a floating playground for the young and young-at-heart, and anyone who enjoys constant stimulation and participation events, together with the three 'Gs' – glitz, glamour, and gambling. This really is cruising Splash Vegas style – and fun, all-American experience. Because it's a large resort ship, there will be lines for things like shore excursions, security control when re-boarding, and disembarkation, as well as sign-up sheets for fitness equipment.

Forget fashion – the sine qua non – of a Carnival cruise is all about having fun. While the cuisine is just so-so, the real fun begins at sundown when Carnival really excels in sound, lights, razzle-dazzle shows, and late-night high volume sounds.

FAMILIES. Children have good facilities, including their own two-level Children's Club, including an outdoor pool, and are well cared for with Camp Carnival, the cruise line's extensive children's program.

ACCOMMODATION. There are numerous price categories, depending on grade, location and size. Over half of all cabins are outside and, at 225 sq ft/21 sq m, are among the largest in the standard market. They are spread over four decks and have private balconies extending from the ship's side; these have glass rather than steel balustrades for unobstructed ocean views, as well as bright fluorescent lighting. The standard cabins are of good size and have all the basics, although the furniture is angular, with no rounded edges. Three decks of cabins – eight per deck, each with private balcony – overlook the stern.

There are eight penthouse suites, each with a large private balcony. Although quite lavish in their appointments, at only 483 sq ft (44.8 sq m), they are really quite small when compared to the best suites even in many smaller ships. There are also 40 other suites that are nothing special, although each has a decent-size bathroom and a good amount of lounge space.

In cabins with balconies, the partition between each balcony is open at top and bottom, so you may well hear noise from neighbors. It is disappointing to see three categories of cabins (both outside and interior) with upper and lower bunk beds – lower beds are far more preferable, but this is how the ships absorb hundreds of extra passengers over and above the lower bed capacity.

The cabins have soft color schemes and more soft furnishings in more attractive fabrics than other ships in the fleet. Interactive Fun Vision technology lets you choose movies on demand, for a fee. The bathrooms, which have good-size showers, have good storage space for toiletries. All grades get a gift basket of toiletry samples.

Book one of the suites and you get Skipper's Club priority check-in at any US homeland port.

DINING. The ship has two main dining rooms, one forward (Lincoln) with windows on two sides and 706 seats, and the other (Washington) aft with windows on three sides and 1,090 seats. Each dining room spans two decks, and incorporates a dozen domes and chandeliers. The aft dining room has a two-deck-high wall of glass overlooking the stern. Tables are for four, six, and eight. There are even a few tables for two that the line tries to keep for honeymooners.

Choose either fixed-time dining (6pm or 8:15pm), or flexible dining (any time between 5:45pm and 9:30pm). This gives you little time to 'dine' – although perhaps it gives you an idea about what to expect from your dining experience. Although the menu choice looks good, the actual cuisine delivered is quite unmemorable. Note that the two main dining rooms are not open for lunch on port days.

The dining room entrances have comfortable drinking areas for pre-dinner cocktails. There are also many options for casual dining, particularly during the day.

Other dining options. An informal international self-serve buffet-style eatery has seating on two levels. Included in this eatery are a New York-style deli (open 11am–11pm), a Chinese restaurant with wok preparation, and a 24-hour pizzeria which typically serves an average of more than 800 pizzas every day.

At night, the Seaview Bistro provides a casual alternative to the main dining rooms, serving pasta, steaks, salads, and desserts. There is also a barbecue for fast grilled foods such as chicken, hamburgers and hot dogs, and a salad bar. Additionally, there is a self-serve ice cream and frozen yoghurt station, at no extra charge. If you want to eat 24 hours a day, you can.

The Steakhouse is one reservations-only, extra-cost dining spot. It features prime USDA steaks and grilled seafood. The restaurant has fine table settings, china, and silverware, as well as leather-bound menus, and a design theme set around Scarlett O'Hara, the heroine of Margaret Mitchell's classic novel *Gone With the Wind*. It's worth the extra cost if you like really good steaks.

ENTERTAINMENT. The three-level showlounges are stunning, with a revolving stage, hydraulic orchestra pit, superb sound, and seating on three levels, the upper levels being tiered through two decks. A proscenium over the stage acts as a scenery loft.

SPA/FITNESS. SpaCarnival spans two decks, with a total area of 13,700 sq ft/1,272 sq m, and is located directly above the navigation bridge in the forward part of the ship; it is accessed from the forward stairway. Facilities on the lower level include a solarium, eight treatment rooms, lecture rooms, sauna and steam rooms for men and women, and a beauty parlor; the upper level consists of a large gymnasium with floor-to-ceiling windows on three sides, including forward-facing ocean views, and an aerobics room with instructor-led classes, some at extra cost.

Carnival Victory
★★★ +

Size:.................................Large Resort Ship	Crew/Passenger Ratio (lower beds/all berths):.......... 2.3/3.0
Tonnage:.. 101,509	Cabins (total):...................................... 1,379
Lifestyle: ....Standard	Size range (sq ft/m): 179.7–482.2/16.7–44.8
Cruise line:......................... Carnival Cruise Lines	Cabins (outside view):................................853
Former names: ....none	Cabins (interior/no view):.............................526
IMO number: 9172648	Cabins (for one person):................................0
Builder: .... Fincantieri (Italy)	Cabins (with private balcony):.........................508
Original cost:...............................$410 million	Cabins (wheelchair accessible): 25
Entered service:............................. Aug 2000	Wheelchair accessibility:............................Good
Registry:....................................... Panama	Cabin voltage: .... 110 volts
Length (ft/m):............................. 893.0/272.2	Elevators:..18
Beam (ft/m):.............................. 116.0/35.3	Casino (gaming tables):............................. Yes
Draft (ft/m): 27.0/8.2	Slot machines:..................................... Yes
Propulsion/Propellers: ...diesel-electric (34,000kW)/2 azimuthing	Swimming pools:.................3 (1 w/sliding glass dome)
pods	Hot tubs (on deck):...................................7
Passenger decks:.................................13	Self-service launderette:............................ Yes
Total crew:.................................... 1,100	Dedicated cinema/seats:.............................No
Passengers (lower beds/alll berths):............. 2,758/3,473	Library: .... Yes
Passenger Space Ratio (lower beds/all berths): 36.8/29.2	Onboard currency: ....US$

Floating fun for a family-friendly first cruise

OVERVIEW. *Carnival Victory* belongs to Carnival Cruise Lines' Destiny class, along with *Carnival Conquest, Carnival Freedom, Carnival Glory,* Carnival Liberty, *Carnival Sunshine, Carnival Valor,* and *Carnival Victory.* The ship is quite stunning to look at, and built to impress at every turn, although it has extremely short bows (the front). The ship is too large to transit the Panama Canal at present.

Berlitz's Ratings

	Possible	Achieved
Ship	500	360
Accommodation	200	144
Food	400	218
Service	400	249
Entertainment	100	76
Cruise	400	255
OVERALL SCORE		
1302 points out of 2000		

THE SHIP. The decor is quite tasteful, and public rooms are given a visual theme. On *Carnival Victory* it's oceans of the world, with seahorses, corals, and shells prominent throughout the design. The layout is logical and fairly easy to navigate.

Amidships on the open deck is a long water slide, about 200ft (60m) long, it travels from just aft of the ship's mast. Tiered sunbathing decks are positioned between two small swimming pools and several hot tubs.

The terraced pool deck is cluttered, and there are no cushioned pads for the deck chairs. Although the outdoor deck space has been improved, there is still much crowding when the ship is full and at sea. Getting away from people and noise is extremely difficult. The photo gallery becomes extremely congested when photographs are on display.

There are three decks full of lounges, 10 bars, and lots of rooms to play in. Like their smaller (though still large) predecessors, this ship has a doublewide indoor promenade, nine decks high, with statues of Neptune at both ends, and a glass-domed rotunda atrium lobby. On the lowest deck of the atrium lobby is a square-

shaped bar, which faces forward to glass-walled panorama elevators and sits under the 10-deck-high dome. A sports bar has tables displaying sports memorabilia.

From a safety viewpoint, passengers can embark directly into the lifeboats from their secured position without having to wait for them to be lowered, thus saving time in the event of a real emergency.

Carnival Victory is a floating playground for the young and young-at-heart, and anyone who enjoys constant stimulation and lots of participation events, together with the three 'Gs' – glitz, glamour, and gambling. This really is cruising Splash Vegas style – and fun, all-American experience. Because it's a large resort ship, there will be lines for things like shore excursions, security control when re-boarding, and disembarkation, as well as sign-up sheets for fitness equipment.

Forget fashion – the sine qua non – of a Carnival cruise is all about having fun. While the cuisine is just so-so, the real fun begins at sundown when Carnival really excels in sound, lights, razzle-dazzle shows, and late-night high volume sounds.

FAMILIES. Children have good facilities, including their own two-level Children's Club, including an outdoor pool, and are well cared for with Camp Carnival, the cruise line's extensive children's program.

ACCOMMODATION. There are a number of different price categories. The price you pay depends on the grade, location and size you choose. Over half of all cabins have outside views and, at 225 sq ft/21 sq m, are quite large. They are spread over four decks and have private balconies extending from the ship's side; these have glass rather than steel balustrades for unobstructed ocean views, as well as bright fluorescent lighting. The standard cabins are of good size and have all the basics, although the furniture is angular, with no rounded edges. Three decks of cabins – eight per deck, each with private balcony – overlook the stern.

There are eight penthouse suites, each with a large private balcony. Although quite lavish in their appointments, at only 483 sq ft (44.8 sq m), they are really quite small when compared to the best suites even in many smaller ships. There are also 40 other suites that are nothing special, although each has a decent-size bathroom and a good amount of lounge space.

In cabins with balconies, the partition between each balcony, is open at the top and bottom, so you may well hear noise from neighbors or smell their cigarettes. It is disappointing to see three categories of cabins (both outside and interior) with upper and lower bunk beds – lower beds are far more preferable, but this is how the ships absorb hundreds of extra passengers over and above the lower bed capacity.

The cabins have soft color schemes and more soft furnishings in more attractive fabrics than other ships in the fleet. Interactive Fun Vision technology lets you choose movies on demand, for a fee. The bathrooms, which have good-size showers, have good storage space for toiletries. All grades get a gift basket of toiletry samples.

Book one of the suites (Category 11 or 12 in the Carnival Cruise Lines brochure), and you get Skipper's Club priority check-in at any US homeland port.

DINING. The ship has two main dining rooms, the Atlantic – forward – with windows on two sides and 706 seats, and the Pacific – aft – with windows on three sides and 1,090 seats. Each dining room spans two decks, and incorporates a dozen domes and chandeliers. The aft dining room has a two-deck-high wall of glass overlooking the stern. Tables are for four, six, and eight. There are even a few tables for two. The dining room entrances have comfortable drinking areas for pre-dinner cocktails.

Choose either fixed-time dining (6pm or 8:15pm) or flexible dining (any time between 5:45 and 9:30pm). This gives you very little time to 'dine' – although it should give you some idea of what to expect from your dining experience. Although the menu choice looks good, the actual cuisine delivered is adequate, but quite unmemorable. Note that the two main dining rooms are not open for lunch on port days.

Other dining options. An informal 'international' self-serve buffet-style eatery (the rather fancily-named Mediterranean Lido Restaurant) has seating on two levels. Included in this eatery are a New York-style deli (open 11am–11pm), a Chinese restaurant (Yangtze Wok) with wok stir-fry preparation, an East Close deli, a Mississippi BBQ, and a 24-hour pizzeria (Pizzeria Arno) which typically serves an average of more than 800 pizzas every day.

At night, the venue morphs into Seaview Bistro to provide a casual alternative to the main dining rooms, serving pasta, steaks, salads, and desserts. There is also a barbecue for fast-grilled foods such as chicken, hamburgers and hot dogs, and a salad bar. In addition, there is a self-serve ice cream and frozen yoghurt station, at no extra charge. If you want to eat 24 hours a day, you can (sort of).

The one reservations-only, extra-cost dining spot is The Steakhouse. It features prime USDA steaks and grilled seafood items (it's worth paying the extra cost). It has fine table settings, china, and silverware, as well as leather-bound menus, and a design theme set around Scarlett O'Hara, the heroine of Margaret Mitchell's classic novel *Gone With the Wind*.

ENTERTAINMENT. The three-level Caribbean Main Lounge, the ship's showlounge, is quite a stunning room, with a revolving stage, hydraulic orchestra pit, superb sound, and seating on three levels, the upper levels being tiered through two decks. A proscenium over the stage acts as a scenery loft.

SPA/FITNESS. SpaCarnival spans two decks, with a total area of 13,700 sq ft/1,272 sq m, and is located directly above the navigation bridge in the forward part of the ship; it is accessed from the forward stairway. Facilities on the lower level include a solarium, eight treatment rooms, lecture rooms, sauna and steam rooms for men and women, and a beauty parlor; the upper level consists of a large gymnasium with floor-to-ceiling windows on three sides, including forward-facing ocean views, and an aerobics room with instructor-led classes, some at extra cost.

Celebrity Century
★★★★

Size:.	.Large Resort Ship	Cabins (total):.	.907
Tonnage:	71,545	Size range (sq ft/m):	.168.9–1,514.5/15.7–140.7
Lifestyle:	.Premium	Cabins (outside view):	.590
Cruise line:.	Celebrity Cruises	Cabins (interior/no view):.	.317
Former names:	.Century	Cabins (for one person):.	.0
IMO number:	.9072446	Cabins (with private balcony):	.386
Builder:	Meyer Werft (Germany)	Cabins (wheelchair accessible):	.8
Original cost:	.$320 million	Wheelchair accessibility:	.Good
Entered service:.	Dec 1995	Cabin voltage:	.110 and 220 volts
Registry:.	Malta	Elevators:	.9
Length (ft/m):.	807.1/246.0	Casino (gaming tables):.	Yes
Beam (ft/m):.	105.6/32.2	Slot machines:.	Yes
Draft (ft/m):	24.6/7.5	Swimming pools:.	.2
Propulsion/Propellers:	diesel (29,250kW)/2	Hot tubs (on deck):.	.4
Passenger decks:.	10	Self-service launderette:	.No
Total crew:.	.858	Dedicated cinema/seats:	Yes/190
Passengers (lower beds/alll berths):	1,814/2,150	Library:	Yes
Passenger Space Ratio (lower beds/all berths):	39.4/33.2	Onboard currency:	.US$
Crew/Passenger Ratio (lower beds/all berths):	2.0/2.5		

A stylish modern ship with understated decor and good food

OVERVIEW. *Celebrity Century* suits well-traveled baby-boomer couples, solo travelers, and families with children seeking a ship with reasonable quality, style, and character. It is a decent, but dated vessel for a big-ship cruise vacation. Sloppy maintenance can be found in some areas, although general cleanliness is excellent. Gratifyingly, there are few annoying announcements.

THE SHIP. The exterior profile is well balanced despite a squared-off stern. It carries the distinctive brand 'X' funnel (X being the Greek letter C – for Chandris, the former owning company, before it was purchased by Royal Caribbean Cruises Ltd.). With a high passenger space ratio, there is no sense of crowding anywhere, the passenger flow throughout the ship is efficient, and the high crew number provides a sound basis for attentive passenger service.

There is a good amount of open deck space, a three-quarter, two-level teak wood promenade deck, and a walking/jogging track atop the ship. The interior decor is elegant, but contemporary and understated. A small, dedicated cinema doubles as a conference and meeting center with the latest audio-visual technology. The atrium lobby is calm and refreshing, due to its high ceiling, and not at all glitzy.

Michael's Club, a former cigar smoking lounge/bar is now a piano/jazz lounge, and features fine whiskies, cognacs, bourbons and scotches. This triangular room, a favorite watering hole, has large and really comfortable chairs, and the feel of a real gentlemen's club. An-

Berlitz's Ratings

	Possible	Achieved
Ship	500	363
Accommodation	200	157
Food	400	278
Service	400	294
Entertainment	100	72
Cruise	400	285

OVERALL SCORE
1449 points out of 2000

yone who like gambling will find a large casino tightly packed with slot machines and gaming tables.

Outstanding are the 500 pieces of art that adorn the ship – a $3.8 million art collection and some fascinating contemporary sculptures (look for the colored violins on Deck 7). The collection includes a comprehensive survey of the most important artists and trends since the 1960s, and embraces Abstract Expressionism, Pop, Conceptualism, Minimalism, and Neo-Expressionism.

Gratuities are charged to your account daily, and a 15 percent gratuity is added to all bar and wine accounts.

Niggles include the fact that the interactive TV system is frustrating to use, and the larger suites have three remotes for TV/audio equipment (one would be better).

In 2006, *Celebrity Century* had a $55 million makeover that added 314 balconies, 14 new 'Sky Suites' and 10 other cabins. The self-serve buffet area was expanded; an Acupuncture at Sea facility was added, as was Murano – a specialty extra-charge restaurant – more shop space, an art gallery for art auctions, more Internet-connect computers plus ship-wide Wi-Fi (for a fee), and a neat ice-walled bar that is part of the Martini Bar. In short, the refit made the ship more like the larger Millennium-class ships.

In 2014, another refit is planned to make the ship more in line with the Solstice-class ships, with additional specialty restaurants like QSine, Tuscan Grille and other features, plus Aqua-class cabins.

FAMILIES. Children and teens are well catered to. X-Treme, which exists within the Kid's Fun Factory area, is a neat hangout for teens. Children's counselors are aboard for every cruise.

ACCOMMODATION. There are several different grades. The price depends on the grade, size, and location. The wide variety of cabin types includes 18 family cabins, each with two lower beds, two foldaway beds, and one upper berth. In the 2006 refit, new minimalist washbasins were installed in cabin bathrooms; however, they are not user-friendly as water splashes everywhere.

All cabins have wood cabinetry and accenting, personal safe, mini-bar/refrigerator, and interactive flat-screen TVs and entertainment systems that enable you to shop, book shore excursions, or play casino games interactively in English, German, French, Italian, or Spanish. Bathrooms have hairdryers, 100 percent cotton towels, and large shower enclosures. However, the standard 24-hour cabin menu is disappointing and limited.

The cabins are nicely equipped and decorated, with warm wood-finish furniture, and none of the boxy feel of cabins in many ships, due to the angled placement of vanity and audio-video consoles. In addition, all suites on Deck 10 (and the Sky Deck suites on Deck 12) have butler service and in-cabin dining facilities. Suites with private balconies have floor-to-ceiling windows and sliding doors; a few have outward opening doors.

For the largest space, choose one of two nicely decorated Presidential Suites, each 1,173 sq ft (109 sq m). These are amidships in a desirable position; each can be combined with an adjacent mini-suite via an interconnecting door to provide a living space of 1,515 sq ft (140.7 sq m). Each suite has a marble-floored foyer, a living room with mahogany wood floor, and hand-woven rug. A separate dining area has a six-seat dining table, and there's a butler's pantry with wet bar, a wine bar, refrigerator, and microwave.

A large private balcony has a dining table for two, chaise longues with cushioned pads, hot tub, and dimmer-controlled lighting; master bedroom with king-size bed, dressed with fine fabrics and draperies; and walk-in closet with abundant storage space. The all-marble bathroom has a jet-spray shower and whirlpool bath.

All accommodation grades feature European duvets, fresh flowers, DVD player, and butler service (for suite-grade accommodation only). Electrically operated blinds and other goodies are also standard in some suites.

DINING. A grand staircase connects the upper and lower levels of the Grand Dining Room. Huge windows overlook the stern. Each of the two levels has a separate finishing galley. There are two seatings for dinner (open-seating for breakfast and lunch), at tables for two, four, six, eight, or 10. The design of the two galleys is good, so food that's meant to be hot arrives hot at the table.

All meals, including full dinners, can be served, course-by-course, in all suites and cabins, no matter what grade you choose. Freshly baked boxed pizzas, for anyone who can't live without them, can be delivered to your cabin. However, the food delivered for room-service is below the standard of food featured in the dining room.

Other dining options. Murano, a reservations-only specialty restaurant off the main lobby, is a fine dining experience that takes about three hours, in a small, intimate setting – ideal for celebrating a birthday or anniversary, with refined service and an extensive wine list.

For casual meals, Islands is a large indoor/outdoor, tray-less self-serve buffet venue; there are four self-service lines, plus two-grill serving stations located adjacent to the swimming pools outdoors.

Cova Café is a coffeehouse serving Cova Italian coffee (from Milan), early morning mini-croissants, pastries, and cakes, and Cova chocolates. The café is situated to one side of the main lobby, and makes an excellent place to meet.

ENTERTAINMENT. The Celebrity Theater is the ship's two-level, 1,000-seat showlounge/theatre, with balcony alcoves on two sides. It has a large stage and a split orchestra pit (hydraulic). However, the continuous bar service during shows can be irritating. The ship has a number of bands, although there is very little music for social dancing, other than disco and Latin music.

SPA/FITNESS. The AquaSpa has 9,040 sq ft (840 sq m) of space dedicated to well-being and body treatments, all set in a calming environment. It includes a large fitness/exercise area, complete with all the latest high-tech muscle machines, thalassotherapy pool, and 10 treatment rooms. The spa includes an 'Acupuncture at Sea' clinic, and a Rasul – a mud and gentle steam bathing room (an excellent facility for couples).

The spa is operated by Steiner, a specialist concession whose staff provides a range of treatments. Some fitness classes are free, while others, such as yoga and kick-boxing, cost extra.

Celebrity Constellation
★★★★

Size:	Large Resort Ship	Crew/Passenger Ratio (lower beds/all berths):	1.9/2.4
Tonnage:	90,228	Cabins (total):	975
Lifestyle:	Premium	Size range (sq ft/m):	165.1–2,530.0/15.34–235.0
Cruise line:	Celebrity Cruises	Cabins (outside view):	780
Former names:	*Constellation*	Cabins (interior/no view):	195
IMO number:	9192339	Cabins (for one person):	0
Builder:	Chantiers de l'Atlantique (France)	Cabins (with private balcony):	590
Original cost:	$350 million	Cabins (wheelchair accessible):	26 (17 with private balcony)
Entered service:	May 2002	Wheelchair accessibility:	Best
Registry:	Malta	Cabin voltage:	110 and 220 volts
Length (ft/m):	964.5/294.0	Elevators:	12
Beam (ft/m):	105.6/32.2	Casino (gaming tables):	Yes
Draft (ft/m):	26.2/8.0	Slot machines:	Yes
Propulsion/Propellers:	gas turbine/2 azimuthing pods (19.5MW each)	Swimming pools:	3 (1 w/sliding glass dome)
Passenger decks:	11	Hot tubs (on deck):	4
Total crew:	999	Self-service launderette:	No
Passengers (lower beds/alll berths):	1,950/2,450	Dedicated cinema/seats:	Yes/368
Passenger Space Ratio (lower beds/all berths):	46.2/36.8	Library:	Yes
		Onboard currency:	US$

Understated decor, providing a stylish setting for families

OVERVIEW. A cruise aboard such a large ship provides a wide range of choices and possibilities. If you travel in one of the suites, the benefits include the highest level of personal service, while cruising in non-suite accommodation is almost like in any large ship. One thing really is certain: cruising in a relatively hassle-free environment such as this is hard to beat no matter how much or how little you pay.

THE SHIP. *Celebrity Constellation* is a sister ship to *Celebrity Infinity*, *Celebrity Millennium*, and *Celebrity Summit*, the line's Millennium-class ships. They are among the very best of the ships in the Premium segment of the marketplace, providing a taste of luxury for those who book in the largest suites. Jon Bannenberg, the mega-yacht designer, dreamed up the exterior featuring a royal blue and white hull – although it looks quite ungainly. It has a pod propulsion system coupled with a quiet, smokeless, energy-efficient gas turbine powerplant, for vibration-free cruising.

Facilities outdoors include two outdoor pools, one indoor/outdoor pool, and four hot tubs. Unfortunately, there is no walk-around wooden promenade deck outdoors. There are cushioned pads for poolside deck lounge chairs only, but not for chairs on other outside decks. Passenger participation activities are amateurish and should be upgraded.

Standing in line for embarkation, disembarkation, shore tenders, and for self-serve buffet meals is an inevitable aspect of cruising aboard all large ships (however,

Berlitz's Ratings		
	Possible	Achieved
Ship	500	389
Accommodation	200	161
Food	400	285
Service	400	298
Entertainment	100	74
Cruise	400	287
OVERALL SCORE		
1494 points out of 2000		

more flexible embarkation hours do help to spread the flow), but the worst lines occur when large numbers of passengers return from shore excursions and go through a security check.

Inside, the ship has an understated elegance, with the same high-class decor and materials – including lots of wood, glass and marble – and public rooms that have made other ships in the fleet so popular. The atrium, with separately enclosed room for shore excursions, is four decks high and houses the reception desk, tour operator's desk, and bank. Four glass-walled elevators travel through the ship's exterior (port) side, connecting the atrium with another seven decks, thus traveling through 10 passenger decks, including the tender stations – a nice ride.

New AquaClass veranda staterooms and Blu, a Mediterranean-themed specialty restaurant exclusively for AquaClass passengers, were added in a 'Solsticizing' of the ship in 2013. Also added were a Celebrity iLounge (for the latest Apple products, computer classes, and Internet connection), a Martini Bar with a frosted countertop, a delightful Cellar-Masters wine bar (good for wine-tasting), QSine (an extra-cost fine dining venue with iPad menus), and a Bistro on Five (a crêperie).

The artwork throughout the ship (particularly the sculptures) is eclectic, provocative, thoughtful, and intelligent, and at almost every turn another piece appears to break the monotony associated with large spaces. For example, on one side of Sky Deck, a huge bronze sculpture of a gorilla is holding a fish under its arm. Created by Angus Fairhurst, it is titled A Couple of Differences Between Thinking and Feeling.

Facilities include a combination Cinema/Conference Center, a shopping arcade with 14,447 sq ft (1,300 sq m) of retail store space (with trendy brand name labels such as Fendi, Fossil, Hugo Boss, and Versace), a lavish four-deck-high showlounge with high-tech sound and lighting equipment, a two-level library (one level for English-language books; a second for books in other languages and reference material), card room, music listening room, and an observation lounge/discotheque with outstanding views.

Michael's Club (formerly a cigar smoker's haven) now features over 50 craft beers plus fine whiskies, cognacs, bourbons and scotches) and is a rather nice, comfortable lounge/piano bar. An Internet café has almost 20 computer workstation with custom-made wood-surround monitors and extra-cost Internet connectivity.

Gaming sports include the ship's overly large Fortunes Casino, with blackjack, roulette, and slot machines, and lots of bright lights and action. Families with children will appreciate the Fun Factory (for children) and The Tower (for teenagers). Children's counselors and youth activities staff provide a wide range of supervised activities.

A 15 percent gratuity is added to all bar and wine accounts.

ACCOMMODATION. There are numerous grades from which to choose, depending on your preference for the size and location of your living space. Almost half of the ship's cabins feature a 'private' balcony; approximately 80 percent are outside-view suites and cabins, and 20 percent are interior cabins. The cabins are extremely comfortable throughout this ship, regardless of which cabin grade you choose. Suites, naturally, have more space, butler service (whether you want it or not), more and better amenities and more personal service than if you choose any of the standard cabin grades. There are several categories of suites, but those at the stern of the ship are in a prime location and have huge balconies that are really private and not overlooked from above.

All suites and cabins have wood cabinetry and accenting, interactive television and entertainment systems (you can go shopping, book shore excursions, play casino games interactively, and even watch soft porn movies). The bathrooms have hairdryers and 100 percent cotton towels.

Penthouse Suites (2). These, on Penthouse Deck, are the ship's largest cabins. Each occupies one half of the beam (width) of the ship, overlooking the stern. Each measures a huge 2,530 sq ft (235 sq m), consisting of 1,431.6 sq ft (133 sq m) of living space, plus a huge wraparound terrace measuring 1,098 sq ft (102 sq m) with 180-degree views. This terrace includes a wet bar, hot tub, and whirlpool tub – but much of it can be overlooked by passengers on other decks above. Features include a marble foyer, a separate living room (complete with ebony baby grand piano and a formal dining room).

The master bedroom has a large walk-in closet, dressing room with vanity desk, exercise equipment, marble-clad master bathroom with twin washbasins, deep whirlpool tub, separate shower, toilet and bidet areas, flat-screen televisions (one in the bedroom and one in the lounge), and electronically controlled drapes. Butler service is standard, and a butler's pantry, with separate entry door, has a full-size refrigerator, wine cabinet, microwave oven, and food preparation and storage areas. For even more space, an interconnecting door can be opened into the adjacent suite (ideal for multi-generation families).

Royal Suites (8). These measure 733 sq ft (68 sq m) and are located towards the aft of the ship (four each on the port and starboard sides). Each has a separate living room with dining and lounge areas (with refrigerator, mini-bar, and Bang & Olufsen CD sound system), and a separate bedroom. There are two entertainment centers with DVD players, two flat-screen televisions (one in the living area, one in the bedroom), and a large walk-in closet with vanity desk. The marble-clad bathroom has a whirlpool bathtub with integral shower, and there are also a separate shower enclosure, two washbasins, and toilet. The teakwood decked balcony is large enough for on-deck massage and also has a hot tub.

Celebrity Suites (8). Each measures 467 sq ft (44 sq m) and has floor-to-ceiling windows, a separate living room with dining and lounge areas, two entertainment centers with flat-screen televisions (one in the living room, one in the bedroom), and a walk-in closet with vanity desk. The marble-clad bathroom has a whirlpool tub with integral shower (a window with movable blinds lets you look out of the bathroom through the lounge to the large ocean-view windows). Interconnecting doors allow two suites to be used as a family unit; as there is no balcony, these suites are ideal for families with small children. These suites overhang the starboard side of the ship (they are located opposite a group of glass-walled lifts) and provide stunning ocean views from the glass-walled sitting/dining area, which extends out from the ship's side. A personal computer allows direct Internet connectivity. Butler service is standard.

Sky Suites (30). Each measures 308 sq ft (28.6 sq m), including the private balcony (some balconies are larger than others, depending on the location). Although these are designated as suites, they are really just larger cabins that feature a marble-clad bathroom with bathtub/shower combination. The suites also have a DVD player in addition to a TV set, and have a larger lounge area (than standard cabins) and sleeping area. Butler service is standard.

Butler Service. Butler service in all suites includes full breakfast, in-suite lunch and dinner service (as required), afternoon tea service, evening hors d'oeuvres, complimentary espresso and cappuccino, daily news delivery, shoeshine service, and other personal touches.

Suite occupants in Penthouse, Royal, Celebrity, and Sky suites also get welcome Champagne; a full personal computer in each suite, including a printer and

Internet access (on request in the Sky Suites); choice of films from a video library; personalized stationery; tote bag; priority dining room seating preferences; private portrait sitting, bathrobe; and in-suite massage service.

Concierge Class. In 2003, Celebrity Cruises added a third service 'class' to the accommodation grades. Positioned between the top grade suite grades and standard cabin grades, Concierge Class accommodation features include priority embarkation, disembarkation, tender tickets, specialty dining, and spa reservations. Occupants also get a double bed overlay (no more 'falling between the cracks' for couples); choice of four pillows (goose down pillow, isotonic pillow, body pillow, conformance pillow); throw pillows on sofa; fruit basket; binoculars; golf umbrella; leather telephone notepad; larger beach towels; hand-held hairdryer. The balcony has better furniture than standard balcony grades. In the bathrooms: plush Frette bathrobes, large towels, and a flower in a silver vase. It all adds up to fine value for money for anyone who appreciates the little extras in life.

Aqua Class. 'Aqua Class' cabins (some 70 were converted from 'Concierge Class cabins and 37 new ones were added in 2013), with spa-healthy dining in the exclusive Blu restaurant, and complimentary access to the Persian Garden (thermal suite) and Relaxation Room in the spa, plus daily delivery of bottled water and herbal teas (infusions), and a host of spa-related personal amenities.

Standard Outside-View/Interior Cabins. All other outside-view and interior cabins have a lounge area with sofa or convertible sofa bed, sleeping area with twin beds that can convert to a double bed, a good amount of closet and drawer space, personal safe, mini-bar/refrigerator (extra cost), interactive television, and private bathroom. The cabins are nicely decorated with warm wood-finish furniture, and there is none of the boxy feel of cabins in so many ships, due to the angled placement of vanity and audio-video consoles. Even the smallest cabin has a good-size bathroom and shower enclosure.

Wheelchair-Accessible Suites/Cabins. Wheelchair accessibility is provided in six Sky Suites, three premium outside-view, eight deluxe ocean-view, four standard ocean-view, and five interior cabins measuring 347–362 sq ft (32.2–33.6 sq m). They are located close to elevators for good accessibility – all have wheelchair-accessible doorways and showers. Some cabins have extra berths for up to four occupants.

CUISINE. The 1,198-seat San Marco Restaurant is the ship's formal dining room. It is two decks high, has a grand staircase connecting the two levels (on the upper level of which is a musicians' gallery), and a huge glass wall overlooking the sea at the stern of the ship (electrically operated blinds provide several different backdrops). There are two seatings for dinner (with open seating for breakfast and lunch), at tables for two, four, six, eight, or 10. The dining room, like all large dining halls, can be extremely noisy.

The menu variety is good, the food is tasty, and it is very attractively presented and served in a well-orchestrated operation with European traditions and training. Full service in-cabin dining is also available for all meals, including dinner.

Other dining options. Ocean Liners Restaurant is the ship's alternative dining salon; it is adjacent to the main lobby. The decor includes some lacquered paneling from the famed 1920s French ocean liner *Ile de France*. Fine tableside preparation and classic French cuisine are the features here. This is haute cuisine at the height of professionalism, for this is, indeed, a room for a full savoring, and not merely for dinner, featuring the French culinary arts of découpage and flambé. However, with just 115 seats, not all passengers are able to experience it even once during a one-week cruise (reservations are necessary, and a cover charge applies). There's a wine cellar with more than 200 labels from around the world.

Tuscan Grille is an extra-cost, reservations-required venue that features Kobe beef and premium-quality steaks.

QSine, which features its menus and wine list on iPads, is another extra-cost, fine dining venue (added in 2012). Reservations are required (the food is funky, but tasty – and, fortunately, comes in small bite-sized portions).

The Seaside Café & Grill is a casual self-serve buffet area, with six principal serving lines, and around 750 seats, grill and pizza bar. Each evening, casual meals take place here, with tablecloths and a modicum of service. Reservations are needed, although there's no additional charge.

Café al Bacio and Gelateria. Located on the third level of the atrium lobby, this is the place to see and be seen, for coffees (espresso, cappuccino, latte), pastries, cakes, and gelato, in a trendy setting.

ENTERTAINMENT. The 900-seat Celebrity Theatre is the venue for the ship's production shows and major cabaret acts. Spanning three decks, it is located in the forward part of the ship, with seating on the main level and two balcony levels.

SPA/FITNESS. A large AquaSpa measures 24,219 sq ft (2,250 sq m). It has a large thalassotherapy pool under a solarium dome, complete with health bar for light breakfast and lunch items and fresh squeezed fruit and vegetable juices. There are 16 treatment rooms, plus eight private massage/body treatment rooms and one room designed for wheelchair passengers, an aerobics room, gymnasium with over 40 exercise machines, large male and female saunas – with a large ocean-view porthole window, a unisex thermal suite containing several steam and shower mist rooms, and a beauty salon.

Sports facilities include a full-size basketball court, compact football, paddle tennis and volleyball, golf simulator, shuffleboard (on two different decks) and a jogging track.

Celebrity Eclipse
★★★★ +

Size:.............................Large Resort Ship		Cabins (total):.......................... 1,426
Tonnage: 121,878		Size range (sq ft/m): 182.9–668.4/17.0–155.0
Lifestyle: ....Premium		Cabins (outside view):.................... 1,286
Cruise line:............................ Celebrity Cruises		Cabins (interior/no view):..................140
Former names: ....none		Cabins (for one person):......................0
IMO number: 9404314		Cabins (with private balcony): 1,216
Builder: .... Meyer Werft (Germany)		Cabins (wheelchair accessible): 30
Original cost: .... $641 million		Wheelchair accessibility:.................. Best
Entered service:......................... Jun 2010		Cabin voltage: ....110 and 220 volts
Registry:.............................. Malta		Elevators:................................12
Length (ft/m):.....................1,033.4/315.0		Casino (gaming tables):.................. Yes
Beam (ft/m):..................... 120.7/36.8		Slot machines:.......................... Yes
Draft (ft/m):......................... 27.2/8.3		Swimming pools:..........................3
Propulsion/Propellers: ......diesel (67.2MW)/2 azimuthing pods		Hot tubs (on deck):........................6
Passenger decks:..........................14		Self-service launderette:....................No
Total crew:........................... 1,210		Dedicated cinema/seats:.....................No
Passengers (lower beds/alll berths):............. 2,852/3,145		Library:............................... Yes
Passenger Space Ratio (lower beds/all berths): 42.7/38.7		Onboard currency: ....US$
Crew/Passenger Ratio (lower beds/all berths):......... 2.3/2.5		

A large, stylish, premium ship for family-friendly cruising

OVERVIEW. This is a sister ship to *Celebrity Equinox* (2009), *Celebrity Reflection* (2012), *Celebrity Silhouette* (2011), and *Celebrity Solstice* (2008).

THE SHIP. *Celebrity Eclipse* has a steeply raked stern – which includes a ducktail platform above the propulsion pods; it is attractive, and balances the ship's contemporary profile.

Behind the two funnels is a real grass outdoor area, the Lawn Club. This is the authentic stuff; it seems to like the salty air. The club is open to all, so you can putt, play croquet or bocce ball, or picnic on the grass. Several pool and water-play areas are positioned on Resort Deck: one in a glass-roofed solarium, a sports pool, a family pool, and a wet zone. The deck space around the two pools isn't large enough for the number of passengers carried.

The interior spaces are well designed; most of the entertainment rooms are positioned forward, while dining venues are located in the aft section of the ship. There's a wine bar with a sommelier; a cocktail lounge that reflects the jazz age of the 1930s and '40s; a bar with the look of an ocean-going yacht; Quasar, a bar with large screens that create a nightly light show synchronized to music; and an observation lounge.

Celebrity's signature Martini Bar, with its frosted bar, has a small alcove called Crush with an ice-filled table where you can participate in caviar and vodka tasting, or host a private party. It's very noisy and congested.

The ship also has a delightful two-deck library, though books on the higher of the 12 shelves are im-

Berlitz's Ratings

	Possible	Achieved
Ship	500	416
Accommodation	200	165
Food	400	297
Service	400	306
Entertainment	100	77
Cruise	400	299

OVERALL SCORE
1560 points out of 2000

possible to reach. The card room – located in the center of the ship, with no ocean view windows to distract players – is open, and attracts noise from adjacent areas, so it's almost useless as a serious card playing room. Fortunes Casino (non-smoking) has 16 gaming tables and 200 slot machines.

An innovative Hot Glass Show, housed in an outdoor studio and created in collaboration with Corning Museum of Glass, includes demonstrations of glass-blowing. Three resident glass-blowing artists also host workshops.

One thing that's cool is an Apple 'iLounge' equipped with 26 Apple MacBook Pro work stations. The elevator call buttons are located in a floor-stand 'pod'; when the elevator arrives, a glass panel turns from blue to pink.

Passenger niggles include lack of usable drawer space in cabins; inadequate children's facilities and staff during school holidays; congestion when exiting the showlounge; and noise in all areas of the lobby when the martini bar is busy. Gratuities are automatically charged to your onboard account.

FAMILIES. Play areas include the Fun Factory (for three- to 12-year-olds, featuring Leapfrog Schoolhouse's educational programs); and 'X Club' – a high-tech teens-only chill-out room with coffee bar and a night-time dance club.

During the summer, the ship is based in the UK, when all beverage prices include a service charge, and include the following British beers: Fuller's London

Pride, Old Speckled Hen, Boddingtons, Guinness, Murphy's Stout, and Newcastle Brown Ale. A 'Champagne High Royal Experience' (afternoon tea with white glove service, Wedgwood porcelain, and Forte loose teas) is available for $25 per person.

ACCOMMODATION. From Penthouse Suites to small interior cabins, the accommodation is practical and comfortable. There are numerous price grades, depending on size and location. In standard Interior and Ocean View cabins, there is little space between the bed and the wall, and usable drawer space is poor. .

About 90 percent of the cabins have an outside view, and many of these have a balcony; due to the ship's pencil-slim width, there are few interior cabins. The suite-grade categories are: Royal Suite, Celebrity Suite, Sky Suite, and Penthouse Suite.

All grades of accommodation include: twin beds convertible to a queen-size bed, sitting area, vanity desk with hairdryer, but there's almost no drawer space. Also standard in all cabins: 32-inch flat-screen TVs (larger screens in suites), Wi-Fi Internet access (for a fee), premium bedding. However, although the closets have good hanging space, other storage space is limited. The bathroom has a shower, toilet, and tiny washbasin. Suites have more space, larger balconies with good-quality sunloungers, and more personal amenities.

Some 130 AquaSpa-class cabins share the relaxation room of the AquaSpa itself, incorporate select spa elements into the cabins, and allow for specialized access to the AquaSpa's Thermal Relaxation Room and Persian Garden (with aromatherapy/steam rooms) on the same deck. Features include: a choice of four pillows (conformance, body, goose, Isotonic); express luggage delivery; shoeshine; Frette bathrobes; dining and seating preferences in other specialty dining venues; and early embarkation and disembarkation. Bathrooms have a decent amount of space, and a large shower enclosure. Occupants also get assigned seating at the exclusive 130-seat Restaurant Blu.

Cabins 1551–1597 on the port side and 1556–1602 on the starboard side on Penthouse Deck (Deck 11) suffer from 'aircraft carrier' syndrome because they are directly under the huge overhanging Resort Deck. They have little exposure to sun or light, so private balcony sunbathing is out of the question. Many thick supporting struts ruin the view from these cabins, which are otherwise pleasantly fitted out.

DINING. Moonlight Sonata is the ship's 1,430-seat two-deck main dining room, and is included in the cruise price. It has ocean views on the port and starboard sides, and to the stern (aft). The design is stunning and contemporary. At the forward end, a two-deck-high wine tower provides an eye-catching focal point.

Other dining options. The following dining spots provide an alternative to the main dining room, good for special occasions or just for something different.

Murano is an extra-cost, reservations-required venue offering high-quality traditional dining with a French flair and exquisite table settings, including large Reidel wine glasses. Food and service are very good.

Blu is a 130-seat specialty restaurant just for the occupants of AquaClass cabins. The room has a pleasing, but rather cold, blue decor.

The Tuscan Grille, an extra-cost venue, serves Kobe beef and premium quality steaks, and has beautifully curved archways – it's like walking into a high-tech winery. There are great views from huge aft-view windows.

Qsine is an extra-cost, 90-seat reservations-required, tablecloth-less 'fun-food' restaurant, with trendy interactive iPad food and wine menus that include cute foodie video snaps. The food consists of multi-flavored, multi-colored, quirky small-bite items that provide you with a selection to tease your taste buds. The food is presented in many unusual ways – even on sticks – sort of 'lolipop' or 'circus' cuisine.

Bistro on Five (Deck 5, that is) is for coffee, cakes, crêpes, pastries, and more. It gets busy at times and the serving counter is small, so it's a congested area.

Café al Bacio & Gelateria is a coffeehouse serving Lavazza Italian coffee. It is on one side of the main lobby, but it's small and lines quickly form at peak times. The seating is mostly in large, very comfortable armchairs.

Oceanview Café and Grill is an large, tray-less, casual self-serve buffet venue. There are a number of food 'islands,' and the signage is good. However, it's impossible to get a warm plate for so-called hot food items.

The AquaSpa Café is for light, healthier options (solarium fare), but the selections are not thrilling.

The Mast Bar Grill and Bar is an outside venue offering fast food.

ENTERTAINMENT. The 1,115-seat Eclipse Theater, the main showlounge, stages three circus-themed production shows featuring in-your-face, formulaic acrobatics. Colorful theme nights are held in the Observation Lounge (bland daytime decor comes alive at night thanks to mood lighting effects). The 200-seat Celebrity Central hosts stand-up comedy, cooking demonstrations, lectures, and films. An Entertainment Court showcases street performers, psychics, and caricaturists, and is in the center of the ship. There's also a big-band-era cocktail lounge with live jazz-styled music, set adjacent to the Murano, the specialty restaurant.

SPA/FITNESS. The AquaSpa is laid out over two decks. A large fitness center includes kinesis (pulleys against gravity) workout equipment, plus all the familiar gym machinery.

An extra-cost, unisex thermal suite features several steam and shower mist rooms and a glacial ice fountain, plus a calming relaxation area with heated tiled beds, and an acupuncture center. Massages include fashionable things such as: Herbal Poultice massage and Bamboo Massage.

Celebrity Equinox
★★★★ +

Size:	.Large Resort Ship	Cabins (total):	1,426
Tonnage:	122,000	Size range (sq ft/m):	182.9–1,668.4/17.0–155.0
Lifestyle:	.Premium	Cabins (outside view):	1,286
Cruise line:	Celebrity Cruises	Cabins (interior/no view):	140
Former names:	none	Cabins (for one person):	0
IMO number:	9372456	Cabins (with private balcony):	1,216
Builder:	Meyer Werft (Germany)	Cabins (wheelchair accessible):	30
Original cost:	$641 million	Wheelchair accessibility:	Best
Entered service:	Aug 2009	Cabin voltage:	110 and 220 volts
Registry:	Malta	Elevators:	12
Length (ft/m):	1,033.4/315.0	Casino (gaming tables):	Yes
Beam (ft/m):	120.7/36.8	Slot machines:	Yes
Draft (ft/m):	27.2/8.3	Swimming pools:	3
Propulsion/Propellers:	diesel (67,200kW)/2 azimuthing pods	Hot tubs (on deck):	6
Passenger decks:	14	Self-service launderette:	No
Total crew:	1,210	Dedicated cinema/seats:	No
Passengers (lower beds/alll berths):	2,852/3,145	Library:	Yes
Passenger Space Ratio (lower beds/all berths):	42.7/38.7	Onboard currency:	US$
Crew/Passenger Ratio (lower beds/all berths):	2.3/2.5		

A large ship with contemporary style, for the well traveled

OVERVIEW. This is a sister ship to *Celebrity Eclipse*, *Celebrity Reflection*, *Celebrity Silhouette*, and *Celebrity Solstice*. The steeply sloping stern, with its mega-yacht-style ducktail platform above the propulsion pods, is very attractive, and nicely balances the ship's contemporary profile. The bows are rounded to accommodate a helipad.

THE SHIP. Two rather slim funnels, set one behind the other, distinguish *Celebrity Equinox* from previous single-funnel Celebrity ships. Between the two funnels is a grass outdoor area, the Lawn Club. This grass is real, and seems to like the salty air. The Lawn Club is open to all, so you can go putting, play croquet or bocce ball, or have a picnic on the grass.

There are several pool and water-play areas on Resort Deck: one in a solarium (with glass roof), a sports pool, a family pool, and a wet zone. However, the deck space around the two pools is not large enough for the number of passengers carried.

Inside, the decor is elegant, yet contemporary. Michael's Club is an intimate, quiet lounge with classic English leather chairs, a dramatic black glass chandelier, a grand fireplace, and some contemporary artwork. Rich furnishings help create a warm atmosphere, amidst a backdrop of piano and jazz music, as well as single malt scotch and cognacs for tastings.

Other attractions include a wine bar; a cocktail lounge playing jazz; a bar with the look of an ocean-going yacht; Quasar, a bar with large screens that create

Berlitz's Ratings

	Possible	Achieved
Ship	500	416
Accommodation	200	165
Food	400	297
Service	400	306
Entertainment	100	77
Cruise	400	298

OVERALL SCORE
1559 points out of 2000

a nightly light show synchronized to music; and an observation lounge with dance floor.

Celebrity's signature Martini Bar, which has a frosted bar, includes a small alcove called Crush with an ice-filled table for caviar and vodka tastings.

Fortunes Casino has 16 gaming tables and 200 slot machines. There's a delightful two-deck library, but books on the upper shelves are impossible to reach. An innovative Hot Glass Show, created in collaboration with Corning Museum of Glass, includes demonstrations and a narrated performance of glass-blowing, housed in an outdoor studio on the open deck as part of the Lawn Club.

Passenger niggles include poor drawer space in cabins; inadequate children's facilities and staff; congestion when you exit the showlounge; and noise in all areas of the lobby when the martini bar is busy.

Good points include elevator call buttons located in a floor-stand 'pod' so that, when an elevator arrives, a glass panel above it turns from blue to pink. Also, the ship has a good collection of designer chairs and sunloungers in various locations.

Gratuities are charged to your onboard account.

ACCOMMODATION. From Penthouse Suites to small interior cabins, the accommodation is practical and comfortable. There are many price grades, depending on size and location. In standard Interior and Ocean View cabins, there is little space between the bed and the wall, and usable drawer space is poor. So, if your budget allows, book a suite-category cabin for all the extra benefits – and a lot more drawer space.

About 90 percent of the cabins have an outside view, and many of these have a balcony; due to the ship's pencil-slim width, there are few interior cabins. The suite-grade categories are: Royal Suite, Celebrity Suite, Sky Suite, and Penthouse Suite.

All grades of accommodation include: twin beds convertible to a queen-size bed, sitting area, vanity desk with hairdryer, but there's almost no drawer space. Also standard in all cabins: 32-inch flat-screen TVs (larger screens in suites), Wi-Fi Internet access (for a fee), premium bedding. However, although the closets have good hanging space, other storage space is limited. The bathroom has a shower enclosure, toilet, and tiny washbasin, and the faucet gets in the way when washing your face or brushing your teeth; there's no retractable clothesline for washed small items; and the two hooks on the back of the bathroom door are tiny. In suite-grade accommodation there is more space, larger balconies with good-quality sunloungers, and more personal amenities.

Some 130 AquaSpa-class cabins share the relaxation room of the AquaSpa itself, incorporate select spa elements into the cabins, and allow for specialized access to the AquaSpa's Thermal Relaxation Room and Persian Garden (with aromatherapy/steam rooms) on the same deck. Features include: a choice of four pillows (conformance, body, goose, Isotonic); express luggage delivery; shoeshine; Frette bathrobes; dining and seating preferences in other specialty dining venues; and early embarkation and disembarkation. Bathrooms have a decent amount of space, and a large shower enclosure. Occupants also get assigned seating at the exclusive 130-seat Restaurant Blu.

Other accommodation grades are Veranda-class, Sunset-Veranda-class, Concierge-class, Family Oceanview with veranda, Deluxe Oceanview with veranda, Standard Oceanview, and Standard Interior cabins.

Cabins 1551–1597 on the port side and 1556–1602 on the starboard side on Penthouse Deck (Deck 11) suffer from 'aircraft carrier' syndrome because they are directly under the huge overhanging Resort Deck. They have little exposure to sun or light, so private balcony sunbathing is out of the question. Many thick supporting struts ruin the view from these cabins, which are otherwise pleasantly fitted out.

DINING. Silhouette, the ship's balconied main dining room (included in the cruise price), has ocean views on the port and starboard sides. The design is stunning and contemporary. At the forward end, a two-deck-high wine tower provides an eye-catching focal point. As for the food, it's a bit of a let-down – the decreased quality is all too obvious to repeat Celebrity passengers.

Other dining options. Murano is an extra-cost, reservations-required venue offering high-quality traditional dining with a French flair and exquisite table settings, including large Reidel wine glasses. Food and service are very good.

Blu is a 128-seat specialty restaurant designated just for the occupants of AquaClass cabins. The room has pleasing, but rather cold, blue decor.

The Tuscan Grille, an extra-cost venue, serves Kobe beef and premium quality steaks, and has beautifully curved archways – it's like walking into a high-tech winery. There are great views from huge aft-view windows.

QSine is an extra-cost, reservations-required fine-dining venue, with iPad menus.

Bistro on Five (Deck 5, that is) is for coffee, cakes, crêpes, pastries, and more. It can get busy at times and the serving counter is small.

Café al Bacio & Gelateria is a coffeehouse serving Lavazza Italian coffee. It is on one side of the main lobby, but it's small and lines quickly form at peak times. The seating is mostly in large, very comfortable armchairs.

Oceanview Café and Grill is the expansive, tray-less, casual self-serve buffet venue. There are a number of food 'islands' rather than those awful straight buffet counters, and the signage is reasonably good. However, it's impossible to get a warm plate for so-called hot food items, and condiments are hard to find.

The AquaSpa Café is for light, healthier options (solarium fare), but the selections are bland and boring.

The Mast Bar Grill and Bar is an outside venue offering fast food.

ENTERTAINMENT. The 1,115-seat Equinox Theater, the ship's principal showlounge, has a main level and two balconied sections positioned amphitheater-style around a stage with music lofts set on either side. Three circus-themed production shows highlight in-your-face, formulaic acrobatics.

Colorful theme nights are held in the Sky Observation Lounge, whose daytime decor comes alive at night thanks to mood lighting effects. The 200-seat Celebrity Central hosts comedy, cooking demonstrations, enrichment lectures, and feature films. An Entertainment Court showcases street performers, psychics, and caricaturists, and is in the center of the ship, linked to the Quasar nightclub. The Ensemble Lounge is a big-band-era cocktail lounge with live jazz, next to the Murano restaurant.

SPA/FITNESS. A large, two-deck AquaSpa is operated by concessionaire Steiner Leisure. The fitness center includes kinesis (pulleys against gravity) workout equipment, plus the familiar cardio-vascular machinery. An extra-cost, unisex thermal suite features steam and shower mist rooms, and a glacial ice fountain, plus a calming relaxation area with heated tiled beds. There's also an acupuncture center.

Celebrity Infinity
★★★★

Size:.................................Large Resort Ship	Crew/Passenger Ratio (lower beds/all berths):..........1.9/2.4
Tonnage: 90,228	Cabins (total):.....................................1,035
Lifestyle: ....Premium	Size range (sq ft/m):.............165.1–2,530.0/15.34–235.0
Cruise line:........................... Celebrity Cruises	Cabins (outside view):................................840
Former names: .... *Infinity*	Cabins (interior/no view):.............................195
IMO number: 9189421	Cabins (for one person):................................0
Builder: .... Chantiers de l'Atlantique (France)	Cabins (with private balcony):........................650
Original cost:..............................$350 million	Cabins (wheelchair accessible): 26
Entered service:............................... Mar 2001	Wheelchair accessibility:.......................... Best
Registry:...Malta	Cabin voltage: ....110 and 220 volts
Length (ft/m):.............................. 964.5/294.0	Elevators:..12
Beam (ft/m):................................ 105.6/32.2	Casino (gaming tables):............................. Yes
Draft (ft/m):................................... 26.2/8.0	Slot machines:..................................... Yes
Propulsion/Propellers:. gas turbine/2 azimuthing pods (39,000kW each)	Swimming pools:.................3 (1 w/sliding glass dome)
	Hot tubs (on deck):..................................4
Passenger decks:..................................11	Self-service launderette:............................No
Total crew:......................................999	Dedicated cinema/seats:.......................Yes/368
Passengers (lower beds/alll berths):............. 2,154/2,570	Library: ....Yes
Passenger Space Ratio (lower beds/all berths): 46.2/36.8	Onboard currency: ....US$

A family-friendly, modern ship with a certain style

OVERVIEW. The ship provides a wide range of choices and possibilities. If you travel in one of the suites, you receive the highest level of personal service, while cruising in non-suite accommodation is much like any large ship. It all depends how much you are willing to pay. The two-seating dining and two shows nightly detract from an otherwise excellent product.

THE SHIP. *Celebrity Infinity* is a sister ship to *Celebrity Constellation*, *Celebrity Millennium*, and *Celebrity Summit*. Jon Bannenberg, famous for his mega-yacht designs, designed the exterior. It is fitted with a 'pod' propulsion system coupled with a quiet, smokeless, energy-efficient gas turbine powerplant.

New AquaClass veranda staterooms and a new Mediterranean-themed specialty restaurant, Blu, exclusively for AquaClass passengers, were added in a 'Solsticizing' of the ship in 2011. Also added were a Celebrity iLounge (for Apple products, computer classes, and Internet-connection), a Martini Bar with a frosted countertop, a Tuscan Grill serving steaks, a CellarMasters wine bar, Café al Bacio and Gelateria, and Bistro on Five (a crêperie). Replacing the former conservatory is QSine, a reservations-only, extra-cost 'interactive' dining venue with iPad menus.

There is no walk-around wooden promenade deck outdoors. There are cushioned pads for poolside sunloungers only, but not for chairs on other outside decks. Trying to reach Cabin Service or the Guest Re-

Berlitz's Ratings

	Possible	Achieved
Ship	500	389
Accommodation	200	161
Food	400	285
Service	400	296
Entertainment	100	74
Cruise	400	288

OVERALL SCORE
1493 points out of 2000

lations Desk to answer the phone (to order breakfast, for example, if you don't want to do so via the 'interactive' TV set) is a matter of luck, timing and patience.

The atrium is the focal point inside the ship; it is three decks high and houses the reception desk, tour operator's desk, and bank. Four glass-walled elevators travel through the ship's exterior (port) side, connecting the atrium with another seven decks, thus traveling through 10 passenger decks, including the tender stations – a nice ride.

Facilities include a Cinema and Conference Center, an expansive shopping arcade with a 14,447-sq-ft (1,300-sq-m) retail store space with all the favorites, a four-deck-high showlounge, a two-level library (one level for English-language books; a second level for other languages); card room; compact disc listening room; art auction center (with seating that looks more like a small chapel); Cosmos, a combination observation lounge/discotheque; and a Celebrity iLounge (an Apple store/reseller and computer center).

Michael's Club (which was a cigar smoker's haven when the ship was new) is now a rather nice, comfortable lounge/piano bar. 15 percent gratuity is added to bar and wine accounts. An Internet café has almost 20 computer workstation with custom-made wood-surround monitors and extra-cost Internet connectivity.

Gaming sports include the ship's overly large Fortunes Casino, with blackjack, roulette, and slot machines, and lots of bright lights and action.

FAMILIES. The Fun Factory is designed for young children and The Tower caters to teenagers. Children's counselors and youth activities staff provide a wide range of supervised activities.

ACCOMMODATION. There are numerous grades from which to choose, depending on your preference for the size and location of your living space. Almost half of the ship's accommodation features a "private" balcony; approximately 80 percent are ocean-view suites and cabins, and the rest are interior cabins. All the accommodation is extremely comfortable. Suites, naturally, have more space, butler service (whether you want it or not), more and better amenities and more personal service than standard cabin grades.

There are several categories of suites, but those at the stern are in a prime location and have huge balconies that are very private and not overlooked from above.

All suites and cabins have wood cabinetry and accenting, interactive television and entertainment systems – you can go shopping, book shore excursions, play casino games, interactively, and even watch soft-porn movies. Bathrooms have hairdryers, and 100 percent cotton towels.

Penthouse Suites (2). These suites, on Penthouse Deck, are like apartments. Each occupies one half of the width of the ship, overlooking the stern. Each is a huge 2,530 sq ft (235 sq m): 1,432 sq ft (133 sq m) of living space, plus a huge wraparound balcony of 1,098 sq ft (102 sq m). It includes a wet bar, hot tub, and whirlpool tub, but much of this terrace can be overlooked from other decks above.

Features include a marble foyer, a separate living room complete with ebony baby grand piano, and a formal dining room. The master bedroom has a large walk-in closet; personal exercise equipment; dressing room with vanity desk; exercise equipment; marble-clad master bathroom with twin washbasins; deep whirlpool tub; separate shower; toilet and bidet areas; flat-screen televisions (one in the bedroom and one in the lounge); and electronically controlled drapes. Butler service is standard, and a butler's pantry, with separate entry door, houses a full-size refrigerator, temperature-controlled wine cabinet, microwave oven, and food preparation and storage areas. For even more space, an interconnecting door can be opened into the adjacent suite.

Royal Suites (8). These are located towards the aft (four each on the port and starboard sides). Each measures 733 sq ft (68 sq m) and has a separate living room with dining and lounge areas (with refrigerator, mini-bar, and a Bang & Olufsen audio system) and a separate bedroom. There are two entertainment centers with DVD players, flat-screen TV sets in the living area and in the bedroom, and a large walk-in closet with vanity desk. The marble-clad bathroom has a whirlpool tub with integral shower, and there are also a separate shower enclosure, two washbasins, and toilet. The

teakwood decked balcony is extensive – large enough for on-deck massage – and has a hot tub.

Celebrity Suites (8). These measure 467 sq ft (44 sq m) and have floor-to-ceiling windows, a separate living room with dining and lounge areas, two entertainment centers with flat-screen TV sets in the living room and in the bedroom, and a walk-in closet with vanity desk. The marble-clad bathroom has a whirlpool tub with integral shower; a window with movable shade lets you look out of the bathroom through the lounge to the large ocean-view windows. Balconies were added in the 2011 refit.

Interconnecting doors allow two suites to be used as a family unit. These suites, located opposite a group of glass-walled elevators, overhang the ship's starboard side, and provide stunning ocean views from the lounge/dining area. A personal computer with wood-surround screen connects to the Internet.

Sky Suites (30). Each is 308 sq ft (29 sq m), including the private balcony – some balconies may be larger than others, depending on the location. Although these are designated as suites, they are really just larger cabins that have a marble-clad bathroom with tub/shower combination. The suites also have a video player in addition to a TV set, and have a larger lounge area and sleeping area than standard cabins.

Butler Service. Provided in all accommodation designated as suites, this includes full breakfast, in-suite lunch and dinner service (as required), afternoon tea service, evening hors d'oeuvres, complimentary espresso and cappuccino, daily news delivery, and shoe-shine service.

Suite occupants in Penthouse, Royal, Celebrity, and Sky suites also get welcome Champagne; a personal computer in each suite, including a printer and Internet access (on request in the Sky Suites); choice of films; personalized stationery; tote bag; priority dining room seating preferences; private portrait sitting; bathrobe; and in-suite massage service.

Concierge Class. In 2003, Celebrity Cruises added a third service 'class' to the accommodation grades. Positioned between the top grade suite grades and standard cabin grades, Concierge Class offers added value to these 'middle-class' cabins, as does a new 'Aqua Class,' added in 2012, with spa-healthy dining in the exclusive Blu restaurant, and complimentary access to the Persian Garden (thermal suite) and Relaxation Room in the spa, plus daily delivery of bottled water and herbal teas (infusions), and a host of spa-related personal amenities.

Enhanced facilities include priority embarkation, disembarkation, tender tickets, specialty dining, and spa reservations. Concierge Class cabin occupants get double bed overlay (no more 'falling between the cracks' for couples); choice of four pillows (goose down pillow, isotonic pillow, body pillow, conformance pillow); eight-vial flower vase on vanity desk; throw pillows on sofa; fruit basket; binoculars; golf umbrella;

leather telephone notepad; larger beach towels; hand-held hairdryer. The balcony gets better furniture. In the bathrooms: plusher Frette bathrobes; larger towels in sea green and pink (alternating days); flower in silver vase. It all adds up to excellent value for money.

Standard Outside-View/Interior Cabins. All other outside-view and interior cabins have a lounge area with sofa or convertible sofa bed, sleeping area with twin beds that can convert to a double bed, a good amount of closet and drawer space, personal safe, mini-bar/refrigerator (extra cost), interactive television, and private bathroom. The cabins are nicely decorated with warm wood-finish furniture, and there is none of the boxy feel of cabins in so many ships, due to the angled placement of vanity and audio-video consoles. Even the smallest cabin has a good-size bathroom and shower enclosure.

Wheelchair-Accessible Accommodation. This is available in various grades and practical locations, close to elevators. All doorways and bathroom doorways and showers are wheelchair-accessible. Some cabins have extra berths for third or third and fourth occupants. There is only one safe for personal belongings, which must be shared.

DINING. The Thellis Restaurant is a 1,170-seat formal dining room. It is two decks high and has a grand staircase connecting the two levels, a huge glass wall overlooking the sea at the stern of the ship (electrically operated shades provide several different backdrops), and a musician's gallery on the upper level, typically for a string quartet or quintet. There are two seatings for dinner (open seating for breakfast and lunch), at tables for two, four, six, eight, or 10. The dining room, like all large dining halls, can be extremely noisy. The menu variety is good, the food has taste, and it is attractively presented and served in a well-orchestrated fashion that displays European traditions and training. Full service in-cabin dining is also available for all meals, including dinner.

Other dining options. The United States Restaurant is adjacent to the main lobby. It has actual glass paneling from the former United States Lines liner *United States*, which in 1952 made the fastest transatlantic crossing by a passenger ship, taking the famed Blue Riband from the Cunard's *Queen Mary*. This restaurant is not as luxurious as the specialty dining salons aboard sister ships *Celebrity Constellation*, *Celebrity Millennium*, or *Celebrity Summit*.

A team of chefs prepares the cuisine exclusively for this restaurant. Fine tableside preparation is the attraction, and both the classic French cuisine (but including some menu items from the United States) and service are very good. This is haute cuisine at the height of professionalism, for this is a room for a full dégustation, and not just a dinner. However, with only 134 seats, not all passengers will be able to experience it even once during a one-week cruise; reservations are necessary, and a per-person cover charge applies. There's a dine-in wine cellar and a demonstration galley.

QSine, which features its menus and wine list on iPads, is another extra-cost, fine dining venue (added in 2011), and reservations are required.

Tuscan Grille is an extra-cost, reservations required venue that features Kobe beef and premium-quality steaks.

Las Olas Café and Grill is a casual self-serve buffet area, with six principal serving lines, and seating for 754; there is also a grill and pizza bar. For Champagne and caviar lovers, not to mention martinis, Carlisle's is the place to see and be seen.

Café al Bacio and Gelateria, on the third level of the atrium lobby, is the place to see and be seen, for coffees (espresso, cappuccino, and specialty coffees), pastries, cakes, and gelato, in a trendy setting. Bistro on Five is a new crêperie.

ENTERTAINMENT. The 900-seat Celebrity Theater is the three-deck-high venue for production shows and major cabaret acts. It is located in the forward part of the ship, with seating on main, and two balcony levels. The large stage has a full fly loft behind its traditional proscenium.

SPA/FITNESS. The AquaSpa measures 24,219 sq ft (2,250 sq m). It includes a large thalassotherapy pool under a solarium glass dome, complete with health bar for light breakfast and lunch items and fresh squeezed fruit and vegetable juices.

Spa facilities include 16 massage/body treatment rooms, plus eight treatment rooms with showers and one treatment room specifically designed for wheelchair passengers, aerobics room, gymnasium with over 40 exercise machines, large men's and women's saunas (with large ocean-view porthole window), a beauty salon, and a unisex thermal suite containing several steam and shower mist rooms with different fragrances such as chamomile, eucalyptus, and mint, and a glacial ice fountain. The spa is operated by Steiner, a specialist concession.

Sports facilities include a full-size basketball court, compact football, paddle tennis and volleyball, golf simulator, shuffleboard on two different decks, and a jogging track.

Celebrity Millennium
★★★★

Size:....................................Large Resort Ship	Cabins (total):......................................975
Tonnage:.......................................90,228	Size range (sq ft/m):..............170.0–2,350.0/15.7–235.0
Lifestyle:......................................Premium	Cabins (outside view):................................780
Cruise line:............................. Celebrity Cruises	Cabins (interior/no view):.............................195
Former names:.............................. Millennium	Cabins (for one person):................................0
IMO number:..................................9189419	Cabins (with private balcony):.........................590
Builder:.................. Chantiers de l'Atlantique (France)	Cabins (wheelchair accessible):.....26 (17 with private balcony)
Original cost:..............................$350 million	Wheelchair accessibility:............................ Best
Entered service:.............................. Jun 2000	Cabin voltage:.........................110 and 220 volts
Registry:...Malta	Elevators:..12
Length (ft/m):...............................964.5/294.0	Casino (gaming tables):.............................. Yes
Beam (ft/m):................................105.6/32.2	Slot machines:...................................... Yes
Draft (ft/m):....................................26.2/8.0	Swimming pools:..................3 (1 w/sliding glass dome)
Propulsion/Propellers:. gas turbine (39,000kW)/2 azimuthing pods	Hot tubs (on deck):....................................4
Passenger decks:....................................11	Self-service launderette:..............................No
Total crew:.......................................999	Dedicated cinema/seats:......................... Yes/368
Passengers (lower beds/alll berths):.............1,950/2,450	Library:.. Yes
Passenger Space Ratio (lower beds/all berths):.......46.2/36.8	Onboard currency:.................................US$
Crew/Passenger Ratio (lower beds/all berths):..........1.9/2.4	

A large, family-friendly ship with a touch of class

OVERVIEW. *Celebrity Millennium* delivers a well-defined North American cruise vacation at a very modest price. A zero-announcement policy means there is little intrusion. Although two-seating dining and two nightly shows detract from an otherwise good product, this ship (like its sisters *Celebrity Constellation*, *Celebrity Infinity*, and *Celebrity Summit*) provides a premium cruise experience that's hard to beat.

Berlitz's Ratings

	Possible	Achieved
Ship	500	389
Accommodation	200	161
Food	400	285
Service	400	298
Entertainment	100	74
Cruise	400	288
OVERALL SCORE		
1495 points out of 2000		

THE SHIP. This was the first Celebrity Cruises ship to be fitted with a pod propulsion system coupled with a gas turbine powerplant. Indeed, this was the first cruise ship in the world to be powered by quiet, smokeless, energy-efficient gas turbines (two GE gas turbines provide engine power while a single GE steam turbine drives the electricity generators).

Facilities outdoors include two outdoor pools, one indoor/outdoor pool, and four hot tubs. Unfortunately, there is no walk-around wooden promenade deck outdoors. There are cushioned pads for poolside deck lounge chairs only, but not for chairs on other outside decks. Passenger participation activities are mostly amateurish.

Inside, the ship has an understated elegance, with the same high-class decor and materials (including lots of wood, glass and marble) and public rooms that have made other ships in the fleet so popular. The atrium, with separately enclosed room for shore excursions, is four decks high and houses the reception desk, tour operator's desk, and bank. Four glass-walled elevators travel through the ship's exterior (port) side, connecting the atrium with another seven decks, thus traveling through 10 passenger decks, including the tender stations.

A 70-person capacity sports bar, Extreme, just doesn't, somehow, belong; it is located directly in front of the main funnel and has glass walls overlooking the ship's side.

Other facilities include a cinema/conference center; an expansive shopping arcade with more than 14,450 sq ft (1,300 sq m) of retailing space; a lavish four-deck-high showlounge with the latest in high-tech staging and lighting equipment; two-level library (one level for English-language books, a second for other languages); card room; CD listening room; art auction center with seating that makes it look like a small chapel; Cosmos, a combination observation lounge/discotheque; and an Internet Center containing 19 computers with wood-surround flat screens.

Gaming sports include the ship's overly large Fortunes Casino, with blackjack, roulette, and slot machines, bright lights, and action. New AquaClass veranda cabins and Blu, a Mediterranean-themed specialty restaurant exclusively for AquaClass passengers, were added in a 'Solsticizing' of the ship in 2012. Also added were a Celebrity iLounge (for the latest Apple products, computer classes and internet connection); a Martini Bar with a frosted bar top, a Cellar-Masters wine bar; QSine, an extra-cost fine dining venue with iPad menus; a Bistro on Five, and a crêperie.

Michael's Club (which was a cigar smoker's haven when the ship was new, but now features over 50 craft beers plus fine whiskies, cognacs, bourbons and scotches) is now a rather nice, comfortable lounge/piano bar. 15 percent gratuity is added to bar and wine accounts. An Internet café has almost 20 computer workstation with custom-made wood-surround monitors and extra-cost Internet connectivity.

FAMILIES. The Fun Factory is designed for young children and The Tower caters to teenagers. Children's counselors and youth activities staff provide a wide range of supervised activities. Interconnecting doors on two Celebrity Suites allow them to be used as one unit; as there is no balcony, they are ideal for those with small children.

ACCOMMODATION. There are numerous grades from which to choose, depending on your preference for the size and location of your living space. The accommodation is extremely comfortable. Suites, naturally, have more space, butler service, and more amenities. There are several categories of suites, but those at the stern are in a prime location and have huge balconies that really are private and not overlooked from above. My advice is to book a suite-category cabin for its many extra benefits.

The suites and cabins have wood cabinetry and accenting, interactive television and entertainment systems. Bathrooms have hairdryers, and cotton towels.

Penthouse Suites (2). On Penthouse Deck, these are the largest suites. Each occupies one half of the ship's beam, and overlooks the stern. Each measures a huge 2,530 sq ft (235 sq m): 1,432 sq ft (133 sq m) of living space, plus a huge wrap-around balcony measuring 1,098 sq ft (102 sq m) with 180° views plus a wet bar, hot tub, and whirlpool tub. Much of this terrace, however, can be overlooked by passengers on decks above, so it's not exactly private.

Features include a marble foyer, a separate living room complete with ebony baby grand piano, and a formal dining room. The master bedroom has a large walk-in closet; personal exercise equipment; dressing room with vanity desk, exercise equipment; marble-clad master bathroom with twin washbasins; deep whirlpool tub; separate shower; toilet and bidet areas; flat-screen televisions (one in the bedroom, one in the lounge); and electronically controlled drapes. Butler service is standard, and a butler's pantry, with separate entry door, has a full-size refrigerator, temperature-controlled wine cabinet, microwave oven, and good-size food preparation and storage areas. For even more space, an interconnecting door can be opened into the adjacent suite.

Royal Suites. These suites, each 733 sq ft (68 sq m), are located towards the ship's aft (four each on the port and starboard sides). The decor in each is different and is geographically themed: Africa, China, Mexico,

France, India, Italy, Morocco, and Portugal. Each has a separate living room with dining and lounge areas (with refrigerator, mini-bar, and Bang & Olufsen CD audio system), and a separate bedroom. There are two entertainment centers with DVD players, and TVs in the living area and bedroom, and a large walk-in closet, with vanity desk. The marble-clad bathroom has a whirlpool tub with integral shower, and there is also a separate shower enclosure, two washbasins and toilet. The teak balcony is extensive – large enough for on-deck massage – and also has a whirlpool hot tub.

Celebrity Suites. These suites, each 467 sq ft (44 sq m), have floor-to-ceiling windows, a separate living room with dining and lounge areas, two entertainment centers with flat-screen televisions (one in the living room, one in the bedroom), and a walk-in closet with vanity desk. The marble-clad bathroom has a whirlpool tub with integral shower – a window with movable shade lets you look out of the bathroom through the lounge to the large ocean-view windows.

These suites, located opposite a group of glass-walled elevators, overhang the starboard side of the ship and provide stunning ocean views from the glass-walled sitting/dining area, which extends out from the ship's side. A computer with wood-surround screen connects directly to the Internet. Butler service is standard.

Sky Suites. Each is 308 sq ft (28.6 sq m), including the private balcony – some balconies may be larger than others, depending on location. Although designated as suites, they are really just larger cabins with a marble-clad bathroom with tub/shower combination. The suites also have a video player in addition to a TV set, and have a larger lounge area than standard cabins, and sleeping area. Butler service is standard.

Butler Service. This service, in all suite-grade accommodation, includes full breakfast, in-suite lunch and dinner service (as required), afternoon tea service, evening hors d'oeuvres, free espresso and cappuccino, daily news delivery, shoeshine, and other personal touches. Suite occupants in Penthouse, Royal, Celebrity, and Sky suites also get welcome Champagne; a full personal computer in each suite, including a printer and Internet access (on request in the Sky Suites); choice of films from a video library; personalized stationery; tote bag; priority dining room seating preferences; private portrait sitting, and bathrobe; and in-suite massage service.

Concierge Class. In 2003, Celebrity Cruises added a third service 'class' to the accommodation grades. Positioned between the top grade suite grades and standard cabin grades, Concierge Class offers added value to these 'middle-class' cabins, as does a new 'Aqua Class,' added in 2012, with spa-healthy dining in Blu Restaurant, and complimentary access to the Persian Garden (thermal suite) and Relaxation Room in the spa, plus daily delivery of bottled water and herbal teas (infusions), and a host of spa-related personal amenities.

Other features include priority embarkation, disembarkation, tender tickets, specialty dining, and spa reservations. Concierge Class cabin occupants get a double bed overlay (no more 'falling between the cracks' for couples); choice of four pillows (goose down pillow, isotonic pillow, body pillow, conformance pillow); eight-vial flower vase on vanity desk; throw pillows on sofa; fruit basket; binoculars; golf umbrella; leather telephone notepad; larger beach towels; hand-held hairdryer. The balcony gets better furniture. In the bathrooms: plusher Frette bathrobes; larger towels in sea green and pink (on alternate days); flower in silver vase.

Standard Outside-View/Interior Cabins. All other outside-view and interior cabins not designated as suites have a lounge area with sofa or convertible sofa bed, sleeping area with twin beds that convert to a double, good closet and drawer space, personal safe, mini-bar/refrigerator (all items cost extra), interactive television, and bathroom. The cabins are nicely decorated with warm wood-finish furniture, and there is none of the boxy feel of cabins in so many ships, due to the angled placement of vanity and audio-video consoles. Even the smallest interior cabin has a good-size bathroom and shower enclosure.

Wheelchair-Accessible Accommodation. This is provided in six Sky Suites, three premium outside-view cabins, eight deluxe ocean-view cabins, four standard ocean-view, and five interior cabins measuring 347 sq ft to 362 sq ft (32.2 to 33.6 sq m). They are located in the most practical parts of the ship, close to elevators for good accessibility. All have doorways and bathroom doorways and showers that are wheelchair-accessible.

DINING. The Metropolitan Restaurant, seating 1,224, is the ship's principal, large dining hall. Two decks high, it has a grand staircase connecting the two levels, a huge glass wall at the stern overlooking the sea, and a small 'musician's gallery' on the upper level, typically for a string quartet or quintet. There are two seatings for dinner (open seating for breakfast and lunch), at tables for two, four, six, eight, or 10. The menu variety is good, the food has taste, and it is attractively presented. Full service in-cabin dining is also available for all meals, including dinner, with menu items from the Metropolitan Restaurant.

Other dining options. Celebrity Cruises created its first true alternative restaurant aboard this ship. The Olympic Restaurant is named after White Star Line's transatlantic ocean liner (sister ship to *Titanic*). It is adjacent to the atrium lobby, and has a dining lounge that is rather like an anteroom that contains figured French walnut wood paneling from the à la carte dining room of the 1911 ship, which was decorated in Louis XVI splendor. When the paneling, sold by the scrapyard, was found in a house in Southport, northern England, Celebrity Cruises bought the house in order to obtain it.

A team of chefs prepares the cuisine exclusively for this restaurant. Tableside preparation is the attraction of this alternative dining room, whose classic French cuisine and service are very good; this is, indeed, a room for a full dégustation, and not just a dinner. The wine list is extensive, with more than 400 labels, but the real treat for connoisseurs is an additional list of rare vintage wines. However, with just 134 seats, not all passengers will be able to experience this restaurant even once during a one-week cruise; reservations are needed, and there's a cover charge. There's also a dine-in wine cellar and a demonstration galley.

QSine, which features its menus and wine list on iPads, is another extra-cost, fine dining venue (added in 2010), and reservations are required.

Tuscan Grille is an extra-cost, reservations required venue that features Kobe beef and premium-quality steaks.

Ocean Café is a self-serve buffet-style eatery – an extensive area that can seat 754. At the aft end of the Ocean Buffet, a separate pasta bar, sushi counter, grill/rotisserie, and pizza station provide freshly created items. Pizzas are made on board from pizza dough and do not come ready made for reheating, as with many cruise lines. On selected evenings, alternative dinners can be taken here (reservations needed). There is also an outdoor grill, adjacent to the swimming pool, for fast food items.

Café al Bacio and Geleteria, located on the third level of the atrium lobby, is the place to see and be seen, for coffees, pastries, cakes, and gelato – all in a trendy setting.

ENTERTAINMENT. The 900-seat Celebrity Theater is a three-deck-high showlounge for presenting the production shows and major cabaret acts. It is located in the forward part of the ship, with seating on main, and two balcony levels. The large stage is equipped with a full fly loft behind its traditional proscenium.

SPA/FITNESS. Wellness facilities (operated by specialist concession Steiner) include a large AquaSpa measuring 24,219 sq ft (2,250 sq m). It has a large thalassotherapy pool under a large solarium dome, complete with health bar for light breakfast and lunch items and fresh squeezed fruit and vegetable juices. There are 16 massage/body treatment rooms, plus eight more with showers and one designed for wheelchair passengers, an aerobics room, gymnasium with over 40 exercise machines, large men's and women's saunas, a unisex thermal suite (containing several steam and shower mist rooms with fragrances such as chamomile, eucalyptus, and mint, and a glacial ice fountain), and a beauty salon.

Sports facilities include a full-size basketball court, compact football, paddle tennis and volleyball, golf simulator, shuffleboard (on two different decks) and a jogging track.

Celebrity Reflection
★★★★ +

Size:.....................................Large Resort Ship	Cabins (total):.....................................1,523
Tonnage: 125,366	Size range (sq ft/m): 182.9–668.4/17.0–155.0
Lifestyle: ....Premium	Cabins (outside view):.....................................1,369
Cruise line:........................... Celebrity Cruises	Cabins (interior/no view):.....................................154
Former names: ....none	Cabins (for one person):.....................................0
IMO number: 9506459	Cabins (with private balcony):.....................................1,216
Builder: .... Meyer Werft (Germany)	Cabins (wheelchair accessible): 30
Original cost:.....................................$641 million	Wheelchair accessibility:..................................... Best
Entered service:.....................................Oct 2012	Cabin voltage: ....110 and 220 volts
Registry:..................................... Malta	Elevators:.....................................12
Length (ft/m):.....................................1,047.2/319.2	Casino (gaming tables):..................................... Yes
Beam (ft/m):..................................... 120.7/36.8	Slot machines:..................................... Yes
Draft (ft/m):..................................... 27.2/8.3	Swimming pools:.....................................3
Propulsion/Propellers: ..... diesel (70,500kW)/2 azimuthing pods	Hot tubs (on deck):.....................................6
Passenger decks:.....................................14	Self-service launderette:.....................................No
Total crew:..................................... 1,271	Dedicated cinema/seats:.....................................No
Passengers (lower beds/all berths):............. 3,046/3,609	Library: ....Yes
Passenger Space Ratio (lower beds/all berths): 41.1/34.7	Onboard currency: ....US$
Crew/Passenger Ratio (lower beds/all berths):.......... 2.3/2.8	

A premium-quality ship for stylish, family-friendly cruising

OVERVIEW. Celebrity Reflection is a sleek-looking ship, with two slim funnels. It is a close sister ship to *Celebrity Eclipse* (2010), *Celebrity Equinox* (2009), *Celebrity Silhouette* (2011), and *Celebrity Solstice* (2008). Behind the two funnels, the ship recreates the great outdoors with a Lawn Club, an area with real Bermudan (not fake) grass. You can go putting, play croquet or bocce ball (think passengers against officers!), or picnic on the grass, and it's a nice place to walk barefoot.

THE SHIP. *Celebrity Reflection* has a steeply sloping stern that includes a mega-yacht-style ducktail platform above the propulsion pods (using the latest Azipod XO system). The ship is attractive, and nicely balanced (the hull is two feet wider, and has an additional deck, although the ship's superstructure is the same width, as Celebrity Silhouette), with two slim funnels set one behind the other. On the open deck, 'The Alcoves' are extra-cost 'private' Wi-Fi-equipped cabanas, and cost $149 per day on sea days and $99 on port days.

Although *Celebrity Reflection* is a close sister to *Celebrity Silhouette*, it has an additional deck. This houses 78 more suites, and more seating is provided in the showlounge, the main dining room, and other restaurants and eateries. With more passengers (but the same number of elevators), the Passenger Space Ratio is therefore slightly reduced. The ship's name is positioned directly under the navigation bridge and not

Berlitz's Ratings

	Possible	Achieved
Ship	500	416
Accommodation	200	165
Food	400	301
Service	400	307
Entertainment	100	80
Cruise	400	302

OVERALL SCORE
1571 points out of 2000

forward on the bows (for space reasons), and the rounded bows accommodate a helicopter winch pad.

Behind the ship's two slim funnels is a real grass outdoor area, the Lawn Club. This is authentic, not fake, grass, and, despite being trampled on by all and sundry, it seems to like the salty air, although it does need constant and copious care by specialists. The club is open to all, so you can go putting, play croquet or bocce ball (like bowling or French boules), ring toss; you can also picnic on the grass, or even sleep on it.

Several pool and water-play areas are positioned on Resort Deck: one under a glass-roofed solarium (with Aqua Café for light healthy bites). There's also a sports pool, a family pool, and a wet zone. The open deck and sunning space around the main pool, however, isn't really large enough for the number of passengers carried , although there are several other outdoor areas for sunbathing, including a music-free Solstice Deck high atop the ship – a very nice space in which to relax.

The interior spaces are really well designed and passenger flow is good; most of the entertainment rooms are positioned forward, while dining venues are located in the aft section of the ship.

Celebrity's signature Martini Bar has a frosted bar and carries over 100 varieties of vodka, as well as martinis. It's lively (noisy) and can get congested, but it can be a lot of fun, as can the Molecular Bar, with its special mixologist concoctions, including fruits and ingredients, aided by liquid nitrogen.

Cellar Masters provides a cozy space for drinking wines. It is hosted by a proper sommelier; the wine list is extensive, and Reidel glasses are featured here. The room has several alcoves, so you really can hide away.

A two-deck library is a delightful open-ended space (operated on an 'honor' system – so you can check out a book 24/7), though books on the upper of 12 shelves are impossible to reach (actually, they are really only for show).

Fortunes Casino is a non-smoking gaming house with multiple gaming tables for serious players, and 235 slot machines. It is open sided, which means that anyone passing is subject to noise from the slot machines.

Elevator call buttons are located in a floor-stand 'pod' and, when an elevator arrives, a glass panel above it turns from blue to pink – neat! Also notable is a collection of designer chairs and sunloungers in various locations, although some are a little on the impractical side of comfort.

Public rooms include an Art Studio, for the budding artist in you (classes and projects are at extra cost).

And speaking of art, when on board, do take a look along the 'dining walkway' where several specialty restaurants are located –two pieces of art stand out. One is a delightful total optical illusion, by Anthony James (Kiln-dried birch trees, glass and steel mirrors 2,350 x 1,680 x 279mm); another is a fascinating video art piece that tells a story about a man, his flashlight, a forest, and things that happen in the forest – I won't tell you more – you'll simply have to experience it for yourself.

Passenger niggles include lack of usable drawer space in standard-grade cabins; congestion when exiting the showlounge after a show; and the noise level in all areas of the lobby (which has a marble dance floor), particularly when the Martini Bar on the deck above is busy. Gratuities are automatically charged to your onboard account.

FAMILIES. Play areas include the Fun Factory (for three- to 12-year-olds, featuring Leapfrog Schoolhouse's educational programs; and video game room; and 'X' Club – a teens-only chill-out room with a night-time dance club. Plenty of additional counsellors are provided during peak holiday periods.

ACCOMMODATION. From Penthouse Suites to small interior cabins, the accommodation is practical and comfortable. There are numerous price grades, depending on size and location. A wide range of accommodation includes 34 Aqua-class suites, plus a Reflection Suite (not aboard other Solstice-class ships). Suite-grade occupants get small bottles of Bulgari toiletries; everyone else doesn't. If your budget allows, book a suite-category cabin for all the extra benefits – and a lot more drawer space.

About 90 percent of the accommodation is in outside-view cabins. Of these, 85 percent have a balcony –

due to its slender width, there are very few interior cabins. There are seven suite-grade categories (compared to five aboard other Solstice-class ships): Reflection, Signature, Aqua, Penthouse, Royal, Celebrity, and Sky.

In the standard Interior and Ocean View cabins, there is little space between the bed and the wall, and the usable drawer space is poor, so, if you can afford it, book suite-grade accommodation for the extra benefits and perks it brings.

All grades of accommodation include: twin beds convertible to a queen-size bed, sitting area, vanity desk with hairdryer, but there's almost no drawer space. Also standard in all cabins: 32-inch flat-screen TVs (larger screens in suites), Wi-Fi Internet access (for a fee), premium bedding. However, although the closets have good hanging space, there are no shelves on which to place folded items, and drawers in the vanity desk can't accommodate such items. The bathroom has a shower enclosure, toilet, and tiny washbasin but no soap dish, and the faucet gets in the way when washing your face or brushing your teeth; there's no retractable clothesline for washed small items; and the two hooks on the back of the bathroom door are tiny. In suite-grade accommodation there is more space, larger balconies with good-quality sunloungers, and more personal amenities.

For the ultimate accommodation aboard this ship, book the Refection Suite. It is a stunning, high-ceilinged abode with two separate bedrooms, large balcony along the port side. The lounge is decorated in creams, beiges and chocolate, and the furniture is large and extremely comfortable, but it's the high ceiling, and infusion of natural light, because of its location, that really makes one feel special. The suite – together with five Signature-class suites – is located in a private, key-card access-only location almost atop the ship (it's next to the Sky Observation Lounge – the ship's disco at night). However, some noise can intrude from the basketball court on the deck above – when it's in use.

DINING. Meals in Opus, the ship's expansive two-level, 1,454-seat principal dining room, are included in the cruise price. It has ocean views on the port and starboard sides, and two seating times, and for anyone choosing 'Celebrity Select Dining' usually assigned to the upper level, which helps to keep the dining room running smoothly. The design is stunning, contemporary, and, despite the size of the restaurant, is extremely comfortable. A two-deck-high wine tower- located towards the aft of the room – provides a great focal point.

Celebrity Cruises prides itself on its cuisine, and rightly so. The company has placed more focus on providing the right kind of menu offerings for today's passengers.

Other dining options. Celebrity Cruises has been a lot more focus on providing cuisine choices that are creative, trendy, and slightly more health-oriented (i.e. reduced use of salt and food modifiers). If you like to dine in different venues rather than only in the main dining room, several dining packages are available, so you really can 'dine around.' The following venues provide an alternative to the main dining room, good for special occasions or just for something different (including a self-serve casual eatery, the Oceanview Café.

Murano is an extra-cost, 72-seat, reservations-required dinner venue (with tablecloths), offering high-quality traditional dining with a real French flair and fine table settings, including large Reidel wine glasses. The food, its preparation and presentation, and the service are outstanding – worth every cent.

Blu is a 156-seat specialty restaurant, with tablecloths, designated exclusively for occupants of Aqua-Class suites/cabins. The room has pleasing, cool ice white décor. The cuisine focuses slightly more on healthy combinations that are nicely presented.

Tuscan Grille is a 146-seat, extra-cost ($35 when I last sailed), no tablecloth informal restaurant, which presents both traditional and trendy fare with an Italian focus, but includes Kobe beef, premium quality steaks and seafood. Its entrance is shaped like a barrel, with nicely curved archways – it's like walking into a high-tech winery. Large aft-facing windows offer a great view over the ship's wake.

Qsine is an extra-cost, 92-seat reservations-required, tablecloth-less 'fun-food' restaurant, with trendy interactive iPad food and wine menus that include cute foodie video snaps. The food consists of multi-flavored, multi-colored, quirky small-bite items that provide you with a selection to tease your taste buds. The food is presented in many unusual ways – even on sticks – sort of 'lolipop' or 'circus' cuisine. It's a delightful experience that I can recommend.

Not a dining venue, but a wine tasting and enjoyment lounge, the 72-seat Cellar Masters features several alcoves for intimate discussions about wine. A wide choice is available, and a wine sommelier will make suggestions (about wine).

Bistro on Five (Deck 5, that is) is for coffee, cakes, crêpes, pastries, and more – it's a sort of French-style bistro-crêperie. It gets busy at times and the serving counter is small, so it can become congested, but the seating is comfortable.

Café al Bacio & Gelateria is a coffeehouse serving (extra cost) Lavazza Italian coffees and Tea Fort é teas and herbal infusions. It is on one side of the main lobby; it's quite small, and extremely popular. The seating is mostly in large, very comfortable armchairs.

And now, for something different – the Lawn Club. It's a patio-style outdoors (glass-covered) lean-to-style venue overlooking the lawn and reserve-able cabanas), and it's the place to go for beautifully grilled steaks, lamb chops, and seafood dishes. You can even grill the food to your liking – with a chef at your side, of course, just in case you burn your fingers!

Close by is The Porch, another enclosed venue, on the starboard side, with 48 seats, particularly for paninis and light bites throughout the day (including breakfast, with delightful fruit muffins and pastry items).

Oceanview Café and Grill is an expansive, tray-less, casual self-serve buffet venue. A number of food 'islands' help to prevent lines, and the flow is good; the signage is clear and concise. A wide variety of food items is available, and plates are available at each of the 'islands' and cooking stations (such as 'Eggs and More' for breakfast). However, it is challenging to get a warm plate for hot food items.

The AquaSpa Café is for light, healthier options – low-salt solarium dishes, including a choice of salad items – even a few sprouts, together with grilled items such as salmon and chicken; all are attractively presented.

The Mast Bar Grill, an outside venue above the main pool deck, provides comfort fast food items like burgers.

I do recommend that you try the Elegant Champagne High Tea in Murano. Presented only once each cruise (usually on a sea day), it comes with a choice of seven teas and tisanes, three-tier stand full of finger sandwiches and pastry items, plus scones and real clotted cream, and a glass of Perrier Jouet Champagne.

ENTERTAINMENT. The 1,160-seat Reflection Theater, the ship's main showlounge, has a main level and two balconied sections that are positioned amphitheater-style around the stage.

Colorful nights are held in the Sky Observation Lounge, whose daytime relaxing minimalist decor comes alive at night thanks to mood lighting effects.

Meanwhile, the 200-seat Celebrity Central hosts adult-only stand-up comedy, cooking demonstrations, enrichment lectures, and feature films.

Ensemble Lounge is a big-band-era-style cocktail lounge with live jazz-styled music, and is located close to specialty restaurant, Murano.

SPA/FITNESS. The AquaSpa is laid out over two decks. A large fitness center includes kinesis equipment, plus all the familiar muscle-pumping machinery.

An extra-cost (it's free to occupants of AquaSpa-grade accommodation) unisex thermal suite contains several steam and shower mist rooms with fragrances such as chamomile, eucalyptus, and mint, and a glacial ice fountain, plus a calming relaxation area with heated tiled beds.

Additionally a small fitness 'suite' (big enough for two persons), each with a selection of cardio-vascular machines, treadmills, etc. can be rented, so you can exercise in complete privacy. The spa is operated by Steiner Leisure.

Celebrity Silhouette
★★★★ +

Size:.	Large Resort Ship
Tonnage:	122,210
Lifestyle:	Premium
Cruise line:	Celebrity Cruises
Former names:	none
IMO number:	9451094
Builder:	Meyer Werft (Germany)
Original cost:	$641 million
Entered service:	Jul 2011
Registry:	Malta
Length (ft/m):	1,047.2/319.2
Beam (ft/m):	120.7/36.8
Draft (ft/m):	27.2/8.3
Propulsion/Propellers:	diesel (67.2MW)/2 azimuthing pods
Passenger decks:	14
Total crew:	1,210
Passengers (lower beds/alll berths):	2,886 /3,179
Passenger Space Ratio (lower beds/all berths):	42.3/38.4
Crew/Passenger Ratio (lower beds/all berths):	2.3/2.5

Cabins (total):	1,443
Size range (sq ft/m):	182.9–668.4/17.0–155.0
Cabins (outside view):	1,303
Cabins (interior/no view):	140
Cabins (for one person):	0
Cabins (with private balcony):	1,216
Cabins (wheelchair accessible):	30
Wheelchair accessibility:	Best
Cabin voltage:	110 and 220 volts
Elevators:	12
Casino (gaming tables):	Yes
Slot machines:	Yes
Swimming pools:	3
Hot tubs (on deck):	6
Self-service launderette:	No
Dedicated cinema/seats:	No
Library:	Yes
Onboard currency:	US$

Premium large ship with contemporary decor and style

OVERVIEW. *Celebrity Silhouette* is quite a sleek-looking ship, with two slim funnels, behind which, the ship recreates the great outdoors with the Lawn Club, an area with real Bermudan (not fake) grass. You can go putting, play croquet or bocce ball, or picnic on the grass, and it's a nice place to walk barefoot.

THE SHIP. *Celebrity Silhouette* is a sister ship to *Celebrity Eclipse, Celebrity Equinox, Celebrity Reflection* and *Celebrity Solstice.* Resort Deck is where you'll find several water-play areas: one within a glass-roofed solarium. However, the deck space around the two pools isn't large enough for the number of passengers carried. For open deck privacy, try 'The Alcoves'; these are garden cabanas for two to four persons, positioned on the lawn. They cost $149 per day on sea days and $99 on port days.

A favorite spot is Michael's Club, an intimate lounge with classic English leather club chairs and a handsome fireplace, plus more than 50 types of beer, whiskeys, and cognacs.

Part of the Lawn Club is an interactive Lawn Club Grill, while The Porch is a 48-seat eatery overlooking the lawn, for complimentary breakfast and lunches, plus specialty coffees, wine, and beer (at extra cost).

Near the Lawn Club entrance is The Art Studio, for art demonstrations and classes on various topics. Some are free; others cost extra.

Most of the entertainment rooms are positioned forward, while dining venues are located aft. There's

Berlitz's Ratings

	Possible	Achieved
Ship	500	416
Accommodation	200	165
Food	400	301
Service	400	307
Entertainment	100	78
Cruise	400	300

OVERALL SCORE
1567 points out of 2000

a wine bar with a sommelier; a jazz-age cocktail lounge; a bar with the look of an ocean-going yacht; Quasar, a bar with a nightly light show synchronized to music; and an observation lounge with a dance floor.

The two-deck library is a delightful open-ended space. The card room – located, unusually, in the center of the ship, with no ocean view windows to distract players – is open, and attracts noise from adjacent areas, so it's almost useless as a serious card playing room. Fortunes Casino (non-smoking) has 16 gaming tables and 200 slot machines.

Celebrity's signature Martini Bar carries over 100 varieties of vodka, as well as martinis. There's also a small alcove called Crush with an ice-filled table where you can participate in caviar and vodka tasting, or host a private party. It's very noisy and congested, but can be a lot of fun.

Passenger niggles include lack of usable drawer space in cabins; inadequate children's facilities and staff in school holidays; congestion when you exit the showlounge; and noise in all areas of the lobby when the martini bar is busy.

Gratuities are charged to your onboard account.

FAMILIES. Play areas include the Fun Factory (for three- to 12-year-olds, featuring Leapfrog School-house's educational programs); and 'X Club' – a high-tech teens-only chill-out room with coffee bar and dance club.

ACCOMMODATION. From Penthouse Suites to small interior cabins, the accommodation is practical and comfortable. There are numerous price grades, depending on size and location. In standard Interior and Ocean View cabins, there is little space between the bed and the wall, and usable drawer space is poor. So, if your budget allows, book a suite-category cabin for all the extra benefits – and a lot more drawer space.

The suite-grade categories are: Royal Suite, Celebrity Suite, Sky Suite, and Penthouse Suite. Most of the balcony cabins on Penthouse Deck and Sky Deck suffer from permanent shade because they are just under the wide deck overhang – the large suites surrounding the aft elevator foyers get much more sunlight.

All grades of accommodation include: twin beds convertible to a queen-size bed, sitting area, vanity desk with hairdryer. Also standard in all cabins: 32-inch flat-screen TVs (larger screens in suites), Wi-Fi Internet access (for a fee), premium bedding. However, although the closets have good hanging space, other storage is limited. The rather cramped bathroom has a shower enclosure, toilet, and tiny washbasin. In suite-grade accommodation there is more space, larger balconies and more personal amenities.

Some 130 'AquaSpa'-class cabins incorporate spa elements into the cabins, and allow access to the AquaSpa's Thermal Relaxation Room and a Persian Garden (with aromatherapy/steam rooms) on the same deck, and other spa amenities. Occupants get assigned seating in Blu Restaurant. Facilities include: a choice of four pillows (conformance, body, goose, isotonic); express luggage delivery; shoeshine; Frette bathrobes; dining and seating preferences in other specialty dining venues; and early embarkation and disembarkation. Bathrooms include a tub plus a separate shower.

Other accommodation grades are Veranda-class, Sunset-Veranda-class, Concierge-class, Family Oceanview with veranda, Deluxe Oceanview with veranda, Standard Oceanview, and Standard Interior cabins.

DINING. Grand Cuvée is the ship's 1,430-seat main dining room – included in the cruise price – is spread over two decks and has ocean views on the port and starboard sides and at the stern. The design is stunning and contemporary. Towards the aft section, a two-deck-high wine tower provides an eye-catching focal point (I'd like to have dinner inside it!).

Other dining options. Murano is an extra-cost, reservations-required, 70-seat dinner venue (with tablecloths), offering high-quality traditional dining with a French flair and gorgeous table settings. The cuisine and service are extremely good.

Blu is a 128-seat specialty restaurant, with tablecloths, exclusively for the occupants of AquaClass cabins. The room has pleasing, but rather cool decor.

The 144-seat Tuscan Grille, an extra-cost, tablecloth-less venue, serves Italian cuisine, Kobe beef and premium quality steaks, and has nicely curved archways – it's like walking into a high-tech winery. Large aft-facing windows offer a great view over the ship's wake.

Qsine is a 90-seat 'fun-food' venue. The food consists of multi-flavored, multi-colored, quirky small-bite items. The food is presented in many unusual ways – even on sticks – sort of 'lolipop' cuisine. It's a delightful experience.

Bistro on Five (Deck 5, that is) is for coffee, cakes, crepes, pastries, and more. The serving counter becomes congested at busy times.

Café al Bacio & Gelateria is a coffeehouse featuring Lavazza Italian coffee, situated on one side of the main lobby, lines quickly form at peak times.

Oceanview Café and Grill is a tray-less, casual self-serve buffet venue. There are a number of food 'islands' and the signage is reasonable.

The AquaSpa Café is for light, healthier options (solarium fare), but the selections are uninspiring.

The Mast Bar Grill and Bar is an outside fast-food venue.

ENTERTAINMENT. The 900-seat Celebrity Theater is the three-deck-high venue for production shows and major cabaret acts.

Colorful theme nights are held in the Observation Lounge (whose daytime bland and minimalist decor comes alive at night thanks to mood lighting effects). The 200-seat Celebrity Central hosts comedy, cooking demonstrations, lectures, and films.

An Entertainment Court showcases street performers, psychics, and caricaturists, and is in the center of the ship, linked to Quasar, a high-pulse, high-volume nightclub. The Ensemble Lounge is a big-band-era cocktail lounge with live music.

SPA/FITNESS. The AquaSpa measures 24,219 sq ft (2,250 sq m). It includes a large thalassotherapy pool under a solarium glass dome, complete with health bar for light food and fresh squeezed juices.

Spa facilities include 25 treatment rooms, including one specifically designed for wheelchair passengers. There's also an aerobics room, a gymnasium, large men's and women's saunas with a sizable ocean-view window, and a beauty salon.

An extra-cost (it's free to occupants of AquaSpa-grade accommodation) unisex thermal suite contains several steam and shower mist rooms with fragrances such as chamomile, eucalyptus, and mint, and a glacial ice fountain, plus a calming relaxation area with heated tiled beds.

Celebrity Solstice
★★★★ +

Size:.....................................Large Resort Ship	Cabins (total):....................................... 1,426
Tonnage: 121,878	Size range (sq ft/m): 182.9–1,668.4/17.0–155.0
Lifestyle: ....Premium	Cabins (outside view):................................ 1,286
Cruise line:............................. Celebrity Cruises	Cabins (interior/no view):................................140
Former names: ....none	Cabins (for one person):...................................0
IMO number: 9362530	Cabins (with private balcony):........................ 1,216
Builder: .... Meyer Werft (Germany)	Cabins (wheelchair accessible): 30
Original cost:.................................. $641 million	Wheelchair accessibility:........................... Best
Entered service:............................... Nov 2008	Cabin voltage:.........................110 and 220 volts
Registry:.. Malta	Elevators:..12
Length (ft/m):............................1,033.4/315.0	Casino (gaming tables):............................... Yes
Beam (ft/m):............................... 120.7/36.8	Slot machines:....................................... Yes
Draft (ft/m): 27.2/8.3	Swimming pools:...2
Propulsion/Propellers:..... diesel (67,200kW)/2 azimuthing pods	Hot tubs (on deck):.....................................6
Passenger decks:....................................14	Self-service launderette:............................. Yes
Total crew:...................................... 1,210	Dedicated cinema/seats:...............................No
Passengers (lower beds/alll berths):............. 2,852/3,145	Library:... Yes
Passenger Space Ratio (lower beds/all berths): 42.7/38.7	Onboard currency: ....US$
Crew/Passenger Ratio (lower beds/all berths):.......... 2.3/2.5	

Elegant, understated decor in a premium setting

OVERVIEW. *Celebrity Solstice* is a sleek-looking ship, with two slim funnels.

THE SHIP. *Celebrity Solstice* has a steeply sloping stern, which includes a mega-yacht-style duck-tail platform above the propulsion pods, and is quite attractive. The ship's name is positioned directly under the navigation bridge and not forward on the bows (for space reasons), and the rounded bows accommodate a helicopter winch pad. An unusual feature is a outdoor grass area called the Lawn Club. The 'club' is open to all, so you can go putting, play croquet or bocce ball, or have a picnic on the grass, and it's a nice place to walk barefoot.

Several pool and water-play areas are positioned on Resort Deck: one within a glass-roofed solarium, a sports pool, a family pool, and a wet zone. The deck space around the two pools, however, isn't large enough for the number of passengers carried.

The interior spaces are well designed, and the decor is elegant yet contemporary; most of the entertainment rooms are positioned forward, while dining venues are mostly located in the aft section of the ship.

There's a wine bar with a sommelier; a pre-dinner cocktail lounge that reflects the jazz age of the 1930s and '40s; a bar with the look of an ocean-going yacht; Quasar, a retro bar with large screens that create a nightly light show synchronized to music; and an observation lounge with a dance floor.

Celebrity's signature Martini Bar carries over 100 varieties of vodka, as well as martinis. There's also a

Berlitz's Ratings

	Possible	Achieved
Ship	500	406
Accommodation	200	165
Food	400	297
Service	400	306
Entertainment	100	78
Cruise	400	299
OVERALL SCORE		
1551 points out of 2000		

small alcove called Crush with an ice-filled table where you can participate in caviar and vodka tasting, or host a private party. It's very noisy and congested, but can be a lot of fun.

A two-deck library is a delightful open-ended space, though books on the upper shelves are impossible to reach. The card room – located in the center of the ship, with no ocean view windows to distract players – is open and attracts noise from adjacent areas, so it's useless as a serious card playing room. Fortunes Casino (non-smoking) has 16 gaming tables and 200 slot machines.

An innovative Hot Glass Show, housed in an outdoor studio on the open deck as part of the Lawn Club and created in collaboration with Corning Museum of Glass, includes demonstrations of glass-blowing. However, it's a novelty, which may be why *Celebrity Reflection* and *Celebrity Silhouette* have replaced the glass show with an interactive Lawn Club Grill.

Public rooms include an Art Studio, for your artistic needs. Meanwhile The Alcoves are extra-cost 'private' Wi-Fi-equipped cabanas on deck, and cost $149 per day on sea days and $99 on port days.

Passenger niggles include lack of usable drawer space in cabins; inadequate children's facilities and staff during school holidays; congestion when you exit the showlounge; and noise in the lobby when the martini bar is busy.

Gratuities are automatically charged to your onboard account.

FAMILIES. Play areas include the Fun Factory (for three- to 12-year-olds, featuring Leapfrog Schoolhouse's educational programs); and 'X Club' – a high-tech teens-only chill-out room with coffee bar and a night-time dance club.

ACCOMMODATION. From Penthouse Suites to small interior cabins, the accommodation is practical and comfortable. There are many different price grades, depending on size and location. In standard Interior and Ocean View cabins, there is little space between the bed and the wall, and usable drawer space is poor. So, if your budget allows, book a suite-category cabin for all the extra benefits – and a lot more drawer space.

About 90 percent of the accommodation is in outside-view cabins. Of these, 85 percent have a balcony, and, due to the ship's slender width, there are few interior cabins. There are four suite-grade categories: Royal Suite, Celebrity Suite, Sky Suite, and Penthouse Suite.

All grades of accommodation include: twin beds convertible to a queen-size bed, sitting area, vanity desk with hairdryer, but almost no drawer space. Also standard in all cabins: 32-inch flat-screen TVs (larger screens in suites), Wi-Fi Internet access (for a fee), premium bedding. Although the closets have good hanging space, storage space is limited. The bathroom is small, with a shower, toilet, and tiny washbasin, and there's no retractable clothesline.

Some 130 AquaSpa-class cabins share the relaxation room of the AquaSpa itself, incorporate select spa elements into the cabins, and allow for specialized access to the AquaSpa's Thermal Relaxation Room and Persian Garden (with aromatherapy/steam rooms) on the same deck. Features include: a choice of four pillows (conformance, body, goose, Isotonic); express luggage delivery; shoeshine; Frette bathrobes; dining and seating preferences in dining venues; and early embarkation and disembarkation. In suite-grade accommodation there is more space, larger balconie and bathrooms, and more personal amenities. Occupants also get assigned seating at the exclusive 130-seat Restaurant Blu.

Other accommodation grades are Veranda-class, Sunset-Veranda-class, Concierge-class, Family Oceanview with veranda, Deluxe Oceanview with veranda, Standard Oceanview, and Standard Interior cabins.

Cabins 1551–1597 on the port side and 1556–1602 on the starboard side on Penthouse Deck (Deck 11) suffer from 'aircraft carrier' syndrome because they are directly under the huge overhanging Resort Deck. They have little exposure to sun or light, and thick supporting struts ruin the view from these cabins, which are otherwise pleasantly fitted out.

DINING. Grand Epernay, the principal dining room that's included in the cruise price, is located towards the aft of the ship, and has ocean views on both sides. The design is stunning and contemporary; however, the almost-backless tub-style chairs are not comfortable. At the forward end, a two-deck high wine tower provides a stunning focal point. The food is disappointing; the decreased quality is all too obvious to repeat Celebrity passengers.

Other dining options. Murano is an extra-cost, reservations-required venue offering high-quality traditional dining with a French flair and fine table settings.

Blu is a 130-seat specialty restaurant designated for occupants of AquaClass cabins. The room has pleasing (but rather cold) blue decor. The ambience is cool.

The Tuscan Grille, an extra-cost, reservations-required venue, serves Kobe beef and premium quality steaks.

Silk Harvest is a Southeast Asian extra-cost dining venue serving unmemorable pan-Asian fusion cuisine.

Bistro on Five (Deck 5, that is) is for coffee, cakes, crêpes, pastries, and more. It gets busy at times and the serving counter is small, so it's a congested area.

Café al Bacio & Gelateria is a small coffeehouse serving Lavazza Italian coffee, situated on one side of the main lobby; lines quickly form at peak times.

Oceanview Café and Grill is the expansive, tray-less, casual self-serve buffet venue. There are a number of food 'islands' rather than those awful straight buffet counters. The signage is reasonable, but condiments are hard to find.

The AquaSpa Café is for light, healthier options (solarium fare), but the selections need improvement.

ENTERTAINMENT. The 1,115-seat Solstice Theater, the main showlounge, stages three circus-themed production shows. Colorful theme nights are held in the Observation Lounge. The 200-seat Celebrity Central hosts comedy, cooking demonstrations, enrichment lectures, and feature films. Quasar is a high-pulse, high-volume nightclub. An Entertainment Court showcases street performers, psychics, and caricaturists, and is in the center of the ship. The Ensemble Lounge is a big-band-era cocktail lounge with live jazz, next to the Murano restaurant.

SPA/FITNESS. The AquaSpa is laid out over two decks. A large fitness center includes kinesis (pulleys against gravity) workout equipment, plus all the familiar muscle-pumping cardio-vascular machinery. An extra-cost, unisex thermal suite features several steam and shower mist rooms with fragrances such as chamomile, eucalyptus, and mint, and a glacial ice fountain, plus a calming relaxation area with heated tiled beds. There's also an acupuncture center. Massages include fashionable things such as Herbal Poultice massage and Bamboo massage.

Celebrity Summit
★★★★

Size:.	.Large Resort Ship
Tonnage:	91,000
Lifestyle:	.Premium
Cruise line:	Celebrity Cruises
Former names:	.Summit
IMO number:	9192387
Builder:	Chantiers de l'Atlantique (France)
Original cost:	$350 million
Entered service:	Nov 2001
Registry:	Malta
Length (ft/m):	964.5/294.0
Beam (ft/m):	105.6/32.2
Draft (ft/m):	26.2/8.0
Propulsion/Propellers: . gas turbine (39,000kW)/2 azimuthing pods	
Passenger decks:	11
Total crew:	999
Passengers (lower beds/alll berths):	1,950/2,450
Passenger Space Ratio (lower beds/all berths):	46.6/37.1
Crew/Passenger Ratio (lower beds/all berths):	1.9/2.4

Cabins (total):	975
Size range (sq ft/m):	165.1–2,530.0/15.34–235.0
Cabins (outside view):	780
Cabins (interior/no view):	195
Cabins (for one person):	0
Cabins (with private balcony):	590
Cabins (wheelchair accessible):	26 (17 with private balcony)
Wheelchair accessibility:	Best
Cabin voltage:	110 and 220 volts
Elevators:	12
Casino (gaming tables):	Yes
Slot machines:	Yes
Swimming pools:	3 (1 w/sliding glass dome)
Hot tubs (on deck):	4
Self-service launderette:	No
Dedicated cinema/seats:	Yes/368
Library:	Yes
Onboard currency:	US$

A premium-quality ship for family-friendly cruising

OVERVIEW. *Celebrity Summit* is a sister ship to *Celebrity Constellation*, *Celebrity Infinity* and *Celebrity Millennium*. The accommodation is extremely comfortable in all grades, and only the two sittings for dining and for the nightly shows detract from an otherwise excellent product.

THE SHIP. Jon Bannenberg, designer of mega-yachts, was responsible for the exterior that has a royal blue and white hull, although it has actually turned out to look extremely ungainly. In early 2012, the ship underwent a 'Solsticizing' program which added more cabins, more facilities and more dining options to match the newer ships in the fleet.

Inside, the ship has a similar standard of decor and materials, and public rooms that make ships in the fleet so user-friendly. The atrium is three decks high and houses the reception desk, tour operator's desk, and bank. Four dramatic glass-walled elevators travel through the ship's exterior (port) side, connecting the atrium with another seven decks, thus traveling through 10 passenger decks, including the tender stations – a nice ride.

Facilities include a combination Cinema/Conference Center, an expansive shopping arcade with 14,447 sq ft (1,300 sq m) of retail store space (with brand name labels such as Fendi, Fossil, Hugo Boss, and Versace), a lavish four-deck-high showlounge with high-tech sound and lighting, a two-level library (one level for English-language books; a second for other languages and reference material), card room, music

Berlitz's Ratings

	Possible	Achieved
Ship	500	389
Accommodation	200	161
Food	400	285
Service	400	290
Entertainment	100	74
Cruise	400	288
OVERALL SCORE		
1487 points out of 2000		

listening room, and an observation lounge/discotheque with fine views.

Michael's Club, formerly a cigar smoker's haven, is now a rather nice lounge/piano bar offering over 50 craft beers plus fine whiskies and cognacs. An Internet café has almost 20 computers and extra-cost Internet connectivity.

The artwork throughout the ship (particularly the sculptures) is eclectic, provocative, thoughtful, and intelligent, and at almost every turn another piece appears to break the monotony associated with large spaces.

Gaming sports include the ship's overly large Fortunes Casino, with lots of bright lights and action. Families with children will appreciate the Fun Factory (for children) and The Tower (for teenagers). Children's counselors and youth activities staff provide a wide range of supervised activities.

Note that there is, sadly, no walk-around wooden promenade deck outdoors. Standing in line for embarkation, disembarkation, shore tenders, and for self-serve buffet meals is an inevitable aspect of cruising aboard all large ships (however, more flexible embarkation hours do help to spread the flow), but the worst time is when large numbers of passengers return from shore excursions and have to go through a security check, resulting in long lines outside the ship. Also, passengers have to fit their evening schedules around the ship's two sittings for dining and shows. All in all though, this ship – together with sister ships *Celebrity Constellation*, *Celebrity Infinity*, and *Celebrity Millen-*

nium – are among the very best of the ships in the Premium segment of the marketplace.

A 15 percent gratuity is added to all bar and wine accounts.

ACCOMMODATION. There are many different grades from which to choose, depending on your preference for the size and location of your living space. Almost half of the ship's accommodation features a "private" balcony; approximately 80 percent are ocean-view suites and cabins, and the rest are interior cabins. All the accommodation is extremely comfortable. Suites, naturally, have more space, butler service (whether you want it or not), more and better amenities and more personal service than standard cabin grades.

There are several categories of suites; those at the stern are in a prime location and have huge balconies that are very private and not overlooked. All suites and cabins have wood cabinetry and accenting, interactive television and entertainment systems – you can shop, book shore excursions, play games, and even watch soft-porn movies. Bathrooms have hairdryers, and 100 percent cotton towels.

Penthouse Suites (2). These suites, on Penthouse Deck, are like apartments. Each occupies one half of the width of the ship, overlooking the stern. Each is a huge 2,530 sq ft (235 sq m): 1,432 sq ft (133 sq m) of living space, plus a huge wraparound balcony of 1,098 sq ft (102 sq m). It includes a wet bar, hot tub, and whirlpool tub, but much of this terrace can be overlooked from other decks above.

Features include a marble foyer, a separate living room complete with ebony baby grand piano, and a formal dining room. The master bedroom has a large walk-in closet; personal exercise equipment; dressing room with vanity desk; marble-clad master bathroom with twin washbasins; separate shower; toilet and bidet areas; flat-screen televisions (one in the bedroom and one in the lounge); and electronically controlled drapes. Butler service is standard, and a butler's pantry, with separate entry door, houses a full-size refrigerator, temperature-controlled wine cabinet, microwave oven, and food preparation and storage areas. For even more space, an interconnecting door can be opened into the adjacent suite.

Royal Suites (8). These are located towards the aft (four each on the port and starboard sides). Each measures 733 sq ft (68 sq m) and has a separate bedroom, dining and lounge areas (with refrigerator, mini-bar, and a Bang & Olufsen audio system). There are two entertainment centers with DVD players, flat-screen TV sets in the living area and in the bedroom, and a large walk-in closet with vanity desk. The marble-clad bathroom has a whirlpool tub with integral shower, and there are also a separate shower enclosure, two washbasins, and toilet. The teakwood decked balcony is extensive – large enough for on-deck massage – and has a hot tub.

Celebrity Suites (8). These measure 467 sq ft (44 sq m) and have floor-to-ceiling windows, a separate living room with dining and lounge areas, two entertainment centers with flat-screen TV sets in the living room and in the bedroom, and a walk-in closet with vanity desk. The marble-clad bathroom has a whirlpool tub with integral shower; a window with movable shade lets you look out of the bathroom through the lounge to the large ocean-view windows. Balconies were added in the 2011 refit.

Interconnecting doors allow two suites to be used as a family unit. These suites, located opposite a group of glass-walled elevators, overhang the ship's starboard side, and provide stunning ocean views from the lounge/dining area. A personal computer with wood-surround screen connects to the Internet.

Sky Suites (30). Each is 308 sq ft (29 sq m), including the private balcony – some balconies may be larger than others, depending on the location. Although these are designated as suites, they are really just larger cabins that have a marble-clad bathroom with tub/shower combination.

Butler Service. Provided in all suite accommodation, this service includes full breakfast, in-suite lunch and dinner (as required), afternoon tea, evening hors d'oeuvres, complimentary espresso and cappuccino, daily news delivery, and shoeshine.

Suite occupants in Penthouse, Royal, Celebrity, and Sky suites also get welcome Champagne; a personal computer in each suite, including a printer and Internet access (on request in the Sky Suites); choice of films; personalized stationery; tote bag; priority dining room seating preferences; private portrait sitting; bathrobe; and in-suite massage service.

Concierge Class. In 2003, Celebrity Cruises added a third service 'class' to the accommodation grades. Positioned between the top grade suite grades and standard cabin grades, Concierge Class offers added value to these 'middle-class' cabins, as does a new 'Aqua Class,' added in 2012, with spa-healthy dining in the exclusive Blu Restaurant, and complimentary access to the Persian Garden (thermal suite) and Relaxation Room in the spa, plus daily delivery of bottled water and herbal teas (infusions), and a host of spa-related personal amenities.

Enhanced facilities include priority embarkation, disembarkation, tender tickets, specialty dining, and spa reservations. Concierge Class cabin occupants get double bed overlay (no more 'falling between the cracks' for couples); choice of four pillows (goose down pillow, isotonic pillow, body pillow, conformance pillow); eight-vial flower vase on vanity desk; throw pillows on sofa; fruit basket; binoculars; golf umbrella; leather telephone notepad; larger beach towels; hand-held hairdryer. The balcony gets better furniture. In the bathrooms: plusher Frette bathrobes; larger towels in sea green and pink (alternating days); flower in silver vase. It all adds up to excellent value for money.

Standard Outside-View/Interior Cabins. All other outside-view and interior cabins have a lounge area with sofa or convertible sofa bed, sleeping area with twin beds that can convert to a double bed, ample closet and drawer space, personal safe, mini-bar/refrigerator (extra cost), and interactive TV. The cabins are nicely decorated with warm wood-finish furniture, and there is none of the boxy feel of cabins in so many ships, due to the angled placement of vanity and audio-video consoles. Even the smallest cabin has a good-size bathroom and shower.

Wheelchair-Accessible Accommodation. This is available in various grades and practical locations, close to elevators. All doorways and bathroom doorways and showers are wheelchair-accessible. Some cabins have extra berths for third or third and fourth occupants.

Concierge Class. In 2003, Celebrity Cruises added a third service 'class' to some of this ship's accommodation grades. Positioned between the top grade suite grades and standard cabin grades, Concierge Class offers added value to these 'middle-class' cabins, as does a new 'Aqua Class,' added in 2012, with spa-healthy dining in the exclusive Blu restaurant, and complimentary access to the Persian Garden (thermal suite) and Relaxation Room in the spa, plus daily delivery of bottled water and herbal teas (infusions), and a host of spa-related personal amenities.

Enhanced facilities include priority embarkation, disembarkation, tender tickets, specialty dining, and spa reservations. Concierge Class cabin occupants get double bed overlay (no more 'falling between the cracks' for couples); choice of four pillows (goose down pillow, isotonic pillow, body pillow, conformance pillow); eight-vial flower vase on vanity desk; throw pillows on sofa; fruit basket; binoculars; golf umbrella; leather telephone notepad; larger beach towels; handheld hairdryer. The balcony gets better furniture. In the bathrooms: plusher Frette bathrobes; larger towels in sea green and pink (alternating days); flower in silver vase. It all adds up to excellent value for money.

DINING. The Cosmopolitan Restaurant is a 1,170-seat main dining room. It is two decks high and has a grand staircase connecting the two levels, a huge glass wall overlooking the sea at the stern of the ship (electrically operated shades provide several different backdrops), and a musician's gallery on the upper level, typically for a string quartet or quintet. As a tribute to the French Line ship *Normandie*, a statue created by Leon-Georges Baudry, called *La Normandie*, that once overlooked the ship's grand staircase and for the past 47 years graced Miami's Fontainebleu Hotel, was bought for $250,000 and can now be seen here. There are two seatings for dinner (it's an open seating for breakfast and lunch), at tables for two, four, six, eight, or 10.

The dining room, like all large dining halls, can be extremely noisy. The menu variety is good, the food has taste, and it is attractively presented and served in a well-orchestrated fashion that displays European traditions and training. Full service in-cabin dining is also available for all meals, including dinner (with items from the Cosmopolitan Restaurant menu).

Other dining options. The extra-cost, reservations-only specialty dining option is the 134-seat Normandie Restaurant, with gold-lacquered paneling from the smoking room of the original French Line ship.

A team of chefs prepares the cuisine exclusively for this restaurant. Fine tableside preparation is the attraction and both the classic French cuisine and service are good. This is haute cuisine at the height of professionalism, for this is a room for a full dégustation, and not just a dinner. However, with only 134 seats, not all passengers will be able to experience it; reservations are necessary, and a per-person cover charge applies. A dine-in wine cellar is located at one end of the restaurant, and a demonstration galley is at the other.

QSine, which features its menus and wine list on iPads, is another extra-cost, fine dining venue, and reservations are required.

Tuscan Grille is an extra-cost, reservations required venue that features premium-quality steaks.

There are several other options in more casual settings.

The Waterfall Café and Grill is a casual self-serve buffet area, with six principal serving lines, and seating for 754; there is also a grill and pizza bar. For Champagne and caviar lovers, and martinis, Carlisle's is the place to see and be seen.

Café al Bacio and Gelateria, on the third level of the atrium lobby, is the place for coffees, pastries, cakes, and gelato, in a trendy setting. Meanwhile, Bistro on Five is a popular French crêperie.

ENTERTAINMENT. The 900-seat Celebrity Theater is the three-deck-high venue for the ship's production shows and major cabaret acts. It is located in the forward part of the ship, with seating on main, and two balcony levels. The large stage is equipped with a full fly loft behind its traditional proscenium.

SPA/FITNESS. A large AquaSpa measures 24,219 sq ft (2,250 sq m). It has a large thalassotherapy pool under a solarium dome, complete with health bar for fresh squeezed fruit and vegetable juices. There are 16 treatment rooms, plus eight treatment rooms with showers and one treatment room designed for wheelchair passengers, an aerobics room, gymnasium with over 40 machines, male and female saunas (with a large ocean-view porthole window), a unisex thermal suite containing steam and shower mist rooms, and a salon. The spa is operated by Steiner, a specialist concession.

Sports facilities include a full-size basketball court, compact football, paddle tennis and volleyball, golf simulator, shuffleboard on two different decks, and a jogging track.

Celebrity Xpedition
★★★+

Size:........................Boutique Ship			
Tonnage:..........................2,842			
Lifestyle:.........................Premium			
Cruise line:...............Celebrity Cruises			
Former names:.....................Sun Bay			
IMO number:......................9228368			
Builder:...............Cassens-Werft (Germany)			
Original cost:...............DM 35 million			
Entered service:............Jun 2001/Jun 2004			
Registry:.......................The Bahamas			
Length (ft/m):.................290.3/88.5			
Beam (ft/m):......................45.9/14.0			
Draft (ft/m):.......................11.4/3.5			
Propulsion/Propellers:........diesel (3,000kW)/2			
Passenger decks:........................4			
Total crew:............................64			
Passengers (lower beds/alll berths):.........90/95			
Passenger Space Ratio (lower beds/all berths):.......31.5/29.9			
Crew/Passenger Ratio (lower beds/all berths):.........1.4/1.4			

Cabins (total):..............................45
Size range (sq ft/m):.........156.0–460.0/14.5–42.7
Cabins (outside view):.........................45
Cabins (interior/no view):.......................0
Cabins (for one person):........................0
Cabins (with private balcony):....................8
Cabins (wheelchair accessible):...................0
Wheelchair accessibility:.....................None
Cabin voltage:..........................220 volts
Elevators:...................................0
Casino (gaming tables):........................No
Slot machines:...............................No
Swimming pools:..............................No
Hot tubs (on deck):............................1
Self-service launderette:.......................No
Dedicated cinema/seats:........................No
Library:....................................Yes
Onboard currency:...........................US$

A comfortable ship for exploring the Galápagos Islands

OVERVIEW. This was the first specialist boutique ship for Celebrity Cruises and is like a small private club, providing ecotourism of the best kind. It will suit mature adults who want an intimate and casual cruise experience, to see the Galápagos Islands.

THE SHIP. *Celebrity Xpedition* has a surprisingly good amount of open deck space –much of it with teakwood decking, as well as teak sunloungers and patio furniture. Although there is no swimming pool, there is a whirlpool tub. Stabilizers were installed in 2004.

All accommodation is located forward half, with public rooms aft. The ambience is unhurried, yet subtly elegant. Except for the dining room, which can double as a conference room, there is only one public room: the main lounge, complete with bar, dance floor, and bandstand.

Shore excursions by Zodiac inflatable boats are in small groups led by Ecuadorian guides. On your return, waiters greet you with refreshing drinks and towels. Included in the fare: excursions, gratuities to shipboard staff, beverages including house wine, Champagne, liquor, beer, and soda.

ACCOMMODATION. There are four price categories in two cabin types: nine Suites measuring 247 sq ft (23 sq m); 34 Comfort Cabins, 172 sq ft (16 sq m); and three Comfort cabins, 156 sq ft (14.5 sq m). All suites and cabins have twin beds (four comfort cabins

Berlitz's Ratings

	Possible	Achieved
Ship	500	334
Accommodation	200	140
Food	400	272
Service	400	290
Entertainment	100	62
Cruise	400	252

OVERALL SCORE
1350 points out of 2000

have a double bed), TV, sofa, drinks table, vanity desk with hairdryer, mini-bar/refrigerator, and personal safe. Bathrooms all have a good-size shower enclosure (there are no tubs) with soap/shampoo dispenser, black granite washbasin, and white marble-clad walls.

The largest accommodation is in nine suites, each with a private balcony. One suite is located forward, with forward-facing views, and has a sloping ceiling with character. Balcony partitions are almost private; the balcony deck is teak covered. Two of the suites can be joined together. One bedroom has two pull-down Murphy beds.

DINING. The Darwin Dining Room operates on an open-seating basis. A self-serve buffet offers salads, cold cuts, and cheeses. House wines and beer are included in the fare; a few better wines can be bought. The cuisine depends on local suppliers; fish seafood and fruits are good, but vegetables are inconsistent. The casual, self-serve Seagull Buffet is just behind the main lounge, with teak tables and chairs.

ENTERTAINMENT. Dinner and after-dinner conversation with fellow passengers is the main entertainment.

SPA/FITNESS. There is a small fitness room, and adjacent unisex sauna located inside on the uppermost deck, while a small beauty salon is located on the lowest deck.

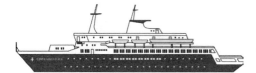

Clipper Adventurer
★★

Size:. . . . . Boutique ship	Cabins (total):. 61
Tonnage: 5,750	Size range (sq ft/m): 119.0–211.0/
Lifestyle: . . . . .Standard	Cabins (outside view): 61
Cruise line:. . . . . Quark Expeditions	Cabins (interior/no view):. 0
Former names: . . . . Alla Tarasova	Cabins (for one person):. 0
IMO number: 7391422	Cabins (with private balcony):. 0
Builder: . . . . Brodgradiliste Uljanik, (Yugoslavia)	Cabins (wheelchair accessible): 0
Original cost: . . . . n/a	Wheelchair accessibility:. . . . . .None
Entered service:. 1976/2011	Cabin voltage: . . . . 220 volts
Registry:. . . . . The Bahamas	Elevators:. 0
Length (ft/m):. 328.0/100.0	Casino (gaming tables):. . . . . .No
Beam (ft/m):. 53.2/16.2	Slot machines:. . . . . .No
Draft (ft/m): 15.2/4.6	Swimming pools:. 0
Propulsion/Propellers: . . . . .diesel (3,884kW)/2	Hot tubs (on deck):. 0
Passenger decks:. 5	Self-service launderette:. . . . . .No
Total crew:. 72	Dedicated cinema/seats:. . . . . .No
Passengers (lower beds/alll berths):. 122/122	Library:. . . . . Yes
Passenger Space Ratio (lower beds/all berths): 47.1/47.1	Onboard currency: . . . . .US$
Crew/Passenger Ratio (lower beds/all berths):. 1.4/1.4	

A hardy expedition ship suited to the Arctic and Antarctica

OVERVIEW. *Clipper Adventurer* is a solidly-built small ship. It has an ice-strengthened (A-1 ice classification), and a royal blue hull and white funnel, bow-thruster, and stabilizers.

THE SHIP. *Clipper Adventurer* is best suited to couples and single travelers who enjoy nature and wildlife up close and personal. However, even with an ice classification, the ship got stuck in an ice field in the Bellingshausen Sea in 2000. It also ran aground in 2010 in the Canadian Arctic. But all is now back to normal, helped by the ship's very tough, deep-draft hull.

There are 10 Zodiac rigid inflatable craft for landings and in-depth excursions, and a covered promenade deck. This cozy ship caters to travelers rather than mere passengers. The dress code is casual during the day, although at night many passengers wear jacket and tie. The public spaces are a little limited, with just one main lounge and bar. There is a small library, with high wingback chairs.

There is no observation lounge with forward-facing views, although there is an outdoor observation area directly below the bridge. Until 2015, the ship is operated under charter by Quark Expeditions, which provides its own expedition staff and experienced geologists. Naturalist lecturers accompany all cruise expeditions. Smoking is permitted only on the outside decks.

The passageways are narrow, and outer deck stairways are steep.

Berlitz's Ratings

	Possible	Achieved
Ship	500	219
Accommodation	200	99
Food	400	190
Service	400	211
Entertainment	100	40
Cruise	400	186
OVERALL SCORE		
945 points out of 2000		

ACCOMMODATION. There are seven grades of cabin, including a dedicated price for single occupancy. All cabins have outside views and twin lower beds, with private bathroom with shower, and toilet. The bathrooms are really tiny, although they are tiled, and have all the basics. Several double-occupancy cabins can be booked by single travelers, but special rates apply.

All cabins have a lockable drawer for valuables, telephone, and individual temperature control. Some have picture windows, while others have portholes. Two larger cabins (called suites in the brochure, which they really are not) are quite well equipped for the size of the vessel.

DINING. The dining room, with deep ocean-view windows, accommodates all passengers at a single seating. The food, a combination of American and Continental cuisine, is prepared freshly by chefs trained at some of America's finest culinary institutions. The food, however, is quite disappointing. There are limited menu choices, and far too much use of canned fruits and juices, particularly for breakfasts, which are repetitive. Casual, self-service breakfast and luncheon buffets are taken in the main lounge.

ENTERTAINMENT. After-dinner conversation in the lounge/bar is the main evening event.

SPA/FITNESS. There is a small sauna.

Clipper Odyssey
★★★

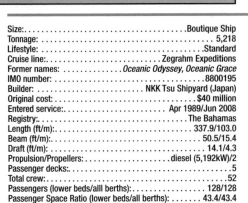

Size:.....................................Boutique Ship	Cabins (total):.......................................64
Tonnage:...5,218	Size range (sq ft/m):...................182.9–258.3/17–24
Lifestyle:.......................................Standard	Cabins (outside view):................................64
Cruise line:............................Zegrahm Expeditions	Cabins (interior/no view):..............................0
Former names:..............Oceanic Odyssey, Oceanic Grace	Cabins (for one person):................................0
IMO number:...................................8800195	Cabins (with private balcony):..........................8
Builder:.........................NKK Tsu Shipyard (Japan)	Cabins (wheelchair accessible):........................1
Original cost:..............................$40 million	Wheelchair accessibility:............................Fair
Entered service:.....................Apr 1989/Jun 2008	Cabin voltage:.................................115 volts
Registry:....................................The Bahamas	Elevators:...1
Length (ft/m):............................337.9/103.0	Casino (gaming tables):..............................No
Beam (ft/m):..............................50.5/15.4	Slot machines:.......................................No
Draft (ft/m):..............................14.1/4.3	Swimming pools:.....................................1
Propulsion/Propellers:..................diesel (5,192kW)/2	Hot tubs (on deck):..................................1
Passenger decks:.....................................5	Self-service launderette:.............................No
Total crew:...52	Dedicated cinema/seats:..............................No
Passengers (lower beds/alll berths):.................128/128	Library:...Yes
Passenger Space Ratio (lower beds/all berths):.......43.4/43.4	Onboard currency:..................................US$
Crew/Passenger Ratio (lower beds/all berths):..........2.4/2.4	

A small expedition-style ship for discovery cruises

OVERVIEW. *Clipper Odyssey* is liked by couples and single travelers who enjoy nature and wildlife up close and personal, and who wouldn't dream of cruising in the mainstream sense aboard ships with large numbers of people.

THE SHIP. It has a contemporary profile. Designed in Holland and built in Japan, it tried to copy the *SeaDream* small ship/ultra-yacht concept for the Japanese market. Operated by Japan's Showa Line, it wasn't suited to Japan's often choppy seas. After 10 years, the company sold it to Clipper Cruise Line (owned by Denmark's Clipper Group, but managed by International Shipping Partners), and in 2008 it began a five-year charter to Seattle-based Zegrahm Expeditions.

Considering its size, there are expansive areas outdoors, excellent for sunbathing or for viewing wildlife. The small swimming pool is just a 'dip' pool. There is a wide teakwood outdoor jogging track. Free snorkeling equipment is available, as is a small fleet of Zodiacs.

Inside, nothing jars the senses, as the interior design concept balances East-West color combinations with some Indonesian accents. The ambience is warm and intimate. There are many pillars in almost all public areas, which spoil the decor and sight lines.

ACCOMMODATION. There are six cabin categories. The ship has all-outside cabins quite tastefully furnished with blond wood cabinetry, twin- or queen-

Berlitz's Ratings

	Possible	Achieved
Ship	500	311
Accommodation	200	135
Food	400	237
Service	400	261
Entertainment	100	57
Cruise	400	235
OVERALL SCORE		
1236 points out of 2000		

size beds, living area with sofa, personal safe, mini-bar/refrigerator, TV set and VCR, and three-sided mirror. All bathrooms have a deep, half-size tub. Some cabins have private balconies; but these are very small, with awkward door handles. The bathroom toilet seats are extremely high.

There is one suite, which is the size of two cabins. It provides more room, of course, with a lounge area, and more storage space.

DINING. The dining room has large ocean-view picture windows. It is quite warm and inviting, and all passengers eat in a single seating. The unmemorable cuisine includes fresh foods from local ports, in a mix of regional and some Western cuisine, with open seating. There is much use of canned fruits and other cheap ingredients. A young, friendly American staff provides the service.

ENTERTAINMENT. There is no formal entertainment, although dinner and after-dinner conversation with fellow passengers in the ship's lounge/bar really becomes the entertainment each evening. Otherwise, it might be a good idea to bring a good book or two.

SPA/FITNESS. There is a tiny beauty salon, and an adjacent massage/body treatment room. A small fitness room is located on a different deck.

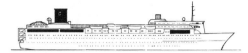

Club Harmony
★★ +

Size:. . . . . Mid-size Ship	Cabins (total):. 386
Tonnage: 25,441	Size range (sq ft/m): 104.4–264.8/9.7–24.6
Lifestyle: . . . . .Standard	Cabins (outside view):. 183
Cruise line:. . . . . Harmony Cruises	Cabins (interior/no view):. 205
Former names: . . . . .Costa Marina, Axel Johnson	Cabins (for one person):. 0
IMO number: 6910544	Cabins (with private balcony):. 8
Builder: . . . . Mariotti Shipyards (Italy)	Cabins (wheelchair accessible): .0
Original cost: . . . . $130 million	Wheelchair accessibility:. . . . . .None
Entered service:. .Jul 1990/Feb 2012	Cabin voltage: . . . . .110 and 220 volts
Registry:. . . . . South Korea	Elevators:. 8
Length (ft/m):. 571.8/174.2	Casino (gaming tables):. . . . . Yes
Beam (ft/m):. 84.6/25.7	Slot machines:. . . . . Yes
Draft (ft/m):. 26.1/8.2	Swimming pools:. 1
Propulsion/Propellers: . . . . .diesel (19,152kW)/2	Hot tubs (on deck):. 3
Passenger decks:. 8	Self-service launderette:. . . . . .No
Total crew:. 400	Dedicated cinema/seats:. . . . . .No
Passengers (lower beds/alll berths):. 772/1,005	Library: . . . . Yes
Passenger Space Ratio (lower beds/all berths): 32.9/25.3	Onboard currency: . . . . .South Korean Won (KRW)
Crew/Passenger Ratio (lower beds/all berths):. 1.9/2.5	

A basic ship for casual, frugal Korean-speaking cruisers

OVERVIEW. *Club Harmony*, originally a container ship, was converted in 1990 to become a cruise vessel. It was chartered for three years from Costa Cruises by new Korean start-up company Harmony Cruises. The ship is for young and young-at-heart Korean-speaking couples and singles who enjoy the vibrant city life, plenty of activities, and loud entertainment.

THE SHIP. This angular-looking vessel was originally built as the container ship Axel Johnson in 1969 and converted in 1988. It has a contemporary, cutaway stern that is virtually replaced by a glass wall – in fact, the dining room windows – and a stark cluster of three white upright funnels. Today the design seems dated.

Most public rooms are above the accommodation decks and include several bars and lounges. There is generally good passenger flow, although congestion occurs between first and second dinner seatings. Although there is a casino, only non-Korean nationals are allowed to gamble.

Open deck and sunbathing space is very limited but is not really needed by Asian passengers, and there is no observation lounge with forward-facing views. The swimming pool is very small. There are simply too many interior cabins.

ACCOMMODATION. There are several categories, ranked by grade, size, and location. Both the outside-view and interior cabins are quite comfortable, but

Berlitz's Ratings

	Possible	Achieved
Ship	500	272
Accommodation	200	117
Food	400	189
Service	400	219
Entertainment	100	55
Cruise	400	216

OVERALL SCORE
1068 points out of 2000

have plain, almost clinical, decor. Bathrooms are functional, but there is little space for toiletries.

DINING. The 452-seat Cristal Restaurant is fairly spacious, with expansive glass windows overlooking the stern, while port and starboard sides have large portholes. There are two seatings but few tables for two, most being for four, six, or eight. Romantic candlelight dining is typically featured on a formal night. The cuisine is Korean (think, lots of kimchee).

ENTERTAINMENT. The Tropicana Showroom is a single-level room. However, 14 pillars obstruct many sight lines from many seats. The room is adequate as a cabaret lounge.

SPA/FITNESS. The spa/fitness facilities are not large, but they include a solarium, several massage/body treatment rooms, sauna and steam rooms for men and women, beauty salon, and gymnasium with floor-to-ceiling windows on three sides. There is a jogging track outdoors.

Club Med 2
★★★+

Size:..................................... Small Ship			

Size:... Small Ship
Tonnage: 14,983
Lifestyle: ....Premium
Cruise line:............................Club Med Cruises
Former names: ....*none*
IMO number: 9007591
Builder: ....Ateliers et Chantiers du Havre
Original cost:.............................$125 million
Entered service:............................. Dec 1992
Registry:..............................Wallis & Fortuna
Length (ft/m):............................. 613.8/187.1
Beam (ft/m):................................. 65.6/20.0
Draft (ft/m): 16.4/5.0
Propulsion/Propellers: ....diesel (9,120kW)/2
Passenger decks:.....................................8
Total crew:.......................................200
Passengers (lower beds/alll berths):......... 394/409
Passenger Space Ratio (lower beds/all berths): 38.0/36.6
Crew/Passenger Ratio (lower beds/all berths):..........1.9/2.0

Cabins (total):....................................197
Size range (sq ft/m): 193.8–322/18–30
Cabins (outside view):.............................197
Cabins (interior/no view):............................0
Cabins (for one person):..............................0
Cabins (with private balcony):........................0
Cabins (wheelchair accessible): 0
Wheelchair accessibility:..........................None
Cabin voltage:........................110 and 220 volts
Elevators:..2
Casino (gaming tables):.............................No
Slot machines:......................................No
Swimming pools:.....................................2
Hot tubs (on deck):..................................0
Self-service launderette:............................No
Dedicated cinema/seats:.............................No
Library: .... Yes
Onboard currency: .... Euros

OVERVIEW. This ship appeals to youthful French-speaking couples and singles who want contemporary facilities and water sports in a casual but chic setting that's different from 'normal' cruise ships, with good food and service, and little or no entertainment.

THE SHIP. *Club Med 2* is one of a pair of the world's largest high-tech sail-cruisers (the other is *Wind Surf*), part-cruise ship, part-yacht. Five huge masts rise 221ft (67.5m) above sea level; they carry seven triangular, self-furling Dacron sails with a total surface area of 26,881 sq ft (2,497 sq m). No human hands touch the sails, as everything is controlled by computer from the bridge. This also keeps the ship on an even keel via the movement of a hydraulic ballast system, so there is no rolling over 6°. When the ship is not using the sails, four diesel-electric motors propel it at up to 12 knots. The ship was refurbished in 2008, when 10 new cabins were added.

An array of water sports facilities is provided (all except scuba gear are included in the cruise fare), and equipment on the aft marina platform includes 12 windsurfers, three sailboats, two waterski boats, several kayaks, 20 single scuba tanks, snorkels, and four motorized water sport boats. There are two small saltwater swimming pools (really 'dip' pools).

Inside, facilities include a main lounge, meeting room, and an extra-charge golf simulator, plus a fitness and beauty center, and piano bar. No gratuities are expected.

Berlitz's Ratings		
	Possible	Achieved
Ship	500	372
Accommodation	200	150
Food	400	272
Service	400	274
Entertainment	100	67
Cruise	400	260
OVERALL SCORE		
1395 points out of 2000		

ACCOMMODATION. There are five suites and 192 standard cabins, all of equal size. All cabins are nicely equipped and very comfortable, and have an inviting decor that includes much blond wood cabinetry. They have a mini-bar/refrigerator, 24-hour room service (but you pay for food), a personal safe, color television, plenty of storage space, bathrobes, and a hairdryer. There are six, four-person cabins, and some 35 doubles are fitted with an extra Pullman berth.

DINING. The two main dining rooms are Le Mediterranée and Le Magellen. Both have tables for two, for, six, or eight. There is open seating, so you can sit with whom you wish. The Grand Bleu Restaurant has a delightful open terrace for informal meals. Complimentary wines and beers are available with lunch and dinner; there is also an à la carte wine list, at a price. Afternoon tea is a delight. The cuisine provides French, Continental, and Japanese specialties, and the creativity and presentation are good.

ENTERTAINMENT. Apart from occasional cabaret acts, there is live music each evening.

SPA/FITNESS. The Health Spa has a sauna, beauty salon, and treatment rooms for massage, facials, and body wraps. There is also a decent fitness room and a beauty salon. The spa facilities are split on three separate decks.

Coral Princess
★★★★

Size:. . . . . .Large Resort Ship	Cabins (total):. 987
Tonnage:. 91,627	Size range (sq ft/m):. 156–470.0/14.4–43.6
Lifestyle: . . . . .Standard	Cabins (outside view):. 879
Cruise line:. . . . . Princess Cruises	Cabins (interior/no view):. 108
Former names: . . . . none	Cabins (for one person):. 0
IMO number: 9229659	Cabins (with private balcony):. 727
Builder: . . . . Chantiers de l'Atlantique (France)	Cabins (wheelchair accessible): 20
Original cost:. . . . . $360 million	Wheelchair accessibility:. . . . . .Good
Entered service:. . . . . Dec 2002	Cabin voltage: . . . . 110 volts
Registry:. . . . . Bermuda	Elevators:. 14
Length (ft/m):. 964.5/294.0	Casino (gaming tables):. . . . . Yes
Beam (ft/m):. 105.6/32.2	Slot machines:. . . . . Yes
Draft (ft/m): 26/7.9	Swimming pools:. . . . . 2 (+ 1 splash pool)
Propulsion/Propellers:. . . . . gas turbine, diesel (40,000kW)/2	Hot tubs (on deck):. 5
Passenger decks:. 11	Self-service launderette:. . . . . Yes
Total crew:. 900	Dedicated cinema/seats:. . . . . .No
Passengers (lower beds/alll berths):. 1,974/2,590	Library: . . . . Yes
Passenger Space Ratio (lower beds/all berths): 46.4/35.3	Onboard currency: . . . . .US$
Crew/Passenger Ratio (lower beds/all berths):. 2.1/2.8	

A comfortable, if bland, large ship for mature-age cruisers

OVERVIEW. For a large ship, the layout is quite user-friendly, and less disjointed than many ships of a similar size. Because of its slim width, the ship can transit the Panama Canal, thus providing greater flexibility in deployment than the Grand Princess-class ships. In a 2009 refit, an adults-only 'Sanctuary' area was added to provide a quiet zone, comfortable, padded sunloungers, and 'Serenity' steward service. Although there's a daily fee, it's worth it.

THE SHIP. *Coral Princess* has an instantly recognizable funnel due to two jet engine-like pods that sit high up on its structure, but these really are mainly for decoration. Four diesel engines provide the generating power. Electrical power is provided by a combination of four diesel and one gas turbine (CODAG) unit; the diesel engines are located in the engine room, while the gas turbine unit is located in the ship's funnel housing. The ship also has three bow thrusters and three stern thrusters.

The interior layout is similar to that of the *Grand*-class ships, but with two decks full of public rooms, lounges and bars instead of just one. Sensibly, it has three major stair towers. There's a large Movies Under the Stars screen in the second pool area just forward of the funnel. Unlike many modern ships, *Coral Princess* has a walk-around open promenade deck, a feature much appreciated by many.

Adjacent is the Wedding Chapel, from which a live web-cam can relay ceremonies via the Internet. The

Berlitz's Ratings		
	Possible	Achieved
Ship	500	378
Accommodation	200	146
Food	400	256
Service	400	290
Entertainment	100	77
Cruise	400	294
OVERALL SCORE		
1441 points out of 2000		

ship's captain can legally marry (American) couples, thanks to the ship's registry and a special dispensation – though this may depend on where you live and should be verified when in the planning stage. The Wedding Chapel can also host renewal of vows ceremonies, for a fee.

This ship has lots of nooks and crannies – so you can hide away and just read a book if you want to. Also, at the forward end of decks 10 and 11, doors open onto a large observation terrace. There are also several self-service launderettes; these are much appreciated during longer cruises.

Niggles include the fact that the forward elevators go between decks 15-7, but you will need to change elevators to get down to the dining rooms on deck 5.

ACCOMMODATION. With many different price categories, in six types, there's a good choice: 16 Suites with balcony (470 sq ft/43.6 sq m); 184 Mini-Suites with balcony (285–302 sq ft/26.4–28.0 sq m); eight Mini-Suites without balcony (300 sq ft/27.8 sq m); 527 Outside-View Cabins with balcony (217–232 sq ft/20–21.5 sq m); 144 Standard Outside-view Cabins (162 sq ft/15 sq m); Interior Cabins (156 sq ft/144.5 sq m). There are 20 wheelchair-accessible cabins (217–374 sq ft/20–34.7 sq m). All measurements are approximate. Almost all outside-view cabins have a private balcony. Some cabins can accommodate a third, or third and fourth person – good for families with children. Some cabins on Emerald Deck (Deck 8) have a view obstructed by lifeboats.

Suites. There are just 16 suites and, although none are really large when compared to such ships as *Norwegian Dawn* and *Norwegian Star*, where the largest suites measure a whopping 5,350 sq ft/497 sq m, for example, each has a private balcony. All are named after islands – mostly coral-based islands in the Indian and Pacific oceans. All suites are located on either Deck 9 or Deck 10. In a departure from many ships, *Coral Princess* doesn't have any suites or cabins with a view over the stern. There are also four Premium Suites, located sensibly in the ship's center, adjacent to a bank of six elevators. Six other suites, called Verandah Suites, are located further aft.

All suites and cabins are equipped with a refrigerator, personal safe, TV set with audio channels, hairdryer, satellite-dial telephone, and twin beds that convert to a queen-size bed (there are a few exceptions). All accommodation has a bathroom with shower enclosure and toilet. Accommodation designated as suites and mini-suites (there are seven price categories) has a bathtub and separate shower enclosure, and two TV sets.

All passengers receive turndown service and chocolates on pillows nightly, bathrobes on request, and toiletries (larger kits, naturally, for suite/mini-suite occupants). Cabin attendants have many cabins to look after – typically 20 – which does not translate to fine personal service.

DINING. The two main dining rooms, Bordeaux and Provence, are in the forward part of the ship on the two lowest passenger decks. The galley is all the way forward so it doesn't intersect public spaces. Both are almost identical in design and layout. The ceilings are quite low and make the rooms appear confined. They have plenty of intimate alcoves, and tables are for two, four, six, or eight. There are two seatings for dinner (or you can opt for 'Anytime' Dining in the Bordeaux Restaurant), while breakfast and lunch are on an open-seating basis; you may have to wait for some while at peak times, just as in many large restaurants ashore.

Other dining options. Horizon Court, a casual 24-hour eatery, is located in the forward section of Lido Deck, with superb ocean views. Several self-serve counters provide an array of food for breakfast and lunch buffets, and offer bistro-style casual dinners in the evening. The venue is a bit short on seating, however.

There are two specialty dining rooms Sabatini's and the Bayou Café. Both cost extra and you need to make a reservation. Sabatini's is an Italian eatery, with colorful tiled Mediterranean-style decor; it is named after Trattoria Sabatini, the 200-year-old institution in Florence. It has Italian-style pizzas and pastas, with a variety of sauces, as well as Italian-style entrées – all provided with flair and entertainment by the waiters. The food is both creative and tasty, with seriously sized portions. Sabatini's is by reservation only, and there's a cover charge.

The Bayou Café, open for lunch and dinner, has a cover charge that includes a Hurricane cocktail. It evokes the charm of New Orleans' French Quarter, with wrought-iron decoration, and features Cajun/Creole cuisine. Platters include Peel 'n' Eat Shrimp Piquante, Sausage Grillades, Oysters Sieur de Bienville. Popular entrées include premium steaks (the Porterhouse and New York Strip are good), Seafood Gumbo, and Chorizo Jambalaya, plus Alligator Ribs, Corn Meal Fried Catfish, Chicken Brochette, and Red Pepper Butter Broiled Lobster. Desserts include sweet potato pie and banana whiskey pound cake. The venue has a small stage with baby grand piano, and live jazz is part of the evening dining scenario.

ENTERTAINMENT. The Princess Theatre is two decks high, and, unusually, there is much more seating in the upper level than on the main floor below. There are typically two production shows on a seven-day cruise, and three on a 10-day cruise. These are colorful, glamorous shows with well-designed costumes and good lighting.

A second entertainment lounge (Universe Lounge) is designed more for cabaret-style features. It also has two levels – a first for a Princess Cruises ship – and three separate stages, enabling nonstop entertainment to be provided without constant set-ups. The room, which has a full kitchen set, is also used for cooking demonstrations and other life-enrichment participation activities. There is a good mix of music in the various bars and lounges.

For self-improvement, Princess Cruises' Scholar Ship@Sea program offers about 20 courses each cruise. Although introductory classes are free, there's a charge if you want to continue any chosen subject in a smaller setting.

SPA/FITNESS. The Lotus Spa is located aft on one of the uppermost decks. It contains men's and women's saunas, steam rooms, changing rooms, relaxation area, beauty salon, an aerobics exercise room and gymnasium with ocean-views and the latest high-tech muscle-pumping, cardio-vascular equipment. There are several large rooms for individual treatments.

Sports enthusiasts will find a nine-hole golf putting course, two computerized golf simulators, and a sports court.

Costa Atlantica
★★★+

Size:...............................Large Resort Ship		Crew/Passenger Ratio (lower beds/all berths):..........2.3/2.9	
Tonnage: 85,700		Cabins (total):....................................1,056	
Lifestyle: ....Standard		Size range (sq ft/m): 161.4–387.5/15.0–36.0	
Cruise line:.............................. Costa Cruises		Cabins (outside view):...............................843	
Former names: ....none		Cabins (interior/no view):............................213	
IMO number: 9187796		Cabins (for one person):................................0	
Builder: .... Kverner Masa-Yards (Finland)		Cabins (with private balcony):........................742	
Original cost: ....$335 million		Cabins (wheelchair accessible): 8	
Entered service:...............................Jul 2000		Wheelchair accessibility:............................Good	
Registry:....................................... Italy		Cabin voltage: .... 110 volts	
Length (ft/m):............................... 959.6/292.5		Elevators:..12	
Beam (ft/m):................................ 105.6/32.2		Casino (gaming tables):............................. Yes	
Draft (ft/m): 25.5/7.8		Slot machines:.................................... Yes	
Propulsion/Propellers:...diesel-electric (34,000kW)/2 azimuthing pods		Swimming pools:.................2 (1 w/sliding glass dome)	
Passenger decks:...................................12		Hot tubs (on deck):..................................4	
Total crew:......................................920		Self-service launderette:.............................No	
Passengers (lower beds/alll berths):.............2,112/2,680		Dedicated cinema/seats:..............................No	
Passenger Space Ratio (lower beds/all berths): 40.5/31.9		Library: .... Yes	
		Onboard currency: .... Euros	

A contemporary Italian ship with volume everywhere

OVERVIEW. This ship is designed to wow the trendy as well as pay homage to many of Italy's great art and past masters. *Costa Atlantica* is aimed at young (and young at heart) couples and singles plus families with children who enjoy big-city life. The international clientele are offered constant activity accompanied by Italian ambience and loud entertainment.

THE SHIP. *Costa Atlantica* is a sister (or close sister) to *Costa Deliziosa, Costa Favolosa, Costa Fascinosa, Costa Luminosa* and *Costa Mediterranea*. There are two centrally located swimming pools outdoors, one with a retractable glass dome cover that can be used in poor weather conditions. A bar abridges two adjacent hot tubs. There's a smaller pool for children, and a winding water slide spanning two decks in height – it starts on a platform bridge aft of the funnel.

The deck names are inspired by Federico Fellini movies (Roma Deck, Le Notte di Cabiria, La Voce della Luna, La Strada, La Luci del Varieta). One deck is named after a Fellini TV movie, Ginger and Fred. The interior design is bold and brash – a mix of classical Italy and contemporary features. Good points include the fact that the interior design allows efficient passenger flow from one public space to another, and there are several floor spaces for dancing, and a wide range of bars and lounges for socializing.

The lobby spans eight decks. Take a drink from the lobby bar and look upwards – the surroundings are visually stunning.

Berlitz's Ratings

	Possible	Achieved
Ship	500	379
Accommodation	200	142
Food	400	241
Service	400	265
Entertainment	100	64
Cruise	400	270

OVERALL SCORE
1361 points out of 2000

A small chapel is located forward of the uppermost level. Other facilities include a winding shopping street with boutique stores (Fendi, Gianni Versace, Paul & Shark Yachting – as well as a shop dedicated to selling Caffè Florian products), a photo gallery, a video games room, an observation balcony, a casino, and a library with Internet access.

All printed materials (room service folio, menus, etc.) are in six languages (Italian, English, French, German, Portuguese, and Spanish).

Some tables in the Tiziano Dining Room have a less than comfortable view of the harsh lighting of the escalators between the galley and the two decks of the dining room.

Niggles! Several pillars obstruct passenger flow and sight lines throughout the ship. The fit and finish of some interior decoration is quite poor, and the décor is a bit overdone. The hospitality levels and service are inconsistent, and below the standard of several other major cruise lines.

ACCOMMODATION. There are a variety of price categories, and a healthy (78 percent) proportion of outside-view to interior cabins. All cabins have twin beds that can be converted into a queen-size bed, individually controlled air conditioning (but it can't be turned off), TV set, and telephone. Many cabins have views obstructed by lifeboats on Deck 4 (Roma Deck), the lowest of the accommodation decks, as well as some cabins on Deck 5. Some cabins have pull-down

(Pullman-style) berths that are fully hidden in the ceiling when not in use. There is much use of fluorescent lighting in the suites and cabins, and the soundproofing could be much better. Some bathroom fixtures – bath and shower taps in particular – are frustrating to use at first.

Some of the most desirable suites and cabins are those with private balconies on five aft-facing decks (decks 4, 5, 6, 7, and 8) with views overlooking the stern and ship's wash. Other cabins with private balconies will find the balconies not so private – the partition between one balcony and the next is not a full partition – so you might be able to hear your neighbors.

However, balcony occupants all have good views through glass and wood-topped railings, and the deck is made of teak. The cabins are well laid out, typically with twin beds that convert to a queen-size bed, vanity desk with built-in hairdryer (but you'll need to hold down the on button continuously), large TV set, and personal safe. One closet has moveable shelves, providing more space for storing luggage. However, the lighting is fluorescent, and much too harsh. The bathroom is a simple, modular unit that has shower enclosures with soap dispenser.

The largest suites are designated Penthouse Suites, although they are really quite small when compared with suites aboard other ships of a similar size. However, they do at least offer more space to move around in, and a slightly larger, better bathroom.

DINING. The 1,320-seat Tiziano Dining Room is in the aft section of the ship on two levels, with a spiral stairway between them. There are two seatings, with tables for two, four, six, or eight. Dinner on European cruises is typically scheduled at 7pm and 9pm to accommodate the later eating habits of Europeans. Themed evenings are a part of the Costa Cruises tradition, and three different window blinds help create a different feel. However, the artwork is placed at table height, so the room seems more closed-in than it should.

This cuisine is traditional cruise fare that is best described as banquet-style food. Note that there are no real sommeliers, so the waiters (who are young) serve the wine (which is also young). They also dance at the tables during the cruise – it's a little bit of show business.

Other dining options. A reservations-only 125-seat dinner venue, Ristorante Club Atlantica, with menus by Gualtiero Marchesi, has a cover charge, but suite-grade occupants get a free pass for one evening. It's a smaller, quieter venue, and the food, though nothing special is cooked to order and is decidedly better than in the main dining room.

Casual breakfast and luncheon self-serve buffet-style meals can be taken in the Botticelli Buffet Restaurant, adjacent to the swimming pools, with seating both indoors and outdoors. A grill (for hamburgers and hot dogs) and a pasta bar are conveniently adjacent to the second pool, while indoors is the Napoli Pizzeria. Excellent cappuccino and espresso coffees are always available in various bars around the ship, served in the right-sized china cups.

One place to see and be seen is in the informal Caffè Florian – a replica of the famous indoor/outdoor café that opened in 1720 in Venice's St Mark's Square. There are four separate salons (Sala delle Stagioni, Sala del Senato, Sala Liberty, and Sala degli Uomini Illustri) and the same fascinating mosaic, marble and wood floors, opulent ceiling art, and special lampshades. Even the espresso/cappuccino machine is a duplicate of that found in the real thing. The only problem is that the chairs are much too small.

ENTERTAINMENT. A three-deck-high, 949-seat showlounge (Caruso Theater) is an imposing room, with just over 1,000 seats. Spiral stairways at the back of the lounge connect all levels. Stage shows are best seen from the upper three levels, from where the sight lines are reasonably good.

Directly underneath the showlounge is the large Coral Lounge, complete with its own bar. An onboard resident troupe of singers and dancers provides the cast members for colorful, high-energy production shows – though these shows are loud and poor. For nights when there are no big shows, the showlounge presents cabaret acts such as singers, comedy jugglers, magicians, and ventriloquists.

A number of bands and small musical units provide a variety of live music in many lounges and bars, and there is a discotheque.

SPA/FITNESS. The Ischia Spa spans two decks. Facilities include a solarium, eight treatment rooms, lecture rooms, sauna and steam rooms for men and women, and a beauty parlor. A large gymnasium has floor-to-ceiling windows on three sides, including forward-facing ocean views, and an aerobics room with instructor-led classes. There is a jogging track outdoors.

The spa is operated by Steiner, a specialist concession, whose young staff will try to sell you Steiner's own-brand Elemis beauty products. Some fitness classes are free, while some (yoga, for example), cost extra.

Massages (including exotic massages such as Aroma Stone massage, and other well-being massages), facials, pedicures, and beauty salon treatments are at extra cost. Make any appointments as early as possible since time slots go quickly.

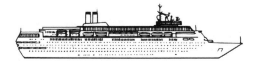

Costa Classica
★★★

Size:.	Mid-size Ship	Cabins (total):.	654
Tonnage:	52,950 tons	Size range (sq ft/m):	185.1–430.5/17.2–40.0
Lifestyle:	Standard	Cabins (outside view):	438
Cruise line:.	Costa Cruises	Cabins (interior/no view):.	216
Former names:	none	Cabins (for one person):.	0
IMO number:	8716502	Cabins (with private balcony):	10
Builder:	Fincantieri (Italy)	Cabins (wheelchair accessible):	6 (interior)
Original cost:	$287 million	Wheelchair accessibility:	Good
Entered service:.	Jan 1992	Cabin voltage:	110 and 220 volts
Registry:.	Italy	Elevators:.	8
Length (ft/m):.	718.5/220.61	Casino (gaming tables):.	Yes
Beam (ft/m):.	98.4/30.80	Slot machines:.	Yes
Draft (ft/m):	25.0/7.60	Swimming pools:.	2
Propulsion/Propellers:	diesel (22,800kW)/2	Hot tubs (on deck):.	4
Passenger decks:.	10	Self-service launderette:	No
Total crew:.	650	Dedicated cinema/seats:.	No
Passengers (lower beds/alll berths):.	1,308/1,766	Library:.	Yes
Passenger Space Ratio (lower beds/all berths):	40.4/29.9	Onboard currency:	Euros
Crew/Passenger Ratio (lower beds/all berths):.	2.0/2.7		

An elegant Italian-style ship for mature passengers

OVERVIEW. This ship, which brought Costa into the mainstream of cruising, Italian-style, has a contemporary design and styling best described as befitting European tastes. It attracts a multinational group of young (and young at heart) couples and singles who enjoy big-city life with constant activity and lots of noise.

THE SHIP. *Costa Classica* is an all-white ship, now over 20 years old, with a slab-sided unflattering profile, which is topped by an unmistakable trio of tall yellow funnels. Lifeboats positioned in an upper location make the high-sided ship look ungainly, with no line to separate the upper from the lower hull section.

The interior design, however, incorporates much use of circles – large portholes instead of windows can be found in cabins on lower decks, and in the dining room, self-serve buffet area, coffee bar, and discotheque, for example. There is an excellent range of public rooms, lounges, and bars, plus a number of specially designed business and meeting facilities; the rooms provide multi-flexible configurations.

Some fascinating artwork includes six hermaphrodite statues in one lounge. The multi-level atrium is stark, angular, and cold. The marble-covered staircases look pleasant, but are uncarpeted and a little dangerous if water or drinks are spilled on them when the ship is moving.

Perhaps the interior is best described as an innovative design project that almost works. A forward observation lounge/nightclub sits atop ship like a lump of cheese, and, unfortunately, fails to work well as a nightclub.

Berlitz's Ratings

	Possible	Achieved
Ship	500	331
Accommodation	200	133
Food	400	214
Service	400	261
Entertainment	100	60
Cruise	400	238

OVERALL SCORE
1237 points out of 2000

Internet access is available from one of several computer terminals in an Internet café.

Gratuities are charged to your onboard account. Although Costa Cruises is noted for its 'Italian' style, ambience and spirit, there are few Italian crew members on board. Although many officers are Italian, most of the crew members, particularly the dining room and housekeeping staff, are from the Philippines. But the lifestyle on board is perceived to be Italian – lively, noisy, with lots of love for life and a love of all things casual, even on so-called formal nights.

Note that all printed material – room service folio, menus, etc. – will typically be in six languages: Italian, English, French, German, Portuguese, and Spanish. During peak European school holiday periods, particularly Christmas and Easter, you can expect to be cruising with a lot of children of all ages.

As aboard other Costa ships, note that for embarkation, few staff members are on duty at the gangway when you arrive; they merely point you in the direction of your deck, or to the ship's elevators and do not escort you to your cabin. Also, note that 'wallpaper' music is played 24 hours a day in all accommodation hallways and elevators, so you may well hear it if you are a light sleeper.

Niggles include the fact that there is no walk-around promenade deck outdoors. The ship's rather slow service speed (19.5 knots) means that itineraries have to be carefully chosen, as the ship cannot compete with the newer ships with faster speeds. Also, the air-conditioning system in the Tivoli Dining Room is noisy.

There are too many loud, repetitious, and irritating announcements. Shore excursions are very expensive.

ACCOMMODATION. There are 11 categories. These include 10 suites, while other cabins are fairly standard in size, shape, and facilities, a higher price being asked for cabins on the highest decks. All suites and cabins have twin lower beds, color TV set, and telephone.

Suites. The 10 suites, located in the center of Portofino Deck, all have a private rounded balcony, marble-clad bathroom with Jacuzzi tub, and separate shower enclosure. There is plenty of space in the living and sleeping areas, and for storing luggage, as these really are very spacious suites.

Standard Outside-View/Interior Cabins. In general, the cabins are of a fairly generous size, and are laid out in a practical manner. They have cherry wood veneered cabinetry and accenting, and include a vanity desk unit with a large mirror. There are useful (unusual, for a cruise ship) sliding doors to the bathroom and closets, and the cabin soundproofing is poor. The soft furnishings are of good quality, but the room service menu is disappointing. The suites have more space – although they are not large by any means – and hand-woven bedspreads.

Some cabins have one or two extra pull-down (Pullman-style) berths – useful for families with small children.

DINING. The Tivoli Dining Room has a lovely, indented, clean white ceiling, although it is extremely noisy. There are two seatings, and a number of tables for 2-8, assigned according to your chosen accommodation grade. Changeable wall panels help create a European Renaissance atmosphere, albeit at the expense of blocking off windows – but during dinner, it's dark outside anyway unless you're in the far North.

The cuisine is traditional cruise fare that is best described as banquet-style food. Note that there are no real sommeliers, so the young waiters serve the (mostly Italian) wine (which is also young). They also dance at the tables during the cruise – it's a little bit of show business that you get caught up in – whether you like it or not.

Other dining options. For casual outdoor eating, the Alfresco Café has teak decking and traditional canvas sailcloth awning. Breakfast and luncheon buffets are repetitious and uncreative, and the source of many passenger complaints.

Excellent (extra-cost) Italian cappuccino and espresso coffees are always available in various bars around the ship, served in the right-sized china cups.

ENTERTAINMENT. The Colosseo Theater, the main showlounge, has an interesting amphitheater-like design. However, the seats are bolt upright, and quite uncomfortable for any length of time. A Galileo discotheque, located atop the ship, for the young at heart, late of night, and hard of hearing.

SPA/FITNESS. The Caracalla Spa, on one of the uppermost decks, contains a gymnasium with good forward-facing views over the ship's bows and high-tech muscle-pump machines, an aerobics exercise area, two hot tubs, Roman bath, health bar, sauna and steam rooms, and beauty salon. The spa is operated by Steiner, a specialist concession, whose young staff will try to sell you Steiner's own-brand Elemis beauty products.

Some fitness classes are free, while some, such as yoga and kick-boxing, cost extra. Massage (including exotic massages such as Aroma Stone massage, Chakra Balancing massage, and other well-being massages), facials, pedicures, and beauty salon treatments cost extra. Make appointments as early as possible as time slots can go quickly.

Nautical Expressions

If you've ever wondered where some terms or phrases came from, you have only to look to the sea, ships, and seamen.

Bamboozle. Today, when you intentionally deceive someone, usually as a joke, you are said to have bamboozled them. The word also was used in the days of sail, but then it meant to deceive a passing vessel as to your ship's origin or nationality by flying an ensign other than your own – a common practice by pirates. From the 17th century, it described the Spanish custom of hoisting false flags to deceive (bamboozle) enemies.

Batten down the hatches. The real hatches are the things that cover the hatchways: gratings and close-hatches. A great deal of water can come aboard either from the sea of the sky or both, so they used to cover those hatches with tarpaulins. The crew typically took battens – stout laths of wood that fit against the coaming (the raised rim of the hatchway) – and pinned the tarpaulin down to cleats on the deck, drum tight.

Barge in. The word barge has two nautical meanings. First as a term applied to a flag officer's boat or highly decorated vessel used for ceremonial occasions. The second usage refers to the more common, flat-bottomed work boat which is hard to maneuver and difficult to control. Hence the term 'barge in.'

Bigwigs. The senior officers in the English Navy, who once wore huge wigs, were referred to as 'bigwigs.'

Bitter End. If a sailor were to lay out all of the anchor warp (chain or rope) until he reached the bitter end, then he would have no more to give out. The bitter end also refers to the end of the 'starter' (a short rope knotted at one end) used for punishment. Today we talk of having reached the 'bitter end' when we mean that we can go no further in a task. The landlubber's phrase 'stick it to the bitter end' and 'faithful to the bitter end' are derivations of the nautical term and refer to anyone who insists in adhering to a course of action without regard to consequences.

Costa Deliziosa
★★★+

Size:.	Large Resort Ship	Cabins (total):.	1,130
Tonnage:.	92,700	Size range (sq ft/m):.	134.5–534.0/12.5–49.6
Lifestyle:.	Standard	Cabins (outside view):.	951
Cruise line:.	Costa Cruises	Cabins (interior/no view):.	179
Former names:.	none	Cabins (for one person):.	0
IMO number:.	9398917	Cabins (with private balcony):.	772
Builder:.	Fincantieri (Italy)	Cabins (wheelchair accessible):.	12
Original cost:.	€548 million	Wheelchair accessibility:.	Good
Entered service:.	Mar 2010	Cabin voltage:.	110 volts
Registry:.	Italy	Elevators:.	12
Length (ft/m):.	958.0/292.0	Casino (gaming tables):.	Yes
Beam (ft/m):.	111.5/34.0	Slot machines:.	Yes
Draft (ft/m):.	26.2/8.0	Swimming pools:.	2
Propulsion/Propellers:.	diesel-electric (4.2MW)/2 azimuthing pods	Hot tubs (on deck):.	4
Passenger decks:.	13	Self-service launderette:.	No
Total crew:.	1,050	Dedicated cinema/seats:.	No
Passengers (lower beds/all berths):.	2,260/2,826	Library:.	Yes
Passenger Space Ratio (lower beds/all berths):.	41.0/32.7	Onboard currency:.	Euros
Crew/Passenger Ratio (lower beds/all berths):.	2.1/2.6		

It's Italy afloat in this casual big-ship setting

OVERVIEW. This ship, sister to *Costa Luminosa*, was named in Dubai, the first new cruise ship to be named in an Arab city – so, instead of Champagne a bottle of fig juice was used to name it. Most passengers are Italian, with a sprinkling of other nationalities. Printed materials are usually in a variety of European languages.

THE SHIP. *Costa Deliziosa* has a nicely balanced profile and a single large funnel in the Costa colors of yellow and blue. A two-deck midships Lido area swimming pool can be covered with a sliding glass roof in poor weather. A large 194-sq-ft (18-sq-m) poolside movie screen often plays lots of Costa Cruises commercials.

The interior decor, which includes marble and gold, pays tribute to the senses, although sensory overkill might be a better description; in any event, it's a lot of overdone bling. The focal point (and always a good meeting place) is the atrium lobby, which features a large sculpture, *Sphere*, by Arnaldo Pomodoro.

The public rooms include 11 bars (one of the largest is Grand Bar Mirabilis), a large casino (Casino Gaius, for table gaming and slot machines), lots of lounges and entertainment venues to enjoy, including a piano bar (Excite), card room, a small screening room (Cinema Etoiles – a 4D cinema highlights sound and lighting effects, with scent pumped in to heighten the experience), a cigar lounge (Tabac Blonde), and a shopping arcade (Galleria Shops).

Gratuities are charged to your onboard account. Although Costa Cruises is noted for its 'Italian' style,

Berlitz's Ratings		
	Possible	Achieved
Ship	500	391
Accommodation	200	143
Food	400	246
Service	400	274
Entertainment	100	65
Cruise	400	275
OVERALL SCORE		
1394 points out of 2000		

ambience and spirit, there are few Italian crew members on board. Although many officers are Italian, most of the crew members, particularly the dining room and housekeeping staff, are from the Philippines. But the lifestyle on board is perceived to be Italian – lively, noisy, with lots of love for life and a love of all things casual, even on so-called formal nights.

Note that all printed material – room service folio, menus, etc. – will typically be in six languages. During peak European school holiday periods, particularly Christmas and Easter, you can expect to be cruising with a lot of children of all ages.

As aboard other Costa ships, note that for embarkation, few staff members are on duty at the gangway when you arrive; they merely point you in the direction of your deck, or to the ship's elevators and do not escort you to your cabin. Also, note that 'wallpaper' music is played 24 hours a day in all accommodation hallways and elevators, so you may well hear it if you are a light sleeper.

ACCOMMODATION. About 68 percent of all accommodation suites and cabins have an ocean view, and there are 772 balcony cabins. Four suites and 52 Samsara Spa cabins are adjacent to (and considered part of) the designated wellness area. Samsara suite/cabin occupants get unlimited access to the spa plus two treatments and fitness or meditation lessons as part of their package, and dine in one of the two Samsara restaurants.

A pillow menu, with five choices, is available to suite-grade occupants, who also get bathrobes, better amenities, a shaving mirror, and walk-in closets. Background music is played 24 hours a day in all hallways and elevators, so you may well be aware of it if you are a light sleeper.

DINING. The Albatross Restaurant is the ship's large, main dining hall. It is located at the aft of the ship and you eat at one of two seatings for dinner, at tables for 2-8 assigned according to your grade of accommodation. This dining room offers traditional cruise fare that is best described as banquet-style food that shows little finesse. Note that there are no real sommeliers, so the waiters (who are young) serve the wine (which is also young). They also dance at the tables during the cruise – it's a little bit of show business.

A Samsara Restaurant is adjacent to the Albatros Restaurant; it is a smaller venue that is more intimate and much quieter. It features healthier food with reduced calories, fat and salt content. Menu creations are under the direction of dietary consultant and Michelin-starred chef Ettore Boccia, known for molecular Italian cuisine. These venues are open for lunch and dinner to those in Samsara-grade suites and cabins, and to anyone else for dinner only at an extra daily or weekly charge.

Other dining options. The Club Restaurant is a reservations-only, specialty restaurant that features à la carte dining with a pristine show kitchen. The food is cooked à la minute and so it is fresher, looks better, and has more taste than food served in the main dining room, and menus are under the direction of Italy's molecular cooking master, Ettore Bocchia, Costa's consulting chef.

Buffet Andromeda is the self-serve casual eatery, but its disjointed layout invites congestion. While there appears to be a decent choice of food, it is extremely repetitive (particularly for breakfast), and a major source of passenger complaints. Also, after it closes in the afternoon, only slices of pizza are available.

One event not to be missed, however, is an 'Elegant Teatime,' during which rather nice cakes and sandwiches are served, together with a choice of teas or tisanes, in one of the lounges.

ENTERTAINMENT. The Theater Duse, with over 800 seats, spans three decks (with seating on all three levels) and is the ship's main showlounge, with the latest computer-controlled lighting and high-volume sound equipment. High-energy production shows are performed here, with Costa's own song and dance troupe.

SPA/FITNESS. The Samsara Spa area occupies some 37,674 sq ft (3,500 sq m) of Samsara Spa space, and spans two decks in height. Facilities include a large fitness room (with all the techno gym muscle-pumping equipment you could ever want), separate saunas, steam rooms, UVB solarium, changing rooms for men and women, and 10 private massage/body treatment rooms. Two VIP treatment rooms, available to couples as a half-day rental, are located on the upper level.

The facilities are staffed and operated by Steiner Leisure, a specialist spa/beauty concession. Some fitness classes are free, while some, such as Pathway to Yoga, and Pathway to Pilates, cost extra. It's wise to make any treatment appointments early as time slots can go quickly.

You can buy a day pass in order to use the sauna/steam rooms, thermal suite and relaxation area, at a cost of €35 per person. However, there's an additional free (no charge) sauna for men and women, but to access it you must walk through an active fitness area, maybe with your bathrobe on – not comfortable for everyone, especially women.

For the sports-minded, a Grand Prix Formula One simulator is housed in a glass enclosure close to the spa. A golf simulator provides a choice of 37 18-hole courses.

Did you know...

...that Quark Expeditions made maritime history in July/August 1991, when its chartered Russian icebreaker, *Sovetskiy Soyuz*, made a spectacular 21-day voyage to negotiate a passage from Murmansk, Russia, to Nome, Alaska, across the North Pole? Although the polar ice cap had been navigated by the US nuclear submarines *Skate* and *Nautilus*, as well as by dirigible and airplane, this was the first passenger ship to make the hazardous crossing.

...that in 1984, Salen Lindblad Cruising made maritime history by negotiating a westbound voyage through the Northwest Passage, a 41-day epic that started from St John's, Newfoundland, in Canada, and ended at Yokohama, Japan? The search for a Northwest Passage to the Orient attracted brave explorers for more than four centuries. Despite numerous attempts and loss of life, including Henry Hudson in 1610,

a 'white passage' to the East remained an elusive dream. Amundsen's 47-ton ship *Gjoa* eventually navigated the route in 1906, taking three years to do so. It was not until 1943 that a Canadian ship, *St Roch*, became the first vessel in history to make the passage in a single season. *Lindblad Explorer* became the 34th vessel, and the first cruise vessel, to complete the Northwest Passage.

...that the most expensive expedition cruise excursion was a cruise/dive to visit the resting place of *RMS Titanic* aboard the two deep-ocean submersibles *Mir I* and *Mir II* used in James Cameron's Hollywood blockbuster. Just 60 participants went as observers in 1998, and another 60 were taken in 1999.

...that a passenger once asked the operations director of a well-known expedition cruise ship where the best shops were in Antarctica? His reply: 'On board, madam!'

Size:.	Large Resort Ship		Cabins (total):.	1,854
Tonnage:	114,500		Size range (sq ft/m):	179.7–482.2/16.7–44.8
Lifestyle:	Standard		Cabins (outside view):	1,167
Cruise line:.	Costa Cruises		Cabins (interior/no view):.	687
Former names:	none		Cabins (for one person):.	0
IMO number:	9479864		Cabins (with private balcony):	913
Builder:	Fincantieri (Italy)		Cabins (wheelchair accessible):	8
Original cost:.	$510 million		Wheelchair accessibility:.	Good
Entered service:.	Nov 2013		Cabin voltage:	110 and 220 volts
Registry:.	Italy		Elevators:.	19
Length (ft/m):.	952.0/290.2		Casino (gaming tables):.	Yes
Beam (ft/m):.	122.0/37.2		Slot machines:.	Yes
Draft (ft/m):	27.2/8.3		Swimming pools:.	2
Propulsion/Propellers:	diesel-electric (75,600kW)/2		Hot tubs (on deck):.	8
Passenger decks:.	13		Self-service launderette:.	No
Total crew:.	1,090		Dedicated cinema/seats:.	No
Passengers (lower beds/alll berths):	3,016/3,800		Library:.	Yes
Passenger Space Ratio (lower beds/all berths):	38.0/30.1		Onboard currency:	Euros
Crew/Passenger Ratio (lower beds/all berths):	2.9/3.9			

Family-friendly Italian ship for contemporary cruising

OVERVIEW. *Costa Diadema* is the newest, largest, and grandest ship in the growing Costa Cruises fleet of family-friendly ships, and becomes the company's new flagship. This is all about casual cruising for a youthful clientele who enjoy the Italian flair for life.

THE SHIP. The ship has a well-proportioned profile with a rounded front, and bolt-upright Costa yellow funnel. The lifeboats are mounted lower down, and this position gives a sense of balance to the ship's towering superstructure. *Costa Diadema* is equipped with a cold ironing facility, allowing it to plug into shore side electric power, and all solid waste is collected for recycling rather than being dumped overboard.

The central focal point is the atrium lobby, which features four panoramic elevators and a lobby bar that often has live music. Look upwards from the lobby bar area and you'll see the inner part of the multi-deck atrium studded with diamonds – well, lighting that looks like diamonds (you'll find them in the ceiling of other public areas, too). The reception desk and shore excursion desk are located tone side, while comfortable seating is set around the lobby and adjacent areas. There is little open deck space, however, so you can expect that seating around the main swimming pool will be busy, crowded and noisy.

ACCOMMODATION. Details of the ship's accommodation were not available when this book was completed.

Berlitz's Ratings

	Possible	Achieved
Ship	500	NYR
Accommodation	200	NYR
Food	400	NYR
Service	400	NYR
Entertainment	100	NYR
Cruise	400	NYR
OVERALL SCORE		
NYR points out of 2000		

DINING. The ship's main dining room is a cavernous room that is two decks high. Seating, which is allocated according to your accommodation grade and location, is at banquettes and individual chairs with armrests. Samsara Restaurant is for occupants of Samsara-grade accommodation. The cuisine focuses more on healthy items, reduced calories, fat and salt, and menus are created under the direction of dietary consultant and Michelin-star chef Ettore Boccia and his molecular Italian cuisine

ENTERTAINMENT. The Main Lounge – the ship's showlounge – has over 1,500 seats, many of which have stark upright backs, a large stage with proscenium arch, and the latest in LED lighting technology. Costa Cruises' revue-style shows – performed by a troupe of resident onboard singers/dancers – are all about color, lights, high-energy action, and volume.

SPA/FITNESS. Samsara Spa is a large facility that includes a large gymnasium with the latest in muscle-training equipment, saunas, steam rooms, a thermal area, and several massage/body treatment rooms. VIP treatment rooms are also available to couples for half-day rentals. You can purchase a day pass in order to use the sauna/steam rooms, thermal suite and relaxation area. Some fitness classes are free, while others cost extra.

Costa Fascinosa
★★★+

Size:................................Large Resort Ship			Cabins (total):.....................................1,508	
Tonnage:.......................................114,500			Size range (sq ft/m):.................179.7–482.2/16.7–44.8	
Lifestyle:......................................Standard			Cabins (outside view):..............................928	
Cruise line:...............................Costa Cruises			Cabins (interior/no view):...........................580	
Former names:.....................................none			Cabins (for one person):..............................0	
IMO number:.................................9479864			Cabins (with private balcony):......................650	
Builder:...............................Fincantieri (Italy)			Cabins (wheelchair accessible):.......................12	
Original cost:..............................€510 million			Wheelchair accessibility:..........................Good	
Entered service:...........................May 2012			Cabin voltage:............................110/220 volts	
Registry:..Italy			Elevators:..14	
Length (ft/m):................................952.0/290.2			Casino (gaming tables):.............................Yes	
Beam (ft/m):................................116.4/35.5			Slot machines:.....................................Yes	
Draft (ft/m):.....................................26.9/8.2			Swimming pools:.....................................2	
Propulsion/Propellers:...........diesel-electric (75,600kW)/2			Hot tubs (on deck):..................................5	
Passenger decks:...................................13			Self-service launderette:...........................No	
Total crew:.......................................1,090			Dedicated cinema/seats:.............................No	
Passengers (lower beds/all berths):.............3,016/3,800			Library:...Yes	
Passenger Space Ratio (lower beds/all berths):.......38.0/30.1			Onboard currency:...............................Euros	
Crew/Passenger Ratio (lower beds/all berths):.........2.7/3.4				

Upbeat Italian decor and style, for family cruising

OVERVIEW. Costa Cruises is for those who want to enjoy the casual life to the full. It does a good job of providing first-time cruise passengers with a packaged seagoing vacation – particularly for families with children – that's a mix of sophistication and chaos, accompanied by loud music everywhere. Most passengers are Italian, with a sprinkling of other European nationals.

THE SHIP. With an instantly recognizable single, large yellow funnel, *Costa Fascinosa* is a sister to *Costa Favolosa*, *Costa Fortuna*, *Costa Magica*, *Costa Pacifica* and *Costa Serena*. On the open decks, two pool areas can be covered with retractable glass domes – useful for inclement weather conditions; one pool has a long water slide, much liked by children; there is also a large poolside movie screen. However, the open deck space is pretty cramped when the ship is full, the plastic sunloungers are crammed together, and do not have cushioned pads.

With three decks packed with 13 bars and lounges and other public rooms, there's a place for all tastes. The decor throughout is on the wild side. The focal social point is a three-deck-high atrium lobby, with four glass panoramic elevators providing a neat view over the lobby bar – a good place for espresso/cappuccino and people-watching. The Casino is large and very colorful, but the slot machines occupy a separate area from the gaming tables, so serious gamers can concentrate. Other public rooms include a small library, an Internet-connection center, 4D cinema, card room, art gallery, and video

Berlitz's Ratings		
	Possible	Achieved
Ship	500	385
Accommodation	200	143
Food	400	246
Service	400	272
Entertainment	100	65
Cruise	400	270
OVERALL SCORE		
1381 points out of 2000		

game room, plus a chapel – a standard aboard all Costa Cruises' ships.

Families like Costa Cruises for its perceived 'Italian' style, ambience and spirit, and most passengers will be Italian, with a sprinkling of other European nationals. However, you won't find many Italian hotel service staff on board – although many of the officers are Italian, most crew members, particularly the dining room and housekeeping staff, are from the Philippines. But the lifestyle on board is decidedly Italian – lively, noisy, and full of sparkle. Naturally, during peak European school-holiday periods, especially during Christmas and Easter, you can expect to be cruising with a lot of children of all ages.

Printed material such as the cabin service folio and menus, are provided in six languages – Italian, English, French, German, Portuguese, and Spanish – and announcements are also made in several languages.

As aboard other Costa ships, few staff members are on duty at the gangway when you arrive for embarkation; they merely point you in the direction of your deck, or to the ship's elevators and do not escort you to your cabin.

ACCOMMODATION. There are many accommodation price grades, from two-bed interior cabins to grand suites with private balcony, although in reality there are only three different sizes: suites with 'private' balcony – which are really not particularly large in comparison with some other large ships; two- or four-bed outside view cabins; and two- or four-bed interior cabins. Fortunately, no cabins have views obstructed by lifeboats or other safety equipment views, and, in most cabins, twin beds can be changed to a double/queen-bed configuration.

Eight Grand Suites, in the center of the ship on one of the uppermost decks, comprise the largest accommodation. They have a queen-size bed and larger living area with vanity desk; the bathrooms have a tub and two washbasins.

A total of 103 Samsara Spa Suites are designated as Samsara-grade. Occupants get unlimited spa access plus two treatments, and fitness or meditation lessons as part of the package. These grades have an Oriental decorative theme, special Samsara bathroom personal amenities, and can eat in one of two designated Samsara Restaurants.

Suite-grade occupants get bathrobes and better amenities, shaving mirror, a pillow menu, and walk-in closets – although the hangars are plastic. Music is played 24 hours a day in all accommodation hallways and elevators, so you may well hear it if you are a light sleeper.

DINING. There are two principal dining rooms, Il Gattopardo and Otto e Mezza. One is aft, the other in the ship's center. Tables for 2-8 are allocated according to your accommodation grade and location, in one of two seating times. These dining rooms offer traditional cruise fare that is best described as banquet-style food. Note that there are no real sommeliers, so the waiters serve the wine. They also dance at the tables during the cruise – for a bit of show business.

Two Samsara Restaurants – open for lunch and dinner to those in Samsara-grade suites and cabins, and to anyone else for dinner only at an extra charge – have separate entrances. While the two main restaurants offer traditional cruise fare, these 'spa cuisine' spots feature healthier food – reduced calories, fat and salt, with menu creations under the direction of dietary consultant and Michelin-star chef Ettore Boccia.

Other dining options. A reservations-required, extra-cost restaurant, Club Fascinosa, has fine table settings and leather-bound menus. The self-serve, buffet-style eatery, Tulipano Nero Buffet, is open for breakfast, lunch, afternoon pizzas, and coffee or tea at any time. A balcony level provides additional seating, but you'll need to carry your own food plates because there are no trays, which makes it difficult to carry both food and a beverage at the same time. The food in this venue is extremely repetitive, and a major source of passenger complaints.

Additionally, a venue called Caffeteria is the place to go for decent, extra-cost coffees and Italian sweet pastries.

ENTERTAINMENT. The Fascinosa Showlounge seats over 800. It's three decks high and is the venue for all production shows and large-scale cabaret acts, with a revolving stage, hydraulic orchestra pit, good sound, and seating on three levels, the upper levels being tiered through two decks.

High-energy revue-style shows are performed by a small troupe of resident onboard singers/dancers), with fast-moving action and busy lighting and costume changes.

SPA/FITNESS. The Samsara Spa is a large facility occupying some 64,585 sq ft (6,000 sq m) of space, including relaxation areas, spread over two decks. It has a large fitness room, separate saunas, steam rooms, UVB solarium, changing rooms for men and women, and 10 body treatment rooms. Two VIP treatment rooms, available to couples for half-day rentals, are located on the upper level.

The Spa/fitness facilities are staffed and operated by Steiner Leisure, a specialist spa/beauty concession. Some fitness classes are free, while some, such as Pathway to Yoga, Pathway to Pilates, and Pathway to Meditation, cost extra. It's wise to make appointments early as time slots can go quickly.

You can buy a day pass in order to use the sauna/steam rooms, thermal suite and relaxation area, at a cost of €35 per person. However, there's an additional no-charge sauna for men and women, but to access it you must walk through an active fitness area, maybe with your bathrobe on – not comfortable for everyone.

Nautical expressions

Brass monkeys. Ever wondered where the expression 'Cold enough to freeze the balls off a brass monkey' came from? Well, maritime history tells us that in the days when war ships and most freighters carried cannons (and round cannon balls) made of iron, that in order to keep a supply of cannon balls near each cannon, a method of keeping them from rolling around had to be found.

The best storage device consisted of a square-based pyramid. One cannon ball rested on top of four others, which rested on top of nine other, which rested on a base of sixteen. Thus, a supply of 30 cannon balls could be stacked in a small area. There was, however, a small problem – how to prevent the bottom layer from rolling out from under the others on a moving ship. The solution was a metal plate called a 'monkey.' It had 16 round indentations – one for each of the 16 'base layer' of cannon balls.

If the 'monkey' were made of iron, the cannon balls placed on it would rust to it; the solution was to make the 'monkey' out of brass. However, brass contracts more than iron when it is chilled. Unfortunately, when the temperature dipped too far, the brass indentations would shrink so much that the iron cannon balls would come adrift from the 'monkey.' It was, thus, a case of being 'cold enough to freeze the balls off a brass monkey.'

Costa Favolosa
★★★+

Size:.	.Large Resort Ship	Cabins (total):.	1,506
Tonnage:	114,500	Size range (sq ft/m):	179.7–482.2/16.7–44.8
Lifestyle:	Standard	Cabins (outside view):	926
Cruise line:.	Costa Cruises	Cabins (interior/no view):	580
Former names:	none	Cabins (for one person):	0
IMO number:	9479852	Cabins (with private balcony):	579
Builder:	Fincantieri (Italy)	Cabins (wheelchair accessible):	12
Original cost:	€510 million	Wheelchair accessibility:	Good
Entered service:	Jul 2011	Cabin voltage:	110 and 220 volts
Registry:	Italy	Elevators:	14
Length (ft/m):	952.0/290.2	Casino (gaming tables):	Yes
Beam (ft/m):	116.4/35.5	Slot machines:	Yes
Draft (ft/m):	26.9/8.2	Swimming pools:	2
Propulsion/Propellers:	diesel-electric (75,600kW)/2	Hot tubs (on deck):	5
Passenger decks:	13	Self-service launderette:	No
Total crew:	1,110	Dedicated cinema/seats:	No
Passengers (lower beds/alll berths):	3,012/3,800	Library:	Yes
Passenger Space Ratio (lower beds/all berths):	38.0/30.1	Onboard currency:	Euros
Crew/Passenger Ratio (lower beds/all berths):	2.7/3.4		

Upbeat Italian decor and style, for family cruising

OVERVIEW. Costa Cruises is a line for those who like to party. It does a good job of providing first-time cruise passengers with a packaged seagoing vacation – particularly for families with children – that is a mix of sophistication and chaos, accompanied by loud music everywhere. Most passengers are Italian, with a sprinkling of other European nationals.

THE SHIP. Displaying a single, large funnel, *Costa Favolosa* is a close sister to *Costa Serena*. Two pool areas can be covered with retractable glass domes – useful in case of bad weather. One has a long water slide – great for kids. There is a large poolside movie screen and, on one of the upper decks, a Grand Prix simulator. However, the open deck space can be pretty cramped when the ship is full, so the sunloungers, which don't have cushioned pads, will be crammed together.

There are three decks full of bars and lounges plus many other public rooms. This ship has a glass-domed rotunda atrium lobby that is nine decks high, with great upward views from the lobby bar, as well as from its four glass panoramic elevators.

The Casino is large and glitzy, but always lively and entertaining – slot machines occupy a separate area to gaming tables, so serious gamers can concentrate. There's a very small library, an Internet center, card room, art gallery, 4D cinema (Belphegor), and a video game room, plus a small chapel – a standard aboard all Costa Cruises' ships.

Berlitz's Ratings		
	Possible	Achieved
Ship	500	385
Accommodation	200	143
Food	400	246
Service	400	271
Entertainment	100	65
Cruise	400	269
OVERALL SCORE		
1379 points out of 2000		

Although Costa Cruises is noted for its 'Italian' style, ambience and spirit, there are few Italian crew members on board. Although many officers are Italian, most of the crew members, particularly the dining room and housekeeping staff, are from the Philippines. But the lifestyle on board is perceived to be Italian – lively, noisy, with lots of love for life and a love of all things casual, even on so-called formal nights.

All printed material – room service folio, menus, etc. – will typically be in six languages: Italian, English, French, German, Portuguese, and Spanish. During peak European school holiday periods, particularly Christmas and Easter, you can expect to be cruising with a lot of children of all ages.

As aboard other Costa ships, note that for embarkation, few staff members are on duty at the gangway when you arrive; they merely point you in the direction of your deck, or to the ship's elevators and do not escort you to your cabin. Also, note that 'wallpaper' music is played 24 hours a day in all accommodation hallways and elevators, so you may well hear it if you are a light sleeper.

ACCOMMODATION. There are numerous accommodation price grades, from two-bed interior cabins to grand suites with private balcony although in reality there are only three different sizes: suites with 'private' balcony – which are really not particularly large in comparison with some other large ships; two- or four-bed outside view cabins; and two- or four-bed interior cabins. Fortunately, no cabins have views obstructed by lifeboats or other safety equipment views, and, in most cabins, twin beds can be changed to a double/queen-bed configuration.

Two Grand Suites comprise the largest accommodation, and include a large balcony with hot tub. They have a queen-size bed and larger living area with vanity desk; the bathrooms have a tub and two washbasins.

If you are into wellness treatments, there are 12 Samsara Spa Suites just aft of the spa itself, although 99 cabins, including the 12 suites, are designated as Samsara-grade. Samsara suite/cabin occupants get unlimited access to the spa plus two treatments and fitness or meditation lessons as part of their package, and dine in one of the two Samsara restaurants. All Samsara-designated accommodation grades have an Oriental decorative theme, and special Samsara bathroom personal amenities.

A pillow menu, with five choices, has been introduced in all suite-grade accommodation. Only suite grades get bathrobes and better amenities, shaving mirror, and walk-in closets – although the hangers are plastic. Music is played 24 hours a day in all hallways and elevators, so you may well hear it if you are a light sleeper.

DINING. There are two principal dining rooms, Duke of Burgundy and Duke of Orleans. One is aft, the other in the ship's center. Tables for 2-8 are allocated according to your accommodation grade and location, in one of two seating times. These dining rooms offer traditional cruise fare that is best described as banquet-style food. Note that there are no real sommeliers, so the waiters serve the wine. They also dance at the tables during the cruise – it's a little bit of show business.

Two 100-seat Samsara Restaurants (spa cuisine spots) are provided with separate entrances. These are for those seeking healthier food with reduced calories, fat and salt content. Menu creations are under the direction of dietary consultant and Michelin-starred chef Ettore Boccia, known for his molecular Italian cuisine. These venues are open for lunch and dinner to those in Samsara-grade suites and cabins, and to anyone else for dinner only at an extra daily or weekly charge.

Other dining options. The intimate Favolosa Club Restaurant sits under a huge glass dome and Murano glass decorative elements. Fine table settings, china, silverware and leather-bound menus are provided. There's a cover charge and reservations are required.

The self-service Ca d'Oro buffet restaurant offers breakfast, lunch, afternoon pizzas, and coffee and tea at any time. A balcony level provides additional seating, but you'll need to carry your own food plates since there are no trays. The food in this venue is extremely repetitive, and a major source of passenger complaints.

Additionally, the Caffeteria is a good place to go for decent (extra-cost) coffees and Italian pastries, but all bars have coffee machines, at extra cost.

ENTERTAINMENT. The Favolosa showlounge, which seats more than 800, utilizes the latest in LED technology. Three decks high, it is decorated in a Baroque style, with warm colors and a Murano glass chandelier. It is the venue for all production shows and large-scale cabaret acts, is stunningly glitzy, and has a revolving stage, hydraulic orchestra pit, superb sound, and seating on three levels – the upper levels are tiered through two decks.

Revue-style shows are performed by a small troupe of resident onboard singers and dancers. Their fast-moving action, busy lighting and costume changes all add up to a high-energy performance.

SPA/FITNESS. The Samsara Spa is a large facility that occupies 23,186 sq ft (2,154 sq m), spread over two decks. It includes a large fitness room, separate saunas, steam rooms, UVB solarium, changing rooms for men and women, and 10 body treatment rooms. Two VIP treatment rooms, available to couples as a half-day rental, are located on the upper level.

The Spa/fitness facilities are staffed and operated by Steiner Leisure, a specialist spa/beauty concession. Some fitness classes are free, while some, such as Pathway to Yoga, Pathway to Pilates, and Pathway to Meditation, cost extra. It's wise to make appointments early as time slots can go quickly.

You can buy a day pass in order to use the sauna/steam rooms, thermal suite and relaxation area, at a cost of €35 per person. However, there's an additional no-charge sauna for men and women, but to access it you must walk through an active fitness area, maybe with your bathrobe on – not comfortable for everyone, especially women.

Did you know...

...that the average time for a ship to pass through the Panama Canal is eight hours? The fastest transit time was set by the USS *Manley* at 4 hours and 38 minutes.

...that the Pacific Ocean has a tide of 22ft (6.7m) and the Atlantic has a tide of only 8ins (20.3cm)?

...that permits for cruise ships to enter Glacier Bay National Park (June–September) are awarded as part of a competitive bidding process, tied to proposals for emissions and pollution control, as well as fees?

...that more than 400,000 cruise passengers a year visit Glacier Bay National Park?

...that Alaska has two time zones? Most of Alaska is one hour behind Pacific Standard Time, whereas the Aleutian Islands are two hours behind Pacific Standard Time.

...that the Wallace Line is not a new cruise line, but the scientific demarcation separating the Asian and Oceanic bio-geographical zones?

Costa Fortuna
★★★+

Size:.................................Large Resort Ship		Crew/Passenger Ratio (lower beds/all berths):.........2.5/3.2	
Tonnage:.......................................102,587		Cabins (total):....................................1,358	
Lifestyle:......................................Standard		Size range (sq ft/m):.................179.7–482.2/16.7–44.8	
Cruise line:...............................Costa Cruises		Cabins (outside view):..............................857	
Former names:..................................none		Cabins (interior/no view):..........................501	
IMO number:..................................9239783		Cabins (for one person):..............................0	
Builder:.....................Cantieri Sestri Navale (Italy)		Cabins (with private balcony):......................522	
Original cost:..............................$381 million		Cabins (wheelchair accessible):........................8	
Entered service:............................Nov 2003		Wheelchair accessibility:.........................Good	
Registry:..Italy		Cabin voltage:.........................110 and 220 volts	
Length (ft/m):..............................892.3/272.0		Elevators:...14	
Beam (ft/m):...............................124.6/38.0		Casino (gaming tables):..........................Yes	
Draft (ft/m):...................................27.2/8.3		Slot machines:....................................Yes	
Propulsion/Propellers:...diesel-electric (34,000kW)/2 azimuthing pods		Swimming pools:....................................2	
Passenger decks:...................................13		Hot tubs (on deck):................................6	
Total crew:.....................................1,068		Self-service launderette:...........................No	
Passengers (lower beds/all berths):.............2,716/3,470		Dedicated cinema/seats:............................No	
Passenger Space Ratio (lower beds/all berths):.......37.7/29.5		Library:...Yes	
		Onboard currency:...............................Euros	

A large, colourful family-friendly Italian-style ship

OVERVIEW. *Costa Fortuna – now over 10 years old –* is built to impress trendy city-dwellers at every turn, and the ship absorbs passengers quite well, with a good passenger space ratio. While a variety of nationalities are carried, most of the passengers are Italian, so the ship is lively but quite noisy, with lots of children running around, particularly during the main European school holiday periods.

Berlitz's Ratings		
	Possible	Achieved
Ship	500	384
Accommodation	200	143
Food	400	246
Service	400	270
Entertainment	100	64
Cruise	400	271
OVERALL SCORE		
1378 points out of 2000		

THE SHIP. The ship's name is an interesting one: in Greek mythology, Fortuna is the daughter of Poseidon (God of the sea), as well as being associated with the Temple Fortuna, located along one of Pompeii's conserved streets.

The aft decks are well tiered, with cut-off quarters that make the ship's stern look a little less square than it otherwise would. There are three pools, one of which can be covered by a sliding glass dome in case of inclement weather, while one pool (Barcelona Pool) features a long water slide. There is not a lot of open deck space considering the number of passengers carried, so sunloungers tend to be crammed together (there's a lack of small tables for drinks – or for somewhere to place those small items you always take to the pool), and they lack cushioned pads.

The interior decor focuses on the Italian passenger ships of yesteryear, so much of the finishing detail replicates the Art Deco interiors fitted aboard ocean liners such as the Conte de Savoia, Michelangelo, Neptunia, Rafaello, Rex, etc., although in the kind of contemporary colors not associated with such ships, whose interiors were rather subdued. There are surprisingly few Italians among the crew, however (except in key positions), though the Philippines is well represented.

The deck names are those of major cities in Europe and South America (Barcelona, Buenos Aires, Caracas, Lisbon, Genoa, Miami). The passenger flow is generally good, with few congestion points.

There are three decks full of lounges, and 11 bars to enjoy, and almost all have espresso coffee machines – a must for Italian families. The interior focal point is a nine-deck high, glass-domed atrium lobby: it houses a Costa Bar on the lower level, a bank of four glass-walled (panoramic) elevators, and, in a tribute to ship buffs, 26 models of Italian ships past and present are glued upside down on the ceiling – it's a bit of a strange feeling to look at them and then look at your feet. The lowest three decks connect the public rooms, the upper levels being mainly for accommodation (plus the pool deck).

For those who like to gamble, the Neptunia 1932 Casino is the place to go (if you want to get from the center to the aft lounges you have to walk through it). There are plenty of gaming tables plus an array of slot machines to entertain you. There's also a chapel – standard aboard Costa ships – and a small library that's a bit of a token gesture, an Internet center, card room, art gallery, and video games room.

Although Costa Cruises is noted for its 'Italian' style, ambience and spirit, there are few Italian crew members on board. Although many officers are Italian, most of the crew members, particularly the dining room and housekeeping staff, are from the Philippines. But the lifestyle on board is perceived to be Italian – lively, noisy, with lots of love for life and a love of all things casual, even on so-called formal nights.

All printed material – room service folio, menus, etc. – will typically be in six languages: Italian, English, French, German, Portuguese, and Spanish. During peak European school holiday periods, particularly Christmas and Easter, you can expect to be cruising with a lot of children of all ages.

As aboard other Costa ships, note that for embarkation, few staff members are on duty at the gangway when you arrive; they merely point you in the direction of your deck, or to the ship's elevators and do not escort you to your cabin. Also, note that 'wallpaper' music is played 24 hours a day in all accommodation hallways and elevators, so you may well hear it if you are a light sleeper.

ACCOMMODATION. There are 15 price grades, from two-bed interior cabins to grand suites with private balcony, although in reality there are only three different sizes: suites with balcony, two- or four-bed outside-view cabins (some 335 of which have portholes rather than windows), and two- or four-bed interior cabins. There are also two single cabins – quite unusual for a large ship. In an example of good design, no cabins have lifeboat-obstructed views; this is something not easy to design in large ships such as this.

The largest accommodation can be found in eight Grand Suites, located in the center of the ship on one of the higher decks. They have a queen-size bed; bathrooms have a tub and two washbasins.

Note that 12 of the most desirable (outside-view) wheelchair-accessible cabins are rather idiotically located a long way from elevators, while eight interior cabins are located close to elevators.

DINING. There are two dining rooms: the Michelangelo 1965 Restaurant (aft), whose ceiling features frescoes by the Great Masters, and the Rafaello 1965 Restaurant (midships) are both two decks high and have two seatings. Note that dinner on European cruises is typically scheduled at 7pm and 9pm. Costa Cruises prides itself on the more than 50 types of pasta it uses during a typical one-week cruise. There is a wine list, although there are no wine waiters, and nearly all the wines (mostly Italian) are rally very young.

Other dining options. The Conte Grande 1927 Club is the more intimate upscale dining venue with seating for around 150 under a huge glass dome – if the lights were turned out, you might be able to see the stars. In its show kitchen, chefs can be seen preparing their masterpieces. Fine table settings, china, silverware and leather-bound menus are used. Reservations

are required and there is a cover charge. The Christoforo Columbus 1954 Buffet Restaurant is a self-serve eatery for breakfast, lunch, afternoon pizzas, and beverages at any time. The food in this venue is extremely repetitive, and a major source of passenger complaints. Also, good cappuccino and espresso coffees are always available in the various bars.

ENTERTAINMENT. The Rex 1932 Theater spans three decks in the ship's forward-most section. It is a stunning setting for all production shows and large-scale cabaret acts, and has a revolving stage, hydraulic orchestra pit, excellent (but usually loud) sound system, and seating on three levels – the upper levels being tiered through two decks.

Typical fare consists of revue-style shows performed by a small troupe of resident onboard singers/dancers, with fast-moving action and busy lighting and costume changes that all add up to a high-energy performance.

SPA/FITNESS. Facilities in the two-deck high Saturnia Spa, to which is assigned about 14,424 sq ft/1,340 sq m. It includes a large solarium, eight private massage/body treatment rooms, sauna and steam rooms for men and women, and a beauty parlor. A gym has floor-to-ceiling windows on three sides, including forward-facing ocean views, and there's an aerobics section with instructor-led classes (some, such as yoga, cost extra). The spa/fitness facilities are staffed and operated by Steiner Leisure, a specialist spa/beauty concession. Some fitness classes are free; others, such as Pathway to Yoga, and Pathway to Pilates, cost extra. Make appointments early as time slots can go quickly. If you like being near the spa, note that there are 18 two-bed cabins with ocean-view windows, located adjacent (just aft of it).

Costa Luminosa
★★★+

Size:.................................Large Resort Ship		Crew/Passenger Ratio (lower beds/all berths):.........2.1/2.6	
Tonnage: 92,700		Cabins (total):....................................1,130	
Lifestyle: ....Standard		Size range (sq ft/m): 134.5–534.0/12.5–49.6	
Cruise line:...............................Costa Cruises		Cabins (outside view):..............................951	
Former names: ....none		Cabins (interior/no view):..........................179	
IMO number: 9398905		Cabins (for one person):..............................0	
Builder: ....Fincantieri (Italy)		Cabins (with private balcony):.....................772	
Original cost:..............................€420 million		Cabins (wheelchair accessible): 12	
Entered service:..............................Jun 2009		Wheelchair accessibility:.........................Good	
Registry:..Italy		Cabin voltage: ....110 and 220 volts	
Length (ft/m):..............................958.0/292.0		Elevators:...12	
Beam (ft/m):...............................111.5/34.0		Casino (gaming tables):............................Yes	
Draft (ft/m):..................................26.2/8.0		Slot machines:....................................Yes	
Propulsion/Propellers: ...diesel-electric (42,000kW)/2 azimuthing pods		Swimming pools:....................................2	
		Hot tubs (on deck):.................................4	
Passenger decks:..................................13		Self-service launderette:...........................No	
Total crew:.....................................1,050		Dedicated cinema/seats:............................No	
Passengers (lower beds/alll berths):..............2,260/2,826		Library: ....Yes	
Passenger Space Ratio (lower beds/all berths): 41.0/32.7		Onboard currency: ....Euros	

Bold decor and big-ship facilities for families

OVERVIEW. While various nationalities are carried, most passengers are Italian, so the ship is lively but quite noisy, with lots of children running around, particularly during school holidays. The interior decor, which includes marble, wood and mother of pearl, pays tribute to light and lighting – hence the name *Costa Luminosa*, so it feels like cruising in a stunning special-effects bubble.

THE SHIP. *Costa Luminosa* was constructed as what is termed a Vista-class ship – although it is slightly larger than *Costa Atlantica* and *Costa Mediterranea*. A 4D cinema highlights sound and lighting effects, with scent pumped in to heighten the experience.

Its two-deck mid-ships Lido area swimming pool can be covered with a sliding glass roof. There's also a large 194-sq-ft (18-sq-m) poolside movie screen.

The public rooms include 11 bars, a large Vega Casino, and lots of lounges and entertainment venues. Sony Playstation fans can enjoy Play Station World. Playstations are also available in cabins, on the pool-deck movie screen, and in the children's and teens' clubs.

One thing not to miss is a fascinating – and rather large, at 346cm long (11ft) – *Reclining Woman 2004* bronze sculpture by Fernando Bolero, in the Atria Supernova, the atrium lobby. Weighing 910kg (2,000 lbs), the suntanned, rather voluminous woman is depicted staring into the atrium space, with her legs in a dynamic position of movement.

Although Costa Cruises is noted for its 'Italian' style, ambience and spirit, there are few Italian crew

Berlitz's Ratings

	Possible	Achieved
Ship	500	384
Accommodation	200	143
Food	400	242
Service	400	271
Entertainment	100	65
Cruise	400	271
OVERALL SCORE		
1376 points out of 2000		

members on board. Although many officers are Italian, most of the crew members, particularly the dining room and housekeeping staff, are from the Philippines. But the lifestyle on board is perceived to be Italian – lively, noisy, with lots of love for life and a love of all things casual, even on so-called formal nights.

All printed material – room service folio, menus, etc. – are usually in six languages: Italian, English, French, German, Portuguese, and Spanish. During peak European school holiday periods, particularly Christmas and Easter, you can expect to be cruising with a lot of children of all ages.

As aboard other Costa ships, note that for embarkation, few staff members are on duty at the gangway when you arrive; they merely point you in the direction of your deck, or to the ship's elevators and do not escort you to your cabin. Also, note that 'wallpaper' music is played 24 hours a day in all accommodation hallways and elevators – so you may well hear it if you are a light sleeper.

ACCOMMODATION. There are numerous price grades. About 68 percent of all accommodation suites and cabins have an ocean view, and there are 772 balcony cabins. Four suites and 52 Samsara Spa cabins are located adjacent to (and considered part of) the designated wellness area. As part of their package, Samsara suite and cabin occupants get unlimited access to the spa plus two treatments and fitness or meditation lessons, and can dine in one of the two Samsara restaurants. All Samsara-designated accommodation grades receive Samsara bathroom amenities.

A pillow menu, with five choices, is available to suite-grade accommodation occupants, who also get bathrobes, better amenities than standard-grade cabin occupants, a shaving mirror, and walk-in closets – although the hangers are plastic. Background music is played 24 hours a day in all hallways and elevators, so you may well be aware of it if you are a light sleeper.

All of the cabins have twin beds that can be converted into a queen-size bed, individually controlled air conditioning, television, and telephone. Some many cabins have their views obstructed by lifeboats – on Deck 4 (Roma Deck), the lowest of the accommodation decks, as well as some cabins on Deck 5. Some cabins have pull-down Pullman berths that are fully hidden in the ceiling when not in use.

Some of the most desirable suites and cabins are those with private balconies on the five aft-facing decks (decks 4, 5, 6, 7, and 8) with views overlooking the stern and ship's wash. Passengers in other cabins with private balconies will find the balconies not so private – the partition between one balcony and the next is not a full partition, so you will be able to hear your neighbors. However, these balcony occupants all have good views through glass and wood-topped railings, and the deck is made of teak.

The cabins are well laid out, typically with twin beds that convert to a queen-size bed, vanity desk with built-in hairdryer, large TV set, personal safe, and one closet that has moveable shelves – thus providing useful space for storing luggage.

The largest suites are those designated as Penthouse Suites, although they are really quite small when compared with suites aboard other ships of a similar size. However, they do at least offer more space to move around in, and a slightly larger, better bathroom.

DINING. The Taurus Restaurant is the large, main restaurant. It is located at the aft of the ship. There are two seatings, with assigned tables for 2-8, according to your chosen accommodation grade. Dinner on European cruises is typically scheduled at 7pm and 9pm. Some tables have a less than comfortable view of the harsh lighting of the escalators between the galley and the two decks of the dining room. Also, a number of support pillars provide a bit of an obstacle course for the waiters.

A Samsara Restaurant is for occupants of the Samsara-grade cabins, and is located adjacent to the Taurus Restaurant; because it's small, it provides a quieter environment in which to dine. Healthier food with reduced calories, fat and salt content is featured.

Other dining options. The Club Restaurant is a reservations-only, intimate restaurant that features à la carte dining with a pristine show kitchen as part of the venue. The food is cooked to order and so it is fresher, looks better, and tastes better than food in the main dining room, and menus are under the direction of Italy's molecular cooking master, Ettore Bocchia, Costa's consulting chef. It's a good idea to go for a meal in this venue, particularly to celebrate a special occasion, because it's different, and portions are small, and cooked to order rather than prepared en masse.

The Andromeda Buffet is the self-serve casual eatery. While there appears to be a decent choice of food, it is extremely repetitive (particularly for breakfast), and is a major source of passenger complaints. Its layout invites congestion because of some narrow passageways between the indoor seating and the food dispensing areas.

ENTERTAINMENT. The Phoenix Theater, with over 800 seats, spans three decks and is the ship's main showlounge. It appears as if it is lit by a rainbow of lighting effects, using the latest computer-controlled lighting. Typical fare consists of revue-style shows performed by a small troupe of resident onboard singers/dancers, with fast-moving action and busy lighting and costume changes that all add up to a high-energy performance.

SPA/FITNESS. This area contains 37,700 sq ft (3,500 sq m) of Samsara Spa space. Included are a Venus beauty salon, saunas for men and women, several private massage/body treatment rooms, a fitness center, and relaxation area.

The spa/fitness facilities are staffed and operated by Steiner Leisure, a specialist spa/beauty concession. Some fitness classes are free, while some, such as Pathway to Yoga, Pathway to Pilates, and Pathway to Meditation, cost extra. It's wise to make appointments early as time slots can go quickly.

Close by, a Grand Prix Formula One simulator is housed in a glass enclosure. For tee-time, a golf simulator provides a choice of 37 18-hole courses. Other sporting facilities include a roller-skating track.

Costa Magica
★★★+

Size:.................................Large Resort Ship	Crew/Passenger Ratio (lower beds/all berths):.........2.5/3.2
Tonnage: 102,587	Cabins (total):.....................................1,359
Lifestyle: ....Standard	Size range (sq ft/m): 179.7–482.2/16.7–44.8
Cruise line:.................................Costa Cruises	Cabins (outside view):...............................857
Former names: ....none	Cabins (interior/no view):..........................501
IMO number: 9239795	Cabins (for one person):..............................0
Builder: ....Fincantieri (Italy)	Cabins (with private balcony):.......................522
Original cost:..............................$418.5 million	Cabins (wheelchair accessible): 8
Entered service:.............................. Nov 2004	Wheelchair accessibility:............................Good
Registry:..Italy	Cabin voltage: ....220 volts
Length (ft/m):.............................. 893.3/272.3	Elevators:..14
Beam (ft/m):..................................124.6/38	Casino (gaming tables):...............................Yes
Draft (ft/m):................................. 27.2/8.3	Slot machines:......................................Yes
Propulsion/Propellers:...diesel-electric (34,000kW)/2 azimuthing pods	Swimming pools:.....................................3
Passenger decks:...................................13	Hot tubs (on deck):...................................
Total crew:......................................1,068	Self-service launderette:............................No
Passengers (lower beds/all berths):.............2,718/3,788	Dedicated cinema/seats:.............................No
Passenger Space Ratio (lower beds/all berths):.......37.7/27.0	Library:...Yes
	Onboard currency: ....Euros

A family-friendly large ship with bright Italian decor

OVERVIEW. *Costa Magica* is a ship that is built to impress.

THE SHIP. There is not a lot of open deck space for the number of passengers carried, so sunloungers tend to be crammed together. The décor is quite chic, but not overly glitzy. There are three decks full of lounges and 11 bars to choose from. A nine-deck-high, glass-domed atrium lobby houses the Costa Bar on the lowest level, and panoramic elevators provide pleasant views of the atrium.

The Sicilia Casino is full of shiny armor, helmets and shields as decoration. There's also a chapel. The Bressanone Library is a nice room, although it is rarely open.

ACCOMMODATION. There are numerous price grades, and accommodation ranges from two-bed interior cabins to grand suites with private balcony. There are two single-occupancy cabins (unusual for a large ship). No cabins have lifeboat-obstructed views, due to the smart design. The largest accommodation can be found in eight Grand Suites, in the center of the ship on Perugino Deck 7. These feature a queen-size bed, while the bathrooms have a tub, two washbasins, and more storage space for personal toiletry items. Note that 12 of the most desirable (outside-view) wheelchair-accessible cabins are located a long way from elevators.

DINING. The two dining rooms, Costa Smeralda Restaurant (aft) and the Portofino Restaurant (mid-ships), are both two decks high and have two seatings. Dinner on

Berlitz's Ratings

	Possible	Achieved
Ship	500	384
Accommodation	200	143
Food	400	245
Service	400	272
Entertainment	100	64
Cruise	400	271

OVERALL SCORE
1379 points out of 2000

European cruises is typically scheduled at 7pm and 9pm at assigned tables. Almost all the wines are young, and there are no sommeliers.

Other dining options. The intimate Club Vincenza is a more upscale dining spot with seating for around 150 under a huge glass dome. There is a cover charge, and reservations are required. The Bellagio Buffet Restaurant is a self-serve eatery for breakfast, lunch, afternoon pizzas, and beverages at just about any time. The food here is extremely repetitive, and a major source of passenger complaints.

ENTERTAINMENT. The Urbino Theater spans three decks in the forwardmost section of the ship. It is the setting for all production shows and large-scale cabaret acts, is quite stunning, and has a revolving stage, hydraulic orchestra pit, excellent (but overly loud) sound, and seating on three levels.

SPA/FITNESS. Facilities in the two-deck high Saturnia Spa include a large solarium, eight treatment rooms, sauna and steam rooms for men and women, and a beauty parlor.

A gymnasium has floor-to-ceiling windows on three sides, and there's an aerobics section with instructor-led classes.

Costa Mediterranea
★★★+

Size:. . . . . .Large Resort Ship		Crew/Passenger Ratio (lower beds/all berths):. 2.2/2.9		
Tonnage:. 85,700		Cabins (total):. 1,056		
Lifestyle: . . . . .Standard		Size range (sq ft/m): 161.4–387.5/15.0–36.0		
Cruise line:. . . . . .Costa Cruises		Cabins (outside view):. 843		
Former names:. . . . . .none		Cabins (interior/no view):. 213		
IMO number:. 9237345		Cabins (for one person):.. 0		
Builder:. . . . . Kvaerner Masa-Yards (Finland)		Cabins (with private balcony):. .742		
Original cost:. . . . .$335 million		Cabins (wheelchair accessible): .8		
Entered service:. . . . . May 2003		Wheelchair accessibility:. . . . . .Good		
Registry:. . . . . Italy		Cabin voltage:. . . . . .110 and 220 volts		
Length (ft/m):. 959.6/292.5		Elevators:. 12		
Beam (ft/m):. 105.6/32.2		Casino (gaming tables):. . . . . Yes		
Draft (ft/m): 25.5/7.8		Slot machines:. . . . . Yes		
Propulsion/Propellers:. . .diesel-electric (34,000kW)/2 azimuthing		Swimming pools:. . . . . .3 (1 w/sliding glass dome)		
pods (17.6MW each)		Hot tubs (on deck):. 4		
Passenger decks:. 11		Self-service launderette:. . . . . .No		
Total crew:. 920		Dedicated cinema/seats:. . . . . .No		
Passengers (lower beds/alll berths):. 2,112/2,680		Library: . . . . Yes		
Passenger Space Ratio (lower beds/all berths): 40.5/31.9		Onboard currency: . . . . Euros		

Upbeat Italian decor and style, suitable for families

OVERVIEW. The interior design is bold and brash – a mix of classical Italy and contemporary features. There is good passenger flow, several spaces for dancing, and a range of bars and lounges for socializing. The appeal is to young and young-at-heart couples and singles, plus families with children, who enjoy big-city life, loud entertainment, and an international mix of passengers.

THE SHIP. *Costa Mediterranea* is one of a series of ships with the same layout and design, the others are: *Costa Atlantica, Costa Deliziosa, Costa Fascinosa, Costa Favolosa,* and *Costa Luminosa*). There are two centrally located swimming pools outdoors, one with a retractable glass dome – so it can be covered in poor weather conditions or when t's cold. Two hot tubs are adjacent. Another smaller pool is for children. There is a winding water slide spanning two decks in height, starting on a platform bridge well aft of the funnel.

The main interior focal point is a dramatic eight-deck atrium lobby, with two grand stairways. It features a stunning wall decoration which consists of two huge paintings and *Danza*, a 25-piece wall sculpture by Gigi Rigamonte – best seen from any of the multiple viewing balconies on the decks above the main lobby-floor level. The squid-shaped wall lighting sconces are neat, too.

The decor itself is inspired by many Italian palaces (some known, many not) and by a love of art and architecture. It is extremely upbeat, bright, glitzy, and quite

Berlitz's Ratings

	Possible	Achieved
Ship	500	374
Accommodation	200	142
Food	400	240
Service	400	271
Entertainment	100	64
Cruise	400	270
OVERALL SCORE		
1361 points out of 2000		

in-your-face wherever you go. I was amused by one of three larger-than-life digital faces of Dionisio in the Dionisio Lounge, with a door handle sticking out of his mouth – in a style recalling Monty Python rather than an Italian palace!

A small chapel is located forward of the uppermost level. Other facilities include a winding shopping street with some of the fashionable brand name stores such as Fendi, Fossil, Paul & Shark Yachting. There's also a photo gallery, video games room, observation balcony, a large Grand Canal Casino with gaming tables as well as an array of slot machines – and a rarely-open library with Internet access, but not many books. Printed material such as room service folio and menus are in six languages (Italian, English, French, German, Portuguese, Spanish).

Expect lots of announcements – especially for revenue activities such as art auctions, bingo, horse racing – and much hustling for drinks.

ACCOMMODATION. There are several different price grades; this includes a healthy 78 percent proportion of outside-view to interior cabins. All cabins have twin beds that convert into a queen-size bed, individually controlled air-conditioning, TV set, and telephone. Some cabins have views obstructed by lifeboats – on deck 4 (Roma Deck), the lowest of the accommodation decks, as well as some cabins on deck 5. Some cabins have pull-down Pullman berths that are fully hidden in the ceiling when not in use.

There is too much use of fluorescent lighting in the suites and cabins, and the soundproofing could be better. Some of the bathroom fixtures such as the bath and shower taps can be frustrating to use at first.

Some of the most desirable suites and cabins are those with private balconies on the five aft-facing decks (decks 4, 5, 6, 7, and 8) with views overlooking the stern and ship's wash. Those in other cabins with 'private' balconies will find the balconies not so private – the partition between them is not a full partition, so you'll be able to hear your neighbors (and smell their smoke, or hear their mobile phone conversations).

However, these balcony occupants all have good views through glass and wood-topped railings, and the deck is teak. The cabins are well laid out, typically with twin beds that convert to a queen-size bed, vanity desk (with built-in hairdryer), large television, personal safe, and one closet with moveable shelves – to provide more space for storing luggage. However, the lighting is fluorescent and too harsh. The bedside control is for a master switch only – other lights cannot be controlled.

The bathroom is a simple, modular unit (it's a little on the bland, minimalist side) that has shower enclosures with soap dispenser; there is a good amount of stowage space for personal toiletries.

The largest suites are the Penthouse Suites, although they are small when compared with suites aboard other ships of a similar size. At least they do offer more space to move around in, and a slightly larger, better bathroom.

In 2008, some 44 cabins were converted to become Samsara Spa cabins. Occupants get special spa amenities and access to the spa. You pay a little extra for these cabins, but you get more, and it may be worth it if you want to spend time in wellness moments.

DINING. The 1,320-seat Ristorante degli Argentiere, the ship's main dining room, is a very large venue. It is located in the aft section of the ship on two levels with a spiral stairway between them. There are two seatings, with assigned tables for two, four, six or eight. Dinner on European cruises is typically scheduled at 7pm and 9pm. Some tables have a less than comfortable view of the harsh lighting of the escalators between the galley and the two decks of the dining room. Also, a number of support pillars provide a bit of an obstacle course for waiters.

Other dining options. The Club Medusa is a more upscale dining spot that spans two of the uppermost decks under a large glass dome that is adjacent to the ship's funnel. It seats around 125 and has a menu by Zeffirino, a well-respected restaurant in Genoa. An open kitchen provides a view into the cooking area, so you can watch the chefs preparing their masterpieces. Fine table settings, china and silverware are used, and menus are leather-bound. Reservations are needed and there's a cover charge. You may think it's worth it in order to have dinner in a setting that's quieter and much more refined than the main dining room.

The Perla del Lago Buffet is an extensive eatery forming the aft third of Deck 9, with part of it wrapping around the upper section of the multi-deck atrium. It includes a central area with several small buffet counters; there are salad counters, a dessert counter, and a 24-hour Posillipo Pizzeria counter, all creating a large eatery with both indoor and outdoor seating. Movement around the buffet area is very slow, and requires you to stand in line for everything. Venture outdoors and you'll find a grill for hamburgers and hot dogs, and a pasta bar, both conveniently located adjacent to the second of two swimming pools on the lido deck.

The place most people will want to see and be seen is the ultra-casual Oriental Café; it features four separate 'salons,' which provide intimate spaces for drinks, conversation, and people-watching.

Excellent Italian cappuccino and espresso coffees are always available in various bars around the ship, and these are always served in the right-sized china cups.

ENTERTAINMENT. The 949-seat Osiris Theater is the venue for the Splash-Vegas-style production shows and major cabaret acts. It spans three decks, with seating on all three levels. Sightlines to the stage are, however, a little better from the second and third levels. Curving stairways at the back of the showlounge connect all levels.

SPA/FITNESS. The expansive Ischia Spa spans two decks, is located directly above the navigation bridge in the forward part of the ship (accessed by the forward stairway elevators), and has around 13,700 sq ft (1,272 sq m) of space. Lower-level facilities include a solarium, eight private massage/body treatment rooms, sauna and steam rooms for men and women, and a beauty parlor. The upper level has a large gymnasium with floor-to-ceiling windows on three sides, and an aerobics room with instructor-led classes (some, such as yoga, may cost extra).

For sporty types, there's a jogging track outdoors, around the ship's mast and the forward third of the ship, as well as a multi-purpose court for basketball, volleyball and deck tennis.

Costa neoRomantica
★★★

Size:....................................Large Resort Ship	Cabins (total):.....................................789
Tonnage:...57,150	Size range (sq ft/m):..................185.1–430.5/17.2–40.0
Lifestyle:..Standard	Cabins (outside view):..............................479
Cruise line:................................Costa Cruises	Cabins (interior/no view):...........................224
Former names:...............................Romantica	Cabins (for one person):..............................0
IMO number:..................................8821046	Cabins (with private balcony):.......................86
Builder:...............................Fincantieri (Italy)	Cabins (wheelchair accessible):.......................6
Original cost:..............................$325 million	Wheelchair accessibility:..........................Good
Entered service:.............................Nov 1993	Cabin voltage:.........................110 and 220 volts
Registry:..Italy	Elevators:..8
Length (ft/m):............................718.5/220.6	Casino (gaming tables):............................Yes
Beam (ft/m):...............................98.4/30.8	Slot machines:.....................................Yes
Draft (ft/m):...................................25.0/7.6	Swimming pools:.....................................2
Propulsion/Propellers:..............diesel (22,800kW)/2	Hot tubs (on deck):..................................2
Passenger decks:...................................10	Self-service launderette:............................No
Total crew:.......................................662	Dedicated cinema/seats:.............................No
Passengers (lower beds/alll berths):...........1,578/1,800	Library:..Yes
Passenger Space Ratio (lower beds/all berths):.......36.2/31.7	Onboard currency:...............................Euros
Crew/Passenger Ratio (lower beds/all berths):..........2.3/2.7	

An elegant Italian-style ship for a mature audience

OVERVIEW. Being Italian, the ship is chic and very tasteful, and will appeal to the sophisticated. The layout and flow are somewhat disjointed, however. The ship's multi-level atrium is open and spacious, and has a revolving mobile sculpture as its focal point. The décor is contemporary and minimalist in style.

THE SHIP. *Costa neoRomantica* (a play on the ship's original name of *Costa Romantica*) is now over 20 years old, but is a fairly contemporary-looking ship, and is easily recognizable by its cluster of three upright yellow funnels. There is, however, no walk-around promenade deck outdoors, so contact with the sea is minimal, although there's some good open space on several of the upper decks.

In 2011–12, the ship was given an extensive €90 million refit, refurbishment and renewal program that added more public rooms, two half-deck extensions, 111 new cabins, 120 suites and cabins with balcony, wine and cheese bar, a chocolate confectionary bar, new Pizzeria Capri (with its black and white tiled decor), a cabaret lounge and nightclub, and LED lighting. However, no additional elevators were installed for the additional growth in passenger numbers.

Facilities also include a Monte Carlo Lido indoor/outdoor bar; Vienna cabaret lounge; Piazza Italia Grand Bar (arguably the best place to see and be seen); a new atrium (with minimalist design features); a new neoRomantica Club Restaurant; Casino Excelsior; a wine and cheese bar, coffee and chocolate bar, and a

Berlitz's Ratings		
	Possible	Achieved
Ship	500	333
Accommodation	200	135
Food	400	214
Service	400	267
Entertainment	100	60
Cruise	400	240
OVERALL SCORE		
1249 points out of 2000		

Caffeteria that forms part of the Via Condotti shopping area. Out on the pool deck (Lido Saint-Tropez) several 'private' cabanas, adjacent to the pool, can be rented.

Although Costa Cruises is noted for its 'Italian' style, ambience and spirit, there are few Italian crew members on board. Although many officers are Italian, most of the crew members, particularly the dining room and housekeeping staff, are from the Philippines. But the lifestyle on board is perceived to be Italian – lively, noisy, with lots of love for life and a love of all things casual, even on so-called formal nights.

All printed material – room service folio, menus, etc. – will typically be in six languages: Italian, English, French, German, Portuguese, and Spanish. During peak European school holiday periods, particularly Christmas and Easter, you can expect to be cruising with a lot of children of all ages.

As aboard other Costa ships, note that for embarkation, few staff members are on duty at the gangway when you arrive; they merely point you in the direction of your deck, or to the ship's elevators and do not escort you to your cabin. Also, note that 'wallpaper' music is played 24 hours a day in all accommodation hallways and elevators, so you may well hear it if you are a light sleeper.

ACCOMMODATION. There are several different price categories. These include 16 suites, 10 of which have a private semi-circular balcony, while six suites command views over the ship's bows. The other cabins are fairly standard in size, shape, and facilities; the ones on the highest decks cost more.

A whole 'wedge' of cabins with half-moon-shaped balconies, as well as normal balconies, has been added in the mid-section of the ship.

Samsara Suites/Cabins. Occupants of these 6 suites and 50 cabins have access to the Samsara Spa and its facilities, located at the front of the ship. Samsara accommodation provides organic cotton bedlinen, purifying shower filter, and a selection of ayervedic teas.

Suites/Mini-Suites. The 16 suites (with floor-to-ceiling windows) and 18 mini-suites are quite pleasant, except for the rounded balconies of the 10 suites on Madrid Deck where a solid steel half-wall blocks the view. A sliding door separates the bedroom from the living room, and bathrooms are of a decent size. Cherry wood walls and cabinetry help make these suites warm and attractive.

The six suites at the forward section of Monte Carlo Deck are the largest, and have huge glass windows with commanding forward views, but no balconies.

Standard Outside-View/Interior Cabins. All other cabins are of a moderately generous size, and all have nicely finished cherry wood cabinetry and walls. However, the cabin bathrooms and shower enclosures are quite small. There is a good number of triple and quad cabins, ideal for families with children. The company's in-cabin food service menu is extremely basic.

DINING. The 728-seat Botticelli Restaurant is of a fine design. There are tables for 2-8 persons. You eat at one of two are two seatings (dinner on European cruises is typically at 7pm and 9pm). Romantic candlelight dining is typically featured on 'formal' night. Traditional cruise fare is served, and best described as banquet-style food. Note that there are no real sommeliers, so the waiters are expected to serve the wine. They also dance in the restaurant during the cruise – in a little bit of Costa Cruises show business style.

Other dining options. Samsara Restaurant is the venue for occupants of the 56 Samsara-grade suites/cabins. The restaurant is located at the aft of the ship on the port side of Vienna Deck. The cuisine is more health-oriented, and the venue is quieter and more intimate than the main dining room.

Club neoRomantica Restaurant is an extra-cost, reservations required, à la carte, cozy and intimate dining venue. While the banquette seating is unbecoming of 'fine' dining, it's a rather pleasant spot for an intimate dinner, and features contemporary French and Italian fare that is worth the extra cost.

For casual meals and snacks, the self-serve Giardino Buffet is a small, cramped buffet. The buffet food items are very much standard fare (repetitive breakfast items are a major source of passenger complaints),

with the exception of some good commercial pasta dishes. One would expect Italian waiters, but most hail from elsewhere.

Pizzeria Capri has something unusual for any cruise ship – a real wood-burning oven – used for making 'genuine' Neapolitan-style pizzas (the venue makes 15 different one).

Enoteco Verona is a wine and cheese bar that features more than 100 different wines, and 80 cheeses from around the world. Italian coffee machines are provided in all bars (coffees are at extra cost, however), so there's never a shortage of espressos and cappuccinos.

ENTERTAINMENT. The Cabaret Vienna is the ship's main showlounge. It is an interesting amphitheater-like design that spans two decks, with seating on both levels. However, the seats are quite upright and uncomfortable, and 10 large pillars obstructing the sight lines from many seats. Typical fare consists of revue-style shows performed by a small troupe of resident onboard singers/dancers, with fast-moving action and busy lighting and costume changes that all add up to a high-energy performance.

SPA/FITNESS. A Samsara Spa is spread over two decks in the forward section of the ship. It contains a gymnasium with some high-tech muscle-pump machines, an aerobics exercise area, thalassotherapy pool, Turkish baths, health bar, sauna and steam rooms, a solarium, and a beauty salon. Occupants of the 56 adjacent Samsara Spa cabins also have a dedicated Samsara Restaurant.

The spa/fitness facilities are staffed and operated by Steiner Leisure, a specialist spa/beauty concession. Some fitness classes are free, while some, such as Pathway to Yoga, Pathway to Pilates, and Pathway to Meditation, cost extra. It's wise to make appointments early as time slots can go quickly.

Costa Pacifica
★★★+

Size:.................................Large Resort Ship	Crew/Passenger Ratio (lower beds/all berths):......... 2.7/3.4
Tonnage: 114,500	Cabins (total):................................... 1,506
Lifestyle: ....Standard	Size range (sq ft/m): 179.7–482.2/16.7–44.8
Cruise line:...............................Costa Cruises	Cabins (outside view):..............................926
Former names: ....none	Cabins (interior/no view):...........................580
IMO number: 9378498	Cabins (for one person):..............................0
Builder: .... Fincantieri (Italy)	Cabins (with private balcony):......................579
Original cost:............................€510 million	Cabins (wheelchair accessible): 12
Entered service:............................Apr 2009	Wheelchair accessibility:...........................Good
Registry:.. Italy	Cabin voltage: ....110 and 220 volts
Length (ft/m):........................... 952.0/290.0	Elevators:......................................14
Beam (ft/m):............................. 116.4/35.5	Casino (gaming tables):............................ Yes
Draft (ft/m):.............................. 27.2/8.3	Slot machines:................................. Yes
Propulsion/Propellers:...diesel-electric (34,000kW)/2 azimuthing pods	Swimming pools:.....................................2
	Hot tubs (on deck):..................................5
Passenger decks:...................................13	Self-service launderette:...........................No
Total crew:................................... 1,110	Dedicated cinema/seats:............................No
Passengers (lower beds/alll berths):............. 3,012/3,780	Library: .... Yes
Passenger Space Ratio (lower beds/all berths): 38.0/30.2	Onboard currency: .... Euros

A large, colorful family-friendly Italian-style ship

OVERVIEW. Costa Cruises does a good job of providing first-time cruise passengers with a well-packaged holiday, particularly for families with children. It's a mix of sophistication and chaos, accompanied by loud music. This ship has a musical design theme featuring 'greatest hits.' The lobby, for example, is covered in musical symbols and instruments.

Berlitz's Ratings		
	Possible	Achieved
Ship	500	386
Accommodation	200	143
Food	400	242
Service	400	268
Entertainment	100	65
Cruise	400	271
OVERALL SCORE		
1375 points out of 2000		

THE SHIP. Sporting a single, large funnel, *Costa Pacifica* is a sister to the popular *Costa Serena*. Two pool areas can be covered with retractable glass domes – good in case of poor weather – and one of the pools has a water slide that's great for kids. There is also a huge screen for poolside movies. A Grand Prix simulator is positioned on one of the upper decks.

However, the open deck space is cramped when the ship is full, so sunloungers tend to be crammed together, and they don't have cushioned pads.

There are three decks full of bars and lounges plus many other public rooms. This ship has a glass-domed atrium lobby nine decks high, with great upward views from the lobby bar, as well as from its four glass panoramic elevators. The passenger flow inside is quite good, and the ship absorbs passengers reasonably well. It also provides a decent passenger space ratio, which means that it won't feel too crowded.

The casino is large and glitzy, but always lively and entertaining; slot machines occupy a separate area from gaming tables, so serious gamers can concentrate. There's also a very small library, an Internet-connection center, card room, art gallery, and video game room, together with several other bars and lounges. A chapel is a standard aboard all Costa ships.

Although Costa Cruises is noted for its 'Italian' style, ambience and spirit, there are few Italian crew members on board its ships. While many of the officers are Italian, most of the crew members – particularly the dining room and housekeeping staff – are from the Philippines. The lifestyle on board is, however, perceived to be Italian – lively, noisy, and embracing a casual lifestyle – even on so-called formal nights. Most passengers will be Italian, with a sprinkling of other European nationals.

Printed material such as room service folio and menus will typically be in six languages (Italian, English, French, German, Portuguese, and Spanish). During peak European school holiday periods, particularly Christmas and Easter, expect to be cruising with a lot of children of all ages. Sony PlayStation fans can enjoy PlayStation World. PlayStations are also available in cabins, in the children's and teens' clubs, and can be used with the poolside movie screen.

As aboard other Costa ships, few staff members are on duty at the gangway when you embark; they merely point you in the direction of your deck, or to the ship's elevators and do not escort you to your cabin.

ACCOMMODATION. There are numerous price grades, from two-bed interior cabins to grand suites with private balcony, although in reality there are only three different sizes: Suites with 'private' balcony (which are really not large when compared with many other large ships), two- or four-bed outside view cabins, and two- or four-bed interior cabins. No cabins have views obstructed by lifeboats or other safety equipment, and, in all cabins, twin beds can be changed to a double/queen-bed configuration.

A total of eight Grand Suites comprise the largest accommodation. These are in the center of the ship on one of the uppermost decks. They have a queen-size bed and larger living area with vanity desk; the bathrooms have a tub and two washbasins.

If you like wellness treatments, 12 Samsara Spa Suites are located just aft of the spa – although 99 cabins, including the 12 suites, are designated as Samsara-grade. Samsara suite/cabin occupants get unlimited access to the spa plus two treatments and fitness or meditation lessons as part of their package, and dine in one of the two Samsara restaurants. All Samsara-designated accommodation grades have an Oriental decorative theme, and special Samsara bathroom amenities.

A pillow menu, with five choices, is available in all suite accommodation grades. Only suite grades get bathrobes and better amenities, shaving mirror, and walk-in closets – although the hangars are plastic. Music is played 24 hours a day in all hallways and elevators, so you may well hear it if you are a light sleeper.

DINING. There are two main dining rooms (New York, New York, and My Way), allocated according to your accommodation grade and location. There are two seatings in each for dinner.

Two 100-seat Samsara Restaurants have separate entrances, adjacent to the My Way restaurant. Unlike the main restaurants that offer traditional cruise fare, these are for people seeking spa food – this means reduced calories, fat and salt, with menus created under the direction of dietary consultant and Michelin-star chef Ettore Boccia and his molecular Italian cuisine. These dining venues are open for lunch and dinner to those in Samsara-grade suites and cabins, and to anyone else (for dinner only) for an extra charge.

Other dining options. Club Blue Moon (reservations required) is an elegant, intimate venue with seating under a huge glass dome. Fine table settings, china, silverware and leather-bound menus are provided. There's a cover charge of $20 per person, for service and a gratuity.

La Paloma Buffet Restaurant is a self-serve eatery for breakfast, lunch, afternoon pizzas, and coffee and tea at any time. A balcony level provides additional seating. You'll need to carry your own food plates – there are no trays. Decent quality cappuccino and espresso coffees are always available in various bars, at extra cost.

Additionally, the Caffeteria is the place to go for decent Italian coffees and Italian pastries, at extra cost (coffee machines are in all bars).

ENTERTAINMENT. The Stardust Theater seats more than 800 and utilizes the latest in LED technology. It is three decks high and is decorated in a Baroque style, with warm colors and a Murano glass chandelier. It is the venue for all production shows and large-scale cabaret acts, is quite stunningly glitzy, and has a revolving stage, hydraulic orchestra pit, superb sound, and seating on three levels (the upper levels are tiered through two decks).

Typical fare consists of revue-style shows performed by a small troupe of resident onboard singers/dancers, with fast-moving action and busy lighting and costume changes that all add up to a high-energy performance.

SPA/FITNESS. The Samsara Spa is a large facility that occupies 23,186 sq ft (2,154 sq m) of space, spread over two decks. It includes a large fitness room, separate saunas, steam rooms, UVB solarium, changing rooms for men and women, and 10 body treatment rooms. On the upper level, two VIP treatment rooms are available to couples for half-day rentals.

The spa/fitness facilities are staffed and operated by Steiner Leisure, a specialist spa/beauty concession. Some fitness classes are free; others, such as Pathway to Yoga, and Pathway to Pilates, cost extra. Make appointments early as time slots can go quickly.

You can buy a day pass in order to use the sauna/steam rooms, thermal suite and relaxation area, at a cost of €35 per person. However, there's an additional no-charge sauna for men and women, but to access it you must walk through an active fitness area, perhaps wearing your bathrobe – an arrangement with which some women may not feel comfortable.

Costa Serena
★★★+

Size:	Large Resort Ship	Crew/Passenger Ratio (lower beds/all berths):	2.7/3.4
Tonnage:	114,147	Cabins (total):	1,500
Lifestyle:	Standard	Size range (sq ft/m):	482.2–179.7/44.8–16.7
Cruise line:	Costa Cruises	Cabins (outside view):	914
Former names:	none	Cabins (interior/no view):	586
IMO number:	9343132	Cabins (for one person):	0
Builder:	Fincantieri (Italy)	Cabins (with private balcony):	575
Original cost:	€475 million	Cabins (wheelchair accessible):	12
Entered service:	May 2007	Wheelchair accessibility:	Good
Registry:	Italy	Cabin voltage:	110 and 220 volts
Length (ft/m):	952.0/290.2	Elevators:	14
Beam (ft/m):	116.4/35.5	Casino (gaming tables):	Yes
Draft (ft/m):	27.2/8.3	Slot machines:	Yes
Propulsion/Propellers:	diesel-electric (34,000kW)/2 azimuthing pods	Swimming pools:	4
		Hot tubs (on deck):	5
Passenger decks:	13	Self-service launderette:	No
Total crew:	1,090	Dedicated cinema/seats:	No
Passengers (lower beds/alll berths):	3,000/3,780	Library:	Yes
Passenger Space Ratio (lower beds/all berths):	38.0/30.1	Onboard currency:	Euros

Upbeat Italian decor and style, for family cruising

OVERVIEW. Costa Cruises does a good job of providing first-time cruise passengers with a well-packaged holiday that is a mix of sophistication and basic fare.

THE SHIP. *Costa Serena* absorbs passengers well and won't feel too crowded – except on the open decks. The delightful interior design is themed around the heavens and astrology.

As aboard other Costa ships, note that for embarkation, few staff members are on duty at the gangway when you arrive; they merely point you in the direction of your deck, or to the ship's elevators and do not escort you to your cabin. Also, note that 'wallpaper' music is played 24 hours a day in all accommodation hallways and elevators, so you may well hear it if you are a light sleeper.

ACCOMMODATION. There are numerous price grades, from two-bed interior cabins to grand suites with private balcony, although in reality there are only three different sizes: Suites with balcony, two- or four-bed outside view cabins, and two- or four-bed interior cabins. Eight Grand suites comprise the largest accommodation.

DINING. There are two main dining rooms: Ceres, located aft, and Vesta, amidships. Tables for 2-8 are allocated according to your accommodation grade and location, in one of two seating times. These dining rooms offer traditional cruise fare that is best described as

Berlitz's Ratings		
	Possible	Achieved
Ship	500	387
Accommodation	200	143
Food	400	245
Service	400	267
Entertainment	100	64
Cruise	400	269
OVERALL SCORE		
1375 points out of 2000		

banquet-style food. Note that there are no real sommeliers.

Two 100-seat Samsara Restaurants are for those seeking spa food with reduced calories, fat and salt. This venue is open for lunch and dinner to those in Samsara-grade suites and cabins, and to anyone else for dinner only at an extra daily or weekly charge.

Other dining options. Club Bacco is an upscale, intimate, extra-cost, reservations required restaurant. The Promotea Buffet Restaurant is a self-serve eatery. The food in this venue is repetitive, and a source of passenger complaints.The Caffeteria is the place to go for decent Italian coffees and Italian pastries (extra-cost).

ENTERTAINMENT. The three-deck high 1,287-seat Giove Theater is the venue for all production shows and large-scale cabaret acts. Typically, it presents revue-style shows performed by a small troupe of resident artists.

SPA/FITNESS. Samsara Spa occupies 23,186 sq ft (2,154 sq m) of space, spread over two decks. It includes a fitness room, saunas, steam rooms, UVB solarium, changing rooms, and treatment rooms.

You can buy a day pass in order to use the sauna/steam rooms, thermal suite and relaxation area, at a cost of €35 per person. However, there's an additional no-charge sauna for men and women, but to access it you walk through a fitness area.

Costa Victoria
★★★ +

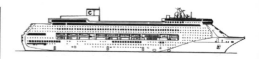

Size:................................Large Resort Ship		Cabins (total):.................................964	
Tonnage:..75,200		Size range (sq ft/m):.................120.0–430.5/11.1–40.0	
Lifestyle:...Standard		Cabins (outside view):..............................573	
Cruise line:................................Costa Cruises		Cabins (interior/no view):...........................391	
Former names:......................................none		Cabins (for one person):..............................0	
IMO number:..................................9109031		Cabins (with private balcony):.....................246	
Builder:.........................Bremer Vulkan (Germany)		Cabins (wheelchair accessible):......................6	
Original cost:..............................$388 million		Wheelchair accessibility:..........................Good	
Entered service:................................Jul 1996		Cabin voltage:.........................110 and 220 volts	
Registry:..Italy		Elevators:...12	
Length (ft/m):.............................823.0/251.0		Casino (gaming tables):............................Yes	
Beam (ft/m):.............................105.5/32.2		Slot machines:.....................................Yes	
Draft (ft/m):.................................25.6/7.8		Swimming pools:.....................................2	
Propulsion/Propellers:..................diesel (30,000kW)/2		Hot tubs (on deck):..................................4	
Passenger decks:....................................10		Self-service launderette:...........................Yes	
Total crew:..800		Dedicated cinema/seats:.............................No	
Passengers (lower beds/all berths):..............1,928/2,464		Library:..Yes	
Passenger Space Ratio (lower beds/all berths):.......39.0/30.5		Onboard currency:................................Euros	
Crew/Passenger Ratio (lower beds/all berths):.........2.4/3.0			

Bland decor in an Italian setting for mature-age cruisers

OVERVIEW. Where this vessel differs from most large ships is in its distinct interior decor, with decidedly Italian styling.

THE SHIP. *Costa Victoria* features an outdoor walk-around promenade deck, although it tends to be full of sunloungers. Inside is a charming four-deck-high observation lounge with a glass elevator; in the center is a cone-shaped waterfall. A seven-deck-high 'planetarium' atrium is the ship's focal point. The uppermost level of the atrium is the deck where two outdoor swimming pools are located, together with four blocks of showers, a grill, and an ice cream bar.

ACCOMMODATION. There are 13 price categories. The six large Panorama suites (each with third/fourth Pullman berths in tiny, train-like compartments) and 14 mini-suites have butler service; 65 percent of all other cabins have outside views (portholes and not windows), but they are extremely small for two persons. While the suites aren't large, all other cabins are of mean dimensions. Only 16 of the interior cabins accommodate four people, while all other cabins are for two or three.

All cabins have wood cabinetry, mini-bar/refrigerator, and electric blackout window blind, but the storage space is very limited. The ocean-view cabins have large picture windows. Bathrooms are small but quite well appointed.

Berlitz's Ratings		
	Possible	Achieved
Ship	500	339
Accommodation	200	132
Food	400	219
Service	400	262
Entertainment	100	62
Cruise	400	246
OVERALL SCORE		
1260 points out of 2000		

DINING. This ship has two main dining rooms: the 594-seat Sinfonia Restaurant and the 506-seat Fantasia Restaurant. There are two seatings, with assigned tables for 2-8, according to your chosen accommodation grade. Some tables have a less than comfortable view of the harsh lighting of the escalators between the galley and the two decks of the dining room. Also, a number of support pillars provide a bit of an obstacle course for the waiters.

Other dining options. Ristorante Magnifico by Zeffirino (reservations only) is available six nights each week, with an additional service charge. Passengers occupying suites receive a free pass for one evening. The ship also has casual buffets, although the displays and food variety are poor (and a source of passenger complaints).

ENTERTAINMENT. The entertainment consists of revue-style shows performed by a small troupe of resident onboard singers/dancers.

SPA/FITNESS. The congested spa/fitness area, on a lower deck, is much too small for the size of the ship. It has a beauty salon, tiny indoor swimming pool, treatment rooms, sauna and steam room, but cramped changing areas. Sporting facilities include a covered walking/jogging track and a tennis court.

Costa Voyager
★★★ +

Size:... Mid-size Ship	Cabins (total):......................................420
Tonnage:... 24,391	Size range (sq ft/m):.................. 140.0–375.0/13.0–34.8
Lifestyle: .... Standard	Cabins (outside view):..............................294
Cruise line:................................. Costa Cruises	Cabins (interior/no view):...........................126
Former names: *Grand Voyager, Olympia Voyager, Olympic Voyager*	Cabins (for one person):...............................0
IMO number:...................................9183506	Cabins (with private balcony):........................12
Builder: .... Blohm & Voss (Germany)	Cabins (wheelchair accessible): 4
Original cost:........................... $150.8 million	Wheelchair accessibility:.........................Good
Entered service:......................Jul 2000/Nov 2011	Cabin voltage: ....110 and 230 volts
Registry:.. Italy	Elevators:..4
Length (ft/m):............................. 590.5/180.0	Casino (gaming tables):............................ Yes
Beam (ft/m):................................. 83.6/25.5	Slot machines:.................................... Yes
Draft (ft/m): 23.2/7.1	Swimming pools:.....................................1
Propulsion/Propellers: .... diesel (37,800kW)/2	Hot tubs (on deck):..................................0
Passenger decks:......................................8	Self-service launderette:...........................No
Total crew:.......................................360	Dedicated cinema/seats:.............................No
Passengers (lower beds/alll berths):................ 840/920	Library: .... Yes
Passenger Space Ratio (lower beds/all berths): 29.0/26.5	Onboard currency: .... Euros
Crew/Passenger Ratio (lower beds/all berths):.......... 2.3/2.5	

A small, high-density ship, with some Italian style

OVERVIEW. *Costa Voyager* is best suited to Italian-speaking couples and single travelers who want to see as much as possible of their destinations in contemporary, comfortable, but not luxurious surroundings, and with food and service that are acceptable but nothing special, all at a decent cruise fare.

THE SHIP. The exterior hull design, called a 'fast monohull,' is similar to that of naval frigates, with a slender fore-body, and two engine rooms (forward and mid-ships) that could provide a speed of up to 28 knots. The ship is well suited to destination-intensive, port-hopping itineraries, giving passengers more time in each port – or more ports per cruise. Its funnel is of a streamlined, swept-back design, with the signature 'C' logo of Costa Cruises in blue on yellow.

There is a limited amount of open deck space, and there aren't many sunloungers. All exterior railings are made – unusually – of stainless steel, topped with thick, beautifully polished wood. A small seawater swimming pool is located aft; adjacent are two shower enclosures.

The interior design combines contemporary touches with restrained decor, intended to remind one of the Mediterranean region the ship is designed for, with warm colors and an abundance of wood and opaque glass paneling. Perhaps the most striking, yet subtle, features in terms of design and decoration can be found in the artwork. Of particular note are two flowing poems, from Greece and Cyprus, etched in backlit opaque glass panels on the stairways. To read the poems, you'll

Berlitz's Ratings

	Possible	Achieved
Ship	500	347
Accommodation	200	133
Food	400	237
Service	400	256
Entertainment	100	62
Cruise	400	259

OVERALL SCORE
1294 points out of 2000

need to walk down a complete set of stairways. One poem, Ithaca, from 1911 by the Greek poet Constantinos Petrou Kavafis, complements the other poem, *Let's Say*, by Cypriot poet Yannis Papadopoulos.

Most public rooms are located on one principal deck in a horizontal-flow layout that makes it easy to quickly find your way around. A slightly winding open passageway links several leisure lounges in one neat 'street scene.' There's a smoking room, adjacent to the main showlounge, for cigar and cognac devotees, with a black fireplace from the 1890s. In the popular Piano Bar, three ship models are cleverly displayed behind large glass wall panels. There's a nightclub, a small library, and a card room. A casino has its own bar as well as table games and slot machines. Children have a dedicated Squok Club.

Niggles include the fact that there is no full walk-around promenade deck, although you can walk around parts of the vessel outdoors. There is considerable vibration when the ship is underway at high speed, and when maneuvering at slow speeds. None of the public toilets is accessible by wheelchair.

ACCOMMODATION. There are five categories – suite with balcony, suite with bay window, junior suite with window but no balcony, outside cabin, and interior cabin – and nine price grades, including one for wheelchair accessible cabins with spacious bathrooms and roll-in showers. The price will depend on grade, location, and size.

Standard Cabins. The standard interior and outside-view cabins are quite compact but practically laid-out, and the decor includes warm blond wood cabinetry, accents, and facings, and pleasing soft furnishings. The bathrooms are small, but have a decent-size shower enclosure, and good storage facilities for toiletries. All cabins include TV set, hairdryer, mini-bar/refrigerator, and personal safe. Only one personal safe is provided in each cabin, although there could be as many as four persons sharing a cabin.

Outside-View Superior Cabins. These simply have a little more room than the standard interior and outside-view cabins, and some have bay windows that extend over the side of the ship. The bathrooms are small, but have a decent-size shower enclosure, and good storage for toiletries.

Balcony Suites. The largest accommodation is in 12 Sky Suites high atop the ship in the forwardmost section. They have large private balconies (some are more like large terraces) and floor-to-ceiling windows.

Some suites have walk-in closets, while others have closets facing the entranceway, but all have an abundance of drawer and hanging space, and a chrome pull-out shoe rack and tie rack. The bathroom has a combination tub/shower – although the tub is extremely small and is really only for sitting in – and a retractable clothesline.

All suites have wood-paneled walls with vanity desk, mini-bar/refrigerator, sofa, drinks table (it's fixed, and can't be raised), and sleeping area partly separated from the lounge area by a wood/glass divider. Four of the suites have large structures above their balconies that are the port side and starboard side gangway lowering mechanisms; they are noisy in ports of call and anchor ports, and so the balconies cannot be considered very private.

When the ship is traveling, considerable wind sweeps across the balconies, rendering them almost useless. The balconies have expensive stainless-steel railings instead of glass, topped with a thick wood railing. Outside-view and interior cabins located aft on Deck 3 (Neptune Deck: Numbers 3120–3138, and 3121–3151) are subject to a substantial amount of throbbing noise from the diesel engines, and should be avoided – unless you like throbbing engine noise, that is.

DINING. The 470-seat Main Restaurant, located aft, is one deck below the main 'street' of public rooms and thus out of the main flow. It has picture windows on three sides and a semi-circular walkway, with minimalist decor, as its entrance. There are two seatings, with assigned tables for 2-8 persons. The interior decor is warm and welcoming, and quite tasteful, finished in what is best described as a minimalist style. The chairs, however, don't have armrests.

Note that a few tables close to the entrance to the galley's escalators suffer due to noise from the service area, and because of the single-deck ceiling height and open waiter stations, the noise level can be considerable.

Other dining options. For casual breakfast and lunch self-service buffets, the Garden Buffet is a pleasant but basic room, with large picture windows and an open feel. It has seating for 210 indoors and about 200 outdoors (where smokers congregate), and a bar outdoors is covered with a sailcloth-style cover. Two small self-service buffet lines have a user-unfriendly layout that invites congestion.

Additional munching outlets include a pizza serving area/salad bar, and an ice cream bar.

ENTERTAINMENT. The Main Lounge is the venue for entertainment events. It is a single-level room with 420 seats, although several pillars obstruct the sight lines from many seats – about 40 percent are almost useless. Entertainment is limited aboard this ship, whose showlounge is best for cabaret-style shows. There's also a disco, and a piano bar.

SPA/FITNESS. One of the nicest and most useful facilities can be found in the Samsara Spa. It includes a large fitness room, several massage/treatment rooms, sauna, steam room, and a rest/changing area.

Crown Princess
★★★★

Size:.	Large Resort Ship
Tonnage:	116,000
Lifestyle:	Standard
Cruise line:.	Princess Cruises
Former names:	none
IMO number:	9293399
Builder:	Fincantieri (Italy)
Original cost:	$500 million
Entered service:.	May 2006
Registry:.	Bermuda
Length (ft/m):.	951.4/290.0
Beam (ft/m):.	118.1/36.0
Draft (ft/m):	26.2/8.0
Propulsion/Propellers: . gas turbine (25,000kW)/2 azimuthing pods	
Passenger decks:.	15
Total crew:	1,163
Passengers (lower beds/alll berths):.	3,114/3,782
Passenger Space Ratio (lower beds/all berths):	37.2/30.6
Crew/Passenger Ratio (lower beds/all berths):.	2.6/3.2

Cabins (total):.	1,557
Size range (sq ft/m):	163–1,279/15.1–118.8
Cabins (outside view):.	1,105
Cabins (interior/no view):.	452
Cabins (for one person):.	0
Cabins (with private balcony):	881
Cabins (wheelchair accessible):	25
Wheelchair accessibility:.	Best
Cabin voltage:	110 volts
Elevators:.	14
Casino (gaming tables):.	Yes
Slot machines:.	Yes
Swimming pools:.	4
Hot tubs (on deck):.	9
Self-service launderette:.	Yes
Dedicated cinema/seats:.	No
Library:	Yes
Onboard currency:	US$

A large ship with sedate decor, for mature-age cruisers

OVERVIEW. *Crown Princess* is a grand resort playground, and Princess Cruises delivers a consistently fine, well-packaged product, always with a good degree of style, at a competitive price. With many choices and 'small' rooms (a relative term) to enjoy, the ship has been extremely well designed, and the odds are that you'll have an enjoyable vacation.

Berlitz's Ratings

	Possible	Achieved
Ship	500	372
Accommodation	200	145
Food	400	251
Service	400	289
Entertainment	100	78
Cruise	400	292

OVERALL SCORE
1427 points out of 2000

THE SHIP. If you are not used to large ships, it'll take you some time to find your way around, despite the company's claim that it offers passengers a 'small ship feel, big ship choice.' One nice feature is The Sanctuary, an extra-cost adults-only retreat located forward on the uppermost deck.

There is a good sheltered teakwood promenade deck, which almost wraps around, and a walkway that leads to the enclosed bow of the ship. The outdoor pools have various beach-like surroundings. Movies Under the Skies and major sporting events are shown on a 300-sq-ft (28-sq-m) movie screen located at the pool in front of the large funnel.

Atop the stern is a ship-wide glass-walled disco, Skywalkers, with spectacular views from the extreme port and starboard side windows.

The interior decor is attractive, with lots of earth tones. An extensive collection of artworks complements the interior design and colors well.

Crown Princess also includes a Wedding Chapel with a live web-cam relaying ceremonies via the Internet. The ship's captain can legally marry American couples,

thanks to the ship's Bermuda registry and a special dispensation.

A large casino has with more than 260 slot machines, and black-jack, craps, and roulette tables, plus games such as Let It Ride Bonus, Spanish 21, and Caribbean Draw Progressive.

Other facilities include a decent library/computer room. Ship lovers should enjoy the wood-paneled Wheelhouse Bar, finely decorated with memorabilia and ship models tracing part of parent company P&O's history.

FAMILIES. There is a two-deck-high playroom, teen room, and a host of trained counselors. Children have their own pools, hot tubs, and open deck area at the stern, thankfully away from adult areas. There are good netted-in areas; one section has a dip pool, while another has a mini-basketball court. There's a video games arcade, too.

Two family suites consist of two suites with an interconnecting door, plus a large balcony. These sleep up to 10 (if at least four are children) or up to eight adults.

ACCOMMODATION. There are six principal types of cabins and configurations: (a) grand suite, (b) suite, (c) mini-suite, (d) outside-view double cabins with balcony, (e) outside-view double cabins, and (f) interior double cabins. These come in a bewildering choice of 35 different brochure price categories.

(a) The Grand Suite has a large bedroom with queen-size bed, huge walk-in closets, two bathrooms, a lounge with fireplace, sofa bed, wet bar, and refrigerator, and a large private balcony on the port side with hot tub that can be accessed from both balcony and bedroom.

(b/c) Suites have a separate living room (with sofa bed) and bedroom, with a TV set in each. The bathroom is quite large and has both a tub and shower stall. The mini-suites also have a private balcony, and a separate living and sleeping area (with a TV set in each). The differences between the suites and mini-suites are basically in the size and appointments. All suite occupants receive greater attention, including priority embarkation and disembarkation, but what's not good is that the most expensive accommodation has only semi-private balconies.

(d/e/f) Both interior and outside-view cabins are functional, although almost no drawers are provided. They are quite attractive, with warm, pleasing decor and fine soft furnishing fabrics; 80 percent of outside-view cabins have a private balcony. Interior cabins measure 163 sq ft (15 sq m).

The 28 wheelchair-accessible cabins measure 250–385 sq ft (23.2–35.7 sq m); surprisingly, there is no mirror for dressing, and no full-length hanging space for long dresses (yes, some passengers in wheelchairs do also use mirrors and full-length clothing).

Cabin bath towels are small, and drawer space is very limited. There are no butlers, even for top-grade suites. Cabin attendants have too many cabins to look after (typically 20), which does not translate to fine personal service. All cabins receive toiletry kits and have a hairdryer.

Most outside-view cabins on Emerald Deck have views obstructed by lifeboats. There are no cabins for singles. There is 24-hour room service, but some items on the room service menu are not available during early morning hours.

Some cabins can accommodate a third and fourth person in upper berths. However, in some cabins, the lower beds cannot then be pushed together to make a queen-size bed.

Almost all balcony suites and cabins can be overlooked both from the navigation bridge wing, as well as from the port and starboard sections of the ship's discotheque – high above the ship at the stern. Cabins with balconies on Dolphin, Caribe, and Baja decks can also be overlooked.

Perhaps the least desirable balcony cabins are eight located forward on Emerald Deck, as the balconies do not extend to the side of the ship and can be passed by walkers and gawkers on the adjacent Upper Promenade walkway so occupants need to keep their curtains closed most of the time. Passengers occupying some the most expensive suites with balconies at the ship's stern may experience considerable vibration during certain maneuvers.

DINING. Of the three principal formal dining rooms, one has traditional two-seating dining, while the other two offer 'anytime dining.' All are no-smoking and split into multi-tier sections in a non-symmetrical design that breaks what are quite large spaces into smaller sections. While six elevators go to Fiesta Deck, where two of the restaurants are located, only four go to Plaza Deck 5, where the Michelangelo Restaurant is located – this can lengthen waits at peak times, particularly for those in wheelchairs.

Other dining options. Sabatini's and Crown Grill are both are open for dinner on days at sea. Sabatini's has Italian-style pizzas and pastas, with a variety of sauces, as well as Italian-style entrées including tiger prawns and lobster tail – all provided with flair and entertainment from by the staff of waiters. Reservations are needed and there's a cover charge for lunch or dinner.

The 160-seat Crown Grill (a steakhouse, for premium-quality steaks, grilled meat and seafood items), also with cover charge, is in a wide promenade area, to tempt you as you pass by – it's worth the extra cost to get food cooked to order.

Casual eateries include a poolside hamburger grill and pizzeria. Some items cost extra at the International Café coffee bar/patisserie in the atrium lobby.

Vines, in the atrium lobby, features sushi and cheese at no extra charge, and extra-cost wine. Other casual meals can be taken in the Horizon Court, open 24 hours a day, with ocean views.

For something different, however, you could try a private dinner on your balcony ('Ultimate Balcony Dinner/Breakfast'), an all-inclusive evening featuring cocktails, fresh flowers, Champagne, and a deluxe four-course meal including Caribbean lobster tail.

ENTERTAINMENT. The Princess Theater spans two decks and has comfortable seating on both main and balcony levels. It has $3 million worth of sound and light equipment, plus a nine-piece orchestra. The ship carries a resident troupe of almost 20 singers and dancers.

Club Fusion, a second entertainment lounge located aft, features cabaret acts at night, and lectures, bingo, and horse racing by day. Explorers, a third entertainment lounge, can also host cabaret acts and dance bands. A variety of other lounges and bars have live music, and a number of male dance hosts act as partners for women traveling alone.

SPA/FITNESS. The Lotus Spa has separate facilities for men and women include a sauna, steam room, and changing rooms; common facilities include a relaxation/waiting zone, body-pampering treatment rooms, and a gymnasium with great ocean views and the latest high-tech equipment. Some fitness classes are free, others cost extra.

Crystal Serenity
★★★★★

Size:.................................... Mid-size Ship	Cabins (total):...................................545
Tonnage: 68,870	Size range (sq ft/m): 226–1,345.5/21–125
Lifestyle: ....Luxury/Premium	Cabins (outside view):..............................545
Cruise line:.............................Crystal Cruises	Cabins (interior/no view):............................0
Former names: ....none	Cabins (for one person):.............................0
IMO number: 9243667	Cabins (with private balcony):......................465
Builder: .... Chantiers de l'Atlantique (France)	Cabins (wheelchair accessible): 8
Original cost: ....$350 million	Wheelchair accessibility:......................... Best
Entered service:............................ Jun 2003	Cabin voltage: ....110 and 220 volts
Registry:................................The Bahamas	Elevators:.......................................8
Length (ft/m):............................. 820.2/250.0	Casino (gaming tables):............................ Yes
Beam (ft/m):................................ 111.5/34.0	Slot machines:.................................... Yes
Draft (ft/m): 24.9/7.6	Swimming pools:.................2 (1 w/sliding glass dome)
Propulsion/Propellers: ....diesel/2 azimuthing pods	Hot tubs (on deck):................................2
Passenger decks:....................................9	Self-service launderette:.......................... Yes
Total crew:..650	Dedicated cinema/seats:......................... Yes/202
Passengers (lower beds/alll berths):............. 1,090/1,210	Library:.. Yes
Passenger Space Ratio (lower beds/all berths): 62.6/56.9	Onboard currency: ....US$
Crew/Passenger Ratio (lower beds/all berths):.......... 1.7/1.8	

An elegant, spacious ship with good food and service

OVERVIEW. *Crystal Serenity* is best suited to sophisticated travelers, typically over 50, who seek contemporary ship surroundings, with fine quality fittings and furnishings, a wide range of public rooms and facilities, and excellent food and service from a well trained staff. This ship has just about everything for its target clientele, including an excellent program of guest lecturers.

THE SHIP. *Crystal Serenity* is the slightly larger but still mid-size close sister ship to *Crystal Symphony*, and has a similar look and profile. While some might not like the exterior's 'apartment block' look, it is in fashion today. The ship was given an extensive $25 million refit and refurbishment in 2011 and looks almost new again.

It achieves a high rating because of its fine facilities, high-ceilinged public rooms, well-trained crew, service, and the attention to detail. It provides announcement-free cruising in a well-tuned, very professionally run, service-oriented ship, roughly the equivalent of a Four Seasons or Ritz Carlton hotel.

Crystal Cruises also provides excellent, cultural lecturers, and the 'Passport to Music' keyboard learning center is a real bonus for anyone wanting to learn how to play a keyboard instrument, and to read music (Yamaha digital keyboards are provided). The passenger mix is usually 85 percent North American (half from California) and 15 percent other nationalities.

Pod propulsion is provided. Electrical power is provided by the latest generation of environmentally friendly diesel engines .

The ship has a very good amount of open deck, sunbathing space, and sports facilities. The aft of two outdoor swimming pools can be covered by a retractable glass dome in poor weather. There is no sense of crowding anywhere (although the self-service buffet can get very busy). There is also a really wide walk-around teakwood deck for walking, pleasingly uncluttered by sunloungers.

The decor in most areas is warm, inviting and contemporary. There is much use of rich wood paneling and detailing throughout the ship. The main lobby houses the 24-hour reception desk, concierge and shore excursion desks, and a popular lounge/bar (Crystal Cove) with 'glass' (some call it 'clearview') baby grand piano.

Some of the most elegant public rooms include Palm Court, evoking images of Colonial-style grand hotel lounge; the Avenue Saloon, a favorite watering hole of the late-night crowd and a throwback to traditional gentlemen's clubs; the Connoisseur Club, for cigar and cognac enthusiasts; and the Stardust Club, a lounge/nightclub. There are new shops and a private jewelry room, a computer-learning center with 24 terminals, and an Internet center. One neat feature is a Vintage Room, a private dining room where 12 invited diners can enjoy exclusive vintages, paired with food, in special wine-tasting dinners. Another is a Yamaha keyboard learning center for the excellent 'Passport to Music' program, which gives you a chance to learn how to play a keyboard instrument (and you get to take home

Berlitz's Ratings

	Possible	Achieved
Ship	500	434
Accommodation	200	168
Food	400	341
Service	400	339
Entertainment	100	86
Cruise	400	346

OVERALL SCORE
1714 points out of 2000

a manual, so you can carry on learning); the program is free – a great value indeed.

The centrally located casino has no outside views to distract gamers. Instead, the location is adjacent to lifeboats on both sides; in this arrangement, the lifeboats do not obstruct views from cabins or public rooms.

Your evenings will be necessarily structured due to the fact that there are two seatings for dinner, unless you eat in one of the specialty dining spots or choose 'open dining by reservation,' whereby you can dine at different or set times each evening in the Crystal Dining Room, and two shows (the showlounge cannot seat all passengers at once). This detracts from the ship's otherwise fine setting and the professionalism of its staff. However, many older passengers do want to eat early, while the line's younger passengers prefer to dine later, so there is some balance.

In May 2012, *Crystal Serenity* became an all-inclusive ship whose fare includes all gratuities, decent wines for lunch and dinner, and bar drinks – which means no more signing or paying extra for drinks (and no pushing by bar staff to sell drinks and wines that bring greater commission). Also, Crystal Cruises has a fine lecture program, and professional bridge instructors are on board every cruise. Effective with the first cruise in 2014, *Crystal Serenity* has eliminated smoking from all indoor areas, except for the Connoisseur Lounge (cigar lounge), but maintained designated smoking areas on open decks.

ACCOMMODATION. This consists of: four Crystal Penthouses with large balcony; 32 Penthouse Suites with Balcony; 72 Penthouses with balcony; 78 superior outside-view cabins with balcony; 286 outside-view cabins with balcony; 84 outside-view cabins without balcony but with large picture windows. Two whole decks of accommodation are designated as suites (decks 10 and 11), while all other accommodation is located on decks 7, 8, and 9. All suites/cabins were completely refurbished in 2011. They are now more elegant, and tasteful, and each has an electronic 'Do Not Disturb' and doorbell system.

Duvets and down pillows are provided, as are lots of other niceties, including a data socket for connecting a laptop computer. All accommodation has a refrigerator and mini-bar, TV set, satellite-linked telephone, and hairdryer. There's a full range of Aveda toiletries (suite-grade occupants get personalized stationery on request, plus a larger list of 'inclusive' brands to choose from), a plush, cotton bathrobe, and plenty of cotton towels, the largest a generous 70 by 34-ins (180 by 85cm). The in-cabin TV programming is excellent – although why it starts at Channel 53 is unclear – and close-captioned videos are provided for the hearing-impaired. The air conditioning in bathrooms and walk-in closets is quite loud and cannot be turned off. In suites/cabins with 'private' balcony, the balcony partition is of the partial, not full, type,

and so noisy neighbors, particularly if using mobile phones in ports of call, can prove intrusive. The balcony decking is teak.

Butlers provide excellent service in all the top category suites on decks 10 and 11, where room service food arrives on silver trays. Afternoon tea trolley service and evening hors d'oeuvres are delivered in butler-service suites.

Crystal Penthouses (with balcony). There are four, each 1,345 sq ft (125 sq m). These are ideally located in the center of the ship on Penthouse Deck 11, each with outstanding views and large private balconies with outside lighting. There is a lounge with audio-visual entertainment center, separate master bedroom with king-size bed and electric curtains, large walk-in closets, and large vanity desk. The marble-clad bathrooms have ocean views; they come with a whirlpool tub and shower, two washbasins, separate shower enclosure, bidet and toilet, and ample storage space for toiletries. They will be completely redesigned and rebuilt in November 2013.

Penthouse Suites (with balcony). These measure 538 sq ft (50 sq m) and are on Penthouse Deck 11. Each has a separate bedroom, walk-in closet and en-suite bathroom with full-size tub with integral shower, two washbasins, separate shower enclosure, bidet, toilet, and ample space for toiletries. The lounge has a large couch, coffee table, and several armchairs, and there is a dining table and four chairs.

Penthouse Deck Cabin (with balcony). Located on Penthouse Decks 10 and 11, these measure 404 sq ft (38 sq m). All have a private balcony, and the eight located at the aft of Deck 11 have larger balconies. They have a sleeping area that can be curtained off from the lounge area, with its large, long vanity desk. The bathroom is large, and has a full-size tub with integral shower, separate shower enclosure, and a bidet and toilet.

Superior Deluxe Outside-View Cabins (with balcony). Measuring 269 sq ft (25 sq m), these really are standard outside-view cabins – but larger than standard cabins aboard most ships. Longer than cabins without a private balcony, they have a sleeping area with clothes closets, small couch, and drinks table, vanity desk with hairdryer. The bathroom has a tub with integral shower, two washbasins, and toilet. Large patio doors open onto a private balcony.

Deluxe Outside-View Cabins (with balcony). These measure 269 sq ft (25 sq m). The 286 cabins, about the same size and shape as the 'Deluxe' version but on a 'superior' deck (Penthouse Deck 10), are longer than cabins that don't have a private balcony. They have a sleeping area with clothes closets, small couch, and drinks table, vanity desk with hairdryer. The bathroom has a tub with integral shower, two basins, and toilet. Patio doors open to a private balcony.

Deluxe Outside-View Cabins (no balcony). These are standard outside-view cabins; they are located on Deck 7, with a walk-around promenade deck outside each cabin. They measure 226 sq ft (21 sq m) and have a large window, sleeping area with clothes closets, small sofa and drinks table, and vanity desk with hairdryer. The small bathroom has a tub with integral shower, two washbasins, and toilet.

Wheelchair-accessible accommodation. This includes two penthouse grades, two cabins with balconies, and four cabins with large picture windows.

DINING. There is one main dining room (the Crystal Dining Room), two specialty, reservations-required dining rooms. The Crystal Dining Room is quite elegant, with a crisp, clean style that includes plenty of space around each table. It is well laid-out and has a raised, circular central section, although it is noisy at times and not conducive to a fine dining experience. There are tables for two, many positioned adjacent to large ocean-view windows, and for four, six, or eight.

The food is attractively presented on large plates, and well served, using both plate service and silver service. It is of a high standard with fine quality ingredients. European dishes are predominantly featured, but in an American style. The menus are extremely varied, and include a fine selection of meat, fish, and vegetarian dishes. Off-menu orders are available, as is caviar. Kosher meals are also available (frozen when brought on board); Kosher pots, pans, and utensils are sterilized in salt water, and all plates used during service are hand-washed separately.

Overall, the food is really good for the size of ship, and, with the choice of the two specialty dining spots, receives high praise. Dining is in two seatings, unless you choose 'open dining by reservation,' whereby you can dine at different or set times each evening.

While the early seating is simply too rushed for many, with two specialty restaurants, off-menu choices, a hand-picked European staff and excellent service, dining is often memorable. Fresh pasta and dessert flambé specialties are made at the table each day by accommodating headwaiters.

Other dining options. There are two, one Italian and one Asian, both requiring reservations but making no extra charge. They are aft on Deck 7, with ocean-view windows. Prego is for Italian food from a menu created by Piero Selvaggio, Italian wines, and service with fine flair. Silk Road has Asian-California 'fusion' food. Although there is no extra charge, a small 'gratuity' is suggested. The alternative dining spots provide an excellent standard of culinary fare with food cooked to order at no extra charge.

A semi-separate sushi bar with counter stools is part of Silk Road, which serves items selected by superb Los Angeles-based Japanese super-chef Nobuyuki 'Nobu' Matsuhisa, and skillfully prepared on board by Nobu-trained chefs; the high-cost ingredients are flown regularly to the ship. Note that to eat in a Nobu restaurant ashore would cost a considerable amount of money, but aboard the ship, this outstanding food is free.

The Bistro, located on the upper level of the two-deck-high lobby, is the delightful casual spot for coffees and pastries, served in the style and atmosphere of a European street cafe. The Bistro has some splendid Crystal Cruises-logo china that can be bought in one of the ship's boutiques.

For informal eats, the Lido Café has an extensive self-serve buffet area. It's high up in the ship, with great views from its large picture windows. For casual poolside lunches, there is also Trident Grill, as well as an ice cream/frozen yoghurt counter (no extra charge). A Chinese street food zone has popular favorites like steamed dumplings.

ENTERTAINMENT. The Galaxy Lounge is the ship's principal showlounge. It is quite a large room with a high ceiling, but on one level, with a nicely sloping floor, for good visibility. Indeed, the sight lines are good from almost all seats. Both banquette and individual seating is provided. The stage, lighting, and sound equipment are all excellent.

The shows are elegant, with excellent costuming (though not much in the way of scenery), but some are seriously dated, too long, and Crystal Cruises' many repeat passengers know them too well. In addition, many nights feature cabaret acts and classical artistes that are of a good standard, and constantly changing. The bands and musical units are also, for the most part, of a high caliber, and there's plenty of music for social dancing. The ship also provides dance hosts, called Ambassador Hosts, for the many single women who enjoy traveling with Crystal Cruises.

SPA/FITNESS. The Crystal Spa is located aft on Lido Deck 12, one of the ship's uppermost decks. Facilities include men's and women's changing rooms with sauna (which has a large porthole-shaped window) and steam rooms, gymnasium with high-tech muscle-pumping equipment, an aerobics exercise area, and reception/relaxation area.

Treatments are provided under the aegis of Steiner Platinum Service (Steiner being the concession). Facilities include one room dedicated to yoga and Pilates classes (no extra charge), an aerobics/exercise room, plus separate sauna, steam rooms, and changing rooms for both men and women. There are seven treatment rooms (including one for couples, and one with a 'dry float bed') for massage, facials, and other treatments, and a separate beauty salon.

The ship has excellent open deck and sunbathing space, and sports facilities that include two full-size paddle tennis courts, electronic golf simulator, and golf driving range. One of two outdoor swimming pools has a retractable glass dome, while the other is one of the longest aboard any ship today. Anyone trying to sunbathe quietly on the deck under and close to the paddle tennis courts will hear the noise of bat against ball when the court is in use.

Crystal Symphony
★★★★★

Size:.......................................Mid-size Ship		Cabins (total):.....................................480		
Tonnage: 51,044		Size range (sq ft/m): 201.2–981.7/18.7–91.2		
Lifestyle: ....Luxury/Premium		Cabins (outside view):.............................480		
Cruise line:..............................Crystal Cruises		Cabins (interior/no view):...........................0		
Former names: ....none		Cabins (for one person):.............................0		
IMO number: 9066667		Cabins (with private balcony):.......................276		
Builder: ....Masa-Yards (Finland)		Cabins (wheelchair accessible): 7		
Original cost:...............................$300 million		Wheelchair accessibility:.......................... Best		
Entered service:............................... Mar 1995		Cabin voltage: ....110 and 220 volts		
Registry:...................................The Bahamas		Elevators:..8		
Length (ft/m):............................... 777.8/237.1		Casino (gaming tables):.......................... Yes		
Beam (ft/m):.................................. 98.0/30.2		Slot machines:.................................... Yes		
Draft (ft/m):...................................... 24.9/7.6		Swimming pools:.................2 (1 w/sliding glass dome)		
Propulsion/Propellers:...........diesel-electric (33,880kW)/2		Hot tubs (on deck):..................................2		
Passenger decks:......................................8		Self-service launderette:......................... Yes		
Total crew:..545		Dedicated cinema/seats:..................... Yes/143		
Passengers (lower beds/all berths):...............960/1,010		Library: .... Yes		
Passenger Space Ratio (lower beds/all berths): 53.1/50.5		Onboard currency: ....US$		
Crew/Passenger Ratio (lower beds/all berths):......... 1.7/1.8				

A highly comfortable ship with elegant, refined decor

OVERVIEW. *Crystal Symphony* is best suited to discerning adult travelers, typically over 50, who seek contemporary ship surroundings, with fine-quality fittings and furnishings, a wide range of public rooms and facilities, and excellent food and service.

THE SHIP. *Crystal Symphony* was given a $23 million refurbishment in 2007–8 that included making the main entertainment deck more contemporary. All suites and cabins received flat-screen TV sets, Murano bedside table lamps and Rubelli fabrics, and oval glass washbasins set in granite surrounds were introduced, together with a raft of other behind-the-scenes improvements. The ship went through further refurbishment in 2012, which increased the bistro-style eatery in the former Trident Pool area.

This is announcement-free cruising in a well-tuned, very professionally run, service-oriented ship.

Crystal Symphony has a nicely raked clipper bow and well-balanced lines. While some might not like the 'apartment block' look of its exterior, it is the contemporary look, balconies having become standard aboard almost all new cruise ships. This one has an excellent amount of open deck, sunbathing space, and sports facilities. The aft of two outdoor pools can be covered by a glass dome in poor weather. There is no sense of crowding anywhere. It combines big ship facilities with the intimacy of rooms found aboard many small vessels. There is a wide walk-around teakwood deck for strolling, uncluttered by lounge chairs.

Berlitz's Ratings		
	Possible	Achieved
Ship	500	430
Accommodation	200	163
Food	400	341
Service	400	340
Entertainment	100	84
Cruise	400	344
OVERALL SCORE		
1702 points out of 2000		

Outstanding is the Palm Court, an observation lounge with forward-facing views over the ship's bows – it is tranquil, one of the nicest rooms afloat, and larger than its equivalent aboard sister ship, Crystal Serenity.

There is an excellent book, video, and CD-ROM library, combined with a business center. The cinema has high-definition video projection and headsets for the hearing-impaired. Useful self-service launderettes are provided on each deck.

The Connoisseurs Club, adjacent to the Avenue Saloon, serves fine premium brands of liquor and cigars. The Computer Learning Center, with more than 20 stations, is a popular venue. Private lessons are available but expensive.

The ship achieves a high rating because of its fine facilities, service, and crew. It is the extra attention to detail that really counts. Crystal Cruises also provides impressive, cultural lecturers, and the 'Passport to Music' keyboard learning center is excellent. The passenger mix is approximately 85 percent North American (typically half will be from California) and 15 percent other nationalities.

In March 2012, *Crystal Symphony* became an all-inclusive ship, with all gratuities to staff, decent wines for lunch and dinner, and bar drinks included. This means no more signing or paying extra for drinks, which makes for a more enjoyable cruise experience. Effective with the first cruise in 2014, *Crystal Symphony* has eliminated smoking from all indoor areas, except for the Connoisseur Lounge (cigar lounge), but maintained designated smoking areas on open decks.

ACCOMMODATION. There are eight categories, with the most expensive suites located on the highest accommodation deck (Deck 10). There are two Crystal Penthouses with private balcony; 18 Penthouse Suites with private balcony; 44 Penthouse Cabins with balcony; 214 Cabins with balcony; 202 Cabins without balcony. Some cabins (grades G and I) have obstructed views. Except for the suites on Deck 10, most other cabin bathrooms are compact, but very comfortable. Interconnecting doors were added to 18 in 2013 – good for families with children.

Duvets and down pillows are provided in all cabins, as are lots of other niceties, together with a data socket for connecting a computer. All accommodation has a refrigerator and mini-bar, TV set, satellite-linked telephone, and hairdryer. A full range of Aveda toiletries is provided, plus a plush cotton bathrobe and plenty of cotton towels, the largest of which measures a generous 70 by 34ins (180 by 85cm). Suite-grades get a larger choice of drinks as well as personalized stationery on request. Excellent in-cabin television programming, including CNN, is transmitted, as well as close-captioned videos for the use of the hearing-impaired.

Deck 10 Penthouses. Two delightful Crystal Penthouses measure 982 sq ft (91 sq m) and have a huge private balcony, a lounge with audio-visual entertainment center, separate master bedroom with king-size bed and electric curtains, large walk-in closets, and stunning ocean-view marble bathrooms with a Philippe Stark whirlpool tub. These really are among the best in fine, private, pampered living spaces at sea, and come with all the best perks, including laundry service.

Other Deck 10 Suites. All of the other suites on this deck have plenty of space and a private balcony. They have a lounge with large sofa, coffee table and chairs, a sleeping area, and walk-in closet. Rich wood cabinetry provides a warm decor. The bathrooms are extremely well appointed, with full-size tub and separate shower, two washbasins, bidet, and toilet.

Five butlers provide the best in personal service in all the top category suites on Deck 10 (with a total of 132 beds). Afternoon tea and evening hors d'oeuvres are standard and the food arrives on silver trays.

Decks 5/6/7/8/9. More than 50 percent of all cabins have private balconies. All cabins are well equipped and extremely comfortable, with excellent sound insulation. The balcony partitions, however, do not go from floor to ceiling, so you can hear your neighbors. Even in the lowest category of standard cabins, there is plenty of drawer space, but the closet hanging space is limited. European stewardesses provide excellent service and attention.

DINING. The Crystal Dining Room is quite elegant, with crisp design and plenty of space around each table, although it is noisy at times.

The food, of a high standard, is always attractively presented and well served, using a mix of plate service and silver service. European dishes are predominantly featured, but in an American style. The menus include a fine selection of meat, fish, and vegetarian dishes. Off-menu orders are available, as is caviar.

Kosher meals are also available (frozen when brought on board); Kosher pots, pans, and utensils are sterilized in salt water, and all plates used during service are hand-washed separately.

Overall, the food is really good for the size of ship and, with the choice of the two specialty dining spots, receives high praise. Dining is in two seatings, unless you choose 'open dining by reservation,' whereby you can dine at different or set times each evening. While the early seating may be too rushed for many, with two specialty restaurants, off-menu choices, a hand-picked European staff and excellent service, dining is often memorable. Dessert flambé specialties are made at the table each day by accommodating headwaiters.

Other dining options. Prego is a 75-seat restaurant, featuring fine Italian cuisine created by Piero Selvaggio, with good Italian wines, and service with flair.

Silk Road features Asian-California 'fusion' food provided by Nobu Matsuhisa-trained chefs. The high-cost ingredients are flown regularly to the ship. To eat in a Nobu restaurant ashore costs a considerable amount; aboard the ship, this outstanding food is free.

Afternoon tea in the Palm Court is a pleasant, civilized daily event, but do try the 'Mozart Teatime,' in which the waiters all dress in period costume.

For informal eats, the Lido Café has great views from its large windows. For casual poolside lunches, there is also Trident Bar & Grill, as well as an ice cream/frozen yoghurt counter (no extra charge). A Chinese street food zone has favorites like steamed dumplings.

ENTERTAINMENT. The Galaxy Lounge is quite large, with a high ceiling, but it's on one level with a tiered floor, for good visibility. A few pillars obstruct sight lines from some seats. Both banquette and individual seating is provided. The stage, lighting, and sound equipment are all excellent.

The shows are elegant, with excellent costuming and scenery, but they are too long, and too familiar to Crystal Cruises' many repeat passengers. On the plus side, the cabaret acts are of a good caliber, and constantly changing. The bands are also good, and there's plenty of music for social dancing. The ship also provides male hosts for single female passengers.

SPA/FITNESS. Facilities include one room for yoga and Pilates (no extra charge), an aerobics/exercise room, plus sauna and steam rooms. There are seven treatment room and a beauty salon.

Dawn Princess
★★★★

Size:.....................................Large Resort Ship	Cabins (total):.....................................975
Tonnage: 77,499	Size range (sq ft/m): 135.0–635.0/12.5–59.0
Lifestyle: ....Standard	Cabins (outside view):.................................603
Cruise line:............................. Princess Cruises	Cabins (interior/no view):..............................372
Former names: ....none	Cabins (for one person):...............................0
IMO number: 9103996	Cabins (with private balcony):.........................446
Builder: .... Fincantieri (Italy)	Cabins (wheelchair accessible): 19
Original cost:.............................. $300 million	Wheelchair accessibility:............................Good
Entered service:........................... May 1997	Cabin voltage: ....110 and 220 volts
Registry:.................................... Bermuda	Elevators:...11
Length (ft/m):............................. 857.2/261.3	Casino (gaming tables):...............................Yes
Beam (ft/m):.................................. 105.6/32.2	Slot machines:.......................................Yes
Draft (ft/m): 26.5/8.1	Swimming pools:.......................................5
Propulsion/Propellers:............ diesel-electric (46,080kW)/2	Hot tubs (on deck):...................................5
Passenger decks:...................................10	Self-service launderette:.............................Yes
Total crew:..900	Dedicated cinema/seats:...............................No
Passengers (lower beds/alll berths):............. 1,950/2,250	Library: ....Yes
Passenger Space Ratio (lower beds/all berths): 39.7/34.4	Onboard currency: ....US$
Crew/Passenger Ratio (lower beds/all berths):......... 2.1/2.5	

A large ship with warm decor for mature-age cruisers

OVERVIEW. *Dawn Princess*, like sister ship *Sun Princess*, is dedicated to the Australian cruise region. As aboard most large ships, if you live in the top suites, you'll be well cared for; if not, you'll just be one of a large number of passengers. The collection of artwork is good, and helps make the ship feel smaller than it is.

THE SHIP. *Dawn Princess*, an all-white ship, has a decent contemporary profile balanced by a large funnel containing a deck tennis/basketball/volleyball court in its sheltered aft base. There is a wide, teak walk-around promenade deck outdoors, some real teak steamer-style deck chairs complete with royal blue cushioned pads, and 93,000 sq ft (8,640 sq m) of space outdoors. A great amount of glass area on the upper decks provides plenty of light and connection with the outside world. There's a large poolside movie screen and an adults-only Sanctuary relaxation area.

The interiors are pretty and warm, with attractive colors and the welcoming decor includes some attractive wall murals and other artwork. The signage could be better, however. There are a number of dead ends in the interior layout, so it's not as user-friendly as a ship this size could be. The cabin numbering system is illogical, with numbers going through several hundred series on the same deck.

The wide range of public rooms includes several intimate rooms so that you don't get the feel of being overwhelmed by large spaces. The interior focal point

Berlitz's Ratings

	Possible	Achieved
Ship	500	376
Accommodation	200	148
Food	400	247
Service	400	278
Entertainment	100	77
Cruise	400	285

OVERALL SCORE
1411 points out of 2000

is a four-deck-high atrium lobby with winding, double stairways, and two panoramic glass-walled elevators.

There are two showlounges, one at each end of the ship; one is a 550-seat, theater-style space that also screens movies, and the other is a 480-seat cabaret-style lounge, with bar.

The library, a warm room with ocean-view windows, has six large butter-colored leather chairs for listening to audio discs. There is a conference center for up to 300, as well as a business center with computers and copiers. The casino, while large, is not really in the main passenger flow and so doesn't generate the 'walk-through' factor found aboard so many ships.

The most traditional room is the Wheelhouse Lounge/Bar, decorated in the style of a late 19th-century gentleman's club, with wood paneling and comfortable seating. The focal point is a large ship model, *Kenya*, from the P&O collection archives.

The captain's cocktail party is typically held in the four-deck-high main atrium so that you can come and go as you please without having to stand in line to have your photograph taken with the captain. However, cruising aboard large ships such as this one has become increasingly an onboard revenue-based product. In-your-face art auctions are overbearing, and the paintings, lithographs and framed pictures strewn throughout the ship clash irritatingly with the interior decor. This is an annoying intrusion into what should be a vacation, not a cruise inside a floating 'art' emporium. Also, bazaar-like tables filled with trinket junk clutter the area outside the shops.

The swimming pools are small, given the number of passengers, and the pool deck is cluttered with white, plastic sunloungers, without cushioned pads. Waiting for tenders in anchor ports can prove irritating, but is typical of large ship operations. Charging for use of the machines and washing powder in the self-service launderette is trifling.

ACCOMMODATION. There are many, many different cabin price grades. Although the standard cabins are a little small, they are well designed and functional in layout, and have earth tone colors accentuated by splashes of color from the bedspreads. Proportionately, there are quite a lot of interior cabins. Many outside-view cabins have private balconies, and all seem to be quite well soundproofed, although the balcony partition is not the floor-to-ceiling type, so you can hear your neighbors clearly, or smell their smoke. The balconies are very narrow, only just large enough for two small chairs, and there is no dedicated lighting.

All cabins have a reasonable amount of closet and abundant drawer and other storage space – adequate for a seven-night cruise – plus a TV set and refrigerator. The bathrooms are practical, although they really are tight spaces, best described as one person at-a-time units. But they do have a decent shower enclosure, a small amount of shelving for toiletries, real glasses, a hairdryer and a bathrobe.

The largest accommodation is in six suites, two on each of three decks located at the stern, and measure 536–754 sq ft (49.8–21.3 sq m), including large private balcony). They are well laid out, and have large bathrooms with two washbasins, a Jacuzzi tub, and a separate shower enclosure. The bedroom has generous amounts of wood accenting and detailing, indented ceilings, and TV sets in both bedroom and lounge areas. The suites also have a dining room table and four chairs.

The 32 mini-suites (374–536 sq ft/34.7–49.7 sq m) typically have two lower beds that convert to a queen-size bed. There is a separate bedroom/sleeping area with vanity desk, and a lounge with sofa and coffee table, indented ceilings with generous amounts of wood accenting and detailing, walk-in closet, and larger bathroom with Jacuzzi bathtub and separate shower enclosure.

There are 19 wheelchair-accessible cabins, which measure 213–305 sq ft (19.7–28.2 sq m) and are a mix of seven outside view and 12 interior cabins.

DINING. There are two main dining rooms of asymmetrical design, Florentine and Venetian, each with about 500 seats. They are located adjacent to the two lower levels of the atrium lobby. Each has its own galley and each is split into multi-tier sections, which help create a feeling of intimacy, although there is a lot of noise from the waiter stations adjacent to many tables. Breakfast and lunch are provided in an open-seating arrangement, while dinner is in two seatings. The wine list is reasonable, but not good, and there are no wine waiters. Note that 15 percent is added to all beverage bills, including wines.

Other dining options. The Horizon Buffet is open 24 hours a day, and, at night, has an informal dinner setting with sit-down waiter service; a small bistro menu is also available. The buffet displays are, for the most part, quite repetitious, but better than they have been in the past. There is no real finesse in presentation, however, as oval plastic plates are provided, instead of trays. The cabin service menu is very limited, and presentation of the food items featured is poor.

For some good meat, try the Sterling Steakhouse; it's for those who want to taste four different cuts of Angus beef from the popular 'Sterling Silver' brand of USDA prime meats – Filet Mignon, New York Strip, Porterhouse, and Rib-Eye – all presented on a silver tray. There is also a barbecue chicken option, plus the usual baked potato or french fries as accompaniments. This is available as an alternative to the dining rooms, between 6.30pm and 9.30pm only, at extra cost. However, it is not, as you might expect, a separate, intimate dining room, but is located in a section of the Horizon Buffet, with its own portable bar and some decorative touches to set it apart from the regular buffet.

There is also a patisserie for cappuccino/espresso coffees and pastries, a wine/caviar bar, and a pizzeria with cobblestone floors, wrought-iron decorative features, and a choice of six excellent pizzas.

ENTERTAINMENT. There are two showlounges, both theatre and cabaret style. The main one, Princess Theater, has a sloping floor, with aisle-style seating (as found in shoreside movie theaters) that is well tiered, and with good sight lines to the raised stage from most of the 500 seats.

A second showlounge, Vista Lounge, located at the aft end of the ship, has cabaret entertainment, and also acts as a lecture and presentation room. Princess Cruises has a good stable of regular cabaret acts to draw from, so there should be something for most tastes.

SPA/FITNESS. A glass-walled health spa complex located high atop the ship includes a gymnasium with the latest high-tech machines. One swimming pool is 'suspended' aft between two decks. There are two other pools, although they are not large for the size of the ship.

Sports facilities are located in an open-air sports deck positioned inside the funnel and adaptable for basketball, volleyball, badminton, or paddle tennis. Joggers can exercise on the walk-around open Promenade Deck.

Delphin
★★★

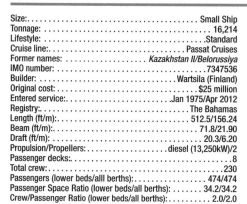

Size:	Small Ship	Cabins (total):	237
Tonnage:	16,214	Size range (sq ft/m):	150.0–492.0/14.0–45.7
Lifestyle:	Standard	Cabins (outside view):	130
Cruise line:	Passat Cruises	Cabins (interior/no view):	107
Former names:	Kazakhstan II/Belorussiya	Cabins (for one person):	0
IMO number:	7347536	Cabins (with private balcony):	0
Builder:	Wartsila (Finland)	Cabins (wheelchair accessible):	0
Original cost:	$25 million	Wheelchair accessibility:	None
Entered service:	Jan 1975/Apr 2012	Cabin voltage:	220 volts
Registry:	The Bahamas	Elevators:	2
Length (ft/m):	512.5/156.24	Casino (gaming tables):	No
Beam (ft/m):	71.8/21.90	Slot machines:	No
Draft (ft/m):	20.3/6.20	Swimming pools:	1
Propulsion/Propellers:	diesel (13,250kW)/2	Hot tubs (on deck):	0
Passenger decks:	8	Self-service launderette:	Yes
Total crew:	230	Dedicated cinema/seats:	No
Passengers (lower beds/alll berths):	474/474	Library:	Yes
Passenger Space Ratio (lower beds/all berths):	34.2/34.2	Onboard currency:	Euros
Crew/Passenger Ratio (lower beds/all berths):	2.0/2.0		

A friendly ship for casual, frugal, destination-busy cruises

OVERVIEW. *Delphin* is best suited to German-speaking couples and single travelers of mature years who seek good value for money in a ship with traditional, quite comfortable surroundings, at a modest price, with in-depth itineraries.

THE SHIP. *Delphin* is a fairly smart-looking all-white cruise ship, topped by a square funnel. The ship's original car decks have long been converted into useful public rooms and additional cabins. But the single circular swimming pool is small and is best described as a 'plunge' pool. This is a basic product that represents very good value for money. The interiors are clean and tidy, and the decor is tasteful and warm.

One negative point is the many pillars throughout the public rooms. The ceiling height is low in most of these rooms, and the stairways are steep. There's no walk-around promenade deck outdoors and no observation lounge/bar with forward-facing views over the ship's bows.

ACCOMMODATION. There are several grades of accommodation. Typically, the higher the deck, the more expensive the cabin.

Boat Deck suites (located forward) are spacious and well equipped, with an abundance of drawers and good closet space, and all feature blond wood furniture, and a refrigerator. The bathrooms are large, and have full-size bathtubs and large toiletries cabinet; bathrobes are also provided.

Berlitz's Ratings

	Possible	Achieved
Ship	500	262
Accommodation	200	111
Food	400	229
Service	400	230
Entertainment	100	60
Cruise	400	235

OVERALL SCORE
1127 points out of 2000

All the other outside-view and interior cabins are very compact units, yet adequate. All beds have European duvets. The bathrooms are small, but there's a decent amount of space for toiletries.

DINING. The single main dining room, the Pacific Restaurant, has 554 seats. It has a high ceiling, large ocean-view picture windows, pleasing decor, and accommodates all passengers in one seating.

The food is attractively presented. The choice is good, with a heavy reliance on meat and game dishes. The wine list has a good selection at moderate prices, and Sekt (sparkling wine) is provided at breakfast. The gala buffet is very good.

For casual meals, breakfast and lunch buffets can be taken in The Lido. The food provided is decent enough, with reasonable choice.

ENTERTAINMENT. The showlounge is a single-level room designed for cabaret-style entertainment, not big production shows. Sight lines are quite good from most seats, although pillars obstruct some views.

SPA/FITNESS. The spa facilities are on the lowest deck of the ship, while a fitness room and beauty salon are located on different decks, so there's no cohesive spa as such. However, in the facility on the lowest deck is a sauna, steam room, solarium, and massage rooms. There is a dialysis station for special cruises; dialysis technicians are provided.

Deutschland
★★★★ +

Size:.	Small Ship	Cabins (total):.	294
Tonnage:	22,400	Size range (sq ft/m):	129.1–365.9/12.0–34.0
Lifestyle:	Premium	Cabins (outside view):	220
Cruise line:.	Peter Deilmann Cruises	Cabins (interior/no view):.	74
Former names:	none	Cabins (for one person):.	36
IMO number:	9141807	Cabins (with private balcony):.	2
Builder:	Howaldswerke Deutsche Werft	Cabins (wheelchair accessible):	1
Original cost:	DM 212 million	Wheelchair accessibility:.	Fair
Entered service:.	May 1998	Cabin voltage:	230 volts
Registry:.	Germany	Elevators:.	3
Length (ft/m):.	574.1/175.0	Casino (gaming tables):.	No
Beam (ft/m):.	75.4/23.0	Slot machines:.	No
Draft (ft/m):.	19.0/5.8	Swimming pools:.	2
Propulsion/Propellers:	diesel (12,300kW)/2	Hot tubs (on deck):.	0
Passenger decks:.	7	Self-service launderette:	No
Total crew:.	270	Dedicated cinema/seats:.	Yes/83
Passengers (lower beds/alll berths):.	552/560	Library:.	Yes
Passenger Space Ratio (lower beds/all berths):	40.8/40.0	Onboard currency:	Euros
Crew/Passenger Ratio (lower beds/all berths):.	2.0/2.0		

A crowded ship with a heavily traditional Germanic style

OVERVIEW. *Deutschland* is a fine, traditional ship best suited to German-speaking couples and single travelers of mature years looking for a very traditional cruise ship with appealing itineraries and destinations, good food and attentive service.

THE SHIP. *Deutschland*, now over 15 years old but in fine condition, has an angular, low-in-the-water profile that is not particularly handsome, and a large, single, squat, traditional

Berlitz's Ratings

	Possible	Achieved
Ship	500	400
Accommodation	200	155
Food	400	318
Service	400	321
Entertainment	100	80
Cruise	400	308
OVERALL SCORE		
1582 points out of 2000		

funnel. The ship, built in sections by four shipyards, was assembled in Kiel, Germany. It is well maintained and kept very clean.

Although there is no walk-around promenade deck outdoors as such – it's full of chairs around the central section where a swimming pool is located – you can walk along some of the open space, although there are windbreakers to negotiate. There are also port and starboard midship walking decks under the inboard lifeboats. There is a decent amount of open deck and sunbathing space for a ship of this size, including three aft decks for open-air lovers, and real teakwood deck chairs with thick royal blue cushioned pads.

The Lido Deck has sides covered by canvas shading and white support pillars – like the ones you would find on seaside piers in England – as a setting for the outdoor swimming pool. This is a self-contained deck that has not only the pool but also the casual Lido Buffet restaurant and Lido Terrasse Café. One could spend all day outdoors on this deck without having to dress to go indoors to eat. There is also a small waterfall aft of the pool.

The ship is laid out in a classic symmetrical pattern, and the interior decor has been successfully designed to re-create the atmosphere of 1920s ocean liners. The ship is finely decorated throughout (some might say overly so), with rich, dark woods and intricate brass and wrought-iron staircases that remind one of an old-style gentleman's club. There is so much detail in the decoration work, and especially in the ornate ceilings, and cleaning it all is rather labor-intensive. There are quite a number of real statues, which don't seem to fit well aboard a cruise ship, but there are also many works of art on display.

There's a good range of public rooms and spaces, although these have been possible only by making the cabins smaller than one would expect of a ship of this size. The ship has an interesting, eclectic decor from different periods, as well as a wide assortment of cabin sizes, configurations and grades.

There are two favorite drinking places: Zum Alten Fritz (Old Fritz) Bar, with dark wood interiors and belle-époque ambience; and the Lili Marleen Salon, adjacent to the Berlin Restaurant, with mahogany channeled ceiling. Another nice public room is the Lido Terrace, which would have made a superb observation lounge had the designers extended it to the forward extremes of the deck. It is reminiscent of the winter gardens aboard the early transatlantic liners, and a delightful place to read or take afternoon tea.

The late Peter Deilmann's personal touch in the heavily detailed interiors is evident everywhere. Although *Deutschland* is registered under the German flag, the company is able to emply non-German staff. Thus you will find Filipinos and other nationalities in the hotel service areas. The friendliness of the staff is good. The ship operates cashless cruising – charges must be settled on the last day of the cruise, when all purchases must, inconveniently, be made in cash.

Although the ship absorbs passengers well, the space ratio could be better. The onboard product is generally sound, with attentive service, but the food and catering side of the operation could be improved. While the interiors are very attractive, the vessel does not come close to ships such as *Europa, Europa 2, Silver Shadow,* and *Silver Whisper*, with their much larger suites/cabins, open-seating dining (except *Europa*, which has open seating for breakfast and lunch, and assigned tables for dinner), and their abundance of cabins with private balconies. Smoking is permitted only on open decks. There is no Internet center.

Just two suites have private balconies; most other cabins are very small when compared to other ships in the luxury and premium sectors of the international market. Refreshingly, there's no bingo, horse racing, or line dancing.

ACCOMMODATION. There are 10 categories (the higher the deck, the higher the cost). There are 18 outside-view suites, 189 outside-view doubles, 17 outside-view single cabins; 12 interior doubles, and 50 interior single cabins.

While many cabins are disappointingly small, all are furnished in fancy bird's-eye maple, and all ceilings are one-piece units, unlike the metal strip ceilings of most cruise ships, and come with molded coving and ornamentation. The closet and drawer space is quite generous, and the attention to detail is very good. All beds have duvets and pillows. All cabins have a TV set, direct-dial satellite telephone, mini-bar/refrigerator, and real cabin keys (not plastic cards) are provided. Many cabins have only one electrical outlet.

The bathrooms are also generously appointed, with a pink marble sink, gold anodized fittings, gilt-edged mirrors, hairdryer, and ample space for one's toiletries. There is an electrical power outlet for shavers, with both 110 and 230 volts. Bathrobes are provided for all passengers.

Accommodations designated as suites (there are two grades) are reasonably large, with a living area that contains a couch, coffee table, and two chairs; the bathroom has a full-size tub (all other cabins have showers only). Only the Executive Suites and Owner's Suites are, sensibly, located in the center of the ship, and each has a small private balcony. There is one wheelchair-accessible cabin (8042).

DINING. Berlin, the 300-seat main restaurant, is a homely room. All the chairs have armrests, although space for serving at window-side tables is limited, and

the hard chair backs are not really very comfortable.

There are tables for two, four, six, or eight, and two seatings for dinner. Two cold buffet bars for cold cuts of meat, cheese, and salad items – either your waiter can obtain the food for you or you can choose it yourself – are featured for breakfast and lunch. Overall, the cuisine is quite creative, with lots of courses, small portions of nouvelle cuisine, and a wide variety of choice and good taste. It's not really memorable, though the desserts are extremely good. The place settings are extensive.

The Restaurant Vierjahreszeiten (Four Seasons), with 104 seats, is an intimate dining room, principally for suite occupants and for à la carte dining, for which a reservation is necessary. There is much detailing and ornamentation in the decor, and the ornate ceiling lamps and indented ceiling coving create an elegant ambience that is relatively intimate. There are tables for two, four, or six.

There is also a small private dining room, the Chancellor Room, with a large oval table seating 10 to 12 – ideal for special occasions and celebrations.

The extensive wine list includes a fine selection of wines from Germany and Austria, although the choice of wines from other countries is very limited. Eating in this restaurant takes considerably longer than in the Berlin Restaurant, and is best for those seeking an evening of fine dining and conversation.

Other dining options. The Lido Restaurant is a casual dining venue. It has large ocean-view windows on two sides and a centrally located, multi-section self-serve buffet station. Additionally, there is a Lido Terrasse, at the stern, with large windows on three sides. It is set on two slightly different levels, houses the ship's library, and has statuary and a relaxing garden in a conservatory-like setting. This Lido Restaurant also has a bar, plus elegant tea and coffee service.

ENTERTAINMENT. The Kaisersaal (Emperor's Saloon) is the main showlounge. It is a galleried period room with red velveteen chairs and is more like a ballroom than showlounge. It is reminiscent of a small opera house and has a beautiful, huge central chandelier. However, sight lines are obstructed from some seats on both upper and lower seating levels by many large marble-effect pillars. The entertainment is geared to German tastes, and is mostly in German.

SPA/FITNESS. The main spa area is on Deck 3, and this includes a small indoor swimming pool with a statue of a female diver at one end, sauna, solarium, thalassotherapy baths, and massage/body therapy rooms; there is also a dialysis station. Deck 6 has a fitness/sport center with a few exercise machines, a sauna with a sea view, and a steam room. A beauty salon is on Deck 7.

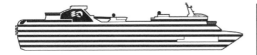

Diamond Princess
★★★★

Size:.................................Large Resort Ship	Cabins (total):................................... 1,337
Tonnage: 115,875	Size range (sq ft/m): 168–1,329.3/15.6–123.5
Lifestyle: ....Standard	Cabins (outside view): 1,000
Cruise line:............................ Princess Cruises	Cabins (interior/no view):...........................337
Former names: ....none	Cabins (for one person):..............................0
IMO number: 9228198	Cabins (with private balcony):.....................750
Builder: .... Mitsubishi Heavy Industries (Japan)	Cabins (wheelchair accessible): 28
Original cost: .... $400 million	Wheelchair accessibility:..........................Good
Entered service:........................... Feb 2004	Cabin voltage: .... 110 volts
Registry:.................................... Bermuda	Elevators:..14
Length (ft/m):............................ 951.4/290.0	Casino (gaming tables):........................... Yes
Beam (ft/m):............................... 123.0/37.5	Slot machines:.................................... Yes
Draft (ft/m): 26.4/8.0	Swimming pools:....................................3
Propulsion/Propellers:............ diesel-electric (42,000kW)/2	Hot tubs (on deck):.................................9
Passenger decks:...................................13	Self-service launderette:......................... Yes
Total crew:..................................... 1,238	Dedicated cinema/seats:...........................No
Passengers (lower beds/alll berths):............. 2,674/3,100	Library:.. Yes
Passenger Space Ratio (lower beds/all berths): 43.3/37.3	Onboard currency: ....US$
Crew/Passenger Ratio (lower beds/all berths):.......... 2.1/2.5	

A large ship with relaxing decor, for mature-age cruisers

OVERVIEW. If you are not used to large ships, it may take you some time to find your way around this one, despite the company's claim that this vessel offers passengers a 'small ship feel, big ship choice.' The passenger flow has been well thought-out, and works with little congestion. The decor is attractive, with lots of earth tones.

THE SHIP. *Diamond Princess*, sister to *Sapphire Princess* (both built in Japan), has an instantly recognizable funnel due to two jet engine-like pods that sit high up on its structure but really are mainly for decoration.

Four areas focus on swimming pools. One has a giant poolside movie screen, and another is two decks high and is covered by a retractable glass dome, itself an extension of the funnel housing. One pool lies within The Sanctuary – an adults-only, extra-cost (it's worth it) relaxation area.

There is plenty of space inside the ship – but there are also plenty of passengers – and a wide array of public rooms, with many 'intimate' – this being a relative word – spaces and places to enjoy. The passenger flow is well thought-out, and there is little congestion anywhere, except perhaps for waiting at elevators at peak times (usually each evening, before dinner).

The interior focal point is a piazza-style atrium lobby, with Vines (wine bar), an International Café (for coffee, pastries, panini sandwiches, etc.) library/Internet-connect center, and Alfedo's sit-down Pizzeria.

Berlitz's Ratings

	Possible	Achieved
Ship	500	384
Accommodation	200	147
Food	400	251
Service	400	293
Entertainment	100	78
Cruise	400	295

OVERALL SCORE
1448 points out of 2000

A Wedding Chapel has a webcam that can relay ceremonies via the Internet. The ship's captain can legally marry American couples, due to the ship's Bermuda registry and a special dispensation (which should be verified when in the planning stage, according to where you reside). Princess Cruises offers three wedding packages – Pearl, Emerald, Diamond; the fee includes registration and official marriage certificate. The Hearts & Minds chapel is useful for renewal of vows ceremonies.

The large Grand Casino has more than 260 slot machines; there are blackjack, craps, and roulette tables, plus other table games. Linked slot machines provide a combined payout.

Other facilities include a library/computer room and a card room. Ship lovers should enjoy the wood-paneled Wheelhouse Bar, housing memorabilia and ship models tracing part of parent company P&O's history. Aft of the International Dining Room is the Wake View Bar, with a spiral stairway leading down to a great viewing spot for watching the ship's wake; it is reached from the back of Club Fusion, on Promenade Deck. Skywalkers Nightclub is set around the base of the funnel structure and has a view overlooking the aft-facing cascading decks and children's pool.

There are many extra-charge items such as ice cream, and freshly squeezed orange juice. There's an hourly charge for group babysitting services and a charge for using the washers and dryers in the self-service launderettes.

In 2014 the ship will be based in Japan for a series of 9- and 10-day cruises from Tokyo (Yokohama), these being targeted to Japanese passengers. Japanese-speaking staff will be employed in key positions, and additional Japanese food items will be available. These include an a la carte sushi bar, a noodle bar, regional tea tastings, and a special sake menu. Non-Japanese passengers will find all the usual Princess Cruises

FAMILIES. There is a two-deck-high playroom, teen chill-out room, and a host of specially trained counselors. Children have their own pools, hot tubs, and open deck area at the stern of the ship (away from adult areas).

ACCOMMODATION. All passengers receive turndown service and pillow chocolates each night, as well as bathrobes on request and toiletry kits (larger for suite/mini-suite occupants). A hairdryer is located at the vanity desk unit in the living area. The tiled bathrooms have a decent amount of open shelf storage space for toiletries. Princess Cruises has BBC World, CNN, CNBC, ESPN, and TNT on the in-cabin TV system (when available, depending on cruise area).

Many outside cabins on Emerald Deck have views obstructed by the lifeboats. There are no cabins for singles. Your name is typically placed outside your suite or cabin – making it simple for delivery service personnel but limiting your privacy. There is 24-hour room service, but some items on the room service menu are not available during early morning hours. Most balcony suites and cabins can be overlooked both from the navigation bridge wing. Cabins with balconies on Baja, Caribe, and Dolphin decks are also overlooked by passengers on balconies on the deck above.

Note that the bath towels are small, and drawer space is limited. The top-grade suites are not really large in comparison to similar suites aboard some other ships of a similar size. Cabin attendants (and their helpers) have a lot of cabins to look after (typically 20), which translates to service that's a bit rushed.

DINING. There are five principal dining rooms with themed decor and cuisine – International (the largest, located aft, with two seatings and 'traditional' cuisine), Sterling Steakhouse for steak and grilled meats, Vivaldi for Italian fare, Santa Fe for south-western USA cuisine, and Pacific Moon for Asian cuisine. These offer a mix of two seatings, with seating assigned according to your cabin location, and 'anytime dining,' where you choose when and with whom you want to eat.

All dining rooms are split into sections in a non-symmetrical design that breaks what are quite large spaces into many smaller sections, for better ambience and less noise pollution. Specially designed dinnerware and good quality linens and silverware are used: Dudson of England (dinnerware), Frette Egyptian cotton table linens, and silverware by Hepp of Germany.

Other dining options. Sabatini's is an informal eatery (reservations needed; cover charge). It serves an eight-course meal, including Italian-style pizzas and pastas, with a variety of sauces, as well as Italian-style entrées, all provided with flair and entertainment by the waiters. The cuisine here is better than in the other dining rooms, with better quality ingredients and more attention to presentation, taste and delivery.

A poolside hamburger grill and pizza bar (no additional charge) are additional dining spots for casual bites, while extra charges will apply if you order items to eat at either the coffee bar/patisserie or the caviar/Champagne bar.

Other casual meals can be taken in the Horizon Court, open 24 hours a day, with large ocean-view on port and starboard sides and direct access to the two main swimming pools and lido deck. There is no finesse in presentation, however, and plastic plates, not trays, are provided.

ENTERTAINMENT. The Princess Theatre spans two decks and has comfortable seating on both main and balcony levels. Princess Cruises prides itself on its glamorous all-American production shows, performed by its resident troupe of singers/dancers.

A second large entertainment lounge, Club Fusion, presents cabaret acts acts at night, and lectures, bingo, and horse racing during the day. A third entertainment lounge can also host cabaret acts and dance bands. Many other lounges and bars have live music, and a number of male dance hosts act as partners for women traveling alone.

SPA/FITNESS. The Lotus Spa complex, with Japanese-style decor, surrounds one of the swimming pools – you can have a massage or other spa treatment in an ocean-view treatment room. Lotus Spa treatments include Chakra hot stone massage, Asian Lotus ritual (featuring massage with reflexology, reiki, and shiatsu massage), deep-tissue sports therapy massage, lime and ginger salt glow, wild strawberry back cleanse, and seaweed mud wraps.

Activities such as yoga, group exercise bicycling, and kick boxing classes cost extra. For exercise, there is a good sheltered faux-teak promenade deck (it's actually painted steel) which almost wraps around the ship (three times around equals one mile).

Discovery
★★★

Size:.. Small Ship	Crew/Passenger Ratio (lower beds/all berths):......... 2.4/2.6	
Tonnage: 21,186	Cabins (total):................................... .355	
Lifestyle: ....Standard	Size range (sq ft/m): 125.9–441.3/11.7–41.0	
Cruise line:.................... Cruise & Maritime Voyages	Cabins (outside view):............................. .283	
Former names: *Platinum, Hyundai Pungak, Island Princess, Island Venture*	Cabins (interior/no view):...........................72	
	Cabins (for one person):.............................0	
IMO number: 7108514	Cabins (with private balcony):........................0	
Builder: .... Rheinstahl Nordseewerke (Germany)	Cabins (wheelchair accessible): 2	
Original cost:............................... $25 million	Wheelchair accessibility:...........................Fair	
Entered service:...................... Feb 1972/May 2003	Cabin voltage: ....110 and 220 volts	
Registry:.................................... Bermuda	Elevators:...4	
Length (ft/m):............................. 553.6/168.7	Casino (gaming tables):..............................No	
Beam (ft/m):................................. 80.7/24.6	Slot machines:.....................................No	
Draft (ft/m):................................. 25.2/7.7	Swimming pools:...................................2	
Propulsion/Propellers:................ diesel (13,400kW)/2	Hot tubs (on deck):.................................2	
Passenger decks:...................................8	Self-service launderette:.............................No	
Total crew:.....................................350	Dedicated cinema/seats:............................ Yes	
Passengers (lower beds/alll berths):............... 710/796	Library: .... Yes	
Passenger Space Ratio (lower beds/all berths): 29.8/26.6	Onboard currency: ....UK£	

Sedate, tired decor lets down an otherwise comfortable ship

OVERVIEW. The ship, well maintained and elegant, provides comfort for older passengers who want space but dislike larger ships. It has limited entertainment and a casual dress code. The decor is tasteful. The ship was refurbished in 2012.

THE SHIP. *Discovery*, has a traditional ship profile and well-balanced, somewhat rounded exterior styling. As the former Island Princess, it was one of the original stars in the American TV series *The Love Boat*.

There is a walk-around promenade deck outdoors. Inside, the public areas are spacious, and there are public rooms with reasonably wide passageways; these include a lobby with mezzanine level and curved staircase. The Discovery Lounge, located aft, has a two-deck high glass wall overlooking the aft deck.

Niggles include tacky plastic flowers, particularly in the dining room, and the tired appearance of parts of the ship. Gratuities are automatically charged to your onboard account.

ACCOMMODATION. There are 15 price categories – a lot for a small ship. There are five suites; these are of quite a decent size, and well designed, with plenty of space to move around in. Two are located forward, just under the navigation bridge, and command good views. Most other cabins have ample room, are quite well appointed, and there is sufficient storage space. The top category cabins have a full bathtub, while all others have a shower. Many have obstructed views.

Berlitz's Ratings		
	Possible	Achieved
Ship	500	226
Accommodation	200	102
Food	400	275
Service	400	253
Entertainment	100	51
Cruise	400	205
OVERALL SCORE		
1112 points out of 2000		

All cabins and suites have a TV set, telephone, personal safe, and hairdryer. Some cabins have interconnecting doors, and some can accommodate a third/fourth person. But some have an 'L' bed configuration, and the beds are rather narrow, at 30ins (76cm).

DINING. The Seven Continents Dining Room is a dated, 1970s-style space with a low ceiling and a slightly sunken center section. There are two seatings for dinner (and fresh flowers), but few tables for two, most being for four, six, or eight people. Many chairs have very low backs. There are separate tables as well as banquette seating, but the banquette seating is uncomfortable, and waiters need to reach over to serve and clear dishes.

Other dining options. Casual breakfasts and lunches can be taken in the Yacht Club, an observation lounge with ocean views on three sides, or outdoors on the Lido Deck. Dinner can also be taken in the Yacht Club, with its observation lounge views.

ENTERTAINMENT. The Carousel Showlounge has banquette-style seating in tiers, set around a thrust stage. The entertainment is low-key. There is live music, and a range of specialist lecturers.

SPA/FITNESS. The Spa Atlantis is positioned aft on two of the uppermost decks. A salon is on the upper deck, while a gym with aft-facing ocean-view windows, treatment rooms, and saunas are on the lower level.

Disney Dream
★★★★

Size:.................................Large Resort Ship		Cabins (total):.....................................1,250	
Tonnage: 129,690		Size range (sq ft/m): 169–1,781/15.7–165.5	
Lifestyle: ....Standard		Cabins (outside view):............................1,100	
Cruise line:............................. Disney Cruise Line		Cabins (interior/no view):...........................150	
Former names: ....none		Cabins (for one person):...............................0	
IMO number: 9434254		Cabins (with private balcony):.....................901	
Builder: .... Meyer Werft (Germany)		Cabins (wheelchair accessible): 37	
Original cost:............................... €600 million		Wheelchair accessibility:..........................Good	
Entered service:............................... Jan 2011		Cabin voltage: .... 110 volts	
Registry:................................The Bahamas		Elevators:...14	
Length (ft/m):.............................1,113.8/339.5		Casino (gaming tables):............................No	
Beam (ft/m):................................. 120.7/36.8		Slot machines:......................................No	
Draft (ft/m): 26.0/7.0		Swimming pools:......................................3	
Propulsion/Propellers:............ diesel-electric (72,000kW)/2		Hot tubs (on deck):...................................4	
Passenger decks:....................................14		Self-service launderette:..........................No	
Total crew:...................................... 1,458		Dedicated cinema/seats:..........................No	
Passengers (lower beds/all berths):............. 2,500/5,007		Library:..No	
Passenger Space Ratio (lower beds/all berths): 51.8/47.8		Onboard currency: ....US$	
Crew/Passenger Ratio (lower beds/all berths):.......... 1.7/3.4			

The ultimate family-friendly floating theme park

OVERVIEW. *Disney Dream* is ideal for families with children or grandchildren. Couples and singles are also welcome, though there are few activities for couples in the daytime, but enough entertainment at night. You will, however, need to be a real Disney fan, as everything revolves around Disney characters and the family theme.

Berlitz's Ratings		
	Possible	Achieved
Ship	500	422
Accommodation	200	159
Food	400	220
Service	400	293
Entertainment	100	91
Cruise	400	337
OVERALL SCORE		
1522 points out of 2000		

THE SHIP. Made of pieces of steel and pixie dust, the ships' exterior is about 40 percent larger than the first two Disney ships, *Disney Magic* and *Disney Wonder*. It also has two extra decks, although the design is similar – a tribute to the grand ocean liners of the 1930s. Like all Disney ships, there are two large funnels. The bows have handsome gold scrollwork more typically seen adorning yesteryear's tall ships (the stern is reminiscent of one of those lovely Airstream trailers). The ship's exterior colors are also those of Mickey himself: red, white, yellow, and black. The lifeboats are yellow, and not the normal orange, by special dispensation.

The biggest outdoor 'wow' factor is definitely going to be the AquaDuck, a 765-ft (233-m) shipboard 'watercoaster' spanning four decks in height – two-and-a-half times the length of a football field. It's pure Disney, really splash-tastic, and beyond anything aboard any other cruise ship dedicated to family cruising.

Disney whimsy and Art Deco style are the hallmarks of the stunning interior decor, too. In the main three-deck-high lobby stands a bronze statue of none other than Admiral Donald (Duck). The decor is enhanced by original paintings, statues, and woodwork all bearing the characteristic Disney attention to detail.

Most public rooms have high ceilings, and the Art Deco theme of the old ocean liners or New York's Radio City Music Hall has been tastefully carried out. Have a look at the stainless steel/pewter Disney detailing on the handrails and balustrades in the atrium lobby.

Grown-ups can inhabit their own area of the ship – away from the kids. Known as The District, it includes five different adults-only venues, including Evolution (a lounge with dance floor and bar), a cozy Skyline Lounge, Pink, 687 Lounge, and District Lounge. There's also a centrally located Concierge Lounge, for occupants of accommodation designated as Concierge Class, all on Deck 12, plus a dedicated private sundeck for Concierge-class occupants.

Other venues include: Mickey's Mainsail, Sea Treasure, Whitecaps, and Whozits and Whatsits (retail shops); District Bar, Pink Champagne Bar, Skyline Bar, Waves Bar, Bon Voyage, Meridian Bar, 687 (sports bar), Currents Bar, and Arr-cade. The best place for a quiet drink, however, is in the ship's delightful Observation Bar.

During the winter, *Disney Dream* sails on three- and four-day cruises to the Bahamas as part of a seven-night vacation package that includes a three- or four-day stay at a Walt Disney World resort hotel in Orlando; the cruise then forms the second half of the vacation. The ship calls at Castaway Cay, Disney's excellent private beach island, whose facilities are constantly being enhanced. American Express cardholders get special treatment and extra goodies. Members of Disney's Vacation Club can exchange points for cruises.

Gratuities are extra, and 15 percent is added to all bar/drinks purchases.

FAMILIES. Almost one entire deck is devoted to catering for children and teens. With names of places to play in like Animator's Studio and Nemo's, it's no wonder that kids have a great time.

It's a Small World Nursery is for children aged from three months to three years. The Oceaneer Lab and Oceaneer Club both have an interactive play floor – a sort of down-to-earth Wii, where team actions translate to movement, a novel idea.

'Edge' is for 11–13 year olds, a tween pad inside the forward funnel that's a chill-out zone including karaoke with green-screen technology. 'Vibe' is for the real teens, an indoor/outdoor space for 14–17s that is almost 9,000 sq ft (830 sq m), accessed by a teen-only swipe card.

ACCOMMODATION. There are nine types of suites and cabins, but many more price grades, depending on the size and location of the accommodation.

Interior cabins have a virtual porthole that gives you the feeling that you are in an outside cabin. It's done with high-definition cameras positioned on the outside decks to feed live video to each virtual porthole. You almost expect one or more Disney characters to pop by your porthole.

One feature that's different from *Disney Magic* and *Disney Wonder*: all bathrooms have round tubs with a pull-down seat and hand-held shower hose – practically perfect for washing babies and small children. The bed frames have been elevated so that luggage can easily be stored underneath.

The largest accommodation can be found in the Concierge Royal Suite (1,781 sq ft/166 sq m, including balcony), with hot tub. It can sleep five and has one master bedroom with a large walk-in closet, a living room (with one additional pull-down wall double bed and one pull-down single bed), two bathrooms (one has two washbasins), dining room, media library, pantry, and wet bar, plus a large balcony. These suites are located in the best possible position in the ship, with great ocean views.

If you opt for one of the 21 Concierge Class suites, you'll get higher quality bed linen (Frette 300-thread count Egyptian cotton), feather and down duvets, cotton bathrobe, and H2O Plus bath and spa products.

DINING. There are three main dining rooms, each with a different decor. Passengers rotate through all three, together with their regular waiter (server in Disney-speak).

Expect to see the surfer-dude sea turtle from Finding Nemo swimming around Animator's Palate, making special appearances and interacting with passengers; the room transforms into a coral reef during dinner. It's all about 'foodertainment,' which Disney does well, but the noise level can sometimes be a little intense.

Royal Palace has decor inspired by the classic Disney films *Cinderella*, *Snow White and the Seven Dwarfs*, *Beauty and the Beast*, and *Sleeping Beauty*.

The Enchanted Garden is a whimsical main dining room inspired by the gardens of Versailles, and the lighting magically transforms from day to night (the central glass panel ceiling is almost covered in what can only be magical foliage).

Other dining options. Cabanas is open to all. At night, it becomes another restaurant where meals from the main dining room menu are available in an even more casual setting but with waiter service.

For something different, and as an escape to the big dining rooms, Remy is an upscale French restaurant with menus created by Michelin-starred French chef Arnaud Lallement from l'Asiette Champagne, close to Reims in France, in conjunction with Scott Hunnel from Victoria & Albert's at Walt Disney World. An extra-cost, reservations-only venue, it offers leisurely European-style dining – ideal for an evening out (without the kids, of course), but at $75 a head for dinner (plus wine) it's not cheap. The design is rather ratty, too (think Disney's Ratatouille); in fact, rats are everywhere in the 'fine dining' venue – though not on your plate.

Palo is an Italian-cuisine themed adults-only restaurant, with à la carte items cooked to order. On days at sea, high tea is also served here, and there's a cover charge.

ENTERTAINMENT. Live shows are presented at the Walt Disney Theater, the ship's 1,340-seat showlounge. It has a star-studded ceiling and proscenium arch stage.

Villains Tonight, which premiered in 2010 aboard Disney Dream and features the baddies in Disney's films, is one of the shows being presented, along with other Disney favorites.

The Buena Vista Theater – which is not to be confused with the Walt Disney Theater – is the ship's movie house, with 399 seats.

There's live evening entertainment on deck including a Pirate Night, with visual and lighting effects, and live fireworks. Everyone's favorite Disney characters will be on board in many different locations, so make sure you have your camera with you (there are lots of photo opportunities).

SPA/FITNESS. Senses Spa and Salon has 17 treatment rooms and private outdoor verandahs. Rainforest features steam heat, misty showers, and hydrotherapy for relaxation. Teens can also have specially tailored spa treatments in their own chill-out zone.

Disney Fantasy
★★★★

Size:.	.Large Resort Ship	Cabins (total):.	1,250
Tonnage:	129,690	Size range (sq ft/m):	169–1,781/15.7–165.5
Lifestyle:	.Standard	Cabins (outside view):	1,100
Cruise line:.	Disney Cruise Line	Cabins (interior/no view):.	.150
Former names:	none	Cabins (for one person):.	.0
IMO number:	.9445590	Cabins (with private balcony):	.901
Builder:	Meyer Werft (Germany)	Cabins (wheelchair accessible):	.37
Original cost:	€600 million	Wheelchair accessibility:	.Good
Entered service:.	.Apr 2012	Cabin voltage:	110 volts
Registry:.	The Bahamas	Elevators:.	.14
Length (ft/m):.	.1,113.8/339.5	Casino (gaming tables):.	.No
Beam (ft/m):.	120.7/36.8	Slot machines:.	.No
Draft (ft/m):	26.0/7.9	Swimming pools:	.3
Propulsion/Propellers:.	diesel-electric (42,000kW)/2	Hot tubs (on deck):.	.4
Passenger decks:.	14	Self-service launderette:.	.No
Total crew:.	1,458	Dedicated cinema/seats:.	.No
Passengers (lower beds/alll berths):.	2,500/5,007	Library:	.No
Passenger Space Ratio (lower beds/all berths):	51.8/47.8	Onboard currency:	.US$
Crew/Passenger Ratio (lower beds/all berths):.	1.7/3.4		

The ultimate family-friendly floating theme park

OVERVIEW. *Disney Fantasy* is ideal for families with children or grandchildren. Couples and singles are also welcome, though there are few activities for couples in the daytime, but enough entertainment at night.

THE SHIP. Made of pieces of steel and pixie dust, the ships' exterior is about 40 percent larger than the first two Disney ships, *Disney Magic* and *Disney Wonder*. It also has two extra decks, although the design is similar – a tribute to the grand ocean liners of the 1930s. Like all Disney ships, there are two large funnels. The bows have handsome gold scrollwork more typically seen adorning yesteryear's tall ships (the stern is reminiscent of one of those lovely Airstream trailers). The ship's exterior colors (red, white and black) are also those of Mickey himself. The lifeboats are yellow, and not the normal orange, by special dispensation.

No doubt the biggest outdoor 'wow' factor is Aqua-Duck, a 765-ft (233-m) AquaDuck shipboard 'water-coaster' spanning four decks in height – two-and-a-half times the length of a football field.

Disney whimsy and Art Deco style are the hallmarks of the stunning interior decor, too. In the main three-deck-high lobby stands a bronze statue of none other than Admiral Donald (Duck). A chandelier is the atrium's focal point. The art Nouveau decor is enhanced by original paintings, statues, and woodwork all bearing the characteristic Disney attention to detail.

Most public rooms have high ceilings, and the Art Nouveau theme has been tastefully carried out. All the

Berlitz's Ratings

	Possible	Achieved
Ship	500	422
Accommodation	200	159
Food	400	220
Service	400	294
Entertainment	100	91
Cruise	400	338

OVERALL SCORE
1524 points out of 2000

artwork in public areas comes from Disney films or animation features.

Grown-ups inhabit their own area of the ship, in an area known as The District. It includes five different adults-only venues, including The Tube (lounge with dance floor and bar), a cozy Skyline Lounge, O'Gill's Pub, La Piazza, and Ooh La La. There's also a centrally located Concierge Lounge, for occupants of accommodation designated as Concierge Class, all on Deck 12, plus a dedicated private sundeck for Concierge-class occupants.

Other venues include: Mickey's Mainsail, Sea Treasure, Whitecaps, and Whozits and Whatsits (retail shops); District Bar, Pink Champagne Bar, Skyline Bar, Waves Bar, Bon Voyage, Meridian Bar, 687 (sports bar), Currents Bar, and Arr-cade. The best place for a quiet drink, however, is in the ship's delightful Observation Bar.

Disney has its own private island, Castaway Cay, whose facilities are constantly being enhanced. American Express cardholders get special treatment and extra goodies. Members of Disney's Vacation Club can exchange points for cruises.

At Port Canaveral, the Disney terminal was inspired by the original Ocean Terminal in Southampton, England, from which the famous ocean liners *Queen Elizabeth*, *Queen Mary*, and the ill-fated *Titanic* once sailed.

Gratuities are extra, and 15 percent is added to all bar/drinks purchases.

FAMILIES. Almost one entire deck is devoted to catering for children and teens. With names of places to play in like Animator's Studio and Nemo's, it's no wonder that kids have a great time.

It's a Small World Nursery is for children aged from three months to three years. The Oceaneer Lab and Oceaneer Club both have an interactive play floor – a sort of down-to-earth Wii, where team actions translate to movement, a novel idea.

'Edge' is for 11–13 year olds, a tween pad inside the forward funnel that's a chill-out zone including karaoke with green-screen technology. 'Vibe' is for the real teens, an indoor/outdoor space for 14–17s that is almost 9,000 sq ft (830 sq m), accessed by a teen-only swipe card.

ACCOMMODATION. There are nine types of suites and cabins, but many more price grades, depending on the size and location of the accommodation.

Interior cabins have a virtual porthole that gives you the feeling that you are in an outside cabin. It's done with high-definition cameras positioned on the outside decks to feed live video to each virtual porthole. You almost expect one or more Disney characters to pop by your porthole.

One feature that's different from *Disney Magic* and *Disney Wonder*: all bathrooms have round tubs with a pull-down seat and hand-held shower hose – practically perfect for washing babies and small children. The bed frames have been elevated so that luggage can easily be stored underneath.

The largest accommodation can be found in the Concierge Royal Suite (1,781 sq ft/166 sq m, including balcony), with hot tub. It can sleep five and has one master bedroom with a large walk-in closet, a living room (with one additional pull-down wall double bed and one pull-down single bed), two bathrooms (one has two washbasins), dining room, media library, pantry, and wet bar, plus a large balcony. These suites are located in the best possible position in the ship, with great ocean views.

If you opt for one of the 21 Concierge Class suites, you'll get higher quality bed linen (Frette 300-thread count Egyptian cotton), feather and down duvets, cotton bathrobe, and H2O Plus bath and spa products.

DINING. There are three main dining rooms, each with a different decor. Passengers rotate through all three, together with their regular waiter (server in Disney-speak).

Expect to see the surfer-dude sea turtle from Finding Nemo swimming around Animator's Palate, making special appearances and interacting with passengers; the room transforms into a coral reef during dinner. It's all about 'foodertainment,' which Disney does well, but the noise level can sometimes be a little intense.

Royal Court has decor inspired by the classic Disney films *Cinderella*, *Snow White and the Seven Dwarfs*, *Beauty and the Beast*, and *Sleeping Beauty*.

The Enchanted Garden is a whimsical main dining room inspired by the gardens of Versailles, and the lighting magically transforms from day to night (the central glass panel ceiling is almost covered in what can only be magical foliage).

Other dining options. Cabanas, is open to all. At night, it becomes another restaurant where meals from the main dining room menu are available in an even more casual setting but with waiter service.

For something different, and as an escape to the big dining rooms, Remy is an upscale French restaurant with menus created by Michelin-starred French chef Arnaud Lallement from l'Asiette Champagne, close to Reims in France, in conjunction with Scott Hunnel from Victoria & Albert's at Walt Disney World. An extra-cost, reservations-only venue, it offers leisurely European-style dining – ideal for an evening out (without the kids, of course), but at $75 a head for dinner (plus wine) it's not cheap. The design is rather ratty, too (think Disney's Ratatouille); in fact, rats are everywhere in the 'fine dining' venue – though not on your plate.

Palo is an Italian-cuisine themed adults-only restaurant, with à la carte items cooked to order. On days at sea, high tea is also served here, and there's a cover charge.

ENTERTAINMENT. Live shows are presented at the Walt Disney Theater, the ship's 1,340-seat showlounge. It has a star-studded ceiling and proscenium arch stage.

Villains Tonight, which premiered in 2010 aboard Disney Dream and features the baddies in Disney's films, is one of the shows being presented, along with other Disney favorites.

The Buena Vista Theater – which is not to be confused with the Walt Disney Theater – is the ship's movie house, with 399 seats.

There's live evening entertainment on deck including a Pirate Night, with visual and lighting effects, and live fireworks. Everyone's favorite Disney characters will be on board in many different locations, so make sure you have your camera with you (there are lots of photo opportunities).

SPA/FITNESS. Senses Spa and Salon has 17 treatment rooms and private outdoor verandahs. Rainforest features steam heat, misty showers, and hydrotherapy for relaxation. Teens can also have specially tailored spa treatments in their own chill-out zone.

Disney Magic
★★★★

Size:	.Large Resort Ship	Cabins (total):	.875
Tonnage:	83,338	Size range (sq ft/m):	180.8–968.7/16.8–90.0
Lifestyle:	Standard	Cabins (outside view):	.720
Cruise line:	Disney Cruise Line	Cabins (interior/no view):	.155
Former names:	none	Cabins (for one person):	.0
IMO number:	9126807	Cabins (with private balcony):	.388
Builder:	Fincantieri (Italy)	Cabins (wheelchair accessible):	.12
Original cost:	$350 million	Wheelchair accessibility:	Good
Entered service:	Jul 1998	Cabin voltage:	110 volts
Registry:	The Bahamas	Elevators:	.12
Length (ft/m):	964.5/294.00	Casino (gaming tables):	.No
Beam (ft/m):	105.7/32.22	Slot machines:	.No
Draft (ft/m):	26.2/8.0	Swimming pools:	.3
Propulsion/Propellers:	diesel-electric (38,000kW)/2	Hot tubs (on deck):	.6
Passenger decks:	11	Self-service launderette:	Yes
Total crew:	945	Dedicated cinema/seats:	Yes/270
Passengers (lower beds/all berths):	1,750/3,325	Library:	.No
Passenger Space Ratio (lower beds/all berths):	47.6/25.0	Onboard currency:	.US$
Crew/Passenger Ratio (lower beds/all berths):	1.8/3.5		

Ultra family-friendly cruising in a casual, big ship setting

OVERVIEW. *Disney Magic* is like a floating version of Disney's incredibly popular theme parks – seagoing Never-Never Lands. In reality, they provide a highly programmed, well organized, strictly timed and regimented onboard experience, with tickets, lines, and reservations necessary for almost everything. Children of all ages (minimum 12 weeks old) will have a great time aboard this ship.

THE SHIP. Disney Cruise Line's first ship's profile is sleek, and combines streamlining with tradition and nostalgia, a black hull and two large red and black funnels designed to remind you of the ocean liners of the past – *Disney Magic* was the first cruise ship built with two funnels since the 1950s. The forward funnel is a dummy containing various public spaces, including a teen center, Aloft.

The ship was constructed in two halves, which were then joined together in the shipyard in Venice, Italy. The ship's whistle even plays a version of 'When You Wish Upon a Star.' The bows have handsome gold scrollwork that more usually was seen adorning the tall sailing ships of yesteryear. There is a walk-around promenade deck outdoors for strolling – just as passengers did aboard the classic ocean liners.

Disney Cruise Line didn't add ostentatious decoration to the exterior. However, although Mickey Mouse's face and ears are painted on the funnels, there is also a special 85-ft (26-m) paint stripe that cleverly incorporates Disney characters into the whimsical yellow paintwork along each side of the

Berlitz's Ratings

	Possible	Achieved
Ship	500	397
Accommodation	200	155
Food	400	201
Service	400	287
Entertainment	100	90
Cruise	400	318

OVERALL SCORE
1448 points out of 2000

hull at the bow. It's really cute. The exterior colors are those of Mickey, too. Also of note is a 15-ft (4.5-m) Goofy hanging upside down in a bosun's chair, painting the stern of the ship, whose nicely rounded design may remind you of one of those retro Airstream trailers.

There are three outdoor pools: one pool for adults only (in theory), one for families, and one for children. One has a large poolside movie screen, and you can guess which one has Mickey's face and ears painted into the bottom.

The children's pool has a long yellow water slide (available at specified times), held up by Mickey's giant hand, although the pool itself is inadequate given the number of children usually aboard.

Inside, the ship is quite stunning. Most public rooms have high ceilings, and the Art Deco theme of the old ocean liners or New York's Radio City Music Hall has been tastefully carried out. Have a look at the stainless steel/pewter Disney detailing on the handrails and balustrades in the three-deck-high lobby. The lobby provides a real photo opportunity, with a 6-ft (1.8-m) bronze statue of Mickey Mouse in the role of a ship's helmsman.

Added in a 2005 refit were additional spaces for spa/fitness facilities, and Ocean Quest, the ship's fifth dedicated space for children; it contains a scale replica of the ship's bridge and LCD screen 'windows' that let youngsters look out over the bridge via live video feed from the actual navigation bridge. Kids can sit in a captain's chair and play a simulation game where they steer into and out of various ports. Teens can go to Aloft, a teens-only dorm-like chill-out zone in the base of the dummy forward funnel; it has big-screen TV, MP3 players, computers with hi-tech games, and video games, and its decor is a cross between a college dorm and a coffee shop.

Two large shops sell an abundance of Disney-theme clothing, soft toys, collectibles and specialty items. Other public rooms include a superb, 977-seat Walt Disney Theater with tiered seating over four decks, piano bar, adults-only nightclub-cum-disco, a family lounge, and a dedicated cinema where classic Disney films are shown, as well as first-run movies.

Apart from the ports of call, the highlight for most is a day spent on Disney's private island, Castaway Cay in the Bahamas. It is an outstanding private island – perhaps the benchmark for all private islands for families with children. It has its own pier so that the ship can dock alongside. Water sports equipment – floats, paddle-boats, kayaks, hobie cats, aqua fins, aqua trikes, and snorkels – can be rented.

Take mainly casual clothing (casual with a capital C), although there are two 'formal' nights on the seven-day cruises. Members of Disney's Vacation Club can exchange points for cruises, and American Express cardholders get special treatment and extra goodies. It is expensive – but so is a stay at any Disney resort. Gratuities are extra, suggested at about $10 per person, per day, and 15 percent is added to all bar/beverage/wine and spa accounts.

Lines at various outlets can prove irritating – some creative Disney Imagineering is needed – as can trying to get through to Guest Services by telephone. Gripes include: poky elevators; lines and signing up for activities; the food product and delivery falls short of less expensive cruise products; there is no proper library; and the early-morning disembarkation and customs inspection is a definite turn-off for many.

FAMILIES. The ship has three main zones: one for adults only, one for families with children, and one for families or single parents with toddlers. Each group has its own swimming pool and open deck/sunbathing areas – adults only at the front of the ship. A 24 x 14-ft (7 x 4-m) Goofy Pool Jumbo Screen is positioned by the family pool area, just behind the forward funnel; it shows classic Disney animated and live-action movies, TV shows, and sporting events.

The children's entertainment areas measure 13,000 sq ft (1,200 sq m), and more than 40 children's counselors run the extensive programmes. All registered children must wear an ID bracelet showing name, cabin number, and muster station number, and parents are given pagers for emergencies. There are also separate teen clubs, tween clubs, and a video game arcade.

A child drop-off service is available in the evenings, and private babysitting services are available at around $11 an hour, as are character 'tuck-ins' for children, and character breakfasts and lunches – all at extra cost. Free strollers are available, and parents can be provided with beepers in order to enjoy their time alone, away from their offspring for much of the day.

ACCOMMODATION. There are 12 grades, but just six different cabin layouts; the price will depend on the grade, size, and location chosen, and are linked to the resort accommodation for those taking a combined resort/cruise vacation. Spread over six decks, all suites and cabins have been designed for practicality and have space-efficient layouts.

Most cabins have common features such as a neat vertical steamer trunk for clothes storage, illuminated closets, a hairdryer located at a vanity desk or in the bathroom, and bathrobes for all passengers. Many cabins have third and fourth pull-down berths that rise and are totally hidden in the ceiling when not in use, but the standard interior and outside cabins, while acceptable for two, are extremely tight with three or four. Some cabins can also accommodate a fifth person. Cabins with refrigerators can have them stocked, at extra cost, with one of several drinks/soft drinks packages.

Bathrooms, although compact due to the fact that the toilet is separate, are really functional units, designed with split-use facilities so that more than one person can use them at the same time – good for families. Many have bathtubs, which are really shower tubs.

Accommodation designated as suites offers much more space, and extra goodies such as CD and DVD players, large-screen TVs, and extra beds (useful for larger families). Some suites are beneath the pool deck, teen lounge, or informal café, so there could be noise as the ceiling insulation is poor – although cabin-to-cabin insulation is good.

The two largest suites, the Walter E. Disney Suite and the Roy O. Disney Suite, are located beside the central bank of elevators. These are luxurious living spaces, each with two bedrooms, and all the Disney trimmings you'd expect.

Wheelchair-bound passengers have a variety of cabin sizes and configurations, including suites with a private balcony – unfortunately you can't get a wheelchair through the balcony's sliding door – and extra-large bathrooms with excellent roll-in showers, and good closet and drawer space. Almost all the vessel is accessible. For the sight-impaired, cabin numbers and elevator buttons are braille-encoded.

A 24-hour room service is available, and suites also get 'concierge service.' But the room service menu and cabin breakfast menu are limited. A 15 percent service charge applies to beverage deliveries, including tea and coffee.

DINING. There are three main dining rooms – non-smoking of course – each with over 400 seats, two seatings, and unique themes. Lumiere's (in the center of the ship on Deck 3) has Beauty and the Beast; Parrot Cay (Deck 4) has a tacky, pseudo-Caribbean theme; also on Deck 4 aft, with great ocean views over the stern, is Animator's Palate, the most visual of the three with food and electronic art that makes the evening decor change from black and white to full-color (this author's signature is on a hidden wall panel in this venue – it was done in the shipyard at Disney Cruise Line's invitation).

You eat in all three dining rooms in rotation – twice per seven-day cruise – and move with your assigned waiter and assistant waiter to each dining room in turn, thus providing the variety of different decor and different menus. It's a great concept – and unique in the cruise industry. As you will have the same waiter in each of the three restaurants, any gratuities go only to 'your' waiter. Parrot Cay and Lumiere's have open seating for breakfast and lunch, but the lunch menu is pitiful.

Other dining options. Palo is a 140-seat reservations-only alternative restaurant with a small cover/gratuity charge, serving Italian cuisine. It has a 270-degree view and is for adults only; the à la carte cuisine is cooked to order, and the wine list is good, although prices are high. Make your reservations as soon as you board or you will miss out on the ship's only decent food. Afternoon High Tea is presented here, on days at sea.

Topsider's (incorporating Beach Blanket Buffet) is an indoor/outdoor café serving low-quality self-serve breakfast and lunch buffets with limited choice and presentation, and a buffet dinner, consisting mostly of fried foods, for children. But the venue is often overcrowded at lunchtime, so it may be better to go to the Parrot Cay dining room, which offers breakfast and lunch buffet, too. A poolside Goofy's Galley has grilled panini and wraps, and soft drinks are complimentary.

Scoops, an ice cream and frozen yogurt bar, opens infrequently; other fast-food outlets include Pluto's for hamburgers, hot dogs, and Pinocchio's, which is open all day but not in the evening, for basic pizza and sandwiches.

On one night, there is also an outdoor self-serve Tropicalifragilisticexpialidocious buffet.

A casual Outlook Café, installed in 2010, has fine views from Deck 10, just forward of the first funnel housing. Vegetarians and those looking for light cuisine will be underwhelmed by the lack of green vegetables. Guest chefs from Walt Disney World Resort prepare signature dishes each cruise, and also host cooking demonstrations.

ENTERTAINMENT. The entertainment and activities programs for families and children are extremely good. There are three large-scale stage shows in the stunning 977-seat showlounge, presenting original Disney musi-cals and the latest comedy productions, bring together a cast of Disney baddies from many Disney films. Sadly, there is no live orchestra, although the lighting, staging, and technical effects are excellent. There is also a Disney-themed Trivia Game Show.

For grown-ups, Route 66 is an adults-only entertainment zone that includes a wacky Hollywood-style 'street,' and three entertainment rooms. Sessions is a jazz piano lounge, with private headphones for listening to music of all types when no live music is scheduled. The Rockin' Bar D provides noisy rock 'n' roll and country music. Barrel of Laughs offers improvisational comedy with audience participation. During the day.

Once each cruise, a late-night 'Pirates In the Caribbean' poolside party includes fireworks. Special equipment installed in the Walt Disney Theatre and the Buena Vista Theatre allows participants to view Disney Digital 3D movies.

One Disney exclusive is the game show 'Who Wants to be a Mouseketeer?' Prizes include free cruises and onboard credits of up to $1,000 and Tea with Wendy Darling from Disney's version of *Peter Pan*. Naturally, all the Disney characters are aboard for all cruises and there are lots of photo opportunities when they come out to play – typically when children's activities are scheduled.

SPA/FITNESS. The Vista Spa is the ship's fitness/wellbeing complex measuring 10,700 sq ft/994 sq m. The fitness/workout room, with high-tech Cybex muscle-toning equipment, has ocean-view windows overlooking the navigation bridge one deck below. There are 11 rooms for spa/beauty treatments – but note that the pounding from the basketball court on the sports deck directly overhead makes spa treatments less than relaxing. Three spa 'villas' have indoor treatment suites connected to private outdoor verandas with personal hot tub, open-air shower and chaise longue. There are a couple of private salons for Pilates instruction and one-on-one beauty and fitness consultations.

A Thermal Zone features a 'tropical rain shower,' sauna, mild steam room, aromatic steam room, and a fog shower. Aromatic scents such as eucalyptus, lime, peppermint, rose, and sage can be infused into the mild steam room, while chamomile is used in the aromatic steam room.

Exotic massages, aromatherapy facials, pedicures, and beauty salon treatments cost extra. The Rasul mud and steam room is a must for couples, but make appointments early. For something extra special, consider booking a massage at Castaway Cay in a private beach hut on the beach that is open to the sea. It's magical.

A sports deck has a paddle tennis court, table tennis, basketball court, shuffleboard, and golf driving range.

Disney Wonder
★★★★

Size:................................Large Resort Ship	Cabins (total):....................................875
Tonnage:....................................... 85,000	Size range (sq ft/m):.............. 180.8–968.7/16.8–90.0
Lifestyle:....................................Standard	Cabins (outside view):............................720
Cruise line:.......................... Disney Cruise Line	Cabins (interior/no view):.........................155
Former names:...................................none	Cabins (for one person):............................0
IMO number:.............................91216819	Cabins (with private balcony):.....................388
Builder:........................... Fincantieri (Italy)	Cabins (wheelchair accessible):.....................12
Original cost:.............................$350 million	Wheelchair accessibility:.........................Good
Entered service:........................... Aug 1999	Cabin voltage:............................ 110 volts
Registry:................................The Bahamas	Elevators:.......................................12
Length (ft/m):............................ 964.5/294.00	Casino (gaming tables):...........................No
Beam (ft/m):............................. 105.7/32.2	Slot machines:...................................No
Draft (ft/m):............................. 26.2/8.0	Swimming pools:...................................3
Propulsion/Propellers:........... diesel-electric (38,000kW)/2	Hot tubs (on deck):.................................6
Passenger decks:..................................11	Self-service launderette:...................... Yes (3)
Total crew:.....................................945	Dedicated cinema/seats:..................... Yes/270
Passengers (lower beds/alll berths):.............. 1,750/3,325	Library:...No
Passenger Space Ratio (lower beds/all berths):....... 48.5/25.5	Onboard currency:...............................US$
Crew/Passenger Ratio (lower beds/all berths):.......... 1.8/3.5	

Theme-park casual cruising for the whole family

OVERVIEW. *Disney Wonder* is like floating versions of Disney's incredibly popular theme parks – seagoing Never-Never Lands. In reality, the ship provides a highly programmed, well organized, strictly timed and regimented cruise experience, with tickets, lines, and reservations necessary for almost everything. But for children of all ages (minimum 12 weeks old), it's hard to beat Disney's entertainment.

Berlitz's Ratings

	Possible	Achieved
Ship	500	397
Accommodation	200	155
Food	400	201
Service	400	287
Entertainment	100	90
Cruise	400	320

OVERALL SCORE
1450 points out of 2000

THE SHIP. *Disney Wonder is the second of an identical pair of ships (first was the* 1998-built *Disney Magic).* The ship's profile is sleek, and combines streamlining with tradition and nostalgia, a black hull and two large red and black funnels designed to remind you of the ocean liners of the past – *Disney Magic* was the first cruise ship built with two funnels since the 1950s. One funnel is a dummy containing various public spaces, including a teen center, Aloft.

The ship was constructed in two halves, which were then joined together in the shipyard in Venice, Italy. The whistle even plays a sort of sickly version of 'When You Wish Upon a Star.' The bows have handsome gold scrollwork that more usually was seen adorning the tall sailing ships of yesteryear. There is a walk-around promenade deck outdoors for strolling – just as passengers did aboard the classic ocean liners.

Disney Cruise Line didn't add ostentatious decoration to the exterior. However, although Mickey Mouse's face and ears are painted on the funnels, there

is also a special 85-ft (26-m) paint stripe that cleverly incorporates Disney characters into the whimsical yellow paintwork along each side of the hull at the bow. Cute. The exterior colors are those of Mickey, too. Also of note are a 15-ft (4.5-m) Donald Duck and Huey Goofy hanging upside down in a bosun's chair, painting the ship's stern.

There are three outdoor pools: one pool for adults only (in theory), one for families, and one for children. One has a large poolside movie screen, and you can guess which one has Mickey's face and ears painted into the bottom.

A children's pool has a long yellow water slide (available at specified times), held up by Mickey's giant hand, although the pool itself is inadequate given the number of small children usually aboard.

Inside, the ship is quite stunning. Most public rooms have high ceilings, and the Art Deco theme of the old ocean liners or New York's Radio City Music Hall has been tastefully carried out. Have a look at the stainless steel/pewter Disney detailing on the handrails and balustrades in the three-deck-high lobby.

One Disney exclusive is the game show 'Who Wants to be a Mouseketeer?' The prizes include free cruises and onboard credits of up to $1,000 and Tea with Wendy Darling from Disney's version of *Peter Pan*. Naturally, all the Disney characters are aboard for all cruises and there are lots of photo opportunities when they come out to play – typically when children's activities are scheduled.

Added in a 2005 refit were additional spaces for spa/fitness facilities, and Ocean Quest, the ship's fifth dedicated space for children; it contains a scale replica of the ship's bridge and LCD screen 'windows' that let youngsters look out over the bridge via live video feed from the actual navigation bridge. Kids can sit in a captain's chair and play a simulation game where they steer into and out of various ports. Teens can go to Aloft, a teens-only dorm-like chill-out zone in the base of the dummy forward funnel; it has big-screen TV, MP3 players, computers with hi-tech games, and video games, and its decor is a cross between a college dorm and a coffee shop.

Two large shops sell an abundance of Disney-theme clothing, soft toys, collectibles and specialty items. Other public rooms include a superb, 977-seat Walt Disney Theater with tiered seating over four decks, piano bar, adults-only nightclub-cum-disco, a family lounge, and a dedicated cinema where classic Disney films are shown, as well as first-run movies.

Apart from the ports of call, the highlight for most is a day spent on Disney's private island, Castaway Cay in the Bahamas. It is an outstanding private island – perhaps the benchmark for all private islands for families with children. It has its own pier so that the ship can dock alongside. There is a post office with its own special Bahamas/Disney postage stamp and a whole host of dedicated, well thought-out attractions and amenities for all ages. These include a large adults-only beach, complete with massage cabanas. Water sports equipment – floats, paddle-boats, kayaks, hobie cats, aqua fins, aqua trikes, and snorkels – can be rented.

Take mainly casual clothing (casual with a capital C), although there are two 'formal' nights on the seven-day cruises. Members of Disney's Vacation Club can exchange points for cruises, and American Express cardholders get special treatment and extra goodies. It is expensive – but so is a stay at any Disney resort. Gratuities are extra, suggested at about $10 per person, per day, and 15 percent is added to all bar/beverage/wine and spa accounts.

Lines at various outlets can prove irritating – some creative Disney Imagineering is needed – as can trying to get through to Guest Services by telephone. Gripes include: poky elevators; lines and signing up for activities; the food product and delivery falls short of less expensive cruise products; there is no proper library; and the early-morning disembarkation and customs inspection is a definite turn-off for many.

FAMILIES. The ship has three main zones: one for adults only, one for families with children, and one for families or single parents with toddlers. Each group has its own swimming pool and open deck/sunbathing areas – adults only at the front of the ship. A 24 x 14-ft (7 x 4-m) Goofy Pool Jumbo Screen is positioned by the family pool area, just behind the forward funnel; it shows classic Disney animated and live-action movies, TV shows, and sporting events.

The children's entertainment areas measure 13,000 sq ft (1,200 sq m), and more than 40 children's counselors run the extensive programmes. All registered children must wear an ID bracelet showing name, cabin number, and muster station number, and parents are given pagers for emergencies. There are also separate teen clubs, tween clubs, and a video game arcade.

A child drop-off service is available in the evenings, and private babysitting services are available at around $11 an hour, as are character 'tuck-ins' for children, and character breakfasts and lunches – all at extra cost. Free strollers are available, and parents can be provided with beepers in order to enjoy their time alone, away from their offspring for much of the day.

ACCOMMODATION. There are 12 grades, but just six different cabin layouts; the price will depend on the grade, size, and location chosen, and are linked to the resort accommodation for those taking a combined resort/cruise vacation. Spread over six decks, all suites and cabins have been designed for practicality and have space-efficient layouts.

Most cabins have common features such as a neat vertical steamer trunk for clothes storage, illuminated closets, a hairdryer located at a vanity desk or in the bathroom, and bathrobes for all passengers. Many cabins have third and fourth pull-down berths that rise and are totally hidden in the ceiling when not in use, but the standard interior and outside cabins, while acceptable for two, are extremely tight with three or four. Some cabins can also accommodate a fifth person. The cabin decor is practical, creative, and colorful, with lots of neat styling touches. Cabins with refrigerators can have them stocked, at extra cost, with one of several drinks/soft drinks packages.

Bathrooms, although compact due to the fact that the toilet is separate, are really functional units, designed with split-use facilities so that more than one person can use them at the same time – good for families. Many have bathtubs, which are really shower tubs.

Accommodation designated as suites offers much more space, and extra goodies such as CD and DVD players, large-screen TVs, and extra beds (useful for larger families). Some suites are beneath the pool deck, teen lounge, or informal café, so there could be noise as the ceiling insulation is poor – although cabin-to-cabin insulation is good.

The two largest suites, the Walter E. Disney Suite and the Roy O. Disney Suite, are located beside the central bank of elevators. These are luxurious living spaces, each with two bedrooms, and all the Disney trimmings you'd expect.

Wheelchair-bound passengers have a variety of cabin sizes and configurations, including suites with a private balcony – unfortunately you can't get a wheelchair through the balcony's sliding door – and extra-large bathrooms with excellent roll-in showers, and good closet and drawer space. Almost all the vessel is accessible. For the sight-impaired, cabin numbers and elevator buttons are braille-encoded.

A 24-hour room service is available, and suites also get 'concierge service.' But the room service menu and cabin breakfast menu are limited. A 15 percent service charge applies to beverage deliveries, including tea and coffee.

DINING. There are has three main dining rooms, all non-smoking, each with over 400 seats, two seatings, and unique themes. Lumiere's (in the center of the ship on Deck 3) has Beauty and the Beast; Parrot Cay (Deck 4) has a tacky, pseudo-Caribbean theme; also on Deck 4 aft, with great ocean views over the stern, is Animator's Palate, the most visual of the three with food and electronic art that makes the evening decor change from black and white to full-color.

You will eat in all three dining rooms in rotation – twice per seven-day cruise – and move with your assigned waiter and assistant waiter to each dining room in turn, thus providing the variety of different decor and different menus. It's a great concept – and unique in the cruise industry. As you will have the same waiter in each of the three restaurants, any gratuities go only to 'your' waiter. Parrot Cay and Lumiere's have open seating for breakfast and lunch, but the lunch menu is pitiful.

Other dining options. Palo is a 140-seat reservations-only alternative restaurant with a cover/gratuity charge, serving Italian cuisine. It has a 270-degree view and is for adults only; the à la carte cuisine is cooked to order, and the wine list is good, although prices are high. Make your reservations as soon as you board or you will miss out on the ship's only decent food. Afternoon High Tea is presented here, on days at sea.

Topsider's (incorporating Beach Blanket Buffet) is an indoor/outdoor café serving low-quality self-serve breakfast and lunch buffets with limited choice and presentation, and a buffet dinner, consisting mostly of fried foods, for children. But the venue is often overcrowded at lunchtime, so it may be better to go to the Parrot Cay dining room, which offers breakfast and lunch buffet, too. A poolside Goofy's Galley has grilled panini and wraps, and soft drinks are complimentary.

Scoops, an ice cream and frozen yogurt bar, opens infrequently; other fast-food outlets include Pluto's for hamburgers, hot dogs, and Pinocchio's, which is open all day but not in the evening, for basic pizza and sandwiches.

On one night, there is also an outdoor self-serve Tropicalifragilisticexpialidocious buffet.

A casual Outlook Café, installed in 2010, has fine views from Deck 10, just forward of the first funnel housing. Vegetarians and those looking for light cuisine will be underwhelmed by the lack of green vegetables. Guest chefs from Walt Disney World Resort prepare signature dishes each cruise, and also host cooking demonstrations.

ENTERTAINMENT. The entertainment and activities programs for families and children are extremely good. There are three large-scale stage shows in the stunning 977-seat showlounge, presenting original Disney musicals and comedy productions, bringing together a cast of Disney characters (both good and bad) from many Disney films. Sadly, there is no live orchestra, although the lighting, staging, and technical effects are excellent. There is also a Disney-themed Trivia Game Show.

For grown-ups, Beal Street is an adult entertainment area that includes a wacky Hollywood-style 'street,' complete with three entertainment rooms. Cadillac is a jazz piano lounge, with private headphones for listening to music of all types when no live music is scheduled.

Wavebands, provides loud rock 'n' roll and country music. Meanwhile, Barrel of Laughs offers improvisational comedy with audience participation. During the day, creative enrichment programs have been added.

SPA/FITNESS. The Vista Spa is a fitness/wellbeing complex measuring 10,700 sq ft/994 sq m. The fitness/workout room, with high-tech Cybex muscle-toning equipment, has ocean-view windows overlooking the navigation bridge one deck below.

There are 11 rooms for spa/beauty treatments – but note that the pounding from the basketball court on the sports deck directly overhead makes spa treatments less than relaxing. Three spa 'villas' have indoor treatment suites connected to private outdoor verandas with personal hot tub, open-air shower and chaise longue. There are a couple of private salons for Pilates instruction and one-on-one beauty and fitness consultations.

A Thermal Zone features a 'tropical rain shower,' sauna, mild steam room, aromatic steam room, and a fog shower. Aromatic scents such as eucalyptus, lime, peppermint, rose, and sage can be infused into the mild steam room, while chamomile is used in the aromatic steam room.

Exotic massages, aromatherapy facials, pedicures, and beauty salon treatments cost extra – massage, for example, costs about $2 per minute, plus gratuity. The Rasul mud and steam room is a must for couples, but make appointments early. For something extra special, consider booking a massage at Castaway Cay in a private beach hut on the beach that is open to the sea. It's magical.

A sports deck has a paddle tennis court, table tennis, basketball court, shuffleboard, and golf driving range.

Emerald Princess
★★★★

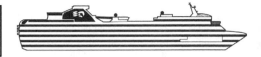

Size:.	.Large Resort Ship	Cabins (total):.	1,557
Tonnage:	113,561	Size range (sq ft/m):	163–1,279/15.1–118.8
Lifestyle:	.Standard	Cabins (outside view):	1,105
Cruise line:.	Princess Cruises	Cabins (interior/no view):.	452
Former names:	none	Cabins (for one person):.	0
IMO number:	9333151	Cabins (with private balcony):.	881
Builder:	Fincantieri (Italy)	Cabins (wheelchair accessible):	25
Original cost:	$500 million	Wheelchair accessibility:	Good
Entered service:.	May 2007	Cabin voltage:	110 volts
Registry:.	Bermuda	Elevators:	14
Length (ft/m):	951.4/290.0	Casino (gaming tables):	Yes
Beam (ft/m):.	118.1/36.0	Slot machines:.	Yes
Draft (ft/m):	26.2/8.0	Swimming pools:.	3
Propulsion/Propellers:	diesel-electric (42,000kW)/2	Hot tubs (on deck):.	9
Passenger decks:.	15	Self-service launderette:	Yes
Total crew:.	1,200	Dedicated cinema/seats:.	No
Passengers (lower beds/alll berths):	3,114/3,782	Library:	Yes
Passenger Space Ratio (lower beds/all berths):	36.2/29.8	Onboard currency:	US$
Crew/Passenger Ratio (lower beds/all berths):	2.5/3.1		

Very comfortable, family-oriented large resort ship

OVERVIEW. The ship is a fine resort playground in which to roam when you are not ashore, and Princess Cruises consistently delivers a well-packaged product, always with a good degree of style, at an attractive, highly competitive price. With many choices and 'small' rooms to enjoy, the ship has been extremely well designed, and you should have an enjoyable time.

THE SHIP. *Emerald Princess* has the same profile as sister *Crown Princess* (similar to half-sisters *Diamond Princess, Golden Princess, Grand Princess, Ruby Princess, Sapphire Princess,* and *Star Princess*). Although the ship takes over 500 more passengers than the half-sisters, the outdoor deck space remains the same, as do the number of elevators, so waiting time will increase at peak periods. The Passenger Space Ratio is also considerably reduced.

One nice feature worth booking on days at sea is The Sanctuary, an extra-cost adults-only retreat located forward on the uppermost deck. It provides a 'private' place to relax and unwind and includes attendants to provide chilled face towels and deliver light bites; there are also two outdoor cabanas for massages. It's worth the extra charge, calculated by the half-day.

There is a good sheltered faux teak promenade deck – it's actually painted steel – which almost wraps around (three times round is equal to one mile) and a walkway which goes to the enclosed, protected bow of the ship. The outdoor pools have various beach-like surroundings, and Movies Under the Skies and

Berlitz's Ratings

	Possible	Achieved
Ship	500	382
Accommodation	200	147
Food	400	250
Service	400	285
Entertainment	100	80
Cruise	400	298

OVERALL SCORE
1442 points out of 2000

major sporting events are shown on a 300-sq-ft (28-sq-m) movie screen at the pool in front of the large funnel structure.

Unlike the outside decks, there is plenty of space inside – but there are also plenty of passengers – and a wide array of public rooms, with many 'intimate' (this being a relative term) spaces and places to play. The passenger flow has been well thought-out, and there is little congestion.

Just aft of the funnel housing is a ship-wide glass-walled disco called Skywalkers. It's in a lower position than in some of the half-sister ships, but still has fine views from the port and starboard side windows – it would make a great penthouse.

The interior decor is attractive, with lots of earth tones. An extensive collection of artworks complements the interior design and colors well. If you see something you like, you will probably be able to purchase it on board.

Emerald Princess also has a wedding chapel, with a live web-cam to relay ceremonies via the Internet. The captain can legally marry (American) couples, thanks to the ship's Bermuda registry and a special dispensation (which should be verified when in the planning stage, according to where you reside). But to get married and take your close family members and entourage with you on your honeymoon may prove expensive. The Hearts & Minds chapel is also useful for renewal of vows ceremonies.

Gamblers should enjoy the large Gatsby's Casino, with more than 260 slot machines, and blackjack, craps, and roulette tables, plus games such as Let It Ride Bonus, Spanish 21, and Caribbean Draw Progressive. But the highlight could well be the linked slot machines that provide a combined payout.

Other features include a small library, and a decent internet-connect room. Ship lovers should enjoy the wood-paneled Wheelhouse Bar (a good place for cocktails and beer), finely decorated with memorabilia and ship models tracing part of parent company P&O's history. A sports bar has two billiard tables, and several television screens.

As with any large resort ship it will take you some time to find your way around, despite the company's claim that it offers passengers a 'small ship feel, big ship choice.' There are several points of congestion, particularly outside the shops when bazaar tables are set up outside on the upper level of the atrium lobby.

FAMILIES. There's a two-deck-high playroom, teen room, and a host of trained counselors. Children have their own pools, hot tubs, open deck, and sports court area at the stern of the ship, away from the adults.

ACCOMMODATION. There are six principal types of cabins and configurations: (a) grand suite, (b) suite, (c) mini-suite, (d) outside-view double cabins with balcony, (e) outside-view double cabins, and (f) interior double cabins. These come in 35 different brochure price categories – the choice is bewildering for both travel agents and passengers – and pricing depends on size and location.

For a comprehensive description of the facilities available in each type of cabin, see the entry for *Crown Princess*.

DINING. Of the three main dining rooms – Botticelli, Da Vinci, and Michelangelo – one has two-seating dining and the other two have 'anytime dining' that allows you to choose when and with whom you want to eat. All three are split into multi-tier sections in a non-symmetrical design that breaks what are quite large spaces into smaller sections for better ambience.

While four elevators go to the deck where two of the restaurants are located, only two go to Plaza Deck 5, where the Michelangelo Dining Room is located – this can cause waiting problems at peak times, particularly for anyone in a wheelchair.

Specially designed dinnerware, high-quality linens and silverware, Frette Egyptian cotton table linens, and silverware by Hepp of Germany are used in the main dining rooms. Note that 15 percent is added to all beverage bills, including wines.

Other dining options. There are two extra-cost venues: Sabatini's and Crown Grill. Both are open for lunch and dinner on days at sea. Sabatini's is an Italian eatery located on a high deck aft of the funnel housing, with colorful tiled Mediterranean-style decor; it is named after Trattoria Sabatini, the 200-year-

old institution in Florence. It includes Italian-style multi-course antipasti and pastas, as well as Italian-style entrées, including tiger prawns and lobster tail. All are provided with flair and entertainment by the staff of waiters. It's by reservation only and has a cover charge.

The Crown Grill, located aft on Promenade Deck, is a reservation-only, extra-cost steakhouse, offering premium-quality American steaks and seafood.

These include a poolside hamburger grill and pizza bar (no additional charge), while extra charges apply if you order items to eat either at the International Café (a coffee bar/patisserie) or in Vines seafood/wine bar in the atrium lobby. Other casual meals can be taken in the Horizon Court (open 24 hours a day). It has large ocean-view on port and starboard sides and direct access to the two principal swimming pools and lido deck. Although there is a wide variety of food, there is no finesse in presentation, however, as plastic plates are provided.

For something different, you could try a private dinner on your balcony, an all-inclusive evening featuring cocktails, fresh flowers, Champagne, and a deluxe four-course meal including Caribbean lobster tail – all served by a member of the dining staff on your private balcony. Of course, it costs extra.

ENTERTAINMENT. The 800-seat Princess Theater is the main entertainment venue; it spans two decks and has comfortable seating on both main and balcony levels. It has $3 million worth of sound and light equipment, plus a nine-piece orchestra. The ship has a resident troupe of almost 20 singers and dancers.

A second entertainment lounge, Club Fusion, is located aft. It features cabaret acts and karaoke contests at night, and lectures, bingo, and horse racing during the day. Explorers Lounge, a third entertainment lounge, can also host cabaret acts and dance bands.

A variety of other lounges and bars have live music, including a string quartet, and street performers who appear in the main atrium lobby.

SPA/FITNESS. The Lotus Spa is located forward on Sun Deck, one of the uppermost decks. Separate facilities for men and women include a sauna, steam room, and changing rooms; common facilities include a relaxation/waiting zone, body-pampering treatment rooms, and a gymnasium with packed with the latest high-tech muscle-pumping, cardio-vascular equipment, and great ocean views. Some fitness classes are free, while others cost extra.

Empress
★★★

Size:	Mid-size Ship	Cabins (total):	800
Tonnage:	48,563 tons	Size range (sq ft/m):	117.0–818/10.8–76
Lifestyle:	Standard	Cabins (outside view):	471
Cruise line:	Pullmantur Cruises	Cabins (interior/no view):	329
Former names:	Empress of the Seas, Nordic Empress	Cabins (for one person):	0
IMO number:	8716899	Cabins (with private balcony):	69
Builder:	Chantiers de l'Atlantique (France)	Cabins (wheelchair accessible):	4
Original cost:	$170 million	Wheelchair accessibility:	Fair
Entered service:	Jun 1990/May 2008	Cabin voltage:	110 volts
Registry:	The Bahamas	Elevators:	7
Length (ft/m):	692.2/211.0	Casino (gaming tables):	Yes
Beam (ft/m):	100.7/30.7	Slot machines:	Yes
Draft (ft/m):	24.9/7.6	Swimming pools:	1
Propulsion/Propellers:	diesel)16,200kW)/2	Hot tubs (on deck):	4
Passenger decks:	9	Self-service launderette:	No
Total crew:	685	Dedicated cinema/seats:	No
Passengers (lower beds/alll berths):	1,600/2,020	Library:	No
Passenger Space Ratio (lower beds/all berths):	30.2/24.0	Onboard currency:	Euros
Crew/Passenger Ratio (lower beds/all berths):	2.3/2.9		

A large but dated family-friendly ship for Spanish speakers

OVERVIEW. *Empress* is best suited to young Spanish-speaking couples and singles seeking an all-inclusive cruise, and those who want a good basic getaway cruise aboard a ship that offers some good drinking places.

THE SHIP. This modern ship has a polished wood walk-around promenade deck outdoors. Although the outdoor pool is decent enough, the two swimming pools are very small for the number of passengers. There's not much open deck space, so sunloungers are crammed together.

A nine-deck-high atrium is the focal point of the interior design, which has many Scandinavian influences. Passenger flow is generally good. A three-level casino has a sailcloth ceiling, but it is a noisy room. The Viking Crown Lounge, aft of the funnel, is a two-level nightclub-disco.

Empress is a fairly smart ship with a high passenger density, and you won't be bored. But you may be overwhelmed by the public spaces, and underwhelmed by the size of the cabins.

ACCOMMODATION. There are 15 price categories. The largest accommodation, the Royal Suite, has a queen-size bed, walk-in closet, separate living area with bar, refrigerator, and entertainment center; the bathroom has a whirlpool tub and vanity dressing area. There is a private balcony.

Nine cabins have private balconies overlooking the stern; these consist of two large owner's suites and

Berlitz's Ratings

	Possible	Achieved
Ship	500	321
Accommodation	200	121
Food	400	216
Service	400	257
Entertainment	100	64
Cruise	400	241
OVERALL SCORE		
1220 points out of 2000		

seven 'superior' ocean-view cabins. The other cabins with private balconies also have a decent amount of living space, and a small sofa, coffee table and chair, and vanity desk. Almost all the other cabins are really small, and only moderately comfortable. All cabins have twin beds that convert to a queen-size configuration. The bathrooms are nicely laid-out.

DINING. The Miramar Restaurant is two decks high, but it really is a noisy room. There are two seatings, at tables for four, six, eight, or 10. The cuisine is typical of mass banquet catering that offers standard fare.

There is one à la carte extra-charge restaurant; reservations required. Its intimacy makes it a romantic place, with a good number of tables for two.

For casual breakfasts and lunches, the Panorama Buffet provides an alternative to the dining room.

ENTERTAINMENT. The two-level Broadway Showroom has poor sight lines in the upper lateral balconies. The sight lines from the balcony are ruined by railings. The entertainment throughout is upbeat – in fact, it is difficult to get away from music. There is even background music in all corridors and lifts, and constant music on the pool deck.

SPA/FITNESS. A gymnasium has some good equipment. Sports fans will like the climbing wall at the stern of the ship.

Enchantment of the Seas
★★★+

Size:. . . . . .Large Resort Ship	Cabins (total):. 1,126
Tonnage: 81,500	Size range (sq ft/m):. 158.2–1,267.0/14.7–117.7
Lifestyle: . . . . .Standard	Cabins (outside view):. 663
Cruise line:. . . . . Royal Caribbean International	Cabins (interior/no view):. 463
Former names: . . . . none	Cabins (for one person):. 0
IMO number: 9111802	Cabins (with private balcony):. 248
Builder: . . . . Kvaerner Masa-Yards (Finland)	Cabins (wheelchair accessible): 20
Original cost:. . . . . $300 million	Wheelchair accessibility:. . . . . .Good
Entered service:. . . . . .Jul 1997	Cabin voltage: . . . . .110 and 220 volts
Registry:. . . . . The Bahamas	Elevators:. 9
Length (ft/m):. 990.1/301.8	Casino (gaming tables):. . . . . Yes
Beam (ft/m):. 105.6/32.2	Slot machines:. . . . . Yes
Draft (ft/m): 25.5/7.6	Swimming pools:. . . . . .3 (1 w/sliding glass dome)
Propulsion/Propellers:. . . . . diesel-electric (50,400kW)/2	Hot tubs (on deck):. 4
Passenger decks:. 11	Self-service launderette:. . . . . .No
Total crew:. 840	Dedicated cinema/seats:. . . . . .No
Passengers (lower beds/alll berths):. 2,252/2,730	Library:. . . . . Yes
Passenger Space Ratio (lower beds/all berths): 36.1/29.8	Onboard currency: . . . . .US$
Crew/Passenger Ratio (lower beds/all berths):. 2.6/3.2	

A large ship with elegant decor, for mature-age cruisers

OVERVIEW. This ship has quite attractive interiors and will provide you with a good cruise vacation. It is good particularly for first-time passengers seeking comfortable surroundings similar to those in a Hyatt Hotel, with fabrics and soft furnishings that blend together. This company provides a well-organized but rather homogenous cruise experience, with the same decades-old passenger participation activities and events.

Berlitz's Ratings

	Possible	Achieved
Ship	500	379
Accommodation	200	142
Food	400	238
Service	400	262
Entertainment	100	74
Cruise	400	263
OVERALL SCORE		
1358 points out of 2000		

THE SHIP. *Enchantment of the Seas*, sister to *Grandeur of the Seas*, has a fairly sleek profile, with a single funnel located well aft – almost a throwback to the designs of the 1950s. The stern is nicely rounded, and a Viking Crown Lounge is set amidships. This, together with the forward mast, provides three distinct focal points in the ship's exterior profile. There is a walk-around promenade deck outdoors, but no cushioned pads for the tacky home patio-style plastic sunloungers.

A large Viking Crown Lounge, a trademark lounge aboard all Royal Caribbean International ships, sits between the funnel and mast at the top of the atrium lobby, and overlooks the forward section of the swimming pool deck, with access provided from a stairway off the central atrium.

The principal interior focal point is a seven-deck-high Centrum (atrium lobby), which provides a good meeting point; the Purser's Desk (reception desk) and Shore Excursion Desk are located on one of the lower levels. Several of the public entertainment rooms, lounges and facilities are located off the atrium.

This ship has a decent passenger flow. There's a varied collection of artworks, including several sculptures, principally by British artists, with classical music, ballet, and theater themes. The casino is large and glitzy, and has a fascinating, theatrical glass-covered, but underfloor exhibit. The children's and teens' facilities are not large, but they are enough to cope with the number of families traveling with children.

A Champagne terrace bar sits forward of the lower level of the two-deck-high dining room. There is a good use of tropical plants throughout the public rooms, which helps to counteract the rather plain and clinical pastel wall colors, while huge murals of opera scenes adorn several stairways.

In 2005, the ship underwent a $60 million 'chop-and-stretch' operation that added a 72.8-ft (22.2-m) mid-section, increasing its overall length to 990.1ft (301.8m) and its gross tonnage to 81,500.

The modification added another 151 passenger cabins, including two 'family' cabins that can sleep six, and some public rooms were given a make-over. Sports facilities were augmented; these included two 'ball zones,' each with three basketball hoops of different heights to accommodate youth, teen, and adult shooters. The pool deck was given more space plus soaring 'suspension' bridges. Special handicap lifts were provided for the two pools, as was a new Splash Deck (children will love the 64 water jets) with a decorative night-time fiber-optic light show. Bungee trampolines were added to Deck 10 (above the Windjammer Café).

The main dining room and Windjammer Café casual eatery were enlarged to handle the extra capacity, and so was the art auction gallery.

ACCOMMODATION. There are multiple price grades, with location and grade perhaps the most important determining factor, given that so many of the cabins are of the same or very similar size. All grades of suites and cabins are provided with a hairdryer. The room service menu has only the most basic selection.

The five grades of suites are well appointed and have pleasing decor, best described as Scandinavian Moderne, with good wood and color accenting.

Royal Suite. The largest accommodation, which contains a baby grand piano, is the Royal Suite, located directly aft of the ship's navigation bridge on the starboard side. It has a separate bedroom with kind-size bed, walk-in closet and vanity dressing area, living room with queen-size sofa bed, refrigerator and wet bar, dining table, entertainment center, and large private balcony. The bathroom has a whirlpool tub, separate shower enclosure, two washbasins, and toilet.

Owner's Suite. The five owner's suites are at the forward end of the ship, just behind the navigation bridge, close to the Royal Suite. They have a queen-size bed, separate living area with queen-size sofa bed, vanity dressing area, refrigerator, and wet bar. The bathroom has a full-size tub, separate shower enclosure, toilet, and two washbasins.

Royal Family Suite. These four suites have two bedrooms with twin beds that convert to queen-size beds, living area with double sofa bed and Pullman bed, refrigerator, two bathrooms (one with tub), and private balcony. This suite can accommodate eight and might suit families.

Grand Suite. Features of these 12 suites include twin beds that convert to a queen-size bed, vanity dressing area, lounge area with sofa bed, refrigerator, and a bathroom with tub. There's also a private balcony.

Superior Suite. Features of these 44 suites, which include two superior suites for the disabled, have twin beds that convert to a queen-size bed, vanity dressing area, lounge area with sofa bed, refrigerator, a bathroom with tub, and private balcony. Although these are called suites, they really are little more than a larger standard cabin with balcony.

Other grades. All standard cabins have twin beds that convert to a queen-size bed, ample closet space for a one-week cruise, and a good amount of drawer space, although under-bed storage space is not good for large suitcases. The bathrooms have nine mirrors. Plastic buckets are provided for Champagne /wine and are really tacky.

DINING. The 1,195-seat My Fair Lady Dining Room spreads over two decks, connected by a grand, sweeping staircase. When you book, choose one of two seatings, or 'My Time Dining' (eat when you want, during dining hours).

Other dining options. The extra-cost, reservations-needed Chops Grill Steakhouse is an à la carte steakhouse serving steaks and veal chops. Think big steaks, better service, and more comfortable dining.

Casual, self-serve breakfasts and luncheons can be taken in the 790-seat informal Windjammer Marketplace. It has a great expanse of ocean-view glass windows, the decor is bright and cheerful, and buffet 'islands' contain food from around the world. An intimate Champagne/Caviar Bar terrace is forward of the lower level of the two-deck-high dining room and just off the atrium for those who might like to taste something a little bit out of the ordinary, in a setting that is both bright and contemporary.

ENTERTAINMENT. The 875-seat Orpheum Theater, the main showlounge, is a grand room at the forward part of the ship. This is where the big production shows are staged, as well as the major cabaret acts.

A second showlounge, the 575-seat Carousel Lounge, is located aft, and is for smaller shows and adult cabarets, including late-night adults-only comedy. A variety of other lounges and bars have almost constant live music; in fact, there's no bar without music to have a quiet drink in. There's even background music in all corridors and elevators, and constant music outdoors on the pool deck. If you want a quiet relaxing holiday, choose another ship.

SPA/FITNESS. The ShipShape Spa is aft of the funnel and spans two decks. Facilities include a large gymnasium (with all the latest techno- and cardio muscle pumping machines), aerobics exercise room, sauna and steam rooms, a beauty salon, and 13 private massage/body treatment rooms, including a couples massage room.

The Spa/fitness facilities are staffed and operated by Steiner Leisure, a specialist spa/beauty concession. Some fitness classes are free, while some, such as Pathway to Yoga, and Pathway to Pilates, cost extra. It's wise to make appointments early as time slots can go quickly.

Eurodam
★★★★

Size:.....................................Large Resort Ship		Cabins (total):....................................1,052	
Tonnage:.....................................86,273		Size range (sq ft/m):...............170.0–1,318.6/15.7–122.5	
Lifestyle:.....................................Premium		Cabins (outside view):.................................897	
Cruise line:.........................Holland America Line		Cabins (interior/no view):.............................155	
Former names:.....................................none		Cabins (for one person):...............................0	
IMO number:.....................................9378448		Cabins (with private balcony):.........................708	
Builder:.............................Fincantieri (Italy)		Cabins (wheelchair accessible):........................30	
Original cost:.....................................$450 million		Wheelchair accessibility:............................Good	
Entered service:.....................................Jul 2008		Cabin voltage:............................110/220 volts	
Registry:.....................................The Netherlands		Elevators:.....................................14	
Length (ft/m):.....................................935.0/285.0		Casino (gaming tables):...............................Yes	
Beam (ft/m):.....................................105.6/32.2		Slot machines:....................................Yes	
Draft (ft/m):.....................................25.5/7.8		Swimming pools:.................2 (1 w/sliding glass dome)	
Propulsion/Propellers:.......diesel-electric (34,000kW)/2 pods		Hot tubs (on deck):....................................5	
Passenger decks:.....................................12		Self-service launderette:.............................No	
Total crew:.....................................929		Dedicated cinema/seats:..........................Yes/170	
Passengers (lower beds/alll berths):.............2,104/2,671		Library:.....................................Yes	
Passenger Space Ratio (lower beds/all berths):.......41.2/32.4		Onboard currency:....................................US$	
Crew/Passenger Ratio (lower beds/all berths):..........2.2/2.8			

A large, spacious ship with family-friendly Dutch-style interiors

OVERVIEW. The ship has a bright interior decor designed to appeal to younger, more vibrant, multi-generational holidaymakers. In keeping with the traditions of Holland America Line, a large collection of artwork is a standard feature, and pieces reflect the former Dutch East Indies.

THE SHIP. *Eurodam* has two funnels, positioned close together – one behind the other instead of side by side – the result of the machinery configuration. The ship has, in effect, two engine rooms – one with three diesels, and one with two diesels. A pod propulsion system is provided, so there's virtually no vibration.

There are 22 rent-by-the-day cabanas, with goodies such as Champagne, chocolate strawberries, an iPod pre-stocked with music, bathrobes, fresh fruit, and chilled towels. These are designed for two adults and two children, so they may not be the promised 'quiet' spaces, after all. They are located in an area on observation deck and around the Lido Pool.

There is a complete walk-around exterior teak promenade deck, real teak steamer-style sunloungers, and a jogging track around the forward third of the ship.

Exterior glass elevators, mounted midships on both port and starboard sides, provide fine ocean views from all 11 passenger decks. There are two centrally located pools outdoors, one of which has a retractable glass roof, plus a children's pool.

The lobby spans three decks. Adjacent are interior and glass wall elevators with exterior views. The in-

Berlitz's Ratings		
	Possible	Achieved
Ship	500	394
Accommodation	200	150
Food	400	270
Service	400	272
Entertainment	100	71
Cruise	400	291
OVERALL SCORE		
1448 points out of 2000		

formation desk (on the lobby's lowest level) is small and somewhat removed from the main passenger flow on the two decks above it.

There are two decks of entertainment and public rooms. Perhaps the most dramatic room is the showlounge, spanning four decks in the forward section of the ship. Other facilities include a winding shopping street with several boutique stores, card room, an art gallery, photo gallery, and several meeting rooms.

The casino is large and equipped with all the usual gaming paraphernalia and slot machines. One of the most popular public rooms is Explorations – a combination coffee bar (all drinks are at extra cost), lounge, library, and Internet center, all in one attractive, open 'lifestyle' environment, adjacent to the Crows Nest Lounge.

On other decks (lower down), you'll find a Queens Lounge, which acts as a lecture room, a Culinary Arts Center, where cooking demonstrations and classes are held. There are a number of other bars and lounges, including an Explorer's Lounge (with live music and warm hors d'oeuvres at cocktail hour). The ship also has a small movie screening room – a nice feature.

Gratuities are automatically added to your onboard account. Passenger niggles? These include noisy cabin air conditioning – the flow can't be turned off, the only regulation being for temperature control. Also, several pillars obstruct the passenger flow and lines of sight throughout the ship.

FAMILIES. For families with children, Club HAL's KidZone provides a whole area dedicated to children's facilities and extensive programming for different age groups (five to 17), with one counselor for every 30 children. Ice cream is free at certain hours. There are no self-service launderettes – something many families with children miss, although special bulk laundry packages are available.

ACCOMMODATION. There are 24 price categories. Most of the total 1,022 suites/cabins have an outside view or 'private' balcony. Note that many of cabins on Upper Promenade Deck have lifeboat- or safety equipment-obstructed views. Avoid cabins directly under the aft pool deck because deck chair dragging noises can be really irritating.

Some cabins that can accommodate a third and fourth person have very little closet space, and only one personal safe. Occupants of suites get exclusive use of the Neptune Lounge and concierge service, priority embarkation and disembarkation, and other benefits. In many of the suites/cabins with private balconies, the balconies can be overlooked from various public locations.

Penthouse Verandah Suites. These offer the largest accommodation (1,318 sq ft/123 sq m, including balcony). They have a separate bedroom with a king-size bed; there's also a walk-in closet, dressing room, living room, dining room, butler's pantry, mini-bar and refrigerator, and balcony. The main bathroom has a large whirlpool tub, and two washbasins. Personalized stationery and free dry cleaning are included, as are hot hors d'oeuvres and other goodies daily.

DeLuxe Verandah Suites. These suites measure 563 sq ft (53 sq m). They have twin beds that convert to a king-size bed, vanity desk, lounge area, walk-in closet, mini-bar and refrigerator, and bathroom with full-size tub, washbasin, and toilet. Personalized stationery and complimentary dry cleaning are included, as are hot hors d'oeuvres and other goodies.

Verandah Suites. Actually they are cabins, not suites, and measure 284 sq ft (26 sq m). Twin beds can convert to a queen-size bed. There is also a lounge area, mini-bar, and refrigerator, while the bathroom has a tub, washbasin, and toilet. Floor-to-ceiling windows open onto a private balcony.

Outside-view Cabins. Standard outside cabins (197 sq ft/18 sq m) have twin beds that can convert to a queen-size bed. There's a small sitting area, while the bathroom has a tub/shower combination. The interior cabins are slightly smaller (183 sq ft/17 sq m).

A total of 37 cabins have interconnecting doors. All balconies have solid steel lower sections instead of glass – so your view is a little restricted when seated).

All suites/cabins have 'Signature of Excellence' premium amenities: plush Mariner's Dream beds, waffle/terry cloth robes, Egyptian cotton towels, flat panel TVs, DVD players, make-up mirrors with halo lighting, massage shower heads, large hair dryers, fresh flowers, and fruit baskets.

DINING. The bi-level Rembrandt Dining Room – a stunning room – is at the stern. Both open seating (you may have to wait a considerable time for a table), and fixed (assigned tables and times) seating are available. It provides a traditional Holland America Line dining experience, with friendly service from Indonesian and Filipino stewards.

The waiter stations in the dining room can be noisy for anyone seated adjacent to them. Live music is provided for dinner each evening. Once each cruise, there's a Dutch Dinner (hats are provided), and an Indonesian Lunch. 'Lighter option' meals are always available. Holland America Line can provide kosher meals, although these are prepared ashore, frozen, and brought to your table sealed in their original containers.

Other dining options. The 130-seat Pinnacle Grill is a slightly more upscale, more intimate restaurant, with higher-quality ingredients and better presentation than in the larger main dining room. It is on Lower Promenade Deck and fronts onto the second level of the atrium lobby. Pacific Northwest cuisine is featured, plus an array of premium-quality steaks. There are fine table settings, china and silverware, and leather-bound menus. The wine bar offers mostly American wines. Reservations are required and there's a cover charge (but the prime steaks are really worth it).

There's also Tamarind, a 144-seat Pan-Asian (fusion cuisine) restaurant; there's no charge for lunch, but there is a cover charge for dinner.

For more casual eats, there's an extensive Lido Café. It includes a pizzeria/Italian specialties counter, a salad bar, Asian stir-fry counter, deli sandwiches, and desserts. Movement through the buffet area can be very slow. In the evenings, one side of this venue is turned into an extra-cost Canaletto Restaurant – a quasi-Italian informal eatery with waiter service.

There's an outdoor self-serve buffet, serving fast food, as well as two smaller buffets adjacent to the mid-ships swimming pool area. An extra-cost Windsurf Café in the atrium lobby (open 20 hours a day) serves coffee and snacks.

ENTERTAINMENT. Theater-style seating is provided in The Mainstage Showlounge – the venue for colourful Las Vegas-style revues and major cabaret shows. Stage shows are best seen from the upper levels, from where the sight lines are quite good.

SPA/FITNESS. The Greenhouse Spa, the largest yet for HAL, includes a thermal suite, hydropool, several private rooms for body pampering treatments, and a large fitness center. Sports enthusiasts can enjoy a basketball court, volleyball court, and a golf simulator.

Europa
★★★★★ +

Size:.................................... Small Ship	Crew/Passenger Ratio (lower beds/all berths):.......... 1.4/1.6
Tonnage:....................................... 28,890	Cabins (total):..204
Lifestyle:....................................... Luxury	Size range (sq ft/m):..................355.2-914.9/33.0-85.0
Cruise line:........................ Hapag-Lloyd Cruises	Cabins (outside view):................................204
Former names:.................................... none	Cabins (interior/no view):..............................0
IMO number:..................................8224422	Cabins (for one person):................................0
Builder:.................. Kvaerner Masa-Yards (Finland)	Cabins (with private balcony):........................168
Original cost:........................... DM260 million	Cabins (wheelchair accessible):........................2
Entered service:............................. Sep 1999	Wheelchair accessibility:...........................Good
Registry:................................... The Bahamas	Cabin voltage:........................110 and 120 volts
Length (ft/m):............................. 651.5/198.6	Elevators:...4
Beam (ft/m):................................. 78.7/24.0	Casino (gaming tables):................................No
Draft (ft/m):.................................. 20.0/6.1	Slot machines:..No
Propulsion/Propellers:...diesel-electric (21,600kW)/2 azimuthing pods	Swimming pools:.................1 (1 w/sliding glass dome)
Passenger decks:.....................................7	Hot tubs (on deck):....................................2
Total crew:..280	Self-service launderette:............................ Yes
Passengers (lower beds/alll berths):................ 408/450	Dedicated cinema/seats:.......................... Yes/60
Passenger Space Ratio (lower beds/all berths):....... 70.4/64.2	Library: .... Yes
	Onboard currency: .... Euros

A truly sophisticated ship for formal longer cruises

OVERVIEW. *Europa* is arguably the most luxurious of all the smaller formal cruise ships, and for the German-speaking market, nothing else comes close. The crew also speaks English and more cruises are designated as bilingual English/German language voyages. Combined with an enthusiastic and well-trained crew, the tradition of luxury cruising is taken to its highest expression, with superb food and a wide range of creature comforts.

Berlitz's Ratings

	Possible	Achieved
Ship	500	471
Accommodation	200	183
Food	400	373
Service	400	360
Entertainment	100	91
Cruise	400	373

OVERALL SCORE
1851 points out of 2000

THE SHIP. *Europa* has a sleek appearance, with a really graceful profile, and Hapag-Lloyd's signature orange/blue funnel. Look down from the aft Lido Deck fantail and you will see a rounded, gracefully-shaped stern – unlike the box-like rears of so many contemporary ships. This is a very stable ship in the open sea, with no vibration or noise – thanks partly to its pod propulsion system. Europa carries 14 Zodiac landing craft for use during close-up shore excursions; and boot-washing areas are also provided. Twenty bicycles are available free for use ashore and are offloaded on to the dock in each port (where possible).

There is an outdoor walking/jogging area with rubberized deck (plus a walk-around teak promenade deck), as well as a small FKK (Frei-KörperKultur) deck for nude sunbathing. The sunloungers are aluminum with teak armrests, and have thick cushioned pads.

There is one long, rectangular swimming pool outdoors (actually, half is indoors, and half is outdoors). While not the widest, it is longer than the pools aboard many other cruise ships, measuring 56.7 by 16.8ft (17.3 by 5.15m). Movies are screened poolside on selected evenings, and themed social events are held here.

With this ship, Hapag-Lloyd has long been judged to reach and maintain the high standards that its passengers demand, due to the fact that most of *Europa*'s hotel service crew is German-speaking nationals who understand the culture and can talk in depth about German, Swiss, and Austrian life.

The space per passenger is high, there is never a hint of a line, and both restaurant and show lounge seat a full complement of passengers. *Europa* is one of the world's most spacious purpose-built cruise ships – an exquisite retreat, an intensely welcoming world of stylish cruising.

The ship is finely appointed, in the contemporary style described in hotel-speak as 'minimalism.' Only the very best quality soft furnishings are used, subtly blending traditional with modern designs and materials. Most public rooms and hallways have extremely high ceilings, providing an enhanced sense of space and grandeur. The colors used in the interior decor are light and contemporary, with no hint of glitz or neon.

The central interior focal point is a seven-deck-high central atrium; included are two glass-walled elevators (these are operated by 'piccolos' on embarkation day). The lower level features a white Steinway grand piano and atrium bar, reception desk, concierge desk, and shore excursion desk. It's a cozy, but open space for stand-up and mingle social parties, and it works well on nights designated as 'formal,' when passengers dress accordingly. Ticked away in one corner is a business center – also good for small group meetings.

Forward of the atrium lobby is the Europa Lounge, with its U-shaped seating configuration and a proper (raised) stage, although several pillars obstruct the sight lines.

Several of the main public rooms are located along a curved 'street' leading aft from the atrium. These include the Clipper Lounge/Bar, which has an extremely high ceiling. The room is a multi-function room, with small stage and wood dance floor.

What was originally designed to be a casino is now a multi-function space for small cocktail parties, and also serves as a high-class art gallery showcasing modern German culture artists.

There is also a fine sidewalk Havana Bar cigar lounge. This clubby room has three large glass-fronted, fully temperature-controlled and conditioned humidor cabinets, and carries an extensive range of cigars from Cuba and other countries. Cigars stocked include a range (from 102mm to 232mm) of top brands. The bar also serves a fine range of armagnacs, calvados, and cognacs, all poured tableside, as well as Cuban beer. Embedded in a wall adjacent to the bar is a digital MP3 jukebox, with a push-button selection of literally thousands of songs – and instrumental music. What's really nice in this intimate spot, with its buttery soft leather chairs and sofas, is Irish Coffee, correctly made (the glass should be rotated while the sugar is blended with the alcohol and heated gently over a candle flame, the liquor set alight before coffee and cream are added). Next door is the ship's jeweler/clothing boutique (Wempe).

On a higher deck, the Club Belvedere stands out – for afternoon tea and intimate music recitals. It is simply a lovely room, with its own bar. Afternoon tea here is a delightful tradition, with a selection of about 30 teas (loose tea, of course, never teabags). There are also several types of coffee and impeccably made liqueur coffees, heated in a hand-turned glass enclosure, and a superb selection of cakes, made fresh every day.

A library has an illuminated globe of the world, numerous book shelves and is open 24 hours a day (books are taken out on the honor system). Opposite is a small cinema/meeting/function room.

There are dedicated rooms for hobbies (arts and crafts), and for children. Although a children's playroom is provided, *Europa* really is a ship for adults seeking a quiet, refined setting.

For wheelchair-bound passengers, a special ramp is provided from the outdoor lido/pool deck down to where the lifeboats are located; only three other ships have such a ramp (*Asuka II, Crystal Serenity* and *Crystal Symphony*).

There is a children's center, and parents with infants receive a 'Baby Welcome Package.' Staff can provide diapers and baby food of your choosing, so you don't need to bring excessive luggage – a service included in the fare. Also, Hapag-Lloyd Cruises has

teamed up with Steiff to create the exclusive Captain Knopf teddy bear.

Hapag-Lloyd Cruises hosts the annual Stella Maris operatic competition, which attracts top-notch up-and-coming operatic singers from around the world compete annually for the prestigious Young Talent Development Prize. A top prize of €15,000 is offered, as well as a Deutsche Grammophon recording contract. Hapag-Lloyd Cruises also sponsors an annual Ocean Sun Festival – for classical/chamber music devotees, and concerts are often held ashore as part of the program.

ACCOMMODATION. This is provided in five configurations and 10 price categories. It consists of all-outside-view suites: two Penthouse Grand Suites (Hapag and Lloyd) and 10 Penthouse Deluxe Suites (Bach, Beethoven, Brahms, Handel, Lehár, Haydn, Mozart, Schubert, Strauss, Wagner; each suite contains a large framed picture of the composer), 156 suites with private balcony, and 36 standard suites. There are two suites (with private balcony) for the disabled and eight suites with interconnecting doors – good for families.

Almost all suites have a private balcony with wide teak deck and lighting, and a smoked glass screen topped by a teak rail. The 12 suites overlooking the stern are among the most sought-after accommodation – six on each of two decks, each suite having a balcony with canvas 'ceiling' for shade and privacy.

General Information. Each suite has a wood floor entryway, and a sleeping area with twin beds that can convert to a queen-size bed, and two bedside tables with lamps and two drawers. There is a separate lounge area with curtain divider and bird's-eye maple wood cabinetry and accenting with rounded edges. Facilities include a refrigerator/mini-bar (beer and soft drinks are supplied at no extra charge), a writing/vanity desk, and couch with large table in a separate lounge area. An illuminated walk-in closet provides ample hanging rail space, six drawers, personal safe that can be opened with a credit card, umbrella, shoehorn, and clothes brush. European duvets are provided, as is a full-color free daily newspaper (there's a wide choice). Almost all suites have totally unobstructed views and excellent soundproofing. All passengers receive a practical shoulder travel bag, an insulated lunch bag for shore excursions, leather keycard holder, and a generous supply of personal toiletry items.

A Media4Cruises system includes 24 hours per day video and audio on-demand. You choose when you want to watch any one of up to 100 movies, or when you want to listen to any of the 1,000+ compact audio discs. The system includes a large flat-screen television and direct, 24-hour Internet connection via a wireless keyboard. The system displays menus, ship's position and chart, deck plan, shore excursion video clips, plus other informational videos. You get a dedicated personal email address (provided with your tickets and other documentation in a proper leather document holder); there is no charge for incoming or outgoing emails, only for attachments and for general Internet access. A data socket is provided should you decide to bring your own laptop computer (the ship has a small number of laptop computers you can borrow), and WLAN sockets are provided on each deck.

All suites have a 100 percent air-circulation system, illuminated walk-in closets, and a generous amount of hanging and storage space. Western European butlers and cabin stewardesses are employed (butlers for the 12 premium suites on Deck 10, cabin stewardesses for all other suites).

The white/gray/sea green marble-tiled bathrooms are very well designed, have light decor, and include two good-size cabinets for toiletries. All bathrooms have a full bathtub plus an integral shower and a retractable clothesline, and separate glass-fronted shower enclosure. Thick, 100 percent cotton bathrobes are provided, as are slippers and an array of toiletries. Parents with babies get a video baby phone (camera via PDA with vibration alarm, and wireless access).

Penthouses (Deck 10). There are two Penthouse Grand suites, redesigned in 2011, and 10 Penthouse Deluxe suites, refurbished in 2009, when electronically adjustable beds and Nespresso coffee machines were added. These have a teakwood entrance hall, spacious living room with full-size dining table and four chairs, fully stocked drinks cabinet with refrigerator butler service, complimentary bar set-up (replenished with whatever you need), laundry and ironing service included, priority spa reservations, caviar or other canapés daily before dinner, hand-made chocolates, petit-fours and other niceties at no extra charge. Balconies have teakwood decking, and white canvas ceiling shades. For the ultimate in exclusivity, the two Penthouse Grand suites have even larger bathrooms (each with a private sauna and specially angled bathtubs), and extensive forward views from their prime, supremely quiet location one deck above the navigation bridge; a large wraparound private balcony; larger walk-in closet (with a window), large flat-screen TVs, and Robbe and Berking silver Champagne goblets. Well-trained butlers provide the highest level of unobtrusive service.

Spa suites. Four 'spa suites' are located just forward of the Futuresse Spa on Deck 7. These incorporate a large private teak-decked balcony (good for massages); twin or queen-size bed; walk-in closet; dark wood cabinetry housing a refrigerator stocked with fruit juices and different mineral waters, and bar set-up. There's a flat-screen TV, and storage space including a jewelry drawer, with pull-around doors that can close off everything to view, a writing/vanity desk, and floor-to-ceiling windows. Decor colors are warm reds, yellow, and gold. There is a large window between the living/sleeping area and the bathroom. The bathroom itself has warm Asian decor, underwa-

ter lighted Jacuzzi bath, separate large shower enclosure (with rain shower), toilet and gold, thick-glass washbasin, hand-held hairdryer, and plenty of storage space. Special teas and other services are provided by spa personnel. For cruises longer than 10 days, a customized spa package, including treatments, is included in the price.

Suites for the Disabled (Deck 7). These spacious suites have one electronically operated bed with hydraulic elevator plus one regular bed, while a non-walk-in closet with drawers replaces the walk-in closet in all other suites. The bathroom has a roll-in shower area. All fittings are at the correct height, and there are several grab handles, plus an emergency call-for-help button. Wheelchair-accessible public toilets are provided on the main restaurant/entertainment deck.

DINING. With over 5,000 separate food ingredients carried at any one time, the executive chef can produce menus that don't repeat even for around-the-world and other long voyages for which this ship excels. The cuisine is outstanding, always full of surprises. Seasonal and regional ingredients are featured, with much totally fresh fish and seafood as standard. Plated presentation of food is provided for entrées with silver service for additional vegetables, as well as tableside flambé dishes. The size of portions is sensible, never overwhelming. There are four restaurants.

The Europa Restaurant is a beautiful two-deck-high formal dining room that can accommodate all passengers in one seating, with tables assigned for dinner only (breakfast and lunch are open seating). Passengers thus keep their favorite waiter for dinner throughout each cruise. In common with most German ships, a small smoking section is provided. There are tables for two (quite a few), four, six, or eight. For superb service, there is a *chef de rang* and an assistant waiter system, so that the *chef de rang* is always at the station, with the assistant waiter acting as runner.

On days at sea, in addition to the regular, extensive breakfast, a Gourmet Breakfast menu includes items such as beef tartare, carpaccio of smoked tuna with wasabi cream, gooseliver tureen with orange confit, and other specialties rarely found aboard cruise ships today. A Cuisine Légère menu provides light, healthy, but tasty spa cuisine.

Table settings include Dibbern china, 150g weight Robbe & Berking silverware, and Riedel wine glasses. The cuisine is very international, but includes German favorites as well as regional dishes from around the world. The quality of food is extremely high. Although top-grade Iranian Ossetre caviar is found on dinner menus at least once each week, it is always available on request, at extra cost. Otherwise, most of the excellent caviar comes from French farmed sturgeon.

An extensive wine list includes a good selection of vintage French wines, as well as a well-balanced selection of Austrian, German, and Swiss wines.

Other dining options. In a first for the cruise industry, three Michelin-starred chef Dieter Müller has his first Dieter Müller at Sea Restaurant, a pocket-sized 26-seat intimate restaurant featuring a personally designed five-course menu (it's three courses for lunch). The menu changes three times during a world cruise, and seasonally during the rest of the year. He participates in about 15 cruises a year – about half of *Europa*'s annual program. The restaurant, which is open for dinner nightly and for lunch on sea days, can be reserved once per cruise by all passengers – and there's no extra charge.

Venezia, a second specialty dining spot, is a much loved, popular for its fine Italian cuisine – and a wide variety of olive oils and grappa. It is open for lunch and dinner, and at no extra charge.

Both venues are adjacent to and forward of the main restaurant, and provide the setting for a truly intimate dining experience, by reservation only.

For more casual dining, try the elegant Lido Café for serve-yourself breakfasts – the ship even makes its own preserves – luncheons and dinners, with both indoor and outdoor seating (under heat lamps when needed) and adjacent indoor/outdoor bar. Themed evening dining is also featured here, with full waiter service. There is a wide variety of food, and many special lunch buffets have a number of popular themes and regional specialties.

Above the Lido Café is the indoor/outdoor Sansibar, with great aft-facing views. It's liked by the late-night set.

Europa is known for its real German sausages, available in the Clipper Bar and at a typical Bavarian Früschoppen featured once each cruise in the Lido Café. Also, late each night, 'light bites,' beautifully presented on silver trays, are taken around the various bars and lounges.

Nautical tradition is maintained with bouillon service each morning at sea, and other daily niceties include fresh waffles and ice cream each afternoon around the pool.

ENTERTAINMENT. The Europa Lounge, whose decor is a rich red, is the main showlounge; it has a sloping floor, providing good sight lines from most seats. The ship excels in its fine, intellectual entertainment program – tailored to the theme of the cruise – which includes a constant supply of high-quality classical and contemporary musical artistes, a variety of cabaret acts, as well as a programme of expert lecturers and poetry readers. There's the occasional colorful production show, plus local shows brought on board in various ports.

The smaller, more intimate Clipper Lounge is the setting for late-night cabaret. The ship carries a main showband, plus small musical units to provide live music for listening or dancing. Classical concerts and recitals are provided in the Belvedere Lounge, with its dropped central circular floor.

SPA/FITNESS. The Ocean Spa has a wide range of beauty services and treatments, including hot stone massage, and an array of other rejuvenating treatments, including full-day spa packages. Shiseido cosmetics are the featured cosmetic/spa products for sale. The entire spa area is a well-integrated and very welcoming wellness and treatment area.

Facilities include a steam room and sauna (mixed), two shower enclosures and two foot-washing stations, relaxation room with three hot tiled beds, three wicker relax beds, male and female changing/dressing rooms, and beauty salon. A Japanese Room includes a two-tatami mat relaxation area; treatments include a cream body massage. A nice touch is that treatment rooms have music menus, so you can choose what music you wish to hear. The gymnasium is located one deck above the swimming pool, and includes a 'miha' bodytec training machine and personal trainer.

On cruises with more than four sea days, *Europa*'s shore-based wellness partner provides specialists for lectures and wellness regimes, in addition to the ship's own fitness team.

An electronic golf simulator room complements a golf driving range; a PGA golf pro is carried on all cruises. Shuffleboard courts can be found on the open deck.

Europa 2
★★★★★ +

Size:.	Small	Crew/Passenger Ratio (lower beds/all berths):	1.3/1.3
Tonnage:	42.830	Cabins (total):	258
Lifestyle:	Luxury	Size range (sq ft/m):	376.7-1,227.1/35.0-114.0
Cruise line:	Hapag-Lloyd Cruises	Cabins (outside view):	258
Former names:	none	Cabins (interior/no view):	0
IMO number:	9616230	Cabins (for one person):	0
Builder:	STX France	Cabins (with private balcony):	258
Original cost:	$360 million	Cabins (wheelchair accessible):	2
Entered service:	May 2013	Wheelchair accessibility:	Best
Registry:	Malta	Cabin voltage:	110 volts
Length (ft/m):	738.1/225.4	Elevators:	4
Beam (ft/m):	87.5/26.7	Casino (gaming tables):	No
Draft (ft/m):	20.6/6.3	Slot machines:	No
Propulsion/Propellers: . . . diesel-electric (24,000kW)/2 azimuthing pods		Swimming pools:	1 (1 w/sliding glass dome)
Passenger decks:	8	Hot tubs (on deck):	2
Total crew:	370	Self-service launderette:	No
Passengers (lower beds/alll berths):	516/516	Dedicated cinema/seats:	Yes/75
Passenger Space Ratio (lower beds/all berths):	83.0/83.0	Library:	Yes
		Onboard currency:	Euros

Stunningly spacious, top-notch informal ship for stylish internationals

OVERVIEW. *Europa 2* is the superb new, elegant, contemporary but informal sister to the much-loved and much-acclaimed *Europa*. This all-suite, all-balcony ship, with the highest passenger space ratio in the cruise industry, is the ultimate space ship – the benchmark in contemporary cruising. It is aimed squarely at youthful but sophisticated cosmopolitan travellers and their families.

THE SHIP. *Europa* 2, like smaller sister *Europa*, has a sleek profile and appearance, balanced by Hapag-Lloyd's signature orange-and-blue funnel. Look down from an upper aft deck and you'll see a nicely rounded stern. It represents a stunning example of detail and finesse in design, with a touch of the whimsical, and boasts a number of firsts. The ship operates in English and German, for its international clientele.

The ship has one additional deck than *Europa*, but has 40 percent more space. In fact, it's the spaciousness and natural light that is so evident. There is a complete walk-around deck – wide enough to walk around even if deck lounge chairs also inhabit the space – a really user-friendly and unusual feature aboard a ship of this size. Teak decking is everywhere (no artificial turf aboard this ship), as are teak handrails on all balconies and outdoor stairways.

The two-level pool deck is a stunning space. It features a 15-meter rectangular saltwater pool, which can be either indoors or outdoors, or both, thanks to a large moveable glass roof (Magrodome) that can completely cover the area in cool or inclement weather conditions

Berlitz's Ratings	Possible	Achieved
Ship	500	476
Accommodation	200	185
Food	400	373
Service	400	360
Entertainment	100	91
Cruise	400	375
OVERALL SCORE		
1860 points out of 2000		

(when closed the area is like a winter garden). A real hot spot, five Balinese sleep beds are on the upper level (another seven can be found on a separate secluded aft deck), contemporary sun beds and drinks tables, as well as a bar, a separate food bar (think waffles and made-on-board ice cream in the afternoon), and a removable movie screen complete the picture (you can even lie down in the Balinese beds in the upper section and watch movies).

A fleet of 12 Zodiacs – all named after Hamburg suburbs – is carried for landings in small harbors and isolated bays away from more familiar routes, as well as 20 bicycles for passenger use (at no charge).

Europa 2 is beautifully appointed, and the quality of the fit and finish is high, due to the demands of the detail-oriented operator. Hamburg-based interior designers PartnerShipDesign did an outstanding job in creating something really contemporary and slightly edgy in a ship setting that also includes some traditional Hapag-Lloyd characteristics from yesteryear, yet is completely different to the more formal *Europa*.

The atrium lobby has grey, black and chrome décor that is chic but minimalist (cool), with plenty of armchair-style seating, a long bar, and a superb specially commissioned grey Steinway grand piano. The high ceiling sets it all off, together with what look like several huge grey and black distillery-like features. A glass viewing wall in the centre on both sides of the main elevator foyer provides multi-deck contact with the sea outside – unusual for this size of ship, and lets natural outside light flood in. These glass walls also provide a connection with the sea (isn't this why people go cruising, after all)? Adjacent to the atrium lobby and reception desk is a large, upscale boutique (Wempe) and jewelry store.

There are seven restaurants (plus one extra-cost 16-seat venue with nautical décor – good for private family functions), two lounges, and six bars – some with familiar names carried over from the tradition of *Europa*, and easily identified by regular Hapag-Lloyd's passengers (Club Belvedere and Sansibar). Like her sister ship several public rooms are located off a main high-ceilinged hallway, and connect at the central atrium lobby.

Then L-shaped, but elegant Club Belvedere provides a refined setting for chamber concerts and poetry readings. It is also a fine, relaxing venue for afternoon tea, and incorporates a pastry and cake counter, and a bar.

Herrenzimmer (a 'gentleman's club'), is a cigar lounge with three large glass-fronted, temperature-controlled and conditioned cabinets. The bar features a wide range of armagnacs, calvados, and cognacs, all poured tableside, as well as Cuban beer, and the largest collection of premium and trendy artisan gins of any cruise ship – over 30 – from several countries.

Sansibar, a firm favorite with Hapag-Lloyd regulars, is a sea-going outpost of the famous, trendy seafood/wine restaurant located on the north German island of Sylt. This popular aft hangout has indoor seating, a dance floor, and plenty of seating outdoors (in fact all the room's floor-to-ceiling windows open to the outside). It features an a la carte menu, plus tapas-style nibbles, wine selections, and a great club-like atmosphere. It's definitely the 'in' place to be at night. It also offers a proper 'late riser's breakfast.'

The Jazz Club is a trendy dedicated lounge featuring live jazz (a seven-piece band plus two vocalists when I sailed), soul music, poetry readings, and other artistic presentations. There's also an auditorium with a stage for presentations as well as 3D movies, a library full of fiction, reference and destination books, and a Miele Culinary Arts School.

Europa 2 sails seven-day, combinable routes in the Western Mediterranean during spring and summer. Autumn itineraries include Eastern Mediterranean destinations, and in winter the ship heads to the Arabian Gulf and Southeast Asia.

There are bound to be comparisons with sister ship Europa, but although they are similar in a few respects, they are vastly different ships – and cater to a very different set of passengers. *Europa 2* features shorter-length cruises for the time-challenged (7-day cruises, although different itineraries can be combined into a longer cruise), and a host of delightful dining venues and other features exclusive to this ship.

Shore excursions and travel services are in small, comfortable one-on-one private booking offices (human interfacing), so there are no lines – anywhere.

Examples of the services aboard this ship: shore excursions feature additional – later – departures for late-risers (very civilized); an Audio-vox instant language translation system is provided for international passengers on shore excursions; shore excursions that can be tailored to your personal tastes.

Something that distinguishes this ship is the fact that human contact is valued much more – for making restaurant and shore excursion bookings rather than those generated by the interactive television systems found aboard many ships today. This is 'soft' (no tie) gratuities-included luxury. Alcoholic beverages are not included – so non-drinkers don't have to subsidize those that do (that's fair). *Europa 2* also provides a host of small details that often go unnoticed, such as the fresh flower displays, wide range of personal toiletry items in the suites, and superb range of wines and spirits.

It really is the crew that really provides the discreet personal service touches and hospitality that so many ships have lost, plus the outstanding sense of space that pervades the public areas. The ship contains an exceptional €2 million collection of 890 pieces of contemporary art, including some by Damien Hirst, David Hockney, Gerhard Richter, Jeppe Hein and other well-known contemporary artists (I'll leave you to discover where they are).

There is no traditional captain's dinner, because the ship is aimed at a more youthful clientele seeking high quality in a relaxed, but luxurious setting, although senior officers will dine occasionally with passengers in varying venues. The ship is on a 12-year charter from its investors and is a lusciously contemporary interpretation of the company's renowned and highly rated *Europa – and then some*.

Europa 2 is the first cruise ship to be equipped with catalysts; these reduce the emission of nitrogen oxides (including nitrogen dioxide) by almost 95 percent. The ship is technologically advanced and extremely eco- and environmentally friendly.

The dress code is strictly smart (no tie) casual at all times, and all gratuities are included, as are soft drinks and beer in all suites.

The hospital has fully-equipped dialysis stations for special cruises, when a dialysis technician is carried.

FAMILIES. There are more facilities and programs for families with children aboard this ship than aboard its more formal sister. There are three special areas for kids and teens: an extra-charge Knopf Club (a new 'Cap'n Knopf' bear was created specially by Steiff – and available for sale in the shop – only aboard *Europa 2*) for children aged from two to three; a Kids' Club for four to 10-year-olds; and a separate Teens' Club for 11–15s – with iPod chairs, table football, and chill-out area. Special (parent-free) shore excursions for children are also available.

Additionally, childcare by trained European nannies is available for children aged two years and above, while parents with children younger than three receive a Baby Welcome Package. Seven 'Family Apartments' – comprised of two (shower only) separate suites with interconnecting doors and interconnecting balcony – are also available.

ACCOMMODATION. There are 13 price categories and eight accommodation grades (sizes given include balcony).

There are two Owners Suites (1,227 sq ft/114 sq m); two Grand Penthouses (947 sq ft/88 sq m); 16 Spa Suites (560 sq ft/52 sq m); 24 Grand Suites (559.7 sq m/52s sq m), including two for the disabled; 59 Ocean Suites; seven Family Apartments (581 sq ft/54 sq m); and 141 Ocean Suites (376.7 sq ft/35 sq m). Even the smallest balcony measures 75.3 sq ft/7 sq m, and all except the 'Family Apartments' have Jacuzzi bathtubs. All Penthouse Deck suite occupants can choose their favourite bottles of spirits at no extra cost and come with butler service.

The two Owners Suites (the price is not listed in the brochure, but available on request) are truly luxurious apartments (like a villa, but with hotel attached), with double-wide balconies. The standout feature, though, is a huge ocean-view wet room (bathroom) with a private steam sauna, a huge 'rain' shower with built-in chromo-therapy lighting, and a separate hand-held shower hose; there's also a separate circular whirlpool tub for two, window-side daybed, two large washbasins, and floor-to-ceiling windows. The spacious living area has walk-in closets, a fully stocked refrigerator, full dining table and chair set, butler service, and an Eames lounge chair. There are multiple TV sets, including one integrated in a bathroom mirror adjacent to the whirlpool bath.

'Spa Suites' have a rain-shower and steam sauna combination, whirlpool bathtub, and a large window between sleeping/living area and bathroom (with a wooden blind for complete privacy), and separate toilet. One cool feature is a television screen integrated into the bathroom mirror.

Two specially outfitted suites for the disabled each has a large bathroom with roll-in shower, three washbasins, and an integrated 'mirror' TV.

Facilities in even the smallest standard suite (28 sq m/301 sq ft plus 75.3 sq ft/7.0 sq m balcony) are excellent, and both the layout is well designed and practical. The overall suite decor is relaxing but not boring – with brown, beige, and cream the underlying colors. The beds have an adjustable torsion arrangement so you can vary it from hard to soft. Both head and body/foot sections can be raised for optimum comfort and best sleeping levels.

A wide choice of large-size, full-color daily newspapers is available (at extra cost except for Penthouse Deck 10 suites), and all accommodation grades feature a Nespresso coffee machine and associated items. An interactive TV can be positioned for viewing from the

bed or lounge seating area. Other practical features include a refrigerator/mini-bar cabinet (beer and soft drinks are supplied at no extra charge) with several 'quiet-close' integral storage trays for glasses, cups and other wet bar amenities – all contained in a superbly-designed anti-rattle cabinet. There's also a writing/vanity desk, and couch with large table in a separate lounge area, and a leather keycard holder (the door unlocks when you touch the keycard against the lock).

An integrated color TV/computer monitor and Media4Cruises system includes 24 hours per day video and audio on-demand. You choose when you want to watch any of up to 100 movies, or when you want to listen to any of the 1,000+ compact audio discs. The system includes a large flat-screen television and direct, 24-hour Internet connection via a wireless keyboard or tablet. The system displays the menus, ship's position and chart, deck plan, shore excursion video clips, plus other informational videos. You get a dedicated personal email address (provided with your tickets and other documentation in a proper leather document holder); there is no charge for incoming or outgoing emails, only for attachments and for general Internet access. A data socket is provided should you decide to bring your own laptop computer, and the ship is Wi-Fi enabled throughout.

The changeable mood lighting – with four different programs and settings – is a really good, user-friendly feature, as is a floor-based nightlight. Adjacent to the floor-to-ceiling windows are three sets of curtains (including a blackout curtain). The layout is extremely practical and user-friendly.

DINING. *Europa 2* really is all about lifestyle and a wide choice when it comes to food, dining experiences, and culinary adventures. The open-seating concept in all restaurants makes it easy for families with children to choose when to eat. Dibbern china and Schott Zwiesel glassware are provided. What's nice is that (unusually for a ship of this size) some 40 percent of all tables are for two – the others are for four, six or eight. What makes most of these double-deck height restaurants special is their décor, individuality, and the different cuisines featured.

Weltmeere: This 266-seat restaurant (its huge, pink "octopus" tentacle-like glass chandeliers are whimsical) features a wide range of international cuisine favourites, and the contemporary chairs have armrests. Open for breakfast, lunch, and dinner.

Other dining options. Yachtclub: This 276-seat (142 indoor and 134 outdoor seats) restaurant is open for breakfast, lunch, and dinner. It includes a self-serve multi-section buffet (including an Ayervedic 'bio-food' section), rotisserie and two active cooking stations – plus one of those wonderful manual Berkel meat slicing machine for wafer-thin prosciutto. Outside on deck is a fine Pasta Bar (several types of pasta are made on board, as are six different sauces daily), and a Grill Bar.

A Canvas-like canopy incorporates heaters for cool-weather areas or conditions.

Tarragon: This extremely chic, tile-floored 44-seat French-style bistro restaurant specializes in tableside carvings (the steak tartare is exceptional, and you can choose the accompanying ingredients), regional/seasonal food, and a focus on fresh herbs – real French 'Bistronomie.' It is open for dinner (and on selected days for lunch). Reservations are required.

Grand Réserve: This 12-seat wine bar/dining venue features special tasting events. Reservations are required. It is adjacent to Tarragon, and open only for dinner.

Serenissima: This 56-seat Italian restaurant has open seating for lunch and dinner (reservations are required for dinner). The large white columns add to the feeling of grandeur.

Elements, is a reservations-required 48-seat pan-Asian food themed restaurant, open for lunch and dinner.

Sakura, is a 58-seat sushi restaurant (part of the Yacht Club, but open only for dinner) featuring the best in Japanese cuisine (a favourite here is the 'Black Spider Man" – tempura soft shell crab with avocado – and other 'secret' ingredients); it incorporates a sit-up sushi counter. Reservations are required.

Speisezimmer, is a 16-seat dining venue for private dining. It has nautically-themed décor, costs €1,500, and can be reserved for breakfast, lunch, or dinner.

Although reservations are required for dinner in several venues, there's no extra cost in any of them (unlike the specialty dining venues aboard many other ships). Hapag-Lloyd Cruises has long been known for its culinary creativity and extremely high quality of food and service. This ship won't disappoint those who seek the best.

Sansibar is a trendy indoor-outdoor venue featuring special drinks and items from the venue of the same name in Sylt. It features special wines, has an a la carte late-riser's breakfast, and constantly-changing tapas-style eats. It has a dance floor, and is the champion late-night disco-style venue, and is a great place to see and be seen.

Guest chefs also conduct cooking lessons, with 12 Miele-brand cooking stations and the kind of equipment found in a typical domestic kitchen, in a dedicated Culinary Center.

ENTERTAINMENT. The Theater is the ship's two-level showlounge; it has good sightlines from almost all seats. It has the latest in LED lighting for superb show backdrops and scenery changes, and a thrust stage for cabaret acts, or concerts. The multi-faceted entertainment is provided by the company's own production team, with 16 different shows scheduled each year. The shows are designed to be more visual to accommodate the bilingual international clientele.

Live music can be found around the ship, but the Jazz Club is a standout venue for the cool stuff. Meanwhile light classical and chamber concerts take place in various venues throughout the ship.

SPA/FITNESS. The Ocean Spa is, without doubt, the largest wellness and spa zone for this size of ship, with indoor and outdoor zones measuring a combined 10,764 sq ft (1,000 sq m) that does justice to the trend for combining holidays and well-being.

The calming, beautifully crafted wellness facilities are outstanding for a ship of this size, and include a beauty salon, eight massage/body treatment rooms; a dry-ice wall; a steam sauna and three dry saunas with differing temperatures (Finnish, Herbal, and Bio), one of which overlooks the stern; two foot-washing stations (with different temperatures), two relaxation rooms (one with three hot, tiled beds), male and female changing/dressing rooms, showers, and two Dr Kneipp basins for foot baths and water walks.

A 'Personal Spa Room' (extra-charge, reservations required) has facilities that include a private treatment room with two beds, hot tub, steam sauna, and relaxing sofa – ideal for a couple seeking exclusivity for a morning or afternoon of wellness together (great for honeymooners).

The fitness area has cardio/strength equipment and an extra group fitness room for spinning, yoga, Pilates, etc. The fitness room is equipped with Technogym equipment, including a Kinesis wall, Hypoxi (atmospheric pressure) training cabinet and 'miha bodytech'-brand equipment.

For golfers, almost 700 sq ft (65 sq m) is devoted to a fitting station with two electronic golf simulators. *Europa 2* is the first ship to combine state-of-the-art golf-simulator with a full-body video analysis – and a golf driving range. The golf simulators are the latest type from the USA's Full Swing Golf. There's also a separate storage room for golf clubs.

The ship also has a fully equipped dialysis room (on selected cruises a dialysis doctor/technician will be carried).

Explorer of the Seas
★★★+

Size:.................................Large Resort Ship	Crew/Passenger Ratio (lower beds/all berths):.........2.6/3.2
Tonnage: 137,308	Cabins (total):......................................1,557
Lifestyle: ....Standard	Size range (sq ft/m): 151.0–1,358.0/14.0–126.1
Cruise line:.................. Royal Caribbean International	Cabins (outside view):................................939
Former names: ....none	Cabins (interior/no view):............................618
IMO number: 9161728	Cabins (for one person):................................0
Builder: .... Kvaerner Masa-Yards (Finland)	Cabins (with private balcony):........................757
Original cost:...............................$500 million	Cabins (wheelchair accessible): 26
Entered service:..............................Oct 2000	Wheelchair accessibility:.............................Best
Registry:................................The Bahamas	Cabin voltage:.................................110 volts
Length (ft/m):.............................1,020.6/311.1	Elevators:..14
Beam (ft/m):............................. 155.5/47.4	Casino (gaming tables):................................No
Draft (ft/m): 28.8/8.8	Slot machines:......................................No
Propulsion/Propellers:......diesel-electric (75,600kW)/3 pods (2	Swimming pools:.....................................3
azimuthing, 1 fixed)	Hot tubs (on deck):...................................6
Passenger decks:...................................14	Self-service launderette:..............................No
Total crew:...................................... 1,181	Dedicated cinema/seats:...............................No
Passengers (lower beds/alll berths):............. 3,114/3,840	Library: ....Yes
Passenger Space Ratio (lower beds/all berths): 44.0/35.7	Onboard currency: ....US$

A large resort ship designed to entertain the whole family

OVERVIEW. In terms of sheer size, this large floating leisure resort exceeds many cruise ships, but in terms of personal service, the reverse is the case, unless you occupy one of the top suites. Although it's a large ship, the cabin hallways are warm and attractive, with artwork and wavy lines to break up the monotony.

THE SHIP. *Explorer of the Seas* is sister to *Adventure of the Seas, Mariner of the Seas, Navigator of the Seas*, and *Voyager of the Seas*. With its large proportions, it provides an abundance of facilities and options, yet it has a healthy amount of space per passenger.

A four-deck-high Royal Promenade, 394-ft (120-m) long and the main interior focal point, is a good place to hang out or to arrange to meet someone. The length of two American football fields, it has two internal lobbies that rise as many as 11 decks high. Restaurants, shops, and entertainment locations front this winding street, and interior 'with-view' cabins look into it from above. The Guest Reception and Shore Excursion counters are located at the aft end of the promenade, as is an ATM machine. Look up to see the large moving, asteroid-like sculpture (constantly growing and contracting), parades and street entertainers.

Arched across the promenade is a captain's balcony. A stairway in the center of the promenade connects you to the deck below, where you'll find Schooner Bar (a piano lounge that's a feature of all RCI ships) the colorful Casino Royale, and several shops. At times, street entertainers appear, and parades happen.

Berlitz's Ratings		
	Possible	Achieved
Ship	500	392
Accommodation	200	142
Food	400	222
Service	400	266
Entertainment	100	74
Cruise	400	264
OVERALL SCORE		
1360 points out of 2000		

There is an ice-skating rink (Studio B), with real ice, and seating for up to 900, plus high-tech broadcast facilities. Ice Follies shows are also presented here. Slim pillars obstruct clear-view arena stage sightlines, however. If ice-skating in the Caribbean doesn't appeal (it has actually become extremely popular), perhaps you'd like reading in the two-deck library, open 24 hours a day. A grand $12 million was spent on permanent artwork.

Drinking places include a neat Aquarium Bar, which comes with 50 tons of glass and water in four large aquariums (no you can't swim in them!). Other drinking places include an intimate Champagne Bar, Crown & Anchor Pub, a Sidewalk Café (for Continental breakfast, pizzas, coffee, and desserts), Weekend Warrior (a sports bar), and a Connoisseur Club (for cigars and cognacs). Jazz fans will head for Dizzy's, an intimate room within the Viking Crown Lounge, or the Schooner Bar piano lounge. Golfers might also enjoy the 19th Hole, a golf bar, as they play the Explorer Links.

A TV studio is adjacent to rooms for trade show exhibitions, with a conference center and a multimedia screening room. You can tie the knot in the Skylight Chapel, which even has wheelchair access via an electric stairlift. Outdoors, the pool and open deck areas provide a resort-like environment.

Passenger gripes: cabin bath towels and noisy (vacuum) toilets; few quiet places to sit and read – almost everywhere there is intrusive background music. And if you have a cabin with an interconnecting door to another cabin, be aware that you'll be able to hear everything your next-door neighbors say and do.

FAMILIES. Facilities for children and teenagers are quite extensive. Aquanauts is for three- to five-year-olds; Explorers (six to eight); Voyagers (nine to 12). Optix is a dedicated area for teenagers, including a daytime club with computers, soda bar, and disco. Challenger's Arcade has the latest video games. Paint and Clay is an arts and crafts center for younger children. Adjacent to these indoor areas is Adventure Beach, an area for all the family to enjoy.

ACCOMMODATION. There are numerous cabin categories, in four major groupings: Premium oceanview suites and cabins, Promenade-view (interiorview) cabins, Ocean-view cabins, and Interior cabins. Many cabins are of a similar size – good for incentives and large groups – and 300 have interconnecting doors, good for families.

Some 138 interior cabins have bay windows look into a central shopping plaza –and into your neighbor's cabin unless you keep the curtains closed. All cabins except for the Royal Suite and Owner's Suite have twin beds that convert to a queen-size unit, TV set, radio and telephone, personal safe, vanity unit, mini-bar, hairdryer, and bathroom.

The largest accommodation includes luxurious penthouse suites; occupants have sole access to a concierge club. The grandest is the Royal Suite, on the port side of the ship, and measures 1,146 sq ft (107 sq m). It has a king-size bed in a large bedroom, a living room with an additional queen-size sofa bed, baby grand piano, refrigerator/wet bar, dining table, entertainment center, and large bathroom.

There are similar facilities in the slightly smaller, but still highly desirable Owner's Suites – there are 10, all in the center of the ship, on both port and starboard sides, each measuring 468 sq ft (43 sq m), and four Royal Family suites, each measuring 574 sq ft (53 sq m). The Royal Family suites, which have two bedrooms (including one with third/fourth upper Pullman berths), are at the stern and have magnificent views over the ship's wake and the accompanying seagulls.

All cabins have a private bathroom with shower enclosure (towels are 100 percent cotton), plus interactive television and pay-per-view movies. Note that cabins with 'private' balconies aren't so private, because the partitions are only partial.

DINING. The huge main dining room is set on three levels, and each is named after an explorer: Columbus, Da Gama, and Magellan. All three have the same menus. Choose one of two seatings, or My Time Dining (eat when you want, during dining room hours), when you book. The place settings, china, and cutlery are of good quality.

Other dining options. Portofino, the ship's upscale Euro-Italian restaurant. It's open for dinner only, reservations are required, and there's a cover charge. The food and its presentation are better than the food in the dining room, although the restaurant isn't large enough for all passengers to try even once during a cruise.

Windjammer Café: this is a really large, sprawling venue for buffet-style, self-help breakfast (this tends to be the busiest time of the day), lunch, and light dinners (but not on the last night of the cruise); it's often difficult to find a table and by the time you do your food could be cold.

The Island Grill (it's actually a section inside the Windjammer Café), for casual dinner (no reservations needed), with a grill and open kitchen.

Johnny Rockets, a retro 1950s all-day, all-night diner-style eatery, has hamburgers, malt shakes (at extra cost), and jukebox hits, with both indoor and outdoor seating.

Promenade Café: for Continental breakfast, all-day pizzas, and speciality coffees (provided in paper cups).

Sprinkles, located on the Royal promenade, is for round-the-clock ice cream and yogurt, pastries and coffee.

ENTERTAINMENT. The stunning 1,350-seat Palace Showlounge spans five decks, with only a few slim pillars and almost no disruption of sight lines – an example of fine design and shipbuilding.

Explorer of the Seas also carries an array of cabaret acts. Although many are not what you'd call headliners, they regularly travel the cruise ship circuit. The strongest cabaret acts are presented in the main showlounge, while others appear in the Maharaja's Lounge, which is also the venue for adult-only late-night comedy. The best shows are the Ice Spectaculars.

Royal Caribbean International's entertainment is always upbeat. There is background music in all corridors and elevators, and constant music outdoors on the pool deck. If you want a quiet relaxing vacation, this is probably not the ship you should choose.

SPA/FITNESS. The Vitality at Seas Spa is reasonably large, and measures 15,000 sq ft (1,400 sq m). It includes an aerobics room, fitness center, treatment rooms, and men's and women's sauna/steam rooms. Another 10,000 sq ft (930 sq m) of space is devoted to a Solarium (with sliding glass-dome roof) to relax in after you've exercised.

On the back of the funnel is a 32.8-ft (10-m) rock-climbing wall, with five climbing tracks. It's a great buzz being 200ft (60m) above the ocean while the ship is moving. Other sports facilities include a roller-blading track, a dive-and-snorkel shop, a full-size basketball court, and a nine-hole, par 26 golf 'course.' A dive-and-snorkel shop provides equipment for rental, and diving classes.

Fifty Years of Victory
★★★★

Size:.....................................Boutique Ship	Crew/Passenger Ratio (lower beds/all berths):.......... 0.9/0.9
Tonnage: 23,439	Cabins (total):..66
Lifestyle: ....Standard (Expedition)	Size range (sq ft/m): 148.5–367.0/13.8–34.1
Cruise line:........................... Quark Expeditions	Cabins (outside view):...66
Former names: ....*Ural*	Cabins (interior/no view):......................................0
IMO number: 9152959	Cabins (for one person):..0
Builder: .... Baltic Works, St Petersburg (Russia)	Cabins (with private balcony):..................................0
Original cost:....................................... n/a	Cabins (wheelchair accessible): 0
Entered service:....................................2009	Wheelchair accessibility:...................................None
Registry:... Russia	Cabin voltage: ....110 volts
Length (ft/m):................................ 523.6/159.6	Elevators:..1
Beam (ft/m):................................... 98.4/30.0	Casino (gaming tables):...0
Draft (ft/m):..................................... 36.3/11.0	Slot machines:..0
Propulsion/Propellers:.... 2 x nuclear reactors, with 3 propulsion	Swimming pools:..1
motors (75,000 hp)	Hot tubs (on deck):...0
Passenger decks:....................................6	Self-service launderette:.....................................Yes
Total crew:......................................140	Dedicated cinema/seats:.......................................No
Passengers (lower beds/alll berths):................ 132/132	Library: ....Yes
Passenger Space Ratio (lower beds/all berths): 177.5/177.5	Onboard currency: ....US$

Nuclear-powered, it's the ultimate expedition ship

OVERVIEW. An advanced vessel of the *Arktika*-class of icebreaking ships, Fifty Years of Victory is an outstanding polar expedition cruise ship that carries adventurous, hardy outdoors types of mature years. It is powered by two nuclear reactors, and carries enough fuel to power it for four years. Experienced lecturers are carried on each sailing.

THE SHIP. This dramatic, incredibly impressive vessel (*Let Pobedy* in Russian, or *50 Years of Victory* or *Fiftieth Anniversary of Victory*) is the world's largest and most powerful icebreaker, capable of breaking through ice up to 8ft (2.5m) thick. While the noise created by the ice-crushing capability of this marine machine is intense, it is all part of the great adventure.

There are more crew members than passengers, giving a most impressive Passenger Space Ratio. The ship is comfortable, and it carries a fleet of Zodiac inflatable landing craft, as well as two helicopters for passenger use, and expedition leaders. The crew is experienced in challenging conditions.

Fifty Years of Victory typically leaves from its northern Russian base city of Murmansk before heading across the Barents Sea. Approaching the North Pole – 90° north and 1,000 miles (1,600km) from the closest tree – aboard a Russian icebreaker is the ultimate prize of a true Arctic Expedition voyage. It's really one of the most spectacular voyages to be made by ship.

The ship has a library that is stocked with books about polar exploration, nature, and wildlife. Because

Berlitz's Ratings		
	Possible	Achieved
Ship	500	367
Accommodation	200	143
Food	400	260
Service	400	273
Entertainment	100	80
Cruise	400	307
OVERALL SCORE		
1430 points out of 2000		

there are so few voyages to the North Pole, places sell out quickly. Yellow parkas and rubber boots are provided, but you should take waterproof trousers and thermal wear.

Gratuities to the staff are left to your discretion, but a suggestion is about $10 per day, per person.

ACCOMMODATION. There are two 'suite' grades and three cabin grades. The suites have a spacious bedroom and separate lounge room, while the bathroom has a tub. Suites also have a coffee-making machine, and fresh fruit is replenished daily. All suites/cabins have windows that open. Each has private bathroom facilities (with shower, except the suites with bathtub), TV/DVD player, and a decent amount of storage space. Only two cabins (46 and 48) have obstructed views.

DINING. The dining room operates in a single, open seating, so you sit with whomever you wish. Expect the food to be carbohydrate-rich, hearty fare that will provide the energy you need for the adventures ahead.

ENTERTAINMENT. There isn't any as such: dinner and conversation among all participants being the main event each day, as well as evening recaps, and, of course, wildlife spotting.

SPA/FITNESS. Sauna, fitness center, basketball and indoor volleyball court. There is a small 'dip' pool at the stern, underneath the helicopter deck.

Fram
★★★ +

Size:.	Small Ship	Cabins (total):.	132
Tonnage:	11,647	Size range (sq ft/m):	
Lifestyle:	Standard	Cabins (outside view):	108
Cruise line:.	Hurtigruten	Cabins (interior/no view):.	24
Former names:	none	Cabins (for one person):.	0
IMO number:	9370018	Cabins (with private balcony):.	6
Builder:	Fincantieri (Italy)	Cabins (wheelchair accessible):	2
Original cost:	€68.6 million	Wheelchair accessibility:.	Fair
Entered service:.	Apr 2007	Cabin voltage:	110 volts
Registry:.	Norway	Elevators:.	2
Length (ft/m):.	374.0/114.0	Casino (gaming tables):.	No
Beam (ft/m):.	66.2/20.2	Slot machines:.	No
Draft (ft/m):	5.1	Swimming pools:.	0
Propulsion/Propellers:.	diesel (4.6MW)/2	Hot tubs (on deck):.	2
Passenger decks:.	6	Self-service launderette:.	No
Total crew:.	75	Dedicated cinema/seats:.	No
Passengers (lower beds/alll berths):.	264/318	Library:	No
Passenger Space Ratio (lower beds/all berths):	44.1/36.5	Onboard currency:	Norwegian krona
Crew/Passenger Ratio (lower beds/all berths):	3.3/4.3		

Expedition-style cruising in a modern, minimalist ship

OVERVIEW. Designed to operate in polar waters, *Fram* sails from Reykjavik, Iceland, operating Greenland and Spitzbergen cruises from May through September, and winter cruises to Antarctica. It suits mature adults who like exploring independently.

THE SHIP. *Fram* features Norway and Greenlandic culture, using an extensive mix of wool, leather, and oak. The interior decor is decidedly Inuit. The few public rooms include the Quilac observation lounge, an Internet café, board room, and a small shop. There is no walk-around promenade deck. Hurtigruten doesn't have a great culture of hospitality and service, so many passengers feel they are traveling with a ferry company rather than a cruise line. The crew to passenger ratio is low, which does not equate to a high level of service or attention to detail.

In Antarctica, the ship is a fairly capable expedition vessel, but can still get stuck in heavy pack-ice. Mv Fram was assisted in January 2013 by the British Royal Navy's ice patrol ship HMS Protector. An Expedition Leader organizes everything to do with a specific voyage. Expedition specialists provide daily lectures. Boots are provided; they come in European sizes – so it helps to know yours before you go.

Life on board is very relaxed, so formal attire is never needed. Smoking is allowed only on the open deck – and not at all when *Fram* is in port. The ship operates in Norwegian and English. There are no safety deposit boxes. Hurtigruten operates a no-tipping-required policy.

Berlitz's Ratings

	Possible	Achieved
Ship	500	356
Accommodation	200	130
Food	400	242
Service	400	246
Entertainment	100	72
Cruise	400	269
OVERALL SCORE		
1315 points out of 2000		

ACCOMMODATION. There are 13 price categories (too many), according to size and location. The good thing is that no cabins have obstructed views. The largest accommodation is one Owner's Suite, which consists of a bedroom, living room, and bathroom with Jacuzzi tub. Six cabins at the aft of the ship, overlooking the stern and the ship's wake, have a shared balcony.

DINING. Restaurant Imaq, the main dining room, is located at the stern, and connects with the main lobby via an arcade.However, several meals are of the self-help buffet variety only – not what one would expect for the cruise prices charged. An extra-charge bistro and self-serve buffet is available for casual snack food items. Dessert items are particularly good. Be aware that alcohol prices are very high.

ENTERTAINMENT. There isn't any. Guides and lecturers organize talks and informative briefings based on the cruise area.

SPA/FITNESS. Saunas are located one deck above the exercise area. There are no other spa facilities, other than a small, but well-equipped exercise room, which can become hot because there's not enough air conditioning.

Freedom of the Seas
★★★★

Size:.	.Large Resort Ship	Crew/Passenger Ratio (lower beds/all berths):.	2.6/3.1
Tonnage:	154,407	Cabins (total):.	1,817
Lifestyle:	.Standard	Size range (sq ft/m):	.153.0–2,025.0/14.2–188.1
Cruise line:.	Royal Caribbean International	Cabins (outside view):.	1,084
Former names:	.none	Cabins (interior/no view):.	733
IMO number:	9304033	Cabins (for one person):.	0
Builder:	Kvaerner Masa-Yards (Finland)	Cabins (with private balcony):	842
Original cost:.	$590 million	Cabins (wheelchair accessible):	32
Entered service:.	Jun 2006	Wheelchair accessibility:.	Best
Registry:.	The Bahamas	Cabin voltage:	110 volts
Length (ft/m):.	1,112.2/339.0	Elevators:.	14
Beam (ft/m):.	183.7/56.0	Casino (gaming tables):.	Yes
Draft (ft/m):	27.8/8.5	Slot machines:.	Yes
Propulsion/Propellers:.	diesel-electric (75,600kW)/3 pods	Swimming pools:.	2
	(42,000kW)	Hot tubs (on deck):.	6
Passenger decks:.	15	Self-service launderette:.	No
Total crew:.	1,397	Dedicated cinema/seats:.	No
Passengers (lower beds/alll berths):.	3,634/4,375	Library:	Yes
Passenger Space Ratio (lower beds/all berths):	42.0/35.32	Onboard currency:	.US$

A large floating theme park – good for the whole family

OVERVIEW. *Freedom of the Seas* is a lively large resort ship, with tasteful decor and many bars and lounges. It is certainly a fine ship for young, active families with children, as long as you don't mind lines and signing up for popular activities like the Flowrider surf area, rock-climbing wall, and full-size boxing ring.

THE SHIP. *Freedom of the Seas* (with sisters *Independence of the Seas* and *Liberty of the Seas*) is an extension of the highly successful Voyager-class of ships, which Royal Caribbean International introduced in 1999 beginning with *Voyager of the Seas*. For this ship, the length and beam were extended, and this enabled an increase in the number of cabins and passenger capacity, as well as a combined pool area that is 43 percent larger than the Voyager-class – but with 500 more passengers, yet the same number of elevators. At 1,112ft/339m, the ship is the length of 37 London double-decker buses; and with a beam of 185ft/56m.

Neat features include two 16-person hot tubs cantilevered 12ft (3.7m) over the sides of the ship in an adults-only Solarium area – although the Solarium's pool itself is small. The ship's pod propulsion system virtually eliminates vibration

Perhaps the 'wow' factor aboard this ship (particularly for younger cruisers) is its connection with water – and this includes a 40ft x 32ft (12.2 x 9.7m) Flowrider surfing zone at the stern. This wave simulator creates a wall of water, flowing at 35,000 gallons per minute,

Berlitz's Ratings		
	Possible	Achieved
Ship	500	399
Accommodation	200	142
Food	400	235
Service	400	283
Entertainment	100	74
Cruise	400	270
OVERALL SCORE		
1403 points out of 2000		

for board or body surfers – but no more than two at a time.

Then there's the H2O Zone forward of the funnel, an interactive water-themed play area for families that includes a pool fed by a waterfall, and two hot tubs. Also included are water cannons and spray fountains, water jets and ground gushers; by night the water park turns into a colorfully lit Sculpture Garden. The twin central pools consist of a main pool and a sports pool, with grandstand-style seating and competitive games including pole jousting.

Other active sports facilities include a rock-climbing wall, in-line skating area, an ice-skating rink, and golf simulators. Then there's a full-size boxing ring in the spa, with sparring partners included in the extra-cost session.

The same facilities (public rooms, bars, and lounges) featured in the *Voyager*-class ships were incorporated, but with the addition of substantial conference facilities, extensive Wi-Fi coverage.

The four elements – earth, air, fire, and water – provide the decorative theme for the artwork aboard this ship. Although this is a large resort ship, the cabin hallways have a warm, attractive feel, with some neat interactive artwork cabinets and asymmetrical flow that leads you along and breaks up the monotony.

There are 16 bars and lounges to enjoy, and a whole promenade of shops and munching and drinking spots along an indoor mall-like environment called the Royal Promenade. This is four decks high, and some interior cabins have great views into it. The Royal Promenade is home to fashion, jewelry and perfume shops, a general store, logo shop, Promenade Café, Ben & Jerry's ice cream outlet, a Book Nook, a 'classic' barber shop called A Close Shave (a razor shave 'experience' costs more than $70), a pizzeria, and an English pub – The Bull and Bear. Look out for the stilt walkers and inflatable elephants when the circus is in town. Look at the ceiling in this large atrium and you'll see Vittoria Alata (Winged Victory) flowing down towards you – an exact replica of the sculpture in the Piazza Venetia in Rome.

The forward section of this large space leads into a large nightclub called Pharaoh's Palace, usually used for late-night adult-only comedy. One deck down from the Royal Promenade is a large Casino Royale (full of gaming tables and slot machines), The Crypt discotheque, Schooner Bar (piano bar), Boleros (Latin hangout), and a photo gallery, while the forward section leads into the three-deck-high Arcadia Theatre.

A regulation-size ice-skating rink called Studio B has real, not fake, ice, with 'bleacher' seating, and the latest in broadcast facilities. Superb Ice Follies shows are presented here, but a number of slim pillars obstruct clear-view arena stage sight lines.

Almost at the top of the ship is RCI's trademark Viking Crown Lounge, the cutely named Olive or Twist jazz lounge, and a wedding chapel. Other facilities include a cigar smoker's lounge, conference center, a concierge lounge (for suite occupants only), and the comfortable 3,600-book Wilhemsen Library.

Freedom of the Seas is an exciting and very comfortable ship, with tasteful decor and many bars and lounges to enjoy. However, there are only four banks of elevators (two forward and two aft) totaling 14, so if you have a cabin in the center of the ship, you'll need to walk forward or aft in order to travel vertically between decks; and there are only two major stairways – one forward, one aft – for such a large ship. On disembarkation day, you'll need to allow plenty of time to get an elevator.

FAMILIES. Children are well catered to, with Adventure Ocean (on Deck 12) for kids of six months to 17 years of age (teens get their own chill-out room). Children will love this ship and all the fun activities and sports activities – not to mention meeting other kids. Adventure Ocean is where new friends are made easily.

ACCOMMODATION. There is a wide range of suites and cabins in several categories and different price grades, from a Presidential Family Suite that can sleep up to 14 to twin-bed two-person interior cabins, and interior cabins that look into an interior shopping/strolling atrium promenade. The price you pay depends on the size, grade, and location. There are many family-friendly cabins, good for reunions,

but no single occupancy cabins. All outside-view cabins have even numbers; all interior cabins have odd numbers.

Presidential Family Suite. Located in the aft section, this suite comprises five rooms. These include two master bedrooms, each with twin beds that convert to a queen-size bed and en suite bathroom with tub/shower (the toiletries cabinets are the same as in all other cabins); two other very small bedrooms that can sleep four; private balcony with sand-colored rubberized decking (not teak), with loungers, tables, chairs, a bar, and a decent view aft – although part of the balcony is overlooked by balconies on the decks above, and there is a lot of wasted space aft of the balcony because it doesn't extend to the very stern. There's also a lounge with two sofa beds, bar. The suite can accommodate eight to 14 (that's odd numbers breathing in, even numbers breathing out!), located aft, at the opposite end of the ship to the show-lounge. Size: 1,215 sq ft (113 sq m) plus Balcony: 810 sq ft (75 sq m). It's a pleasant enough apartment, but nothing special – it's really quite cramped and the ceilings are plain – but it could be good value for a large family, provided everyone gets on well in a confined space.

Owner's Suite. Features include a queen-size bed, private balcony, separate living area with queen-size sofa bed, wet bar, vanity area, walk-in closet; bathroom with tub and shower. Sleeps up to five. Size: 506 sq ft (46 sq m) plus Balcony: 131 sq ft (12 sq m).

Royal Suite. Perhaps the nicest decor of all the suites, the Royal Suite has a very spacious lounge, with black baby grand player piano, queen-size sofa and entertainment center, wet bar, and dining table. The bedroom is quite spacious and has a queen-size bed; the bathroom has a whirlpool jet bath, large walk-in shower, and two (rather gaudy) gold washbasins. Sleeps up to four. Size: 1,406 sq ft (130.6 sq m) plus 377 sq ft (35 sq m).

Grand Suite. This has two twin beds convertible to queen-size, a private balcony, sitting area (some with sofa bed), vanity area; bathroom with tub and shower. Sleeps up to four. Size: 381 sq ft (35.3 sq m) plus Balcony: 89 sq ft (8.2 sq m).

Junior Suite. Two twin beds convertible to queen-size, a private balcony, sitting area (some with sofa bed), vanity area; bathroom with tub and shower. Sleeps up to four. Size: 277 sq ft (25.7 sq m) plus Balcony: 65 sq ft (6 sq m).

Superior Oceanview Cabin. Two twin beds convertible to queen-size, a private balcony, sitting area (some with sofa bed), vanity area; bathroom with shower. Sleeps two (some rooms sleep three or four). Size: 202 sq ft (18.7 sq m) plus Balcony: 42 sq ft (3.9 sq m).

Deluxe Oceanview Cabin. Two twin beds convertible to queen-size, a private balcony, sitting area (some with sofa bed), vanity area; bathroom with shower.

Sleeps two (some rooms sleep three or four). Size: 173 sq ft (16.0 sq m) plus Balcony: 46 sq ft (4.2 sq m).

Interior (promenade-view) Cabin. These 172 cabins, on three decks, are interior cabins but with bay windows that allow occupants to look into the Royal Promenade. They have two twin beds convertible to queen-size; private bathroom with shower.

Interior Cabin. Two twin beds convertible to queen-size; there's a private bathroom with shower. Sleeps two (some rooms sleep three or four). Size: 160 sq ft (14.8 sq m).

Family Ocean-view Cabin. Located at the front of the ship, it contains two twin beds (convertible to queen-size), sofa and/or Pullman beds, sitting area; bathroom, with shower. Accommodates six, and has 48-in (122-cm) round windows. Size: 265 sq ft (24.6 sq m).

All grades of accommodation have a private bathroom with tub and shower, or shower only, washbasin, and toiletries cabinet. There's a vanity desk with hairdryer, mini-bar, personal safe, flat-screen TV, radio, satellite-dial telephone, and nine-inch (23-cm) thick mattresses and duvets. A room service menu is provided. Occupants of suite-grade accommodation gain access to a Concierge Lounge, for more personal service.

DINING. The extremely large main dining room is set on three levels. Each has a theme and different name – Leonardo, Isaac, and Galileo – but all have the same menus and food. A dramatic staircase connects the three levels, but huge support pillars obstruct the sight lines from many seats. When you book, choose from one of two seatings – tables are for 4-12 – or My Time Dining (eat when you want, during dining hours). The place settings, porcelain, and cutlery are of good quality.

Other dining options. Chops Grill for premium steaks, chops, and special seafood, set in a great location. Open for dinner only, reservations required; cover charge.

Portofino: this Euro-Italian restaurant is open for dinner only. Reservations required; cover charge. Choices include: antipasti, soup, salad, pasta, main dish, dessert, cheese, and coffee, and the menu doesn't change during the cruise.

Promenade Café: for Continental breakfast, all-day pizzas, sandwiches, and coffees provided in paper cups.

Sprinkles: for round-the-clock ice cream and yoghurt, pastries and coffee.

Windjammer Café: this is a really large, sprawling venue for casual buffet-style, self-help breakfast (this tends to be the busiest time of the day), lunch, and light dinners (but not on the last night of the cruise); it's often difficult to find a table and by the time you do your food could be cold.

Jade 'Restaurant' (it's actually a section of the Windjammer Café), for casual Asian-themed food.

Johnny Rockets, a retro 1950s all-day, all-night diner-style eatery that serves hamburgers, hot dogs, and other fast-food items, malt shakes and sodas (at extra cost) with indoor and outdoor seating. All indoor tables have a mini-jukebox, and dimes are provided for you to make your selection of vintage records. The waitresses are all-singing and all-dancing. There's a cover charge.

You'll need to make reservations for Chops Grill or Portofino as early as you can in the cruise, because seating is limited and sells out quickly – not surprising when there are typically over 4,000 passengers on each cruise.

ENTERTAINMENT. A stunning 1,350-seat Arcadia Theater is located on three decks at the forward end of the ship. It actually spans five decks – including the orchestra pit and scenery storage space. A well-designed showlounge, it has only a small number of pillars to disrupt the sight lines to the stage. The room has a hydraulic orchestra pit and huge stage areas, together with sonic-boom loud sound, and some superb lighting equipment. The cast usually performs three production shows each cruise.

Most of the cabaret acts are not what you would call headliners. The strongest acts perform in the main showlounge, while others are presented in the Nightclub, the venue for late-night adults-only comedy. The most entertaining shows are the Ice Spectaculars. There is also a TV studio, adjacent to rooms that can also be used for trade show exhibit space – good for conventions at sea.

Royal Caribbean's production shows are colorful spectaculars that will remind you of Las Vegas casino hotels, fast-moving, razzle-dazzle shows that have little or no story line, and often poor linkage between themes and scenes, and choreography that is more stepping in place rather than dancing.

One 'show' not to be missed is the Greatest Show at Sea Parade – a superbly executed 15-minute fun extravaganza that bumbles along the Royal Promenade at turtle speed; it replicates the parade of stars and animals at a circus of yesteryear (Barnum and Bailey's meets cruise ship).

SPA/FITNESS. The large Steiner-operated ShipShape health spa includes a large aerobics room, fitness center (with stairmasters, treadmills, stationary bikes, weight machines, and free weights), several treatment rooms, and men's and women's sauna/steam rooms, and relaxation areas. Some basic exercise classes are free, but the good ones such as yoga and personal training cost extra.

More active passengers can go bodyboarding, boxing (in the full-size boxing ring in the middle of the spa (at extra cost for a personal session, or as part of a power-boxing class), climb the rock-climbing wall at the back of the funnel housing, jog, putt, swim, skate, step, surf, workout, and more (including play basketball and volleyball) in the sports area of the ship, located mostly aft of the funnel.

FTI Berlin
★★★

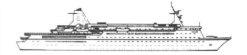

Size:.	Small Ship	Cabins (total):.		206
Tonnage:.	9,570	Size range (sq ft/m):		92.5–191.6/8.6–17.8
Lifestyle:.	Standard	Cabins (outside view):.		158
Cruise line:.	FTI Cruises	Cabins (interior/no view):.		48
Former names:	Spirit of Adventure, Berlin, Princess Mahsuri	Cabins (for one person):.		0
IMO number:.	7904889	Cabins (with private balcony):.		0
Builder:	Howaldtswerke Deutsche Werft (Germany)	Cabins (wheelchair accessible):		2
Original cost:.	n/a	Wheelchair accessibility:.		None
Entered service:.	Jun 1980/May 2012	Cabin voltage:		220 volts
Registry:.	The Bahamas	Elevators:.		1
Length (ft/m):.	457.0/139.3	Casino (gaming tables):.		No
Beam (ft/m):.	57.5/17.52	Slot machines:.		No
Draft (ft/m):.	15.7/4.8	Swimming pools:.		2
Propulsion/Propellers:.	diesel (7,060kW)/2	Hot tubs (on deck):.		0
Passenger decks:.	7	Self-service launderette:.		Yes
Total crew:.	168	Dedicated cinema/seats:.		No
Passengers (lower beds/all berths):.	412/456	Library:		Yes
Passenger Space Ratio (lower beds/all berths):	23.2/20.9	Onboard currency:		Euros
Crew/Passenger Ratio (lower beds/all berths):	2.4/2.7			

A small, comfortable ship for 'destination-a-day' cruising

OVERVIEW. This ship is best suited to German-speaking couples and solo travelers seeking a vacation in a ship that is unpretentious and provides a reasonable standard.

THE SHIP. *FTI Berlin*, a somewhat angular ship, has an all-white ice-strengthened hull and a balanced profile. As *Berlin*, it starred for many years in the long-running German TV show *Traumschiff* (Dream Ship). FTI Cruises bought the ship from Saga Cruises (who operated her for several years) in 2011.

The interiors are crisp, contemporary and well-appointed, with tasteful European decor and furnishings. The Library occupies an expansive space; Internet access is provided at four computer stations.

The swimming pool, located aft, is just a 'dip' pool. The surrounding open-deck and sunbathing space is cramped, because it's in the same area as the outdoor seating for the Verandah Restaurant. There is only one elevator and it doesn't go to the two topmost decks or to the Spa Aquarius on the lowermost deck. The passenger accommodation hallways are rather narrow.

ACCOMMODATION. There are four types: Superior Suite, Junior Suite, Standard outside-view, and Standard interior cabins, in 12 price categories. Most of the cabins are small, but comfortable enough for short cruises. There are no balcony cabins. While most cabins have fixed twin beds, more than 60 cab-

Berlitz's Ratings		
	Possible	Achieved
Ship	500	275
Accommodation	200	109
Food	400	267
Service	400	247
Entertainment	100	62
Cruise	500	261
OVERALL SCORE		
1221 points out of 2000		

ins do have a double bed. The bathrooms have showers but no tubs, and storage space for toiletries is really limited. All cabins have a refrigerator, and TV/DVD player. Cabins nearest the engine room suffer from more noise.

The largest accommodation is in two Owner's Suites (Rhapsody and Sonata); both have a double bed, lounge area, more closet and drawer space, larger bathroom, binoculars, and shoe horn/clothes brush.

DINING. The 280-seat Restaurant has large, ocean-view picture windows and dark wood accents. There are tables for four or six, and dining is in one seating.

Casual breakfasts, lunches and dinners can be taken in the Verandah Restaurant, a self-serve buffet-style venue with both indoor and outdoor seating areas. A variety of well prepared and presented items is the norm, with of cold cuts, cheeses, bread and pastry items.

ENTERTAINMENT. The 250-seat Main Lounge is a single-level venue designed for cabaret performances, but used mainly for concerts, lectures and guest speakers. The Yacht Club Lounge/Bar is the evening/late-night gathering place.

SPA/FITNESS. Spa Aquarius is the indoor health spa. It includes a shallow swimming pool, small fitness area, massage room, sauna, and relaxation room. A beauty salon is adjacent to the Library.

Golden Princess
★★★★

Size:.............................Large Resort Ship	Cabins (total):.....................................1,312
Tonnage: 108,865	Size range (sq ft/m): 161.4–764.2/15.0–71.0
Lifestyle: ....Standard	Cabins (outside view):...............................940
Cruise line:.............................Princess Cruises	Cabins (interior/no view):............................372
Former names: ....none	Cabins (for one person):................................0
IMO number: 9192351	Cabins (with private balcony):........................720
Builder: ....Fincantieri (Italy)	Cabins (wheelchair accessible): ......28 (18 outside/10 interior)
Original cost: ....$450 million	Wheelchair accessibility:.............................Best
Entered service:..............................May 2001	Cabin voltage: ....110 and 220 volts
Registry:......................................Bermuda	Elevators:...14
Length (ft/m):..............................951.4/290.0	Casino (gaming tables):..............................Yes
Beam (ft/m):...............................118.1/36.0	Slot machines:.....................................Yes
Draft (ft/m):..................................26.2/8.0	Swimming pools:.....................................3
Propulsion/Propellers: ....diesel-electric (42,000kW)/2	Hot tubs (on deck):....................................9
Passenger decks:...................................13	Self-service launderette:............................Yes
Total crew:.....................................1,100	Dedicated cinema/seats:.............................No
Passengers (lower beds/alll berths):............2,624/3,124	Library: ....Yes
Passenger Space Ratio (lower beds/all berths): 41.4/34.8	Onboard currency: ....US$
Crew/Passenger Ratio (lower beds/all berths):.........2.1/2.8	

A comfortable family-friendly large ship with an informal style

OVERVIEW. Golden Princess, with its bold, forthright profile, provides a wide variety of choices and 'small-ish' rooms to enjoy – a veritable playground.

THE SHIP. Golden Princess, sister to Grand Princess and Star Princess, has a racy 'spoiler' at the stern that is an observation lounge with aft-facing views by day, and a discotheque by night. The ship has a rather flared snub-nosed bow and a galleon-like transom stern.

There is a good sheltered faux teak promenade deck – it's actually painted steel – which almost wraps around (three times round is equal to one mile) and a walkway that goes to the enclosed bow of the ship. The outdoor pools have various beach-like surroundings, plus a large poolside movie screen. One lap pool has a pumped 'current' to swim against.

High atop the stern of the ship is a ship-wide glass-walled disco pod, with spectacular views from the extreme port and starboard side windows; it's a good place to read a book in the daytime, but at night it's a discotheque. It could well be removed soon, following in the footsteps of sister Grand Princess. The Sanctuary is adult passengers only; it has plush padded lounge chairs, two private massage cabanas, and dedicated Serenity Stewards.

There is plenty of space inside the ship and a wide array of public rooms. The passenger flow has been well thought-out, with little congestion, except at the photo gallery. The decor is attractive and warm, with

Berlitz's Ratings		
	Possible	Achieved
Ship	500	370
Accommodation	200	147
Food	400	250
Service	400	285
Entertainment	100	76
Cruise	400	292
OVERALL SCORE		
1420 points out of 2000		

lots of earth tones.

The main lobby, La Piazza, has live 'street' entertainment; an International café for coffees, fresh cookies, pastries, panini, and tapas; and Vines, a wine bar. The ship has an extensive collection of art works complement the elegant, non-glitzy interior design and colors, and most of the paintings are for sale.

This ship has a Wedding Chapel, with a web-cam to relay ceremonies via the Internet. The ship's captain can legally marry (American) couples, thanks to the ship's Bermuda registry and a special dispensation (this should, however, be verified when in the planning stage, and may vary according to where you reside).

The large casino, on Deck 7, has more than 260 slot machines, plus blackjack, craps, and roulette tables for the more serious gamers. The wood-paneled Wheelhouse Bar is finely decorated with memorabilia and ship models tracing part of parent company P&O's history. There is an Internet café – which isn't a café, though it does have computer workstations.

The automated telephone system is frustrating to use, and luggage delivery is inefficient. Lines can form at the Passenger Services Desk, and for open-seating breakfast and lunch. There is a charge for using the washers and dryers in the self-service launderettes (coins are needed).

FAMILIES. A two-deck-high playroom and teen room is located in the forward section of the ship, and a video games room is located at the opposite end of the ship.

There is a host of trained counselors. Many cabins have additional upper berths (there are 609), good for families. Group babysitting services are available for an hourly charge.

ACCOMMODATION. There are six principal types of cabins and configurations but a bewildering number of price categories. The price depends on grade, size, and location.

(a) The largest, most lavish suite is the Grand Suite (B748), at the stern. It has a large bedroom with a queen-size bed, huge walk-in closets, a large bathroom with full-size tub and separate shower enclosure, toilet, and washbasin, and a hot tub (accessed from the bedroom), a lounge with sofa bed, dining table and chairs, wet bar and refrigerator, a guest bathroom, and a large private balcony.

(b/c) Suites (with a semi-private balcony) have a separate living room with sofa bed and a bedroom (with a TV in each). The bathroom is quite large and has both a tub and shower stall. The mini-suites also have a semi-private balcony, and a separate living and sleeping area (with a TV in each). The bathroom is also spacious, with both a bathtub and separate shower enclosure. Passengers occupying the best suites receive greater attention, including priority embarkation and disembarkation. What is not good is that some of the most expensive accommodation has only semi-private balconies that can be seen from above, so there is no privacy (suites C401, 402, 409, 410, 414, 415, 420, 421, 422, 423, 424, and 425 on Caribe Deck in particular). Also, the extremely large suites D105 and D106 (Dolphin Deck) have balconies that can be seen from above.

(d/e/f) The standard interior and outside-view cabins (the outsides come either with or without private balcony) are of a functional, practical, design, although almost no drawers are provided. They are very attractive, with warm, pleasing decor and fine soft furnishing fabrics.

Two family suites consist of two suites with an interconnecting door, plus a large balcony. These can sleep up to 10 (if at least four are children), or up to eight adults.

The views from most outside cabins on Emerald Deck are obstructed by lifeboats. Some cabins can accommodate a third and fourth person in upper berths. However, in such cabins, the lower beds cannot then be pushed together to make queen-size bed.

Cabins with balconies on Dolphin, Caribe, and Baja decks are overlooked by passengers on balconies on the deck above; they are, therefore, not at all private. However, perhaps the least desirable balcony cabins are the eight located forward on Emerald Deck, as the balconies don't extend to the side of the ship and can be passed by walkers and gawkers on an adjacent walkway (so occupants need to keep their curtains closed most of the time). Those in expensive suites with balconies at the stern may experience some considerable vibration during certain slow-speed ship maneuvers.

Cabin attendants have too many cabins to look after (typically 20), which cannot translate to fine personal service.

DINING. For 'formal' meals there are three principal dining rooms (Bernini, Canaletto, and Donatello). There are two seatings in one restaurant, and the others have 'anytime dining' where you choose your time and companions. All are split into multi-tier sections in a non-symmetrical design that breaks what are quite large spaces into many smaller sections, for better ambience. Each dining room has its own galley. While four elevators go to Fiesta Deck for Canaletto and Donatello, only two go to Plaza Deck 5 for Bernini, which can mean long wait problems at peak times, particularly for anyone in a wheelchair). Note that 15 percent is added to all beverage bills, including wines, coffees, etc.

Other dining options. There are two extra-cost dining venues: Sabatini's and Crown Grill. Sabatini's features Italian-style pizzas and pastas, with a variety of sauces, as well as Italian-style entrées, including tiger prawns and lobster tail. Sabatini's is by reservation only, for lunch or dinner on sea days only. Crown Grill has an open galley, and features premium-quality steaks and grilled seafood items. Reservations are required and a cover charge applies in both restaurants, but it's worth it for food that is cooked to order.

A poolside hamburger grill and pizza bar (no extra charge) offer casual bites. Other casual meals can be taken in the 24-hour Horizon Court, with large ocean-view windows and direct access to the two main swimming pools and lido deck, and outdoor seating. Plastic plates are provided instead of trays.

ENTERTAINMENT. The 748-seat Princess Theatre spans two decks and has comfortable seating on both main and balcony levels. It has a nine-piece orchestra. Princess Cruises prides itself on its glamorous and colourful, all-American production shows.

The Vista Lounge is a second entertainment venue and multi-function room. It presents cabaret acts at night, and lectures, bingo, and horse racing during the day.

Explorers, is a third entertainment lounge that features cabaret acts and dance bands, and it has a decent sized dance floor. Many other lounges and bars have live music, and there are male dance hosts as partners for women traveling alone.

SPA/FITNESS. The Lotus Spa is a complex that surrounds one of the swimming pools at the forward end of the ship. It comprises a large fitness room with all the high-tech workout machinery, an aerobics room, sauna and steam rooms, beauty salon, treatment rooms, and a relaxation area.

Grand Celebration
★★★

Size:.	Mid-size Ship	Cabins (total):.	747
Tonnage:	47,262	Size range (sq ft/m):	184.0/17.1
Lifestyle:	Standard	Cabins (outside view):	453
Cruise line:.	Iberocruceros	Cabins (interior/no view):.	296
Former names:	Celebration	Cabins (for one person):.	0
IMO number:	8314134	Cabins (with private balcony):.	10
Builder:	Kockums (Sweden)	Cabins (wheelchair accessible):	14
Original cost:	$130 million	Wheelchair accessibility:	Fair
Entered service:.	Mar 1987/Jun 2008	Cabin voltage:	110 and 220 volts
Registry:.	Panama	Elevators:.	8
Length (ft/m):	732.6/223.3	Casino (gaming tables):.	Yes
Beam (ft/m):.	92.5/28.2	Slot machines:.	Yes
Draft (ft/m):	25.5/7.8	Swimming pools:.	3
Propulsion/Propellers:	diesel (23,520kW)/2	Hot tubs (on deck):.	2
Passenger decks:.	10	Self-service launderette:	Yes
Total crew:	620	Dedicated cinema/seats:	No
Passengers (lower beds/alll berths):	1,494/1,896	Library:	Yes
Passenger Space Ratio (lower beds/all berths):	31.6/24.9	Onboard currency:	Euros
Crew/Passenger Ratio (lower beds/all berths):	2.4/3.0		

A child-friendly ship for Spanish-speaking families

OVERVIEW. This ship is a floating playground for young, Spanish-speaking active adults who enjoy stimulation. There is a wide range of entertainment and passenger participation activities, and it should prove a good choice for families with children.

THE SHIP. *Grand Celebration*, now more than 25 years old, has extremely short bows. It also has a distinctive, large, swept-back wing-tipped blue funnel just aft of the center of the ship. The swimming pools are smaller than one would expect, and the open deck space can be extremely crowded.

It has a double-width indoor promenade and a good selection of public rooms, including a large casino. Facilities include a library and Internet center. Children are split into two age categories, with facilities for each: Club 5 (five- to 10-year-olds), or Club 10 (10 years and older).

ACCOMMODATION. There are four accommodation grades, and several price categories: suite with balcony; junior suite with balcony; outside-view; and interior cabins. The cabins are quite standard, are of fairly generous proportions, except for the interior cabins, which are quite small. A 24-hour room service menu is provided. The best living spaces on board are in 10 suites, each of which has much more space, its own private balcony, a larger bathroom and more closet, drawer, and storage space.

Berlitz's Ratings

	Possible	Achieved
Ship	500	291
Accommodation	200	121
Food	400	216
Service	400	247
Entertainment	100	66
Cruise	400	235

OVERALL SCORE
1176 points out of 2000

DINING. There are two dining rooms: Vista Hermoza, with 550 seats, and Riazor, with 450 seats. They are quite cramped when full, and extremely noisy. There are tables for four, six, or eight (none for two). The decor is bright and extremely colorful. Dining is in two seatings: 8:30pm and 10:30pm. Meals for vegetarians and special children's menus are available, as is a snack at midnight.

The presentation of the dishes is simple, and few garnishes are used. Some meat and fowl dishes are disguised with gravies and sauces. There is much use of canned fruit and jellied desserts. This is all about banquet catering, with all its standardization and production cooking. There is a decent wine list, but no wine waiters. For casual meals, there's the 280-seat, self-serve Buffet Triana, although the meals are basic and repetitive.

ENTERTAINMENT. The Astoria Showlounge is the main venue for large-scale, high-volume production shows and major European cabaret acts. Almost every lounge/bar has live bands and musical units, so there's always plenty of live music in the evening.

SPA/FITNESS. The Spa is located on the ship's uppermost deck. It has a gymnasium with muscle-pumping cardiovascular machines, men's and women's changing rooms, and saunas. The beauty salon is elsewhere. Massages, facials, pedicures, and beauty treatments cost extra.

Grand Holiday
★★★

Size:.	Mid-size Ship	Cabins (total):.		726
Tonnage:.	46,052	Size range (sq ft/m):	189.2–420.0/17.0–39.0	
Lifestyle:.	Standard	Cabins (outside view):.		447
Cruise line:.	Iberocruceros	Cabins (interior/no view):.		279
Former names:.	Holiday	Cabins (for one person):.		0
IMO number:.	8217881	Cabins (with private balcony):.		10
Builder:.	Aalborg Vaerft (Denmark)	Cabins (wheelchair accessible):.		15
Original cost:.	$170 million	Wheelchair accessibility:.		None
Entered service:.	Jul 1985/May 2010	Cabin voltage:.		110 volts
Registry:.	The Bahamas	Elevators:.		8
Length (ft/m):.	726.9/221.5	Casino (gaming tables):.		Yes
Beam (ft/m):.	92.4/28.1	Slot machines:.		Yes
Draft (ft/m):.	25.5/7.7	Swimming pools:.		3
Propulsion/Propellers:.	diesel (22,360kW)/2	Hot tubs (on deck):.		2
Passenger decks:.	9	Self-service launderette:.		No
Total crew:.	660	Dedicated cinema/seats:.		No
Passengers (lower beds/all berths):.	1,452/1,800	Library:.		Yes
Passenger Space Ratio (lower beds/all berths):.	31.7/25.5	Onboard currency:.		Euros
Crew/Passenger Ratio (lower beds/all berths):.	2.2/2.7			

A casual, family-friendly ship for Spanish-speaking cruisers

OVERVIEW. This ship is best suited to young Spanish-speaking couples seeking their first cruise experience, single passengers, and families. The passenger flow is good, although the ship does have a high density and always feels crowded.

THE SHIP. *Grand Holiday* used to be *Holiday*, a Carnival Cruise lines ship. It is a bold, high-sided, all-white contemporary vessel with a very short, rakish bow and stubby stern typical of so many ships built in the 1980s. It has a distinctive swept-back wing-tipped funnel. Iberocruceros spent €55 million to refurbish the ship in 2010.

The decks are named after cities and towns – Seville, Valencia, Lugo, Pamplona, Avila, Elche, Barcelona, Madrid, and Ronda. There are numerous public rooms on two entertainment decks to choose from, and these flow from a double-width indoor promenade. A real red-and-cream bus is located right in the middle of one of the two promenades, and this is used as a snack café.

ACCOMMODATION. There are just four cabin categories: Suite with balcony; Junior Suite with balcony; exterior cabins, and interior cabins, in 13 different price grades. The standard outside and interior cabins are plain but functional units that provide all the basics including a small vanity/writing desk. TV sets are typically placed high in one corner and are not easy to watch. The bathrooms are practical, with decent-size shower enclosures. Wall-mounted dispensers provide body soap and shampoo.

Berlitz's Ratings

	Possible	Achieved
Ship	500	289
Accommodation	200	123
Food	400	214
Service	400	241
Entertainment	100	64
Cruise	400	225
OVERALL SCORE		
1156 points out of 2000		

DINING. There are two main restaurants: Cantabrico and Alboran. Both are large, have low ceilings and raised center sections, and feel cramped.

The food is presented well, but few garnishes are used. Do remember that this really is banquet-style catering, with families and children in mind, so standardization and production cooking is the norm. Although there is a decent wine list, there are no wine waiters.

The Ensenada Buffet is a self-serve buffet area that provides all the basics (except service) although its layout is old in style and makes the venue seem more like a canteen than a restaurant. Still, it's good for that quick meal when the ship is in port and the family and kids want to be out and about.

ENTERTAINMENT. The Grand Theater Bazan is the principal venue for large-scale production shows and major cabaret acts – although pillars obstruct the views from several seats. It has a main and upper level.

Most lounges and bars have live music, so there's always plenty of life. There are two discos – one large, one small overlooking the ship's single swimming pool.

SPA/FITNESS. Some fitness classes are free, while some may cost extra. Do make early appointments for massages, facials, or other beauty treatments such as manicures and pedicures), because time slots go quickly.

Grand Mistral
★★★+

Size:.	Mid-size Ship	Cabins (total):.	598
Tonnage:.	48,200	Size range (sq ft/m):	139.9–236.8/13.0–22.0
Lifestyle:.	Standard	Cabins (outside view):.	375
Cruise line:.	Iberocruceros	Cabins (interior/no view):.	223
Former names:.	Mistral	Cabins (for one person):.	0
IMO number:.	9172777	Cabins (with private balcony):.	80
Builder:.	Chantiers de l'Atlantique (France)	Cabins (wheelchair accessible):.	2
Original cost:.	$245 million	Wheelchair accessibility:.	Fair
Entered service:.	Jul 1999/May 2005	Cabin voltage:.	110 and 220 volts
Registry:.	Marshall Islands	Elevators:.	6
Length (ft/m):.	709.9/216.4	Casino (gaming tables):.	Yes
Beam (ft/m):.	94.6/28.8	Slot machines:.	Yes
Draft (ft/m):.	22.4/6.8	Swimming pools:.	2
Propulsion/Propellers:.	diesel-electric (31,680kW)/2	Hot tubs (on deck):.	2
Passenger decks:.	8	Self-service launderette:.	No
Total crew:.	470	Dedicated cinema/seats:.	No
Passengers (lower beds/all berths):.	1,196/1,600	Library:.	Yes
Passenger Space Ratio (lower beds/all berths):.	39.5/30.1	Onboard currency:.	Euros
Crew/Passenger Ratio (lower beds/all berths):.	2.4/3.4		

Child-friendly, casual cruising for Spanish-speaking families

OVERVIEW. *Grand Mistral* is best suited to youthful Spanish-speaking couples and singles, and families with children that enjoy big-city life and outdoor cafés, constant activity accompanied by lots of noise, late nights, loud entertainment, and food that focuses on quantity rather than quality.

THE SHIP. *Grand Mistral* is owned by a consortium of French investors and banks, and operates under charter to Iberocruceros, a vibrant tour operator for Spanish-speaking passengers that's part of the giant Carnival Corporation. Its profile is similar to that of most new cruise ships, although the built-up stern makes it look bulky and is less than handsome.

The lido deck surrounding the outdoor swimming pools – which are small, and regulated for use by various age groups in several time of day zones – has whirlpool tubs and a large bandstand is set in raised canvas-covered pods. The sunloungers, however, do have cushioned pads. There is no full walk-around promenade deck outdoors, although there is a partial walking deck on port and starboard sides under the lifeboats, plus an oval jogging track atop ship.

The interior layout and general passenger flow is good, as are the 'you are here' deck signs, and the ship absorbs passengers quite well. It is light and cheerful without being glitzy in any way – there's not even a hint of colored neon – and there's much use of blonde/cherry wood paneling and rich, textured soft furnishings.

Berlitz's Ratings

	Possible	Achieved
Ship	500	355
Accommodation	200	132
Food	400	240
Service	400	252
Entertainment	100	58
Cruise	400	259

OVERALL SCORE
1296 points out of 2000

Public rooms, bars, and lounges have names inspired by European places or establishments such as San Remo Casino, San Marco Lounge, Cafe Guon, and Richlieu Library. There is a smoking room (Le Diplomate); it has all the hallmarks of a traditional gentleman's club, a piano bar, and a library that has real writing desks – something many ships seem to omit.

Atop the ship is an observation lounge with a twist – it faces aft, instead of forward; it doubles as a discotheque for the late-night set. There's a video games room for teens, and a children's center. A conference center provides facilities for meetings.

Smokers are difficult to avoid, towels are small, and the square chairs in the Café Navona are uncomfortable and impractical. Standing in line for embarkation, disembarkation, shore tenders, and for self-serve buffet meals is inevitable aboard all ships of this size. The onboard currency is the euro except when the ship operates in Brazil during that country's summer season, when the Brazilian Real is used. Gratuities are included.

An optional drinks package (standard drink brands) can be bought for €16 per person, per day or €8 for a non-alcoholic drinks package for minors.

ACCOMMODATION. There are three basic cabin types, in several different price grades. These include 80 'suites' (each with a private balcony, although partitions are of the partial, and not the full type), ocean-view standard cabins, and interior standard cabins. The price you pay will depend on grade, size and location.

The cabins on Deck 10 are subject to noise from the Lido Deck above. Good planning and layout means that no outside-view cabins have lifeboat-obstructed views. The cabin numbering system goes against maritime tradition, where even-numbered cabins are on the port side and odd-numbered cabins on the starboard; in Grand Mistral, the opposite is the case.

All cabins have twin beds that convert to a queen-size unit, bold, colorful bedspreads (with blankets and sheets, not duvets), a personal safe, a TV, and a good amount of closet and drawer space for a one-week cruise. The bathrooms, although not large, do have a good-size shower enclosure, and there is a decent amount of stowage space for toiletries.

Accommodation designated as suites – which are really only larger cabins and not suites, as there is no separation of lounge and sleeping space – have more space, larger (walk-in) closets, more drawers and better storage space, plus a two-person sofa, coffee table and additional armchair, vanity desk, floor-to-ceiling mirrors, and hairdryer; bathrooms have a tub/shower combination.

Six Grand Suites are well-designed units that have a separate bedroom with flat-screen TV, bedside tables, vanity desk, floor-to-ceiling windows, and door to balcony; the lounge has an audio-visual center, sofa, dining table, and lots of space, plus a balcony door. A large bathroom has contemporary styling, two Villeroy & Boch washbasins, dark hardwood storage cabinets, large Jacuzzi tub, separate shower enclosure (hand-held shower), and bathrobes.

In addition, there are two interior wheelchair accessible cabins for the handicapped, which provide more spacious interiors than standard cabins.

DINING. There are two dining rooms (and two seatings for meals), which can be configured in any of several different ways. Both have ocean-view windows. The principal dining room – Restaurant Mallorca, with 610 seats – has round tables for two, four, six, or eight, and a small podium with baby grand piano.

Restaurant Formentor, a second dining venue seating 380 in chairs with no armrests, is on a different deck. Smaller and more intimate, it is for passengers occupying Deck 10 accommodation; it has tables for two, four, or six, and ocean-view windows.

The food is quite sound, and, with varied menus and decent presentation, should prove a highlight for most passengers. The wine list features a good variety of standard wines at reasonable prices, but almost all are young.

There's a casual Bahia de Palma cafeteria for al-fresco self-serve buffet-style breakfasts and lunches, with ocean-view windows, but the flow is awkward and cramped. Additionally, there's an outdoor pool bar; plus a pleasant little coffee bar (Café Navona, which serves Brazilian coffee) on the upper level of the two-deck high lobby, which, unfortunately, has lifeboat-restricted ocean views.

ENTERTAINMENT. The Grand Theatre Ibiza, the showlounge, spans two decks, has a sloping floor, and good sight lines from most seats (the seating is in banquettes), and there is a small balcony level at the rear. Sadly, the designer forgot to include space for a live band (so all shows are performed to pre-recorded backing tracks), and the lighting facilities are anything but high-tech.

There's also a bar/lounge (Salon Formentera) on the lower level at the entrance to the showlounge. Entertainment is, without doubt, one of the weakest links in the chain for passengers.

SPA/FITNESS. The Santai Spa health/fitness facilities, located forward of the mast, are quite decent. Included is a gymnasium with high-tech muscle-pump equipment, lifecycles, and life-rowing machines and a view over the bow of the ship through large floor-to-ceiling windows.

Other facilities include a thalassotherapy room, and beauty salon, six rooms for massage and other body treatments, as well as a sauna each for men and women, plus an aerobics exercise room. It's best to make appointments early, as the best time slots can go fairly quickly.

Grand Princess
★★★★

Size:.................................Large Resort Ship	Cabins (total):.................................... 1,300
Tonnage: 108,806	Size range (sq ft/m): 161.4–764.2/15.0–71.0
Lifestyle: ....Standard	Cabins (outside view):...............................928
Cruise line:............................. Princess Cruises	Cabins (interior/no view):............................372
Former names: ....none	Cabins (for one person):..............................0
IMO number: 9104005	Cabins (with private balcony):........................710
Builder: .... Fincantieri (Italy)	Cabins (wheelchair accessible): 28
Original cost: ....$450 million	Wheelchair accessibility:........................... Best
Entered service:............................... May 1998	Cabin voltage: ....110 and 220 volts
Registry:.. Bermuda	Elevators:..14
Length (ft/m):............................... 951.4/290.0	Casino (gaming tables):............................. Yes
Beam (ft/m):................................. 118.1/36.0	Slot machines:..................................... Yes
Draft (ft/m): 26.2/8.0	Swimming pools:......................................3
Propulsion/Propellers: .... diesel-electric (42,000kW)/2	Hot tubs (on deck):...................................9
Passenger decks:....................................13	Self-service launderette:........................... Yes
Total crew:....................................... 1,100	Dedicated cinema/seats:..............................No
Passengers (lower beds/all berths):............. 2,600/3,100	Library: .... Yes
Passenger Space Ratio (lower beds/all berths): 41.8/35.0	Onboard currency: ....US$
Crew/Passenger Ratio (lower beds/all berths):.......... 2.3/2.8	

A multi-choice large ship for informal family cruising

OVERVIEW. Whether *Grand Princess* provides a genuinely relaxing holiday is a moot point, but with many choices and 'small' rooms to enjoy, it is an extremely well designed ship – particularly for families with children. The odds are that you'll have a fine time, in a controlled, well-packaged way.

THE SHIP. *Grand Princess* was first in a series of Grand-class ships, whose interior design and configuration evolved with each new ship in the series. It has a flared dolphin-like bow and a galleon-like transom stern. The ship was refreshed following an extensive 2011 refit. There is a good sheltered faux teak promenade deck – it's actually painted steel – which almost wraps around, and a walkway that goes right to the enclosed, protected bow. The outdoor pools have various beach-like surroundings. One lap pool has a pumped 'current' to swim against.

Unlike the outside decks, there is plenty of space inside the ship – but also plenty of passengers – and a wide array of public rooms, with many 'intimate' (this being a relative word) spaces. The decor is attractive and warm, with lots of earth tones, and an extensive collection of art complements the interior design and colors well.

Four areas center on swimming pools, one of which is two decks high and can be covered by a retractable glass dome. The former Skywalkers Nightclub was repositioned to a lower deck (Deck 15) in 2011. Now called One5 (cute), it has improved the ship's former shopping-cart look.

Berlitz's Ratings

	Possible	Achieved
Ship	500	370
Accommodation	200	147
Food	400	249
Service	400	285
Entertainment	100	76
Cruise	400	292

OVERALL SCORE
1419 points out of 2000

Other facilities include a new Piazza Atrium, with an integral International Café, Vines wine bar (including tapas and sushi items and wines for purchase); and Leaves Tea Lounge and Library (with 'tea sommelier' to create personalized 'artisan' teas). There's a Wedding Chapel with a web-cam to relay ceremonies via the Internet. The ship's captain can legally marry US citizens, due to the ship's Bermuda registry and a special dispensation.

Another neat feature is the motion-based 'virtual reality' room with its enclosed motion-based rides, and a blue-screen studio, where passengers can star in their own videos. There is an excellent library/computer room, and a separate card room. Youngsters have a two-deck-high playroom, teen room, and trained counselors.

Gamblers should enjoy the large casino, with more than 260 slot machines with dolphin-shaped handles; there are blackjack, craps, and roulette tables.

Ship enthusiasts will savor the wood-paneled Wheelhouse Bar, decorated with memorabilia and ship models tracing part of the history of sister company P&O.

The dress code has been simplified to formal or smart casual. Gratuities are automatically added to your account, and tips for children are charged at the same rate. If you want to pay less, you'll have to line up at the reception desk.

ACCOMMODATION. There are six types of cabins and configurations but there is a bewildering choice of price categories. Many cabins have additional upper berths (there are 609 of them), which is good for families with children. Many balcony cabins overhang the ship's lower hull section.

(a) The plushest accommodation is the Grand Suite, with a hot tub accessible from both the private balcony and from the bedroom, two bedrooms, lounge, two bathrooms, a huge walk-in closet, and lots of drawer and storage space.

(b/c) Suites, with a semi-private balcony, have a separate living room with sofa bed, and bedroom – with a TV set in each. The bathroom is quite large and has both a tub and shower stall. The mini-suites also have a private balcony, and a separate living and sleeping area, with a TV set in each. The differences between the suites and mini-suites are basically in the size and appointments. Passengers in both receive priority attention, including speedy embarkation and disembarkation. What is unacceptable is that the most expensive accommodation has only semi-private balconies that can be seen from above, so there is no privacy (suites C401, 402, 409, 410, 414, 415, 420, 421/422, 423, 424, and 425 on Caribe Deck). The suites D105 and D106 (Dolphin Deck) are extremely large, but their balconies can be seen from above.

(d/e/f) Both interior and outside-view cabins – the outsides come either with or without private balcony – are functional and practical, although there are almost no drawers. They are attractive, with warm, pleasing decor and fine soft furnishing fabrics. The tiled bathrooms have a good amount of open shelf storage space for toiletries.

There are also two family suites. These consist of two suites with an interconnecting door, plus a large balcony, and can sleep up to 10 (if at least four are children), or up to eight adults.

Most outside cabins on Emerald Deck have views obstructed by lifeboats. Sadly, there are no cabins for singles. Your name is placed outside your suite or cabin – making it simple for delivery service personnel but compromising privacy. Some cabins can accommodate a third and fourth person in upper berths – but in such cabins, the lower beds cannot then be pushed together to make a queen-size bed.

Perhaps the least desirable balcony cabins are the eight located forward on Emerald Deck, as the balconies do not extend to the side of the ship and can be passed by walkers and gawkers on the adjacent Upper Promenade walkway. Also, passengers occupying some the most expensive suites with balconies at the stern may experience considerable vibration during certain ship maneuvers.

The cabin bath towels are small, and drawer space is limited. There are no butlers – even for the top-grade suites. Cabin attendants have many cabins to look after (typically 20), which cannot translate to fine personal service.

DINING. For formal meals, there are three main dining rooms, Botticelli (504 seats), Da Vinci (486), and Michelangelo (486). There are two seatings in one restaurant, while the other two have 'anytime dining' where you choose when, and with whom, you want to eat. All three split into multi-tier sections in a non-symmetrical design that breaks what are quite large spaces into many smaller sections. Each dining room has its own galley. While four elevators go to Fiesta Deck for the Botticelli and Da Vinci restaurants, only two go to Plaza Deck 5 for the Michaelangelo Restaurant – this can cause long waits at peak times, especially for wheelchair users.

Other dining options. There are several informal dining areas, open for lunch and dinner. The food is mostly prepared and cooked to order, and so there is much more taste, and it is perhaps worth paying the extra cost to get better food.

Sabatini's is an extra-cost, reservations required Italian eatery, with colorful tiled Mediterranean-style decor. It has Italian-style pizzas and pastas, with a variety of sauces, as well as Italian-style entrées that include tiger prawns and lobster tail.

A Crown Grill is an extra-cost steakhouse – featuring premium American steaks and seafood in a very pleasant setting, with plenty of space around diner's tables. There's a cover charge (worth it), and reservations are required.

Painted Desert is an open area that features 'Southwestern' American food for lunch or dinner – but only on sea days.

The poolside hamburger grill and pizza bar (no additional charge) are additional dining spots for casual bites, while extra charges apply if you order items to eat at either the coffee bar/patisserie, or the caviar/Champagne bar.

Other casual meals can be taken in the Horizon Court buffet – open 24 hours a day, with large ocean-view on port and starboard sides and direct access to the two main swimming pools and lido deck. Oval, plastic plates are used (there are no trays).

ENTERTAINMENT. The 748-seat Princess Theater spans two decks and has comfortable seating on both main and balcony levels. Princess Crusies has long been known and liked for its colourful Hollywood-style (rather than Las-Vegas-style) production shows.

The Vista Lounge, a second entertainment lounge, presents cabaret acts at night, and lectures, bingo, and horse racing during the day. Explorers, a third lounge, can also host cabaret acts and dance bands.

SPA/FITNESS. The Lotus Spa is a large complex that surrounds one of the swimming pools at the forward end. It comprises a large gymnasium with all the usual equipment, an aerobics room, sauna and steam rooms, salon, ocean-view treatment rooms, and a relaxation area. It is operated by Steiner Leisure.

Grande Caribe
★★

Size:.....................................Boutique Ship		Cabins (total):....................................50	
Tonnage:...99		Size range (sq ft/m):.................72.0–96.0/6.6–8.9	
Lifestyle:...Standard		Cabins (outside view):............................41	
Cruise line:...................Blount Small Ship Adventures		Cabins (interior/no view):..........................9	
Former names:...................................none		Cabins (for one person):...........................0	
IMO number:.................................8978631		Cabins (with private balcony):......................0	
Builder:...................Blount Industries (USA)		Cabins (wheelchair accessible):.....................0	
Original cost:................................$8 million		Wheelchair accessibility:........................None	
Entered service:...........................Jun 1997		Cabin voltage:..............................110 volts	
Registry:...USA		Elevators:...0	
Length (ft/m):.............................183.0/55.7		Casino (gaming tables):............................No	
Beam (ft/m):...............................40.0/12.1		Slot machines:.....................................No	
Draft (ft/m):......................................6.5/1.9		Swimming pools:....................................0	
Propulsion/Propellers:...................diesel (1,044kW)/2		Hot tubs (on deck):................................0	
Passenger decks:.....................................3		Self-service launderette:..........................No	
Total crew:..17		Dedicated cinema/seats:...........................No	
Passengers (lower beds/all berths):................100/100		Library:..Yes	
Passenger Space Ratio (lower beds/all berths):.......0.99/0.99		Onboard currency:.................................US$	
Crew/Passenger Ratio (lower beds/all berths):..........5.8/5.8			

A tiny ship for coastal cruising, with minimal facilities

OVERVIEW. This ship is best for mature-age couples and single travelers who enjoy nature and wildlife up close, and who wouldn't dream of cruising in the mainstream sense aboard warehouse-size ships and who don't demand a high standard of service. It's a basic, no-glitz vessel, providing an all-American cruise experience, albeit at a high price, and is not for children.

THE SHIP. *Grande Caribe* is the largest, most contemporary Blount-built vessel. Like sister ship *Grande Mariner*, it has stabilizers. During emergency drill, passengers are taught how to use fire extinguishers – a useful piece of training.

The ship's shallow draft enables it to cruise into off-the-beaten-path destinations well out of reach of larger ships. It also has a retractable navigation bridge – practical for those low bridges along inland waterways. An underwater video camera allows passengers, while seated in comfort in the lounge, to view on large-screen TV monitors what a scuba diver might see underneath the ship. Underwater lights, which attract fish and other marine life, are fitted. There are two 24-passenger launches, one of which is a glass-bottomed boat, and snorkeling equipment.

There is one lounge/bar, located on a different deck to the dining room. The style is casual – no jackets or ties – by day and night. An electric stairway chairlift is provided for those whose mobility is restricted. Gratuities given by passengers (high at the suggested $10–$15 per person, per day) are pooled and shared by all the staff.

Berlitz's Ratings

	Possible	Achieved
Ship	500	164
Accommodation	200	67
Food	400	180
Service	400	198
Entertainment	100	35
Cruise	400	175
OVERALL SCORE		
819 points out of 2000		

ACCOMMODATION. The cabins are all extremely small, relatively utilitarian units, with very little closet space but just enough drawers. The very small bathrooms have new vacuum toilets. The twin beds convert to queen-size beds, with good storage space under them. There is no room service menu, and only soap is supplied – bring your own toiletries. Each cabin has its own air conditioner, so passengers don't have to share air with the rest of the ship. Refreshingly, there are no cabin keys. Be prepared for noise from the generators.

DINING. The dining room seats all passengers in one open seating, so you dine with whomever you wish, making new friends each day – it is also good for small groups. The tables convert to card tables for use between meals. Passengers are welcome to bring their own alcohol, as the company doesn't sell it aboard ship. Effervescent, young American waitresses provide the service, although there is no finesse.

A hand-held colonial bell is rung to summon passengers to the dining room.

ENTERTAINMENT. There is no formal entertainment, so conversation with fellow passengers in the ship's lounge/bar becomes the entertainment each evening. If that isn't appealing, take a good book.

SPA/FITNESS. There are no facilities.

Grande Mariner
★★

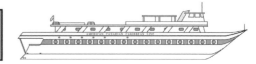

Size:..Boutique Ship	Cabins (total):...50
Tonnage: 99	Size range (sq ft/m): 72.0–96.0/6.6–8.9
Lifestyle: ....Standard	Cabins (outside view):.......................................41
Cruise line:....................Blount Small Ship Adventures	Cabins (interior/no view):.....................................9
Former names: ....none	Cabins (for one person):.......................................0
IMO number: 8978643	Cabins (with private balcony):................................0
Builder: ....Blount Industries (USA)	Cabins (wheelchair accessible): 0
Original cost:..$8 million	Wheelchair accessibility:................................None
Entered service:....................................Jun 1998	Cabin voltage: ....110 volts
Registry:...USA	Elevators:...0
Length (ft/m):....................................183.0/55.7	Casino (gaming tables):......................................No
Beam (ft/m):.......................................40.0/12.1	Slot machines:...No
Draft (ft/m): 6.5/1.9	Swimming pools:..0
Propulsion/Propellers:...................diesel (1,044kW)/2	Hot tubs (on deck):..0
Passenger decks:..3	Self-service launderette:.....................................No
Total crew:..17	Dedicated cinema/seats:.....................................No
Passengers (lower beds/alll berths):...............100/100	Library:...Yes
Passenger Space Ratio (lower beds/all berths): 0.99/0.99	Onboard currency: ....US$
Crew/Passenger Ratio (lower beds/all berths):..........5.8/5.8	

A US coastal cruise ship with basic food and facilities

OVERVIEW. This ship is best for mature-age couples and single travelers who enjoy nature and wildlife up close, who wouldn't dream of cruising in the mainstream sense aboard warehouse-size ships and who don't demand a high standard of service. It's a basic, no-glitz vessel, providing an all-American cruise experience, albeit at a high price, and is not for children.

THE SHIP. *Grande Mariner* is the second of two almost identical Blount-built vessels. Like sister ship *Grande Caribe*, it has stabilizers. During emergency drill, passengers are taught how to use fire extinguishers – a useful piece of training.

The ship's shallow draft enables it to cruise into off-the-beaten-path destinations well out of reach of larger ships. It also has a retractable navigation bridge – practical for those low bridges along inland waterways. An underwater video camera allows passengers, while seated in comfort in the lounge, to view on large-screen TV monitors what a scuba diver might see underneath the ship. Underwater lights, which attract fish and other marine life, are fitted. There are two 24-passenger launches, one of which is a glass-bottomed boat, and snorkeling equipment.

There is one lounge/bar, located on a different deck to the dining room. The style is casual – no jackets or ties – by day and night. An electric stairway chairlift is provided for those with restricted mobility. Gratuities (high at the suggested $10–$15 per person, per day) are pooled and shared by all the staff.

Berlitz's Ratings	Possible	Achieved
Ship	500	159
Accommodation	200	67
Food	400	180
Service	400	194
Entertainment	100	35
Cruise	400	169
OVERALL SCORE		
804 points out of 2000		

ACCOMMODATION. The cabins are all extremely small, relatively utilitarian units, with very little closet space but just enough drawers. The very small bathrooms have new vacuum toilets. The twin beds convert to queen-size beds, with good storage space under them. There is no room service menu, and only soap is supplied – bring your own toiletries. Each cabin has its own air conditioner, so passengers don't have to share air with the rest of the ship. Refreshingly, there are no cabin keys. Be prepared for noise from the generators.

DINING. The dining room seats all passengers in one open seating, so you dine with whomever you wish, making new friends each day – it is also good for small groups. The tables convert to card tables for use between meals. Passengers should bring their own alcohol, as the company doesn't sell it aboard ship. Effervescent, young American waitresses provide the service, although there is no finesse.

A hand-held colonial bell is rung to summon passengers to the dining room.

ENTERTAINMENT. There is no formal entertainment, so conversation with fellow passengers in the ship's lounge/bar becomes the entertainment each evening. If that isn't appealing, take a good book.

SPA/FITNESS. There are no facilities.

Grandeur of the Seas
★★★+

Size:.	.Large Resort Ship	Cabins (total):.	.975
Tonnage:.	74,137	Size range (sq ft/m):	.158.2–1,267.0/14.7–117.7
Lifestyle:.	.Standard	Cabins (outside view):.	.576
Cruise line:.	Royal Caribbean International	Cabins (interior/no view):.	.399
Former names:.	.none	Cabins (for one person):.	.0
IMO number:.	9102978	Cabins (with private balcony):.	.212
Builder:.	Kvaerner Masa-Yards (Finland)	Cabins (wheelchair accessible):.	.14
Original cost:.	.$300 million	Wheelchair accessibility:.	.Good
Entered service:.	Dec 1996	Cabin voltage:.	.110 and 220 volts
Registry:.	The Bahamas	Elevators:.	.9
Length (ft/m):.	916.0/279.6	Casino (gaming tables):.	.Yes
Beam (ft/m):.	105.6/32.2	Slot machines:.	.Yes
Draft (ft/m):.	25.5/7.6	Swimming pools:.	.2 (1 w/sliding glass dome)
Propulsion/Propellers:.	diesel-electric (50,400kW)/2	Hot tubs (on deck):.	.6
Passenger decks:.	.11	Self-service launderette:.	.No
Total crew:.	.760	Dedicated cinema/seats:.	.No
Passengers (lower beds/alll berths):.	1,950/2,446	Library:.	.Yes
Passenger Space Ratio (lower beds/all berths):.	38.0/30.3	Onboard currency:.	.US$
Crew/Passenger Ratio (lower beds/all berths):.	2.5/3.2		

Big family-friendly ship with multiple-choice dining

OVERVIEW. Grandeur of the Seas has a good interior passenger flow. It also features a varied collection of artworks including several sculptures, principally by British artists, with classical music, ballet, and theater themes. Huge murals of opera scenes adorn several stairways. The children's and teens' facilities are quite decent – good for families.

THE SHIP. *Grandeur of the Seas* (sister ships are *Enchantment of the Seas, Legend of the Seas, Rhapsody of the Seas, Splendor of the Seas* and *Vision of the Seas*) has an attractive contemporary profile, with a single funnel located well aft – it's almost a throwback to some ship designs used in the 1950s. The ship also has a nicely rounded stern. A large Viking Crown Lounge, a trademark of Royal Caribbean International ships, sits between funnel and mast at the top of the atrium lobby, and overlooks the forward section of the swimming pool deck, with access provided from stairway off the central atrium. This, together with the forward mast, provides three distinct focal points of the ship's exterior profile. There is a walk-around promenade deck outdoors, but there are no cushioned pads for the tacky home patio-style plastic sunloungers.

The principal interior focal point is a seven-deck-high Centrum (atrium lobby), which is a good meeting point – the Purser's Desk and Shore Excursion Desk are on one of the lower levels. Many public entertainment rooms and facilities connect with the atrium. The large, glitzy casino (on deck 5) has a fascinating,

Berlitz's Ratings

	Possible	Achieved
Ship	500	377
Accommodation	200	140
Food	400	238
Service	400	262
Entertainment	100	73
Cruise	400	263
OVERALL SCORE		
1353 points out of 2000		

somewhat theatrical glass-covered but underfloor exhibit. Two conference rooms also provide space card- and board game players; there's also a small library.

There is a good use of tropical plants throughout the public rooms, which helps counteract the otherwise rather plain and clinical pastel wall colors.

Niggles include the fact that RCI charges for shuttle buses in many ports of call; the cost of bottles water is high; and receipts show an extra line 'for additional gratuity' when a gratuity has been added automatically.

ACCOMMODATION. There are numerous price grades, including five grades for suites. The price depends on grade, size, and location, with location and grade perhaps more important since so many of the cabins are of the same, or a very similar size. All are well appointed and have pleasing decor, best described as Scandinavian Moderne, with good wood and color accenting. There are, however, a huge number of interior (no view) cabins.

Royal Suite. This is the largest accommodation, located directly aft of the navigation bridge on the starboard side. It has a separate bedroom with king-size bed, walk-in closet and vanity dressing area, living room with queen-size sofa bed, baby grand piano, refrigerator and wet bar, dining table, entertainment center, and large private balcony. The bathroom has a whirlpool tub, separate shower enclosure, two washbasins, and toilet.

Owner's Suites (5). These suites are at the forward end of the ship, just behind the navigation bridge. They have a queen-size bed, separate living area with queen-size sofa bed, vanity dressing area, refrigerator and wet bar. The bathroom has a full-size tub, separate shower enclosure, toilet and two washbasins.

Royal Family Suites (4). These suites include two bedrooms with twin beds that convert to queen-size beds, living area with double sofa bed and Pullman bed, refrigerator, two bathrooms (one with tub), and private balcony. They can accommodate eight, and so might suit families.

Grand Suites (12). These have twin beds that convert to a queen-size bed, vanity dressing area, lounge area with sofa bed, refrigerator, and a bathroom with tub, plus a private balcony.

Superior Suites (44). These suites, including two suites for the disabled, have twin beds that convert to a queen-size bed, vanity dressing area, lounge area with sofa bed, refrigerator, plus private balcony, and a bathroom with tub. Although they are called suites, they really are little more than larger standard cabins with a balcony.

Other grades. All standard cabins have twin beds that convert to a queen-size bed, ample closet space for a one-week cruise, and a good amount of drawer space, although under-bed storage space is not good for large suitcases. The bathrooms have nine mirrors. Plastic buckets are provided for Champagne or wine and are really tacky.

All grades of suite/cabin include a hairdryer. The room service menu is really minimal, with only the most basic selection – there are no hot items for breakfast, for example.

DINING. The 1,195-seat Great Gatsby Dining Room is spread over two decks, with both levels connected by a grand, sweeping staircase. When you book, choose one of the two seatings for dinner or 'My Time Dining' – so you can eat when you want, during dining room hours. A neat Champagne terrace bar sits forward of the lower level of the two-deck-high dining room.

Other dining options. A cavernous, 790-seat, glass-walled Windjammer Café is a rather non-descript casual, eatery for self-serve breakfast, lunch and dinner buffet items. Note that there are no cups and saucers for tea – only paper cups or plastic mugs.

For decent (extra-cost) Seattle's Best espresso/cappuccino, head for Caffe Latte-tudes on Deck 6.

In an extensive refit in 2012, extra dining options were added. These include Giovanni's Table, an Italian trattoria (a service charge applies); Izumi (located in a delightful spot just forward of the funnel) for pan-Asian cuisine including hot-rock cooking (service charge and à la carte menu pricing apply); Park Café outdoor market; Chops Grille steakhouse; and Chef's Table – an exclusive hosted event (it is located on the starboard side aft, within the dining room) with a five-course, wine-paired menu – worth it to celebrate a birthday or special event, perhaps.

ENTERTAINMENT. The 875-seat Palladium Theater is the ship's principal showlounge. It is located at the forward part of the ship, and is used for big production shows. It has excellent sight lines from 98 percent of the seats.

Another showlounge, the 575-seat South Pacific Lounge, is used for smaller shows and cabaret acts, including smutty late-night adult-only comedy.

SPA/FITNESS. The Vitality at Sea spa is aft of the funnel and spans two decks. Facilities include a gymnasium with all the latest muscle-pumping exercise machines, aerobics exercise room, sauna and steam rooms, a beauty salon, and a clutch of private massage/body treatment rooms. The spa is staffed and operated by specialist Steiner Leisure.

For the sporting, there is activity galore – including a rock-climbing wall with several separate climbing tracks. It is located outdoors at the aft end of the funnel (just behind the Vitality at Sea spa). A jogging track takes you around most of the ship (it's outside, on Deck 10)

Hamburg
★★★ +

Size:. . . . . Small Ship		Cabins (total):. 205	
Tonnage: 14,903		Size range (sq ft/m): 139.9–339.0/13.0–31.5	
Lifestyle: . . . . .Standard		Cabins (outside view):. 158	
Cruise line:. . . . . .Plantours Cruises		Cabins (interior/no view):. 47	
Former names: . . . .*Columbus*		Cabins (for one person):. 2	
IMO number: 9138329		Cabins (with private balcony):. 2	
Builder: . . . . MTW Schiffswerft (Germany)		Cabins (wheelchair accessible): 2	
Original cost:. . . . . $69 million		Wheelchair accessibility:. . . . . .Fair	
Entered service:. . . . . .Jul 1997/Jun 2012		Cabin voltage: . . . . 220 volts	
Registry:. . . . . The Bahamas		Elevators:. 2	
Length (ft/m):. 472.8/144.1		Casino (gaming tables):. . . . . .No	
Beam (ft/m):. 70.5/21.5		Slot machines:. . . . . .No	
Draft (ft/m):. 16.8/5.1		Swimming pools:. 1	
Propulsion/Propellers:. . . . . diesel (10,560kW)/2		Hot tubs (on deck):. 0	
Passenger decks:. 6		Self-service launderette:. . . . . .No	
Total crew:. 170		Dedicated cinema/seats:. . . . . .No	
Passengers (lower beds/alll berths):. 408/421		Library: . . . . .Yes	
Passenger Space Ratio (lower beds/all berths): 36.5/35.3		Onboard currency: . . . . Euros	
Crew/Passenger Ratio (lower beds/all berths):. 2.4/2.4			

A small ship for worldwide port-intensive cruising

OVERVIEW. This ship will appeal to youthful-minded German-speaking couples and single travelers seeking good value for money on a first cruise, aboard a ship with contemporary, comfortable but not pretentious surroundings, and good itineraries, at a very modest price.

THE SHIP. Hamburg has an ice-strengthened hull, useful for cold-weather cruise areas. While it's a comfortable, trendy ship, the swimming pool is small – it's really a 'plunge' pool – as is the open deck space, and there is no walk-around promenade deck outdoors.

The delightful Palm Garden doubles as anobservation lounge and has four Internet-connect computers. Shipwide Wi-Fi is also available. The fit and finish of the interiors is a little utilitarian – the mottled gray walls are somewhat cold, but a contrast to the splashes of color found in carpeting and other decorative touches.

ACCOMMODATION. The standard cabins are really small. All but 10 cabins have lower berths. Except for two forward-facing suites, there are no balcony cabins, and no room service except for accommodation designated as suites. There are several single-occupancy cabins. Note that 16 cabins on Deck 4 have lifeboat-obstructed views. The cabin decor is bright and upbeat, and there's a good amount of closet and shelf space. All cabins have a mini-bar/refrigerator, flat-screen TV, personal safe, and hairdryer.

Berlitz's Ratings

	Possible	Achieved
Ship	500	343
Accommodation	200	145
Food	400	267
Service	400	288
Entertainment	100	60
Cruise	400	262

OVERALL SCORE
1365 points out of 2000

There are eight suites, each at least double the size of a standard cabin and each with a curtained partition between its lounge and sleeping areas. Two suites at the bows each have a narrow private veranda, a bedroom and lounge area separated by a curtain, two TV sets, and an excellent amount of storage space.

DINING. There's one large main dining room, at the stern, with large ocean-view windows on three sides. All passengers can be seated in a single seating, at assigned tables, although breakfast is open-seating. There are just two tables for two, but other tables can accommodate up to 16. The unstuffy cuisine is good, though the choice is small. Themed dinners make dining a treat. Breakfast and lunch can also be taken in the bright, but casual, setting of the self-serve Palm Garden, which doubles as a comfortable observation lounge. Light dinners can also be taken there; a small dance floor adds another dimension.

ENTERTAINMENT. The showlounge is a single-level, H-shaped room, with banquette and individual seating in tub chairs, and a bar, which is located at the back of the room. Because the apron stage is in the center of the room, the sight lines from many seats aren't good.

SPA/FITNESS. A fitness room is located forward on the uppermost deck of the ship. There's a sauna on the lowest passenger deck, next to the beauty salon. Massage and facial treatments are available.

Hanseatic
★★★★★

Size:	Boutique Ship
Tonnage:	8,378
Lifestyle:	Luxury
Cruise line:	Hapag-Lloyd Expedition Cruises
Former names:	Society Adventurer
IMO number:	5321679
Builder:	Rauma Yards (Finland)
Original cost:	$68 million
Entered service:	Mar 1993
Registry:	The Bahamas
Length (ft/m):	402.9/122.8
Beam (ft/m):	59.1/18.0
Draft (ft/m):	16.1/4.9
Propulsion/Propellers:	diesel (5,880kW)/2
Passenger decks:	7
Total crew:	122
Passengers (lower beds/all berths):	184/194
Passenger Space Ratio (lower beds/all berths):	45.5/43.1
Crew/Passenger Ratio (lower beds/all berths):	1.5/1.5

Cabins (total):	92
Size range (sq ft/m):	231.4–470.3/21.5–43.7
Cabins (outside view):	92
Cabins (interior/no view):	0
Cabins (for one person):	0
Cabins (with private balcony):	0
Cabins (wheelchair accessible):	2
Wheelchair accessibility:	None
Cabin voltage:	220 volts
Elevators:	2
Casino (gaming tables):	0
Slot machines:	0
Swimming pools:	1
Hot tubs (on deck):	1
Self-service launderette:	No
Dedicated cinema/seats:	Yes
Library:	Yes
Onboard currency:	Euros

A delightful, small and stylish expedition ship for discovery

OVERVIEW. *Hanseatic* provides destination-intensive, nature cruises and expeditions in elegant but un-stuffy surroundings at a suitably handsome price that ensures good food and service. It is at its best in the Arctic and Antarctic, but passengers should be wary of the difficult conditions for shore landings in these areas.

THE SHIP. *Hanseatic*, operated by Hapag-Lloyd Cruises, was designed for worldwide expedition-style cruises in contemporary, but quite luxurious, surroundings. It is extremely environmentally friendly, and is one of few ships that allow you to tour the engine room. It has a fully enclosed bridge and an ice-hardened hull with the highest passenger vessel ice classification, plus a helicopter pad and the very latest in high-tech navigation equipment.

A fleet of 14 Zodiac inflatable craft, each named after a famous explorer, is used for in-depth shore landings (including one named David Fletcher, the celebrated expedition leader who spent 16 years working with the British Antarctic Expedition – he loves being aboard Hanseatic). These craft provide the ship with tremendous flexibility in itineraries, with excellent possibilities for up-close wildlife viewing in natural habitats. Rubber boots, parkas, boot-washing and storage rooms are provided. For warmer climes, a Bike Box, with 10 bicycles for passenger use at no charge, is offloaded in each port the ship is alongside, where possible.

Berlitz's Ratings

	Possible	Achieved
Ship	500	446
Accommodation	200	173
Food	400	348
Service	400	346
Entertainment	100	88
Cruise	400	364

OVERALL SCORE
1765 points out of 2000

Inside, the ship is equipped with fine-quality luxury fittings and soft furnishings, and exudes a microclimate of good taste. There is a choice of several public rooms – most located aft, with accommodation forward. All are well-furnished and decorated, and all have high ceilings which help make the ship feel much larger than its actual size. The library/observation lounge provides a good selection of hardback books in English and German, including many geographical, travel, wildlife, and archaeology titles; it has a sunken bar, and a warm, inviting atmosphere, and two Internet-access computer stations. A large lecture hall, with excellent audio-visual facilities, on a lower deck, can accommodate almost all passengers.

The passenger count is generally kept to about 150, which means plenty of comfort, no lines, and lots of space. In passageways and suites/cabins, 400 large, framed, black and white photographs depict wildlife and expedition experiences. Bouillon is always served at 11am.

Safety is paramount, particularly in Antarctica, and here the ship excels with professionalism, pride, and skilled seamanship. Most of each day is taken up with being ashore, and evenings consist mainly of dinner and daily recaps. Lectures, briefings, and the amount of information provided about the itinerary, ports of call and expedition landings are excellent. Well-qualified lecturers and naturalists accompany each cruise, and a discreet crew and service staff are hallmarks of this ship.

Hanseatic operates in two languages, English and German, though many staff speak several languages, and it caters well to both sets of passengers. All port taxes, insurance, staff gratuities, and Zodiac trips are included. A relaxed ambience and informal dress code prevail.

There are few negatives. The ship is marketed mainly to German and English speakers, so other nationalities may find it hard to integrate. Hapag-Lloyd publishes its own excellent handbooks (in both English and German) on expedition regions such as the Arctic, Antarctica, Amazonia, and the South Sea Islands, as well as exclusive maps.

ACCOMMODATION. There are no bad cabins, and accommodation is priced in seven grades. The all-outside cabins, located in the forward section, are large and very well equipped, and include a separate lounge area next to a large picture window (which has a pull-down blackout blind as well as curtains).

All furniture is in warm woods such as beech, and everything has rounded edges. Wood trim accents the ceiling perimeter, and acts as a divider between bed and lounge areas. Each cabin has a mini-bar, flat-screen interactive TV with Internet access, when available, and wireless keyboard. A complete infotainment system includes movies and audio tracks on demand at no extra charge. There's a separate bedside three-channel radio, two locking drawers, a retro alarm clock, and plenty of closet and drawer space, as well as two separate cupboards and hooks for all-weather outerwear. One useful feature of all cabins is a blue, night/safety light, nicely hidden in each bathroom. A privacy curtain between the cabin door and the sleeping area of the cabin would be useful – you can be seen from the hallway when the cabin door is opened.

All cabin bathrooms have a large shower enclosure with curved glass wall, toiletries cabinets, hairdryer, and bathrobe. There are only two types of cabins; 34 have double beds, others have twin beds. The bath-size towels are large, bed linens and pillowcases are 100 percent cotton, and individual cotton-filled duvet covers are provided. Laundry, dry cleaning, and pressing services are available.

Suites and cabins on Bridge Deck have impeccable butler service and in-cabin dining privileges, plus stationery and a larger flat-screen TV. Free soft drinks in the refrigerator are replenished daily, but all liquor costs extra. Bulgari and Crabtree & Evelyn amenities are provided.

DINING. The 186-seat Marco Polo restaurant is elegant, warm, and welcoming, with large picture windows on two sides as well as aft. There is one seating for dinner, and open seating for breakfast and lunch, although many passengers like to be seated at their 'regular' table. On embarkation day, waiters introduce themselves after the meal, so hungry passengers won't be delayed by small talk.

The cuisine and service are absolutely first-rate, but are slightly more informal than, for example, aboard the larger Europa, which is at or close to the same price level. Top-quality ingredients are always used, and most items are bought fresh when available. In some ports, passengers can go shopping with the chef to source local, regional ingredients and fresh fish.

The meals are very creative and nicely presented, each being appealing to the eye as well as to the palate. There is always an outstanding selection of breads, cheeses, desserts, and pastry items. In the Arctic or Antarctic, table setups are often minimal, due to possible movement of the ship – stabilizers can't be used in much of the Antarctic – so cutlery is provided and changed for each course. Three types of sugar are presented when coffee or tea is ordered – it should never be placed on the table during meal service.

An alternative dining spot is the Bistro Lemaire, with 74 seats and leather-topped tables indoors, as well as copious seating at outdoor tables. An informal, open seating, self-serve (or waiter service) buffet-style eatery by day, it changes into a second dining room at night, with themed dinners and barbeques featuring region-specific food. Reservations are required – you make them in the morning of the day you want to dine there – but there is no extra charge and no tipping.

The Bistro features four different breakfast themes: the well-named Zodiac breakfast (quick and easy before Zodiac landing); Small Hanseatic Breakfast; Big Hanseatic Breakfast; Gourmet Breakfast; Healthy Breakfast. Each cruise also includes a full Viennese teatime, as well as a daily teatime with a selection of cakes, pastries, and finger sandwiches befitting a Viennese coffeehouse.

ENTERTAINMENT. There is no showlounge as such, although there is a lecture room. Entertainment is certainly not a priority aboard this ship, but the itinerary and destinations are the main show. There is no formal entertainment – except on some summer cruises, when a small classical music ensemble might be on board – nor does the ship normally carry a band.

SPA/FITNESS. The spa facilities include a decent-size gymnasium (with up-to-date cardio-vascular and muscle-toning equipment, treadmills, and exercycles) and sauna, all located forward on the Sun Deck in an area that also includes a solarium and hot tub. There's also a cosmetics/make-up room. Massage is available in a rather clinical room within the medical facility, on a lower deck.

Hebridean Princess
★★★★ +

Size:.....................................Boutique Ship	Cabins (total):...30
Tonnage: 2,112	Size range (sq ft/m):.................144.0–340.0/13.4–31.6
Lifestyle: ....Luxury	Cabins (outside view):......................................24
Cruise line:.....................Hebridean Island Cruises	Cabins (interior/no view):...................................6
Former names: ....Columba	Cabins (for one person):....................................10
IMO number:................................6409351	Cabins (with private balcony):................................4
Builder: ....Hall Russell (Scotland)	Cabins (wheelchair accessible): 0
Original cost:..n/a	Wheelchair accessibility:................................None
Entered service:.........................1964/May 1989	Cabin voltage: ....240 volts
Registry:...................................Great Britain	Elevators:..0
Length (ft/m):...............................235.0/71.6	Casino (gaming tables):...................................No
Beam (ft/m):................................46.0/14.0	Slot machines:...No
Draft (ft/m):.................................10.0/3.0	Swimming pools:...0
Propulsion/Propellers:.....................diesel (1,790kW)/2	Hot tubs (on deck):......................................0
Passenger decks:.....................................5	Self-service launderette:..................................No
Total crew:...38	Dedicated cinema/seats:..................................No
Passengers (lower beds/alll berths):..................50/50	Library:...Yes
Passenger Space Ratio (lower beds/all berths):.......42.2/42.2	Onboard currency: ....UK£
Crew/Passenger Ratio (lower beds/all berths):..........1.3/1.3	

This English country inn afloat is the real McCoy

OVERVIEW. This charming little ship has a warm, totally cosseted, traditional Scottish country house ambience and a stately home service that's unobtrusive but always at hand when you need it. It suits mature-age adult couples and single travelers who enjoy learning about the natural sciences, geography, history, gardening, art, architecture, and enjoy a very small ship with almost no entertainment.

THE SHIP. Small and old can be chic and comfortable. *Hebridean Princess*, originally one of three Scottish ferries built for David MacBrayne Ltd – although actually owned by the British government – was skillfully converted into a gem of a cruise ship in order to operate island-hopping itineraries in Scotland, together with the occasional jaunt to Norway and an occasional sailing around the UK coast. It was renamed in 1989 by the Duchess of York.

There is an outdoors deck for occasional sunbathing and alfresco meals, as well as a bar where occasional formal cocktail parties are held when weather conditions are right. There is no walk-around promenade deck, although there is an open deck atop ship. The ship carries two Zodiac inflatable runabouts (Calgary and Kiloran) and two Hardy shore tenders (*Sanda* and *Shona*).

Use of the ship's small boats, speedboat, a dozen or so bicycles, and fishing gear are included in the price, as are entrance fees to gardens, castles, other attractions, and the occasional coach tour, depending on the itinerary. The destination-intensive cruises have very creative itineraries and there's plenty to do, despite the

Berlitz's Ratings		
	Possible	Achieved
Ship	500	410
Accommodation	200	174
Food	400	349
Service	400	342
Entertainment	100	84
Cruise	400	319
OVERALL SCORE		
1678 points out of 2000		

lack of big-ship features. Specialist guides, who give daily talks about the destinations to be visited and some fascinating history and the local folklore, accompany all cruises.

What passengers appreciate is the fact that the ship does not have photographers or some of the trappings found aboard larger ships. They also love the fact that there is no bingo, art auctions, or mindless parlor games.

The principal public room inside the ship is the charming Tiree Lounge, which has a real brick-walled inglenook fireplace, plus a very cozy bar with a wide variety of whiskies – the selection of single malts is excellent – and cognacs for connoisseurs. Naturally, the ship specializes in Scottish spirits.

Agatha Christie's Inspector Hercule Poirot would be very much at home here, particularly in the Tiree Lounge. Who needs megaships when you can take a retro-cruise aboard this little gem? Direct bookings are accepted.

Hebridean Princess has UK officers and an excellent Lithuanian service crew; all are discreet and provide unobtrusive service. This little ship remains one of the world's best-kept travel secrets, although Queen Elizabeth II chartered the ship for a family-only celebration of her 80th birthday in 2006, and again for a family holiday in 2010.

A roughly polished gem, it is especially popular with single passengers. More than half the passengers are repeaters. Children under nine are not accepted. Despite the shortcomings of the ship itself, it's the food that rates highly.

If you cruise from Oban, you can be met at Glasgow station (or airport) and taken to/from the ship by private motor coach. Passengers are piped aboard at embarkation by a Scottish bagpiper – a neat touch. All drinks (except premium brands, which incur a small charge), soft drinks, and bottled Scottish mineral water are included in the fare, as are gratuities – the company requests that no additional gratuities be given.

Although this vessel is strong, it does have structural limitations and noisy engines that cause some vibration. However, the engines do not run at night because the ship anchors before bedtime, providing soul-renewing tranquility – except for the sound of a single generator. The ship doesn't have an elevator, so anyone with walking disabilities may find it challenging – and there may be several tender ports on each itinerary. It is often cold and very wet in the Scottish highlands and islands, so take plenty of warm clothing for layering.

ACCOMMODATION. All cabins have different color schemes and names – there are no numbers, and, refreshingly, no door keys, although cabins can be locked from the inside. No two cabins are identical – they are individually created, with delightfully eclectic curtains, sweeping drapes over the beds, and lots of cushions. They really are quite different from almost all other cruise ships, and come in a wide range of configurations (some with single, some with double, some with twin beds), including four with a private balcony – a private and self-indulgent bonus.

All cabins have a private bathroom with bath or shower (two cabins share a bathroom). All have a refrigerator, ironing board with iron, trouser press, brass clock, and tea/coffee-making set – there's something magical about getting up in the morning, making fresh tea in your cabin using mineral water and organic teas, and sitting outside on a protected balcony watching Scotland's islands come and go. All seems right with the world.

Cabins have Victorian-style bathroom fittings, many gold-plated, and some have brass cabin portholes or windows that actually open. Three of the newest cabins are outfitted in real Scottish Baronial style. All towels and bathrobe are 100 percent cotton, as is the bed linen. Some cabins in the front of the ship are subject to the noise of the anchor being weighed each morning.

Each cabin has Villeroy and Boch china, fair trade coffee, organic teas, and fresh milk – not the irradiated long-life milk or chemical milk found aboard many ships these days.

DINING. The Columba Restaurant has ocean-view windows and tables laid with crisp white linen. Classic white Schonwald china is provided. There is a single seating at assigned tables. Some chairs have armrests

while some do not. While days are casual, dinner means jackets and ties, and formal attire typically twice per cruise.

The cuisine is extremely creative, and at times outstanding – and about the same quality and presentation as *SeaDream I* and *SeaDream II*, although, usually, menus offer just one meat and one fish dish (a different fish each day), plus an alternative, casual option. Fresh, taste-filled ingredients are sourced and purchased locally, supporting Scottish suppliers – a welcome change from the mass catering of most ships. Although there are no flambé items – the galley has electric, not gas, ranges – what is created is beautifully presented and of the highest standard. The desserts are also worth saving space for.

The breakfast menu is standard each day, although you can always ask for any favorites, and each day there's a specialty item, plus a help-yourself buffet table. Try the porridge and a 'wee dram' (Scotch whisky – single malt, of course) – it's lovely on a cold morning, and it sets you up for the whole day.

Not to be missed is the exclusive theatrical treat 'a tasting o' haggis wi' bashed neeps an champit tatties,' accompanied by bagpipe music and an 'address to the haggis' ceremony, traditionally given by the captain. Although there is waiter service for most things, there is also a good buffet table display during breakfast and luncheon. Wines are provided at lunch and dinner, although an additional connoisseur's list is available for those seeking fine vintage wines. Highly personal and attentive service from an attentive staff completes the picture.

ENTERTAINMENT. The Tiree Lounge is the equivalent of a main lounge aboard this very small ship. Dinner is the entertainment of the evening. Occasionally, there might be after-dinner drinks, poetry readings, and an occasional storyteller, but little else (passengers neither expect nor need it).

SPA/FITNESS. There is no spa, as the ship is too small. The only concessions to fitness are an exercycle and treadmill.

Henna
★★ +

Size:.. Mid-size Ship		Cabins (total):..743	
Tonnage: 47,252		Size range (sq ft/m): 182.9-419.8/17.0-39.0	
Lifestyle: ....Standard		Cabins (outside view):..453	
Cruise line:................................HNA Tourism		Cabins (interior/no view):....................................290	
Former names: .... Pacific Sun, Jubilee		Cabins (for one person):.......................................0	
IMO number: 8314122		Cabins (with private balcony):................................10	
Builder: .... Kockums (Sweden)		Cabins (wheelchair accessible): 14	
Original cost:...............................$134 million		Wheelchair accessibility:....................................Fair	
Entered service:.....................Jul 1986/Jan 2013		Cabin voltage: .... 110 volts	
Registry:................................. The Bahamas		Elevators:..8	
Length (ft/m):............................. 733.0/223.4		Casino (gaming tables):....................................Yes	
Beam (ft/m):................................. 92.5/28.2		Slot machines:..Yes	
Draft (ft/m): 24.7/7.5		Swimming pools:..3	
Propulsion/Propellers:................ diesel (23,520kW)/2		Hot tubs (on deck):..2	
Passenger decks:..................................9		Self-service launderette:....................................Yes	
Total crew:.....................................670		Dedicated cinema/seats:....................................No	
Passengers (lower beds/alll berths):.............. 1,486/1,896		Library: ....Yes	
Passenger Space Ratio (lower beds/all berths): 31.8/24.9		Onboard currency: .... Chinese Yuan	
Crew/Passenger Ratio (lower beds/all berths):.......... 2.2/2.8			

Casual, family-friendly older ship for Chinese-speakers

OVERVIEW. *Henna* is aimed at the Chinese-language cruiser seeking a basic cruise with good drinking places and lots of noise.

THE SHIP. This ship has a bold, forthright, angular all-white profile, short bows, and a pencil-slim funnel. Most of the public rooms are arranged on one deck. A double-wide indoor promenade acts as a boulevard. The decor consists of contemporary colors in all the public rooms. One of the major attractions is the casino, with multiple gaming tables, and lots of slot machines. The ship is designed for passenger participation in a party-like setting for families with children, and active adults who enjoy constant stimulation. There's plenty for kids to do; facilities include a children's club and activity center. Passenger niggles: there is no walk-around promenade deck outdoors.

ACCOMMODATION. There are several different price categories for ocean-view and interior cabins and two categories for suites. Quite nice are 10 large suites on Verandah Deck, each with a private balcony, although there are obstructed views from four of them. Almost all other cabins are spacious units that are neatly appointed and have utilitarian decor. The ocean-view cabins have large picture windows, and you should try to book one of these cabins. There are many interior cabins, although they are actually fairly spacious. They have two lower beds, a small vanity unit, and a reasonable-sized bathroom. Some cabins

Berlitz's Ratings

	Possible	Achieved
Ship	500	282
Accommodation	200	109
Food	400	208
Service	400	207
Entertainment	100	55
Cruise	400	200
OVERALL SCORE		
1061 points out of 2000		

have additional upper berths, and even rollaway beds.

DINING. There are two dining rooms: Burgundy, located amidships, and Bordeaux, located aft. They are cramped and noisy, and they have low ceilings. There are tables for four, six, or eight, but none for two, and many banquette seats (individual chairs don't have armrests). Window-side tables are for six and are typically the quietest. The Lido Deck poolside self-serve Grill offers casual meals. At night, it provides a dress-down alternative to eating in the main dining rooms, serving pasta, steaks, salads and desserts. For casual food there's also a sushi bar and a poolside pizzeria.

ENTERTAINMENT. The Showlounge, the principal venue for production shows, is two decks high, decorated in glitz, and has seating on both main and balcony levels. However, pillars obstruct the sight lines on the main level, and railings obstruct sight lines from many seats on the balcony level. The entertainment is all-Chinese. The room also doubles as a cinema for big-screen movies.

SPA/FITNESS. The Spa is on the ship's uppermost deck, just aft of the mast, and accessed by the center stairway and lifts. The facility is small by today's standards, but a former gym is now a relaxation area, while a new gym with has views over the stern. There are changing rooms and saunas.

Horizon
★★★ +

Size:.	Mid-size Ship	Cabins (total):.	721
Tonnage:.	47427	Size range (sq ft/m):.	172.2–500.5/16–46.5
Lifestyle:.	Standard	Cabins (outside view):.	573
Cruise line:.	CDF Croisieres de France	Cabins (interior/no view):.	148
Former names:.	Pacific Dream, Island Star, Horizon	Cabins (for one person):.	0
IMO number:.	8807088	Cabins (with private balcony):.	68
Builder:.	Meyer Werft (Germany)	Cabins (wheelchair accessible):.	Good
Original cost:.	$185 million	Wheelchair accessibility:.	Good
Entered service:.	May 1990/Apr 2012	Cabin voltage:.	110 and 220 volts
Registry:.	Malta	Elevators:.	7
Length (ft/m):.	682.4/208.0	Casino (gaming tables):.	Yes
Beam (ft/m):.	95.1/29.0	Slot machines:.	Yes
Draft (ft/m):.	23.6/7.2	Swimming pools:.	2
Propulsion/Propellers:.	diesel (19,960kW)/2	Hot tubs (on deck):.	3
Passenger decks:.	10	Self-service launderette:.	No
Total crew:.	620	Dedicated cinema/seats:.	No
Passengers (lower beds/alll berths):.	1,442/1,534	Library:.	Yes
Passenger Space Ratio (lower beds/all berths):.	32.8/30.5	Onboard currency:.	Euros
Crew/Passenger Ratio (lower beds/all berths):.	2.0/2.4		

A family-friendly casual ship for French-speakers

OVERVIEW. This ship is quite suited to young (and young at heart) French-speaking couples, singles, and families with children of all ages who want a first cruise experience in a smart, almost elegant ship, with plenty of public rooms, a lively atmosphere, and a French cruise experience.

THE SHIP. *Horizon* was originally built for, owned and operated by Celebrity Cruises. Although now well over 20 years old, it still has a fairly contemporary, though angular profile that gives the impression of power and speed thanks to its blue hull (the hull itself was designed by mega-yacht designer Jon Bannenberg). CDF Croisieres de France took over the ship – from Pullmantur Cruises – in April 2012.

The exterior pool deck features one large pool and another for children, plus a couple of hot tubs, and in-built shower enclosures.

Inside, there is a similar interior layout to its sister ship – *Pullmantur Cruises' Zenith*, with décor that is quite restrained, even elegant. The feeling is one of uncluttered surroundings, and the ship features some interesting artwork. Soothing, pastel colors and high-quality soft furnishings are used throughout the interiors. The decks are named after colors (cobalt, turquoise, indigo, etc.).

An elegant Art Deco-style hotel-like lobby, reminiscent of Miami Beach hotels, has a two-deck-high ceiling and a spacious feel, and is the contact point for the reception desk, shore excursions, and onboard accounts counters.

Berlitz's Ratings

	Possible	Achieved
Ship	500	365
Accommodation	200	140
Food	400	236
Service	400	264
Entertainment	100	61
Cruise	400	258

OVERALL SCORE
1324 points out of 2000

The principal deck that houses many of the public entertainment rooms (located two decks above the lobby, has a double-width indoor promenade – good for strolling and people watching. There is a decent-size library. Other facilities include a large Zephyr Lounge Bar; a Jame's Piano Bar – with quasi-fireplace and Internet-connect center; and a Café Moka – for coffee and chat (téte a téte). A large, elegantly appointed Monte Carlo Casino has its own bar.

CDF Croisiers de France changed some of the public rooms and open areas, and has added splashes of bright colors, motifs, and new signage. The hospitality and the range and variety of food have been tailored to its French-speaking family clientele. Expect to find an abundance of children during the peak holiday periods, when the passenger rmix becomes younger.

Passenger niggles? Lines for embarkation, disembarkation, shore tenders, and for self-serve buffet meals. The doors to the public restrooms and the outdoor decks are very heavy. The public restrooms are clinical and need some refreshing décor change. There are no cushioned pads for the poolside sunloungers.

FAMILIES. CDF Croisieres de France has a good program for children and teenagers, with specially trained youth counselors, and a decent range of activities, although the children's play areas are not extensive (because this is a mid-size ship and not a large resort ship). Children under 3 travel free. All drinks are included, which makes things simpler for families with children.

ACCOMMODATION. There are several price grades, including outside-view suites and cabins, and interior cabins. Note that many of the outside-view cabins on the safety equipment deck have lifeboat-obstructed views.

Standard Cabins. The outside-view and interior cabins have good-quality fittings with lots of wood accenting, are tastefully decorated and of an above-average size, with an excellent amount of closet and drawer space and reasonable insulation between cabins. All have twin beds that convert to a queen-size bed, and a good amount of closet and drawer space. The cabin soundproofing is quite good although this depends on location – some cabins are located opposite crew access doors, which can be busy and noisy. The bathrooms have a generous shower area, and a small range of toiletries is provided, although towels are a little small, as is storage space for toiletries. The lowest priced outside-view cabins have a porthole, but all others have picture windows.

Royal Suites. The largest accommodation is in two Royal Suites midships on Atlantic Deck (Deck 10), and forward on Marina Deck. These have a large private balcony and a separate bedroom and lounge, a dining area with glass dining table, plus CD and DVD players in addition to a large television. The bathroom is also large and has a whirlpool tub with integral shower.

Another 20 suites, also on Atlantic Deck, are very tastefully furnished, although they are really just larger cabins rather than suites. They do have a generous amount of drawer and other storage space, however, and a sleeping area with European duvets on the beds instead of sheets and blankets, plus a lounge area. They also have good bathrooms. All accommodation designated as suites suffers from noise generated on the swimming pool deck directly above.

DINING. Le Splendide Restaurant (the main dining room) features a raised section in its center. It has several tables for two, as well as for four, six, or eight (in banquettes), although the chairs don't have armrests. There are two seatings for dinner and open seating for breakfast and lunch, at tables for two, four, six, eight, or 10. The cuisine, its presentation, and service are quite decent, now that the menus are overseen by Francis Leveque, chef of the Restaurant du Marché in Paris. Menus include a choice of four appetizers, four main dishes and four desserts.

Other dining options. For informal meals, the Marché Gourmand has a traditional single-line self-service buffet for breakfast and lunch, and includes a pasta station, rotisserie, and pizza ovens. At peak times, the buffet is simply too small, too crowded, and noisy. It is also open (as Bistro Gourmand) for casual dinner between 6:30pm and 11pm.

The Terrace and Grill, located outdoors adjacent to the Bistro, serves typical fast food items such as burgers and hot dogs.

ENTERTAINMENT. The two-level Broadway Theater, with main and balcony levels, has good sight lines from almost all seats, except where the railing at the front of the balcony level impedes sight lines. It has a large stage for this size of ship, and decent lighting and sound equipment.

The shows consist of a troupe of showgirl dancers, whose routines are reminiscent of high-school shows. Cabaret acts are the main feature; these include singers, magicians, and comedians, among others, and very much geared to the family audience that this ship carries on most cruises. There is also plenty of live – and loud – music for dancing to in various bars and lounges, plus the Saphir Dance Club (disco). Participation activities tend to be quite amateurish.

SPA/FITNESS. The Salle de Fitness is located high in the ship, just aft of the funnel. It has a gymnasium with ocean-view windows and high-tech muscle-pump equipment, an exercise area, several therapy treatment rooms including a rasul (mud treatment) room, and men's/women's saunas.

Independence
★★★+

Size:	Boutique Ship	Cabins (total):	52
Tonnage:	2,300	Size range (sq ft/m):	204.0–240.0/18.9–22.2
Lifestyle:	Standard	Cabins (outside view):	52
Cruise line:	American Cruise Lines	Cabins (interior/no view):	0
Former names:	none	Cabins (for one person):	7
IMO number:	1223608	Cabins (with private balcony):	40
Builder:	Chesapeake Shipbuilding (USA)	Cabins (wheelchair accessible):	1
Original cost:	n/a	Wheelchair accessibility:	None
Entered service:	Jun 2010	Cabin voltage:	110 volts
Registry:	USA	Elevators:	1
Length (ft/m):	223.0/67.9	Casino (gaming tables):	No
Beam (ft/m):	51.0/15.5	Slot machines:	No
Draft (ft/m):	8.2/2.5	Swimming pools:	0
Propulsion/Propellers:	diesel/2	Hot tubs (on deck):	0
Passenger decks:	4	Self-service launderette:	No
Total crew:	27	Dedicated cinema/seats:	No
Passengers (lower beds/alll berths):	97/100	Library:	Yes
Passenger Space Ratio (lower beds/all berths):	23.7/23.0	Onboard currency:	US$
Crew/Passenger Ratio (lower beds/all berths):	3.5/3.7		

A very small US coastal ship for mature-age cruisers

OVERVIEW. This ship is for couples and single travelers of mature years sharing a cabin and wishing to cruise in an all-American environment, with destinations more important than food, service, or entertainment. It is extremely expensive for what you get – although this is a new ship and the cabins are larger and marginally better equipped than those in comparable ships.

THE SHIP. *Independence* is the fourth vessel in this cruise line's growing fleet (sister ships: *American Glory*, *American Spirit*, *American Star*). The company builds the ships in its own shipyard in Chesapeake, Maryland. *Independence* is built specifically for coastal and inland cruising, in a casual, unregimented setting, to destinations unreachable by large cruise ships.

The uppermost deck is open – good for views – behind a forward windbreaker; plenty of sunloungers are provided, as is a small golf putting green.

The public rooms include an observation lounge, with views forward and to port and starboard side; a library/lounge; a small midships lounge; and an elevator that goes to all decks, including the outdoor sun deck.

Cruises are typically seven to 14 days long. The ship docks in the center, or within walking distance of most towns and ports. The dress code is 'no ties casual.' There are no additional costs, except for gratuities and port charges, because it's all included – quite different from big-ship cruising.

Berlitz's Ratings

	Possible	Achieved
Ship	500	292
Accommodation	200	127
Food	400	210
Service	400	180
Entertainment	100	10
Cruise	400	145
OVERALL SCORE		
964 points out of 2000		

ACCOMMODATION. There are five cabin price grades – four are doubles, one is for singles. All cabins have twin beds that convert to a king-size bed, a small desk with chair, flat-screen television, DVD player, and clothes hanging space. All also have Internet access, a private (modular) bathroom with separate shower, washbasin and toilet (no cabin has a bathtub), windows that open, and satellite-feed TV sets. Accommodations incorrectly designated as suites (23) have a private balcony; although narrow, it does have two chairs and a small drinks table.

DINING. The dining salon, in the latter third of the vessel, has large, panoramic picture windows on three sides. Everyone eats in a single, open seating, so you can get to know your fellow passengers. The cuisine is mainstream American: simple, honest food highlighting regional specialties. The choice of entrées, appetizers, and soups is limited. There is no wine list, although basic white and red American table wines are included. On the last morning of each cruise, Continental breakfast only is available.

ENTERTAINMENT. Dinner and after-dinner conversation with fellow passengers in the ship's lounge/bar are the entertainment each evening. Otherwise, take a good book.

SPA/FITNESS. There is a tiny fitness room with a few bicycles and other exercise machines.

Independence of the Seas
★★★+

Size:..................................Large Resort Ship	Crew/Passenger Ratio (lower beds/all berths):.......... 2.6/3.1
Tonnage: 154,407	Cabins (total):.................................... 1,817
Lifestyle: ....Standard	Size range (sq ft/m): 149.0–2,025.0/13.8–188.1
Cruise line:.................. Royal Caribbean International	Cabins (outside view):............................... 1,084
Former names: ....none	Cabins (interior/no view):..............................733
IMO number: 9349681	Cabins (for one person):.................................0
Builder: .... Kvaerner Masa-Yards (Finland)	Cabins (with private balcony):..........................842
Original cost:................................. $590 million	Cabins (wheelchair accessible): 32
Entered service:............................... May 2008	Wheelchair accessibility:..........................Good
Registry:.................................The Bahamas	Cabin voltage: .... 110 volts
Length (ft/m):.............................1,112.2/339.0	Elevators:...14
Beam (ft/m):................................ 184.0/56.0	Casino (gaming tables):............................. Yes
Draft (ft/m):.................................... 27.8/8.5	Slot machines:..................................... Yes
Propulsion/Propellers:......diesel-electric (75,600kW)/3 pods (2	Swimming pools:......................................2
azimuthing, 1 fixed/14MW each)	Hot tubs (on deck):..................................6
Passenger decks:....................................15	Self-service launderette:............................No
Total crew:...................................... 1,397	Dedicated cinema/seats:.............................No
Passengers (lower beds/alll berths):............. 3,634/4,376	Library: .... Yes
Passenger Space Ratio (lower beds/all berths): 42.0/35.2	Onboard currency: ....US$

This ship provides abundant family facilities and entertainment

OVERVIEW. This ship's 'wow' factor is its connection with water in the design of a dramatic water theme park on the pool deck – recommended for families with children. It is now based year-round in the UK for cruises from Southampton, although the onboard currency remains the US dollar, which makes drinks about twice the cost of those aboard the P&O Cruises vessels, also Southampton-based. There is, however, something for everyone.

Berlitz's Ratings		
	Possible	Achieved
Ship	500	391
Accommodation	200	142
Food	400	235
Service	400	284
Entertainment	100	75
Cruise	400	269
OVERALL SCORE		
1396 points out of 2000		

THE SHIP. *Independence of the Seas* – with the same layout and facilities as *Freedom of the Seas* and *Liberty of the Seas* – is an extension of the slightly smaller Voyager-class of ships, which RCI introduced in 1999 with *Voyager of the Seas*. Extending its length and beam enabled an increase in the number of cabins and passenger capacity, as well as a combined pool area 43 percent larger than the *Voyager*-class (but with 500 more passengers). Two 16-person hot tubs are cantilevered 12ft (3.7m) over the ship's sides in an adults-only Solarium area – neat. The ship's 'pod' propulsion system virtually eliminates vibration.

This *Freedom*-class ship is essentially split into three separate areas, rather like the Disney cruise ships: adults-only, family, and main.

The ship's 'wow' factor (particularly for children) is its connection with water in the design of a dramatic water theme park afloat. By day, an H2O Zone (in the center of the pool deck, has an interactive water-themed play area for families that includes water

cannons and spray fountains, water jets and ground gushers; by night the 'water park' turns into a colorfully lit sculpture garden. Adjacent is a 'sports' pool – with grandstand-style seating – for things like jousting contests and other sports-related pool games, plus a 'main' pool.

Note that, during winter cruises, it's too cold to use some of the outdoor facilities – things like the Flow Rider, for example – so the ship can become quite crowded at times, with too many bingo games and quizzes programmed.

There are 16 bars and lounges to enjoy, plus a whole promenade of shops and munching and drinking spots along an indoor mall-like environment called the Royal Promenade. This is four decks high, and some interior cabins have great views into it. The Royal Promenade is home to fashion, jewelry and perfume shops, a general store, logo shop, Promenade Café, Ben & Jerry's ice cream outlet, a Book Nook, a 'classic' barber shop called A Clean Shave (a razor shave 'experience' costs more than $70), a pizzeria, and an English pub – the Dog & Badger. Just remember to look out for the stilt walkers and inflatable elephants when the circus is in town (promenades will be announced in the daily program).

One deck down from the Royal Promenade is a large Casino Royale (full of gaming tables and slot machines), The Raven disco, Schooner Bar (piano bar), Boleros Lounge (a Latin hangout), and a photo gallery and shop, while the forward section leads into the three-deck-high Alhambra Theatre.

A regulation-size ice-skating rink called Studio B has real, not fake, ice, with 'bleachers'-style seating, and good broadcast facilities Outstanding Ice Follies shows are presented here, but note that a number of slim pillars obstruct clear-view arena stage sight lines.

Almost at the top of the ship is RCI's trademark Viking Crown Lounge, the cutely named Olive or Twist jazz lounge, and a wedding chapel (this is actually on the deck above). Other facilities include a cigar smoker's lounge, conference center, a concierge lounge (for suite occupants only), and a comfortable 3,600-book library – located at the aft end of the Royal Promenade, on Deck 7.

Independence of the Seas is an exciting and very comfortable ship, with contemporary, yet tasteful decor. However, there are only four banks of elevators (two forward and two aft) totaling 14, so if you have a cabin in the center of the ship, you'll need to walk forward or aft in order to travel vertically between decks; and there are only two major passenger stairways – one forward, one aft (not many for such a large ship).

FAMILIES. Children are well catered to, with Adventure Ocean (on Deck 12) for kids of six months to 17 years of age (teens get their own chill-out room). Children will love this ship and all the fun activities and sports activities – not to mention meeting other kids. Adventure Ocean is where new friends are made easily.

ACCOMMODATION. There is a wide range of suites and cabins in several categories and different price grades, from a Presidential Family Suite that can sleep up to 14 to twin-bed two-person interior cabins, and interior cabins that look into an interior shopping/strolling atrium promenade. The price you pay depends on the size, grade, and location you choose. There are many family-friendly cabins, good for reunions, but no single occupancy cabins. All outside-view cabins have even numbers; all interior cabins have odd numbers.

Presidential Family Suite. Located in the aft section, this suite comprises five rooms. These include two master bedrooms, each with twin beds that convert to a queen-size bed and en suite bathroom with tub/shower (the toiletries cabinets are the same as in all other cabins); two other very small bedrooms that can sleep four; private balcony with sand-colored rubberized decking (not teak), with loungers, tables, chairs, a bar, and a decent view aft – although part of the balcony is overlooked by balconies on the decks above, and there is a lot of wasted space aft of the balcony because it doesn't extend to the very stern. There's also a lounge with two sofa beds, bar. The suite can accommodate eight to 14 (that's odd numbers breathing in, even numbers breathing out!), located aft, at the opposite end of the ship to the showlounge. Size: 1,215 sq ft (113 sq m) plus Balcony:

810 sq ft (75 sq m). It's a pleasant enough apartment, but nothing special – it's really quite cramped and the ceilings are plain – but it could be good value for a large family, provided everyone gets on well in a confined space.

Owner's Suite. Features include a queen-size bed, private balcony, separate living area with queen-size sofa bed, wet bar, vanity area, walk-in closet; bathroom with tub and shower. Sleeps up to five. Size: 506 sq ft (46 sq m) plus Balcony: 131 sq ft (12 sq m).

Royal Suite. Perhaps the nicest decor of all the suites, the Royal Suite has a very spacious lounge, with black baby grand player piano, queen-size sofa and entertainment center, wet bar, and dining table. The bedroom is quite spacious and has a queen-size bed; the bathroom has a whirlpool jet bath, large walk-in shower, and two (rather gaudy) gold washbasins. Sleeps up to four. Size: 1,406 sq ft (130.6 sq m) plus 377 sq ft (35 sq m).

Grand Suite. This has two twin beds convertible to queen-size, a private balcony, sitting area (some with sofa bed), vanity area; bathroom with tub and shower. Sleeps up to four. Size: 381 sq ft (35.3 sq m) plus Balcony: 89 sq ft (8.2 sq m).

Junior Suite. Two twin beds convertible to queen-size, a private balcony, sitting area (some with sofa bed), vanity area; bathroom with tub and shower. Sleeps up to four. Size: 277 sq ft (25.7 sq m) plus Balcony: 65 sq ft (6 sq m).

Superior Oceanview Cabin. Two twin beds convertible to queen-size, a private balcony, sitting area (some with sofa bed), vanity area; bathroom with shower. Sleeps two (some rooms sleep three or four). Size: 202 sq ft (18.7 sq m) plus Balcony: 42 sq ft (3.9 sq m).

Deluxe Oceanview Cabin. Two twin beds convertible to queen-size, a private balcony, sitting area (some with sofa bed), vanity area; bathroom with shower. Sleeps two (some rooms sleep three or four). Size: 173 sq ft (16.0 sq m) plus Balcony: 46 sq ft (4.2 sq m).

Interior (promenade-view) Cabin. These 172 cabins, on three decks, are interior cabins but with bay windows that allow occupants to look into the Royal Promenade. They have two twin beds convertible to queen-size; private bathroom with shower.

Interior Cabin. Two twin beds convertible to queen-size; there's a private bathroom with shower. Sleeps two (some rooms sleep three or four). Size: 160 sq ft (14.8 sq m).

Family Ocean-view Cabin. Located at the front of the ship, it contains two twin beds (convertible to queen-size), sofa and/or Pullman beds, sitting area; bathroom, with shower. Accommodates six, and has 48-in (122-cm) round windows. Size: 265 sq ft (24.6 sq m).

All grades of accommodation have a private bathroom with tub and shower, or shower only, washbasin, and toiletries cabinet. However, they are really basic, modular and akin to bathrooms found in caravans and mobile homes. There's a vanity desk with hairdryer, mini-bar, personal safe, flat-screen TV, radio, satellite-dial telephone, and nine-inch (23-cm) thick premium-quality mattresses and duvets. A room service menu is provided, although it's quite limited. Occupants of suite-grade accommodation gain access to a Concierge Lounge, for more personal service, which saves going down to the reception desk and standing in line when you need information or help in making restaurant or spa bookings.

DINING. The huge Shakespeare-themed main dining room is set on three levels, each with a different name: King Lear, Macbeth, and Romeo and Juliet. A dramatic staircase connects all three levels, and fat support pillars obstruct many sight lines. All three have the same menus and food. When you book, choose one of two seatings, or 'My Time Dining' (eat when you want, during dining room hours). Tables are for four, six, eight, 10, or 12, and place settings, china, and cutlery are of good quality.

Other dining options. Promenade Café: for Continental breakfast, all-day pizzas (Sorrento's), sandwiches, and coffee in paper cups or plastic mugs.

Windjammer Café: this is a really large, sprawling venue for casual buffet-style, self-help breakfast (this tends to be the busiest time of the day), lunch, and light dinners (but not on the last night of the cruise); it's often difficult to find a table and by the time you do your food could be cold. This venue bears the brunt of many passenger complaints regarding poor, lukewarm food and non-caring staff.

Jade 'Restaurant' (it's actually a section of the Windjammer Café) is the spot to go for casual Asian-themed food.

Portofino: an upscale Euro-Italian specialty restaurant, open for dinner only. Reservations are required, and a there's a cover charge. The menu, which doesn't change during the cruise, includes antipasti, soup, salad, pasta, main dish, dessert, cheese, and coffee.

Chops Grill: an intimate specialty restaurant for steaks and seafood. There's a cover charge.

Johnny Rockets: a retro 1950s all-day, all-night diner-style eatery that serves hamburgers, hot dogs, and other fast-food, and malt shakes, with both indoor and outdoor seating. All indoor tables have a mini-jukebox; dimes are provided for you to make your selection of vintage records. The all-singing, all-dancing waitresses will knock your socks off, if you can stand the volume. There's a cover charge, and it's located near Adventure Ocean on the starboard side of Deck 12.

Sprinkles: for round-the-clock ice cream and yoghurt, pastries and coffee.

ENTERTAINMENT. The Alhambra Theater – the ship's stunning showounge – is located at the forward end of the ship. It spans five decks in height, with only a few slim pillars and almost no disruption of sight lines. The room has a hydraulic orchestra pit and huge stage area, together with sonic-boom loud sound, and superb lighting equipment.

The entertainment includes an array of cabaret acts. The strongest of them perform in the main showlounge, while others are presented in the Pyramid Lounge (nightclub), the venue for smutty late-night adults-only comedy. The most entertaining shows are the Spectaculars on Ice. There is also a television studio, adjacent to rooms that could be used, for example, for trade show exhibit space – good for conventions at sea.

SPA/FITNESS. A large Independence Day Spa includes an aerobics room, fitness center (with stairmasters, treadmills, stationary bikes, weight machines, and free weights), private massage/body treatment rooms, men's and women's sauna/steam rooms, and relaxation areas. Some basic exercise classes are free, but the good ones such as yoga and personal training cost extra. More active passengers can bodyboard, climb the rock wall aft the funnel housing, jog, putt, swim, skate, step, surf, or workout.

Sports enthusiasts and active types will find plenty of facilities. Basketball and volleyball are available in the sports area of the ship, located aft of the funnel (on Deck 13), as is a rock-climbing wall (this one is 10ft/3m taller than aboard the Voyager-class ships), and an in-line skating area. Other active facilities include an ice-skating rink, golf course (Independence Dunes), and the Flow Rider surfing spot, for which you'll need to sign up for a time slot. Go forward, and in the middle of the spa you'll find a full-size boxing ring.

Insignia
★★★★

Size:.	Small Ship	Cabins (total):.	342
Tonnage:	30,277	Size range (sq ft/m):	145.3–968.7/13.5–90.0
Lifestyle:	Premium	Cabins (outside view):	317
Cruise line:.	Oceania Cruises	Cabins (interior/no view):.	25
Former names:	*Columbus 2, R One*	Cabins (for one person):.	0
IMO number:	9156462	Cabins (with private balcony):	232
Builder:	Chantiers de l'Atlantique	Cabins (wheelchair accessible):	3
Original cost:	$150 million	Wheelchair accessibility:	Good
Entered service:.	Jul 1998/Apr 2014	Cabin voltage:	110 and 220 volts
Registry:.	Marshall Islands	Elevators:.	4
Length (ft/m):.	593.7/181.0	Casino (gaming tables):.	No
Beam (ft/m):.	83.5/25.5	Slot machines:.	No
Draft (ft/m):	19.5/6.0	Swimming pools:.	1
Propulsion/Propellers:	diesel (18,600kW)/2	Hot tubs (on deck):.	2
Passenger decks:.	9	Self-service launderette:	Yes
Total crew:	386	Dedicated cinema/seats:	No
Passengers (lower beds/alll berths):	684/824	Library:	Yes
Passenger Space Ratio (lower beds/all berths):	44.2/36.7	Onboard currency:	US$
Crew/Passenger Ratio (lower beds/all berths):	1.7/2.1		

A compact contemporary ship, good for worldwide cruising

OVERVIEW. This ship is suitable for couples who like good food and style, but want informality, and interesting itineraries at a price well below what the luxury ships charge. Oceania Cruises provides a high level of food and service in an informal setting that's elegant yet comfortable and welcoming, with almost no announcements.

THE SHIP. *Insignia* was one of a series of almost identical ships built for the now-defunct Renaissance Cruises. The all-white ship has a large, square funnel. Teak overlaid decking and teak lounge chairs enhance the pool deck outdoors, giving it an elegant look.

Although there's no walk-around promenade deck outdoors, there is a jogging track around the perimeter of the swimming pool, and on the port and starboard side of a lower deck.

The interior decor is quite lovely, a throwback to the ship decor of the ocean liners of the 1920s and '30s, with dark woods and warm colors, all in fine taste – though a bit 'faux' in places. This includes detailed ceiling cornices, both real and faux wrought-iron staircase balustrades, leather-paneled walls, trompe l'oeil ceilings, rich carpeting in hallways, and many other interesting expensive-looking decorative touches. The decor is reminiscent of an old-world country club.

The public rooms are spread over three decks. The reception hall has a staircase with an intricate wrought-iron balustrade, a scaled-down version of *Titanic*'s First-class staircase. A large Horizon Lounge

Berlitz's Ratings		
	Possible	Achieved
Ship	500	404
Accommodation	200	153
Food	400	310
Service	400	295
Entertainment	100	74
Cruise	400	309
OVERALL SCORE		
1545 points out of 2000		

is located high atop ship; it's a long bar with forward ocean views (at least for the barman), lots of seating, and a dance floor.

There are plenty of bars – including one in each of the restaurant entrances. Perhaps the nicest is The Club, a lovely room reminiscent of Europe's grand hotels. It has an inviting marble fireplace, comfortable sofas, individual armchairs, and a dance floor.

The Library is a stunning Regency-style room, with a fireplace, a high, indented, trompe l'oeil ceiling, and an excellent selection of books, plus very comfortable wingback chairs with footstools, and sofas you could sleep on.

There may not be marble bathroom fittings, but the value for money is really good. The ship also carries 20 bicycles for passenger use, at no extra cost. The dress code is informal. Note that *Insignia* starts cruising again for Oceania Cruises in mid-April 2014 following a two-year charter to Hapag-Lloyd Cruises as *Columbus 2*.

ACCOMMODATION. There are several cabin categories and price grades. The standard interior and outside-view cabins (the lowest four grades) are rather compact units – tight for two persons, particularly for longer cruises. They have twin beds or queen-size bed, with good under-bed storage areas, personal safe, vanity desk with large mirror, good closet and drawer space in rich, dark woods, 100 percent cotton bathrobe and towels, slippers, clothes brush, and shoe horn.

Suite occupants get Bulgari bathroom amenities and other goodies, complimentary shoeshine, and cashmere throw blanket, bottle of Champagne on arrival, hand-held hairdryer, and priority restaurant reservations.

Owner's Suites (6): Measuring 968.7 sq ft (90 sq m), these are the most spacious accommodation. They are outstanding, decadent, and exclusive living spaces located aft overlooking the stern on decks 6, 7, and 8. Each has extensive teak-floor private balconies that really are private and can't be overlooked from the decks above. Each has an entrance foyer, living room, separate bedroom (the bed faces the sea, which can be seen through the floor-to-ceiling windows and sliding glass door), CD player, fully tiled bathroom with Jacuzzi tub, and a small guest bathroom.

Vista Suites (4): Measuring 785.7 sq ft (73 sq m), these are located forward on decks 5 and 6. They have extensive teak-floor private balconies that can't be overlooked from the decks above. The layout is similar to the Owner's Suites except that there is no guest bathroom.

Penthouse Suites (52): These measure about 322.9 sq ft (30 sq m). They are not really suites, but large cabins because the bedrooms aren't separate from the living areas. They have a good-size teak-floor balcony with sliding glass door (but with partial, and not full, balcony partitions) and teak deck furniture. The lounge area has a proper dining table and there is ample clothes storage space. The bathroom has a tub, shower enclosure, washbasin, and toilet.

Cabins with Balcony: Cabins with private balconies (about 216 sq ft/20 sq m) comprise about two-thirds of all cabins. They have partial, not full, balcony partitions and sliding glass doors, and 14 cabins on Deck 6 have lifeboat-obstructed views and no balcony. The living area has a refrigerated mini-bar, lounge area with breakfast table, and a balcony with teak floor, two teak chairs, and a drinks table. The bathrooms, with tiled floors and plain walls, are compact, standard units, and include a shower stall with a strong, removable hand-held shower unit, hairdryer, toiletries storage shelves, and retractable clothesline.

Outside View and Interior Cabins: These measure around 160–165 sq ft (14.8–15.3 sq m) and have twin beds (convertible to a queen-size bed), vanity desk, small sofa and coffee table, and bathroom with a shower enclosure with a strong, removable hand-held shower unit, hairdryer, toiletries storage shelves, retractable clothesline, washbasin, and toilet. Although they are not large, they are quite comfortable, with decent storage space.

DINING. Flexibility and choice are what the dining facilities are about. There are four restaurants:

The Restaurant has around 320 seats and a raised central section. There are large ocean-view windows on three sides, with prime tables overlooking the stern. The chairs are comfortable and have armrests.

Toscana Italian Restaurant has 96 seats, windows along two sides, and a set menu.

Polo Grill has 98 seats, windows along two sides, and a set menu including prime steaks and seafood.

The Lido Café, a self-serve buffet venue, seats 154 indoors and 186 outdoors, and is open for breakfast, lunch, and casual dinners. It has a small pizzeria and grill.

All restaurants have open-seating dining, so you can dine when you want, with whom you wish. Reservations are needed in Toscana Restaurant and Polo Grill, where there are mostly tables for four or six; there are few tables for two. Unlike other same-size ships in the same class, there's no extra charge. There is also a Poolside Grill outdoors. On days at sea, afternoon teatime is presented in the Horizon Lounge, with formally dressed staff, cake display trolleys, and a selection of different teas.

ENTERTAINMENT. The Insignia Lounge presents entertainment, lectures, and some social events. There is also live music in several bars and lounges.

SPA/FITNESS. A lido deck has a swimming pool and good sunbathing space, plus a thalassotherapy tub. A jogging track encircles the swimming pool deck (one deck above). The uppermost outdoors deck includes a golf driving net and shuffleboard court. The spa consists of a beauty salon, three treatment rooms, men's and women's changing rooms, steam room (but no sauna), and a good range of body treatments. Note that an 18 percent gratuity is added for spa and beauty treatments and services.

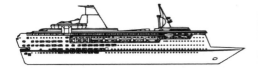

Island Escape
★★ +

Size:.	Mid-size Ship	Cabins (total):.	757
Tonnage:.	40,132	Size range (sq ft/m):.	143.1–398.2/13.3–37.0
Lifestyle:.	Standard	Cabins (outside view):.	462
Cruise line:.	Island Cruises	Cabins (interior/no view):.	295
Former names:	Viking Serenade, Stardancer, Scandinavia	Cabins (for one person):.	0
IMO number:.	8002597	Cabins (with private balcony):.	5
Builder:.	Dubigeon-Normandie (France)	Cabins (wheelchair accessible):.	3
Original cost:.	$100 million	Wheelchair accessibility:.	None
Entered service:.	Oct 1982/Apr 2009	Cabin voltage:.	110 volts
Registry:.	Bahamas	Elevators:.	5
Length (ft/m):.	623.0/189.8	Casino (gaming tables):.	Yes
Beam (ft/m):.	88.6/27.0	Slot machines:.	Yes
Draft (ft/m):.	23.6/7.2	Swimming pools:.	1
Propulsion/Propellers:.	diesel (19,800kW)/2	Hot tubs (on deck):.	0
Passenger decks:.	10	Self-service launderette:.	No
Total crew:.	540	Dedicated cinema/seats:.	No
Passengers (lower beds/alll berths):.	1,504/1,710	Library:.	Yes
Passenger Space Ratio (lower beds/all berths):	26.6/23.4	Onboard currency:	UK£
Crew/Passenger Ratio (lower beds/all berths):.	2.7/3.1		

Family-friendly, low budget, no-frills cruise ship

OVERVIEW. This is 'all-inclusive' cruising in comfortable, unpretentious surroundings that are dated but comfortable, with a totally relaxed ambience that appeals to anyone looking for a casual first cruise with plenty of life and entertainment, food that is quantity rather than quality, and a modest price. In summer the ship operates one-week cruises specifically for the British family market.

THE SHIP. *Island Escape*, originally built for a cruise-ferry service between New York and Freeport, Bahamas, was extensively reconstructed in 1991 to become a full-fledged cruise ship. Today it is run by Island Cruises, which itself is owned and operated by Thomson Cruises, part of the TUI group. This is the company's most laid-back ship.

It has only a token bow, a fairly decent amount of open deck and sunbathing space, and a pool (more a 'dip' pool) with a sliding glass dome that can be used in case of inclement weather. It suffers from having an extremely boxy, angular shape with a short, stubby funnel, and has a 'sponson' skirt that goes around the stern at the waterline – this is required for stability reasons.

Inside, the accommodation is mostly located forward, while the public rooms are mostly in the aft third of the ship. There is a decent amount of public rooms and facilities, including six bars, and a lounge/discotheque is cantilevered around the funnel with good ocean views. The decor employs tasteful colors and furnishings of decent quality, though some have seen better days. Other facilities include an Internet-con-

Berlitz's Ratings		
	Possible	Achieved
Ship	500	270
Accommodation	200	108
Food	400	200
Service	400	235
Entertainment	100	56
Cruise	400	229
OVERALL SCORE		
1098 points out of 2000		

nection center, and a coffee/pastry shop with three Internet computer stations. The ceilings in many public areas and accommodation hallways are quite low – a legacy of the ship's original role as a cruise-ferry.

Vacations can be extended with a 'cruise-and-stay' package, with special pricing to make an extended break more affordable. If you book two cruises back-to-back, some entertainment may be repeated for the second week. Children should enjoy themselves with Palmy, a character they can eat with, and there are well-supervised activities.

Background music is played almost everywhere inside the ship and on deck around the pool, making it difficult to find quiet spots to relax, chill out, or simply read a book. Passenger participation events tend to be quite amateurish. Standing in line for embarkation, disembarkation, shore tenders, and for self-serve buffet meals can be frustrating.

In March 2013, the ship became an 'all-inclusive' product, with drinks, gratuities, and all service charges included, which makes it easier for families with children – no worries. Cruise-and-stay vacations were introduced at the same time. In my professional view, this ship does what it says on the tin.

Niggles include the fact that excursions and bingo cards are expensive.

ACCOMMODATION. There are just six categories, so choosing the right one shouldn't be difficult. The price will depend on grade, size, and location. The cabins, however, are quite small, with little closet space, so take as few changes of clothes as possible. They are moderately appointed with soft furnishings that are very cheerful, with upbeat colors.

Almost all cabins have twin beds that can be pushed together to form a queen-size bed; some cabins have an L-shaped arrangement, with immovable beds. All grades have a TV set, telephone, and three-channel radio, dressing table, and mirror. There are many interior cabins, and drawers and other storage space is extremely limited. If you'd like more space, it's best to go for one of the suite categories. Room service is available 24 hours a day, at extra cost.

The cabin bathrooms are really small, so you can expect to dance with the shower curtain, particularly if you are bigger than average – only some of the accommodation designated as suites have a bathtub. Eleven outside-view cabins have even numbers, and all interior cabins have odd numbers. Also, if you are cruising with young children, there's almost no space for baby strollers. If, after looking at the deck plans, you want to book a specific cabin number, it currently costs £35 per cabin extra.

Some cabins have extra Pullman upper berths – good for families with young children. An in-cabin room service menu is available, but all items cost extra.

Island Suite. Towards the aft on the port side, this is the largest accommodation. Although it doesn't have a balcony, it's relatively spacious. There's a walk-in closet, and mini-bar/refrigerator. The bathroom has a tub and shower.

Club Suites. Five other cabins with balconies at the stern are designated as suites. These have great views over the wash created by the ship's propellers, although they may be subject to a little vibration now and then. A tub and shower are provided in the marble-clad bathroom, and there's a walk-in closet in the sleeping area, and mini-bar/refrigerator and entertainment center in the living room. Additionally, another two suites (without balcony or bathtub) are located in the forward third of the ship one deck lower than the aft-facing suites, but with the same facilities.

DINING. The Island Restaurant, the main dining room, has ocean-view windows on two sides, and upbeat decor. There are tables for two, four, six, or eight. It is open for breakfast, lunch, and dinner; you can serve yourself from the buffets, or be served by a waiter. It's a very casual open-seating arrangement, and so waiters do not get to know your preferences. Although there is much repetition of salad items for lunch, there are plenty of main dish and dessert choices. The menus contain a fair variety of British-style food.

Other dining options. Oasis is a smaller, more intimate, quieter restaurant, one deck below the Island Restaurant. This à la carte, extra-cost dining spot, with seats for two or four, is open only for dinner (reservations required), with full waiter service for all courses. The wine list is typical of a high-street eatery, with European prices that provide decent value for money.

The ceiling is low in both venues, which provides a sense of intimacy, but the noise level is intense.

For breakfast, lunch, and dinner – in fact, 24 hours a day – there is another place to go: the Beachcomber Café. This is really casual, and is ideal for grabbing a bite to eat while taking the sun on the open decks. Again, it's a self-serve buffet, with food being constantly refreshed. Tea and coffee are provided at a beverage station, with plastic cups and mugs. Additionally, there's the Café Brazil for pastries, extremely sinful cakes and pastries, and a range of espresso and cappuccino coffees, all at extra cost.

ENTERTAINMENT. The Ocean Theater is a single-level showlounge, with banquette and individual seating surrounding a thrust stage. Although it is a comfortable room, several pillars obstruct sight lines from some seats.

A resident troupe of young, enthusiastic singer/dancers provide the low-budget revue-style 'shows' that are, at best, amateurish, with weak recorded tracks but lots of color. In addition, visiting cabaret acts – typically strong singers, magicians, and smutty comedians – are presented, both in their own shows and as the middle of a 'pie' that includes the ship's resident troupe.

There is a ship's band, and several small musical units and pianists provide live music for dancing and listening in the bars and lounges. There's a throbbing discotheque.

SPA/FITNESS. The Ship Shape Hair and Beauty Spa is surprisingly good for the size of the ship. There are treatment rooms for massage, separate saunas and changing rooms for men and women, and a large beauty salon. The gymnasium itself is quite large and contains lots of muscle-pumping, body toning equipment. It is located just aft of the main swimming pool on the port side of the ship.

The spa staff are provided by Harding Brothers, and treatments offered include massages, aromatherapy facials, manicures, pedicures, and hair beautifying treatments. Do book appointments early, as time slots go quickly.

Island Princess
★★★★

Size:................................Large Resort Ship		Cabins (total):....................................987	
Tonnage:.......................................91,627		Size range (sq ft/m):.................156–470.0/14.4–43.6	
Lifestyle:.....................................Standard		Cabins (outside view):............................879	
Cruise line:............................ Princess Cruises		Cabins (interior/no view):.........................108	
Former names:.................................none		Cabins (for one person):..............................0	
IMO number:................................9230402		Cabins (with private balcony):.....................727	
Builder:................. Chantiers de l'Atlantique (France)		Cabins (wheelchair accessible):.....................20	
Original cost:...............................$360 million		Wheelchair accessibility:.........................Good	
Entered service:............................. Jun 2003		Cabin voltage:..............................110 volts	
Registry:...................................... Bermuda		Elevators:.......................................14	
Length (ft/m):............................. 964.5/294.0		Casino (gaming tables):...........................Yes	
Beam (ft/m):.............................. 105.6/32.2		Slot machines:..................................Yes	
Draft (ft/m):.....................................26/7.9		Swimming pools:.........................2 (+ 1 splash pool)	
Propulsion/Propellers:......... gas turbine, diesel (40,000kW)/2		Hot tubs (on deck):................................5	
Passenger decks:...................................11		Self-service launderette:..........................Yes	
Total crew:.....................................900		Dedicated cinema/seats:...........................No	
Passengers (lower beds/alll berths):.............1,974/2,590		Library:..Yes	
Passenger Space Ratio (lower beds/all berths):.......46.4/35.3		Onboard currency:..............................US$	
Crew/Passenger Ratio (lower beds/all berths):..........2.1/2.8			

A comfortable contemporary ship for mature-age cruisers

OVERVIEW. For a large ship, the layout is user-friendly, and less disjointed than many similar ships. Cecause of its pencil-slim beam, it can transit the Panama Canal.

THE SHIP. *Island Princess* has an instantly recognizable funnel due to two jet engine-like pods that sit high up on its structure, but these really are mainly for decoration. Four diesel engines provide the generating power. Electrical power is provided by a combination of four diesel and one gas turbine (CODAG) unit; the diesel engines are located in the engine room, while the gas turbine unit is located in the ship's funnel housing. The ship also has three bow thrusters and three stern thrusters.

Island Princess has two decks full of public rooms, lounges, and bars instead of just one. Sensibly, there are three major stair towers for passengers with plenty of elevators for easy access.

A large "Movies Under the Stars" screen is located in the second of two pool areas on the open deck just forward of the funnel. Adults using the 'Sanctuary' area have their own splash pool. Walkers will like the ship's full walk-around exterior promenade deck.

The captain can legally marry American couples, thanks to the ship's registry and a special dispensation. The Wedding Chapel can host renewal of vows ceremonies, for a fee.

This ship has lots of nooks and crannies – so you can hide away and just read a book if you want to. Also, at the forward end of decks 10 and 11, doors open onto

Berlitz's Ratings		
	Possible	Achieved
Ship	500	381
Accommodation	200	146
Food	400	256
Service	400	290
Entertainment	100	77
Cruise	400	292
OVERALL SCORE		
1442 points out of 2000		

a large observation terrace. There are also several self-service launderettes.

Niggles include the fact that the forward elevators go between decks 15-7, but you will need to change elevators to get down to the dining rooms on deck 5 (strangely, the 'panoramic' elevators go only between decks 5 and 8; passengers do find this a trifle confusing, but it's all about the way the layout and flow has to work – from a designer's point of view, that is).

ACCOMMODATION. There are numerous price categories, in six types: 16 Suites with balcony (470 sq ft/43.6 sq m); 184 Mini-Suites with balcony (285–302 sq ft/26.4–28 sq m); eight Mini-Suites without balcony (300 sq ft/27.8 sq m); 527 Outside-View Cabins with balcony (217–232 sq ft/20.1–21.5 sq m); 144 Standard Outside-view Cabins (162 sq ft/15 sq m); 108 Interior Cabins (156 sq ft/144.5 sq m). There are also 20 wheelchair-accessible cabins (217–374 sq ft/20.1–34.7 sq m).

Almost all outside-view cabins have a private balcony. Some cabins can accommodate a third, or third and fourth person. Some cabins on Emerald Deck (Deck 8) have a view obstructed by lifeboats. The décor is earth tones. All cabins have a personal safe, hair dryer, small 'fridge, television, and premium quality bedding.

Suites (16). Each has a private balcony. All suites are located on either Deck 9 or Deck 10. In a departure from many ships, *Island Princess* doesn't have any suites or cabins with a view of the stern. There are four Premium Suites, located sensibly in the center of the ship, adjacent to a bank of six elevators. Farther aft are six other suites (Veranda Suites).

All Accommodation. Suites and cabins have a refrigerator, personal safe, TV set with audio channels, hairdryer, satellite-dial telephone, and twin beds that convert to a queen-size bed (there are a few exceptions). All accommodation has a bathroom with shower enclosure and toilet. Accommodation designated as suites and mini-suites (there are seven price categories) have a bathtub and separate shower enclosure, and two TV sets.

All passengers receive turndown service and chocolates on pillows each night, bathrobes on request, and toiletry kits. Most outside-view cabins on Emerald Deck have views obstructed by lifeboats. There are no cabins for singles. Nor are there butlers – even for the top-grade suites. Cabin attendants have too many cabins to look after (typically 20).

DINING. The two main dining rooms, Bordeaux and Provence, are in the forward section of the ship on the two lowest passenger decks. Both are almost identical – the ceilings are quite low, and have plenty of intimate alcoves and cozy dining spots, with tables for two, four, six, or eight. There are two seatings for dinner (or you can opt for 'Anytime' Dining in the Bordeaux Restaurant), while breakfast and lunch are on an open-seating basis; you may have to wait for some while at peak times.

Other dining options. There are two extra-charge restaurants: Sabatini's and the Bayou Café, both enclosed and both requiring reservations. Sabatini's, with colorful tiled Mediterranean-style decor, has Italian-style pizzas and pastas, with a variety of sauces, as well as Italian-style entrées including tiger prawns and lobster tail, all provided with flair and entertainment by the waiters. The food is both creative and tasty. There is a cover charge for lunch or dinner on sea days only.

The Bayou Café, open for lunch and dinner, has a cover charge that includes a Hurricane cocktail. It evokes the charm of New Orleans' French Quarter, with wrought-iron decoration, and features Cajun/Creole cuisine. Platters include Peel 'n' Eat Shrimp Piquante, Sausage Grillades, Oysters Sieur de Bienville. Popular entrées include premium steaks, Seafood Gumbo, and Chorizo Jambalaya, plus Alligator Ribs, Corn Meal Fried Catfish, Blackened Chicken Brochette, and Red Pepper Butter Broiled Lobster. Desserts include sweet potato pie and banana whiskey pound cake. The venue has a small stage, with baby grand piano and live jazz is part of the evening dining scenario.

Horizon Court, a casual 24-hour eatery, is in the forward section of Lido Deck with superb ocean views. Self-serve counters provide food for breakfast and lunch buffets, and bistro-style casual dinners are available each evening. Sadly, there's just not enough seating for the number of passenger using the facility.

Also, La Pâtisserie, in the reception lobby, is a coffee, cakes, and pastries spot and good for informal meetings. There's also a pizzeria, hamburger grill, and an ice cream bar (extra charge for the ice cream).

ENTERTAINMENT. The Princess Theatre is two decks high, and, unusually, there is much more seating in the upper level than on the main floor below. Princess Cruises prides itself on its colourful Hollywood-style production shows.

A second entertainment venue, Universe Lounge, is designed more for cabaret-style features. It also has two levels, and three separate stages, enabling non-stop entertainment to be provided without constant set-ups. Some 50 of the room's seats are equipped with a built-in laptop computer. The room is also used for cooking demonstrations (it has a full kitchen set), and other participation activities.

Princess Cruises always provides plenty of live music in bars and lounges, with a wide mix of light classical, jazz, and dance music, from solo entertaining pianists to showbands, and volume is normally kept to an acceptable level.

Those craving education can learn aboard ship with the ScholarShip@Sea program, which includes about 20 courses per cruise (six on any given day at sea). Although all introductory classes are free, fees apply if you want to continue any chosen subject in a smaller setting. There are four core subjects: culinary arts, visual/creative arts, photography, and computer technology. A full culinary demonstration kitchen set is built into the Universe Lounge, which is also used for wine tastings, and there's a pottery studio with kiln.

SPA/FITNESS. The Lotus Spa is located aft on one of the ship's uppermost decks. It contains men's and women's saunas, steam rooms, changing rooms, relaxation area, beauty salon, aerobics exercise room, and gymnasium with aft-facing ocean views packed with the latest high-tech muscle-pumping, cardiovascular equipment. There are several large rooms for individual treatments.

Sports enthusiasts will find a nine-hole golf putting course, two computerized golf simulators, and a sports court.

Island Sky
★★★★ +

Size:.	Boutique Ship	Cabins (total):.	59
Tonnage:	4,280	Size range (sq ft/m):	234.6–353.0/21.8–32.8
Lifestyle:	Standard	Cabins (outside view):	59
Cruise line:.	Noble Caledonia	Cabins (interior/no view):.	0
Former names:	Sky, Renai II, Renaissance VIII	Cabins (for one person):.	0
IMO number:	8802894	Cabins (with private balcony):	4
Builder:	Nuovi Cantieri Appaunia (Italy)	Cabins (wheelchair accessible):	0
Original cost:.	$25 million	Wheelchair accessibility:	None
Entered service:.	Dec 1991/May 2004	Cabin voltage:	110 volts
Registry:.	The Bahamas	Elevators:.	1
Length (ft/m):.	297.2/90.6	Casino (gaming tables):.	No
Beam (ft/m):.	50.1/15.3	Slot machines:.	No
Draft (ft/m):	12.9/2.95	Swimming pools:.	0
Propulsion/Propellers:	diesel (5000kW)/2	Hot tubs (on deck):.	1
Passenger decks:.	5	Self-service launderette:	No
Total crew:.	66	Dedicated cinema/seats:	No
Passengers (lower beds/alll berths):	122/122	Library:	Yes
Passenger Space Ratio (lower beds/all berths):	35.0/35.0	Onboard currency:	UK£
Crew/Passenger Ratio (lower beds/all berths):	1.7/1.7		

A delightful small ship for life-enrichment cruises

OVERVIEW. This comfortable, intimate ship operates in areas devoid of large cruise ships. Although not quite matching the standard of Seabourn or Silversea vessels, it provides a good cruise experience at a moderate cost. It suits seasoned travelers who like a relaxed lifestyle, good food and service, and an itinerary that promises 'get away from it all, but in comfort.'

THE SHIP. *Island Sky* has contemporary mega-yacht looks and handsome styling, with twin flared funnels that give it a smart profile, and a 'ducktail' (sponson) stern that provides stability and seagoing comfort. This ship was originally built as one of a series of eight similar ships for the now-defunct Renaissance Cruises. It was completely refurbished in 2010.

There is a teak walk-around promenade deck outdoors, and a reasonable amount of open deck and sunbathing space. A 'baby island' tender hangs off the aft deck and acts as ship-to-shore transportation. Some equipment for watersports is carried, together with a fleet of Zodiac inflatables for shore landings.

Inside, the interior design is elegant, with polished wood-finish paneling throughout. There is a very small library with two Internet-connect workstations. Gratuities are included, as are house wine, beer, and soft drinks during lunch and dinner.

ACCOMMODATION. The spacious cabins combine highly polished imitation rosewood paneling with lots

Berlitz's Ratings		
	Possible	Achieved
Ship	500	396
Accommodation	200	161
Food	400	317
Service	400	307
Entertainment	100	70
Cruise	400	316
OVERALL SCORE		
1567 points out of 2000		

of mirrors and hand-crafted furniture, lighted walk-in closets, three-sided vanity mirrors – in fact, there are a lot of mirrored surfaces in the decor – and just about everything you need, including a refrigerator, a TV set and player, and Wi-Fi access. The bathrooms are extremely compact; they have real teakwood floors and marble vanities, and shower enclosures, but none have tubs, not even the owner's suite. All were replaced in the 2010 refit.

DINING. The dining room operates with open seating for all meals. Small but quite smart, it has tables for two, four, six, and eight. You sit where you like, with whom you like, and at what time you like. The meals are self-service, buffet-style foods for breakfast and lunch, with hot foods chosen from a table menu and served properly. The dining room operation works well. The food quality, choice, and presentation are all very decent.

ENTERTAINMENT. There is no formal entertainment in the main lounge, the venue for all social activities. Anyway, six pillars obstruct sight lines to the small stage area.

SPA/FITNESS. Water sports facilities include an aft platform, and Zodiacs.

Jewel of the Seas
★★★+

Size:......................................Large Resort Ship			Cabins (total):...1,055	
Tonnage:..90,090			Size range (sq ft/m):...............165.8–1,216.3/15.4–113.0	
Lifestyle:...Standard			Cabins (outside view):....................................817	
Cruise line:...................Royal Caribbean International			Cabins (interior/no view):.................................238	
Former names:....................................none			Cabins (for one person):.....................................0	
IMO number:................................9228356			Cabins (with private balcony):............................577	
Builder:..........................Meyer Werft (Germany)			Cabins (wheelchair accessible):............................14	
Original cost:................................$350 million			Wheelchair accessibility:...............................Good	
Entered service:................................Jun 2004			Cabin voltage:...................................110 volts	
Registry:.......................................The Bahamas			Elevators:...9	
Length (ft/m):...............................961.9/293.2			Casino (gaming tables):.................................Yes	
Beam (ft/m):................................105.6/32.2			Slot machines:..Yes	
Draft (ft/m):....................................27.8/8.5			Swimming pools:..2	
Propulsion/Propellers:. gas turbine (39,000kW)/2 azimuthing pods			Hot tubs (on deck):..3	
Passenger decks:......................................12			Self-service launderette:................................No	
Total crew:...858			Dedicated cinema/seats:.................................Yes	
Passengers (lower beds/all berths):.............2,110/2,500			Library:...Yes	
Passenger Space Ratio (lower beds/all berths):.......42.9/36.0			Onboard currency:......................................US$	
Crew/Passenger Ratio (lower beds/all berths):..........2.4/2.9				

A large resort ship for family-friendly casual cruising

OVERVIEW. This ship is best suited to young-minded adult couples and singles, families with toddlers, tots, children, and teenagers who like to mingle in a large ship setting with plenty of city-like life and high-energy entertainment. The food is acceptable, stressing quantity rather than quality unless you pay extra to dine in the specialty restaurant.

THE SHIP. *Jewel of the Seas* is a streamlined, contemporary ship, with a two-deck-high wraparound structure in the forward section of the funnel. Along the starboard side, a central glass wall protrudes, giving great views – cabins with balconies occupy the space directly opposite on the port side. The gently rounded stern has nicely tiered decks, which gives the ship an extremely well-balanced look.

As aboard almost all new cruise ships today, the navigation bridge is of the fully enclosed type. In the very front of the ship is a helipad, which also acts as a viewing platform. Pod propulsion power is provided.

Inside, the decor is contemporary, yet elegant, bright and cheerful, designed for young, active types. The artwork is quite eclectic and provides a spectrum and a half of color works. The interior focal point is a nine-deck high atrium lobby with glass-walled elevators that travel through 12 decks, face the sea, and provide a link with nature and the ocean. The Centrum, as the atrium is called, has several public rooms connected to it: the guest relations and shore excursions desks, a lobby bar, Champagne bar, a small library, Royal Caribbean Online (an Internet center with 12 computers), a Con-

Berlitz's Ratings

	Possible	Achieved
Ship	500	381
Accommodation	200	142
Food	400	242
Service	400	287
Entertainment	100	74
Cruise	400	270

OVERALL SCORE
1396 points out of 2000

cierge Club, and a Crown & Anchor Lounge. A great view can be had of the atrium by looking down through the flat glass dome high above it.

Other facilities include a large Schooner Bar that houses maritime art in an integral art gallery, and a rather large, noisy, and colorful Casino Royale. There's also a small dedicated screening room for movies (with space for two wheelchairs), as well as a 194-seat conference center, and a business center.

This ship also contains a Viking Crown Lounge, a large structure set around the base of the ship's funnel. It functions as an observation lounge during the daytime, with views forward over the swimming pool. In the evening, the space becomes a futuristic, high-energy dance club, as well as a more intimate and relaxed entertainment venue for softer mood music and 'black box' theater.

The onboard product delivery is casual and unstructured. While the ship is quite delightful in many ways, the onboard operation suffers from a lack of service staff. *Jewel of the Seas* offers more space, more comfortable public areas and several more intimate spaces, slightly larger cabins, and more dining options than most of the larger ships in the RCI fleet. A 15 percent gratuity is automatically added to all bar and spa bills.

Niggles? There are no cushioned pads for sun-loungers, and the deck towels are quite thin and small. It is virtually impossible to escape background music anywhere (it's even played in the hallway outside your cabin).

FAMILIES. Youth facilities include Adventure Ocean, an 'edutainment' area with four separate age-appropriate sections for junior passengers: Aquanaut Center (for ages three to five); Explorer Center (six to eight); Voyager Center (nine to 12); and the Optix Teen Center (13–17). There is also Adventure Beach, which includes a splash pool complete with waterslide; Surfside, with computer lab stations with entertaining software; and Ocean Arcade, a video games hangout.

ACCOMMODATION. There's a wide range of suites and standard outside-view and interior cabins to suit different tastes, requirements, and depth of wallet, in 10 different categories and numerous price groups. There are 14 wheelchair-accessible cabins, 8 of which have a private balcony.

Apart from the largest suites (six owner's suites), which have king-size beds, almost all other cabins have twin beds that convert to a queen-size bed. All cabins have rich but faux wood cabinetry, including a vanity desk with hairdryer, faux wood drawers that close silently (hooray), television, personal safe and three-sided mirrors. Some cabins have ceiling-recessed, pull-down berths for a third and fourth person, although closet and drawer space would be extremely tight for four (even if two are children). Some cabins have interconnecting doors, allowing families with children to cruise together in adjacent cabins. Audio channels are available through the TV set, so you can't switch off its picture while listening. Data ports are provided in all cabins.

Many 'private' balcony cabins aren't very private, as they can be overlooked by anyone standing in the port and starboard wings of the Solarium, and from other locations.

Most cabin bathrooms have tiled accenting and a terrazzo-style tiled floor, and a shower enclosure in a half-moon shape (it is rather small, however, considering the size of some passengers), Egyptian cotton towels, a small cabinet for toiletries and a small shelf. There is little space to stow toiletries for two or more.

The largest accommodation consists of a family suite with two bedrooms. One bedroom has twin beds that convert to a queen-size bed, while a second has two lower beds and two upper Pullman berths, a combination that can sleep up to eight persons – this would be suitable for large families.

Occupants of accommodation designated as suites also get the use of a private Concierge Lounge where priority dining room reservations, shore excursion bookings, and beauty salon/spa appointments can be made.

DINING. Reflections – the main dining room – spans two decks; the upper deck level has floor-to-ceiling windows, while the lower deck level has picture windows. It is a fine, but inevitably noisy dining hall and eight huge, thick pillars obstruct the sight lines. It seats 1,104, and the decor has a cascading water theme.

There are tables for 2-10, in two seatings for dinner. Two small private dining rooms (Illusions and Mirage) are located off the main dining room. There is an adequate wine list, with moderate prices.

Other dining options. Extra-cost venues include Portofino, with 112 seats, offers Italian cuisine, and Chops Grille Steakhouse, with 95 seats and an open 'show' kitchen, serves premium meats in the form of chops and steaks. Both have food that is of a higher quality than in the main dining room and are typically open 6–11pm. There is a cover charge, and reservations are required.

Casual breakfasts, lunches, and dinners can be taken in the self-serve, buffet-style Windjammer Café, which can be accessed directly from the pool deck. It has about 400 seats, and islands dedicated to specific foods, and indoor and outdoor seating. Additionally, there is the Seaview Café, open for lunch and dinner. You can choose from the self-serve buffet, or from the menu for casual, fast-food seafood items including fish sandwiches, popcorn shrimp, fish 'n' chips, as well as non-seafood items such as hamburgers and hot dogs.

ENTERTAINMENT. Facilities include the three-level Coral Reef Theater, the ship's large showlounge, with 874 seats, including 24 wheelchair stations. The sight lines are good from most seats due to steep tiers. A second entertainment venue is the Safari Club, which hosts cabaret shows, late-night adult comedy, and dancing to live music. All the ship's entertainment is upbeat – so much so that it's virtually impossible to get away from music and noise.

SPA/FITNESS. The Day Spa health and fitness facilities have themed decor, and include a 10,176-sq-ft (945-sq-m) solarium with whirlpool and counter current swimming under a retractable glass roof, a gymnasium with 44 cardiovascular machines, a 50-person aerobics room, sauna and steam rooms, and private massage/body treatment rooms. The facility is staffed and operated by Steiner Leisure.

For the sports-oriented, there are activities galore – including a rock-climbing wall that's 30ft (9m) high, with five separate climbing tracks. It's free, and all safety gear is included, but you'll need to sign up.

Other sports facilities include a nine-hole miniature golf course, and an indoor/outdoor country club with computer-controlled golf simulator, a jogging track, and basketball court. Want to play pool? You can, thanks to two special tables whose gyroscopic technology adjusts to the movement of the ship.

Kristina Katarina
★★ +

Size:.	Small Ship	Cabins (total):.	193
Tonnage:	12,688	Size range (sq ft/m):	96.8–322.9/9.0–30.0
Lifestyle:	Standard	Cabins (outside view):	74
Cruise line:.	Kristina Cruises	Cabins (interior/no view):.	119
Former names:	The Iris, Francesca, Konstantin Simonov	Cabins (for one person):.	0
IMO number:	7625811	Cabins (with private balcony):	0
Builder:	Szczesin Stocznia (Poland)	Cabins (wheelchair accessible):	1
Original cost:	n/a	Wheelchair accessibility:	None
Entered service:.	Apr 1982/Mar 2011	Cabin voltage:	220 volts
Registry:.	Finland	Elevators:	2
Length (ft/m):.	452.7/138.0	Casino (gaming tables):	Yes
Beam (ft/m):.	72.1/22.0	Slot machines:	Yes
Draft (ft/m):	19.0/5.8	Swimming pools:	1
Propulsion/Propellers:	diesel (12,800kW)/2	Hot tubs (on deck):.	1
Passenger decks:.	7	Self-service launderette:	Yes
Total crew:	170	Dedicated cinema/seats:	No
Passengers (lower beds/alll berths):	380/386	Library:	No
Passenger Space Ratio (lower beds/all berths):	33.3/33.3	Onboard currency:	Euros
Crew/Passenger Ratio (lower beds/all berths):	2.7/4.8		

A modestly comfortable older ship with Finnish style

OVERVIEW. *Kristina Katarina* can easily handle harsh winter northern weather when necessary. Although it doesn't compare to today's new ships, it does have a welcoming, homely feel and ambience.

THE SHIP. The dark-hulled ship has a rather angular profile with a square stern, short bows, and a low, squat funnel placed amidships. Although built for a different purpose, it has undergone several extensive refit and refurbishment programs for use as a cruise ship.

Some interior and exterior staircases are quite steep, the open deck is quite limited, particularly if the ship is full, and a swimming pool is really just a 'dip' pool. Public rooms include a Veranda Bistro coffee lounge, Nautilus main lounge, Meridian Club (nightclub/disco), a shop, and a children's playroom called Pelagus.

Overall, the ship has a rather disjointed feel. The ambience is casual, and the decor includes blond woods and minimalist design, which all helps to make it feel more spacious.

ACCOMMODATION. There are several price grades, depending on size and location, but there are no balcony cabins. Except for the large Columbus suites, cabins are pretty small, although they are practically appointed. All grades have a telephone and TV set. Some cabins have interconnecting doors. There's little drawer space or under-bed space for luggage storage. Many are fitted with two lower

Berlitz's Ratings

	Possible	Achieved
Ship	500	233
Accommodation	200	110
Food	400	238
Service	400	233
Entertainment	100	42
Cruise	400	196
OVERALL SCORE		
1052 points out of 2000		

beds and two upper berths. All cabins have a private bathroom, with shower, washbasin, and toilet; some of the larger grades have a cabinet for personal toiletries. The cabin hallways are quite plain.

The two Columbus suites have a separate bedroom with plenty of closet and drawer space, and a larger bathroom with tub and shower combination (two other cabins also have bathtubs).

DINING. The Aurora Restaurant has large ocean-view windows, and tables for four, six, or eight. The cuisine is Finnish, but with an international flair, and relies heavily on seafood. The wine glasses are small – very small.

The Aurora Restaurant, with its white tablecloth setting, is an à la carte, extra-cost venue. There's also a Polaris Buffet self-serve venue, and a Veranda Bistro for coffee and tea and light snacks.

ENTERTAINMENT. The entertainment is limited to cabaret acts in the L-shaped Nautilus main lounge. It's strange to see a railing in front of the band – a throwback to the days of ocean liners. There is live music for dancing and listening.

SPA/FITNESS. There is a really spacious sauna (with ocean-view window) and a small fitness room. A massage room is available in a separate location.

L'Austral
★★★★

Size:.	Small Ship	Cabins (total):.	132
Tonnage:.	10,944	Size range (sq ft/m):.	215.2–301.3/20.0–28.0
Lifestyle:.	Premium	Cabins (outside view):.	132
Cruise line:.	Ponant Cruises	Cabins (interior/no view):.	0
Former names:.	none	Cabins (for one person):.	0
IMO number:.	9502518	Cabins (with private balcony):.	125
Builder:.	Fincantieri (Italy)	Cabins (wheelchair accessible):.	3
Original cost:.	$100 million	Wheelchair accessibility:.	Fair
Entered service:.	May 2011	Cabin voltage:.	110 and 220 volts
Registry:.	Wallis & Fortuna	Elevators:.	2
Length (ft/m):.	465.8/142.0	Casino (gaming tables):.	No
Beam (ft/m):.	9.0/18.0	Slot machines:.	Yes
Draft (ft/m):.	15.4/4.7	Swimming pools:.	2
Propulsion/Propellers:.	diesel-electric (4,600kW)/2	Hot tubs (on deck):.	0
Passenger decks:.	6	Self-service launderette:.	No
Total crew:.	140	Dedicated cinema/seats:.	No
Passengers (lower beds/alll berths):.	224/264	Library:.	Yes
Passenger Space Ratio (lower beds/all berths):.	48.8/41.4	Onboard currency:.	Euros
Crew/Passenger Ratio (lower beds/all berths):.	1.5/1.8		

A contemporary ship and style to suit French speakers

OVERVIEW. *L'Austral* is best suited to young-minded couples and singles who want sophisticated facilities in a relaxed but chic yacht-like environment quite different to most cruise ships, with very good food and decent service. The ship is often chartered or part-chartered by 'premium' travel organizers who prefer smaller ships, such as Abercrombie & Kent, Gohagen, and Tauck Tours.

THE SHIP. One of three identical sister ships (the others are *Le Boreal* and *Le Soléal*) catering to French speakers, *L'Austral* (South Wind) is a gem of contemporary design – chic and uncluttered. With a dark grey hull and sleek white superstructure, it looks like a large private yacht rather than a traditional cruise ship. The Passenger Space Ratio, a healthy 53.5, decreases if the 40 suites that convert into 20 are all occupied by two persons.

L'Austral has a smart 'sponson' skirt built-in at the stern for operational stability, and carries a fleet of 12 Zodiac landing craft for soft expedition voyages. For Antarctic voyages, passenger numbers are kept to a maximum of 199, although the ship does not have boot storage lockers.

There is some sunbathing space outdoors forward of the funnel and around the small pool – aft of the casual eatery one deck below – together with one shower enclosure. Aft of the funnel is an outdoor bar (Copernico) and grill, but seating is limited.

Almost all public rooms are aft, with accommodation located forward; the elevators go to all decks except the uppermost one (Deck 7).

Berlitz's Ratings		
	Possible	Achieved
Ship	500	404
Accommodation	200	155
Food	400	284
Service	400	299
Entertainment	100	72
Cruise	400	293
OVERALL SCORE		
1507 points out of 2000		

The decor is minimalist and super-yacht chic – relaxing and pleasant, with lots of browns and creams and a splash of red here and there. Glitz is entirely absent, although there are many reflective surfaces and the overall feeling of the decor is cool rather than warm.

The focal point is the main lobby, with a central, circular seating and tiled floor surround; its small central section spans two decks. The other flooring is wood, which can be noisy. The lower decks of the main stairway are made of faux gray wood, while the upper decks are carpeted – a strange combination that somehow works.

This is all-inclusive cruising – except for spa treatments – with drinks, table wine for lunch and dinner, bottled mineral water, port charges, and Zodiac excursions on expedition-style cruises all included in the fare. The crew is English- and French-speaking, with many hotel service staff from Asia.

Passenger niggles? There's no outside walking or jogging deck. The interior stairways are a quite steep and have short steps. The restaurant is noisy. The entertainment system is not user-friendly and internet connection is slow and expensive. Overall, it's difficult for French-speaking and non-French-speaking passengers to mix.

ACCOMMODATION. Of the 132 suites/cabins, there are three Prestige Suites with a 301 sq ft plus 54 sq ft balcony (28 plus 5 sq m). Forty of the 94 deluxe cabins – 200 sq ft plus 43 sq ft balcony (18.6 plus 4 sq m) – can be combined into 20 larger suites, each with two bathrooms, and separate living area and bedroom. All cabinetry is made in elegant dark woods. A real plus is that there are no interior (no view) cabins – all cabins have a view of the outside, and cabin insulation is good.

Each deluxe and standard cabin has a large ocean-view window, two beds that convert to a queen-size bed, and a long vanity desk with good lighting. Facilities include a TV set, DVD player, refrigerator, and personal safe. The marble-appointed bathrooms have large, rather heavy hand-held shower hoses. Amenities include a mini-bar, personal safe, hairdryer, bathrobe, and French bathroom products. Wi-Fi costs extra.

All other cabins have good-size beds, although the bedframe corners are square, so you need to be careful when passing between bed and a storage unit that's quite large, with two deep drawers, refrigerator, television, and wall mirror. Other facilities include good-size wardrobe-style closet (armoire) with personal safe, and a vanity desk with drawer and a small shelf.

The small cabin bathrooms (the entrance door is only 20½ins/52cm wide) also have a sliding partition window that enables you to see through the cabin to the ocean, and a deep, half-size tub/shower combination. The lip between floor and bathroom is just over 6ins (16cm) high. Bottles of L'Occitaine toiletry items are provided.

There are no shelves for toiletries, but there are two drawers under the washbasin – although they are not really practical in use. A separate cubicle houses the vacuum toilet. Balconies have faux-wood decking and a fine (real) wood handrail, although solid paneling obstructs views when seated and makes the cabin seem dark – glass panels would have been nicer; the balconies are also narrow. The closet space is quite good, but, although the doors, with excellent white leather handles, are wide – at 31ins (79cm), they are wider than the cabin door, and can't be opened without first closing the bathroom and toilet doors which are directly opposite.

Good quality bed linen, overlays and cushions are provided, although there is no choice of pillows.

DINING. The main restaurant is chic but not pretentious. It accommodates all passengers in an open-seating arrangement and has two integral wine display cabinets (not temperature-controlled). The chairs are square and have thin armrests and low backs – but they look good. And the food? While appetizers and main course items are reasonably good but nothing special, the cakes and desserts are delightful.

A casual indoor/outdoor Grill (although there is no actual grill) has seating for up to 130, with self-serve buffet set-up for breakfast and lunch, and a 'fast grill' dinner in an alfresco setting. But the layout is disjoint-ed, and the port and starboard sides are separated by two elevators. There are two main buffet display units (one for cold food, one for hot), and a separate table set-up for bread, and an active cooking station (eggs for breakfast, pasta dishes at lunchtime).

ENTERTAINMENT. French Line, the showlounge/lecture hall, has amphitheater-style seating for 260, and a raised stage suited to concerts and cabaret. The production shows are weak, repetitive, and loud. The venue is also used for expert specialist lecturers, and expedition-style recaps. Two large pillars obstruct the sight lines from several seats.

SPA/FITNESS. The Yacht Spa facilities include a fitness room with starboard-side ocean views, adjacent kinetic wall, and a steam room, but there's no changing room. A wide range of massage and body treatments are provided by Carita of Paris, which staffs and oversees the facility.

Le Boreal
★★★★

Size:. . . . . Small Ship			
Tonnage: 10,700			
Lifestyle: . . . . .Premium			
Cruise line:. . . . . .Ponant Cruises			
Former names: . . . . .none			
IMO number: 9502506			
Builder: . . . . Fincantieri (Italy)			
Original cost:. . . . .$100 million			
Entered service:. . . . . May 2010			
Registry:. . . . . .Wallis & Fortuna			
Length (ft/m):. 465.8/142.0			
Beam (ft/m):. 9.0/18.0			
Draft (ft/m):. 15.4/4.7			
Propulsion/Propellers:. . . . . diesel-electric (4,600kW)/2			
Passenger decks:. 6			
Total crew:. 140			
Passengers (lower beds/alll berths):. 264/264			
Passenger Space Ratio (lower beds/all berths): 41.4/41.4			
Crew/Passenger Ratio (lower beds/all berths):. 1.5/1.8			

Cabins (total):. 132
Size range (sq ft/m): 215.2–301.3/20.0–28.0
Cabins (outside view):. 132
Cabins (interior/no view):. 0
Cabins (for one person):. 0
Cabins (with private balcony):. .125
Cabins (wheelchair accessible): 3
Wheelchair accessibility:. . . . . .Fair
Cabin voltage: . . . . .110 and 220 volts
Elevators:. 2
Casino (gaming tables):. . . . . .No
Slot machines:. . . . . Yes
Swimming pools:. 2
Hot tubs (on deck):. 0
Self-service launderette:. . . . . .No
Dedicated cinema/seats:. . . . . .No
Library: . . . . Yes
Onboard currency: . . . . Euros

Exudes French ambience and super-yacht chic

OVERVIEW. *Le Boréal* is best suited to young-minded couples and singles who want sophisticated facilities in a relaxed but chic yacht-like environment quite different to most cruise ships, with very good food and decent service. The ship is often chartered or part-chartered by 'premium' travel organizers who prefer smaller ships, such as Abercrombie & Kent, Gohagen, and Tauck Tours.

Berlitz's Ratings

	Possible	Achieved
Ship	500	404
Accommodation	200	155
Food	400	284
Service	400	299
Entertainment	100	72
Cruise	400	292

OVERALL SCORE
1506 points out of 2000

THE SHIP. One of two identical new ships catering to French speakers, *Le Boréal* (North Wind) is a gem of contemporary design – chic and uncluttered. The ship has a smart 'sponson' skirt built-in at the stern for operational stability, and carries a fleet of 12 Zodiac landing craft for soft expedition voyages.

There is some sunbathing space outdoors forward of the funnel and around the small pool – aft of the casual eatery one deck below – together with one shower enclosure. Aft of the funnel is an outdoor bar/grill, but not much seating.

Almost all public rooms are aft, with accommodation located forward; the elevators go to all decks except the uppermost one (Deck 7). The decor is minimalist and super-yacht chic – relaxing and pleasant, with lots of browns and creams and a splash of red here and there. Glitz is entirely absent, although there are many reflective surfaces and the overall feeling of the decor is cool rather than warm.

The focal point is the main lobby, with a central, circular seating and tiled floor surround; its small cen-

tral section spans two decks. The other flooring is wood, which can be noisy. The lower decks of the main stairway are made of faux gray wood, while the upper decks are carpeted – a strange combination that somehow works.

This is all-inclusive cruising – except for spa treatments – with drinks, table wine for lunch and dinner, bottled mineral water, port charges, and Zodiac excursions on expedition-style cruises all included in the fare. The crew is English- and French-speaking, with many hotel service staff from Asia.

Passenger niggles? There's no outside walking or jogging deck. The interior stairways are a quite steep and have short steps. The restaurant is noisy. The entertainment system is not user-friendly and internet connection is slow and expensive. Overall, it's difficult for French-speaking and non-French-speaking passengers to mix.

Passenger niggles. There's no outside walking or jogging deck. The interior stairways are a quite steep and have short steps. The restaurant is noisy. The entertainment system is not user-friendly and internet connection is slow and expensive. Overall, it's difficult for French-speaking and non-French-speaking passengers to mix.

ACCOMMODATION. Of the 132 suites/cabins, there are three Prestige Suites with a 301 sq ft plus 54 sq ft balcony (28 plus 5 sq m). Forty of the 94 deluxe cabins – 200 sq ft plus 43 sq ft balcony (18.6 plus 4 sq

m) – can be combined into 20 larger suites, each with two bathrooms, and separate living area and bedroom. All cabinetry is made in elegant dark woods. A real plus is that there are no interior (no view) cabins – every cabin has an outside view, and the cabin insulation is good.

Each deluxe and standard cabin has a large ocean-view window, two beds that convert to a queen-size bed, and a long vanity desk with good lighting. Facilities include a TV set, DVD player, refrigerator, and personal safe. The marble-appointed bathrooms have heavy hand-held shower hoses. Amenities include a mini-bar, personal safe, hairdryer, bathrobe, and French bathroom products. Wi-Fi costs extra.

All other cabins have good-size beds, although the bedframe corners are square, so you need to be careful when passing between bed and a storage unit that's quite large, with two deep drawers, refrigerator, television, and wall mirror. Other facilities include good-size wardrobe-style closet (armoire) with personal safe, and a vanity desk with drawer and a small shelf.

The small cabin bathrooms (the entrance door is only 20½ins/52cm wide) also have a sliding partition window that enables you to see through the cabin to the ocean, and a deep, half-size tub/shower combination. The lip between floor and bathroom is just over 6ins (16cm) high. Bottles of L'Occitaine toiletry items are provided.

There are no shelves for toiletries, but there are two drawers under the washbasin – although they are not really practical in use. A separate cubicle houses the vacuum toilet. Balconies have faux-wood decking and a fine (real) wood handrail, although solid paneling obstructs views when seated and makes the cabin seem dark – glass panels would have been nicer; the balconies are also very narrow. The closet space is quite good, but, although the doors, with excellent white leather handles, are wide – at 31ins (79cm), they are wider than the cabin door, and can't be opened without first closing the bathroom and toilet doors which are directly opposite.

Good quality bed linen, overlays and cushions are provided, although there is no choice of pillows.

DINING. The main restaurant, La Licorne, is chic but not pretentious. It accommodates all passengers in an open-seating arrangement and has two integral wine display cabinets (not temperature-controlled). The chairs are rather square and have very thin armrests and low backs – but they certainly look good. And the food? While appetizers and main course items are reasonably good but nothing special, the cakes and desserts are delightful.

La Boussole, an indoor/outdoor Grill (though there's no grill), has casual seating for up to 130, with self-serve buffet setup for breakfast and lunch, and a 'fast grill' dinner in an alfresco setting. But the layout is quite disjointed, and the port and starboard sides are separated by two elevators. There are two main buffet display units – one for cold food, one for hot – and a separate table setup for bread, and an active cooking station (eggs for breakfast, pasta at lunchtime).

ENTERTAINMENT. French Line, the show lounge/lecture hall, has amphitheater-style seating for 260, and a raised stage suited to concerts and cabaret presentations. The production shows are weak, repetitive, and loud. The venue is also used for expert specialist lecturers and expedition-style recaps. Two large pillars obstruct the sight lines from several seats, however.

SPA/FITNESS. The Yacht Spa facilities include a fitness room with starboard-side ocean views, adjacent kinetic wall, and a steam room, but no changing room. A wide range of massage and body treatments are provided by Carita of Paris, which staffs and oversees the facility.

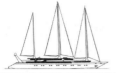

Le Ponant
★★★ +

Size:.................................Boutique Ship	Cabins (total):....................................32
Tonnage: 1,489	Size range (sq ft/m): 139.9/13.0
Lifestyle: ....Premium	Cabins (outside view):.............................32
Cruise line:..............................Ponant Cruises	Cabins (interior/no view):...........................0
Former names: ....none	Cabins (for one person):............................0
IMO number: 8914219	Cabins (with private balcony):.......................0
Builder: .... SFCN (France)	Cabins (wheelchair accessible): 0
Original cost: .... n/a	Wheelchair accessibility:.........................None
Entered service:................................1991	Cabin voltage: ....220 volts
Registry:..................................... France	Elevators:..No
Length (ft/m):..............................288.7/88.0	Casino (gaming tables):............................No
Beam (ft/m):................................39.3/12.0	Slot machines:....................................No
Draft (ft/m):.................................13.1/4.0	Swimming pools:....................................0
Propulsion/Propellers: ....diesel/sail power/1	Hot tubs (on deck):................................0
Passenger decks:...................................3	Self-service launderette:..........................No
Total crew:.......................................32	Dedicated cinema/seats:...........................No
Passengers (lower beds/alll berths):..................64/64	Library: ....Yes
Passenger Space Ratio (lower beds/all berths): 23.2/22.2	Onboard currency: .... Euros
Crew/Passenger Ratio (lower beds/all berths):.......... 2.1/2.2	

Chic decor, and for relaxed cruising for French-speakers

OVERVIEW. *Le Ponant* is best suited to young-minded couples and singles who want contemporary, sophisticated facilities in a very relaxed but chic setting, with good food and service, no entertainment, and plenty of time for quiet relaxation.

THE SHIP. Ultra sleek, and very efficiently designed, this contemporary sail-cruise ship has three masts that rise 54.7ft (16.7m) above the water line, and electronic winches assist in the furling and unfurling of the sails. The total sail area measures approximately 16,140 sq ft (1,500 sq m). This captivating ship has plenty of room on its open decks for sunbathing. Although they have padded cushions, somehow the off-white plastic sunloungers are not at all elegant.

The interior design is clean, stylish, functional, and high-tech. Three public lounges have pastel decor, soft colors and great flair. One price fits all. The ship is marketed mainly to young, sophisticated French-speaking passengers who love yachting and the sea. The company also has three mega-yacht cruise ships. Gratuities are 'not required', but they are expected.

ACCOMMODATION. There are five cabins on Antigua Deck (the open deck) and 27 on Marie Galante Deck (the lowest deck). Crisp, clean blond woods and pristine white cabins have twin beds that convert to a double. There's a mini-bar, personal safe, and a bathroom. All cabins have portholes, artwork, and a refrig-

Berlitz's Ratings		
	Possible	Achieved
Ship	500	371
Accommodation	200	143
Food	400	266
Service	400	282
Entertainment	100	70
Cruise	400	225
OVERALL SCORE		
1357 points out of 2000		

erator. There is limited storage, however, and few drawers – they are also very small. The cabin bathrooms are quite small, but efficient.

DINING. The lovely Karukera dining room has an open-seating policy. There is fresh fish daily, when available, and dinner is always treated as a true *affaire gastonomique*. The chef goes out to buy fresh local food items, including fresh fish, produce, and fruit. Free wines are included for lunch and dinner, and the cuisine is, naturally, classic French. That Frenchness also means the selection of cheeses, breads, and breakfast croissants is good. There are free cappuccinos and espressos. For casual breakfasts and luncheons, there is a charming outdoor café under a canvas sailcloth awning.

ENTERTAINMENT. There is no professional entertainment as such, although occasionally the crew may put on a little soirée. Dinner is the main event each evening, and, being a French product, dinner can provide several hours' worth of entertainment in itself.

SPA/FITNESS. There is no spa, fitness room, sauna, or steam room. However, for recreation, there are water sports facilities, and these include an aft marina platform from which you can swim, windsurfers, waterski boat, and scuba and snorkel equipment. Scuba diving costs extra, charged per dive.

Le Soleal
★★★★

Size:. . . . . Small Ship		Cabins (total):. 132		
Tonnage: 10,944		Size range (sq ft/m): 215.2–301.3/20.0–28.0		
Lifestyle: . . . . .Premium		Cabins (outside view):. 132		
Cruise line:. . . . . Ponant Cruises		Cabins (interior/no view):. 0		
Former names: . . . . .none		Cabins (for one person):. 0		
IMO number: 9641675		Cabins (with private balcony): 125		
Builder: . . . . Fincantieri (Italy)		Cabins (wheelchair accessible): 3		
Original cost:. . . . . $100 million		Wheelchair accessibility:. . . . . .Fair		
Entered service:. . . . . .Jul 2013		Cabin voltage: . . . . .110 and 220 volts		
Registry:. . . . . .Wallis & Fortuna		Elevators:. 2		
Length (ft/m):. 465.8/142.0		Casino (gaming tables):. . . . . .No		
Beam (ft/m):. 9.0/18.0		Slot machines:. . . . . Yes		
Draft (ft/m):. 15.4/4.7		Swimming pools:. 2		
Propulsion/Propellers:. . . . . diesel-electric (4,600kW)/2		Hot tubs (on deck):. 0		
Passenger decks:. 6		Self-service launderette:. 0		
Total crew:. 140		Dedicated cinema/seats:. . . . . .No		
Passengers (lower beds/alll berths):. 264/264		Library: . . . . Yes		
Passenger Space Ratio (lower beds/all berths): 41.4/41.4		Onboard currency: . . . . Euros		
Crew/Passenger Ratio (lower beds/all berths):. 1.5/1.8				

French ambience and small mega-yacht chic

OVERVIEW. *Le Soléal* is geared to young-minded couples and singles who want semi-sophisticated facilities in a relaxed but stylish yacht-like environment quite different from most cruise ships, with reasonably good food and service. The ship is often chartered or part-chartered by 'premium' travel organizers who prefer smaller ships, such as Abercrombie & Kent, Gohagen, and Tauck Tours.

Berlitz's Ratings		
	Possible	Achieved
Ship	500	404
Accommodation	200	155
Food	400	284
Service	400	299
Entertainment	100	72
Cruise	400	295
OVERALL SCORE		
1509 points out of 2000		

THE SHIP. One of a trio of identical sister ships catering mainly to French speakers, *Le Soléal* is contemporary – chic and uncluttered. With a dark grey hull and sleek white superstructure, the ship looks more like a large private yacht rather than a traditional cruise ship.

The ship has a smart 'sponson' skirt built-in at the stern – this is for operational stability – and carries a fleet of 12 Zodiac landing craft for soft expedition voyages. There is some sunbathing space outdoors forward of the funnel and around the small pool – aft of a casual eatery located one deck below – together with a shower enclosure.

Almost all the public rooms are located in the aft section, with accommodation located forward; the elevators go to all decks except the uppermost one (Deck 7). The decor is minimalist and super-yacht chic – relaxing and pleasant, with lots of browns and creams and a splash of red here and there. However, there are many reflective surfaces and the overall feeling of the decor is cool rather than warm and cosseting.

The focal point of the interior is the main lobby, with a central, circular seating and tiled floor surround; its small central section spans two decks. The other flooring is wood, which can be noisy. The lower decks of the main stairway are made of faux gray wood, while the upper decks are carpeted – a strange combination that somehow works.

This is all-inclusive cruising – except for spa treatments – with drinks, table wine for lunch and dinner, bottled mineral water, port charges, and Zodiac excursions on expedition-style cruises included in the fare. The crew is English- and French-speaking, with many hotel service staff from Asia.

Passenger niggles? There's no outside walking or jogging deck. The interior stairways are a quite steep and have short steps. The restaurant is noisy. The entertainment system is not user-friendly and internet connection is slow and expensive. Overall, it's difficult for French-speaking and non-French-speaking passengers to mix.

ACCOMMODATION. Of the 132 suites/cabins, there are three Prestige Suites with a 301 sq ft plus 54 sq ft balcony (28 plus 5 sq m). Forty of the 94 deluxe cabins – 200 sq ft plus 43 sq ft balcony (18.6 plus 4 sq m) – can be combined into 20 larger suites, each with two bathrooms, and separate living area and bedroom. All cabinetry is made in elegant dark woods. A real plus is that there are no interior (no view) cabins – every cabin has an outside view. Cabin insulation is also good, so you won't hear your neighbour easily.

The deluxe and standard cabins have a large ocean-view window, two beds that convert to a queen-size bed, and a long vanity desk with good lighting. Facilities include a TV set, DVD player, refrigerator, and personal safe. The bathrooms are marble-appointed, but they have very heavy hand-held shower hoses. Amenities include a mini-bar, personal safe, hairdryer, bathrobe, and French (L'Occitaine) personal bathroom products. Wi-Fi costs extra.

All other cabins have good-size beds, although the bedframe corners are square, – so be careful when passing between bed and a storage unit that's quite large, with two deep drawers, refrigerator, television, and wall mirror. Other facilities include good-size wardrobe-style closet (armoire) with personal safe, and a vanity desk with drawer and a small shelf.

The small cabin bathrooms (the entrance door is only 20½ins/52cm wide) also have a sliding partition window that enables you to see through the cabin to the ocean, and a deep, half-size tub/shower combination. The lip between floor and bathroom is just over 6ins (16cm) high. Bottles of L'Occitaine toiletry items are provided.

There are no shelves for toiletries, but there are two drawers under the washbasin – although they are not really practical in use. A separate cubicle houses the vacuum toilet. Balconies have faux-wood decking and a fine (real) wood handrail, although solid paneling obstructs views when seated and makes the cabin seem dark – glass panels would have been nicer; the balconies are also narrow. The closet space is decent enough, but, although the doors, with nice white leather handles, are wide – at 31ins (79cm), they are wider than the cabin door, and can't be opened without first closing the bathroom and toilet doors which are directly opposite.

Good quality bed linen, overlays and cushions are provided, although there is no choice of pillows.

DINING. The main restaurant is chic but not pretentious – or even warm. It accommodates all passengers in an open-seating arrangement and has two integral wine display cabinets (not temperature-controlled). The chairs are rather square and have very thin armrests and low backs – but they look good. And the food? While appetizers and main course items are reasonably good but nothing special, the cakes and desserts are delightful.

An indoor/outdoor Grill has casual seating for up to 130, with self-serve buffet setup for breakfast and lunch, and a 'fast grill' dinner in an alfresco setting. The layout is disjointed, and port and starboard sides are separated by two elevators. There are two main buffet display units – one for cold food, one for hot, plus a separate table setup for bread and an active cooking station (eggs for breakfast, pasta at lunchtime, for example).

ENTERTAINMENT. The showlounge, which doubles as a lecture hall, has amphitheater-style seating for 260, and a raised stage for concerts and cabaret-style entertainment. The production shows are weak, repetitive, and loud, but they do have a sort of French flair about them. The venue is also used for expedition-style recaps and lecturers, but two large pillars obstruct the sight lines from several seats.

SPA/FITNESS. The Yacht Spa facilities include a fitness room with starboard-side ocean views, adjacent kinetic wall, and a steam room, but there is no changing room. A wide range of massage and body treatments are provided by Carita of Paris, which staffs and oversees the facility.

Did you know...

...that most of the major cruise lines have replaced Champagne with sparkling wine for the captain's welcome aboard cocktail party?

...that the liner *Amerika* in 1938 was the first ship to have an alternative restaurant open separately from the dining saloons? It was named the Ritz Carlton.

...that the first à la carte restaurant aboard a passenger ship was in the German ship *Amerika* of 1905?

...that Hapag-Lloyd Cruises' *Europa 2* and TUI Cruises' *Mein Schiff 1*, *Mein Schiff 2* and *Mein Schiff 3* are the only ships with an espresso coffee machine in every cabin?

...that a whole county in Iowa raises all its beef cattle for sale to Carnival Cruise Lines?

...that the first single-berth cabins built as such were also aboard the *Campania*?

...that the whole disc of the sun is visible for 24 hours a day at some points north of the Arctic Circle? North Cape (May 14–July 29); Hammerfest (May 16–July 27); Tromso (May 20–July 22); Harstad (May 26–July 19); Bodo (June 4–July 8).

Legend of the Seas
★★★+

Size:	.Large Resort Ship	Cabins (total):	900
Tonnage:	69,130	Size range (sq ft/m):	137.7–1,147.4/12.8–106.6
Lifestyle:	Standard	Cabins (outside view):	575
Cruise line:	Royal Caribbean International	Cabins (interior/no view):	325
Former names:	none	Cabins (for one person):	0
IMO number:	9070620	Cabins (with private balcony):	231
Builder:	Chantiers de l'Atlantique (France)	Cabins (wheelchair accessible):	17
Original cost:	$325 million	Wheelchair accessibility:	Good
Entered service:	May 1995	Cabin voltage:	110 and 220 volts
Registry:	The Bahamas	Elevators:	11
Length (ft/m):	867.0/264.2	Casino (gaming tables):	Yes
Beam (ft/m):	105.0/32.0	Slot machines:	Yes
Draft (ft/m):	23.9/7.3	Swimming pools:	2 (1 with sliding glass dome)
Propulsion/Propellers:	diesel (40,200kW)/2	Hot tubs (on deck):	4
Passenger decks:	11	Self-service launderette:	No
Total crew:	720	Dedicated cinema/seats:	No
Passengers (lower beds/all berths):	1,800/2,076	Library:	Yes
Passenger Space Ratio (lower beds/all berths):	38.3/33.2	Onboard currency:	US$
Crew/Passenger Ratio (lower beds/all berths):	2.5/2.8		

Refined European decor for mature-age cruisers

OVERVIEW. Royal Caribbean International has designed a ship with much larger standard cabins than in any of its previous vessels except *Splendour of the Seas*. The ship is based in Britain in summer, and operates Europe/Med cruising for American and British passengers. It can be difficult to find relaxation areas without music, except for the Viking Crown Lounge during the day.

THE SHIP. *Legend of the Seas* has a contemporary profile and a nicely tiered stern, although the stern was fitted with a 'duck-tail' in 2013 to aid stability. The pool deck amidships overhangs the hull to provide an extremely wide deck, while still allowing the ship to navigate the Panama Canal. With engines placed midships, there is little noise and no noticeable vibration, and the ship has an operating speed of up to 24 knots.

The interior decor is colorful, if slightly glitzy for European tastes. The outside light is brought inside in many places, with over 2 acres (8,000 sq m) of glass. There's an innovative single-level sliding glass roof over the more formal setting of one of two swimming pools, providing a multi-activity, all-weather indoor-outdoor area called the Solarium. The glass roof provides shelter for the Roman-style pool and the health and fitness facilities (which are good) and slides aft to cover the miniature golf course when required – both cannot be covered at the same time, however.

Golfers are offered an 18-hole, 6,000-sq-ft (560-sq-m) miniature golf course. It has the topography of a

Berlitz's Ratings

	Possible	Achieved
Ship	500	381
Accommodation	200	140
Food	400	238
Service	400	262
Entertainment	100	74
Cruise	400	262

OVERALL SCORE
1357 points out of 2000

real course, complete with trees, foliage, grass, bridges, water hazards, and lighting for play at night. The holes themselves are 155–230 sq ft (14.3–21.3 sq m).

Inside, two full entertainment decks are sandwiched between five decks full of cabins, so there are plenty of public rooms to lounge and drink in. A multi-tiered seven-deck-high atrium lobby, complete with a huge stainless steel sculpture, connects with the impressive Viking Crown Lounge via glass-walled lifts. The casino is expansive, disorientingly glitzy but usually packed. The library, outside of which is a bust of Shakespeare, is a nice facility, with around 2,000 books. There is, sadly, no separate cinema.

ACCOMMODATION. There are many different cabin price grades. Some cabins on Deck 8 also have a larger door for wheelchair access in addition to the 17 cabins for the physically disabled, and the ship is very accessible, with ample ramped areas and sloping decks.

All cabins have a sitting area and beds that convert to double configuration, and there is ample closet and drawer space. There is not much space around the bed, though, and the showers could have been better designed. Those cabins with balconies have glass railings rather than steel/wood to provide less intrusive sightlines.

The largest accommodation is the Royal Suite, which is beautifully designed, finely decorated, and has a baby grand piano and whirlpool bathtub. Several quiet sitting areas are located adjacent to the best cabins amidships.

DINING. The Romeo and Juliet Dining Room has dramatic two-deck-high glass side walls, so many passengers both upstairs and downstairs can see both the ocean and each other in reflection; it is quite noisy when full, and would perhaps have been even better located at the stern. When you book, choose one of two seatings, or 'My Time Dining' (eat when you want, during dining room hours).

Other dining options. A cavernous indoor-outdoor Windjammer Café, located towards the bow and above the bridge, has good views on three sides from large ocean-view windows. A good-size snack area provides even more informal eating options.

A Park Café, Chef's Table, Chops Grille, and Izumi Asian Cuisine were added in a 2013 refit, and these venues provide more dining choices (most at extra cost).

ENTERTAINMENT. The, That's Entertainment Theatre seats 802 and is a single-level showlounge with tiered seating levels: sight lines are generally good from almost all seats. Strong cabaret acts are also presented here. A second entertainment lounge, the Anchors Aweigh Lounge, is where cabaret acts, including late-night adult comedy are presented. Other lounges and bars have live music for listening and dancing, and arial entertainment is featured in The Centrum – the atrium lobby.

Entertainment throughout the ship is upbeat – in fact, it is difficult to get away from music and noise – but is typical of the kind of resort hotel found ashore in Las Vegas. There is even background music in all corridors and elevators, and constant music outdoors on the pool deck. If you want a quiet relaxing holiday, choose another ship.

SPA/FITNESS. The ShipShape Fitness Center has a gymnasium, located on the port side of the ship, aft of the funnel, and has a small selection of high-tech muscle-pumping equipment. There is also an aerobics studio (classes are offered in a variety of keep-fit regimes), a beauty salon, and a sauna, as well as treatment rooms for such pampering procedures as massages and facials. While the facilities are quite small when compared with those aboard the company's newer ships, they are adequate for the short cruises that this ship operates.

For more sporting passengers, there is activity galore – including a rock-climbing wall with several separate climbing tracks. It is located outdoors at the aft end of the funnel.

Fun facts

Cruise ship design is interesting. The beauty of design lies in curves, not in straight lines. Today's large resort ships, designed merely for cruising in warm weather regions and not for voyaging across the North Atlantic (heaven forbid, the delivery voyage was enough), are made of straight lines. They are boxy and cold in appearance, although they provide much more usable space inside the ship (some call it warehouse cruising). Take a look at *Disney Magic* and you won't find many straight lines. Then look at the boxy, angular *Carnival Imagination* and compare the two.

Beatrice Muller, now in her 80s, makes her permanent home at sea. She lives almost year-round aboard Cunard Line's *Queen Victoria,* paying a set amount to reside in her chosen cabin. She prefers being aboard the ship rather than sit around in a retirement home in Britain's damp climate, and proves that the world is her oyster. She loves it because she doesn't have to deal with the daily drudgery of shopping, doesn't need a car, or pay electric, gas or telephone bills. She communicates with her family by using the computer center's email service.

Cruise lines and charity go hand in hand (or hand in pocket), giving back to the community. The cruise industry holds fundraising events and makes huge donations to help natural disaster relief efforts, and to various charitable foundations. New ship debuts are almost always accompanied by gala evenings in the name of a well-deserved charity (often for children) or medical research organization (usually connected with cancer), Cunard donated 1,500 pieces of classic furniture from the 1994 refit of *QE2* to the Salvation Army for its adult rehabilitation program. Crew aboard the same ship donate money to buy guide dogs for the blind, or an ambulance for the St John's Ambulance Brigade in the UK. Cunard also collects money from passengers for The Prince's Trust, headed by the Prince of Wales. Princess Cruises made a 'sizeable' contribution to UNICEF following the death of Audrey Hepburn in 1993 (she named the company's former *Star Princess*). Passengers of Hapag-Lloyd's *Europa* have donated more than 1 million euros to children's homes in Vietnam.

Both Holland America Line and Princess Cruises have contributed heavily to the Raptor Center in Juneau, Alaska. MSC Cruises has raised more than $2 million for UNICEF; meanwhile, small ship company Fred. Olsen Cruise Lines' purchased its fourth lifeboat for the Royal National Lifeboat Institution funded by passenger donations. For the relief effort following the earthquake in Haiti in 2010, various cruise companies donated close to $10 million in financial aid, goods and services (Carnival Corporation and its brands alone donated $5 million). In 2011, Mitsui OSK Line (one of three Japanese cruise lines) donated its cruise ship *Fuji Maru* to the Japanese government in the aftermath of the great east Japan earthquake and tsunami.

Someone forgot to 'score' the Champagne bottle when Dame Judi Dench named *Carnival Legend* in Harwich, England, on August 21, 2002. On the first two tries, the bottle didn't break. Then Dame Judi took the bottle in her own hands and smashed it against the side of the ship. It broke, and the foam and champagne went all over her.

In the mid-1960s there were 12 'bell boys' ('piccolos' in hotelspeak) aboard the Cunard Line's *RMS Queen Elizabeth* and *Queen Mary*. They manned the elevators and opened the doors to the various restaurants. Each day, before they were allowed to work, they all lined up and their fingernails were inspected. Those were the days.

Liberty of the Seas
★★★+

Size:.....................................Large Resort Ship	Crew/Passenger Ratio (lower beds/all berths):..........2.6/3.1
Tonnage:......................................154,407	Cabins (total):.....................................1,817
Lifestyle:.....................................Standard	Size range (sq ft/m):.............149.0–2,025.0/13.8–188.1
Cruise line:..................Royal Caribbean International	Cabins (outside view):............................1,084
Former names:.....................................none	Cabins (interior/no view):............................733
IMO number:...................................9330032	Cabins (for one person):................................0
Builder:..................Kvaerner Masa-Yards (Finland)	Cabins (with private balcony):........................842
Original cost:.............................$590 million	Cabins (wheelchair accessible):........................32
Entered service:............................May 2007	Wheelchair accessibility:............................Best
Registry:..................................The Bahamas	Cabin voltage:.............................110 volts
Length (ft/m):............................1,112.2/339.0	Elevators:.......................................14
Beam (ft/m):.............................184.0/56.0	Casino (gaming tables):..............................Yes
Draft (ft/m):...............................27.8/8/5	Slot machines:.....................................Yes
Propulsion/Propellers:......diesel-electric (75,600kW)/3 pods (2	Swimming pools:.....................................2
azimuthing, 1 fixed)	Hot tubs (on deck):...................................6
Passenger decks:...................................15	Self-service launderette:............................No
Total crew:....................................1,397	Dedicated cinema/seats:.............................No
Passengers (lower beds/alll berths):..............3,634/4,375	Library:...Yes
Passenger Space Ratio (lower beds/all berths):.......42.0/35.3	Onboard currency:.................................US$

A large resort ship for family-friendly cruising

OVERVIEW. *Liberty of the Seas* is a large, Las Vegas-style floating resort city. The facilities (such as public rooms, bars, and lounges) of the Voyager-class ships have been incorporated in this larger version, but with more conference and meetings facilities, Wi-Fi capabilities, and connectivity for cell phones.

THE SHIP. *Liberty of the Seas* is a fine ship for families with children. The ship's 'pod' propulsion system virtually eliminates vibration. The ship's 'wow' factor is the H2O Zone, a water-themed play area for families; by night it turns into a colorfully lit sculpture garden. Adjacent is a 'sports' pool. Two 16-person hot tubs are cantilevered 12ft (3.7m) over the ship's sides in an adults-only Solarium area.

There are 16 bars and lounges to enjoy, plus a whole promenade of shops, munching and drinking spots along the Royal Promenade. One deck down from the Royal Promenade is a large Casino Royale, The Catacombs disco, Schooner Bar, Boleros Lounge, and a photo gallery and shop, while the forward section leads into the three-deck-high Platinum Theatre.

A regulation-size ice-skating rink called Studio B has real, not fake, ice, with bleachers seating, and good broadcast facilities. Outstanding Ice Follies shows are presented here, but note that a number of slim pillars obstruct clear-view arena stage sight lines.

Almost at the top of the ship is RCI's trademark Viking Crown Lounge, the cutely named Olive or Twist jazz lounge, and a wedding chapel. Other facilities in-

Berlitz's Ratings

	Possible	Achieved
Ship	500	390
Accommodation	200	141
Food	400	236
Service	400	283
Entertainment	100	74
Cruise	400	267

OVERALL SCORE
1391 points out of 2000

clude a cigar smoker's lounge, conference center, a concierge lounge (for suite occupants only), and a comfortable 3,600-book library.

Liberty of the Seas is an exciting and very comfortable ship, with contemporary decor. However, there are only four banks of elevators (two forward and two aft) totaling 14, so if you have a cabin in the center of the ship, you'll need to walk in order to travel vertically between decks; and there are only two major passenger stairways – one forward, one aft.

FAMILIES. Children are well catered to, with Adventure Ocean (on Deck 12) for kids of six months to 17 years of age (teens get their own chill-out room). Children will love this ship and all the fun activities and sports activities.

ACCOMMODATION. There is a wide range of cabins in 14 categories and 21 price grades. There are many family-friendly cabins, good for family reunions.
Presidential Family Suite. Two master bedrooms each have twin beds that convert to queen-size, a private balcony, sofa bed, bar, private bathroom, bathtub, vanity, hair-dryer, flat screen TV, and phone. The suite has great views over the ship's stern, and occupants have access to the Concierge Club lounge and services. There is only one Presidential Family Suite, which can sleep up to 14, though this would be quite cramped. Size: 1,215 sq ft (113 sq m) plus Balcony: 810 sq ft (75 sq m), set with lounge area and dining table.

Royal Suite. Features a separate bedroom with king-size bed, private balcony, living room with queen-size sofa bed, and private bathroom. Size: 1,406 sq ft (131 sq m) plus Balcony: 377 sq ft (35 sq m).

Royal Family Suite. There are two bedrooms with twin beds that convert to queen-size beds (one room has third and fourth Pullman beds), a private balcony, two bathrooms, and living area with double sofa bed. Size: 588 sq ft (54.6 sq m) plus Balcony: 234 sq ft (21.7 sq m).

Owners Suite. There's a queen-size bed, private balcony, separate living area with queen-size sofa bed, wet bar, vanity area, walk-in closet; bathroom with tub and shower, plus access to the Concierge Club lounge and attendant services. Sleeps up to five. Size: 506 sq ft (46 sq m) plus Balcony: 131 sq ft (12.1 sq m).

Grand Suite. Two twin beds convert to queen-size. There's a private balcony, sitting area (some with sofa bed), vanity area; bathroom with tub and shower. Access to the Concierge Club lounge and services. Sleeps up to four. Size: 381 sq ft (35.3 sq meters) plus Balcony: 89 sq ft (8.2 sq m).

Junior Suite. Two twin beds convertible to queen-size, private balcony, sitting area (some with sofa bed), vanity area; bathroom with tub and shower. Sleeps up to four. Size: 285.2 sq ft (26.5 sq m) plus Balcony: 101 sq ft (9.3 sq m).

Superior Oceanview Cabin. Two twin beds convertible to queen-size, a private balcony, sitting area (some with sofa bed), vanity area; bathroom with shower. Sleeps two (some rooms sleep three or four). Size: 202 sq ft (18.7 sq m) plus Balcony: 42 sq ft (3.9 sq m).

Deluxe Oceanview Cabin. Same facilities as Superior Oceanview cabins, but size is different: 173 sq ft (16.0 sq m) plus Balcony: 46 sq ft (4.2 sq m).

Promenade Cabin (interior, but overlooking the Royal Promenade). A view of the Royal Promenade with bay windows, two twin beds that convert to queen-size, and private bathroom. Size: 149 sq ft (13.8 sq m).

Promenade Family Cabin. There are two twin beds that convert to queen-size, and private bathroom. Size: 300 sq ft (27.8 sq m).

Interior Cabin. Two twin beds convertible to queen-size; private bathroom with shower. Sleeps two (some rooms sleep three or four). Size: 152 sq ft (14.1 sq m).

Family Ocean-view Cabin. Located at the front of the ship, it contains two twin beds (convertible to queen-size), sofa and/or Pullman beds, sitting area; bathroom, with shower. Accommodates six and has 48-in (122-cm) round windows. Size: 265 sq ft (24.6 sq m).

All cabins have a private bathroom (with tub and shower, or shower only), vanity desk with hairdryer, mini-bar, safe, flat-screen TV, iPod dock, radio, and satellite telephone. A room service menu is provided. Suite occupants have access to a Concierge Lounge, for more personal service – this saves standing in line at the reception desk.

DINING. The main dining room is large and is set on three levels. A dramatic staircase connects all three, and huge support pillars obstruct the sight lines. When you book, choose one of two seatings, or 'My Time Dining'. Tables are for 4-12. The place settings, porcelain, and cutlery are of good quality.

Other dining options. Promenade Café: for Continental breakfast, all-day pizzas (Sorrento's), sandwiches, and coffees (in paper cups).

Windjammer Café: this is a really large, sprawling venue for casual buffet-style, self-help breakfast (this tends to be the busiest time of the day), lunch, and light dinners (but not on the last night of the cruise); it's often difficult to find a table and by the time you do your food could be cold.

Jade 'Restaurant' (it's actually a section of the Windjammer Café), for casual Asian-themed food.

Portofino: this is an upscale Euro-Italian restaurant, open for dinner only. Reservations are required, and there's gratuity. Choices include: antipasti, soup, salad, pasta, main dish, dessert, cheese, and coffee (the menu does not change during the cruise).

Chops Grill: an intimate restaurant for steaks and seafood. There's a cover charge.

Johnny Rockets: a retro 1950s all-day, all-night diner-style eatery that has hamburgers, hot dogs and other fast-food items, and malt shakes, with both indoor and outdoor seating (indoor tables have a mini-jukebox), and singing waitresses. There's a cover charge.

Sprinkles: for round-the-clock ice cream and yoghurt, pastries and coffee.

ENTERTAINMENT. The Platinum Theatre is a stunning, well-designed showlounge located at the forward end of the ship, with only a few slim pillars and almost no disruption of sight lines. The showlounge has a hydraulic orchestra pit and huge stage areas, as well as superb lighting equipment.

A performance not to be missed is the Greatest Show at Sea Parade – a 15-minute extravaganza that bumbles along the Royal Promenade; it replicates the parade of stars and animals at a circus of yesteryear. This is when it's really good to have one of those interior-view atrium cabins. Otherwise, get a position early along the Royal Promenade.

SPA/FITNESS. The Steiner-operated Day Spa is large. It includes a large aerobics room, fitness center, treatment rooms, and sauna/steam rooms and relaxation areas. Some basic exercise classes are free, but others cost extra. Active types can go body-boarding, go boxing in the full-size boxing ring, go rock-climbing, in-line skating, jog, putt, swim, surf, or play in the golf simulators.

Louis Aura
★★ +

Size:..................................... Mid-size Ship	Cabins (total):..414	
Tonnage:.. 16,916	Size range (sq ft/m): 111.9–324.0/10.4–30.1	
Lifestyle: ....Standard	Cabins (outside view):...............................192	
Cruise line:............................... Louis Cruises	Cabins (interior/no view):.............................200	
Former names: .... Orient Queen, Bolero, Starward	Cabins (for one person):................................0	
IMO number: 6821080	Cabins (with private balcony):............................0	
Builder: .... A.G. Weser (Germany)	Cabins (wheelchair accessible): 2	
Original cost:..na	Wheelchair accessibility:...........................None	
Entered service:...................... Dec 1968/Aug 2006	Cabin voltage: ....110 and 220 volts	
Registry:..................................... Greece	Elevators:..4	
Length (ft/m):............................. 525.9/160.3	Casino (gaming tables):............................... Yes	
Beam (ft/m):............................... 74.9/22.8	Slot machines:..................................... Yes	
Draft (ft/m): 22.5/6.8	Swimming pools:......................................2	
Propulsion/Propellers:.................. diesel (12,950kW)/2	Hot tubs (on deck):...................................9	
Passenger decks:......................................7	Self-service launderette:.............................. Yes	
Total crew:..400	Dedicated cinema/seats:.............................. Yes	
Passengers (lower beds/alll berths):................. 828/910	Library: .... Yes	
Passenger Space Ratio (lower beds/all berths): 26.3/18.5	Onboard currency: .... Euros	
Crew/Passenger Ratio (lower beds/all berths):.......... 2.4/2.9		

A traditional small, casual ship for frugal cruisers

OVERVIEW. *Louis Aura* (ex-*Orient Queen*) will suit adult couples and single travelers who want to cruise aboard a smaller ship, in modest, fairly cramped, but quite comfortable surroundings, at a modest price.

THE SHIP. The open deck and sunbathing space is very limited and some of the decks are of plain, painted steel. On the aft decks, there's a clutter of wooden sunloungers, and sun-shade umbrellas. Forward of the twin funnels is an enclosed sports facility. Aft of the mast is a solarium-style shielded housing, with a multi-level lounge/bar/disco that's adjacent to one of the ship's small swimming pools. The dress code is casual.

There's a decent choice of public rooms, including six bars, all with clean, contemporary furnishings, upbeat fabric colors, and a mix of traditional and fairly contemporary decor. However, the diesel engines tend to throb in some parts of the vessel and can be a little noisy, particularly for occupants of cabins on the lower decks close to the engine casing.

ACCOMMODATION. There are four Royal Suites, and 54 other 'suites' (they are not really suites, because there is no separate bedroom). The other cabins are very compact units that are moderately comfortable and decorated in soft colors. While closet space is limited, there are plenty of drawers, although they are metal and tinny.

The bathrooms are small, compact units, and the towels provided are not large. Toilets are of the gentle

Berlitz's Ratings		
	Possible	Achieved
Ship	500	273
Accommodation	200	94
Food	400	216
Service	400	244
Entertainment	100	55
Cruise	400	206
OVERALL SCORE		
1088 points out of 2000		

flush (non-vacuum) variety. Unfortunately, the soundproofing between the cabins is poor, and air conditioning is noisy.

The four Royal suites have decent space. There is ample floor space, a king-size bed, vanity desk, closet, plenty of drawer and storage space, a lounge with a sofa that converts into an additional bed, drinks table, and two chairs. A large pillar obstructs movement. The bathroom has a small but deep tub with hand-held shower. Operates Cuba cruises under charter during the winter.

DINING. There are four eateries. The 444-seat Mermaid Restaurant is cheerful, even almost charming, and has some prime tables that overlook the stern. Seating is at tables for four, six, or eight, with two seatings. The cuisine is Mediterranean, with some Greek specialties, while the wine list consists mainly of young wines.

Breakfast and lunch buffets are provided indoors at the casual self-serve Horizon Café, with outdoor seating at tables around the aft swimming pool, but space is tight.

ENTERTAINMENT. The 420-seat El Cabaret Show-lounge is a single-level room, and provides poor entertainment. There's also a nightclub.

SPA/FITNESS. There is a beauty salon and massage/body treatment room – on two different decks.

Louis Cristal
★★★

Size:..................................... Mid-size Ship	Crew/Passenger Ratio (lower beds/all berths):......... 2.4/3.1
Tonnage:....................................... 25,611	Cabins (total):..483
Lifestyle:....................................Standard	Size range (sq ft/m):................. 107.6–462.8/10.0–43.0
Cruise line:.............................. Louis Cruises	Cabins (outside view):................................318
Former names: .... Silja Opera, SuperStar Taurus, Leeward, Sally	Cabins (interior/no view):.............................165
Albatross, Viking Saga	Cabins (for one person):................................0
IMO number:................................7827213	Cabins (with private balcony):.........................10
Builder:............................. Wartsila (Finland)	Cabins (wheelchair accessible): 6
Original cost:...................................... n/a	Wheelchair accessibility:...........................None
Entered service:......................... 1980/Jul 2007	Cabin voltage: ....110 and 220 volts
Registry:.................................... Malta	Elevators:..4
Length (ft/m):............................. 530.5/161.7	Casino (gaming tables):..............................Yes
Beam (ft/m):............................. 100.0/30.5	Slot machines:.......................................Yes
Draft (ft/m):............................... 20.1/6.1	Swimming pools:......................................1
Propulsion/Propellers:................. diesel (19,120kW)/2	Hot tubs (on deck):...................................0
Passenger decks:....................................7	Self-service launderette:............................No
Total crew:.......................................400	Dedicated cinema/seats:..............................Yes
Passengers (lower beds/alll berths):...............966/1,278	Library: .... Yes
Passenger Space Ratio (lower beds/all berths): 26.5/20.0	Onboard currency: .... Euros

A casual ship and friendly crew for port-intensive cruises

OVERVIEW. This ship will appeal to first-time passengers who simply want to cruise the Greek Islands in a modicum of comfort, and at a bargain price. The dress code is casual throughout, with no formal nights. The ship is due to be refitted/refurbished.

THE SHIP. *Louis Cristal* has undergone a number of changes, modifications, and mishaps during its busy life. Originally built as a Viking Line passenger ferry, it was extensively reconstructed in 1995 to the tune of $60 million, after which it operated under charter to Norwegian Cruise Line as *Leeward*.

The ship has a smart wedge-shaped profile with a squared-off stern and short, stubby bows, and the enclosed bridge looks like it's really one deck lower than it should be. But *Louis Cristal* does benefit from a good, walk-around teakwood promenade deck. The pool deck is very cramped, although the pool itself can be covered by a sliding glass dome. There is no forward-facing observation lounge atop the ship, but there is a reasonable array of public rooms, lounges, bars, and meeting places. Note that gratuities are not included in the fare.

ACCOMMODATION. There are three suite categories (Grand, Imperial, and Royal, plus an interior 'suite'), and a mix of several outside-view cabins (some of which have balconies) and interior cabins in 19 price grades.

The top-grade suites have neatly-angled private bal-

Berlitz's Ratings

	Possible	Achieved
Ship	500	322
Accommodation	200	133
Food	400	230
Service	400	246
Entertainment	100	65
Cruise	400	243
OVERALL SCORE		
1239 points out of 2000		

conies and provide a decent amount of space for short cruises; the bathrooms have a tub, separate shower, and good storage facilities for toiletries. Most of the standard cabins are really quite small. The bathrooms really are dimensionally challenged – dancing with the shower curtain comes to mind. Also, note that some cabins have views obstructed by safety equipment.

DINING. There are two principal dining rooms, plus a number of other dining spots and casual eateries. There are two seatings for dinner on most nights (typically an open seating for the first night), and open seating for breakfast and lunch. Your seating and table assignments for dinner are made by the maître d' during embarkation.

The cuisine is predominantly Continental, with some Greek specialties. All tables are laid with crisp white linen. Spa and vegetarian dishes are available on lunch and dinner menus. Louis Cruises makes all its own breads, soups, pâtés, jams, pizzas, and beef burgers on board from scratch.

ENTERTAINMENT. The show lounge has tiered seating and decent sight lines, but entertainment is a weak link in the overall cruise experience.

SPA/FITNESS. Facilities include a beauty salon, fitness room, and sauna. Massages, aromatherapy facials, manicures, pedicures, and hair treatments are available.

Louis Olympia
★★★

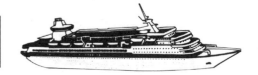

Size:............................... Mid-size Ship		Cabins (total):....................................725	
Tonnage:..37,773		Size range (sq ft/m):......... 118.4–425.1/11.0–39.5	
Lifestyle:.......................................Standard		Cabins (outside view):............................425	
Cruise line:...............................Louis Cruises		Cabins (interior/no view):........................300	
Former names: ..... Thomson Destiny, Sunbird, Song of America		Cabins (for one person):............................0	
IMO number:.................................8814744		Cabins (with private balcony):......................9	
Builder:.............................Wartsila (Finland)		Cabins (wheelchair accessible): 0	
Original cost:...........................$140 million		Wheelchair accessibility:.........................Fair	
Entered service:.....................Dec 1982/May 2012		Cabin voltage: .... 110 volts	
Registry:.....................................The Bahamas		Elevators:..7	
Length (ft/m):............................ 705.0/214.8		Casino (gaming tables):............................ Yes	
Beam (ft/m):................................. 93.1/28.4		Slot machines:.................................... Yes	
Draft (ft/m):................................. 22.3/6.8		Swimming pools:.....................................2	
Propulsion/Propellers:..................diesel (16,480kW)/2		Hot tubs (on deck):...................................0	
Passenger decks:..................................11		Self-service launderette:...........................No	
Total crew:...540		Dedicated cinema/seats:............................No	
Passengers (lower beds/alll berths):............. 1,450/1,664		Library: .... Yes	
Passenger Space Ratio (lower beds/all berths): 26.0/23.4		Onboard currency: .... Euros	
Crew/Passenger Ratio (lower beds/all berths):.......... 2.6/2.9			

A family-friendly ship for casual cruising

OVERVIEW. *Louis Olympia* is best suited to adult couples and singles taking their first or second cruise, and families with children, all seeking a modern but not glitzy ship with a wide array of public lounges and bars, a middle-of-the-road lifestyle, and decent food and service. It operates in the Greek Islands and Mediterranean.

THE SHIP. Originally built for Royal Caribbean International, the all-white ship is smart-looking, with nicely rounded lines, sharply raked bow, and a single funnel with a cantilevered, wraparound lounge – a fine place from which to observe the world around and below you.

There's a decent amount of open deck and sunbathing space – but it will be crowded when the ship sails full, which is most of the time. There are some nicely polished wooden decks and rails and two swimming pools – the aft one designated for children, the forward one for adults.

The interior decor is bright and breezy. There's a good array of public rooms, most with high ceilings. All are located one deck above the dining room and include the main showlounge, casino, and nightclub. There's also a small conference center for meetings, as well as an Internet café with several computer terminals.

There are no cushioned pads for the sunloungers. Standing in line for embarkation, disembarkation, shore tenders, and for self-serve buffet meals is an inevitable aspect of cruising aboard all large ships. Passenger niggles include the dated look of the ship's interiors.

Berlitz's Ratings

	Possible	Achieved
Ship	500	310
Accommodation	200	118
Food	400	242
Service	400	251
Entertainment	100	63
Cruise	400	262
OVERALL SCORE		
1246 points out of 2000		

The best part of cruising aboard *Louis Olympia* lies in the destinations, and not the ship – although it is perfectly comfortable, and Louis Cruises provides a consistent, well-tuned, and well-packaged product.

ACCOMMODATION. This is provided in several categories and price bands: Interior Cabins (parallel or L-shaped bed arrangement), Outside View Cabins (parallel or L-shaped bed arrangement), Deluxe Cabins (with parallel twin beds that can convert to a queen-size bed), Suites, and Grand Suites.

Most cabins are of a similar size – dimensionally challenged when compared to today's newer ships – and insulation between them is poor. The cabins also have mediocre closets and little storage space, yet somehow everyone seems to manage. They are just about adequate for a one-week cruise, as you'll require only a small selection of mainly casual clothes. You'll probably need to store your shoes and luggage under the bed.

Most bathrooms contain a washbasin, toilet, and shower, with very little space for toiletries. Although they are reasonably cheerful, the shower enclosure is small, and has a curtain that you will probably end up dancing with.

In some cabins, twin beds are fixed in a parallel mode – some are moveable and can be made into a queen-size bed – while others may be in an L-shape. In almost all cabins there is a threshold of about nine inches (23cm) at the bathroom door to step over.

You can get more space and a larger cabin if you book one of the 21 slightly more expensive deluxe-grade cabins on Promenade Deck. These have twin beds that convert to a queen-size bed, set diagonally into a sleeping area adjacent to outside-view windows. There's more drawer space, more closet space, and the bathroom has a half-size tub and shower combination. Bathrobes are also provided. The largest of these deluxe-grade cabins is Cabin 7000.

For even more exclusivity, you can book one of nine suites. All are located in a private area, have fine wood paneling and trim, and come with additional space and better, more personalized service.

The additional space includes a lounge area with sofa (this converts to a double bed – making it ideal for families with children), coffee table and two chairs, a vanity desk, combination TV/DVD, an abundance of drawers, illuminated closets with both hanging space and several shelves, excellent storage space, king-size bed, and bathrobes. The bathroom is fully tiled and has a full-size enamel tub (rare in ships today) with shower, pink granite-look washbasin, and plenty of storage space for toiletries.

Suite occupants also get a semi-private balcony – whose door is extremely heavy and hard to open – with drinks table and two teak chairs. Book one of the two Grand Suites, and you'll get even more room – plus views over the bows and a larger balcony (these can be overlooked from the open deck above), more floor space, and a walk-in closet. Missing are a bedside telephone and a bathroom telephone.

The accommodation deck hallways are also very narrow on some decks.

DINING. The Seven Seas Restaurant, a large room, consists of a central main section and two long, narrow wings – the Magellan Room and Galileo Room – with large, ocean-view windows. The low ceiling creates a high level of ambient noise. There are two seatings. There are tables for two (but only 14), four, six, or eight, and window tables are for two or six.

If you enjoy eating out adventurously, you could be disappointed. The menus are standard and deviation is difficult. Bottled water costs extra. There is an adequate wine list. Wine prices are quite modest, as are the prices for most alcoholic drinks.

Other dining options. For casual, self-serve breakfasts and lunches, the Veranda Café is the alternative choice, although the tables and seats outdoors are of metal and plastic, and the buffets are basic and old-fashioned. The low cruise fare dictates the use of plastic cups and plastic stirrers – teaspoons are unheard of. At night you can 'dine' under the steel and canvas canopy, where the café becomes a pleasant, outdoors alternative to the dining room – and includes waiter service.

The excellent Italian illy coffee brand is featured aboard this ship, together with a selection of fine teas, in several bars and lounges.

ENTERTAINMENT. The Can Can Lounge, the venue for all entertainment events and social functions, has a stage and hardwood dance floor. It is a single-level room, designed more for cabaret acts than for large-scale production shows. The revue-style shows are typically of the end-of-pier variety type, with an energetic, well-meaning cast of young people who also double as cruise staff during the day, together with some professional cabaret acts.

Another, smaller room, the Oklahoma Lounge, has a stage and dance floor, and is often used to present late-night comedy and other acts.

SPA/FITNESS. Although the Ocean's Spa facilities are not exactly generous, there is a gymnasium, sauna but no steam room, changing rooms for men and women, and a beauty salon. You can book a massage, an aromatherapy facial, manicure, and pedicure, among other treatments. Sports facilities include basketball, badminton, and table tennis.

About name badges

Should staff name badges be on the left or right side of the body? In the hospitality industry, name badges are worn on the left side of the body. There are two principal reasons for this:

Typically 81 percent of humans are right-handed, and the human eye naturally goes towards the right (that is, the left side of the body of the person facing you).

The right side of the body is considered reserved for the military, whose name badges are always worn on the right side of the body (medals being worn on the left, or most important, side). You may also notice that when cameras pan in a documentary film made by painstaking professionals (such as in nature films), it is normal to pan from right to left.

Maasdam
★★★+

Size:..................................... Mid-size Ship	Cabins (total):....................................632
Tonnage:.. 55,451	Size range (sq ft/m):..............186.2–1,124.8/17.3–104.5
Lifestyle:.......................................Premium	Cabins (outside view):..............................502
Cruise line:.......................... Holland America Line	Cabins (interior/no view):...........................131
Former names:......................................none	Cabins (for one person):..............................0
IMO number:................................... 8919257	Cabins (with private balcony):.......................150
Builder:............................. Fincantieri (Italy)	Cabins (wheelchair accessible):........................6
Original cost:.............................. $215 million	Wheelchair accessibility:..........................Good
Entered service:............................. Dec 1993	Cabin voltage:........................110 and 220 volts
Registry:.................................The Netherlands	Elevators:..8
Length (ft/m):............................... 719.3/219.3	Casino (gaming tables):............................. Yes
Beam (ft/m):................................. 101.0/30.8	Slot machines:..................................... Yes
Draft (ft/m):................................... 24.6/7.5	Swimming pools:....................2 (1 w/sliding glass dome)
Propulsion/Propellers:........... diesel-electric (34,560kW)/2	Hot tubs (on deck):...................................2
Passenger decks:....................................10	Self-service launderette:.......................... Yes
Total crew:..557	Dedicated cinema/seats:........................... Yes
Passengers (lower beds/alll berths):........... 1,266/1,627	Library:.. Yes
Passenger Space Ratio (lower beds/all berths):....... 43.8/34.0	Onboard currency:................................US$
Crew/Passenger Ratio (lower beds/all berths):......... 2.2/2.9	

Dutch-style decor for mature-age regular cruisers

OVERVIEW. Holland America Line constantly fine-tunes its performance, and its regular passengers, almost all North American, find its ships comfortable and well-run. HAL continues its strong maritime traditions and keeps its vessels clean and tidy, although the food and service components still let the rest of the cruise experience down.

THE SHIP. *Maasdam* is one of four almost identical ships, along with *Statendam*, *Ryndam*, and *Veendam*. Although the exterior styling is rather angular (some would say boxy – the funnel certainly is), it is softened and balanced somewhat by the black hull. There is a full walk-around teak promenade deck outdoors – excellent for strolling, and, thankfully, there's no sign of synthetic turf. The sunloungers on the exterior promenade deck are wood, and have comfortable cushioned pads, while those at the swimming pool on Lido Deck are of white plastic. There is good passenger flow throughout the public areas.

In the interiors of this 'S'-class ship, an asymmetrical layout helps to reduce bottlenecks and congestion. Most of the public rooms are concentrated on two decks, Promenade Deck and Upper Promenade Deck, which creates a spacious feel to the ship's interiors. In general, the interior styling is restrained, using contemporary materials combined with traditional woods and ceramics. There is, thankfully, little glitz anywhere.

Some $2 million worth of artwork was assembled and nicely displayed to represent HAL's fine Dutch

Berlitz's Ratings		
	Possible	Achieved
Ship	500	352
Accommodation	200	142
Food	400	247
Service	400	283
Entertainment	100	68
Cruise	400	265
OVERALL SCORE		
1357 points out of 2000		

heritage and to present a balance between standard itineraries and onboard creature comforts. Several oil paintings of the line's former ships by Stephen Card, a former captain, adorn stairway landings. Also noticeable are the fine flower arrangements in the public areas and foyers – used to good effect to brighten up what to some is dull decor. Atop the ship, with forward facing views that wrap around the sides, is the Crow's Nest Lounge. By day it is a decent observation lounge, with large ocean-view windows; by night it turns into a nightclub with extremely variable lighting.

The atrium foyer is three decks high, although its light-catching green glass sculpted centerpiece (*Totem* by Luciano Vistosi, composed of almost 2,000 pieces of glass) makes it look a little crowded, and leaves little room in front of the Front Office. A hydraulic glass roof covers the reasonably sized swimming pool/hot tubs and central Lido area – whose focal point is a large dolphin sculpture – so that this can be used in either fine or poor weather.

This ship has a large, relaxing Leyden Library; a card room, an Explorer's Lounge (good for afternoon tea and after-dinner coffee), an intimate Piano Bar, and a casino. The casino features gaming tables and slot machines. However, note that part of the casino is open, and passers-by can be subject to cigarette smoke (yes, smoking is still permitted), so non-smokers should hold their breath.

Holland America Line's many repeat passengers seem to enjoy the fact that social dancing is always on the menu. In the final analysis, however, the score for this ship ends up a tad under what it could be if the food and food service staff were more memorable – more professional training might help.

Niggles? An escalator travels between two of the lower decks, one of which was originally planned to be the embarkation point, but it is almost pointless. The charge to use the washing machines and dryers in the self-service launderette is petty, particularly for suite occupants, who pay high prices for their cruises. The men's urinals in public restrooms are unusually high. Sadly, the ship is now looking decidedly tired and dated, like the towels.

Perhaps the ship's best asset is its friendly, personable Filipino and Indonesian crew, although communication can prove frustrating and service is inconsistent.

ACCOMMODATION. The accommodation ranges from small interior cabins to a large penthouse suite, in 17 price categories. The interior and outside standard cabins have twin beds that convert to a queen-size bed, and there is a separate living space with sofa and coffee table. Although the drawer space is generally good, the closet space is very tight, particularly for long cruises, although more than adequate for a seven-night cruise. Bathrobes are provided for all suites and cabins, as are hairdryers, and a small range of toiletries. The bathrooms are quite well laid out, but the tubs are small units better described as shower tubs.

On Navigation Deck, 28 suites have accommodation for up to four. These have in-suite dining as an alternative to the dining room, for private meals. These are spacious, tastefully decorated and well laid-out, and have a separate, good-size living room, a bedroom with two lower beds that convert to a king-size bed, dressing room, plenty of closet and drawer space (walk-in closet), marble bathroom with Jacuzzi tub, and separate toilet/washroom with bidet.

Penthouse Suite. The largest accommodation, this is located on the starboard side of Navigation Deck at the forward staircase. It has a king-size bed and vanity desk; large walk-in closet with superb drawer space, oversize whirlpool bath (it could seat four) and separate shower enclosure, separate washroom with toilet, bidet, and washbasin; living room with writing desk, large TV set, and full set of audio equipment; dressing room, large private balcony (with teak lounge chairs and drinks tables, dining table and four chairs), mini-bar/refrigerator, a pantry with large refrigerator, toaster unit, and full coffee/tea-making facilities and food preparation area. There's a separate entrance from the hallway, a guest toilet, and floor-to-ceiling windows.

DINING. The Rotterdam Dining Room, spanning two decks, is located aft. It is quite large, and has a grand staircase, panoramic views on three sides, and a music balcony. Both open seating and assigned seating are available, while breakfast and lunch are open-seating – you'll be seated by restaurant staff when you enter. The waiter stations are very noisy for anyone seated near them.

Other dining option. The 66-seat Pinnacle Grill is located just forward of the balcony level of the main dining room on the starboard side. It serves Pacific Northwest cuisine such as Dungeness crab, Alaska salmon, halibut, and other regional specialties (reservations needed, cover charge applies). A Bulgari show plate, Rosenthal china, Reidel wine glasses, and Frette table linen are used. The Pinnacle Grill is a much better, more relaxed dining experience than the main dining room and worth it for that special celebration.

For more casual evening eating, the Lido Buffet is open for casual dinners on all except the last night of each cruise, in an open-seating arrangement. Tables are set with crisp linens, flatware, and stemware. A set menu includes a choice of several entreés. The buffet is also open for casual breakfasts and lunches. Again there is much use of canned fruits and packeted items, although there are several commercial low-calorie salad dressings. The beverage station lets it down, for it is no better than those found in family outlets ashore in the United States. In addition, a poolside grill provides basic American hamburgers and hot dogs.

Passengers have to use the Lido Buffet on days when the dining room is closed for lunch, which is typically once or twice per cruise, depending on the itinerary.

ENTERTAINMENT. The Showroom at Sea, in the forward part of the ship, spans two decks, with banquette seating on both main and upper levels. It is basically a well-designed room, but the ceiling is low and the sight lines from the balcony level are quite poor. The production shows are passé, but individual cabaret acts are sometimes good.

SPA/FITNESS. The Ocean Spa is located one deck below the navigation bridge at the very forward part of the ship. It has ocean views and includes a gymnasium with all the latest muscle-pumping exercise machines, including an abundance of treadmills. There's also an aerobics exercise area, large beauty salon with ocean-view windows to the port side, several treatment rooms, and men's and women's sauna, steam room, and changing areas.

Majesty of the Seas
★★★

Size:...................................Large Resort Ship				

Size:..................................Large Resort Ship
Tonnage: 73,941
Lifestyle: ....Standard
Cruise line:................... Royal Caribbean International
Former names: ....*none*
IMO number: 8819512
Builder: .... Chantiers de l'Atlantique (France)
Original cost: ....$300 million
Entered service:................................Apr 1992
Registry:...................................The Bahamas
Length (ft/m):...............................879.9/268.2
Beam (ft/m):................................ 105.9/32.3
Draft (ft/m):.................................... 24.9/7.6
Propulsion/Propellers: ....diesel (21,844kW)/2
Passenger decks:.....................................11
Total crew:...827
Passengers (lower beds/alll berths):............. 2,380/2,774
Passenger Space Ratio (lower beds/all berths): 30.8/26.3
Crew/Passenger Ratio (lower beds/all berths):.......... 2.8/3.3

Cabins (total):................................... 1,190
Size range (sq ft/m): 118.4–670.0/11.0–62.2
Cabins (outside view):...............................732
Cabins (interior/no view):...........................458
Cabins (for one person):................................0
Cabins (with private balcony):.........................62
Cabins (wheelchair accessible): 4
Wheelchair accessibility:............................Fair
Cabin voltage: .... 110 volts
Elevators:..11
Casino (gaming tables):.............................Yes
Slot machines:.....................................Yes
Swimming pools:.......................................2
Hot tubs (on deck):...................................2
Self-service launderette:............................No
Dedicated cinema/seats:.............................No
Library: ....Yes
Onboard currency: ....US$

A well-worn large ship for casual family cruising

OVERVIEW. This fairly smart-looking resort ship provides well-tuned, yet impersonal, short cruises (three- and four-day Bahamas cruises year-round from Miami) for a lot of passengers. The dress code is casual and sloppy. You will probably be overwhelmed by the public spaces, and underwhelmed by the size of the cabins.

THE SHIP. When first introduced, Majesty of the Seas (together with her sisters *Monarch of the Seas* and *Sovereign of the Seas* – now operated by Spain-based Pullmantur Cruises) was an innovative vessel. Royal Caribbean International's trademark Viking Crown lounge and bar surrounds the funnel and provides a great view, but it has no soul and looks dated. The open deck space is very cramped when full, as aboard any large ship, although there seems to be plenty of it. There is a basketball court.

The interior layout is a little awkward, as it is designed in a vertical stack, with most public rooms located aft, and the accommodation located forward, which ensures quiet areas. There's an impressive array of spacious and elegant public rooms, although the decor calls to mind the Ikea school of interior design, despite a revitalization in 2007 when cabins were refreshed and more casual eating options introduced. A rather pleasant five-deck-high Centrum lobby has cascading stairways and two glass-walled elevators.

There is a decent two-level showlounge and a selection of shops, albeit with lots of tacky merchandise, and an 'All items at $10' store – good for souvenirs.

Berlitz's Ratings		
	Possible	Achieved
Ship	500	306
Accommodation	200	117
Food	400	221
Service	400	258
Entertainment	100	63
Cruise	400	247
OVERALL SCORE		
1212 points out of 2000		

Casino gamers will find blackjack, craps, Caribbean stud poker, and roulette tables, plus an array of slot machines in Casino Royale.

Among the public rooms, the library is a nice feature for quiet relaxation, and there is a decent selection of books. An Internet center has 10 workstations, but the cost is quite high; the ship is also Wi-Fi enabled – but there's a charge. The entertainment program is quite sound, and there's a decent range of children's and teens' programs (teens have their own chill-out room – adults not allowed) and cheerful youth counselors.

Because the public rooms are mostly located aft, with accommodation in the forward section, there is often a long wait for elevators, particularly at peak times after dinner, shows, and talks. But at least the restrooms are quite welcoming.

Niggles include the nickel and diming that goes on everywhere you turn. But, this is a bit of a party ship, with lots of karaoke, smutty comedy and silly participation games.

ACCOMMODATION. There are several categories, priced by grade, size, and location.

Suites. Thirteen suites on Bridge Deck are reasonably large and nicely furnished (the largest is the Royal Suite), with separate living and sleeping spaces. They provide more space, with better service and more perks than standard-grade accommodation.

Standard Cabins. The standard outside-view and interior cabins are incredibly small, although an arched window treatment and colorful soft furnishings give an illusion of more space. Almost all cabins have twin beds that convert to a queen-size or double-bed configuration, together with moveable bedside tables, and flat-screen TV sets. All standard cabins have very little closet and drawer space – you will need some luggage engineering to stow your cases. You should, therefore, think of packing only minimal clothing – all you really need for a short cruise.

All cabins have a private bathroom, with shower enclosure, toilet, and washbasin. All cabins are provided with good mattresses and duvets.

DINING. There are two main dining rooms: Moonlight, located on the lowest level of the atrium lobby, and Starlight, one deck higher. When you book, choose one of two seatings, or 'My Time Dining' (eat when you want, during dining room hours at tables for two to eight). The dining operation is well orchestrated, with emphasis on highly programmed, extremely hurried service that many find insensitive and intrusive. If you want a premium-quality all-American filet steak, you can have it for an extra cost.

For casual breakfasts and lunches, there's Windjammer Marketplace (the source of most complaints received from passengers). It is split into various specialty areas including American, Asian, Latin, and Mediterranean fare. Compass Deli is a bar in which you can make up your own sandwich.

Johnny Rockets is a 1950s retro diner for fast foods such as hamburgers and hot dogs, sodas and shakes, located on an upper deck section of the Windjammer Marketplace (a cover charge applies, and there's an additional cost if you want a classic milkshake to go with your JR burger).

In Sorrento's (for American-Italian pizzas) there is no extra cost.

Café Lattetudes serves Seattle's Best Coffee brand (extra-cost) in paper cups. And for ice cream lovers, there's Freeze Ice Cream.

ENTERTAINMENT. A Chorus Line is the ship's principal showlounge; it has both main and balcony levels, with banquette seating, but many pillars supporting the balcony level provide less than good sight lines from the side seats on the lower level.

Royal Caribbean's large-scale production shows are extremely colorful spectaculars with high-energy hype, presentation, and glitz. They are fast-moving, razzle-dazzle shows that rely a lot on lighting and special effects, but have little or no storyline, often poor linkage between themes and scenes, and choreography that's more stepping in place than dancing. Strong cabaret acts are also presented in the main showlounge.

The entertainment throughout is upbeat but is typical of the kind of resort hotel found in Las Vegas. There is even background music in all corridors and elevators, and constant music outdoors on the pool deck.

Live music is provided in a number of bars and lounges by solo entertainers and small musical units.

SPA/FITNESS. The Majesty Day Spa has a gymnasium with aft-facing views and high-tech muscle-pumping equipment. There is an aerobics studio, and classes are offered in a variety of keep-fit regimes. There is also a beauty salon, and a sauna, and 10 treatment rooms for pampering massages, facials, and so on. While the facilities are not as extensive as those aboard the company's newer ships, they are adequate for the short cruises that this ship operates.

For the more sporting, there is activity galore – including a rock-climbing wall with several separate climbing tracks. It is located outdoors at the aft end of the funnel.

Marco Polo
★★ +

Size:. . . . . Mid-size Ship		Cabins (total):. 425	
Tonnage:. 22,080		Size range (sq ft/m):. 93.0–484.0/8.6–44.9	
Lifestyle:. . . . . .Standard		Cabins (outside view):. 292	
Cruise line:. . . . . .Cruise and Maritime Voyages		Cabins (interior/no view):. 133	
Former names:. . . . . Aleksandr Pushkin		Cabins (for one person):. . . . . . . .many doubles are sold for single	
IMO number:. 5112195		occupancy	
Builder:. . . . . VEB Mathias Thesen Werft (Germany)		Cabins (with private balcony):. 0	
Original cost:. . . . . n/a		Cabins (wheelchair accessible):. 2	
Entered service:. . . . . .Apr 1966/Apr 2008		Wheelchair accessibility:. . . . . .Fair	
Registry:. . . . . The Bahamas		Cabin voltage:. . . . . .110 and 220 volts	
Length (ft/m):. 578.4/176.2		Elevators:. 4	
Beam (ft/m):. 77.4/23.6		Casino (gaming tables):. . . . . .No	
Draft (ft/m):. 26.8/8.1		Slot machines:. . . . . .No	
Propulsion/Propellers:. . . . . diesel(14,444kW)/2		Swimming pools:. 1	
Passenger decks:. 8		Hot tubs (on deck):. 3	
Total crew:. 356		Self-service launderette:. . . . . .No	
Passengers (lower beds/alll berths):. 848/915		Dedicated cinema/seats:. . . . . .No	
Passenger Space Ratio (lower beds/all berths):. 26.0/24.1		Library:. . . . . Yes	
Crew/Passenger Ratio (lower beds/all berths):. 2.3/2.5		Onboard currency:. . . . . .UK£	

A modest ship, food, and service, for frugal cruisers

OVERVIEW. This is a comfortable ship with classic looks, and, with its deep draft, rides well in unkind sea conditions. It appeals to couples and single travelers of mature years who enjoy visiting interesting destinations in the comfort of a ship that is unpretentious yet pleasing, without much entertainment or organized parlor games, but with plenty of old-world charm.

THE SHIP. *Marco Polo* was built as one of five sister ships for the Russian/Ukrainian fleet. Originally designed in 1966 to re-open the Leningrad to Montreal transatlantic route in 1966, inoperative since 1949, it has a traditional 'real ship' profile, an extremely strong ice-strengthened hull, and huge storage spaces for long voyages.

The ship passed to Norwegian Cruise Line in 1998, and in 2007 to Greek owners. In 2008, it was operated under charter to Transocean Tours of Germany, which sub-chartered it to Cruise & Maritime Voyages, the UK's newest cruise line. It received a £3 million refit/refurbishment in 2009. It operates adults-only cruises from the UK (although during school vacation periods anyone 16 and over is an eligible passenger) with Tilbury (London International Cruise Terminal) as its home port.

Marco Polo is fitted with the latest navigational aids and biological waste treatment center, and carries 10 Zodiac landing craft for in-depth shore trips in eco-sensitive areas. There are two large, forward-facing open-deck viewing areas, and a helicopter pad. The

Berlitz's Ratings		
	Possible	Achieved
Ship	500	272
Accommodation	200	120
Food	400	198
Service	400	223
Entertainment	100	56
Cruise	400	213
OVERALL SCORE		
1082 points out of 2000		

teakwood-decked aft swimming pool/lido deck area is kept in good condition. Joggers and walkers can circle around the ship – not on the promenade deck, but one deck above, although this goes past vast air intakes that are noisy, and the walkway is narrow.

As soon as you walk aboard, you feel a warm, welcoming, homely ambience. There is a wide range of public rooms, most of which are arranged on one deck. A sense of spaciousness pervades, as most have high ceilings. The interior decor is quite tasteful, with careful use of mirrored surfaces and colors that do not clash but aren't boring. The subdued lighting helps maintain an air of calmness and relaxation.

Now more than 45 years old, the ship is still in decent shape. Indeed, it's in better shape than many ships only 10 years old, and its interiors are constantly being refurbished and refreshed. It operates well-planned destination-intensive cruises and offers really good value for money in very comfortable, unpretentious but tasteful surroundings, while an accommodating crew helps to make a cruise a pleasant, no-hassle experience. Gratuities are automatically applied to your onboard account.

Passenger niggles? There is no observation lounge with forward-facing views over the bows. There are many raised thresholds, so you need to be on your guard when walking through the ship and particularly when negotiating the exterior stairways, which could prove difficult for mobility-limited passengers.

ACCOMMODATION. The cabins, which come in 15 price grades, depending on location and size, are a profusion of different sizes and configurations. All are pleasingly decorated, practical units with good, solid, rich wood cabinetry, wood and mirror-fronted closets, adequate drawer and storage space, TV set, thin cotton bathrobe (upper grades only), and bathroom-mounted hairdryer and non-vacuum, non-noisy toilets. Carpets, curtains, and bedspreads are all nicely color-coordinated. Weak points include extremely poor sound insulation between cabins – you can probably hear your neighbors brushing their hair – and the fact that the bathrooms are small, with little storage space for toiletries, which is a particular concern during long cruises.

The largest accommodation is found in two suites: Dynasty and Mandarin, on Columbus Deck. These have a separate living room, and marble bathroom with tub/shower, walk-in closet, refrigerator, and a TV set/DVD unit. Slightly smaller are two Junior Suites on Pacific Deck. All suites have superior locations with forward-facing views over the ship's bow.

Also quite comfortable are the Superior Deluxe ocean-view cabins that have two lower beds (some can be converted to a queen-size bed), marble bathroom with tub/shower, and refrigerator.

Some cabins on Upper Deck and Sky Deck have lifeboat-obstructed views. It would be advisable to avoid cabins 310/312 as these are located close to the engine room doorway and the noise level is considerable. No cabins have a balcony because the ship was built for long-distance ocean/sea crossings before they became popular.

DINING. The Waldorf, in the ship's center, is nicely decorated in soft pastel colors, practical in design, and functions well, but it has a low ceiling, is noisy, and the tables are very close together. There are two seatings, with tables for two to 10, and good place settings/china. The food itself is of a modest standard, and presentation, quality, and taste could certainly be improved. The wine and prices are reasonable, although most wines are young.

Other dining options. Marco's Restaurant is for informal self-serve breakfasts and lunches – there is seating inside as well as outdoors around the ship's single, aft swimming pool. On some evenings during each cruise, it also becomes an alternative dining spot for about 75 people. Reservations are required, but there is no extra charge. A 15 percent gratuity is added to all bar and wine accounts.

ENTERTAINMENT. The Ambassador Lounge is the principal venue for shows, cabaret acts, and lectures. A single-level room, it has banquette seating and fairly decent sight lines, although several pillars obstruct the view from some seats. Entertainment is low-key and low-budget, and consists of cabaret acts such as singers, magicians, and comedians. There's live music for social dancing and listening in several bars and cocktail lounges.

SPA/FITNESS. This is an older ship that was built when spa and wellbeing facilities were not really thought about. A Health Spa was added in a later refit. It is located aft on Upper Deck, and contains a gymnasium – it's not large, but there are a few treadmills, exercycles, and some muscle-toning equipment. There's also a beauty salon, a sauna, changing facilities, and treatment rooms for massages, facials, and other body pampering treatments.

The spa is operated by Mandara Spa, and treatments have an Asian flavor – Indonesian facials, coconut body polish, aromatherapy massages.

Did you know...

...that Silvio Berlusconi, Italy's former premier, was once a cruise ship entertainer? He sang, and accompanying him on piano was his oldest buddy, Fedele Confalonieri, who became president of Berlusconi's Mediaset empire.

...that the cruise ship used in the 1974 movie *Juggernaut*, in which seven bombs in oil drums were placed aboard, was *Maxim Gorkiy*? The film starred Richard Harris, Omar Sharif, David Hemmings, and Anthony Hopkins.

...that the first cruise line to provide tickets for shows was Celebrity Cruises in 1991?

...that the Cunard White Star Line's *Queen Mary* was the first ship to have a system of colored lights that varied according to

music (chromosonics)?

...that the 212-passenger *Seabourn Legend* was the star of the 1997 film *Speed 2: Cruise Control*? The film was shot on location in Marigot, the capital of the French side of the tiny two-nation Caribbean island of St Martin/St Maarten. The filming called for the building of almost a complete 'town' at Marigot, into which the ship crashes.

...that Verdi wrote an opera to commemorate the opening of the Suez Canal? Its name is *Aïda*.

...that *Titanic*, the stage musical, cost $10 million to mount in New York in 1997? That's $2.5 million more than it cost to build the original ship that made its one and only voyage in 1912.

Marina
★★★★+

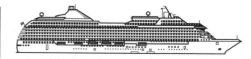

Size:............................Mid-size Ship		Cabins (total):.................................629	
Tonnage: 66,048		Size range (sq ft/m): 172.2–2,000/16.0–185.0	
Lifestyle: ....Premium		Cabins (outside view):............................611	
Cruise line:............................Oceania Cruises		Cabins (interior/no view):..........................18	
Former names: ....none		Cabins (for one person):............................0	
IMO number: 9438066		Cabins (with private balcony):....................593	
Builder: .... Fincantieri (Italy)		Cabins (wheelchair accessible): 6	
Original cost:............................$530 million		Wheelchair accessibility:............................Good	
Entered service:............................ Jan 2011		Cabin voltage: ....110 and 220 volts	
Registry:............................Marshall Islands		Elevators:...................................6	
Length (ft/m):............................776.5/236.7		Casino (gaming tables):............................Yes	
Beam (ft/m):............................ 105.3/32.1		Slot machines:............................Yes	
Draft (ft/m): 24.2/7.4		Swimming pools:............................1	
Propulsion/Propellers:....................diesel-electric/2		Hot tubs (on deck):............................3	
Passenger decks:............................11		Self-service launderette:............................Yes	
Total crew:............................800		Dedicated cinema/seats:............................No	
Passengers (lower beds/alll berths):............1,258/1,258		Library: ....Yes	
Passenger Space Ratio (lower beds/all berths): 51.6/51.6		Onboard currency: ....US$	
Crew/Passenger Ratio (lower beds/all berths):.......... 1.5/1.5			

Premium country club style for mature-age cruisers

OVERVIEW. *Marina* is really comfortable, although you will need to walk a little more. It will suit mature-age adults who appreciate quality and style, with plenty of space, plus excellent cuisine and service, in an informal setting with realistic pricing.

THE SHIP. Built in 55 blocks, *Marina* is the first newbuild for this growing small cruise line. Its profile is quite handsome, with a nicely rounded front and topped by a swept-back funnel. Able to cruise at a speed 25 percent faster than the other three ships in the fleet, it can operate cruises over longer distances.

Oceania Cruises has been careful to try to keep the warm and tasteful 'country house' decor style for which it has become known – the smaller ships were designed by the Scottish designer John McNeece – together with an uncomplicated layout that's easy to master quickly.

The interior focal point is the stunning wrought-iron and Lalique glass horseshoe-shaped staircase in the main lobby. Public rooms include nine bars and lounges. There is a 2,000-book library, set on the port side of the funnel housing. The Monte Carlo Casino has its own soft lavender-colored Casino Bar.

Something new for Oceania Cruises is the Culinary Center, a cooking demonstration kitchen with 24 workstations run in conjunction with the US-based *Bon Appétit* magazine – there's a fee for each of several cookery classes, but at least you get to eat your creations. An Artist's Loft hosts constantly changing artists – bring

Berlitz's Ratings

	Possible	Achieved
Ship	500	442
Accommodation	200	179
Food	400	333
Service	400	316
Entertainment	100	82
Cruise	400	328
OVERALL SCORE		
1680 points out of 2000		

your own paintbrushes. If you like art, look for the genuine Picassos on board; there are 16 of them, including six in the casino.

The dress code is country club– no pyjamas or track suits, but no ties either. Despite uneven service in some of the dining venues, the ship just manages to squeeze into the Berlitz 5-Star Club. A 15 percent gratuity is added to bar and spa accounts.

In late 2012, some of the modifications made when building its close sister *Riviera* will be incorporated in its first drydocking. These include better lighting and and deeper drawers in suites and cabins, teak decking, plus hand-held shower hoses in suites with bathtubs, and chandeliers in public rooms.

ACCOMMODATION. There are several different price categories, with four suite grades: Owner's suite; Oceania suite; Vista suite; Penthouse suite – and four cabin grades: Concierge-Level Veranda cabin; Veranda cabin; Deluxe Ocean-View cabin; and Interior cabin. Price depends on size and location, but all have one thing in common – a good-size bathroom with tub and separate but small shower enclosure.

Around 96 percent of all accommodation has teak-decked balconies. All suites/cabins have a bathtub and shower, and two toiletry cabinets. There's no tie rack in the closets because the dress code is casual. The decor includes chocolate brown, cream, and white – the sort of earthy colors that don't jar the senses. All suites and cabins have dark wood cabinetry with rounded edges.

Standard Veranda Cabins. measure 282 sq ft (26 sq m). Veranda and Concierge-level cabins have a sitting area and teak balcony with faux wicker furniture. Concierge-level grades get L'Occitane toiletries.

Penthouse Suites. measure 420 sq ft (39 sq m) with living/dining room separate from the sleeping area, walk-in closet, and bathroom with a double vanity. The large veranda has a hot tub.

Oceania Suites. measure about 1,030 sq ft (96 sq m) and have a living room, dining room, separate bedroom, walk-in closet, teak-decked balcony with Jacuzzi tub, main bathroom, and a second bathroom for guests.

Vista Suites. range from 1,200–1,500 sq ft (111–139 sq m) and offer the same features as Oceania Suites but add floor-to-ceiling windows overlooking the bow.

The Owner's Suite. at more than 2,000 sq ft (186 sq m), spans the ship's entire beam. It is decked out in furniture, fabrics, lighting, and bedding from the Ralph Lauren Home collection with design by New York-based Tocar, Inc. It is outfitted with a Yamaha baby grand piano, private fitness room, laptop computers, Bose audio system, and a teak-decked balcony with Jacuzzi tub.

Suite-category occupants get niceties like Champagne on arrival, 1,000-thread-count bed linen, 42-in plasma TV sets, Hermès and Clarins bath amenities, butler service and en suite delivery from any of the ship's restaurants. Amenities include Tranquility beds, Wi-Fi laptop computer, refrigerated mini-bar with unlimited free soft drinks and bottled water replenished daily, personal safe, writing desk, cotton bathrobes, slippers, and marble and granite bathroom. Priority check-in and early embarkation and priority luggage delivery are extra perks.

Occupants of Owner's, Vista, Oceania, and Penthouse suites can have in-suite course-by-course dining from any restaurant menu, making private dining possible as a change to being in the restaurants.

Some grades get access to an Executive Lounge or Concierge Lounge. These are great little hideaways, with sofas, Internet-connect computers, Continental breakfast items, soft drinks, and magazines.Self-service launderettes are on each accommodation deck – useful for long voyages.

DINING. Six main open-seating dining venues provide plenty of choice, enough even for long cruises, although banquette seating in some venues does not evoke the image of premium dining as much as individual seating does. Also, it would be hard to describe some of the specialty dining venues as intimate. This is, however, a foodie's ship, with really high-quality ingredients and effectively fancy presentation. Particularly notable are the delicious breads, rolls, croissants, and brioches – all made on board from French flour and d'Isigny butter.

The Grand Dining Room has 566 seats, and a domed, or raised, central ceiling. Versace bone china, Christo-fle silver, and fine linens are used. Canyon Ranch spa dishes are available for all meals.

Other dining options. French celebrity chef Jacques Pépin, Oceania's executive culinary director, has his first sea-going restaurant, Jacques, with 124 seats. It has antique oak flooring, antique flatware, and Lalique glassware, and offers fine dining in an elegant but informal setting, with roast free-range meats, nine classic French dessert items, and a choice of 12 AOC cheeses.

Polo Grill, with 134 seats, serves steaks and seafood, including Oceania's signature 32-oz bone-in King's Cut prime rib. The setting is classic traditional steakhouse, with dark wood paneling and classic white tablecloths, although the tables are a little close together.

The 124-seat Toscana features Italian-style cuisine, served on Versace china.

Privée, with seating for up to 10 in a private setting, invites exclusivity for its seven-course dégustation menu.

La Réserve offers a choice of two seven-course small-portion dégustation menus (Discovery and Explorer), paired with wines. With just 24 seats, it's really intimate.

The Terrace Café is the casual self-serve buffet-style venue; outdoors, as an extension of the café, is Tapas on the Terrace – good for light bites (although the ceiling is low and it can be very noisy).

Red Ginger is a specialty restaurant which offers 'classic and contemporary' Asian cuisine; the setting is visually refined, with ebony and dark wood finishes, but the banquette-style seating lets the venue down. Your waiter will ask you to choose your chopsticks from a lacquered presentation box.

The poolside Waves Grill, shaded from the sun, serves Angus beef burgers, fishburgers, veggie burgers, Reuben sandwiches, seafood, and other fast food, cooked to order.

Baristas coffee bar overlooks the pool deck and has excellent – and free – *illy* Italian coffee. However, in the bars the tonic mixed with gin and vodka is too sweet and of inferior quality.

ENTERTAINMENT. The 600-seat Marina Lounge spans two decks, with tiered amphitheater-style seating. It's more cabaret-style entertainment than big production shows, in keeping with the cruise line's traditions, which suits the passenger clientele just fine.

SPA/FITNESS. The Canyon Ranch Spa Club provides wellness and personal spa treatments. The facility includes a fitness center, beauty salon, several treatment rooms, thalassotherapy pool, and sauna and steam rooms. A jogging track is located aft of the funnel, above two of the specialty restaurants.

Mariner of the Seas
★★★+

Size:...................................Large Resort Ship	Crew/Passenger Ratio (lower beds/all berths):..........2.6/3.2
Tonnage:......................................137,276	Cabins (total):.....................................1,557
Lifestyle:......................................Standard	Size range (sq ft/m):..............151.0–1,358.0/14.0–126.1
Cruise line:...................Royal Caribbean International	Cabins (outside view):...............................939
Former names:....................................none	Cabins (interior/no view):............................618
IMO number:...................................9227516	Cabins (for one person):...............................0
Builder:...................Kvaerner Masa-Yards (Finland)	Cabins (with private balcony):........................765
Original cost:...............................$500 million	Cabins (wheelchair accessible):.......................26
Entered service:............................Nov 2004	Wheelchair accessibility:...........................Best
Registry:...................................The Bahamas	Cabin voltage:.................................110 volts
Length (ft/m):.............................1,020.6/311.1	Elevators:..14
Beam (ft/m):................................155.5/47.4	Casino (gaming tables):.............................Yes
Draft (ft/m):..................................28.8/8.8	Slot machines:....................................Yes
Propulsion/Propellers:......diesel-electric (75,600kW)/3 pods (2	Swimming pools:.....................................3
azimuthing, 1 fixed)	Hot tubs (on deck):..................................6
Passenger decks:..................................14	Self-service launderette:............................No
Total crew:....................................1,185	Dedicated cinema/seats:.............................No
Passengers (lower beds/alll berths):..............3,114/3,840	Library:...Yes
Passenger Space Ratio (lower beds/all berths):.......44.0/35.7	Onboard currency:..................................US$

A large resort ship for family-friendly casual cruising

OVERVIEW. This ship dwarfs most other cruise ships in size, but not in terms of personal service unless you happen to reside in a top suite. Royal Caribbean International tries to provide a good standard of programmed service from its hotel service staff.

THE SHIP. *Mariner of the Seas* is a stunning, large, floating leisure resort. It has a healthy passenger space ratio and extensive facilities such as a regulation-size ice-skating rink.

A four-deck-high Royal Promenade, 394-ft (120-m) long and the main interior focal point, is a good place to hang out or to arrange to meet someone. It has two internal lobbies that rise through 11 decks. Casual eateries, shops, and entertainment locations front this winding street and interior 'with-view' cabins look into it from above. The Guest Reception and Shore Excursion counters are located at the aft end of the promenade, as is an ATM machine.

Arched across the promenade is a captain's balcony. A stairway in the center of the promenade connects you to the deck below, where you'll find Schooner Bar and the colorful Casino Royale. Several shops line the Royal Promenade, including a jewelry store, gift shop, and liquor store.

There is a regulation-size ice-skating rink (Studio B), with real ice, and stadium-style seating for up to 900, plus high-tech broadcast facilities. Ice Follies shows are also presented here. Slim pillars obstruct clear-view arena stage sightlines, however. You can

Berlitz's Ratings

	Possible	Achieved
Ship	500	393
Accommodation	200	141
Food	400	223
Service	400	267
Entertainment	100	74
Cruise	400	264
OVERALL SCORE		
1362 points out of 2000		

also read in the two-deck library, open 24 hours a day.

Drinking places include an intimate Champagne Bar, Wig & Gavel Pub, a Sidewalk Café, Sprinkles, a sports bar, and a Connoisseur Club. Jazz fans might like the intimate Jazz Club. Golfers might also enjoy the 19th Hole, a golf bar, as they play the Explorer Links.

Passenger niggles: cabin bath towels and noisy (vacuum) toilets; few quiet places to sit and read – almost everywhere there is intrusive background music. If you have a cabin with an interconnecting door to another cabin, you'll be able to hear everything they do.

FAMILIES. Facilities for children and teenagers are quite extensive. Aquanauts is for three- to five-year-olds; Explorers (six to eight); Voyagers (nine to 12). Optix is a dedicated area for teenagers, including a daytime club with computers, soda bar, disco with disc jockey and dance floor. Challenger's Arcade has the latest video games. Paint and Clay is an arts and crafts center for younger children. Adjacent to these indoor areas is Adventure Beach.

ACCOMMODATION. There is a wide range of cabin price grades, in four major groupings. Premium ocean-view suites and cabins, Interior (atrium-view) cabins, Ocean-view cabins, and Interior cabins. Many cabins are of a similar size and 300 have interconnecting doors.

Some 138 interior cabins have bay windows that look into an interior horizontal atrium. Regardless of what cabin grade you choose, all except for the Royal Suite and Owner's Suite have twin beds that convert to a queen-size unit, TV set, radio and telephone, personal safe, vanity unit, hairdryer, and private bathroom. However, you'll need to keep the curtains closed in the bay windows, because you can be seen easily from adjacent bay windows.

Royal Suite (Deck 10). At around 1,146 sq ft (107 sq m), the Royal Suite is the largest private living space, located almost at the top of the Centrum lobby on the port side. It has a king-size circular bed in a separate large bedroom that can be closed off; a living room with an additional queen-size sofa bed, baby grand piano, refrigerator/wet bar, dining table and four chairs, expansive entertainment center, and a reasonably large bathroom.

Royal Family Suite. The four Royal Family suites (two aft on Deck 9, two aft on Deck 8, each measuring around 574 sq ft/53 sq m) have two separate bedrooms. The main bedroom has a large vanity desk; the second, smaller bedroom also includes two beds and third/fourth upper Pullman berths. There's a lounge with dining table and four chairs, wet bar, walk-in closet; and large bathroom with Jacuzzi tub, washbasin, and separate shower enclosure. The suites, at the stern, have large balconies with views out over the ship's wash.

Owner's Suites. Ten slightly smaller but desirable Owner's Suites (around 468 sq ft/43 sq m) are in the center of the ship, on both port and starboard sides, adjacent to the Centrum lobby on Deck 10. Each has a bedroom with queen-size bed or twin beds; lounge with large sofa; wet bar; bathroom with Jacuzzi tub, washbasin and separate shower enclosure. There's also a private balcony, although it's not very large.

Standard Outside-View and Interior Cabins. All cabins have a private bathroom, as well as interactive TV and pay-per-view movies, including an X-rated channel. Cabin bathrooms really are compact, but at least they have a proper shower enclosure instead of a shower curtain.

Some accommodation grades have a refrigerator/mini-bar, although there is no space left because it is crammed with 'take-and-pay' items. If you take anything from the mini-bar/refrigerator on the day of embarkation in Miami, Florida, sales tax will be added to your bill.

Cabins with 'private balconies' aren't so private. The balcony decking is made of Bolidt – a sort of rubberized sand – and not wood, though the balcony rail is of wood. Cabin bath towels are small and skimpy. Room service food menus are very basic.

DINING. The main dining room, with a seating capacity of 1,919, is set on three levels: Rhapsody in Blue, Top Hat and Tails, and Sound of Music, all offering exactly the same menus and food. A dramatic staircase connects all three levels, and huge, fat support pillars obstruct the sight lines from many seats. When you book, choose one of two seatings, or 'My Time Dining'. Tables are for four, six, eight, 10, or 12. The place settings, porcelain, and cutlery are of good quality.

Other dining options. Alternative dining options for casual and informal meals at all hours (according to company releases) include: Promenade Café: for Continental breakfast, all-day pizzas, and speciality coffees – which are only available in paper cups. Windjammer Café: this is a really large, sprawling venue for casual buffet-style, self-help breakfast (this tends to be the busiest time of the day), lunch, and light dinners (but not on the last night of the cruise); it's often difficult to find a table and by the time you do your food could be cold. Island Grill: (actually this is a section within the Windjammer Café), for casual grilled meat and seafood items (no reservations necessary) featuring a grill and open kitchen. Portofino: the ship's upscale Italian restaurant, open for dinner only. Reservations are required, and there's a gratuity per person. The food and its presentation are better than the food in the dining room. The menu does not change throughout the cruise. Johnny Rockets, a retro 1950s eatery, has hamburgers, malt shakes (at extra cost), and jukebox hits, with both indoor and outdoor seating. Sprinkles, located on the Royal Promenade, is for round-the-clock ice cream and yogurt, pastries and coffee.

ENTERTAINMENT. The 1,350-seat Savoy Showlounge is a stunning room that could well be the equal of many showrooms on land. It has a hydraulic orchestra pit and a huge stage area, and superb lighting equipment. Mariner of the Seas also has an array of cabaret acts. The best shows of all are the Ice Spectaculars. Note that Royal Caribbean International's entertainment is always upbeat. There is even background music in all corridors and elevators, and constant music outdoors on the pool deck.

SPA/FITNESS. The Vitality at Sea Spa is reasonably large, and measures 15,000 sq ft (1,400 sq m). It includes an aerobics room, fitness center, treatment rooms, and sauna/steam rooms. Another 10,000 sq ft (930 sq m) of space is devoted to a Solarium (with sliding glass-dome roof) to relax in.

On the back of the funnel is a 32.8-ft (10-m) rock-climbing wall, with five climbing tracks. It gives you a great buzz being 200ft (60m) above the ocean while the ship is moving. Other facilities include a roller-blading track, a dive-and-snorkel shop, a full-size basketball court, and a nine-hole, par 26 golf course. A dive-and-snorkel shop provides equipment for rental, and diving classes.

Mein Schiff 1
★★★★

Size:.................................Large Resort Ship			

Size:.................................Large Resort Ship
Tonnage:..77,713
Lifestyle:..Standard
Cruise line:.................................TUI Cruises
Former names:.................Celebrity Galaxy, Galaxy
IMO number:...................................9106297
Builder:..........................Meyer Werft (Germany)
Original cost:............................$320 million
Entered service:.................Dec 1996/May 2009
Registry:..Malta
Length (ft/m):..............................865.8/263.9
Beam (ft/m):...............................105.6/32.2
Draft (ft/m):..................................25.2/7.7
Propulsion/Propellers:................diesel (31,500kW)/2
Passenger decks:.................................10
Total crew:.......................................780
Passengers (lower beds/alll berths):............1,948/2,725
Passenger Space Ratio (lower beds/all berths):.......39.8/28.5
Crew/Passenger Ratio (lower beds/all berths):.........2.0/3.4

Cabins (total):...................................974
Size range (sq ft/m):..............169.0–1,219.0/15.7–113.2
Cabins (outside view):...........................665
Cabins (interior/no view):.......................309
Cabins (for one person):...........................0
Cabins (with private balcony):...................430
Cabins (wheelchair accessible):....................8
Wheelchair accessibility:.........................Good
Cabin voltage:.........................110 and 220 volts
Elevators:..10
Casino (gaming tables):..........................Yes
Slot machines:...................................Yes
Swimming pools:....................................2
Hot tubs (on deck):................................4
Self-service launderette:..........................No
Dedicated cinema/seats:.....................Yes/200
Library:...Yes
Onboard currency:..............................Euros

Contemporary style for family-friendly cruising

OVERVIEW. *Mein Schiff 1* is for German-speaking families with children who want to cruise aboard a large ship with a contemporary environment, good itineraries and food, and European-style service from a well-trained crew that delivers a product that's fresh and surprisingly good. The product is worth more than the cruise fare charged when compared with several other large-ship cruise lines.

Berlitz's Ratings

	Possible	Achieved
Ship	500	415
Accommodation	200	165
Food	400	282
Service	400	309
Entertainment	100	71
Cruise	400	305

OVERALL SCORE
1547 points out of 2000

THE SHIP. *Mein Schiff*, originally built for Celebrity Cruises as *Galaxy*, was transferred in 2009 to newcomer TUI Cruises (part of TUI Travel – Europe's largest tour operator) specifically for German-speaking passengers, in a joint venture with Royal Caribbean Cruises, parent of Royal Caribbean International. The ship underwent a major conversion at that time. Its name ('My Ship') was suggested by several entrants to a magazine competition; the winner, whose name was drawn from a hat, was Oliver Krimmel, a Stuttgart designer.

This large, all-inclusive resort ship has just about all you need for an enjoyable and rewarding cruise experience, and provides competition for AIDA Cruises, whose ships, by comparison, do not have a traditional dining room, and have few service staff. TUI Cruises has got the onboard product just about right for German-speaking passengers, with many more dining and eating choices and more class and style than AIDA's ships, and with far better food and plenty of snappily dressed service personnel. With 10 bars, four restaurants, six bistros, and good facilities for families, *Mein Schiff 1* has become the benchmark for a high-value, full-service cruise vacation in Germany.

The ship has good tender loading platforms. But, although there are more than 4.5 acres (1.8 hectares) of space on the open decks, it can appear to be a little small and cramped when the ship is full. Ten charming two-person cabanas can be rented on an upper, outside deck, with great ocean views, but insulated from the life that goes on around the ship.

Inside, a four-deck-high main foyer houses the reception desk and shore excursion station. There's a small, dedicated cinema, which doubles as a conference and meeting center with all the latest audio-visual technology, including simultaneous translation and headsets for the hearing-impaired.

Relaxation is a key element of the product, and *Mein Schiff 1* is equipped with individual hammocks in various locations, including on cabin balconies as well as in public areas. Additionally, 'Meditation Islands' are installed on deck: the ship's rail is fitted with mini-balconies, equipped with special blinds. Here, passengers are able to enjoy a private space for relaxation.

Making it even more user-friendly for families is the all-inclusive pricing introduced in 2010, though this excludes the extra-cost restaurants Richard's Fines Essen, Blaue Welt Sushi Bar, and the Surf 'n' Turf steakhouse and also excursions and spa treatments. The dress code throughout the ship is smart casual.

ACCOMMODATION. There are 10 price grades, depending on the size and location of your living space, but the accommodation is very comfortable throughout. Every cabin has its own Nespresso coffee machine, which takes pre-portioned packets of espresso coffee. The first two are included, but any additional packets cost €1 each. All accommodation grades are designated no-smoking.

Most suites with private balconies have floor-to-ceiling windows and sliding doors to balconies, and a few have outward opening doors. Suite-grade accommodation gets European duvets on the beds, instead of sheets and blankets. A balcony massage service is also available – it's worth it. Suite occupants get special cards to open their doors, plus priority service throughout the ship and for embarkation and disembarkation, free cappuccino/espresso coffees served by a butler, welcome Champagne, flowers, video recorder, and picnic baskets as required. Suite occupants also get a private, 100-seat concierge lounge/bar and social venue (the 'X' Lounge) atop the ship, with great ocean views – a good place for reading a book during the day.

Penthouse Suites. These two suites, located amidships, are the largest. Each is 1,173 sq ft (108.9 sq m) and has its own butler's pantry. There is an interconnecting door so that it can link to the suite next door to become a 1,515-sq-ft (141-sq-m) apartment.

Most of the Deck 10 suites and cabins are of generous proportions, are beautifully equipped, and have balconies with full floor-to-ceiling partitions and large flat-screen TV sets. The Sky Deck suites are also excellent, and most of them have huge balconies; unfortunately, the partitions are not quite of the floor-to-ceiling type, so you can hear your neighbors. Also included are wall clock, large floor-to-ceiling mirrors, marble-topped vanity/writing desk, excellent closet and drawer space, and dimmer-controlled ceiling lights.

Standard Outside-view/Interior Cabins. All of these are of a good size – larger than those aboard the ships of AIDA Cruises, for example – and come nicely furnished with twin beds that convert to a queen-size unit. The bathrooms are spacious and well equipped, and have generous-size showers, hair-dryers, and space for personal toiletries. Baby-monitoring telephones are provided in all cabins. There are no cabins for single occupancy.

DINING. Restaurants and bistros range from self-serve buffet style to service, with a focus on healthy eating. There is no pre-defined seating, so you can dine when you want, and with whomever you want – good for multi-generational families. The emphasis is on healthy food, including power food, brain food, soul food, erotic food, new food (quinoa, soya, and tofu dishes), including fresh fish.

The Atlantik Restaurant is a stunning, two-level dining hall – somewhat reminiscent of the dining halls aboard the ocean liners of the 1930s – with a grand staircase that flows between both levels and perimeter alcoves that provide more intimate dining spaces. However, there's one big difference, in that this restaurant has two-meter-wide trapeze bars built into its center (talk about swinging food – or is that food for swingers?). Tables are for two, four, six, eight, or 10.

Other dining options. Richard's Gourmet Restaurant is an à la carte, reservations-only venue, with a calming, restful wood-laden interior where high-quality fine dining and service can be found.

Surf 'n' Turf Steakhouse serves premium steaks and grilled seafood, with aged beef commanding different price points.

In a venue covered by a retractable glass dome, in the aft section of the ship, three eateries, combined with a communal bar, provide completely different food experiences: Bistro La Vela for Italian cuisine, including an 'active' pasta cooking station, and pizza; Gosch Sylt, for fresh fish and seafood; and Tapas Y Mas, for tapas-tasting dishes. This venue is a most popular place to meet the fashionable set.

Other dining spots around the ship include: La Vida Sana, for wellness cuisine; Blaue Welt (Blue World) Sushi Bar, on the upper level of the atrium; Vino, a wine tasting bar; and a coffee lounge set around the atrium lobby, for specialty coffees and pastries.

For informal breakfasts and lunches, the two-level self-serve Anckelmannsplatz Buffet – the name comes from the road on which the TUI Cruises offices are located in Hamburg – is the place to go. There are several serving counters and 'active' food islands; the venue has warm wood-accented decor, and eight bay windows provide some prime seating spots. There are also two poolside grills – one located adjacent to the midships pools, the other wedged into an area aft of the swimming pool/hot tub cluster.

ENTERTAINMENT. The Theater is a 927-seat show-lounge spanning two decks, with seating on both main and cantilevered balcony levels. There are good sightlines from all seats. The large-scale production shows are excellent. It has a revolving stage, 'hard' curtain, and large fly tower.

SPA/FITNESS. The Spa and More, located at the front of the ship one deck above the navigation bridge, has 18,299 sq ft (1,700 sq m) of space. It includes a large fitness/exercise area with all the latest muscle machines and video cycles; beauty salon; thalassotherapy pool; seven treatment rooms; and a Rasul room for Mediterranean mud and gentle steam bathing. Private 'spa suites' with fine, relaxing views are located above the ship's navigation bridge and can be rented for the morning, afternoon, or the whole day. Atop the ship at the front is a healthy FKK (freikörperkulture) deck for naked sunbathing.

Mein Schiff 2
★★★★

Size:. . . . . .Large Resort Ship		Cabins (total):. 935		
Tonnage: 77,713		Size range (sq ft/m): 171.0–1,219.0/15.8–113.2		
Lifestyle: . . . . .Standard		Cabins (outside view):. 639		
Cruise line:. . . . . TUI Cruises		Cabins (interior/no view):. 296		
Former names: . . . . Celebrity Mercury, Mercury		Cabins (for one person):. 0		
IMO number: 9106302		Cabins (with private balcony):. 220		
Builder: . . . . Meyer Werft (Germany)		Cabins (wheelchair accessible): 8		
Original cost:. . . . .$320 million		Wheelchair accessibility:. . . . . .Good		
Entered service:. . . . . .Nov 1997/May 2011		Cabin voltage: . . . . .110 and 220 volts		
Registry:. . . . . Malta		Elevators:. 10		
Length (ft/m):. 865.8/263.9		Casino (gaming tables):. . . . . Yes		
Beam (ft/m):. 105.6/32.2		Slot machines:. . . . . Yes		
Draft (ft/m):. 25.2/7.7		Swimming pools:. . . . . .3 (1 w/sliding glass dome)		
Propulsion/Propellers:. . . . . .diesel (31,500kW)/2		Hot tubs (on deck):. 4		
Passenger decks:. 10		Self-service launderette:. . . . . .No		
Total crew:. 909		Dedicated cinema/seats:. Yes/183		
Passengers (lower beds/alll berths):. 1,870/2,681		Library:. . . . . Yes		
Passenger Space Ratio (lower beds/all berths): 41.5/28.9		Onboard currency: . . . . Euros		
Crew/Passenger Ratio (lower beds/all berths):. 2.0/2.9				

A large and stylish premium large ship for family-friendly cruising

OVERVIEW. *Mein Schiff 2* is for German-speaking families with children who want to cruise aboard a large ship with a contemporary environment, good itineraries, great food, and good European-style service from a well-trained crew that delivers a cruise that's fresh and surprisingly good. The product really is excellent value for money.

THE SHIP. *Mein Schiff 2*, originally built as *Mercury* for Celebrity Cruises, was transferred in 2011 to newcomer TUI Cruises (part of TUI Travel, Europe's largest tour operator) specifically for German-speaking passengers, in a joint venture with Royal Caribbean Cruises, parent of Royal Caribbean International. The ship underwent a major conversion at that time.

This large, all-inclusive resort ship has just about all you need for an enjoyable and rewarding cruise experience. There are 10 bars, four restaurants, six bistros, and good facilities for families with children. Indeed, *Mein Schiff 2* is on track to become the benchmark for a premium cruise vacation in Germany since the decor and finish are even smarter than they are aboard sister ship *Mein Schiff 1*.

The ship has good tender loading platforms. But, although there are more than 4.5 acres (1.8 hectares) of space on the open decks, it can become crowded when the ship is full. Charming two-person cabanas can be rented on an upper, outside deck, with great ocean views, but insulated from shipboard life.

Inside, a four-deck-high main foyer houses the re-

Berlitz's Ratings

	Possible	Achieved
Ship	500	416
Accommodation	200	165
Food	400	282
Service	400	309
Entertainment	100	71
Cruise	400	306
OVERALL SCORE		
1549 points out of 2000		

ception desk and shore excursion station. There's a small cinema, which doubles as a conference and meeting center with the latest audio-visual technology, including simultaneous translation and headsets for the hearing-impaired. There's a large shopping center, including ultra-smart shops like Svaorovski, while cigar smokers will appreciate the private club-like cigar lounge and bar.

The interior decor is at once contemporary in style, but with many restful colors and combinations throughout and nothing is garish – except, perhaps, for the starkly contrasting wall covering of blood-red capillaries in the Blue World Bar.

Mein Schiff 2 has individual hammocks in various outdoor locations, including on some suite-grade balconies. 'Meditation Islands' are also installed on the open deck: the ship's rail is fitted with mini-balconies, equipped with special blinds, for private relaxation space.

Making it even more user-friendly for families is the all-inclusive pricing, though this excludes spa treatments, excursions, and the extra-cost restaurants: Richard's Fines Essen, Blaue Welt Sushi Bar, and Surf 'n' Turf steakhouse. The dress code is smart casual.

FAMILIES. Younger children are well catered for, with a playroom and an outdoor paddling pool, while teens have their own adult-free chill-out lounge. There's also a character called Captain Sharky.

ACCOMMODATION. There are 10 price grades, depending on the size and location of your living space, but the accommodation is very comfortable. Every cabin has its own Nespresso coffee machine, which takes pre-portioned packets of espresso coffee. The first two are included, but any additional packets cost €1 each (free in suites). All accommodation grades are designated no-smoking.

Most suites with private balconies have floor-to-ceiling windows and sliding doors to large balconies – 12 have balconies measuring 258.3 sq ft (24 sq m), with a hammock, two sunloungers and a dining table, and a few have outward opening doors. Suite-grade accommodation gets European duvets on the beds instead of sheets and blankets. A balcony massage service is also available – it's worth it. Suite occupants get special cards to open their doors, plus priority service throughout the ship and for embarkation and disembarkation, free cappuccino and espresso coffees, welcome Champagne, flowers, and picnic baskets as required. Suite occupants also get keycard access to a private, 100-seat concierge lounge/bar and social venue – the 'X' Lounge, with a selection of cold food, including some rather nice caviar for breakfast.

Penthouse Suites. These two suites, located amidships, are the largest. Each is 1,173 sq ft (108.9 sq m) and has its own butler's pantry. There is an interconnecting door so that it can link to the suite next door to become an impressive 1,515-sq ft (141-sq m) apartment.

Most of the Deck 10 suites and cabins are generously proportioned, beautifully equipped, and have balconies with full or almost-full floor-to-ceiling partitions, and large flat-screen TV sets. Also included are a wall clock, large floor-to-ceiling mirrors, a well-stocked minibar, a marble-topped vanity/writing desk, excellent closet and drawer space, and large shower enclosure. Suite occupants get newspapers, chocolates, Champagne, and access to the exclusive X Lounge, next door to the Himmel und Meer Lounge. Look out for the phrase 'Wood Thrust Into Brine' in large letters above the bar – you'll have to look up to see it.

Standard Outside-view/Interior Cabins. All of these are of a good size – larger than those aboard the ships of AIDA Cruises, for example – and come nicely furnished with twin beds that convert to a queen-size unit. The bathrooms are spacious and well equipped, and have generous-size showers, hairdryers, and space for toiletries. Baby-monitoring telephones and personal safes are provided in all cabin. A box containing three crystal-mineral stones provides special filtration for the ship's own bottled water. There are no cabins for single occupancy.

DINING. Restaurants and bistros range from self-serve buffet style to service. There is no pre-defined seating. The emphasis is on healthy food, including power food, brain food, soul food, erotic food, and fresh fish. The Atlantik Restaurant is a lovely, two-level art deco grand dining hall with a grand staircase. Tables are for two, four, six, eight, or 10.

Other dining options. Richard's Gourmet Restaurant, a specialty dining venue, is à la carte and reservations-only, with a restful wood-laden interior and high-quality fine dining and service. A dégustation menu and three specialty vegetarian menus are also available, and the wine list is extensive.

Surf 'n' Turf Steakhouse serves premium steaks and grilled seafood, with aged beef, displayed in a 'proving' or maturing cabinet – a cruise industry first.

In an area covered by a retractable glass dome in the aft section of the ship, three eateries and a communal bar provide very different food experiences (all included in the cruise price): Bistro La Vela for Italian cuisine, including an 'active' pasta cooking station with your choice of six pastas, and freshly made pizza; Gosch Sylt for fresh fish and seafood, with daily specials (it's hugely popular, so make a reservation early); and Tapas Y Mas for tapas-tasting dishes. This venue is a most popular place to meet the fashionable set, with both indoor and outdoor seating and bar.

Others include Blaue Welt (Blue World) Sushi Bar, on the upper level of the atrium; Vino, a wine tasting bar specializing in Austrian and German wines; Cliff 24, a 24-hour poolside grill with different food items throughout the day; and the TUI Bar, a coffee lounge set around the atrium lobby for specialty coffees and pastries, and a separate praline chocolate counter.

For informal breakfasts and lunches, the two-level self-serve Anckelmannsplatz Buffet is the place to go. There are several serving counters and 'active' food islands. There are also two poolside grills – one adjacent to the midships pools, the other wedged into an area aft of the swimming pool/hot tub cluster.

ENTERTAINMENT. The Theater is a 927-seat showlounge spanning two decks, with seating on both main and cantilevered balcony levels. There are good sightlines from all seats. The large-scale production shows are excellent.

SPA/FITNESS. The Spa and More, located at the front of the ship one deck above the navigation bridge, has 18,299 sq ft (1,700 sq m) of space. It includes a large exercise area with the machines and cycles; a beauty salon; a thalassotherapy pool; 15 treatment rooms; a Rasul room for mud and steam bathing, and a sauna.

Private 'spa suites,' bookable for an hour or two, or half- or full-day, are extremely large, and include a steam/shower cabinet, thalassotherapy bath, two hydraulic massage/relaxation tables, relaxation seating, and great floor-to-ceiling windows. A balcony adjacent to the sauna is designated as a *freikörperkulture* (FKK) deck for nude sunbathing.

Mein Schiff 3
Not Yet Rated

Size:.....................................Large Resort Ship	Cabins (total):....................................1,250
Tonnage: 99,300	Size range (sq ft/m): 182.9-581.2/17.0-54.0
Lifestyle: ....Standard	Cabins (outside view):............................1,130
Cruise line:...................................TUI Cruise	Cabins (interior/no view):...........................123
Former names: ....none	Cabins (for one person):.............................1
IMO number: ....na	Cabins (with private balcony):....................1,033
Builder: ....STX Europe (Finland)	Cabins (wheelchair accessible): 10
Original cost:................................€390 million	Wheelchair accessibility:.........................Good
Entered service:............................May 2014	Cabin voltage: ....110 and 220 volts
Registry:..Malta	Elevators:..10
Length (ft/m):..............................967.8/295.0	Casino (gaming tables):.............................Yes
Beam (ft/m):...............................118.1/36.0	Slot machines:....................................Yes
Draft (ft/m):..................................26.2/8.0	Swimming pools:.................3 (1 w/sliding glass dome)
Propulsion/Propellers:...........diesel-electric (28,000kW)/2	Hot tubs (on deck):..................................4
Passenger decks:..................................12	Self-service launderette:............................No
Total crew:.....................................1,000	Dedicated cinema/seats:............................Yes
Passengers (lower beds/alll berths):.........2,506/2,790	Library: ....Yes
Passenger Space Ratio (lower beds/all berths): 39.7/35.5	Onboard currency: ....Euros
Crew/Passenger Ratio (lower beds/all berths):..........2.5/2.7	

This ship has it all for youthful German-speaking families

OVERVIEW. *Mein Schiff 3* is the new kid on the block for expanding TUI Cruises. This new ship, for German-speaking families, takes the best parts of the all-inclusive brand further.

THE SHIP. Slightly larger than *Mein Schiff 1* and *Mein Schiff 2*, this ship incorporates all the best of the previous two ships, and has added more facilities and tailored the design to its passengers' needs.

A 25-meter lap pool is featured outdoors – together with a large-scale movie screen and sports area for basketball and volleyball – while a second, indoor pool and adjacent hot tubs provides plenty of choice for families with children.

High up on Deck 14 is what's known as the Blue Balcony, an 11sq m (118.4 sq ft) glass-floored platform some 37m (121.3 ft) above the sea, which gives the sensation of floating over the ocean.

Public rooms are plentiful, and include a real concert hall (auditorium) which has been designed to really high acoustic specifications.

What makes a cruise aboard *Mein Schiff 3* really user-friendly for families is the all-inclusive pricing, though this excludes spa treatments, excursions, and the extra-cost restaurants: Richard's Fines Essen, Blaue Welt Sushi Bar, Fish House Gosch Sylt, and a Surf 'n' Turf steakhouse, among others. The dress code is smart casual.

FAMILIES. Younger children are well catered for, with a playroom and an outdoor paddling pool, while teens have their own adult-free chill-out lounge. There's also

Berlitz's Ratings		
	Possible	Achieved
Ship	500	NYR
Accommodation	200	NYR
Food	400	NYR
Service	400	NYR
Entertainment	100	NYR
Cruise	400	NYR
OVERALL SCORE		
NYR points out of 2000		

a character called Captain Sharky (perhaps he's 'driving' the ship?).

ACCOMMODATION. About 82 percent of all cabins feature private balconies, and each one features a hammock – now a signature item for all ships in the TUI Cruises fleet. Likewise, every cabin comes with a Nespresso coffee machine.

Combination balcony cabins allow for interconnecting balconies, and a 'holiday home' package provides a *Mein Schiff 3* chef to prepare a barbecue on the balcony grill.

Spa accommodations are located near the spa and part of a package that includes a massage for two in one of the most extensive wellness spa environments at sea.

A Captain's Suite, at 54 sq.m (581.2 sq.ft) is the largest suite aboard ship, and is located near the navigation bridge. Meanwhile, Sea & Sky suites give access to a large roof terrace with private sunbathing areas. Premium veranda cabins offer large, diagonal terraces, and there are three suite categories. Also, 10 cabins are designated as wheelchair-accessible.

Family-friendly suites sleep up to 6 (they come in three different types). One example measures about 42 sq.m (452.0 sq.ft) but there's also a huge balcony measuring 47 sq.m (505.9 sq ft). The total adds up to a delightfully large 89 sq.m (958.0 sq.ft). All come with Xbox game consoles.

DINING. With a choice of 11 dining venues, there really is plenty of choice. The Atlantic Restaurant is the ship's main restaurant. It is divided into three sections, and focuses on three styles of food: Classic – for dishes such as steak with roasted shallots and a chili-chocolate reduction); Mediterranean – for choices like homemade pastas, grilled fish and lamb with herbs of Provence; and Eurasian – for items such as sweet and sour vegetables with fried jasmine rice. Five course menus include home-made pastas, grilled fish or antipasti, as well as Asian dishes and is part of the inclusive offering.

Other dining options. At the aft of the ship, a 167sq m (1,797.6 sq.ft) multifaceted glass structure (nicknamed The Diamond) spans two decks. Inside the 'diamond,' are two restaurants that became extremely popular aboard *Mein Schiff 1* and *Mein Schiff 2* – Richards Essen for fine dining and Surf & Turf Steakhouse, which features a glass-enclosed meat dry-ageing cabinet.

Hanami is a Japanese restaurant, which incorporates a sushi bar. The venue offers sushi creations and other specialties of Japanese cuisine at an additional cost.

A real bakery, an adjunct of the self-serve buffet restaurant Anckelmannsplatz, features freshly baked (all day long) crispy rolls, panini and cakes. The venue contains a partially covered outdoor area which provides an opportunity to eat outside.

Already appearing aboard *Mein Schiff 1* and *Mein Schiff 2*, the popular informal restaurant Fish House Gosch Sylt now has about 130 seats (vs 88 seats aboard *Mein Schiff 1* and *Mein Schiff 2*, and features fresh fish and well-prepared seafood dishes, with daily specials listed on a blackboard.

For the still hungry, the Day & Night Bistro provides regional and international snacks around the clock, while in a modern coffee lounge a barista brews international coffees and presents *Mein Schiff 3*'s own handcrafted pralines and chocolates.

ENTERTAINMENT. The Theatre is the ship's show-lounge. It is a three-deck venue with 949 seats, and features colourful, razzle-dazzle production shows and major cabaret acts.

Additionally, a small concert hall/movie theatre – called Klanghaus (literally: small concert hall) was developed in conjunction with renowned acoustics experts from leading opera houses and concert halls. It provides a really fine setting for live classical and jazz cncerts, theatrical readings, lectures and movies with surround sound.

Numerous bands, small musical units and solo musical entertainers provide live music in several of the lounge venues throughout the ship.

SPA/FITNESS. Sports facilities include a large arena in the aft section of the ship for volleyball, basketball and football.

Ship talk

Abeam. Off the side of the ship, at a right angle to its length.

Aft. Near, toward, or in the rear of the ship.

Ahead. Something that is ahead of the ship's bow.

Alleyway. A passageway or corridor.

Alongside. Said of a ship when it is beside a pier or another vessel.

Amidships. In or toward the middle of the ship; the longitudinal center portion of the ship.

Anchor Ball. Black ball hoisted above the bow to show that the vessel is anchored.

Astern. The opposite of Ahead (i.e., meaning something behind the ship).

Backwash. Motion in the water caused by the propeller(s) moving in a reverse (astern) direction.

Bar. Sandbar, usually caused by tidal or current conditions near the shore.

Beam. Width of the ship between its two sides at the widest point.

Bearing. Compass direction, expressed in degrees, from the ship to a particular objective or destination.

Below. Anything beneath the main deck.

Berth. Dock, pier, or quay. Also means bed on board ship.

Bilge. Lowermost spaces of the infrastructure of a ship.

Boat Stations. Allotted space for each person during lifeboat drill or any other emergency when lifeboats are lowered.

Bow. The forward most part of the vessel.

Bridge. Navigational and command control center.

Bulkhead. Upright partition (wall) dividing the ship into compartments.

Bunkers. The space where fuel is stored; 'bunkering' means taking on fuel.

Cable Length. A measured length equaling 100 fathoms (or 600ft/180m).

Chart. A nautical map used for navigating.

Colors. Refers to the national flag or emblem flown by the ship.

Companionway. Interior stairway.

Course. Direction in which the ship is headed, in degrees.

Davit. A device for raising and lowering lifeboats.

Deadlight. A ventilated porthole cover, to prevent light from entering.

Disembark (also debark). To leave a ship.

Dock. Berth, pier, or quay.

Draft (or draught). Measurement in feet from the ship's waterline to the lowest point of its keel.

Embark. To join a ship.

Fantail. The rear or overhang of the ship.

Fathom. Distance equal to 6ft.

Flagstaff. A pole at the stern of a ship where the flag of its country of registry is flown.

Minerva
★★★★

Size:	Small Ship	Crew/Passenger Ratio (lower beds/all berths):	2.1/3.0
Tonnage:	12,892	Cabins (total):	190
Lifestyle:	Standard	Size range (sq ft/m):	139.9–360.6/13.0–33.5
Cruise line:	Swan Hellenic Discovery Cruises	Cabins (outside view):	144
Former names:	Explorer II, Alexander von Humboldt, Saga Pearl,	Cabins (interior/no view):	46
	Minerva, Okean	Cabins (for one person):	0
IMO number:	9144196	Cabins (with private balcony):	44
Builder:	Mariotti (Italy)	Cabins (wheelchair accessible):	4
Original cost:	na	Wheelchair accessibility:	Fair
Entered service:	Apr 1996/May 2008	Cabin voltage:	220 volts
Registry:	Bahamas	Elevators:	2
Length (ft/m):	436.3/133.0	Casino (gaming tables):	No
Beam (ft/m):	65.6/20.0	Slot machines:	No
Draft (ft/m):	19.6/6.0	Swimming pools:	1
Propulsion/Propellers:	diesel (6,960kW)/2	Hot tubs (on deck):	0
Passenger decks:	6	Self-service launderette:	Yes
Total crew:	157	Dedicated cinema/seats:	No
Passengers (lower beds/alll berths):	380/380	Library:	Yes
Passenger Space Ratio (lower beds/all berths):	33.9/33.9	Onboard currency:	UK£

A homely ship with a focus on discovery and learning

OVERVIEW. *Minerva* passengers, called 'Swanners,' are couples and single travelers of a mature age who seek to cruise off the beaten track in comfortable surroundings, and who don't need the highly organized entertainment provided by larger ships. This 'soft expedition' vessel is highly valued for its excellent food, friendly service, and fine library. It is not recommended for children.

Berlitz's Ratings

	Possible	Achieved
Ship	500	340
Accommodation	200	145
Food	400	305
Service	400	303
Entertainment	100	77
Cruise	400	285

OVERALL SCORE
1455 points out of 2000

THE SHIP. Originally intended as a spy ship (*Okean*) for the Soviet navy, the strong, 1989-built ice-strengthened hull was built at the Nikolajev shipyard on the River Ingul in Ukraine; it had a stern ramp for launching submersibles for submarine tracking (now removed). It was later converted for 'discovery' cruising and tailored to suit British tastes. The ship now operates for Swan Hellenic Discovery Cruises, part of the UK's All Leisure Group.

After an extensive refit in 2011–12, the ship's former angular profile has been improved. The refit included the addition of 32 wide balconies to existing cabins; remodeled bathrooms in all cabins; a new, large Orpheus (observation) Lounge above the navigation bridge; an extended Shackleton's Lounge; a larger, dedicated Internet-connect lounge; and an expanded library. The changes reflect the financial commitment of Swan Hellenic Cruises to its loyal clientele, and provide a better sense of space, more public rooms, and more comfort. There's ample open and shaded deck space too, particularly in the aft section, and there is also a new, wide teak walk-around promenade deck atop ship.

Four rubber inflatable Zodiac craft are carried for excursions ashore, useful for inhospitable locations such as in Antarctica without landing piers or formal docking arrangements. The interior decor is homely and restrained, like a country house hotel, not in the slightest bit glitzy, for passengers with good taste, although cushions would be a welcome addition to the many sofas. Lectures and briefings take place in the Darwin Lounge, the main lounge. Fine wool carpets inhabit the passageways and public rooms, and furniture is decidedly 'colonial' in style.

Perhaps the most appreciated and used public area is the excellent 5,000-book library with its classical 'armchair' decor and a fine range of reference books, many of academic standard. Shackleton's Lounge and Wheeler's Bar (in which is displayed fine glass-cased half-cut model of the *SS Caledonia*) exude a country-house atmosphere, and are good for socializing, as is the new Orpheus Observation Lounge atop ship. The ship also has a small shop, and an in-port kiosk for basic items.

The ship absorbs passengers well and maintains a feeling of intimacy. A great benefit of a cruise with Swan Hellenic is the quality and diversity of the lecturers and guest speakers. The open space is very good for the size of the ship. Wine is included with lunch and dinner, as are shore excursions. All gratuities are also included, although port charges are extra.

While the ship is not new and the cabins are small,

the refurbishment has added new features, and all cabin bathrooms were replaced. The food and service are extremely good, and so the score just tips the ship into the four-star category.

ACCOMMODATION. There are eight different cabin price grades, in 12 price categories. The price depends on grade and location rather than any great difference in size. Most standard cabins really are quite small, particularly when compared to the 'standard' cabin size on the latest ships today.

Owner's Suites (2). These Bridge Deck suites measure 372.4 sq ft (34.6 sq m). Facilities include a queen-size bed, bedside reading lights, an extra-large double closet and ample drawer space; separate lounge area with sofa, table and chair, and vanity table/writing desk, TV set with movie and audio channels, refrigerator, hairdryer, and binoculars; floor-to-ceiling patio doors leading to a private balcony (with green turf-covered deck); bathroom with bath/shower combination and toilet.

Deluxe Balcony Suites (22). These suites on Bridge Deck measure 336 sq ft (31 sq m), including an extra-large balcony. Facilities include twin beds or queen-size bed, two double closets and ample drawer space; separate lounge area with sofa, table and chair, and vanity table/writing desk, small TV set with movie and audio channels, refrigerator, hairdryer and binoculars; floor to ceiling patio doors and private balcony; bathroom with tub/shower and toilet.

Deluxe Balcony Suites. These new Sun Deck suites measure 340 sq ft (32 sq m), including a large balcony. Facilities include twin beds or queen-size bed, bedside reading lights, two double closets and ample drawer space; separate lounge area with sofa, table and chair, and vanity table/writing desk, TV set, refrigerator, hairdryer, and binoculars; large picture window; bathroom with bath/shower and toilet.

Standard Outside-View or Interior Cabins. These 'standard' cabins are small (140 sq ft/13 sq m) when compared to the 182-sq-ft (17-sq-m) cabins aboard today's newest ships. Facilities include twin beds or queen-size bed, two double closets and ample drawer space; separate lounge area with sofa, table and chair, and vanity table/writing desk, TV set, refrigerator, hairdryer, and binoculars; large picture window (outside-view cabins only; or porthole, depending on deck and price category); bathroom with shower enclosure and toilet.

The bathrooms have a raised 'lip' to step over, are totally white, and have small shower enclosures (except for some suites, which have bathtubs and marble tiled floors).

All grades have a hairdryer, 100 percent cotton bathrobe, cotton duvets, binoculars, passenger list, direct-dial telephone, fresh fruit basket, and L'Occitane toiletries and soap, but bottled mineral water costs extra. All bathrooms have hygienic hand-held, flexible shower hoses, and large bath-size towels.

The TV set includes movie and music channels, although the quality leaves much to be desired. There is little space for hanging outerwear parkas and other gear for any of the 'soft' expedition-style cruises, and some cabins on B Deck aft are subject to noise and vibration from the ship's engines/generators.

DINING. The Swan restaurant has open-seating dining, allowing you to eat with whomever you wish. The menus are quite extensive and feature many traditional British favourite dishes. The food itself is of a high quality. It's also creative, attractively presented, and has plenty of taste. The wine list is very decent (it includes the Chairman's Rothschild wine selection), and so is the special Champagne. The service staff are very pleasant, friendly, and willing.

Coffees and teas are available 24 hours a day from a beverage station in the self-serve Veranda Café, in which you can have casual breakfasts, luncheons, and dinners in an open-seating arrangement; for dinner, items from the menu in the Swan Restaurant are available, in addition to lighter fare.

ENTERTAINMENT. Although there is a main lounge (Darwin Lounge), this is used principally for lectures, for classical music ensembles, and poetry readings. The ship has a small band and solo entertaining musicians to provide live music for dancing and listening.

SPA/FITNESS. There is a small fitness room on Aegean Deck, and a beauty salon, but no sauna or steam room. Massages and aromatherapy facials, manicures, pedicures, and hair beautifying treatments are available, provided by the Ocean Spa company.

Monarch
★★★

Size:.................................Large Resort Ship			Cabins (total):.....................................1,192	
Tonnage: 73,937			Size range (sq ft/m): 118.4–670.0/11.0–62.2	
Lifestyle: ....Standard			Cabins (outside view):..................................732	
Cruise line:.............................Pullmantur Cruises			Cabins (interior/no view):..............................460	
Former names: ....Monarch of the Seas			Cabins (for one person):.................................0	
IMO number: 8819500			Cabins (with private balcony):..........................62	
Builder: ....Chantiers de l'Atlantique (France)			Cabins (wheelchair accessible): 4	
Original cost:................................£300 million			Wheelchair accessibility:...............................Fair	
Entered service:.....................Nov 1991/Apr 2013			Cabin voltage: ....110 volts	
Registry:.....................................The Bahamas			Elevators:...11	
Length (ft/m):............................879.9/268.2			Casino (gaming tables):...............................Yes	
Beam (ft/m):...............................105.9/32.3			Slot machines:.......................................Yes	
Draft (ft/m):...................................24.9/7.6			Swimming pools:......................................2	
Propulsion/Propellers:..................diesel (21,844kW)/2			Hot tubs (on deck):....................................2	
Passenger decks:......................................11			Self-service launderette:................................No	
Total crew:...858			Dedicated cinema/seats:.................................No	
Passengers (lower beds/alll berths):...............31.0/26.6			Library:..Yes	
Passenger Space Ratio (lower beds/all berths):.......31.0/26.6			Onboard currency: ....Euros	
Crew/Passenger Ratio (lower beds/all berths):.........2.8/3.3				

A modestly large, busy ship, good for a first cruise

OVERVIEW. This floating resort provides the basics for a well-tuned, but somewhat impersonal, short cruise experience for Spanish-speaking families. The range of facilities is decent enough, with consistently sound, highly programmed service from a reasonably attentive young staff. In April 2013, the ship was transferred from Royal Caribbean International to Pullmantur Cruises to operate family-friendly cruises for Spanish speakers, and renamed, simply, Monarch (ex-Monarch of the Seas).

THE SHIP. Monarch is almost identical in size and appearance to sister ship Sovereign but actually has a slightly improved internal layout and better public room features, and passenger flow. The ship, whose hull is painted a deep blue, sports a lounge and bar that is wrapped around the blue funnel and provides a stunning view (it's a great place to sit and enjoy a decent coffee from one of its 320-plus seats). The open deck space itself, however, is very cramped when the ship is full, as aboard any large ship, although there seems to be plenty of it. There is a basketball court aft for sports lovers.

The interior layout is a little awkward, as it is designed in a vertical stack, with most public rooms located aft, and the accommodation forward. There's an impressive array of spacious and elegant public rooms to play in, although the decor brings to mind the IKEA school of interior design. A spacious five-deck-high Centrum lobby has cascading stairways

Berlitz's Ratings		
	Possible	Achieved
Ship	500	302
Accommodation	200	117
Food	400	223
Service	400	260
Entertainment	100	64
Cruise	400	245
OVERALL SCORE		
1211 points out of 2000		

and two glass-walled elevators. You may be overwhelmed by the public spaces, but underwhelmed by the size of the cabins.

The ship has a good array of spacious, smart public rooms, including a conference room, library, and card players' room, plus a Monte Carlo Casino for the more serious gamers, as well as shops and an internet-connect center. The décor is accented with wood paneling, and some bright color splashes. Children and teens are well catered for, and there's a whole team of youth activity staff, together with a range of rooms for children and teens, including a chill-out lounge and an open aft sundeck with a dance floor.

The dress code is ultra-casual. All gratuities and port taxes are included in the cruise fare. Passengers can embark at Panama's Colón, Colombia's Cartagena or Venezuela's La Guaira on a seven-night year-round itinerary that also includes Aruba and Curaçao. Although Pullmantur Cruises markets this ship in Europe it focuses more on Latin America, where it provides a visa-free alternative for many nationalities. This provides an opportunity for South Americans to cruise the Caribbean in their winter.

ACCOMMODATION. There are numerous categories, priced by grade, size, and location. Note that there are no cabins with private balconies.

Suites. Thirteen suites on Bridge Deck are fairly large and nicely furnished (the largest is the Royal

Suite), with separate living and sleeping spaces. These provide more space, with better service and more perks than standard-grade accommodation.

Standard Cabins. The standard outside-view and interior cabins are very small, although an arched window treatment and colorful soft furnishings do give the illusion of more space.

Almost all cabins have twin beds that convert to a queen-size or double bed configuration, together with moveable bedside tables. However, when in a queen-bed configuration, the bed is typically flush against the wall, and access is from one side only. All standard cabins have very little closet and drawer space. You should, therefore, pack only minimal clothing, which is all you really need for a short cruise.

All cabins have a private bathroom, with a shower enclosure, toilet, and washbasin.

DINING. The two large dining rooms, Claude's and Vincent's, are located off the Centrum lobby. There are tables for four, six, or eight, but none for two. There are two seatings, and the dining operation is well-orchestrated, with emphasis on well-timed, programmed service. The cuisine is typical of mass banquet catering that offers standard fare comparable to that found in family-style eateries ashore. While menu descriptions are tempting, the actual food may be somewhat disappointing and unmemorable. Many items are pre-prepared ashore to keep costs down.

A decent selection of light meals is provided, and a vegetarian choice is also available. The selection of breads, rolls, and pastry items is good. The wine list is not extensive, but the prices are moderate.

For casual breakfasts and lunches, the Café is the place to go, although there are often long lines at peak times. On the aft of the upper level of the venue is a pizzeria.

ENTERTAINMENT. The Sound of Music is the principal showlounge; it has both main and balcony levels, with banquette seating, although sight lines from many of the balcony seats are poor.

A smaller entertainment venue, the April in Paris Lounge, is where cabaret acts, including late-night adult comedy are featured, as well as music for dancing.

The entertainment throughout is upbeat – in fact, it's difficult to get away from music and noise. There's even background music in all corridors and elevators, and constant music outdoors on the pool deck. If you want a quiet relaxing holiday, choose another ship.

SPA/FITNESS. The Spa del Mar features a gymnasium with aft-facing views and a selection of muscle-pumping equipment. There is also an aerobics studio, and classes are offered in a variety of keep-fit regimens, a beauty salon, and a sauna, as well as treatment rooms for pampering massages and facials. While the facilities aren't extensive, they're adequate.

For the sports-inclined, there is activity galore – including a rock-climbing wall with several separate climbing tracks. It is located outdoors aft of the blue funnel and wrap-around panoramic lounge.

Did you know...

...that the first regular steamship service across the North Atlantic was inaugurated on March 28, 1838, when the 703-ton steamer *Sirius* left London for New York via Cork, Ireland?
...that the winter of 1970–71 was the first time since 1838 that there was no regular passenger service on the North Atlantic?
...that the first scheduled transatlantic advertisement appeared in the New York Evening Post on October 27, 1817, for the 424-ton sailing packet *James Monroe* to sail from New York to Liverpool on January 5, 1818, and for *Couvier* to sail from Liverpool to New York on January 1?
...that Cunard Line held the record from 1940 to 1996 for the largest passenger ship ever built (*RMS Queen Elizabeth*)?

...that the Dollar Steamship Line featured a round-the-world cruise that started October 15, 1910, from New York, aboard the *ss Cleveland?* The cruise was advertised as 'one-class, no overcrowding' voyage. The cost was '$650 and up,' according to an advertisement.
...that a round-the-world cruise was made in 1922–23 by Cunard's *Laconia* (19,680 grt), a three-class ship that sailed from New York? The itinerary included many ports of call that are still popular with world cruise passengers today. The vessel accommodated 350 persons in each of its first two classes, and 1,500 in third class – giving a total capacity of 2,200 passengers, more than many current ships.

MSC Armonia
★★★ +

Size:................................... Mid-size Ship		Crew/Passenger Ratio (lower beds/all berths):.......... 2.2/3.1	
Tonnage: 58,625		Cabins (total):.....................................783	
Lifestyle: ....Standard		Size range (sq ft/m): 139.9–236.8/13.0–22.0	
Cruise line:................................MSC Cruises		Cabins (outside view):...............................511	
Former names: .... European Vision		Cabins (interior/no view):............................272	
IMO number: 9210141		Cabins (for one person):...............................0	
Builder: .... Chantiers de l'Atlantique (France)		Cabins (with private balcony):........................132	
Original cost:............................... $245 million		Cabins (wheelchair accessible): 2	
Entered service:.................... Jun 2001/May 2004		Wheelchair accessibility:..........................Good	
Registry:.. Italy		Cabin voltage: ....110 and 220 volts	
Length (ft/m):............................. 823.4/251.0		Elevators:..9	
Beam (ft/m):............................... 94.4/28.8		Casino (gaming tables):............................. Yes	
Draft (ft/m): 22.4/6.85		Slot machines:.................................... Yes	
Propulsion/Propellers: ...diesel-electric (31,680kW)/2 azimuthing pods		Swimming pools:....................................2	
Passenger decks:...................................10		Hot tubs (on deck):..................................1	
Total crew:.......................................710		Self-service launderette:............................No	
Passengers (lower beds/alll berths):.............. 1,566/2,223		Dedicated cinema/seats:.............................No	
Passenger Space Ratio (lower beds/all berths): 37.4/26.3		Library: .... Yes	
		Onboard currency: .... Euros	

A comfortable large ship for pan-European cruisers

OVERVIEW. *MSC Armonia* will suit those comfortable with multilingual fellow passengers, although the staff is more focused on Italian passengers. It is best for adult couples and solo travelers, and families with children, who enjoy constant activity accompanied by lots of noise, late nights, entertainment that is loud.

THE SHIP. As *European Vision*, the ship began its working life auspiciously, having been selected to be a floating hotel to accommodate the leaders and staff of the G8 summit in 2001. When its owner, Festival Cruises, ceased operations in 2004, it was bought by MSC Cruises for €215 million and renamed *MSC Armonia*. It is fitted with a high-tech azimuthing pod propulsion system. The exterior deck space is barely adequate for the number of passengers carried. The lido deck surrounding the outdoor swimming pool also has whirlpool tubs and a large bandstand is set in raised canvas-covered pods. All sunloungers have cushioned pads.

Inside, the layout and passenger flow is good, as are the 'you are here' deck signs. The decks are named after European cities – e.g., Oxford Deck (with British public room names), Venice Deck (with Italian names), and Biarritz Deck (with French names). The decor is 'European Moderne' – whatever that means – but it does include crisp, clean lines, minimalism in furniture designs – including some chairs that look interesting but are totally impractical. However, the interior colors are good; nothing jars the senses, but rather

Berlitz's Ratings		
	Possible	Achieved
Ship	500	381
Accommodation	200	153
Food	400	233
Service	400	294
Entertainment	100	55
Cruise	400	270
OVERALL SCORE		
1386 points out of 2000		

calms them, unlike the effect aboard many ships.

Facilities include Amadeus, a nightclub; Ambassador, a cigar smoking room with all the hallmarks of a gentleman's club; and Vivaldi, a piano lounge. The Goethe Library/Card Room has real writing desks – something many ships omit. There is an extensive Internet café, and an English pub, the White Lion. The Lido Casino has blackjack, poker and roulette games, plus an array of slot machines.

Standing in line for embarkation, disembarkation, shore tenders, and self-serve buffet meals is part of cruising aboard large ships. Announcements are in several languages.

Wheelchair-bound passengers should note that there is no access to the uppermost forward and aft decks, although access throughout most of the interior is good. The passenger hallways are a little narrow on some accommodation decks to pass when housekeeping carts are in place.

The company keeps prices low by providing air transportation that may be at inconvenient times, or that involves long journeys by bus. In other words, be prepared for a little discomfort in getting to and from your cruise in exchange for low cruise rates. Note that 15 percent is added to all drinks and beverage orders.

ACCOMMODATION. There are numerous categories, the price depending on the grade, size, and location you choose. These include 132 'suites' with private balcony (whose partitions are only of the partial and not the full type), outside-view cabins and interior (no view) cabins.

Suite grade accommodation – they are not true suites, as there's no separate bedroom and lounge – has more room, a larger lounge area, walk-in closet, wall-to-wall vanity counter, a bathroom with combination tub and shower, toilet, and private balcony with light. Bathrobes are provided. In general, the 'suites' are practical and nicely furnished. However, except for the very highest category, the bathrooms are very plain, with white plastic washbasins and white walls, and mirrors that steam up.

Even the smallest interior cabins are acceptable, with plenty of space between two lower beds. All grades of accommodation have a TV, mini-bar/refrigerator, personal safe cleverly positioned behind a vanity desk mirror, hairdryer, and bathroom with shower and toilet. But standard grade cabins, at a modest 140 sq ft (13 sq m), are quite small when compared to many other ships.

DINING. The principal dining room, the 610-seat Marco Polo Restaurant, has two seatings for dinner, and an open seating (meaning you'll be seated when you turn up when the dining room is open) for breakfast and lunch. However, during an open seating, you may well be seated with others with whom you may not be able to communicate very satisfactorily, given the wide mix of nationalities and languages on board.

In general, the cuisine is acceptable, although it is rather unmemorable. Even so, the menus are varied and the presentation is generally sound, and should prove a highlight for most passengers. Regional and seasonal specialties are also sometimes presented. The wine list has quite wide variety of wines at fairly reasonable prices, although most of the wines are very young.

La Pergola, the most formal restaurant, has stylish Italian cuisine. It is assigned to all passengers occupying accommodation designated as suites, although other passengers can dine in it too, on a reservations-only basis.

Other dining options. Chez Claude, on the starboard side aft, adjacent to the ship's funnel, is a grill area for fast-food. La Brasserie is a casual, self-serve buffet eatery, open 20 hours a day (including a sit-down, casual dinner each evening with waiter service). The selections are quite standardized – i.e., minimal. Café San Marco, on the upper, second level of the main lobby, serves extra-cost Sagafredo coffees, and pastry items.

ENTERTAINMENT. La Gondola Theater, which is two decks high, is the main venue for production shows, cabaret acts, plays, and other theatrical presentations. It is a well-designed room, except for the fact that no space was allocated for a live showband. Consequently, production shows are performed to pre-recorded backing tracks. The sight lines from most seats are good, and four entrances allow easy access and exit.

Other shows consist of unknown cabaret acts such as singers, magicians, mimes, and comedy jugglers. A number of bands and small musical units provide live music for dancing or listening.

SPA/FITNESS. The Atlantica Spa has numerous body-pampering treatments, a gymnasium with ocean views, and high-tech, muscle-toning and strengthening equipment. A thermal suite has different kinds of steam rooms combined with aromatherapy infusions such as chamomile and eucalyptus, and a rasul chamber provides a combination of two or three kinds of application mud and gentle steam shower. The spa, operated by the Italian concession OceanView, offers a wide range of well-being treatments. Gratuities to spa staff are at your discretion.

For active types there's a simulated climbing wall outdoors aft of the ship's funnel, as well as a volleyball/basketball court, and mini-golf.

Did you know...

...that motion pictures' most famous on-screen odd couple, Jack Lemmon and Walter Matthau, played gentlemen dance hosts intent on defrauding rich widows aboard a Caribbean cruise ship (*Westerdam*)? Out to Sea – a 1997 Martha Coolidge film – also starred Dyan Cannon, Gloria DeHaven, and Elaine Stritch. The 'cruise ship' interior was filmed at Raleigh Studios in Hollywood.

...that Epirotiki Line's *Jupiter* was used to carry the 61 finalists of the 1976 Miss Universe contest (Epirotiki Line became part of the now defunct Royal Olympia Cruises)?

...that on Valentine's Day, 1998, some 5,000 couples renewed their vows aboard the ships of Princess Cruises?

...that a 15-ft-high model of Goofy hangs upside down over the

stern of *Disney Magic*? He's painting the ship.

...that Carnival Cruise Lines and Mattel teamed up to produce a nautical-themed Barbie Doll? She can be found in the gift shops aboard all the company's ships.

...that the spa aboard the now withdrawn *Queen Elizabeth 2* was the first afloat to have a fully functional thalassotherapy pool? It was installed in 1994.

...that Steiner Leisure spa employees at sea massage over 30,000 bodies, deep cleanse 15,000 faces, blow dry 6,000 heads of hair, and manicure approximately 6,000 pairs of hands?

...that in 2002 Steiner Leisure purchased Mandara Spas and the Greenhouse Spas? Each brand continues to maintain its own identity.

MSC Divina
★★★★ +

Size:.................................Large Resort Ship	Cabins (total):.................................... 1,751
Tonnage: .... 139,400 tons	Size range (sq ft/m): 148.5–568.3/13.8–52.8
Lifestyle: ....Standard	Cabins (outside view):............................ 1,166
Cruise line:................................MSC Cruises	Cabins (interior/no view):...........................405
Former names: ....none	Cabins (for one person):.............................0
IMO number:.................................9585285	Cabins (with private balcony):..................... 1,125
Builder: ....STX France	Cabins (wheelchair accessible): 45
Original cost:............................$760 million	Wheelchair accessibility:...........................Good
Entered service:............................ Jun 2012	Cabin voltage: ....110 and 220 volts
Registry:.....................................Panama	Elevators:..17
Length (ft/m):.......................1,093.5/333.3	Casino (gaming tables):............................. Yes
Beam (ft/m):............................ 124.6/38.0	Slot machines:...................................... Yes
Draft (ft/m):............................. 27.72/8.45	Swimming pools:......................................3
Propulsion/Propellers:.............. diesel-electric (40MW)/2	Hot tubs (on deck):...................................13
Passenger decks:....................................13	Self-service launderette:............................No
Total crew:...................................... 1,388	Dedicated cinema/seats:..............................No
Passengers (lower beds/all berths):.............. 3,502/4,345	Library: .... Yes
Passenger Space Ratio (lower beds/all berths):....... 39.8/32.0	Onboard currency: .... Euros
Crew/Passenger Ratio (lower beds/all berths):.......... 2.5/3.1	

A really stunning large family-friendly ship for Europeans

OVERVIEW. This large, really elegantly attired resort ship has a trendy infinity pool and 'beach' zone, and will appeal to young adult couples, singles, and families with children and teens who enjoy an urban Mediterranean lifestyle, with a mix of many European nationalities.

THE SHIP. *MSC Divina*, together with sister ship MSC Preziosa are the largest ships yet for MSC Cruises. This ship features the latest in green-technology engines. Its exclusive area, the MSC Yacht Club, includes an expanded Top-Sail Lounge (an observation/lifestyle lounge and social meeting place), private sunbathing with integral dip pool, two hot tubs, and concierge services. Even more desirably, it has a private Yacht Club-only restaurant, Le Muse. Only Yacht Club-grade occupants are escorted to their cabins by their butlers. Housekeeping staff point passengers in the right direction, but no longer escort them to their cabins.

The interior décor is quite stunning. There are basically two decks full of public lounges, bars, and eateries, including a large two-deck-high theater-style showlounge, a nightclub/discotheque, library, card room, an internet center, virtual reality center, shopping gallery, and large casino (inhabited by many people who can smoke at the bar). Drinking places include many lounges and bars, most with live music. One lounge in the aft section is for adults only, as is an aft swimming pool and relaxation deck. For a little music, the Golden Jazz Bar is a must (the walls are 'stoned').

Berlitz's Ratings

	Possible	Achieved
Ship	500	422
Accommodation	200	162
Food	400	276
Service	400	308
Entertainment	100	76
Cruise	400	308

OVERALL SCORE
1552 points out of 2000

Additionally, there are conference and small group meeting facilities.

The ship's focal point, however, is its gorgeous five-deck high atrium lobby with shimmering Hollywood Swarovski crystal stairways and elegant, Art Deco-ish decor. The reception desk and financial services desk are located on the lower level, which also has a stage and seating in oh-so-comfortable oversized armchairs.

You can drive an F1 Ferrari racing car in a simulator, and experience seat-of-your pants rides in a 4D theatre.

Niggles include the fact that all the lounges flow' into each other, and so the music from each one bleed into the adjacent room. For a more general idea of the ship's features, see the entries for *MSC Fantasia* and *MSC Splendida*.

FAMILIES. The ship is well designed to cater for families with children, who have their own play centers (a children's club and jungle adventure playground), youth counselors, and activity programs. Facilities include a water slide, video arcade, and a 4D cinema.

ACCOMMODATION. There are nine types of accommodation, in numerous cabin price grades. Included are two Royal Suites, three Executive/Family Suites, and a mix of outside-view (with or without balconies) and interior cabins. The price you pay depends on the grade, size, and location you choose.

The 'Yacht Club' exclusive accommodation consists of some 67 'suites,' housed in a key-operated access only area of the ship. Included in the suites is number 16007 – the Sophia Loren Suite, in rich reds, specially designed lamps, and stunning photos of her great movie roles, together with a replica of the dressing table that Ms Loren uses in her home) and comes with full butler service, interactive TV, minibar, personal safe, hairdryer, and satellite-link telephone.

DINING. There are two main restaurants. The two-level Black Crab has 626 seats on one level and 529 on the other, and assigned tables and seating for dinner. The second is the 766-seat Villa Rossa Restaurant. The focus of the cuisine is on Mediterranean fare, with regional and seasonal fare when available. Light 'always available' choices are also provided. The ship makes all its pasta on board, and prides itself on its Italian flair.

Occupants of Yacht-Club accommodation grades eat in Le Muse, a private, quite intimate restaurant which looks out onto the aft infinity pool area. The service here is less hurried and much more personalized.

Other dining options. A Sacramento Tex-Mex and Burger specialty venue (serving large portions of burritos, fajitas, enchiladas, tacos, tortillas and more, together with a choice of several Mexican beers) provides an alternative to the main dining room.

Two very large Lido-style self-serve buffet cafeterias (Calumet and Manitou – named after native Indian peace pipes and spirits; each has about 400 seats) are for breakfasts and lunches, and served, casual dinners. The buffets are open for up to 20 hours daily – so there's always something to eat whenever you're hungry).

Additional foodie-type places include La Cantina di Bacco (a wine bar and pizzeria), Piazza del Doge (for Italian pastries, coffees, and huge selection of gelato), an Italia Bar for coffees (the Italian Sagafredo brand is featured) and pastries, and Galaxy (an extra cost a la carte eatery located as part of the discotheque, it overlooks the entire mid-ship pool deck, and is good for a late-riser's brunch (featuring several trendy tapas-like dishes).

A Sports and Bowling Diner features a classic American food experience (including sandwiches and burgers).

ENTERTAINMENT. The 1,603-seat Pantheon Theater is spread over two decks. Because passengers really are multinational, the entertainment concentrates on shows that are highly visual, such as mime, magic, dancing, and acrobatics, and are performed to recorded music. A number of bands and small musical units provide live music for dancing or listening to in most lounges and bars.

SPA/FITNESS. The large Aurea Spa and Wellbeing Center houses a beauty salon, numerous body treatment rooms (with Balinese therapists and 21 types of massage), a bar (for fruit drinks and smoothies), relaxation room, solarium, and a gymnasium with great ocean views. A thermal suite contains two steam rooms and four saunas combined with herbal aromatherapy infusions. This is the first cruise ship to have a halotherapy (Himalayan salt crystal) bed for body detoxing. There's also a Shu Uemura Art of Hair Cabin. Sports facilities include basketball, tennis court, volleyball, a power-walking track, bowling, and shuffleboard. Gratuities to spa staff are at your discretion.

MSC Fantasia
★★★★

Size:.................................Large Resort Ship	Cabins (total):.................................... 1,637
Tonnage: 137,936	Size range (sq ft/m): 161.4-699.6/15-65
Lifestyle: ....Standard	Cabins (outside view):............................. 1,354
Cruise line:.................................MSC Cruises	Cabins (interior/no view):.........................283
Former names: ....none	Cabins (for one person):...............................0
IMO number:.................................5515738	Cabins (with private balcony):.................... 1,260
Builder: ....STX Europe (France)	Cabins (wheelchair accessible): 43
Original cost:.............................$550 million	Wheelchair accessibility:.......................... Best
Entered service:............................... Dec 2008	Cabin voltage: ....110 and 220 volts
Registry:.................................... Panama	Elevators:...14
Length (ft/m):.........................1,093.5/333.3	Casino (gaming tables):............................. Yes
Beam (ft/m):................................. 124.3/37.9	Slot machines:..................................... Yes
Draft (ft/m): 27.72/8.45	Swimming pools:..................3 (1 w/sliding glass dome)
Propulsion/Propellers:............... diesel-electric (40MW)/2	Hot tubs (on deck):.................................13
Passenger decks:.....................................13	Self-service launderette:...........................No
Total crew:...................................... 1,325	Dedicated cinema/seats:............................No
Passengers (lower beds/all berths):............. 3,274/4,363	Library: .... Yes
Passenger Space Ratio (lower beds/all berths): 42.1/31.6	Onboard currency: .... Euros
Crew/Passenger Ratio (lower beds/all berths):.......... 2.5/3.0	

Comfort, space and a Mediterranean lifestyle for families

OVERVIEW. This ship appeals to young adult couples, singles, and families with children and teens that enjoy big ships and a big-city lifestyle with a mix of nationalities, mostly European. You can drive an F1 Ferrari racing car in a simulator, and experience hair-raising, seat-of-your pants rides in a 4D theater. Note that only Yacht Club-grade occupants are escorted to their cabins by their butlers. Housekeeping staff point passengers in the right direction, but no longer escort them to their cabins.

THE SHIP. Built in 67 blocks, some more than 600 tons, *MSC Fantasia* is one of the largest ships built for a European cruise company. It is 10 meters longer than the Eiffel Tower is high, and the propulsion power is the equivalent of 120 Ferraris. There are four swimming pools, one of which can be covered by a glass dome.

The interior design is an enlargement and extension of MSC's smaller *Musica*- and *Orchestra*-class ships, but with the addition of an exclusive area called the MSC Yacht Club for occupants of the 99 suites. This 'club' includes a Top-Sail Lounge, private sunbathing with integral dip pool, two hot tubs, and concierge services such as making dining reservations, and booking excursions and spa treatments.

It's worth paying extra to stay in one of the 'suites' in the Yacht Club accommodation. You'll get silver-tray room service by a team of well-trained butlers, a reserved (quieter) section of the Il Cerchio d'Oro

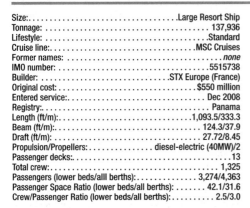

Berlitz's Ratings		
	Possible	Achieved
Ship	500	418
Accommodation	200	162
Food	400	271
Service	400	306
Entertainment	100	74
Cruise	400	306
OVERALL SCORE		
1537 points out of 2000		

restaurant, plus keycard access to a members-only sundeck sanctuary area that includes its own bar and food counters, a small dip pool, two hot tubs, and expansive open but sheltered lounging deck. It's a world away from the hustle and bustle of the main pool decks and solarium on the decks below.

The interior décor is quite stunning. There are basically two decks full of public lounges, bars, and eateries, including a large two-deck-high theater-style showlounge, a nightclub/discotheque, library, card room, an internet center, virtual reality center, shopping gallery, and large casino (inhabited by many people who can smoke at the bar). Shopping becomes a city-like environment. The Monte Carlo Casino features blackjack, poker, and roulette games, plus an array of slot machines.

Drinking places include a pub-like venue and several comfortable lounges with live music. Note that 15 percent is added to all drinks/beverage orders. A neat mini-golf course is on the port side of the funnel, and a walking and jogging track encircles the two swimming pools.

Niggles include the fact that all the lounges 'flow' into each other, and so the music from each one bleeds into any adjacent room.

FAMILIES. The ship is designed to accommodate families with children, who have their own play centers (a children's club and jungle adventure playground), a teens arcade, youth counselors, and activity programs.

ACCOMMODATION. Eighty percent of cabins have an outside view, and 95 percent of these have a balcony – a standard balcony cabin will measure almost 172 sq ft (16 sq m), plus bathroom and balcony. There are 72 suites in a MSC Yacht Club VIP section; each measures 312 sq ft (29 sq m) and comes with full butler service. The price you pay depends on the grade, size, and location you choose.

In a 2011 refit, 28 Aurea Suites were created with direct access to the Aurea Spa. The spa suites come with amenities and 'extras,' including a non-alcoholic cocktail at the Aurea Spa Bar, unlimited access to the Thermal Suite (sauna and steam room) and a private consultation with the spa doctor. Also part of the price are a Balinese massage, a facial relax treatment using skin-firming cream, and a solarium session for full-body tanning.

A black marble floor leads to a magnificent Swarovski glass staircase that connects the concierge facilities between decks 15 and 16 under a glass-domed ceiling.

DINING. There are four dining venues. The two-deck-high Red Velvet, the main restaurant, is in the aft section. It has a ship-wide balcony level, with a stairway to connect its two levels. The focus of the cuisine is on Mediterranean fare, with regional and seasonal fare when available. Light 'always available' choices are also provided. The ship makes all its pasta on board, and prides itself on its Italian flair.

Il Cerchio d'Oro is a single-level specialty restaurant, with a different menu each evening devoted to a different region of Italy. The Murano chandeliers are quite lovely, and definitely really worth noticing.

Other dining options. L'Etoile is a classic French restaurant, with decor reminiscent of the Belle Epoque era. Menus focus on one of three themes: the sea, the countryside, and the kitchen garden, and change seasonally. There's also an extra-charge Tex-Mex restaurant, El Sombrero, serving large portions of burritos, fajitas, enchiladas, tacos, tortillas and more, together with a choice of several Mexican beers.

Casual breakfasts, lunches, and sit-down, served, but casual dinners can be taken in the large self-serve L'Africana Café, a self-serve buffet-style eatery that is open 20 hours daily – so you can always find something to eat.

Another casual spot for people-watching is the Il Cappuccino coffee bar. Located two decks above the main reception area, it serves all types of coffees and teas, as well as fine chocolate delicacies.

La Cantina Toscana is a neat wine bar that pairs wines with food from several regions of Italy, in a setting that includes alcove seating, and L'Africana, which has a decor of dark African hardwoods.

A Sports and Bowling Diner features a classic American food experience (including sandwiches and burgers).

ENTERTAINMENT. L'Avanguardia, the main show-lounge, has 1,603 seats, and facilities that rival almost any to be found on land. Additionally, live music is provided in most lounges by small musical units and solo musicians.

SPA/FITNESS. The Aurea Spa has a beauty salon, several treatment rooms, and a gymnasium with great ocean views. A thermal suite contains different kinds of steam rooms combined with herbal aromatherapy infusions, in a calming Asia-themed environment. The spa is operated by OceanView, a specialist spa provider.

Sports facilities include deck quoits, shuffleboard courts, large tennis/basketball court, mini-golf, and a jogging track.

Gratuities are not included, but left to your own discretion.

Nautical Expressions

If you've ever wondered where some terms or phrases came from, you have only to look to the sea, ships, and seamen.

Square meal. This derives from the meals served on square wooden platters used on board ship. The platters could be easily stowed in racks between meals. Any substantial meal is now described as a 'square meal.'

Three sheets to the wind. A term said of a man who is clearly behaving under the influence of drink. A ship with three sheets in the wind would 'stagger to and fro like a drunken man.' Conversely, a drunken man behaves like a ship with three sheets in the wind.

To know the ropes. There were miles and miles of cordage in the rigging of a square rigged ship. The only way of keeping track of and knowing the function of all of these lines was to know their locations. It took an experienced seaman to know the ropes.

Under the weather. Refers to a sailor being in the uncomfortable position of having his station at the weather bow, subject to the pitching of the boat with spray constantly blown in his face. It is used today to mean feeling unwell.

MSC Lirica
★★★★

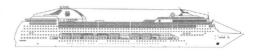

Size:.................................. Mid-size Ship		Cabins (total):...............................780	
Tonnage: 59,058		Size range (sq ft/m): 139.9–302.0/13.0–28.0	
Lifestyle: ....Standard		Cabins (outside view):..........................504	
Cruise line:...............................MSC Cruises		Cabins (interior/no view):.......................276	
Former names: ....none		Cabins (for one person):..........................0	
IMO number: 9246102		Cabins (with private balcony):......................132	
Builder: .... Chantiers de l'Atlantique (France)		Cabins (wheelchair accessible): 4	
Original cost:..............................$266 million		Wheelchair accessibility:..........................Good	
Entered service:...........................Mar 2003		Cabin voltage: ....110 and 220 volts	
Registry:.................................. Panama		Elevators:.......................................9	
Length (ft/m):............................. 830.7/253.2		Casino (gaming tables):.......................... Yes	
Beam (ft/m):.............................. 94.4/28.8		Slot machines:................................. Yes	
Draft (ft/m):............................... 22.4/6.8		Swimming pools:.................................2	
Propulsion/Propellers:..... diesel (31,680kW)/2 azimuthing pods		Hot tubs (on deck):...............................	
Passenger decks:................................10		Self-service launderette:..........................No	
Total crew:......................................701		Dedicated cinema/seats:..........................No	
Passengers (lower beds/alll berths):............. 1,560/2,069		Library: .... Yes	
Passenger Space Ratio (lower beds/all berths): 37.5/28.5		Onboard currency: .... Euros	
Crew/Passenger Ratio (lower beds/all berths):.......... 2.2/2.9			

A large, Euro-style, informal, family-friendly ship.

OVERVIEW. MSC Lirica is best suited to young adult couples, singles, and families with tots, children and teens who enjoy big-ship surroundings and facilities, and passengers of different nationalities and languages (mostly European). The decor has many Italian influences, including clean lines, minimalism in furniture design, and an eclectic collection of colors and soft furnishings that somehow work well together without any hint of garishness.

Berlitz's Ratings		
	Possible	Achieved
Ship	500	388
Accommodation	200	150
Food	400	236
Service	400	299
Entertainment	100	55
Cruise	400	279
OVERALL SCORE		
1407 points out of 2000		

THE SHIP. MSC Lirica, sister to MSC Opera, was the first of a pair of newbuilds for Mediterranean Shipping Cruises (MSC), Italy's largest privately owned cruise line. The ship's deep blue funnel is quite sleek; it has a swept-back design. The ship is fitted with an azimuthing pod propulsion system.

Inside, the layout and passenger flow is quite good with the exception of a couple of points of congestion – typically when first seating passengers exit the dining room and second seating passengers are waiting to enter.

An abundance of real woods and marble are used extensively in the interiors, and the high quality reflects MSC's commitment to high quality. The interior fit and finish is good.

Facilities include a large main showlounge, a nightclub/discotheque, multiple lounges and bars, an Internet center, a virtual reality center, a children's club, and a shopping gallery named Rodeo Drive with stores that have an integrated bar and entertainment area so that

shopping becomes a city-like environment where you can shop, drink, and be entertained all in one convenient area. The Las Vegas Casino offers blackjack, poker, and roulette games, together with an array of slot machines. There is also a card room, but the integral library is small and disappointing and there are no hardback books.

The ship is designed to accommodate families with children, who have their own play center, youth counselors, and activity programs. Anyone wheelchair-bound should note that there is no access to the uppermost forward and aft decks, although access throughout most of the interior is very good and there are also several wheelchair-accessible public restrooms. But passenger hallways are a little narrow on some decks for you to pass when housekeeping carts are in place.

Some things that passengers find irritating: the ship's photographers always seem to be in your face; the telephone numbering system to reach such places as the information bureau (2224) and hospital (2360) are not easy to remember – single digit numbers would be better. Gratuities are extra even though bar drinks already include a 15 percent service charge added to all drinks/beverage orders.

ACCOMMODATION. There are several different price levels for accommodation, depending on grade and location: one suite category, five outside-view cabin grades, and five interior cabin grades. Included are 132 'suites' with private balcony (though partitions between balconies are of the partial type), outside-view cabins, and interior cabins.

All cabins have a mini-bar and personal safe, satellite-linked television, several audio channels, and 24-hour room service. While tea and coffee are complimentary, snacks for room service have a delivery charge of €2.50.

Accommodation designated as suites – they are not true suites, as there is no separate bedroom and lounge – has more room, a larger lounge area, walk-in closet, wall-to-wall vanity counter, a bathroom with combination tub and shower, toilet, and semi-private balcony with a light but partitions that are partial, not full. The bathrobes are 100 percent cotton. However, except for the very highest category, the suite bathrooms are very plain, with white plastic washbasins and white walls, and mirrors that steam up.

Some cabins on Scarlatti Deck have views obstructed by lifeboats, while those on Deck 10 aft (10105–10159) can be subject to late-night noise from the discotheque on the deck above.

DINING. There are two dining rooms: La Bussola Restaurant, and the smaller, slightly more intimate L'Ippocampo Restaurant, located one deck above. Both have large ocean-view picture windows at the aft end of the ship. There are two seatings for meals, in keeping with all other ships in the MSC fleet, and tables are for two, four, six, or eight.

La Pergola is the most formal restaurant, offering stylish Italian cuisine. It is assigned to passengers in accommodation designated as suites, although other passengers can dine in it, too, on a reservations-only basis. The food and service are superior to that in the main dining room.

Other dining options. Casual, self-serve buffets for breakfast and lunch can be taken in Le Bistrot Cafeteria, which is also open for 20 hours a day, for sit-down, served, but casual dinners each evening. For fast foods, there is also a grill and a pizzeria, both located outside, adjacent to the swimming pool and ship's funnel.

Coffee Corner, located on the upper, second level of the main lobby, is the place for coffees and pastry items – as well for people-watching throughout the day and evening. Although there are windows, the view is not of the ocean, but of the stowed gangways and associated equipment.

ENTERTAINMENT. The Broadway Theater, the main showlounge, is located in the forward section. It has tiered seating set in a sloping floor, and sightlines are good from most seats. The room can also serve as a venue for large social functions. There is no separate bandstand, and the shows work with recorded music; hence there is little consistency in orchestration and sound balance.

High-quality entertainment has not, to date, been part of MSC's mindset. Hence, production shows and variety acts tend to be adequate at best. The Lirica Lounge, one deck above the showlounge, is the place for social dancing, with live music. For the young and lively set, there is The Blue Club, the ship's throbbing, ear-melting discotheque.

Additionally, live music is provided in most lounges by small musical units and solo musicians.

SPA/FITNESS. The Lirica Health Center is located one deck above the navigation bridge at the forward end of the ship. The complex has a beauty salon, several private massage/body treatment rooms, plus a fitness center with ocean views and an array of cardio-vascular equipment. There's also a thermal suite, containing different kinds of steam rooms combined with aromatherapy infusions, available at extra cost.

The health center is run as a concession by the Italian company OceanView, and has European hairstylists and Balinese massage and body treatment staff. Gratuities to spa staff are not included, but left to your discretion.

MSC Magnifica
★★★★

Size:.................................Large Resort Ship	Cabins (total):.................................... 1,275
Tonnage:....................................... 92,409	Size range (sq ft/m):................. 150.6–301.3/14.0–28.0
Lifestyle:.......................................Standard	Cabins (outside view):........................... 1,000
Cruise line:...............................MSC Cruises	Cabins (interior/no view):...........................275
Former names:...................................none	Cabins (for one person):.............................0
IMO number:...............................9387085	Cabins (with private balcony):.......................827
Builder:........................... Aker Yards (France)	Cabins (wheelchair accessible):......................17
Original cost:....................................... n/a	Wheelchair accessibility:.........................Good
Entered service:............................. Mar 2010	Cabin voltage:.........................110 and 220 volts
Registry:.....................................Panama	Elevators:...13
Length (ft/m):............................... 963.9/293.8	Casino (gaming tables):........................... Yes
Beam (ft/m):................................ 105.6/32.2	Slot machines:.................................... Yes
Draft (ft/m):.................................. 25.2/7.7	Swimming pools:.....................................2
Propulsion/Propellers:.................diesel (31,680kW)/2	Hot tubs (on deck):..................................4
Passenger decks:.....................................13	Self-service launderette:............................No
Total crew:.......................................987	Dedicated cinema/seats:............................No
Passengers (lower beds/alll berths):.............. 2,550/3,013	Library:... Yes
Passenger Space Ratio (lower beds/all berths):....... 37.0/30.9	Onboard currency:............................... Euros
Crew/Passenger Ratio (lower beds/all berths):.......... 2.5/3.0	

A large, family-friendly ship with bright decor

OVERVIEW. This large resort ship is designed to accommodate families with children, who have their own play center, video games room, youth counselors, and activity programs. The interior layout and passenger flow are quite good, and decks are named after Mediterranean destinations like Capri, Positano, Porto Venere, Ischia. Some of the artwork is quite whimsical, but it suits the ship's contemporary design.

THE SHIP. *MSC Magnifica* is one of a quartet of the same class, the others being *MSC Musica, MSC Poesia,* and *MSC Orchestra*. The ship sports a dark blue funnel, which has a swept-back design that balances an otherwise large-ship profile. The hull itself has large circular porthole-style windows instead of square or rectangular ones. The ship is powered by diesel motors driving electric generators to provide power to two conventional propellers.

The interior decor has an abundance of Italian and general Mediterranean influences. These include clean lines, minimalism in furniture design, and a collection of colors, soft furnishings, and fabrics that work well together. Real wood and marble have been used extensively in the Italianate interiors, and the high quality reflects the commitment that MSC Cruises has in the vessel's future.

The focal point is a main three-deck-high lobby; it has a water-feature backdrop and a crystal (glass) piano on a small stage that appears to float on a pond. Facilities include a large main showlounge (Royal

Berlitz's Ratings

	Possible	Achieved
Ship	500	403
Accommodation	200	155
Food	400	242
Service	400	298
Entertainment	100	62
Cruise	400	292
OVERALL SCORE		
1452 points out of 2000		

Theatre), a nightclub, Atlantic City Casino, a discotheque that incorporates two bowling lanes, numerous lounges and bars (including L'Olimpiade sports/wine/food bar), a library, a card room, an Internet center, a 4D virtual reality center, children's club, and a dedicated cigar lounge (Cuba Lounge) with specialized smoke extraction and stocking a selection of Cuban, Dominican, and Italian smokes.

One of the most popular venues is the Tiger Lounge/Bar. It features animal-themed decor and sumptuous but heavy chairs, and a long curvy bar. A shopping area, which includes an electronics store, is a well-integrated bar and entertainment area that flows through the main lobby so that shopping becomes a city-like environment where you can shop, drink, and be entertained all in one convenient area.

Drinking places include a pub-like venue as well as several comfortable lounges with live music. Note that 15 percent is added to all bar drink prices. Although access throughout most of the interior is very good, wheelchair-bound passengers should note that accommodation hallways are narrow on some decks for you to pass when housekeeping carts are in place. Sadly, there is no walk-around open promenade deck.

ACCOMMODATION. There are numerous different price levels, depending on grade and location: suites, outside-view cabins, and interior cabins. Included are 18 'suites' with private balcony, mini-suites, outside-view cabins, and interior cabins. Contrary to nautical convention, the cabin numbering system has even numbered cabins on the starboard side, and odd numbered cabins on the port side.

All cabins have high-quality Italian bed linen (400-count cotton for suites, 300-count cotton for all other cabins), a mini-bar, safe, satellite flat-screen TV set, several audio channels, and 24-hour room service. Continental breakfast is complimentary in cabins from 7:30am to 10am, and room service snacks are available at extra cost at any other time.

Accommodation designated as 'suites' – they are not true suites, as there is no separate bedroom and lounge – also has more space, although they are small compared to suites on some other major cruise lines. They have a larger lounge area, walk-in closet, and vanity desk with drawer-mounted hairdryer; a bathroom with combination tub and shower, toilet, and semi-private balcony with light. The partitions between each balcony are of the partial, not full, type. The bathrobes and towels are 100 percent cotton, and a pillow menu with a choice of five pillows is available.

Views from many cabins on Camogli Deck are obstructed by lifeboats. Some of the most popular cabins are those at the aft section of the ship, with views over the stern from the balcony cabins. The 17 cabins for the disabled are spacious and well-equipped.

DINING. There are two principal dining rooms: L'Edera and Quattro Venti. Both are located aft – on different decks – with large ocean-view picture windows. There are two seatings for meals, at assigned tables for 2-8. Seating is both banquette-style and in individual chairs – although the chairs are slim and do not have armrests.

Other dining options. Casual, self-serve buffets for breakfast and lunch are set out in the Sahara Cafeteria (open 20 hours every day), where you can also enjoy sit-down and be served dinners in a casual setting each evening. There's also a pool deck fast-food eatery for burgers. Coffee/tea and pastries are available in several bars adjacent to the mid-ships atrium lobby.

Enclosed in the ship's center, on Amalfi Deck, Shanghai is a Chinese à la carte extra-cost restaurant. It's a popular place, and reservations are required.

L'Oesi is a reservation-required, extra charge, à la carte dining spot that, by day, forms the aft section of the Sahara Cafeteria, complete with Moroccan-style decor. Dinners are cooked to order from the adjacent galley.

A Sports Bar is the venue for light-bite snack foods (examples: chicken breast and rocket salad; eggs stuffed with salmon roe; smoked salmon rosettes; assorted sole rolls – all at a small additional cost).

Silver trays full of late-night snacks are taken throughout the ship by waiters, and on some days, special late-night desserts, such as flambé items, are showcased in various lounges. Ice cream is made on board.

All sorts of coffees, available in the many bars and lounges, cost extra but are still good value.

ENTERTAINMENT. The Royal Theater is the large, principal show lounge, and the tiered seating spans three decks in the forward section of the ship, with good sightlines from most of the plush, comfortable seats. The room can also serve as a venue for large groups or social functions. All the large-scale production shows are performed to prerecorded music – there is no showband.

The L'Amethista Lounge is the place for social dancing and functions such as cooking demonstrations, with live music provided by a band. For the young and lively crowd, there's the ear-melting T32 discotheque. With its floor-to-ceiling windows, it is a quiet, pleasant place to relax and read during sea days.

Additionally, big-screen movies are shown on a mega-screen above the forward pool, just behind the ship's mast, and live music is provided in most lounges and bars.

SPA/FITNESS. The Aurea Spa is one deck above the navigation bridge at the forward end of the ship. The complex has a beauty salon, several treatment rooms offering massage and other body-pampering treatments, and a gymnasium with forward ocean views and an array of muscle-toning and strengthening equipment. There's also a Middle East-themed thermal suite, containing steam rooms and saunas with aromatherapy infusions, and a relaxation/hot tub room; there's an extra charge for using these facilities.

Sports facilities include table tennis, a tennis court, mini-golf course, golf practice net, two shuffleboard courts, and a jogging track.

Note that gratuities to staff are not included, but left to your discretion.

MSC Musica
★★★★

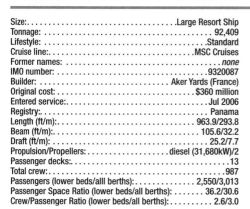

Size:.................................Large Resort Ship		Cabins (total):............................ 1,275	
Tonnage: 92,409		Size range (sq ft/m): 150.6–301.3/14.0–28.0	
Lifestyle:....................................Standard		Cabins (outside view):......................... 1,000	
Cruise line:...............................MSC Cruises		Cabins (interior/no view):.......................275	
Former names: .... none		Cabins (for one person):..........................0	
IMO number: 9320087		Cabins (with private balcony):....................827	
Builder: .... Aker Yards (France)		Cabins (wheelchair accessible): 17	
Original cost:.............................$360 million		Wheelchair accessibility:......................Good	
Entered service:............................Jul 2006		Cabin voltage: ....110 and 220 volts	
Registry:..................................... Panama		Elevators:..13	
Length (ft/m):........................... 963.9/293.8		Casino (gaming tables):......................... Yes	
Beam (ft/m):............................ 105.6/32.2		Slot machines:.................................. Yes	
Draft (ft/m): 25.2/7.7		Swimming pools:...................................2	
Propulsion/Propellers: ....diesel (31,680kW)/2		Hot tubs (on deck):................................4	
Passenger decks:....................................13		Self-service launderette:..........................No	
Total crew:..987		Dedicated cinema/seats:...........................No	
Passengers (lower beds/alll berths):............. 2,550/3,013		Library:.. Yes	
Passenger Space Ratio (lower beds/all berths): 36.2/30.6		Onboard currency: .... Euros	
Crew/Passenger Ratio (lower beds/all berths):.......... 2.6/3.0			

Lively Italian decor and style for family cruising

OVERVIEW. *MSC Musica* suits young adult couples, singles, and families with tots, children, and teens who enjoy big-ship surroundings and a noisy, big-city life-style, with different nationalities and languages, mostly European. The ship is designed to accommodate families with children, who have their own play center, video games room, youth counselors, and activity programs.

THE SHIP. *MSC Musica* is an extension and evolution of the slightly smaller (and earlier) *MSC Lirica* and *MSC Opera*. The ship's deep blue funnel is sleek, and features a swept-back design that carries the MSC logo in gold lettering. The overall profile is quite well-balanced. The hull has large circular porthole-style windows instead of square or rectangular windows. From a technical viewpoint, the ship is powered by diesel motors driving electric generators that provide power to two conventional propellers.

Real wood and marble have been used extensively in the ship's interiors, and the high quality reflects the commitment that MSC Cruises has in the cruise industry.

The interior focal point is a main three-deck high lobby, with a water-feature backdrop and a crystal (glass) piano on a small stage that appears to float on a pond. Other principal facilities include a large main show lounge, a nightclub, discotheque, numerous lounges and bars (including a wine bar), library, card room, an Internet center, virtual reality center, children's club, and cigar lounge with specialized smoke extraction and

Berlitz's Ratings

	Possible	Achieved
Ship	500	403
Accommodation	200	155
Food	400	242
Service	400	298
Entertainment	100	62
Cruise	400	289
OVERALL SCORE		
1449 points out of 2000		

a selection of Cuban, Dominican, and Italian (Toscana) smokes.

A shopping gallery has an integrated bar and entertainment area that flows through the main lobby so that shopping becomes a city-like environment where you can shop, drink, and be entertained all in one convenient area. The expansive San Remo Casino has blackjack, poker, and roulette games, and an array of slot machines for entertainment.

Drinking places include a pub-like venue as well as several comfortable lounges with live music. A gratuity of 15 percent is added to all drinks/beverage orders. Some of the artwork is whimsical, but fishermen will appreciate the stuffed head from a blue marlin caught by Pierfrancesco Vago, president of MSC Cruises in 2004; it weighs 588lbs (267kg) and stands at the Blue Marlin Bar on the pool deck. And do check out the 'restroom with a view' – the toilets have a great ocean view if you leave the door open.

Although access throughout most of the interior of the ship is very good, anyone who is wheelchair-bound should note that the passenger hallways are a narrow on some decks. There is no walk-around open promenade deck.

Although the interior layout and passenger flow is good, a congestion point occurs when first seating passengers exit the two main dining rooms and passengers on the second seating are waiting to enter.

ACCOMMODATION. There are several price levels, depending on grade and location. There are suites with private balcony, mini-suites, outside-view cabins, and interior (no view) cabins. Contrary to nautical convention, the cabin numbering system has even-numbered cabins on the starboard side, and odd-numbered cabins on the port side.

All cabins have a mini-bar and personal safe, satellite flat-screen TV with audio channels, and 24-hour room service. Continental breakfast is complimentary from 7:30 to 10am, but room service snacks cost extra at any other time.

Accommodation designated as 'suites' – they are not true suites, as there is no separate bedroom and lounge – also has more room, although they are small compared to suites on some on other cruise lines. They have a larger lounge area, walk-in closet, and vanity desk with drawer-mounted hairdryer, and a bathroom with combination tub and shower. There is a semi-private balcony with light, but the partitions between each balcony are of the partial, not full, type. The suite bathrooms are plain, with white plastic washbasins and white walls, and mirrors that steam up.

Many cabins on Forte Deck have views obstructed by lifeboats. Cabins on the uppermost accommodation deck (Cantata Deck) may be subject to the noise of sunloungers being dragged across the deck above when it is set up or cleaned early in the morning. Some of the most popular cabins are those at the aft end of the ship, with views over the ship's stern from the balcony cabins (on Virtuoso, Adagio, Intermezzo, and Forte decks). The 17 cabins for the disabled are spacious and well-equipped.

DINING. There are two main dining rooms, L'Oleandro and Le Maxim's, both located aft, with large ocean-view picture windows. There are two seatings for meals, and tables are for two, four, six, or eight. Seating is both banquette-style and in individual chairs; the chairs, however, are slim and lack armrests. All dining venues are managed by Italians.

Passengers occupying accommodation designated as suites and deluxe grades are typically assigned the best tables in the quietest sections of Le Maxim's restaurant, which is quieter than L'Oleandro, the main dining room.

Other dining options. The Gli Archi Cafeteria (a section of which forms the reservations-only Il Giardino) is the place for casual, self-serve buffets for breakfast and lunch and for sit-down, served, but casual dinners each evening – it's actually open for 20 hours daily – so there's always something available. There's also an outside fast-food eatery on the pool deck for burgers and other grilled food items. Several bars adjacent to the mid-ships atrium lobby, serve extra-cost Segafredo Italian coffees, or tea, and pastries.

Il Giardino is an à la carte dining spot that costs extra and requires reservations.

Kaito is a Japanese sushi bar with counter and table seating and a menu that has a fine array of extra-cost à la carte sashimi pieces, nigiri and temaki sushi and maki rolls, tempura and teriyaki items, and a choice of several types of cold or hot sake, and Japanese beer. Reservations are needed and a la carte pricing is in effect.

Enoteca Wine Bar, a very creative wine bar, provides a selection of famous regional Italian cheeses, hams, honey, and wines in a relaxing and entertaining bistro-style setting.

Silver trays full of late-night snacks are taken throughout the ship by waiters, and on some days, special late-night desserts, such as flambé items, are showcased in various lounges like the Il Tucana Lounge. The ship makes ice cream freshly on board.

ENTERTAINMENT. The Theatro La Scala, the large, principal showlounge, is in the ship's forward section. It has tiered seating on two levels, and the sight lines are good from most of the plush, comfortable seats. The room can also serve as a venue for large groups or social functions.

High-quality entertainment has not, to date, been a priority for MSC Cruises. Production shows and the variety acts could be better. However, due to the multi-national passenger mix, almost all entertainment needs to be visual rather than vocal. There is no space for a showband in the showlounge, and so all shows are performed to recorded music pre-recorded tracks.

The Il Tucano Lounge, aft of the showlounge, is the place for social dancing and functions such as cooking demonstrations, with live music provided by a band. Another nightclub, the Crystal Lounge, provides music for social dancing. The young and lively crowd have the ear-melting G32 discotheque; with its floor-to-ceiling windows, it is a quiet, pleasant place to relax and read by day.

Big-screen movies are shown on a large screen above the forward pool, just behind the ship's mast.

SPA/FITNESS. The Aloha Beauty Farm is located one deck above the navigation bridge at the forward end of the ship. The complex has a beauty salon, several treatment rooms offering massage and other body-pampering treatments, and a gymnasium with forward ocean views and an array of high-tech, muscle-toning and strengthening equipment. There's also a Middle East-themed thermal suite, containing steam rooms and saunas with aromatherapy infusions, and a relaxation/hot tub room; it costs extra to use these facilities.

The spa is run as a concession by Steiner Leisure, with European hairstylists and massage/body treatment staff. Gratuities to spa staff are at your discretion.

Sports facilities include table tennis, a tennis court mini-golf course, golf practice net, two shuffleboard courts, and a walking/jogging track.

MSC Opera
★★★★

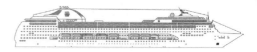

Size:.....................................Large Resort Ship	Cabins (total):....................................878
Tonnage:.. 59,058	Size range (sq ft/m):..............139.9–302.0/13.0–28.0
Lifestyle:.......................................Standard	Cabins (outside view):.............................602
Cruise line:..................................MSC Cruises	Cabins (interior/no view):..........................276
Former names:....................................none	Cabins (for one person):............................0
IMO number:...................................9240464	Cabins (with private balcony):......................200
Builder:.................Chantiers de l'Atlantique (France)	Cabins (wheelchair accessible):.......................4
Original cost:..............................$266 million	Wheelchair accessibility:..........................Good
Entered service:.............................Mar 2004	Cabin voltage:.........................110 and 220 volts
Registry:..Italy	Elevators:..9
Length (ft/m):...........................830.7/256.2	Casino (gaming tables):............................Yes
Beam (ft/m):................................94.4/28.8	Slot machines:....................................Yes
Draft (ft/m):...............................22.4/6.8	Swimming pools:....................................2
Propulsion/Propellers:.....diesel (31,680kW)/2 azimuthing pods	Hot tubs (on deck):................................2
Passenger decks:...................................10	Self-service launderette:..........................No
Total crew:......................................740	Dedicated cinema/seats:............................No
Passengers (lower beds/alll berths):...... 1,756/2,200	Library:...Yes
Passenger Space Ratio (lower beds/all berths):.......33.6/26.8	Onboard currency:..............................Euros
Crew/Passenger Ratio (lower beds/all berths):.........2.3/2.9	

A large family-friendly ship with pan-European decor

OVERVIEW. *MSC Opera* suits young adult couples, singles, and families with tots, children, and teens who enjoy big-ship surroundings and a noisy, big-city life-style, with different nationalities and languages, mostly European. The ship is designed to accommodate families with children, who have their own play center, video games room, youth counselors, and activity programs.

Berlitz's Ratings		
	Possible	Achieved
Ship	500	404
Accommodation	200	155
Food	400	234
Service	400	298
Entertainment	100	62
Cruise	400	285
OVERALL SCORE		
1438 points out of 2000		

THE SHIP. *MSC Opera* was the second of the new ships built for MSC Cruises, Italy's largest privately owned cruise line – the first was *MSC Lirica*, which had almost 100 fewer cabins than *MSC Opera*. The deep blue funnel is quite sleek, and features a swept-back design that carries the MSC logo. Although similar in size and structure to *MSC Lirica*, there are many modifications, mostly in technical spaces, and an improved layout in public rooms.

All decks are named after operas. The interior layout and passenger flow are quite good, except for a couple of points of congestion, typically when the first seating exits the dining room and passengers on second seating are waiting to enter. The decor has many Italian and other Mediterranean influences, including clean lines, minimalism in furniture design, and a collection of colors, soft furnishings, and fabrics that work well together, and without any hint of garishness. Real wood and marble have been used extensively in the interiors, whose fit and finish is very good.

Facilities include the ship's main showlounge, a nightclub/discotheque, several lounges and bars, an Internet center with 10 terminals, a virtual reality center, a children's club, a shopping gallery named Via Conditti with shops that have an integrated bar and entertainment area so that shopping becomes a city-like environment where you can shop, drink, and be entertained all in one convenient area. The Monte Carlo Casino provides blackjack, poker, and roulette games, together with an array of slot machines. There is also a card room, but the integral library is small, uncared for and disappointing, and there are no hardback books.

Drinking places include the Sotto Vento Pub (under the showlounge) and the La Cabala lounge. A 15 percent gratuity is added to all drinks/beverage orders. The ship is designed to accommodate families with children, who have their own play center, youth counselors, and programming.

Anyone who is wheelchair-bound should note that there is no access to the uppermost forward and aft decks, although access throughout most of the interior of the ship is very good and there are several wheelchair-accessible public restrooms. In passenger hallways it can be a squeeze to get past housekeeping carts at certain hours.

Minor niggles include the in-your-face photographers; constant music in every lounge; and the fact that standing in line for embarkation, disembarkation, shore tenders, and for self-serve buffet meals is an inevitable aspect of cruising aboard all large ships. There is no forward observation lounge.

ACCOMMODATION. There are several different price levels, depending on grade and location: one suite category, five outside-view cabin grades, and five interior cabin grades. Included are 172 'suites' with private balcony, outside-view cabins, and interior cabins. The cabin numbering system has even-numbered cabins on the starboard side, and odd-numbered cabins on the port side – contrary to nautical convention.

All cabins have a mini-bar and personal safe, satellite TV, several audio channels, and 24-hour room service. Tea and coffee are complimentary, but snacks delivered by room service cost extra.

Accommodation designated as suites – they are not true suites, as there is no separate bedroom and lounge – has more room, a larger lounge area, walk-in closet, wall-to-wall vanity counter, a bathroom with combination tub and shower, toilet, and semi-private balcony with a light but partitions between each balcony that are partial, not full. Cotton bathrobes are provided. Except for the very highest category, the suite bathrooms are very plain, with white plastic washbasins and white walls, and mirrors that steam up.

Some cabins on Othello Deck and Rigoletto Deck have views obstructed by lifeboats, while those on Turandot Deck aft (10192–10241) may be subject to late-night and early morning noise from the cafeteria on the deck above. Cabins on the uppermost accommodation deck are subject to deck chairs and tables being dragged across the deck when it is set up or cleaned early in the morning.

DINING. There is one principal dining room, La Caravella Restaurant, with large ocean view picture windows in the aft section of the ship. There are two seatings for meals, in keeping with other ships in the MSC Cruises fleet, and tables are for two, four, six, or eight.

L'Approdo Restaurant is assigned to all passengers occupying accommodation designated as suites, although other passengers can dine in it, too, on a reservations-only basis. As you might expect, the food and service are superior to that in the main dining room.

Other dining options. Casual, self-serve buffets for breakfast and lunch can be taken in Le Vele Cafeteria, although the serving lines on both port and starboard sides are quite cramped and the food is quite basic, or at the pool deck outside the fast food eatery, with grill and pizzeria. Le Vele is also open for sit-down, served, but casual dinners each evening – it's actually open for 20 hours a day – so even in the middle of the night you can find something to eat. Extra-cost coffee/tea and pastries are served in the Aroma Café, on the upper level of the two-deck-high atrium lobby, but annoying videos constantly play on TV sets in the forward section of the area.

ENTERTAINMENT. The 713-seat Theatre dell Opera is the ship's main showlounge, located in the forward section of the ship. It has tiered seating set in a sloping floor, and the sight lines are good from most seats, which are plush and comfortable. The room can also serve as a venue for large social functions. There is no separate bandstand and the shows use recorded music, so there's little consistency in orchestration and sound balance.

High-quality entertainment has not, to date, been a priority for MSC Cruises. As a result, production shows and variety acts tend to be amateurish at best when compared to some other major cruise lines.

The Opera Lounge, one deck above the show lounge, is used extensively for social dancing, and features a live band. Meanwhile, for the young and lively set, there is the Byblos Discotheque, the ship's throbbing, ear-melting discotheque.

A number of bands provide live music in the various bars and lounges.

SPA/FITNESS. The Opera Health Center is one deck above the navigation bridge at the forward end of the ship. The complex has a beauty salon, several treatment rooms offering massage and other body-pampering treatments, as well as a gymnasium with ocean views and an array of high-tech, muscle-toning and strengthening equipment. There's also a thermal suite, containing different kinds of steam rooms combined with aromatherapy infusions, at extra cost.

The health center is run as a concession by the excellent Italian company OceanView, with European hairstylists and Balinese massage and body treatment staff. Gratuities are not included, and are at your discretion.

Outside on deck, sports fans will appreciate a neat eight-hole mini-golf course that wraps around the funnel, while a walking/jogging track encircles the two swimming pools in the center of the ship.

MSC Orchestra
★★★★

Size:.....................................Large Resort Ship		Cabins (total):.....................................1,275		
Tonnage:.......................................92,409		Size range (sq ft/m):...............150.6–301.3/14.0–28.0		
Lifestyle:.....................................Standard		Cabins (outside view):..............................1,000		
Cruise line:..................................MSC Cruises		Cabins (interior/no view):.............................275		
Former names:.....................................none		Cabins (for one person):................................0		
IMO number:...................................9320099		Cabins (with private balcony):.........................827		
Builder:...........................Aker Yards (France)		Cabins (wheelchair accessible):.........................17		
Original cost:................................$360 million		Wheelchair accessibility:.............................Good		
Entered service:..............................May 2007		Cabin voltage:...........................110 and 220 volts		
Registry:...Italy		Elevators:...13		
Length (ft/m):...............................963.9/293.8		Casino (gaming tables):...............................Yes		
Beam (ft/m):.................................105.6/32.2		Slot machines:.....................................Yes		
Draft (ft/m):....................................25.2/7.7		Swimming pools:.......................................2		
Propulsion/Propellers:..........diesel-electric (40,4000kW)/2		Hot tubs (on deck):....................................4		
Passenger decks:.....................................13		Self-service launderette:.............................No		
Total crew:...987		Dedicated cinema/seats:...............................No		
Passengers (lower beds/alll berths):..............2,550/3,013		Library:..Yes		
Passenger Space Ratio (lower beds/all berths):.......36.2/30.6		Onboard currency:..................................Euros		
Crew/Passenger Ratio (lower beds/all berths):.........2.6/3.0				

A large, family-friendly ship with elegant decor

OVERVIEW. *MSC Orchestra* will suit young adult couples, singles, families with tots, children, and teens who enjoy big-ship surroundings and a noisy, big-city lifestyle, with different nationalities and languages, mostly European. The ship accommodates families with children, who have their own meeting and play centers, video games room, youth counselors, and fun programs.

THE SHIP. The ship's deep blue funnel is sleek, and features a swept-back design that carries the MSC logo in gold lettering. The overall profile is quite well-balanced. The hull has large circular porthole-style windows instead of square or rectangular windows. From a technical viewpoint, the ship is powered by diesel motors driving electric generators to provide power to two conventional propellers.

MSC Orchestra is a sister to *MSC Musica* and *MSC Poesia*, though the fabrics and furnishings used in the ship's interiors are nicer and softer. Among the numerous lounges and bars, the Out of Africa Savannah Lounge is stunning. A delightful four-piece classical ensemble regularly performs in the atrium lobby.

Plenty of real wood and marble have been used in the interiors, and the high quality reflects the commitment that MSC Cruises has in the vessel's future.

The focal point of the ship is the main three-deck high lobby, with a water-feature backdrop and a crystal piano on a small stage that appears to float on a pond. Other facilities include a large main show lounge, a

Berlitz's Ratings

	Possible	Achieved
Ship	500	403
Accommodation	200	155
Food	400	242
Service	400	298
Entertainment	100	62
Cruise	400	291

OVERALL SCORE
1451 points out of 2000

nightclub, discotheque, numerous lounges and bars (including a wine bar), library, card room, an Internet center, virtual reality center, children's club, and cigar lounge with specialized smoke extraction and a selection of Cuban, Dominican, and Italian (Toscana) smokes.

A shopping gallery, which includes an electronics store, has an integrated bar and entertainment area that flows through the main lobby so that shopping becomes a city-like environment where you can shop, drink, and be entertained all in one convenient area. The expansive San Remo Casino has blackjack, poker, and roulette games, and an array of slot machines.

Drinking places include a pub-like venue as well as several comfortable lounges with live music. A 15 percent gratuity is added to all drinks/beverage orders. Some of the artwork is whimsical. And, speaking of whimsical, take a look at the 'restrooms with a view' – the men's/ladies toilets adjacent to the forward pool deck bar have a great ocean view and you can even watch the passing scenery while sitting on the toilet – if you leave the door open.

The themed decor has many Italian influences, including clean lines, minimalism in furniture design, and a collection of colors, soft furnishings, and fabrics that work well together, although it's a little more garish than one would expect.

Access throughout most of the interior of the ship is good, but wheelchair-bound passengers should note that the accommodation hallways are narrow on some decks for you to pass the housekeeping carts. Note that there is no walk-around open promenade deck.

Although the interior layout and passenger flow is good, a congestion point occurs when first seating passengers exit the two main dining rooms and second seating passengers are waiting to enter.

The MSC Cruises crew really does try their best to provide good service to a multi-national clientele, and the ship exudes a noticeable 'feel-good' factor.

ACCOMMODATION. There are several price levels, depending on grade and location. There are suites with private balcony, mini-suites, outside-view cabins, and interior (no view) cabins. Contrary to nautical convention, the cabin numbering system has even-numbered cabins on the starboard side, and odd-numbered cabins on the port side.

All cabins have a mini-bar and personal safe, satellite flat-screen TV with audio channels, and 24-hour room service. Continental breakfast is complimentary from 7:30 to 10am, but room service snacks cost extra at any other time.

Accommodation designated as 'suites' – they are not true suites, as there is no separate bedroom and lounge – also has more room, although they are small compared to suites on some on other cruise lines. They have a larger lounge area, walk-in closet, and vanity desk with drawer-mounted hairdryer, and a bathroom with combination tub and shower. There is a semi-private balcony with light, but the partitions between each balcony are of the partial, not full, type. The suite bathrooms are plain, with white plastic washbasins and white walls, and mirrors that steam up.

Many cabins on Forte Deck have views obstructed by lifeboats. Cabins on the uppermost accommodation deck (Cantata Deck) may be subject to the noise of sunloungers being dragged across the deck above when it is set up or cleaned early in the morning. Some of the most popular cabins are those at the aft end of the ship, with views over the ship's stern from the balcony cabins (on Virtuoso, Adagio, Intermezzo, and Forte decks). The 17 cabins for the disabled are spacious and well-equipped.

DINING. There are two main dining rooms, Villa Borghese Restaurant and L'Ibiscus, located in the aft section of the ship, and with large ocean-view picture windows. There are two seatings for dinner, and open seating for breakfast and lunch. Tables are for 2-8, as well as some alcove banquette-style seating. Anyone occupying upper-grade accommodation typically gets the better tables in quieter areas.

Other dining options. Shanghai Chinese Restaurant makes a change from the main restaurants. This was the first real Chinese restaurant aboard any cruise ship – mainly because of the challenges of providing high-temperature wok and deep fryer preparation. Dim sum steamed dishes are also served, typically

for lunch. The food embraces four main cuisines – Beijing, Cantonese, Shanghai, and Szechzuan – and there's Tsing Tao beer.

The Four Seasons Restaurant offers extra-cost à la carte Italian cuisine in a garden-like setting with fine china, and a menu reflecting regional and seasonal fare. Food is cooked to order, and so it tends to taste better than in the main dining room. Reservations are required, and there's a cover charge.

La Piazzetta Café is open 20 hours a day for casual, self-serve buffet-style breakfasts and for sit-down, served dinners in a relaxed environment.

ENTERTAINMENT. Covent Garden is the ship's stunning large show lounge. The Opera Lounge, one deck above, is the place for social dancing, with live music. The G32 discotheque is for the more energetic. A large poolside movie screen provides moviegoers with more choices. All the activities are provided by an energetic multilingual cruise staff. Also, live music is provided in almost all bars and lounges.

SPA/FITNESS. The Orchestra Health Center, operated by the Italian company OceanView, includes a beauty salon, several treatment rooms offering massage and other body-pampering treatments, and a fitness center with ocean views and high-tech muscle-toning equipment.

There's also a thermal suite, containing different kinds of steam rooms combined with aromatherapy infusions, at extra cost. There's a neat juice and smoothie bar opposite the reception desk. Gratuities are at your discretion.

For the sports-minded, there is deck quoits, as well as shuffleboard courts, tennis and basketball courts, mini-golf, and a jogging track.

MSC Poesia
★★★★

Size:. . . . . .Large Resort Ship	Cabins (total):. 1,275
Tonnage: 92,490	Size range (sq ft/m):. 150.6–301.3/14.0–28.0
Lifestyle: . . . . .Standard	Cabins (outside view):. 1,000
Cruise line:. . . . . .MSC Cruises	Cabins (interior/no view):. 275
Former names: . . . . .none	Cabins (for one person):. 0
IMO number: 930373	Cabins (with private balcony):. 827
Builder: . . . . Fincantieri (Italy)	Cabins (wheelchair accessible): 17
Original cost: . . . .$360 million	Wheelchair accessibility:. . . . . .Good
Entered service:. . . . . .Oct 2008	Cabin voltage: . . . . .110 and 220 volts
Registry:. . . . . Panama	Elevators:. 13
Length (ft/m):. 963.9/293.8	Casino (gaming tables):. . . . . Yes
Beam (ft/m):. 105.6/32.2	Slot machines:. . . . . Yes
Draft (ft/m): 26.2/8.0	Swimming pools:. 2
Propulsion/Propellers:. . . . . diesel (58,000kW)/2	Hot tubs (on deck):. 4
Passenger decks:. 13	Self-service launderette:. . . . . .No
Total crew:. 987	Dedicated cinema/seats:. . . . . .No
Passengers (lower beds/alll berths): 2,550/3,013	Library: . . . . Yes
Passenger Space Ratio (lower beds/all berths): 36.2/30.6	Onboard currency: . . . . Euros
Crew/Passenger Ratio (lower beds/all berths):. 2.6/3.0	

A large Euro-style informal and family-friendly ship

OVERVIEW. *MSC Poesia* will suit young adult couples, singles, families with tots, children, and teens who enjoy big-ship surroundings and a noisy, big-city life-style, with many different nationalities and languages, mostly European. The ship is designed to accommodate families with children, who have their own playcenters, video games room, youth counselors, and plenty of activity programs.

THE SHIP. *MSC Poesia* is a sister ship to *MSC Musica* and *MSC Orchestra*. The ship's deep blue funnel is sleek, and has a swept-back design that carries the MSC logo in large lettering. The hull has large circular porthole-style windows instead of square or rectangular windows. From a technical viewpoint, the ship is powered by diesel motors driving electric generators to provide power to two conventional propellers.

The interior layout and passenger flow is good – with the exception of a couple of points of congestion, typically when the first seating exits the two main dining rooms and passengers on the second seating are waiting to enter.

The interior focal point is a main three-deck high lobby, which has a grand water-feature backdrop and a crystal (glass) piano on a small stage that appears to float on a pond. Other facilities include a large main show lounge, a nightclub, discotheque, numerous lounges and bars – including a wine bar – library, card room, Internet center, virtual reality center, children's club, and cigar lounge with specialized smoke

Berlitz's Ratings

	Possible	Achieved
Ship	500	403
Accommodation	200	155
Food	400	242
Service	400	298
Entertainment	100	62
Cruise	400	292

OVERALL SCORE
1452 points out of 2000

extraction and a selection of Cuban, Dominican, and Italian (Toscana) smokes.

The musically themed decor has many Italian influences, including clean lines, minimalism in furniture design, and a collection of colors, soft furnishings, and fabrics that work well together, although it's a little more garish than one would expect.

Real wood and marble have been used extensively in the interiors and the high quality reflects the commitment that MSC Cruises has in the vessel's future.

A shopping gallery, which includes an electronics store, has an integrated bar and entertainment area that flows through the main lobby so that shopping becomes a city-like environment where you can shop, drink, and be entertained all in one convenient area. The expansive Casino Royale has blackjack, poker, and roulette tables, and an array of slot machines.

Drinking places include several comfortable lounges – all with live music. A 15 percent gratuity is added to all drinks/beverage orders. A mini-golf course is on the port side of the funnel, while a walking/jogging track encircles an upper level above the two swimming pools.

Some of the artwork is whimsical. Do check out the 'restroom with a view' – the men's/ladies toilets adjacent to the Blue Marlin pool deck bar have a great ocean view and you can even watch the passing scenery while sitting on the toilet if you leave the door open.

Although access throughout most of the interior of the ship is good, wheelchair-bound passengers should note that the passenger hallways are a little narrow on some decks for you to pass when housekeeping carts are in place. There is no walk-around open promenade deck.

ACCOMMODATION. There are several price levels, depending on grade and location. Included are 18 'suites' with private balcony, mini-suites, outside-view cabins, and interior cabins. Contrary to nautical convention, the cabin numbering system has even-numbered cabins on the starboard side, and odd-numbered cabins on the port side.

All cabins have a mini-bar and personal safe, satellite flat-screen TV with audio channels, and 24-hour room service. Continental breakfast is complimentary from 7:30 to 10am; room service snacks cost extra at any other time.

Accommodation designated as 'suites' – they are not true suites, as there is no separate bedroom and lounge – also has more room, although they are small compared to suites on some on other cruise lines. They have a larger lounge area, walk-in closet, and vanity desk with drawer-mounted hairdryer, and a bathroom with combination tub and shower. There is a semi-private balcony with light but the partitions between each balcony are of the partial, not full, type. The suite bathrooms are plain, with white plastic washbasins and white walls, and mirrors that steam up.

Many cabins on Forte Deck have views obstructed by lifeboats. Cabins on the uppermost accommodation deck (Cantata Deck) may be subject to the noise of sunloungers being dragged across the deck above when it is set up or cleaned early in the morning. Some of the most popular cabins are those at the aft end of the ship, with views over the ship's stern from the balcony cabins on four of the aft decks. The 17 cabins for the disabled are spacious and well-equipped.

DINING. There are two principal dining rooms, both of them located aft (on different decks), with large ocean-view picture windows. There are two seatings for meals, as aboard other ships in the MSC Cruises fleet, and tables are for 2-8; seating is both banquette-style and in individual armless chairs.

Other dining options. Kaito is a delightful, extra-cost Japanese restaurant, with a sushi bar and an extensive à la carte menu. Reservations are needed, but the cuisine is worth the extra cost.

A Tex-Mex Restaurant is an extra-cost à la carte dining spot, and reservations are necessary.

The Wine Bar (Enoteca) provides a selection of famous regional cheeses, hams, and a variety of wines in a bistro-style setting that is relaxing and entertaining.

The Villa Pompeina Cafeteria is for casual, self-serve buffets for breakfast and lunch and for sit-down, served, but casual dinners (it's actually open for 20 hours a day – so there's always something available to eat – even in the middle of the night). Outside, there's a fast-food eatery on the pool deck for burgers and other grilled fast-food items. Extra-cost Segafredo coffees, together with a variety of teas and pastry items are also available in several bars adjacent to the atrium mid-ships lobby.

Silver trays full of late-night snacks are taken throughout the ship by waiters, and on some days, special late-night desserts, such as flambé items, are showcased in various lounges.

ENTERTAINMENT. The Teatro Carlo Felice is the ship's principal showlounge; it is in the forward section of the ship, with tiered seating on two levels, and the sight lines are good from most of the plush, comfortable seats. The room can also be a venue for large group meetings or social functions. There is no showband, so all shows are performed to pre-recorded music tracks.

High-quality entertainment has not, to date, been a priority for MSC Cruises. Production shows and the variety acts could be better. However, due to the multinational passenger mix, almost all entertainment needs to be visual rather than vocal. There is no space for a showband in the showlounge, and so all of the shows are performed to recorded music pre-recorded tracks.

Another large lounge (Zebra Bar), aft of the showlounge, is the place for social dancing and functions such as cooking demonstrations, with live music provided by a band.

Big-screen movies are shown on a large screen above the forward pool, just behind the ship's mast.

Live music is provided in the various bars and lounges throughout the ship.

SPA/FITNESS. The Poesia Health Center is run by OceanView, and Italian spa specialist. The complex features a beauty salon, several treatment rooms offering massage and other body-pampering treatments, and a gymnasium with forward ocean views and an array of high-tech, muscle-toning and strengthening equipment. There's also a Middle East-themed thermal suite, containing steam rooms and saunas with aromatherapy infusions, and a relaxation/hot tub room; it costs extra to use these facilities.

The spa is run as a concession by Steiner Leisure, with European hairstylists and massage/body treatment staff. Gratuities to spa staff are at your discretion.

Sports facilities include table tennis, a tennis court mini-golf course, golf practice net, two shuffleboard courts, and a jogging track.

MSC Preziosa
★★★★ +

Size:................................Large Resort Ship		Cabins (total):.................................... 1,751	
Tonnage: .... 140,000 tons		Size range (sq ft/m): 148.5–568.3/13.8–52.8	
Lifestyle: ....Standard		Cabins (outside view):............................. 1,166	
Cruise line:...............................MSC Cruises		Cabins (interior/no view):............................405	
Former names: ....none		Cabins (for one person):...............................0	
IMO number: 9595321		Cabins (with private balcony):..................... 1,125	
Builder: ....STX France		Cabins (wheelchair accessible): 45	
Original cost:.............................$760 million		Wheelchair accessibility:..........................Good	
Entered service:.............................. Mar 2013		Cabin voltage: ....110 and 220 volts	
Registry:....................................... Panama		Elevators:...16	
Length (ft/m):..............................1,093.5/333.3		Casino (gaming tables):...........................Yes	
Beam (ft/m):............................... 124.6/38.0		Slot machines:....................................Yes	
Draft (ft/m):................................... 27.72/8.4		Swimming pools:.............3 (1 w/sliding glass dome)	
Propulsion/Propellers:.......... diesel-electric (40,000kW)/2		Hot tubs (on deck):.................................13	
Passenger decks:....................................13		Self-service launderette:............................No	
Total crew:.................................. 1,390		Dedicated cinema/seats:.............................No	
Passengers (lower beds/alll berths):............. 3,502/4,345		Library: ....Yes	
Passenger Space Ratio (lower beds/all berths): 39.9/32.2		Onboard currency: ....Euros	
Crew/Passenger Ratio (lower beds/all berths):.......... 2.5/3.1			

A fine large family-friendly ship designed for Europeans

OVERVIEW. This large resort ship, a close sister to *MSC Divina*, *MSC Fantasia* and *MSC Splendida*, will appeal to young-at-heart adult couples, singles, and families with children and teens enjoying an urban lifestyle, with a mix of mostly European nationalities and style.

THE SHIP. *MSC Preziosa* was originally ordered by the Libyan government-owned shipping company GNMTC (the contract was signed by Captain Hannibal Muammar Gaddafi – fifth eldest son of Muammar Gaddafi) before Europe-based cruise line MSC Cruises acquired the hull and configured the ship as the fourth in its Fantasia class. It has the very latest in green-technology engines.

Outside on the expansive main pool deck, there is a main swimming pool, together with a whole Aqua Park with raised sections, hot tubs, and numerous water features. Slightly forward of the pool deck is a family swimming pool; it's open well into the late evening, and can be covered by a sliding glass dome in case of inclement weather.

Facilities for all passengers include a large three-deck-high theater-style showlounge, a nightclub/discotheque, library, card room, an Internet center, a 4D virtual reality center, multi-deck shopping gallery, a large Millennium Star Casino with gaming tables and an array of slot machines and a nicely-shaped stairway, and, in the aft section, an 'infinity' pool that overlooks the stern, and 'beach club' area. Drinking places include numerous lounges and bars (including a trendy 'Green

Berlitz's Ratings

	Possible	Achieved
Ship	500	423
Accommodation	200	162
Food	400	276
Service	400	308
Entertainment	100	76
Cruise	400	308
OVERALL SCORE		
1553 points out of 2000		

Sax' jazz lounge/bar), most with live music. One lounge in the aft section of the ship is for adults only.

An area called the MSC Yacht Club – an exclusive community 'suite-grade' accommodation, includes a Top Sail Lounge – an observation/lifestyle lounge and social meeting place, private sunbathing with integral dip pool, hot tubs, and concierge services for making dining reservations, booking excursions and spa treatments, and arranging private parties. A marble floor leads to a shiny Swarovski glass staircase that connects the concierge facilities between decks 15 and 16 under a glass-domed ceiling.

FAMILIES. The ship is designed to cater well for families with children, who sail free and have their own extensive collection of play centers, including a children's club and jungle adventure playground, plus two waterslides in an area called the Doremi Castle Aqua Park, youth counselors, and activity programs tailored to specific age groups. One coveted feature is a 120-meter-long Vertigo waterslide, with twists and turns and a 9-meter transparent section that shoots off the side of the ship. Riders travel at an average speed of six metres per second (note that only children over 120 cm – about 47.2 inches – tall are allowed on the slide).

ACCOMMODATION. It's worth paying extra to stay in one of the 'suites' in the Yacht Club accommodation. You'll get silver-tray room service by a team of well-trained butlers, who are good. The suites have a minibar, interactive TV, personal safe, hairdryer, and satellite-link telephone.

DINING. There are two main restaurants – Golden Lobster, on Deck 5 – and l'Arabesque, on Deck 6. There are two seatings for dinner, and open seating for breakfast and lunch. Tables are for two, four, six, or eight, and include some cozy alcove banquette seating (although it's challenging for waiters to serve these alcove tables properly). Both restaurants feature Mediterranean cuisine.

Occupants of Yacht Club-grade accommodation have their own, intimate La Palmeraie Restaurant, with rather Moorish décor, Moroccan-style arches and hanging brass lamps. Dining is in an open seating arrangement.

Other dining options. A 115-seat Eataly Restaurant – a specialty dining spot (together with a 30-seat Ristorante Italia), provides tastes of Italy (the 'slow food' way, with a choice of 18 items). The chairs in the Ristorante Italia section of the Eataly Restaurant, however, are see-through plastic, and grossly uncomfortable. MSC Cruises, in partnership with Eataly, the popular Turin-based chain founded in 2007 by Oscar Farinetti, places its major emphasis on local, artisanal producers, food education, accessibility and affordability, sustainable sourcing and production.

The Galaxy Restaurant is an extra-charge venue that sits high above the main pool – and has great views. It has a trendy vibe (it forms part of the discotheque), and the food – with Mediterranean fusion food – including steaks and seafood items – is good.

Casual serve-yourself buffet-style meals can be taken in the huge Inca and Maya buffet venue (it's open 20 hours daily) for breakfasts and lunches, and waiter-served dinners in a relaxed, but always busy, setting. A bakery corner provides freshly-baked breads and rolls throughout the day.

A Sports and Bowling Diner features a classic American food experience (including sandwiches and burgers).

ENTERTAINMENT. The 1,600-seat Platinum Theater is the ship's vast showlounge – it's really more like a concert theatre and auditorium. It is spread over three decks, and there are good sight lines from almost all seats except for a few rows at the back on port and starboard sides. It is a well-designed room, except for the fact that no space is allocated for a live showband.

Because passengers are multi-national, the shows concentrate more on visual entertainment such as mime, magic, dancing, and acrobatics, and are performed with recorded music (known as a 'click-track'). Introductions are done at breakneck speed by the multi-lingual cruise director.

There is live music in almost all the other lounge/bar venues – one of the most popular of which is the Golden Jazz Bar.

SPA/FITNESS. The Aurea Wellbeing Center is large and houses a beauty salon, body treatment rooms, and a gymnasium with great ocean views. A thermal suite contains different kinds of steam rooms combined with herbal aromatherapy infusions, in a calming Asia-themed environment. Features include a She Uemura Art of Hair cabin, a vintage barbershop, and a Himalayan salt crystal 'bed.' The spa is operated by OceanView, a specialist spa provider, and most of the therapists are from the island of Bali.

Sports facilities include deck quoits, shuffleboard courts, large tennis/basketball court, mini-golf, and a jogging track.

Did you know...

...that Fred. Olsen Cruise Lines' entire fleet is comprised of ships that have been 'stretched'? It's only the second line that can claim so; the first was Royal Viking Line, with all three of its ships having been stretched (Fred. Olsen Cruise Lines operate two of the former Royal Viking Line ships, and the third is operated by Phoenix Reisen).

...that shore power hook-ups have been available in Juneau since 2001 and in Seattle since 2005?

...that the first cruise ship to have an outdoor laser light show was the original AIDA (since renamed *AIDAcara*, which debuted in 1996?

...that tickets for production shows were first issued by Celebrity Cruises in the early 1990s? They were given out by the waiters in the dining rooms aboard *Century*, *Galaxy*, and *Mercury*.

...that the first passenger ship to have a children's carousel was the *Ile de France*?

...that Cunard introduced the first gymnasium and health center aboard a ship (*Franconia*, 1911)?

...that Cunard Line's *Aquitania* of 1913 was the first ship to have an indoor swimming pool?

...that Nowegian America Line's *Sagafjord* was the first ship to have a central plug-in vacuum system?

...that Karin Stahre Janson was the first female cruise ship captain? Born in Sweden, she took command of RCI's *Monarch of the Seas* in 2007 at the age of 38.

...that when sailing from England to the Caribbean in 'the old days' a rule of thumb was to sail south until the butter melts, then proceed west?

...that the word 'buccaneer' comes from the French word *boucanier*, which means: 'to cure meat on a bucan (barbeque)?' Since pirates often used this method of cooking, they became known as buccaneers. The word buccaneer, strictly speaking, was used to denote pirates in the Caribbean.

...that in 1992 Carnival Cruise Lines used its original ship *Mardi Gras* as an accommodation ship? It was for senior executives and staff who were made homeless when Hurricane Andrew hit Miami in August that year.

MSC Sinfonia
★★★ +

Size:.......................................Mid-size Ship	Cabins (total):...777
Tonnage:.. 58,600	Size range (sq ft/m):................... 139.9–236.8/13–22
Lifestyle:.......................................Standard	Cabins (outside view):....................................511
Cruise line:...............................MSC Cruises	Cabins (interior/no view):.................................272
Former names:............................European Stars	Cabins (for one person):.....................................0
IMO number:................................9210153	Cabins (with private balcony):.............................132
Builder:................. Chantiers de l'Atlantique (France)	Cabins (wheelchair accessible):..............................2
Original cost:............................. $245 million	Wheelchair accessibility:................................Good
Entered service:...................... Apr 2002/Mar 2005	Cabin voltage:.........................110 and 220 volts
Registry:... Italy	Elevators:..9
Length (ft/m):............................. 823.4/251.0	Casino (gaming tables):................................... Yes
Beam (ft/m):................................. 94.4/28.8	Slot machines:.. Yes
Draft (ft/m):.................................. 22.4/6.8	Swimming pools:..2
Propulsion/Propellers:..... diesel (31,680kW)/2 azimuthing pods	Hot tubs (on deck):..1
Passenger decks:.................................10	Self-service launderette:.................................No
Total crew:......................................710	Dedicated cinema/seats:..................................No
Passengers (lower beds/alll berths):............. 1,564/3,087	Library:.. Yes
Passenger Space Ratio (lower beds/all berths):....... 37.4/27.6	Onboard currency:................................... Euros
Crew/Passenger Ratio (lower beds/all berths):.......... 2.2/3.1	

A large Euro-style, informal and family-friendly ship

OVERVIEW. *MSC Sinfonia* is best for adult couples and solo travellers, and families with children, who enjoy lots of activity, accompanied by lots of noise and late nights, in a setting that exudes Mediterranean family vacation values.

THE SHIP. *MSC Sinfonia* is a sister ship to *MSC Armonia*, with a decor that's decidedly 'European Moderne.' The international mix of passengers adds to the overall ambience of the cruise experience.

The exterior deck space is barely adequate for the number of passengers carried. The lido deck surrounding the outdoor swimming pool also has whirlpool tubs and a large bandstand is set in raised canvas-covered pods. All sunloungers have cushioned pads.

The decor is 'European Moderne' – whatever that means – but it does include crisp, clean lines, minimalism in furniture designs – including some chairs that look interesting but are totally impractical. However, the interior colors are good; nothing jars the senses, but rather calms them, unlike the effect aboard many ships.

Standing in line for embarkation, disembarkation, shore tenders, and self-serve buffet meals is an inevitable aspect of cruising aboard large ships. Announcements are in several languages.

Wheelchair-bound passengers should note that there is no access to the uppermost forward and aft decks, although access throughout most of the interior is good. Also, passenger hallways are a little narrow on some accommodation decks to pass when housekeeping

Berlitz's Ratings		
	Possible	Achieved
Ship	500	380
Accommodation	200	149
Food	400	233
Service	400	295
Entertainment	100	55
Cruise	400	271
OVERALL SCORE		
1383 points out of 2000		

carts are in place.

The company keeps prices low by providing air transportation that may be at inconvenient times, or that involves long journeys by bus. In other words, be prepared for a little discomfort in getting to and from your cruise in exchange for low cruise rates. Note that 15 percent is added to all drinks and beverage orders.

ACCOMMODATION. There are numerous categories, the price depending on the grade, size, and location you choose. These include 132 'suites' with private balcony (whose partitions are only of the partial and not the full type), outside-view cabins and interior (no view) cabins.

Suite grade accommodation – they are not true suites, as there's no separate bedroom and lounge – has more room, a larger lounge area, walk-in closet, wall-to-wall vanity counter, a bathroom with combination tub and shower, toilet, and private balcony with light. Bathrobes are provided. In general, the 'suites' are practical and nicely furnished. However, except for the very highest category, the bathrooms are very plain, with white plastic washbasins and white walls, and mirrors that steam up.

Standard grade cabins, at a modest 140 sq ft (13 sq m), are quite small when compared to many other ships, but they are reasonably comfortable, with plenty of space between two lower beds. All grades of accommodation have a TV, mini-bar/refrigerator, personal safe cleverly positioned behind a vanity desk mirror, hairdryer, and bathroom with shower and toilet.

DINING. There are two main dining rooms, the 610-seat Il Galeone Restaurant and the Il Covo Restaurant; both have two seatings and share the same menu. The cuisine is reasonably sound, and, with varied menus and good presentation, should prove a highlight for most passengers. The wine list has a wide variety of wines at fairly reasonable prices, although almost all are very young.

Other dining options. La Terrazza is a casual, self-serve buffet eatery that is open 20 hours a day, including sit-down, waiter-served dinners in a very relaxed setting. The selections are very standardized and could be better. Café del Mare, adjacent to one of two swimming pools and to the ship's funnel, is a grill area for burgers and other fast food items.

Extra-cost coffee/tea and pastries are available in Le Baroque Café, set around the upper level of the two-deck-high atrium lobby. It's a good location for people-watching, but annoying music videos are constantly played on TV monitors in the forward sections.

ENTERTAINMENT. The two-deck-high Gondola Theater is the main showlounge; it is the venue for pro-duction shows, cabaret acts, plays, and other theatrical presentations. Entertainment consists mainly of visual shows, because of the mix of nationalities carried. Other shows consist of cabaret acts such as singers, magicians, mimes, and comedy jugglers.

The ship carries a number of bands and small musical units that provide live music for dancing or listening in various lounges and bars throughout the ship.

SPA/FITNESS. The spa features a gymnasium with ocean views, and high-tech, muscle-toning and strengthening equipment. A thermal suite has different kinds of steam rooms combined with aromatherapy infusions such as chamomile and eucalyptus, and a rasul chamber provides a combination of two or three kinds of application mud and gentle steam shower. The spa, operated by the Italian concession OceanView, offers a wide range of body-pampering well-being treatments.

For active types there's a simulated climbing wall outdoors aft of the ship's funnel, as well as a volleyball/basketball court, and mini-golf.

Environmental issues

There are three types of waste water: bilge water, black water (or sewage), and grey water.

Bilge water is oily engine run-off and condensation that collects in the bilge, a compartment at the bottom of a vessel's hull where water is collected and later pumped out. Grey water comes from showers and sinks. Black water, perhaps the most damaging to the environment, comes from the toilets and from the drains and sinks of the medical center. When water is treated to reduce its oil content below 15 parts of oil per million parts of water, international law allows it to be discharged virtually anywhere.

Few accidents have happened, and most cruise ships' environmental standards meet or surpass all international laws; the cruise industry represents only 0.2 percent of all oceangoing vessels worldwide.

Cruise ship owners are working toward stricter emission limits for particulate matter and sulfur oxides, and reducing nitrogen oxide levels (compared to existing emissions levels) that will probably be imposed within the next few years. Older engines (those built before January 1, 2000) are required to achieve a 20 percent reduction in nitrogen oxides.

The latest generation of propulsion machinery (engines) is, however, much more fuel efficient than older ships. For example, RCI's *Freedom*-class ships are 10 percent more fuel efficient than the *Voyager*-class ships, and the company's *Oasis*-class ships, introduced in 2009, are 15 percent more fuel efficient than the *Freedom*-class ships.

In the past 10 years, cruise ships have spent huge sums of money in new technology; the result is that waste and garbage have been almost cut in half, while sustaining cruise capacity growth just approaching around eight percent annually. The latest hull coatings increase fuel efficiency; the coating, which reduces surface resistance in the water, is completely non-toxic. Many large resort ships now have environmental officers on board to oversee compliance with environmental regulations and requirements.

Cruise lines reduce the solid waste they generate by purchasing in bulk, encouraging suppliers to use more efficient packaging, reusing packaging when possible and packaging more environmentally friendly materials. Other examples:

Advanced purification systems treat all onboard wastewater.

Ships actively recycle glass, metals, wood, cardboard, and paper.

Excess heat from engine boilers is rerouted to power evaporators used in the process of turning sea water into potable water.

Special high-tech compactors process garbage (the one aboard *Queen Mary 2*, for example, is four decks high).

Dry cleaning machines now use non-hazardous detergents formulated with soy, banana, and orange extracts.

Materials printed on board can be produced using soy-based inks.

Some ships 'plug in' to clean, local hydroelectric when they dock in ports cities such as Seattle and Juneau.

The only solid waste discharged to sea is food waste, considered safe because, either fish consume it or natural elements break it down in the water. And some use only seafood farmed from sustainable sources. NCL ships offload their used cooking oil for recycling to bio-diesel fuel.

What you can do to help

Specially marked garbage containers are scattered throughout each ship for you to use.

MSC Splendida
★★★★

Size:.................................Large Resort Ship			Cabins (total):.....................................1,637	
Tonnage:..137,936			Size range (sq ft/m):....................161.4–699.6/15–65	
Lifestyle:...Standard			Cabins (outside view):................................1,354	
Cruise line:...................................MSC Cruises			Cabins (interior/no view):..............................283	
Former names:..................................none			Cabins (for one person):................................0	
IMO number:..................................9359806			Cabins (with private balcony):.......................1,260	
Builder:.............................Aker Yards (France)			Cabins (wheelchair accessible):........................43	
Original cost:..............................$550 million			Wheelchair accessibility:...........................Good	
Entered service:................................Jul 2009			Cabin voltage:...........................110 and 220 volts	
Registry:..Panama			Elevators:...14	
Length (ft/m):..............................1,093.5/333.3			Casino (gaming tables):.............................Yes	
Beam (ft/m):...............................124.6/38.0			Slot machines:....................................Yes	
Draft (ft/m):...................................27.2/8.4			Swimming pools:.............3 (1 w/sliding glass dome)	
Propulsion/Propellers:...............diesel (40,000kW)/2			Hot tubs (on deck):..................................13	
Passenger decks:....................................13			Self-service launderette:.............................No	
Total crew:......................................1,313			Dedicated cinema/seats:.............................No	
Passengers (lower beds/all berths):............3,274/3,900			Library:..Yes	
Passenger Space Ratio (lower beds/all berths):......42.1/31.6			Onboard currency:...............................Euros	
Crew/Passenger Ratio (lower beds/all berths):.........2.4/2.9				

A large, family-friendly ship with tasteful, elegant decor

OVERVIEW. *MSC Splendida* will appeal to young adult couples, singles, and families with children and teens that enjoy big ships with a mix of nationalities, mostly European. Children appreciate Virtual World's five white-knuckle 4D rides in a 10-seat thrill room. It all feels rather like a European city center, and is full of large and small rooms, nooks and crannies, and places to play in.

THE SHIP. A sister ship to *MSC Fantasia*, *MSC Splendida* is a stunning ship, and one of the largest ships built for a European cruise company. It is 10 meters longer than the Eiffel Tower is high, and the propulsion power is the equivalent of 120 Ferraris. There are four swimming pools, one of which can be covered by a glass dome.

The interior includes an exclusive area called the MSC Yacht Club for occupants of some 99 'suites.' This 'club' includes a Top-Sail Lounge (with butler service, canapés and little bit-sized food items), private sunbathing with an integral dip pool, two hot tubs, and concierge services such as making dining reservations, and booking excursions and spa treatments.

It's worth paying extra to stay in one of the 'suites' in the Yacht Club accommodation. You'll get silver-tray room service by a team of butlers, a reserved (quieter) section of the Villa Verde Restaurant, and keycard access to a members-only sundeck sanctuary area that includes its own bar and food counters, a small dip pool, two hot tubs, and expansive open but sheltered lounging deck. It's a world away from the hustle and

Berlitz's Ratings

	Possible	Achieved
Ship	500	413
Accommodation	200	161
Food	400	271
Service	400	306
Entertainment	100	74
Cruise	400	305

OVERALL SCORE
1530 points out of 2000

bustle of the main pool decks and solarium on the decks below.

The interior décor is quite stunning. There are basically two decks full of public lounges, bars, and eateries, including a large two-deck-high theater-style showlounge, a nightclub/discotheque, library, card room, an internet center, virtual reality center, shopping gallery, and large casino (inhabited by many who can smoke at the bar). Shopping becomes a city-like environment. The Royal Palm Casino features blackjack, poker, and roulette games, plus an array of slot machines.

Public rooms include a large showlounge (The Strand), a nightclub/disco (The Aft Lounge), many lounges and bars (most with live music), library, card room, an Internet center, and an extensive shopping gallery. The ship is well designed to accommodate families with children. A 15 percent gratuity is added to all drinks/beverage orders.

Niggles include the fact that all the lounges 'flow' into each other, and so the music from each one bleed into the adjacent room. Note that Only Yacht Club-grade occupants are escorted to their cabins by their butlers. Housekeeping staff point passengers in the right direction, but no longer escort them to their cabins.

ACCOMMODATION. Eighty percent of the cabins are outsides, and 95 percent of these have a balcony – the standard balcony cabin is almost 172 sq ft (16 sq m), plus bathroom and balcony. It's worth paying extra to stay in one of the 72 'suites' (each 312 sq ft/29 sq m) in the Yacht Club area at the top, front end of the ship. Here, you'll get silver-tray room service, a reserved section of the Villa Verde restaurant, plus access to a 'members only' sundeck sanctuary area that includes its own bar and food counters, small 'dip' pool, two hot tubs, and open lounging deck. It's a world away from the hustle and bustle of the main pool decks.

In a 2011 refit, 28 Aurea Suites (from former Yacht Club accommodation) were created, with direct access to the Aurea Spa. The spa suites include unlimited access to the sauna and steam room, a private consultation with the spa doctor, a Balinese massage, a facial relax treatment, and a solarium session.

The Yacht Club has its own serene concierge lounge, small library, and reception desk. A Svarovski glass stairway leads to the Yacht Club suites, and a private elevator accesses the Aurea Spa, located one deck below. The lounge has its own galley and dedicated chef.

DINING. La Reggia is the ship's main restaurant. It spans two decks, and has two seatings for dinner, and an open seating for both breakfast and lunch. Tables are for two, four, six, or eight, and there's some alcove banquette seating on both main and balcony levels. A second restaurant, the single-level Villa Verde, is for occupants of suite-grade accommodation and has panoramic windows at the stern of the ship.

Other dining options. L'Olivo is an Italian/Mediterranean extra-cost à la carte venue that is located in a smaller, more intimate setting aft, overlooking a small pool and relaxation area. The food is cooked to order, and dining here is a pleasant, unhurried experience. Reservations are required.

Santa Fe is an extra-cost, L-shaped Tex-Mex restaurant with food items cooked to order.

Bora Bora Cafeteria is a large casual self-serve lido buffet-style eatery. It is open 20 hours a day, for breakfast, and lunch and for sit-down, casual, waiter-served dinners each evening.

ENTERTAINMENT. The Strand Theater has plush seating in tiers for as many as 1,700, and good sight lines. Because of the multi-national background of passengers, the shows concentrate on more visual entertainment such as mime, magic, dancing, and acrobatics, and are performed with recorded music – because there is no orchestra pit.

Live music for dancing or listening to is provided by a number of bands.

SPA/FITNESS. The Aurea Spa (16,000 sq ft/1,485 sq m) has a beauty salon, well-equipped treatment rooms, and a large gymnasium with ocean views. Included is a large thermal suite, and saunas. The decor is welcoming and restful. The spa is run by OceanView. Gratuities to spa staff are at your discretion. Sports facilities include deck quoits, large tennis/basketball court, mini-golf, and a jogging track.

Ship Talk

Free Port. Port or place free of customs duty and regulations.

Funnel. Chimney from which the ship's combustion gases are propelled into the atmosphere.

Galley. The ship's kitchen.

Gangway. The stairway or ramp that provides the link between ship and shore.

Helm. The apparatus for steering a ship.

House Flag. The flag denoting the company owning a ship.

Hull. The frame and body of the ship exclusive of masts or superstructure.

Leeward. The side of a ship that is sheltered from the wind.

Luff. The side of a ship facing the wind

Manifest. A list of the ship's passengers, crew, and cargo.

Nautical Mile. One-sixtieth of a degree of the circumference of the Earth.

Pilot. A person licensed to navigate ships into or out of a harbor or through difficult waters, and to advise the captain on handling the ship during these procedures.

Pitch. The rise and fall of a ship's bow that may occur when the ship is underway.

Port. The left side of a ship when facing forward.

Quay. Berth, dock, or pier.

Rudder. A finlike device astern and below the waterline, for steering the vessel.

Screw. A ship's propeller.

Stabilizer. A gyroscopically operated retractable 'fin' extending from either or both sides of the ship below the waterline in order to provide a more stable ride.

Starboard. The right side of a ship when facing forward.

Stern. The aftmost part of the ship that is opposite the bow.

Tender. A smaller vessel, often a lifeboat, used to transport passengers between ship and shore when the vessel is at anchor.

Wake. The track of agitated water left behind a ship when in motion.

Waterline. The line along the side of a ship's hull corresponding to the water surface.

Windward. The side of a ship facing the direction in which the wind blows.

Yaw. The erratic deviation from the ship's set course, usually caused by a heavy sea.

National Geographic Endeavour
★★★+

Size:	Boutique Ship	Cabins (total):	62
Tonnage:	3,132	Size range (sq ft/m):	191.6–269.1/17.8–25.0
Lifestyle:	Standard	Cabins (outside view):	62
Cruise line:	National Geographic	Cabins (interior/no view):	0
Former names:	Caledonian Star, North Star, Lindmar, Marburg	Cabins (for one person):	14
IMO number:	6611863	Cabins (with private balcony):	0
Builder:	A.G. Weser Seebeckwerft (Germany)	Cabins (wheelchair accessible):	0
Original cost:	n/a	Wheelchair accessibility:	None
Entered service:	1966/1984	Cabin voltage:	110 and 220 volts
Registry:	The Bahamas	Elevators:	0
Length (ft/m):	292.6/89.20	Casino (gaming tables):	No
Beam (ft/m):	45.9/14.0	Slot machines:	No
Draft (ft/m):	20.3/6.2	Swimming pools:	1
Propulsion/Propellers:	diesel (3,236kW)/1	Hot tubs (on deck):	9
Passenger decks:	6	Self-service launderette:	No
Total crew:	64	Dedicated cinema/seats:	No
Passengers (lower beds/all berths):	113/124	Library:	Yes
Passenger Space Ratio (lower beds/all berths):	27.7/25.2	Onboard currency:	US$
Crew/Passenger Ratio (lower beds/all berths):	1.7/1.9		

A very small ship, for nature and wildlife cruises

OVERVIEW. *National Geographic Endeavour* and its type of soft exploration cruising are best suited to adventurous, hardy types who enjoy being with nature and wildlife in some of the most interesting places, but cosseted aboard a small, modestly comfortable ship. Specialized lecturers accompanying each cruise make this a real life-enrichment experience.

THE SHIP. Renamed in 2005, the former *Endeavour* was built as a stern factory fishing trawler for North Sea service. Today, *National Geographic Endeavour* is a tidy and well-cared-for discovery-style cruise vessel operating 'soft' expedition cruises. There is an open bridge policy for all passengers. It carries 10 Zodiac landing craft for excursions, and has a helicopter pad and an enclosed shore tender. A steep aft stairway leads down to the landing craft platform. This small ship has a reasonable number of public rooms and facilities, including a lecture room/lounge/bar/library, where videos are also stocked for in-cabin use. There's a good book selection.

This likeable, homey ship runs well organized, destination-intensive, soft expedition-style cruises, at a very reasonable price. It attracts loyal repeat passengers who don't want to sail aboard ships that look like apartment blocks. The itineraries include Antarctica, where this ship has been operating since 1998.

The interior stairways are a little steep, as is the exterior stairway to the Zodiac embarkation points.

Berlitz's Ratings

	Possible	Achieved
Ship	500	201
Accommodation	200	94
Food	400	194
Service	400	216
Entertainment	100	54
Cruise	400	205

OVERALL SCORE
964 points out of 2000

Noise from the diesel engines can be irksome, particularly on the lower decks. Recommended gratuities are $10 per person, per day.

ACCOMMODATION. There are five categories of cabins: one suite category and four non-suite categories. The all-outside-view cabins are compact, but reasonably comfortable, and they are decorated in warm, muted tones. All cabins have a minibar/refrigerator, video player, and a decent amount of closet and drawer space – though it's tight for long voyages. The bathrooms are tight, with little space for storing toiletries. Four 'suites' are basically double the size of a standard cabin, and have a wood partition separating the bedroom and lounge area. The bathroom is still small, however.

DINING. The open-seating dining room is small and charming, but the low-back chairs are not comfortable. The cuisine is reasonably high quality, fresh ingredients, but not a lot of choice. Salad items lack variety, as do international cheeses. Service is attentive and friendly.

ENTERTAINMENT. The main lounge is the venue for lectures, slide shows, and occasional film presentations. There are no shows.

SPA/FITNESS. There is a small fitness room and a tiny sauna.

National Geographic Explorer
★★★

Size:.. Small Ship	Cabins (total):...81
Tonnage: 6,471	Size range (sq ft/m): .... n/a
Lifestyle: ....Standard	Cabins (outside view): 81
Cruise line:...........................National Geographic	Cabins (interior/no view):............................0
Former names: .... *Lyngen, Midnatsol II, Midnatsol*	Cabins (for one person):.............................14
IMO number: 8019356	Cabins (with private balcony):.......................13
Builder: .... Ulstein Hatlo (Norway)	Cabins (wheelchair accessible): 1
Original cost: .... n/a	Wheelchair accessibility:...........................None
Entered service:......................1982/Jun 2008	Cabin voltage: .... 110 volts
Registry:...............................The Bahamas	Elevators:..1
Length (ft/m):........................... 367.4/112.0	Casino (gaming tables):.............................No
Beam (ft/m):............................. 54.1/16.5	Slot machines:..No
Draft (ft/m): 15.0/4.5	Swimming pools:......................................0
Propulsion/Propellers: diesel/2	Hot tubs (on deck):..................................0
Passenger decks:....................................6	Self-service launderette:............................No
Total crew:..70	Dedicated cinema/seats:............................No
Passengers (lower beds/alll berths): 148/181	Library: .... Yes
Passenger Space Ratio (lower beds/all berths): 43.7/35.7	Onboard currency: ....US$
Crew/Passenger Ratio (lower beds/all berths):.......... 2.1/2.5	

A small, sturdy ship for nature and wildlife cruises

OVERVIEW. *National Geographic Explorer* suits hardy, adventurous types who enjoy being with nature and wildlife in some of the most interesting and occasionally inhospitable places on earth, cosseted aboard a small but comfortable ship.

THE SHIP. Originally built as *Midnatsol* for Hurtigruten, the ship was purchased by Lindblad Expeditions in 2007 and extensively refitted and outfitted well for expedition-style cruising, with some really good facilities and expedition equipment.

The ship has an ice-strengthened hull and is quite stable due to the stabilizers, so movement is minimized. Twin funnel uptakes are located almost at the very stern – an unusual design. There is little outdoor deck space, but it's not needed in cold-weather areas.

The main facilities include a lecture room and bistro bar with espresso machine adjacent to the restaurant, and boot washing stations. An expedition voyage aboard this ship is all about learning and exploration. The dress code is totally casual; layered clothing and sturdy outer wear is recommended. Gratuities to staff are not included in the price.

ACCOMMODATION. The price you pay depends on size and location. The cabins are small, as are the bathrooms, although they are nicely designed, practical units. Some have a fixed queen-size bed configuration, others have twin beds (some can be pushed together, some are fixed). There are several cabins for single

Berlitz's Ratings		
	Possible	Achieved
Ship	500	281
Accommodation	200	110
Food	400	195
Service	400	232
Entertainment	100	60
Cruise	400	232
OVERALL SCORE		
1110 points out of 2000		

occupancy. The tiled bathrooms have shower enclosures, and small shelves for toiletries. Suites have two washbasins, premium bedding, and feather-fluffy duvets.

There is a decent supply of electrical outlets and an ethernet connection for laptops. Closet doors are of the sliding type instead of the outward opening type, to minimize noise and banging when the ship is in tough weather conditions. Naturally, a National Geographic Atlas is provided.

DINING. There is one main dining room, as well as areas for self-serve buffet-style food. The food is hearty and fairly healthy, although you should not expect to find fresh greens in some of the more out-of-the-way areas.

ENTERTAINMENT. Lectures, briefings and recaps, plus after-dinner conversation with fellow participants are the main entertainment – if you're not too tired after exhausting days of landings and other adventures.

SPA/FITNESS. There are two body treatment rooms – with skylights, for wildlife-inspired wellness, facials, and massage, including a special 'ice-bear massage,' as well as a fitness/workout room.

National Geographic Sea Bird
★ +

Size:.....................................Boutique Ship	Cabins (total):.......................................36
Tonnage: 630	Size range (sq ft/m): 73.0–202.0/6.7–18.7
Lifestyle:.....................................Standard	Cabins (outside view):.................................36
Cruise line:.........................National Geographic	Cabins (interior/no view):..............................0
Former names: .... Sea Bird, Majestic Explorer	Cabins (for one person):................................2
IMO number: 8966444	Cabins (with private balcony): 0
Builder: ....Whidbey Island (USA)	Cabins (wheelchair accessible): 0
Original cost:..................................... n/a	Wheelchair accessibility:............................None
Entered service:...................................1981	Cabin voltage: .... 110 volts
Registry:..USA	Elevators:...0
Length (ft/m):................................ 151.9/46.3	Casino (gaming tables):................................No
Beam (ft/m):.................................... 30.8/9.4	Slot machines:.......................................No
Draft (ft/m):..................................... 8.0/2.4	Swimming pools:.......................................0
Propulsion/Propellers:............................ diesel/2	Hot tubs (on deck):...................................0
Passenger decks:....................................4	Self-service launderette:..............................No
Total crew:.......................................22	Dedicated cinema/seats:...............................No
Passengers (lower beds/alll berths):.................. 70/70	Library: ....No
Passenger Space Ratio (lower beds/all berths): 9.0/9.0	Onboard currency: ....US$
Crew/Passenger Ratio (lower beds/all berths):.......... 3.1/3.1	

A basic smaller, older ship for nature-watching

OVERVIEW. *National Geographic Sea Bird* is best suited to senior-age couples and single travelers who enjoy learning about nature, geography, history, and other life sciences in casual, non-dressy surroundings with no pretension. They are likely to be hardy, outdoors types who don't need a lot of entertainment or parlor games. Lectures and recap sessions are held daily.

THE SHIP. *National Geographic Sea Bird* carries a fleet of motorized Zodiac landing craft for use as shore tenders and for up-close shore exploration. A number of sea kayaks are also carried. An open-bridge policy means you can go to the navigation bridge at any time. The vessel is small enough to operate in ports and narrow inlets inaccessible to larger ships.

This small craft – sister to *National Geographic Sea Lion* – is adequate for looking at nature and wildlife close-up, in modest but comfortable surroundings that provide an alternative to big-ship cruising. Cruises visit Alaska, Baja California, and the Sea of Cortés. Tipping is suggested at about $7 per person per day.

In the cabins, the mattresses are enclosed in a wood frame with sharp corners, which you bang into constantly.

ACCOMMODATION. All cabins have rudimentary furniture, but all have an outside view through picture windows, except for those on the lowest deck, which have portholes but no view. Some cabins have double beds, and some have twin beds that can be pushed to-

Berlitz's Ratings		
	Possible	Achieved
Ship	500	141
Accommodation	200	71
Food	400	150
Service	400	185
Entertainment	100	43
Cruise	400	154
OVERALL SCORE		
744 points out of 2000		

gether to form a queen-size bed. Some are for singles, at a surcharge of 50 percent. There is just enough room to stow your luggage.

All cabins have a private bathroom, although it really is tiny. There is no room service for food or beverages.

DINING. The dining room, which has ocean-view picture windows, is large enough to accommodate all passengers in a single seating. The tables are not assigned, and so you can sit with whoever you like. The food is unpretentious, good, and wholesome, although its presentation is very plain, with no frills, and features regional specialties.

The wine list is very limited, and is comprised mostly of wines from California.

ENTERTAINMENT. There is no formal entertainment, although dinner and after-dinner conversation with fellow passengers in the ship's lounge/bar really becomes the entertainment. So, if you're not in the mood to talk to your fellow passengers, you can retire with a good book, or go outside, where you'll usually find that nature provides varied entertainment.

SPA/FITNESS. There are no spa or fitness facilities aboard this very small cruise vessel.

National Geographic Sea Lion
★ +

Size:..Boutique Ship	Cabins (total):.......................................37
Tonnage:..630	Size range (sq ft/m):..................73.0–202.0/6.7–18.7
Lifestyle:..Standard	Cabins (outside view):................................37
Cruise line:...........................National Geographic	Cabins (interior/no view):..............................0
Former names:...............Sea Lion, Great Rivers Explorer	Cabins (for one person):...............................2
IMO number:...................................8966456	Cabins (with private balcony):..........................0
Builder:...........................Whidbey Island (USA)	Cabins (wheelchair accessible):.........................0
Original cost:..n/a	Wheelchair accessibility:............................None
Entered service:...................................1982	Cabin voltage:................................110 volts
Registry:..USA	Elevators:...0
Length (ft/m):.................................151.9/46.3	Casino (gaming tables):...............................No
Beam (ft/m):..................................30.8/9.4	Slot machines:.......................................No
Draft (ft/m):..................................8.0/2.4	Swimming pools:......................................0
Propulsion/Propellers:...........................diesel/2	Hot tubs (on deck):...................................0
Passenger decks:.....................................4	Self-service launderette:..............................No
Total crew:...22	Dedicated cinema/seats:..............................No
Passengers (lower beds/alll berths):..................72/76	Library:...No
Passenger Space Ratio (lower beds/all berths):.........8.7/8.2	Onboard currency:.................................US$
Crew/Passenger Ratio (lower beds/all berths):..........3.2/3.4	

A small, older ship for wildlife and nature watching

OVERVIEW. This ship is best suited to older couples and single travelers who enjoy learning about nature, geography, and history, in casual, non-dressy surroundings without a hint of pretension. They are likely to be hardy, outdoors types who don't need entertainment. The ship is small enough to operate in ports and narrow inlets inaccessible to larger vessels.

THE SHIP. The close-to-the-water *National Geographic Sea Lion* carries a fleet of motorized Zodiac landing craft for use as shore tenders and for up-close shore exploration. A number of sea kayaks are also carried. An open-bridge policy means that you are allowed to go to the navigation bridge at any time.

This small craft is adequate for looking at nature and wildlife up close, in modest but comfortable surroundings that provide an alternative to big-ship cruising. Lectures and recap sessions are held each day.

Cruises visit Alaska, Baja California, and the Sea of Cortés. Tipping is suggested at about $7 per person per day.

Note that in the cabins, the mattresses are enclosed in a wood frame with sharp corners, which you can all too easily bang into constantly.

ACCOMMODATION. All the cabins aboard this little ship have an outside view through picture windows, except for those on the lowest deck, which have portholes. Some cabins have double beds, some have twin beds that can be pushed together to form a queen-size

Berlitz's Ratings		
	Possible	Achieved
Ship	500	141
Accommodation	200	71
Food	400	150
Service	400	185
Entertainment	100	43
Cruise	400	154
OVERALL SCORE		
744 points out of 2000		

bed. Some are for singles, at a surcharge of 15 percent. There is plenty of room to stow your luggage.

All cabins have a private bathroom, although it really is tiny. There is no room service for food or beverages.

DINING. The dining room, which has ocean-view picture windows, is large enough to accommodate all passengers in a single seating. The tables are not assigned, and so you can sit with whoever you like. The food is unpretentious, good, and wholesome, although its presentation is very plain, with no frills, and features regional specialties.

The wine list is very limited, and is comprised mostly of wines from California.

ENTERTAINMENT. There is no formal entertainment, although dinner and after-dinner conversation with fellow passengers in the ship's lounge/bar really becomes the entertainment each evening. So, if you don't want to talk to your fellow passengers, take a good book, or go outside, where you'll find nature provides the rest of the entertainment.

SPA/FITNESS. There are no spa or fitness facilities aboard this very small cruise vessel.

Nautica
★★★★

Size:... Small Ship	Cabins (total):.....................................342
Tonnage: 30,277	Size range (sq ft/m): 145.3–968.7/13.5–90.0
Lifestyle: ....Premium	Cabins (outside view):.................................317
Cruise line:............................... Oceania Cruises	Cabins (interior/no view):...............................25
Former names: ....R Five	Cabins (for one person):..................................0
IMO number: 9200938	Cabins (with private balcony):..........................232
Builder: .... Chantiers de l'Atlantique	Cabins (wheelchair accessible): 3
Original cost:..............................£150 million	Wheelchair accessibility:............................Good
Entered service:...................... Dec 1998/Nov 2005	Cabin voltage: ....110 and 220 volts
Registry:..............................Marshall Islands	Elevators:..4
Length (ft/m):............................ 593.7/181.0	Casino (gaming tables):................................Yes
Beam (ft/m):................................ 83.5/25.5	Slot machines:.......................................Yes
Draft (ft/m): 19.5/6.0	Swimming pools:.......................................1
Propulsion/Propellers:..................diesel (18,600kW)/2	Hot tubs (on deck):....................................2
Passenger decks:.......................................9	Self-service launderette:..............................Yes
Total crew:...386	Dedicated cinema/seats:................................No
Passengers (lower beds/all berths):................. 684/824	Library: ....Yes
Passenger Space Ratio (lower beds/all berths): 44.2/36.7	Onboard currency: ....US$
Crew/Passenger Ratio (lower beds/all berths):.......... 1.7/2.1	

A stylish premium ship for mature-age cruisers

OVERVIEW. *Nautica* is best suited to couples who like good food and style, but want informality and interesting itineraries, all at a very reasonable price.

THE SHIP. *Nautica*, almost identical to *Insignia* and *Regatta*, is an all-white ship with a large, square white funnel. The addition of teak overlaid decking and teak lounge chairs has greatly improved what was once a bland pool deck outdoors, but the front rows of double sunloungers ('cabanas') cost $100 a day.

The interior decor is quite stunning, a throwback to ship decor of the ocean liners of the 1920s and '30s, with dark woods and warm colors, all carried out in fine taste, although a bit faux in places. This includes detailed ceiling cornices, both real and faux wrought-iron staircase railings, leather-paneled walls, trompe l'oeil ceilings, rich carpeting in hallways with an Oriental rug-look center section, and many other interesting and expensive-looking decorative touches. It feels like an old-world country club.

The public rooms are spread over three decks. The lobby has a staircase with intricate wrought-iron railings. A large observation lounge, the Horizon Bar, is high atop ship.

There are plenty of bars – including one in each of the restaurant entrances. Perhaps the nicest is the casino bar/lounge, a beautiful room reminiscent of London's grand hotels and includes a martini bar. It has an inviting marble fireplace, comfortable sofas, and individual chairs.

Berlitz's Ratings

	Possible	Achieved
Ship	500	402
Accommodation	200	153
Food	400	308
Service	400	295
Entertainment	100	74
Cruise	400	308
OVERALL SCORE		
1540 points out of 2000		

The Library is a grand Regency-style room, with a fireplace, a high, indented, trompe l'oeil ceiling, and excellent selection of books, plus very comfortable wingback chairs.

Gratuities are automatically added to your onboard account. Accommodations designated as suites pay more, for the butler. A 15 percent gratuity is added to bar and spa accounts.

The stairways, though carpeted, are tinny. Passenger niggles include all the highly irritating extra charges that can be incurred. What's nice is the fact that there are almost no announcements.

ACCOMMODATION. There are six cabin categories, and several price grades: three suite price grades, five outside-view cabin grades, and two interior cabin grades. All of the standard interior and outside-view cabins – the lowest four grades – are very compact units, and tight for two persons. They have twin beds or queen-size bed, with good under-bed storage areas, personal safe, vanity desk with large mirror, good closet and drawer space in rich, dark woods, cotton bathrobe and towels, slippers, clothes brush, and shoe horn. TV sets carry a major news channel, where obtainable, plus a sports channel and round-the-clock movie channels.

About 100 cabins qualify as 'Concierge Level' accommodation, and occupants get extra goodies such as enhanced bathroom amenities, complimentary shoeshine, tote bag, cashmere throw blanket, bottle of Champagne on arrival, hairdryer, priority restaurant reservations, priority embarkation, and dedicated check-in desk.

Owner's Suites. The six Owner's Suites, measuring 962 sq ft/89.3 sq m, are the most spacious accommodation. They are fine, large living spaces located aft overlooking the stern on decks 6, 7, and 8 – they are, however, subject to movement and vibration. They have teak-floor private balconies that really are private and can't be overlooked. Each has an entrance foyer, living room, separate bedroom (the bed faces the sea, which can be seen through the floor-to-ceiling windows), fully tiled bathroom with tub, and a small guest bathroom.

Vista Suites. There are four, each around 786 sq ft/73 sq m, and located forward on decks 5 and 6. They have teak-floor private balconies that can't be overlooked. Each has an entrance foyer, living room, separate bedroom with similar layout to that in the owner's suites, CD player plus audio discs, and a fully tiled bathroom with Jacuzzi tub.

Penthouse Suites. There are 52 of these – though they are not suites at all but large cabins because the bedrooms aren't separate from the living areas. They measure around 323 sq ft (30 sq m) and have a good-size teak-floor balcony with sliding glass door (but with partial, and not full, balcony partitions) and teak deck furniture. The lounge area has a proper dining table and there is ample clothes storage space. The bathroom has a tub, shower enclosure, washbasin, and toilet.

Cabins with Balcony. Cabins with private balconies (around 216 sq ft/20 sq m) comprise about two-thirds of all cabins. They have partial, not full, balcony partitions and sliding glass doors, and 14 cabins on Deck 6 have lifeboat-obstructed views and no balcony. The living area has a refrigerated mini-bar, lounge area with breakfast table, and a balcony with teak floor, two teak chairs, and a drinks table. The bathrooms, with tiled floors and plain walls, are compact, standard units, and include a shower stall with a strong, removable hand-held shower unit, hairdryer, toiletries storage shelves, and retractable clothesline.

Outside View and Interior Cabins. These measure around 160–165 sq ft (14.8–15.3 sq m) and have twin beds that convert to a queen-size bed, vanity desk, small sofa and coffee table, and bathroom with a shower enclosure with a strong, removable hand-held shower unit, hairdryer, toiletries storage shelves, retractable clothesline, washbasin, and toilet. Although they are not large, they are quite comfortable, with decent storage space.

All suites/cabins located at the stern may suffer from vibration and noise, particularly when the ship is proceeding at or close to full speed, or maneuvering in port.

DINING. Flexibility and choice are what the dining facilities aboard the Oceania ships are all about. There are four different restaurants:

The Grand Dining Room has around 340 seats and a raised central section, but the problem is the noise level: it's atrocious when the dining room is full – the effect of the low ceiling height. Being located at the stern, there are large ocean-view windows on three sides – prime tables overlook the stern. The chairs are comfortable and have armrests. The menus change daily for lunch and dinner.

Other dining options. The Toscana Italian Restaurant has 96 seats, windows along two sides, and a set menu plus daily chef's specials.

The cozy Polo Grill has 98 seats, windows along two sides and a set menu including prime steaks and seafood.

The Terrace Café has seats for 154 indoors – not enough during cruises to cold-weather areas – and 186 outdoors. It is open for breakfast, lunch, and casual dinners, when it has tapas (Tapas on the Terrace) and other Mediterranean food. As the ship's self-serve buffet restaurant, it incorporates a small pizzeria and grill. There are basic salads, a meat carving station, and a reasonable selection of cheeses.

All restaurants have open-seating dining, so you can dine when you want, with whom you wish. Reservations are needed in Toscana Restaurant and Polo Grill (but there's no extra charge), where there are mostly tables for four or six; there are few tables for two. There is a Poolside Grill Bar. All cappuccino and espresso coffees cost extra.

The food and service staff is provided by Apollo, a respected maritime catering company with an interest in Oceania Cruises. The consultant chef is Jacques Pépin, well-known in the United States as a television chef. This is a foodie's ship, with really high-quality ingredients, and a wide selection of dining venues. Particularly notable are the delicious breads, rolls, croissants, and brioches – all made on board from French flower and d'Isigny butter.

On sea days, an elegant teatime is presented in the Horizon Lounge, with formally dressed staff, cake display trolleys, and an excellent array of cake and scones. Sadly, teabags – not loose tea – prevail.

ENTERTAINMENT. The Nautica Lounge has entertainment, lectures, and some social events. There is little entertainment because of the intensive nature of the itineraries. However, there is live music in several bars and lounges.

SPA/FITNESS. A lido deck has a swimming pool, and good sunbathing space, plus a thalassotherapy tub. A jogging track circles the swimming pool deck, but one deck above. The uppermost outdoors deck includes a golf driving net and shuffleboard court. The Canyon Ranch SpaClub consists of a beauty salon, three treatment rooms, men's and women's changing rooms, and steam room. There is no sauna. An 18 percent gratuity applies to massages and treatments.

Navigator of the Seas
★★★+

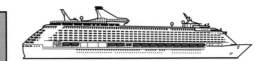

Size:................................Large Resort Ship		Crew/Passenger Ratio (lower beds/all berths):.........2.6/3.2	
Tonnage:...137,276		Cabins (total):..1,557	
Lifestyle:.......................................Standard		Size range (sq ft/m):..............151.0–1,358.0/14.0–126.1	
Cruise line:...................Royal Caribbean International		Cabins (outside view):.................................939	
Former names:.....................................none		Cabins (interior/no view):.............................618	
IMO number:..................................9227506		Cabins (for one person):................................0	
Builder:...................Kvaerner Masa-Yards (Finland)		Cabins (with private balcony):.........................765	
Original cost:................................$500 million		Cabins (wheelchair accessible):.........................26	
Entered service:...............................Dec 2002		Wheelchair accessibility:..............................Best	
Registry:....................................The Bahamas		Cabin voltage:...................................110 volts	
Length (ft/m):................................1,020.6/311.1		Elevators:...........................14 (6 glass-enclosed)	
Beam (ft/m):................................155.5/47.4		Casino (gaming tables):................................Yes	
Draft (ft/m):.....................................28.8/8.8		Slot machines:.......................................Yes	
Propulsion/Propellers:......diesel-electric (75,600kW)/3 pods (2		Swimming pools:.......................................3	
azimuthing, 1 fixed)		Hot tubs (on deck):....................................6	
Passenger decks:....................................14		Self-service launderette:...............................No	
Total crew:.......................................1,185		Dedicated cinema/seats:...............................No	
Passengers (lower beds/alll berths):............3,114/3,835		Library:...Yes	
Passenger Space Ratio (lower beds/all berths):.......44.0/35.7		Onboard currency:....................................US$	

A colorful, fun-filled ship for family-friendly cruising

OVERVIEW. *Navigator of the Seas* is a large, floating leisure resort. It provides a host of facilities, rather like a small town, with plenty of entertainment for all ages, yet offers a healthy amount of space per passenger. The food focuses on quantity rather than quality unless you are prepared to pay extra in the specialty restaurant.

THE SHIP. The first ship in the RCI fleet to receive 'virtual balconies' for all interior (no view) cabins – a neat feature installed during a 2013 refurbishment, *Navigator of the Seas* is a sister to *Adventure of the Seas, Explorer of the Seas, Mariner of the Seas,* and *Voyager of the Seas.* Embarkation and disembarkation usually take place through two access points, designed to minimize lines. Once inside the ship, spending your first few hours exploring the facilities and public spaces will be time well spent.

A stunning four-deck-high Royal Promenade is the main interior focal point; it's a fun place to hang out, or to arrange to meet someone. The length of two American football fields, it has two internal lobbies rising through 11 decks. Cafés, shops, and entertainment locations from this winding street and interior 'with-view' cabins look into it from above. It is an imaginative piece of design work, and fans of shopping malls enjoy it immensely.

The long super-atrium houses a 'traditional' pub. There's also a Champagne Bar, a Sidewalk Café (for Continental breakfast, all-day pizzas, specialty coffees, and desserts), Sprinkles (for round-the-clock ice

Berlitz's Ratings

	Possible	Achieved
Ship	500	392
Accommodation	200	141
Food	400	223
Service	400	267
Entertainment	100	75
Cruise	400	264
OVERALL SCORE		
1362 points out of 2000		

cream and yoghurt), and a sports bar. There are also several shops – for jewelry, gifts, liquor, perfumes, and souvenirs.

The Guest Reception and Shore Excursion counters are located at the aft end of the promenade, as is an ATM machine. At times (given in the daily program), street entertainers appear, and parades are staged, while at other (carefully orchestrated) times it's difficult to walk through the area as it's filled to the brim with tacky shopping items – like a cheap bazaar.

Arched across the promenade is a captain's balcony, and in the center of the promenade a stairway connects you to the deck below, where you'll find the Schooner Bar (a piano lounge common to all RCI ships) and a flashy Casino Royale. Gaming includes blackjack, Caribbean stud poker, roulette, and craps, plus 300 slot machines. Aft of the casino is the neat Champagne Bar.

There's a regulation-size ice-skating rink (Studio B), with real ice, with 'bleacher' seating for up to 900, and the latest in broadcast facilities. Superb Ice Follies shows are presented here. A fine two-deck library is open 24 hours a day.

Other drinking places include the small and intimate Two Poets Pub, and Connoisseur Club – for cigars and cognacs. There is a TV studio ('Studio B') with high-tech broadcast facilities, located adjacent to rooms that can be used for trade show exhibit space, with a conference center seating 400 and a multi-media 60-seat screening room.

High atop the ship, you can tie the knot in a wedding chapel in the sky, the Skylight Chapel; located on the upper level of the Viking Crown Lounge, it has wheelchair access via an electric stairlift. Outdoors, the pool and open deck areas provide a resort-like setting. If you can, it's worth visiting the Helicopter Deck at the front of the ship for great starry-sky views at night (and neat photo opportunities).

Passenger niggles include having to negotiate 'sale' bazaar tables along the Royal Promenade; the lunchtime chaos in the Windjammer Café on embarkation day (before you have access to your cabin); and the problem of getting a table in the extra-cost dining venues.

FAMILIES. Facilities for children and teenagers are quite extensive (actually, they are larger than aboard the sister ships). Aquanauts is for three- to five-year-olds; Explorers is for six- to eight-year-olds; Voyagers is for nine- to 12-year-olds. Optix is a dedicated area for teenagers, including a daytime club with several computers, a soda bar, and a dance floor. Challenger's Arcade has an array of video games. Paint and Clay is an arts and crafts center for younger children. Adjacent is Adventure Beach, an area for all the family to enjoy; it includes swimming pools, a water slide, and outdoor game areas.

ACCOMMODATION. There is a wide range of cabin price grades, in four major groupings: Premium oceanview suites and cabins, Interior (atrium-view) cabins, Ocean-view cabins, and Interior cabins (which now have 'virtual balconies' projected on a formerly blank wall – a really neat feature). Many cabins are of a similar size – good for incentives and large groups – and 300 have interconnecting doors (good for families).

Some 138 interior cabins have bay windows that look into an interior horizontal atrium – a cruise industry first when the ship debuted. Regardless of what cabin grade you choose, all except for the Royal Suite and Owner's Suite have twin beds that convert to a queen-size unit, TV set, radio and telephone, personal safe, vanity unit, hairdryer, and private bathroom. However, you'll need to keep the curtains closed in the bay windows if you wear little clothing, because you can be seen easily from adjacent bay windows.

The accommodation hallways are warm and attractive, with artwork cabinets and wavy lines to lead you along and break up the monotony. In fact, there are plenty of colorful, even whimsical, decorative touches to avoid what could be a very clinical environment.

Royal Suite (Deck 10). At around 1,146 sq ft (107 sq m), the Royal Suite is the largest private living space, located almost at the top of the Centrum lobby on the port side. It is a nicely appointed penthouse suite, whose occupants, sadly, must share the rest of the ship with everyone else, except for access to their own exclusive concierge club. It has a king-size circu-

lar bed in a separate large bedroom that can be fully closed off; a living room with an additional queen-size sofa bed, baby grand piano, refrigerator/wet bar, dining table and four chairs, expansive entertainment center, and a reasonably large bathroom.

Royal Family Suite. The four Royal Family suites (two aft on Deck 9, two aft on Deck 8, each measuring around 574 sq ft/53 sq m) have two separate bedrooms. The main bedroom has a large vanity desk; the second, smaller bedroom also includes two beds and third/fourth upper Pullman berths. There's a lounge with dining table and four chairs, wet bar, walk-in closet; and large bathroom with Jacuzzi tub, washbasin, and separate shower enclosure. The suites, at the stern, have large balconies with views out over the ship's wash.

Owner's Suites. Ten slightly smaller but desirable Owner's Suites (around 468 sq ft/43 sq m) are in the center of the ship, on both port and starboard sides, adjacent to the Centrum lobby on Deck 10. Each has a bedroom with queen-size bed or twin beds; lounge with large sofa; wet bar; bathroom with Jacuzzi tub, washbasin and separate shower enclosure. There's also a private balcony, although it's not very large.

Standard Outside-View and Interior Cabins. All cabins have a private bathroom, as well as interactive TV and pay-per-view movies, including an X-rated channel. Cabin bathrooms really are compact, but at least they have a proper shower enclosure instead of a shower curtain.

Some accommodation grades have a refrigerator/mini-bar, although there is no space left because it is crammed with 'take-and-pay' items. If you take anything from the mini-bar/refrigerator on the day of embarkation in Miami, Florida, sales tax will be added to your bill.

Cabins with 'private balconies' aren't so private, however. The balcony decking is made of Bolidt – a sort of rubberized sand – and not wood, though the balcony rail is of wood. If you have a cabin with a connecting door to another cabin, be aware that you'll probably be able to hear everything your next-door neighbors say and do. Bathroom toilets are explosively noisy, based on the vacuum system. Cabin bath towels are small and skimpy. Note that room service food menus are very basic.

DINING. The main dining room has a total capacity of 1,919. It is close to being massive, and consists of three levels, each of which is named after a famous composer: Mozart, Strauss, and Vivaldi. The menu is the same on all three levels. A dramatic staircase connects all three levels, and huge, fat support pillars obstruct sight lines from a number of seats. However, the ambiance is good and there's always a good buzz when the ship is full dinner is in progress.

Two small private wings serve private groups: La Cetra and La Notte, each with 58 seats. When you book, choose one of two seatings, or 'My Time Dining' (eat when you want during dining room hours). Tables are for four, six, eight, 10, or 12. The place settings, china, and cutlery are of good quality.

Other dining options. Portofino, the ship's upscale Euro-Italian restaurant. It's open for dinner only, reservations are required, and there's a cover charge. The food and its presentation are better than the food in the dining room, although the restaurant isn't large enough for all passengers to try even once during a cruise. Choices include antipasti, soup, salad, pasta, main dish, dessert, cheese, and coffee.

Windjammer Café: this is a really large, sprawling venue for casual buffet-style, self-help breakfast (this tends to be the busiest time of the day), lunch, and light dinners (but not on the last night of the cruise); it's often difficult to find a table and by the time you do your food could be cold.

The Island Grill (it's actually a section inside the Windjammer Café), for casual dinner (no reservations needed), with a grill and open kitchen.

Johnny Rockets, a retro 1950s all-day, all-night diner-style eatery, has hamburgers, malt shakes (at extra cost), and jukebox hits, with both indoor and outdoor seating.

Promenade Café: for Continental breakfast, all-day pizzas, and speciality coffees – which are provided in paper cups.

Sprinkles, located on the Royal Promenade is for round-the-clock ice cream and yogurt, pastries and coffee.

ENTERTAINMENT. The 1,350-seat Lyric Theater, the principal showlounge, is a stunning room located at the forward end of the ship. It has Art Nouveau themed décor, spans the height of five decks, with only a few slim pillars and almost no disruption of sight lines. Production shows are presented here by a large cast and a live band. There's also an array of up-and-coming cabaret acts and late-night adults-only comedy.

In addition, the ship has an array of cabaret acts. Although many are not what you'd call headliners, they regularly travel the cruise ship circuit. The strongest cabaret acts are presented in the main showlounge, while others appear in the Imperial Lounge (it's on the deck above), which is also the venue for adult-only late-night comedy. The best shows of all, for many, are, however, the Ice Spectaculars.

There is also a TV studio that can be used, for example, for trade show exhibit space – good for conventions at sea.

Entertainment is always upbeat. There is even background music in all corridors and elevators, and constant music outdoors on the pool deck. If you want a quiet relaxing vacation, this is not the right ship for you.

SPA/FITNESS. The ShipShape health spa is reasonably large, and measures 15,000 sq ft (1,400 sq m). It includes an aerobics room, fitness center (with the usual stairmasters, treadmills, stationary bikes, weight machines, and free weights), treatment rooms, and men's and women's sauna/steam rooms. Another 10,000 sq ft (930 sq m) of space is devoted to a Solarium (with sliding glass-dome roof) to relax in after you've exercised.

On the aft of the funnel is a 32.8-ft (10-m) rock-climbing wall, with five climbing tracks. It's a great buzz being 200ft (60m) above the ocean while the ship is moving. Other sports facilities include a roller-blading track, a dive-and-snorkel shop, a full-size basketball court, and a nine-hole, par 26 golf 'course.' A dive-and-snorkel shop provides equipment for rental and diving classes.

Nieuw Amsterdam
★★★★

Size:.................................Large Resort Ship	Crew/Passenger Ratio (lower beds/all berths):..........2.2/2.8
Tonnage:.......................................86,700	Cabins (total):..................................1,053
Lifestyle:.....................................Premium	Size range (sq ft/m):.............170.0–1,318.6/15.7–122.5
Cruise line:.......................Holland America Line	Cabins (outside view):..............................897
Former names:..................................none	Cabins (interior/no view):..........................156
IMO number:...............................9378450	Cabins (for one person):..............................0
Builder:...........................Fincantieri (Italy)	Cabins (with private balcony):......................708
Original cost:..............................$400 million	Cabins (wheelchair accessible):......................30
Entered service:...............................Jul 2010	Wheelchair accessibility:.........................Good
Registry:................................The Netherlands	Cabin voltage:........................110 and 220 volts
Length (ft/m):............................935.0/285.0	Elevators:..14
Beam (ft/m):..............................105.6/32.2	Casino (gaming tables):............................Yes
Draft (ft/m):................................25.5/7.8	Slot machines:....................................Yes
Propulsion/Propellers:...diesel-electric (34,000kW)/2 azimuthing pods	Swimming pools:................2 (1 w/sliding glass dome)
	Hot tubs (on deck):..................................5
Passenger decks:.................................12	Self-service launderette:............................No
Total crew:......................................929	Dedicated cinema/seats:........................Yes/170
Passengers (lower beds/all berths):............2,106/2,671	Library:...Yes
Passenger Space Ratio (lower beds/all berths):.......41.1/32.4	Onboard currency:.................................US$

Dutch decor, traditions and comfort for mature-age cruisers

OVERVIEW. The ship is designed to appeal to younger, more vibrant, multi-generational holidaymakers. Neat little tented cabanas on the aft deck provide private shaded space. They are filled with goodies such as Champagne, chocolate strawberries, bathrobes, fresh fruit, and chilled towels for two adults and two children.

THE SHIP. *Nieuw Amsterdam* is a Vista-class ship, sister to *Eurodam*, *Noordam*, *Oosterdam*, *Westerdam*, and *Zuiderdam*. It is named for the Dutch name for New York City and the interior design reflects the great city. The ship, the latest in a line of HAL ships to carry this name, has two upright 'dustbin lid' funnels in a close-knit configuration. The twin working funnels are the result of the slightly unusual machinery configuration; the ship has, in effect, two engine rooms – one with three diesels, and one with two diesels and a gas turbine. There's a pod propulsion system, so there's no vibration.

There is a complete walk-around exterior teak promenade deck, with teak steamer-style sunloungers. A jogging track outdoors is located around the mast and the forward third of the ship. Exterior glass elevators, mounted mid-ships on both port and starboard sides, provide fine ocean views from any one of 10 decks. One of the two centrally located swimming pools outdoors can be used in inclement weather due to its retractable sliding glass roof. Two hot tubs, adjacent to the swimming pools, are abridged by a bar. There's also a small swimming pool for children.

Berlitz's Ratings		
	Possible	Achieved
Ship	500	392
Accommodation	200	150
Food	400	270
Service	400	274
Entertainment	100	71
Cruise	400	286
OVERALL SCORE		
1443 points out of 2000		

There are two whole entertainment/public room decks, the most dramatic space being a showlounge spanning four decks in the forward section. Other facilities include a winding shopping street with several boutique stores and logo shops, card room, an art gallery, photo gallery, and several small meetings rooms. The large casino is equipped with an array of gaming paraphernalia and slot machines, and you have to walk through it to get from the restaurant to the showlounge.

Explorations – perhaps the most popular public room – is a combination coffee bar (where coffees and other drinks cost extra), lounge, extensive library, and Internet-connect center, all contained in one attractive, open 'lifestyle' environment – it's a popular area for relaxation and reading, although noise from the coffee machine can interrupt concentration.

On other decks (lower down), you'll find a Queens Lounge, which acts as a lecture room a Culinary Arts Center, where cooking demonstrations and cooking classes are held. Naturally, a bar is close at hand – it's at the back of the room. There are also a number of other bars and lounges, including an Explorer's Lounge (live string and piano music is appropriate for cocktails in the evenings, when warm hors d'oeuvres are provided). The ship also has a small movie screening room.

The information desk in the lobby is small and somewhat removed from the main passenger flow on the two decks above it. Many pillars obstruct the passenger flow and lines of sight throughout the ship.

There are no self-service launderettes – something families with children miss, although special laundry packages are available.

Gratuities are automatically added to your onboard account. Passenger niggles? These include noisy cabin air conditioning – the flow can't be regulated or turned off.

FAMILIES. Club HAL's KidZone provides a whole area dedicated to children's facilities and extensive programming for different age groups (five to 17), with one counselor for every 30 children. Free ice cream is provided at certain hours, plus hot hors d'oeuvres in all bars. Some cabins have interconnecting doors.

ACCOMMODATION. There are 24 price categories: 16 outside-view and eight interior. The views from some cabins on the lowest accommodation deck (Main Deck) are obstructed by lifeboats. Some cabins that can accommodate a third and fourth person have very little closet space, and only one personal safe. Occupants of suites get exclusive use of the Neptune Lounge and concierge service, priority embarkation and disembarkation, and other benefits. In many of the suites/cabins with private balconies, the balconies are not so private and can be overlooked from various public locations.

Penthouse Verandah Suites (2). These offer the largest accommodation (1,318 sq ft/123 sq m, including balcony). These have a separate bedroom with a king-size bed; there's also a walk-in closet, dressing room, living room, dining room, butler's pantry, minibar and refrigerator, and private balcony. The main bathroom has a large whirlpool tub, two washbasins, toilet, and plenty of storage space for toiletries. Personalized stationery and free dry cleaning are included, as are hot hors d'oeuvres and other goodies daily.

DeLuxe Verandah Suites (60). These suites measure 563 sq ft (53 sq m). They have twin beds that convert to a king-size bed, vanity desk, lounge area, walk-in closet, mini-bar and refrigerator, and bathroom with full-size tub, washbasin, and toilet. Personalized stationery and complimentary dry cleaning are included, as are hot hors d'oeuvres and other goodies.

Verandah Suites (100). Actually they are cabins, not suites, and measure 284 sq ft (26 sq m). Twin beds can convert to a queen-size bed. There is also a lounge area, mini-bar, and refrigerator, while the bathroom has a tub, washbasin, and toilet. Floor-to-ceiling windows open onto a private balcony.

Outside-view Cabins. Standard outside cabins (197 sq ft/18 sq m) have twin beds that can convert to a queen-size bed. There's a small sitting area, while the bathroom has a tub/shower combination. The interior cabins are slightly smaller (183 sq ft/17 sq m).

DINING. The 1,045-seat Rembrandt Dining Room spans two decks at the stern, with seating at tables for two, four, six, or eight on both main and balcony levels.

It provides a traditional Holland America Line dining experience, with friendly service from smiling Indonesian and Filipino stewards. Both open seating and assigned seating are available for dinner, while breakfast and lunch are open-seating – you'll be seated by restaurant staff when you enter.

Holland America Line can provide Kosher meals (if requested when you book), although these are prepared ashore, then frozen, and brought to your table sealed in their original containers.

The 148-seat Pinnacle Grill is a more upscale dining spot, with higher quality ingredients and better presentation than in the larger main dining room. On Lower Promenade Deck, it fronts onto the second level of the atrium lobby; tables along its outer section are open to it and can suffer from noise from the Atrium Bar one deck below, though these tables are good for those who like to see and be seen. Pacific Northwest cuisine is featured, with items such as sesame-crusted halibut with ginger-miso, and an array of premium-quality steaks. The wine list includes some fine wines from around the world, including many gorgeous Bordeaux reds. Reservations are required, and there is a cover charge.

Other dining options. For casual eating, there is an extensive Lido Café, an eatery that wraps around the funnel, with indoor-outdoor seating and ocean views. It includes several sections including a salad bar, Asian stir-fry and sushi section, deli sandwiches, and a separate dessert buffet, although lines can form for made-to-order items such as omelets for breakfast and pasta for lunch.

An outdoor grill bar adjacent to the Lido pool has fast food such as hamburgers, veggie burgers, hot dogs, chicken, and fries. On certain days, barbecues and other culinary specialties are available poolside.

ENTERTAINMENT. The 867-seat Mainstage Lounge is the venue for Las Vegas-style revues and major cabaret shows. The main floor level includes a bar in its aft section. Spiral stairways at the back of the showlounge connect all levels. Stage shows are best seen from the upper levels, from where the sight lines are quite good.

SPA/FITNESS. The Greenhouse Spa, a large, two-decks-high health spa, is located directly above the navigation bridge. Facilities include a solarium, hydrotherapy pool, unisex thermal suite – a unisex area incorporating a Laconium (gentle sauna), Hammam (mild steam), and Chamomile Grotto (small aromatic steam room).

There is a beauty salon, 11 private massage/body treatment rooms (including one for couples), and a large gymnasium with floor-to-ceiling windows on three sides and forward-facing ocean views, and the latest high-tech muscle-toning equipment. Sports enthusiasts can enjoy a basketball court, volleyball court, and a golf simulator.

Nippon Maru
★★★★

Size:.. Small Ship	Cabins (total):.....................................204
Tonnage:..................................... 22,472	Size range (sq ft/m): 150.6–430.5/14.0–40.0
Lifestyle: ....Standard	Cabins (outside view):................................184
Cruise line:.................... Mitsui OSK Passenger Line	Cabins (interior/no view):..............................18
Former names: ....none	Cabins (for one person):................................6
IMO number: 8817631	Cabins (with private balcony):..........................27
Builder: ....Mitsubishi Heavy Industries	Cabins (wheelchair accessible): 2
Original cost:............................. $59.4 million	Wheelchair accessibility:.............................Fair
Entered service:............................... Sep 1990	Cabin voltage: .... 100 volts
Registry:..Japan	Elevators:...5
Length (ft/m):............................. 546.7/166.6	Casino (gaming tables):...............................Yes
Beam (ft/m):................................ 78.7/24.0	Slot machines:.....................................No
Draft (ft/m): 21.4/6.5	Swimming pools:.....................................1
Propulsion/Propellers: ....diesel (15,740kW)/2	Hot tubs (on deck):..................................4
Passenger decks:...................................7	Self-service launderette:.............................Yes
Total crew:.......................................230	Dedicated cinema/seats:..............................Yes
Passengers (lower beds/all berths):................ 408/607	Library: ....Yes
Passenger Space Ratio (lower beds/all berths): 55.0/37.0	Onboard currency: ....Japanese Yen
Crew/Passenger Ratio (lower beds/all berths):.......... 2.5/3.7	

Modern styling for Japanese mature-age cruisers

OVERVIEW. *Nippon Maru* is best suited to Japanese-speaking couples and single travelers who want very comfortable surroundings, and who enjoy decent food and good service, all at a decent cost.

THE SHIP. *Nippon Maru* had an ambitious four-month refit in 2009–10, when a new hydraulic tender loading platform was created. Deck extensions created space for more public rooms such as a new dining room for suite-class and deluxe-grade passengers, a piano lounge, and a health/fitness facility.

The interior's focal point is an atrium lobby that spans six decks. Public rooms include a showlounge, piano lounge, a 54-seat screening room/lecture room (Mermaid Theatre), a gaming corner with give-aways rather than cash prizes, and a Chashitsu tatami room within the Horizon Lounge. The Neptune Bar has probably the most extensive assortment of Scotch whiskies at sea.

ACCOMMODATION. The newer suites, on Deck 6, are large and have a separate sleeping and living areas. A sofa, two chairs, and coffee table occupy one section of the lounge; there is also a writing desk with Nespresso machine and tea-making facilities. The two beds can be pushed together. The bathroom includes a 'washlet,' but the step into the bathroom is high, at 8ins (21cm). Slippers and bathrobes are provided. Nine new suites include two with huge balconies. Suites and deluxe-grade cabins are nicely decorated, and the living area has a table and two chairs, and two beds; there's also a personal computer.

All standard cabins have blond wood cabinetry and good drawer space. Many have a third (or third and fourth) pull-down upper Pullman berth.

Berlitz's Ratings

	Possible	Achieved
Ship	500	377
Accommodation	200	147
Food	400	307
Service	400	301
Entertainment	100	78
Cruise	400	288

OVERALL SCORE
1498 points out of 2000

DINING. The Mizuho dining room, which seats around 320, serves both traditional Japanese cuisine and Western dishes. There is one open seating. The ship is known for its high-quality food. A premium dining room, Kasuga, has been added for suite- and deluxe-grade occupants; adjacent is the excellent Shiosai sushi bar.

ENTERTAINMENT. The Dolphin Hall has a proscenium-arched stage, wooden dance floor, and seating on both the main and balcony levels of this two-deck-high room. There's social dancing, with gentlemen hosts available as partners, and a rich program of lecturers and musicians.

SPA/FITNESS. The Terraké Spa includes beauty and nail treatment rooms, three body treatment rooms, and a small fitness room. There's a traditional Japanese Grand Bath (one for women, one for men, open until 1am), with washing stations and a sauna. Adjacent is a sports massage room.

Noordam
★★★★

Size:................................Large Resort Ship	Crew/Passenger Ratio (lower beds/all berths):.........2.3/2.9
Tonnage: 82,318	Cabins (total):......................................959
Lifestyle: ....Premium	Size range (sq ft/m): 170.0–1,318.6/15.7–122.5
Cruise line:...................... Holland America Line	Cabins (outside view):...............................806
Former names: ....none	Cabins (interior/no view):...........................153
IMO number: 9230115	Cabins (for one person):..............................0
Builder: .... Fincantieri (Italy)	Cabins (with private balcony):.......................641
Original cost:..............................$400 million	Cabins (wheelchair accessible): 28
Entered service:......................... Feb 2006	Wheelchair accessibility:..........................Good
Registry:..........................The Netherlands	Cabin voltage: .... 110 volts
Length (ft/m):........................... 935.0/285.0	Elevators:..14
Beam (ft/m):............................. 105.6/32.25	Casino (gaming tables):.............................Yes
Draft (ft/m): 25.5/7.8	Slot machines:....................................Yes
Propulsion/Propellers: ...diesel-electric (34,000kW)/2 azimuthing	Swimming pools:.................. 2 (1/sliding glass dome)
pods (17.6MW each)	Hot tubs (on deck):..................................5
Passenger decks:.................................11	Self-service launderette:...........................No
Total crew:.......................................820	Dedicated cinema/seats:............................Yes
Passengers (lower beds/alll berths):............. 1,918/2,457	Library:...Yes
Passenger Space Ratio (lower beds/all berths): 42.9/33.4	Onboard currency: ....US$

Dutch decor, traditions, and comfort for mature-age cruisers

OVERVIEW. *Noordam* offers a wide range of public rooms with a reasonably intimate atmosphere and the overall feel of the ship is quite homely and comforting, with fresh flowers everywhere, as well as some nicely showcased Dutch artifacts from the 16th and 17th centuries.

THE SHIP. *Noordam*, with 35 cabins more than its close sisters *Oosterdam*, *Westerdam*, and *Zuiderdam*, is one of the Vista-class of ships in the Holland America Line fleet, designed to appeal to multi-generational holidaymakers. The twin working funnels are the result of the slightly unusual machinery configuration; the ship has, in effect, two engine rooms – one with three diesels, and one with two diesels and a gas turbine. A pod propulsion system is provided, so there's no vibration.

There is a complete walk-around exterior teak promenade deck, with teak steamer-style sunloungers. A jogging track outdoors is located around the mast and the forward third of the ship. Exterior glass elevators provide fine ocean views from any one of 10 decks. One of the two swimming pools outdoors can be used in inclement weather due to its retractable sliding glass roof. Two hot tubs, adjacent to the swimming pools, are abridged by a bar. There's also a small swimming pool for children.

The intimate lobby spans three decks, and is topped by a beautiful, rotating, Waterford Crystal globe of the world. Adjacent are interior and glass wall elevators with exterior views. The information

Berlitz's Ratings

	Possible	Achieved
Ship	500	391
Accommodation	200	150
Food	400	270
Service	400	274
Entertainment	100	71
Cruise	400	288

OVERALL SCORE
1444 points out of 2000

desk (on the lobby's lowest level) is small and somewhat removed from the main passenger flow on the two decks above it.

The interior decor is bright in many areas, and the ceilings are particularly noticeable. A large collection of artwork is a standard feature, and pieces reflect the history of the former Dutch East Indies.

There are two whole entertainment/public room decks, the most dramatic space being a showlounge spanning four decks in the forward section. Other facilities include a winding shopping street with several boutique stores and logo shops, card room, an art gallery, photo gallery, and several small meetings rooms. The large casino is equipped with an array of gaming paraphernalia and slot machines, and you have to walk through it to get from the restaurant to the showlounge.

Explorations is a combination coffee bar (where coffees and other drinks cost extra), lounge, extensive library, and Internet center – it's a popular area for relaxation and reading, although noise from the coffee machine can interrupt concentration.

On other decks (lower down), you'll find a Queens Lounge, which acts as a lecture room a Culinary Arts Center, where cooking demonstrations and cooking classes are held. Naturally, a bar is close at hand – it's at the back of the room.

Gratuities are automatically added to your onboard account. Passenger niggles? These include noisy cabin air conditioning – the flow can't be regulated or turned off, the only regulation being for temperature control. Also, several pillars obstruct the passenger flow and lines of sight throughout the ship. There are no self-service launderettes, although special laundry packages are available.

FAMILIES. Club HAL's KidZone provides a whole area dedicated to children's facilities and extensive programming for different age groups (five to 17), with one counselor for every 30 children. Free ice cream is provided at certain hours, plus hot hors d'oeuvres in all bars. Some cabins have interconnecting doors.

ACCOMMODATION. There are numerous price categories: 16 outside-view and eight interior. The views from some cabins on the lowest accommodation deck (Main Deck) are obstructed by lifeboats. Some cabins that can accommodate a third and fourth person have very little closet space, and only one personal safe. Occupants of suites get exclusive use of the Neptune Lounge and concierge service, priority embarkation and disembarkation, and other benefits. In many of the suites/cabins with private balconies, the balconies are not so private and can be overlooked from various public locations.

Penthouse Verandah Suites (2). These offer the largest accommodation (1,318 sq ft/123 sq m, including balcony). These have a separate bedroom with a king-size bed; there's also a walk-in closet, dressing room, living room, dining room, butler's pantry, mini-bar and refrigerator, and private balcony. The main bathroom has a large whirlpool tub, two washbasins, toilet, and plenty of storage space for toiletries. Personalized stationery and free dry cleaning are included, as are hot hors d'oeuvres and other goodies daily.

DeLuxe Verandah Suites (60). These suites measure 563 sq ft (53 sq m). They have twin beds that convert to a king-size bed, vanity desk, lounge area, walk-in closet, mini-bar and refrigerator, and bathroom with full-size tub, washbasin, and toilet. Personalized stationery and complimentary dry cleaning are included, as are hot hors d'oeuvres and other goodies.

Verandah Suites (100). Actually they are cabins, not suites, and measure 284 sq ft (26 sq m). Twin beds can convert to a queen-size bed. There is also a lounge area, mini-bar, and refrigerator, while the bathroom has a tub, washbasin, and toilet. Floor-to-ceiling windows open onto a private balcony.

Outside-view Cabins. Standard outside cabins (197 sq ft/18 sq m) have twin beds that can convert to a queen-size bed. There's a small sitting area, while the bathroom has a tub/shower combination. The interior cabins are slightly smaller (183 sq ft/17 sq m).

Niggles include noisy cabin air conditioning – the flow can't be regulated or turned off; the only regulation is for temperature control.

DINING. The 1,045-seat Vista Dining Room is two decks high, with seating at tables for two, four, six, or eight on both main and balcony levels, and is at the stern. It provides a traditional Holland America Line dining experience, with friendly service from smiling Indonesian and Filipino stewards. Both open seating and assigned seating are available for dinner, while breakfast and lunch are open-seating – you'll be seated by restaurant staff when you enter.

Holland America Line can provide Kosher meals (if requested when you book), although these are prepared ashore, then frozen, and brought to your table sealed in their original containers.

Other dining options. The 148-seat Pinnacle Grill is a more upscale dining spot, with higher quality ingredients and better presentation than in the larger main dining room. On Lower Promenade Deck, it fronts onto the second level of the atrium lobby; tables along its outer section are open to it and can suffer from noise from the Atrium Bar one deck below, though these tables are good for those who like to see and be seen. Pacific Northwest cuisine is featured, with items such as sesame-crusted halibut with ginger-miso, and an array of premium-quality steaks. The wine list includes some fine wines from around the world, including many gorgeous Bordeaux reds. Reservations are required, and there is a cover charge.

For casual eating, there is an extensive Lido Café, an eatery that wraps around the funnel, with indoor-outdoor seating and ocean views. It includes several sections including a salad bar, stir-fry and sushi section, deli sandwiches, and a dessert buffet, although lines can form for made-to-order items.

An outdoor grill bar adjacent to the Lido pool has fast food such as hamburgers, veggie burgers, hot dogs, chicken, and fries. On certain days, barbecues and other culinary specialties are available poolside.

ENTERTAINMENT. The 867-seat Vista Lounge is the venue for Las Vegas-style revues and major cabaret shows. The main floor level has a bar in its starboard aft section. Spiral stairways at the back of the lounge connect all levels. Stage shows are best seen from the upper levels, from where the sight lines are quite good.

SPA/FITNESS. The Greenhouse Spa, a large, two-decks-high health spa, is located directly above the navigation bridge. Facilities include a solarium, hydrotherapy pool, unisex thermal suite – a unisex area incorporating a Laconium (gentle sauna), Hammam (mild steam), and Chamomile Grotto (small aromatic steam room).

There is a beauty salon, 11 private massage/therapy rooms (including one for couples) for body pampering treatments, and a large gymnasium with floor-to-ceiling windows on three sides and forward-facing ocean views, and the latest high-tech muscle-toning equipment. Sports enthusiasts can enjoy a basketball court, volleyball court, and a golf simulator.

Norwegian Breakaway
★★★★

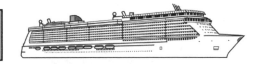

Size:.	.Large Resort Ship	Cabins (total):.	1,994
Tonnage:	145,655	Size range (sq ft/m):	n/a
Lifestyle:	Standard	Cabins (outside view):	1,545
Cruise line:.	Norwegian Cruise Line	Cabins (interior/no view):.	449
Former names:	none	Cabins (for one person):.	59
IMO number:	9606912	Cabins (with private balcony):.	1,252
Builder:	Meyer Werft (Germany)	Cabins (wheelchair accessible):	40
Original cost:	€600 million	Wheelchair accessibility:	Good
Entered service:.	Apr 2013	Cabin voltage:	110 volts
Registry:.	The Bahamas	Elevators:.	16
Length (ft/m):.	1,066.2/325.0	Casino (gaming tables):.	Yes
Beam (ft/m):.	133.0/40.5	Slot machines:.	Yes
Draft (ft/m):	27.8/8.5	Swimming pools:.	5
Propulsion/Propellers:.	diesel-electric (79,800kW)/2	Hot tubs (on deck):.	9
Passenger decks:.	15	Self-service launderette:	No
Total crew:.	1,595	Dedicated cinema/seats:.	No
Passengers (lower beds/all berths):	3,998	Library:	No
Passenger Space Ratio (lower beds/all berths):	36.4/36.4	Onboard currency:	US$
Crew/Passenger Ratio (lower beds/all berths):	2.5/3.1		

Über-casual, multi-choice playground for the family

OVERVIEW. *Norwegian Breakaway* really is a ship for young, trendy, and edgy urbanites. It provides families with children, single parents, couples, and solo travelers with a mountain of entertainment choices, in an environment that is a pure playground for an active, entertaining cruise vacation.

THE SHIP. *Norwegian Breakaway* has a more streamlined and a better, more balanced profile than its slightly larger sister ship, *Norwegian Epic*, with a less boxy look to its front upper forward section. The colorful, signature artwork on the lower front section of the hull depicting the city of New York was created by Peter Max, the popular American illustrator and graphic artist.

Families with children really enjoy the pool deck facilities like the Aqua Park, with five huge water slides, a large rock-climbing wall and rappelling wall, and a rope and scaffold-like walking course – with a small section that extends over the side of the ship. Aft is a large movie screen with amphitheater-style seating in an adults-only area called Spice H20.

Despite the ship's size, however, the open deck space for sunbathing is rather tight, and made smaller by the 'exclusive' 'Haven' area in the forward section, whose suites-only occupants (pay more, get more) are given enough sunbathing space, bar, pool, hot tubs, all in a beach-club-like setting. The rest of the ship shares multiple pools and water-fun exterior decks, designed for families and children.

Berlitz's Ratings

	Possible	Achieved
Ship	500	391
Accommodation	200	149
Food	400	248
Service	400	275
Entertainment	100	82
Cruise	400	285

OVERALL SCORE
1430 points out of 2000

Lower down, on an outdoor promenade deck, a 'Waterfront' boardwalk-style outdoor area with bar and eateries brings you more in contact with the sea. It forms part of the outdoor experience, and away from the hubbub of the family-friendly sun/sports action deck atop the ship.

Inside, the decor is decidedly more traditional and provides a more restful, relaxed feel and ambience – although this is all relative and it's still rather upbeat and jazzy.

Careful planning and time management will be needed to make the most of this large resort ship and all it has to offer. So it's really worth spending time to decide what you want to get out of your cruise vacation before you board the ship – which sort of negates the 'freestyle' aspect of a large resort ship cruise – still, it's all about choice.

Most of the public rooms, shops, entertainment spots, the large casino (gaming tables and slots), and a number of the 12 bars and 17 themed dining venues are located on decks 6, 7 and 8 – a three-deck area complex called 678 Ocean Place.

A venue that proved popular aboard other NCL ships is Bliss Ultra Lounge, a decadent venue (think late-night SoHo, minus the muggers and deadbeats).

The ship's home port is New York. Indeed, Norwegian Breakaway is the largest cruise ship ever to home-port in the Big Apple. Gratuities (called a 'service charge') are charged to your onboard account, or you can pre-pay on-line. Bar purchases incur a 15 percent gratuity; spa treatments are an eye-popping 18 percent.

FAMILIES. Facilities for kids and teens are pretty large and varied, and are spread over two decks; there's Splash Academy for kids and a separate Entourage space for teens. Nickelodeon is the family entertainment brand on all cruises, as part of NCL's children's programming.

Splash Academy is close to the family-friendly accommodation and provides areas for three age groups. Babies and toddlers have their own play space and parent-involving activities. At the Splash Academy reception area, tablet-based electronic registration allows parents to swipe their keycard and input a password to sign in their children.

Just past the reception area, the three- to five-year-olds (Guppies) have their own brightly decorated space, complete with child-sized furniture. In a separate zone, six- to nine-year-olds (Turtles) have building block activity centers, an interactive dance mat with corresponding large video screen, video game stations and a video viewing lounge.

Upstairs, 10- to 12-year-olds (Seas) get a multipurpose dance space with a touch-screen jukebox, moveable tables for activities, and bean bags for lounging; an activity zone includes arts and crafts items, and a 'hang out' area stocked with the latest video games.

Entourage, for ages 13–17 (Dolphins) has air hockey, foosball, and an arcade with five separate large-screen areas to play the latest video games while lounging on sofas. It becomes a teen nightclub with a dance floor and video jukebox in the evenings.

ACCOMMODATION. Having learned a lot from its innovative big sister *Norwegian Epic*, NCL has made some sensible changes that should please many of its regulars. The 'wavy' cabin design has been modified, and the former separated bathroom has been reworked into a more traditional design, which is much more practical.

The Haven. The more exclusive accommodation is located in a two-deck-high section called The Haven – really a 'ship within a ship.' It consists of 42 suites on decks 15 and 16 forward, and includes a private restaurant, a cocktail bar, and a concierge desk where passengers can relax, have a drink, and make dining, entertainment, and spa reservations through the dedicated concierge. There is a private pool, changing areas, two hot tubs, gym, saunas, two private massage rooms, and sun deck with bar. The Haven occupants get private access to the spa and fitness center, as well as 24-hour butler service, and in-suite, white-tablecloth dining service. Suite occupants get a platinum key card and priority reservations for all the restaurants, spa, and entertainment venues.

The top suites within The Haven are two Deluxe Owner's Suites, with their contemporary skyscraper apartment look – including an elegant living room and dining area with wet bar. The bedroom has a king-size bed with pillow-top mattress that faces floor-to-ceiling windows and an extra-spacious wraparound private balcony. The bathroom has an oversize tub, two vanity sinks, and a luxury shower. The Deluxe Owner's Suites can be joined to the Owner's Suites, creating one grand suite that can sleep up to eight.

The 21 two-bedroom Family Villas have two bathrooms as well as two bedrooms. The separate living room and dining area includes a single sofa bed, writing desk, and bar. The master bedroom has a king-size bed, floor-to-ceiling windows, and a private balcony. The master bath includes an oversize oval tub that looks out to the sea. The second bedroom includes a double sofa bed and bathroom.

Also in The Haven are 17 Courtyard Penthouses, with a king-size bed, living and dining area, a single sofa bed, writing desk, and ample storage spaces. On other (non-Haven) decks throughout the ship are eight aft-facing penthouses and 10 forward-facing penthouses.

Other accommodation. There are 15 Spa mini-suite rooms and 28 Spa balcony cabins, all with easy access to the adjacent spa and its facilities. While most outside-view cabins have a balcony, some have only windows, but all have flat-screen televisions, satellite-linked telephone, and private bathroom. There are also 42 Family 'suites' with ocean views.

Balcony suites/cabins have rich wood-look paneling with warm tones and accent colors. Each balcony cabin has a king-size bed that can be made into twins, with a pillow-top mattress set against a chestnut leather headboard cushioned and tufted to make reading and sitting up in bed more comfortable. There's a lighted recess above the bed for books, magazines, tablet computers, or electronic reading devices. Each room has a sofa bed with additional storage. A built-in 26-inch flat-screen television is mounted on the wall and tilts so it can be seen from the sofa or the bed. Underneath the television is another recessed nook to hold cruise information, books, and magazines. A built-in vanity area has shelving and abundant storage space. LED lighting surrounds the perimeter of the ceiling to give the room warmth. There is also a full-size closet that is easily accessible with sliding doors. The cabins are energy-efficient, using key card access to control lighting in the room.

The balcony bathroom features a contemporary, clean design, ensuring more generous and comfortable space. There are several rich-wood shelves to help reduce clutter and keep everything within easy reach. There's an enclosed vanity underneath the washbasin that hides the trash bin, along with more storage. The built-in washbasin is size-generous and has an easy-to-use faucet. A private shower with a shaving bar for ladies completes the picture. Mini-suite bathrooms get a rain shower plus a hand-held shower hose.

There are 59 studio (single-occupancy) cabins. They are colorful, hip, trendy, and capsule-hotel small, with minimalist design – especially for closet space. Still this is a neat way to cruise solo – just don't bring many clothes

The many interior cabins also have one or two additional upper berths, while the lower beds are twins that convert to a queen-size bed – good for families with young children.

DINING. There are many food-themed restaurants (the largest of which, Savor, and Taste are like main dining rooms), dining venues, and casual eateries to choose from. This means that you'll need to make reservations in whichever venue you want to eat, so you'll need to be prepared for a bit of planning and waiting – just like you would ashore. However, if you want to see a show in the evening, then your dining time will really be dictated by the time of the show, which rather limits your choice. The good news is that the wall-based touch-screen reservations systems work well, so you see instantly how long you may have to wait if your chosen restaurant is fully booked.

Other dining options. The Manhattan Room is the ship's equivalent of a main restaurant (it is included in the fare); it is large, with an integral dance floor and large ocean-view windows aft. Other dining venues (Cagney's Steakhouse and Moderno Currascaria) are located one deck above, and have a view into the Manhattan Room.

Because the lifeboats hang over the side of the ship's hull, and not inboard (as is normal), a whole promenade deck has become an oceanfront extension of the eateries on the inside, thus creating a New York sidewalk-style experience, called The Waterfront.

Inside, Geoffrey Zakarian's 678 Ocean Place (meaning decks 6, 7, and 8) connects with several interior extra-cost dining venues as well as the extensive Breakaway Casino, cigar smoking room, and several entertainment venues. These include Moderno Churrascaria, a Brazilian-style steakhouse with table-side carved meat service by 'passadores,' and a salad bar; Cagney's Steakhouse, a classic American steakhouse, with open kitchen; La Cucina, for Italian family food with a focus on Tuscany, with inside seating; or for alfresco eating on The Waterfront, Maltings (bar) and Ocean Blu by Geoffrey Zakarian – NCL's first à la carte all-seafood and raw bar eatery – designed and overseen by the popular Food Network chef. The ingredients and techniques that he employs in his land-based establishments are featured here, too.

Other venues include Le Bistro, for classic French-style cuisine; a 96-seat Teppanyaki restaurant with 12 flat-top grills and a lot of show (yes, food can be entertaining), complete with Japanese rock garden with bamboo plants and bonsai trees; and Cirque Dreams and Dinner, a big-top, circus-like dining spot with a Cirque Dreams and Dinner show (it's a lively, action-filled supper club). All are extra-cost, and reservations are required.

Casual eateries, at no extra cost, include O'Sheehan's Neighborhood Bar & Grill, a sports bar and popular fast-food joint, with a big screen for sporting events, miniature bowling alley, pool and air hockey tables, and interactive games; the Atrium Café and Bar, for coffees and pastries; and Shanghai's Noodle Bar, for Chinese-style noodle dishes.

Garden Café is an extremely large, self-serve buffet, with indoor and outdoor seating. It's open round the clock. Many different counters provide themed and ethnic food varieties, and there's a special section for kids, too.

ENTERTAINMENT. The two-deck-high Breakaway Theater, located at the front of the ship, is a fine large showlounge, where all the major production shows and mainline cabaret acts are presented.

NCL has always been at the forefront for creativity in entertainment. So, in a cruise industry first, the company has pulled out of its hat an 'Illusionarium' – a theatre of magic and illusions. This envelopes you in the fascinating and mystical world of magic and invites you to experience the astonishing illusions of world-class magicians and fascinating special effects. The experience is the result of a collaboration between NCL's entertainment department and Broadway director/choreographer Patricia Wilcox, Tony Award winning scenic designer David Gallo and veteran magician Jeff Hobson. The show's design is inspired by the science fiction of Jules Verne, the artistry of legendary magicians such as Houdini and the popularity of recent blockbusters featuring supernatural characters. Whether you can get your water changed into wine remains to be seen.

Meanwhile, the popular Blue Man group, first introduced aboard *Norwegian Epic* to great acclaim and very entertaining for the whole family, forms part of the offering here, too.

Celebrity look-alike shows are presented in the Manhattan Room. These conjure up the likes of Elvis, Janet Jackson, Madonna, Neil Diamond, Tina Turner, and others, are also part of the entertainment line-up. They are produced by Legends in Concert, a Las Vegas company that has provided shows for The Strip for over 25 years.

Jazz and blues devotees should enjoy the Fat Cats Jazz & Blues Club – an intimate room that's often standing room only – when the live jazzers are jammin' away in a really cool place.

SPA/FITNESS. The spa and fitness center is spread over two decks and houses a warehouse-size gymnasium. The complex includes an extra-cost thermal suite (herbal rainshowers, saunas and steam rooms, relaxation area with hot-tile beds), a salt room, a beauty salon, and multiple body treatment rooms, including massage rooms for couples.

Norwegian Dawn
★★★+

Size:.	.Large Resort Ship
Tonnage:	91,740
Lifestyle:	Standard
Cruise line:	Norwegian Cruise Line
Former names:	none
IMO number:	9195169
Builder:	Meyer Werft (Germany)
Original cost:	$400 million
Entered service:	Oct 2002
Registry:	Bahamas
Length (ft/m):	964.9/294.1
Beam (ft/m):	105.6/32.2
Draft (ft/m):	26.9/8.2
Propulsion/Propellers:	diesel-electric/2 azimuthing pods
Passenger decks:	11
Total crew:	1,069
Passengers (lower beds/alll berths):	2,476/3,072
Passenger Space Ratio (lower beds/all berths):	36.7/29.6
Crew/Passenger Ratio (lower beds/all berths):	2.3/2.8

Cabins (total):	1238
Size range (sq ft/m):	142.0–5,350.0/13.2–497.0
Cabins (outside view):	847
Cabins (interior/no view):	393
Cabins (for one person):	0
Cabins (with private balcony):	511
Cabins (wheelchair accessible):	20
Wheelchair accessibility:	Best
Cabin voltage:	110 volts
Elevators:	12
Casino (gaming tables):	Yes
Slot machines:	Yes
Swimming pools:	3
Hot tubs (on deck):	2
Self-service launderette:	No
Dedicated cinema/seats:	No
Library:	Yes
Onboard currency:	US$

A large casual ship for lively, family-friendly cruising

OVERVIEW. Plenty of choices, including many dining options, add up to a very attractive holiday package, particularly suitable for families with children, in a contemporary floating leisure center that provides ample facilities for you to have an enjoyable time. Despite the company's name, Norwegian Cruise Line, there's almost nothing Norwegian about this product, except for some senior officers.

Berlitz's Ratings

	Possible	Achieved
Ship	500	370
Accommodation	200	145
Food	400	240
Service	400	273
Entertainment	100	67
Cruise	400	275
OVERALL SCORE		
1370 points out of 2000		

THE SHIP. *Norwegian Dawn*, sister to *Norwegian Star*, was built in 64 sections and has a pod propulsion system. The hull displays interesting logos on top of its white paint, depicting the ship's itineraries: the port side features the cruise itinerary from New York to the Bahamas and Florida, while the starboard side features the winter itinerary from Miami to the Caribbean. Dolphins, the Statue of Liberty, and representations of the four original paintings displayed on board: the Impressionists Matisse, Renoir, and Van Gogh, and the pop artist Andy Warhol. It is a colorful concept, and makes the ship easy to spot in a sea of similar-sized ships in port.

In 2011, some 58 additional suites/cabins were added, which makes the ship more crowded and dining venues a little busier. In general, the ship absorbs passengers well, but the open deck space has become more congested.

Facilities include a large Dawn Club Casino gaming area, an Internet café with 24 computers, a 1,150-seat showlounge, a 3,000-book library, a card room, a writing and study room, a business center, conference and meeting rooms, and a large retail shopping complex.

While the initial cruise fare seems very reasonable, the extra costs and charges soon mount up if you want to sample more than the basics. With many dining choices, some costing extra, your overall experience will be determined by how much you are prepared to spend. You will need to plan where to eat well in advance, and make reservations. The dress code is very casual – no jacket and tie needed, although you are welcome to dress formally if you so wish.

The ship is full of revenue centers designed to help part you from your money. You can expect to be subjected to a stream of flyers advertising daily art auctions, 'designer' watches, 'inch of gold/silver,' and other promotions.

A non-changeable per person service charge is automatically added to your account daily for staff gratuities; 15 percent is also added for bar charges, and a whopping 18 percent for spa treatments.

Music played in some areas bleeds through into others; for example, Latin music played in Salsas on the second level of the lobby is heard throughout the lobby and the Internet café on the third level of the lobby and is most disconcerting. Communication, particularly between passengers and some of the Asian staff, is weak. Standing in line for embarkation, disembarkation, shore tenders, and for self-serve buffet meals is an inevitable aspect of cruising aboard all large ships.

FAMILIES. A good deal of space is devoted to children's facilities such as the T-Rex Kids' Center and Teen Club. All are tucked well away from adult recreation areas, at the aft end. Children of all ages will get to play in a superb wet 'n' wild space-themed water park, complete with large pool, water slide, and paddle pool. There's a room full of cots for toddlers to use for sleepovers, and even the toilets are at a special low height. Teens, too, are well catered for, and get their own cinema (with DVD movies), discotheque with dance floor, and their own hot tub. Some cabins have interconnecting doors – good for families with children.

ACCOMMODATION. Although the suites and junior suites are quite spacious, the standard interior and outside-view cabins are very small when compared to those of other major cruise lines such as Carnival or Celebrity, particularly when occupied by three or four persons; the bathrooms, however, are decently sized and have large shower enclosures. There are many different price grades.

All cabins have tea- and coffee-making sets – but only coffee creamer is provided, so tea drinkers who want fresh milk need to arrange this with their steward, or call room service. All cabins also have rich cherry wood cabinetry, bathroom with sliding door and separate toilet, shower enclosure and washbasin compartments, and European duvets. The private balconies of the top suites have teak decks, while most other cabins with balconies have a Bolidt (rubberized sand-like) deck, and smoked glass/wood rail panels that provide good sight lines. Audio channels are on the in-cabin TV system, but you cannot turn off the picture. Elemis personal amenities are provided.

Garden Villas (2). The largest living spaces, Vista and Horizon, sit high atop the ship in a pod located forward of the funnel, and overlooking the main swimming pool and recreation deck. These villas have huge glass walls and landscaped private roof gardens for outdoor dining – with whirlpool tubs, naturally – and huge private sunbathing areas completely shielded from anyone. Each has three bedrooms and bathrooms, and a large living room overlooking the lido/pool deck. These units have their own private elevator access and private stairway. Each measures 5,350 sq ft (497 sq m) and can be combined to create a huge, double-size 'house' measuring 10,700 sq ft (994 sq m), including a private outdoor Italian garden. Butler service is provided.

Owner's Suites (4). Located in the very front of the ship, each measures 750 sq ft (70 sq m). Two are nestled under the enclosed navigation bridge wings on Deck 11, and the other two are in the equivalent space on the deck below. They have an entrance with wooden door front, large lounge/dining room, and separate bedroom with king-size bed beneath a mirrored ceiling, and TV set with integral DVD player.

The bathroom – almost as large as a standard cabin – has a full-size tub with shower and TV; separate shower enclosure, separate toilet, and a dressing area with his-and-hers walk-in closets. There are forward-facing (open) and side-facing (enclosed) private balconies. Butler service is provided. If you don't need the entertaining space of the Garden Villas, these suites are delightful living spaces. However, they do suffer occasionally from noise generated in Spinnaker's nightclub/disco on the deck above. Each Owner's Suite can also be interconnected to a Penthouse Suite and balcony cabin – useful for large families when parents value privacy.

Penthouse Suites (30). Each measures 366 sq ft/34 sq m. Facilities include a bedroom with queen-size bed, walk-in closet, living room with dining table, and bathroom with separate shower enclosure and tub. Penthouse Suites on Deck 11 can be interconnected to a children's cabin with double sofa bed and a pull-down Pullman-style bed, separate bathroom and shower enclosure. These suites also have a private balcony and butler service.

Romance Suites (4). Each measures 288 sq ft (27 sq m). They include a separate bedroom with queen-size bed, a sitting area with double sofa bed, and living and dining areas. The bathroom has a full-size tub and shower. There is a private balcony.

Mini Suites (107). These measure 229 sq ft (21 sq m), and each has two lower beds that convert to a queen-size bed, and a sitting area with double sofa bed. The bathroom has a full-size tub and shower. Floor-to-ceiling windows open onto a private balcony.

All suites are well furnished, most in rich cherry wood, although closet space in some of the smaller units is tight. Some suites have extras like a trouser press, and a full range of toiletries. Suites also get butlers, who can serve all meals en suite from the menus of a number of restaurants.

Although nicely furnished and quite well equipped, the standard outside-view and interior cabins are quite small, particularly for three or four people. Many cabins have third- and fourth-person pull-down berths or trundle beds.

A small room service menu is available; non-food items cost extra, and a 15 percent service charge and a gratuity are added to your account. Bottled water is placed in each cabin, but you are charged if you open the bottle.

DINING. With Freestyle Dining, you can choose which restaurant to eat in, at what time, and with whom – there are no assigned dining rooms, tables, or seats. While this is fine in theory, in practice it means that you have to make reservations for a specific time, so 'freestyle dining' actually turns out to be programmed dining.

Other dining options. Apart from three principal dining rooms, there are a number of other themed eateries, giving a wide range of choice – though some cost extra and require advance reservations. Two entire decks are filled with 10 restaurants and eateries. NCL's dress code states that 'jeans, T-shirts, tank tops, and bare feet are not permitted in restaurants.'

Venetian: the first main dining room (seats 472) offers traditional six-course dining (open 5:30pm–midnight). It is located aft, with good views over the ship's stern – at least in the daytime – although the sight lines from some seats are obstructed by 14 pillars. The room has a baby grand piano. If you want a quieter table, choose one of two wings in the forward section near the entrance/steps.

Aqua: the second main dining room seats 344 and offers traditional six-courses from 5:30pm to midnight.

Impressions: the third main dining room, seating 236, offers lighter cuisine from 5:30pm to midnight. The waiter stations are too close to the tables and are very noisy.

Bamboo (a Taste of Asia): a Japanese/Thai/Chinese restaurant, with 140 seats, has a sit-up conveyor-belt style sushi/sashimi bar, sake bar, show galley, and separate room with a teppanyaki grill. In the evenings, music from Gatsby's lounge/bar on the deck below completely fills the restaurant through an open lobby-like well, and a quiet meal is almost impossible. All items cost extra and there is an 'all you can eat' sushi charge of $10.

Le Bistro: a French restaurant with 72 seats, serving nouvelle cuisine. The decor includes four Impressionist paintings on loan from the private collection of the chairman of Star Cruises, NCL's parent company, although they don't really match the room's decor. There's a cover charge and also a line for you to add an extra gratuity – very cheeky. But it's the best food on board and worth the extra cost.

Blue Lagoon: a food court-style eatery with 68 seats serves hamburgers, fish and chips, pot pies, and wok fast dishes.

Garden Café: an indoor/outdoor self-serve buffet (seats 490). It includes 'action stations' with made-to-order omelets, waffles, fruit, soups, ethnic specialties, and pasta.

Salsa: a Spanish tapas eatery and bar (seats 112) with a selection of hot and cold tapas dishes and authentic entertainment, located on the second level of the atrium lobby.

La Trattoria: located inside the indoor/outdoor buffet (seats 162); serves pasta, pizza, and other Italian fare.

Cagney's Steak House: arranged atop the ship seats 112, incorporates a show kitchen, and serves US prime steaks and seafood. Be prepared for large portions. Reservations are required and a cover charge applies.

Other eating/drinking spots include the Pearly Kings, an English pub for draft beer and perhaps a game of darts; Havanas, a cigar and cognac lounge;

Java, an atrium lobby café and bar (hot and frozen coffees, teas, and pastries); a Beer Garden (grilled foods); a Gelato Bar (ice cream); and a Gym and Spa Bar (health food snacks and drinks).

ENTERTAINMENT. The 1,037-seat Stardust Theatre is the venue for colorful Las Vegas-style production shows and major cabaret acts. It is designed in the style of an opera house, spans three decks, and has a steeply tiered main floor and port and starboard balconies. There are three production shows in a typical seven-day cruise, ably performed by the Jean Ann Ryan Company. These are very colorful, high-energy, razzle-dazzle shows with much use of pyrotechnics, lasers, and color-mover lighting. They're not particularly memorable but they are very entertaining.

A number of bands and solo entertaining musicians provide live music for listening and dancing in several lounges and bars. Throughout the ship, loud Latin music prevails. In Spinnakers Lounge nightclub, a Pachanga Party (a Miami South Beach rave) is held each cruise.

SPA/FITNESS. Wellness devotees should enjoy the two-deck-high El Dorado health spa complex, operated by the Steiner-owned and Hawaii-based Mandara Spa. Located at the stern, it has large ocean-view windows on three sides. There are many facilities and services, almost all at extra cost, including Thai massage in the spa, outdoors on deck, in your cabin, or on your private balcony.

There is an indoor lap pool measuring 37 ft (11 m), a hydrotherapy pool, two sit-in deep tubs, aromatherapy and wellness centers, and mud treatment rooms (there are 15 treatment rooms in all, including one specifically designed for couples). The fitness and exercise rooms, with the latest Cybex muscle-pumping equipment, are located not within the spa, but at the top of the glass-domed atrium lobby. Included is a room for exercycle classes. Some classes, such as Pathway to Yoga, Body Cycling Class, and Body Beat Class (cardio kickboxing), cost extra.

Recreational sports facilities include a jogging track, golf driving range, basketball and volleyball courts, as well as four levels of sunbathing decks.

Norwegian Epic
★★★★

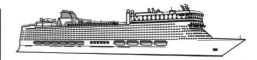

Size:..................................Large Resort Ship			Cabins (total):....................................... 2,100	
Tonnage: 155,873			Size range (sq ft/m): 850.3–100.1/79–9.3	
Lifestyle: ....Standard			Cabins (outside view):................................ 1,415	
Cruise line:.........................Norwegian Cruise Line			Cabins (interior/no view):...............................685	
Former names: ....none			Cabins (for one person):................................128	
IMO number: 9410569			Cabins (with private balcony):........................ 1,415	
Builder: ....STX Europe (France)			Cabins (wheelchair accessible): 42	
Original cost:............................... $735 million			Wheelchair accessibility:............................Good	
Entered service:................................. Jun 2010			Cabin voltage: .... 110 volts	
Registry:.. Panama			Elevators:...16	
Length (ft/m):.............................1,080.7/329.4			Casino (gaming tables):............................... Yes	
Beam (ft/m):................................ 133.0/40.5			Slot machines:....................................... Yes	
Draft (ft/m):.................................... 28.5/8.6			Swimming pools:..5	
Propulsion/Propellers:............ diesel-electric (79,800kW)/2			Hot tubs (on deck):....................................9	
Passenger decks:.....................................15			Self-service launderette:...............................No	
Total crew:...................................... 1,730			Dedicated cinema/seats:...............................No	
Passengers (lower beds/alll berths): 4,200/5,400			Library: ....Yes	
Passenger Space Ratio (lower beds/all berths): 37.1/28.8			Onboard currency: ....US$	
Crew/Passenger Ratio (lower beds/all berths):.......... 2.4/3.1				

An epic-sized, family-friendly, multiple-choice ship

OVERVIEW. *Norwegian Epic* is a blast for youthful adults, and kids alike. It's all about lifestyle – bistro eateries, lots of dining choices, color and noise, the perceived über-chic South Beach nightlife at sea, stuffed with entertainment.

THE SHIP. *Norwegian Epic* is perhaps the most extreme example of 'all-exclusive' cruising, and is a throwback to the days when First Class, Cabin Class, and Tourist Class meant passengers could not access certain areas of the ship – the familiar 'pay more, get more' philosophy.

The largest ship ever constructed in STX Europe's French shipyard, in St Nazaire, *Norwegian Epic* is just a tad larger than *Queen Mary 2*. Its profile isn't very handsome because several decks above the navigation bridge make it look really top-heavy, like a square lump of cheese. But the two side-by-side funnels – between which is a 60-ft (18-m) wide rock climbing wall – bring some semblance of balance. The ship is about 30 percent wider than the Norwegian Jewel-class ships, and is a prototype for NCL.

The pool deck has an Aqua Park, with three major water slides – one involves inner tubes that give you a spin before spitting you out into a big bowl, reminiscent of a washing machine. Aft is a large movie screen with amphitheater-style seating, and a nightclub within an area called Spice H2O, which also includes a sun deck. However, despite the ship's size, the open deck space for sunbathing is extremely small and cramped – much diminished by the 'exclusive'

Berlitz's Ratings		
	Possible	Achieved
Ship	500	384
Accommodation	200	145
Food	400	248
Service	400	275
Entertainment	100	82
Cruise	400	285
OVERALL SCORE		
1419 points out of 2000		

Courtyard block in the forward section, whose occupants do have enough sunbathing space.

The three lowest passenger decks contain the main entertainment venues, restaurants and other dining venues, show lounges, and a large casino. Some spaces open to two or three decks in height to create an illusion of space – like mini-atriums, but the overall flow is disjointed and invites congestion, particularly around a casino walk-through area. A dramatic three-deck-high chandelier in the lobby is the largest at sea.

Two escalators do nothing to diminish congestion – they even encourage gridlock at peak times. Sandwiched between these three lower entertainment decks and the upper entertainment decks are seven decks mainly comprised of accommodation units. Something new for NCL is a bridge viewing room, just behind the navigation bridge.

NCL will extract more money from you with a number of 'exclusive' experiences, including a members-only POSH Beach Club, above the more exclusive Courtyard area atop the ship. This has a Miami South Beach vibe and includes four pay-extra experiences: (1) POSH Vive, 6–9am, when you can participate in yoga classes and treatments in private cabanas; (2) POSH Rehab until noon, so you can recover from a hard night, with Bloody Marys and chill-out music; (3) POSH Sol, noon–6pm, when you can lounge on day beds and enjoy a beach-themed atmosphere; and (4) Pure POSH, echoing Caesar's

Palace in Las Vegas, where you can drink and dance under the stars.

Other ship features include a novel Ice Bar, a chill-out, chat-up venue inspired by the original ice bars and ice hotels of Scandinavia. In this frozen chamber of iced vodka, the centerpiece is a giant ice cube that glows and changes color. The Ice Bar accommodates 25 passengers who are given fur coats, gloves, and hats because the room's temperature does not rise above –8°C (around 17°F). Naturally, there's a cover charge, but it includes two drinks. Svedka vodka and Canada's Inniskillin ice wine are featured.

Then there's Halo, an über-bar, where garden and courtyard villa occupants, who pay a premium for much better accommodation, have exclusive access, although other passengers can use it by paying a cover charge. This bar sits at the top of the ship on Deck 16 and showcases art and jewelry, 'modeled' by shop staff.

Spice H2O is a tiered pool, stage, and movie screen complex for adults only, at the stern. It's a smaller version of the AquaTheatre aboard RCI's Oasis-class ships. With all-day-long music and a huge screen, different themes prevail: (1) Sunny Spice 8am–11am, including spicy drinks and breakfast; (2) Daytime Aqua Spice with sun and water and Chinese take-away food items; (3) Evening Sunset Spice, with a perfect sunset every day; and (4) All Spice at night, offering a show of aqua ballet and dancing. A Beyond the Velvet Rope package for all clubs is available at extra cost.

It's a big ship, but the elevators are forward and aft – there are none in the middle of the ship, which is tough for mobility-limited passengers. Yet *Norwegian Epic* has more elevators than the much larger *Oasis of the Seas*.

A 'ship within a ship' two-deck complex provides a private courtyard/pool area, male and female steam rooms, concierge lounge, and private dining rooms and lounge for those willing to pay more for exclusivity.

Niggles include the cigarette smokers in the casino, a walk-through area. The ship sails on alternating seven-day eastern and western Caribbean itineraries during the winter season, and operates Mediterranean cruises in summer.

A non-changeable per person service charge is automatically added to your account daily; 15 percent is also added for bar charges, and a whopping 18 percent for spa treatments.

FAMILIES. Family-friendly cabins are within easy access to the Kid's Crew facilities, in two zones: for Kids two to nine, and tweens of 10–12. Nickleodeon is the family entertainment brand on all cruises, as part of NCL's children's programming. Activities include: Slime Time Live, an interactive game; Nick Live, with poolside entertainment; Character ('Pajama Jam') breakfast, at extra charge; and meet and greet. There's also a Nickleodeon in-cabin TV channel.

ACCOMMODATION. There are many, many different accommodation price levels in 13 accommodation grades, including the first Loft Suites at sea – although upstairs/downstairs suites have been available for years aboard ships such as *Saga Ruby* and the now withdrawn *QE2*. In true nautical tradition, even-numbered cabins are on the port side (red carpet), with odd-numbered cabins on the starboard side (blue carpet); if you're color-blind, forget it.

The Courtyard Suites (decks 16 and 17) are located in the 'block of cheese' in the forward section called The Haven, above the navigation bridge. There are six courtyard 'villas' – two face forward, while six overlook the central pool section, although none has a private balcony. Occupants, however, have access to a four-deck gated-community style grouping of facilities, including a concierge lounge, private courtyard and pool, his-and-her steam rooms, and private sunbathing areas – so no need to go to the rest of the ship underneath you, except to disembark or go out to the entertainment decks to play, or escape.

All outside-view suites/cabins have a 'private' balcony. In a New Wave concept, the designers introduced curved walls in a wave shape for a contemporary look and feel to cabins. LED lighting, backlit domed ceiling, comfortable sofa seating (except Standard Cabins), vanity desk, and minibar. A palette of soft, warm colors in each cabin melds beautifully with walnut and rosewood colored veneers and stark white surfaces. See-through bathrooms have a separate toilet; tub or tub/shower combination, and separate vanity washbasin (few people like the see-through toilet).

Although they are about the same size as current standard industry cabins, there's an efficient use of space, achieved by separating the toilet and shower unit to either side of the entryway, and by curving the bulkheads and furniture to give the cabins a more open, wavy, and contemporary feel. However, space at the foot of the beds is poor. There's absolutely no privacy between what would normally be a bathroom, and the rest of the cabin. Also, you'll need to grab a towel before you step into the shower, because they are in a different location – adjacent to the tiny washbasin.

Eight Spa Suites have private key-card entry to the adjacent Mandara Spa, and complimentary 24-hour access to the inner Thermal Spa. These have more space and larger balconies.

Solo travelers can take one of the 128 Studio cabins, many of which are interconnecting – reminiscent of a capsule hotel. A small window looks out into the passageway. On decks 11 and 12, these are priced for single occupancy – although they can be occupied by two persons (and two toothbrushes only) since there is a double bed. They measure 100 sq ft (9.3 sq m) and occupants have access to a common lounge with hostess, and free espressos/cappuccinos. In Interior Cabins and Studio categories, the bed faces the cabin door, so there's no privacy.

DINING. There are certainly plenty of dining choices. With 21 restaurants, dining venues, and casual eateries, it will take some planning in order to eat where you want, when you want, despite NCL's claim to Freestyle Dining. Actually, there is no 'main' dining room as such. In other words, just like in a city or town, you choose where to eat – unless, of course, there are no tables available, which is possible at peak times when everyone wants to see a show simultaneously, and you'll have to wait for a table. There is also no Lido self-service buffet as aboard almost all other large resort ships. Instead, different food outlets have been created in numerous locations – 11 are included in the cruise fare, while the others have a per person cover charge. Because gratuities are automatically added to your onboard account, if you change dining venues every time you eat, you don't need to think about tips.

Cagney's Steakhouse & Churrascaria, with 276 seats, expands the New York-style favorite of earlier NCL ships to include Argentine churrasco offerings of skewered meats presented by tableside waiters. The spot adds a large self-help salad bar in its center.

Taste, in the atrium on Deck 5, is touted as a European retro-chic restaurant with brick details and floor-to-ceiling velvet curtains. The menu includes traditional and contemporary cuisine for breakfast, lunch, and dinner.

The Manhattan Room, located aft, is two decks high and reminiscent of an elegant Art Deco supper club, with dance floor and live Celebrity Look-Alike shows. It's the closest thing to a main dining room and has a spectacular glass window wall aft.

La Cucina is from Tuscany, of course. It's at the front of the ship, providing great ocean views, one deck above the navigation bridge.

The 124-seat Le Bistro serves French cuisine; there has been a Le Bistro aboard all NCL ships since the first one was installed aboard the now scrapped Norway.

Multiple Asian-themed venues include Shanghai's for Chinese dishes and noodle bar specialties with an open kitchen and 133 seats; the 20-seat Wasabi for sushi and sakes; and a showy, food-chopping venue, the adjacent Teppanyaki Grill, with 115 seats.

The Epic Club and Courtyard Grill, in the Courtyard Villas complex, is exclusive to suite and villa occupants and split between an elegant, private club-style restaurant with a large wine display and a casual outdoor area for breakfast and lunch. It can accommodate 127.

O'Sheehan's is a neighborhood-style sports bar and grill, open 24 hours (no extra charge). It is adjacent to a bowling alley, though I'm not sure why – it disturbs the ambience.

Café Jardin (Garden Café) is a large self-serve buffet venue, with 728 seats, and is modeled on an English country garden conservatory – but with a French name and excellent ocean views. The casual venue includes 'action' stations where chefs prepare pasta and other items, made to order – join the line. The outdoor seating area, the Great Outdoors, looks over the Aqua Park.

A section for children, the Kids Café, has low height tables and seats.

ENTERTAINMENT. The two-deck-high Epic Theater, at the front of the ship, presents major production shows and mainline cabaret acts. Another entertainment venue is the Bliss Ultra Lounge, a decadent venue that contains a bowling alley or two – there's another one in Sheehan's on the deck above. This is where late-night comedy and some cabaret acts are presented.

Celebrity look-alike shows, conjuring up the likes of Elvis, Janet Jackson, Madonna, Neil Diamond, and Tina Turner, is part of the entertainment offering. They are produced by Legends in Concert, the Las Vegas company that has provided shows for The Strip for over 25 years.

The Spiegel Tent is a two-deck-high Cirque-like space, combining a show with dinner, similar to the Teatro ZinZanni dinner theatre in San Francisco and Seattle. It's a mix of in-your-face street theatre, acrobatics, and Berlin-style 'foodertainment,' with lots of clowning and satire during a poorly scripted two-hour show. There's a cover charge.

As part of NCL's creative Check In, Rock Out program, guitar enthusiasts can, for a daily fee, rent a real Gibson guitar and a set of headphones to play in the comfort of their cabin.

SPA/FITNESS. The Smile Spa and Pulse Fitness Center complex is possibly the largest at sea (31,000 sq ft/2,880 sq m). Operated by the Steiner-owned Mandara Spa, it is in the center of the ship, and some of the 24 treatment rooms have no view. The Fitness Center has port-side ocean views; the aerobics room has no view. Numerous facilities and services are offered, almost all at extra charge.

Sports facilities include six bowling lanes in two venues (O'Sheehans Neighborhood Bar & Grill and Bliss Ultra Lounge). There's also a full-size basketball court, volleyball, soccer, dodge ball, a batting cage, bungee trampoline, a 24-ft (7.3-m) tall climbing cage called the spider web, and an abseiling wall. Walkers should note that only 2.2 laps around the walking track equals 1 mile.

Norwegian Gem
★★★+

Size:.................................Large Resort Ship	Cabins (total):.....................................1,197
Tonnage:......................................93,530	Size range (sq ft/m):...............142.0–4,390.0/13.2–407.8
Lifestyle:.....................................Standard	Cabins (outside view):................................792
Cruise line:.......................Norwegian Cruise Line	Cabins (interior/no view):............................405
Former names:....................................none	Cabins (for one person):................................0
IMO number:.................................9355733	Cabins (with private balcony):........................540
Builder:.........................Meyer Werft (Germany)	Cabins (wheelchair accessible):.........................27
Original cost:...............................$390 million	Wheelchair accessibility:............................Good
Entered service:.............................Oct 2007	Cabin voltage:...............................110 volts
Registry:......................................Panama	Elevators:.......................................12
Length (ft/m):.............................964.8/294.1	Casino (gaming tables):...............................Yes
Beam (ft/m):..............................105.6/32.2	Slot machines:...................................Yes
Draft (ft/m):...............................26.9/8.2	Swimming pools:....................................2
Propulsion/Propellers:........diesel-electric/2 azimuthing pods	Hot tubs (on deck):....................................6
Passenger decks:..................................12	Self-service launderette:.............................Yes
Total crew:....................................1,126	Dedicated cinema/seats:...............................No
Passengers (lower beds/alll berths):.............2,394/2,846	Library:..Yes
Passenger Space Ratio (lower beds/all berths):.......39.0/32.8	Onboard currency:................................US$
Crew/Passenger Ratio (lower beds/all berths):..........2.1/2.5	

A large, family-friendly ship with multiple eating venues

OVERVIEW. A multitude of choices, including many dining options, add up to a very attractive vacation package, highly suitable for families with children, in a floating leisure center that provides ample facilities for enjoyment.

THE SHIP. The design and layout of *Norwegian Gem* is similar to that of *Norwegian Pearl*, and there is a pod propulsion system for vibration-free cruising. The white hull has a colorful string of gems along its sides as a design. There are plenty of deck lounge chairs – more than the total of passengers. Water slides are included for the adult swimming pools. Children have their own pools at the ship's stern.

Inside the ship is an entertaining mix of bright, warm colors and decor that you probably wouldn't have in your home, and yet somehow they all work well.

The dress code is ultra-casual: no jacket and tie needed, although you are welcome to dress formally – but jeans are probably essential. Although service levels and finesse may be inconsistent, the level of hospitality aboard Norwegian Cruise Line ships is good. There's plenty of lively music, constant activity, entertainment, and food that is mainstream and acceptable but nothing more – even when you pay extra to eat in the specialty dining spots.

There are 11 bars and lounges, including Bar Central, four specialty bars: martini bar, Champagne and wine bar, beer and whiskey bar, and a cigar lounge; these interconnect with the lobby, yet have distinct per-

Berlitz's Ratings		
	Possible	Achieved
Ship	500	371
Accommodation	200	145
Food	400	240
Service	400	272
Entertainment	100	66
Cruise	400	275
OVERALL SCORE		
1369 points out of 2000		

sonalities. The lobby houses a Java Bar, plus a two-deck-high movie screen, typically used to show sports events and Wii activities. One neat room is the Bliss Ultra Lounge & Night Club, at the aft end of the ship; it houses a 24-hours a day V-shaped sports bar and lounge complex, including a bowling alley with four real bowling lanes – the cost is $5 per person, including special playing shoes, and it is limited to six persons per lane. The lounge doesn't have many seats, but does have a couple of decadent beds.

The casino is typical of larger resort ship casinos, with plenty of gaming tables, slot machines, noise, and smoke. So, if you walk through the casino to get from the showlounge to other public rooms, you'll be subject to cigarette smoke. A new twist in the onboard casino scene has appeared, with poolside blackjack now established in its own 'open-air casino' on the pool deck.

The ship is full of revenue centers designed to help you part with even more money than you paid for your cruise ticket. Expect to be subjected to a stream of flyers advertising art auctions, 'designer' watches, gold and silver chain by the inch, and other promotions – and the cruise director's long program announcements three times a day. This pre-paid tipping has led to unmotivated service.

A per person service charge that can't be changed is automatically added to your account daily; 15 percent is also added for bar charges, and a whopping 18 percent for spa treatments.

FAMILIES. Because NCL is all about cruising with families of all ages, much space is devoted to children's facilities, all thoughtfully tucked well away from adult recreation areas, at the aft end of the ship. Children of all ages can play in the wet 'n' wild space-themed water park (the Aqua Kid's Club), complete with large pool, water slide, and paddle pool. There's a 30-ft by 19-ft (9m by 6m) climbing wall at the funnel. Teens are well catered for, and have their own cinema, discotheque with dance floor, and hot tub. There's a room full of cots for toddlers to use for sleepovers. And Nickelodeon characters are onboard, so young ones can enjoy a Pajama Jam Breakfast.

More than 250 cabins have interconnecting doors – good for families with children. That means interior cabins can connect; outside-view cabins can connect; and outside-view and balcony cabins can connect. Also for families, many cabins also have third- and fourth-person pull-down berths or trundle beds.

ACCOMMODATION. There are many, many different price grades, from small interior cabins to lavish suites in a private courtyard setting.

Although they are nicely furnished and quite well equipped, the standard outside-view and interior cabins are quite small, particularly when occupied by three or four people. A small room service menu is available – all non-food items cost extra cost, and a 15 percent service charge is automatically added to your account. Bottled water is placed in each cabin, but you will be charged if you open the bottle.

The following suites, part of The Haven, are available:

Courtyard Villas/Garden Villas. The two Garden Villa Suites, each measuring 4,390 sq ft (408 sq m), and 10 Courtyard Villas share a private courtyard with its own small pool, hot tub, and small fitness room, and have butler service. These units enjoy exclusivity – rather like accommodation in a gated community – where others cannot live unless they pay the asking price.

Deluxe Owner's Suites. These two suites, Black Pearl and Golden Pearl, are set high atop all other accommodation, have stunning ocean views, and consist of a master bedroom with king-size bed, a dining/lounge area, a decent-size balcony, and access to the private courtyard.

Penthouse Suites. Located at the front of the ship, they have a partly private balcony under the navigation bridge.

DINING. There are two main dining rooms: the 304-seat Grand Palace, with its minimalist decor; and the 558-seat Magenta Restaurant. There are several other themed eating spots, giving a wide range of choice; some cost extra, and require advance reservations, particularly for dinner. All are part of NCL's Freestyle Dining – there are no assigned dining rooms, tables, or seats, so you'll need to plan your meals and times accordingly.

With 17 video screens located around the ship, you can check how busy each dining spot is and make a booking and find out whether, or how long, you'll need to wait for a table; pagers are also available, so you can go bar-hopping while you wait for a table in your chosen venue. The system generally works well, with colored bars to indicate whether a restaurant is 'full,' 'moderately busy,' or 'empty.' This has cut down the frustration of waiting a long time for a table, although on formal nights, when you may want to see the production shows, congestion certainly does occur. Note that NCL's dress code states that 'jeans, T-shirts, tank tops, and bare feet are not permitted in restaurants.'

Other dining options. include Cagney's Steak House (serving steaks from 5oz to 48oz); Blue Lagoon (for trendy fast-food street snacks); Le Bistro for classic French cuisine; Orchid Garden, an Asian eatery complete with sushi bar and Teppanyaki grill (where the chef puts on a display in front of you); La Cucina, serving Italian cuisine; Latin Restaurant; the Garden Café, a large self-serve buffet-style restaurant, for casual meals; Kids' Café; and a Java Café, which serves Lavazza coffee, in the lobby.

ENTERTAINMENT. The Stardust Theater, seating 1,042, is the venue for colorful Las Vegas-style production shows and major cabaret acts. It is designed in the style of an opera house, spans three decks, and has a steeply tiered main floor and port and starboard balconies.

There are three production shows in a typical seven-day cruise, all ably performed by the Jean Ann Ryan Company. They are always colorful and high-energy shows.

SPA/FITNESS. Wellness devotees should enjoy the two-deck-high Yin-Yang Health Spa complex, open until 10pm and operated by the Steiner-owned and Hawaii-based Mandara Spa. It is located in the front of the ship, with large ocean-view windows on three sides. There are many facilities and services to pamper you, and 18 treatment rooms. There's also a 37-ft (11-m) indoor lap pool, hydrotherapy pool, two sit-in deep tubs, aromatherapy and wellness centers, and mud treatment room.

The Body Waves fitness and exercise rooms are within the spa and have the latest Cybex muscle-pumping equipment. Most classes, such as Pathway to Yoga, Body Cycling Class, and Body Beat Class (cardio kickboxing), cost extra.

Recreational sports facilities include a jogging track, golf driving range, and basketball and volleyball courts, as well as several levels of sunbathing decks, plus the four bowling lanes and a funnel-mounted rock-climbing wall.

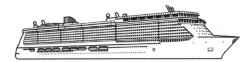

Norwegian Getaway
Not Yet Rated

Size:.	Large Resort Ship	Cabins (total):.	1,994
Tonnage:.	145,655	Size range (sq ft/m):.	n/a
Lifestyle:.	Standard	Cabins (outside view):.	1,545
Cruise line:.	Norwegian Cruise Line	Cabins (interior/no view):.	449
Former names:.	none	Cabins (for one person):.	59
IMO number:.	9606912	Cabins (with private balcony):.	1,252
Builder:.	Meyer Werft (Germany)	Cabins (wheelchair accessible):.	40
Original cost:.	$600 million	Wheelchair accessibility:.	Good
Entered service:.	Apr 2013	Cabin voltage:.	110 volts
Registry:.	The Bahamas	Elevators:.	16
Length (ft/m):.	1,066.2/325.0	Casino (gaming tables):.	Yes
Beam (ft/m):.	133.0/40.5	Slot machines:.	Yes
Draft (ft/m):.	27.8/8.5	Swimming pools:.	5
Propulsion/Propellers:.	diesel-electric (79,800MW)/2	Hot tubs (on deck):.	9
Passenger decks:.	15	Self-service launderette:.	No
Total crew:.	1,595	Dedicated cinema/seats:.	No
Passengers (lower beds/alll berths):.	3998	Library:.	No
Passenger Space Ratio (lower beds/all berths):.	36.4	Onboard currency:.	US$
Crew/Passenger Ratio (lower beds/all berths):.	2.5/3.1		

multi-choice, Über-casual playground for the family

OVERVIEW. *Norwegian Getaway* really is a ship for young and trendy urbanites. It will provide families with children, single parents, couples, and solo travelers with a mountain of entertainment choices, in an environment that is a pure playground for an active, entertaining cruise vacation. This is 'South Beach Miami' at sea.

Berlitz's Ratings

	Possible	Achieved
Ship	500	NYR
Accommodation	200	NYR
Food	400	NYR
Service	400	NYR
Entertainment	100	NYR
Cruise	NYR	NYR
OVERALL SCORE		
NYR points out of 2000		

THE SHIP. *Norwegian Getaway* (sister to *Norwegian Breakaway*) has a more streamlined and a much more balanced profile than its slightly larger close-sister ship, *Norwegian Epic*, with less of a less boxy look to its forward section.

Families with children can enjoy the pool deck facilities like the Aqua Park, with multiple water slides and a large rock-climbing wall and rappelling wall. Aft is a large movie screen with amphitheater-style seating. But, despite the ship's size, the open deck space for sunbathing is rather tight, and made smaller by the 'exclusive' 'Haven' area in the forward section, whose suites-only occupants (pay more, get more) are given enough sunbathing space, bar, pool, hot tubs, and beach-club-like setting. The rest of the ship shares multiple pools and water-fun exterior decks, designed for families and children. Still, the pool deck is where all the family action will be – particularly on sea days – and the kids will love it.

Lower down, on an outdoor promenade deck, a 'Waterfront' boardwalk-style outdoor area with bar and eateries brings you more in contact with the sea. It forms part of the outdoor experience, and away from the hubbub of the family-friendly sun/sports action deck atop the ship.

Inside, the decor is decidedly more traditional and provides a more restful, relaxed feel and ambience – although this is all relative and still rather upbeat. Careful planning and time management will be needed to make the most of this large resort ship and all it has to offer. So it's worth spending time to decide what you want to get out of your cruise vacation before you board the ship – which sort of negates the 'freestyle' aspect of a large resort ship cruise. You'll be sharing the ship with about 4,000 others, so there's no doubt it will be a lively travel experience.

Most of the public rooms, shops, entertainment spots, the casino, and a number of the 12 bars and 17 themed dining venues are located on decks 6, 7 and 8 – a three-deck area complex called 678 Ocean Place.

Norwegian Getaway is scheduled to homeport in Miami. Gratuities are charged to your onboard account, or you can pre-pay on-line. Bar purchases incur a 15 percent gratuity; spa treatments are 18 percent.

FAMILIES. Facilities for kids and teens are spread over two decks (Splash Academy for kids and a separate Entourage space for teens).

Splash Academy is located adjacent to the ship's family-friendly accommodation and provides areas for three age groups. Babies and toddlers under three will also have their own dedicated play space and parent-involving activities. At the Splash Academy reception area, tablet-based electronic registration allows parents to swipe their keycard and input a password to sign in their children.

Just past the reception area, the three- to five-year-olds (Guppies) have their own brightly decorated space, complete with child-sized furniture. In a separate zone, six- to nine-year-olds (Turtles) have building block activity centers, an interactive dance mat with corresponding large video screen, video game stations and a video viewing lounge.

Upstairs, 10- to 12-year-olds (Seas) get a multipurpose dance space with a touch-screen jukebox, moveable tables for activities, and bean bags for lounging. An activity zone includes arts and crafts items, and a 'hang out' area stocked with the latest video games.

Entourage, the dedicated space for ages 13–17 (Dolphins) has air hockey, foosball, and an arcade with five separate large-screen areas to play the latest video games while lounging on sofas. In becomes a teen nightclub with a dance floor and video jukebox in the evenings. Adjacent is a video arcade and an outdoor eatery.

Nickelodeon is the family entertainment brand on all cruises, as part of NCL's children's programming. Activities include: Slime Time Live, an interactive game; Nick Live, with poolside entertainment; Character breakfast, at extra charge; and meet and greet. There's also a Nickelodeon in-cabin TV channel. So, expect to see Sponge Bob, Dora the Explorer, Patrick Star, and Diego as part of the family-themed entertainment.

ACCOMMODATION. Having learned a lot from its innovative big sister *Norwegian Epic*, NCL made sensible changes that now please many of its regulars. The 'wavy' cabin design (unloved by women) has been modified, and the former separated bathroom has been reworked into a more traditional design format, which is much more practical.

The Haven. The more exclusive accommodation is located in a two-deck-high section called The Haven – really a 'ship within a ship.' It consists of 42 suites on decks 15 and 16 forward, and includes a private restaurant, a cocktail bar, and a concierge desk where passengers can relax, have a drink, and make dining, entertainment, and spa reservations through the dedicated concierge. There is a private pool (with a deep end for swimming and a shallow area for relaxing), changing areas, two hot tubs, gym, saunas, two private massage rooms, and sun deck with bar. The Haven occupants have private access to the spa and fitness center, as well as 24-hour butler service, and in-suite, white-tablecloth dining service. Suite occupants get a platinum key card (better recognition in the rest of the ship – who said the 'class' system was dead?) and priority reservations for all the restaurants, spa, and entertainment venues.

The top suites within The Haven are two Deluxe Owner's Suites, with their contemporary skyscraper apartment look – including an elegant living room and dining area with wet bar. The bedroom has a king-size bed with pillow-top mattress that faces floor-to-ceiling windows and an extra-spacious wraparound private balcony. The bathroom has an oversize tub, two vanity sinks, and a luxury shower. The Deluxe Owner's Suites can be joined to the Owner's Suites, creating one grand suite that can sleep up to eight.

The 21 two-bedroom Family Villas have two bathrooms as well as two bedrooms. The separate living room and dining area includes a single sofa bed, writing desk, and bar. The master bedroom has a king-size bed, floor-to-ceiling windows, and a private balcony. The master bath includes an oversize oval tub that looks out to the sea. The second bedroom includes a double sofa bed and bathroom.

Also in The Haven are 17 Courtyard Penthouses, with a king-size bed, living and dining area, a single sofa bed, writing desk, and ample storage spaces. On other (non-Haven) decks throughout the ship are eight aft-facing penthouses and 10 forward-facing penthouses.

Other accommodation. There are 15 Spa mini-suite rooms and 28 Spa balcony cabins, all with easy access to the adjacent spa and its facilities. While most outside-view cabins have a balcony, some have only windows, but all have flat-screen televisions, satellite-linked telephone, and private bathroom. There are also 42 Family 'suites' with ocean views.

Balcony suites/cabins have rich wood-look paneling with warm tones and accent colors. Each balcony cabin has a king-size bed that can be made into twins, with a pillow-top mattress set against a chestnut leather headboard cushioned and tufted to make reading and sitting up in bed more comfortable. There's a lighted recess above the bed for books, magazines, tablet computers, or electronic reading devices. Each room has a sofa bed with additional storage. A built-in 26-inch flat-screen television is mounted on the wall and tilts so it can be seen from the sofa or the bed. Underneath the television is another recessed nook to hold cruise information, books, and magazines. A built-in vanity area has shelving and abundant storage space. LED lighting surrounds the perimeter of the ceiling to give the room warmth. There is also a full-size closet that is easily accessible with sliding doors. The cabins are energy-efficient, using key card access to control lighting in the room.

The balcony bathroom features a contemporary, clean design, ensuring more generous and comfortable space. There are several rich-wood shelves to help reduce clutter and keep everything within easy reach. There's an enclosed vanity underneath the washbasin that hides the trash bin, along with more storage. The built-in washbasin is size-generous and has an easy-to-use faucet. A private shower with a shaving bar for ladies completes the picture. Mini-suite bathrooms get a rain shower plus a hand-held shower hose.

There are 59 studio (single-occupancy) cabins. They are colorful, hip, trendy, and small, with a minimalist design – especially the closet space. Still this is a neat way to cruise solo – just don't bring many clothes.

The many interior cabins also have one or two additional upper berths, while the lower beds are twins that convert to a queen-size bed – good for families with young children.

DINING. Freestyle Dining has no assigned dining rooms, tables or seats, so you can choose which restaurant to eat in, at what time, and with whom. In practice, the wealth of choices means that you'll need to make reservations in whichever venue you want to eat, so you'll need to be prepared for a bit of planning and waiting – just like you would ashore. But, if you want to see a show in the evening, then your dining time will really be dictated by the time of the show, which rather limits your choice.

Other dining options. The Manhattan Room is the ship's equivalent of a main restaurant (it is included in the fare); it is large, with an integral dance floor and large ocean-view windows aft. Other dining venues (Cagney's Steakhouse and Moderno Currascaria) are located one deck above, and have a view into the Manhattan Room.

The Waterfront is a boardwalk-style outdoor area with bar and eateries, while Geoffrey Zakarian's 678 Ocean Place (meaning decks 6, 7, and 8) connects it with several interior extra-cost dining venues as well as the extensive Breakaway Casino, cigar smoking room, and several entertainment venues. These include Moderno Churrascaria, a Brazilian-style steakhouse with table-side carved meat service by passadores and a salad bar); Cagney's Steakhouse, a classic American steakhouse, with open kitchen; La Cucina, for Italian family food with a focus on Tuscany, with inside seating; or for alfresco eating on The Waterfront, Maltings and Ocean Blu by Geoffrey Zakarian (designed and overseen by Food Network's popular Geoffrey Zakarian). The celebrity chef uses ingredients and techniques that he employs in his land-based establishments.

Other venues include Le Bistro, for classic French-style cuisine; a 96-seat Teppanyaki restaurant with 12 flat-top grills and a lot of show (yes, food can be entertaining), complete with Japanese rock garden with bamboo plants and bonsai trees; and Cirque Dreams and Dinner, a big-top, circus-like dining spot with show (it's a lively, action-filled supper club). All are extra-cost, and reservations are required.

Casual eateries, at no extra cost, include O'Sheehan's Neighborhood Bar & Grill, a sports bar and popular fast-food joint, with a big screen for sporting events, miniature bowling alley, pool and air hockey tables, and interactive games; the Atrium Café and Bar, for coffees and pastries; and Shanghai's Noodle Bar, for Chinese-style noodle dishes.

The Garden Café is an extremely large, self-serve buffet, with indoor and outdoor seating. It's open round the clock. Many different counters provide themed and ethnic food varieties, and there's a special section for kids, too.

ENTERTAINMENT. The two-deck-high Getaway Theater, located at the front of the ship, is a stunning showlounge where the major production shows and mainline cabaret acts are presented. A specially produced version of *Legally Blonde* will be one of the highlights. Another entertainment venue is the Bliss Ultra Lounge, a decadent venue that contains a bowling alley or two, as well as other diversions.

NCL has always been at the forefront for creativity in entertainment. The Blue Man group, first introduced aboard *Norwegian Epic* to great acclaim and very entertaining for the whole family, forms part of the line-up here, too.

Celebrity look-alike shows are presented in the Manhattan Room. These conjure up the likes of Elvis, Janet Jackson, Madonna, Neil Diamond, Tina Turner, and others, are also part of the entertainment line-up. They are produced by Legends in Concert, a Las Vegas company that has provided shows for The Strip for over 25 years.

SPA/FITNESS. The spa and fitness center, spread over two decks, houses a warehouse-size gymnasium. The complex includes a thermal suite (herbal rain-showers, saunas and steam rooms, relaxation area with hot-tile beds), a beauty salon, and multiple body treatment rooms, including massage rooms for couples.

Norwegian Jade
★★★+

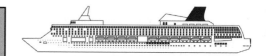

Size:.................................Large Resort Ship	Crew/Passenger Ratio (lower beds/all berths):.........2.2/2.6
Tonnage:..93,558	Cabins (total):..................................1,233
Lifestyle:......................................Standard	Size range (sq ft/m):............142.0–4,390.0/13.2–407.8
Cruise line:........................Norwegian Cruise Line	Cabins (outside view):............................834
Former names:..........................*Pride of Hawaii*	Cabins (interior/no view):.........................425
IMO number:.................................9304057	Cabins (for one person):.............................0
Builder:........................Meyer Werft (Germany)	Cabins (with private balcony):......................763
Original cost:.............................$390 million	Cabins (wheelchair accessible):......................27
Entered service:....................May 2006/Mar 2008	Wheelchair accessibility:..........................Good
Registry:................................The Bahamas	Cabin voltage:..............................110 volts
Length (ft/m):...........................964.8/294.1	Elevators:.......................................12
Beam (ft/m):............................105.6/32.2	Casino (gaming tables):............................Yes
Draft (ft/m):..............................26.9/8.2	Slot machines:...................................Yes
Propulsion/Propellers:...diesel-electric (40,000kW)/2 azimuthing pods	Swimming pools:....................................2
	Hot tubs (on deck):.................................6
Passenger decks:..................................12	Self-service launderette:...........................No
Total crew:.....................................1,076	Dedicated cinema/seats:.............................No
Passengers (lower beds/alll berths):.............2,466/2,890	Library:...Yes
Passenger Space Ratio (lower beds/all berths):.......37.9/32.3	Onboard currency:...............................US$

Entertainment and a casual lifestyle for the whole family

OVERVIEW. *Norwegian Jade* best suits youthful adult couples, single passengers, and families with children and teenagers who want upbeat surroundings, good facilities, a wide range of entertainment lounges and bars, and high-tech sophistication – all in a neat, highly programmed, and well-packaged cruise. But, although the initial fare seems very reasonable, the extra costs and charges can soon mount up.

THE SHIP. Built from 67 blocks, this is a sister ship to *Norwegian Jewel*. After service as *Pride of Hawaii*, it underwent a small transformation, gained a casino, and became *Norwegian Jade* for cruising in Europe and the Caribbean – though some interior decor elements from the ship's former life in Hawaii remain. The interior decor is decidedly bright and cheerful, and it has a pod propulsion system.

Norwegian Jade's interior focal gathering place is Bar Central – three specialty bars (Magnum's Champagne/Wine Bar, Mixers' Martini/Cocktail Bar, and Tankard's Beer/Whiskey Bar) that are connected but have distinct personalities. They are located on the deck above the reception lobby. All told, there are a dozen bars and lounges on board. Other facilities include a casino, three meeting rooms, a chapel, card room, bridge viewing room, and the *SS United States* Library with original photography and material about America's last ocean liner.

The dress code is very casual; no jacket and tie are needed, although you are welcome to dress formally if you wish. The ship is full of revenue centers designed

Berlitz's Ratings

	Possible	Achieved
Ship	500	371
Accommodation	200	145
Food	400	240
Service	400	273
Entertainment	100	66
Cruise	400	276

OVERALL SCORE
1371 points out of 2000

to help you part with more of your money. You can expect to be subjected to a stream of flyers advertising daily art auctions, 'designer' watches, and many other promotions including poolside 'inch of gold' sales outlets.

A non-negotiable per person service charge is automatically added to your account daily; 15 percent is also added for bar charges.

Passenger niggles include waiting to use the interactive dining reservation screens in the public areas; lines for breakfast in the main dining spots, particularly before the shore excursions start; and poor service and hospitality in some areas.

FAMILIES. Children are well provided for, and have their own facilities, including a Kids' Club; teens have their own disco, the Wipe-Out Club. More than 250 cabins have interconnecting doors – good for families with children. That means interior cabins can connect; outside-view cabins can connect; and outside-view and balcony cabins can connect. Also for families, many cabins also have third- and fourth-person pull-down berths or trundle beds.

ACCOMMODATION. There are many, many different price grades, determined by size and location. Although they are nicely furnished and quite well equipped, the standard outside-view and interior cabins are quite small, particularly when occupied by three or four people.

A small room service menu is available; all non-food items cost extra, and a 15 percent service charge is added to your account. Bottled water is placed in each cabin, but a charge is made to your account if you open the bottle.

Garden Villas. Two multi-room villas have great views over the pool deck and ocean. Each has a roof terrace and private garden, with open-air dining, hot tub, and private sunning and relaxation areas. They are among the most extravagant suites at sea today. Each has a living room with Bose audio-visual equipment (including a CD/DVD library), grand piano, wet bar, and refrigerator. Each has three bedrooms (king- or queen-size bed) with en suite bathroom and walk-in closet. Each Garden Villa measures approximately 4,390 sq ft/408 sq m – the ultimate in living space, exclusivity and privacy.

Courtyard Villas. 10 Courtyard Villas (up to 660 sq ft/61 sq m) share a private courtyard with its own small pool, hot tub, massage bed, and fitness room – all in a setting that is distinctly Asian. They also share a private concierge lounge with the two largest villas, as well as butler and concierge service. These units enjoy exclusivity – rather like accommodation in a gated community. The two Garden Villas each have three bedrooms with en suite bathroom, living room, dining room, and stunning views.

Owner's Suites. Each of these five units (approximately 1,195 sq ft/111 sq m) has a large bedroom with king-size bed and audio-visual entertainment center, and a living room with dining area. The bathroom has a tub, separate shower enclosure, and powder room. Some Owner's suites can interconnect with Penthouse Suites.

Penthouse Suites. There are 24 of these, measuring up to 600 sq ft (56 sq m). They have a bedroom with queen-size bed, and living room with dining area. The bathroom has a tub/shower or separate shower enclosure. Some can be interconnect to a kid's room with double sofa bed and a Pullman bed with separate bathroom with shower.

All villas and suites have a private balcony, walk-in closet, rich cherry wood cabinetry, tea/coffee/espresso/cappuccino makers, plus butler and concierge service.

DINING. Freestyle Dining has no assigned dining rooms, tables, or seats, so you can choose which restaurant to eat in, at what time, and with whom. In practice, this means you have to make reservations for a specific time, so 'freestyle dining' turns out to be programmed dining. Ten restaurants and eateries are spread over two entire decks. Some are included in the cruise fare, others cost extra.

The two main restaurants, included in the cruise fare, are Alizar (310 seats) and Grand Pacific (486 seats). Favorite NCL specialty dining venues include Cagney's Steak House (176 seats), Blue Lagoon (a casual eatery serving American food and seating 94), and Le Bistro (a classic French restaurant, with 129 seats

– check out the beautiful, and real, Van Gogh painting).

Paniola (100 seats) offers trendy tapas and salsa fare. Jade Garden (including a sushi counter, sake bar, and a 32-seat Teppanyaki Grill) has Southeast Asian cuisine. The 70-seat Papa's Italian Kitchen has a long wooden table that creates a farmhouse ambience. Self-serve buffet-style meals can be taken in the Garden Café and its outdoor section. Extra-cost Lavazza (Italian) coffees can be found in the Aloha Café.

You can make reservations through the Freestyle Dining information system; plasma screens showing waiting times for the various venues are located in high-traffic areas.

ENTERTAINMENT. The 1,042-seat Stardust Theatre is the venue for colorful Las Vegas-style production shows and major cabaret acts. It is designed in the style of an opera house, spans three decks, and has a steeply tiered main floor and port and starboard balconies. Colorful, high-energy, razzle-dazzle production shows are ably performed by the Jean Ann Ryan Company.

Bands and solo entertaining musicians provide live music for listening and dancing in several lounges and bars. Throughout the ship, loud music prevails. In Spinnakers Lounge, a nightclub located high atop the ship with great ocean views on three sides, a Pachanga Party (a Miami South Beach rave) is held during each cruise.

SPA/FITNESS. The two-deck-high Yin and Yang health spa complex, operated by the Steiner-owned Mandara Spa, is at the stern, with large ocean-view windows on three sides. There are many facilities and services, almost all costing extra. In addition, there is a 37-ft (11-m) indoor lap pool, hydrotherapy pool, two sit-in deep tubs, aroma-therapy and wellness centers, and mud treatment rooms, including one for couples. Spa treatments incur an 18 percent gratuity.

The fitness and exercise rooms, with the latest Cybex muscle-pumping equipment, are located not within the spa, but at the top of the glass-domed atrium lobby. Included is a room for exercycle classes.

Recreational sports facilities include a jogging track, two golf driving nets (there's a golf pro shop, too), basketball and volleyball courts, paddle tennis, mini-golf, oversize chess, and several sunbathing decks.

Norwegian Jewel
★★★+

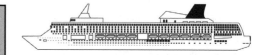

Size:.................................Large Resort Ship	Crew/Passenger Ratio (lower beds/all berths):..........2.1/2.6
Tonnage: 93,000	Cabins (total):................................ 1,188
Lifestyle: ....Standard	Size range (sq ft/m): 142.0–4,390.0/13.2–407.8
Cruise line:.......................Norwegian Cruise Line	Cabins (outside view):...............................783
Former names: ....none	Cabins (interior/no view):............................405
IMO number:.................................9304045	Cabins (for one person):..............................0
Builder: .... Meyer Werft (Germany)	Cabins (with private balcony):.......................540
Original cost:................................$390 million	Cabins (wheelchair accessible): 27
Entered service:.............................. Aug 2005	Wheelchair accessibility:............................Good
Registry:.. Panama	Cabin voltage:................................ 110 volts
Length (ft/m):............................... 964.8/294.1	Elevators:...12
Beam (ft/m):................................. 105.6/32.2	Casino (gaming tables):............................. Yes
Draft (ft/m): 26.9/8.2	Slot machines:..................................... Yes
Propulsion/Propellers: . . . diesel-electric (40,000kw)/2 azimuthing pods	Swimming pools:.....................................2
	Hot tubs (on deck):..................................6
Passenger decks:....................................12	Self-service launderette:.............................No
Total crew:...................................... 1,089	Dedicated cinema/seats:.............................No
Passengers (lower beds/alll berths):............. 2,376/2,846	Library: .... Yes
Passenger Space Ratio (lower beds/all berths): 39.1/32.6	Onboard currency: ....US$

A large, casual ship for lively, family-friendly cruising

OVERVIEW. A multitude of choices, including many dining options, add up to a very attractive vacation package, highly suitable for families with children, in a floating leisure center that provides ample facilities for enjoyment. The dress code is very casual – no jacket and tie needed – although you are welcome to dress formally if you wish.

THE SHIP. *Norwegian Jewel*, assembled from 67 blocks, has a basic design and layout similar to that of *Norwegian Gem* and *Norwegian Pearl*, and a pod propulsion system. The white hull has a colorful, funky design on its sides featuring sparkling jewels. There are plenty of sunloungers – in fact, more than the number of passengers carried. Water slides are included for the adult swimming pools. Children have their own pools at the stern, out of sight of adult areas.

Inside the ship, you'll be met by an eclectic mix of colors and decor that you probably wouldn't have in your home, and yet somehow it works extremely well in this large resort ship setting designed to attract the young, active, and trendy.

There are 13 bars and lounges, including Bar Central, three specialty bars that are connected but have distinct personalities. Shakers Martini and Cocktail Bar is a 1960s-inspired lounge; Magnum's Champagne and Wine Bar recalls Paris of the 1920s and the liner *Normandie*; and Maltings Beer and Whiskey Pub is a contemporary bar with artwork themed around whiskey and beer production.

Berlitz's Ratings

	Possible	Achieved
Ship	500	371
Accommodation	200	145
Food	400	240
Service	400	273
Entertainment	100	66
Cruise	400	276
OVERALL SCORE		
1371 points out of 2000		

Despite the company's name, there's little that's Norwegian about this product, except for some senior officers. There's plenty of lively music, constant activity, entertainment, and food that is mainstream and acceptable but nothing more, unless you pay extra to eat in the specialty dining spots. All this is delivered by a smiling, friendly service staff that lacks polish but is willing.

The ship is full of revenue centers designed to part you from your cash. Expect to be subjected to a stream of flyers advertising daily art auctions, 'designer' watches, and 'inch of gold/silver.'

The initial cruise fare is reasonable, but extra costs soon mount up if you want to sample more than the basics. A mandatory per person service charge is added to your account daily; 15 percent is also added for bar charges, and a whopping 18 percent for spa treatments.

FAMILIES. A good deal of space is devoted to children's facilities, which are all tucked well away from adult recreation areas, at the aft end of the ship. Children of all ages get to play in a superb wet 'n' wild space-themed water park complete with large pool, water slide, and paddle pool. There's a room full of cots for toddlers to use for sleepovers, and even the toilets are at a special low height. Teens, too, are well catered for, and have their own cinema, discotheque with dance floor, and hot tub.

More than 250 cabins have interconnecting doors – good for families with children. That means interior cabins can connect; outside-view cabins can connect; and outside-view and balcony cabins can connect. Also for families, many cabins also have third- and fourth-person pull-down berths or trundle beds.

ACCOMMODATION. There are numerous accommodation price grades, so there's something for all tastes, from small interior cabins to lavish penthouse suites in a private courtyard setting – part of The Haven complex. Although they are nicely furnished and quite well equipped, the standard outside-view and interior cabins are quite small, particularly when occupied by three or four people.

A small room service menu is available; all non-food items are at extra cost, and a 15 percent service charge is added to your account. Bottled water is placed in each cabin, but you will be charged if you open the bottle.

Courtyard Penthouses/Suites. Two Garden Villas (each measures 4,390 sq ft/408 sq m), and 10 Courtyard Villas share a private courtyard with its own small pool, hot tub, massage bed, and fitness room – all in a setting that is distinctly Asian. They also share a private concierge lounge with the two largest villas, as well as butler and concierge service. These units enjoy exclusivity – rather like accommodation in a gated community – where others cannot live unless they pay the asking price. The two largest are duplex apartments, with a spiral stairway between the upper and lower quarters.

DINING. Freestyle Dining has no assigned dining rooms, tables or seats, so you can choose which restaurant to eat in, at what time, and with whom. In practice, this means you have to make reservations for a specific time, so 'freestyle dining' turns out to be programmed dining. Ten restaurants and eateries are spread over two entire decks. Some are included in the cruise fare, others cost extra.

There are two main dining rooms: the 552-seat Tsar's Palace, designed to look like the interior of Catherine the Great's St Petersburg palace in Russia, and the 310-seat Azura. There are also a number of other themed eating establishments, giving a wide range of choice – though some cost extra, and require advance reservations.

The 17 video screens around the ship enable you to check how long you'll have to wait for a table at each dining spot. Pagers are available, so you can go bar-hopping while you wait for a table. The system works well, although on formal nights when you may want to see the show, congestion can occur. NCL's dress code states that 'jeans, T-shirts, tank tops, and bare feet are not permitted in restaurants.'

Other dining options. Cagney's House (for fine steaks and seafood), Blue Lagoon (Asian street food), and Le Bistro (French cuisine) are NCL favorites. Tango is a contemporary spot with bright colors and Latin/tapas fare. Chin Chin is an Asian eatery with a Teppanyaki Grill and sushi counter. Mama's Italian Kitchen is novel in that it has a long wooden table running through the room to create the ambience of a Tuscan farmhouse. For really casual (self-serve) buffet-style eating, there's the light, airy Great Outdoors. Finally, the Garden Café incorporates an ice cream bar, and Kid's Café, with its own kid-height counter, is wisely located opposite the children's play areas. For coffee, head to the Java Café in the lobby – it's a great place for people watching. Three of the specialty restaurants incur a cover charge, while others are free.

ENTERTAINMENT. The Stardust Theatre, seating 1,037, is the venue for colorful Las Vegas-style production shows and major cabaret acts. It is designed in the style of an opera house, spans three decks, and has a steeply tiered main floor and port and starboard balconies.

There are two or three production shows in a typical seven-day cruise, all ably performed by the Jean Ann Ryan Company. These are all very colorful, high-energy, razzle-dazzle shows with much use of pyrotechnics, lasers, and color-mover lighting. By the end of the evening, you may well be too tired to remember much about the shows, which are nevertheless very entertaining.

A number of bands and solo entertaining musicians provide live music for listening and dancing in lounges and bars. In Spinnakers Lounge, a nightclub, a Pachanga Party is held each cruise (a Miami South Beach rave).

SPA/FITNESS. Wellness devotees should enjoy the two-deck-high Bora Bora health spa complex, operated by the Hawaii-based Mandara Spa, located in the front of the ship with large ocean-view windows on three sides. There are many facilities and services to pamper you, almost all at extra charge, including Thai massage in the spa, outdoors on deck, in your cabin or on your private balcony.

In addition, there is a 37-ft (11-m) indoor lap pool, hydrotherapy pool, two sit-in deep tubs, aromatherapy and wellness centers, and mud treatment rooms. There are 15 treatment rooms in all, including one specifically designed for couples, and heated tile loungers in a relaxation area.

The fitness and exercise rooms, with the latest Cybex muscle-pumping equipment, are located not within the spa, but at the top of the glass-domed atrium lobby. Included is a room for exercycle classes. Some classes, such as Pathway to Yoga, Body Cycling Class, and Body Beat Class (cardio kick-boxing), cost extra.

Recreational sports facilities include a jogging track, golf driving range, basketball and volleyball courts, as well as four levels of sunbathing decks.

Norwegian Pearl
★★★+

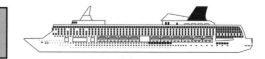

Size:.................................Large Resort Ship	Crew/Passenger Ratio (lower beds/all berths):.........2.2/2.6
Tonnage:.......................................93,530	Cabins (total):...................................1,197
Lifestyle:....................................Standard	Size range (sq ft/m):...............142.0–4,390.0/13.2–407.8
Cruise line:............................Norwegian Cruise Line	Cabins (outside view):...............................792
Former names:...................................none	Cabins (interior/no view):............................405
IMO number:.................................9342281	Cabins (for one person):..............................0
Builder:..........................Meyer Werft (Germany)	Cabins (with private balcony):........................540
Original cost:..............................$390 million	Cabins (wheelchair accessible):........................27
Entered service:...........................Dec 2006	Wheelchair accessibility:..........................Good
Registry:......................................Panama	Cabin voltage:...............................110 volts
Length (ft/m):.............................964.8/294.1	Elevators:.......................................12
Beam (ft/m):..............................105.6/32.2	Casino (gaming tables):.............................Yes
Draft (ft/m):................................26.9/8.2	Slot machines:....................................Yes
Propulsion/Propellers:...diesel-electric (39,000kW)/2 azimuthing	Swimming pools:....................................2
pods	Hot tubs (on deck):.................................6
Passenger decks:...................................12	Self-service launderette:...........................Yes
Total crew:....................................1,087	Dedicated cinema/seats:.............................No
Passengers (lower beds/alll berths):.............2,394/2,846	Library:...Yes
Passenger Space Ratio (lower beds/all berths):.......39.0/32.8	Onboard currency:.................................US$

A casual, family-friendly multi-choice ship

OVERVIEW. Plenty of choices, including many dining options, add up to an attractive vacation package, highly suitable for families with children, in a floating leisure center that provides ample facilities for enjoyment. The dress code is very casual – no jacket and tie needed – although you are welcome to dress formally if you wish.

THE SHIP. The ship's white hull has a colorful, funky design on its sides featuring sparkling jewels. There are plenty of sunloungers – in fact, more than the number of passengers carried. Water slides are included for the adult swimming pools. Children have their own pools at the stern, out of sight of adult areas.

Inside the ship, you'll be met by an eclectic mix of colors and decor that you probably wouldn't have in your home, and yet somehow it works extremely well in this large resort ship setting designed to attract the young, active, and trendy.

There are 13 bars and lounges, including Bar Central, three specialty bars that are connected but have distinct personalities. Shakers Martini and Cocktail Bar is a 1960s-inspired lounge; Magnum's Champagne and Wine Bar recalls Paris of the 1920s and the liner *Normandie*; and Maltings Beer and Whiskey Pub is a contemporary bar with artwork themed around whiskey and beer production.

Despite the company's name, there's little that's Norwegian about this product, except for some senior officers. There's plenty of lively music, constant ac-

Berlitz's Ratings		
	Possible	Achieved
Ship	500	371
Accommodation	200	145
Food	400	240
Service	400	272
Entertainment	100	66
Cruise	400	275
OVERALL SCORE		
1369 points out of 2000		

tivity, entertainment, and food that is mainstream and acceptable but nothing more, unless you pay extra to eat in the specialty dining spots. All this is delivered by a smiling, friendly service staff that lacks polish but is willing.

The ship is, however, full of revenue centers designed to part you from your cash. Expect to be subjected to a stream of flyers advertising daily art auctions, 'designer' watches, and 'inch of gold/silver.'

The initial cruise fare is reasonable, but extra costs soon mount up if you want to sample more than the basics. A mandatory per person service charge is added to your account daily; 15 percent is also added for bar charges, and a whopping 18 percent for spa treatments.

FAMILIES. A good deal of space is devoted to children's facilities, which are all tucked well away from adult recreation areas, at the aft end of the ship. Children of all ages will get to play in a superb wet 'n' wild space-themed water park complete with large pool, water slide, and paddle pool. There's a room full of cots for toddlers to use for sleepovers, and even the toilets are at a special low height. Teens, too, are well catered for, and have their own cinema, discotheque with dance floor, and hot tub.

More than 250 cabins have interconnecting doors – good for families with children. That means interior cabins can connect; outside-view cabins can connect; and outside-view and balcony cabins can connect. Also for families, many cabins also have third- and fourth-person pull-down berths or trundle beds.

ACCOMMODATION. There are numerous accommodation price grades, so there's something for all tastes, from small interior cabins to lavish penthouse suites in a private courtyard setting – part of The Haven complex. Although they are nicely furnished and quite well equipped, the standard outside-view and interior cabins are quite small, particularly when occupied by three or four people.

A small room service menu is available; all non-food items are at extra cost, and a 15 percent service charge is added to your account. Bottled water is placed in each cabin, but you will be charged if you open the bottle.

Courtyard Penthouses/Suites. Two Garden Villas (each measures 4,390 sq ft/408 sq m), and 10 Courtyard Villas share a private courtyard with its own small pool, hot tub, massage bed, and fitness room – all in a setting that is distinctly Asian. They also share a private concierge lounge with the two largest villas, as well as butler and concierge service. These units enjoy exclusivity – rather like accommodation in a gated community – where others cannot live unless they pay the asking price. The two largest are duplex apartments, with a spiral stairway between the upper and lower quarters.

Deluxe Owner's Suites. Two suites are set high atop all other accommodation, have stunning ocean views, and consist of a master bedroom with king-size bed, a dining/lounge area, a decent-size balcony, and access to the private courtyard.

DINING. Freestyle Dining has no assigned dining rooms, tables or seats, so you can choose which restaurant to eat in, at what time, and with whom. In practice, this means you have to make reservations for a specific time, so 'freestyle dining' turns out to be programmed dining. Ten restaurants and eateries are spread over two entire decks. Some are included in the cruise fare, others cost extra.

The two principal dining rooms are the 304-seat Indigo, with its minimalist decor; and the 558-seat Summer Palace, plus eight other themed eating spots. The 17 video screens around the ship enable you to check how long you'll have to wait for a table at each dining spot. Pagers are available, so you can go bar-hopping while you wait for a table. The system works well, although on formal nights when you may want to see the show, congestion can occur. NCL's dress code states that 'jeans, T-shirts, tank tops, and bare feet are not permitted in restaurants.'

Other dining options. Cagney's House (for fine steaks and seafood), Blue Lagoon (Asian street food), and Le Bistro (French cuisine) are NCL favorites. Mambo's is a contemporary spot with bright colors and Latin/tapas fare. Lotus Garden is an Asian eatery featuring a Teppanyaki Grill and sushi counter. A La Cucina Italian Restaurant is novel in that it has a long wooden table running through the room to create the ambience of a Tuscan farmhouse. For really casual (self-serve) buffet-style eating, there's the light, airy Great Outdoors. Finally, the Garden Café incorporates an ice cream bar, and Kid's Café, with its own kid-height counter, is wisely located opposite the children's play areas. For coffee, head to the Java Café in the lobby – it's a great place for people watching. Three of the specialty restaurants incur a cover charge, while others are free.

ENTERTAINMENT. The 1,037-seat Stardust Theatre is the venue for colorful Las Vegas-style production shows and major cabaret acts. It is designed in the style of an opera house, spans three decks, and has a steeply tiered main floor and port and starboard balconies.

There are two or three production shows in a typical seven-day cruise, all ably performed by the Jean Ann Ryan Company. These are all very colorful, high-energy, razzle-dazzle shows with much use of pyrotechnics, lasers, and color-mover lighting. By the end of the evening, you may well be too tired to remember much about the shows, which are nevertheless very entertaining.

A number of bands and solo entertaining musicians provide live music for listening and dancing in lounges and bars. In Spinnakers Lounge, a nightclub, a Pachanga Party is held each cruise (a Miami South Beach rave).

SPA/FITNESS. Bodywaves is the name of the spa/fitness center. It is operated by the Hawaii-based Mandara Spa (Steiner Leisure), located in the front of the ship with large ocean-view windows on three sides. There are lots of facilities and services to pamper you, almost all at extra charge, including Thai massage in the spa, outdoors on deck, in your cabin or on your private balcony.

In addition, there is a 37-ft (11-m) indoor lap pool, hydrotherapy pool, two sit-in deep tubs, aromatherapy and wellness centers, and mud treatment rooms. There are 15 private massage/body treatment rooms, including one just for couples.

The fitness and exercise rooms, with the latest muscle-pumping equipment, are located not within the spa, but at the top of the glass-domed atrium lobby. Included is a room for exercycle classes. Some classes, such as Pathway to Yoga, Body Cycling Class, and Body Beat Class, cost extra.

Recreational sports facilities include a jogging track, golf driving range, basketball and volleyball courts, as well as four levels of sunbathing decks.

Norwegian Sky
★★★ +

Size:.....................................Large Resort Ship	Cabins (total):................................... 1,001
Tonnage: 77,104	Size range (sq ft/m): 120.5–488.6/11.2–45.4
Lifestyle: ....Standard	Cabins (outside view):...............................574
Cruise line:........................Norwegian Cruise Line	Cabins (interior/no view):............................427
Former names: ....Pride of Aloha, Norwegian Sky	Cabins (for one person):..............................0
IMO number: 9128532	Cabins (with private balcony):......................252
Builder: .... Lloyd Werft (Germany)	Cabins (wheelchair accessible): 6
Original cost: ....$332 million	Wheelchair accessibility:..........................Good
Entered service:........................ Aug 1999/Jun 2008	Cabin voltage: .... 110 volts
Registry:................................The Bahamas	Elevators:..12
Length (ft/m):.............................. 853.0/260.0	Casino (gaming tables):............................ Yes
Beam (ft/m):............................... 105.8/32.2	Slot machines:................................... Yes
Draft (ft/m): 26.2/8.0	Swimming pools:.....................................2
Propulsion/Propellers:........... diesel-electric (50,000kW)/2	Hot tubs (on deck):..................................5
Passenger decks:....................................12	Self-service launderette:............................No
Total crew:.....................................914	Dedicated cinema/seats:.............................No
Passengers (lower beds/alll berths):............. 2,002/2,450	Library: ....Yes
Passenger Space Ratio (lower beds/all berths): 38.5/31.4	Onboard currency: ....US$
Crew/Passenger Ratio (lower beds/all berths):......... 2.1/2.6	

A multi-choice ship for upbeat, family-friendly cruising

OVERVIEW. *Norwegian Sky*, a resort at sea, caters well to a multi-generational clientele, with lots of choices for dining and entertainment. It provides a fine, comfortable base from which to explore. The outdoor space is quite generous, including an extra wide pool deck with two swimming pools and four hot tubs.

THE SHIP. In 2004 *Norwegian Sky* was 'Hawaiianized' and morphed into *Pride of Aloha* for NCL's Hawaii cruise operation. It withdrew from that market in May 2008 and was transferred to NCL for short cruises in the Caribbean. The interior decor reflects its operating area, and the focal point is an eight-deck-high atrium lobby, with spiral sculptures and rainbow-colored sails.

Public rooms include a shopping arcade, children's playroom, Internet center with 14 terminals and coffee available from an adjacent bar, several lounges and bars, small conference room, the Mark Twain library; and Captain Cook's for cigars and cognac. Those with a black belt in shopping may seek out the Black Pearl Gem Shop.

The hustling for passengers to attend art auctions is aggressive and annoying, as is the constant bombardment for revenue activities and the daily junk mail that arrives at one's cabin door. There are many announcements – particularly annoying are those that state what is already written in the daily program. There is little connection to the sea from many public rooms. Passenger hallways are quite plain.

Berlitz's Ratings

	Possible	Achieved
Ship	500	370
Accommodation	200	145
Food	400	240
Service	400	266
Entertainment	100	74
Cruise	400	272

OVERALL SCORE
1367 points out of 2000

A per person service charge you can't change is added to your account daily; 15 percent is also added for bar charges, and a whopping 18 percent for spa treatments.

ACCOMMODATION. There are numerous price categories, including 13 for outside-view suites and cabins, and six for interior cabins. All the standard cabins have two lower beds that convert to a queen-size bed, a small lounge area with sofa and table, and a decent amount of closet space, but very little drawer space, and the cabins themselves are disappointingly small. However, each is decorated in colorful Hawaiian style, with an explosion of floral themes and vibrant colors.

More than 200 outside-view cabins have their own private balcony. Each cabin has a small vanity/writing desk, color TV set, personal safe, climate control, and a laptop computer connection socket. Audio can be obtained only through the TV set. Bottled water is placed in each cabin – but your account will be charged if you open it.

The largest accommodation is four Owner's Suites. Each has a hot tub, large teak table, two chairs and two sunloungers outside on a huge, very private, forward-facing teakwood floor balcony just under the ship's navigation bridge, with large floor-to-ceiling windows. Each suite has a separate lounge and bedroom. The lounge has a large dining table and four chairs, two two-person sofas, large TV set, DVD/CD unit, coffee table, queen-size pull-down Murphy's bed, guest closet, writing desk, wet bar with two bar stools, refrigerator and sink, several cupboards for glasses, and several drawers and other cupboards for storage. The bedroom, which has sliding wood half-doors that look into the lounge, has a queen-size bed (with European duvet) under a leaf-glass chandelier, vanity desk, TV, walk-in closet with plenty of hanging rail space, five open shelves, and large personal safe. The white-tiled bathroom, although not large, has a full-size tub with retractable clothesline, separate shower enclosure with glass doors, deep washbasin, and toiletries cabinets.

There are 10 Junior Suites, each with a private teak decked balcony; these suites face aft in a secluded position and overlook the ship's wash. They have almost the same facilities as those in the owner's suites, except for the outdoor hot tub, and the fact that there is less space.

DINING. Freestyle Dining has no assigned dining rooms, tables or seats, so you can choose which restaurant to eat in, at what time, and with whom. In practice, this means you have to make reservations for a specific time, so 'freestyle dining' turns out to be programmed dining.

The main dining rooms – Palace Restaurant, with 510 seats, and Crossings Restaurant, with 556 seats – have tables for four, six, or eight and an open-seating arrangement. The cuisine in both includes regional specialties. However, it's best to have dinner in one of the specialty restaurants, as the food in these two large dining rooms is just so-so.

Other dining options. A smaller eatery, the 83-seat Plantation Club Restaurant, is an à la carte, light-eating option serving 'healthy' spa dishes and tapas. It has half-moon-shaped alcoves and several tables for two. The wine list is quite decent and well arranged, with moderate prices, although you won't find many good vintage wines. The cutlery is very ordinary and there are no fish knives.

For classic and nouvelle French cuisine, the 102-seat Bistro has an à la carte menu. The decor is inspired by royal and aristocratic gardens. For premium steaks and lamb chops, there's Cagney's Restaurant, with 84 seats, intimate seating alcoves, and good food, at extra cost.

Other eateries include Pacific Heights, a casual Pacific Rim/Asian Fusion eatery that has steaks plus local fish and seafood. Casual, self-serve buffet-style meals can be taken in the Garden Café.

ENTERTAINMENT. The 1,000-seat, two-deck-high (main and balcony levels) Stardust Theater is the venue for production shows and major cabaret acts, although the sight lines are quite poor from some seats. A number of bands and solo entertaining musicians provide live music for listening and dancing in several lounges and bars.

SPA/FITNESS. Body Waves is a large health/fitness spa – including an aerobics room and a separate gymnasium, and several treatment rooms. Mandara Spa, headquartered in Honolulu but owned by Steiner Leisure, operates it and provides all staff and treatments as the concession. A whopping 18 percent gratuity is added to spa treatments.

Sports fans will appreciate the large basketball/volleyball court, baseball-batting cage, golf-driving net, platform tennis, shuffleboard, and table tennis facilities. A sports bar, with baseball and surfing themes, has live satellite television coverage of sports events and major games on several TV screens. Joggers can take advantage of a walk-around indoor/outdoor jogging track.

Norwegian Spirit
★★★+

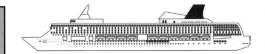

Size:................................Large Resort Ship		Cabins (total):.....................................988	
Tonnage: 75,338		Size range (sq ft/m): 150.6–638.3/14.0–59.3	
Lifestyle: ....Standard		Cabins (outside view):..............................609	
Cruise line:.........................Norwegian Cruise Line		Cabins (interior/no view):..........................379	
Former names: .... *SuperStar Leo*		Cabins (for one person):.............................0	
IMO number: 914106		Cabins (with private balcony):......................374	
Builder: .... Meyer Werft (Germany)		Cabins (wheelchair accessible): 4	
Original cost:..............................$350 million		Wheelchair accessibility:..........................Good	
Entered service:..................... Oct 1998/May 2004		Cabin voltage: .... 240 volts	
Registry:...................................... Panama		Elevators:.......................................9	
Length (ft/m):............................... 879.2/268.0		Casino (gaming tables):............................ Yes	
Beam (ft/m):................................. 105.6/32.2		Slot machines:.................................. Yes	
Draft (ft/m):.................................. 25.9/7.9		Swimming pools:...................................2	
Propulsion/Propellers:.............. 2 diesels (50,400kW)/2		Hot tubs (on deck):................................4	
Passenger decks:....................................10		Self-service launderette:...........................No	
Total crew:.......................................948		Dedicated cinema/seats:............................No	
Passengers (lower beds/alll berths):.............. 1,976/2,475		Library:.. Yes	
Passenger Space Ratio (lower beds/all berths): 38.1/30.4		Onboard currency: ....US$	
Crew/Passenger Ratio (lower beds/all berths):.......... 2.0/2.6			

A casual and lively lifestyle in a large resort ship

OVERVIEW. Because Norwegian Spirit is quite a stunning ship and offers a wide choice of dining venues, keeping consistency of product delivery will depend on the quality of the staff. There are many extra-cost items in addition to the extra-charge dining spots, and announcements that never end.

THE SHIP. A full walk-around promenade deck outdoors is good for strolling and has lots of space, including a whole area devoted to children's outdoor activities and pool. Inside, there are two indoor boulevards and a large, stunning, two-deck-high central atrium lobby with three glass-walled lifts and ample space to peruse the shops and cafés that line its inner sanctum. The lobby itself is modeled after the lobby of Hong Kong's Hyatt Hotel, with little clutter from the usual run of desks found aboard other cruise ships.

The interior design theme revolves around art, architecture, history, and literature. The ship has a mix of both eastern and western design and decor details. Three stairways are each carpeted in a different color, which helps new passengers find their way around.

A 450-seat room atop the ship functions as an observation lounge during the day and a nightclub at night, with live music. From it, a spiral stairway takes you down to a navigation bridge viewing area, where you can see the captain and bridge officers at work.

There is a business and conference center – good for small groups – and writing room, and a smoking room for those who enjoy cigars and cognac. A shopping

Berlitz's Ratings		
	Possible	Achieved
Ship	500	371
Accommodation	200	145
Food	400	240
Service	400	274
Entertainment	100	66
Cruise	400	274
OVERALL SCORE		
1370 points out of 2000		

concourse is set around the second level of the lobby.

The casino complex is at the forward end of the atrium boulevard on Deck 7 (not between showlounge and restaurant as in most Western ships). This includes Maharajah's, a large general-purpose, brightly lit casino, with gaming tables and slot machines.

The dress code is extremely casual – no jacket and tie needed. With many dining choices, some of which cost extra, to accommodate different tastes and styles, your cruise and dining experience will largely depend on how much you are prepared to spend.

Standing in line for embarkation, disembarkation, shore tenders, and for self-serve buffet meals is an inevitable aspect of cruising aboard all large ships. Note that a non-changeable per person service charge is added to your account daily; 15 percent is also added for bar charges, and a whopping 18 percent for spa treatments.

FAMILIES. Teens have their own huge video arcade, while younger children get to play in a wet 'n' wild aft pool (complete with pirate ship and caves) and two whirlpool tubs. Plus there's all the fun and facilities of Charlie's childcare center, which includes a painting room, computer learning center, and small cinema. Even the toilets are at a special low height, and there's a room full of cots for toddlers. Over 15,000 sq ft (1,400 sq m) is devoted to children's facilities – all tucked well away from adult recreation areas.

ACCOMMODATION. Three whole decks of cabins have private balconies, while two-thirds of all cabins have an outside view. Both the standard outside-view and interior cabins really are very small – particularly given that all cabins have extra berths for a third/fourth person – although the bathrooms have a good-size shower enclosure. So, take only the least amount of clothing you can get away with. All cabins have a personal safe, 100 percent cotton towels, and 100 percent cotton duvets or sheets. In cabins with balconies, the balconies are extremely narrow, and the cabins themselves are very small – the ship was originally constructed for three- and four-day cruises.

Choose one of the six largest Executive Suites (named Hong Kong, Malaysia, Shanghai, Singapore, Thailand, and Tokyo) and you'll have an excellent amount of private living space, with separate lounge and bedroom. Each has a large en suite bathroom that is part of the bedroom and opens onto it. It has a gorgeous mosaic tiled floor, kidney bean-shaped whirlpool tub, two sinks, separate shower enclosure with floor-to-ceiling ocean-view window, and separate toilet with glass door. There are TV sets in the lounge, bedroom, and bathroom. The Singapore and Hong Kong suites and the Malaysia and Thai suites can be combined to form a double suite – good for families with children. Butler service and a concierge come with the territory.

The 12 Zodiac suites, each named after an astrological sign, are the second largest accommodation, and also have a butler and concierge. Each has a separate lounge, bedroom, and bathroom, and an interconnecting door to an ocean-view cabin with private balcony – good for families. All cabinetry features richly lacquered woods, large (stocked) wet bar with refrigerator, dining table with a top that flips over to reveal a card table, and four chairs, plus sofa, drinks table, and trouser press. The bedrooms are small but have a queen-size bed; there is a decent amount of drawer space, although the closet space is rather tight because it contains two personal safes.

A small room service menu is available; all non-food items cost extra, and both a 15 percent service charge as well as a gratuity are added to your account.

DINING. There are eight places to eat, two at extra cost, so you need to plan where you want to eat well in advance or you may be disappointed.

Windows Restaurant: The equivalent of a main dining room; it seats 632 in two seatings, is two decks high at the aft-most section, and has huge cathedral-style windows set in three sections overlooking the ship's stern and wake. Waiter stations are tucked neatly away in side wings, which help to keep down noise levels.

Other dining options. The Garden Room Restaurant: This venue has 268 seats.

Raffles Terrace Café: a large self-serve buffet restaurant with indoor/outdoor seating for 400 and pseudo-Raffles Hotel-like decor, with rattan chairs, overhead fans, etc.

Moderno Churrascaria: Installed in a 2011 refit, this Brazilian steakhouse has passadors who serve skewered meats tableside. Reservations are required and there's a cover charge.

Taipan: a Chinese Restaurant, with traditional Hong Kong-themed decor and items such as dim sum made from fresh, not frozen, ingredients. Cover charge, reservations needed.

Shogun Asian Restaurant: a Japanese restaurant and sushi bar, for sashimi, sushi, and tempura. A section can be closed off to make the Samurai Room, with 22 seats, while a traditional Tatami Room has seats for eight. There's also a teppanyaki grill, with 10 seats, where the chef cooks in front of you.

Maxim's: a small à la carte restaurant with ocean-view windows; fine cuisine in the classic French style. Cover charge applicable, reservations necessary.

Blue Lagoon Café: a small, casual street café with about 24 seats, featuring noodle dishes, fried rice, and other Southeast Asian cuisine. Adjacent is a street bar called The Bund.

In addition, The Café, in the atrium lobby, is a pâtisserie serving several types of coffees, teas, cakes, and pastries, at extra cost.

ENTERTAINMENT. The Moulin Rouge Showlounge, with 973 seats, is the main venue. It is two decks high, with a main and balcony levels. The room has almost no support columns to obstruct the sight lines, and a revolving stage for Broadway-style reviews and other production shows – typically to recorded music since there's little space for an orchestra. The showlounge is also used as a large-screen cinema, and has excellent surround sound.

SPA/FITNESS. The Roman Spa and Fitness Center is on one of the uppermost decks, just forward of the Tivoli Pool. It has a gymnasium full of high-tech muscle-toning equipment, and aerobics exercise room, hair and beauty salon, and saunas, steam rooms, and changing rooms for men and women, as well as several treatment rooms, and aqua-swim pools that provide counter-flow jets (swimming against the current). The spa facility is operated by the Hawaii-based Mandara Spa, owned by Steiner Leisure.

The fitness and exercise rooms, with the latest Cybex muscle-pumping equipment, are located not within the spa, but at the top of the glass-domed atrium lobby. Included is a room for exercycle classes. Sports facilities include a jogging track, golf driving range, basketball and tennis courts, and there are four levels of sunbathing decks.

Norwegian Star
★★★+

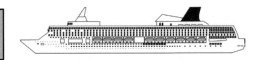

Size:......................................	.Large Resort Ship	Crew/Passenger Ratio (lower beds/all berths):.........	2.1/2.6
Tonnage:..................................	91,740	Cabins (total):..................................	1,122
Lifestyle:.................................	.Standard	Size range (sq ft/m):..............142.0–5,350.0/13.2–497.0	
Cruise line:..............................	Norwegian Cruise Line	Cabins (outside view):..............................	787
Former names:.............................	none	Cabins (interior/no view):...........................	335
IMO number:..............................	9195157	Cabins (for one person):.............................	0
Builder:..........................	Meyer Werft (Germany)	Cabins (with private balcony):........................	509
Original cost:.............................	$400 million	Cabins (wheelchair accessible):.......................	20
Entered service:...........................	Dec 2001	Wheelchair accessibility:...........................	Best
Registry:.................................	Panama	Cabin voltage:..............................	110 volts
Length (ft/m):.............................	964.9/294.1	Elevators:....................................	12
Beam (ft/m):..............................	105.6/32.2	Casino (gaming tables):.............................	Yes
Draft (ft/m):..............................	26.9/8.2	Slot machines:..................................	Yes
Propulsion/Propellers:...diesel-electric (39,000kW)/2 azimuthing pods		Swimming pools:.................................	3
		Hot tubs (on deck):..............................	5
Passenger decks:...........................	12	Self-service launderette:...........................	No
Total crew:...............................	1,063	Dedicated cinema/seats:............................	Yes
Passengers (lower beds/alll berths):...........	2,244/2,846	Library:......................................	Yes
Passenger Space Ratio (lower beds/all berths):.......	40.8/32.0	Onboard currency:...............................	US$

A family-friendly, multi-choice ship for active types

OVERVIEW. Many more choices, including lots of dining options, add up to a very attractive package, particularly suitable for families with children, in a very contemporary floating leisure center that really does provide ample facilities for enjoyment.

THE SHIP. *Norwegian Star*, a sister ship to *Norwegian Dawn*, has a pod propulsion system. A large structure located forward of the funnel houses a children's play center, and, one deck above, the two outstanding 'villa' suites. The hull is adorned with a decal consisting of a burst of colorful stars and streamers.

There are plenty of sunloungers. Water slides are included for the adult swimming pools. Children have their own pools at the ship's stern.

Facilities include an Internet café with 17 computer stations, a 1,150-seat showlounge with main floor and two balcony levels, 3,000-book library, card room, writing and study room, business center, karaoke lounge, conference and meeting rooms, a large retail shopping complex, and a casino.

With so many dining choices, some costing extra. The dress code is very casual – no jacket and tie needed, although you are welcome to dress formally if you wish. Although service levels and finesse are sometimes inconsistent, the level of hospitality is very good. But the hustling for passengers to attend art auctions is aggressive and annoying. Reaching room service tends to be an exercise in frustration.

Berlitz's Ratings

	Possible	Achieved
Ship	500	381
Accommodation	200	145
Food	400	240
Service	400	272
Entertainment	100	67
Cruise	400	273

OVERALL SCORE
1378 points out of 2000

A mandatory per person service charge is added to your account daily; 15 percent is also added for bar charges.

FAMILIES. Children of all ages will get to play in a superb wet 'n' wild space-themed water park complete with large pool, water slide, and paddle pool. They also get their own dedicated cinema in which DVD movies are featured all day long, a jungle gym, painting area, and computer center. Even the toilets are at a special low height. Teens get their own cinema with DVD movies, discotheque with dance floor, and whirlpool tub.

ACCOMMODATION. With 29 price grades, this is a mix that includes something for everyone. There are 36 suites, including two of the largest aboard any cruise ship, 372 balcony-class standard cabins, 415 outside-view cabins (no balcony), 363 interior cabins, and 20 wheelchair-accessible cabins. Suites and cabins with private balconies have easy-to-use sliding glass doors.

All have a powerful hairdryer, and a tea and coffee making sets, rich cherry wood cabinetry, and a bathroom with a sliding door and a separate toilet, and shower enclosure and washbasin compartments. There is plenty of wood accenting in all accommodation, including wood frames surrounding balcony doors.

The largest accommodation is in two huge Garden Villas (Vista and Horizon), located high atop the ship in a pod that is located forward of the ship's funnel, and overlooks the main swimming pool. Each measures 5,350 sq ft (497 sq m) and can be combined to create a huge, double-size 'house.' These villas have huge glass walls and landscaped private roof gardens (one has a Japanese-style garden, the other a Thai-style garden) for outdoor dining (with whirlpool tubs, naturally), and huge private sunbathing areas that are completely shielded.

Each suite has three bedrooms, one with a sliding glass door that leads to the garden, and bathrooms. One bathroom has a large corner tub, and two washbasins set in front of large glass walls that overlook the side of the ship as well as the swimming pool, although most of the view is of the overlarge waterslide, and a large living room with Yamaha baby grand piano, glass dining table, and eight chairs. These units have their own private elevator and private stairway.

There are many suites (the smallest measures 290 sq ft/27 sq m) in several different configurations. Some overlook the stern, while others are in the forward part of the ship. All are lavishly furnished, although closet space in some of the smaller units is tight.

Although the suites and junior suites are quite spacious, the standard interior and outside-view cabins are very small when compared to those of other major cruise lines such as Carnival or Celebrity, particularly when occupied by three or four people. The bathrooms, however, are of quite a decent size and have large shower enclosures. Some cabins have interconnecting doors – good for families with children – and many cabins have third- and fourth-person pull-down berths or trundle beds.

A small room service menu is available; all non-food items cost extra, and a 15 percent service charge are added to your account. Bottled water is placed in each cabin, but a charge is made if you open the bottle.

DINING. NCL operates Freestyle Dining, so you can choose which restaurant to eat in, at what time, and with whom. Ten restaurants and eateries, with 11 different menus nightly, are spread over two decks. Overall, the food is best described as adequate, but lacking in taste and presentation, although the menus make the dishes sound good. The wine list is quite good and moderately priced, though the glasses are small.

Versailles, the ornate 375-seat first main dining room, is decorated in brilliant red and gold. This offers traditional six-course dining experience and has excellent views through windows that span two decks.

Other dining options. Aqua: a contemporary-styled 374-seat second main dining room, offering lighter cuisine, and an open galley where you can view the preparation of pastries and desserts.

Soho: Pacific Rim mixes Californian and Asian cuisine. It has a live lobster tank – the first aboard a ship outside Southeast Asia. A main dining area seats 132, and private dining rooms each seat 10.

Ginza: a Japanese restaurant, with 193 seats, a sit-up sushi bar, tempura bar, show galley, and separate 'teppanyaki grill' room.

Le Bistro: a French restaurant, with 66 seats, serving nouvelle cuisine and six courses.

Blue Lagoon: a funky food-court-style eatery with 88 seats, both indoors and outdoors, with hamburgers, fish and chips, potpies, and fast (wok stir-fried) dishes.

Market Café: a large indoor/outdoor self-serve buffet eatery, with almost 400ft (120m) of buffet counter space. 'Action Stations' has made-to-order omelets, waffles, fruit, soups, ethnic specialties, and pasta dishes.

La Trattoria, an Italian, evening-only dining spot within the buffet area, has pasta, pizza, and other Italian fare.

Steakhouse: prime USDA beef steaks and lamb chops.

Endless Summer: a Hawaiian themed restaurant, incorporating a performance stage and a large movie screen.

Other spots include the Red Lion, an English pub for draft beer and a game of darts; Havana Club, a cigar and cognac lounge; Java Café, an atrium lobby bar-café for hot and frozen coffees, teas, and pastries; a Beer Garden for grilled foods; a Spinkles, an ice cream bar; a Gym and Spa Bar for health food snacks and drinks; and Gatsby's wine bar.

A lavish chocoholics buffet is available once each cruise – a firm favorite among the regulars.

ENTERTAINMENT. The Stardust Theatre, seating 1,037, is the venue for colorful Las Vegas-style production shows and major cabaret acts. Two or three production shows are presented in a typical seven-day cruise, all ably performed by the Jean Ann Ryan Company. They're very entertaining if not particularly memorable.

A number of bands and solo entertainers provide live music for listening and dancing in several lounges and bars.

SPA/FITNESS. The two-deck-high Barong health spa complex, operated by the Steiner-owned and Hawaii-based Mandara Spa, is at the stern, with large ocean-view windows on three sides.

The many facilities and services, almost all cost extra, include Thai massage. There is an indoor lap pool measuring 37ft (11m), hydrotherapy pool, aromatherapy and wellness centers, and 15 treatment rooms. A gratuity of 18 percent is automatically added for spa and beauty treatments.

The fitness and exercise rooms, with the latest equipment, are at the top of the atrium lobby. Recreational sports facilities include a jogging track, golf driving range, basketball and volleyball courts, as well as four levels of sunbathing decks.

Norwegian Sun
★★★ +

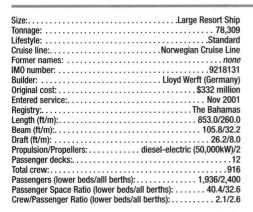

Size:....................................Large Resort Ship	Cabins (total):.......................................968
Tonnage: 78,309	Size range (sq ft/m): 120.5–488.6/11.2–45.4
Lifestyle: ....Standard	Cabins (outside view):................................676
Cruise line:.......................Norwegian Cruise Line	Cabins (interior/no view):..............................292
Former names: ....*none*	Cabins (for one person):.................................0
IMO number: 9218131	Cabins (with private balcony):........................252
Builder: .... Lloyd Werft (Germany)	Cabins (wheelchair accessible): 6
Original cost:................................ $332 million	Wheelchair accessibility:..........................Good
Entered service:.............................. Nov 2001	Cabin voltage: .... 110 volts
Registry:....................................The Bahamas	Elevators:...12
Length (ft/m):............................... 853.0/260.0	Casino (gaming tables):...............................Yes
Beam (ft/m):................................ 105.8/32.2	Slot machines:......................................Yes
Draft (ft/m): 26.2/8.0	Swimming pools:......................................2
Propulsion/Propellers:........... diesel-electric (50,000kW)/2	Hot tubs (on deck):...................................4
Passenger decks:...................................12	Self-service launderette:..............................No
Total crew:..916	Dedicated cinema/seats:..............................No
Passengers (lower beds/all berths):............. 1,936/2,400	Library: ....Yes
Passenger Space Ratio (lower beds/all berths): 40.4/32.6	Onboard currency: ....US$
Crew/Passenger Ratio (lower beds/all berths):.......... 2.1/2.6	

Big-ship casual cruising in a family-friendly ship

OVERVIEW. What this offers is plenty of bars and lounges to play in, and multiple dining and snacking options. But the food in the large dining rooms is a weak point, and the ship is full of revenue centers, designed to help you part you from your money.

THE SHIP. *Norwegian Sun* is a close sister ship to *Norwegian Sky*, but has better outfitting and finishing detail, plus one extra deck of balcony cabins and additional cabins to accommodate the extra 200 crew needed for the Freestyle dining concept. The outdoor space is quite good, especially the ultra-wide pool deck, with two swimming pools and four Jacuzzi tubs, and plenty of sunloungers, albeit arranged in camp-style rows.

A separate cabaret venue, Dazzles Lounge, has an extremely long bar. A large casino operates 24 hours a day. There's a shopping arcade, children's playroom, and a video arcade. Other facilities include a small conference room, library and beauty salon, a lounge for smoking cigars and drinking cognac, and an Internet café with 20 computers. You can expect to be subjected to a stream of flyers advertising daily art auctions, 'designer' watches, and other promotions, while 'artworks' for auction are strewn throughout the ship.

A mandatory per person service charge is added to your account daily; 15 percent is also added for bar charges, and a whopping 18 percent for spa treatments.

The standard interior and outside-view cabins are very small when compared to those of other major cruise lines. There are many plastic plates, Styrofoam

Berlitz's Ratings		
	Possible	Achieved
Ship	500	371
Accommodation	200	145
Food	400	240
Service	400	266
Entertainment	100	74
Cruise	400	271
OVERALL SCORE		
1367 points out of 2000		

and plastic cups, and plastic stirrers in use in the casual eateries.

FAMILIES. Young passengers will find an array of facilities, which include a children's playroom called Kid's Corner for 'junior sailors' (ages three to five); First Mates (six to nine); Navigators (10–12); and Teens (13–17).

ACCOMMODATION. There are many, many different categories, including six grades of suites, 15 grades of outside-view cabins, and nine grades of interior cabins.

All of the standard outside-view and interior cabins have common facilities, such as two lower beds that can convert to a queen-size bed, a small lounge area with sofa and table, and a decent amount of closet and drawer space, although the cabins themselves are disappointingly small. Over 200 outside-view cabins have a private balcony. There are two Honeymoon/Anniversary Suites, each with a separate lounge and bedroom.

The largest accommodation is in two Owner's Suites – each with a hot tub, large teak table, two chairs and two sunloungers outside on a huge, private, forward-facing teak floor balcony just under the navigation bridge, with large floor-to-ceiling windows. There are a number of other suites, each with a private teakwood balcony. They share some facilities with the owner's suites, except for the outdoor hot tub and the fact that there's less space.

All cabins have tea/coffee-making sets, a safe, satellite-linked telephone, and bathroom with bath or shower.

DINING. NCL has Freestyle Dining, so you can choose which restaurant you would like to eat in, at what time, and with whom. Apart from two large dining rooms, there are a number of other themed eating establishments – although it would be wise to plan in advance, particularly for dinner. Some incur an extra charge. The dress code states that: 'jeans, T-shirts, tank tops and bare feet are not permitted in restaurants.'

The two main dining rooms – the 564-seat Four Seasons Dining Room and the 604-seat Seven Seas Dining Room – have tables for two, four, six, or eight. Sandwiched between the two (rather like a train carriage) is a third, 84-seat Italian Restaurant, Il Adagio, available as an à la carte (extra charge, reservations required) option, with window-side tables for two or four persons. Reservations are necessary.

Overall, the food is adequate, but lacks taste and presentation quality, although the menus make the dishes sound good. There's a reasonably decent selection of breads, rolls, cheeses, and fruits. The wine list is quite good and moderately priced, though the glasses are small.

Other dining options. Most are located on one of the uppermost decks, with great views from large picture windows, and include:

Le Bistro: a 90-seat dining spot for French-style meals, including tableside cooking. Reservations required.

Las Ramblas: a Spanish/Mexican style eatery serving tapas (light snack items).

Ginza: a Japanese Restaurant, with a sushi bar and a teppanyaki grill (show cooking in a U-shaped setting where you sit around the chef). Reservations required.

East Meets West: a Pacific Rim Fusion Restaurant, featuring à la carte California/Hawaii/Asian cuisine. Reservations are necessary for dinner.

Moderna Churrascaria: Brazilian steakhouse and salad bar, with tableside meat carving. Reservations required.

Garden Café: a busy 24-hour restaurant indoor/outdoor self-serve buffet-style eatery with fast foods and salads.

Although the menus make meals sound appetizing, overall the food is rather unmemorable, lacking taste, and mostly overcooked. However, the presentation is generally quite good. There is a reasonable selection of breads, rolls, and pastry items, but the selection of cheeses is very poor.

The wine list is well balanced, and there is also a connoisseur list of premium wines, although the vintages tend to be young. There are many types of beer (including some on draught in the popular Sports Bar & Grill).

There is no formal afternoon tea, although you can make your own at beverage stations (but it's difficult to get fresh milk as non-dairy creamers are typically supplied). The service is, on the whole, adequate, nothing more.

A lavish chocoholics buffet is featured once each cruise – a firm favorite among NCL passengers.

ENTERTAINMENT. The Stardust Theater is a two-level showlounge with more than 1,000 seats and a large proscenium stage. However, the sight lines are obstructed in a number of seats by several slim pillars. Two or three production shows are presented in a typical seven-day cruise (all ably performed by the Jean Ann Ryan Company). These are very colorful, high-energy, high-volume razzle-dazzle shows with much use of pyrotechnics, lasers, and color-mover lighting.

The ship carries a number of bands and solo entertaining musicians. These provide live music for listening and dancing in several of the lounges and bars, including the loud Dazzles, home to musical groups.

SPA/FITNESS. Bodywaves, at the top of the atrium, is a large health/fitness spa (including an aerobics room and separate gymnasium), several treatment rooms, and men's and women's saunas/steam rooms and changing rooms.

There is an indoor-outdoor jogging track. a large basketball/volleyball court, baseball batting cage, golf driving range, platform tennis, shuffleboard and table tennis facilities, and sports bar with 24-hour live satellite TV coverage of sports events and major games.

Oasis of the Seas
★★★★

Size:....................................Large Resort Ship	Crew/Passenger Ratio (lower beds/all berths):..........2.4/2.9
Tonnage:......................................222,900	Cabins (total):...................................2,704
Lifestyle:.....................................Standard	Size range (sq ft/m):................................n/a
Cruise line:..................Royal Caribbean International	Cabins (outside view):............................2,210
Former names:.....................................none	Cabins (interior/no view):...........................494
IMO number:...................................9383936	Cabins (for one person):...............................0
Builder:.............................Aker Yards (Finland)	Cabins (with private balcony):......................1,956
Original cost:................................$1.5 billion	Cabins (wheelchair accessible):.......................46
Entered service:..............................Dec 2009	Wheelchair accessibility:...........................Good
Registry:..................................The Bahamas	Cabin voltage:..............................110 volts
Length (ft/m):..............................1181.1/360.0	Elevators:.......................................24
Beam (ft/m):................................216.5/66.0	Casino (gaming tables):.............................Yes
Draft (ft/m):...................................30.0/9.1	Slot machines:....................................Yes
Propulsion/Propellers:.... diesel-electric (97,200kWW)/3 pods (2	Swimming pools:.....................................3
azimuthing, 1 fixed)	Hot tubs (on deck):.................................10
Passenger decks:..................................16	Self-service launderette:............................No
Total crew:.....................................2,164	Dedicated cinema/seats:.............................No
Passengers (lower beds/alll berths):..............5,408/6,360	Library:...Yes
Passenger Space Ratio (lower beds/all berths):.......41.6/35.4	Onboard currency:..................................US$

A huge floating resort for families with boundless energy

OVERVIEW. *Oasis of the Seas* is large, but it provides a fine all-round cruise and wide range of choices for young adults and families with children, though the service is notably better in suite-class accommodation. The large resort ship is packed with innovative design elements – none more so than the dramatic Central Park, the first real park at sea.

THE SHIP. *Oasis of the Seas*, the first cruise ship in the world measuring over 200,000 tons – essentially a large block of apartments sitting on a white hull – is a benchmark for all floating self-contained resorts. Technically, it's no longer the world's largest cruise ship because its sister, *Allure of the Seas*, is almost 2ins (5cm) longer. In almost every other way, however, the ships are identical.

Built as a 'Moveable Resort Vacation' for families with children, it is a stunning ship and a credit to Royal Caribbean International's design team. There is a lot of outdoor and indoor/outdoor space for aqua-bathing and sports, although there's not much actual space for sunbathing. There are several swimming pools, and an H2O Zone. Two large hot tubs are cantilevered over the ship's side.

While the design of *Oasis of the Seas* from the front aspect is quite handsome, if rather bulky, the aft end looks as if it's been chopped off and unfinished when viewed from the side.

The public spaces are arranged as seven 'neighborhoods': Central Park, the Boardwalk, the Royal

Berlitz's Ratings

	Possible	Achieved
Ship	500	409
Accommodation	200	147
Food	400	236
Service	400	290
Entertainment	100	83
Cruise	400	293
OVERALL SCORE		
1458 points out of 2000		

Promenade, the Pool and Sports Zone, Vitality at Sea Spa/Fitness Center, Entertainment Place, and Youth Zone. The most popular are the Boardwalk and Central Park, both open to the air, and the indoor Royal Promenade.

The Boardwalk. Its design is reminiscent of New York's Coney Island. The Boardwalk contains shops and an art gallery. Art is displayed in Central Park's Art Artists who contributed to the ship's multi-million dollar collection can sell items to passengers.

Eateries include the Boardwalk Donut Shop; Johnny Rockets, a burger/milk shake diner; and a covered Seafood Shack for fish and seafood. If you are in a Central Park cabin, you'll need to take the elevator to get to the closest pool.

Central Park. This space is 328ft (100m) long. The vegetation is real, with 27 trees and almost 12,000 plants, including a vertical 'living' plant wall. But, unlike its New York inspiration, it includes, at its lower level, a 'town center.' At night, it's just about the only quiet and serene area, and is best for couples. Vintages wine bar is a great place to chill-out, and there are several reservations-required, extra-charge dining venues; arguably the nicest is 150 Central Park, while Chops Grille and Giovanni's Table are favorites for South Beach types. There's also Vintages wine and tapas bar, a nice place to relax in the late afternoon.

The Royal Promenade really is the equivalent of a floating shopping mall, with casual food eateries (including a Starbucks coffee store, located at the forward end), shops with all kinds of merchandise, video screens, and changing color lights at every step. But one thing not to be missed is the 'Move On! Move On!' parade, a 15-minute circus-like extravaganza that includes characters from DreamWorks Animation's Madagascar. A hydraulic, oval-shaped Rising Tide Bar moves slowly through three floors and links the double-width Royal Promenade with Central Park.

The ship is so large that it doesn't feel so crowded in most areas, except for the pool deck and in the Windjammer Café (particularly on days when the ship is in port and everyone is scrambling to get breakfast at the same time). Don't be concerned about long lines at check-in – there aren't any, because RCI has a custom-built terminal in Fort Lauderdale (Port Everglades) designed to get you on board in about 15 minutes.

The Passenger Space Ratio is actually good for such a large vessel, so there's not generally the hugely crowded feeling you might expect. The design concept is a continuum of the Freedom-class ships (*Oasis* of the Seas is, however, 30 percent more energy-efficient), themselves an extension of the Voyager-class ships – and then some. The increase in size has meant that RCI has been able to incorporate more of the facilities that young families seek for action-packed cruise vacations, including 37 bars and more than 20 places to eat or snack.

The ship is remarkably well designed, with large public spaces made possible by the split aft superstructure design – the idea of Harri Kulovaara, who first achieved this with Silja Serenade in 1986. This gives the ship the interior space needed to provide the 'seven neighborhoods' concept. Large touch-screen information screens provide electronic maps at each stairway, and elevators are color-coordinated in either pink or blue for the fore and aft sections of the ship. There are no elevators in the center of the ship; all are in forward and aft locations, but there are enough of them, and they are speedy.

Because Central Park and the Boardwalk are open to the elements – so you could hide under a tree – but better take an umbrella just in case it rains in the sunny Caribbean.

The Pool and Sports Zone forward of the twin funnels is a real adventurous fun place for families. An adults-only open-air solarium and rentable cabanas are part of the outdoor scene today, and Oasis provides several. Two Flow-Riders are part of the sports line-up; these are located atop the ship around the aft exhaust mast, together with basketball courts and golf. The ship also has the largest jogging track at sea.

The Solarium is the most welcoming large, light-filled and restful (despite the background music) space. High atop ship, it is frequented by few children – so adults can 'escape' the Las Vegas–like atmosphere of most other parts of the ship. On the subject of casinos, the roulette tables are stunning – all electronic and touch-buttony (no need to place chips on the table –

simply touch a screen with your finger). There are also blackjack, craps, Caribbean Stud Poker, and 450 slot machines, plus a player's club and poker room – but this really can be a smoke-filled place, even in the 'no-smoking' area.

The Caribbean itinerary for this ship includes a 'private' beach day at Labadee, the company's leased island. RCI built its own 800-ft (244-m) pier, making it a logistically simple matter for anyone to access the ship and beach several times during the day-long stay. Do try the zipline – it's one of the world's longest, and a real blast. Other fun things: an alpine coaster, a beach club with 20 private cabanas, a large artisans' market, and a Haitian Cultural Center.

A cruise aboard *Oasis of the Seas* should provide a fine family vacation experience, with a wide range of choices – many at extra cost. This means you'll need to plan how you will spend your time, and where you would like to eat, well in advance of your cruise. Overall, if you are in suite-grade accommodation, you'll be treated well, while those in anything else receive second-class service, and will hear the word 'no' a lot. But that's part and parcel of a large resort ship.

Passenger Niggles. If all 5,400 passengers want a sunlounger at the same time, forget it! Anyone able to secure one will find them so tightly packed together that there's little space to put any belongings. Exterior wooden railings have mostly been replaced by fibreglass railings – this is particularly noticeable on the balconies.

Live or recorded music is everywhere, 24 hours a day, whether inside or outside the ship, including elevators and accommodation hallways. Ordering room service is complicated – you can't do it by phone, only by using the interactive touch-screen television in your suite/cabin. Standing in line to make reservations for the main shows can be time-consuming and frustrating (the reservation booth is in the middle of the Royal Promenade). You could make them online before your cruise.

Getting reservations in one of the specialty restaurants takes a bit of effort, unless you are occupying suite-grade accommodation. Smoking is permitted in several bars and lounges aboard this ship and the smell of stale smoke permeates several areas. Cigar smokers will probably be underwhelmed by the cigar lounge.

The sense of being aboard a cruise ship is somewhat lost in all the large spaces to play in, but what this ship offers is a moveable resort full of facilities. There are few quiet nooks and crannies – except for a small, cramped library, with oversize leather chairs, and perhaps the Solarium.

Oasis of the Seas operates from a purpose-built $75 million Terminal 18 in Port Everglades (Fort Lauderdale), whose restroom facilities are minimal. Getting to the terminal is where people experience delays and frustration.

Disembarkation. If the two 'flybridge' gangways are working, disembarkation is relatively speedy. However, when only one is working, a line forms in the Royal Promenade, in which case it's better to sit somewhere until the line gets shorter. Disembarkation for non-US citizens can be appallingly slow.

ACCOMMODATION. There are many, many accommodation price grades, reflecting the choice of location and size. Suite occupants get access to a concierge lounge and associated services. There are many family-friendly cabins, good for family reunions, but there are no single-occupancy cabins. The cabin numbering system is a bit awkward to get used to. In a first for RCI, cabin doors open outwards (towards you), as in most European and Scandinavian hotels. In many of the lower grade accommodation, access to the closet is awkward – often with small sofas in the way. Most cabins feel extremely small, given the size of the ship. All cabins have an iPod dock.

Some 395 interior balcony cabins have either Central Park or Royal Promenade views from their curved interior balconies, four of which are wheelchair-accessible, plus 80 cabins with windows (no balconies) and views of Central Park. But you'll need to keep your curtains closed for privacy, which rather defeats the object. Noise could be generated along the inner promenades, particularly late at night with street parades and non-stop music.

Loft suites. Although a few ships such as the now withdrawn Saga Rose and Saga Ruby had upstairs/downstairs suites, RCI introduced its 'loft' suites to the Oasis-class ships. These offer spectacular ocean views, with floor-to-ceiling, double-height windows. Each has a lower living area plus a private balcony with sun chairs, and a stairway that connects to the sleeping area which overlooks the living area and has extended ocean views. Modern designs are dotted with abstract, modern art pieces.

There are 28 Loft Suites, with 25 Crown Loft suites measuring 545 sq ft (51 sq m). Three more spacious Loft Suites (called Royal Loft Suites) measure 1,524 sq ft (141 sq m). Each sleeps up to six, and each a baby grand piano, indoor and outdoor dining areas, a private wet bar, a library, and an extended 843-sq-ft (78.3-sq-m) balcony with flat-screen TV set, entertainment area, and Jacuzzi. Two large Sky Loft Suites measure 722 sq ft (67 sq m) and 770 sq ft (71 sq m), and a 737-sq-ft (68-sq-m) Crown Accessible Loft Suite includes an elevator to aid disabled passengers.

Standard Cabins (balcony and non-balcony class). Electrical sockets are located below the vanity desk unit in a user-unfriendly position. This is quite poor for anyone trying to use the hairdryer in the 50 percent of cabins where the sockets are positioned on the right side. Also, it's difficult to watch television from the bed.

The washbasins in non-suite grade cabins are very small and low, at just 30½ins (77.5cm) above the floor

level. Be careful – it's easy to hit your head on the mirror above. Small soap bars are provided, while shampoo is provided in a dispenser in the shower enclosure. Unfortunately, the shower head is fixed, making it difficult to wash yourself thoroughly. Although there is no soap dish or indentation in the washbasin surround for soap, useful touches include a blue ceiling bathroom nightlight.

Cabins are exposed to noise and whatever is happening on the Boardwalk itself, including rehearsals and sports activities in the Aqua Theater aft, bells from the carousel (whose animal figures took six weeks to carve), rowdy revelers on the Boardwalk late at night, plus screaming zip-lining participants high above during the day, not to mention loud music from bands playing at one of the pools, and exceedingly loud announcements by the cruise director repeating what's already printed in the daily program.

Boardwalk-view balcony cabin occupants need to close their curtains for privacy at times. However, the curved balconies – good for storing luggage to free up space inside the cabin – connect you with the open air and provide a community feeling, as you look across at balconies on the opposite side. Almost all have a sea view aft (just); those close to the aft Aqua Theater can use their balconies for a great view of any shows or events. The lowest deck of Boardwalk-view cabins has windows but no balcony – and actually the view is mainly of the top of things such as the carousel or beach hut-like structures. The best Boardwalk balcony cabins are, in my view, located on decks 8–12. For more privacy, however, it might be best to book a sea-facing balcony cabin, not one that overlooks the Boardwalk.

Many suite-grade cabins have bathrooms with granite-look washbasin counter tops, and two washbasins. Some have bidets, Jacuzzi tubs, and a separate shower enclosure. Some Family Suite grades have a separate, small room with bunk beds; some, not all, have curtains to separate them.

DINING. Because *Oasis of the Seas* is an extra-large resort ship, the main meals in the main dining room, which is spread over three decks, are all about well-timed production cooking and fast delivery – essentially a banquet catering operation. Almost inevitably, the food is tasteless (except for salt) and mostly underwhelming. When you book, choose one of two seatings, or 'My Time Dining' (eat when you want, during dining room hours). There are tables of all sizes, including large ones for family reunions.

Other dining options. 150 Central Park: The most exclusive restaurant aboard the ship, combines cutting-edge cuisine with interesting design. An observation window into the kitchen allows passers-by to watch the chefs in action. KeriAnn Van Raesfeld offers a multi-course tasting menu. It's open for dinner only, reservations are required and there's an extra charge.

Chops Grille, RCI's popular 'signature' steakhouse is open for dinner only, and offers premium-cut meats. There's a cover charge, and reservation are required.

Chef's Table, on the upper level of the Concierge lounge, is available to anyone. At $70 per person for dinner, and offers a six-course meal with wine. It is hosted by the executive chef, but, with just 14 seats, trying to get a reservation could be difficult.

Giovanni's Table ($20 for dinner – and well worth it if you're hungry): This casual Italian dining spot has a rustic feel, yet modern flair. It offers toasted herb breads, pizzas, salads, pastas, sandwiches, braised meat dishes, and stews. It's all rather good.

Central Park Café, a casual dining spot with a high level of variety and flexibility, is an indoor/outdoor food market with line-up counters and limited waiter service. Items include freshly prepared salads, made-to-order sandwiches, panini, crêpes, and hearty soups. You order directly from the chefs behind the food stations.

Rita's Cantina, on the Boardwalk, is a noisy canteen offering quasi-Mexican fare. The cover charge is high for what it is, and you'll need to a wait to get a table-cloth-less table. But then it is a bit of a cantina – so it lives up to its name.

Vintages, is a wine bar with a robust selection of decent wines, accompanied by cheese and tapas (with an à la carte item charge).

Other Boardwalk spots for snacking include: Boardwalk Dog House (for hot dogs, wieners, bratwurst, and sausages), the Donut Shop, and Ice Cream Shoppe.

Elsewhere, dining venues/eateries include Izumi, offering Japanese-style cuisine, at an à la carte price; Sorrento's Pizzeria; Park Café (for salads and light bites); and Wipe Out Café. For those with a sweet tooth, there's a 1940s-style Cupcake Shop. Naturally, if you're thinking of getting married, you could have a cupcake wedding cake. For lighter, more health-conscious fare, there's a self-serve section in the Solarium Bistro for breakfast and lunch – it's usually the quietest place, too.

The Windjammer Café is the (free) casual, self-serve eatery common to all RCI ships. However, note that no trays are provided, only oval plates, so if you are disabled or have mobility difficulties you may need to ask for help. Also, because they're plastic, it's impossible to get a hot plate. The venue is simply too small to handle the number of people that can invade it at peak times – my advice is to try some of the other venues to avoid the overcrowding. The food varies from acceptable to less than acceptable – fresh fruit tends to be hard and unripe – and it's best to arrive early, when things have just been cooked and displayed. Although there's a decent enough variety, the quality of some of the meat is poor and overcooked.

Regular coffee is available free in many venues, but espresso and cappuccino (in paper cups) costs extra – in Starbucks.

The longest waiting lines are usually for Johnny Rockets and Rita's Cantina. Note that the cover charges quoted above are subject to change – check with RCI's website or your travel provider for the latest cover charges.

Reservation-only evening 'parties' in Rita's Cantina and the Seafood Shack include popular food items and drinks. Also, three dining packages (Central Park, Chef's, and Choice) for several specialty restaurants are available. The packaged pricing is confusing.

ENTERTAINMENT. The 1,380-seat main show-lounge, spread over three decks, stages the popular musical Hairspray – an excellent, 90-minute-long production, just like a Broadway show, and is performed four times during each cruise. Frozen in Time is a stunning, must-see ice show at the ice-skating rink.

There's no charge for any of the shows, and bookings can be made at www.royalcaribbean.com up to three months before your cruise, although reservations are not required. It is, however, quite difficult to change any reservations.

The 750-seat AquaTheater, located outside at the ship's stern with a 6,000-sq-ft (560-sq-m) stage, is a stunning combination show theatre, sound stage, and events space (some great viewing places can be found high in the aft wings of the ship on both sides). The stern has some 'overhang,' to accommodate the venue. A DreamWorks Animation aquatic acrobatic and dive show is also presented.

DreamWorks Animation Studios also provides interactive shows featuring characters from popular animation such as *Shrek*, *King Fu Panda*, *Madagascar*, and *How to Train Your Dragon*.

SPA/FITNESS. The Vitality at Sea Spa includes a Vitality Café for extra-cost health drinks and snacks. The fitness center includes 158 cardio and resistance machines. An extra-cost thermal suite includes saunas, steam rooms, and heated tiled loungers. You can't just take a sauna for 10 minutes without paying for a one-day pass, at $30 per person. Steiner Leisure provides the staff and treatments, and gratuities are at your discretion.

The facility really is not that large, given the number of passengers carried. It's best not to book a massage when the ship is due to arrive or leave an anchor port because some treatment rooms experience immense vibration when the anchor chain is in use. Sports facilities include two surfboard pools, golf putting course, ziplining (screaming is mandatory), and an ice-skating rink that has proven to be extremely popular for kids.

Ocean Diamond
★★★

Size:.....................................Boutique Ship	Cabins (total):......................................113
Tonnage: 8,282	Size range (sq ft/m): 183.0–398.0/17.0–37.0
Lifestyle: ....Standard	Cabins (outside view):...............................113
Cruise line:........................... Quark Expeditions	Cabins (interior/no view):...............................0
Former names: ... Le Diamant, Song of Flower, Explorer Starship	Cabins (for one person):................................0
IMO number:.................................7325629	Cabins (with private balcony):.........................10
Builder: ....KMV (Norway)	Cabins (wheelchair accessible):.........................0
Original cost:..n/a	Wheelchair accessibility:...........................None
Entered service:..............................1986/2012	Cabin voltage: .... 220 volts
Registry:.......................... Wallis and Fortuna	Elevators:..2
Length (ft/m):.............................. 407.4/124.2	Casino (gaming tables):............................. Yes
Beam (ft/m):................................ 52.4/16.0	Slot machines:..................................... Yes
Draft (ft/m):..................................16.0/4.9	Swimming pools:.....................................1
Propulsion/Propellers: .... diesel (5,500kW)/2 (CP)	Hot tubs (on deck):..................................1
Passenger decks:......................................6	Self-service launderette:...........................No
Total crew:..144	Dedicated cinema/seats:...........................No
Passengers (lower beds/alll berths):................ 226/240	Library: .... Yes
Passenger Space Ratio (lower beds/all berths): 36.6/34.5	Onboard currency: ....US$
Crew/Passenger Ratio (lower beds/all berths):.......... 1.6/1.7	

'Soft' discovery cruising aboard a small, tired ship

OVERVIEW. *Ocean Diamond* is for discovery-minded participants who enjoy a comfortable travel environment. It will provide a good base for learning and 'soft' expedition cruises, and there's a fairly decent amount of sheltered open-deck space.

THE SHIP. *Le Diamant* was originally built as the ro-ro vessel *Begonia* in 1974 and converted for cruising in 1986. Operated for many years by Radisson Seven Seas Cruises (now Regent Seven Seas Cruises), the ship was acquired in 2011 by Miami-based ISP (International Shipping Partners), who chartered it to Quark Expeditions, and it has been modified for expedition cruise service. It has tall, twin funnels (with a platform between them) that give a somewhat squat profile. If only the foredeck and bow could be a little longer, the ship would look less ungainly.

The interior decor is warm, with pastel colors accented by splashes of color. Good-quality soft furnishings and fabrics make the ship feel chic and comfortable. The crew is caring and tries hard to make you feel at home during your cruise adventure.

ACCOMMODATION. There are 10 very comfortable suites. All other accommodation grades are nicely equipped, but dated. All come with good closet and drawer space. Some cabins have bathtubs, but they are tiny – deep shower tubs would be a better description.

DINING. The dining room is quite charming and has warm colors, a welcoming ambience, and one seating,

Berlitz's Ratings		
	Possible	Achieved
Ship	500	281
Accommodation	200	123
Food	400	234
Service	400	236
Entertainment	100	58
Cruise	400	237
OVERALL SCORE		
1169 points out of 2000		

with no assigned tables. Tables are for two, four, or six.

ENTERTAINMENT. The well-tiered main lounge is ideal as a comfortable lecture hall, and there are good sight lines from almost all the banquette-style seats.

SPA/FITNESS. The health spa facility is very compact and short on space, but is adequate, and includes a beauty salon and sauna.

Ocean Princess
★★★★

Size:.. Small Ship	Cabins (total):....................................344
Tonnage:.. 30,277	Size range (sq ft/m):................. 145.3–968.7/13.5–90.0
Lifestyle:.....................................Standard	Cabins (outside view):...............................317
Cruise line:............................ Princess Cruises	Cabins (interior/no view):.............................27
Former names:.................. Tahitian Princess, R Four	Cabins (for one person):................................0
IMO number:....................................9187899	Cabins (with private balcony):........................232
Builder: .... Chantiers de l'Atlantique (France)	Cabins (wheelchair accessible): 3
Original cost:..............................$150 million	Wheelchair accessibility:...........................Good
Entered service:..................... Nov 1999/Dec 2002	Cabin voltage:.........................110 and 220 volts
Registry:..................................... Bermuda	Elevators:..4
Length (ft/m):............................. 593.7/181.0	Casino (gaming tables):............................. Yes
Beam (ft/m):................................. 83.5/25.5	Slot machines:..................................... Yes
Draft (ft/m): 19.5/6.0	Swimming pools:.....................................1
Propulsion/Propellers:........... diesel-electric (18,600kW)/2	Hot tubs (on deck):..................................3
Passenger decks:...................................9	Self-service launderette:........................... Yes
Total crew:.......................................373	Dedicated cinema/seats:.............................No
Passengers (lower beds/alll berths):................. 688/826	Library: .... Yes
Passenger Space Ratio (lower beds/all berths): 44.1/36.6	Onboard currency: ....US$
Crew/Passenger Ratio (lower beds/all berths):.......... 1.8/2.2	

An informal smaller ship for mature-age cruisers

OVERVIEW. This ship is best suited to young and not-so-young couples, and older singles who like to mingle in a small ship setting with pleasing, sophisticated surroundings and lifestyle, reasonably good entertainment and fairly decent food and service, all at an affordable price.

THE SHIP. *Ocean Princess* (known as *Tahitian Princess* until 2009) and its sister ship Pacific Princess are an ideal size for smaller ports. The value for money is extremely good, and gives you with a chance to cruise in comfort aboard a mid-size ship with some interesting dining choices. There's very little entertainment, but it is not really needed in its main cruise areas such as Europe and Australasia. *Ocean Princess* is much more about relaxation than the larger ships in the Princess Cruises fleet, and would make a good child-free vessel.

The interior decor is stunning and elegant, a throwback to ship decor of the ocean liners of the 1920s and '30s. This includes detailed ceiling cornices, both real and faux wrought-iron staircase railings, leather and cherry wood paneled walls, trompe l'oeil ceilings, rich carpeting in hallways with an Oriental rug-look center section, and many other interesting and expensive-looking decorative touches. The overall feel is of an old-world country club. The staircase in the main, two-deck-high foyer may remind you of the one in the 1998 movie *Titanic*.

The public rooms are spread over three decks. The reception hall has a staircase with intricate wrought-

Berlitz's Ratings		
	Possible	Achieved
Ship	500	392
Accommodation	200	150
Food	400	252
Service	400	287
Entertainment	100	71
Cruise	400	288
OVERALL SCORE		
1440 points out of 2000		

iron railings. The Nightclub, with forward-facing views, sits high in the ship and has Polynesian-inspired decor and furniture.

There are plenty of bars – including one in the entrance to each restaurant. Perhaps the nicest can be found in the casino bar/lounge, a beautiful room reminiscent of London's grand hotels and understated gaming clubs. It has an inviting marble fireplace, comfortable sofas, and individual chairs. There is also a large card room, which incorporates an internet center, with eight stations.

The Library, a grand room designed in the Regency style by the Scottish interior designer John McNeece, has a fireplace, a high, indented, trompe l'oeil ceiling, and an excellent selection of books, plus some comfortable wing-back chairs with footstools, and sofas you can easily fall asleep on – it's the most relaxing room aboard.

There is no walk-around promenade deck outdoors, though there's a small jogging track around the perimeter of the swimming pool, and port and starboard side decks. There are no wooden decks outdoors; instead, they are covered by a sand-colored rubberized material. There is no sauna. Stairways, although carpeted, are tinny. To keep prices low, the air routing to get to and from your ship is often not the most direct. There is a charge for using machines in the self-service launderette and you have to obtain tokens from the reception desk – a change machine in the launderette itself would be better.

Drinks prices are moderate, while beer prices are high. As with all Princess Cruises ships, 15 percent is added to bar and spa accounts and a standard gratuity is added to your onboard account. To reduce the amount, you must visit the reception desk.

ACCOMMODATION. There are about eight different cabin types. All of the standard interior and outside-view cabins (the lowest four grades) are extremely tight for two persons, particularly for cruises longer than seven days. Cabins have twin beds (or queen-size bed), with good under-bed storage areas, personal safe, vanity desk with large mirror, good closet and drawer space in rich, dark woods, and bathrobe. Color TVs carry a major news channel, where obtainable, plus a sports channel and several round-the-clock movie channels. The bathrooms, which have tiled floors and plain walls, are compact, standard units, and include a shower enclosure with a removable, strong hand-held shower unit, hairdryer, 100 percent cotton towels, toiletries storage shelves, and a retractable clothesline.

The suites/cabins that have private balconies (66 percent of all suites/cabins, or 73 percent of all outside-view suites/cabins) have partial, and not full, balcony partitions, sliding glass doors, and, due to good design and layout, only 14 cabins on Deck 6 have lifeboat-obstructed views. The balcony floor is covered in thick plastic matting – teak would be nicer – and some awful plastic furniture.

Mini-Suites. The 52 accommodation units designated as mini-suites are in reality simply larger cabins than the standard varieties, as the sleeping and lounge areas aren't divided. While not overly large, the bathrooms have a good-size tub and ample space for storing toiletries. The living area has a refrigerated mini-bar, lounge area with breakfast table, and a balcony with two plastic chairs and a table.

Owner's Suites. The 10 Owner's Suites, the most spacious accommodation, are fine, large living spaces in the forward-most and aft-most sections of the accommodation decks – particularly nice are those that overlook the stern, on decks 6, 7, and 8. They have more extensive balconies that can't be overlooked by anyone from the decks above. There is an entrance foyer, living room, bedroom, CD player, bathroom with Jacuzzi tub, as well as a small guest bathroom. The bed faces the sea, which can be seen through the floor-to-ceiling windows and sliding glass door.

Be aware that all suites/cabins located at the stern may suffer from vibration and noise, particularly when the ship is close to full speed, or maneuvering in port.

DINING. Flexibility and choice are what this mid-size ship's dining facilities are all about. There is a choice of four different dining spots, including a self-serve buffet:

The Club Restaurant has 338 seats, all with armrests, and a large raised central section. There are large ocean-view windows on three sides, several prime tables overlooking the stern, and a small bandstand for occasional live dinner music. The noise level can be high, due to its single deck height ceiling. This restaurant is operated in two seatings, with dinner typically at 6pm and 8:15pm – the others have an open dining hours.

Sabatini's Trattoria is an extra-charge, reservations-required Italian restaurant, with 96 seats (all with armrests), windows along two sides, and a set 'Bellissima' three-hour dégustation menu.

Sterling Steakhouse is an extra-charge, reservations-required American-style steak house with 98 seats (all with armrests), and windows along two sides. There's a set menu, plus the chef's daily specials. The cover charge is $8 per person. There are few tables for two.

The Lido Café has seating for 154 indoors and 186 outdoors with white plastic patio furniture. It is open for breakfast, lunch, and casual dinners. As the ship's 24-hour self-serve buffet restaurant, it incorporates a small pizzeria and grill. Basic salads, a meat carving station, and a reasonable selection of cheeses are served daily. There is also a Poolside Grill and Bar for fast food items.

ENTERTAINMENT. The 345-seat Cabaret Lounge has a stage, and circular hardwood dance floor with banquette and individual tub chair seating, and raised sections on port and starboard sides. It is not large, and not really designed for production shows, so cabaret acts form the main focus, with mini-revue style shows presented by a troupe of resident singer/dancers in a potted version of what you might experience aboard the large ships of Princess Cruises.

A band, small musical units, and solo entertaining pianists provide live music for shows and dancing in the various lounges and bars before and after dinner.

SPA/FITNESS. A gymnasium has ocean-view windows, high-tech muscle-toning equipment and treadmills, steam rooms (no sauna), changing areas for men and women, and a beauty salon with ocean views. The spa is operated by Steiner, a specialist concession. A lido deck has a swimming pool, and good sunbathing space, while an aft deck has a thalassotherapy pool. A jogging track circles the pool deck, but one deck above. The uppermost outdoors deck includes a golf driving net and shuffleboard court.

Oceana
★★★+

Size:.................................Large Resort Ship	Cabins (total):.......................................975
Tonnage:..77,499	Size range (sq ft/m):.................158.2–610.3/14.7–56.7
Lifestyle:..Standard	Cabins (outside view):..............................603
Cruise line:..................................P&O Cruises	Cabins (interior/no view):..........................372
Former names:...........................Ocean Princess	Cabins (for one person):................................0
IMO number:..................................9169550	Cabins (with private balcony):......................410
Builder:.............................Fincantieri (Italy)	Cabins (wheelchair accessible):.......................19
Original cost:............................$300 million	Wheelchair accessibility:............................Good
Entered service:.....................Feb 2000/Nov 2002	Cabin voltage:........................110 and 220 volts
Registry:.......................................Bermuda	Elevators:..11
Length (ft/m):.............................857.2/261.3	Casino (gaming tables):..............................Yes
Beam (ft/m):...............................105.6/32.2	Slot machines:......................................Yes
Draft (ft/m):..................................25.9/7.9	Swimming pools:.......................................4
Propulsion/Propellers:...........diesel-electric (28,000kW)/2	Hot tubs (on deck):...................................5
Passenger decks:...................................10	Self-service launderette:............................Yes
Total crew:.......................................850	Dedicated cinema/seats:..............................No
Passengers (lower beds/all berths):.............1,950/2,272	Library:..Yes
Passenger Space Ratio (lower beds/all berths):.......39.7/34.1	Onboard currency:...................................UK£
Crew/Passenger Ratio (lower beds/all berths):.........2.2/2.5	

Family-friendly cruising in a comfortable environment

OVERVIEW. This ship is all about British-ness and will be comfortingly familiar for families with children who want to go abroad but take their British traditions and food with them. It is best suited to adults of all ages and families with children of all ages, and offers excellent value for money to first-time cruisers who enjoy reading tabloids.

THE SHIP. The all-white *Oceana* has a pleasing profile for a large ship and is well balanced by its large funnel, which contains a deck tennis/basketball/volleyball court in its sheltered aft base. There is 93,000 sq ft (8,600 sq m) of open deck space and a wide, teakwood walk-around promenade deck outdoors. A great amount of glass area on the upper decks provides plenty of light and connection with the outside world. The ship underwent a few changes to make it more user-friendly for British passengers, although it is looking tired in places.

The ship, while large, absorbs passengers well, although its open lounge architecture means bleed-through music and little sense of intimacy. Its interiors are pretty and warm, with attractive colors and welcoming decor that includes some attractive wall murals and other artwork.

There is a wide range of public rooms, with several intimate rooms and spaces, so that you don't feel overwhelmed by large spaces. The interior focal point is a large four-deck-high atrium lobby with winding, double stairways and two panoramic glass-walled lifts.

Berlitz's Ratings

	Possible	Achieved
Ship	500	374
Accommodation	200	148
Food	400	245
Service	400	278
Entertainment	100	71
Cruise	400	272

OVERALL SCORE
1388 points out of 2000

There is plenty of space throughout the public areas, and the traffic flow is quite good. The library is a warm room with ocean-view windows and has six large buttery leather chairs for listening to audio discs.

The collection of artwork is decent, particularly on the stairways, and this helps make the ship feel smaller than it really is. The Monte Carlo Club Casino, while large, is not in the main passenger flow and so does not generate the walk-through factor found aboard so many ships. The most traditional room is the Yacht and Compass Bar, decorated in the style of a turn-of-the-century gentleman's club, with wood paneling and comfortable seating.

Ballroom dance fans will be pleased to note that there are several good-size wooden dance floors. The ship usually carries a professional dance couple as hosts and teachers, and there is plenty of dancing time included in the entertainment programming.

As is the case aboard most large ships, if you live in the best accommodation – a suite – you will be well attended. Otherwise, you will merely be one of a large number of passengers aboard a ship that caters to families with children – lots of them in peak vacation periods. Most cabin stewards and dining room personnel are from India, and provide service with a well-balanced smile and warmth that many other nationals find difficult to equal.

One nice feature is a traditional Captain's cocktail party, held in the four-deck-high main atrium so you can come and go as you please, with no standing in line to have your photograph taken with the captain if you don't want to.

There are a number of dead ends in the interior layout, so it's not as user-friendly as it should be. There will be lines for disembarkation, shore tenders, and for self-serve buffet meals – an inevitable aspect of cruising aboard large ships.

The swimming pools are really quite small and will be crowded when the ship is full; also the pool deck is cluttered with white, plastic deck lounge chairs, which don't have cushioned pads. The rule about not leaving sunloungers unattended for more than half an hour is flouted by most British passengers, who are keen to keep their favored position.

While the ship's interior space is a non-smoking environment, smoking is permitted on cabin balconies and in designated spots on the open decks.

In the quest for increased onboard revenue and shareholder value, even birthday cakes are an extra-cost item, as are espressos and cappuccinos (fake ones, made from instant coffee, are available in the dining rooms). Also at extra cost are ice cream and bottled water – items that can add up to a considerable amount. Expect to be subjected to a stream of flyers advertising daily art auctions, 'designer' watches, and other promotions. Gratuities are automatically charged to your onboard account.

A small brass band welcomes passengers arriving at the terminal for sailings from Southampton. Other touches include church bells that sound throughout the ship for the interdenominational Sunday church service. A coach service for passengers embarking or disembarking in Southampton covers much of the UK. Car parking is also available – there is one rate for undercover parking, and another rate for parking in an open compound.

FAMILIES. Children have their own Treasure Chest (for ages two to five), The Hideout (six to nines), and for older children (10–13) there is The Buzz Zone. P&O Cruises provides an abundance of staff to look after the children, as well as many activities to keep them out of adult areas. A night nursery is available 6pm–2am, with a per-child charge after midnight. While many children don't like organized clubs, they will probably find they make new friends quickly during a cruise.

ACCOMMODATION. There are 19 different cabin grades, designated as: suites with private balcony, mini-suites with private balcony, outside-view twin-bedded cabin with balcony, outside-view twin bedded cabin, and interior twin-bedded cabins. Although the standard outside-view and interior cabins are a little small, they are well designed and functional in layout, and have earth tone colors accentuated by splashes of color from the bedspreads. Proportionately, there are quite a lot of interior cabins.

The cabin numbering system is illogical, with numbers going through several hundred series on the same deck. The walls of the passenger accommodation decks are very plain – some artwork would be an improvement.

Many of the outside-view cabins have private balconies, and all seem to be quite well soundproofed, although the balcony partition is not of the floor-to-ceiling type, so you can hear your neighbors clearly. The balconies are very narrow – just large enough for two small chairs – and there is no dedicated outdoor balcony lighting. Many cabins have third- and fourth-person upper bunk beds – good for families with children. All cabins have tea- and coffee-making facilities – a comforting addition.

There is a reasonable amount of closet and abundant drawer and other storage space in all cabins; although this is adequate for a seven-night cruise, it could prove to be quite tight for longer. Also provided are a color TV set, and refrigerator, and each night a chocolate will appear on your pillow. The cabin bathrooms are practical, and come complete with all the details one needs – although, again, they really are tight spaces, best described as one person at a time units. Fortunately, they have a shower enclosure of a decent size, a small amount of shelving for your toiletries, real glasses, and a hairdryer.

High-quality toiletries are by Temple Spa; suite occupants get larger bottles and a wider selection.

Also standard in all cabins are Slumberland eight-inch sprung mattresses, 10.5 tog duvets (blankets and pillows if you prefer), Egyptian cotton towels, improved tea/coffee-making facilities with speciality teas (long-life is provided), and a Nick Munro-designed bespoke tray.

Suites. The largest accommodation is in six suites, two on each of three decks at the aft of the ship, with a private balcony giving great views over the stern. Each of these suites – Oronsay, Orcades, Orion, Orissa, Orsova, Orontes, all P&O ships of yesteryear – has a large private balcony. They are well laid out, and have large, marble-clad bathrooms with two washbasins, a Jacuzzi tub, and a separate shower enclosure. The bedroom has generous amounts of wood accenting and detailing, indented ceilings, and TV sets in both bedroom and lounge areas, which also have a dining room table and four chairs.

Mini-Suites. Mini-suites typically have two lower beds that convert to a queen-size bed. There is a separate bedroom/sleeping area with vanity desk, and a lounge with sofa and coffee table, indented ceilings with generous amounts of wood accenting and detailing, walk-in closet, and a larger, marble-clad bathroom with Jacuzzi tub and a separate shower enclosure. There is a private balcony.

Standard Outside-view/Interior Cabins. A reasonable amount of closet and abundant drawer and other storage space is provided in all cabins – adequate for seven nights but a little tight for longer cruises. There's a TV set and refrigerator. Each night a chocolate will appear on your pillow. The cabin bathrooms are practical, and come with all the details one needs, although they really are tight spaces. But they do have a decent shower enclosure, a small amount of shelving for toiletries, real glasses, and a hairdryer.

You can receive BBC World channel on the in-cabin color television system (when available, depending on cruise area), as well as movies – the ship doesn't have a dedicated theater. The cabin service menu is rather limited, and presentation of the food items could be better.

DINING. There are two principal asymmetrically designed dining rooms, Adriatic and Ligurian, each seating about 500, located adjacent to the two lower levels of the four-deck-high atrium lobby. One has open seating and the other has two seatings. Each has its own galley and is split into multi-tier sections, which help create a feeling of intimacy, although there is a lot of noise from the waiter stations adjacent to many tables. Breakfast and lunch are provided in an open-seating arrangement, while dinner is in two seatings.

The cuisine is decidedly British – a little adventurous at times, but always with plenty of curry dishes and other standard British items. Don't expect exquisite dining – this is British hotel catering that doesn't pretend to gourmet standards. What it does present is attractive and tasty, with some excellent gravies and sauces to accompany meals.

In keeping with the British aspect of P&O Cruises, the desserts are always good. A statement in the onboard cruise folder states that P&O Cruises does not knowingly purchase genetically modified foods, though it makes no mention of all those commercial American cereals.

The service is provided by a team of friendly stewards – most from India, with which P&O has had a long relationship. The wine list is quite reasonable.

The Plaza, a self-serve buffet, is located above the navigation bridge, with some commanding views. At night, this large room (there are two food lines – one each on both port and starboard sides) is transformed into an informal dinner setting with sit-down waiter service. For an extra £9.50 you can experience the Tasting Menu – a selection of small cosmopolitan dishes, with three different menus per cruise.

Outdoors on deck, with a sheltered view over the Riviera Pool, the Horizon Grill has fast-food items for those who don't want to change from their sunbathing attire.

For other informal eats, there is Café Jardin, with a Frankie's Bar & Grill-style menu serving Italian-inspired dishes such as antipasti, glazed belly pork Marco Polo, and rib-eye steak alla rosmarino. Upgraded in a March 2008 refit, it is on the uppermost level of the four-deck-high atrium lobby.

Explorer's serves for cappuccino, espressos, and pastries, and Magnums is a Champagne/caviar bar.

ENTERTAINMENT. There are two showlounges – Footlights Theatre, and Starlights – one at each end of the ship. The Footlights, located at the forward end, is a superb 550-seat, theater-style showlounge, for production shows and theater events; movies can also be shown here. Starlights is a 480-seat cabaret-style lounge with bar.

P&O Cruises places a big emphasis on a decent quality of entertainment. To this end, there's a resident group of actors, singers, and dancers who provide theater-style presentations such as cut-down versions of well-known musicals. In addition, the ship features a whole array of cabaret acts. Although many of these aren't what you would call headliners, they do regularly travel the cruise ship circuit. Classical concerts are scheduled for many cruises.

The ship has several good-size wooden dance floors for ballroom dancing. P&O Cruises carries a professional dance couple as hosts and teachers, and there's plenty of dancing time included in the entertainment programming.

SPA/FITNESS. The Ocean Spa has facilities that are contained in a glass-walled complex on one of the highest decks at the aft part of the ship. It includes a gymnasium, with all the associated high-tech muscle-pumping equipment, a combination aerobics/exercise class room, sauna, steam room, and several treatment rooms.

The spa is operated by Harding Brothers, a UK concession that provides the staff and range of beauty and wellness treatments. Examples of treatments include: Body Toning (detox for the body); Body Bien Etre (body scrub and massage); Seaweed Wrap; and Collagen Velvet Facial Mask.

One swimming pool is 'suspended' aft between two decks, forming part of the spa complex, and two other pools are located in the ship's center. They are not large for the size of the vessel. Sports facilities are located in an open-air sports deck positioned inside the ship's funnel structure and can be adapted to basketball, volleyball, badminton, or paddle tennis. Joggers can exercise on the walk-around open Promenade Deck. There's an electronic golf simulator, so no need to bring your own clubs.

Oosterdam
★★★★

Size:.................................Large Resort Ship		Crew/Passenger Ratio (lower beds/all berths):......... 2.3/2.9		
Tonnage: 82,305		Cabins (total):.....................................924		
Lifestyle: ....Premium		Size range (sq ft/m): 185.0–1,318.6/17.1–122.5		
Cruise line:.......................... Holland America Line		Cabins (outside view):.............................788		
Former names: ....none		Cabins (interior/no view):..........................136		
IMO number: 9221281		Cabins (for one person):............................0		
Builder:............................. Fincantieri (Italy)		Cabins (with private balcony):......................623		
Original cost:...............................$400 million		Cabins (wheelchair accessible): 28		
Entered service:............................. Aug 2003		Wheelchair accessibility:..........................Good		
Registry:.................................The Netherlands		Cabin voltage: .... 110 volts		
Length (ft/m):.............................. 935.0/285.0		Elevators:..14		
Beam (ft/m):.............................. 105.6/32.25		Casino (gaming tables):............................Yes		
Draft (ft/m): 25.5/7.8		Slot machines:....................................Yes		
Propulsion/Propellers: . . .diesel-electric (34,000kW)/2 azimuthing		Swimming pools:.................2 (1 w/sliding glass door)		
pods		Hot tubs (on deck):.................................5		
Passenger decks:...................................11		Self-service launderette:...........................No		
Total crew:......................................800		Dedicated cinema/seats:............................Yes		
Passengers (lower beds/alll berths):............. 1,918/2,387		Library: ....Yes		
Passenger Space Ratio (lower beds/all berths): 42.9/34.4		Onboard currency: ....US$		

A contemporary, family-friendly ship with Dutch decor

OVERVIEW. *Oosterdam* offers a range of public rooms with an intimate atmosphere. In keeping with the traditions of Holland America Line, there's a large collection of Dutch artwork and artifacts.

THE SHIP. *Oosterdam* (sister ships: *Eurodam, Nieuw Amsterdam, Noordam, Westerdam,* and *Zuiderdam*) is one of the new generation of Vista-class ships for Holland America Line, designed to appeal to younger, more vibrant, multi-generational, family-oriented holidaymakers.

Berlitz's Ratings		
	Possible	Achieved
Ship	500	391
Accommodation	200	149
Food	400	261
Service	400	268
Entertainment	100	71
Cruise	400	286
OVERALL SCORE		
1426 points out of 2000		

The twin working funnels are the result of the slightly unusual machinery configuration; the ship has, in effect, two engine rooms – one with three diesels, and one with two diesels and a gas turbine. A pod propulsion system is provided, powered by a diesel-electric system, with a small gas turbine located in the funnel for the reduction of emissions.

There's a complete walk-around exterior teak promenade deck, with teak steamer-style sunloungers. An outdoor jogging track is located around the mast and the forward third of the ship. Exterior glass elevators, mounted midships on both port and starboard sides, provide ocean views. There are two centrally located swimming pools outdoors, and one can be used in poor weather thanks to its retractable sliding glass roof. Two whirlpool tubs, adjacent to the swimming pools, are abridged by a bar. Another smaller pool is available for children.

The intimate lobby spans just three decks, but it is topped by a beautiful, rotating, Waterford crystal globe of the world. The interior decor is bright, yet comfortable. The ceilings are particularly noticeable in the public rooms. The cast-aluminum elevator doors are interesting – the design being inspired by the deco designs from New York's Chrysler Building.

There are two decks of entertainment/public rooms. A winding shopping street has several boutiques, and there's an Internet center, library, card room, an art gallery, photo gallery, and several small meetings rooms. The casino is large, but you have to walk through it to get from the restaurant to the showlounge. Ice cream is free at certain hours, and a selection of warm hors d'oeuvres is provided in all bars.

On other decks, you'll find a Queens Lounge, which acts as a lecture room a Culinary Arts Center. There are also a number of other bars and lounges, including an Explorer's Lounge. The ship also has a small movie screening room.

The information desk in the lobby is small and somewhat removed from the main passenger flow on the two decks above it. Many pillars obstruct passenger flow and lines of sight throughout the ship. There are no self-service launderettes – something families with children might miss, although special laundry packages are available.

FAMILIES. Children have KidZone, an indoor/outdoor facility, and Cub Hal for ages five to 12, with a number of dedicated youth counsellors (a ratio of one for every 30 children). Teenagers get to use WaveRunner, which includes a dance floor, special lighting effects, and a booming sound system. There's also a video game room, and big-screen television for movies. There are no self-service launderettes, though special laundry packages are available.

ACCOMMODATION. There are many price categories: 16 outside-view and eight interior. Lifeboats obstruct the view from some cabins on the lowest accommodation deck (Main Deck). Some cabins that can accommodate a third and fourth person have very little closet space, and only one personal safe. Occupants of suites get exclusive use of the Neptune Lounge and concierge service, priority embarkation and disembarkation, and other benefits. In many of the suites/cabins with private balconies the balconies are not so private and can be overlooked from various public locations.

Penthouse Verandah Suites (2). These measure 1,318 sq ft (123 sq m), including balcony. Each has a separate bedroom with a king-size bed; there's also a walk-in closet, dressing room, living room, dining room, butler's pantry, mini-bar and refrigerator, and private balcony. The main bathroom has a large whirlpool tub, two washbasins, toilet, and plenty of storage space for toiletries. Personalized stationery and free dry cleaning are included, as are hot hors d'oeuvres and other goodies daily.

DeLuxe Verandah Suites (60). These measure 563 sq ft (53 sq m). They have twin beds that convert to a king-size bed, vanity desk, lounge area, walk-in closet, mini-bar and refrigerator, and bathroom with full-size tub, washbasin, and toilet. Personalized stationery and complimentary dry cleaning are included, as are hot hors d'oeuvres and other goodies.

Verandah Suites (100). Actually, they are cabins, not suites, and measure 284 sq ft (26 sq m). Twin beds can convert to a queen-size bed; there is also a lounge area, mini-bar, and refrigerator, while the bathroom has a tub, washbasin, and toilet. Floor-to-ceiling windows open onto a private balcony.

Outside-view Cabins. Standard outside cabins measure 197 sq ft (18 sq m) and have twin beds that convert to a queen-size bed. There's a small sitting area, while the bathroom has a tub/shower combination. The interior cabins are slightly smaller (183 sq ft/17 sq m).

Niggles include noisy air conditioning – the flow in cabins and bathrooms can't be turned off and the only regulation is for temperature control.

DINING. The 1,045-seat Vista Dining Room is located at the stern. It spans two decks, and is quite a stunning room, with seating on both main and balcony levels. Both open seating, and fixed seating are available. Breakfast and lunch is is an open-seating arrangement where you'll be seated by restaurant staff when you enter. There are tables for two, four, six, or eight. The waiter stations in the dining room can be noisy for anyone seated adjacent to them. Live music is provided for dinner each evening. Once each cruise, there's a Dutch Dinner (hats are provided), and an Indonesian Lunch. 'Lighter option' meals are always available for the nutrition-conscious and the weight-conscious. Holland America Line can provide kosher meals, although these are prepared ashore, frozen, and brought to your table sealed in their original containers.

Other dining options. The 130-seat Pinnacle Grill is slightly more upscale, with higher-quality ingredients and better presentation than in the larger main dining room. It is on Lower Promenade Deck and fronts onto the second level of the atrium lobby. Pacific Northwest cuisine is featured, with items such as sesame-crusted halibut with ginger-miso, Peking duck breast with blackberry sauce, and an array of premium-quality steaks. There are fine table settings, china and silverware, and leather-bound menus. The wine bar offers mostly American wines. Reservations are needed and there's a cover charge.

For casual eating, there's an extensive Lido Café, a self-serve eatery that wraps around the funnel housing and extends aft; there are also some fine views over the ship's central multi-deck atrium. Movement through the buffet area can be very slow, particularly at peak times. In the evenings, one side of this venue is turned into an extra-cost, 72-seat Canaletto Restaurant – a quasi-Italian informal eatery with waiter service.

An outdoor self-serve buffet – adjacent to the fantail pool – provides fast food such as hamburgers and hot dogs, chicken and fries, as well as two smaller buffets adjacent to the midships swimming pool area. An extra-cost Windsurf Café in the atrium lobby (open 20 hours a day) serves coffee, pastries, snack foods, deli sandwiches, and, in the evenings, liqueur coffees.

ENTERTAINMENT. The 867-seat Vista Lounge is the principal venue for Las Vegas-style revues and major cabaret shows. The main-floor level has a bar in its starboard aft section. Spiral stairways at the back of the lounge connect all levels. Stage shows are best seen from the upper levels, from where the sight lines are quite good.

SPA/FITNESS. The Greenhouse Spa is a large, two-deck-high health spa, located directly above the navigation bridge. Facilities include a solarium, hydrotherapy pool, unisex thermal suite – a unisex area incorporating a Laconium, Hammam, and Camomile Grotto. There is also a salon, 11 private massage/body treatment rooms including one for couples, and a large gym with floor-to-ceiling windows, and the latest equipment. Sports enthusiasts can enjoy a basketball court, volleyball court, and golf simulator.

Oriana
★★★★

Size:.	Large Resort Ship	Cabins (total):.	936
Tonnage:.	69,153	Size range (sq ft/m):.	150.6–500.5/14.0–46.5
Lifestyle:.	Standard	Cabins (outside view):.	592
Cruise line:.	P&O Cruises	Cabins (interior/no view):.	317
Former names:.	none	Cabins (for one person):.	2
IMO number:.	6821080	Cabins (with private balcony):.	118
Builder:.	Meyer Werft (Germany)	Cabins (wheelchair accessible):.	8
Original cost:.	£200 million	Wheelchair accessibility:.	Good
Entered service:.	Apr 1995	Cabin voltage:.	110 and 220 volts
Registry:.	Bermuda	Elevators:.	10
Length (ft/m):.	853.0/260.0	Casino (gaming tables):.	Yes
Beam (ft/m):.	105.6/32.2	Slot machines:.	Yes
Draft (ft/m):.	25.9/7.9	Swimming pools:.	3
Propulsion/Propellers:.	diesel (47,750kW)/2	Hot tubs (on deck):.	5
Passenger decks:.	10	Self-service launderette:.	Yes
Total crew:.	760	Dedicated cinema/seats:.	Yes/189
Passenger (lower beds/alll berths):.	1,870/2,231	Library:.	Yes
Passenger Space Ratio (lower beds/all berths):.	36.9/30.9	Onboard currency:.	UK£
Crew/Passenger Ratio (lower beds/all berths):.	2.4/2.9		

British decor, style and food for adults-only cruising

OVERVIEW. Anyone cruising aboard *Oriana*, an adults-only ship, will get a well-organized cruise experience. It suits mature adults seeking to cruise aboard a large ship with the facilities of a small resort.

THE SHIP. Although well over 15 years old, this ship has a feeling of timeless elegance. There's a good amount of outdoor space, with enough (white plastic) sunloungers for all passengers, and there's an extra-wide, traditional walk-around outdoor promenade deck. The stern superstructure is nicely rounded, with several tiers that overlook a swimming pool and hot tub. In 2011, a refit transformed *Oriana* from a ship for family cruising to an adults-only ship – and, as such, much better suited to long cruises. Some 27 new cabins were added, which lowered the space ratio and crew to passenger ratio. A sponson skirt was added to the hull, as a stability aid. However, vibration at the stern still persists (it has been a problem for years).

Inside, the design provides good horizontal passenger flow and wide passageways, with decor that is gentle and welcoming. Of note are some fine, detailed ceiling treatments. The interior focal point is a four-deck-high atrium. It is quite elegant but not glitzy, and is topped by a dome of Tiffany glass. The many public rooms provide plenty of choice.

The L-shaped Anderson's Lounge – named after Arthur Anderson, founder of the Peninsular Steam Navigation Company in the 1830s – contains an attractive series of 19th-century marine paintings and is deco-

Berlitz's Ratings		
	Possible	Achieved
Ship	500	393
Accommodation	200	155
Food	400	244
Service	400	294
Entertainment	100	77
Cruise	400	285
OVERALL SCORE		
1448 points out of 2000		

rated in the manner of a fine British gentleman's club.

Atop the ship and forward is the Crow's Nest, a U-shaped observation lounge with one small wing that can be closed off for small groups. A long bar includes a model of the former P&O ship *Ranpura* in a glass case. Two small stages are set into the forward port and starboard sections, and there is a wooden dance floor. Smoking is permitted only on cabin balconies and in designated spots on the open decks.

The library is a fine room, with a good range of hardback books and a librarian, inlaid wood tables and bookcases crafted by Lord Linley's company, and some comfortable chairs. By the second day of almost any cruise, the library will have been almost stripped of books by word-hungry passengers. Adjacent is Thackeray's, a reading/writing room named after the novelist William Makepeace Thackeray, a P&O passenger in 1844. Lord's Tavern, decorated with cricket memorabilia, is the most sporting place to pitch a beverage or two, or take part in a singalong. There's also a small casino with table games and slot machines, and, unusually for ships today, not only a small cinema/lecture room but also a large room for card players.

The carpeting throughout is of a high quality, much of it custom designed and made from 100 percent wool. Some fine pieces of sculpture add the feeling of a floating museum, and original artworks by all-British artists include several tapestries and sculptures.

There's a wide variety of mainly British entertainment. P&O Cruises has a successful program of theme cruises covering areas such as antiques, art appreciation, classical music, comedy, cricket, gardening, jazz, motoring, popular fiction, Scottish dance.

Most cabin stewards and dining room personnel are from India, and provide service with a warm smile. However, in the quest for increased onboard revenue, even birthday cakes cost extra, as do real espressos and cappuccinos – fake ones, made from instant coffee, are available in the dining rooms. Ice cream and bottled water also cost extra.

A small British brass band unit usually welcomes passengers to the cruise terminal on sailings from Southampton. Other touches include church bells sounded for the interdenominational Sunday service. Gratuities are charged to your onboard account daily.

ACCOMMODATION. With the change to an adults-only ship, the former children's playrooms were converted into additional cabins. There are 14 price categories, priced according to size and location.

Standard interior cabins and outside-view cabins are well equipped, but compact. There is much use of rich, warm limed oak or cherry wood, which makes even the least expensive interior cabin quite inviting. All cabins have good closet and drawer space, a small refrigerator, full-length mirror, and blackout curtains (essential for North Cape cruises). All cabins have premium Slumberland mattresses, duvets, and high-quality bedlinen. Some can accommodate a third or third/fourth person, so sharing with friends can make for an economical cruise. Satellite television typically includes BBC World. Cabin soundproofing could be better.

There are a number of cabins for passengers traveling alone. Singles who share a cabin should note that only one personal safe is provided in most twin-bedded cabins.

The modest-size standard cabin bathrooms have mirror-fronted cabinets, although the lighting is quite soft; all have a wall-mounted hairdryer. High-quality toiletries are by Temple Spa; suite occupants get larger bottles and more of a choice.

There are eight suites, each measuring 500 sq ft (46 sq m), with butler service. Facilities include a separate bedroom with two lower beds convertible to a queen-size bed, walk-in dressing area, two double closets, and plenty of drawer space. The lounge area has a sofa, armchairs and table, writing desk, binoculars, umbrella, trouser press, iron and ironing board, two TV sets, video player, personal safe, hairdryer, and refrigerator. The bathroom has a whirlpool bath, shower, and toilet, and there's also a guest bathroom. All in all, the suites, and particularly the bathrooms, are disappointing when compared with similarly sized suites in other ships. The private balcony has two sunloungers, tables, and chairs. Suite occupants get priority embarkation and their own lounge in the Southampton cruise terminal.

Other balcony cabins (called outside deluxe) measure 210 sq ft (19 sq m). There is plenty of closet and drawer space. The bathrooms are somewhat disappointing and dated, and have a very small, plain washbasin. One would expect marble or granite units in these grades.

DINING. Peninsula (located amidships) and Oriental (aft) are the two restaurants, each with two seatings and with one galley between them. Both are moderately handsome, with tables for two, four, six, or eight. But in the aft dining room the noise level can be high at many tables, because of the room's position above the propellers, and vibration at almost any speed. The meals are mostly of the 'Middle-England' variety, and the presentation generally lacks creativity. Curries and other Indian-style dishes are heavily featured, particularly on luncheon menus. Afternoon tea is disappointing. The typical menu cycle is 14 days; anyone on a long voyage may find it quite repetitive.

Other dining options. The former Oriana Rhodes (a Gary Rhodes at Sea) restaurant has been changed into a delightful Marco Pierre White venue, called the Ocean Grill (Marco Pierre White also has restaurants aboard *Adonia* and *Arcadia*). Reservations are required and there's a per-person cover charge. An adjacent Tiffany's Bar serves as a pre-dinner anteroom for drinks. The menu is uncomplicated, but preparation and presentation are good.

The 50-seat Sorrento's, added in the 2011 refit, serves Italian fare and has ocean views from its upper-level location at the aft portside section of the buffet venue (there is mainly outdoor seating).

The Conservatory is for casual self-serve breakfast and luncheon buffets, and 24-hour self-serve beverage stands, although the selection of teas is poor, and the coffee is … well, let's not talk about that.

ENTERTAINMENT. The Theatre Royal, a well-designed room, has a sloping floor and good sightlines from almost all seats. The fare is mainly British, from production shows staged by a resident company to top British 'names' and lesser artists. A second, smaller Pacific Lounge is a multi-function venue for cabaret acts, including late-night comedy, and can also be used as a lecture room. However, pillars obstruct the stage from a number of seats.

Ballroom dance fans will appreciate the four good-sized wood dance floors aboard his ship, and a professional dance couple acts as hosts and teachers (social dancing time is always included in the programming).

SPA/FITNESS. The Oasis Spa is reasonably large, and provides the latest alternative treatment therapies. A gymnasium has high-tech muscle toning equipment. The unisex sauna is a large facility; there is also a steam room each for men and women, and several massage/body treatment rooms, an aerobics room with wood floor, plus a relaxation area incorporating a hot tub.

Orient Queen
★★+

Size:.............................. Mid-size Ship	Cabins (total):................................414
Tonnage: 16,916	Size range (sq ft/m): 111.9–324.0/10.4–30.1
Lifestyle: ....Standard	Cabins (outside view):...........................192
Cruise line:............................. Louis Cruises	Cabins (interior/no view):........................200
Former names: .... Orient Queen, Bolero, Starward	Cabins (for one person):............................0
IMO number:................................6821080	Cabins (with private balcony):.......................0
Builder: .... A.G. Weser (Germany)	Cabins (wheelchair accessible): 2
Original cost:......................................n/a	Wheelchair accessibility:............................None
Entered service:...................... Dec 1968/Aug 2006	Cabin voltage: ....110 and 220 volts
Registry:.....................................Greece	Elevators:..4
Length (ft/m):.............................. 525.9/160.30	Casino (gaming tables):............................ Yes
Beam (ft/m):................................. 74.9/22.84	Slot machines:.................................... Yes
Draft (ft/m):................................. 22.5/6.86	Swimming pools:....................................2
Propulsion/Propellers:.................. diesel (12,950kW)/2	Hot tubs (on deck):.................................0
Passenger decks:....................................7	Self-service launderette:...........................No
Total crew:.......................................400	Dedicated cinema/seats:....................... Yes/210
Passengers (lower beds/alll berths): 828/910	Library: .... Yes
Passenger Space Ratio (lower beds/all berths): 26.3/18.5	Onboard currency: .... Euros
Crew/Passenger Ratio (lower beds/all berths):......... 2.4/2.9	

A traditional small, casual ship for frugal cruisers

OVERVIEW. *Orient Queen* suits adult couples and single travelers who want to visit the Greek Islands in some comfort. It provides a good basic cruise experience in rather crowded, but moderately comfortable surroundings, at a modest price. The dress code is casual.

THE SHIP. The open deck and sunbathing space is very limited and some of the decks are of plain, painted steel. On the aft decks, there's a clutter of wooden sunloungers and sun-shade umbrellas. Just forward of the twin funnels is an enclosed sports facility. Aft of the mast is a large solarium-style shielded housing, with multi-level lounge/bar/disco that's adjacent to one of the ship's small swimming pools.

There's a decent choice of public rooms, including six bars, all with clean, contemporary furnishings, upbeat fabric colors, and a mix of traditional and contemporary decor. The noisy diesel engines tend to throb in cabins on the lower decks.

ACCOMMODATION. There are four Royal Suites, and 54 'suites.' The other cabins are very compact units that are moderately comfortable, and decorated in soft colors. But they are adequate for a short cruise, particularly as the ship is in port each day. While closet space is very limited, there are plenty of drawers.

The bathrooms are small and tight, and the towels are not large. Toilets are of the gentle flush (non-vacuum) variety. Soundproofing between cabins is poor, and the air conditioning is quite noisy.

Berlitz's Ratings

	Possible	Achieved
Ship	500	273
Accommodation	200	94
Food	400	216
Service	400	244
Entertainment	100	55
Cruise	400	206

OVERALL SCORE
1088 points out of 2000

The four Royal suites have decent space for the size of the ship. There is ample floor space, a king-size bed, vanity desk, curtained-off closet, plenty of drawer and storage space for luggage, a lounge with a sofa that converts into an additional bed, drinks table, and two chairs. A large pillar obstructs the room's flow. A bathroom has a small but deep Jacuzzi tub with integral hand-held shower. All accommodation has flat-screen TV sets, refrigerator, and telephone.

CUISINE. There are four eateries. The 444-seat Mermaid Restaurant is cheerful, even almost charming, and has some prime tables that overlook the stern. Seating is at tables for four, six, or eight, with two seatings. The cuisine is Mediterranean, with some Greek specialties, while the wine list consists mainly of young wines.

Breakfast and lunch buffets are provided indoors at the casual self-serve Horizon Café, with outdoor seating at tables around the aft swimming pool, but space is tight.

ENTERTAINMENT. The 420-seat El Cabaret showlounge, a single-level room, provides 'low budget, low quality' entertainment. There's also a nightclub/discotheque. A casino operates during cruises from Beirut.

SPA/FITNESS. There is a beauty salon and massage/body treatment room – on two different decks.

Orion
★★★★ +

Size:................................Boutique Ship	Cabins (total):....................................53
Tonnage:.......................................4,050	Size range (sq ft/m):.................175.0–345.0/16.3–32.1
Lifestyle:.....................................Premium	Cabins (outside view):................................53
Cruise line:....................Orion Expedition Cruises	Cabins (interior/no view):..............................0
Former names:......................................none	Cabins (for one person):...............................0
IMO number:...............................9273076	Cabins (with private balcony):..........................9
Builder:....................Cassens-Werft (Germany)	Cabins (wheelchair accessible):..........................0
Original cost:.......................................n/a	Wheelchair accessibility:...........................None
Entered service:....................Nov 2003/Mar 2006	Cabin voltage:.......................110 and 220 volts
Registry:.................................The Bahamas	Elevators:..1
Length (ft/m):...............................337.0/102.7	Casino (gaming tables):..............................No
Beam (ft/m):.................................46.0/14.0	Slot machines:.....................................No
Draft (ft/m):...................................12.6/3.8	Swimming pools:.....................................0
Propulsion/Propellers:...........................diesel/1	Hot tubs (on deck):..................................1
Passenger decks:....................................5	Self-service launderette:.............................No
Total crew:..75	Dedicated cinema/seats:............................Yes
Passengers (lower beds/all berths):.............106/125	Library:...Yes
Passenger Space Ratio (lower beds/all berths):.......38.2/32.4	Onboard currency:.........................Australian $
Crew/Passenger Ratio (lower beds/all berths):.........1.4/1.6	

For Australia-based 'soft' expedition and adventure cruising

OVERVIEW. This small ship is enjoyed by mature couples and single travelers that like learning about nature and wildlife in an up close and personal way. Cruising is really the wrong word for this type of eco-travel; it's more like having a magic carpet whisk to you to destinations most people have never heard of – particularly on the spectacular Papua New Guinea or Kimberley region itineraries.

THE SHIP. *Orion* is an attempt in the quest to build the ideal expedition cruise ship, offering life enrichment in high-class surroundings and the company of well-traveled people. It has all the comforts of home, and then some – as well as specialist equipment for expedition cruising. Although small, it has stabilizers, bow and stern thrusters for maximum maneuverability, and a fleet of 10 heavy-duty Zodiac inflatable landing craft and a fishing boat, BeeKay. There is also an aft marina platform for swimming off.

There is no swimming pool, nor is one needed, but there is a hot tub set amid an open deck, which also houses a bar and a small rock garden/water feature. All outdoor tables, chairs, and real steamer-style sunloungers are made of tropical hardwood.

The interior decor is really warm and inviting, providing a cozy, cosseting atmosphere far removed from the majority of today's larger expedition-style cruise ships. Public rooms include an observation lounge (Galaxy Lounge), which opens onto a walk-around open promenade deck; it also connects with the small Vega Health Spa.

Berlitz's Ratings

	Possible	Achieved
Ship	500	415
Accommodation	200	163
Food	400	308
Service	400	300
Entertainment	100	88
Cruise	400	329

OVERALL SCORE
1603 points out of 2000

Other public rooms include Leda Lounge (main lounge), a boutique, and a dedicated Cosmos Lecture Hall with surround sound system for lectures and movies. Typically, five expedition, culture, history, and marine biology lecturers are carried on each expedition.

The reception desk is open 24 hours a day, and there's an Internet-connect computer (A$50 for two hours) in the library, which has green leather seating). Some rooms are clustered around a glass-walled atrium and the single elevator. A special 'mud room,' complete with boot washing stations, is adjacent to a Zodiac/tender loading platform on the port side. The artwork focuses on exploration and myths associated with exploration. According to one myth, Neptune was Orion's father, for example, while Queen Eurayle of the Amazon was his mother.

This is about as far away from big cruise ships as you can get, with well-planned itineraries to some of the southern hemisphere's most remote regions, including the islands of Papua New Guinea, Australia's Kimberly region, 'Wild' Tasmania, and Antarctica's McMurdo Sound and Ross Sea regions. If you want magic moments in soft adventure travel, wrapped in the comfort of some fine, contemporary surroundings and good food, it would be hard to beat Orion. But make sure you can walk well – some expeditions are quite demanding.

When the ship operates in Australian waters – on Kimberly itineraries, for example – an Australian sales tax is added to all wine and beverage accounts. Drinks really should be included with this kind of product. However, bottled water is provided for all passengers at no charge.

Note that Orion Expedition Cruises and Orion were acquired in 2013 by the USA's Lindblad Expeditions. Orion will be renamed *National Geographic Orion* and transferred to the new operator in March 2014, when it will become part of the Lindblad Expeditions/ National Geographic fleet. Lindblad Expeditions will add more snorkeling gear and enough diving gear for 24 diving program participants, as well as an ROV (remote operated vehicle) able to descent up to 1,000 feet (305 meters).

ACCOMMODATION. There are four suite grades, and two cabin grades; the facilities in all of them are top-rate. All have twin beds that convert to a queen-size bed, a TV set, a DVD/CD player, a mini-refrigerator, ample closet space, and a small personal safe.

The marble-clad bathroom has a small toiletries cabinet, single washbasin, and a large shower enclosure, with a retractable clothes line. Toiletries are by Escada. All the cabinetry was custom-made, and the bathrooms were fitted individually, which is rare in today's modular-fit world.

There are 13 suites, nine of which have a small 'French' balcony (meaning you can just about step out onto it), four Owner's suites, six balcony suites, two Deluxe suites, and one rather odd-shaped but delightful Junior suite. These have more space, and some share a narrow communal balcony (meaning there is no partition between them), sofa, glass drinks table, and good-size vanity desk. Only the four Owners' suites have a bathtub; all other suites/cabins have large shower enclosures.

All cabins display black and white photographs of yachts, by Beken of Cowes.

DINING. The Constellation Restaurant has oceanview picture windows, artwork based on the astrological signs, and operates one space seating. Its low ceiling, however, makes it rather noisy. The cuisine is extremely good and varied, and, in addition to an à la carte menu, each dinner includes a four-course signature menu by one of Australia's new breed of high-profile chefs, Serge Dansereau of The Bathers' Pavilion in Sydney.

While portions are not large, they are colorful and creative. You can expect to find Tasmanian oysters, crocodile, emu, and kangaroo among the offerings. Place settings include Bauscher china and Hepp silverware.

The ship carries a decent range of mostly Australian wines, including delightful reds such as Wolf Blass Black Label, and Yalumba's The Octavius Old Vine Shiraz; and whites such as Leeuwin Estate's Art Series Chardonnay, and Devil's Lair 5th Leg Chardonnay-Sauvignon. There are less-pricey alternatives whites such as the Bunnamagoo Estate Chardonnay, and the Chain of Ponds Unwooded Chardonnay; and reds such as the Penfolds Bin 389, and the perfectly acceptable Bunnamagoo Merlot. If you want Champagne, several are available, such as the top of the range Krug Grande Cuvée, or the tasty Veuve Clicquot. There is no sommelier on board, but the wines are well served by the waiters or maître d' hotel.

Delphinus Outdoor Café, an open deck aft of the Leda Lounge, serves as an alfresco dining spot for casual breakfasts, lunches, and occasional barbecue dinners.

Continental breakfast and afternoon tea are also served in the Galaxy Lounge. Espressos and cappuccinos are available at no extra charge in two lounges/ bars and restaurant, and do try the delicious brownies on the bar counter.

The service staff is Filipino; they are warm and communicate well with passengers.

ENTERTAINMENT. There is no formal entertainment, although the ship typically carries an entertaining duo. Each evening, lecturers provide daily recaps and fascinating, in-depth talks on marine or plant biology.

SPA/FITNESS. The Vega Health Spa consists of a fitness center, sauna, shower enclosure, and a private treatment room (for massages). A beauty salon is located two decks below. Four 90-minute top-to-toe massage experiences are called Top End, Island and Reef, Tasmania, and Antarctica, and include an aromatherapy massages.

The ship carries a range of personal beauty products used on board and also for sale; creams, oils, and other ingredients are mixed by the therapist and tailored to your own needs.

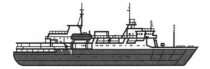

Ortelius
★★ +

Size:.	Boutique Ship	Cabins (total):.	45
Tonnage:	4,575	Size range (sq ft/m):	n/a
Lifestyle:	Standard	Cabins (outside view):	45
Cruise line:.	Oceanwide Expeditions	Cabins (interior/no view):.	0
Former names:	*Marina Svetaeva*	Cabins (for one person):.	0
IMO number:	8509181	Cabins (with private balcony):	0
Builder:	Gdynia Shipyards (Poland)	Cabins (wheelchair accessible):	0
Original cost:	n/a	Wheelchair accessibility:	none
Entered service:.	1989/Dec 2011	Cabin voltage:	110 volts
Registry:.	Belize	Elevators:.	0
Length (ft/m):	299.3/91.2	Casino (gaming tables):.	No
Beam (ft/m):.	57.7/17.6	Slot machines:.	No
Draft (ft/m):	19.0/5.8	Swimming pools:.	0
Propulsion/Propellers:	diesel/2	Hot tubs (on deck):.	0
Passenger decks:.	3	Self-service launderette:	0
Total crew:.	49	Dedicated cinema/seats:	0
Passengers (lower beds/alll berths):	90/100	Library:	Yes
Passenger Space Ratio (lower beds/all berths):	50.8/45.7	Onboard currency:	US$
Crew/Passenger Ratio (lower beds/all berths):	n/a		

A capable specialist ship for polar adventures

OVERVIEW. With a strong, ice-strengthened hull, this ship provides a good base for expedition adventures, and has accommodation and facilities that are quite comfortable.

THE SHIP. This smart-looking specialist expedition ship was built in Poland for the Russian Academy of Science (as Marina Svetaeva). After being acquired by Oceanwide Expeditions, it was reflagged and renamed *Ortelius* – after Abraham Ortelius, a Dutch/Flemish cartographer credited with publishing the first modern world atlas.

Except for the dining rooms, the only public room is a bar, which also acts as the lecture room and a reception area. The decor is plain and utilitarian. Parkas are provided. Smoking is allowed only on the open deck – but not near the Zodiacs or fuel storage. With Russian nautical crew, international catering staff, expedition staff and lecturers, it's an international mix. A total of 11 Zodiac rigid inflatable shore landing craft are carried. Gratuities are not included, but are suggested at about US$10 per person, per day, and are pooled by all the crew.

ACCOMMODATION. There are six different cabin categories and price grades. At the cheap end, there are five shared-bathroom cabins with two beds and two upper berths for low-cost voyaging; 14 twin cabins with two lower berths and shared facilities. There are also nine twin cabins with portholes, private shower and toilet, and two single lower beds; 10 twin cabins with windows, private toilet and shower, and two single low-

Berlitz's Ratings

	Possible	Achieved
Ship	500	231
Accommodation	200	90
Food	400	205
Service	400	191
Entertainment	100	45
Cruise	400	200

OVERALL SCORE
962 points out of 2000

er berths; six larger cabins with double beds, private toilet and shower, and separate day room; and one suite with double bed, private toilet and shower, and a separate day room. Although storage space is minimal, at least all cabins either have a window or a porthole. The bathrooms

DINING. The ship has two small restaurants, and both are quite cozy and intimate, although a little lacking in decor. The food is best described as hearty, down-to-earth fare, which is welcome after a day's tiring adventures. However, don't expect a wide selection of vegetables in the polar region – all the food has to be sent to the ships in containers.

ENTERTAINMENT. Recaps, after-dinner conversation, and catching up on some book reading is all you need.

SPA/FITNESS. There's a small sauna. That's it – but you won't have much time for anything else, because being busy and discovering things is what expedition cruising is all about.

Pacific Dawn
★★★ +

Size:.	Mid-size Ship	Cabins (total):.	798
Tonnage:	70,285	Size range (sq ft/m):	189.4–586.6/17.6–54.5
Lifestyle:	Standard	Cabins (outside view):	620
Cruise line:.	P&O Cruises (Australia)	Cabins (interior/no view):.	178
Former names:	Regal Princess	Cabins (for one person):.	0
IMO number:	8521232	Cabins (with private balcony):	148
Builder:	Fincantieri Navali (Italy)	Cabins (wheelchair accessible):	13
Original cost:	$276.8 million	Wheelchair accessibility:	Fair
Entered service:	Aug 1991/Nov 2007	Cabin voltage:	110 and 220 volts
Registry:.	Great Britain	Elevators:.	9
Length (ft/m):	811.0/247.2	Casino (gaming tables):	Yes
Beam (ft/m):.	105.6/32.2	Slot machines:	Yes
Draft (ft/m):	25.5/7.8	Swimming pools:.	2
Propulsion/Propellers:	diesel (24,000kW)/2	Hot tubs (on deck):.	4
Passenger decks:.	11	Self-service launderette:	Yes
Total crew:	725	Dedicated cinema/seats:.	No
Passengers (lower beds/alll berths):	1,596/2,020	Library:	Yes
Passenger Space Ratio (lower beds/all berths):	44.0/34.7	Onboard currency:	Australian $
Crew/Passenger Ratio (lower beds/all berths):	2.2/2.7		

This dated large ship is good for family-friendly cruising

OVERVIEW. *Pacific Dawn* provides a very pleasant cruise in elegant and comfortable surroundings, and a friendly staff will make you feel really welcome. Sunbathing space is rather limited when the ship is full. But, overall, *Pacific Dawn* performs well and is excellent value for money.

THE SHIP. There is no walk-around promenade deck outdoors – the only walking space being along the sides of the ship. Inside, the understated decor of soft pastel shades is highlighted by some colorful artwork. A striking, elegant three-deck-high atrium has a grand staircase with fountain sculpture. The Dome, an observation dome set high atop the ship, houses a multipurpose lounge/comedy club with live music.

FAMILIES. Children have their own play areas: Turtle Cove (ages three to six); Shark Shack (ages seven to 10); HQ (11–13); and HQ+ (14–17). Each age group has dedicated counselors to keep them occupied.

ACCOMMODATION. There are numerous different price grades, ranked by location and size. In the most recent refit, some 282 cabins had upper berths fitted to accommodate two adults and two children. In general, the cabins are well designed, with large bathrooms and good soundproofing. All cabins have walk-in closets, refrigerator, personal safe, and TV set. Twin beds convert to queen-size beds in standard cabins. Lifeboats obstruct the view from the outside-view cabins for

Berlitz's Ratings

	Possible	Achieved
Ship	500	313
Accommodation	200	135
Food	400	263
Service	400	276
Entertainment	100	72
Cruise	400	271

OVERALL SCORE
1330 points out of 2000

disabled passengers.

The 14 most expensive suites, each with a large private balcony, are very well equipped, and storage space is generous, adequate even for long cruises.

DINING. The Waterfront Restaurant has open seating for all meals. The food has good taste thanks to the use of fresh produce. A large 'always available' selection is combined with multiple daily additions; vegetable and potato side orders are always provided.

For more intimate dining, with food prepared to order, try the specialty venue Salt Grill by Luke Mangan. The fish specialties include barramundi and fresh oysters. There's a cover charge (Aus$40 for dinner, Aus$30 for lunch; reservations are needed. The downside is the intrusive background music.

There is a Trattoria (nominal fee) for informal meals; this is particularly popular at lunchtime and in the afternoons. There's also an extra-cost patisserie, Charlie's Bar, in the spacious lobby.

ENTERTAINMENT. The Marquee Showlounge spans two decks. There's plenty of live music for the bars and lounges, with a wide mix of classical, jazz, and dance, from solo pianists to showbands. Three times during each cruise, a stunning laser light and sound show is presented in the atrium.

SPA/FITNESS. The Aqua Spa and fitness center has a gymnasium, exercise room, steam room, and sauna.

Pacific Jewel
★★★ +

Size:	Mid-size Ship		Crew/Passenger Ratio (lower beds/all berths):	2.5/2.9
Tonnage:	70,310		Cabins (total):	
Lifestyle:	Standard		Size range (sq ft/m):	188.3–538.2/17.5–50.0
Cruise line:	P&O Cruises (Australia)		Cabins (outside view):	628
Former names:	Ocean Village Two, AIDAblu, A'RosaBlu, Crown Princess		Cabins (interior/no view):	197
			Cabins (for one person):	0
IMO number:	8521220		Cabins (with private balcony):	198
Builder:	Fincantieri Navali (Italy)		Cabins (wheelchair accessible):	10
Original cost:	$276.8 million		Wheelchair accessibility:	Fair
Entered service:	Jul 1990/Dec 2009		Cabin voltage:	110 and 220 volts
Registry:	Great Britain		Elevators:	9
Length (ft/m):	805.7/245.6		Casino (gaming tables):	Yes
Beam (ft/m):	105.8/32.2		Slot machines:	Yes
Draft (ft/m):	26.9/8.2		Swimming pools:	2
Propulsion/Propellers:	diesel-electric (24,000kW)/2		Hot tubs (on deck):	2
Passenger decks:	11		Self-service launderette:	Yes
Total crew:	621		Dedicated cinema/seats:	No
Passengers (lower beds/alll berths):	1,708/2,014		Library:	Yes
Passenger Space Ratio (lower beds/all berths):	41.1/34.9		Onboard currency:	Australian $

This large ship provides family-friendly Aussie cruising

OVERVIEW. *Pacific Jewel* is best suited to young Australian couples, single travelers, families, and single parent families with children seeking a good-value-for-money first cruise in a large, casual ship setting, with appealing itineraries and destinations, and a range of fun-filled activities. The young, vibrant staff makes passengers feel welcome.

THE SHIP. Originally ordered by Sitmar Cruises, this ship debuted in 1990 as *Crown Princess* but has since assumed many identities. It was moved to the A'Rosa Cruises brand and, as *A'Rosa Blu*, began operating cruises for the German-speaking family market in 2002. Two years later, it was refitted and renamed *AIDAblu* for AIDA Cruises, then became *Ocean Village Two* for the UK's Ocean Village brand. In 2009 it turned into *Pacific Jewel*, specifically for the Australian market.

It has a dolphin-like upper front structure made of lightweight aluminum alloy, originally designed to keep the weight down in line with stability requirements. It was designed by Renzo Piano, the renowned Italian architect behind Paris's revolutionary Centre Georges Pompidou and Japan's Kansai International Airport, Osaka. A large swept-back funnel, also made from aluminum alloy, is placed aft.

Facilities are in line with the tastes of young, active Aussie families, single parents with children, and single travelers. The interior layout is a bit disjointed, however. Some innovative and elegant styling is mixed with traditional features and a reasonably spacious in-terior layout. An understated decor of soft pastel shades is highlighted by splashes of color, as well as some colorful artwork.

The oval-shaped atrium lobby is three decks high and has a grand staircase as its focal point; it provides a good meeting and gathering point. Shops, bars, and lounges span out from the lobby on three decks. Other facilities include an Internet café, Mix Bar, and Charlie's Bar. Child-free areas include Oasis, a sunbathing quiet zone aft on Deck 10, and the Aqua Spa and Health Center.

There is no decent outdoor or indoor forward observation viewpoint, and no walk-around promenade deck outdoors, the only walking space being along the port and starboard sides of the ship. In fact, there's little contact with the outdoors, and sunbathing space is quite limited. Other niggles include the many support pillars throughout the public rooms which obstruct sightlines and impede passenger flow.

P&O Cruises (Australia) scrapped automatic tipping from October 2010, so tips are at your discretion. P&O provides really good value for money, particularly when compared to most land-based resorts in Australia. Some cruises have special themes, such as food and wine. The onboard product is playful and casual; its delivery is highly targeted to the Australian lifestyle, and nobody does it better. The crew are extremely friendly and service is better than you can find in many parts of Australia.

FAMILIES. There is a good range of facilities for children, who are split into four age groups, with separate

Berlitz's Ratings

	Possible	Achieved
Ship	500	350
Accommodation	200	140
Food	400	261
Service	400	276
Entertainment	100	72
Cruise	400	268
OVERALL SCORE		
1367 points out of 2000		

facilities and staff for each: Turtle Cove (ages three to six); Shark Shack (ages seven to 10); HQ (11–13s); HQ+ (14–17s). A paddling pool for toddlers is included.

ACCOMMODATION. There are 19 price categories, including mini-suites with private balconies, outside view cabins and interior cabins, and special cabins for the disabled. Generally, accommodation on the higher decks will cost more because, aboard ship, location is everything. Occupants of mini-suites (there are 36) get more space, a larger bathroom, and premium bathroom amenities.

Single-parent families comprise an increasing number of today's cruise passengers, so a good number of two-bed cabins also have a third (or third/fourth) pull-down berth.

In general, the well-designed cabins have large bathrooms as well as decent soundproofing. Walk-in closets, refrigerator, personal safe, and color TV are provided in all of them. Twin beds convert to queen-size beds in most cabins. Bathrobes and toiletries are provided. Views from the outside-view cabins for the disabled are obstructed by lifeboats, as are some other cabins on the same deck (Deck 8).

Suites: The most expensive suites have a private balcony, and are quite well laid out to a practical design. The bedroom is separated from the living room by a heavy wooden door; there are TV sets in both rooms, and closet and drawer space are generous.

DINING. There are two principal restaurants, several decks apart: Plantation and The Waterfront. There are a few tables for two, but most are for four, six, or eight. Plantation is open 24 hours a day, while The Waterfront is open for à la carte breakfasts, lunches, and dinner at times given in the daily program. There's a neat table for 10 persons in the Wine Room, part of the Waterfront Restaurant, for use as a Chef's Table, complete with dégustation menu.

The Waterfront's menu is really varied and caters to the multi-cultural, multi-ethnic passenger mix. The food has great taste, thanks to the use of fresh Australian produce and meat and other items of Australian origin. It is perhaps best described as modern Australian fare. A large 'always available' selection is combined with multiple daily additions, plus vegetable and potato side orders ('sides' in Aussie-English).

Other dining options. For a treat or special celebration, extra-charge full service dining is available in the intimate bistro-style restaurant, Salt Grill by Luke Mangan (think: Sydney crab omelet with miso mustard broth). It is located forward of the main pools, on the starboard side, accessed by the forward stairway. The cover charge is worth it because the meals have more taste and neat flavor combinations.

La Luna, a small, casual deck restaurant adjacent to the aft pool and funnel, serves Asian-style cuisine.

For coffee, tea, chocolate, and sweet snacks during the day, and drinks in the evening, Charlie's Bar is an extra-cost patisserie/bar on the lower level of the spacious lobby.

ENTERTAINMENT. The Marquee Theatre, the venue for main entertainment events, spans two decks, with seating on both main and balcony levels. Several support pillars obstruct sightlines from a number of seats. There's plenty of colorful entertainment, including a song and dance troupe, and a good stable of Aussie cabaret acts. A high-energy acrobatic-and-dance deck show is provided for warm nights under the stars, on a stage and acrobatic archway fitted during one of the ship's refits.

Connexions (lounge/bar) is an adults-only comedy venue that doubles as a karaoke and live music venue. Also, if you like country and western music, hoedowns, and line dancing, you'll find your tastes are catered for.

SPA/FITNESS. The Aqua Spa and Health Club, an extensive wellness center, spans two decks and measures almost 14,000 sq ft (1,300 sq m); a staircase connects two levels. Located at the top of the ship at the forward stairway, it occupies the space in the 'dolphin head' section. With its curved surfaces, walking the treadmills or exercycling and facing out to sea (albeit on the port side) makes you feel you're doing so in the upper deck of a Boeing 747.

Panoramic saunas and Hammam steam room are on the lower level; a seven-day pass for the sauna and steam rooms costs extra. The reception area has a waterfall and cypress trees, and there are 11 treatment rooms for facials, massages (including hot stones and couples massage), manicure and pedicure, dry float and hydrobath. There is also a solarium, and a four-person relaxation room. It's a very nice spa facility.

The spa is operated by a specialist concession. Some exercise classes and health talks are free; others may incur a charge.

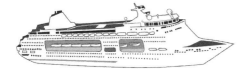

Pacific Pearl
★★★ +

Size:	Mid-size Ship
Tonnage:	63,524
Lifestyle:	Standard
Cruise line:	P&O Cruises (Australia)
Former names:	Ocean Village, Arcadia, Star Princess, FairMajesty
IMO number:	9048081
Builder:	Chantiers de L'Atlantique (France)
Original cost:	$200 million
Entered service:	Mar 1989/May 2010
Registry:	Great Britain
Length (ft/m):	810.3/247.0
Beam (ft/m):	105.6/32.2
Draft (ft/m):	26.9/8.2
Propulsion/Propellers:	diesel-electric (39,000kW)/2
Passenger decks:	12
Total crew:	514
Passengers (lower beds/all berths):	1,624/1,692
Passenger Space Ratio (lower beds/all berths):	39.1/37.5
Crew/Passenger Ratio (lower beds/all berths):	3.1/3.2

Cabins (total):	812
Size range (sq ft/m):	148.0–538.2/13.7–50.0
Cabins (outside view):	622
Cabins (interior/no view):	190
Cabins (for one person):	0
Cabins (with private balcony):	64
Cabins (wheelchair accessible):	8
Wheelchair accessibility:	Good
Cabin voltage:	220 volts
Elevators:	9
Casino (gaming tables):	Yes
Slot machines:	Yes
Swimming pools:	3
Hot tubs (on deck):	2
Self-service launderette:	Yes
Dedicated cinema/seats:	No
Library:	Yes
Onboard currency:	Australian $

A dated, very family-friendly ship for casual cruising

OVERVIEW. *Pacific Pearl* is best suited to young couples, singles of all ages, and families with children and teenagers who like to mingle in a mid-size ship with plenty of life, music, and entertainment for everyone, with food that is quantity rather than quality, and a price that's attractive.

THE SHIP. *Pacific Pearl* was originally designed and built as *FairMajesty* for Sitmar Cruises just as the company was absorbed into Princess Cruises. In 2003, after a refurbishment that brightened the interior passageways, public rooms, and dining spots, it morphed into *Ocean Village*, a trendy ship designed for younger couples and families.

Several new cabins were added during that refit. The casino was also relocated, displacing the library, and a former casino became an Internet center/bar. In 2010, the ship was transferred to P&O Cruises (Australia) to become *Pacific Pearl* for Australasian passengers, and further refurbished to suit Australian cruise tastes.

Pacific Pearl is a well-proportioned ship, with a decent amount of open deck and sunbathing space – and an adults-only quiet zone decks (The Oasis, with two hot tubs, but no shower) on the aft, tiered decks. On the open leisure deck are two pools, one with sloping steps, the other with vertical steps, and one has a sit-in 'splash' bar. An archway over the aft pool provides a platform for aerial acrobatic shows, and there's also a poolside screen for those important rugby games – and movies. An Oasis adults-only quiet zone with daybeds, and a hot tub is located at the aft of Deck 8.

Berlitz's Ratings

	Possible	Achieved
Ship	500	359
Accommodation	200	138
Food	400	262
Service	400	277
Entertainment	100	74
Cruise	400	278

OVERALL SCORE
1388 points out of 2000

The interiors are quite elegant, with much attention paid to lighting. But they also include a few items that have a link with the past, such as the Art Deco stainless steel balustrades and the soulless stainless steel elevators. There aren't a lot of public rooms, although one nice feature is the fact that they have ceilings higher than the average for contemporary cruise ships. My favorite bar: Mix.

The focal point of the interior is a three-deck-high atrium lobby and a multi-deck dual staircase. The Dome, an observation lounge, sits atop the ship, forward of the mast. It is a lounge for cocktails; at night it turns into a night-spot/discotheque with a sunken, circular wooden dance floor.

For retail therapy, several shops are clustered around the second and third levels of the atrium lobby. Other facilities include a small casino, aft of the upper level of the two-deck-high showlounge, a Victorian pub called Oriana (with Fat Yak, Hoegaarden, Carlsberg, and Bulmers Cider on tap), Connexions Bar (for adult-only comedy, karaoke, and trivia quizzes), and Mix Bar, a more traditional cocktail bar/drinking lounge with cool blue decor.

There's no full walk-around promenade deck outdoors, but open port and starboard walking areas stretch partly along the sides. There is, however, a walking track on the uppermost open deck.

Some cruises have special themes, such as food and wine. The onboard product is playful and casual; its delivery is highly targeted to the Australian lifestyle, and nobody does it better. The crew are extremely friendly, and service is better than you can find in many parts of Australia. So hats off to P&O, who made tipping discretionary in 2010.

FAMILIES. The children's facilities and playrooms are quite extensive. At the aft of the ship, there's an indoor play area – Turtle Cove for three- to six-year-olds, and Shark Shack for seven- to 10-year-olds. An exterior aft deck has a paddling pool and games area. Tweens and teenagers have their own areas (HQ Club for ages 11–14, and HQ+ for 15–17s, including a good chill-out zone). A children's dinner is offered for ages three to 10, with babysitting available until 1am.

A number of cabins have third- and fourth person berths – good for families with children, but the drawer and storage space is tight.

ACCOMMODATION. There are four basic types, mini-suites, outsides with balcony, outside-view, and interior, in 22 different price grades, depending on location and size. These include 36 mini-suites with small private balcony, walk-in closet, masses of storage space, and wood-floored bathroom with bathtub and shower. All other accommodation consists of standard outside-view and interior grade cabins, almost all of which are of a decent size. If you like to fall asleep with soft music playing, note that because music is available only through the TV set, you can't access any of the music channels without having a TV picture on.

Standard Outside-view/Interior Cabins. All are equipped with twin beds that can, in most cases, be put together to form a queen-size bed. All have a good amount of storage, including wooden drawer units, plus some under-bed space for luggage, and a walk-in closet. Sound insulation between cabins could be better – TV sound late at night can be irritating. High-quality bed linen, duvets, and pillows are provided.

The bathrooms are of a modular design and have good-size shower enclosures and a retractable clothesline. None have tubs except for the mini-suites, as the ship was originally built for American passengers, who prefer showers. However, shower heads are affixed to the wall, denying you the ease of a flexible shower hose. Soap is provided.

Room-service items cost extra, and incur an additional delivery charge.

DINING. The main restaurant is the 812-seat, open-seating Waterfront; it has large ocean-view windows, sit-down, tablecloth dining, and tables for two, four, six, or eight persons. It has a high ceiling, and seating sections help divide the room into comfortable spaces, so it doesn't feel as large as it actually is.

The Waterfront's menu is really varied and caters to the multi-cultural, multi-ethnic passenger mix. The food has great taste, thanks to the use of fresh Australian produce and meat and other items of Australian origin. It is perhaps best described as modern Australian fare. A large 'always available' selection, including vegetarian dishes, is combined with multiple daily additions, and vegetable and potato side orders are always provided. The food is straightforward, unfussy, and unpretentious, with little use of garnishes. The service is attentive, warm, and lighthearted. Bar snacks such as peanuts or crisps cost extra.

For more intimate dining and food prepared to order, try the specialty venue Salt Grill by Luke Mangan. This small dining spot with open kitchen serves really excellent New World cuisine. The steaks are extremely good, and the fish specialties include barramundi and fresh oysters. There's a cover charge (Aus$40 for dinner, Aus$30 for lunch – and absolutely worth it), and reservations are needed; the downside is the intrusive, unnecessary vocal background 'music.'

Plantation is a self-serve buffet, open for breakfast, lunch, and dinner, but setting is limited. It's typically slow-going along straight buffet lines, so patience is needed. A wide selection of tea is provided at the smart beverage stations, as is coffee.

The Café, for coffees, hot chocolate, and chocolate snacks, is adjacent to the forward swimming pool. Charlie's, a neat little coffee bistro, located on the lowest lobby level opposite the reception desk, serves coffees, teas, pastries, and snacks (at extra cost). A new ice cream bar has been added to the pool.

ENTERTAINMENT. The Marquee Theatre is the venue for all principal entertainment events. A horseshoe-shaped room, with main and balcony levels (there's a bar at the back on the main level), it has adequate sight lines from most of the banquette-style seating, but sight lines from the front row seats on the upper level are obstructed by the required balcony railing.

Although the ship isn't young and doesn't have the latest bells and whistles, the stage has an excellent LED lighting backdrop. There is a good variety of entertainment, from production shows to cabaret-style acts and comedians. There is also live music throughout the many lounges and bars – in fact, there's no bar without music, so sitting down for a quiet drink or two isn't an option. Fans of country and western music, hoedowns, and line dancing are well catered for.

SPA/FITNESS. The attractive Aqua Spa facilities include a beauty salon, gymnasium, and an extra-cost thermal/relax area that includes a unisex sauna, steam room, herbal showers, and two body-shaped tiled hot beds. It is located on the lowest passenger deck.

It is wise to book treatments such as massages and facials as soon as possible after you embark, as time slots fill quickly. Some exercise classes are free, but most incur a charge.

Pacific Princess
★★★★

Size:.	Small Ship	Cabins (total):.	344
Tonnage:	30,277	Size range (sq ft/m):	145.3–968.7/13.5–90.0
Lifestyle:	Standard	Cabins (outside view):	317
Cruise line:.	Princess Cruises	Cabins (interior/no view):.	27
Former names:	R Three	Cabins (for one person):.	0
IMO number:	9187887	Cabins (with private balcony):	232
Builder:	Chantiers de l'Atlantique (France)	Cabins (wheelchair accessible):	3
Original cost:	$150 million	Wheelchair accessibility:	Good
Entered service:.	Aug 1999/Nov 2002	Cabin voltage:	110 and 220 volts
Registry:.	Bermuda	Elevators:.	4
Length (ft/m):.	593.7/181.0	Casino (gaming tables):.	Yes
Beam (ft/m):.	83.5/25.5	Slot machines:.	Yes
Draft (ft/m):	19.5/6.0	Swimming pools:.	1
Propulsion/Propellers:	diesel-electric (18,600kW)/2	Hot tubs (on deck):.	3
Passenger decks:.	9	Self-service launderette:	Yes
Total crew:	373	Dedicated cinema/seats:	No
Passengers (lower beds/alll berths):.	688/826	Library:	Yes
Passenger Space Ratio (lower beds/all berths):	44.1/36.6	Onboard currency:	US$
Crew/Passenger Ratio (lower beds/all berths):.	1.8/2.2		

English country house decor for mature-age cruisers

OVERVIEW. *Pacific Princess* appeals to mature adults seeking value for money aboard a comfortable mid-size ship with plenty of dining choices and limited entertainment.

THE SHIP. *Pacific Princess* has an all-white, instead of a black hull, – this makes the ship appear larger than it is – and a large, square-ish funnel. A lido deck has a swimming pool and good sunbathing space, while one of the aft decks has a thalassotherapy pool. A jogging track circles the swimming pool deck, but one deck above. The uppermost outdoors deck includes a golf driving net and shuffleboard court.

There is no walk-around promenade deck outdoors, although there is a small jogging track around the perimeter of the swimming pool, and port and starboard side decks. Instead of wooden decks outdoors, they are covered by Bollidt, a sand-colored rubberized material. There is no sauna. The room service menu is extremely limited. Stairways, although carpeted, are tinny. In order to keep the prices low, often the air routing to get to/from your ship is not the most direct.

The interior decor is quite stunning and elegant, a throwback to ship decor of the ocean liners of the 1920s and '30s, executed in fine taste. This includes detailed ceiling cornices, both real and faux wrought-iron staircase railings, leather- and cherry wood-paneled wall, trompe l'oeil ceilings, and rich carpeting in hallways with an Oriental rug-look center section. The overall feel echoes that of an old-world country club.

Berlitz's Ratings

	Possible	Achieved
Ship	500	392
Accommodation	200	150
Food	400	252
Service	400	287
Entertainment	100	71
Cruise	400	290

OVERALL SCORE
1442 points out of 2000

The staircase in the main, two-deck-high foyer recalls the staircase in the 1997 movie *Titanic*.

The public rooms are spread over three decks. The reception hall has a staircase with intricate wrought-iron railings. The Nightclub, with forward-facing views, sits high in the ship and has some Polynesian-inspired decor and furniture.

There are plenty of bars – including one in the entrance to each restaurant. Perhaps the nicest of all bars and lounges are in the casino bar/lounge that is a beautiful room reminiscent of London's grand hotels and understated gaming clubs. It has an inviting marble fireplace – in fact, there are three such fireplaces aboard – and comfortable sofas and individual chairs. There is also a large Card Room, which incorporates an internet center with eight stations.

The Library is a beautiful, grand Regency-style room, with a fireplace, a high, indented, trompe l'oeil ceiling, and an excellent selection of books, plus very comfortable wingback chairs with footstools, and sofas you could sleep on; it's the most relaxing room aboard. There's very little entertainment, but it is not needed in the cruise areas featured. *Pacific Princess* is much more about relaxation than the larger Princess ships.

As with all Princess Cruises ships, 15 percent is added to all bar and spa accounts – drink prices are moderate, but beer prices are high. A standard gratuity is automatically added to onboard accounts – to reduce the amount, you'll need to go to the reception desk.

There is a charge – tokens must be obtained from the reception desk – for using the machines in the self-service launderette. A change machine in the launderette itself would be more user-friendly.

ACCOMMODATION. There is a variety of about eight different cabin types to choose from, with prices linked to grade, location and size.

All of the standard interior and outside-view cabins are extremely compact units, and extremely tight for two persons – especially for cruises longer than seven days. Cabins have twin beds or queen-size bed, with good under-bed storage areas, personal safe, vanity desk with large mirror, good closet and drawer space in rich, dark woods, and bathrobe. Color TVs carry a major news channel, where obtainable, plus a sports channel and several round-the-clock movie channels. The bathrooms, which have tiled floors and plain walls, are compact, standard units, and include a shower enclosure with a removable, strong hand-held shower unit, hairdryer, 100 percent cotton towels, toiletries storage shelves, and a retractable clothesline.

The suites/cabins that have private balconies (66 percent of all suites/cabins, or 73 percent of all outside-view suites/cabins) have partial, and not full, balcony partitions, and sliding glass doors. Thanks to good design and layout, only 14 cabins on Deck 6 have lifeboat-obstructed views. The balcony floor is covered in thick plastic matting – teak would be nicer – and some awful plastic furniture.

Mini-Suites (52). Units designated as mini-suites are in reality simply larger cabins than the standard varieties, as the sleeping and lounge areas are not divided. While not overly large, the bathrooms have a good-size tub and ample space for storing toiletries. The living area has a refrigerated mini-bar, lounge area with breakfast table, and a balcony with two plastic chairs and a table.

Owner's Suites (10). The most spacious accommodation, these are fine, large living spaces in the forward-most and aft-most sections of the accommodation decks. Particularly nice are those that overlook the stern, on decks 6, 7, and 8. They have more extensive balconies that really are private and cannot be overlooked by anyone from the decks above. There is an entrance foyer, living room, bedroom, CD player, bathroom with Jacuzzi tub, as well as a small guest bathroom. The bed faces the sea, which can be seen through the floor-to-ceiling windows and sliding glass door.

All suites/cabins located at the stern may suffer from vibration and noise, particularly when the ship is proceeding at or close to full speed, or maneuvering in port.

DINING. There are four different dining spots – three restaurants and one casual self-serve buffet:

The Club Restaurant has 338 seats, all with armrests, and includes a large raised central section. There are large ocean-view windows on three sides, and some prime tables that overlook the stern, as well as a small bandstand for occasional live dinner music. However, the noise level can be high because of the single-deck-height ceiling.

Sabatini's Trattoria, an extra-cost Italian restaurant, has 96 seats (all chairs have armrests), windows along two sides, and a set 'Bellissima' three-hour dégustation menu.

The Sterling Steakhouse is an 'American steak house' with a good selection of large, prime steaks and other meats. It has 98 comfortable seats, all with armrests, and windows along two sides. It has a set menu, together with added daily chef's specials. There is a cover charge.

The Lido Café has seating for 154 indoors and 186 outdoors, with white plastic patio furniture. It is open for breakfast, lunch, and casual dinners. The ship's self-serve buffet restaurant, it is open 24 hours a day and has a small pizzeria and grill.

All restaurants have open-seating dining, so you dine when you want, although reservations are necessary for Sabatini's Trattoria and Sterling Steakhouse, where there are mostly tables for four or six – there are few tables for two. In addition, there is a Poolside Grill and Bar for fast food.

ENTERTAINMENT. The 345-seat Cabaret Lounge, in the forward part of the ship on Deck 5, is the main venue for entertainment events and some social functions. The single-level room has a stage, and circular hardwood dance floor with adjacent banquette and individual tub chair seating, and raised sections on port and starboard sides. It is not a large room, and not really designed for production shows, so cabaret acts and local entertainment form the main focus. Mini-revue style shows with colorful costumes are presented by a troupe of resident singer/dancers in a potted version of what you might experience aboard the large ships of Princess Cruises. Inevitably, art auctions and bingo are pushed almost daily.

SPA/FITNESS. Facilities, which are located in the forward part of the ship on a high deck (Deck 9) include a gymnasium with ocean-view windows and some high-tech muscle-toning equipment and treadmills. There are steam rooms but no sauna, changing areas for men and women, and a beauty salon with ocean-view windows.

The spa is operated by Steiner, a specialist concession whose retail products will be pushed. Some fitness classes, such as Stepexpress, Power Walk, Total Body Conditioning, Xpress Circuit, are free. Others, such as yoga and kick-boxing, cost extra, as do massage, facials, pedicures, and beauty salon treatments.

Pacific Venus
★★★★

Size:.	Small Ship	Cabins (total):.	238
Tonnage:	26,518	Size range (sq ft/m):	164.6–699.6/15.3–65.0
Lifestyle:	Standard	Cabins (outside view):	238
Cruise line:.	Venus Cruise	Cabins (interior/no view):.	0
Former names:	none	Cabins (for one person):.	0
IMO number:	9160011	Cabins (with private balcony):	20
Builder:	Ishikawajima Heavy Industries (Japan)	Cabins (wheelchair accessible):	1
Original cost:	$114 million (13 billion yen)	Wheelchair accessibility:	Fair
Entered service:.	Apr 1998	Cabin voltage:	110 volts
Registry:.	Japan	Elevators:.	4
Length (ft/m):.	601.7/183.4	Casino (gaming tables):	Yes
Beam (ft/m):	82.0/25.0	Slot machines:.	Yes
Draft (ft/m):	21.3/6.5	Swimming pools:.	1
Propulsion/Propellers:	diesel (13,636kW)/2	Hot tubs (on deck):.	1
Passenger decks:.	7	Self-service launderette:	Yes
Total crew:	220	Dedicated cinema/seats:	Yes
Passengers (lower beds/alll berths):	476/620	Library:	Yes
Passenger Space Ratio (lower beds/all berths):	55.7/42.7	Onboard currency:	Japanese yen
Crew/Passenger Ratio (lower beds/all berths):	2.1/2.8		

Comfortable decor and style for Japanese cruisers

OVERVIEW. *Pacific Venus* is best suited to Japanese-speaking couples and single travelers of mature years who appreciate very comfortable surroundings and good food and service, all at a moderate cost. The ship is often operated under charter to travel organizations, so drinks aren't always included in the fare; when operated by Venus Cruise, alcoholic drinks are not included.

Berlitz's Ratings

	Possible	Achieved
Ship	500	388
Accommodation	200	147
Food	400	310
Service	400	310
Entertainment	100	75
Cruise	400	301
OVERALL SCORE		
1531 points out of 2000		

THE SHIP. The company Venus Cruise is part of Japan Cruise Line, which is itself part of SHK Line Group, a joint venture between the Shin Nohonkai, Hankyu, and Kanpu ferry companies, which operate more than 20 ferries. There is a decent amount of open deck space aft of the funnel – good for deck sports – while protected sunbathing space is provided around the small swimming pool. All sunloungers have cushioned pads. The open walking promenade decks are rubber-coated steel – teak would be more desirable.

The base of the funnel itself is the site of a day/night lounge, which overlooks the swimming pool – it is slightly reminiscent of Royal Caribbean International's funnel-wrapped Viking Crown lounges aboard its first ships. There is plenty of space per passenger. The decor is clean and fresh, with much use of pastel colors and blond woods, giving the interiors a feeling of warmth.

The dining rooms are located off Deck 7, which has a double-width indoor promenade, with high ceiling height. The three-deck-high atrium has a crystal chandelier as its focal point, and a white baby grand piano on its lower level, where the Reception Desk is situated.

There are special rooms for meetings and conference organizers, for times when the ship is chartered. A piano salon has colorful low-back chairs, and a large main hall has a finely sculptured high ceiling and over 700 moveable seats and hosts production shows. There's a 350-seat main lounge for cabaret shows and ballroom dancing, a small movie theater, and a library/writing room and card room.

A casino gaming area is located as part of the Top Lounge set at the front of the funnel (winners receive prizes instead of cash, under Japanese law). There's also a smoking room, Chashitsu (tatami mat) room, karaoke room (for rent) and card room/mahjong room, free self-service launderettes on each accommodation deck, and two (credit card/coin) public telephone booths.

Overall, this company provides a well-packaged cruise in a ship that has a very comfortable, serene environment. The dress code is relaxed, and no tipping is allowed.

The ship has two classes: Salon Class and Standard Class. Salon Class passengers pay more, but get suite-grade accommodation, eat in the Grand Siècle private dining room, and are given lots of extra goodies and services, including a welcome embarkation basket, more toiletries, and priority tickets for shows and shore tenders.

ACCOMMODATION. There are four types: royal suites, suites, deluxe cabins, state cabins (in four price grades), and standard cabins. All are located from the uppermost to lowermost decks, respectively. All suites and cabins have an outside view, but few cabins have a private balcony.

The four Royal Suites (Archaic, Elegant, Modern, and Noble) are decorated in two different styles – one contemporary, one in a more traditional Japanese style. Each has a private balcony (with a drinks table and two chairs) with sliding door, an expansive lounge area with large sofa and plush armchairs, coffee table, window-side chairs and drinks table, floor-to-ceiling windows, and a large flat-screen TV set, with separate DVD unit. There is a separate bedroom, with twin- or queen-size bed, vanity/writing desk, a large walk-in closet with personal safe. Also provided are high-quality binoculars, camera tripod, humidifier, coffee/tea-making set, and free mini-bar setup. The large bathroom has ocean-view windows, Jacuzzi tub, a separate shower enclosure, and his/her washbasins.

Sixteen other suites have private balconies (with teak table and two chairs), a good-size living area with vanity/writing desk, dining table, chair and curved sofa, separate sleeping area, and bathroom with deep tub slightly larger than the Royal suites, and single large washbasin. There is ample lighted closet and drawer space (two locking drawers instead of a personal safe), and a DVD unit.

There are 20 Deluxe cabins; these have large picture windows fronted by a large, curtained arch, sleeping area with twin or queen beds, plus a daytime sofa that converts into a third bed.

The so-called 'state' cabins, many with upper berths for third passengers, are in three price levels, have decor that is best described as basic, with reasonable closet space, but very little drawer space.

The standard cabins, however, are really plain, but can accommodate three persons – useful for families – although the drawer and storage space is a bit tight.

All accommodation grades have a tea set with electric hot water kettle, TV set, telephone, and stocked mini-bar/refrigerator – all items included in the cruise price. Bathrooms have a hairdryer and lots of Shiseido toiletries, particularly in the suites. All room-service menu items cost extra – this is typical of all Japanese cruise ships – except for Salon-class suite-grade accommodation. All passengers receive a yukata (a Japanese-style light cotton robe). Suite occupants also get a plush bathrobe, and all accommodation grades have electric, automatic toilets (washlets) with heated seats.

DINING. The Primavera Restaurant is located aft, with ocean views on three sides, and has a high ceiling. Passengers dine in one seating, and tables are for six, 10, or 12. The food consists of both Japanese and Western items; the menu is varied and the food is attractively presented. For breakfast and lunch it includes a self-serve buffet, while dinner is typically a fully served set meal.

A separate, intimate 42-seat restaurant, Grand Siècle, is reserved for occupants of suite-grade (Salon Class) accommodation; it is tastefully decorated in Regency style, with fine wood-paneling and a detailed, indented ceiling. It has mostly tables for two (with plenty of space for correct service), better quality chopsticks, nori seaweed, and better quality and variety of fine china. Cold and hot towels are provided, and the whole dining experienced is far better than in the Primavera.

ENTERTAINMENT. Le Pacific Main Lounge is the venue for all shipboard entertainment and also functions as a lecture and activities room during the day. It is a single-level room with seating clustered around a thrust stage so that entertainers are in the very midst of their audience.

On most cruises, special featured entertainers such as singers, instrumentalists, storytellers, and dance champions are brought on board from ashore.

SPA/FITNESS. Spa facilities include male and female Grand Baths, which include two bathing pools and health/cleansing stations, ocean-view windows, a steam room, a gymnasium with ocean-view windows (in a different location just aft of the funnel); and a sauna.

Japanese massage is available, as are hairdressing and barber services in the small salon, located on the lowest passenger-accessible deck of the ship.

Paul Gauguin
★★★★ +

Size:.. Small Ship	Cabins (total):.....................................166
Tonnage: 19,200	Size range (sq ft/m):.......... 200.0–588.0/18.5–54.6
Lifestyle: ....Premium	Cabins (outside view):..............................166
Cruise line:........................... Paul Gauguin Cruises	Cabins (interior/no view):..............................0
Former names: ....none	Cabins (for one person):................................0
IMO number: 9111319	Cabins (with private balcony):.........................89
Builder: .... Chantiers de l'Atlantique (France)	Cabins (wheelchair accessible): 1
Original cost:............................... $150 million	Wheelchair accessibility:............................Fair
Entered service:....................... Jan 1998/Jan 2010	Cabin voltage: .... 110 volts
Registry:.................................... The Bahamas	Elevators:..4
Length (ft/m):............................... 513.4/156.5	Casino (gaming tables):.............................. Yes
Beam (ft/m):.................................. 72.1/22.0	Slot machines:...................................... Yes
Draft (ft/m):.................................... 16.8/5.1	Swimming pools:......................................1
Propulsion/Propellers: .... diesel-electric (9,000kW)/2	Hot tubs (on deck):....................................0
Passenger decks:......................................7	Self-service launderette:.............................No
Total crew:..215	Dedicated cinema/seats:..............................No
Passengers (lower beds/alll berths):................ 332/332	Library:.. Yes
Passenger Space Ratio (lower beds/all berths): 57.8/57.8	Onboard currency: ....US$
Crew/Passenger Ratio (lower beds/all berths):.......... 1.5/1.5	

An elegant, cool ship for chic warm-weather cruising

OVERVIEW. *Paul Gauguin* is best suited to couples and single travelers, typically over 50, seeking specialized itineraries, good regional cuisine and service, with almost no entertainment. Where the ship really shines is in its variety of water-sports equipment, and its shallow draft that allows it to navigate and anchor in lovely little places that larger ships couldn't possibly reach.

THE SHIP. Built by a French company specifically to operate in shallow waters, *Paul Gauguin* is now under long-term charter to Pacific Beachcombers of Tahiti, which also own the Intercontinental Tahiti, Intercontinental Bora Bora Le Moana, Intercontinental Bora Bora, and Intercontinental Moorea. The ship cruises around French Polynesia and the South Pacific and, while it could carry many more passengers, it is forbidden to do so by French law. It had a $9 million refurbishment in 2009, has a well-balanced, all-white profile, and a single funnel.

This smart ship also has a retractable aft marina platform, and carries two water-skiing boats and two inflatable craft for water sports. Windsurfers, kayaks, plus scuba and snorkeling gear are available for your use; all except scuba gear, are included in the cruise fare. Islands, beaches, and water sports are what *Paul Gauguin* is good at. Perhaps the best island experience is in Bora Bora. Its shallow draft means there could be some movement, as the ship is a little high-sided for its size.

Inside, there is a pleasant array of public rooms, and both the artwork and the decor have a real French

Berlitz's Ratings

	Possible	Achieved
Ship	500	402
Accommodation	200	169
Food	400	304
Service	400	320
Entertainment	100	71
Cruise	400	285

OVERALL SCORE
1551 points out of 2000

Polynesia look and feel. The interior colors are quite restful, although a trifle bland, but the new deck and direction signage has been improved, and the ship was refreshed during a 2011 refurbishment. The 'tub' chairs in some of the public rooms are uncomfortable.

Expert lecturers on Tahiti and Gauguin accompany each cruise, and a Fare (pronounced *foray*) Tahiti Gallery – a vestibule featuring books, videos, and other materials on the unique art, history, and culture of the islands. Three original Gauguin sketches are displayed under protective glass.

The dress code is totally relaxed – every day. The standard itinerary means the ship docks only in Papeete, and shore tenders are used in all other ports. There is little entertainment, as the ship stays overnight in several ports – so little is needed. The high crew-to-passenger ratio translates to a high level of personalized service. The ship has become a favorite of travelers to these climes, and the quiet, refined atmosphere on board makes it clubby, with passengers getting to know each other easily. Wi-Fi spots are provided, but Internet charges are high. Le Casino has blackjack and roulette tables, while slot players will find 13 machines in an adjacent area.

A cruise aboard Paul Gauguin is all about connecting with French Polynesia, and the ship carries lecturers to inform you about the life, history, and sea life of the region.

All in all, the ship will provide you with a delightful, intimate cruise and product that most will really enjoy, and gratuities are included. Soft drinks and mineral water are included in the cruise price. Note that if you fly out to Tahiti a day or so before our cruise, and stay in a hotel, that bugs (insects) are a problem encountered by many travelers (so it may be wise to take some insect repellent).

ACCOMMODATION. There are eight suite/cabin grades, priced according to location and size. The outside-view cabins, half of which have private balconies, are nicely equipped, although they are strictly rectangular and none have more interesting shapes. Most have large windows, except those on the lowest accommodation deck, which have portholes. Each has queen- or twin-size beds convertible to queen, and wood-accented cabinetry with rounded edges. A mini-bar/refrigerator stocked with complimentary soft drinks, a DVD player, personal safe, hairdryer, and umbrellas are standard. A selection of L'Occitaine personal toiletry items is provided.

The marble-look bathrooms are large and pleasing and have a tub as well as a separate shower enclosure. All passengers are provided with 100 percent cotton bathrobes and cotton slippers. The two largest suites have a private balcony at the front and side of the vessel. Although there's a decent amount of in-cabin space, with a beautiful long vanity unit and plenty of drawer space, the bathrooms are disappointingly small and plain, and too similar to all other standard cabin bathrooms.

Butler service is provided in all accommodation designated as Owners Suite, Grand Suites, Ocean-view 'A' and 'B' category suites.

DINING. L'Etoile, the main dining room, is open for dinner only, while La Veranda, an alternative dining spot, serves breakfast, lunch, and dinner. Both have open seating, which means you can choose when you want to dine and with whom. This provides a good opportunity to meet new people for dinner each evening. The chairs have armrests, making it more comfortable for a leisurely mealtime. La Veranda provides dinner by reservation, with alternating French and Italian menus; the French menus are provided by Jean-Pierre Vigato, a two-star Michelin chef with his own restaurant, Apicius, in Paris.

The dining operation is well orchestrated, with cuisine and service of a reasonably high standard. Select wines and liquor are included in the fare, while the limited selection of premium wines cost extra.

The 134-seat La Verandah Restaurant provides an alternative to the main dining room, and is one deck above it. There is both indoor and outdoor seating. This is a self-serve buffet venue for breakfast and lunch. The breakfast buffets tend to be extremely repetitive (especially the boxed cereals), and lunch buffets are often a disappointment (but there is a decent selection of olive

oils and sauces made on board). At night, the venue provides better, more creative fare, in very pleasant surroundings (reservations are required, but there's no extra charge, and the capacity is limited to 75 persons).

An outdoor (but covered) Le Grill provides informal café fare on deck aft of the pool, with up 100 seats. Each evening it becomes Pacific Grill and serves Polynesian cuisine; although reservations are required there is no extra charge.

For something different, it is possible to have dinner on the Marina platform on certain nights (when it's calm, of course).

ENTERTAINMENT. Le Grand Salon is the venue for shows and cabaret acts. It is a single-level room, and seating is in banquette and individual tub chairs. Sight lines are quite good from most seats, although there are some obstructions. Don't expect lavish production shows (there aren't any), as the main entertainment consists of local Polynesian shows brought on board from ashore, plus the odd cabaret act. A piano lounge was added in a 2006 refit.

SPA/FITNESS. The Deep Nature Spa, on Deck 6 in the ship's center, is the wellbeing space. It includes a fitness centre with muscle-pumping and body-toning equipment (in a windowless room), a steam room, several treatment rooms, changing area (very small), and beauty salon. Spa/beauty services and staff are provided by Algotherm. There is no sauna, but use of the steam room is complimentary. Body pampering treatments include various massages, aromatherapy facials, manicures, pedicures, and hairdressing services.

Polar Pioneer
★★+

Size:. . . . . .Boutique Ship	Cabins (total):. 29
Tonnage: 1,753	Size range (sq ft/m): 105.4-242.1/9.8-22.5
Lifestyle: . . . . .Standard	Cabins (outside view): 29
Cruise line:. . . . . .Aurora Expeditions	Cabins (interior/no view):. 0
Former names: . . . . Marine Spirit, Akademik Shuleykin	Cabins (for one person):. 0
IMO number: 8010324	Cabins (with private balcony): 0
Builder: . . . . Rauma Shipyard (Finland)	Cabins (wheelchair accessible): 0
Original cost: . . . . n/a	Wheelchair accessibility:. . . . . .none
Entered service:. 1985/2011	Cabin voltage: . . . . .110 and 220 Volts
Registry:. . . . . Russia	Elevators:. 0
Length (ft/m):. 234.9/71.6	Casino (gaming tables):. . . . . .No
Beam (ft/m):. 41.9/12.8	Slot machines:. . . . . .No
Draft (ft/m): 15.0/4.5	Swimming pools:. 1
Propulsion/Propellers: . . . . .diesel (2,330kW)/2	Hot tubs (on deck):. 0
Passenger decks:. 3	Self-service launderette:. . . . . .No
Total crew:. 25	Dedicated cinema/seats:. . . . . .No
Passengers (lower beds/alll berths):. 58/63	Library: . . . . .Yes
Passenger Space Ratio (lower beds/all berths): 30.2/27.8	Onboard currency: . . . . .US$
Crew/Passenger Ratio (lower beds/all berths):. 2.3/2.5	

Hardy but comfortable ship for expeditions to Antarctica

OVERVIEW. *Polar Pioneer*, with its dark blue hull – originally constructed for the former Soviet Union's polar and oceanographic research program – was converted in the early 1990s to carry passengers. It is best suited to hardy outdoors couples and single travelers who enjoy being with nature in one of the most interesting regions on earth.

THE SHIP. This is the sister ship to *Akademik Shokalskiy*, and is operated under charter to Aurora Expeditions. It was refurbished in 1996 and fitted out specifically for expedition cruising. The navigation officers and most crew members are Russian. The ship has an ice-strengthened steel hull, which makes the vessel ideally suited to cruising in Antarctica. Its strengths are its strong hull, and maneuverability. There is an open-bridge policy, giving passengers access to the navigation bridge. There are several Zodiac landing craft for close-in shore excursions and nature observation trips. The ship has a seawater swimming pool outdoors, but it is really small – more a 'dip' pool.

Inside, the public rooms consist simply of a library, lounge/bar, and reception area. The dining rooms also serve as a lecture room. This ship does have medical facilities.

This is expedition-style cruising, in a very small ship with limited facilities and a basic product delivery. However, it provides a genuine sense of adventure. Bigger ships can't get this close to Antarctica, but this little vessel will get you there in basic comfort. Credit

Berlitz's Ratings

	Possible	Achieved
Ship	500	204
Accommodation	200	103
Food	400	203
Service	400	212
Entertainment	100	40
Cruise	400	222

OVERALL SCORE
984 points out of 2000

card payments for onboard expenditure incur a surcharge.

ACCOMMODATION. This is arranged over three decks, in five price grades. Except for a single Captain's Suite – quite large for the ship's size – almost all cabins are extremely small, utilitarian, and simply furnished, although there's a reasonable amount of closet space. There are two-berth (one upper, one lower) cabins with shower and toilet, as well as two-bed cabins on the lowest deck.

DINING. There are two dining rooms, with the galley located between them, and all participants dine in a single seating. The food consists of basic but hearty fare, with no frills. European chefs oversee the food operation.

ENTERTAINMENT. The lounge is for recaps, after-dinner talks, and forward planning.

SPA/FITNESS. As one might expect, these facilities are minimal, due to the fact that this is an expedition cruise vessel.

Pride of America
★★★

Size:...............................Large Resort Ship	Crew/Passenger Ratio (lower beds/all berths):......... 2.2/2.5
Tonnage:.. 81,439	Cabins (total):.................................... 1,104
Lifestyle:.....................................Standard	Size range (sq ft/m):..............129.1–1,377.8/12.0–128.0
Cruise line:......................Norwegian Cruise Line	Cabins (outside view):................................871
Former names:...................................none	Cabins (interior/no view):..........................232
IMO number:.................................9209221	Cabins (for one person):..............................0
Builder:.......Ingalls Shipbuilding (USA)/Lloyd Werft (Germany)	Cabins (with private balcony):......................665
Original cost:..............................$450 million	Cabins (wheelchair accessible):......................22
Entered service:...........................Jul 2005	Wheelchair accessibility:..........................Good
Registry:...USA	Cabin voltage:.............................. 110 volts
Length (ft/m):............................ 921.9/281.0	Elevators:..10
Beam (ft/m):............................. 106.6/32.2	Casino (gaming tables):............................Yes
Draft (ft/m):............................... 26.25/8.0	Slot machines:....................................Yes
Propulsion/Propellers:...diesel-electric (32,000kW)/2 azimuthing pods	Swimming pools:....................................2
Passenger decks:.................................11	Hot tubs (on deck):.................................0
Total crew:.................................... 1,000	Self-service launderette:...........................No
Passengers (lower beds/alll berths):............. 2,202/2,500	Dedicated cinema/seats:............................No
Passenger Space Ratio (lower beds/all berths):....... 36.5/32.1	Library:...Yes
	Onboard currency:................................US$

A large, family-friendly resort ship for Hawaiian cruises

OVERVIEW. The ship suits first-time young couples, single passengers, children, and teenagers who enjoy city night-life and who want contemporary, upbeat surroundings, plenty of entertainment lounges and bars, and high-tech sophistication – all in one well-packaged cruise vacation, with constant music, participation activity, and entertainment. But don't expect good service – most of the crew simply don't cut it.

THE SHIP. *Pride of America*, which sank during its dockside reconstruction at Germany's Lloyd Werft shipbuilders, sails on inter-island cruises, focusing on Hawaii's islands. The 85,850-sq-ft (7,975-sq-m) open deck space includes a sunbathing/pool deck inspired by Miami's South Beach – think Ocean Drive/Lincoln Mall – and an Art Deco area.

The stunning interior design is modeled after a 'Best of America' theme, with public rooms named after famous Americans. Facilities include the Capitol Atrium (a lobby spanning eight decks and said to be inspired by the Capitol Building and White House), a large casino, a conservatory complete with tropical landscaped garden and live exotic birds, Soho Art Gallery (holding art auctions), Washington Library, and Newbury Shopping Center.

Six dedicated meetings rooms range in size from boardrooms for 10 people to an auditorium for up to 250. The ship has a mainly Hawaiian crew.

A non-changeable service charge (as distinct from a gratuity) for staff is added to your onboard account at $12

Berlitz's Ratings

	Possible	Achieved
Ship	500	371
Accommodation	200	148
Food	400	214
Service	400	206
Entertainment	100	68
Cruise	400	237

OVERALL SCORE
1244 points out of 2000

per person ($6 for children aged three to 12) per day; this is pooled for all crew and provides payment when they are on vacation. You will be expected to provide gratuities. In addition, a 15 percent gratuity plus Hawaii's sales tax (because of the ship's US registry) is added to all bar (and 18 percent for spa treatment) accounts.

Although the islands are pleasant enough, a cruise aboard this ship is likely to test your patience. *Pride of America* is a good example of how not to run a cruise ship, and cabin cleanliness in particular is poor.

ACCOMMODATION. Of the 982 cabins, about 75 percent have outside views. There are also a large number of family-friendly interconnecting cabins. Many cabins have third/fourth upper berths, and some family-special cabins can accommodate as many as six. Some suites have king-size beds, while most cabins have twin beds that can be placed together to make a queen-size bed. In 2013, four Studio-grade cabins were added, as were 24 'suites' and four interior (no view) cabins (in the space previously used as a conference center.

A number of cabins are wheelchair-accessible, while some are equipped for the hearing-impaired.

Grand Suite. The largest accommodation is in the Grand Suite, with around 1,400 sq ft (130 sq m) of living space. It is located high atop the ship forward of the sun deck and offers sweeping views from its walk-around outdoor terrace. It has a large living room with Bang & Olufsen entertainment center (television, DVD/CD player with library), Internet-access computers, and wet bar, separate dining room with dining table and six chairs. A butler is included. The master bedroom has a king-size bed, large bathroom, with whirlpool tub and separate shower enclosure; dressing area with flat-screen TV, and walk-in closet. At the entrance to the suite is a guest powder room. There is a wraparound veranda, and facilities include open-air dining and a hot tub, plus a private sunbathing and entertainment area.

Owner's Suites (5). Measuring around 870 sq ft (80 sq m), these are named after indigenous flowers in Hawaii such as Bird of Paradise, Gardenia, Orchid, Plumeria. Each has a bedroom with king-size bed, walk-in closet, dressing area, separate living room with Bang & Olufsen entertainment center, and Internet-access computer. The bathroom has a whirlpool tub and separate shower enclosure. There is also a large private balcony with hot tub, outdoor dining facilities, and sun beds.

Deluxe Penthouse Suites (6). These measure around 735 sq ft (68 sq m). They have a separate bedroom with king-size bed and walk-in closet; the bathroom has a whirlpool tub, separate shower enclosure, two washbasins, dressing area; living room with Bang & Olufsen entertainment center, wet bar, and private balcony.

Penthouse Suites (28). These measure 504–585 sq ft (47–55 sq m). They have a separate bedroom with king-size bed and walk-in closet; the bathroom has a whirlpool tub, separate shower enclosure, two washbasins, dressing area; living room with Bang & Olufsen entertainment center, wet bar, and private balcony.

Family Suites (8). These measure around 360 sq ft (34 sq m). Each has a main bedroom with two twin beds that convert to a queen-size bed, a living room with double sofa bed and entertainment center, separate den with single sofa bed. Another four family 'suites,' measuring 330–380 sq ft (30.5–35 sq m), have an interconnecting door between two cabins; there are thus two bathrooms.

Standard Outside-View and Interior Cabins. Outside-view cabins have either a window or porthole, depending on location. All cabins have twin beds that can convert into a queen-size bed, TV, satellite-dial telephone, and personal safe; the bathrooms have a built-in hairdryer.

DINING. NCL ships operate Freestyle Cruising, which means that there are several restaurants and informal dining spots. You can choose from two main dining rooms, and six other à la carte, informal and casual spots, some of which incur a cover charge.

The 628-seat Skyline Restaurant, the first main restaurant, has decor is inspired by the skyscrapers of the 1930s. The 496-seat Liberty Dining Room, the second main restaurant, has two seatings.

Other dining options. The Lone Star Steak House seats 106. It is a contemporary steak house with Texas decor – the artwork includes Houston Space Center, Texas Rangers, and Dallas Cowboys.

China Town is a Pacific Rim/Asian Fusion restaurant that has a sushi/sashimi bar and a Teppanyaki grill room with two tables (food is prepared in front of you with a bit of showmanship) that can accommodate up to 32.

Jefferson's Bistro, which seats 104, is the ship's 'signature' restaurant, with an à la carte menu of classic and nouvelle French cuisine. The decor is inspired by that of Thomas Jefferson's home in Monticello – Jefferson was the US ambassador to France from 1785 to 1789 before becoming America's third president.

Little Italy, a casual Italian eatery, serves pasta, pizza, and other popular light Italian fare. It has 116 seats.

Cadillac Diner accommodates 106 (70 indoors, 36 outdoors) and is open 24 hours a day. It has Cadillac seats and a video jukebox. There's fast food galore, with hamburgers and hot dogs, fish and chips, potpies, and wok dishes.

Aloha Café/Kids Café is an indoor/outdoor self-serve buffet-style eatery with a Hawaiian theme; there are 322 indoor and 310 outdoor seats. A special section for children has counter tops just the right height, as well as chairs and tables that have been shrunk to a child-friendly size.

Other indoor eateries and bars include the Napa Wine Bar (wines by the glass), Pink's Champagne and Cigar Bar (inspired by Hawaii's Pink Palace Hotel on Waikiki Beach), the Gold Rush pub (with karaoke, plus a darts board and bar billiards), and the John Adams Coffee Bar. Outdoor eateries and drinking places include the Key West Bar and Grill, and the Waikiki Bar.

ENTERTAINMENT. The Hollywood Theater seats 840 and stages large-scale production shows and local Hawaiian shows. A 590-seat cabaret lounge, the Mardi Gras Lounge, has cabaret entertainment, including late-night comedy.

SPA/FITNESS. The Santa Fe Spa and Fitness Center, decorated with artifacts from New Mexico, is designed to be a tranquil center for mind and body. It is staffed and operated by Mandara Spa (originating in Bali, now headquartered in Hawaii, but owned by Steiner Leisure), and includes Ayurvedic-style treatments.

While some fitness classes are free, others – such as yoga, and kick-boxing – usually cost extra. Massage (including exotic massages such as Hot Stone, Lomi Lomi, and other well-being massages), facials, pedicures, and beauty salon treatments also cost extra.

Prinsendam
★★★★

Size:.....................................Mid-size Ship		Cabins (total):....................................419	
Tonnage: 38,100		Size range (sq ft/m): 137.7–723.3/12.8–67.2	
Lifestyle: ....Premium		Cabins (outside view):..............................388	
Cruise line:..........................Holland America Line		Cabins (interior/no view):............................31	
Former names: .... Seabourn Sun, Royal Viking Sun		Cabins (for one person):..............................3	
IMO number: 8700280		Cabins (with private balcony): 166	
Builder: ....Wartsila (Finland)		Cabins (wheelchair accessible): 10	
Original cost: ....$125 million		Wheelchair accessibility:..........................Best	
Entered service:......................Dec 1988/May 2002		Cabin voltage: .... 110 volts	
Registry:..............................The Netherlands		Elevators:..4	
Length (ft/m):..............................674.2/205.5		Casino (gaming tables):............................Yes	
Beam (ft/m):................................ 91.8/28.0		Slot machines:...................................Yes	
Draft (ft/m): 23.6/7.2		Swimming pools:...................................2	
Propulsion/Propellers:..................diesel (21,120kW)/2		Hot tubs (on deck):.................................4	
Passenger decks:.....................................9		Self-service launderette:...........................Yes	
Total crew:.......................................443		Dedicated cinema/seats:............................Yes	
Passengers (lower beds/alll berths):................835/915		Library: ....Yes	
Passenger Space Ratio (lower beds/all berths): 45.6/41.6		Onboard currency: ....US$	
Crew/Passenger Ratio (lower beds/all berths):.......... 1.8/1.8			

A very comfortable ship that provides a premium ambience

OVERVIEW. This ship is best suited to older adult couples and singles who like to mingle in a mid-size ship operating longer cruises, in an unhurried setting with some eclectic, antique artwork, good food, and service from a smiling crew. It is a very comfortable vessel – smaller than other Holland America Line ships, but more refined.

THE SHIP. *Prinsendam* is a contemporary, well-designed ship with sleek, flowing lines, a sharply raked bow, and a well-rounded profile, with lots of floor-to-ceiling glass. Having started life as *Royal Viking Sun*, it was bought by Seabourn Cruise Line in 1998 and refitted as *Seabourn Sun*. In 2002, it was transferred to Holland America Line as *Prinsendam*, and the hull color was changed from all-white to a dark blue hull with white superstructure. A 2007 refit added an Explorations Café and expanded the shopping arcade. In 2009 an aft deck, including 21 new cabins, was added.

Wide teak wood decks provide excellent walking areas including a decent walk-around promenade deck outdoors, but there's no jogging track. The swimming pool, outdoors on Lido Deck, is not large, but it is quite adequate, while the deck above has a croquet court and golf driving range. The interior layout is very spacious – it is even more ideal when no more than 600 passengers are aboard. Impressive public rooms and tasteful decor now reign. Two handrails – one of wood, one of chrome – are provided on all stairways, a thoughtful touch.

Berlitz's Ratings		
	Possible	Achieved
Ship	500	393
Accommodation	200	160
Food	400	271
Service	400	291
Entertainment	100	73
Cruise	400	295
OVERALL SCORE		
1483 points out of 2000		

The Crow's Nest, the forward observation lounge, is an elegant, contemporary (at least in decor) space. Pebble Beach is the name of the electronic golf simulator room, complete with wet bar, with play possible on 11 virtual courses.

The Erasmus Library is well organized, although it's simply not large enough for long-distance cruising.

The Oak Room is the ship's cigar/pipe smoker's lounge; it has a marble fireplace, which sadly cannot be used due to United States Coast Guard regulations.

Whether by intention or not, the ship has a two-class feeling, with passengers in 'upstairs' penthouse suites and 'A' grade staterooms gravitating to the quieter Crow's Nest lounge, particularly at night, while other passengers go to the main entertainment deck.

The wide range of facilities includes a concierge, self-service launderettes (useful on long voyages), a varied guest lecture program, 24-hour information office, and true 24-hour cabin service for the discriminating passenger who demands spacious personal surroundings and good food and service, regardless of price. This ship operates mainly long-distance cruises in great comfort, and free shuttle buses are provided in almost all ports of call.

While *Prinsendam* isn't perfect, the few design flaws (for example: poorly designed bar service counters) are minor points. The elegant decorative features include Dutch artwork and memorabilia. Added benefits include a fine health spa facility, spacious, wide teakwood decks and many teak sunloungers.

There are only four elevators, so anyone with walking disabilities may have to wait for some time during periods of peak usage, such as before meals. This spacious ship shows signs of wear and tear in some areas, particularly in the accommodation passageways, despite recent refurbishments. The library is difficult for anyone in a wheelchair to enter. The shore tenders are thoughtfully air conditioned.

ACCOMMODATION. There are several accommodation grades, ranging from Penthouse Verandah Suites to standard interior cabins. All suites and cabins have undergone some degree of refurbishment since the ship was taken over by Holland America Line in 2002.

Penthouse Verandah Suite. The Penthouse Verandah Suite (723 sq ft/67 sq m) is a most desirable living space, although not as large as penthouse suites aboard some other ships. It is light and airy, with two bathrooms, one of which has a large whirlpool tub with ocean views, and anodized gold bathroom fittings. The living room contains a large dining table and chairs, and large sofas. There is also a substantial private balcony, and butler service.

Deluxe Verandah Suites. There are 18 of these (eight on Sports Deck, 10 on Lido Deck). Located in the forward section, they have large balconies, two sofas, and large bar/entertainment center (mini-bar/refrigerator, color television, video and CD players). Bathrooms have separate toilet, sink and toiletries cabinets, connecting sliding door into the bedroom, large mirror, two toiletries cabinets, plenty of storage space, full bathtub, and anodized gold fittings. Each evening the butler brings different goodies – hot and cold hors d'oeuvres and other niceties. If you do choose one of these suites, it might be best on the starboard side where they are located in a private hallway, while those on the port side (including the Penthouse Verandah Suite) are positioned along a public hallway. The 10 suites on Lido Deck are positioned along private port and starboard side hallways.

Passengers in Penthouse and Deluxe Verandah Suites are provided with a private concierge lounge, high tea served in the suite each afternoon, hors d'oeuvres before dinner each evening (on request), complimentary laundry pressing and dry cleaning, private cocktail parties with captain, priority disembarkation, and more.

Other cabin grades. Most of the remaining cabins, spread over six other decks, are of generous proportions and have just about everything you would need, including a video player. About 38 percent have a small, private balcony. All cabins have walk-in closets, lockable drawers, full-length mirrors, hairdryers, and ample cotton towels. A few cabins have third berths, while some have interconnecting doors – good for couples who want two bathrooms and more space or for families with children.

In all grades of accommodation, passengers receive a basket of fresh fruit, fluffy cotton bathrobes, evening turndown service, and a Holland America Line signature tote bag. Filipino and Indonesian cabin stewards and stewardesses provide unobtrusive personal service.

Four well-equipped, L-shaped cabins for the disabled are quite well designed, fairly large, and equipped with special wheel-in bathrooms with shower facilities and closets.

DINING. La Fontaine Dining Room wraps around the aft end of Lower Promenade Deck and has extensive ocean-view windows; along the starboard side is a second, smaller and quieter section. There is plenty of space around tables. A good number of window-side tables are for two persons, although there are also tables for four, six, or eight. Crystal glasses, Rosenthal china, and fine cutlery are provided.

There are two seatings for dinner, at assigned tables, and an open-seating arrangement for breakfast and lunch – you'll be seated by restaurant staff when you enter. On most port days the restaurant is closed at lunchtime, which means using the self-serve buffet or ordering room service.

Other dining options. A small, quiet dining spot on the port side is the Pinnacle Dining Room, with 48 seats, wood-paneled decor that increases the feeling of intimacy and privacy, and fine ocean views. Table settings include Bulgari china, Reidel glassware, and Frette table linens. The venue specializes in fine steaks and seafood. Seating preference is given to suite occupants. Reservations are required, and there is a cover charge. There is a well-chosen wine list, although there's a great deal of emphasis on California wines, with prices that are quite high.

There is also a Lido Restaurant, for decent casual dining and self-serve buffet-style meals. At night, in a section that was formerly outside but is now a wintergarden, this eatery becomes La Canaletto (named after the famous Venetian artist).

ENTERTAINMENT. The Queens showlounge is an amphitheater-style layout, with a well-tiered floor, and both banquette and individual seating. While Holland America Line isn't known for fine entertainment, what it does offer is a consistently good, tried and tested array of cabaret acts. There are male 'dance hosts' who act as partners for women traveling alone.

SPA/FITNESS. The extensive Greenhouse Health Spa includes six treatment rooms with integral showers, a rasul chamber (for mud and gentle steam heat treatments, combined with gentle steam), a gymnasium with views over the stern, and separate sauna, steam room, and changing rooms for men and women. The spa is operated by Steiner.

Quantum of the Seas
Not Yet Rated

Size:.................................Large Resort Ship		Crew/Passenger Ratio (lower beds/all berths):.............n/a	
Tonnage: 167,800		Cabins (total):.......................................2.090	
Lifestyle: ....Standard		Size range (sq ft/m): ....n/a	
Cruise line:...................Royal Caribbean International		Cabins (outside view):.............................1,717	
Former names: ....none		Cabins (interior/no view):...........................373	
IMO number: ....n/a		Cabins (for one person):.............................18	
Builder: ....Meyer Werft (Germany)		Cabins (with private balcony):......................1,570	
Original cost:.................................$936 million		Cabins (wheelchair accessible): 34	
Entered service:................................Oct 2014		Wheelchair accessibility:.........................Good	
Registry:.....................................The Bahamas		Cabin voltage: ....110 and 220 volts	
Length (ft/m):..............................1,145.0/348.0		Elevators:...n/a	
Beam (ft/m):.................................134.5/41.0		Casino (gaming tables):..............................Yes	
Draft (ft/m): ....n/a		Slot machines:....................................Yes	
Propulsion/Propellers: ...diesel-electric (41,000kW)/2 azimuthing pods		Swimming pools:...................................n/a	
Passenger decks:....................................16		Hot tubs (on deck):.................................n/a	
Total crew:...n/a		Self-service launderette:..............................No	
Passengers (lower beds/alll berths):.............4,180/4,905		Dedicated cinema/seats:.............................No	
Passenger Space Ratio (lower beds/all berths): 40.1/34.2		Library: ....Yes	
		Onboard currency: ....US$	

A STATE-OF-THE-ART FAMILY-FRIENDLY FLOATING RESORT

OVERVIEW. *Quantum of the Seas* – a new class and type of ship for popular Royal Caribbean International – has a slender profile – and has lifeboats slung low and over the side, from newly designed davits. Everyone will love it because it incorporates all of the latest features, and then some, for a lot of RCI WOW! And that means the sum of all the parts equals a Quantummation!

Berlitz's Ratings

	Possible	Achieved
Ship	500	NYR
Accommodation	200	NYR
Food	400	NYR
Service	400	NYR
Entertainment	100	NYR
Cruise	400	NYR

OVERALL SCORE
NYR points out of 2000

THE SHIP. The exterior design of Quantum of the Seas looks somewhat like a 'stretched' version of the Celebrity Reflection and employs the latest in hydrodynamics, hull shape, low emissions and, importantly, low fuel consumption. In terms of size, *Quantum of the Seas* is similar to the *Freedom of the Seas*-class, but is designed to carry about 500 more passengers, in a more efficient configuration.

The ship employs the latest ('quantum' physics?) hull-scrubber technology to comply with the 2015 Emission Control Area (ECA) 0.1% sulphur limit, by removing sulphur emissions and harmful particles from the exhaust system.

Several novel features will be incorporated, mostly outdoors. North Star – quite the engineering marvel – is a 14-person glass capsule that lifts you off from the ship's uppermost decks and provides a bird's eye view of all below you (including the sea) as it moves around. It's like a posh giant 'cherry picker' with attitude – and is expected to be quite a ride! It is located in the front section of the ship, just behind the mast. It is complimentary (and wheelchair-accessible), although a charge

will apply for booking at certain times such as Sunrise with Brunch, Sunset and Specialty Dining, and Private Flights – for weddings and other romantic occasions – think: the '300 Feet above Sea Level' club!). Actually, I think it would just make a great suite (naturally, the bed would need to rotate, too)!

The second of the stunners is RipCord by iFly – a skydiving experience in a two-storey vertical wind tunnel that lets you experience the thrill of skydiving – but in a safe, controlled environment. The special in-your-face unit uses a powerful air flow to keep you up in the air – like a giant hairdryer underneath you! It is located aft of the ship's funnel housing. It accommodates 13 persons for each 75-minute class, which includes two 'hovering in the air' experiences, instruction and gear.

Meanwhile, a SeaPlex complex – located just underneath the North Star mobile 'eye-pod'-style observation unit – offers a circus 'school,' adrenalin-boosting bumper car rides, and act as a roller skating rink and basketball court. It's a veritable active interactive sporting venue that replaces the ice rinks of other large RCI ships.

Inside, the 'WOW' factor continues, with more details to be announced after this book goes to press. Naturally, there will be many shops for your retail therapy at sea, including a perfume shop and a logo souvenir shop.

Just aft of the center of the ship, a vertical glass wall provides connection with the sea from each deck, while panoramic elevators whizz you even to the pool deck.

This ship provides the setting for an 'all the fun of the fair' cruise – just don't even bother coming if all you want to do is relax – you won't be allowed to. Quantum of the Seas will be based in New York Harbor (from Cape Liberty in Bayonne, New Jersey).

FAMILIES. Facilities for children and teenagers aboard this family-friendly ship are extensive – as part of the Adventure Ocean program. Royal Babies and Tots Nursery is for the really young ones; Aquanauts, is for 3–5-year-olds; Explorers, is for 6–8-year-olds; Voyagers, is for 9–12-year-olds. Optix is the chill-out zone for teenagers. There's also Adventure Beach, an area for all the family, which includes swimming pools, a water slide and game areas outdoors in the Aqua-Park. DreamWorks events and entertainment will be featured, with live character appearances from Shrek, Kung Fu Panda and Madagascar.

ACCOMMODATION. There are many, many different price grades and categories for accommodation. The price you pay depends on the size and location you choose. Fortunately, every cabin aboard this ship has a view – whether it's real or virtual. The 'virtual' balconies were first introduced aboard Navigator of the Seas in 2013 and are a really neat feature of the interior (no view) cabins; they can provide real-time ocean views.

Several new accommodation categories and types are being introduced aboard this ship. Standard cabins are about 9 percent larger than those aboard the Oasis-class ships.

Loft cabins (including a 975 sq ft/90.5 sq m Owner's Loft) vary in size and configuration, but measure approximately 502 sq ft/46.6 sq m and are located at the ship's stern.

Inter-connecting family cabins are good for multi-generational accommodation. The 15 units consist of a junior suite, balcony cabin, and interior studio connected through a shared vestibule. Together they can create a 575.8 sq ft/53.5 sq m of living space with three bedrooms, three bathrooms, and a 216 sq ft/20.0 sq m balcony.

Studio cabins (there are 16 of them, 12 of which have balconies) for solo occupancy are a first for RCI. As there's no single supplement, they are priced in a new category for solo travelers.

DINING. Details were not available at press time, but Quantum of the Seas will feature more restaurant and eatery choices. These will include:

Portofino: an 'upscale,' extra-cost, reservations-required Euro-Italian restaurant.

Johnny Rockets: the popular retro 1950s all-day, all-night diner-style eatery will feature hamburgers, extra-cost malt shakes, and jukebox hits (all indoor tables feature a mini-jukebox).

ENTERTAINMENT. The entertainment spaces and events are being designed to knock your socks off.

Kristin Chenoweth, Broadway and TV star, will serve as the ship's godmother.

Two 70o is a multi-level room, located at the ship's stern, and includes a food-court-style marketplace, and sit-down ultra-casual eateries, including The Café @ Two 70o. By night, the huge venue morphs into an entertainment house, with aerialists, live performers, digital video 'performances' on 100-inch/254-cm LED screens on robotic arms that descend from the ceiling, and an ice bar.

Music Hall is two-decks high a rock-'n'-roll joint, outfitted with all the right paraphernalia, and will feature DJs and theme nights. The venue features a raised main stage (with unobstructed views) for live 'music,' and host dance classes and improve workshops.

SPA/FITNESS. Facilities include a thermal suite (extra-cost), beauty salon and barber shop, and fitness room with Technogym equipment. Massage and other body pampering treatments will take place in 19 treatment rooms.

Queen Elizabeth
★★★★ +

Size:.	.Large Resort Ship	Crew/Passenger Ratio (lower beds/all berths):.	2.0/2.1
Tonnage:.	90,900	Cabins (total):.	1,046
Lifestyle:.	.Premium	Size range (sq ft/m):.	152.0–1,493 sq.ft/14.0–138.5
Cruise line:.	Cunard Line	Cabins (outside view):.	.892
Former names:.	.none	Cabins (interior/no view):.	.154
IMO number:.	.9477438	Cabins (for one person):.	.0
Builder:.	Fincantieri (Italy)	Cabins (with private balcony):.	.820
Original cost:.	€634 million	Cabins (wheelchair accessible):.	.20
Entered service:.	.Oct 2010	Wheelchair accessibility:.	.Good
Registry:.	Bermuda	Cabin voltage:.	.110 and 220 volts
Length (ft/m):.	964.5/294.0	Elevators:.	.12
Beam (ft/m):.	105.9/32.3	Casino (gaming tables):.	Yes
Draft (ft/m):.	26.2/8.0	Slot machines:.	Yes
Propulsion/Propellers: . . .diesel-electric (64,000kW)/2 azimuthing pods		Swimming pools:.	.2
		Hot tubs (on deck):.	.5
Passenger decks:.	.12	Self-service launderette:.	Yes
Total crew:.	1,003	Dedicated cinema/seats:.	.No
Passengers (lower beds/all berths):.	2,092/2,172	Library:.	Yes
Passenger Space Ratio (lower beds/all berths):.	43.4/41.8	Onboard currency:.	.US$

A delightful interior decor that represents British heritage

OVERVIEW. *Queen Elizabeth*, a cruise ship that longs to be an ocean liner, suits mature adults and solo travelers, and families with children. It's pitched at traditionalists who like to dress more formally for dinner, and sail with a sense of style. Note that Berlitz's Ratings scores are the averages for both Grill Class and Britannia Class.

THE SHIP. Instantly recognizable is the Cunard red funnel aboard this ocean-liner-styled cruise ship. *Queen Elizabeth*, named in the company's 170th year (the company began operations in 1840), is the second largest Cunarder ordered in that long history. But, although Cunard purports to offer a resolutely British experience, the marketing hype is undermined by the use of US dollars as the onboard currency, and trying to find British service staff is challenging.

The ship is a pretend ocean liner, and, with its Vista-class hull design, is susceptible to rolling and pitching, like sister ship *Queen Victoria*. Anyone comparing this ship with the former *Queen Elizabeth 2* can't fail to notice the difference in the design of the stern – *QE2*'s was beautifully rounded, while the new ship's is flat and boxy. However, it does allow for more open lido deck/pool space – good on warm weather cruises. The foredeck is disappointing.

Once you are inside, the ship feels instantly comfortable, rather like a mini-*QE2*. It has less somber colors than *Queen Victoria*, commendably little glitzy brass or chrome surfaces in the public areas, and more of the look and feel of a real ocean liner, including some gor-

Berlitz's Ratings		
	Possible	Achieved
Ship	500	423
Accommodation	200	145
Food	400	300
Service	400	315
Entertainment	100	81
Cruise	400	321
OVERALL SCORE		
1585 points out of 2000		

geous carpeting. The decor is classic and timeless. Unlike *Queen Mary 2*, it can transit the Panama Canal – useful for long voyages.

Nice touches like destination-themed sail-away music, the afternoon tea experience, a wide variety of entertainment – including a varied Cunard Insights lecture program – and decent service, albeit lacking in finesse, help Cunard to stand out from the crowd. It provides a traditional setting for those who enjoy dressing properly for dinner. Passengers get cocktail parties, and enjoy the lecturers and speakers who sail on each voyage – Cunard cunningly calls them voyages, not cruises.

The ship has a few more cabins, and therefore more passengers, than *Queen Victoria*, but the dimensions and number of elevators remain the same. Outdoors facilities include a promenade deck; unfortunately it's not teak, but a rubberized deck covering made to look like wooden planking, which gets hot and stays hot in warm weather areas. You can almost walk around – the forward section is for marine use only – with several deck lounge chairs with comfortable Cunard-logo cushioned pads.

One open deck atop the ship has a life-size chess board, adjacent to the croquet and bowls area.

Other features include a majestic three-deck high Grand Lobby with a sweeping staircase, sculpted balconies and elegant decorative touches, and an adjacent Cunarders' Galleria floating museum whose glass cabinets display memorabilia. The original Asprey silver model of *QE2* is In the Yacht Club, and there's a nice model of the original *Queen Elizabeth* in a cabinet at the back of the Café Carinthia.

One 'wow' factor in the main lobby is a painting of the Queen by Isobel Peachey, at 31 the youngest person to paint the monarch. Commissioned by Cunard, it shows Her Majesty in the yellow drawing room at Buckingham Palace, dressed in blue and wearing Queen Victoria's collet necklace and earrings. Another beautiful piece of art is a stunning 18½-ft (5.6-m) Viscount Linley marquetry panel 'sculpture' that adorns the three-deck grand stairway. Crafted from nine natural woods, it depicts the port bow of the original *Queen Elizabeth* as seen from sea level.

Several public rooms are two decks high; these include the gold-beige Queen's Room, with a large, wooden ballroom dance floor measuring about 1,000 sq ft (93 sq m); above are two huge ceiling-mounted chandeliers. The bandstand is fronted by a large proscenium arch, while cantilevered balconies line the room's starboard side.

Traditional British afternoon tea is served in this Art Deco-style grand room with Twinings tea or premium teas from the Twinings Rituals Collection. Artwork in entrance to this ballroom includes a gold bust of the Queen by Oscar Nemon; a replica of the Cunard-commissioned portrait of Princess Elizabeth and the Duke of Edinburgh displayed in *Caronia*'s main lounge before being moved to *QE2*; and *QE2* launch ceremonies painted by the Italian artist Diego Bormida.

The Royal Arcade is a cluster of several shops, selling goods connected with traditional and modern-day Britain, all set in an arcade-like environment; they include Hackett, Penhaligan's, and Aspinal of London. There's a separate Fortnum & Mason shop.

The Library is a stunning two-deck-high wood-paneled 6,000-book facility serviced by full-time librarians, although there are few chairs in which to sit in and read. Few ships today have such a fine library. There's a good bookshop selling maritime-related books, memorabilia, maps, and stationery.

Gratuities – called a Hotel and Dining charge, of $11.50–13.50 per person, depending on your accommodation grade – are added to your onboard account daily.

There's no escort to your cabin on embarkation (unless you are in certain suite-grade accommodation), leaving a bad first impression for first-timers. The layout is a little disjointed on the uppermost decks, although the general flow is good. Access between the aft deck and the pool area and Winter Garden can be gained mainly by going through the expansive buffet area. This causes congestion at the self-serve buffet as people are constantly passing through, as in a railway carriage. Some formerly free classes now incur a charge (example: the computer class about $30). Despite the hype, afternoon tea in the Queens Room could be better (Cunard must know the British use freshly boiled water). Finally, the size of the chocolate you get on your pillow was reduced by 25 percent in 2012! Despite these minor reservations, *Queen Elizabeth*

provides an elegant setting for a traditional cruise experience, with a wide choice of public rooms, bars and lounges, and a mostly attentive staff that provides the kind of service that's hard to find on land today. But, in the final analysis, the finesse is missing, and the ship's Princess-style cabins are below the standard expected.

Note that smokers inhabit the starboard side of the promenade deck so be aware if you intend to relax in a chair on that deck – it has been the subject of many complaints, as has the area outside Churchill's cigar lounge, where cigarette smokers congregate. Limited smoking is also allowed on cabin balconies.

ACCOMMODATION. There are three class categories of accommodation: Queens Grill, seven price grades; Princess Grill, four price grades; Britannia Accommodation, 21 price grades. That's 32 different price grades! Still, it's all about location, location, location. Yet however much or little you pay, passengers all embark and disembark via the same gangway. In keeping with maritime tradition, even-numbered cabins are on the port side, with odd-numbered cabins on the starboard side. The six top suites are named after former Cunard commodores, all of whom have been knighted by royalty.

The amount of drawer space in the standard cabins is less than one would expect, and there is little room for luggage storage. Note that the air conditioning cannot be turned off in cabins or bathrooms.

Grand Suites. four units, measuring 1,918–2,131 sq ft (178–184 sq m). Named Bisset, Charles, Illingworth, and Rostron, they are located aft, with great ocean views from their private wraparound balconies, which contain a complete wet bar. The suites have two bedrooms with walk-in closets; bathroom with tub and separate shower enclosure; lounge; and dining room with seating for six. In-suite dining from the Queens Grill menus is also available.

Master Suites. Two units, measuring 1,100 sq ft (102 sq m). Named Britten and Thomson, they are located in the center of the ship.

Penthouse Suites. Measuring 520–707 sq ft (48–65 sq m).

Queens Suites. Measuring 508–771 sq ft (47–72 sq m).

Princess Suites. Measuring 342–513 sq ft (32–48 sq m).

Balcony Cabins. Measuring 242–472 sq ft (22–44 sq m).

Outside-View Cabins. Measuring 180–201 sq ft (17–9 sq m).

Interior Cabins. Measuring 151–243 sq ft (14–23 sq m).

All accommodation grades have both British three-pin (240-volt) sockets and American (110-volt) and European-style two-pin (220-volt) sockets. Gilchrist & Soames toiletries are supplied to all passengers, and a hairdryer is stored in the vanity desk units. Some cabins have nicely indented ceilings with suffused lighting.

The regular cabins (Grades C/D) are small, but functional. However, the cabinetry is a bit austere and lacking in character. There's a lack of drawer space in a cabin supposedly designed for two persons – it's noticeable on long voyages, and the additional drawers located under the bed may prove challenging for some to use. The premium mattresses are excellent – as is the bed linen. European duvets are standard.

The bathrooms, too, are rather bland, similar to those found aboard the ships of Princess Cruises, with small washbasins, and little storage space for toiletries. The fixed-head shower doesn't permit the thorough wash that hand-held flexible hoses do. Overall, the standard (lower-grade) cabins are a little underwhelming – so, for more space and quality, consider booking one of the higher-grade cabins, or, better still, go for Grill-class accommodation – the perks and increased attention and service are really worth it. The walls in most accommodation passageways are rather plain, and could do with artwork.

DINING. Cunard Line is respected for its old-world cuisine and service, with a wide variety of well-prepared and presented dishes made from good ingredients. The 878-seat Britannia Restaurant – the name is taken from a former Cunard ocean liner of 1914–50 – is located in the aft section. It is two decks high, with seating on both main and balcony levels, and two seatings for dinner; stairways link both levels. An adjacent restaurant houses Britannia Club passengers, who get single-seat dining.

Exclusive Dining (Queens Grill, Princess Grill). As with its sister ships, there are two special Grill-Class-only restaurants. These have a single-seating arrangement, providing a more intimate and exclusive dining experience than can be found in the two-seating main Britannia Restaurant.

The 142-seat Queens Grill (on the port side), with single-seating dining, is for those in suites and the top accommodation grades, and provides the best cuisine and service aboard the ship. The beloved Cunard Grill experience includes alfresco dining in The Courtyard, a seldom-used courtyard terrace protected from the wind, and access for Grill-class passengers only to an exclusive lounge and bar to their own upper terrace deck, with dedicated staff.

The 132-seat Princess Grill (on the starboard side), with single-seating dining, is for passengers in middle-class accommodation grades.

How Fido and Felix can come, too

You can take your dog along on transatlantic crossings – but not on cruises – and 12 kennels are overseen by a kennel master. Dogs and cats receive a gift pack containing a QM2-logo coat, Frisbee, name tag, food dish, and scoop; a portrait with pet owners; and a crossing certificate and personalized cruise card. Other pet perks include toys, cat posts and scratchers, plus premium pet foods. You can make kennel reservations when you book. The cost: $300–$500. Dogs must be fitted with a microchip, issued with a PETS certificate or official PET passport, and vaccinated against rabies.

Other dining options. The Verandah Restaurant is a beautiful à la carte specialty dining venue, available to all passengers. It has a bar and is on the second level of the three-deck high lobby. The decor and ambience recreate the Verandah Grill restaurant aboard the original *Queen Elizabeth* and *Queen Mary*. The classic French cuisine is exceptionally good and makes for a fine dining experience. Reservations are required, and there's a cover charge for lunch or dinner.

The Lido Café (on Deck 9) has panoramic views, indoor/outdoor seating for approximately 470, and operates a fairly standard multi-line self-serve buffet arrangement. It's a bit downmarket for what is supposed to be a stylish ship – the original *Queen Elizabeth* didn't have such a facility – but then, these are different times. At night, the venue is transformed into three distinct flavors: Asado (South American Grill); Aztec (Mexican cuisine); and Jasmine (Asian cuisine), each with a small cover charge.

For excellent Lavazza-family coffees from Luigi (the name given to the coffee machine), teas, and light bites, there's the Parisian-style Café Carinthia, one deck above the Purser's Desk and adjacent to the popular Veuve Clicquot Champagne bar.

For traditional British pub food, the Golden Lion Pub offers fish 'n' chips, steak and mushroom pie, a ploughman's lunch and, of course, bangers (sausages) and mash, plus a wide range of draft beers and lagers.

ENTERTAINMENT. The 830-seat, three-deck-high Royal Court Theatre is designed in the style of a classic opera house. It has 20 private boxes that can be reserved by anyone for special nights, and a special package includes Champagne, chocolates, and a ticket printed with name and box number – in the tradition of a real London West End theatre. There's a lounge for pre-show drinks.

Colorful, large-cast production shows and a good variety of cabaret entertainment are presented here. The Royal Court Theatre is also used to show big-screen movies. The ship has a number of bands, small combos, and solo entertainers. A Big Band night is sometimes held in the Queens Room, where afternoon tea is served and live music is provided. Some bars and lounges have live jazz.

SPA/FITNESS. The Cunard Royal Health Club and Spa consists of a beauty salon, large gymnasium with high-tech muscle-pumping equipment, and great ocean views; an aerobics area; separate changing rooms for men and women, each with its own ocean-view sauna; a Thermal Area with sauna and steam rooms (extra-cost day passes are available if you don't book a treatment, at $35 per day, or at a lower per-day cost for a multi-use pass); several body treatment rooms; a rasul chamber for private Hammam-style mud/steam bathing; and a relaxation area. A 12.5% gratuity is added to all spa treatment prices.

Sports include paddle tennis, croquet, British bowls, and life-size chess.

Queen Mary 2
★★★★+

Size:.................................Large Resort Ship	Crew/Passenger Ratio (lower beds/all berths):......... 2.0/2.4
Tonnage:...................................... 148,528	Cabins (total):.................................... 1,310
Lifestyle:.....................Luxury/Premium/Standard	Size range (sq ft/m):............... 194.0–2,249.7/18.0–209
Cruise line:................................ Cunard Line	Cabins (outside view):............................. 1,017
Former names:.....................................none	Cabins (interior/no view):..............................293
IMO number:..................................9241061	Cabins (for one person):................................0
Builder:.................Chantiers de l'Atlantique (France)	Cabins (with private balcony):........................953
Original cost:...........................$800 million	Cabins (wheelchair accessible):.......................30
Entered service:.............................. Jan 2004	Wheelchair accessibility:............................ Best
Registry:...................................... Bermuda	Cabin voltage:..........................110 and 220 volts
Length (ft/m):.............................1,131.9/345.0	Elevators:...22
Beam (ft/m):............................ 134.5/41.0	Casino (gaming tables):.............................. Yes
Draft (ft/m):................................. 32.6/9.9	Slot machines:...................................... Yes
Propulsion/Propellers:. gas turbine + diesel-electric (103,000kW)/	Swimming pools:......................................2
4 pods (2 azimuthing, 2 fixed)	Hot tubs (on deck):....................................8
Passenger decks:.....................................12	Self-service launderette:............................. Yes
Total crew:.................................... 1,254	Dedicated cinema/seats:........................ Yes/473
Passengers (lower beds/alll berths):.............. 2,620/3,090	Library:.. Yes
Passenger Space Ratio (lower beds/all berths):....... 56.6/48.0	Onboard currency:..................................US$

A real ocean liner built for transatlantic crossings

OVERVIEW. *Queen Mary 2* offers the pleasures of crossing the North Atlantic comfortably on a regular schedule. It is best suited to couples and single travelers who enjoy the cosmopolitan setting of a floating city at sea with an unequaled maritime heritage. Note that the scores given in the Berlitz's Ratings box apply to Grill Class.

THE SHIP. RMS *Queen Mary 2*, designated a Royal Mail Ship by the British Post Office, is the largest ocean liner ever built – in terms of gross tonnage, length, and beam, though not passengers carried. A powerful propulsion system allows it to go backwards faster than many cruise ships can go forwards. Taller than the Empire State Building, it is the first new ship to be built for Cunard Line since 1969, when *QE2* first sailed from Southampton to New York. In addition to its scheduled transatlantic crossings, *QM2* operates an annual round-the-world cruise.

Its exterior was designed by naval architect Stephen Payne, an ocean liner specialist. This superbly designed ship is able to weather any unkind conditions on the North Atlantic, or anywhere else – hence the long foredeck, extra-thick plating and hull, designed to maintain a high speed and battle against unkind sea conditions. It has a large, contemporary funnel and beautifully tiered stern, but it is too wide to transit the Panama Canal.

The ship is propelled by the world's first four-pod propulsion system (Rolls-Royce), which can power

Berlitz's Ratings		
	Possible	Achieved
Ship	500	438
Accommodation	200	175
Food	400	308
Service	400	335
Entertainment	100	82
Cruise	400	335
OVERALL SCORE		
1673 points out of 2000		

through the waters of the North Atlantic at up to 30 knots – the contracted top speed is 29.3 knots, but the ship can easily exceed this. Each pod weighs 270 tons – more than an empty Boeing 747 jumbo jet – and they are powered by a diesel-electric system.

One of the many delightful features is the ship's Tyfon whistle: (there are two: one is new, and the other a copy of the whistle from the original *Queen Mary*). Both whistles are tuned so that they do not disturb passengers on deck, yet they can be heard 10 miles (16km) away.

Almost everything about the liner is British in style, but with some American decor input and accents, and even the four tender stations have London names: Belgravia, Chelsea, Kensington, and Knightsbridge. There is a wide walk-around promenade deck outdoors, with the forward section under cover from the weather or wind. Three times around is 6,102 ft (1,860 m), or 1.1 miles (1.6km). A full line of teak 'steamer' chairs is provided on the open walk-around promenade deck, with plenty of room for walkers to pass. However, plastic sunloungers are provided on some other open decks.

Robert Tillberg, the interior designer, produced a stylish, elegant interior design, with towering public spaces, sweeping staircases and grand public rooms. High ceilings – typically two decks of *QM2* are the equivalent of three decks in height of a regular cruise vessel – provide a great sense of space and grandeur. While many ships are designed inward with a central atrium, *QM2* is different. You enter the public rooms from a central location and will always be looking out, with the sea in the background. Deck signage is good, and it's quite easy to find one's way around the ship for the most part.

There are a few ostentatious gold pillars and tacky decorative elements, including some awful bas-reliefs in the accommodation passageways, but for the most part the ship's interiors are quite stunning. The use of wood laminate paneling may offend ship buffs, as did the plastic laminates when *QE2* debuted in 1968–69, but is the result of stringent SOLAS regulations.

The atrium lobby, spanning six decks, has an elegant staircase and exclusive works of art. In the main elevator lobby attached to the central atrium, a wall mural of Samuel Cunard welcomes you aboard; it looks like an enlarged photograph, although it is made from almost 700 postage stamp-size digital images of previous Cunard ships.

Here's a deck-by-deck look at the facilities and public rooms, starting at the lowest deck and working our way upward, forward to aft:

Deck 2 has Illuminations (with planetarium), and the Royal Court Theatre, the lower level of the six-deck-high atrium lobby, the Purser's Desk, Video Arcade, Empire Casino, Golden Lion Pub, and the lower level of the two-deck-high Britannia Restaurant.

Deck 3 has the upper level of Illuminations and the Royal Court Theatre, the second level of the six-deck-high atrium lobby, Mayfair Shops, Sir Samuel's, The Chart Room, Champagne Bar (Veuve Clicquot is the house Champagne), the upper level of the Britannia Restaurant, the Queens Room, and the G32 Nightclub.

Decks 4/Deck 5/Deck 6 have accommodation and the third, fourth, and fifth levels of the six-deck-high atrium lobby; at the aft end of Deck 6 are the facilities for children, including an outdoor pool (Minnows Pool).

Deck 7 has the Canyon Ranch Spa, the Winter Garden, the sixth and uppermost level of the six-deck-high atrium lobby, expansive Kings Court Buffet, Queens Grill Lounge, Queens Grill, and Princess Grill dining salons.

Deck 8 (forward) has the upper level of the Canyon Ranch Spa, and the Library and Bookshop. The center section has accommodation. In the aft section are the specialty restaurant Todd English, Terrace Bar, and swimming pool outdoors.

Deck 9 (forward) has the Commodore Club, Boardroom, and the Cigar Lounge (Churchills). The rest of the deck has accommodation and a Concierge Club for suite occupants.

Deck 10 has accommodation only.

Deck 11 (forward) has an outdoors observation area. The rest of the deck has accommodation. The aft section outdoors has a whirlpool tub and sunbathing deck.

Deck 12 (forward) has accommodation. The midsection has an indoor/outdoor pool with sliding glass roof, and golf areas (Fairways), located just aft of the public restrooms. The aft section has the Boardwalk Café, dog kennels, and shuffleboard courts.

Deck 13 has the Sports Centre, Regatta Bar, a splash pool, and extensive outdoor sunbathing space.

There are 14 lounges, clubs, and bars. An observation lounge, the delightful Commodore Club, has commanding views forward over the bows; light jazz is played in this bar, which is connected to the Boardroom, and Cigar Lounge. Other drinking places include a Golden Lion Pub (pub lunches are served here, too), Sir Samuel's (wine bar), a nautically themed cocktail bar (The Chart Room), and a Champagne/Coffee Bar. Outdoor bars include the Regatta Bar and Terrace Bar. The G32 nightclub, which has a main and mezzanine level, is at the aft end of the ship, away from passenger cabins; it is named after the number designated to the ship by its French builder.

The Queens Room is a grand ballroom, and has one of the largest dance floors at sea. It has a dramatic high ceiling, two huge crystal chandeliers, highly comfortable armchairs, and is used for dancing, cocktail parties, and afternoon teas.

Illuminations, the first full-scale planetarium at sea, is a stunning multi-purpose show lounge space that also functions as a 473-seat grand cinema and broadcast studio. As a planetarium, it has tiered seating rows, with 150 comfortable reclining seats, allowing you to sit in a special area under a dome, which is 38ft/11.5m in diameter and almost 20ft/6m deep that forms the setting for the night sky. It's worth reserving a seat for at least one of the four outstanding 20-minute programs. The specially equipped venue also screens 3D movies.

A Maritime Quest Exhibit provides a beautifully constructed Cunard history plus shipbuilding milestones throughout history, including John Brown's shipyard that built the original *Queen Mary* in the 1930s.

Just aft of the Canyon Ranch Spa is a colonial-style Winter Garden reminiscent of London's Kew Gardens, where flowers bloom year-round – because they are artificial (some are downright tacky). This peaceful garden setting is for relaxation.

There are five swimming pools, including one that can be enclosed under a retractable glass roof. A large area of open sunning space includes a sports bar at one end. Sports facilities include an electronic golf simulator, giant chess board, and a paddle tennis court.

The ship's Library and Bookshop is the world's largest floating bookshop and the most popular public room on the transatlantic crossings. Staffed by full-time librarians from Ocean Books, it has a superb display of 10,000 books in several languages, in 150 book cabinets. It takes the staff 25 minutes a day to unlock the cabinets and 25 minutes to lock them again. The area includes leather sofas and armchairs, and a large selection of magazines. It is a delightful facility, but there are few chairs, and the adjacent bookshop is quite small.

ConneXions features seven sophisticated classrooms for Oxford University's 'Oxford Discovery' educational programs. Classes in such things as computer learning, seamanship and navigation, art and wine appreciation, history, languages, and photography are taught. Fast-access Internet connectivity and a many computer terminals are available in the Internet Center, with a choice of connection packages. Ship-wide Wi-Fi connectivity is available (at extra cost).

Children have their own spaces, with a dedicated play area, the Play Zone. English nannies supervise toddlers, while older children use The Zone.

In 2012, Cunard started its Weddings At Sea program. Just one wedding per sea day is permitted on the crossings, with mid-Atlantic weddings proving the most sought-after. The ship carries a wedding coordinator, and the cost is $2,500 plus marriage license fee.

ACCOMMODATION. Although there are four separate categories – Queens Grill, Princess Grill, Britannia Club, and Britannia – QM2 really operates as a two-class ship (Grill Class and Britannia Class), and the restaurant to which you are assigned depends on your accommodation grade. You even get a different cabin breakfast menu depending on whether you travel in Grill Class or Britannia Class accommodation. Twenty-five price grades cover everything from standard outside-view cabins to the most opulent suites.

Perhaps the most noticeable difference between this ship and QE2 is the addition of a large number of cabins with private balconies – 75 percent of all cabins have them, although they are of little use when crossing the North Atlantic and have steel bulkheads that obscure ocean views when you are seated.

All grades have a 20-inch (or larger) TV set, and all beds have fluffy European duvets. There's a mini-fridge, safe, and hand-held hairdryer. All bathrooms have toiletries supplied by Canyon Ranch, the spa/fitness concession. Other features include digital video on demand (English-, French-, and German-language movies are available), music on demand with 3,000 titles, and audio books on demand. One channel covers Cunard Line's eventful history since 1840.

A number of cabins can accommodate a third or fourth person, although they are so small as to be useful only for contortionists. They are, however, the most inexpensive way of experiencing this fine ship.

Beware of cabins on deck 6 located underneath the Kings Court – they can be subject to noise from the casual eatery on the deck above, where almost constant trolley movement adds noise.

For the largest accommodation in the cruise industry, two combinations offer the equivalent of a large house at sea. At the front of the ship, you could, in fact, combine the Queen Elizabeth and Queen Mary suites with the Queen Anne and Queen Victoria suites to produce a mansion measuring 5,016 sq ft (466 sq m). Even this can be eclipsed at the other end of the ship, by joining Grand Duplex apartments at the lower level to the adjacent penthouses to produce an unprecedented 8,288 sq ft (770 sq m).

Balmoral/Sandringham Duplexes (Grade Q1). The largest stand-alone accommodation is in the Balmoral and Sandringham Duplexes (2,249 sq ft/209 sq m), with superb views along the length of the ship. Upstairs is a bedroom with wood-framed king-size bed, and large (not so private) balcony; downstairs is a living room with sofa, coffee table, dining table, and writing desk. There are two marble-clad bathrooms with whirlpool bath and separate shower enclosure, toilet and bidet, and two washbasins.

Queen Elizabeth/Queen Mary Suites (Grade Q2). The Queen Elizabeth Suite and Queen Mary Suite (1,194 sq ft/111 sq m) are located just under the navigation bridge, with good views over the ship's long bows. There are living and dining areas, with a large private balcony (but not as large as the Balmoral/Sandringham duplex balconies). The master, marble-clad bathroom has a whirlpool tub and shower enclosure, and a second bathroom with a shower enclosure (no tub). Each suite has the convenience of private elevator access.

Duplex Apartments (Grade Q2). There are three duplex apartments: Buckingham and Windsor (each 1,291 sq ft/120 sq m), and Holyrood (1,566 sq ft/145 sq m). Each has a gymnasium, balcony, butler and concierge service, and superb views over the stern.

Queen Anne/Queen Victoria Suites (Grade Q3). These two suites (796.5 sq ft/74 sq m) have the most commanding views over the ship's long bows. They consist of a bedroom with master, marble-clad bathroom with whirlpool tub and separate shower enclosure, separate living/dining area, and a second bathroom with a shower enclosure (no tub).

Penthouse Suites (Grade Q4). The six penthouse suites (758 sq ft/70 sq m) have a living and dining area, large private balcony, bedroom, and dressing room with master, marble-clad bathroom with whirlpool tub and separate shower enclosure.

Suites (506 sq ft (Grade Q5/Q6). These 82 suites (506 sq ft/47 sq m) have a large private balcony, living area, dressing room, marble-clad bathroom with whirlpool tub/shower. Beds can be arranged as king-size or twins.

Junior Suites (Grade P1/P2). There are 76 Junior Suites (381 sq ft/35 sq m). Each has a lounge area, large private balcony, and marble-clad bathroom with whirlpool tub and separate shower enclosure. Beds can be arranged in a king-size or twin-bed configuration.

Deluxe/Premium Balcony Cabins. These 782 cabins (248 sq ft/23 sq m) include a sitting area with sofa, and bathroom with shower enclosure. Beds can be arranged in a king-size or twin-bed configuration.

Standard Outside-View/Interior Cabins. There are 62 outside-view cabins and 281 interior cabins measuring 194 sq ft/18 sq m). Beds can be arranged in a king-size or twin-bed configuration.

Atrium View Cabins. Each of these 12 interior cabins (194 sq ft/18 sq m) has an unusual view – into the six-deck high atrium lobby. Beds can be arranged as king-size or twins. An en suite bathroom has a shower enclosure, washbasin, toilet, and toiletries cabinet.

Wheelchair-Accessible Cabins. There are 30 wheelchair-friendly suites and cabins in various categories. All have pull-down closet hanging rails, above-bed emergency pull-cord, and large, well-equipped bathrooms with roll-in showers and handrails. Facilities for blind passengers include Braille signs and tactile room signs. Eight wheelchair-accessible elevators service the dining areas. Additionally, 36 cabins accommodate deaf or hearing-impaired passengers. There are headsets in the Royal Theatre and Illuminations, and closed-caption TV.

DINING. There are 10 dining rooms and eateries (and seven galleys to service them), and all dining venues have ocean-view windows. The wines and Champagnes have been selected by Michael Broadbent, one of the world's top wine experts.

Britannia Restaurant. This main dining room seats 1,347, and spans the ship's full width. A lavish room almost three decks high, it has two grand sweeping staircases which enable you to make your entry in style. Breakfast and lunch are open-seating, while dinner is in two seatings, all with crisp linen and fine china. Vegetarian options are included on all lunch and dinner menus. One downside of open seating for breakfast or lunch is that you'll probably have a different waiter each time, who won't know your preferences. Another is that if you are seated on the lower level underneath the balcony formed along the port and starboard sides of the upper level, you'll feel enclosed in an inferior space. It's better to get a table in the central well or on the upper level.

In 46 cabins graded Category AA, occupants eat in an exclusive private dining area, the Britannia Club. This single-seating venue offers the Britannia Restaurant menu, plus various à la carte options and tableside flambé service.

Queens Grill/Princess Grill. There are two Grill Rooms (the 200-seat Queens Grill and the 178-seat Princess Grill), which are small dining salons. Which you dine in depends on your accommodation grade and fare. Both are located aft and have, in theory, fine ocean-view windows – although walkers passing by on the exterior promenade deck can be disturbing in the daytime, so window blinds are kept down. Canyon Ranch Spaclub recommendations and vegetarian options are provided on all lunch and dinner menus.

The Queens Grill has retained waiter stations, which can be noisy at times. The chairs are comfortable, and many have armrests, and the dining table height is just right. There's an impressive à la carte menu in addition to the regular menu. The excellent dining experience includes free caviar, an extra-cost item in the Princess Grill.

Todd English Restaurant. This 216-seat reservations-only restaurant is named after the American TV chef whose Boston restaurant (Olives) has a fine reputation. With its Moorish decor, it serves his noted Mediterranean cuisine. The room has been designed with intimate detailing and overlooks the Pool Terrace, allowing for alfresco dining. Food presentation from an à la carte menu is excellent, although overly fussy at times, but the venue is disappointing.

Kings Court. This truly nondescript, informal eatery has 478 seats and obnoxious daytime lighting, and is more suited to a land-based shopping mall. It offers self-serve breakfast and lunch. Breakfast is repetitive, but includes British traditional standards: eggs, bacon, kippers, and fried tomatoes. The lunch menu changes daily, and includes Indian dishes such as curried rice and chicken. Pizza, however, cannot be recommended – think cardboard with toppings. The beverage station now has real teaspoons rather than the previous wooden stirrers.

At night, decorated screens transform Kings Court into four extra-cost dining venues: an Italian Trattoria (La Piazza), Asian cuisine (Lotus), a British eatery (The Carvery) for roast meats, and a Chef's Galley; all have full sit-down tablecloth service. The 36-seat Chef's Galley has a live demonstration of your meal's preparation.

Comfort foods are served in the outdoors Boardwalk Café, weather permitting, while pub lovers can find traditional British fare in the popular Golden Lion Pub. You can also order from the restaurant menus and have breakfast, lunch, and dinner served in your own suite or cabin.

ENTERTAINMENT. The Royal Court Theatre, a lovely venue, has tiered seating for 1,094, though some sight lines are less than ideal. It stages lavish West End-style productions and hosts headline entertainers and cabaret acts. The Royal Academy of Dramatic Art (RADA) supplies a company of actors to give Shakespearean performances, lead acting workshops, and take part in street-theater performances.

SPA/FITNESS. Health Spa and Beauty Services are provided in a 20,000-sq-ft (1,850-sq-m) Canyon Ranch Spa Club, arranged on two decks. There's a thalassotherapy pool, whirlpool, and thermal suite. The daily charge for using the facilities is waived if you buy a treatment. There are 20 body and skincare treatment rooms. Treatment prices are slightly less on port days.

A gym has the latest equipment, as well as free weights. In addition, a beauty salon offers a full menu of services for hair and skin, and Canyon Ranch's own range of natural skincare products (Living Essentials) can be purchased. As there are only six hairdressing chairs, appointments should be booked early. The spa, staffed by about 50 Canyon Ranch employees, is operated as a concession.

Queen Victoria
★★★★ +

Size:.....................................Large Resort Ship	Cabins (total):.....................................1,007
Tonnage: 90,049	Size range (sq ft/m):............143.0–2,131.3/13.2–198.0
Lifestyle: ....Premium	Cabins (outside view):...............................864
Cruise line:.................................. Cunard Line	Cabins (interior/no view):.............................143
Former names: ....none	Cabins (for one person):..............................0
IMO number: 9320556	Cabins (with private balcony):.......................718
Builder: .... Fincantieri (Italy)	Cabins (wheelchair accessible): 20
Original cost:...............................$390 million	Wheelchair accessibility:...........................Good
Entered service:.............................. Dec 2007	Cabin voltage: ....110 and 220 volts
Registry:.......................................Bermuda	Elevators:..12
Length (ft/m):............................. 964.5/294.0	Casino (gaming tables):..............................Yes
Beam (ft/m):............................... 105.9/32.3	Slot machines:......................................Yes
Draft (ft/m):................................. 26.2/8.0	Swimming pools:......................................2
Propulsion/Propellers:diesel-electric (64,00kW)/2 azimuthing pods	Hot tubs (on deck):..................................5
Passenger decks:....................................12	Self-service launderette:............................Yes
Total crew: 1,001	Dedicated cinema/seats:..............................No
Passengers (lower beds/alll berths):.............2,014/2,172	Library: ....Yes
Passenger Space Ratio (lower beds/all berths): 44.7/41.4	Onboard currency: ....US$
Crew/Passenger Ratio (lower beds/all berths):..........2.2/2.4	

A pretend ocean liner that suits British tastes

OVERVIEW. *Queen Victoria*, a very comfortable, likeable cruise ship posing as an ocean liner, is best suited to a couples and single travelers who enjoy a ship that offers traditional British ocean liner-style decor, world-wide itineraries, and dressing for dinner. Note that scores given in the Berlitz's Ratings box are the averages for both Grill Class and Britannia Class.

THE SHIP. *Queen Victoria* flies the British Red Ensign for the ship's UK registry, and is aimed at the North American and British markets, but will appeal to any Anglophile, because Cunard is still a resolutely British experience. But the proclaimed Britishness is to some extent marketing hype since British staff are thin on the ground.

Basically a stretched, modified platform and layout as the Vista series of ships (examples: *Arcadia, Carnival Legend, Costa Atlantica, Costa Luminosa, Costa Mediterranea, Oosterdam*), the Cunard version has an additional passenger deck, a specially strengthened hull lengthened by 36ft (11m), giving the ship more of an 'ocean liner' feel. It also has a modified, more traditional interior layout reminiscent of yesteryear's ocean liners.

The promenade deck is not teak but a rubberized deck covering made to look like wooden planking, which gets hot and stays hot in warm weather areas. You can almost walk around – the forward section is for marine use only – and several deck lounge chairs with comfortable Cunard-logo cushioned pads make it a good place to read a book. One open deck atop the

Berlitz's Ratings		
	Possible	Achieved
Ship	500	420
Accommodation	200	145
Food	400	299
Service	400	313
Entertainment	100	81
Cruise	400	321
OVERALL SCORE		
1579 points out of 2000		

ship has a life-size chess board.

Queen Victoria also has a rather classy interior layout that takes the best and most favorite public rooms, bars, and lounges aboard *QM2* and from the now retired *QE2* and sets them into a high-tech ship designed to offer crossings of both the Atlantic and Pacific – but with a maximum speed of 23.7 knots – as well as squeeze through the Panama Canal and offer a mix of short and long voyages.

The interior decor is 'traditional' in Cunard-speak, with many public rooms finely decorated in Edwardian/Victorian styles, with wrought-iron balustrades on the staircases and in some bars. Most rooms have fine wood (veneer) paneling and decorative accents like wrought-iron horseshoe-shaped stairways, scrolled woodwork, and etched-glass panels. The majestic three-deck-high Grand Lobby has a sweeping staircase and sculpted balconies. The Cunardia museum's glass cabinets display models of former Cunard Line ships, old menus, and daily programs.

Several public rooms are two decks high; these include the gold-beige Queen's Room, with a large, proper wooden ballroom dance floor; above are two huge ceiling-mounted chandeliers. The bandstand is fronted by a large proscenium arch, while cantilevered balconies line the room's starboard side. Traditional British afternoon tea is served in this Art Deco-style grand room, although the tea itself is pretty basic – it's made with tea bags, not loose tea, so it's difficult to get the strength you like.

The Royal Arcade houses a cluster of seven shops, including Harrods, Royal Doulton, and Wedgwood, set in an arcade-like environment. At the forward end of the ship is a horseshoe-shaped staircase, above which is a magnificent British-made chiming pillar clock made by Dent of London – the company that created Big Ben at the Houses of Parliament and was official clockmaker to Queen Victoria herself, since 1841.

The Library is a really stunning two-deck-high wood-paneled 6,000-book facility with two full-time librarians. But there are few chairs on which to sit in and read. A bookshop in another location sells maritime-related books, memorabilia, maps, and stationery. The Library is a great place to meet people, quietly, and the carpet is rather special, with the names of great authors scattered throughout.

Golden Lion Pub – a must aboard a Cunarder. This one lies along the starboard side, and is a good gathering place for karaoke, sing-along, and quiz enthusiasts – plus, it has good pub food.

The Commodore Club acts as a large observation lounge, with its ocean views on three sides, and late-night room for low-volume interactive entertainment.

The adjacent Churchill's Cigar Lounge, on the starboard side, is a haven for smokers.

Chart Room Bar, adjacent to the Britannia Restaurant – a place for a quiet drink before dinner.

Hemispheres, positioned aft of the mast and adjacent to the Commodore Club, overlooks the wood-decked Pavilion Pool; this is the high-volume disco and themed nightclub.

There's also a fairly large casino (no smoking) on the port side of the lower level of the Royal Court.

A grand conservatory (Winter Gardens), with central fountain and retractable glass roof, has a moveable glass wall to an open-air swimming pool. Rattan furniture and ceiling fans help to conjure up the area's colonial theme.

Artwork worth more than $2 million, including original etchings by the liner's namesake and her husband Prince Albert, adorn various walls. An Internet Center is adjacent to the Reception Desk on Deck 1.

The layout is a little disjointed on the uppermost decks, although the general flow is reasonably good. Access between the aft deck and the pool area and Winter Gardens can be gained only by going through the expansive buffet area. This makes for congestion at the self-serve buffet as people are constantly passing through, as in a railway carriage; but it's a very popular area and provides a wide choice of food items and special themed buffet food.

The pitiful amount of drawer space in the standard cabins is disappointing, even though new under-bed drawers were added at the end of 2008, leaving almost no space for luggage storage.

Queen Victoria provides a suitable setting for passengers who enjoy dressing properly for dinner, either in formal or semi-formal attire. Passengers get cocktail party invitations, and enjoy the intellectual lecturers and specialist speakers who sail on each voyage – Cunard wisely calls them voyages, not cruises.

A per person, per day gratuity is charged to your onboard account, and a 15 percent gratuity is added to all bar and wine accounts. Gratuities – called a 'Hotel and Dining' charge – of $11.50–$13.50, depending on accommodation grade, are automatically added to your onboard account daily. The onboard currency is the US dollar – another reason to take the Britishness claims with a pinch of salt.

Sadly, there is no escort to your cabin on embarkation unless you are in certain suite-grade accommodation, leaving a bad first impression for first-timers.

Note that smokers inhabit the starboard side of the promenade deck so be aware if you intend to relax in a chair on that deck – it has been the subject of many complaints, as has the area outside Churchill's cigar lounge, where cigarette smokers congregate. Smoking is also allowed on cabin balconies.

ACCOMMODATION. There are numerous price grades but just eight types of accommodation, which ranges from ample to opulent: seven Queens Grill, eight Princess Grill, and 16 Britannia Restaurant grades. In the accommodation hallways, cabins on the port side (left side of the ship, facing forward) will find a red carpet, while those on the starboard (right) side will find a blue carpet. The air conditioning can't be turned off in cabins or bathrooms. In the measurements below, which are approximate, balconies are included. Finally, the size of the chocolate you get on your pillow was reduced by 25 percent in 2012!

Grand Suites. There are four, measuring 1,918–2,131 sq ft (178–197 sq m). They are located aft, with great ocean views from their private wraparound balconies, which contain a complete wet bar. The suites have two bedrooms with walk-in closets; bathroom with bathtub and separate shower enclosure; lounge; dining room (with seating for six). In-suite dining from the Queens Grill menus is also available.

Master Suites. Two, measuring 1,100 sq ft (102 sq m), located in the center of the ship (Deck 7).

Penthouse Suites. 25, measuring 520–707 sq ft (48–66 sq m).

Queens Suites. 35, measuring 508–771 sq ft (47–72 sq m).

Princess Suites. 61, measuring 342–513 sq ft (32–48 sq m).

Balcony Cabins. 581, measuring 242–472 sq ft (22–44 sq m).

Outside-View Cabins. 146, measuring 180–201 sq ft (17–19 sq m).

Interior (no-view) Cabins. 143, measuring 151–243 sq ft (14–19 sq m).

All accommodation grades have both British three-pin (240-volt) sockets and American (110-volt) and European-style two-pin (220-volt) sockets. Gilchrist &

Soames toiletries are supplied to all passengers, and a hairdryer is stored in the vanity desk units. Some cabins have nicely indented ceilings with suffused lighting. However, the flat-screen TV sets are small – not good for bedtime movie watching.

The regular cabins (Grades C/D) are small, but functional, although completely lacking in 'wow' factor. The cabinetry resembles that in an Ibis hotel – a bit austere and lacking character. There is a distinct lack of drawer space in a cabin supposedly designed for two persons – it's very noticeable on long voyages, and the additional drawers located under the bed may prove challenging for some to use. The premium mattresses are, however, excellent, as is the bed linen; European duvets are standard.

The bathrooms, also, are stunningly bland, similar to those found aboard the ships of Princess Cruises, with small washbasins and little storage space for toiletries, and cold, tiled floors. The fixed-head shower doesn't permit the thorough wash that hand-held flexible hoses do. Overall, the standard (lower-grade) cabins are a little underwhelming – so, for more space and quality, consider booking one of the higher-grade cabins, or, better still, go for Grill-class accommodation – the perks and increased attention and service are worth it. The walls in most accommodation passageways are rather plain, and could do with a little artwork.

DINING. Cunard is respected for its cuisine and service, with a wide variety of well-prepared and presented dishes made from good ingredients. The Britannia Restaurant – the name is taken from a former Cunard ocean liner of 1914–50 – is located in the aft section. It is two decks high, with seating on both the main level (two seatings for dinner, but open seating for breakfast and lunch) and balcony level. A horseshoe-shaped stairway links both levels. While the lower level diners have a good sea view through large picture windows, balcony diners get a promenade view. Waterford Wedgwood china is used, and there's a wide range of wines (and prices).

Queens Grill and Princess Grill, two Grill-Class-only restaurants, provide exclusive dining. These have a single-seating arrangement, providing a much more intimate and exclusive dining experience than can be found in the two-seating main Britannia Restaurant.

On the port side, the 142-seat Queens Grill, with its single-seating dining, is for passengers in suites and top category accommodation grades, and provides the best cuisine and service aboard the ship. The famous Cunard Grill experience also includes alfresco dining in a seldom used courtyard terrace (The Courtyard), suitably protected from the wind, and exclusive access for Grill-class passengers to their own upper terrace deck, with dedicated staff as well as the Grills' lounge and bar.

On the starboard side, the 132-seat Princess Grill, with single-seating dining, is for passengers in middle-class accommodation grades.

Other dining options. The 100-seat Verandah Restaurant (it was formerly Todd English Restaurant) focuses on classic French cuisine, and features a choice of seven entrees, 11 *plats principaux*, and six dessert choices. The *plats principaux* includes the popular beef and lobster flambéed with Cognac and truffle with parmesan fries, and baked rack of lamb in pastry with morel mushrooms and Madeira reduction. The extra-charge, à la carte restaurant is on the second level of the three-deck high lobby; reservations are required.

The Lido Café, on Deck 11, has good panoramic views, indoor/outdoor seating for 468, and offers a fairly standard multi-line self-serve buffet arrangement. For excellent Lavazza-family coffees from Maria (the coffee machine), and light bites, there's the Parisian-style Café Carinthia, located one deck above the Purser's Desk and adjacent to the popular Veuve Clicquot Champagne bar.

For traditional British pub food, the Golden Lion Pub serves fish 'n' chips, steak and mushroom pie, ploughman's lunch, and, of course, bangers (sausages) and mash – particularly good at lunchtime – with a nice draft pint of bitter, naturally.

Cabin service is available 24 hours a day, so you can always have extra items when you are feeling peckish.

ENTERTAINMENT. The 830-seat, three-deck-high Royal Court Theatre is designed in the style of a classic opera house. In the tradition of a real London West End theatre, it provides 20 private boxes which can be reserved by any passengers for special nights. A special package includes Champagne and chocolates, and ticket printed with name and box number. There's also a lounge for pre-show drinks.

A Victoriana show is all about good old British tradition. Other production shows include Celtic Heartbeat and Stroke of Genius, and a good variety of cabaret entertainment is presented. The Royal Court Theatre is also used to show large-screen movies. The ship has a number of bands, small combos, and solo entertainers. A Big Band night is sometimes held in the Queens Room.

SPA/FITNESS. The Cunard Royal Health Club and Spa consists of a beauty salon, large gymnasium with high-tech muscle-pumping equipment, and great ocean views; aerobics area; changing rooms for men and women (each with its own ocean-view sauna); a Thermal Area with sauna and steam rooms (extra-cost day passes are available if you don't book a treatment, at $35 per day, or at less per day cost for a multi-use pass); several body treatment rooms; a rasul chamber for private Hammam-style mud/steam bathing; and a relaxation area.

Radiance of the Seas
★★★+

Size:.	.Large Resort Ship	Cabins (total):.	1,072
Tonnage:.	90,090	Size range (sq ft/m):.	.165.8–1,216.3/15.4–113.0
Lifestyle:.	.Standard	Cabins (outside view):.	.829
Cruise line:.	Royal Caribbean International	Cabins (interior/no view):.	.237
Former names:.	.none	Cabins (for one person):.	.0
IMO number:.	.9195195	Cabins (with private balcony):.	.578
Builder:.	Meyer Werft (Germany)	Cabins (wheelchair accessible):.	.14 (8 with private balcony)
Original cost:.	.$350 million	Wheelchair accessibility:.	.Good
Entered service:.	.Apr 2001	Cabin voltage:.	.110 and 220 volts
Registry:.	.The Bahamas	Elevators:.	.9
Length (ft/m):.	961.9/293.2	Casino (gaming tables):.	Yes
Beam (ft/m):.	105.6/32.2	Slot machines:.	Yes
Draft (ft/m):.	27.8/8.5	Swimming pools:.	.2
Propulsion/Propellers:.	.Gas turbine (40,000kW)/2 azimuthing pods	Hot tubs (on deck):.	.3
Passenger decks:.	12	Self-service launderette:.	.No
Total crew:.	858	Dedicated cinema/seats:.	Yes
Passengers (lower beds/alll berths):.	2,146/2,542	Library:.	Yes
Passenger Space Ratio (lower beds/all berths):.	42.0/35.4	Onboard currency:.	.US$
Crew/Passenger Ratio (lower beds/all berths):.	2.5/2.9		

A large, family-friendly ship for casual-style cruising

OVERVIEW. *Radiance of the Seas* offers a decent amount of space, comfortable public areas, and slightly larger cabins than some RCI ships for younger, active travelers. A grand amount of glass provides more contact with the ocean. While the ship is delightful in many ways, the operation does suffer from having too few well trained service staff.

THE SHIP. *Radiance of the Seas* was the first Royal Caribbean International ship to use gas and steam turbine power instead of the more conventional diesel or diesel-electric combination. Pod propulsion is provided. In the very front of the ship is a helipad, which also acts as a viewing platform for passengers.

This is a contemporary ship, with a two-deck-high walk-around structure in the forward section of the funnel. Along the ship's starboard side, a central glass wall protrudes, giving great views – cabins with balconies occupy the space directly opposite on the port side. The gently rounded stern has nicely tiered decks. One of two swimming pools can be covered by a glass dome for use as an indoor/outdoor pool.

Inside, the decor is contemporary, yet elegant, bright, and cheerful. A nine-deck-high atrium lobby has glass-walled elevators that travel through 12 decks, face the sea, and provide a link with nature and the ocean. The Centrum, as the atrium is called, has several public rooms connected to it: the guest relations and shore excursions desks, a Lobby Bar, Cham-

Berlitz's Ratings

	Possible	Achieved
Ship	500	382
Accommodation	200	141
Food	400	242
Service	400	279
Entertainment	100	73
Cruise	400	270

OVERALL SCORE
1387 points out of 2000

pagne Bar, the Library, Royal Caribbean Online, the Concierge Club, and a Crown & Anchor Lounge.

Other facilities include a delightful, but very small library. A large Schooner Bar houses maritime art in an integral art gallery. Casino Royale has a French Art Nouveau decorative theme and 11 crystal chandeliers. There's also a small dedicated screening room for movies, with space for two wheelchairs, plus a 194-seat conference center, and a business center.

The Viking Crown Lounge (a trademark aboard all RCI ships) is a large structure set around the base of the ship's funnel. It functions as an observation lounge during the daytime, with views forward over the swimming pool. In the evening, the space hosts Starquest – a high-energy dance club, and Hollywood Odyssey – for softer mood music.

Royal Caribbean Online is a center with 12 computers, located in a semi-private setting; in addition, shipwide Wi-Fi is available for a fee. More Internet-access terminals are located in Books 'n' Coffee, a bookshop with coffee and pastries, located in an extensive array of shops.

The artwork is eclectic, providing a spectrum of color. It ranges from Jenny M. Hansen's *A Vulnerable Moment* glass sculpture to David Buckland's *Industrial and Russian Constructionism 1920s* in photographic images on glass and painted canvas, to a huge multi-deck high contemporary bicycle-cum-paddle-wheel sculpture design suspended in the atrium.

FAMILIES. Youth facilities include Adventure Ocean, an 'edutainment' area with four separate age-appropriate sections for junior passengers: Aquanaut Center (for ages three to five); Explorer Center (six to eight); Voyager Center (nine to 12); and the Optix Teen Center (13–17). There is also Adventure Beach, which includes a splash pool complete with waterslide; Surfside, with computer lab stations with entertaining software; and Ocean Arcade, a video games hangout.

ACCOMMODATION. There is a wide range of suites and standard outside-view and interior cabins in 10 different categories and numerous price groups.

Apart from the largest suites (six owner's suites), which have king-size beds, almost all other cabins have twin beds that convert to a queen-size bed, All cabins have rich (but faux) wood cabinetry, including a vanity desk with hairdryer, faux wood drawers that close silently (hooray), television, personal safe and three-sided mirrors. Some cabins have ceiling recessed, pull-down berths for third and fourth persons, although closet and drawer space would be extremely tight for four persons even if two of them were children, and some have interconnecting doors – so families with children can cruise together in separate but adjacent cabins. Audio channels are available through the TV set, whose picture cannot be turned off while listening to an audio channel.

Most bathrooms have a terrazzo-style tiled floor, and a small shower enclosure in a half-moon shape, Egyptian cotton towels, a cabinet for toiletries and a shelf. In reality, there is little space to stow toiletries for two (or more).

The largest accommodation consists of a family suite with two bedrooms. One bedroom has twin beds that convert to queen-size bed, while a second has two lower beds and two upper Pullman berths, a combination that can sleep up to eight persons. Many of the 'private' balcony cabins aren't very private, as they can be overlooked.

DINING. Cascades, the main dining room, spans two decks. The upper deck level has floor-to-ceiling windows, while the lower deck level has picture windows. It is a lovely, but noisy, dining hall – reminiscent of those aboard the transatlantic liners in their heyday, although eight huge, thick pillars obstruct the sight lines. It seats 1,104, and has cascading water themed decor. There are tables for two, four, six, eight, or 10. Two small private dining rooms – the 94-seat Breakers and the 30-seat Tides – are located off the main dining room. When you book, choose one of two seatings, or 'My Time Dining' that enables you to eat when you want, during dining room hours.

Other dining options. Several optional dining venues/eateries were added during an extensive refurbishment in 2011:

Boardwalk Dog House, for hot dogs, wieners, brats, sausages, and a variety of toppings to split a long bun (open for lunch and dinner, no added cost).

Giovanni's Table, an Italian trattoria with Italian classics served family-style (open for lunch and dinner; a cover charge applies, and reservations are required).

Izumi has a sushi bar with hot-rock cooking (open for lunch and dinner; a cover charge applies, as well as additional à la carte menu item pricing, and reservations are required).

Park Café, an indoor/outdoor market for salads, sandwiches, soups, and pastries (open for breakfast, lunch and dinner; no added cost, but reservations are required).

Rita's Cantina, a casual indoor/outdoor eatery, for families by day, and adults by night. It offers Mexican fare, and live guitar music (open for lunch and dinner, a cover charge applies, as well as à la carte menu item pricing, and reservations are required).

Samba Grill, a Brazilian churrascaria (steakhouse), for a variety of meats, chicken, and seafood brought to the table ready to slice and serve upon request (a cover charge applies; open for dinner only, and reservations are required).

Chef's Table, a private experience co-hosted by the executive chef and sommelier for a wine pairing dinner of five courses (open for dinner only; a cover charge applies, and reservations are required).

ENTERTAINMENT. The three-level Aurora Theater has 874 seats, including 24 stations for wheelchairs, and good sight lines from most seats. The Colony Club hosts casual cabaret shows, including late-night adult comedy, and provides live music for dancing. The entertainment throughout is very lively and upbeat. There is even background music in all corridors and elevators, and constant music outdoors on the pool deck.

SPA/FITNESS. The Day Spa fitness and spa facilities have themed decor, and include a gymnasium with 44 cardiovascular machines, a 50-person aerobics room, sauna and steam rooms, and therapy treatment rooms. All are located on the uppermost decks, forward of the mast, with access from the forward stairway.

A climate-controlled 10,176-sq-ft (945-sq-m) indoor/outdoor Solarium has a sliding glass roof that can be closed in cool or inclement weather.

More sporting passengers are offered a 30-ft (9-m) rock-climbing wall with five separate climbing tracks. There is also an exterior jogging track. Other sports facilities include a nine-hole miniature golf course with novel 17th-century decorative ornaments, and an indoor/outdoor country club with golf simulator, a jogging track, and basketball court. There are two specially stabilized pool tables.

Regal Princess
Not Yet Rated

Size:................................Large Resort Ship		Cabins (total):....................................... 1,780	
Tonnage: 141,000		Size range (sq ft/m): .... n/a	
Lifestyle: ....Standard		Cabins (outside view):............................... 1,438	
Cruise line:............................ Princess Cruises		Cabins (interior/no view):............................342	
Former names: ....none		Cabins (for one person):................................0	
IMO number: .... n/a		Cabins (with private balcony):...................... 1,438	
Builder: .... Fincantieri (Italy)		Cabins (wheelchair accessible): 36	
Original cost: .... €775 million		Wheelchair accessibility:.......................... Best	
Entered service:........................... May 2014		Cabin voltage: ....110 and 220 volts	
Registry:.................................... Bermuda		Elevators:...14	
Length (ft/m):............................1,082.6/330.0		Casino (gaming tables):............................ Yes	
Beam (ft/m):.............................. 126.3/38.5		Slot machines:.................................... Yes	
Draft (ft/m): 27.8/8.5		Swimming pools:....................................2	
Propulsion/Propellers:........... diesel-electric (52,000kW)/2		Hot tubs (on deck):....................................6	
Passenger decks:.....................................17		Self-service launderette:............................ Yes	
Total crew:....................................... 1,346		Dedicated cinema/seats:..............................No	
Passengers (lower beds/alll berths):............. 3,560/4,610		Library:.. Yes	
Passenger Space Ratio (lower beds/all berths): 39.6/30.5		Onboard currency: ....US$	
Crew/Passenger Ratio (lower beds/all berths):.......... 2.6/3.4			

A large, multi-choice family-friendly resort ship

OVERVIEW. *Regal Princess* is a sister to *Royal Princess*, which debuted in 2013. Princess Cruises delivers a consistent, well-packaged cruise vacation, with a good range of entertainment options, at an attractive price, which is why passengers come back again and again.

THE SHIP. Although large, the ship's profile is quite well balanced, and is an enhancement of the earlier range of Grand-class ships. In terms of practical design, the lifeboats are located outside the main public room areas, so that they don't impair the view from balcony cabins.

An over-the-water SeaWalk, a top-deck glass-bottomed enclosed walkway (first introduced in 2013 aboard sister ship *Royal Princess*) on the starboard side extends almost 30ft (9.1m) beyond the vessel's edge and forms part of a lounge/bar venue. This is the place to go for dramatic views, including to the sea 128ft (39m) below – it reminds me of Gallery 9 in the Titanic museum in Belfast, Northern Ireland, where you stand on a glass floor and look down to the famous ship seemingly lost beneath you – so you really can 'walk' on water (well, over it). On the ship's port side is a similarly unique cantilevered SeaView bar.

There are three main stair towers and elevator banks, with panoramic-view elevators in the central bank. The interior decor is warm and attractive, with an abundance of earth tones that suit both American and European tastes. One of the line's hallmark venues, the Piazza Atrium, has been significantly expanded compared to the older ships. This area is the ship's multi-faceted social hub and combines a specialty dining venue, light meals, snack food items, pastries, beverages, entertainment, shopping, and guest services. It is larger than aboard any other Princess Cruises ship, and has a horseshoe-shaped flowing stairway and lots of mood lighting effects.

The base level includes Vines, a wine bar with sushi and tapas; International Café, for coffees, teas, panini, and pastries; Sabatini's, a Tuscan specialty extra-cost restaurant, with both regular and à la carte menus; and a gift shop. Upstairs, level two includes Alfredo's Pizzeria, Bellini's (a bar serving Bellini drinks) a photo gallery, reception, and shore excursion counters. On the third level, Crooners Bar has glass pianos and dueling pianist entertainers, while a new addition is the Seafood Bar. The Piazza Atrium is all about food, entertainment, and passenger services.

The company provides a number of gentlemen dance hosts to act as partners for women traveling alone.

ACCOMMODATION. There are five main types of accommodation and 35 price grades: (a) grand suite; (b) 40 suites with balcony; (c) 306 mini-suites with balcony; (d) 360 deluxe outside-view balcony cabins; (e) 732 outside-view cabins with balcony; and (e) 342 interior cabins. Pricing depends on two things: size and location. Outside-view cabins account for about 81

Berlitz's Ratings

	Possible	Achieved
Ship	500	NYR
Accommodation	200	NYR
Food	400	NYR
Service	400	NYR
Entertainment	100	NYR
Cruise	400	NYR
OVERALL SCORE		
NYR points out of 2000		

percent of all accommodation, and all have a balcony; those located at the stern are the quietest and most sought-after.

All accommodation grades share energy-efficient lighting and key card readers that automatically turn off lights when occupants leave their cabins. All cabins get beds with upholstered headboards, wall-mounted TV sets, additional 220v electrical socket, turndown service and heart-shaped chocolates on pillows each night, bathrobes (on request unless you are in suite-grade accommodation), and toiletries. A hairdryer is provided in all cabins, sensibly located at the vanity desk unit in the living area. Bathrooms generally have a good amount of open shelf storage space for toiletries, and – in a first for Princess Cruises – all bathrooms have hand-held, flexi-hose showers, and shower enclosures larger than aboard other Princess ships (except sister *Royal Princess*).

Suite and mini-suite grade occupants have their own concierge lounge – useful for making dining, spa, and shore excursion reservations. They also get more amenities and larger TV sets, and suites get two washbasins.

Some of the most sought-after suites are located aft, occupying the corner (port and starboard) positions.

DINING. There are three 'formal' main dining rooms. You can choose either traditional two-seating dining (typically 6pm and 8:15pm for dinner), or 'anytime dining' – which allows you to choose when and with whom you want to eat. If you want to see a show in the evening, however, then your dining time will be dictated by the time of the show, which rather limits your choice.

Other dining options. Extra-cost, reservations-required Sabatini's, located adjacent to Vines Wine Bar on the lower atrium level is an Italian restaurant with colorful Tuscany-themed decor. Named after Trattoria Sabatini, the 200-year-old institution in Florence, it serves Italian-style pasta dishes with a choice of sauces, as well as Italian-style entrées, including tiger prawns and lobster tail, all provided with flair and entertainment by energetic waiters. There's both a table d'hôte and an à la carte menu. This venue, which is all about Tuscany, also hosts Italian wine tasting.

Ocean Terrace, located on the second level of the atrium lobby, is a seafood bar. International Café, on the lowest level of the Piazza Atrium, is the place for extra-cost coffees, pastries, panini, and more. Vines Wine Bar, on the lowest level of the Piazza Atrium, is an escape from all the noise and hubbub elsewhere – for a glass of extra-cost wine, tapas, and sushi bites. This is really a pleasant area in which to while away a late afternoon, trying out new wines.

Crown Grill is an extra-cost à la carte dining venue, adjacent to the Wheelhouse Bar, on the uppermost level of the three-deck-high atrium, and is the place to go for extra-cost steaks and seafood.

For casual meals, the self-serve buffet venue (Horizon Court) seats 900 indoors and 350 outdoors at the Horizon Terrace, and there are multiple active cooking stations. Sections of the eatery highlight specific themes, such as Mediterranean, Asian, and Italian cuisine; there's also a deli section. At night, it becomes Horizon Bistro, for casual dinners. Certain nights will feature special themes and foods, such as British pub food or Brazilian churrascarria (for steaks). Rotisseries, carvings, hibachi grill, and other active cooking station items are all part of the scenario.

The ship's bakery (well, part of it) comes out of the galley and into a separate area of the Horizon Court. Called the Horizon Bistro Pastry Shop, it offers freshly baked bread, croissants, pastry items, waffles, and other pastries throughout the day.

ENTERTAINMENT. The Princess Theater, the ship's main showlounge, is a state-of-the-art, two-deck-high venue for the large-scale production shows that Princess Cruises is renowned for.There's also a 'Princess Live' auditorium for stand-up comedy and other small-audience entertainment features. At the stern of the ship (on the same deck) is a Vista Lounge; this is also an entertainment venue, with a large dance floor. Meanwhile, on the subject of dancing, the ship has a number of gentlemen dance hosts for women without partners.

SPA/FITNESS. The Lotus Spa is located forward on the lower level of the atrium, so it doesn't take away premium outdoor-view real estate space. Separate facilities for men and women include a sauna, steam room, and changing rooms; common facilities include a relaxation/waiting zone, body-pampering treatment rooms, and a gymnasium packed with the latest high-tech, muscle-pumping cardio-vascular equipment, and providing great ocean views. Some fitness classes are free, while others cost extra. Children and teens have their own fitness rooms adjacent to their age-related facilities.

The well-known spa concessionaire Steiner Leisure operates and staffs the Lotus Spa. You can make online reservations for any spa treatments before your cruise, which could be a great time-saver, as long as you can plan ahead.

Regatta
★★★★

Size:. . . . . Small Ship			Cabins (total):. 342	
Tonnage: 30,277			Size range (sq ft/m): 145.3–968.7/13.5–90.0	
Lifestyle: . . . . .Premium			Cabins (outside view):. 317	
Cruise line:. . . . . Oceania Cruises			Cabins (interior/no view):. 25	
Former names: . . . . R Two			Cabins (for one person):. 0	
IMO number: 9156474			Cabins (with private balcony):. 232	
Builder: . . . . Chantiers de l'Atlantique			Cabins (wheelchair accessible): 3	
Original cost:. . . . .£150 million			Wheelchair accessibility:. . . . . .Good	
Entered service:. Dec1998/Dec 2003			Cabin voltage: . . . . .110 and 220 volts	
Registry:. . . . . .Marshall Islands			Elevators:. 4	
Length (ft/m):. 593.7/181.0			Casino (gaming tables):. . . . . Yes	
Beam (ft/m):. 83.5/25.5			Slot machines:. . . . . Yes	
Draft (ft/m):. 19.5/6.0			Swimming pools:. 1	
Propulsion/Propellers:. . . . . diesel (18,600kW)/2			Hot tubs (on deck):. 3	
Passenger decks:. 9			Self-service launderette:. . . . . Yes	
Total crew:. 386			Dedicated cinema/seats:. . . . . .No	
Passengers (lower beds/alll berths):. 684/824			Library:. . . . . Yes	
Passenger Space Ratio (lower beds/all berths): 44.2/36.7			Onboard currency: . . . . .US$	
Crew/Passenger Ratio (lower beds/all berths):. 1.7/2.1				

An informal premium ship for mature-age cruisers

OVERVIEW. Oceania Cruises is a young company that aims to provide a high level of food and service in an informal setting that's elegant yet comfortable. *Regatta* suits couples who like good food and style, but want informality with no formal nights on board, and interesting itineraries, all at a very reasonable price.

THE SHIP. *Regatta* was originally one of eight almost identical ships built for the now-defunct Renaissance Cruises. The exterior design manages to balance the ship's high sides by painting the whole ship white, with a large, square white funnel. The addition of teak overlaid decking and teak lounge chairs have improved the pool deck– but it costs $100 a day to use the front rows of double sunloungers (cabanas).

There is no walk-around promenade deck outdoors as such – there is, however, a small jogging/walking track, above the swimming pool. Stairways, though carpeted, are tinny.

The stunningly elegant interior decor is a throwback to the ocean liners of the 1920s and '30s, with dark woods and warm colors, all carried out in fine taste – if a bit faux in places. It feels like an old-world country club.

The public rooms are spread over three decks. The reception hall has a staircase with intricate wrought-iron railings. A large observation lounge, the Horizon Bar, is located high atop ship. There are plenty of bars, including one in each of the restaurant entrances. Perhaps the nicest is the casino bar/lounge, a beautiful

Berlitz's Ratings

	Possible	Achieved
Ship	500	402
Accommodation	200	153
Food	400	308
Service	400	295
Entertainment	100	74
Cruise	400	309
OVERALL SCORE		
1541 points out of 2000		

room reminiscent of London's grand hotels. It has an inviting marble fireplace, sofas, and chairs.

The Library is a grand Regency-style room, with a fireplace, a high, indented, trompe l'oeil ceiling, and excellent selection of books, plus very comfortable wingback chairs with footstools, and sofas you could sleep on.

The dress code is 'smart casual.' Gratuities are added at $10.50 per person, per day, and accommodation designated as suites have an extra $3 per person charge for the butler. A 15 percent gratuity is added to bar accounts.

Passenger niggles include all the inventive extra charges that can be incurred. What's really nice is the fact that there are almost no intrusive announcements.

ACCOMMODATION. There are six cabin categories, and 10 price grades (three suite price grades; five outside-view cabin grades; two interior cabin grades). All of the standard interior and outside-view cabins (the lowest four grades) are extremely tight for two people, particularly for cruises longer than five days. They have twin beds or a queen-size bed, with good under-bed storage areas, personal safe, vanity desk with large mirror, good closet and drawer space in rich, dark woods, 100 percent cotton bathrobe and towels, slippers, clothes brush, and shoe horn.

Certain cabin categories (about 100 of them) qualify as 'Concierge Level' accommodation, and occupants get extra goodies such as enhanced bathroom amenities, complimentary shoeshine, tote bag, cashmere throw blanket, bottle of Champagne on arrival, a handheld hairdryer, priority restaurant reservations, and priority embarkation.

Owner's Suites (6). Measuring around 962 sq ft (90 sq m), these fine living spaces provide the most spacious accommodation. Located aft overlooking the stern on decks 6, 7, and 8, they are subject to more movement and some vibration. They have extensive teak-floor private balconies that really are private and cannot be overlooked by anyone. Each has an entrance foyer, living room, separate bedroom, CD player, fully tiled bathroom with Jacuzzi tub, and a small guest bathroom. The bed faces the sea, which can be seen through the floor-to-ceiling windows and sliding glass door.

Vista Suites (4). These measure around 786 sq ft (73 sq m), and located forward on decks 5 and 6. They have extensive teak-floor private balconies that can't be overlooked by anyone from the decks above. Each has an entrance foyer, living room, separate bedroom, CD player (with selection of audio discs), and fully tiled bathroom with Jacuzzi tub. The bed faces the sea, visible through the floor-to-ceiling windows and sliding glass door.

Penthouse Suites (52). Actually, these are large cabins rather than suites as the bedrooms aren't separate from the living areas, but they measure around 323 sq ft (30 sq m). They have a good-size teak-floor balcony with sliding glass door – but with partial, not full, balcony partitions. The lounge area has a dining table and there is ample storage space. The bathroom has a tub, shower, washbasin, and toilet.

Cabins with Balcony. Measuring around 216 sq ft (20 sq m), these comprise about two-thirds of all cabins. They have partial, not full, balcony partitions, sliding glass doors, and only 14 cabins on Deck 6 have lifeboat-obstructed views. The living area has a refrigerated mini-bar, lounge area with breakfast table, and a balcony with teak floor, two teak chairs, and a drinks table. The bathrooms, with tiled floors and plain walls, are compact, standard units, and include a shower stall with a strong, removable handheld shower unit, hairdryer, toiletries storage shelves, and retractable clothesline.

Outside View and Interior Cabins. These measure around 160–165 sq ft (14.8–15.3 sq m) and have twin beds that convert to a queen-size bed, vanity desk, small sofa and coffee table, and bathroom with a shower enclosure with a strong, removable hand-held shower unit, hairdryer, toiletries storage shelves, retractable clothesline, washbasin, and toilet. Although they aren't large, they are quite comfortable, with a decent amount of storage space.

All suites/cabins located at the stern may suffer from vibration and noise, particularly when the ship is maneuvering in port.

DINING. Flexibility and choice are what the dining facilities aboard Oceania Cruises ships are all about. There are four different restaurants:

The Grand Dining Room has around 340 seats, and a raised central section, but the problem is the noise level – because of the low ceiling height, it's atrocious when the dining room is full. Being located at the stern, there are large ocean-view windows on three sides, and prime tables overlook the stern). The chairs are comfortable, with armrests. The menus change daily for lunch and dinner.

Toscana Italian Restaurant has 96 seats, windows along two sides, and a set menu plus daily chef's specials.

The cozy Polo Grill has 98 seats, windows along two sides and a set menu including prime steaks and seafood.

The Terrace Café has seats for 154 indoors – not enough during cruises to cold-weather areas – and 186 outdoors. It is open for breakfast, lunch, and casual dinners, when it has excellent tapas and other Mediterranean food. As the ship's self-serve buffet restaurant, it incorporates a small pizzeria and grill.

A poolside Waves Grill serves fishburgers, veggie burgers, and Reuben sandwiches, as well as Angus beef burgers, and hot dogs.

All restaurants have open-seating dining, so you can dine when you want, with whom you wish. Reservations are needed in Toscana Restaurant and Polo Grill (but there's no extra charge), where there are mostly tables for four or six; there are few tables for two. There is a Poolside Grill Bar.

The food and service staff is provided by Apollo, a respected maritime catering company that also has an interest in Oceania Cruises. The consultant chef is American TV chef Jacques Pepin. Oceania Cruises' brochure claims "Cuisine so extraordinary it's unrivaled at sea" is hogwash. This is, however, a foodie's ship, with really high-quality ingredients. Particularly notable are the delicious breads, rolls, croissants, and brioches – all made on board from French flour and d'Isigny butter.

On sea days, teatime is presented in the Horizon Lounge, with formally dressed staff, cake display trolleys, and an array of cake and scones.

ENTERTAINMENT. The Regatta Lounge has entertainment, lectures, some social events, and a mix of production shows and cabaret acts.

SPA/FITNESS. A lido deck has a swimming pool, and good sunbathing space, plus a thalassotherapy tub. The uppermost outdoors deck includes a golf driving net and shuffleboard court. The Canyon Ranch SpaClub consists of a beauty salon, three treatment rooms, changing rooms, and steam room. There is no sauna. Note that 18 percent is added to your spa account.

Rhapsody of the Seas
★★★+

Size:.................................Large Resort Ship		Cabins (total):.................................... 1,000	
Tonnage: 78,491		Size range (sq ft/m): 135.0–1,270.1/12.5–118.0	
Lifestyle: ....Standard		Cabins (outside view):............................... 593	
Cruise line:................... Royal Caribbean International		Cabins (interior/no view):............................407	
Former names: ....*none*		Cabins (for one person):...............................0	
IMO number: 9116864		Cabins (with private balcony):.......................229	
Builder: .... Chantiers de l'Atlantique (France)		Cabins (wheelchair accessible): 14	
Original cost:................................$275 million		Wheelchair accessibility:..........................Good	
Entered service:.............................. May 1997		Cabin voltage: ....110 and 220 volts	
Registry:...................................The Bahamas		Elevators:..9	
Length (ft/m):............................... 915.3/279.0		Casino (gaming tables):............................. Yes	
Beam (ft/m):................................. 105.6/32.2		Slot machines:...................................... Yes	
Draft (ft/m):...................................... 24.9/7.6		Swimming pools:.......................................2	
Propulsion/Propellers:........... diesel-electric (50,400kW)/2		Hot tubs (on deck):....................................6	
Passenger decks:.....................................11		Self-service launderette:...........................No	
Total crew:...765		Dedicated cinema/seats:............................No	
Passengers (lower beds/alll berths):............ 2,000/2,435		Library: .... Yes	
Passenger Space Ratio (lower beds/all berths): 39.2/32.2		Onboard currency: ....US$	
Crew/Passenger Ratio (lower beds/all berths):.......... 2.6/3.1			

OVERVIEW. What makes *Rhapsody of the Seas* feel warm and cozy are the use of fine, light wood surfaces throughout its public rooms, plus the large array of potted plants. There is a large shopping area, although the merchandise is consistently tacky. Throughout the ship, the artwork is upbeat and colorful, with a musical theme: classical, jazz, popular, and rock 'n' roll.

Berlitz's Ratings

	Possible	Achieved
Ship	500	381
Accommodation	200	140
Food	400	238
Service	400	262
Entertainment	100	74
Cruise	400	263
OVERALL SCORE		
1358 points out of 2000		

THE SHIP. This all-white ship, sister to *Vision of the Seas*, shares design features that make many, but not all, Royal Caribbean International ships identifiable, including a Viking Crown Lounge and a multi-level nightspot – the music can be loud and overbearing, however.

The Viking Crown Lounge (it is also the ship's disco) is positioned just aft of the center of the ship, above the central atrium lobby. The funnel is positioned well aft – a departure from many other RCI ships – which positions the Viking Crown lounge around the funnel or at its base. The stern of this ship is beautifully rounded. There is a reasonable amount of open-air walking space, although this tends to become cluttered with sunloungers.

There's a wide range of interesting public rooms, lounges, and bars, and the interiors have been cleverly designed to avoid congestion and aid passenger flow into revenue areas. Speaking of which, for those who enjoy gambling, the astrologically-themed Casino Royale is large and rather glitzy – although not as bold as aboard some of the company's other ships. Again, this is typical of most new large ships; a couple of piec-

es of 'electrostatic' art in globe form provide fascinating relief.

The atrium lobby – called the Centrum – is the social meeting place. It has a large kinetic sculpture, *Diadem*. It is a multi-material construction that spans six decks, and has an astrological theme, as do many of the decorative elements throughout the ship. The interior decor is imaginative and provides a connection between the sea and the stars.

Ship-wide Wi-Fi is provided (yes, there is a cost if you use it), as is a digital direction-finding system, electronic mustering, and an outdoor movie screen. Also, iPads in every cabin contain content about the ship's amenities and activities. In the Centrum, the R Bar has a 1960s vibe, iconic furnishings, and is wild about cocktails.

Ship enthusiasts will like the chair fabric in the Shall We Dance lounge, with its large aft-facing windows, and the glass case-enclosed mechanical sculptures.

FAMILIES. RCI caters to children really well. There is a Royal Babies and Tots nursery (for babies of six months to 36 months). Other ages are grouped as follows; Aquanauts (for three- to five-year-olds); Explorers (six to eight); Voyagers (nine to 12); Navigators (12–14); and Teens (15–17).

ACCOMMODATION. There are numerous accommodation grades, priced by size and location. The standard interior and exterior view cabins are of an adequate size, and have just enough functional facilities to make them comfortable for a one-week cruise, but longer might prove confining. The decor is bright and cheerful, although the ceilings are plain; the soft furnishings make this home away from home look like the inside of a modern Scandinavian hotel – with minimalist tones, and splashes of color. Twin lower beds convert to queen-size beds, and there is a reasonable amount of closet and drawer space, but there is little room to maneuver between the bed and the desk/television unit.

The bathrooms are small but functional. The shower units themselves are small, too, and there is no cabinet for toiletries. The towels should be larger and thicker. In the passageways, upbeat artwork depicts musical themes.

Choose a 'C' grade suite if you want spacious accommodation that includes a curtained-off sleeping area, a good-sized outside balcony with part, not full, partition, a lounge with sofa, two chairs and coffee table, three closets, plenty of drawer and storage space, television and video player. The bathroom is large and has a full-size tub, integral shower, and two washbasins with two toiletries cabinets.

For the best accommodation, choose the Royal Suite. It resembles a Palm Beach apartment, and comes complete with a white baby grand piano. It has a separate bedroom with king-size bed, living room with queen-size sofa bed, refrigerator/mini-bar, dining table, entertainment center, and vanity dressing area. The decor is simple and elegant, with pastel colors, and wood-accented ceiling treatments. Located just under the starboard side navigation bridge wing, it has its own private balcony.

DINING. The two-level Edelweiss Dining Room is attractive and works well as a large dining hall, although the noise level can be high. When you book, choose one of two seatings for dinner or My Time Dining (eat when you want, during dining room hours).

Other dining options. A number of venues were installed or refreshed during the ship's 2011–12 refit. Chops Grille is for steaks and seafood items. Izumi Asian Cuisine sushi bar has hot-rock cooking; it is open for lunch and dinner, with a small cover charge for both plus à la carte menu pricing. Chef's Table is a private experience co-hosted by the executive chef and sommelier for a five-course wine-pairing dinner (it's a little expensive, but worth it for a special occasion). Park Café is a casual no-charge market-style eatery for salads, sandwiches, soups, and pastries.

A drinks package is available at all bars, in the form of cards or stickers. This enables you to pre-pay for a selection of standard soft drinks and alcoholic drinks, but the packages are not exactly easy to understand.

ENTERTAINMENT. The Broadway Melodies Theater is the principal showlounge. It is a large, but well-designed room with main and balcony levels, and good sight lines from most of the banquette seats.

Other cabaret acts are presented in the Shall We Dance Lounge, located aft, and include late-night adult comedy, as well as live music for dancing. A number of other bars and lounges have live music of differing types.

The entertainment, for which Royal Caribbean International always gets plenty of praise, is upbeat. However, it's difficult to escape from the background music provided everywhere – even in the passenger hallways and elevators, and outdoors on the pool deck. If you want a quiet relaxing holiday, choose another ship.

SPA/FITNESS. There are good health spa facilities, set in a spacious environment on one of the uppermost decks. The decor has Egypt as its theme, with pharaohs lining the pool. The spa is operated by Steiner, a specialist concession whose staff provide a wide range of body treatments and hair care.

For the more sporting, there is activity galore – including a rock-climbing wall with several separate climbing tracks. It is located outdoors at the aft end of the funnel.

Riviera

★★★★+

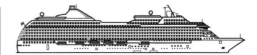

Size:. . . . . Mid-size Ship	Cabins (total):. 629
Tonnage: 66,048	Size range (sq ft/m): 172.2–2,000/16.0–185.0
Lifestyle: . . . . .Premium	Cabins (outside view): 611
Cruise line:. . . . . Oceania Cruises	Cabins (interior/no view):. 18
Former names: . . . . .none	Cabins (for one person):. 0
IMO number: 9438078	Cabins (with private balcony):. 593
Builder: . . . . Fincantieri (Italy)	Cabins (wheelchair accessible): 6
Original cost: . . . .$530 million	Wheelchair accessibility:. . . . . .Good
Entered service:. . . . . .Jul 2012	Cabin voltage: . . . . .110 and 220 Volts
Registry:. . . . . .Marshall Islands	Elevators:. 6
Length (ft/m):. 776.5/236.7	Casino (gaming tables):. . . . . Yes
Beam (ft/m):. 105.3/32.1	Slot machines:. . . . . Yes
Draft (ft/m): 24.2/7.4	Swimming pools:. 1
Propulsion/Propellers:. diesel-electric/2	Hot tubs (on deck):. 2
Passenger decks:. 11	Self-service launderette:. . . . . Yes
Total crew:. 800	Dedicated cinema/seats:. . . . . .No
Passengers (lower beds/all berths): 1,258/1,258	Library:. . . . . Yes
Passenger Space Ratio (lower beds/all berths): 51.6/51.6	Onboard currency: . . . . .US$
Crew/Passenger Ratio (lower beds/all berths):. 1.5/1.5	

A homey, comfortable, mid-size ship with a country-club feel

OVERVIEW. This ship suits mature-age adults who appreciate refined quality and style, plenty of space and comfort (no lines), and excellent cuisine and service, in a semi-casual setting with realistic pricing. Oceania Cruises has succeeded in keeping the warm, tasteful country house decor style for which its ships are known, as well as an uncomplicated layout.

THE SHIP. *Riviera* is the second newbuild (close sister to *Marina*) for this popular, small premium-ship cruise line. Its profile is quite handsome, with a nicely rounded front, and is topped by a swept-back funnel. Able to cruise at a speed 25 percent faster than Oceania Cruises' smaller ships, *Nautica* and *Regatta,* the ship can operate more longer-distance cruises.

The interior focal point is a stunning wrought-iron and Lalique glass horseshoe-shaped staircase in the main lobby. Differences from *Marina* – there are reportedly 727 of them – include better steps on the main lobby staircase, a higher ceiling on one public deck, changes to drawer depth in cabins, a hand-held shower in suites with bathtub, and faster internet speed.

Public rooms include nine bars and lounges. There is a 2,000-book library, set on the port side of the funnel housing, which also contains the staffed Oceania@Sea computer center, and Barista's coffee bar/lounge (serving the excellent illy brand Italian coffee). The ship also showcases a collection of fine Latin artwork by some of

Berlitz's Ratings		
	Possible	Achieved
Ship	500	442
Accommodation	200	179
Food	400	335
Service	400	316
Entertainment	100	82
Cruise	400	328
OVERALL SCORE		
1682 points out of 2000		

the most renowned artists from Cuba's Vanguard Movement (1927–50).

A Monte Carlo Casino is located between two bars – the Grand Bar and Martinis, with its own soft lavender-colored Casino Bar. Martinis houses a beautiful special-edition Steinway baby grand piano. There are also three boutiques, and several dining venues. There aren't that many different lounges as such because most are drinking venues.

A Culinary Center comprises a cooking demonstration kitchen and 24 workstations, with various classes run in conjunction with the US-based *Bon Appétit* magazine – there's a charge for these, but you get to eat your creations.

You can bring your paintbrushes to an Artist's Loft that has constantly changing artists. Other classes may include photography, needlepoint, scrap-booking, drawing and quilting.

The dress code is 'elegant country club attire' – no pyjamas or track suits, but no ties either (so there's no tie rack in the closets). A 15 percent gratuity is added to bar accounts.

ACCOMMODATION. There are 17 price categories, including four suite grades and four cabin grades. Price depends on size and location, but all have one thing in common – a good-sized bathroom with tub and separate shower enclosure, plus his 'n' hers toiletry cabinets. All suites/cabins have dark wood cabinetry with rounded edges. The decor includes chocolate brown, cream, and white – the sort of earthy colors that don't jar the senses. Around 96 percent of all accommodation has teak-decked balconies.

Standard veranda cabins. These measure 282 sq ft (26 sq m). Veranda- and Concierge-level cabins have a sitting area and teak balcony with faux wicker furniture. Concierge-level grades get L'Occitane toiletries.

Penthouse Suites. These measure 420 sq ft (39 sq m) with living/dining room separate from the sleeping area, walk-in closet, and bathroom with a double vanity. The large veranda has a hot tub.

Oceania Suites. These measure about 1,030 sq ft (96 sq m) and have a living room, dining room, separate bedroom, walk-in closet, teak-decked balcony with Jacuzzi tub, main bathroom, and a second bathroom for guests.

Vista Suites. These range from 1,200 to 1,500 sq ft (111–139 sq m) and offer the same features as Oceania Suites plus floor-to-ceiling windows overlooking the bow.

The Owner's Suite. At more than 2,000 sq ft (186 sq m), this spans the entire beam of the ship (about 105ft/32m). It is decked out in furniture, fabrics, lighting, and bedding from the Ralph Lauren Home collection with design by New York-based Tocar Inc. It is outfitted with a Yamaha baby grand piano, private fitness room, laptop computers, Bose audio system, and a teak-decked balcony with Jacuzzi tub.

Suite-category occupants get niceties like Champagne on arrival, 1,000-thread-count bed linen, 42-inch plasma TV sets, Hermès and Clarins bath amenities, butler service, and en suite delivery from any of the ship's restaurants. Amenities include Tranquility beds, Wi-Fi laptop computer, refrigerated mini-bar with unlimited free soft drinks and bottled water replenished daily, personal safe, writing desk, cotton bathrobes, slippers, and marble and granite bathroom. Priority check-in and early embarkation and priority luggage delivery are extra perks.

Occupants of Owner's, Vista, Oceania, and Penthouse suites can have in-suite course-by-course dining from any restaurant menu, allowing private dining as a change from restaurant dining – a nice alternative on longer voyages.

Some grades get access to an Executive or Concierge Lounge. These are great little hideaways, with sofas, Internet-connect computers, Continental breakfast items, soft drinks, magazines, and more. Self-service launderettes are on each accommodation deck – useful for long voyages.

DINING. This really is a food lover's ship that uses high-quality ingredients and has a wide selection of dining venues, providing plenty of choice, even for long cruises. However, banquette seating in some venues does not evoke the image of premium dining as much as individual seating does. Particularly notable are the breads, rolls, croissants, and brioches – all made on board from French flour and d'Isigny butter.

The Grand Dining Room has 566 seats, and a domed, or raised, central ceiling. Versace bone china, Christofle silver, fine linens are used. Canyon Ranch spa dishes are available for all meals.

Jacques, with 124 seats, is the second seagoing restaurant for French celebrity chef Jacques Pépin, Oceania's executive culinary director. It has antique oak flooring, antique flatware and Lalique glassware, and provides fine dining in an elegant but informal setting, with roast free-range meats, nine classic French dessert items, and a choice of 12 A.O.C. cheeses.

Polo Grill, with about 130 seats, serves steaks and seafood, including Oceania's signature 32-ounce bone-in King's Cut prime rib. The setting is classic traditional steakhouse, with dark wood paneling and classic white tablecloths, although the tables are close together.

Toscana is a 124-seat venue serving Italian-style cuisine (including some tasty desserts) and has Versace china.

Privée, with seating for up to 10 in a private setting, invites exclusivity for its seven-course dégustation menu.

La Réserve is the venue for wine and food, offering two different seven-course small-portion, wine-paired dégustation menus. With just 24 seats, it's also really intimate.

The Terrace Café is the ship's casual self-serve buffet-style venue. Outdoors, as an extension of the café, is Tapas on the Terrace, good for light bites – although the ceiling is low, so it can be very noisy.

Red Ginger is a specialty restaurant which offers 'classic and contemporary' Asian cuisine; the setting is visually refined, with ebony and dark wood finishes, but the banquette-style seating lets the venue down. You'll be asked by the waiter to choose your chopsticks from a lacquered presentation box.

The poolside Waves Grill, shaded from the sun, is for burgers (including fishburgers and veggie burgers), seafood and other fast food, cooked to order. Baristas coffee bar overlooks the pool deck and has excellent, free illy Italian coffee – though, sadly, it's served in paper cups.

ENTERTAINMENT. The 600-seat Marina Lounge, spans two decks, with tiered amphitheater-style seating. It's more cabaret-style entertainment than big production shows, in keeping with the cruise line's traditions.

SPA/FITNESS. The Canyon Ranch SpaClub provides wellness and personal spa treatments. The facility includes a fitness center, beauty salon, several treatment rooms (including a couples room), sauna and steam rooms, and a large thalassotherapy pool. A jogging track is located aft of the funnel, above two of the specialty restaurants. All treatments incur an automatic 18 percent gratuity – almost one-fifth of the treatment price.

Rotterdam
★★★★

Size:..............................Mid-size Ship				

Size:..................................... Mid-size Ship
Tonnage: 59,855
Lifestyle: ....Premium
Cruise line:......................... Holland America Line
Former names: ....*none*
IMO number:................................9122552
Builder: .... Fincantieri (Italy)
Original cost:............................. $250 million
Entered service:............................. Dec 1997
Registry:...............................The Netherlands
Length (ft/m):.............................. 777.5/237.0
Beam (ft/m):............................... 105.8/32.2
Draft (ft/m):................................... 25.5/7.8
Propulsion/Propellers:........... diesel-electric (37,500kW)/2
Passenger decks:..................................12
Total crew:.......................................600
Passengers (lower beds/alll berths):............. 1,404/1,802
Passenger Space Ratio (lower beds/all berths): 42.6/33.2
Crew/Passenger Ratio (lower beds/all berths):......... 2.3/3.0

Cabins (total):.....................................702
Size range (sq ft/m):.............184.0–1,124.8/17.1–104.5
Cabins (outside view):..............................577
Cabins (interior/no view):..........................125
Cabins (for one person):..............................0
Cabins (with private balcony):......................192
Cabins (wheelchair accessible): 25
Wheelchair accessibility:......................... Best
Cabin voltage: ....110 and 220 volts
Elevators:...12
Casino (gaming tables):............................ Yes
Slot machines:.................................... Yes
Swimming pools:..................2 (1 w/sliding glass door)
Hot tubs (on deck):..................................2
Self-service launderette:.......................... Yes
Dedicated cinema/seats:........................... Yes
Library: .... Yes
Onboard currency: ....US$

Dutch traditions and decor for senior-age cruisers

OVERVIEW. This is quite a contemporary ship for Holland America Line, with light, bright decor. It is an extremely comfortable vessel with elegant and luxurious decorative features. But these are marred by the poor quality of dining room food and service and a lack of understanding of what it takes to make the 'luxury' cruise experience touted in the company's brochures.

THE SHIP. This latest *Rotterdam*, the sixth Holland America Line ship to bear the name, is capable of 25 knots – useful for longer itineraries. It has been built to look like a slightly larger but much sleeker version of the S-class ships, while retaining the graceful lines of its immediate predecessor, including a nicely raked bow and a more rounded exterior. Also retained are the familiar interior flow and design style, and twin-funnel.

Two decks, Promenade Deck and Upper Promenade Deck, house most of the public rooms, and are sandwiched between several accommodation decks. The layout is quite easy to learn, and the signage is good.

The interior decor is restrained, with much use of wood accenting. As a whole, the decor is extremely refined, with much of the traditional ocean liner detailing so loved by frequent HAL passengers. A three-deck-high atrium has an oval, instead of circular, shape. Its focal point is a huge 'one-of-a-kind' custom-made clock, based on an antique Flemish original that includes an astrolabe, an astrological clock, and 14 other clocks.

Berlitz's Ratings

	Possible	Achieved
Ship	500	404
Accommodation	200	157
Food	400	267
Service	400	268
Entertainment	100	73
Cruise	400	288

**OVERALL SCORE
1457 points out of 2000**

One room has a glass ceiling similar to that aboard a former *Statendam*. The Ambassador's Lounge has an interesting brass dance floor, similar to the dance floor that adorned the Ritz-Carlton room aboard the previous *Rotterdam*.

Instead of just two staircases aboard the S-class ships, *Rotterdam* has three – better from the viewpoint of safety, passenger accessibility, and evacuation. A pool, on the Lido Deck between the mast and the ship's twin funnels, is covered by a glass dome.

Popcorn is available at the Wajang Theatre for moviegoers, while adjacent is the popular Java Café. The casino, located in the middle of a major passenger flow, has blackjack, roulette, poker, and dice tables alongside the requisite rows of slot machines.

Holland America Line has a long legacy in Dutch maritime history. The $2 million worth of artwork here consists of a collection of 17th-century Dutch and Japanese artifacts together with contemporary works specially created for the ship, although there seems little linkage between some of the items.

HAL's Signature of Excellence program has created 'Mix,' a new open area with comfortable sofa and armchair seating in small alcove-like setting adjacent to a shopping area. The trendy, upbeat space combines three specialty theme bars: Champagne (serving Champagne and sparkling wines from around the world), Martinis (in individual shakers), and Spirits & Ales (a sports bar with beer, baseball, and basketball). Microsoft Surface touch-screen technology enhances checkers and chess, air hockey, and other sports games.

With one whole deck of suites – and a dedicated, private concierge lounge, and preferential passenger treatment – the company has in effect created a two-class ship. Passenger niggles include inadequate room service, poor staff communication, and the charge to use the washing machines and dryers in the self-service launderette – petty and irritating, particularly for the occupants of suites, as they pay high prices for their cruises.

In a 2009 refit, 23 Veranda Deck cabins were converted into 'Spa Cabins,' while new lanai-style cabins were created on Lower Promenade Deck.

FAMILIES. The ship has allotted more space to children's and teens' play areas, although these really are token gestures by a company that traditionally doesn't cater well to children. However, grandparents do take their grandchildren with them – pleasing parents, who get a well-deserved break. Enhanced children's programming is brought into play according to the number of children carried.

ACCOMMODATION. There are 17 categories, priced by grade, size and location. Accommodation is spread over five decks, and some cabins have full or partially obstructed views. Interestingly, no cabin is more than 144ft (44m) from a stairway, which makes it easier to get from cabins to public rooms. All cabin doors have a bird's-eye maple look, and hallways have framed fabric panels to make them less clinical. Cabin televisions carry CNN.

All standard inside and outside cabins are tastefully furnished, with twin beds that convert to queen-size, though space is tight for walking between beds and vanity unit. There is a decent amount of closet and drawer space, but this will prove tight for longer voyages.

The fully tiled bathrooms are disappointingly small, particularly for long cruises, and have small shower tubs, utilitarian toiletries cupboards, and exposed under-sink plumbing. There is no detailing to distinguish them significantly from bathrooms aboard the S-class ships.

There are 36 full veranda suites on Navigation Deck, including four penthouse suites, which share a private Concierge Lounge with a concierge to handle such things as special dining arrangements, shore excursions, and special requests – although strangely there are no butlers for these suites, as aboard many ships with similar facilities. Each suite has a separate steward's entrance and separate bedroom, dressing and living areas. Suite passengers get personal stationery, complimentary laundry and ironing, cocktail-hour hors d'oeuvres, and other goodies, as well as priority embarkation and disembarkation. The concierge lounge, with its latticework teak detailing and private library is accessible only by private key-card.

Disabled passengers have a choice of 20 cabins, including two of the large 'penthouse' suites that include concierge services. However, there are different cabin configurations, and it is wise to check with your booking agent.

DINING. The La Fontaine Dining Room seats 747, spans two decks, and has are tables for four, six, or eight, but only nine tables for two. Both open seating and assigned seating are available, while breakfast and lunch are open seating, where you'll be seated by restaurant staff when you enter. Fine Rosenthal china and good cutlery are provided.

Other dining options. Pinnacle Grill is an extra-cost 88-seat restaurant that is more upscale and more intimate than the main dining room. It also features higher-quality ingredients and better presentation than the main dining room. It is on Promenade Deck and fronts onto the second level of the atrium lobby. Pacific Northwest cuisine is featured, together with an array of premium-quality steaks. There are fine table settings, china and silverware, and leather-bound menus. The wine list consists mostly of American wines. Reservations are required and there's a cover charge – but the prime steaks are worth it.

For casual meals, the Lido Restaurant is a self-serve buffet venue. A section of this restaurant turns into the Canaletto Restaurant by night, when Italian dishes are featured (reservations are required and a cover charge applies).

Grilled fast food items (hamburger, hot dogs, etc.) can be obtained outdoors from the Terrace Grill, forward of the Lido Pool.

ENTERTAINMENT. The 577-seat Showroom at Sea is the venue for all production shows, the strongest cabaret, and other entertainment. It is two decks high, with seating on both main and balcony levels. The decor includes umbrella-shaped gold ceiling lamps made from Murano glass (from Venice), and the stage has hydraulic lifts and three video screens, as well as a closed-loop system for the hearing-impaired.

SPA/FITNESS. The Ocean Spa is one deck above the navigation bridge at the very forward part of the ship. It includes a gymnasium with all the latest muscle-pumping exercise machines, including an abundance of treadmills, with forward views over the ship's bows. There's an aerobics exercise area, large beauty salon with ocean-view windows to the port side, several treatment rooms, and men's and women's sauna, steam room, and changing areas.

Royal Clipper
★★★★

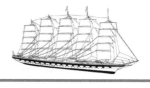

Size:...................................Boutique Ship	Cabins (total):....................................114
Tonnage: 5,061	Size range (sq ft/m): 100.0–320.0/9.3–29.7
Lifestyle: ....Premium	Cabins (outside view):............................108
Cruise line:................................ Star Clippers	Cabins (interior/no view):............................6
Former names: ....none	Cabins (for one person):..............................0
IMO number:................................8712178	Cabins (with private balcony):........................14
Builder: .... De Merwede (Holland)	Cabins (wheelchair accessible): 0
Original cost:............................... $75 million	Wheelchair accessibility:........................None
Entered service:........................... .Oct 2000	Cabin voltage: .... 220 volts
Registry:...................................Luxembourg	Elevators:..0
Length (ft/m):............................ 439.6/134.0	Casino (gaming tables):..............................No
Beam (ft/m):................................. 54.1/16.5	Slot machines:......................................No
Draft (ft/m):..................................... 18.5/5.6	Swimming pools:.....................................3
Propulsion/Propellers:..................diesel (3,700kW)/1	Hot tubs (on deck):...................................0
Passenger decks:.....................................5	Self-service launderette:.............................No
Total crew:...106	Dedicated cinema/seats:.............................No
Passengers (lower beds/alll berths): 228/255	Library: .... Yes
Passenger Space Ratio (lower beds/all berths): 22.1/19.8	Onboard currency: .... Euros
Crew/Passenger Ratio (lower beds/all berths): 2.1/2.4	

The ultimate tall ship, exuding character and charm

OVERVIEW. *Royal Clipper* best suits couples and singles who would probably never even consider a 'normal' cruise ship, but who enjoy sailing and the thrill of ocean and wind, but want a package that includes accommodation, food, like-minded companions, and interesting destinations, and don't want the bother of owning or chartering their own yacht. This is the bee's knees.

Berlitz's Ratings		
	Possible	Achieved
Ship	500	405
Accommodation	200	157
Food	400	288
Service	400	296
Entertainment	100	77
Cruise	400	306
OVERALL SCORE		
1529 points out of 2000		

THE SHIP. The culmination of an owner's childhood dream, *Royal Clipper* is a stunning sight under sail. It's marketed as the world's largest true fully rigged sailing ship – it has five masts – and is a logical addition to the company's two other, smaller, four-mast sail-cruise ships (*Star Clipper* and *Star Flyer*).

Royal Clipper's five-masted design is based on the only other five-masted sailing ship to be built, the 1902-built German tall ship *Preussen*, and has approximately the same dimensions, albeit 46ft (14m) shorter (it is much larger than the famous *Cutty Sark*, for example). It is almost 40ft (12.1m) longer than the largest sailing ship presently in commission – the four-mast Russian barkentine *Sedov*. To keep things in perspective, *Royal Clipper* is the same length overall as *Wind Spirit* and *Wind Star* – the computer-controlled cruise-sail vessels of Windstar Cruises.

The construction time for this ship was remarkably short, owing to the fact that its hull had been almost completed (at Gdansk shipyard, Poland) for another owner but became available to Star Clippers for completion and fitting out. The ship is instantly recogniz-

able due to its geometric blue and white hull markings. Power winches, as well as hand winches, are employed in deck fittings, as well as a mix of horizontal furling for the square sails and hydraulic power assist to roll the square sails along the yardarm. The sail handling system, which was designed by the ship's owner, Mikael Krafft, is such that it can be converted from a full rigger to a schooner in an incredibly short time.

Its masts reach as high as 197ft (60m) above the waterline, and the top 19ft (5.8m) can be hinged over 90° to clear bridges, cable lines, and other port-based obstacles. Watching the sailors manipulate ropes, rigging, and sails is like watching a ballet – the precision and cohesion of a group of men who make it all look so simple.

As a passenger, you are allowed to climb to special lookout points aloft – maybe even for a glass of Champagne. Passengers are also allowed on the bridge at any time – but not in the galley or engine room.

The ship has a large amount of open deck space and sunning space – something most tall ships lack – although, naturally, this is laid with ropes due to the rigging. A marina platform can be lowered at the stern, from where you can use the surfboards, sailing dinghies, take a ride on the ship's own banana boat, or go waterskiing or swimming. Snorkeling gear is available free, but there is a charge for scuba gear. You will be asked to sign a waiver if you wish to use the watersports equipment.

Inside, a midships atrium three decks high sits under one of the ship's three swimming pools, and sunlight streams down through a piano lounge on the uppermost level inside the ship and down into the dining room, which is on the lower level. A forward observation lounge is a real plus, and this is connected to the piano lounge via a central corridor. An Edwardian library/card room is decorated with a belle-époque fireplace. A lounge, the Captain Nemo Club, is where passengers can observe fish and sea life when the ship is at anchor, through thick glass portholes, floodlit from underneath at night to attract the fish.

This delightful, quite spectacular tall ship for tourists operates seven-night and 14-day cruises in the Grenadines and Lower Windward Islands of the Caribbean during the winter and seven-night and 14-night cruises in the Mediterranean in summer. It is good to note that the officers navigate using both traditional (sextant) and contemporary methods (advanced electronic positioning system).

Being a tall ship with true sailing traditions, there is, naturally, a parrot (sometimes kept in a large, gilded cage, but often seen around the ship on someone's shoulder), which is part of the crew, as aboard all Star Clippers' ships. The general ambience is extremely relaxed, friendly and casual – completely unpretentious. The passenger mix is international, often consisting of a good cross-section of yachting types. The dress code is casual at all times (shorts and casual tops are the order of the day – yachting wear), with no ties needed at any time.

There is no doubt that *Royal Clipper* is a superb vessel for the actual experience of sailing – a tall ship probably without equal, as much more time is spent actually under sail than aboard almost any other tall ship, including the smaller *Sea Cloud* and *Sea Cloud II*. However, apart from the sailing experience, it is in the cuisine and service that the lack of professionalism and poor standards of delivery shows. The result is a score that could be higher if the cuisine and service were better.

The suites and cabins are larger than those aboard the tall ships of the Windjammer Barefoot Cruises fleet, while, in general, smaller than aboard *Sea Cloud* and *Sea Cloud II*. While the food and service are far superior to the Windjammers, both are well below the standard found aboard *Sea Cloud* and *Sea Cloud II*. I do not include the Windstar Cruises ships (*Wind Spirit*, *Wind Star*, *Wind Surf*), because they cannot, in any sense of the word, be considered tall ships. *Royal Clipper*, however, is exactly that – a real, working, wind-and-sails-in-your-face tall ship with a highly personable captain and crew that welcome you as if you were part of the team.

This vessel is not for the physically impaired, or for children. The steps of the internal stairs are steep, as in most sailing vessels. Any gratuities you give are pooled and divided among all members of the crew.

What gives the ship a little extra in the scoring department is the fact that many water sports are included in the price of a cruise.

ACCOMMODATION. There are eight accommodation grades, priced according to grade, size, and location: Owner's Suites (2), Deluxe Suites (14), and Categories 1–6. All have polished wood-trimmed cabinetry and wall-to-wall carpeting, personal safe, full-length mirror, small TV set with audio channels and 24-hour text-based news, and private bathroom. All have twin beds (86 of which convert into a queen-size bed, while 28 are fixed queen-size beds that cannot be separated), hairdryer, and satellite-linked telephone. The six interior cabins and a handful of other cabins have a permanently fixed double bed.

Most cabins have a privacy curtain, so that you cannot be seen from the hallway when the cabin attendant opens the door – useful if you're undressed. In addition, 27 cabins sleep three.

The two owner's suites, located at the very aft of the ship, provide the most lavish accommodation, and have one queen-size bed and one double bed, a separate living area with semi-circular sofa, large vanity desk, mini-bar/refrigerator, marble-clad bathroom with whirlpool bathtub, plus one guest bathroom, and butler service. The two suites have an interconnecting door, so that the combined super-suite can sleep eight persons. However, there is no private balcony.

The 14 'Deck Suites' have interesting names: Ariel, Cutty Sark, Doriana, Eagle Wing, Flying Cloud, France, Golden Gate, Gloria, Great Republic, Passat, Pommern, Preussen, and Thermopylae. However, they are not actually suites, as the sleeping area cannot be separated from the lounge – they are simply larger cabins with a more luxurious interior, more storage space, and a larger bathroom. Each has two lower beds convertible to a queen-size, small lounge area, mini-bar/refrigerator, writing desk, small private balcony, and marble-clad bathroom with combination whirlpool tub/shower, washbasin, and toilet, and butler service. The door to the balcony can be opened so that fresh air floods the room; note that there is a 12-inch (30-cm) threshold to step over.

There are no curtains, only roll-down shades for the windows and balcony door. The balcony itself typically has two white plastic chairs and drinks table; however, teak chairs and table would be more in keeping with the nature of the ship. The 14 balconies are not particularly private, and most have ship's tenders or Zodiacs overhanging them, or some rigging obscuring the views.

Two other name cabins (Lord Nelson and Marco Polo – designated as Category 1 cabins) are located aft, but do not have private balconies, although the facilities are similar.

The interior cabins and the lowest grades of outside-view cabins are extremely small and tight, with very little room to move around the beds. So take only the minimum amount of clothing and luggage. When in cabins where beds are linked together to form a double bed, you will have to clamber up over the front of the bed, as both sides have built-in storm barriers (this applies in inclement weather conditions only).

There is a small room service menu (all items cost extra).

DINING. The Dining Room is constructed on several connecting levels (getting used to the steps is not easy), and seats all passengers at one seating under a three-deck-high atrium dome. You can sit with anyone you wish at tables for four, six, eight, or 10. However, it is a noisy dining room, due to the positioning of the many waiter stations. Some tables are badly positioned so that correct waiter service is impossible, and much reaching over has to be done in order to serve everyone.

One corner can be closed off for private parties. Breakfasts and lunches are self-serve buffets, while dinner is a sit-down affair with table service, although the ambience is always friendly and lighthearted. The wine list consists of very young wines, and prices are quite high. The cuisine, although perfectly acceptable, is certainly nothing to write home about.

ENTERTAINMENT. There are no entertainment shows, nor are any expected by passengers aboard a tall ship such as this, where sailing is the main purpose. There is, however, live music, provided by a single lounge pianist/singer. Otherwise, dinner is the main evening event, as well as 'Captain's Storytime,' recaps of the day's interesting events, and conversation with fellow passengers in the lounge or on deck under the stars provides engaging entertainment.

During the day, when the ship is sailing, passengers can learn about the sails, and the captain or chief officer will give briefings as the sails are being furled and unfurled. The closest this tall ship comes to any kind of 'show' is when, one evening towards the end of each cruise, a 'sailor's choir,' comprised of the ship's crew, presents a nautical performance of sea songs, sea shanties, and other light diversions.

SPA/FITNESS. The Royal Spa is located on the lowest passenger deck and, although not large, incorporates a beauty salon, an extra-charge Moroccan steam room, and a small gymnasium with porthole views, several muscle-pump machines, body toning equipment, treadmills, rowing machines, and exercycles. Thai massage as well as traditional massage, aromatherapy facials, and other beauty treatments, are available.

A sails guide to Royal Clipper

Up to 42 square-rigged sails can be used aboard *Royal Clipper*. 26 square sails (fore upper topgallant, fore lower topgallant, fore upper topsail, fore lower topsail, foresail, main royal, main upper topgallant, main lower topgallant, main upper topsail, main lower topsail, mainsail, middle royal, middle upper topgallant, middle lower topgallant, middle upper topsail, middle lower topsail, middle course, mizzen upper topgallant, mizzen lower topgallant, mizzen upper topsail, mizzen lower topsail, mizzen course, jigger topgallant, jigger upper topsail, jigger lower topsail, crossjack), 11 staysails (main royal staysail, main topgallant staysail, main topmast staysail, middle royal staysail, middle topgallant staysail, middle topmast staysail, mizzen royal staysail, mizzen topgallant staysail, mizzen topmast staysail, jigger topgallant staysail, jigger topmast staysail); four jibs (flying jib, outer jib, inner jib, fore topmast staysail); and one gaff-rigged spanker, it looks quite magnificent when under full sail – an area of 55,995 sq ft (5,202 sq m).

Royal Princess
★★★★

Size:.	.Large Resort Ship	Cabins (total):.	1,780
Tonnage:	141,200	Size range (sq ft/m):	n/a
Lifestyle:	.Standard	Cabins (outside view):	1,438
Cruise line:.	Princess Cruises	Cabins (interior/no view):.	.342
Former names:	none	Cabins (for one person):.	0
IMO number:	.9584712	Cabins (with private balcony):	1,438
Builder:	Fincantieri (Italy)	Cabins (wheelchair accessible):	.36
Original cost:	. €775 million	Wheelchair accessibility:	Best
Entered service:.	Jun 2013	Cabin voltage:	.110 and 220 volts
Registry:.	Bermuda	Elevators:.	.14
Length (ft/m):.	.1,082.6/330.0	Casino (gaming tables):.	Yes
Beam (ft/m):.	126.3/38.5	Slot machines:.	Yes
Draft (ft/m):	27.8/8.5	Swimming pools:.	2
Propulsion/Propellers:	diesel-electric (52MW)/2	Hot tubs (on deck):.	.6
Passenger decks:.	17	Self-service launderette:	Yes
Total crew:.	1,346	Dedicated cinema/seats:.	.No
Passengers (lower beds/alll berths):	3,560/4,610	Library:	Yes
Passenger Space Ratio (lower beds/all berths):	39.6/30.6	Onboard currency:	.US$
Crew/Passenger Ratio (lower beds/all berths):	2.6/3.4		

A large, family-friendly, multi-choice resort ship

OVERVIEW. *Royal Princess* really is a grand resort (she was named in Southampton by the Duchess of Cambridge on 13 June 2013 – and the Champagne bottle did break), a playground in which to roam when not ashore. Princess Cruises has taken the best features of its previous large Grand-class ship, fine-tuned them to the latest passenger tastes, and included more hedonistic retreats and food venues. The company delivers a consistent and well-packaged cruise vacation at an attractive price, which is why passengers keep returning.

Berlitz's Ratings		
	Possible	Achieved
Ship	500	412
Accommodation	200	161
Food	400	267
Service	400	295
Entertainment	100	84
Cruise	400	305
OVERALL SCORE		
1524 points out of 2000		

THE SHIP. Royal Princess is a fascinating ship that has quite a streamlined, contemporary look for its size (the Duchess of Cambridge acted as godmother – before she became a mother herself!). It has larger public areas to accommodate the increase in passenger numbers compared to the smaller Grand-class ships, on which the ship's design is loosely based. It is the third time the name *Royal Princess* has been given to a Princess ship (the name Royal Princess was also the former name of *Artania* between 1984 and 2005, and the present *Adonia* between 2007 and 2011).

It has a walk-around deck that is mostly outside (under the lifeboats), but partly inside at the front and stern of the ship – a practical feature. And, in terms of practical design, the lifeboats are located outside the main public room areas, so that they don't impair the view from balcony cabins.

One notable innovation is the superb 'over-the-water' SeaWalk, a top-deck glass-floor enclosed walkway (stiletto heels not advisable!) on the starboard side that extends almost 30ft (9.1m) beyond the vessel's edge and forms part of a lounge/bar venue. This is where you go for dramatic views of the sea – some 128ft (39m) below (you can also see over many of the balcony cabins in the central section below the walkway and bar). It reminds me of Gallery 9 in the *Titanic* museum in Belfast, Northern Ireland, where you stand on a glass floor and look down to the famous ship seemingly lost beneath you. On the ship's port side is a similarly unique cantilevered SeaView bar (maybe it's a good place to have a 'Sea and C'!).

A poolside 'Movies Under the Stars' (it's the largest in the fleet) has a huge high-definition screen, located just forward of the swept-back funnel in a mid-ship position; popcorn is provided, of course. The pool itself (called 'Fountain Pool') has curved wading areas around it that make it appear larger than it is. Adjacent is a 'dip' pool and several hot tubs. At night, the area (known as the 'tropical island') changes into an outdoor dance center with a water and light show.

Other outdoor features include an adult-only 'Retreat Pool' (it's free for everyone) surrounded by six extra-cost 'private' cabanas that appear to be floating on the water.

For real escapees, an extra-cost adults-only retreat called The Sanctuary is larger than aboard the Grand-class ships and has more amenities. It includes four rentable cabanas, two extra-cost Lotus-Spa-operated 'couples' cabanas, and has its own retreat pool and relaxation areas (in both sunny and shaded positions).

There are three main stair towers and elevator banks, with panoramic-view elevators in the central bank. The ship's interior decor is warm and attractive, with an abundance of earth tones that suit both American and European tastes.

One of the line's hallmark areas, the Piazza Atrium is the ship's multi-faceted social hub and combines a specialty dining spot, with light meals, snack food items, pastries, beverages, entertainment, shopping, and guest services all in one area. It is larger than aboard any other Princess Cruises ship, and has multi-level horseshoe-shaped 'flowing' stairways, lots of mood lighting effects, a small dance floor, and a delightful tea tower hosted by a 'tea sommelier.'

The base level of the atrium includes Vines, a wine bar with sushi and tapas; International Café, for coffees, teas, panini, and pastries; Sabatini's, a Tuscan specialty extra-cost restaurant, with both regular and à la carte menus; and a gift shop. Upstairs, level two includes a 121-seat Alfredo's Pizzeria (perhaps the largest pizzeria at sea; pizzas are free), Bellini's (a bar serving Bellini drinks) a photo gallery, and the reception and shore excursion counters. On the third level, Crooners Bar has glass pianos and dueling pianist entertainers; there's also a Seafood Bar.

If you aren't used to large ships, it will take you some time to find your way around. Despite the company's claim that it offers passengers a 'small ship feel, big ship choice' it's a little disjointed on the upper decks. However, Royal Princess is really a comfortable ship in which to take a cruise. Gratuities are added to your onboard account. A sister ship to *Royal Princess (Regal Princess)* debuts in spring 2014.

FAMILIES. Children have their own playrooms (Pelicans, Shockwaves), teens-only chill-out room, pools, fitness and open deck areas, away from adult areas, plus a host of energetic, dedicated children's and youth counselors. There are good sports facilities for younger cruisers, too, so that they can be kept really active. Children can eat in a dedicated section of the Horizon Court buffet area, which is equipped with kid-height tables and chairs. A total of 50 cabins have interconnecting doors – good for families with children.

ACCOMMODATION. There are five main types of accommodation and a bewildering number of different price grades: (a) grand suite; (b) 40 suites with balcony; (c) 306 mini-suites with balcony; (d) 360 deluxe outside-view balcony cabins; (e) 732 outside-view cabins with balcony; and (e) 342 interior cabins. Pricing depends on two things: size and location. Outside-view cabins account for about 81 percent of all accommodation, and have a balcony; those located at the stern are

the quietest and most sought-after.

All accommodation grades share energy-efficient lighting and key card readers that automatically turn off lights when occupants leave their cabins. All cabins get beds with upholstered headboards, wall-mounted TV sets, additional 220v electrical socket, turndown service and heart-shaped chocolates on pillows each night, bathrobes (on request unless you are in suite-grade accommodation), and toiletries. A hairdryer is provided in all cabins, sensibly located at the vanity desk unit in the living area. Bathrooms generally have a good amount of open shelf storage space for toiletries, and – in a first for Princess Cruises – all bathrooms have hand-held, flexi-hose showers, and shower enclosures larger than aboard other Princess ships, although they still have a shower curtain instead of more contemporary glass doors.

Suite and mini-suite grade occupants have their own concierge lounge – useful for making dining, spa, and shore excursion reservations. They also get more amenities and larger TV sets, larger towels, and two washbasins.

Some of the most sought-after suites are located aft, occupying the corner (port and starboard) positions. They have destination names (Dominica, Barbados, Verona, Torino, Santorini, Mykonos, Valencia, Seville, Bora Bora, Tahiti, Kauai, Hilo, Sydney, Auckland).

DINING. There are three 'formal' main dining rooms: Allegro, Concerto, and Symphony. You can choose either traditional two-seating dining (typically 6pm and 8:15pm for dinner), or 'anytime dining' – where you choose when and with whom you want to eat. However, if you want to see a show in the evening, then your dining time will be dictated by the time of the show, which rather limits your choice.

A 12-seat circular table is located within the Wine Cellar of the Allegro and Symphony dining rooms. This extra-cost, reservations-required venue is ideal for private functions and celebrations. Also available is a private exclusive Chef's Table Lumière, located within the Concerto dining room. It has a custom-made glass dining table and fine dining utensils. In both Allegro and Symphony, you can reserve a private table (at extra cost) for up to 12 in each venue's wine room, for meals that are paired with specific wines – ideal for that special celebration and for something different to the norm.

Other dining options. Extra-cost, reservations-required Sabatini's (Vines Wine Bar is located inside), on the lower atrium level, is an Italian restaurant with colorful Tuscany-themed decor. Named after Trattoria Sabatini, the 200-year-old institution in Florence, it serves Italian-style pasta dishes with a choice of sauces, as well as Italian-style entrées, including tiger prawns and lobster tail, all provided with flair and entertainment by energetic waiters. There's both a table d'hôte and an à la carte menu. This venue, which is all about Tuscany, also hosts Italian wine tasting.

Alfredo's is a sit-down pizzeria named after Alfredo Marzi, corporate chef for Princess Cruises, and the venue specializes in 'authentic' family-friendly-size pizzas.

Ocean Terrace, located on the upper level of the three-deck-high atrium lobby, is a seafood bar. International Café, on the lowest level of the Piazza Atrium, is the place for extra-cost coffees, pastries, paninis, and more. Vines Wine Bar, on the lowest level of the Piazza Atrium, is an escape from all the noise and hubbub elsewhere – for a glass of extra-cost wine and tapas. It's a pleasant area in which to while away a late afternoon, trying out new wines.

The Crown Grill is for all-American premium-quality steaks and grilled seafood. It is an extra-cost, reservations-required, à la carte dining venue, adjacent to the Wheelhouse Bar, on the uppermost level of the three-deck-high atrium.

For casual meals, the self-serve buffet venue – Horizon Court – which seats 900 indoors and 350 outdoors at the adjacent Horizon Terrace, and there are multiple active cooking stations. Sections of the eatery highlight specific themes, such as Mediterranean, Asian, and Italian cuisine; there's also a deli section. At night, the aft section becomes the Horizon Bistro, for casual dinners. Certain evenings will feature special themes and foods, such as British pub food or as a Brazilian churrascarria (for Brazilian-style carved meat dishes). Rotisseries, carvings, crab, fondue. A hibachi grill and other 'active' cooking stations (for regional specialties, for example) are part of the scenario. It all translates to a more flexible large-scale eatery – but very useful as a change to the main dining rooms. Additionally, Horizon Court now features its own bakery, as a separate area. Called the Horizon Bistro Pastry Shop, it offers freshly baked bread, croissants, pastry items, waffles, and other pastry items throughout the day.

Outside on the pool deck, the poolside Trident Grill (for hamburgers, hot dogs and other fast-food grilled items during the day) becomes a traditional smokehouse barbecue in the evenings. Meanwhile, Mexican-style eats can be obtained from the Outrigger Bar, where Margaritas will be the evening specialty drink.

ENTERTAINMENT. The 1,000-seat Princess Theater is the ship's main showlounge. The state-of-the-art venue is two decks high, and is designed for the large-scale production shows that Princess Cruises is renowned for, and has fine views from all seats (no pillars to spoil the view - an outstanding achievement in such a large room).

A 'Princess Live' television studio features stand-up comedy and other small-audience entertainment features. Aft on the same deck is Vista Lounge (although there is no view), also an entertainment venue, with a large dance floor (so rare aboard today's large resort ships). And, on the subject of dancing, the ship has a number of gentlemen dance hosts for women without partners.

Club 6 is the place to go for the intimate late-night dance crowd.

SPA/FITNESS. The Lotus Spa is large, and is located forward on the lower level of the atrium, so it doesn't take away premium outdoor-view real estate space (it's adjacent to Sabatini's Italian Restaurant). Separate facilities for men and women include a sauna, steam room, and changing rooms; common facilities include a relaxation/waiting zone, body-pampering treatment rooms. A gymnasium packed with the latest high-tech, muscle-pumping cardiovascular equipment is located aft on a higher deck.

The Enclave is an extra-cost inner area that contains a hydrotherapy pool, warm stone beds and relaxing waterbeds, plus a variety of saunas and steam rooms. There's also a 'Scrub and Shine' bar to prepare you for your booked body treatments in one of the 18 massage/body treatment rooms (including two for couples).

The Lotus Spa is operated by Steiner Leisure. You can make online reservations for any spa treatments before your cruise, which could be a time-saver, if you can plan ahead. Some fitness classes are free, while others cost extra. Children and teens have their own fitness rooms adjacent to their age-related facilities.

For the sporting-inclined, an outdoor area called Sports Central features an outdoor basketball court (called Center Court), table-tennis area, putting green (The Greens), jogging track and a 'shooting range.'

Ruby Princess
★★★★

Size:.....................................Large Resort Ship	Cabins (total):.....................................1,557
Tonnage:...113,561	Size range (sq ft/m):..................163–1,279/15.1–118.8
Lifestyle:...Standard	Cabins (outside view):..............................1,105
Cruise line:...............................Princess Cruises	Cabins (interior/no view):.............................452
Former names:...................................none	Cabins (for one person):...............................0
IMO number:...................................1890038	Cabins (with private balcony):........................881
Builder:..............................Fincantieri (Italy)	Cabins (wheelchair accessible):........................25
Original cost:................................$500 million	Wheelchair accessibility:............................Good
Entered service:...............................Sep 2008	Cabin voltage:...............................110 volts
Registry:..Bermuda	Elevators:...14
Length (ft/m):..............................951.4/290.0	Casino (gaming tables):..............................Yes
Beam (ft/m):................................118.1/36.0	Slot machines:.....................................Yes
Draft (ft/m):..................................26.2/8.0	Swimming pools:.....................................3
Propulsion/Propellers:..........diesel-electric (42,000kW)/2	Hot tubs (on deck):....................................9
Passenger decks:....................................15	Self-service launderette:.............................Yes
Total crew:......................................1,200	Dedicated cinema/seats:...............................No
Passengers (lower beds/alll berths):..........3,114/3,782	Library:..Yes
Passenger Space Ratio (lower beds/all berths):.......36.4/30.0	Onboard currency:..................................US$
Crew/Passenger Ratio (lower beds/all berths):.........2.5/3.1	

> **A large ship with sedate decor, for family-friendly cruising**

OVERVIEW. This ship, among the best in the standard family market, is a veritable resort playground. Princess Cruises delivers a consistently fine, well-packaged vacation product, always with a good degree of style, at a highly competitive price. Passenger flow is well thought-out and, despite its large capacity, there's little congestion.

THE SHIP. *Ruby Princess* has the same profile, interior layout, and public rooms as sister ships *Crown Princess* (2006) and *Emerald Princess* (2007). Although it accommodates over 500 more passengers than earlier half-sisters such as *Diamond Princess*, the outdoor deck space remains the same, as do the number of elevators – so waiting time can be frustrating during peak usage. The Passenger Space Ratio is also considerably reduced.

The Sanctuary, an extra-cost adults-only retreat, is a facility worth paying extra for if you are cruising in a warm-weather area. It is located forward on the uppermost deck, it provides a 'private' place to relax and unwind and includes attendants to provide chilled face towels and deliver water and light bites; there are also two outdoor cabanas for private couples massage.

While The Sanctuary steals space from what used to be a communal passenger area, it is worth the extra cost. There's a good sheltered faux wood promenade strolling deck – it's actually painted steel – which almost wraps around the front and aft sections of the ship; three times round is equal to one mile. The outdoor pools have beach-like surroundings, and Movies

Berlitz's Ratings		
	Possible	Achieved
Ship	500	377
Accommodation	200	147
Food	400	249
Service	400	285
Entertainment	100	81
Cruise	400	295
OVERALL SCORE		
1434 points out of 2000		

Under the Skies and major sporting events are shown on a 300-sq-ft (28-sq-m) movie screen located at the pool in front of the large funnel structure. Movies afloat in the open are a big hit with passengers.

With the interior layout and flow similar to that of the sister ships, the main public bars and lounges are located off one double-wide promenade deck. The main lobby is the focal meeting point. Called La Piazza, it's like a town square. It houses a 44-seat International Café with a patisserie/deli and lots of nice cakes and pastries, and Vines, a wine/cheese corner combined with a sushi/tapas counter.

The library is in a little corner adjacent to the wood-paneled Wheelhouse Bar (a Pub Lunch is offered on sea days; it includes sausages and mash, cottage pie, fish and chips, and ploughman's lunch – at no extra cost); the room is adorned with ship models and nautical memorabilia. There are many other pleasant bars and lounges to enjoy. One intimate lounge is Crooners, a New York-style piano bar, with around 70 seats on the upper level of the lobby, but perhaps the nicest of all is Adagio's.

High atop the stern is a ship-wide glass-walled disco pod. It looks like an aerodynamic spoiler and is positioned high above the water, with spectacular views. It would make a great penthouse, but it is a good place to read a book during the day.

Ruby Princess also has a wedding chapel, Hearts and Minds (also used for renewal of vows ceremonies); a live web-cam can relay ceremonies via the Internet. The ship's captain can legally marry American couples, thanks to the ship's Bermuda registry and a special dispensation.

The casino, Gatsby's, has more than 260 slot machines (linked slot machines provide a combined payout), and blackjack, craps, and roulette tables for serious gamers.

Whether you'll have a relaxing vacation is a moot point. But, with so many choices and 'small' rooms, the ship has been extremely well designed, and odds are you'll enjoy it. If you aren't used to large ships, it will take you some time to find your way around, despite the company's claim that it offers passengers a 'small ship feel, big ship choice.'

FAMILIES. For children, there are several playrooms, a teen room, and a host of trained counselors. Children have their own pools, hot tubs, and open deck area at the stern, away from adult areas. There are good netted-in areas; one section has a dip pool, while another has a mini-basketball court. The Wizard's Academy is an enrichment program from the California Science Center.

ACCOMMODATION. There are six main types of cabins and configurations: (a) grand suite, (b) suite, (c) mini-suite, (d) outside-view double cabins with balcony, (e) outside-view double cabins, and (f) interior double cabins. These come in 35 different brochure price categories. The choice is quite bewildering for both travel agents and passengers, but pricing will depend on two things: size and location. By comparison, the largest suite is slightly smaller, and the smallest interior cabin is slightly larger than the equivalent suites/cabins aboard *Golden*, *Grand*, and *Star Princess*.

Cabin bath towels are small, and drawer space is very limited. There are no butlers – even for the top-grade suites, which are not large in comparison to similar suites aboard some other similarly-sized ships. Cabin attendants have too many cabins to look after – typically 20 – which does not translate to fine personal service.

(a) The largest, most lavish suite is the Grand Suite: A750, located at the stern. It has a large bedroom with queen-size bed, huge walk-in closets, two bathrooms, a lounge with fireplace, sofa bed, wet bar and refrigerator, and a large private balcony on the port side, with a hot tub accessible from both balcony and bedroom.

(b/c) Suites, with a semi-private balcony, have a separate living room with sofa bed, and bedroom, with a TV set in each. The bathroom is quite large and has both a tub and shower stall. The mini-suites also have a private balcony, and a separate living and sleeping area, with a TV set in each. The differences between the suites and mini-suites are basically in the size and appointments, the suite being more of a square shape while mini-suites are more rectangular and have few drawers. Both suites and mini-suites have plush bath-

robes, and fully tiled bathrooms with ample open-shelf storage space. Passengers in both receive greater attention, including priority embarkation and disembarkation privileges. What is not good is that the most expensive accommodation has only semi-private balconies that can be seen from above, so there is little privacy – Suites C401, 402, 404, 406, 408, 410, 412, 401, 405, 411, 415, and 417 on Riviera Deck 14. Also, the suites D105 and D106 (Dolphin Deck 9), which are extremely large, have balconies that are overlooked from above.

(d/e/f) Both interior and outside-view cabins – the outsides come either with or without private balcony – are of a functional, practical, design, although almost no drawers are provided. They are quite attractive, with warm, pleasing decor and fine soft furnishing fabrics; 80 percent of the outside-view cabins have a private balcony. Interior cabins measure 163 sq ft (15 sq m).

The 28 wheelchair-accessible cabins measure 250–385 sq ft (23–35.7 sq m); surprisingly, there's no mirror for dressing, and no full-length hanging space for long dresses – some passengers in wheelchairs do use mirrors and full-length clothing. Additionally, two family suites consist of two suites with an interconnecting door, plus a large balcony. These can sleep up to 10 if at least four are children, or up to eight adults.

All cabins receive turndown service and heart-shaped chocolates on pillows each night, bathrobes (on request unless you are in suite-grade accommodation), and toiletries. A hairdryer is provided in all cabins, sensibly located at the vanity desk unit in the living area. All bathrooms have tiled floors, and there is a decent amount of open-shelf storage space for toiletries, although the plain beige decor is basic.

Most outside-view cabins on Emerald Deck have views obstructed by lifeboats. There are no cabins for singles. Your name is placed outside your suite or cabin in a documents holder, making it simple for delivery service personnel but also reducing privacy. There is 24-hour room service, but some items on the room service menu are not available during early morning hours.

Some cabins can accommodate a third and fourth person in upper berths. However, in such cabins, the lower beds can't then be pushed together to make queen-size bed.

Almost all balcony suites and cabins can be overlooked both from the navigation bridge wing, as well as from the port and starboard sections of the ship's discotheque – high above the ship at the stern. Cabins with balconies on Dolphin, Caribe, and Baja decks can be overlooked by passengers on balconies above; they are, therefore, not at all private.

Passengers occupying some the most expensive suites with balconies at the stern of the vessel may experience some vibration during certain ship manoeuvers. Many cabins on Emerald Deck 8 have a lifeboat-obstructed view.

DINING. As befits the ship's size, there's a lot of dining options. There are three main dining rooms, plus Sterling Steakhouse, and Sabatini's Trattoria.

The three rooms for formal dining are Botticelli, Da Vinci, and Michelangelo. The Botticelli Dining Room has traditional two seating dining (typically 6pm and 8:15pm for dinner), while 'anytime dining' – where you choose when and with whom you want to eat – is offered in Da Vinci and Michelangelo. All are split into various sections in a non-symmetrical design that breaks the large spaces into smaller parts for better ambience, and each restaurant has its own galley.

Dinnerware by Dudson of England, high-quality linens and silverware, Frette Egyptian cotton table linens, and silverware by Hepp of Germany are used in the main dining rooms. Note that 15 percent is added to all beverage bills, including wines.

Other dining options. Sabatini's and Crown Grill, both extra-charge and reservations needed venues, are open for lunch and dinner on days at sea. Sabatini's is a 132-seat Italian eatery with some painted scenes of Tuscan villas and gardens and colorful tiled Mediterranean-style decor; it is named after Trattoria Sabatini, the 200-year-old institution in Florence. It has Italian-style pizzas and pastas, with a variety of sauces, as well as Italian-style entrées, including tiger prawns and lobster tail, all provided with flair and entertainment by the waiters. It is also open for breakfast for suite/mini-suite occupants only – when it really is a quiet haven.

Crown Grill is a 138-seat restaurant that serves an excellent array of premium steaks, chops, and grilled seafood items (with everything cooked to order). It is located off the main indoor Deck 7 promenade. Seating is mainly in semi-private alcoves, and the venue incorporates a show kitchen for those who like to watch the action.

Casual meals can be taken in the 312-seat Horizon Court, with its indoor-outdoor seating, open 24 hours a day. It has large ocean-view windows on port and starboard sides and direct access to the principal swimming pools and lido deck forward, and a more secluded aft pool deck and several terraces. There is no real finesse in presentation, however, as plastic plates are provided and the central display sections are really crowded.

Other casual eateries include a poolside hamburger grill and pizza bar (no additional charge), while extra charges do apply if you order items to eat at the coffee bar/patisserie, or the caviar/Champagne bar.

Also, Café Caribe, provides themed menus (Italian, French, Bavarian, for example) each evening, and may be provide welcome change from the busy main dining venues.

The International Café, on Deck 5 in The Piazza, is the place for coffees and specialty coffees, pastries, light lunches, and delightful afternoon cakes, most at no extra cost.

For something different, you could try a private dinner on your balcony (it's called the 'Ultimate Balcony Dinner/Breakfast'), an all-inclusive evening featuring cocktails, fresh flowers, Champagne, and a deluxe multi-course meal – all served by a member of the dining staff. It costs $50 per person for dinner, or $32 per couple for the Ultimate Balcony Breakfast – superb value for money.

For a $75 per person charge, this exclusive dining experience showcases the talents of the executive chef in a mini-dégustation that includes an array of appetizers in the galley. It really is a fine dining experience that includes good wines paired with high-quality meat and seafood dishes, and extremely creative presentation. It's worth taking the three hours needed to enjoy this special dinner; the slow-cooked roast veal shank is outstanding.

ENTERTAINMENT. The Princess Theater, the main entertainment venue, spans two decks and has comfortable seating on both main and balcony levels. It has $3 million worth of sound and light equipment, plus a nine-piece orchestra for backing the colourful production shows and major cabaret acts. The ship has a resident troupe of singers and dancers, plus an army of audio-visual support staff.

Club Fusion, a second entertainment lounge, is located aft. It presents cabaret acts at night, and lectures, bingo, and horse racing during the day. Explorers, a third entertainment lounge, can also host cabaret acts and dance bands. A variety of other lounges and bars have live music, and Princess Cruises employs a number of male dance hosts as partners for women traveling alone.

SPA/FITNESS. The Lotus Spa is located forward on Sun Deck – one of the uppermost decks. Separate facilities for men and women include a sauna, steam room, and changing rooms; common facilities include a relaxation/waiting zone, body-pampering treatment rooms, and a gymnasium with the latest high-tech muscle-pumping, cardiovascular equipment, accompanied by great ocean views. Some fitness classes are free, while others cost extra.

Ryndam
★★★ +

Size:..................................... Mid-size Ship	Cabins (total):................................633
Tonnage: 55,819	Size range (sq ft/m):.............186.2–1,124.8/17.3–104.5
Lifestyle: ....Premium	Cabins (outside view):..........................502
Cruise line:........................ Holland America Line	Cabins (interior/no view):.......................131
Former names: ....none	Cabins (for one person):...........................0
IMO number: 8919269	Cabins (with private balcony):.........................150
Builder: .... Fincantieri (Italy)	Cabins (wheelchair accessible): 6
Original cost:................................$215 million	Wheelchair accessibility:..........................Fair
Entered service:...............................Nov 1994	Cabin voltage: ....110 and 220 volts
Registry:...............................The Netherlands	Elevators:..8
Length (ft/m):............................... 719.3/219.3	Casino (gaming tables):............................ Yes
Beam (ft/m):.............................. 101.0/30.8	Slot machines:.................................... Yes
Draft (ft/m): 24.6/7.5	Swimming pools:.................1 (1 w/sliding glass dome)
Propulsion/Propellers:.......... diesel-electric (34,560kW)/2	Hot tubs (on deck):..................................2
Passenger decks:....................................10	Self-service launderette:.......................... Yes
Total crew:..557	Dedicated cinema/seats:........................Yes/249
Passengers (lower beds/alll berths):.............. 1,266/1,627	Library:.. Yes
Passenger Space Ratio (lower beds/all berths):........ 44.0/34.3	Onboard currency: ....US$
Crew/Passenger Ratio (lower beds/all berths):.......... 2.2/2.9	

Dutch decor and artifacts to suit senior-age cruisers

OVERVIEW. This ship has fairly decent interior fit and finish. Holland America Line constantly fine-tunes its performance as a cruise operator and regular passengers, almost all North American, find its ships comfortable and well-run, though the food and service are disappointing. The ship is deployed year-round in the Caribbean, where its rather dark interior decor contrasts with the strong sunlight.

Berlitz's Ratings

	Possible	Achieved
Ship	500	350
Accommodation	200	142
Food	400	252
Service	400	281
Entertainment	100	68
Cruise	400	265
OVERALL SCORE		
1358 points out of 2000		

THE SHIP. *Ryndam* is one of a series of four almost identical ships, the others being *Maasdam*, *Statendam*, and *Veendam*. The exterior styling is rather angular – some would say boxy – although it is softened and balanced by the black hull. There is a full walk-around teakwood promenade deck outdoors – excellent for strolling. The sunloungers here are wooden, with comfortable cushioned pads, while those at the swimming pool on Lido Deck are of white plastic. Holland America Line keeps its ships clean and tidy, and there is good passenger flow throughout the public areas.

A 2010 refurbishment created 'Mix,' which combines library, lounge, Internet center, and coffee bar; and 16 cabins near the spa were transformed into 'spa cabins'.

In the interiors of this S-class ship, an asymmetrical layout helps to reduce bottlenecks and congestion. Most public rooms are concentrated on two decks, Promenade Deck and Upper Promenade Deck, which creates a spacious feel. In general, a restrained approach to interior styling is taken, using a mixture of contemporary materials combined with traditional woods and ceramics.

The array of artworks throughout the ship, costing about $2 million, is really good, and is nicely displayed to represent the cruise line's fine Dutch heritage. Also noticeable are the fine flower arrangements throughout the public areas and foyers.

Atop the ship, with forward-facing views that wrap around the sides, is the Crow's Nest Lounge. By day it is a fine observation lounge with large ocean-view windows, while by night it turns into a nightclub with extremely variable lighting. The three-deck-high atrium foyer is attractive, although its sculptured centerpiece makes it look a little crowded and leaves little room in front of the reception office. A hydraulic glass roof covers the reasonably sized swimming pool/whirlpools and central Lido area (whose focal point is a large dolphin sculpture) so that this can be used in all weathers. There is a large and relaxing reference library.

The casino features gaming tables and slot machines. However, note that part of the casino is open, and passers-by can be subject to cigarette smoke (yes, smoking is still permitted), so non-smokers should hold their breath.

Complimentary cappuccino and espresso coffees, and free ice cream are provided during certain hours of the day, as well as hot hors d'oeuvres in all bars – something other major lines seem to have dropped, or charge extra for. However, the score for this ship ends up a tad under what it could be if the food and service staff were better.

An escalator travels between two of the lower decks (one of which was originally planned to be the embarkation point), but it is about as useful as a glass hammer! The charge to use the washing machines and dryers in the self-service launderette is petty, particularly for suite occupants, as they pay steep prices for their cruises. The men's urinals in public restrooms are unusually high.

ACCOMMODATION. This ranges from small interior cabins to a large penthouse suite, in seven types and a large number of different accommodation price categories. All cabin TV sets carry CNN.

The interior and outside-view standard cabins have twin beds that convert to a queen-size bed, and there is a separate living space with sofa and coffee table. However, although the drawer space is generally good, the closet space is very tight, particularly for long cruises – although more than adequate for a seven-night cruise). Bathrobes are provided for all suites/cabins, as are hairdryers, and a small range of personal amenities. The bathrooms are quite well laid out, but the tubs are small units better described as shower tubs. Some cabins have interconnecting doors.

On Navigation Deck, 28 suites have accommodation for up to four. These suites also have in-suite dining as a change to the dining room. These are very spacious, tastefully decorated and well laid-out, with a separate living room, bedroom with two lower beds (convertible to a king-size bed), a good sized living area, dressing room, plenty of storage space, and a marble bathroom with Jacuzzi tub.

The largest accommodation, a single penthouse suite, is on the starboard side of Navigation Deck at the forward staircase. It has a king-size bed, a TV set and video player, and a vanity desk, a large walk-in closet with superb drawer space, oversize whirlpool bath (it could seat four) and separate shower enclosure, and a washroom with toilet, bidet, and basin. The living room has a writing desk, a large TV set, and a full set of audio equipment. There's a dressing room, a large private balcony (with teak lounge chairs and drinks tables, dining table and four chairs), a pantry (with large refrigerator, toaster unit, and full coffee/tea-making facilities and food preparation area, and a separate entrance from the hallway), mini-bar/refrigerator, a guest toilet, and floor-to-ceiling windows.

DINING. The Rotterdam Dining Room, at the stern, spans two decks. It is quite dramatic, with two grand staircases to connect the two levels, panoramic views on three sides, and a music balcony. Both open seating and fixed (assigned tables and times) seating are available, while breakfast and lunch are open-seating (you'll be seated by restaurant staff when you enter). There are tables for two, four, six, or eight.

The waiter stations in the dining room are very noisy for anyone seated adjacent to them. Fine Rosenthal china and cutlery are used, although there are no fish knives. Live music is provided for dinner each evening; once each cruise, there's a Dutch Dinner (hats are provided), as is an Indonesian Lunch.

Other dining options. An intimate restaurant, the Pinnacle Grill, is just forward of the balcony level of the main dining room on the starboard side. The 66-seat dining spot (reservations are necessary, and a cover/service charge applies) serves Pacific Northwest cuisine such as fresh Alaskan salmon and halibut, and other regional specialties, plus a selection of premium steaks such as filet mignon from Black Angus beef. The Pinnacle Grill is a much better dining experience.

For more casual evening eating, the Lido Buffet is open for dinners on all except the last night of each cruise, in an open-seating arrangement; part of it is designated as Canaletto for dinner, featuring Italian fare. Tables are set with crisp linens, flatware, and stemware. The set menu includes a choice of four entrées. The self-serve Lido Buffet is also the place for casual breakfasts and lunches. Again there is much use of canned fruits and packets of items, although there are several commercial low-calorie salad dressings. The choice of cheeses (and accompanying crackers) is very poor. In addition, a poolside grill provides basic American hamburgers and hot dogs.

Passengers will need to eat in the Lido Buffet on days when the dining room is closed for lunch – typically once or twice per cruise, depending on the ship's itinerary.

ENTERTAINMENT. The Showroom at Sea spans two decks, with banquette seating on both main and upper levels. It is basically a well-designed room, but the ceiling is low and the sightlines from the balcony level are poor.

While Holland America Line is not known for its fine entertainment, what the line does offer is a consistently good, tried and tested array of cabaret acts that constantly rove the cruise ship circuit. The production shows, however, while a good attempt, fall short on storyline, choreography, and performance, with colorful costuming and lighting hiding the weak spots.

A number of bands, a string ensemble and solo musicians play live music in many lounges and bars. There's evening dancing in the Crow's Nest, and serenading string music in the Explorer's Lounge and dining room.

SPA/FITNESS. The Greenhouse Spa is one deck below the navigation bridge at the very forward part of the ship. It includes a gymnasium with ocean views, an aerobics exercise area, large beauty salon with ocean-view windows to the port side, several treatment rooms, and men's and women's sauna, steam room, and changing areas. The spa is operated by Steiner, a specialist concession.

Safari Legacy
★★★ +

Size:.....Boutique Ship		Cabins (total):.....45	
Tonnage:.....1,472		Size range (sq ft/m):.....80.0–510.0/7.4–47.3	
Lifestyle:.....Premium		Cabins (outside view):.....45	
Cruise line:.....Un-Cruise Adventures		Cabins (interior/no view):.....0	
Former names: .... *Spirit of '98, Pilgrim Belle, Victorian Empress*		Cabins (for one person):.....0	
IMO number:.....8963703		Cabins (with private balcony):.....0	
Builder:.....Bender Shipbuilding (USA)		Cabins (wheelchair accessible):.....1	
Original cost:.....n/a		Wheelchair accessibility:.....Poor	
Entered service:.....1984/Jun 2013		Cabin voltage:.....110 volts	
Registry:.....USA		Elevators:.....1	
Length (ft/m):.....192.0/58.2		Casino (gaming tables):.....No	
Beam (ft/m):.....40.0/12.1		Slot machines:.....No	
Draft (ft/m):.....9.3/2.8		Swimming pools:.....0	
Propulsion/Propellers:.....diesel (2,012kW)/1		Hot tubs (on deck):.....2	
Passenger decks:.....4		Self-service launderette:.....No	
Total crew:.....35		Dedicated cinema/seats:.....No	
Passengers (lower beds/alll berths):.....88/88		Library:.....Yes	
Passenger Space Ratio (lower beds/all berths): 15.3/15.3		Onboard currency:.....US$	
Crew/Passenger Ratio (lower beds/all berths):.....3.2/3.2			

Unique-looking 1800s-look coastal casual cruising gem

OVERVIEW. This is a rather cute, distinctive-looking ship, built to resemble a late 1800s coastal cruising vessel. It is particularly suited to in-depth glacier spotting, and for close-in cruising along the coastline of Alaska, and will appeal to couples and single travelers who enjoy nature and wildlife up close.

THE SHIP. *Safari Legacy* (the name of the company, American Safari Cruises was changed to Un-Cruise Adventures in 2013) has an all-American crew. It has an outdoor viewing area right at the bow, and the cruising areas are Alaska and the Pacific Northwest. The Gold 'n' Locks Library – perhaps a reference to the Klondyke era? – has books on river lore and American history. The dress code is casual – not even a jacket for men, and no ties needed. But do take comfortable walking shoes, as well as photographic materials for wildlife spotting. Smoking is permitted only on the outside decks. All tips are pooled by all staff.

Because it's a small ship, there's a little bit of throbbing from the diesel engines/generator, but it shouldn't disturb you too much.

ACCOMMODATION. There are six grades of cabin. The two-room Owner's Suite is the biggest accommodation, with large picture windows on three sides. Its lounge/living room has a games table, TV/DVD, and refrigerator. and its separate bedroom has a king-size bed and large bathroom with Jacuzzi tub.

There are four irregular-shaped deluxe cabins at the

Berlitz's Ratings

	Possible	Achieved
Ship	500	343
Accommodation	200	146
Food	400	257
Service	400	263
Entertainment	100	67
Cruise	400	260

OVERALL SCORE
1336 points out of 2000

front of the vessel, with good closet space, a queen-size bed (or twin beds), and a bathroom with a separate shower enclosure. Most cabins are quite small, but are reasonably comfortable, and have a large picture window. While a few have queen-size or double beds, most have single beds that can't be moved together. Each cabin has its own private bathroom, although these really are tiny, with a wall-mounted shower. There is no room service for food or snacks.

DINING. The Klondyke Dining Room, decorated in the style of 100 years ago, is elegant. The cuisine is expected to be premium, taste-rich American fare. Expect lots of seafood. The ingredients are mostly fresh, and local. Wine and full bar services are available.

ENTERTAINMENT. There is no formal entertainment. Dinner and after-dinner conversation with fellow passengers in the lounge/bar is what it's all about.

SPA/FITNESS. There is a sauna, massage room (passengers get one free massage per cruise), and a modicum of exercise facilities.

Saga Pearl II
★★★ +

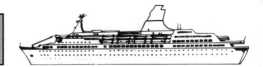

Size:.	Small Ship	Crew/Passenger Ratio (lower beds/all berths):.	1.8/1.8
Tonnage:.	18,591	Cabins (total):.	258
Lifestyle:.	Standard	Size range (sq ft/m):.	150.0–725.0/13.4–65
Cruise line:.	Saga Cruises	Cabins (outside view):.	178
Former names: *Quest for Adventure, Saga Pearl II, Astoria, Arkona, Astor*		Cabins (interior/no view):.	82
		Cabins (for one person):.	60
IMO number:.	7904889	Cabins (with private balcony):.	40
Builder:.	Howaldtswerke Deutsche Werft (Germany)	Cabins (wheelchair accessible):.	0
Original cost:.	$55 million	Wheelchair accessibility:.	Fair
Entered service:.	Dec 1981/May 2013	Cabin voltage:.	220 volts
Registry:.	The Bahamas	Elevators:.	3
Length (ft/m):.	539.2/164.3	Casino (gaming tables):.	No
Beam (ft/m):.	74.1/22.6	Slot machines:.	No
Draft (ft/m):.	20.0/6.1	Swimming pools:.	2
Propulsion/Propellers:.	diesel (13,200kW)/2	Hot tubs (on deck):.	0
Passenger decks:.	8	Self-service launderette:.	Yes
Total crew:.	252	Dedicated cinema/seats:.	No
Passengers (lower beds/all berths):.	456/456	Library:.	Yes
Passenger Space Ratio (lower beds/all berths):.	40.7/40.7	Onboard currency:.	UK£

A comfortable small ship for discovery-style cruising

OVERVIEW. This ship is best suited to English-speaking couples, and single travelers of mature years. Saga Cruises staff go out of their way to ensure you have an excellent time.

THE SHIP. *Saga Pearl II* is a traditional-looking cruise ship. A multi-million pound 2009 refit added a superb 3,000-book library, an array of balcony cabins, and new galleys. There is a good amount of open deck and sunbathing space, with some teakwood decks, polished wood railings, and cushioned pads for sunloungers. There is no walk-around promenade deck outdoors, but a small walking area under the lifeboats exists on both sides. Unusually for this size of ship, there is an indoor swimming pool and wellness center.

ACCOMMODATION. The accommodation consists of 23 price categories, including 10 grades for single-occupancy cabins, and is spread over four decks. Some 40 French balconies were added in the 2009 refit.

Grand Suites. Two Boat Deck suites (725 sq ft/65 sq m) provide really large spaces, and have just about everything needed for refined, private shipboard living. There's a separate bedroom with double bed, and a living room with sofa, dining table, and chairs. The tiled bathroom has a large tub, separate shower, and plenty of storage space for toiletries.

Suites. 34 suites (269 sq ft/25 sq m) have a separate bedroom with twin beds, and a living room with sofa, dining table, and chairs. The tiled bathroom has a large

Berlitz's Ratings

	Possible	Achieved
Ship	500	321
Accommodation	200	134
Food	400	262
Service	400	286
Entertainment	100	72
Cruise	400	273

**OVERALL SCORE
1348 points out of 2000**

tub, separate shower enclosure, and plenty of space for toiletries.

Outside-view Cabins/Interior Cabins. The standard cabins (140 sq ft/13 sq m) are quite well appointed and decorated, and all have crisp, clean colors – some might find them plain. The bathrooms are quite compact units, although there is a decent-size shower. They are fully tiled, and have a decent cabinet for toiletries. Passengers in all grades get 100 percent cotton towels, and bathrobe. The cabin service menu is very limited.

DINING. The Dining Room has ocean-view picture windows. It has dark wood paneling and restful decor. There's a single, open seating, at tables for four, six, or eight. Two small wings, each with one a 12-seat table, can be used for small groups. The wine list has a decent selection of wines from many regions.

ENTERTAINMENT. The Discovery Lounge is the main entertainment space. It is a single-level room, although 14 pillars obstruct the sight lines from many seats. The stage also acts as the dance floor and cannot be raised for shows. The entertainment consists of cabaret-style performances. It can also be used as a lecture room.

SPA/FITNESS. The spa is located on the lowest passenger deck, and contains a sauna (but no steam room), solarium, indoor swimming pool, treatment rooms, and changing areas.

Saga Sapphire
★★★★

Size:.. Small Ship	Crew/Passenger Ratio (lower beds/all berths):.......... 1.7/1.7
Tonnage:.. 37,301	Cabins (total):...................................374
Lifestyle: ....Standard	Size range (sq ft/m): 161.4–678.1/15.0–63.0
Cruise line:.............................. Saga Cruises	Cabins (outside view):..............................309
Former names: . *Bleu de France, Holiday Dream, SuperStar Aries,*	Cabins (interior/no view):...........................65
SuperStar Europe, Europa	Cabins (for one person):.............................56
IMO number: 7822457	Cabins (with private balcony): 19
Builder: .... Bremer Vulkan (Germany)	Cabins (wheelchair accessible): 2
Original cost:................................$120 million	Wheelchair accessibility:...........................Good
Entered service:..................... Jan 1982/Mar 2012	Cabin voltage: ....110 and 220 volts
Registry:.....................................The Bahamas	Elevators:.......................................4
Length (ft/m):.............................. 654.9/199.6	Casino (gaming tables):.............................No
Beam (ft/m):................................. 93.8/28.6	Slot machines:....................................No
Draft (ft/m): 27.6/8.4	Swimming pools:....................................2
Propulsion/Propellers:.................diesel (21,270kW)/2	Hot tubs (on deck):.................................3
Passenger decks:..................................10	Self-service launderette:...........................Yes
Total crew:.....................................415	Dedicated cinema/seats:............................No
Passengers (lower beds/alll berths):................. 706/706	Library: ....Yes
Passenger Space Ratio (lower beds/all berths): 49.6/49.6	Onboard currency: ....UK£

An elegant ship for British cruisers over 50

OVERVIEW. *Saga Sapphire* is best suited to couples and single travelers, almost all British, seeking a holiday afloat in spacious, classy surroundings, and provides decent accommodation, good food, and friendly service, plus interesting itineraries and destinations. Passengers must be over 50, but spouses and partners can be as young as 45.

Berlitz's Ratings		
	Possible	Achieved
Ship	500	385
Accommodation	200	144
Food	400	274
Service	400	289
Entertainment	100	71
Cruise	400	284
OVERALL SCORE		
1447 points out of 2000		

THE SHIP. *Saga Sapphire* was originally built as the fifth incarnation of Europa for Hapag-Lloyd Cruises, and was for many years the pride of the German cruise industry. It was originally to have twin side-by-side funnels, but the idea was dropped in favor of a single funnel. The ship is in remarkably fine shape, despite the fact that it is now just over 30 years old. Saga Cruises tailored the ship to British tastes when it took delivery in April 2012.

It has a deep blue hull and white upper structure, and a sponson stern, a kind of 'skirt' added in order to comply with the latest stability regulations. But it still maintains its moderately handsome, balanced profile. There is a really decent amount of open outdoor deck space. The ship has both outdoor and outdoor/indoor pools. While there is no walk-around outdoors promenade deck, there are half-length teak port and starboard promenades.

The interior focal point is a three-deck high lobby, which has a 'floating' fish sculpture – I counted over 1,000 fish, including one red herring!). There is a good range of good-size public rooms – most of which have high ceilings, and wide interior stairways create a feel-

ing of spaciousness on a grand – but human – scale. Contemporary yet restful colors have been applied to many public rooms and cabins, and subtle, hidden lighting is used throughout, particularly on the stairways. The public rooms are positioned aft in a 'cake-layer' stacking, with all the accommodation located forward, thus separating potentially noisy areas from quieter ones.

Facilities include a delightful observation lounge (The Drawing Room), and an integral, extensive library plus several Internet-connected computer stations (iPads can also be provided), chess and draught tables; light entertainment is presented here in the evenings, and yummy Lavazza coffees are available here at almost any time, with delightful cakes in mid-morning (free). Quirky table lamps are made from old clarinets and fishing rods.

For a delightful, neat hideaway, head to Cooper's, named after the famed British comedy-magician Tommy Cooper (there are numerous black and white photos on the wall of some of the UK's best-known comedians of yesteryear and today, including Spike Milligna – the well-known typing error; the table lamps are topped by Tommy Cooper's trademark – a fez). Then there's Aviators – a cute little pre-dining room bar with models of those splendid Spitfire aircraft (from the Second World War), with, of course, Spitfire draft beer as the featured bar beverage.

The ship, which has some rather amusing and quirky artwork, provides an informal, relaxed, yet elegant setting, with many public rooms that have a high ceiling.

Saga Cruises includes many things other UK-based operators charge extra for – that's why its cruises may appear to cost more – such as private car transfers to the ship (check brochure for details), all gratuities, shuttle buses in ports of call where possible, and newspapers in the library in each port of call, when available.

ACCOMMODATION. There is a wide range of suites and cabins (including many for singles), in a multitude of price grades. All of the original cabins are quite spacious, and have illuminated closets, dark wood cabinetry with rounded edges, full-length mirrors, color TV/DVD player, mini-bar/refrigerator, personal safe, hairdryer, and good cabin insulation. They are also laid out in a very practical design. Some suites/cabins have table lamps made from old cameras like the Kodak Brownie and similar 'box' cameras – delightfully quirky!

Most of the bathrooms (163 to be precise) have deep tubs (cabins without a bathtub have a large shower enclosure), a three-head shower unit, two deep washbasins (not all cabins), large toiletries cabinet, and handsome toiletries – created exclusively for Saga Cruises by Clarity, an organization that provides employment for blind persons. Admirable!

The largest living spaces are the suites. However, because of their location – they were created from former bridge officers' cabins in a 1999 refit – they have lifeboat-obstructed views. Six other suites had private balconies added, and all provide generous living spaces. There is a separate bedroom with either a queen-size or twin beds, illuminated closets, and a vanity/writing desk. The lounge includes a wet bar with refrigerator and glass cabinets and large audio-visual center complete with large-screen TV set and DVD player. The marble-clad bathroom has a large shower enclosure, with retractable clothesline.

Even the standard, lower-priced cabins are very comfortable, the ship having been designed for long voyages.

DINING. Pole to Pole, the main restaurant, seats 620 diners and has ocean-view windows on two sides, yet still manages to have an intimate, clubby feel thanks to different areas styled to the theme of four continents: Africa, Asia, Europe, and the Americas. Both self-serve buffet and full-service meals are provided. There is open seating, so you can dine wherever you choose. For dinner, a number of tables can be reserved for fixed dining times when you book.

Other dining options. The Grill and Verandah, an indoor/outdoor venue, provides lighter, healthier grilled meals, with food cooked to order in a show kitchen. It's open for breakfast, lunch, and relaxed dinner. The 'spider's web' alcove seating partitions are novel (I didn't find any big spiders yet!). One neat feature is a slicing machine to produce cold cuts of meat – so you know it's fresh and has taste.

Asian-fusion cuisine (Indian, Sri Lankan, and Thai) is served in the intimate 64-seat East to West restaurant, whose decor includes traditional wood carvings, reflecting the mood of the East. Adjacent is The Grill, specializing in steaks and seafood, in a room with an open kitchen.

The Beach, adjacent to the indoor/outdoor pool, provides fish and chips and other light British fare, traditional desserts, and ice cream (the machine is inside a blue-white striped beach hut – there are jars and jars of boiled sweets in a second beach hut – all very British and a pleasant throwback to yesteryear.

ENTERTAINMENT. The Britannia Lounge is the venue for major social events and shows. The sight lines are mostly good, although some thin pillars present problems from some seats – the room was originally built more for use as a single-level concert salon than a room for shows – but the setting is elegant. The shows consist of a small troupe of female dancers, plus a number of cabaret acts. There is live music for listening or dancing in various bars and lounges. Male dance hosts are aboard each cruise for the many single women passengers.

SPA/FITNESS. An area of about 8,611 sq ft (800 sq m) is host to a rather nice, homely retreat – an indoor wellness center. It includes an indoor swimming pool (few ships have them today). Adjacent facilities include sauna and steam room, a fitness/exercise area, several treatment rooms, and a beauty salon. Sporting facilities include St Andrews, a crazy-golf course located outdoors atop ship in what was a former FKK – nude – sunbathing spot.

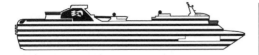

Sapphire Princess
★★★★

Size:. . . . . .Large Resort Ship		Cabins (total):. 1,337	
Tonnage: 115,875		Size range (sq ft/m): 168–1,329.3/15.6–123.5	
Lifestyle: . . . . .Standard		Cabins (outside view): 1,000	
Cruise line:. . . . . Princess Cruises		Cabins (interior/no view):. 337	
Former names: . . . . .none		Cabins (for one person):. 0	
IMO number: 9228186		Cabins (with private balcony):. 750	
Builder: . . . . Mitsubishi Heavy Industries (Japan)		Cabins (wheelchair accessible): 28	
Original cost:. . . . . $400 million		Wheelchair accessibility:. . . . . .Good	
Entered service:. . . . . May 2004		Cabin voltage:. . . . . 110 volts	
Registry:. . . . . Bermuda		Elevators:. 14	
Length (ft/m):. 951.4/290.0		Casino (gaming tables):. . . . . Yes	
Beam (ft/m):. 123.0/37.5		Slot machines:. . . . . Yes	
Draft (ft/m): 26.4/8.0		Swimming pools:. 3	
Propulsion/Propellers: . . . . diesel-electric (42,000kW)/2		Hot tubs (on deck):. 9	
Passenger decks:. 13		Self-service launderette:. . . . . Yes	
Total crew:. 1,238		Dedicated cinema/seats:. . . . . .No	
Passengers (lower beds/all berths):. 2,674/3,100		Library: . . . . Yes	
Passenger Space Ratio (lower beds/all berths): 43.3/37.3		Onboard currency: . . . . .US$	
Crew/Passenger Ratio (lower beds/all berths):. 2.1/2.5			

A multi-choice large ship for informal family cruising

OVERVIEW. *Sapphire Princess* is quite a grand playground in which to roam and play when you're not ashore. Princess Cruises delivers a fine, well-packaged holiday product, with some sense of style, at an attractive, highly competitive price, and this ship will appeal to those who really enjoy big-city life with all the trimmings.

THE SHIP. *Sapphire Princess* has an instantly recognizable funnel due to two jet engine-like pods that sit high up on its structure, but really are mainly for decoration. The ship is similar in size and internal layout to *Golden Princess*, *Grand Princess*, and *Star Princess*, although of a greater beam. Unlike its half-sister ships, , all of which had a 'spoiler' containing a discotheque located aft of the funnel, this has been removed from both *Diamond Princess* and *Sapphire Princess*, being replaced by a more sensible aft-facing nightclub/discotheque, Sky-walkers Nightclub.

Several areas focus on swimming pools. One has a giant poolside movie screen, one is two decks high and is covered by a retractable glass dome, itself an extension of the funnel housing, and one pool lies within The Sanctuary – an adults-only, extra-cost relaxation area.

The interiors were overseen and outfitted by the Okura Group, whose Okura Hotel is one of Tokyo's best. Fit and finish quality is superior to that of the Italian-built *Golden Princess*, *Grand Princess*, and *Star Princess*. Unlike the outside decks, there is plenty

Berlitz's Ratings	Possible	Achieved
Ship	500	378
Accommodation	200	147
Food	400	250
Service	400	289
Entertainment	100	78
Cruise	400	295
OVERALL SCORE		
1437 points out of 2000		

of space inside the ship – but there are also plenty of passengers – and a wide array of public rooms, with many 'intimate' (this being a relative term) spaces and places to enjoy. The passenger flow has been well thought-out, and there's little congestion.

The interior focal point is a piazza-style atrium lobby, with Vines (wine bar), an International Café (for coffee, pastries, panini, etc.) library/Internet-connect center, and Alfedo's sit-down Pizzeria.

A Wedding Chapel has a live web-cam to relay ceremonies via the Internet. The ship's captain can legally marry American couples, due to the ship's Bermuda registry and a dispensation which should be verified in advance according to where you reside. Princess Cruises offers three wedding packages – Pearl, Emerald, Diamond.

The Grand Casino is one of the largest casinos at sea, with over 260 slot machines (some of which are linked and may provide a combined payout), plus blackjack, craps, and roulette tables.

Other facilities include a library/computer room, and a card room. The wood-paneled Wheelhouse Bar is finely decorated with memorabilia and ship models tracing part of the history of sister company P&O. The Wake View Bar has a spiral stairway leading down to a great viewing spot for those who want to watch the ship's wake.

A high-tech hospital has live SeaMed telemedicine linkups to the Cedars-Sinai Medical Center in Los Angeles, with specialists available for emergency help.

The ship is full of revenue centers. Expect to be subjected to flyers advertising daily art auctions, designer watches and the like.

The dress code is formal or smart casual – interpreted by many as jeans and trainers. Gratuities to staff are added to your account, with gratuities for children charged at the same rate. If you want to pay less, you can have these charges adjusted at the reception desk.

Lines form for many things aboard large ships, but particularly so for the information office, and for open-seating breakfast and lunch in the four main dining rooms. Long lines for shore excursions and shore tenders are also a fact of life, as is waiting for elevators at peak times, and embarkation and disembarkation – though an 'express check-in' option is available for embarkation if you fill in some forms 40 days before your cruise.

The many extra-charge items include ice cream and freshly squeezed orange juice. Yoga, group exercise bicycling, and kick boxing classes cost extra. There's an hourly rate for group babysitting services, and a charge for using washers and dryers in the self-service launderettes.

FAMILIES. For youngsters and teenagers there is a two-deck-high playroom, teen room, and a host of specially trained counselors. Children have their own pools, hot tubs, and open deck area at the stern, away from adult areas.

ACCOMMODATION. Everyone receives turndown service and nightly chocolates on pillows, bathrobes on request, and toiletries. A hairdryer is provided in all cabins. All bathrooms are tiled and have a decent amount of open shelf storage space for toiletries.

Most outside cabins on Emerald Deck have views obstructed by the lifeboats. Sadly, there are no cabins for singles. Your name is typically placed outside your suite or cabin – handy for delivery service personnel but eroding your privacy. Most balcony suites and cabins can be overlooked from the navigation bridge wing. There is 24-hour room service, though some menu items aren't available during early morning hours.

Cabins with balconies on Baja, Caribe, and Dolphin decks are overlooked by passengers on balconies on the deck above. Cabin bath towels are small, and drawer space is limited. There are no butlers, even for the top grade suites – which aren't really large in comparison to similar suites aboard some other ships. Cabin attendants have too many cabins to look after – typically 20 – which does not encourage fine personal service.

DINING. All dining rooms are located on one of two decks in the ship's center. There are five principal dining rooms with themed decor and cuisine: Sterling Steakhouse for steak and grilled meats, Vivaldi for Italian fare, Santa Fe for southwestern USA cuisine, Pacific Moon for Asian cuisine, and International, the largest, located aft, with two seatings and 'traditional' cuisine. These offer a mix of two seatings, with seating assigned according to your cabin's location, and 'anytime dining' where you choose when and with whom you want to eat. All dining rooms are split into sections in a non-symmetrical design that breaks what are quite large spaces into many smaller sections, for better ambience and less noise pollution.

Specially designed dinnerware and good-quality linens and silverware are used. Note that 15 percent is added to all beverage bills, including wines.

Other dining options. Sabatini's is an informal eatery (reservations required; cover charge). It offers an eight-course meal, including Italian-style pizzas and pastas, with a variety of sauces, as well as Italian-style entrées including tiger prawns and lobster tail. Its cuisine is potentially better than in all the other dining rooms – better quality ingredients and more attention to presentation and taste.

A poolside hamburger grill and pizza bar (no additional charge) are additional dining spots for casual bites. You have to pay extra if you order items to eat at either the coffee bar/patisserie, or the caviar/Champagne bar.

Other casual meals can be taken in the Horizon Court, open 24 hours a day, with large ocean-view on port and starboard sides and direct access to the two principal swimming pools and lido deck.

ENTERTAINMENT. The Princess Theatre, spanning two decks, has comfortable seating on both main and balcony levels. It has $3 million in sound and light equipment, plus a nine-piece orchestra.

Princess Cruises prides itself on its glamorous all-American production shows, and the two or three shows on a typical seven-day cruise should not disappoint.

A second large entertainment lounge, Club Fusion, presents cabaret acts at night, and lectures, bingo, and horse racing during the day. A third entertainment lounge can also host cabaret acts and dance bands. Many lounges and bars have live music, and a number of male dance hosts act as partners for women traveling alone.

SPA/FITNESS. The Lotus Spa is forward on Sun Deck – one of the uppermost decks. Separate facilities for men and women include a sauna, steam room, and changing rooms; common facilities include a relaxation/waiting zone, body-pampering treatment rooms, and a gymnasium packed with the latest high-tech muscle-pumping, cardiovascular equipment, and providing great ocean views. Some fitness classes are free, while others cost extra.

The Lotus Spa is operated by Steiner Leisure. You can make online reservations for any spa treatments before your cruise.

Sea Cloud
★★★★★

Size:..................................Boutique Ship		Crew/Passenger Ratio (lower beds/all berths):..........1.1/1.1	
Tonnage: 2,532		Cabins (total):.......................................32	
Lifestyle: .... Luxury		Size range (sq ft/m): 102.2–409.0/9.5–38.0	
Cruise line:............................. Sea Cloud Cruises		Cabins (outside view):................................34	
Former names: Sea Cloud of Grand Cayman, IX-99, Antama, Patria,		Cabins (interior/no view):..............................0	
Angelita, Sea Cloud, Hussar		Cabins (for one person):...............................0	
IMO number: 8843446		Cabins (with private balcony):..........................0	
Builder: ....Krupp Werft (Germany)		Cabins (wheelchair accessible): 0	
Original cost:...................................... n/a		Wheelchair accessibility:............................None	
Entered service:..........................Aug 1931/1979		Cabin voltage: .... 220 volts	
Registry:..................................... Malta		Elevators:..0	
Length (ft/m):............................. 359.2/109.5		Casino (gaming tables):...............................No	
Beam (ft/m):....................................... n/a		Slot machines:.......................................No	
Draft (ft/m): 16.8/5.1		Swimming pools:.....................................0	
Propulsion/Propellers:........ sail power + diesel (4,476kW)/2		Hot tubs (on deck):...................................0	
Passenger decks:....................................3		Self-service launderette:..............................No	
Total crew:...60		Dedicated cinema/seats:...............................No	
Passengers (lower beds/alll berths):..................64/64		Library: ....Yes	
Passenger Space Ratio (lower beds/all berths): 39.5/39.5		Onboard currency: .... Euros	

Simply the most beautiful sailing ship in the world

OVERVIEW. *Sea Cloud* is the most romantic sailing ship afloat. It is best suited to couples and singles (not children) who would probably never consider a 'normal' cruise ship, but who enjoy sailing aboard a real tall ship that is packaged to include accommodation, good food, like-minded companions, and interesting destinations. It operates under charter to various travel companies for much of the year.

Berlitz's Ratings

	Possible	Achieved
Ship	500	432
Accommodation	200	173
Food	400	340
Service	400	333
Entertainment	100	95
Cruise	400	329

OVERALL SCORE
1702 points out of 2000

THE SHIP. *Sea Cloud*, a completely authentic 1930s barque whose 80th birthday was celebrated in 2011, is the largest private yacht ever built – three times the size of Captain Cook's *Endeavour* – and a stunningly beautiful ship when under sail in both the Caribbean and European/Mediterranean waters. Its four masts are almost as high as a 20-story building, the main one being 178ft (54m) above the main deck.

This was the largest private yacht ever built when completed in 1931 by Edward F. Hutton for his wife, Marjorie Merriweather Post, the American cereal heiress. Originally constructed for $1 million as *Hussar* in the Germany's Krupp shipyard in Kiel, the steel-hulled vessel saw action during World War II as a weather observation ship, under the code name IX-99.

There is plenty of deck space (but lots of ropes on deck, and other nautical equipment), even under the vast expanse of white sail, and the promenade deck outdoors still has wonderful varnished sea chests. The decks themselves are made of mahogany and teak, and wooden steamer-style sunloungers are provided.

One of the most delightful aspects of sailing aboard this ship is its 'Blue Lagoon,' located at the stern. Weather permitting, you can lie down on the thick blue padding and gaze up at the stars and night sky – it's one of the great pleasures – particularly when the ship is under sail, with engines turned off.

The original engine room, with diesel engines, is still in operation for the rare occasions when sail power can't be used. An open-bridge policy is the norm, except during poor weather or navigational maneuvers.

In addition to its retained and refurbished original suites and cabins, some newer, smaller cabins were added in 1979 when a consortium of German yachtsmen and businessmen bought the ship and spent $7.5 million refurbishing it. The interiors exude warmth and are finely hand-crafted. There is much antique mahogany furniture, fine original oil paintings, gorgeous carved oak paneling, parquet flooring, and burnished brass everywhere, as well as some finely detailed ceilings. Marjorie Merryweather Post had been accustomed to the very finest things in life.

Passengers are not allowed to climb the rigging, as they are aboard some other tall ships. This is because the mast rigging on this vintage sailing ship is of a very different type to more modern sailing vessels such as *Royal Clipper*, *Star Clipper*, *Star Flyer*, and *Sea Cloud II*. However, passengers may be able participate occasionally in the furling and unfurling of the sails.

A cruise aboard the intimate *Sea Cloud* is really exhilarating. A kind of stately home afloat, it remains one of the world's best travel experiences. The activities are few, and so relaxation is the key, in a setting that provides fine service and style, but in an unpretentious way. The only dress-up night is the Captain's Welcome Aboard Dinner, but otherwise, smart casual clothing is all that is needed.

However, mini-skirts would be impractical because of the steep staircases in some places – trousers are more practical. Also bear in mind that a big sailing vessel such as this can heel to one side occasionally, so flat shoes are preferable to high heels.

Sea Cloud sails, for part of each year, under charter to Hapag-Lloyd Cruises. On those occasions, white and red wines and beer are included for lunch and dinner, and soft drinks, espresso and cappuccino coffees are included at any time. Shore excursions are an optional extra, as are gratuities. Details may differ for other charter operators such as Abercrombie & Kent. Gratuities can be charged to your onboard account.

Although now over 80 years young – I doubt if any modern cruise ship will last this long – *Sea Cloud* is so lovingly maintained and operated that anyone who sails aboard it cannot fail to be impressed. The food and service are good, as is the interaction between passengers and crew, many of whom have worked aboard the ship for many, many years. The crew is of mixed nationality, and the sailors who climb the rigging and set the sails include women as well as men. On a cruise's last night, the sailors' choir sings seafaring songs. One bonus is the fact that the doctor on board is available at no charge for medical emergencies or seasickness medication.

Hamburg-based Sea Cloud Cruises also operates the rivercruise vessels *River Cloud* and *River Cloud II* for cruising along the rivers of Europe, and, in 2001 introduced a brand new companion sailing ship, *Sea Cloud II*.

ACCOMMODATION. Because *Sea Cloud* was built as a private yacht, there is a wide variation in cabin sizes and configurations. Some cabins have double beds, while some have twins (side by side or in an L-shaped configuration) that are fixed and cannot be placed together. Many of the original cabins have a fireplace, now with an electric fire.

All the cabins are very comfortable, but those on Main Deck (cabins 1–8) were part of the original accommodation. Of these, the two owner's suites (cabins 1 and 2) are really opulent, and have original Chippendale furniture, fine gilt detailing, a real fireplace, French canopy bed, and large Italian Carrara marble bathrooms with gold fittings.

Owner's Cabin Number 1 is decorated in white throughout, and has a French double bed, a marble fireplace, and Louis Phillippe chairs; the bathroom is appointed in Carrara marble, with cut-glass mirrors, and faucets (taps) in the shape of swans. Owner's Cabin Number 2, completely paneled in rich woods, retains the mahogany secretary used 60 years ago by Edward F. Hutton, its dark wood decor reminiscent of the 1930s.

Other cabins – both the original ones, and some newer additions – are beautifully furnished. All were refurbished in 1993 and are surprisingly large for the size of the ship. There is a good amount of closet and drawer space and all cabins have a personal safe and telephone. The cabin bathrooms, too, are quite luxurious, and equipped with everything you will need, including bathrobes and hairdryer, and an assortment of toiletries. There is a 110-volt AC shaver socket in each bathroom. The 'new' cabins are rather small for two people, so it's best to take minimal luggage.

There is no cabin food or beverage service. Also, if you occupy one of the original cabins on Main Deck you may be subjected to some noise when the motorized capstans are used to raise and lower or trim the sails. On one day each cruise, an 'open-house' cocktail party is held on the Main Deck, with all cabins available for passengers to see.

DINING. The exquisitely elegant dining room, created from the original owner's living room/saloon, is in the center of the vessel, and also houses the ship's library. It has beautiful wood paneled walls and a wood beam ceiling.

There is ample space at each table for open-seating meals. German chefs are in charge, and the high-quality cuisine is very international, with a good balance of nouvelle cuisine and regional dishes, although there is little choice, due to the size of the galley. There is always excellent seafood and fish, purchased locally, when available, as are most other ingredients.

For breakfast and lunch, there are self-serve buffets. European wines accompany lunch and dinner. Soft drinks and bottled water are included in the fare, while alcoholic drinks cost extra. On the last day of each cruise, homemade ice cream is produced.

ENTERTAINMENT. A keyboard player/singer is available for the occasional soirée, but after-dinner conversation constitutes the main entertainment each evening.

SPA/FITNESS. There are no spa or fitness facilities. However, for recreation (particularly at night), there is the Blue Lagoon, an area of seating with blue cushioned pads at the very aft of the ship, where you can lie down and watch the heavens.

Sea Cloud II
★★★★★

Size:. . . . . .Boutique Ship	Cabins (total):. 47
Tonnage: 3,849	Size range (sq ft/m):. 215.2–322.9/20.0–30.0
Lifestyle: . . . . Luxury	Cabins (outside view):. 47
Cruise line:. . . . . Sea Cloud Cruises	Cabins (interior/no view):. 0
Former names: . . . . .none	Cabins (for one person):. 0
IMO number: 9171292	Cabins (with private balcony):. 0
Builder: . . . . Astilleros Gondan, Figueras (Spain)	Cabins (wheelchair accessible): 0
Original cost:. . . . . DM 50 million	Wheelchair accessibility:. . . . . .None
Entered service:. . . . . Feb 2001	Cabin voltage: . . . . .110 and 220 volts
Registry:. . . . . Malta	Elevators:. 0
Length (ft/m):. 383.8/117.0	Casino (gaming tables):. . . . . .No
Beam (ft/m):. 52.9/16.1	Slot machines:. . . . . .No
Draft (ft/m): 17.7/5.4	Swimming pools:. 0
Propulsion/Propellers:. . . . . sail power + diesel (2,500kW)/2	Hot tubs (on deck):. 0
Passenger decks:. 4	Self-service launderette:. . . . . .No
Total crew:. 60	Dedicated cinema/seats:. . . . . .No
Passengers (lower beds/alll berths):. 94/94	Library:. . . . . Yes
Passenger Space Ratio (lower beds/all berths): 40.9/40.9	Onboard currency: . . . . Euros
Crew/Passenger Ratio (lower beds/all berths):. 1.6/1.6	

A fine tall ship providing sail-cruises for couples

OVERVIEW. This is just about as exclusive as it gets – sailing in the lap of luxury aboard one of the world's most luxurious true sailing ships – although your experience will depend on which company is operating the ship under charter when you sail, and exactly what is to be included in the package.

THE SHIP. This three-mast tall ship (called a barque) is slightly longer and beamier than the original *Sea Cloud*, and has the look, ambience, and feel of a 1930s sailing vessel while benefiting from the latest high-tech navigational aids. It complements the company's original, 1931-built *Sea Cloud* in almost every way, including its external appearance – except for a very rounded stern in place of the counter stern of the original ship.

The interior designers have managed to replicate the same beautiful traditional look and special decorative touches, so anyone who has sailed aboard *Sea Cloud* will feel instantly at home. Whether the modern materials used will stand up to 80 years of use like those of the original ship remains to be seen, although they are of a high quality. In any event, comparisons are bound to be made, and if you have sailed aboard the original *Sea Cloud*, you will probably be disappointed with the more limited space and decoration of the equivalent cabins aboard this ship.

The main lounge is truly elegant, with sofa and large individual tub chair seating around oval drinks tables. The ceiling is ornate, with an abundance of wood de-

Berlitz's Ratings

	Possible	Achieved
Ship	500	433
Accommodation	200	173
Food	400	338
Service	400	333
Entertainment	100	95
Cruise	400	329

OVERALL SCORE
1701 points out of 2000

tailing, and an oval centerpiece is set around skylights to the open deck above. A bar is set into the aft port side of the room, which has audio-visual aids built in for lectures and presentations.

A treasured aspect of sailing aboard this ship is its 'Blue Lagoon', at the very stern – part of the outdoor bar and casual dining area. Weather permitting, you can lie on thick blue padding and gaze up at the stars and warm night sky – it's a huge pleasure, particularly when the ship is under sail, with the engines turned off.

In terms of interior design, degree of luxury in appointments, the passenger flow, fabrics, food, and service, the ceiling height of public rooms, larger cabins, great open deck space, better passenger space ratio and crew to passenger ratio, there is none better than *Sea Cloud II*. I have sailed aboard both vessels and I can promise you a memorable sail-cruise experience.

A small water sports platform is built into the aft quarter of the starboard side (with adjacent shower), and the ship carries four inflatable craft for close-in shore landings, as well as snorkeling equipment.

There are three masts and up to 24 sails, measuring a billowing 32,292 sq ft/3,000 sq m. These are: flying jib, outer jib, inner jib; fore royal, fore topgallant, fore upper topsail, fore lower topsail, fore course; main royal staysail, main topgallant staysail, main topmast staysail; sky sail, main royal, main topgallant, main upper topsail, main lower topsail, main sail; mizzen topgallant staysail, mizzen topmast staysail; mizzen gaff topsail, mizzen upper gaff sail, mizzen lower gaff sail, middle gaff, upper gaff.

ACCOMMODATION. The decor in the cabins is very tasteful 1920s retro, with lots of bird's-eye maple wood paneling, brass accenting, and beautiful molded white ceilings. All cabins have a vanity desk, hairdryer, refrigerator (typically stocked with soft drinks and bottled water), and a combination TV/video player.

All cabins have a private bathroom with shower enclosure (or tub/shower combination), and plenty of storage space for toiletries. The cabin current is 220 volts, although all bathrooms also include a 110-volt socket for shavers.

There are two suites. Naturally, these have more space – but not as much space as the two owner's suites aboard Sea Cloud – and comprise a completely separate bedroom, with four-poster bed, and living room, while the marble-clad bathroom has a full-size tub.

There are 16 junior suites. These provide a living area and sleeping area with twin beds that convert to a queen-size bed. The marble-clad bathroom is quite opulent, and has a small tub/shower combination, with lots of cubbyholes to store toiletries.

DINING. The one-seating dining room operates an open-seating policy, so you can dine with whom you wish, when you wish. It is decorated in a light, modern maritime style, with wood and carpeted flooring, comfortable chairs with armrests, and circular light fixtures. The gold-rimmed plates used for the captain's dinner – typically a candlelit affair – have the ship's crest embedded in the white porcelain; they are extremely elegant and highly collectible. The place settings for dinner, also often by candlelight, are navy blue, white, and gold Bauscher china.

There is always excellent seafood and fish, purchased fresh, locally, when available, as are most other ingredients. For breakfast and lunch, there are self-serve buffets. These are really good, and beautifully presented – usually indoors for breakfast and outdoors on the Promenade Deck for lunch. Meal times are announced by the ship's bell.

European wines typically accompany lunch and dinner – mostly young vintages. Soft drinks and bottled water are included in the fare, while alcoholic drinks cost extra. On a cruise's last day, homemade ice cream is produced.

ENTERTAINMENT. There is a keyboard player/singer for the occasional soirée, but nothing else – nothing else is needed since the thrill of sailing is the entertainment. Dinner and after-dinner conversation with fellow passengers really becomes the main activity each evening. So, if you are feeling anti-social and don't want to talk to your fellow passengers, take a good book or two.

SPA/FITNESS. There is a health/fitness area, with a small gymnasium, and sauna. Massage is available.

How to recognize the rigging

For the yachting types among you, the 30 sails (measuring a huge 32,292 sq ft/3,000 sq m) are, in order, from fore to aft mast, top to bottom:
Fore Mast. Flying jib, outer jib, inner jib, fore topmast staysail, fore royal, fore topgallant, fore upper-top sail, fore lower-top sail, foresail.
Main Mast. Main royal staysail, main topgallant staysail, main topmast staysail, skysail, main royal, main topgallant, main upper topsail, main lower topsail, main sail.
Mizzen Mast. Mizzen royal staysail, mizzen topgallant staysail, mizzen topmast staysail, mizzen royal topsail, mizzen topgallant, mizzen upper topsail, mizzen lower topsail, mizzen course.
Spanker Mast. Spanker top mast staysail, spanker staysail, spanker-gaff topsail, spanker.

Sea Explorer
★★★ +

Size:..................................Boutique Ship	Crew/Passenger Ratio (lower beds/all berths):......... 1.7/1.8
Tonnage:.. 4,280	Cabins (total):.......................................61
Lifestyle:......................................Standard	Size range (sq ft/m):................. 234.6–353.0/21.8–32.8
Cruise line:........................... Quark Expeditions	Cabins (outside view):.................................61
Former names: .... Corinthian II, Island Sun, Sun, Renaissance I,	Cabins (interior/no view):..............................0
Regina Renaissance, Renaissance VII	Cabins (for one person):...............................0
IMO number: 8802882	Cabins (with private balcony):..........................4
Builder: ....Nuovi Cantieri Appaunia (Italy)	Cabins (wheelchair accessible): 0
Original cost:................................ $25 million	Wheelchair accessibility:............................None
Entered service:..................... Dec 1991/Nov 2012	Cabin voltage: .... 110 volts
Registry:....................................Marshall Islands	Elevators:..1
Length (ft/m):............................... 297.2/90.6	Casino (gaming tables):..............................No
Beam (ft/m):................................... 50.1/15.3	Slot machines:......................................No
Draft (ft/m): 12.9/2.9	Swimming pools:.....................................0
Propulsion/Propellers:...................diesel (5,000kW)/2	Hot tubs (on deck):..................................1
Passenger decks:....................................5	Self-service launderette:............................No
Total crew:...77	Dedicated cinema/seats:.............................No
Passengers (lower beds/alll berths):................ 112/122	Library: ....Yes
Passenger Space Ratio (lower beds/all berths): 38.2/38.2	Onboard currency: ....US$

OVERVIEW. This really intimate little ship is very comfortable and totally inviting, and operates warm-weather cruises in regions devoid of large cruise ships. It suits mature adults who like to discover small ports in a relaxed lifestyle combined with good food and service, and itineraries that enable you to 'get away from it all, but in comfort.'

THE SHIP. *Sea Explorer* has mega-yacht looks, a smart profile and handsome styling, with twin flared funnels and a 'ducktail' (or sponson), stern to provide fairly decent stability and seagoing comfort. This ship is owned by ISP and was chartered to Polar Latitudes in April 2013 for 'soft' destination-intensive discovery cruises. The ship has a narrow teak walk-around promenade deck outdoors, and a decent amount of open deck space.

A baby shore tender hangs off the aft deck and acts as ship-to-shore transportation. Some equipment for watersports is carried.

The interior design is elegant, with polished wood-finish paneling throughout. There is also a very small book and video library. Although *Sea Explorer* is not up to the standard of a Seabourn or Silversea ship, it will provide a good cruise experience at a moderate cost. Gratuities are appreciated but not required.

ACCOMMODATION. The cabins are quite spacious and combine highly polished imitation rosewood paneling with lots of mirrors and hand-crafted Italian furniture, lighted walk-in closets, and vanity

Berlitz's Ratings

	Possible	Achieved
Ship	500	359
Accommodation	200	157
Food	400	267
Service	400	282
Entertainment	100	60
Cruise	400	272

OVERALL SCORE
1397 points out of 2000

mirrors. In fact, there are a lot of mirrored surfaces in the decor, as well as just about everything you need, including a TV set and DVD player, a refrigerator, and free soft drinks and bottled water. The beds are fixed, so there's no under-bed storage space.

The bathrooms are extremely compact; they have real teakwood floors and marble vanities, and shower enclosures. None have tubs, not even the owner's suite. Cabins with balconies have glass panels topped with a polished wood railing.

DINING. The dining room operates in an open seating arrangement for all meals, so you sit where you like, with whom you like, and at what time you like. It is small but quite smart, with tables for two, four, six, and eight. The meals are self-service, buffet-style cold foods for breakfast and lunch, with hot foods chosen from a table menu and served properly, and sit-down service for dinner. The food quality, choice, and presentation are all very good.

ENTERTAINMENT. There is no formal entertainment in the main lounge, the venue for all social activities. However, six pillars obstruct the sight lines to the small stage area so it's not easy to see a speaker/lecturer.

SPA/FITNESS. Water sports facilities include an aft platform, sailfish, snorkel equipment, and Zodiacs.

Sea Princess
★★★★

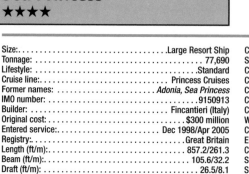

Size:.................................Large Resort Ship	Cabins (total):.......................................1,008
Tonnage: 77,690	Size range (sq ft/m): 158.2–610.3/14.7–56.7
Lifestyle: ....Standard	Cabins (outside view):..................................603
Cruise line:............................. Princess Cruises	Cabins (interior/no view):...............................405
Former names: .... Adonia, Sea Princess	Cabins (for one person):....................................0
IMO number: 9150913	Cabins (with private balcony):..........................411
Builder: .... Fincantieri (Italy)	Cabins (wheelchair accessible): 19
Original cost:.............................. $300 million	Wheelchair accessibility:..............................Good
Entered service:..................... Dec 1998/Apr 2005	Cabin voltage:..........................110 and 220 volts
Registry:...................................Great Britain	Elevators:...11
Length (ft/m):.............................. 857.2/261.3	Casino (gaming tables):................................. Yes
Beam (ft/m):................................ 105.6/32.2	Slot machines:... Yes
Draft (ft/m):.................................... 26.5/8.1	Swimming pools:..3
Propulsion/Propellers:............ diesel-electric (46,080kW)/2	Hot tubs (on deck):.......................................5
Passenger decks:.......................................10	Self-service launderette:............................... Yes
Total crew:..850	Dedicated cinema/seats:.................................No
Passengers (lower beds/all berths):............. 2,016/2,272	Library: .... Yes
Passenger Space Ratio (lower beds/all berths): 39.3/34.1	Onboard currency: ....US$
Crew/Passenger Ratio (lower beds/all berths):......... 2.2/2.5	

A large, family-friendly ship with relaxing decor

OVERVIEW. *Sea Princess* spends most of its time cruising in Australasian and South Pacific waters. As is the case aboard most large ships, you will be well attended if you live in the top-grade cabins; otherwise, you'll be one of a very large number of passengers.

THE SHIP. This all-white ship (sister ships: *Dawn Princess, Sun Princess*) has a profile balanced by a large, swept-back funnel that, in its sheltered base aft contains a deck tennis/basketball/volleyball court. There is a wide, teak walk-around promenade deck outdoors, some real teak steamer-style deck chairs with cushioned pads, and 93,000 sq ft (8,640 sq m) of outdoors space. A large glazed area on the upper decks provides plenty of light and connection with the outside world.

Sea Princess absorbs passengers well and has a decent passenger space ratio for a large ship. Some areas even have an intimate feel to them, which is what the interior designers intended. The interiors are attractive and welcoming with pastel colors and decor that includes countless wall murals and other artwork. There is a wide range of public rooms, including 13 bars, with several intimate rooms and spaces so that you aren't overwhelmed. A large, four-deck-high atrium lobby has winding, double stairways and two panoramic glass-walled elevators.

There is a library, a warm room with ocean-view windows and large buttery leather chairs for listening to CDs and audio books, a card room and reading room.

Berlitz's Ratings

	Possible	Achieved
Ship	500	377
Accommodation	200	148
Food	400	247
Service	400	278
Entertainment	100	77
Cruise	400	287

OVERALL SCORE
1414 points out of 2000

The artwork collection is good, particularly on the stairways, and helps make the ship feel smaller than it is. The Grand Casino is slightly out of the main passenger flow and so doesn't generate the 'walk-through' factor found aboard so many ships. Cyberspace is a lounge and Internet-connect room close to the pools on Riviera Deck.

Perhaps the most popular drinking venue is the Wheelhouse Bar, with decor that is a pleasing mix of traditional and modern, a bandstand and dance floor; it's like a gentleman's club, with its wood paneling and comfortable seating. For families with children, plenty of space is provided in The Fun Zone children's center, on the starboard side of the Riviera Deck.

One nice feature is the fact that the captain's cocktail party is normally held in the four-deck-high open-flow main atrium, so you can come and go as you please. In the quest for increased onboard revenue, even birthday cakes are now an extra-cost item, as are espressos and cappuccinos in the lobby café, though fake ones, made from instant coffee, are available in the dining rooms. Also at extra cost are ice cream, except in the restaurant, and bottled water; these can add up to a considerable amount on a long cruise.

There are a number of dead ends in the interior layout, so it could be more user-friendly. The swimming pools are quite small for the number of passengers carried, and the pool deck is cluttered with plastic sunloungers. The digital voice announcing lift deck stops is annoying for many.

ACCOMMODATION. There are numerous different cabin price grades, designated as suites with private balcony, mini-suites with private balcony, outside-view twin-bedded cabins with balcony, outside-view twin-bedded cabins, and interior twin-bedded cabins. Although the standard outside-view and interior cabins are a little small, they are functional, and have earth tone colors accentuated by splashes of color from the bedspreads. Proportionately, there are quite a lot of interior cabins.

Many outside-view cabins have private balconies, and all seem to be quite well soundproofed, although the balcony partition is not of the floor to ceiling type, so you can hear your neighbors. The balconies are very narrow – just big enough for two small chairs – and there is no outdoor balcony light. Some cabins have third- and fourth-person upper bunk beds – good for families with children.

There is a reasonable amount of closet space and abundant drawer and other storage space in the cabins; although adequate for a seven-night cruise, it can prove challenging for longer cruises. Also provided are a TV set and refrigerator, and each night a chocolate will appear on your pillow. The cabin bathrooms are practical units, and come complete with all the facilities one needs – although, again, they really are tight spaces. Fortunately, they have a shower enclosure of a decent size, real glasses, a hairdryer, and a small amount of shelving for toiletries.

Suites. The largest cabins are six suites, two on each of three decks at the stern, each with its own large private balcony. These suites are well laid-out, and the large bathrooms have two washbasins, a Jacuzzi tub, and separate shower enclosure. The bedroom has generous amounts of wood accenting and detailing, indented ceilings, TV sets in the bedroom and lounge areas, and a dining table and four chairs.

Mini-Suites. These typically have two lower beds that convert into a queen-size bed. There is a separate bedroom/sleeping area with vanity desk, and a lounge with sofa and coffee table, indented ceilings, generous amounts of wood accenting and detailing, walk-in closet; the bathroom has a Jacuzzi tub and separate shower enclosure.

Standard Outside-view/Interior Cabins. The cabin bathrooms are practical, but compact. They do, however, have a decent shower enclosure, real glasses, a hairdryer, and a small amount of shelving for toiletries.

The cabin numbering system is quite illogical, with numbers going through several hundred series on the same deck. The room service menu is very limited.

DINING. Rigoletto and Traviata are the two main, asymmetrically designed dining rooms, each seating about 500 and adjacent to the two lower levels of the four-deck high atrium lobby. Your cabin location determines which you are assigned to. Each has its own galley and each is split into multi-tier sections that help create a feeling of intimacy, although there is a lot of noise from the waiter stations. Breakfast and lunch have open seating, and dinner is in two seatings. The wine list is quite reasonable; 15 percent is added to all beverage bills, including wines.

Other dining options. Horizon Court is the ship's 24-hour casual, self-serve buffet. At night, this large room, which resembles a food court, can be transformed into an informal bistro dinner setting with waiter service. Reservations are necessary and there may be a cover charge.

Outdoors on deck, with a sheltered view over the Riviera Pool, the Terrace Grill serves fast-food items to those who don't want to change from sunbathing attire. In the evening, the grill offers steaks, seafood, and a 'white sisters' mixed grill. There's a cover charge for dining under the stars.

For informal eats, Verdi's, on the uppermost level of the atrium lobby, serves steaks and seafood at extra cost. In addition, there's a patisserie for cappuccino/espresso coffees and pastries opposite the reception desk on the atrium's lowest deck, and a wine/caviar bar, Rendezvous, on Promenade Deck. Coffee or tea from any of the bars costs extra.

ENTERTAINMENT. The Princess Theater, located forward, is a 550-seat, theater-style showlounge, where the main production shows are staged and movies can be shown. The second theater, Vista Lounge, located aft, is a 480-seat lounge and bar for cabaret entertainment and lectures.

In addition, the ship has an array of cabaret acts. Although many are not what you would call headliners, they regularly travel the cruise ship circuit. Classical concerts are scheduled for many cruises throughout the year.

SPA/FITNESS. The Lotus Spa has facilities that are contained in a glass-walled complex located on Lido Deck – one of the highest decks, at the aft section of the ship. It includes a gymnasium with ocean views aft and to port, with all the associated high-tech muscle-pumping and body toning equipment, a combination aerobics/exercise room, sauna and steam room, and several wellbeing treatment rooms. Some fitness and exercise classes may cost extra.

Forming part of the outside area of the spa complex, one swimming pool is 'suspended' aft between two decks. Two other pools are located in another area in the center of the ship, although they are not large for the size of the vessel. Sports facilities are located in an open-air sports deck positioned inside the funnel and adaptable for basketball, volleyball, badminton, or paddle tennis.

Joggers can exercise on the wraparound open Promenade Deck. There's also an electronic golf simulator – no need to bring your own clubs.

Sea Spirit
★★★ +

Size:.....................................Boutique Ship	Crew/Passenger Ratio (lower beds/all berths):..........1.8/4.7
Tonnage:..4,200	Cabins (total):....................................60
Lifestyle:.....................................Standard	Size range (sq ft/m):............215.0–353.0/20.0–32.7
Cruise line:...........................Quark Expeditions	Cabins (outside view):..............................60
Former names: Spirit of Oceanus, MegaStar Sagittarius, Sun Viva,	Cabins (interior/no view):............................0
Renaissance Five	Cabins (for one person):.............................0
IMO number:.................................8802878	Cabins (with private balcony):......................12
Builder:.....................Nuovi Cantieri Apuania (Italy)	Cabins (wheelchair accessible):......................0
Original cost:...............................$25 million	Wheelchair accessibility:..........................None
Entered service:..........................1991/Oct 2011	Cabin voltage:...............................110 volts
Registry:..................................The Bahamas	Elevators:..1
Length (ft/m):.............................294.5/89.7	Casino (gaming tables):............................No
Beam (ft/m):..............................50.1/15.3	Slot machines:....................................No
Draft (ft/m):...............................13.2/4.0	Swimming pools:....................................1
Propulsion/Propellers:..................diesel (5,000kW)/2	Hot tubs (on deck):.................................1
Passenger decks:....................................5	Self-service launderette:..........................No
Total crew:.......................................64	Dedicated cinema/seats:............................No
Passengers (lower beds/alll berths):................120 /127	Library:...Yes
Passenger Space Ratio (lower beds/all berths):.......35.0/33.0	Onboard currency:................................US$

A comfortable ship for exploring Antarctica up close

OVERVIEW. This ship is best suited to couples and single travelers who enjoy nature and wildlife up close in a contemporary small-ship setting, and who wouldn't dream of cruising in the mainstream sense.

THE SHIP. *Sea Spirit* (formerly *Spirit of Oceanus*) has a modern exterior with a private yacht-like look, with twin, flared funnels. There is a narrow teakwood walking deck outdoors, and a reasonable amount of open deck and sunbathing space, and Deck 5 has a hot tub. The deck furniture is also teak, as is a platform at the stern of the ship, used by passengers for passengers to decant into inflatable, rubber expedition landing craft. The main lounge, the focal point for social activities, has six pillars that destroy sightlines to the small stage/floor area. Refitted in 2010, it now includes better equipment to make it suitable for polar expedition cruising.

ACCOMMODATION. There are several price categories. Fine all-outside-view cabins (called 'suites' in the brochure) combine highly polished imitation rosewood paneling with lots of mirrors, and fine, hand-crafted Italian furniture. All suites have twin beds that convert to a queen-size bed, a sitting area with three-person sofa, one individual chair, coffee table, mini-bar/refrigerator (stocked with juices and bottled water), flat-screen TV and DVD player, direct-dial satellite telephone, and a bowl of fresh fruit on embarkation day. While closet space is good, space for stowing

Berlitz's Ratings		
	Possible	Achieved
Ship	500	358
Accommodation	200	157
Food	400	220
Service	400	237
Entertainment	100	50
Cruise	400	234
OVERALL SCORE		
1256 points out of 2000		

luggage is tight, and there is little drawer space. There are no music channels in the cabins, and there is no switch to turn off announcements in your cabin.

The marble bathrooms are compact units that have showers (no bathrooms have a tub) with fold-down (plastic) seat, real teakwood floor, marble vanity, large mirror, recessed towel rail, and built-in hairdryer. There is a high lip into the bathroom.

DINING. The Restaurant, which has an open-seating policy, is bright, elegant, and welcoming. It is on the lowest deck and has portholes rather than windows, due to international maritime construction and insurance regulations. There are tables for two, four, six, or eight. Dinners are normally sit-down affairs, although, depending on the itinerary and length of cruise, there could be an occasional buffet. Breakfast and lunch are typically self-serve buffets and can be taken at the poolside (weather permitting), in your cabin, or in the restaurant.

ENTERTAINMENT. There is no formal entertainment, so dinner and after-dinner conversation with fellow passengers in the ship's lounge/bar is the main diversion.

SPA/FITNESS. There is a small fitness center. Massage is available.

Seabourn Legend
★★★★+

Size:.....................................Boutique Ship	Cabins (total):.....................................106
Tonnage:.......................................9,961	Size range (sq ft/m):.............277.0–575.8/25.7–53.5
Lifestyle:......................................Luxury	Cabins (outside view):..............................106
Cruise line:..................................Seabourn	Cabins (interior/no view):.............................0
Former names:...........Queen Odyssey, Royal Viking Queen	Cabins (for one person):..............................0
IMO number:.................................9008598	Cabins (with private balcony):.........................6
Builder:................Schichau Seebeckwerft (Germany)	Cabins (wheelchair accessible):.......................4
Original cost:..............................$87 million	Wheelchair accessibility:...........................None
Entered service:.....................Mar 1992/Jul 1996	Cabin voltage:.........................110 and 220 volts
Registry:.....................................Bahamas	Elevators:..3
Length (ft/m):...........................442.9/135.0	Casino (gaming tables):...........................Yes
Beam (ft/m):...............................62.9/19.2	Slot machines:....................................Yes
Draft (ft/m):................................16.4/5.0	Swimming pools:....................................1
Propulsion/Propellers:..................diesel (7,280kW)/2	Hot tubs (on deck):................................3
Passenger decks:.................................6	Self-service launderette:.........................Yes
Total crew:......................................160	Dedicated cinema/seats:............................No
Passengers (lower beds/all berths):................212/212	Library:...Yes
Passenger Space Ratio (lower beds/all berths):.......46.9/46.9	Onboard currency:.................................US$
Crew/Passenger Ratio (lower beds/all berths):.........1.3/1.3	

A small, cozy, elegant ship for mature-age cruisers

OVERVIEW. *Seabourn Legend* can cruise to places where large cruise ships can't, thanks to its ocean-yacht size. For a grand, small-ship vacation in fine surroundings, with just over 100 other couples as neighbors and excellent food that approaches gourmet standards, it's hard to beat. It is best suited to sophisticated, well traveled couples, typically over 50, but possibly younger.

THE SHIP. *Seabourn Legend* is a contemporary gem of a ship with a handsome profile, almost identical in looks and size to *Seabourn Pride* and *Seabourn Spirit*, but younger and built to a much higher standard, with streamline 'decorator' bars made by Mercedes-Benz located along the side of the upper superstructure and a slightly different swept-over funnel design. The sunloungers have thankfully been changed to a steel-mesh design, but they are hard-surfaced and need pads to make them comfortable for more than a few minutes. There is no walk-around promenade deck outdoors.

The ship has two fine mahogany water taxis for use as shore tenders. An aft water sports platform and marina can be used in suitably calm warm-water areas. Water sports facilities include a small, enclosed 'dip' pool, sea kayaks, snorkel equipment, windsurfers, waterski boat, and Zodiac inflatable boats.

Inside, a wide central passageway divides port and starboard side accommodation. The finest quality interior fixtures, fittings and fabrics have been combined in its sumptuous public areas to present an outstanding,

Berlitz's Ratings	Possible	Achieved
Ship	500	414
Accommodation	200	171
Food	400	327
Service	400	341
Entertainment	100	77
Cruise	400	324
OVERALL SCORE		
1654 points out of 2000		

elegant decor, with warm color combinations and some fine artwork. There is no glitz anywhere. The dress code, relaxed by day, is a little more formal at night.

All drinks, except premium brands and connoisseur wines, are included in the fare. So are gratuities, fine aromatherapy Molton Brown bath products and large soaps by Bronnley, Chanel, and Hermès, short massages ('massage moments') on deck, open-seating dining, use of watersports equipment, one included Exclusively Seabourn shore excursion per cruise, and movies under the stars.

The three Seabourn ships, which provide a good hotel service product, are still not up to the standard of *Europa*'s better product delivery and hospitality. Indeed, there have been many recent complaints about falling standards aboard the Seabourn ships, particularly in regard to maintenance – they are more than 20 years old.

Niggles? The range of cigars offered is limited. The Club suffers from over-amplified music. Non-American passengers should note that almost all entertainment and activities are geared towards American tastes, despite the increasingly international passenger mix.

DHL can provide luggage pick-up and delivery service. Port charges and insurance are not included in the fare. Note that Seabourn Legend has been sold to Xanterra Parks & Resorts, parent company of Windstar Cruises; it will be transferred in April 2015 and renamed Star Legend. Sister ships Seabourn Pride (to be renamed Star Pride) will be transferred in May 2014, and Seabourn Spirit (to be renamed Star Spirit) will be transferred in May, 2015.

ACCOMMODATION. This is spread over three decks, and there are several price categories. All suites are comfortably large and comprehensively equipped. They are, for example, larger than those aboard the smaller *SeaDream I* and *SeaDream II*, but then the ship is also larger, with almost twice as many passengers.

All suites have a sleeping area with European duvets and Frette linens. A separate lounge area has a Bose wave radio/CD unit, DVD player and flat-screen TV, vanity desk with hairdyer and personalized stationery, world atlas, mini-bar and refrigerator stocked with soft drinks and two bottles of your favorite liquor at embarkation, a large walk-in closet illuminated automatically when you open the door, digital personal safe, and wall-mounted clock and barometer. A full passenger list is provided – a rarity today – as are a fresh fruit basket, replenished daily, and flowers.

Marble-clad bathrooms have one or two washbasins, depending on accommodation grade, a decent but not full-size tub (four suites have a shower enclosure only – no bathtub), plenty of storage areas, 100 percent thick cotton towels, plush terrycloth bathrobe, and designer soaps. A selection of five Molton Brown aromatherapy bath preparations can be ordered from your stewardess, who will prepare your bath for you.

Course-by-course in-cabin dining is available during dinner hours – the cocktail table can be raised to form a dining table – and there is 24-hour room service. Also provided are personalized stationery, and fancy ticket wallet, suitably boxed and nicely packaged before your cruise. Non-smoking cabins are available. Menus for each dinner are delivered to your suite during the day.

In 2001, 36 French (or 'Juliet') balconies were added to suites on two out of three accommodation decks. These are not balconies in the true sense, but have two doors that open wide onto a tiny teakwood balcony that is just 10.6ins (27cm) deep – just enough for toes. The balconies do allow you to have fresh sea air, however, together with some salt spray.

Four Owner's suites (Ibsen/Grieg, each 530 sq ft/49 sq m, and Eriksson/Heyerdahl, each 575 sq ft/53 sq m), and two Classic Suites (Queen Maud/Queen Sonja, each 400 sq ft/37 sq m) are superb, private living spaces. Each has a walk-in closet, second closet, full bathroom plus a guest toilet with washbasin. There is a fully secluded forward- or side-facing balcony, with sun lounge chairs and wooden drinks table (Ibsen and Grieg don't have balconies). The living area has ample bookshelf space, including a complete edition of *Encyclopaedia Britannica*, large refrigerator/drinks cabinet, television and DVD player, plus a second TV set in the bedroom. All windows, as well as the door to the balcony, have manually operated blackout blinds, and a complete blackout is possible in both bedroom and living room.

DINING. The Restaurant is a part-marble, part-carpeted dining room that has portholes and elegant decor but it is not as warm and intimate as that found aboard the smaller SeaDream ships, with their wood paneling. The silverware (150g weight – the best available) is by Robbe & Berking. Open-seating dining means that you can dine when you want, with whom you wish. Course-by-course meals can be served in your cabin.

Dining can be memorable, if you choose the right thing. The menus are creative and well-balanced, with a wide selection of foods, including regional dishes. Seabourn's cuisine is artfully presented, with many items cooked to order. Special orders are available, as is caviar (at extra cost, although it will probably be of the farmed American Hackleback variety). Flaming desserts can be cooked at your table. The selection of exotic fruits and cheeses is good.

Each day, basic table wine is included for lunch and dinner, but the decent ones cost extra. The wine list is quite extensive, with prices ranging from moderate to high; many of the wines come from the smaller, more exclusive vineyards. The European dining room staff is hand-picked and provides excellent, unhurried service.

Relaxed breakfasts until 11am, lunch buffets, and casual, themed candlelight dinners (including a new '2' tasting menu) can be taken in the popular Veranda Café, adjacent to the swimming pool, instead of in the dining room. The Sky Grill provides an above-poolside setting complete with candle-lit dining and specializing in steaks and seafood.

ENTERTAINMENT. The King Olaf Lounge is the venue for shows, cabaret acts, lectures, and most social functions. It has a sloping floor that provides good sightlines from just about every seat. This is a small, upscale ship, so the typically four-person 'production' shows are of limited scope because dinner is almost always the main event. You can, however, expect to see the occasional cabaret act.

Singers also tend to do mini-cabaret performances in The Club, one deck above the showlounge.

SPA/FITNESS. The Spa at Seabourn, a small, well-equipped health spa/fitness center, is located just aft of the navigation bridge. It provides sauna and steam rooms with separate facilities for men and women, and integral changing room; plus a separate exercise room with videotapes for private, individual aerobics workouts; and a beauty salon.

The facility is staffed and operated by concession Elemis by Steiner. Treatment prices are equal to those in an expensive land-based spa. The beauty salon offers hair beautifying treatments, while in the gym, personal training, yoga classes, mat Pilates, and body composition analysis are available at extra cost.

Seabourn Odyssey
★★★★★

Size:.	Small Ship	Cabins (total):.	225
Tonnage:	32,000	Size range (sq ft/m):	295.0–438.1/27.5–133.6
Lifestyle:	Luxury	Cabins (outside view):	225
Cruise line:.	Seabourn	Cabins (interior/no view):.	0
Former names:	none	Cabins (for one person):.	0
IMO number:	9417086	Cabins (with private balcony):.	199
Builder:	Mariotti (Italy)	Cabins (wheelchair accessible):	7
Original cost:	$250 million	Wheelchair accessibility:	Good
Entered service:.	Jun 2009	Cabin voltage:	110 volts
Registry:.	Bahamas	Elevators:.	3
Length (ft/m):.	6450.0/198.1	Casino (gaming tables):.	Yes
Beam (ft/m):.	83.9/25.6	Slot machines:.	Yes
Draft (ft/m):	21.3/6.5	Swimming pools:.	2
Propulsion/Propellers:	diesel-electric (23,040kwW)/2	Hot tubs (on deck):.	6
Passenger decks:.	10	Self-service launderette:.	Yes
Total crew:.	330	Dedicated cinema/seats:.	No
Passengers (lower beds/alll berths):.	450/462	Library:.	Yes
Passenger Space Ratio (lower beds/all berths):	71.1/69.2	Onboard currency:	US$
Crew/Passenger Ratio (lower beds/all berths):.	1.3/1.4		

An elegant, upscale ship for mature-age cruisers

OVERVIEW. This is a ship with a yacht-like ambience. Its strong points are the staff, high service levels, attention to detail, and the fitness/wellness facilities.

THE SHIP. *Seabourn Odyssey*, the first of three larger ships for Seabourn, looks like an up-sized version of its three smaller vessels – *Seabourn Legend*, *Seabourn Pride*, *Seabourn Spirit*. However, this ship and sister ships *Seabourn Quest* and *Seabourn Sojourn* have one of the highest passenger space ratios in the cruise industry – so you will never feel that it's crowded.

There are two outdoor swimming pools, midships and aft; the aft pool is in a more secluded area, although there's not a lot of sunbathing space and the sunloungers are of the steel mesh variety. One of the most pleasing outdoor areas is the Sky Bar. But for stargazing, the hot tub located by the ship's bow is a delight. While real teak is used in most outdoor areas, Flexteak (faux teak) is used in some locations.

All accommodation areas are in the forward section, with most public rooms aft – so accommodation is quiet, but you'll need to pass through several decks to get to some public rooms. An Observation Lounge, which has great views, is a well laid-out, very comfortable room. The Marina, at the stern, has a staging area from which watersports are organized. The interior decor uses light woods, tame colors, and suitably rich soft furnishings to create a contemporary, restrained, and relaxing environment, which is good

Berlitz's Ratings

	Possible	Achieved
Ship	500	438
Accommodation	200	178
Food	400	333
Service	400	343
Entertainment	100	81
Cruise	400	333

OVERALL SCORE
1706 points out of 2000

considering the low ceiling height in most public rooms.

Seabourn Square, a 'concierge lounge,' has a relaxed and club-like ambience designed to encourage sociability. The area includes a library, Internet-connect computers, an outdoor terrace, and a coffee bar that's particularly good for late-riser coffees and pastries. Wi-Fi is available throughout.

Drinks, wines with meals, and all gratuities are included, though premium brands and high-quality wines cost extra.

Passenger niggles include the high charge for Internet-connectivity. The ship's 'vertical stacking' layout is not really user-friendly. The cabin doors are rather narrow; doors within the cabins are of varying heights and sizes, and feel utilitarian. Most public rooms are of a single deck height, which doesn't create a good feeling of spaciousness, and support pillars are everywhere, as well as fire doors that protrude outside bulkheads instead of being integral to them.

ACCOMMODATION. There are several different grades of suites in many price categories, although the smaller 'suites' are really large cabins. However, the ship has many balcony cabins (about 90 percent, in fact), giving you plenty of personal privacy. Even the smallest cabin is a generous 269 sq ft (25 sq m). All cabins have a separate tub and shower enclosure in a granite bathroom setting, twin beds convertible to a queen-size bed, flat-screen TV plus CD and DVD player, minibar, vanity desk with hairdryer, world atlas, personalized stationery, and large walk-in closet with personal safe.

The interior designers have crafted homely, contemporary living spaces in the suites and cabins, although the walls are rather plain and unimaginative. It's good to see that the beds are high enough off the floor to enable even the largest suitcases to be stowed underneath. All drawers are fitted with soft gel, which means they are quiet – no more slamming contests with your next-door neighbor.

The cabins are bathed in soft earthy tones, although a splash of color wouldn't go amiss. The cabinetry has many seams and strips covering joints which suggest that the ship's outfitters would benefit from a joinery course. It's also strange that several internal doors are of different sizes, widths and heights. One neat, very creative feature is a leather-clad vanity stool/table that converts into a backgammon table.

Seabourn Suites and Veranda Suites are quite narrow, and feel cramped, with little space in the passageway between the bed and the opposite wall. However, the bathrooms are generously proportioned, with grey and chocolate-brown decor; there are two washbasins, a bathtub, and a separate shower enclosure.

Some size examples (excluding balcony): Grand Suites 1,135 sq ft (105 sq m), including two-bedrooms; Signature Suites 819 sq ft (76 sq m); Wintergarden Suites 914 sq ft (85 sq m). Rather neat suites within a glass-enclosed solarium, set in front of the funnel, with a side balcony; Owners Suites 611–675 sq ft (57–63 sq m); Penthouse Suite 436–611 sq ft (41–57 sq m); Veranda Suite 269–298 sq ft (25–28 sq m); Seabourn Suite (295 sq ft (27 sq m).

Four 'Penthouse Spa Suites' were added in a 2013 refit. These are located directly above the spa itself (and connect to it via a spiral stairway), and measure between 64 sq m (688 sq ft) and 66 sq m (710 sq ft), including a balcony. The suites have a living and dining area with seating for four, a separate bedroom, walk-in closet, and a bathroom with tub and shower, balcony. Plus, there's free access to the spa's Serene Area.

DINING. There are three dining venues plus a poolside grill: The Restaurant has open-seating dining at tables for 2-8, with menus designed by American celebrity chef Charlie Palmer. It is a large venue that actually feels more clinical than classical with its white-on-white decor and double-height ceiling in its central section. The most-sought-after seats are located in the center, rather than along the port and starboard sides, which have a window, but low ceiling height.

Restaurant 2, with seating for around 50, features regional, seasonal cuisine and tasting menus, for a mini-dégustation. However, the ceiling height is rather low, which makes the feeling cramped. The cuisine is contemporary, with a flirtation with fusion, where taste and flavors are what the experience is all about. This venue shares the same galley as the adjacent The Colonnade.

The Colonnade, located aft, has indoor/outdoor seating and is nicely decorated, although its free-flow design could be better; there's too little outdoor seating for the demand in warm-weather areas, when many passengers like to eat outdoors. During dinner, passengers who are dressed formally on designated formal nights have to share the space with those who are more casually dressed. The venue is also adjacent to one of the fine dining restaurants.

The Patio Grill is located in a casual poolside setting outdoors – and is most enjoyable on balmy evenings, as a change to the air-conditioned interior dining venues. In addition, a 24-hour, in-suite menu offers the à la carte items served in the main dining room during dinner hours. Extra-cost Silver ($225.00) or Gold ($450.00) "connoisseur" wine packages provide a choice of red and white vintage wines for a set amount – perhaps a good idea for a longer cruise.

ENTERTAINMENT. The Grand Salon is the main entertainment venue for shows, cabaret performances, social dancing, and for use as a cinema. However, the stage is small – large enough for a live band, but performers need to use the dance floor area – and the room has nine thick pillars that make it awkward to see anything at all, although the room has a gentle slope. There's also a decorative steel ceiling grating in the central section that is black, cold and unappealing. It has banquette seating in the front and mid-section, and, strangely, sofa-style leather seating along the side walls to the rear, which mean you actually sit with your back to the stage – a rather unhelpful arrangement (particularly for the performers)!

Another venue, The Club, is a large, cool, trendy but high-volume nightclub/disco with a wooden dance floor, large bar and minimalist design. Located beneath the Grand salon, it incorporates a comfortable casino.

SPA/FITNESS. The Spa at Seabourn, operated by Elemis, occupies the aft section of two decks, and is quite large, at 11,500 sq ft (1,068 sq m). It offers full services in a very pleasant setting that includes a two-deck-high waterfall at the entrance and seven indoor/outdoor treatment rooms, as well as a Kneipp 'walk-in-the-water' experience, thermal suite (for which a pass costs extra), and complete salon facilities, while a hot tub and relaxation area on the deck above is accessed by a spiral staircase. Separate saunas and steam rooms for men and women are provided, but are extremely small. In the gymnasium, personal training sessions, yoga classes, mat Pilates, and body composition analysis are available at extra cost, but some basic exercise programs are free.

Seabourn Pride
★★★★+

Size:.....................................Boutique Ship	Cabins (total):.....................................106
Tonnage: 9,975	Size range (sq ft/m): 277.0–575.0/25.7–53.4
Lifestyle:...Luxury	Cabins (outside view):.................................106
Cruise line:.......................................Seabourn	Cabins (interior/no view):................................0
Former names: ....none	Cabins (for one person):.................................0
IMO number: 8797343	Cabins (with private balcony):.............................6
Builder: ....Seebeckwerft (Germany)	Cabins (wheelchair accessible): 4
Original cost: ....$50 million	Wheelchair accessibility:.............................None
Entered service:.............................. Dec 1988	Cabin voltage: ....110 and 220 volts
Registry:..Bahamas	Elevators:...3
Length (ft/m):................................. 439.9/134.1	Casino (gaming tables):................................ Yes
Beam (ft/m):..................................... 62.9/19.2	Slot machines:...................................... Yes
Draft (ft/m): 16.8/5.1	Swimming pools:.......................................1
Propulsion/Propellers: ....diesel (5,355kW)/2	Hot tubs (on deck):....................................3
Passenger decks:......................................6	Self-service launderette:.............................. Yes
Total crew:.......................................160	Dedicated cinema/seats:................................No
Passengers (lower beds/alll berths):................. 212/212	Library: ....Yes
Passenger Space Ratio (lower beds/all berths): 47.09/47.09	Onboard currency: ....US$
Crew/Passenger Ratio (lower beds/all berths):.......... 1.3/1.3	

A small, inclusive ship for compact, stylish cruising

OVERVIEW. *Seabourn Pride* is best for sophisticated, well-traveled couples – typically over 50, but possibly younger – looking for a small ship with excellent food and fine European-style service. The ship's big advantage is being able to cruise where large cruise ships can't, thanks to its ocean-yacht size. You sail with only 100 other couples, and a sense of intimate camaraderie.

THE SHIP. This pleasantly appointed, intimate cruise ship has sleek exterior styling, handsome profile with swept-back, rounded lines, and is an identical twin to *Seabourn Spirit*. It has two fine mahogany water taxis for use as shore tenders. An aft water sports platform and marina can be used in suitably calm warm-water areas. Water sports facilities include a small, enclosed 'dip' pool, sea kayaks, snorkel equipment, windsurfers, waterski boat, and Zodiac inflatable boats.

The sunloungers have thankfully been changed from plastic to a steel mesh design. There is no walk-around promenade deck outdoors. There is only one dryer in the self-service launderette. Non-American passengers should note that almost all entertainment and activities are geared towards American tastes, despite the increasingly international passenger mix.

A wide central passageway divides port and starboard side accommodation. Inviting, sumptuous public areas have warm colors. Fine quality interior fixtures, fittings, artwork, and fabric combine to present an outstanding, elegant decor. For a small ship, there's

Berlitz's Ratings

	Possible	Achieved
Ship	500	409
Accommodation	200	170
Food	400	327
Service	400	335
Entertainment	100	77
Cruise	400	322

OVERALL SCORE
1640 points out of 2000

wide range of public rooms. These include a main lounge that stages small cabaret shows, a nightclub, an observation lounge with bar, large, deep armchairs, and a cigar smoking area complete with cabinet, cigar humidor, and small selection of good cigars. There is a small business center, small meeting room, and a small casino with roulette and blackjack tables, plus a few slot machines.

Not for the budget-minded, this ship is for those desiring supremely elegant, stylish, small-ship surroundings, but is perhaps rather small for long voyages in open waters. During the past few years, there have been complaints about falling standards aboard the Seabourn ships, particularly with regard to maintenance – they are now over 20 years old – and that food, presentation, and service had deteriorated. However, the company has turned things around, and the product delivered is again good.

Seabourn Pride provides a fine level of personal service and an utterly civilized cruise. All drinks except premium brands and connoisseur wines are included. So are gratuities, aromatherapy bath selections from Molton Brown and soaps by Bronnley, Chanel, and Hermès, short massages on deck ('massage moments'), open-seating dining, use of watersports equipment, one included Exclusively Seabourn shore excursion per cruise, and movies under the stars. Port charges and insurance are not included. DHL provides a luggage pick-up and delivery service.

Note that Seabourn Pride has been sold to Xanterra Parks & Resorts, parent company of Windstar Cruises, and will be transferred in May 2014, and will be re-named Star Pride. Sister ships Seabourn Legend and Seabourn Spirit will be transferred in April and May, 2015, and will be named Star Legend and Star Spirit, respectively.

ACCOMMODATION. This is spread over three decks, with several different price categories. The all-outside cabins (called suites in brochure-speak) are comfortably large and beautifully equipped with eve-rything one could reasonably need. Electric blackout blinds are provided for the large windows in addition to curtains. All cabinetry is made of blond woods, with softly rounded edges, and cabin doors are neatly angled away from the passageway.

All the suites have a sleeping area, with European duvets and Frette linens as standard. A separate lounge area has a Bose Wave audio unit, DVD player and flat-screen TV, vanity desk with hairdryer and personal-ized stationery, world atlas, mini-bar, and refrigerator (stocked with soft drinks and two bottles of your fa-vorite liquor when you embark). There's a large walk-in closet illuminated automatically when you open the door, wooden hangers, electronic personal safe, um-brella, and wall-mounted clock and barometer. A full passenger list is also provided – a rarity these days – as are a fresh fruit basket, replenished daily, and flowers.

Marble-clad bathrooms have one or two washbasins, depending on the accommodation grade, a decent but not full-size tub (four suites have a shower enclosure only – no tub), plenty of storage areas, 100 percent thick cotton towels, plush terrycloth bathrobe, designer soaps, and Molton Brown personal amenities. A selec-tion of five Molton Brown aromatherapy bath prepara-tions can be ordered from your stewardess, who will prepare your bath.

In 2001, Seabourn added 36 French balconies to suites on two out of three accommodation decks. These are not balconies in the true sense of the word, but they do have two doors that open wide onto a tiny teakwood balcony that is just 10.6ins (27cm) wide. The balconies allow you to have fresh sea air, together with some salt spray.

Course-by-course in-cabin dining is available dur-ing dinner hours, and the cocktail table can be raised to form a dining table. There is 24-hour room service. Also provided are personalized stationery, and fancy ticket wallet. Non-smoking cabins are available. Men-us for each dinner are delivered to your suite during the day.

Four Owner's suites (King Haakon/King Magnus, each measuring 530 sq ft (49 sq m), and Amundsen/Nansen, each 575 sq ft (53 sq m), and two Classic Suites (King Harald/King Olav), each 400 sq ft (37 sq m) offer superb, private living spaces. Each has a walk-in closet, second closet, full bathroom plus a guest toilet with washbasin. There is a fully secluded forward- or side-facing balcony, with sunloungers and

wooden drinks table. The living area has ample book-shelf space including a complete edition of *Encyclo-paedia Britannica*, large refrigerator/drinks cabinet, television, and DVD player, plus a second TV set in the bedroom. All windows, as well as the door to the balcony, have manually operated blackout blinds, and a complete blackout is possible in both bedroom and living room.

DINING. The Restaurant is a part-marble, part-car-peted dining room with portholes and restful decor. The silverware (150g weight – the best available) is by Robbe & Berking. Open-seating dining means that you can dine when you want, with whom you wish.

The menus are creative and well-balanced, with a wide selection of foods and regional cuisine. Sea-bourn's cuisine is artfully presented, with many items cooked to order. Special orders are also available, and caviar (well, sort of – it's usually the farmed, very salty American Hackleback variety of caviar) is available on request. Flambé desserts can be presented at your table. There is always a good selection of exotic fruits and cheeses.

Each day, basic table wine is included for lunch and dinner, but the decent bottles cost extra. The wine list is quite extensive, with prices ranging from moderate to high; many of the wines come from the smaller, more exclusive vineyards. The European dining room staff provide excellent, unhurried service.

In addition, relaxed breakfasts (available until 11am) and lunch buffets and casual, themed candlelight din-ners, including a '2' tasting menu, can be taken in the popular Veranda Café adjacent to the swimming pool.

The Sky Grill provides an above-poolside setting for candlelit dining. It specializes in sizzling steaks and seafood.

ENTERTAINMENT. The Magellan Lounge has a sloping floor that provides good sight lines from just about every seat. 'Production' shows are of limited scope, as dinner is usually the main event. You can, however, expect to see the occasional cabaret act. Sing-ers also tend to do mini-cabaret performances in The Club, one deck above the showlounge, the gathering place for late-night drinkers.

SPA/FITNESS. The Spa at Seabourn is a small but well-equipped health spa/fitness center. It has sauna and steam rooms (separate facilities for men and wom-en), an equipment-packed gymnasium – but the ceiling height is low – and a beauty salon.

The spa is staffed and operated by concession Elemis by Steiner. Treatment prices equal those in an expensive land-based spa. The beauty salon has hair beautifying treatments and conditioning. In the gym-nasium, personal training sessions, yoga classes, mat Pilates, and body composition analysis are available at extra cost.

Seabourn Quest
★★★★★

Size:. . . . . Small Ship			Cabins (total):. 225	
Tonnage: 32,000			Size range (sq ft/m): 295.0–438.1/27.5–133.6	
Lifestyle: . . . . Luxury			Cabins (outside view): 225	
Cruise line:. . . . . Seabourn			Cabins (interior/no view):. 0	
Former names: . . . . .none			Cabins (for one person):. 0	
IMO number: 9483126			Cabins (with private balcony):. 199	
Builder: . . . . .Mariotti (Italy)			Cabins (wheelchair accessible): 7	
Original cost:. . . . .$250 million			Wheelchair accessibility:. . . . . .Good	
Entered service:. . . . . Jun 2011			Cabin voltage: . . . . 110 volts	
Registry:. . . . . Bahamas			Elevators:. 3	
Length (ft/m):. 650.0/198.1			Casino (gaming tables):. . . . . Yes	
Beam (ft/m):. 83.9/25.6			Slot machines:. . . . . Yes	
Draft (ft/m): 21.3/6.5			Swimming pools:. 2	
Propulsion/Propellers: . . . . diesel-electric (23,040kW)/2			Hot tubs (on deck):. 6	
Passenger decks:. 10			Self-service launderette:. . . . . Yes	
Total crew:. 330			Dedicated cinema/seats:. . . . . .No	
Passengers (lower beds/alll berths):. 450/462			Library: . . . . Yes	
Passenger Space Ratio (lower beds/all berths): 71.1/69.2			Onboard currency: . . . . .US$	
Crew/Passenger Ratio (lower beds/all berths):. 1.3/1.4				

An elegant, all-inclusive ship for trendy cruisers

OVERVIEW. This ship's big attractions are its staff, service levels, and wellness facilities. Like its sister ships *Seabourn Odyssey* and *Seabourn Sojourn*, it has one of the highest passenger space ratios in the cruise industry, so you will never feel crowded.

THE SHIP. *Seabourn Quest* has two small outdoor swimming pools, midships and aft; the aft pool is in a delightful area, although there's not a lot of sunbathing space, and the pool is just a 'dip' pool. One popular outdoor areas is the Sky Bar – good for those balmy evenings in the right cruise areas. But for stargazing, the hot tub located by the ship's bow is a delight, and it's dimly lit and peaceful.

All the accommodation areas are in the forward section, with most public rooms located aft, so the accommodation areas are quiet; however, you'll need to traverse through several decks to get to some of the public rooms. The Marina, at the stern, has a staging area from which watersports are organized. This is being converted during 2013 to provide expedition equipment, zodiac shore landing craft, a boot washing station and storage for boots and parkas – so that the ship can focus more on expedition-style cruising. Four suites will also be added.

Seabourn Square, the focal social gathering point of the ship a 'concierge lounge,' has a relaxed, club-like ambience. The area includes a library, shops, eight computers (Internet use is chargeable – at high cost – a major source of passenger complaints), an outdoor

Berlitz's Ratings

	Possible	Achieved
Ship	500	438
Accommodation	200	178
Food	400	333
Service	400	343
Entertainment	100	81
Cruise	400	334
OVERALL SCORE		
1707 points out of 2000		

terrace, and a coffee bar. Its 'concierges' can provide in-port shopping tips, set up shore excursions, get dinner reservations in ports of call, etc. There's a private diamond showroom, called The Collection. Drinks, wines with meals, and all gratuities are included, though premium brands and high-quality wines cost extra. Wi-Fi is available throughout the ship.

The 'vertical stacking' layout is not user-friendly. While real teak is used in most outdoor areas, Flexteak (faux teak) is used in other areas. The cabin doors are narrow, and doors within the cabins are of varying heights and sizes, and feel utilitarian. Most public rooms are of a single deck height, so there's not such a good feeling of spaciousness, and support pillars are everywhere.

ACCOMMODATION. There are 13 grades of suites in many price categories – while the smaller 'suites' are really large cabins, not suites. However, there are many balcony cabins – good for personal privacy.

All cabins have a separate tub and shower enclosure in a granite bathroom setting, twin beds convertible to a queen-size bed, flat-screen TV plus CD and DVD player, minibar, vanity desk with hairdryer, world atlas, personalized stationery, and large walk-in closet with personal safe.

The interior designers have created very homely, contemporary living spaces in the suites and cabins, although the walls are rather plain and unimaginative. It's good to see that the beds are high enough off the floor to enable even the largest suitcases to be stowed underneath. All drawers are fitted with soft gel, which means they are quiet.

The suites are bathed in soft earthy tones – a splash of color wouldn't go amiss. The cabinetry has many seams and strips covering joints which suggest that the ship's outfitters would benefit from joinery lessons. One neat, creative feature is a leather-clad vanity stool/table that converts into a backgammon table. The design of a 'cube table' that can be inserted under a glass-topped table when not being used as a footrest is a smart idea for making more space.

The Seabourn Suites and Veranda Suites are quite narrow, and feel cramped, with little space in the passageway between the bed and the opposite wall. However, the bathrooms are generously proportioned, with grey and chocolate-brown decor; there are two washbasins, a bathtub, and a separate shower enclosure.

Some size examples (excluding balcony): Grand Suites 1,135 sq ft (105 sq m), including two-bedrooms; Signature Suites 819 sq ft (76 sq m); Wintergarden Suites 914 sq ft (85 sq m). Rather neat suites within a glass-enclosed solarium, set in front of the funnel, with a side balcony; Owners Suites 611–675 sq ft (57–63 sq m); Penthouse Suite 436–611 sq ft (41–57 sq m); Veranda Suite 269–298 sq ft (25–28 sq m); Seabourn Suite (295 sq ft (27 sq m).

Four 'Penthouse Spa Suites' were added in a 2013 refit. These are located directly above the spa itself (and connect to it via a spiral stairway), and measure between 64 sq m (688 sq ft) and 66 sq m (710 sq ft), including balcony. The suites have a living and dining area with seating for four persons, a separate bedroom, walk-in closet, and a bathroom with tub and shower, and balcony. Plus, there's free access to the spa's Serene Area.

DINING. There are three venues, plus a Poolside Grill. The Restaurant has open-seating dining at tables for two, four, six, or eight, with menus designed by American celebrity chef Charlie Palmer. It is a large venue that actually feels more clinical than classical with its white-on-white decor and double-height ceiling in its central section. The most-sought-after seats are in the center rather than along the port and starboard sides, which have a window, but low ceiling height.

Restaurant 2, with around 50 seats, has regional, seasonal cuisine and tasting menus, perhaps for a mini-dégustation; however, the ceiling height is rather low, which makes the feeling cramped. The cuisine is contemporary, with a flirtation with fusion, where taste and flavors are what the experience is all about. This venue shares the same galley as the adjacent The Colonnade.

The Colonnade, located aft, has indoor/outdoor seating and is nicely decorated, although its free-flow design could be better; there's too little outdoor seating for the demand in warm-weather cruising areas, when many passengers like to eat outdoors. During dinner, passengers who are dressed formally on designated formal nights have to share the space with those who are more casually dressed. The venue is also adjacent to one of the fine dining restaurants.

The Patio Grill is in a casual poolside setting outdoors – and most enjoyable on a balmy evening, as a change to the air-conditioned interior dining venues.

In addition, a 24-hour, in-suite menu offers the à la carte items served in the main dining room during dinner hours.

Extra-cost Silver ($225.00) or Gold ($450.00) "connoisseur" wine packages provide a choice of red and white vintage wines for a set amount – perhaps a good idea for a longer cruise.

ENTERTAINMENT. The Grand Salon is the main entertainment venue for shows, cabaret performances, social dancing, and for use as a cinema. However, the stage is small – large enough for a live band, but performers need to use the dance floor area – and the room has nine thick pillars that make it awkward to see anything at all, although the room has a gentle slope. There's also a decorative steel ceiling grating in the central section is black, cold and unappealing. It has banquette seating in the front and mid-section, and, strangely, sofa-style leather seating along the side walls to the rear, which mean you actually sit with your back to the stage – a rather unhelpful arrangement.

Small production shows (remember this is a small ship) are performed well to pre-recorded tracks, and the audio equipment and sound dispersion are extremely good. Another venue, The Club, is a large, cool, trendy but high-volume nightclub/disco with a wooden dance floor, large bar and minimalist design. Located beneath the Grand salon, it incorporates a comfortable casino.

SPA/FITNESS. The Spa at Seabourn, operated by Elemis, occupies the aft section of two decks, and is quite large, at 11,500 sq ft (1,068 sq m). It offers full services in a very pleasant setting that includes a two-deck-high waterfall at the entrance and seven indoor/outdoor treatment rooms, as well a Kneipp 'walk-in-the-water' experience, a thermal suite (for which a pass costs extra), and complete salon facilities, while a hot tub and relaxation area on the deck above is accessed by a spiral staircase. Separate saunas and steam rooms for men and women are provided, but they are very small. In the gymnasium, personal training sessions, yoga classes, mat Pilates, and body composition analysis are available at extra cost, but some basic exercise programs are free.

Seabourn Sojourn
★★★★★

Size:.	Small Ship	Cabins (total):.	225
Tonnage:	32,000	Size range (sq ft/m):	295.0–438.1/27.5–133.6
Lifestyle:	Luxury	Cabins (outside view):	225
Cruise line:.	Seabourn	Cabins (interior/no view):.	0
Former names:	none	Cabins (for one person):.	0
IMO number:	9417098	Cabins (with private balcony):	199
Builder:	Mariotti (Italy)	Cabins (wheelchair accessible):	7
Original cost:.	$250 million	Wheelchair accessibility:.	Good
Entered service:.	Jun 2010	Cabin voltage:	110 volts
Registry:.	Bahamas	Elevators:.	3
Length (ft/m):.	650.0/198.1	Casino (gaming tables):.	Yes
Beam (ft/m):.	83.9/25.6	Slot machines:.	Yes
Draft (ft/m):	21.3/6.5	Swimming pools:.	2
Propulsion/Propellers:	diesel-electric (23,040kW)/2	Hot tubs (on deck):.	6
Passenger decks:.	10	Self-service launderette:	Yes
Total crew:	330	Dedicated cinema/seats:.	No
Passengers (lower beds/alll berths):	450/462	Library:	Yes
Passenger Space Ratio (lower beds/all berths):	71.1/69.2	Onboard currency:	US$
Crew/Passenger Ratio (lower beds/all berths):	1.3/1.4		

An upscale, elegant small ship for the well-traveled

OVERVIEW. This ship's big attractions are its staff and service levels, and the wellness facilities. Like its sister ships *Seabourn Odyssey* and *Seabourn Quest*, it has one of the highest passenger space ratios in the cruise industry, so you'll never get the feeling of it being crowded.

THE SHIP. *Seabourn Sojourn*, the second of Seabourn's three larger ships (the three boutique-sized ships – Seabourn Legend, Seabourn Pride, and Seaboutn Spirit – have been sold and will be delivered in 2014/15), has two small outdoor swimming pools, midships and aft; the aft pool is in a delightful area, although there's not a lot of sunbathing space. One of the most pleasing outdoor areas is the Sky Bar. But for stargazing, the hot tub located on the ship's foredeck is a peaceful delight.

All the accommodation areas are in the forward section, with most public rooms located aft, but you'll need to traverse through several decks to get to some of the public rooms. The Marina, at the stern, has a staging area from which watersports are organized.

Seabourn Square, the focal social gathering point of the ship is a 'concierge lounge,' has a relaxed, club-like ambience. The area includes a library, shops, eight computers (Internet connection is chargeable), an outdoor terrace, and a coffee bar. Its 'concierges' can provide in-port shopping tips, set up shore excursions, get dinner reservations in ports of call, etc. There's a private diamond showroom, called The Collection. Drinks, wines with meals, and all gratuities are in-

Berlitz's Ratings

	Possible	Achieved
Ship	500	437
Accommodation	200	178
Food	400	333
Service	400	342
Entertainment	100	81
Cruise	400	333
OVERALL SCORE		
1704 points out of 2000		

cluded, though premium brands and high-quality wines cost extra. Wi-Fi is available throughout the ship.

Minus points? The 'vertical stacking' layout is not really user-friendly. While real teak is used in most outdoor areas, Flexteak (faux teak) is used in other areas. The cabin doors are rather narrow, and doors within the cabins vary in height and size, and feel utilitarian.

Most public rooms are of a single deck height, so there's not such a good feeling of spaciousness, and support pillars are everywhere – Mariotti, the shipbuilder, should look at Europa to see it's not necessary to have so many pillars.

ACCOMMODATION. There are several grades of suites in multiple price categories. The smaller 'suites' are really large cabins, and not true suites. However, there are many balcony cabins, for personal privacy (about 90 percent of all suites/cabins).

All cabins have a separate tub and shower enclosure in a granite bathroom setting, twin beds convertible to a queen-size bed, flat-screen TV plus CD and DVD player, minibar, vanity desk with hairdryer, world atlas, personalized stationery, and large walk-in closet with personal safe.

The interior designers have created very homely, contemporary living spaces in the suites and cabins, although the walls are rather plain and unimaginative. It's good to see that the beds are high enough off the floor to enable even the largest suitcases to be stowed underneath. All drawers are fitted with soft gel, which means they are quiet – no more slamming contests with your next-door neighbor.

The cabins are bathed in soft earthy tones, although a splash of color wouldn't go amiss. The cabinetry has many seams and strips covering joints which suggest that the ship's outfitters would benefit from a joinery course. It's also strange that several internal doors are of different sizes, widths and heights. One neat, very creative feature is a leather-clad vanity stool/table that converts into a backgammon table. The design of a 'cube table' that can be inserted under a glass-topped table when not being used as a footrest is a smart idea for making more space.

Seabourn Suites and Veranda Suites are quite narrow, and feel cramped, with little space in the passageway between the bed and the opposite wall. However, the bathrooms are generously proportioned, with grey and chocolate-brown decor; there are two washbasins, a bathtub, and a separate shower enclosure.

Some size examples (excluding balcony): Grand Suites 1,135 sq ft (105 sq m), including two-bedrooms; Signature Suites 819 sq ft (76 sq m); Wintergarden Suites 914 sq ft (85 sq m). Rather neat suites within a glass-enclosed solarium, set in front of the funnel, with a side balcony; Owners Suites 611–675 sq ft (57–63 sq m); Penthouse Suite 436–611 sq ft (41–57 sq m); Veranda Suite 269–298 sq ft (25–28 sq m); Seabourn Suite (295 sq ft (27 sq m).

Four 'Spa Suites' were added in a 2013 refit. These are located directly above the spa itself (connected to it via a spiral stairway), and measure between 64 sq m (688 sq ft) and 66 sq m (710 sq ft), including a balcony. The suites have a living and dining area with seating for four, a separate bedroom, walk-in closet, and a bathroom with tub and shower, and balcony. Occupants get free use of the 'Serene' relaxation area of the spa.

DINING. There are three venues, plus a poolside grill. The Restaurant has open-seating dining at tables for two, four, six, or eight, with menus designed by American celebrity chef Charlie Palmer. It is a large venue that actually feels more clinical than classical with its white-on-white decor and double-height ceiling in its central section. The most-sought-after seats are in the center rather than along the port and starboard sides, which have a window, but low ceiling height.

Restaurant 2, with around 50 seats, has regional, seasonal cuisine and tasting menus, perhaps for a mini-dégustation; however, the ceiling height is rather low, which makes the feeling cramped. The cuisine is contemporary, with a flirtation with fusion, where taste and flavors are what the experience is all about. This venue shares the same galley as the adjacent The Colonnade.

The Colonnade, located aft, has indoor/outdoor seating and is nicely decorated, although its free-flow

design could be better; there's too little outdoor seating for the demand in warm-weather areas, when many passengers like to eat outdoors. During dinner, passengers who are dressed formally on designated formal nights have to share the space with those who are more casually dressed. The venue is also adjacent to one of the fine dining restaurants.

The Patio Grill is located in a casual poolside setting outdoors; it is at its most enjoyable on balmy evenings, as a change to the air-conditioned interior dining venues.

In addition, a 24-hour, in-suite menu offers the à la carte items served in the main dining room during dinner hours.

Extra-cost Silver ($225.00) or Gold ($450.00) "connoisseur" wine packages provide a choice of red and white vintage wines for a set amount – perhaps a good idea for a longer cruise.

ENTERTAINMENT. The Grand Salon is the main entertainment venue for shows, cabaret performances, social dancing, and for use as a cinema. However, the stage is small – large enough for a live band, but performers need to use the dance floor area – and the room has nine thick pillars that make it awkward to see anything at all, although the room has a gentle slope. There's also a decorative steel ceiling grating in the central section is black, cold and unappealing. It has banquette seating in the front and mid-section, and, strangely, sofa-style leather seating along the side walls to the rear, which mean you actually sit with your back to the stage – a rather unhelpful arrangement (particularly for the performers)!

Small production shows (remember this is a small ship) are performed well to pre-recorded tracks, and the audio equipment and sound dispersion are extremely good. Just don't expect big ship entertainment, though.

Another venue, The Club, is a large, cool, trendy but high-volume nightclub/disco with a wooden dance floor, large bar and minimalist design. Located beneath the Grand salon, it incorporates a comfortable casino.

SPA/FITNESS. The Spa at Seabourn, operated by Elemis, occupies the aft section of two decks, and is quite large, at 11,500 sq ft (1,068 sq m). It offers full services in a very relaxing setting that includes a two-deck-high waterfall at the entrance and seven indoor/outdoor treatment rooms, as well as a thalassotherapy wave pool; there's also a thermal suite (for which a pass costs extra), and complete salon facilities, while a hot tub and relaxation area on the deck above is accessed by a spiral staircase. Separate saunas and steam rooms for men and women are provided, but are extremely small. In the gymnasium, personal training sessions, yoga classes, mat Pilates, and body composition analysis are available at extra cost, but some of the basic exercise programs are free.

Seabourn Spirit
★★★★+

Size:.....................................Boutique Ship		Cabins (total):......................................106	
Tonnage: 9,975		Size range (sq ft/m): 277.0–575.0/25.7–53.4	
Lifestyle: ....Luxury		Cabins (outside view):..............................106	
Cruise line:.......................................Seabourn		Cabins (interior/no view):..............................0	
Former names: ....none		Cabins (for one person):................................0	
IMO number: 8807997		Cabins (with private balcony):..........................6	
Builder: ....Seebeckwerft (Germany)		Cabins (wheelchair accessible): 4	
Original cost:................................$50 million		Wheelchair accessibility:............................None	
Entered service:............................... Nov 1989		Cabin voltage: ....110 and 220 volts	
Registry:...Bahamas		Elevators:..3	
Length (ft/m):................................ 439.9/134.1		Casino (gaming tables):..............................Yes	
Beam (ft/m):..................................... 62.9/19.2		Slot machines:.......................................Yes	
Draft (ft/m):......................................16.8/5.1		Swimming pools:.......................................1	
Propulsion/Propellers:....................diesel (5,355kW)/2		Hot tubs (on deck):....................................3	
Passenger decks:....................................6		Self-service launderette:..............................Yes	
Total crew:..160		Dedicated cinema/seats:...............................No	
Passengers (lower beds/alll berths):................212/212		Library: ....Yes	
Passenger Space Ratio (lower beds/all berths): 47.0/47.0		Onboard currency: ....US$	
Crew/Passenger Ratio (lower beds/all berths):..........1.3/1.3			

A contemporary small ship for mature-age cruisers

OVERVIEW. The intimate, *Seabourn Spirit* is best suited to sophisticated and well-traveled couples – typically over 50, but possibly younger – looking for a small ship with excellent food and fine European-style service. The ship's big advantage is being able to cruise where large cruise ships can't, thanks to its ocean-yacht size. You sail with only 100 other couples, and a sense of intimate camaraderie.

THE SHIP. This pleasantly appointed cruise vessel has sleek exterior styling, handsome profile with swept-back, rounded lines, and is an identical twin to *Seabourn Pride*. It has two fine mahogany water taxis for use as shore tenders. An aft water sports platform and marina can be used in suitably calm warm-water areas. Water sports facilities include a small, enclosed 'dip' pool, sea kayaks, snorkel equipment, windsurfers, waterski boat, and Zodiac inflatable boats.

The sunloungers are now a steel mesh design. There is no walk-around promenade deck outdoors. There is only one dryer in the self-service launderette. Non-American passengers should note that almost all entertainment and activities are geared towards American tastes, despite the increasingly international passenger mix.

A wide central passageway divides port and starboard side accommodation. Inviting, sumptuous public areas have warm colors. Fine quality interior fixtures, fittings, artwork, and fabric combine to pre-

Berlitz's Ratings

	Possible	Achieved
Ship	500	409
Accommodation	200	170
Food	400	327
Service	400	336
Entertainment	100	77
Cruise	400	323

OVERALL SCORE
1642 points out of 2000

sent an outstanding, elegant decor. For a small ship, there's wide range of public rooms. These include a main lounge that stages small cabaret shows, a nightclub, an observation lounge with bar, large, deep armchairs, and a cigar smoking area complete with cabinet, cigar humidor, and small selection of good cigars. There is a small business center, small meeting room, and a small casino with roulette and blackjack tables, plus a few slot machines.

Not for the budget-minded, this ship is for those desiring supremely elegant, stylish, small-ship surroundings, but is perhaps rather small for long voyages in open waters. During the past few years, there have been complaints about falling standards aboard the Seabourn ships, particularly with regard to maintenance – they are now over 20 years old – and that food, presentation, and service had deteriorated. However, the company has turned things around, and the product delivered is again pretty decent.

Seabourn Spirit provides a fine level of personal service and an utterly civilized cruise. All drinks except premium brands and connoisseur wines are included. So are gratuities, aromatherapy bath selections from Molton Brown and soaps by Bronnley, Chanel, and Hermès, short massages on deck ('massage moments'), open-seating dining, use of watersports equipment, one free Exclusively Seabourn shore excursion per cruise, and movies under the stars. Port charges and insurance are not included.

Note that Seabourn Spirit has been sold to Xanterra Parks & Resorts, parent company of Windstar Cruises, and will be transferred in May 2015, to be renamed Star Spirit. Sister ships Seabourn Legend (to be renamed Star Legend) will be transferred in April 2015, and Seabourn Spirit will be transferred in May, 2015, and renamed Star Spirit.

ACCOMMODATION. This is spread over three decks, with nine price categories. The all-outside cabins (called suites in brochure-speak) are comfortably large and beautifully equipped with everything one could reasonably need. Electric blackout blinds are provided for the large windows in addition to curtains. All cabinetry is made of blond woods, with softly rounded edges, and cabin doors are neatly angled away from the passageway.

All the suites have a sleeping area, with European duvets and Frette linens as standard. A separate lounge area has a Bose Wave audio unit, DVD player and flat-screen TV, vanity desk with hairdryer and personalized stationery, world atlas, mini-bar, and refrigerator (stocked with soft drinks and two bottles of your favorite liquor when you embark). There's a large walk-in closet illuminated automatically when you open the door, wooden hangers, electronic personal safe, umbrella, and wall-mounted clock and barometer. A full passenger list is also provided – a rarity these days – as are a fresh fruit basket, replenished daily, and flowers.

Marble-clad bathrooms have one or two washbasins, depending on the accommodation grade, a decent but not full-size tub (four suites have a shower enclosure only – no tub), plenty of storage areas, 100 percent thick cotton towels, plush terrycloth bathrobe, designer soaps, and Molton Brown personal amenities. A selection of five Molton Brown aromatherapy bath preparations can be ordered from your stewardess, who will prepare your bath.

In 2001, Seabourn added 36 French balconies to suites on two out of three accommodation decks. These are not balconies in the true sense of the word, but they do have two doors that open wide onto a tiny teakwood balcony that is just 10.6ins (27cm) wide. The balconies allow you to have fresh sea air, together with some salt spray.

Course-by-course in-cabin dining is available during dinner hours, and the cocktail table can be raised to form a dining table. There is 24-hour room service. Also provided are personalized stationery, and fancy ticket wallet. Non-smoking cabins are available. Menus for each dinner are delivered to your suite during the day.

Four Owner's suites (King Haakon/King Magnus, each measuring 530 sq ft (49 sq m), and Amundsen/Nansen, each 575 sq ft (53 sq m), and two Classic Suites (King Harald/King Olav), each 400 sq ft (37 sq m) offer superb, private living spaces. Each has a walk-in closet, second closet, full bathroom plus a guest toilet with washbasin. There is a fully secluded forward- or side-facing balcony, with sunloungers and wooden drinks table. The living area has ample bookshelf space including a complete edition of *Encyclopaedia Britannica*, large refrigerator/drinks cabinet, television, and DVD player, plus a second TV set in the bedroom. All windows, as well as the door to the balcony, have manually operated blackout blinds, and a complete blackout is possible in both bedroom and living room.

DINING. The Restaurant is a part-marble, part-carpeted dining room with portholes and restful decor. The silverware (150g weight – the best available) is by Robbe & Berking. Open-seating dining means that you can dine when you want, with whom you wish.

The menus are creative and well-balanced, with a wide selection of foods and regional cuisine. Seabourn's cuisine is artfully presented, with many items cooked to order. Special orders are also available, and caviar (well, sort of) is available on request. Flambé desserts can be presented at your table. There is always a good selection of exotic fruits and cheeses.

Each day, basic table wine is included for lunch and dinner, but the decent bottles cost extra. The wine list is quite extensive, with prices ranging from moderate to high; many of the wines come from the smaller, more exclusive vineyards. The European dining room staff provide excellent, unhurried service.

In addition, relaxed breakfasts (available until 11am) and lunch buffets and casual, themed candlelight dinners, including a '2' tasting menu, can be taken in the popular Veranda Café adjacent to the swimming pool.

The Sky Grill provides an above-poolside setting for candlelit dining. It specializes in sizzling steaks and seafood.

ENTERTAINMENT. The Amundsen Lounge has a sloping floor that provides good sight lines from just about every seat. 'Production' shows are of limited scope, as dinner is usually the main event. You can, however, expect to see the occasional cabaret act. Singers also tend to do mini-cabaret performances in The Club, one deck above the showlounge, the gathering place for late-night drinkers.

SPA/FITNESS. The Spa at Seabourn is a small but well-equipped health spa/fitness center. It has sauna and steam rooms (separate facilities for men and women), an equipment-packed gymnasium – but the ceiling height is low – and a beauty salon.

The spa is staffed and operated by concession Elemis by Steiner. Treatment prices equal those in an expensive land-based spa. The beauty salon has hair beautifying treatments and conditioning. In the gymnasium, personal training sessions, yoga classes, mat Pilates, and body composition analysis are available at extra cost.

SeaDream I
★★★★★

Size:.....................................Boutique Ship	Cabins (total):..56
Tonnage: 4,253	Size range (sq ft/m): 195.0–446.7/18.1–41.4
Lifestyle: ....Luxury	Cabins (outside view):.................................56
Cruise line:.........................SeaDream Yacht Club	Cabins (interior/no view):...............................0
Former names: ....Seabourn Goddess I, Sea Goddess I	Cabins (for one person):.................................0
IMO number: 8203438	Cabins (with private balcony):...........................0
Builder: ....Wartsila (Finland)	Cabins (wheelchair accessible): 0
Original cost:..............................$34 million	Wheelchair accessibility:............................None
Entered service:.......................Apr 1984/May 2002	Cabin voltage: ....110 and 220 volts
Registry:.................................The Bahamas	Elevators:..1
Length (ft/m):..............................343.8/104.8	Casino (gaming tables):...............................Yes
Beam (ft/m):................................47.9/14.6	Slot machines:.......................................Yes
Draft (ft/m): 13.6/4.1	Swimming pools:.......................................1
Propulsion/Propellers:...................diesel (3,540kW)/2	Hot tubs (on deck):...................................1
Passenger decks:....................................5	Self-service launderette:.............................No
Total crew:..95	Dedicated cinema/seats:...............................No
Passengers (lower beds/alll berths):................112/112	Library: ....Yes
Passenger Space Ratio (lower beds/all berths):.......37.9/37.9	Onboard currency: ....US$
Crew/Passenger Ratio (lower beds/all berths):..........1.1/1.1	

Nice mega-yacht for informal but really stylish cruising

OVERVIEW. *SeaDream I* is best suited to sophisticated and well-traveled couples who are typically over 40. Rejecting today's huge standard resort cruise ships, they are looking for a small ship with excellent food approaching gourmet standards, and fine European-style service in surroundings that border on the elegant and refined while remaining trendy.

THE SHIPS. *Seadream I* (and sister ship *SeaDream II*) were originally funded by about 800 investors, and operated under the Norske Cruise banner, and named *Sea Goddess I* and *Sea Goddess II*. They have an ultra-sleek profile, with deep blue hull and white superstructure, and the ambience of a private club. After they were bought by SeaDream Yacht Club in 2001, they were completely refurbished, with many changes to public rooms and outdoor areas, and several new features added to create what are contemporary, chic, and desirable, if aging, vessels.

Note that, because these ships are popular for small company charters, you may find that the date and itinerary you want will not be available, so you may be asked to change to the sister ship and a different itinerary.

A 'Top of the Yacht' bar, crafted in warm wood, was added to both ships. So were eight special alcoves set to the port and starboard sides of the funnel, equipped with two-person sun loungers with thick pads (and two equipped for one person); however, there is quite a bit of noise from the adjacent funnel.

Berlitz's Ratings

	Possible	Achieved
Ship	500	432
Accommodation	200	173
Food	400	355
Service	400	370
Entertainment	100	84
Cruise	400	347

OVERALL SCORE
1761 points out of 2000

You are encouraged to sleep under the stars if you wish, and cotton sleep suits are provided.

At the front part of the deck there are more sun loungers and a couple of large hammocks, as well as a golf simulator with a choice of 30 courses.

Inside, there is a feeling of unabashed but discreet sophistication. Elegant public rooms have flowers and potpourri everywhere. The main social gathering places are the lounge, a delightful library/living room with a selection of about 1,000 books, a piano bar – which can be more like a karaoke bar at times – and a small casino with two blackjack tables and five slot machines.

SeaDream I really is an exclusive boutique vessel – it's like having your own private yacht in which hospitality, anticipation, and personal recognition are art forms practiced to a high level. The staff is delightful and accommodating – 'no' is not in their vocabulary. The dress code is resort (no tie) casual. Fine-quality furnishings and fabrics are used throughout, with marble and blond wood accents that help create a sense of warmth.

A cruise aboard *SeaDream I* is for experienced, independent travelers who don't like regular cruise ships, large ships, glitzy lounges, a platoon of people and kids running around, or dressing up – no tuxedos or gowns are allowed, and ties aren't needed. The ship provides the setting for personal indulgence and refined, unstructured living at sea, in a casual, private setting akin to that on a mega-yacht. One delightful feature of each cruise in warm weather areas is a 'caviar in the surf' beach barbecue.

Life could hardly be better at sea – so, as many regular SeaDream Yacht Club passengers say, why bother with ports of call at all? Embarkation never starts before 3pm, in case you are eager to get aboard.

All drinks (with the exception of premium brands and connoisseur wines), farmed sevruga caviar, and gratuities are included, but port charges and insurance are not. The price of a cruise is just that: the price of a cruise. Air and/or other travel arrangements can be made on your own, or through your own travel agent, or you can use the excellent services of Total Travel Marine, whose offices in London and Miami specialize in air arrangements as partner to SeaDream Yacht Club, with service 24/7.

The SeaDreams were the first of the mega-yacht-style ships when built, and none of the cabins has a private balcony – ships with private balconies made their debut just a couple of years later, and, anyway, yachts don't have balconies (they are too close to the waterline). One not so positive item is the fact that the reception desk is now called the Concierge, although it is doubtful whether the staff has the kind of in-depth knowledge that is expected of a concierge.

ACCOMMODATION. There are four types, and six price categories (depending on location, size, and grade): Yacht Club (standard) Cabin, Commodore Club Suite, Admiral Suite, and Owner's Suite.

Yacht Club Cabins: Incorrectly called 'suites' in the brochure, the standard cabins are, more correctly, fully equipped mini-suites with an outside view through windows or portholes, depending on deck and price category. Each measures 195 sq ft (18 sq m), which isn't large by today's cruise ship standards; however, it is large compared to cabins aboard many private motor yachts, and extremely large when compared to oceangoing racing yachts. The sleeping area has twin beds that can be put together to form a queen-size configuration; the beds are positioned next to the window or porthole so that you can entertain in the living area without going past the sleeping area, as you must aboard the slightly larger Seabourn or Silversea ships, for example; a curtain separates the sleeping and lounge areas. All cabinetry and furniture is of thick blond wood, with nicely rounded edges.

A long vanity desk in the sleeping area has a large mirror above it; however, there is no three-sided mirror for women to check the back of their hair. There are two small drawers for cosmetic items, and a brass clock is positioned on one wall. A mirror is placed opposite the bed, which won't please those who follow feng shui principles.

In the lounge area, a long desk has six drawers, plus a vertical cupboard unit that houses a sensible safe, refrigerator, and drinks cabinet stocked with your choice of drinks. There is also a 20in (52mm) flat-screen television, CD and DVD player, and an MP3 audio player with a choice of more than 100 selections. The beds have the finest linens, including thick cotton duvets, and hypoallergenic pillows are also available. There's little room under the beds for luggage, although this can be taken away and stored.

One drawback is the fact that the insulation between cabins is not particularly good, although rarely does this present a problem as most passengers aboard the *SeaDreams* are generally extremely quiet, considerate types who are allergic to noise. Incidentally, a sleep suit is supplied in case you want to sleep out on deck under the stars in one of the on-deck two-person beds – but more of those later.

When the ships became *SeaDreams I* and *II*, all the bathrooms were totally refurbished. The new cheerful decor is more hip and trendy, with softer colors and large (beige) marble tiles. The former tiny sit-in bathtubs were taken out – these are missed by some passengers – and replaced by a multi-jet power glassed-in shower enclosure. A washbasin set in a marble-look surround and two glass shelves make up the facilities, and an under-sink cupboard provides further space for larger toiletries. Bulgari toiletries are provided. Gorgeously thick, plush, 100 percent cotton SeaDream-logo bathrobes and towels are also supplied.

However, despite their having been completely rebuilt, the bathrooms really are small, particularly for those of larger than average build. Also, the bathroom door opens inward, so space inside is at a premium. The toilet is located in a somewhat awkward position and, unless you close the door, you can see yourself in the mirror facing of the closets, opposite the bathroom door.

Commodore Club Suites. For larger accommodation, choose one of 16 Commodore Club Suites. These consist of two standard cabins with an interconnecting door, thus providing you with a healthy 380 sq ft (36 sq m) of living space. One cabin is made into a lounge and dining room, with table and up to four chairs, while the other becomes your sleeping area. The advantage is that you get two bathrooms. One disadvantage is that the soundproofing between cabins could be better.

Admiral Suite. Added in 2008–09, this suite occupies space previously devoted to the ship's boutique, and adjacent to the piano bar/library. It's a little smaller than the Owner's Suite, but is well laid out and extremely comfortable.

Owner's Suite. For the largest living space, go for the Owner's Suite. This measures a grand 490 sq ft (46 sq m). It's the only accommodation with a bathroom that incorporates a real full-size tub; there's also a separate shower enclosure and lots of space for toiletries.

In all grades of accommodation, passengers receive personalized stationery, a personal email address, a 100 percent cotton sleep suit, Bulgari toiletries, 24-hour room service, and 'sweet dreams' chocolates.

CUISINE. The dining salon, called The Restaurant, is elegant and inviting, and has bird's-eye maple-wood paneled walls and alcoves showcasing beautiful handmade glass creations. It is cozy, yet with plenty of space around each table for fine service, and the ship provides a floating culinary celebration in an open-seating arrangement, so you can dine whenever, and with whomever, you want. Course-by-course meals can also be served out on deck.

Tables can be configured for two, four, six, or eight. They are laid with a classic setting of a real glass base (show) plate, Porsgrund china, pristine white monogrammed table linen, and fresh flowers.

Candlelit dinners are part of the inviting setting. There's even a box of spare spectacles for menu reading in case you forget your own. You get leather-bound menus, and close to impeccable personalized European service.

The SeaDream Yacht Club experience really is all about dining. The ships will not disappoint, and culinary excellence prevails. Only the very freshest and finest quality ingredients are used in the best culinary artistry. Fine, unhurried European service is provided. Additionally, good-quality Champagne is available whenever you want it, and so is caviar – American farmed Hackleback sturgeon malossol caviar, sadly – and not Russian caviar, whose purchase and supply today is challenging. The ice cream, which is made on board, however, is excellent.

In addition to the regular menus, some beautifully prepared and presented 'raw food' menu items have been introduced, in cooperation with Forida's Hippocrates Institute, with nothing cooked at a temperature of more than 115°F (46°C).

Aboard *SeaDream I*, everything is prepared individually to order and the cuisine is extremely creative. Special orders are possible, although the former popular flaming desserts have almost disappeared. You can also dine course by course in your suite for any meal, at any time during meal hours. The dining room isn't open for lunch, which disappoints those who don't want to eat outside, particularly in hot climates.

Good-quality table wines are included in the cruise fare for lunch and dinner. Real wine connoisseurs, however, will appreciate the availability of an extra wine list, full of special vintages and premier crus at extra cost. If you want to do something different with a loved one, you can also arrange to dine one evening on the open (but covered) deck, overlooking the swimming pool and stern – it is a rather romantic setting.

The Topside Restaurant is an informal open-air eatery and has roll-down sides (in case of inclement weather), and is open for breakfast, lunch or the occasional dinner. Teak tables and chairs add a touch of class.

ENTERTAINMENT. There is no evening entertainment as such (it's not needed), other than a duo or solo musician to provide music for listening and dancing in the lounge. Dinner is the main event, and videos are available to take to your cabin.

SPA/FITNESS. The holistic approach to wellbeing plays a big part in relaxation and body pampering aboard *SeaDream I*. To this end, when you enter the Asian Spa/Wellness Centre, which has a good-sized gymnasium and a small beauty salon, you enter another world. There are three massage rooms, a small sauna, and steam shower enclosure.

The spa, located in a private area forward on Deck 4, is staffed and operated as a concession by Universal Maritime Services. Massage on the beach is available when the ship stages its famous beach party.

For golfers, there's an electronic golf simulator, and choice of several golf courses to play. There is a small, retractable, water sports platform at the stern. Equipment carried includes a water-ski boat, sailboat, wave runners (jet skis), kayaks, wake boards, snorkeling equipment, and two Zodiacs. The use of all this equipment is included in the price of a cruise.

The sea conditions have to be just right (minimal swell) for these items to be used, which, on average is once or twice during a typical seven-night cruise. You may be allowed to swim off the stern platform if conditions permit. Ten mountain bikes are also carried, and these can be used on shore visits.

Five Firsts

In 1903 the British liner *Lucania* acquired wireless equipment, which enabled it to keep in touch with both sides of the Atlantic Ocean at the same time.

The first ship-to-shore wireless telegraphy took place on the American passenger ship *St. Paul* in 1899.

The first twin-screw passenger ship was the Compagnie Générale Transatlantique's 3,200-ton *Washington*, built in 1863 and converted in 1868.

The first floating eclipse expedition was led by the US astronomer Ted Pedas in 1972, when 800 passengers sailed to a spectacular rendezvous with a total sun eclipse in the North Atlantic.

The first passenger ship to exceed 80,000 gross tonnage was the Compagnie Générale Transatlantique's *Normandie* (82,799 gross tonnage in 1936).

SeaDream II
★★★★★

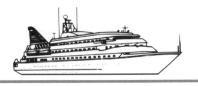

Size:.......................................Boutique Ship	Cabins (total):......................................54
Tonnage: 4,333	Size range (sq ft/m): 195.0–446.7/18.1–41.5
Lifestyle: .... Luxury	Cabins (outside view):................................56
Cruise line:.........................SeaDream Yacht Club	Cabins (interior/no view):..............................0
Former names: ....Seabourn Goddess II, Sea Goddess II	Cabins (for one person):................................0
IMO number: 8203440	Cabins (with private balcony):...........................0
Builder: .... Wartsila (Finland)	Cabins (wheelchair accessible): 0
Original cost: .... $34 million	Wheelchair accessibility:...........................None
Entered service:...................... May 1985/Jan 2002	Cabin voltage: ....110 and 220 volts
Registry:...............................The Bahamas	Elevators:...1
Length (ft/m):............................... 343.8/104.8	Casino (gaming tables):.............................Yes
Beam (ft/m):................................. 47.9/14.6	Slot machines:....................................Yes
Draft (ft/m): 13.6/4.1	Swimming pools:...................................1
Propulsion/Propellers: ....diesel (3,540kW)/2	Hot tubs (on deck):..................................1
Passenger decks:...................................5	Self-service launderette:.............................No
Total crew:.......................................95	Dedicated cinema/seats:..............................No
Passengers (lower beds/alll berths):...............112/112	Library: ....Yes
Passenger Space Ratio (lower beds/all berths): 37.9/37.9	Onboard currency: ....US$
Crew/Passenger Ratio (lower beds/all berths):..........1.1/1.1	

Like having your own mega-yacht for stylish cruising

OVERVIEW. *SeaDream II* is best suited to sophisticated and well-traveled couples who are typically over 40. Rejecting today's huge standard resort cruise ships, they are looking for a small ship with excellent food approaching gourmet standards, and fine European-style service in surroundings that border on the elegant and refined while remaining trendy.

THE SHIPS. *SeaDream II* (and sister ship *Seadream I*) were originally funded by about 800 investors, and operated under the Norske Cruise banner, and named Sea Goddess I and Sea Goddess II. They have an ultra-sleek profile, with deep blue hull and white superstructure, and the ambience of a private club. After they were bought by SeaDream Yacht Club in 2001, they were completely refurbished, with many changes to public rooms and outdoor areas, and several new features added to create what are contemporary, chic, and desirable, if aging, vessels.

Note that, because these ships are popular for small company charters, you may find that the date and itinerary you want will not be available, so you may be asked to change to the sister ship and a different itinerary.

A 'Top of the Yacht' bar, crafted in warm wood, was added to both ships. So were eight special alcoves set to the port and starboard sides of the funnel, equipped with two-person sun loungers with thick pads (and two equipped for one person); however, there is quite a bit of noise from the adjacent funnel. You are encouraged

Berlitz's Ratings		
	Possible	Achieved
Ship	500	428
Accommodation	200	173
Food	400	355
Service	400	370
Entertainment	100	84
Cruise	400	344
OVERALL SCORE		
1754 points out of 2000		

to sleep under the stars if you wish, and cotton sleep suits are provided.

At the front part of the deck there are more sun loungers and a couple of large hammocks, as well as a golf simulator with a choice of 30 courses.

Inside, there is a feeling of unabashed but discreet sophistication. Elegant public rooms have flowers and potpourri everywhere. The main social gathering places are the lounge, a delightful library/living room with a selection of about 1,000 books, a piano bar – which can be more like a karaoke bar at times – and a small casino with two blackjack tables and five slot machines.

SeaDream II really is an exclusive boutique vessel – it's like having your own private yacht in which hospitality, anticipation, and personal recognition are art forms practiced to a high level. The staff is delightful and accommodating – 'no' is not in their vocabulary. The dress code is resort (no tie) casual. Fine-quality furnishings and fabrics are used throughout, with marble and blond wood accents that help create a sense of warmth.

A cruise aboard SeaDream II is for experienced, independent travelers who don't like regular cruise ships, large ships, glitzy lounges, a platoon of people and kids running around, or dressing up – no tuxedos or gowns are allowed, and ties aren't needed. The ship provides the setting for personal indulgence and refined, unstructured living at sea, in a casual, private setting akin to that on a mega-yacht. One delightful feature of each cruise in warm weather areas is a 'caviar in the surf' beach barbecue.

Life could hardly be better at sea – so, as many regular SeaDream Yacht Club passengers say, why bother with ports of call at all? Embarkation never starts before 3pm, in case you are eager to get aboard.

All drinks (with the exception of premium brands and connoisseur wines), farmed sevruga caviar, and gratuities are included, but port charges and insurance are not. The price of a cruise is just that: the price of a cruise. Air and/or other travel arrangements can be made on your own, or through your own travel agent, or you can use the excellent services of Total Travel Marine, whose offices in London and Miami specialize in air arrangements as partner to SeaDream Yacht Club, with service 24/7.

The SeaDreams were the first of the mega-yacht-style ships when built, and none of the cabins has a private balcony – ships with private balconies made their debut just a couple of years later, and, anyway, yachts don't have balconies (they are too close to the waterline). One not so positive item is the fact that the reception desk is now called the Concierge, although it is doubtful whether the staff has the kind of in-depth knowledge that is expected of a concierge.

ACCOMMODATION. There are four types, and six price categories (depending on location, size, and grade): Yacht Club (standard) Cabin, Commodore Club Suite, Admiral Suite, and Owner's Suite.

Yacht Club Cabins. Incorrectly called 'suites' in the brochure, the standard cabins are, more correctly, fully equipped mini-suites with an outside view through windows or portholes, depending on deck and price category. Each measures 195 sq ft (18 sq m), which isn't large by today's cruise ship standards; however, it is large compared to cabins aboard many private motor yachts, and extremely large when compared to ocean-going racing yachts. The sleeping area has twin beds that can be put together to form a queen-size configuration; the beds are positioned next to the window or porthole so that you can entertain in the living area without going past the sleeping area, as you must aboard the slightly larger Seabourn or Silversea ships, for example; a curtain separates the sleeping and lounge areas. All cabinetry and furniture is of thick blond wood, with nicely rounded edges.

A long vanity desk in the sleeping area has a large mirror above it; however, there is no three-sided mirror for women to check the back of their hair. There are two small drawers for cosmetic items, and a brass clock is positioned on one wall. A mirror is placed opposite the bed, which won't please those who follow feng shui principles.

In the lounge area, a long desk has six drawers, plus a vertical cupboard unit that houses a sensible safe, refrigerator, and drinks cabinet stocked with your choice of drinks. There is also a 20in (52mm) flat-screen television, CD and DVD player, and an MP3 audio player with a choice of more than 100 selections. The beds have the finest linens, including thick cotton duvets, and hypoallergenic pillows are also available. There's little room under the beds for luggage, although this can be taken away and stored.

One drawback is the fact that the insulation between cabins is not particularly good, although rarely does this present a problem as most passengers aboard the *SeaDreams* are generally extremely quiet, considerate types who are allergic to noise. Incidentally, a sleep suit is supplied in case you want to sleep out on deck under the stars in one of the on-deck two-person beds – but more of those later.

When the ships became *SeaDreams I* and *II*, all the bathrooms were totally refurbished. The new cheerful decor is more hip and trendy, with softer colors and large (beige) marble tiles. The former tiny sit-in bathtubs were taken out – these are missed by some passengers – and replaced by a multi-jet power glassed-in shower enclosure. A washbasin set in a marble-look surround and two glass shelves make up the facilities, and an under-sink cupboard provides further space for larger toiletries. Bulgari toiletries are provided. Gorgeously thick, plush, 100 percent cotton SeaDream-logo bathrobes and towels are also supplied.

However, despite their having been completely rebuilt, the bathrooms really are small, particularly for those of larger than average build. Also, the bathroom door opens inward, so space inside is at a premium. The toilet is located in a somewhat awkward position and, unless you close the door, you can see yourself in the mirror facing of the closets, opposite the bathroom door.

Commodore Club Suites. For larger accommodation, choose one of 16 Commodore Club Suites. These consist of two standard cabins with an interconnecting door, thus providing you with a healthy 380 sq ft (36 sq m) of living space. One cabin is made into a lounge and dining room, with table and up to four chairs, while the other becomes your sleeping area. The advantage is that you get two bathrooms. One disadvantage is that the soundproofing between cabins could be better.

Admiral Suite. Added in 2008–09, this suite occupies space previously devoted to the ship's boutique, and adjacent to the piano bar/library. It's a little smaller than the Owner's Suite, but is well laid out and extremely comfortable.

Owner's Suite. For the largest living space, go for the Owner's Suite. This measures a grand 490 sq ft (46 sq m). It's the only accommodation with a bathroom that incorporates a real full-size tub; there's also a separate shower enclosure and lots of space for toiletries.

In all grades of accommodation, passengers receive personalized stationery, a personal email address, a 100 percent cotton sleep suit, Bulgari toiletries, 24-hour room service, and 'sweet dreams' chocolates.

DINING. The dining salon, called The Restaurant, is elegant and inviting, and has bird's-eye maple-wood paneled walls and alcoves showcasing beautiful hand-made glass creations. It is cozy, yet with plenty of space around each table for fine service, and the ship provides a floating culinary celebration in an open-seating arrangement, so you can dine whenever, and with whomever, you want. Course-by-course meals can also be served out on deck.

Tables can be configured for two, four, six, or eight. They are laid with a classic setting of a real glass base (show) plate, Porsgrund china, pristine white mono-grammed table linen, and fresh flowers.

Candlelit dinners are part of the inviting setting. There's even a box of spare spectacles for menu reading in case you forget your own. You get leather-bound menus, and close to impeccable personalized European service.

The SeaDream Yacht Club experience really is all about dining. The ships will not disappoint, and culinary excellence prevails. Only the very freshest and finest quality ingredients are used in the best culinary artistry. Fine, unhurried European service is provided. Additionally, good-quality Champagne is available whenever you want it, and so is caviar – American farmed Hackleback sturgeon malossol caviar, sadly – and not Russian caviar, whose purchase and supply today is challenging. The ice cream, which is made on board, however, is excellent.

In addition to the regular menus, some beautifully prepared and presented 'raw food' menu items have been introduced, in cooperation with Forida's Hippo-crates Institute, with nothing cooked at a temperature of more than 115°F (46°C).

SeaDream II provides extremely creative cuisine, and everything is prepared individually to order. Special orders are possible, although the former popular flaming desserts have almost disappeared. You can also dine course by course in your suite for any meal, at any time during meal hours. The dining room isn't open for lunch, which disappoints those who don't want to eat outside, particularly in hot climates.

Good-quality table wines are included in the cruise fare for lunch and dinner. Real wine connoisseurs, however, will appreciate the availability of an extra wine list, full of special vintages and premier crus at extra cost. If you want to do something different with a loved one, you can also arrange to dine one evening on the open (but covered) deck, overlooking the swim-ming pool and stern – it is a rather romantic setting.

The Topside Restaurant is an informal open-air eat-ery and has roll-down sides (in case of inclement weath-er), and is open for breakfast, lunch or the occasional dinner. Teak tables and chairs add a touch of class.

ENTERTAINMENT. There is no evening entertain-ment as such (it's not needed), other than a duo or solo musician to provide music for listening and dancing in the lounge. Dinner is the main event, and videos are available to take to your cabin.

SPA/FITNESS. The holistic approach to wellbe-ing plays a big part in relaxation and body pampering aboard *SeaDream II*. To this end, when you enter the Asian Spa/Wellness Centre, which has a good-sized gymnasium and a small beauty salon, you enter another world. There are three massage rooms, a small sauna, and steam shower enclosure.

The spa, located in a private area forward on Deck 4, is staffed and operated as a concession by Universal Maritime Services. Massage on the beach is available when the ship stages its famous beach party.

For golfers, there's an electronic golf simulator, and choice of several golf courses to play. There is a small, retractable, water sports platform at the stern. Equip-ment carried includes a water-ski boat, sailboat, wave runners (jet skis), kayaks, wake boards, snorkeling equipment, and two Zodiacs. The use of all this equip-ment is included in the price of a cruise.

The sea conditions have to be just right (minimal swell) for these items to be used, which, on average is once or twice during a typical seven-night cruise. You may be allowed to swim off the stern platform if condi-tions permit. Ten mountain bikes are also carried, and these can be used on shore visits.

Serenade of the Seas
★★★+

Size:.....................................Large Resort Ship		Cabins (total):.......................................1,050	
Tonnage: 90,090		Size range (sq ft/m): 165.8–1,216.3/15.4–113.0	
Lifestyle: ....Standard		Cabins (outside view):.................................813	
Cruise line:...................Royal Caribbean International		Cabins (interior/no view):.............................237	
Former names: ....none		Cabins (for one person):................................0	
IMO number: 9228344		Cabins (with private balcony):.........................577	
Builder: ....Meyer Werft (Germany)		Cabins (wheelchair accessible): ......14 (8 with private balcony)	
Original cost:...................................$350 million		Wheelchair accessibility:.............................Best	
Entered service:................................Aug 2003		Cabin voltage: ....110 and 220 volts	
Registry:.......................................The Bahamas		Elevators:...9	
Length (ft/m):................................961.9/293.2		Casino (gaming tables):................................Yes	
Beam (ft/m):..................................105.6/32.2		Slot machines:..Yes	
Draft (ft/m): 27.8/8.5		Swimming pools:...2	
Propulsion/Propellers:. gas turbine (40,000kW)/2 azimuthing pods		Hot tubs (on deck):.....................................3	
Passenger decks:.....................................12		Self-service launderette:................................No	
Total crew:..858		Dedicated cinema/seats:................................Yes	
Passengers (lower beds/alll berths):..............2,100/2,500		Library: ....Yes	
Passenger Space Ratio (lower beds/all berths): 42.9/36.0		Onboard currency: ....US$	
Crew/Passenger Ratio (lower beds/all berths):..........2.4/2.9			

A large resort ship for family-friendly casual cruising

OVERVIEW. Life aboard is more casual and unstructured than is often the case with Royal Caribbean International. This ship offers more space, more comfortable public areas, and several more intimate spaces, slightly larger cabins and more dining options than most of the larger ships in the fleet. But the onboard operation suffers from a lack of service staff.

THE SHIP. *Serenade of the Seas* uses gas and steam turbine power, as do sister ships *Brilliance of the Seas* and *Radiance of the Seas*, instead of the formerly conventional diesel or diesel-electric combination. Pod propulsion power is also provided.

As aboard all RCI vessels, the navigation bridge is of the fully enclosed. In the very front of the ship is a helipad, which also acts as a viewing platform for passengers. One of two swimming pools can be covered by a large glass dome.

Serenade of the Seas is a streamlined contemporary ship, and has a two-deck-high walk-around structure in the forward section of the funnel. Along the starboard side, a central glass wall protrudes, giving great views; cabins with balconies occupy the space directly opposite on the port side. The gently rounded stern has nicely tiered decks, which gives the ship a well-balanced look.

The interior focal point is a nine-deck-high atrium lobby with glass-walled elevators (on the port side of the ship only) that travel through 12 decks, face the sea and provide a link with nature and the ocean. The Cen-

Berlitz's Ratings		
	Possible	Achieved
Ship	500	378
Accommodation	200	141
Food	400	242
Service	400	281
Entertainment	100	74
Cruise	400	268
OVERALL SCORE		
1384 points out of 2000		

trum, as the atrium is called, has several public rooms connected to it: the guest relations office and shore excursions desks, a Lobby Bar, Champagne Bar, the Library, an Internet-connect center, the Concierge Club, and a Crown & Anchor Lounge.

Other facilities include a delightful, but very small library and, in the atrium lobby, a Coffee Shop that also sells pastries and cakes. The large Schooner Bar is popular aboard RCI ships, with nautical riggings, ship replicas, and maritime art. Gamblers should enjoy the large, noisy, and colorful Casino Royale. There's also a small dedicated screening room for movies, as well as a 194-seat conference center and a business center.

This ship has a Viking Crown Lounge, a Royal Caribbean International trademark, set around the base of the funnel. It is an observation lounge by day, with views forward over the swimming pool. In the evening, the space transforms into a dance club, as well as a more intimate and relaxed entertainment venue for softer mood music.

Royal Caribbean Online, located in a semi-private setting, has 12 computers providing high-speed Internet access for sending and receiving email. Four more Internet terminals are located in Books 'n' Coffee, located in an extensive area of shops.

Many 'private' balcony cabins aren't private, as they can be overlooked by anyone standing in the port and starboard wings of the Solarium, and from other locations. There are no cushioned pads for the sunloungers, and the deck towels provided are quite thin and small.

Spa treatments are extravagantly expensive. It is virtually impossible to escape background music.

Standing in lines for embarkation, the reception desk, disembarkation, for port visits, shore tenders, and for the self-serve buffet stations in the Windjammer Café is an inevitable aspect of cruising aboard this large ship.

FAMILIES. Youth facilities include Adventure Ocean, an 'edutainment' area with four separate age-appropriate sections for junior passengers: Aquanaut Center (for ages three to five); Explorer Center (six to eight); Voyager Center (nine to 12); and the Optix Teen Center (13–17). There is also Adventure Beach, which includes a splash pool complete with waterslide; Surfside, with computer lab stations with entertaining software; and Ocean Arcade, a video games hangout.

ACCOMMODATION. There is a wide range of suites and standard outside-view and interior cabins, in many different categories.

Apart from the largest suites (six owner's suites), which have king-size beds, almost all other cabins have twin beds that convert to a queen-size bed. All cabins have rich (but faux) wood cabinetry, including a vanity desk with hairdryer, faux wood drawers that close silently (hooray), a television, personal safe and three-sided mirrors. Some cabins have a recessed ceiling, pull-down berths for third and fourth persons, although closet and drawer space would be extremely tight for four people, even if two of them are children.

Most cabin bathrooms have tiled accenting and a terrazzo-style tiled floor, and a rather small shower enclosure in a half-moon shape, 100 percent Egyptian cotton towels, a small cabinet for toiletries, and a small shelf. In reality, there is little space to stow toiletries for two or more people.

The largest accommodation consists of a family suite with two bedrooms. One bedroom has twin beds that convert to a queen-size bed, while a second has two lower beds and two upper Pullman berths, a combination that can sleep up to eight people – this would suit large families.

Occupants of accommodation designated as suites also get the use of a private Concierge Lounge, where priority dining room reservations, shore excursion bookings, and beauty salon/spa appointments can be made.

DINING. Reflections, the main dining room, spans two decks; the upper deck level has floor-to-ceiling windows, while the lower level has picture windows. It is a pleasant but inevitably noisy dining hall, reminiscent of those aboard the transatlantic liners in their heyday. However, eight huge, thick pillars obstruct sight lines.

Reflections seats 1,104 hungry persons, and its decor features a cascading water theme. There are ta-

bles for two, four, six, eight, or 10. Two small private dining rooms – Illusions with 94 seats and Mirage with 30 seats – are located off the main dining room. When you book, choose one of two seatings, or My Time Dining.

The cuisine is typical of mass banquet catering that offers standard fare comparable to that found in American family-style restaurants ashore. The menu descriptions make the food sound better than it is. The selection of breads, rolls, fruit, and cheese is quite poor, however. Caviar, once a standard menu item, now incurs a hefty extra charge. Menus may include a Welcome Aboard Dinner, French Dinner, Italian Dinner, International Dinner, Captain's Gala Dinner.

One thing RCI does once each cruise is to put on a Galley Buffet whereby passengers go through a section of the galley picking up food for a midnight buffet. There is an adequate wine list, moderately priced.

Other dining options. Extra-cost venues include Portofino, with 112 seats, serves Italian cuisine, and Chops Grill Steakhouse, with 95 seats and an open 'show' kitchen, serves premium meats in the form of veal chops and steaks. The menus don't change throughout the cruise. In both restaurants, a cover charge applies, reservations are required.

ENTERTAINMENT. Facilities include the three-level, 874-seat Tropical Theater, which also has 24 stations for wheelchairs. There are good sight lines from most seats. Strong cabaret acts are also presented in the main showlounge. A second entertainment venue is the Safari Club. This is where more casual cabaret shows, including late-night adult comedy, and live music for dancing are performed. The entertainment is always upbeat – in fact, it is almost impossible to get away from music and noise. There is even background music in all corridors and elevators, and constant music on the pool deck. If you want a quiet holiday, choose another cruise line.

SPA/FITNESS. The ShipShape Spa's health, fitness, and spa facilities have themed decor, and include a 10,176-sq-ft (945-sq-m) solarium, a gym with 44 cardiovascular machines, 50-person aerobics room, sauna and steam rooms, and therapy treatment rooms. The climate-controlled 10,176-sq-ft (945-sq-m) indoor/outdoor Solarium has a sliding glass dome roof that can be closed in cool or inclement weather conditions, and provides facilities for relaxation. It has Balinese-themed decor, and includes a whirlpool and counter-current swimming.

For the more sporting passengers, there is activity galore – including a 30-ft (9-m) rock-climbing wall with five separate climbing tracks. It is located outdoors at the aft end of the funnel. Other sports facilities include a nine-hole miniature golf course, and an indoor/outdoor country club with golf simulator, a jogging track, and basketball court.

Seven Seas Mariner
★★★★ +

Size:. . . . . Small Ship	Crew/Passenger Ratio (lower beds/all berths):. 1.6/1.7
Tonnage: 48,075	Cabins (total):. 354
Lifestyle: . . . . .Luxury/Premium	Size range (sq ft/m): 301.3–2,002.0/28.0–186.0
Cruise line:. Regent Seven Seas Cruises	Cabins (outside view):. 354
Former names: . . . . *none*	Cabins (interior/no view):. 0
IMO number: 9210139	Cabins (for one person):. 0
Builder: . . . . Chantiers de l'Atlantique (France)	Cabins (with private balcony):. 354
Original cost: . . . . $240 million	Cabins (wheelchair accessible): 6
Entered service:. . . . . Mar 2001	Wheelchair accessibility:. . . . . Best
Registry:. . . . . The Bahamas	Cabin voltage: . . . . 110 volts
Length (ft/m):. 713.0/217.3	Elevators:. 6
Beam (ft/m):. 95.1/29.0	Casino (gaming tables):. . . . . Yes
Draft (ft/m): 21.4/6.5	Slot machines:. . . . . Yes
Propulsion/Propellers:. . .diesel-electric (16,000kW)/2 azimuthing	Swimming pools:. 1
pods	Hot tubs (on deck):. 3
Passenger decks:. 9	Self-service launderette:. . . . . Yes (3)
Total crew:. 445	Dedicated cinema/seats:. . . . . .No
Passengers (lower beds/alll berths):. 708/752	Library: . . . . Yes
Passenger Space Ratio (lower beds/all berths): 67.9/63.9	Onboard currency: . . . . .US$

An all-inclusive premium ship for senior-age cruisers

OVERVIEW. *Seven Seas Mariner* is best suited to well-traveled couples and single travelers, typically over 50, who seek excellent itineraries, fine food, and good service, with some entertainment, all wrapped up in a contemporary ship that is elegant and comfortable. Its passenger space ratio is among the highest in the cruise industry.

THE SHIP. The largest ship in the Regent Seven Seas Cruises fleet (with a superb Passenger Space Ratio), this was the first to receive a pod propulsion system, replacing the traditional shaft and rudder system. The ship was extensively refurbished in 2009.

There is a wide range of public rooms, almost all located under the accommodation decks. Three sets of stairways (forward, center, aft) mean it is easy to find your way around. An atrium lobby spans nine decks, with the lowest level opening directly onto the tender landing stage.

Facilities include a very comfortable, large observation lounge, a small casino, a shopping concourse with 'open market' area, a garden lounge/promenade arcade, a large library (incorporating several computer workstations, and adjacent room with 14 Internet-connect computers, coffee lounge (featuring illy coffee) card player's room, conference room, cigar-smoking lounge (Connoisseur Club), and a Park West art gallery (silent auctions are held).

With *Seven Seas Mariner*, the company embraced larger ships that are more economical to operate, and

Berlitz's Ratings		
	Possible	Achieved
Ship	500	432
Accommodation	200	177
Food	400	318
Service	400	310
Entertainment	100	82
Cruise	400	326
OVERALL SCORE		
1645 points out of 2000		

offer more choices in terms of facilities, open deck space, public rooms and dining venues. The company's former smaller ships used to have a more intimate, close-knit ambience and feel; fortunately, some of the personal service of the smaller ships has been absorbed into the larger structure. However, this ship is too large to enter the small harbors and berths that the company's former smaller ships were able to access, and so loses some of the benefits of upscale small-ship cruising. The ship has many good points, such as finely varnished wooden handrails on all stairways and balconies, a 'Meet the Neighbors Block Party,' and a choice of dining venues, and should please the well-traveled.

The same carpeting is used throughout the public areas, with no relief or change of color or pattern on the stairwells. The decor is non-glitzy and restrained, but has a contemporary look and feel. Much of the intimacy and close-knit ambience of smaller vessels is missing, and, because of all those cabins with balconies, the feeling of privacy and relaxation often translates into fewer passengers in public rooms and for entertainment events, depending on the passenger mix.

The ship scores highly in terms of hardware and software, but operationally loses a few points because it can't enter some of the more intimate ports that smaller ships can, and dining service ranges from excellent to spotty and inconsistent. Overall *Seven Seas Mariner* ends up just a tad under the score base needed for it to join the Berlitz Five Star Club.

Basic gratuities are included, as are all alcoholic and non-alcoholic beverages and table wines for lunch and dinner – although premium and connoisseur selections are available at extra cost (and excellent illy brand coffees are also included), and internet-connection charges are high. Shore excursions and pre- or post-cruise hotel stays are also included, depending on the itinerary.

ACCOMMODATION. There are around a dozen accommodation categories. *Seven Seas Mariner* was the cruise industry's first all-suites, all-balconies ship – though that's not technically correct as not all accommodation has sleeping areas completely separated from living areas.

Most grades of accommodation have private, marble-clad bathrooms with tub or half-tub, and all suite entrances are neatly recessed away from the passenger hallways to provide quietness (refreshingly there's no music in the hallways, although there is in the elevators). In comparison with Seven Seas Navigator, the bathrooms aboard this ship are not as large in the lower accommodation grades. Bathrobes and towels by Anichini are provided.

Master Suites. The largest accommodation (1,580 sq ft/147 sq m), in two Master Suites, has two separate bedrooms, living room with TV/DVD and CD player, walk-in closet, dining area, large, two marble-clad bathrooms with tub and separate shower enclosure, and two private teakwood-decked balconies. Butler service is provided, as is an illy espresso machine.

Mariner Suites. Six Mariner Suites (739 sq ft/69 sq m), on the port and starboard sides of the atrium on three separate decks, have a separate bedroom, living room with large audio-visual center, walk-in closet, dining area, large, marble-clad bathroom with tub and separate shower enclosure, and a good-size private balcony. Butler service is provided, as is an illy espresso machine.

Grand Suites. Two Grand Suites (707 sq ft/66 sq m) are located one deck above the ship's navigation bridge. The facilities are similar to those in Mariner Suites. Butler service is provided

Seven Seas Suites. Six spacious suites (697 sq ft/65 sq m) overlook the ship's stern (two suites are located on each of four decks) and have very generous private balcony space and good wraparound views over the ship's stern and to port or starboard. The balconies, however, are only semi-private and can be partly overlooked. Another two are located just aft of the ship's navigation bridge. They are slightly smaller, at 600 sq ft (56 sq m), and have balconies. They have a separate bedroom, living room with audio-visual center, walk-in closet, dining area, and marble-clad bathroom with a combination tub/shower.

Horizon View Suites. The 12 Horizon Suites (627 sq ft/58 sq m) overlook the stern and have a very large balcony and good views. These suites have a separate bedroom, living room with TV/DVD, walk-in closet,

dining area, large, marble-clad bathroom with a combination tub/shower. Butler service is provided.

Penthouse Suite. The 14 Penthouse Suites (categories A-C) measure 449 sq ft (41.7 sq m) and have a bedroom that can be separated from the living area, and twin beds that convert to a queen-size bed. They are wide (highly desirable) rooms, located on the uppermost accommodation deck, and provide plenty of open space. The bathrooms are nicely appointed, and the balcony is quite large. Butler service is provided, as is an illy espresso machine.

Deluxe Suites. Categories D-E and F–H in the brochure, listed as Concierge Suites and Deluxe Suites, these measure approximately 301 sq ft (28 sq m) and have twin beds that convert to a queen-size bed, small walk-in closet, marble-lined bathroom with combination tub/shower, vanity desk, hairdryer, TV/DVD, refrigerator (stocked with soft drinks and bar setup on embarkation), and personal safe. In these suites, the sleeping area is separated from the living area only by partial room dividers, and therefore is a cabin – albeit a good-size one – and not a true suite.

Six wheelchair-accessible suites are located as close to an elevator as one could possibly get, and provide ample living space, together with a large roll-in shower and all bathroom fittings located at the correct height.

While it's nice to have an illy espresso coffee machine in many of the suites, it doesn't work for anyone wanting an espresso macchiato or cappuccino, because there is no milk steaming wand.

DINING. Four different dining venues all operate on an open-seating basis, so that you can dine when you choose and with whomever you choose. Reservations are required in two of the four dining venues. In general, the cuisine is good to very good, with creative presentation and a wide variety of food choices (Kosher meals can be provided).

The main dining room, the 570-seat Compass Rose Restaurant, has a light, fresh decor, and seating at tables for two, four, six, or eight – although tables for six or eight predominate. With a one-and-a-half deck height, the restaurant has a nice open feeling, and there's plenty of space around most tables for decent service to be provided.

Other dining options. The 80-seat Prime 7 Steakhouse is the smallest of the specialty dining venues. It features a range of superb USDA prime, dry-aged steaks as well as chops, oven-roasted half chicken, Alaskan king crab legs, and Maine lobster. It's the most intimate dining spot – though, again, the single-deck ceiling height makes it feel busy – and it can get noisy (call it lively ambiance). There is seating for two, four, or six, and reservations are required.

Signatures is a 120-seat 'supper club' has ocean views along the room's port side. It is directed and staffed by chefs wearing the white toque and blue riband of Le Cordon Bleu, the prestigious culinary society, whose cuisine is classic French. Doors open onto a covered area outdoors, with small stage and dance floor. Seating is at tables of two, four, or six, and reservations are required. However, the single-deck ceiling height robs the room of the grandeur that suits fine classic French cuisine.

For more casual meals, La Veranda is a large self-serve indoor/outdoor café with seats for 450; the decor is fresh and light. This eatery has several food islands and substantial counter display space. At night, it is transformed into Sette Mari – an Italian eatery with some excellent pasta-based dishes.

The outdoor Pool Grill and ice cream bar, adjacent to the swimming pool, is a popular eatery. It features a creative list of burgers (a choice of 11, to be exact, including Black Angus beefburger, Philly beefburger, southwestern beefburger, pestobeefburger, Portobello and feta cheese burger, Asian salmon burger, tofu veggie burger, roasted garlic teriyaki mushroom turkeyburger – and others, as well as various sandwiches.

For privacy, you can also dine in your cabin. There is a 24-hour room service menu, and, during regular dinner hours, the full dining room menu is available.

ENTERTAINMENT. The Constellation Theater spans two decks and is quite stunning, with really good sight lines from almost all seats. The proscenium stage also includes a front thrust stage that's useful for presenting more intimate cabaret acts (or catwalk-style fashion shows). Seven Seas Cruises has an eclectic entertainment program, tailored to each individual ship.

Seven Seas Mariner presents both production shows and cabaret acts. A troupe of eight singers/dancers perform the colorful shows – the cast is, however, small for the size of the stage. Cabaret acts tend to feature vocalists, magicians, and comedy jugglers, among others.

The Horizon Lounge, located aft, is a combination day lounge with bar, and the venue for afternoon tea and daily quizzes. A number of bands, small musical units, and solo pianists provide live music in lounges and bars.

There is also Stars nightclub (with a section for cigarette smokers), with an oval-shaped dance floor, and a stairway that connects it to the casino on the deck above.

SPA/FITNESS. Health and fitness facilities include an extensive health spa with gymnasium and aerobics room, beauty parlor, and separate changing, sauna, and steam rooms for men and women. The spa is located not at the top of the ship, as is common with many other ships today, but just off the atrium in the center of the ship. Canyon Ranch SpaClub operates the spa and beauty services as a concession, and provides the staff. There's a range of clothing, beauty products for the body and wellbeing books for sale. An 18 percent gratuity is included in treatment and beauty salon services prices.

Sports devotees can play in the paddle tennis court, golf driving and practice cages.

Nautical Expressions

If you've ever wondered where some terms or phrases came from, you have only to look to the sea, ships, and seamen.

Above board. This term for honesty originated in the days when pirates would hide most of their crews below decks, to trick an unsuspecting victim. A ship that showed its crew openly on the deck, above board, was obviously an honest merchantman.

All Above Board. This phrase referred to the fact that boards or planking which made up the decks are in plain view; hence, anything that was stored above board was in plain view of everyone and lessened the chances of commercial deception. Today we tend to use 'going overboard' in the sense of going too far in our reaction or in some venture. 'All above board' has come to be synonymous with honest dealings.

All hands on deck. Everyone should gather together to their positions and prepare for action. It is used nowadays to mean 'to gather together for some task or other.'

As the crow flies. British coastal vessels customarily carried a cage of crows. These birds hate wide expanses of water and head, 'as straight as the crow flies,' to the nearest land when released at sea. This was useful to vessels lost in foggy coastal weather before the days of radar. The lookout perch on sailing vessels became known as the crow's nest.

Bale out. The term is typically used in the sense of getting out of some situation – particularly a financial one. However, the verb to bale out, means to remove water, and comes from the old name 'boyle' for a bucket.

Seven Seas Navigator
★★★★ +

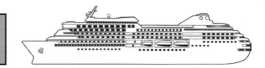

Size:. . . . . Small Ship	Cabins (total):. 245
Tonnage: 28,550	Size range (sq ft/m): 301.3–1,173.3/28.0–109.0
Lifestyle: . . . . .Luxury/Premium	Cabins (outside view): 245
Cruise line:. Regent Seven Seas Cruises	Cabins (interior/no view):. 0
Former names: . . . . .none	Cabins (for one person):. 0
IMO number: 9064126	Cabins (with private balcony): 196
Builder: . . . . .T. Mariotti (Italy)	Cabins (wheelchair accessible): 4
Original cost:. . . . . $200 million	Wheelchair accessibility:. . . . . .Good
Entered service:. . . . . Aug 1999	Cabin voltage: . . . . .110 and 220 volts
Registry:. . . . . Bermuda	Elevators:. 5
Length (ft/m):. 559.7/170.6	Casino (gaming tables):. . . . . Yes
Beam (ft/m):. 71.5/21.8	Slot machines:. . . . . Yes
Draft (ft/m): 21.3/6.5	Swimming pools:. 1
Propulsion/Propellers:. . . . . .diesel (13,000kW)/2	Hot tubs (on deck):. 2
Passenger decks:. 8	Self-service launderette:. . . . . Yes
Total crew:. 325	Dedicated cinema/seats:. . . . . .No
Passengers (lower beds/alll berths):. 490/530	Library: . . . . Yes
Passenger Space Ratio (lower beds/all berths): 58.2/53.8	Onboard currency: . . . . .US$
Crew/Passenger Ratio (lower beds/all berths):. 1.5/1.6	

A premium, all-inclusive ship for mature-age cruisers

OVERVIEW. This ship is best suited to well-traveled couples and single travelers, typically over 50, who seek excellent itineraries, fine food, and good service, with some entertainment, all wrapped up in a contemporary ship that's elegant and comfortable. Designed for worldwide cruise itineraries, this is one of the upscale ships in the diverse Regent Seven Seas Cruises fleet.

THE SHIP. *Seven Seas Navigator* was built using a hull already constructed in St Petersburg, Russia, as the research vessel *Akademik Nikolay Pilyugin*. The superstructure was incorporated into the hull in an Italian shipyard – the result being that, in effect, a new ship was delivered in record time. The result is less than handsome – particularly at the stern – but it's large enough to be stable over long stretches of water, and there is an excellent amount of space per passenger. In 2009, a 'ducktail' stern was added to aid stability and buoyancy.

The interiors have a mix of classical and contemporary Italian styling and decor, with warm, soft colors and fine quality soft furnishings and fabrics. Galileo's, a large piano lounge, has good views over the stern. A Navigator's Lounge has warm mahogany and cherry wood paneling and large, comfortable, mid-back tub chairs. Next door, cigars and cognac can be taken in the delightful Connoisseur's Club – the first aboard a Regent Seven Seas Cruises vessel. The extensive library also has several computers with direct Internet access, for a fee.

Berlitz's Ratings

	Possible	Achieved
Ship	500	401
Accommodation	200	175
Food	400	307
Service	400	304
Entertainment	100	77
Cruise	400	309

OVERALL SCORE
1573 points out of 2000

There is no walk-around promenade deck outdoors, although there's a jogging track high atop the aft section around the funnel housing. Two of the upper, outer decks are laid with green Astroturf, which cheapens the look of the ship – they would be better in teak. The ceilings in several public rooms, including the main restaurant, are quite low, which makes the ship feel smaller and more closed-in than it is. It suffers from a considerable amount of vibration, which detracts from the comfort level when compared with other vessels of the same size.

Basic gratuities are included in the fare, as are alcoholic and non-alcoholic beverages, plus table wines for lunch and dinner. Shore excursions and any pre- or post-cruise hotel stays are also included.

ACCOMMODATION. There are several different price grades, and the company markets this as an 'all-suites' ship. Even the smallest suite is quite large, and all have outside views (all were refreshed in 2012). Almost 90 percent of all suites have a private balcony, with floor-to-ceiling sliding glass doors, while 10 suites are interconnecting, and 38 have an extra bed for a third occupant. By comparison, even the smallest suite is more than twice the size of the smallest cabin aboard the world's largest cruise ships, Royal Caribbean International's *Voyager*-class ships.

All accommodation grades feature a walk-in closet, European king-size bed or twin beds, wooden cabinetry with nicely rounded edges, plenty of drawer space, mini-bar/refrigerator stocked with complimentary soft drinks and bar setup on embarkation, TV/DVD player, and personal safe. The marble-appointed bathroom has a full-size tub, as well as a separate shower enclosure, 100 percent cotton bathrobe and towels, and hairdryer. Balconies benefit from real teak decking.

The largest living spaces are in four Grand and Master suites, with forward-facing views and double-length side balconies. Each suite has a completely separate bedroom with dressing table; the living room has a full dining room table and chairs for up to six persons, wet bar, counter and bar stools, large three-person sofa and six armchairs, an audio-visual console/entertainment center, and an Illy coffee machine. Each suite has a large main, marble-clad, fully tiled bathroom with full-size tub and separate shower enclosure, a separate room with bidet, toilet, and washbasin, with plenty of space for toiletries. There is a separate guest bathroom.

Next in size are the superb Navigator Suites, which have a separate bedroom, walk-in closet, large lounge with mini-bar/refrigerator stocked with complimentary soft drinks and bar setup on embarkation, personal safe, compact disc player, large TV/DVD player, and dining area with large table and four chairs. The marble-clad, fully tiled bathroom has a full-size tub with hand-held shower, plus a separate shower enclosure (although the door is only 18ins/45cm wide), large washbasin, toilet and bidet, and ample toiletries storage space.

Unfortunately, the Navigator Suites are located in the center of the ship, directly underneath the swimming pool deck. They are thus subject to early morning noise attacks – when deck cleaning is carried out – and chairs are dragged across the deck. You are also aware of pool deck stewards dragging and dropping sun-loungers into place. Despite these disadvantages, the Navigator Suites are delightful living spaces.

Four suites for the physically challenged have private balconies, and are ideally located adjacent to the elevators. However, while they are very practical, it is almost impossible to access the balcony because of the high threshold at the bottom of the sliding-glass door.

DINING. The Compass Rose Dining Room has large ocean-view picture windows and open-seating dining, which means that you can choose your companions. There are a few tables for two, but most are for four, six, or eight persons. With a low ceiling height and noisy waiter stations, the overall feeling is cramped and unbecoming in terms of the lack of space and grace. Complimentary wines are served during dinner, and a connoisseur wine list is available at extra cost. The company also promotes 'heart healthy' cuisine.

Other dining options. La Veranda is the casual self-serve eatery for breakfast and lunch. Each evening, it is transformed into Sette Mari, for informal dining, and serves dinners with an emphasis on Italian cuisine (reservations required for dinner). Al fresco dining is also available.

The 70-seat Prime 7 is the place for steaks and seafood, is in an elegant setting for dinner only (reservations required). For fast-food, there is a small outdoor Grill one deck above.

You can also dine in your cabin. There is a 24-hour room service menu and, during regular dinner hours, you can choose from the full dining room menu.

ENTERTAINMENT. The Seven Seas Lounge, a two-deck-high showlounge, has reasonable sight lines from most seats on both main and balcony levels, although pillars obstruct the views from some side balcony seats. Seven Seas Cruises has an eclectic entertainment program tailored to each ship. *Seven Seas Navigator* puts on both production shows and cabaret acts. Bands, small musical units, and solo pianist entertainers provide live music in several lounges and bars.

SPA/FITNESS. The spa, fitness center, and beauty salon are in the most forward part of the top deck. Canyon Ranch SpaClub operates the spa and beauty services as a concession, provides the staff, and sells its own beauty products. An 18 percent gratuity is included in treatment and beauty salon services prices.

Seven Seas Voyager
★★★★ +

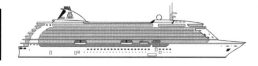

Size:. . . . . Small Ship	Crew/Passenger Ratio (lower beds/all berths):. 1.65/1.6
Tonnage: 42,363	Cabins (total):. 354
Lifestyle: . . . . .Luxury/Premium	Size range (sq ft/m): 356.0-1,399.3/33.0–130.0
Cruise line:. . . . . Regent Seven Seas Cruises	Cabins (outside view): 354
Former names: . . . . .none	Cabins (interior/no view):. 0
IMO number: 9247144	Cabins (for one person):. 0
Builder: . . . . .T. Mariotti (Italy)	Cabins (with private balcony): 354
Original cost:. . . . . $240 million	Cabins (wheelchair accessible): 4
Entered service:. . . . . Mar 2003	Wheelchair accessibility:. . . . . Best
Registry:. . . . . .The Bahamas	Cabin voltage: . . . . 110 volts
Length (ft/m):. 669.2/204.0	Elevators:. 6
Beam (ft/m):. 94.5/28.8	Casino (gaming tables):. . . . . Yes
Draft (ft/m): 23.0/7.0	Slot machines:. . . . . Yes
Propulsion/Propellers:. . .diesel-electric (16,000kW)/2 azimuthing	Swimming pools:. 1
pods	Hot tubs (on deck):. 3
Passenger decks:. 9	Self-service launderette:. . . . . Yes (3)
Total crew:. 445	Dedicated cinema/seats:. . . . . .No
Passengers (lower beds/alll berths):. 708/752	Library: . . . . Yes
Passenger Space Ratio (lower beds/all berths): 59.8/56.3	Onboard currency: . . . . .US$

Premium all-inclusive cruising with space and style

OVERVIEW. Seven Seas Voyage would be ideally suited to well-traveled couples and single travelers, typically over 50, seeking excellent itineraries, fine food, and good service, with some entertainment, in a contemporary ship that's elegant and comfortable.

THE SHIP. *Seven Seas Voyager* was built in 32 blocks, with the same basic hull design as *Seven Seas Mariner*, with a few modifications. It has a pod propulsion system. It has a decent range of public rooms, almost all located under the accommodation decks. Three sets of stairways mean it is easy to find your way around. An atrium lobby spans nine decks, with the lowest level opening directly onto the tender landing stage.

Facilities include a showlounge that spans two decks, an observation lounge, a casino, a shopping concourse, a large library, Internet-connect center, Club.com and business center (Coffee.com), a card room, and a small conference room. There is also a nightclub, Voyager, with an oval-shaped dance floor, a cigar-smoking lounge, the Connoisseur Club for cigars and cognacs, and the usual photo gallery.

Basic gratuities are included, as are all drinks, including table wines for lunch and dinner (premium selections are available at extra cost). Shore excursions and any pre- or post-cruise hotel stays are also included. Service levels have decreased since the introduction of the drinks-inclusive policy, so the overall delivery of a quality onboard experience is on the downward slope.

Berlitz's Ratings

	Possible	Achieved
Ship	500	431
Accommodation	200	177
Food	400	324
Service	400	306
Entertainment	100	82
Cruise	400	324

OVERALL SCORE
1643 points out of 2000

Passenger gripes: there is no walk-around outdoor promenade deck, and there is no forward-viewing exterior deck with views over the ship's bows.

ACCOMMODATION. There are about a dozen different accommodation price grades. As the ship was built with a central corridor design, this has allowed for larger suites and bathrooms than aboard *Seven Seas Mariner*. This is Regent Seven Seas Cruises' second 'all-suites, all-balconies' ship – although that's not strictly correct as not all sleeping areas are completely separated from living areas.

All grades of accommodation have private, marble-clad bathrooms with tub, walk-in closet with personal safe, and most suite entrances are recessed away from passenger hallways (a central corridor), so as to provide extra quietness.

Master Suites. Basically 1,162 sq ft/108 sq m, these two suites, 1100 and 1001, each expand to 1,403 sq ft (130 sq m) when paired with one Grand Suite via an interconnecting door, while 700 and 701 measure 1,335 sq ft (124 sq m). Each has two separate bedrooms, living room with TV/DVD player, walk-in closet with personal safe, dining area, large, two marble-clad bathrooms with tub and separate shower enclosure, and private teakwood-decked balconies. These suites are on the deck under the navigation bridge. Butler service is provided, as is a Nespresso coffee machine. The bathrooms, which are open to the bedroom, have a stand-alone tub with integral shower, separate shower, toilet, bidet, and washbasin. The private balcony, with floor-to-ceiling partitions, has teak decking and teak deck furniture.

Grand Suites. These two suites (1104, 1005) are one deck above the navigation bridge and each is 876 sq ft/81 sq m. They are pleasant living spaces, and have a separate bedroom, living room with TV/DVD player, walk-in closet, dining area, and two marble-clad bathing areas. One bathing area, open to the bedroom, although a curtain can be used to close it off, has a large five-sided sit-in tub placed in a glass walled enclosure on the balcony – but with no access door to the balcony, which can be accessed only from the lounge/dining area. The second is a bathroom with separate shower enclosure, bidet, toilet, and washbasin. The suites have a private balcony with port or starboard views. There is also a guest toilet. Butler service is provided, as is a Nespresso coffee machine. The private balcony is similar to that in the Master Suites.

Voyager Suites. Measuring 603 sq ft/56 sq m, these eight suites, on port and starboard sides of the atrium on three decks, have a separate bedroom, living room with TV/DVD player, walk-in closet, dining area, large, marble-clad bathroom with tub and separate shower enclosure, and a good-size private balcony with either port or starboard views. Butler service is provided. The balcony has teakwood deck, part partitions, and white plastic deck furniture.

Seven Seas Suites, Aft. Measuring 657 sq ft/61 sq m, these six spacious suites overlook the ship's stern and have a generous wraparound balcony. However, the balconies can be partly overlooked. They have teak decking, but white plastic deck furniture. Butler service is provided. Another four Seven Seas Suites, located amidships, measure a slightly smaller 545 sq ft (51 sq m), and have small balconies with either port or starboard views. They have a separate bedroom, living room with audio-visual center, walk-in closet, dining area, large, and marble-clad bathroom with a combination tub/shower.

Penthouse Suites. There are 32 Category 'A' Penthouse Suites and 32 Category 'B' Penthouse Suites – Category 'A' Suites have the better location, but the size is the same at 370 sq ft/34.3 sq m. These have a sleeping area with dressing table and adjacent lounge area, walk-in closet, and bathroom with tub, washbasin, separate shower enclosure, and toilet. The balcony is accessed from the lounge. The balcony has teakwood deck, part partitions, and white plastic deck furniture. Butler service is provided.

Horizon Suites. The 29 Horizon Suites, measuring 522 sq ft/48.4 sq m, overlook the stern, some being sandwiched between the larger Seven Seas Suites, and have a good-size balcony and aft-facing views. They have a separate bedroom, living room with TV/DVD player, walk-in closet, dining area, and a large, marble-clad bathroom with a combination tub/shower. The balcony has teakwood deck, part partitions, and white plastic deck furniture.

All other cabins. Categories C–H in the brochure, listed as Deluxe Suites and measuring 356 sq ft/33 sq m, are larger than those of the same grade aboard Seven Seas Mariner. They have twin beds that convert to a queen-size bed (European duvets are standard), small walk-in closet, marble-lined bathroom with combination tub/shower, 100 percent cotton bathrobe and towels, vanity desk, hairdryer, TV/DVD player, refrigerator stocked with soft drinks and bar setup on embarkation, and personal safe. In these suites, the sleeping area is separated from the living area only by partial room dividers, and therefore they are cabins – albeit good-size ones – rather than suites.

Four wheelchair-accessible suites (761, 762, 859, and 860) are all as close to an elevator as one could possibly get, and provide ample living space, together with a large roll-in shower and all bathroom fittings at the correct height.

DINING. For food entertainment, make a reservation in Latitudes. It has real show business flair and an open 'show' kitchen, also used for Le Cordon Bleu cooking demos. Dinner is at a set time, typically 7:30pm, and consists of a set menu, the only choice being the main course, which is fish or meat. Seating is in alcoves or at open tables.

Other dining options. The 80-seat Prime 7 Steakhouse is the smallest of the specialty dining venues. It features a range of superb USDA prime, dry-aged steaks as well as chops, oven-roasted half chicken, Alaskan king crab legs, and Maine lobster. There is seating for two, four, or six, and reservations are required.

Signatures 'supper club' seats 120, and has ocean views along the room's port side. Doors open onto a covered area outdoors, with small stage and dance floor. Seating is at tables of two, four, or six, and reservations are required.

ENTERTAINMENT. The stunning Constellation Showlounge spans two decks, and sight lines are very good from almost all seats. A troupe of 10 singers/dancers provides colorful mini-Las-Vegas-style revues and production shows. Cabaret acts provide stand-alone evening shows. The ship carries a main showband, several small musical groups and soloists.

SPA/FITNESS. For details of the Canyon Ranch SpaClub and other sporting facilities, see the listing for *Seven Seas Mariner.* An 18 percent gratuity is included in treatment and beauty salon services prices.

Silver Cloud
★★★★ +

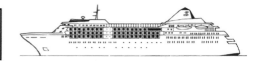

Size:.	Small Ship		Cabins (total):.	148
Tonnage:.	16,927		Size range (sq ft/m):.	240.0–1,314.0/22.2–122.0
Lifestyle:.	Luxury		Cabins (outside view):.	148
Cruise line:.	Silversea Cruises		Cabins (interior/no view):.	0
Former names:.	none		Cabins (for one person):.	0
IMO number:.	8903923		Cabins (with private balcony):.	110
Builder:.	Visentini/Mariotti (Italy)		Cabins (wheelchair accessible):.	2
Original cost:.	$125 million		Wheelchair accessibility:.	Fair
Entered service:.	Apr 1994		Cabin voltage:.	110 and 220 volts
Registry:.	The Bahamas		Elevators:.	4
Length (ft/m):.	514.4/155.8		Casino (gaming tables):.	Yes
Beam (ft/m):.	70.62/21.4		Slot machines:.	Yes
Draft (ft/m):.	17.3/5.3		Swimming pools:.	1
Propulsion/Propellers:.	diesel (11,700kW)/2		Hot tubs (on deck):.	2
Passenger decks:.	6		Self-service launderette:.	Yes
Total crew:.	212		Dedicated cinema/seats:.	Yes/306
Passengers (lower beds/all berths):.	296/329		Library:.	Yes
Passenger Space Ratio (lower beds/all berths):.	57.1/51.4		Onboard currency:.	US$
Crew/Passenger Ratio (lower beds/all berths):.	1.4/1.5			

An all-inclusive luxury small ship for mature-age cruisers

OVERVIEW. *Silver Cloud* is an intimate sort of ship best suited to discerning and well-traveled couples, typically over 50, who seek a small ship with excellent food and fine European-style service in surroundings that border on the elegant. The passenger mix includes many nationalities, although the majority are North American. Children are sometimes seen aboard, although they are not really welcomed by most passengers.

Berlitz's Ratings

	Possible	Achieved
Ship	500	409
Accommodation	200	174
Food	400	333
Service	400	334
Entertainment	100	74
Cruise	400	334
OVERALL SCORE		
1658 points out of 2000		

THE SHIP. *Silver Cloud* has quite a handsome profile, with a sloping stern reminiscent of an Airstream trailer. The size is just about ideal for highly personalized cruising in an elegant environment. The vertical cake-layer stacking of public rooms aft and the location of accommodation forward ensures quiet cabins. There is a synthetic turf-covered walk-around promenade deck outdoors, and a spacious swimming pool deck with teak/aluminum deck furniture. Little Silversea touches such as cold towels, water sprays, and fresh fruit provide poolside pampering on hot days.

The spacious interior is well planned, with elegant decor and fine-quality soft furnishings throughout, accented by the gentle use of brass fittings (some of substandard quality and now showing blotchy patches in several places), fine woods, and creative ceilings. In 2009, an extensive refit saw the addition of a proper observation lounge, with covered passageway to access it – so passengers don't have to go outside to do so. All suites were also refreshed.

There is a business center as well as an audio and hardback book library, open 24 hours a day. An excellent amount of space per passenger means there is no hint of a line anywhere in this unhurried environment. Good documentation is provided before your cruise in a high-quality document wallet.

An elegant, announcement-free onboard ambience prevails, and there is no pressure or hype, and an enthusiastic staff to pamper you, including a high ratio of Europeans. All drinks, gratuities, and port taxes are included, and no further tipping is necessary – though it is not prohibited. This ship is ideal for those who enjoy spacious surroundings, excellent food, and some entertainment. It would be hard not to have a good vacation aboard this ship, albeit at a fairly high price.

Silversea Cruises has 'all-inclusive' fares, including gratuities, but now charges extra for insurance. The fares do not, however, include vintage wines, or massage, or other personal services, but they do include many things that cost extra aboard the ships of many rivals.

The onboard product delivered is very good, particularly the cuisine and its presentation. Shuttle buses are provided in most ports of call, and all the little extras passengers receive makes a cruise an extremely pleasant experience. The surroundings are very comfortable and contemporary without being extravagant, with open seating dining and drinks included, cold canapés and hot hors d'oeuvres served in the bars in the pre-dinner cocktail hour, a captain's welcome aboard and a farewell cocktail party.

Personalized Voyages enable you choose the port of embarkation and disembarkation and the length of cruise you want (minimum five days). While this adds flexibility, the onboard programming is already set, so you may be joining and leaving in the middle of a 'normal' cruise.

Niggles? Some vibration is evident when bow thrusters or the anchors are used, particularly in the forward-most cabins. The self-service launderette is not large enough for longer cruises. Crew facilities are minimal, leading to a high crew turnover which undermines service.

ACCOMMODATION. There are seven price grades in this 'all-suites' ship. The all-outside-view suites, three-quarters of which have fine private teakwood balconies, have convertible queen-to-twin beds and are beautifully fitted out. They have large floor-to-ceiling windows, large walk-in closets, dressing table, writing desk, stocked mini-bar/refrigerator (no charge), and fresh flowers.

The marble-floor bathrooms have a tub, fixed showerhead (not as hygienic as a hand-held unit), single washbasin, and plenty of high-quality towels. Personalized stationery, an eight-pillow menu from soft down to memory foam, bathrobes, and a range of Acqua di Parma bathroom amenities are provided in all suites.

All suites have televisions and DVD players, and top-grade suites also have CD players. However, the walk-in closets don't provide much hanging space, particularly for such items as full-length dresses, and it would be better for the door to open outward instead of inward. The drawers themselves are poorly positioned, but several other drawers and storage areas are provided in the living area.

Although the cabin insulation above and below each cabin is good, the insulation between cabins is not – a privacy curtain installed between entry door and sleeping area would be most useful. Light from the passageway leaks into the cabin, making it hard to achieve a dark room.

Top-grade suites have teak balcony furniture, while other suites do not, but all balconies have teak floors. Suites with balconies on the lowest deck can suffer from sticky salt spray when the ship is moving, so the balconies need lots of cleaning. Each evening, the stewardesses bring plates of canapés to your suite – just right for a light bite with cocktails. In the Grand, Royal, Rossellini, or Owner's Suites, you get unobtrusive butler service from butlers certified by London's Guild of Professional Butlers.

DINING. The Restaurant provides open-seating dining in elegant surroundings. It has an attractive arched gazebo center and a wavy ceiling design as its focal point, and is set with fine Eschenbach china and well-balanced Christofle silverware. Meals are served in an open seating, which means you can eat when you like within the given dining room opening times, and with whom you like.

Standard table wines are included for lunch and dinner, and there is a 'connoisseur list' of premium wines at extra charge. All meals are prepared a la minute, with little of the pre-preparation that used to exist.

Other dining options. La Saletta, adjacent to the main dining room, is an intimate 24-seat specialty dining salon. Dégustation menus include dishes designed for Silversea Cruises by chefs from Relais Châteaux Gourmands, the cuisine-oriented division of Relais & Châteaux, paired with selected wines. Reservations are required, and there's a cover charge.

La Terrazza provides self-serve breakfast and lunch buffets and informal evening dining with different regional Italian dishes nightly. Both indoor and outdoor seating is at teakwood tables and chairs.

There is a 24-hour in-cabin dining service. Full course-by-course dinners are available, although the balcony tables in the standard suites are rather low for dining outdoors.

ENTERTAINMENT. The Showlounge hosts all entertainment events and some social functions. The room spans two decks and has a sloping floor; banquette and individual seating are provided, with good sight lines.

Although Silversea Cruises places more emphasis on food than entertainment, what is provided is quite tasteful and not overbearing, as aboard some larger ships. A decent array of cabaret acts does the Silversea circuit, and small colorful production shows have been reintroduced.

Most of the cabaret acts provide intelligent entertainment that is generally appreciated by the well-traveled international clientele. Also, more emphasis is now placed on classical music ensembles. A band, as well as several small musical units, provide live music in the evenings in The Bar, and Panorama Lounge.

SPA/FITNESS. Although The Spa at Silversea facility is not large, it underwent a sea change in 2007 with re-designed, more welcoming decor, and an updated range of treatments and spa packages for both men and women. Massage and other body pampering treatments, facials, pedicures, and beauty salon treatments cost extra.

Facilities include a separate sauna for men and women, several treatment rooms, and a beauty salon. A separate gymnasium (formerly an observation lounge), located atop the ship, provides sea views.

Silver Explorer
★★★★ +

Size:.	Boutique Ship	Crew/Passenger Ratio (lower beds/all berths):.	1.1/1.4
Tonnage:.	6,072	Cabins (total):.	66
Lifestyle:.	Premium	Size range (sq ft/m):.	172.2–785.7/16.0–73.0
Cruise line:.	Silversea Cruises	Cabins (outside view):.	66
Former names: *Prince Albert II, World Discoverer, Dream 21, Baltic Clipper, Sally Clipper, Delfin Star, Delfin Clipper, World Adventurer*		Cabins (interior/no view):.	0
		Cabins (for one person):.	0
IMO number:	8806747	Cabins (with private balcony):.	20
Builder:	Rauma-Repola (Finland)	Cabins (wheelchair accessible):	0
Original cost:.	$50 million	Wheelchair accessibility:.	None
Entered service:.	Jul 1989/Jun 2008	Cabin voltage:	110 and 220 volts
Registry:.	The Bahamas	Elevators:.	2
Length (ft/m):.	354.9/108.20	Casino (gaming tables):.	No
Beam (ft/m):.	51.1/15.60	Slot machines:.	No
Draft (ft/m):.	13.1/4.00	Swimming pools:.	0
Propulsion/Propellers:.	diesel (4,500kw)/2	Hot tubs (on deck):.	2
Passenger decks:.	5	Self-service launderette:.	No
Total crew:.	111	Dedicated cinema/seats:.	No
Passengers (lower beds/all berths):.	132/158	Library:.	No
Passenger Space Ratio (lower beds/all berths):	46.0/38.4	Onboard currency:.	US$

A small 'soft' expedition ship with premium style

OVERVIEW. *Silver Explorer* is best suited to adventurous couples and single travelers of mature years who enjoy seeing nature at close range, but want an extremely comfortable setting, plus good food and service.

THE SHIP. Twin swept-back outboard funnels highlight the semi-smart exterior design of this small specialist 23-year-old expedition cruise ship. It has a dark ice-hardened hull, carries a fleet of eight Zodiac inflatable landing craft for shore landings and exploration, and has one boot washing station, the Mud Room, with six bays. There is no walk-around promenade deck outdoors.

The accommodation is located forward, with all public rooms aft, an arrangement that helps keep noise to a minimum in accommodation areas. The interior has many European design elements, including warm color combinations. Public rooms include an observation lounge, large lecture room/cinema with bar, and library/Internet center.

This small expedition cruise vessel has many of the creature comforts of much larger vessels. It will provide a very comfortable expedition-style cruise experience in tasteful and elegant surroundings. All passengers receive a pre-cruise amenities package that typically includes a field guide, backpack, carry-on travel bag, and luggage tags.

ACCOMMODATION. There are six types of accommodation, and 11 price grades. The cabins – quite

Berlitz's Ratings

	Possible	Achieved
Ship	500	397
Accommodation	200	172
Food	400	334
Service	400	330
Entertainment	100	50
Cruise	400	334

OVERALL SCORE
1617 points out of 2000

large for such a small ship – are fitted out to a fairly high standard, with ample closet and drawer space. All have outside views and twin beds that convert to a queen-size bed, TV/DVD unit, telephone, hairdryer, refrigerator, and lockable drawer.

Although only six suites have a large private balcony (they're really not needed in cold-weather regions), another 14 cabins have glass doors that open onto a few inches of space outdoors. The suites have whirlpool bathtubs. The owner's suite has two rooms, linked by an interconnecting door, to provide a separate lounge, bedroom, and two bathrooms.

The sizes are: Owner's Suites 538 sq ft (50 sq m); Medallion Suites 358 sq ft (33 sq m); Grand Suites 650 sq ft (60 sq m); Silver Suites 431 sq ft (40 sq m); Veranda Suites 215 sq ft (20 sq m); Explorer Class 190 sq ft (28 sq m); Expedition Suites 431 sq ft (40 sq m).

DINING. The spacious dining room, with pastel-color decor, accommodates all passengers in one seating. Casual alfresco bites can be had at the outdoor grill.

ENTERTAINMENT. Daily recaps; after-dinner conversation.

SPA/FITNESS. Facilities include a small gymnasium, sauna, and treatment room for massage.

Silver Galapagos
★★★★

Size:. . . . . .Boutique Ship	Cabins (total):. 53
Tonnage:. 4,077	Size range (sq ft/m):. 231.4–282.0/21.5–26.2
Lifestyle: . . . . .Standard	Cabins (outside view):. 53
Cruise line:. . . . . Canodros	Cabins (interior/no view):. 0
Former names: . . . . Renaissance Three, Galapagos Explorer II	Cabins (for one person):. 0
IMO number: 8798660	Cabins (with private balcony):. 4
Builder: . . . . Cantieri Navale Ferrari (Italy)	Cabins (wheelchair accessible): 0
Original cost:. . . . .$20 million	Wheelchair accessibility:. . . . . .None
Entered service:. Aug 1990/Sep 2013	Cabin voltage: . . . . 110 volts
Registry:. . . . . Liberia	Elevators:. 1
Length (ft/m):. 293.1/89.3	Casino (gaming tables):. . . . . Yes
Beam (ft/m):. 50.1/15.3	Slot machines:. . . . . Yes
Draft (ft/m): 11.9/3.6	Swimming pools:. 1
Propulsion/Propellers: . . . . .diesel (3,514kW)/2	Hot tubs (on deck):. 1
Passenger decks:. 5	Self-service launderette:. . . . . .No
Total crew:. 72	Dedicated cinema/seats:. . . . . .No
Passengers (lower beds/alll berths):. 106/111	Library: . . . . .No
Passenger Space Ratio (lower beds/all berths): 38.4/36.7	Onboard currency: . . . . .US$
Crew/Passenger Ratio (lower beds/all berths):. 1.4/1.5	

A fine ship to use as a hotel base in the Galápagos

OVERVIEW. *Silver Galápagos* operates two specific Galápagos cruise itineraries year-round from Baltra, Ecuador. It suits couples and single travelers who want to cruise around the primitive islands, but want to do so in comfortable, stylish surroundings.

THE SHIP. This is a comfortable and inviting ship, built as one of a series of eight similar small ships for the defunct Renaissance Cruises. While it is in good condition, maintenance could be better. Its looks are quite contemporary in the style of a mega-yacht. There is a wooden promenade deck outdoors. The limited number of public rooms have smart and restful, non-glitzy decor. The main lounge doubles as a lecture room, but perhaps it is the piano bar that provides the best place to relax after dinner in the evening. A doctor is carried at all times.

This ship (first operated by Silversea Cruises in 2013) provides a destination-intensive, refined, quiet, and relaxed cruise for those who don't like crowds or dressing up. Naturalist guides trained at the Darwin Station lead the shore excursions (included in the fare), and the ship carries two glass-bottom boats, plus wetsuits and snorkeling equipment.

All drinks, bottled water, and soft drinks are included in the fare, but wine and Champagne are not. Also included are guided visits to the islands. The brochure rates may or may not include the Galápagos Islands visitor tax, which must be paid in cash.

Sunbathing space is cramped. The tiny 'dip' pool is not a swimming pool. Plastic wood is everywhere

Berlitz's Ratings

	Possible	Achieved
Ship	500	368
Accommodation	200	157
Food	400	261
Service	400	297
Entertainment	100	50
Cruise	400	282
OVERALL SCORE		
1415 points out of 2000		

(although it looks good). The service lacks finesse, but the crew is willing. The small library is attractive, but the book selection is poor.

ACCOMMODATION. This is located forward, with public rooms aft. Pleasant, all-outside suites have a large picture window and combine gorgeous, highly polished imitation rosewood paneling with lots of mirrors, hand-crafted Italian furniture, and wet bar. All cabins have a queen-size bed, a sitting area, a mini-bar/refrigerator, TV, DVD player, and hairdryer. The small bathrooms have showers with a fold-down seat, real teakwood floors, and marble vanities.

DINING. The small, elegant and intimate dining room has open seating, and tables for two, four, six, and eight. The meals are self-service, buffet-style cold foods for breakfast and lunch (lunch will sometimes be on the open deck), with local Ecuadorian delicacies and meat.

ENTERTAINMENT. Dinner and after-dinner conversation with fellow passengers forms the entertainment each evening.

SPA/FITNESS. There is a small sauna. Water sports facilities include an aft platform, snorkel gear, and Zodiacs.

Silver Shadow
★★★★★

Size:.	Small Ship	Cabins (total):.	.194
Tonnage:	28,258	Size range (sq ft/m):	.287.0–1,435.0/26.6–133.3
Lifestyle:	Luxury	Cabins (outside view):	.194
Cruise line:.	Silversea Cruises	Cabins (interior/no view):.	.0
Former names:	none	Cabins (for one person):.	.0
IMO number:	.9192167	Cabins (with private balcony):	.166
Builder:	Visentini/Mariotti (Italy)	Cabins (wheelchair accessible):	.2
Original cost:	$150 million	Wheelchair accessibility:	.Good
Entered service:.	Sep 2000	Cabin voltage:	.110 and 220 volts
Registry:.	The Bahamas	Elevators:.	.5
Length (ft/m):.	610.2/186.0	Casino (gaming tables):	.Yes
Beam (ft/m):.	81.8/24.8	Slot machines:	.Yes
Draft (ft/m):	19.6/6.0	Swimming pools:.	.1
Propulsion/Propellers:	diesel/2	Hot tubs (on deck):.	.2
Passenger decks:.	.7	Self-service launderette:	.Yes
Total crew:	.295	Dedicated cinema/seats:	.No
Passengers (lower beds/alll berths):	388/429	Library:	.Yes
Passenger Space Ratio (lower beds/all berths):	72.8/65.8	Onboard currency:	.US$
Crew/Passenger Ratio (lower beds/all berths):	1.3/1.3		

An all-inclusive premium ship for mature-age cruisers

OVERVIEW. This ship is best suited to discerning, well-traveled couples, typically over 50, who seek a small ship with excellent food that approaches gourmet standards, and fine service in surroundings bordering on the elegant and luxurious.

THE SHIP. *Silver Shadow* is one of the second generation of vessels in the Silversea Cruises fleet. It is slightly larger than the first two ships, *Silver Cloud* and *Silver Wind*, with a more streamlined forward profile and large, sleek single funnel. However, the stern section is not particularly handsome. There is a generous amount of open deck and sunbathing space, and aluminum/teak deck furniture is provided.

The company's many international passengers react well to the ambience, food, service, and the helpful staff. The cruise line has 'all-inclusive' fares, including gratuities and many things that cost extra aboard many rivals' ships, but the fares don't include vintage wines, massage, or other personal services.

Although the ship shows signs of wear, the onboard product is very good, particularly the cuisine and its presentation. Shuttle buses are provided in most ports of call, and all the little extras that passengers receive make this an extremely pleasant experience, in surroundings that are comfortable and contemporary without being extravagant, with open seating dining and drinks included, cold canapés and hot hors d'oeuvres served in the bars in the pre-dinner cocktail hour, a captain's welcome aboard and farewell cocktail party.

Berlitz's Ratings

	Possible	Achieved
Ship	500	450
Accommodation	200	181
Food	400	341
Service	400	346
Entertainment	100	85
Cruise	400	344
OVERALL SCORE		
1747 points out of 2000		

The swimming pool is surprisingly small, as is the fitness room, although it was expanded in 2007. The Humidor by Davidoff, the cigar lounge, has 25 seats and the style of an English smoking club. There is a Champagne bar and a four-terminal computer center (Wi-Fi costs extra).

Personalized Voyages enable you choose the port of embarkation and disembarkation and the length of cruise you want (minimum five days). While this adds flexibility, the onboard programming is already set, so you may be joining and leaving in the middle of a 'normal' cruise.

ACCOMMODATION. There are eight price grades in this all-suites ship. All suites have double vanities in the marble-floored bathrooms, which also have a tub and separate shower enclosure. All grades receive Silversea monogrammed Frette bed linen, an eight-pillow menu (from soft down to memory foam), 100 percent cotton bathrobes, a range of Acqua di Parma bathroom amenities, and personalized stationery. Stay in the Grand, Royal, Rossellini, or Owner's Suite and you get unobtrusive service from butlers certified by London's Guild of Professional Butlers.

Vista Suites. These 287-sq-ft (27-sq-m) suites don't have a private balcony. Instead there's a large window, twin beds that convert to a queen-size bed, sitting area, TV set and video player, refrigerator, writing desk, personal safe, cocktail cabinet, dressing table with hairdryer, and walk-in closet. The bathroom is marble-clad in gentle colors, and has two washbasins, a full-size tub, separate shower enclosure, and toilet.

Veranda Suites. Each of these suites (really Vista Suites plus a veranda) measures 345 sq ft (33 sq m) and has convertible twin-to-queen beds. They are well fitted-out with just about everything you would need, including large floor-to-ceiling windows, large walk-in closet, dressing table, writing desk, stocked mini-bar/refrigerator with all drinks are included in the fare, and fresh flowers. The marble-clad bathrooms have two washbasins, full-size tub, separate shower enclosure, and toilet.

Silver Suites. These measure 701 sq ft (65 sq m). These are much wider than the Vista Suites or Veranda Suites and have a separate bedroom, an entertainment center with CD player, TV/video player in both bedroom and living room, and much more living space that includes a large dining area with table and four chairs. The marble-clad bathrooms have two washbasins, full size tub, separate shower enclosure, and toilet.

Owner's Suites. These two suites, each measuring 1,208 sq ft (112 sq m), are much larger and include an extra powder room/toilet for guests, as well as more living space. There is a 200-sq-ft (18-sq-m) veranda, two bedrooms with queen-size beds, two walk-in closets, two living rooms, two sitting areas, separate dining area, an entertainment center with flat-screen plasma television in the living room and a TV set/video player player in each bedroom, telephones, refrigerators, cocktail cabinet, writing desk, dressing tables, with hairdryers. There are two marble-clad bathrooms, one with a full-size whirlpool tub and two washbasins, separate toilet, and separate shower, as well as a powder room for guests. Owner's Suites can be configured as one or two bedrooms.

Royal Suites. Stately accommodation can be found in two Royal Suites measuring either 1,312 sq ft (122 sq m) or 1,352 sq ft (126 sq m). These are two-bedroom suites, with two teakwood verandas, two living rooms, sitting areas, dining area, queen-size beds, an entertainment center with flat-screen plasma television in the living room and a TV/video player player in each bedroom, telephones, refrigerators, cocktail cabinet, writing desk, two closets, dressing tables with hairdryers. There are two marble-clad bathrooms, one with a full-size whirlpool tub and two washbasins, separate toilet, and separate shower, as well as a powder room for guests. Royal Suites can be either a one- or two-bedroom configuration.

Grand Suites. There are two of these, one measuring 1,286 sq ft (119 sq m), and the other (including an adjoining suite with interconnecting door) 1,435 sq ft (133 sq m). These have two bedrooms, two large walk-in closets, two living rooms, Bang & Olufsen entertainment centers, and large, forward-facing, private verandas. These really are sumptuous apartments that have all the comforts of home, and then some.

Disabled Suites. There are two suites for the physically disabled (535 and 537), both adjacent to an elevator and next to each other. Measuring a generous 398 sq ft (37 sq m), they are well equipped with an accessible hanging rail, and roll-in bathroom with roll-in shower unit.

DINING. The main dining room, The Restaurant has open-seating in elegant surroundings. Three grand chandeliers provide an upward focal point, while you can dine when you want, and with whom you wish. Meals can also be served, course-by-course, in your suite, although the balcony tables are rather low for dining outdoors. The cuisine is very good, with a choice of formal and informal areas. Standard table wines are included for lunch and dinner, with an extra-cost 'connoisseur list' of premium wines. Once each cruise, there's a Galley Brunch when the galley is transformed into a large 'chef's kitchen.'

Other dining options. For something special, Le Champagne is a more intimate extra-cost venue that allows diners to sample highly specialized dégustation menus marrying international cuisine with vintage wines selection by Relais & Châteaux sommeliers. Reservations are needed, and the wines also cost extra.

For more informal meals, La Terrazza provides self-serve breakfast and lunch buffets; outdoor seating is at teakwood tables and chairs. The buffet design and setup presents flow problems during breakfast, and 'active' stations for cooking eggs or pasta to order would help.

Adjacent to La Terazza is a wine bar and a cigar smoking room. A poolside grill provides a casual alternative daytime bistro-style eatery, for grilled and fast-food items, and becomes The Grill for evening dining, with food cooked on hot stones.

ENTERTAINMENT. The Showlounge, the venue for entertainment and some social functions, spans two decks and has a sloping floor; both banquette and individual seating are provided, with good sight lines from almost all seats.

Although Silversea Cruises places more emphasis on food than entertainment, what is provided is quite tasteful. A decent array of cabaret acts does the Silversea circuit, and small, colorful production shows have been reintroduced. More emphasis is placed on classical music ensembles. There is a band, and several small musical units for live music in the evenings in The Bar, and the Panorama Lounge.

SPA/FITNESS. The Spa at Silversea health/fitness facility, just behind the Observation Lounge, high atop the ship, had a complete make-over in 2007. It includes a gymnasium, beauty salon, and separate saunas and steam rooms for men and women, plus several personal treatment rooms.

Silver Spirit

★★★★★

Size:	Small Ship	Cabins (total):	270
Tonnage:	36,009	Size range (sq ft/m):	312.1–1,614.6/29–150
Lifestyle:	Luxury	Cabins (outside view):	270
Cruise line:	Silversea Cruises	Cabins (interior/no view):	0
Former names:	none	Cabins (for one person):	0
IMO number:	9437866	Cabins (with private balcony):	258
Builder:	Fincantieri (Italy)	Cabins (wheelchair accessible):	4
Original cost:	$250 million	Wheelchair accessibility:	Best
Entered service:	Dec 2009	Cabin voltage:	110 volts
Registry:	The Bahamas	Elevators:	6
Length (ft/m):	642.3/195.8	Casino (gaming tables):	Yes
Beam (ft/m):	86.9/26.5	Slot machines:	Yes
Draft (ft/m):	20.9/6.4	Swimming pools:	1
Propulsion/Propellers:	diesel-electric (26,100kW)/2	Hot tubs (on deck):	4
Passenger decks:	8	Self-service launderette:	Yes
Total crew:	370	Dedicated cinema/seats:	No
Passengers (lower beds/all berths):	540/608	Library:	Yes
Passenger Space Ratio (lower beds/all berths):	66.6/59.2	Onboard currency:	US$
Crew/Passenger Ratio (lower beds/all berths):	1.4/1.6		

An upper-class, stylish ship for sophisticated cruising

OVERVIEW. This ship suits discerning, well-traveled couples, typically over 50, who are looking for a smaller ship setting with fine food and European-style service in surroundings bordering on the elegant and luxurious without being extravagant. Shuttle buses are provided in most ports of call, and all the little extras passengers receive make a cruise an extremely pleasant experience.

THE SHIP. *Silver Spirit*, larger than *Silver Shadow* and *Silver Whisper*, is the newest 'all-inclusive' addition to the Silversea Cruises fleet – although 'all-inclusive' doesn't include the two specialty dining venues. It represents a substantial investment in new tonnage. Sharing its name with a famous Rolls-Royce car, *Silver Spirit* has a similar profile to the smaller *Silver Shadow* and *Silver Whisper*, with a nicely shaped stern with tiered aft decks, but exudes more style and provides more choice than the line's other ships.

Although there's a main pool and hot tub deck, there's little shade, and no hot tubs on any other deck. Also, because there are so many balcony suites/cabins, there's no walk-around outdoor promenade deck.

The interior layout has a cake-layer stacking of almost all the public rooms in the aft section, and the accommodation located forward, so there is minimal noise in passenger accommodation, although it means there are more stairs and no flow-through horizontal deck where passengers can parade. But regular Silversea Cruises passengers are used to this arrangement,

Berlitz's Ratings

	Possible	Achieved
Ship	500	454
Accommodation	200	182
Food	400	343
Service	400	347
Entertainment	100	85
Cruise	400	351
OVERALL SCORE		
1762 points out of 2000		

and it's good exercise. The decor is elegant and understated, but bland (muted colors), a mix of art deco and modern, but not contemporary.

The Observation Lounge, at the front of the ship with access from a central passageway, has fine ocean views, and is a very comfortable place to relax and read. A Panorama Lounge, at the stern, is a comfortable multi-function room. Non-smokers should note that smoking is allowed on the port side. A cigar lounge, with doors that open in to the casino, has a pleasing list of cigars. The casino has five blackjack tables, American Roulette table, and 52 slot machines.

The company's 'all-inclusive' fares include gratuities, drinks with meals, and many things that cost extra on rivals' ships. Vintage wines, massage, and other personal services do cost extra, though. Passengers appreciate open-seating dining, cold canapés and hot hors d'oeuvres served in the bars in the pre-dinner cocktail hour, a captain's welcome aboard and a farewell cocktail party.

The passenger mix includes many nationalities, which makes for a more interesting experience, although most passengers are North American. Children are sometimes seen aboard, but are not really welcomed by most people.

Passenger niggles include the lack of electrical sockets in the cabins; there are almost no shaded outdoor areas; the butler service is sometimes poor, not least because each butler has about 15 cabins to look after.

ACCOMMODATION. *Silver Spirit*, like other Silversea Cruises ships, has 'all-suites' accommodation. Some suites can accommodate a third person. Eight have interconnecting doors, so families and friends can be adjacent.

Accommodation consists of: two Owner's suites, approx. 1,292 sq ft (120 sq m) for one bedroom and 1,614 sq ft (150 sq m) for two bedrooms; four Grand suites in the front of the ship (990 sq ft/92 sq m for one bedroom and 1,302 sq ft/117 sq m for two bedrooms); two Royal suites in the front of the ship, 26 Silver suites (742 sq ft/69 sq m); 166 Midship Veranda suites (376 sq ft/35 sq m); 50 Verandah suites (376 sq ft/35 sq m); and 12 Vista suites (312 sq ft/29 sq m). The Owner's, Grand, and Royal suites all have interconnecting doors for an available second bedroom.

All provide personalized stationery, a menu with a choice of eight pillows from soft down to memory foam, bathrobes, and an array of Bulgari bathroom amenities. All have walk-in closets with personal safe, TV set, DVD unit, and vanity desk with hairdryer. Suite bathrooms are marble-clad, with marble and wood floors, and contain a toilet, one or two washbasins, a full-size tub, and a shower enclosure with a fixed 'rain-shower' and a separate hand-held hose). Occupants of the Owner's Suites or Grand Suites receive unobtrusive service from 21 butlers certified by London's Guild of Professional Butlers.

The suites have recessed lighting in the ceiling – a nice touch that allows a little diffused mood lighting when needed. Balconies have sliding doors that can move if not securely locked when not in use. Non-smokers should be aware that Silversea Cruises allows smoking in cabins.

DINING. There are certainly plenty of dining choices. The Restaurant is the name of the ship's main dining room – a light, airy venue, although its design is quite disappointing – in particular because of its low ceiling height. It seats up to 456, and has an integral dance floor. This is all about open-seating dining in elegant surroundings, with unhurried, unobtrusive service. It is open for breakfast, lunch, and dinner; tables are set with fine china, silverware, and Reidel wine glasses. For complete privacy, meals can also be served, course-by-course, in your suite.

Other dining options. Le Champagne, adjacent to The Restaurant, is an intimate, extra-cost, reservations-required, dinner-only venue offering a six-course mini-dégustation menu based on Relais & Châteaux menus. Sadly, the banquette seating along the outer walls detracts from the otherwise very comfortable, uncluttered, intimate dining spot, which has a small walk-in wine room as its central, focal point.

Seishin Restaurant, also adjacent to The Restaurant, is an extra-cost reservations-required venue, with just 24 seats. It serves Kobe beef, sushi items, and Asian seafood, and an octagonal display counter is the focal point to the venue. It is open for dinner only, and there's a cover charge.

La Terrazza is the venue for self-serve buffet-style items for breakfast and lunch. Each evening, it turns into an Italian-themed dining spot, with waiter service and regional Italian cuisine cooked to order. Reservations are required for dinner (not open for lunch).

Stars Supper Club, with 58 seats and a dance floor, is designed in the manner of an English supper club of the 1920s to provide an intimate, club-like ambience and all-night entertainment – which means volume-intrusive. Reservations are required for dinner (not open for lunch).

The Pool Grill is a casual outside eatery serving steaks, seafood, and pizza. Pizza cannot possibly be considered a luxury food item, but then, this is a ship with Italian connections. Meals are served on hot stones that act as plates, so you can't touch them, but this is more a casual eating novelty than proper dining.

Additionally, a lobby bar serves Lavazza Italian coffees, wines, spirits, and pastries.

ENTERTAINMENT. The Showlounge, in the aft section, has a main stage and two ancillary side stages. It seats about 320 passengers, and there are good sight lines from all seats but no beverage service. It's a lovely room, and seating consists of two-person love seats, and each has a small table for personal items such as ladies' clutch purses for formal evenings. Production shows have been re-introduced, and these, together with cabaret acts, provide a balanced entertainment program.

SPA/FITNESS. The Spa at Silversea, with 8,300 sq ft (770 sq m) of space, is quite large for this size of ship, and includes a sanctuary for total relaxation and detox. Located at the stern of the ship, one deck below La Terrazza, it is a haven for me-time and personal treatments.

Silver Whisper
★★★★★

Size:................................... Small Ship	Cabins (total):...................................194
Tonnage: 28,258	Size range (sq ft/m): 287.0–1,435.0/26.6–133.3
Lifestyle: ....Luxury	Cabins (outside view):...............................194
Cruise line:............................ Silversea Cruises	Cabins (interior/no view):..............................0
Former names: ....none	Cabins (for one person):................................0
IMO number: 9192179	Cabins (with private balcony):........................166
Builder: .... Visentini/Mariotti (Italy)	Cabins (wheelchair accessible): 2
Original cost:............................$150 million	Wheelchair accessibility:............................Good
Entered service:............................Jul 2001	Cabin voltage: ....110 and 220 volts
Registry:................................The Bahamas	Elevators:..5
Length (ft/m):........................... 610.2/186.0	Casino (gaming tables):...............................Yes
Beam (ft/m):.............................. 81.8/24.8	Slot machines:.....................................Yes
Draft (ft/m): 19.6/6.0	Swimming pools:.....................................1
Propulsion/Propellers:...........................diesel/2	Hot tubs (on deck):..................................2
Passenger decks:....................................7	Self-service launderette:.............................Yes
Total crew:......................................295	Dedicated cinema/seats:...............................No
Passengers (lower beds/all berths):................388/429	Library: ....Yes
Passenger Space Ratio (lower beds/all berths): 72.8/65.8	Onboard currency: ....US$
Crew/Passenger Ratio (lower beds/all berths):..........1.3/1.3	

All-inclusive cruising with space, style, and good food

OVERVIEW. This ship suits discerning, well-traveled couples who like a small ship that provides excellent food and fine European-style service in elegant, highly comfortable surroundings. Silversea Cruises promotes its Italian Heritage theme, and its many international passengers respond well to the ambience, food, and the staff, most of whom go out of their way to please.

THE SHIP. *Silver Whisper*, which Russia's Vladimir Putin chartered in 2003 to host guests for the three-day celebrations of St Petersburg's 300th anniversary, is the second generation of vessels in the Silversea Cruises fleet. It is sister to *Silver Shadow*, and is slightly larger than the line's first two ships, *Silver Cloud* and *Silver Wind*, but with a more streamlined profile and a large, sleek single funnel.

The cruise line has 'all-inclusive' fares, including gratuities (although additional tips are not expected, they are not prohibited). The fares do not include vintage wines, or massage, or other personal services, but they do include many things that are at extra cost compared aboard the ships of many other cruise lines. The passenger mix includes many nationalities, although the majority of passengers are North American. Children are sometimes aboard, though they aren't really welcomed by most passengers.

Only a few ships make it to a five-star Berlitz rating, but Silversea Cruises' emphasis on quality has earned it an enviable reputation, particularly for cuisine. Shuttle buses are provided in most ports of call, and all the

Berlitz's Ratings		
	Possible	Achieved
Ship	500	451
Accommodation	200	181
Food	400	341
Service	400	346
Entertainment	100	85
Cruise	400	345
OVERALL SCORE		
1749 points out of 2000		

little extras that passengers receive make this ship an extremely pleasant experience. The surroundings are very comfortable and contemporary without being extravagant, there is open-seating dining with drinks included, cold canapés and hot hors d'oeuvres are served in the bars in the pre-dinner cocktail hour, and there's a captain's welcome aboard and farewell cocktail party.

Aluminum/teak deck furniture is placed by the swimming pool, but the pool itself is quite small. The Humidor, by Davidoff, a 25-seat cigar smoking lounge, has been styled like an English smoking club. There's a wine bar and computer learning center.

ACCOMMODATION. This 'all-suites' ship has eight cabin price categories. All grades have double vanities in the marble-floored bathrooms, plus tub and separate shower enclosure. Silversea-monogrammed Frette bed linen is provided in all grades, as is an eight-pillow menu from soft down to memory foam, 100 percent cotton bathrobes, a fine array of Acqua di Parma bathroom amenities, and personalized stationery. In the Grand, Royal, Rossellini, or Owner's Suites, you get unobtrusive service from butlers certified by London's Guild of Professional Butlers.

Vista Suites. These suites measure 287 sq ft (27 sq m) and don't have a private balcony. Instead there is a large window, twin beds that convert to a queen-size bed, sitting area, TV and video player, refrigerator, writing desk, personal safe, cocktail cabinet, dressing table with hairdryer, and walk-in closet. The bathroom is marble-clad in gentle colors, and has two washbasins, full-size tub, separate shower enclosure, and toilet.

Veranda Suites. Each of the Veranda Suites – which are really Vista Suites plus a veranda – measures 345 sq ft (32 sq m) and has convertible twin-to-queen beds. They are well fitted-out and have large floor-to-ceiling windows, large walk-in closet, dressing table, writing desk, stocked mini-bar/refrigerator (drinks included in the fare), and fresh flowers. The marble-clad bathrooms have two washbasins, full-size tub, separate shower enclosure, and toilet.

Silver Suites. The Silver Suites measure 701 sq ft (65 sq m). Much wider than the Vista Suites or Veranda Suites, they have a separate bedroom, an audio-visual entertainment center in both bedroom and living room, and much more living space, including a large dining area with table and four chairs. The marble-clad bathrooms have two washbasins, full-size tub, separate shower enclosure, and toilet.

Owner's Suites. The two Owner's Suites, each 1,208 sq ft (112 sq m), are much larger units and include an extra bathroom for guests, plus more living space. There is a 200-sq-ft (18-sq-m) veranda, two bedrooms with queen-size beds, two walk-in closets, two living rooms, two sitting areas, separate dining area, an entertainment center with flat-screen plasma television in the living room and TV/DVD player in each bedroom, telephones, refrigerators, cocktail cabinet, writing desk, dressing tables with hairdryers. There are two marble-clad bathrooms, one with a full-size whirlpool tub and two washbasins, separate toilet, and separate shower, plus a powder room for guests. Owner's Suites can be a one- or two-bedroom configuration.

Royal Suites. Stately accommodation can be found in two Royal Suites, measuring 1,312 sq ft (122 sq m) and 1,352 sq ft (126 sq m). These are two-bedroom suites, with two teakwood verandas, two living rooms, sitting areas, dining area, queen-size beds, an entertainment center with flat-screen plasma television in the living room and TV/DVD player in each bedroom, telephones, refrigerators, cocktail cabinet, writing desk, two closets, dressing tables with hairdryers. There are two marble-clad bathrooms, one with a full-size whirlpool tub and two washbasins, separate toilet, and separate shower, as well as a powder room for guests. Royal Suites can be either a one- or two-bedroom configuration.

Grand Suites. There are two, one 1,286 sq ft (119 sq m) and the other, including an adjoining suite with interconnecting door, 1,435 sq ft (133 sq m). These have two bedrooms, two large walk-in closets, two living rooms, Bang & Olufsen entertainment centers, and large, forward-facing, private verandas. These are sumptuous apartments with all the comforts of home, and then some.

Disabled Suites. There are two adjacent suites for the physically disabled (535 and 537), both beside an elevator. They measure a generous 398 sq ft (37 sq m) and are well-equipped with an accessible hanging rail, and roll-in bathroom with roll-in shower unit.

DINING. The main dining room, The Restaurant, offers open-seating dining in elegant surroundings. Three grand chandeliers provide an upward focal point, while you can dine when you want, and with whom you wish within the given opening times. Meals can also be served, course-by-course, in your suite, although the balcony tables are rather low for dining outdoors. The dining is good throughout the ship, with a choice of formal and informal areas, although the cuisine and presentation don't quite match up to that of vessels such as the smaller Seabourn Cruise Line ships. Cristofle silverware is provided. Standard table wines are included for lunch and dinner, and there is an extra-cost 'connoisseur list' of premium wines.

Other dining options. As an alternative to the main restaurant, the extra-cost Le Champagne offers a more intimate, reservation-only dining spot that enables diners to dine from highly specialized dégustation menus marrying international cuisine with vintage wines selected by Relais & Châteaux sommeliers.

La Terrazza has self-serve breakfast and lunch buffets. The buffet design and set-up presents flow problems during breakfast, however, and 'active' stations for cooking eggs or pasta to order would help. In the evening this room serves regional Italian cuisine, and has softer lighting to create a more intimate atmosphere.

Adjacent to the café is a wine bar and a cigar smoking room. A poolside grill provides a casual alternative daytime dining spot; in the evening it turns into The Grill, with food cooked using the Black Rock (hot stone) method.

ENTERTAINMENT. The Showlounge spans two decks and has a sloping floor; both banquette and individual seating are provided, with good sight lines from almost all seats.

A decent array of cabaret acts does the Silversea circuit, most providing intelligent entertainment, and colorful production shows are back. More emphasis is placed on classical music ensembles. A band and small musical units provide music in the evenings in The Bar and the Panorama Lounge.

SPA/FITNESS. The Spa at Silversea health/fitness facility, just behind the Observation Lounge, high atop the ship, includes a gymnasium, beauty salon, and separate saunas and steam rooms for men and women, plus several treatment rooms. A range of body-pampering services is offered to men and women. Massage and other treatments, facials, pedicures, and beauty salon treatments cost extra.

Silver Wind
★★★★ +

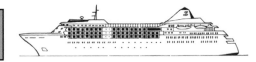

Size:.	Small Ship	Cabins (total):.	151
Tonnage:	17,400	Size range (sq ft/m):.	240.0–1,314.0/22.2–122.0
Lifestyle:	Luxury	Cabins (outside view):	151
Cruise line:.	Silversea Cruises	Cabins (interior/no view):.	0
Former names:	none	Cabins (for one person):.	0
IMO number:	8903935	Cabins (with private balcony):	123
Builder:	Visentini/Mariotti (Italy)	Cabins (wheelchair accessible):	2
Original cost:	$125 million	Wheelchair accessibility:	Fair
Entered service:.	Jan 1995	Cabin voltage:	110 and 220 volts
Registry:.	Bahamas	Elevators:.	4
Length (ft/m):.	514.4/155.8	Casino (gaming tables):	Yes
Beam (ft/m):.	70.62/21.4	Slot machines:.	Yes
Draft (ft/m):	17.3/5.3	Swimming pools:.	1
Propulsion/Propellers:	diesel (11,700kW)/2	Hot tubs (on deck):.	2
Passenger decks:.	6	Self-service launderette:.	Yes
Total crew:.	222	Dedicated cinema/seats:.	Yes/306
Passengers (lower beds/alll berths):	302/336	Library:	Yes
Passenger Space Ratio (lower beds/all berths):	57.6/51.7	Onboard currency:	US$
Crew/Passenger Ratio (lower beds/all berths):	1.3/1.5		

An all-inclusive small ship for mature-age cruisers

OVERVIEW. This ship is best suited to discerning, well-traveled couples, typically over 50, who seek a small ship with fine cuisine, European-style service, and surroundings that border on the elegant. An announcement-free ambience prevails, and there is no pressure or hype, and an enthusiastic staff know how to pamper you.

THE SHIP. *Silver Wind* has a quite handsome profile, with a sloping stern reminiscent of an Airstream trailer. The size is just about ideal for personalized cruising in an elegant environment. The vertical cake-layer stacking of public rooms aft and the location of accommodation units forward ensures quiet cabins. There is a synthetic turf-covered walk-around promenade deck outdoors – which should be upgraded to teak or Bolidt – and a fairly spacious swimming pool and sunbathing deck with teak/aluminum deck furniture. Little Silversea touches such as cold towels, water sprays, and fresh fruit provide poolside pampering on hot days.

The ship had a multi-million dollar makeover in 2003, and a further refit in 2009 made it more user-friendly by adding a proper, if small, observation lounge with bookcases and a covered walkway to access it, as well as a relocated and enlarged health spa. The spacious interior is well-planned, with elegant decor and fine-quality soft furnishings throughout, accented by brass fittings – some of sub-standard quality and showing blotchy patches in several places – fine woods and creative ceilings. There is an excellent

Berlitz's Ratings

	Possible	Achieved
Ship	500	410
Accommodation	200	174
Food	400	333
Service	400	333
Entertainment	100	74
Cruise	400	337

OVERALL SCORE
1661 points out of 2000

amount of space per passenger and no hint of a line anywhere. There is a useful Internet center, a 24-hour library with hardback books and DVDs, and a cigar lounge.

Before your cruise, good documentation is provided in a high-quality document wallet and presentation box. Insurance, once included in the fare, now costs extra. All drinks, gratuities, and port taxes are included, and no further tipping anywhere on board is necessary, though it is not prohibited. It would be hard not to have good cruise aboard this ship, albeit at a fairly high price. The company's many international passengers like the ambience, food, service, and the staff, most of whom go out of their way to please.

The company's 'all-inclusive' fares include gratuities and many things that cost extra aboard the ships of some rivals. Not included, however, are vintage wines, massage, and other personal services. Shuttle buses are provided in most ports of call, and all the little extras that passengers receive aboard this ship makes it an extremely pleasant experience, in surroundings that are very comfortable and contemporary without being extravagant, with open seating dining and drinks included, cold canapés and hot hors d'oeuvres served in the bars in the pre-dinner cocktail hour, a captain's welcome aboard and a farewell cocktail party.

After 10 years, Silversea Cruises re-invented itself with a more defined and refined product based on an Italian Heritage theme. The past few years sometimes saw the delivery of a tarnished service, but this has been recognized and Silversea Cruises is now polishing the silver again.

The passenger mix includes many nationalities, although most passengers are North American. Children are sometimes seen aboard, although they are not really welcomed by most passengers.

Passenger niggles include the fact that some vibration is evident when bow thrusters or the anchors are used, particularly in the forward-most suites. The self-service launderette is poor and not large enough for longer cruises, when passengers like to wash their own small items. Crew facilities are minimal, so crew turnover is quite high, making it difficult to maintaining consistency.

ACCOMMODATION. There are seven price grades. The all-outside suites, 75 percent with fine private teakwood-floor balconies, have convertible queen-to-twin beds and are nicely fitted out. They include large floor-to-ceiling windows, large walk-in closets, dressing table, writing desk, stocked mini-bar/refrigerator (no charge), and fresh flowers. The marble floor bathrooms have a tub, fixed shower head – not as hygienic as a hand-held unit – single washbasin, and plenty of high-quality towels. Personalized stationery, an eight-pillow menu from soft down to memory foam, bathrobes, and an array of Acqua di Parma bathroom amenities are provided in all suites.

In the Grand, Royal, Rossellini or Owner's Suites, you get unobtrusive service from butlers certified by London's Guild of Professional Butlers.

All suites have TV and DVD players (top-grade suites also have CD players). However, the walk-in closets don't actually provide much hanging space, particularly for such items as full-length dresses, and it would be better for the door to open outward instead of inward. The drawers themselves are poorly positioned, although several other drawers and storage areas are provided in the living area. Although the cabin insulation above and below each suite is good, the insulation between them is not – a privacy curtain installed between entry door and sleeping area would be useful – and light from the passageway leaks into the suite, making it hard to achieve a dark room.

The top grades of suites have teak balcony furniture, while others don't – but all balconies have teak floors. Suites with balconies on the lowest deck can suffer from sticky salt spray when the ship is moving, so the balconies need lots of cleaning. Each evening, the stewardesses bring plates of canapés to your suite – just right for a light bite with cocktails.

DINING. The main dining room, The Restaurant, provides open-seating dining in elegant surroundings. It has an attractive arched gazebo center and a wavy ceiling design as its focal point, and is set with fine Li-

moges china and well-balanced Christofle silverware. Meals are served in an open seating, which means you can eat when you like within the given dining room opening times, and with whom you like.

The cuisine/dining experience is good, with a choice of three dining salons. Standard table wines are included for lunch and dinner, but there is also a 'connoisseur list' of premium wines at extra charge. All meals are prepared as à la carte items, with almost none of the pre-preparation that used to exist. Special orders are also possible.

Other dining options. A specialty dining salon, the intimate 24-seat La Saletta, adjacent to the main dining room, has dégustation menus that include dishes designed for Silversea Cruises by chefs from Relais & Châteaux Gourmands, the cuisine-oriented division of Relais & Châteaux, paired with selected wines. Reservations are required, and there's a cover charge.

For more informal dining, La Terrazza offers self-serve breakfast and lunch buffets. In the evening it serves Italian regional dishes and has softer lighting, with both indoors and outdoors seating at teakwood tables and chairs.

There is a 24-hour in-cabin dining service; full course-by-course dinners are available, although the balcony tables in the standard suites are rather low for dining outdoors.

ENTERTAINMENT. The Showlounge is the venue for all entertainment events and some social functions. The room spans two decks and has a sloping floor; both banquette and individual seating are provided, with good sightlines from almost all seats.

Although Silversea Cruises places more emphasis on food than entertainment, what is provided is quite tasteful and not overbearing, as aboard some larger ships. A decent array of cabaret acts does the Silversea circuit. Most of the cabaret acts provide intelligent entertainment.

Also, more emphasis is now placed on classical music ensembles. There is also a band, as well as several small musical units for live music in the evenings in The Bar, and the Panorama Lounge.

SPA/FITNESS. Although The Spa at Silversea facility isn't large, it underwent a sea change in 2007 with redesigned, more welcoming decor, and an updated range of treatments and spa packages for both men and women. Massage and other body pampering treatments, facials, pedicures, and beauty salon treatments cost extra.

Facilities include a mixed sauna for men and women, several treatment rooms, and a beauty salon. A separate gymnasium, formerly an observation lounge, located atop the ship, provides sea views.

Sovereign
★★★

Size:.....................................Large Resort Ship	Cabins (total):.................................. 1,153
Tonnage:...................................... 73,192	Size range (sq ft/m):................ 118.4–670.0/11.0–62.2
Lifestyle:......................................Standard	Cabins (outside view):................................722
Cruise line:...........................Pullmantur Cruises	Cabins (interior/no view):............................431
Former names:.................... Sovereign of the Seas	Cabins (for one person):................................0
IMO number:.................................8512281	Cabins (with private balcony):.........................62
Builder:.................. Chantiers de l'Atlantique (France)	Cabins (wheelchair accessible):.........................6
Original cost:............................ $183.5 million	Wheelchair accessibility:.............................Fair
Entered service:...........................Jan 1988/2008	Cabin voltage:..........................110 and 220 volts
Registry:......................................The Bahamas	Elevators:......................................13
Length (ft/m):............................... 879.9/268.2	Casino (gaming tables):..............................Yes
Beam (ft/m):................................. 105.9/32.3	Slot machines:..................................Yes
Draft (ft/m):................................. 24.9/7.6	Swimming pools:..................................2
Propulsion/Propellers:..................diesel (21,844kW)/2	Hot tubs (on deck):................................2
Passenger decks:....................................11	Self-service launderette:.............................No
Total crew:......................................820	Dedicated cinema/seats:.............................No
Passengers (lower beds/all berths):.............. 2,306/2,733	Library:......................................Yes
Passenger Space Ratio (lower beds/all berths):....... 31.7/26.7	Onboard currency:.............................. Euros
Crew/Passenger Ratio (lower beds/all berths):.......... 2.7/3.4	

A busy big ship for casual, Spanish-speaking family cruising

OVERVIEW. This ship is best suited to Spanish-speaking families, young couples, and singles seeking a first cruise at an all-inclusive price that even includes drinks.

THE SHIP. *Sovereign* has a smart profile and nicely rounded lines. The ship, whose hull is painted a deep blue, sports a lounge and bar that is wrapped around the blue funnel and provides a stunning view. Open deck space isn't generous, but there's a wide walk-around polished wood promenade deck. The interior layout is unusual in that most of the public rooms are located aft in a cake-layer stacking, with the accommodation located forward.

There's an array of spacious public rooms, including a conference room, library, and card players' room, plus a Monte Carlo Casino. The décor is accented with wood paneling, and some bright color splashes. Children and teens are well catered for, and there's a whole team of youth activity staff, together with a range of rooms for children and teens. The dress code is very casual. All gratuities and port taxes are included in the cruise fare.

ACCOMMODATION. There are 16 cabin price grades. Some cabins have interconnecting doors – useful for families.

Suites. Thirteen suites on Bridge Deck, the largest of which is the Royal Suite, are reasonably large and nicely furnished, with separate living and sleeping spaces.

Berlitz's Ratings

	Possible	Achieved
Ship	500	302
Accommodation	200	119
Food	400	228
Service	400	254
Entertainment	100	63
Cruise	400	249
OVERALL SCORE		
1215 points out of 2000		

Standard Cabins. The standard outside-view and interior cabins are very small, although an arched window treatment and colorful soft furnishings give the illusion of more space. Almost all cabins have twin beds that convert to a queen-size or double-bed configuration. There is little closet and drawer space. All cabins have a private bathroom, with shower, toilet, and washbasin.

DINING. El Guardiana and El Duero, two dining rooms off the Centrum (lobby), have tables for four, six, or eight persons but none for two. Both have two seatings, with table wines included in the fare. An à la carte restaurant offers better menus at an extra cost. For casual meals and snacks, the two-level Buffet Panorama is open almost 24 hours a day, although it is usually congested at peak times.

ENTERTAINMENT. The Broadway Showlounge has both main and balcony levels, with banquette seating. On the stage is a video wall with 50 screens. A smaller venue for late-night dancing or chilling out is the Disco Zoom.

SPA/FITNESS. In the Spa del Mar, you'll find a gym with fine ocean views, full of cardiovascular equipment. There's also an aerobics studio, a salon, and sauna, as well as 11 treatment rooms, including one for couples' massages. An outdoor rock-climbing wall, located on the aft of the ship's blue funnel, has several climbing tracks.

Spirit of Enderby
★★

Size:.....................................Boutique Ship		Cabins (total):......................................29		
Tonnage: 1,754		Size range (sq ft/m): .... n/a		
Lifestyle: ....Standard		Cabins (outside view):...............................29		
Cruise line:......................... Heritage Expeditions		Cabins (interior/no view):.............................0		
Former names: ....Professor Khromov		Cabins (for one person):..............................0		
IMO number:.................................8010350		Cabins (with private balcony):.........................0		
Builder: ....Wartsila (Finland)		Cabins (wheelchair accessible): 0		
Original cost:...................................... n/a		Wheelchair accessibility:...........................none		
Entered service:.............................. 1984/2010		Cabin voltage: .... 110 volts		
Registry:...................................... Russia		Elevators:...0		
Length (ft/m):............................... 234.9/71.6		Casino (gaming tables):............................No		
Beam (ft/m):................................ 41.9/12.8		Slot machines:....................................No		
Draft (ft/m): 15.0/4.8		Swimming pools:...................................0		
Propulsion/Propellers: ....diesel (3,120kW)/2		Hot tubs (on deck):.................................0		
Passenger decks:.....................................3		Self-service launderette:...........................Yes		
Total crew:...20		Dedicated cinema/seats:.............................0		
Passengers (lower beds/alll berths):.................. 50/59		Library:..Yes		
Passenger Space Ratio (lower beds/all berths): 35.0/29.7		Onboard currency: ....New Zealand $		
Crew/Passenger Ratio (lower beds/all berths):.......... 2.5/2.9				

A sturdy specialist expedition ship for hardy, intrepid travelers

OVERVIEW. This is expedition-style cruising in a small-ship setting for participants who want to be close to nature and wildlife, accompanied by specialist lecturers and expedition staff. Basic but quite comfortable, this ship will provide a good platform for exploration and learning, along with a sense of adventure.

THE SHIP. *Spirit of Enderby* is named after the two Enderby brothers of London. Both captains, they were for 40 years at the forefront of early Antarctic exploration in the 1800s. Enderby Island is also a sub-Antarctic island.

The ship was originally built for the former Soviet Union's oceanographic research program, but converted in 1992 to carry passengers for 'soft' expedition cruises. Other ships in the same series (original names) are *Akademik Boris Petrov, Akademik Golitsyn, Akademik A. Lauentiev, Akademik Nikolai Strakhov, Akademik Shokalskiy, Livonia, Professor Molchanov,* and *Professor Multanovskiy.*

Heritage Expeditions designed and built its own hovercraft for ice-peditions (hovering over and landing on ice). The ship also has a fleet of RIBs (inflatable rubber landing craft), and ATVs (amphibious all-terrain vehicles). Expedition staff accompany all cruises, while the ship's crew are Russian nationals.

The ship's interior spaces are small but comfortable, and include a main lounge/bar, two small dining rooms, while there is space on the open deck for nature and wildlife viewing.

Berlitz's Ratings

	Possible	Achieved
Ship	500	207
Accommodation	200	102
Food	400	190
Service	400	195
Entertainment	100	40
Cruise	400	199

OVERALL SCORE
933 points out of 2000

ACCOMMODATION. There are six accommodation price grades, spread over the three passenger decks. One of these is a suite; the others are a mix of two- and three-berth cabins. Most have private facilities, but those on the lowest deck have shared facilities. All are pretty basic, but they do have enough storage space for most expedition voyages.

DINING. There are two dining rooms that, between them, can accommodate all passengers at one seating. The chefs are Australian and New Zealanders. Expect hearty carbohydrate-rich fare that will keep you warm in cold-weather conditions.

ENTERTAINMENT. A lecture theatre is the place for learning and recaps.

SPA/FITNESS. There is a sauna.

Splendour of the Seas
★★★+

Size:...............................Large Resort Ship		Cabins (total):.................................902		
Tonnage:..69,130		Size range (sq ft/m):...............137.7–1,147.4/12.8–106.6		
Lifestyle:..Standard		Cabins (outside view):...............................575		
Cruise line:..................Royal Caribbean International		Cabins (interior/no view):.............................327		
Former names:..................................none		Cabins (for one person):.................................0		
IMO number:...................................9070632		Cabins (with private balcony):..........................355		
Builder:..................Chantiers de l'Atlantique (France)		Cabins (wheelchair accessible):..........................17		
Original cost:................................$325 million		Wheelchair accessibility:.............................Good		
Entered service:..............................Mar 1996		Cabin voltage:.........................110 and 220 volts		
Registry:.....................................The Bahamas		Elevators:...11		
Length (ft/m):..............................867.0/264.2		Casino (gaming tables):..............................Yes		
Beam (ft/m):...............................105.0/32.0		Slot machines:.....................................Yes		
Draft (ft/m):....................................24.5/7.3		Swimming pools:..................2 (1/sliding glass dome)		
Propulsion/Propellers:................diesel (40,200kW)/2		Hot tubs (on deck):..................................4		
Passenger decks:...................................11		Self-service launderette:.............................No		
Total crew:..720		Dedicated cinema/seats:............................No		
Passengers (lower beds/all berths):.............1,804/2,064		Library:..Yes		
Passenger Space Ratio (lower beds/all berths):.......38.3/33.4		Onboard currency:..................................US$		
Crew/Passenger Ratio (lower beds/all berths):.........2.5/2.8				

A large, lively ship for family-friendly cruising

OVERVIEW. Realizing that small cabins don't please passengers, Royal Caribbean International set about designing a ship with much larger standard cabins than in its previous vessels (except for sister ship *Legend of the Seas*). The (originally glitzy) interior decor was toned down during a refurbishment of the ship in 2011.

THE SHIP. *Splendour of the Seas* has a contemporary profile that looks somewhat unbalanced – although it grows on you – and it does have a nicely tiered stern. The pool deck amidships overhangs the hull to provide an extremely wide deck, while allowing the ship to navigate the Panama Canal. With engines placed amidships, there's little noise and no noticeable vibration, and the ship has an operating speed of up to 24 knots.

New dining venues and lounges, 124 new balconies, remodeled cabins, and some upgraded technology were all part of a 2011 refurbishment.

The outside light is brought inside in many places, with more than two acres (8,000 sq m) of glass that provides contact with sea and air. There's a single-level sliding glass roof over the more formal setting of one of two swimming pools, providing a large, multi-activity, all-weather indoor/outdoor area, called the Solarium. The glass roof provides shelter for the Roman-style pool and good health and fitness facilities and slides aft to cover the miniature golf course when required – though both can't be covered at the same time.

For golfers, there's an 18-hole, 6,000-sq-ft (557-sq-m) miniature course with the topography of a real

Berlitz's Ratings		
	Possible	Achieved
Ship	500	379
Accommodation	200	141
Food	400	238
Service	400	262
Entertainment	100	73
Cruise	400	270
OVERALL SCORE		
1363 points out of 2000		

golf course, complete with trees, foliage, grass, bridges, water hazards, and lighting to enable play at night. The holes are 155- to 230-sq-ft (14- to 21-sq-m).

Inside, two full entertainment decks are sandwiched between five decks full of cabins. A multi-tiered seven-deck-high atrium lobby, the ship's central social point, has live acrobatics within its entertainment-based environment, plus its iconic 'R' Bar. The Centrum connects with a Viking Crown Lounge via glass-walled elevators. The casino, which has mirrored walls and lights flashing everywhere, is really expansive, glitzy, and absolutely packed. The library, outside which you'll find a bust of Shakespeare, is a decent facility with more than 2,000 books. Ship-wide Wi-Fi is provided, for a fee.

Niggles include the fact that RCI charges for shuttle buses in many ports of call; the cost of bottles water is high; and receipts show an extra line 'for additional gratuity' when a gratuity has been added automatically.

FAMILIES. Royal Babies and Tots Nursery is available for young families, as are youth staff and special family-friendly programs.

ACCOMMODATION. There are 17 cabin price grades. All cabins now have iPads, a sitting area, and beds that convert to double configuration, and there is ample closet and drawer space, although there's not much space around the bed. Also, the showers could have been better designed. Cabins with balconies have glass railings rather than steel/wood to provide less intrusive sight lines.

The largest accommodation, the Royal Suite, is a superb living space for those who can afford the best. It is beautifully designed, finely decorated, and has a baby grand piano and whirlpool bathtub. Quiet sitting areas are located adjacent to the best cabins amidships. There are no cabins for singles.

Some cabins on Deck 8 have a larger door for wheelchair access in addition to the 17 cabins for the disabled, and the ship is very accessible, with ample ramped areas and sloping decks.

DINING. The King and I dining room has dramatic two-deck-high glass side walls, so many passengers both upstairs and downstairs can see both the ocean and each other in reflection. It would, perhaps, have been even better located at the stern, and it is quite noisy when full – call it atmosphere. When you book, choose one of two seatings, or My Time Dining which allows you to eat when you want during dining room hours.

Other dining options. A Chef's Table ($95 cover charge) offers wine and food paired five-course dinners co-hosted by the executive chef and sommelier – a nice treat for a special occasion perhaps.

Chops Grille, added in 2011, is adjacent to the Viking Crown Lounge and features classic American steaks and grilled seafood – all cooked to order. There is a per-person cover charge, and it's open for dinner only.

Close by is Izumi, with items cooked on hot rocks, pan-Asian cuisine, and a sushi bar (open for lunch and dinner).

For casual meals, there are two informal options: Windjammer Café, a self-serve buffet venue (with good forward views, because it's located at the front of the ship). It can get a bit cramped when it's busy, however.

ENTERTAINMENT. The 802-seat 42nd Street Theater is a single-level showlounge with tiered seating levels. The sight lines are good from almost all seats. Strong cabaret acts are also presented here, and the orchestra pit can be raised or lowered as required. Other cabaret acts are featured in the Top Hat Lounge, and these include late-night adult comedy, as well as live music for dancing. A number of other bars and lounges have live music of differing types.

SPA/FITNESS. The Vitality Spa is located on Deck 9, aft of the funnel. It has a fitness center, with a small selection of high-tech muscle-pumping equipment and weights. There is also an aerobics studio where classes in a variety of keep-fit regimes take place, a beauty salon, and a sauna, as well as rooms for such pampering treatments as massages, facials, etc.

While the facilities are quite small, they are adequate for the short cruises this ship operates. The spa is operated by Steiner. For the more sporting, there is a rock-climbing wall, with several separate climbing tracks – outdoors on the aft wall of the funnel.

Nautical Expressions

If you've ever wondered where some terms or phrases came from, you have only to look to the sea, ships, and seamen.

In the doldrums. Doldrums is the name of a place in the ocean that is located either side of, and near, the equator. It is characterized by unstable trade winds or even lack of winds for days, if not weeks, at a time. A sailing ship caught in the Doldrums can be stranded due to lack of wind. If the situation was bad enough, or if danger threatened, the boats might be launched in order to tow the ship until the wind picked up. Today, if we are in the doldrums, we feel stagnated or even morose.

Mind your P's and Q's. Sailors would get credit at the waterfront taverns until they were paid. The innkeeper kept a record of their drinks, and he had to mind that no pints or quarts were left off of their accounts. Today, the term usually refers to manners.

Passed with flying colors. This comes from sailing ships that, when passing other ships at sea, would fly their colors (pennants, flags) if they wanted to be identified. Today we tend to mean by this phrase that a person has passed an exam or test or trial with great marks.

Pipe down. A boatswain's call denoting the completion of an all hands evolution, and that you can go below. This expression is now used to mean 'keep quiet' or 'quiet down.'

Port and Starboard. Originally, the old sailing ships (like the Vikings), didn't have a rudder, and were steered by a board on the right side. This came to be the 'steerboard' side or starboard. The other side was called 'larboard' at first, but since the side with the board could not be against the dock, the left when facing forward, it became known as the 'port' side.

Round robin. The term originated in the British nautical tradition. Sailors wishing to mutiny would sign their names in a circle so the leader could not be identified. Today the term is often used in sports and competitions to denote a series of games in which all members of a league play each other one time.

Star Clipper
★★★+

Size:..............................Boutique Ship		Cabins (total):...............................85		
Tonnage: 2,298		Size range (sq ft/m):.............95.0–225.0/8.8–21.0		
Lifestyle: ....Standard		Cabins (outside view):..........................79		
Cruise line:............................. Star Clippers		Cabins (interior/no view):........................6		
Former names: ....none		Cabins (for one person):..........................0		
IMO number: 9247807		Cabins (with private balcony):.....................0		
Builder: ....Scheepswerven van Langerbrugge (Belgium)		Cabins (wheelchair accessible): 0		
Original cost:.............................$30 million		Wheelchair accessibility:.......................None		
Entered service:...........................May 1992		Cabin voltage: ....110 volts		
Registry:................................Luxembourg		Elevators:...................................0		
Length (ft/m):............................378.9/115.5		Casino (gaming tables):.........................No		
Beam (ft/m):...............................49.2/15.0		Slot machines:................................No		
Draft (ft/m): 17.7/5.6		Swimming pools:...............................2		
Propulsion/Propellers:.........sail power + diesel (1,030kW)/1		Hot tubs (on deck):.............................0		
Passenger decks:..............................4		Self-service launderette:........................No		
Total crew:...................................72		Dedicated cinema/seats:.........................No		
Passengers (lower beds/alll berths):...............170/182		Library: ....Yes		
Passenger Space Ratio (lower beds/all berths):.......13.5/12.6		Onboard currency: ....Euros		
Crew/Passenger Ratio (lower beds/all berths):.........2.3/2.5				

A real tall ship experience to put wind in your sails

OVERVIEW. This tall ship suits couples and singles who would probably never even consider a 'normal' cruise ship, but who enjoy sailing and the thrill of ocean and wind, with everything packaged to include accommodation, decent food, likeminded companions, interesting destinations, and an almost unstructured lifestyle.

THE SHIP. *Star Clipper* is one of a pair of almost identical tall ships – its sister ship is *Star Flyer*, the first clipper sailing ship to be built for 140 years and the first commercial sailing vessel to cross the North Atlantic in 90 years. It is, first and foremost, a sailing vessel with cruise accommodation that evokes memories of the 19th-century clipper sailing ships. This is an accurate four-mast, barkentine-rigged schooner with graceful lines, a finely shaped hull and masts that are 206ft (63m) tall. Some amenities found aboard large cruise vessels are provided, such as air conditioning, cashless cruising, occasional live music, a small shop, and two pools to 'dip' in.

Breathtaking when under full sail, the ship displays excellent sea manners – heeling is kept to a very comfortable 6 degrees. This working sailing ship relies on the wind about 80 percent of the time. During a typical cruise, you'll be able to climb the main mast to a platform 75ft (25m) above the sea and help with the ropes and sails at appropriate times – this could be an unnerving experience if you're not used to heights, but it is exhilarating when the ship is moving under sail. One really neat chill-out pleasure is to lie in the net-

Berlitz's Ratings

	Possible	Achieved
Ship	500	376
Accommodation	200	134
Food	400	249
Service	400	271
Entertainment	100	88
Cruise	400	278

OVERALL SCORE
1396 points out of 2000

ting at the front of the ship's bows, watching the bow wake as it streams along the ship's sides.

A diesel engine is used as the main propulsion engine when the ship is not under sail (in poor wind conditions), and two generators supply electrical power and help desalinate 40 or so tons of seawater each day for shipboard needs. The crew performs almost every task, including hoisting, trimming, winching, and repairing the sails, helped by electric winches. Water sports facilities include a waterski boat, sunfish, scuba and snorkel equipment, and eight Zodiac inflatables. Sports directors provide basic dive instruction for a fee.

Inside the vessel, classic Edwardian nautical decor throughout is clean, warm, intimate, and inviting. The paneled library has a fireplace and comfortable chairs. There are no lines and no hassle. Sailing a Square Rigger and other nautical classes are a part of every cruise, as is stargazing at night.

Depending on the itinerary and region, passengers may gather for 'captain's story time,' normally held on an open deck area adjacent to the bridge, or bar – which, incidentally, has a collection of single malt whiskies. The captain may explain sailing maneuvers when changing the rigging or directing the ship as it sails into port, and notes the important events of the day.

The sail-ship promotes total informality and provides a carefree sailing experience in an unstructured and relaxed setting at a fair price. Take minimal clothing: short-sleeved shirts and shorts for men, shorts and tops for women are the order of the day (smart casual at night). No jackets, ties, high-heeled shoes, cocktail dresses, or formal wear are needed. Take flat shoes because there are lots of ropes and sailing rig to negotiate on deck, not to mention the high thresholds to climb over and steps to negotiate – this is, after all a tall ship, not a cruise ship. The deck crew consists of real sailors, brought up with yachts and tall ships – most wouldn't set foot aboard a 'normal' cruise ship.

The steps of the internal stairways are short and steep, as in all sailing vessels, and so this ship cannot be recommended for anyone with walking disabilities. Also, there is no doctor on board, although there is a nurse.

For yachting enthusiasts, sailing aboard *Star Clipper* is like finding themselves in heaven, as there is plenty of sailing during a typical one-week cruise. The whole experience evokes the feeling of sailing aboard some famous private yacht, and even the most jaded passenger should enjoy the feel of the wind and sea close at hand. Just don't expect fine food to go with what is decidedly a fine sailing experience – which is what *Star Clipper* is all about. Note that a 12.5 percent gratuity is added to all beverage purchases.

For the nautically minded, the sailing rig consists of 16 manually furled sails, measuring a billowing 36,221 sq ft (3,365 sq m). These include: fore staysail, inner jib, outer jib, flying jib, fore course, lower topsail, upper topsail, lower topgallant, upper topgallant, main staysail, upper main staysail, mizzen staysail, main fisherman, jigger staysail, mizzen fisherman, and spanker. The square sails are furled electronically by custom-made winches.

ACCOMMODATION. There are six cabin price grades plus one owner's suite. Generally, the higher the deck, the more expensive a cabin. The cabins are quite well equipped and comfortable; they have rosewood-trimmed cabinetry and wall-to-wall carpeting, two-channel audio, color TV and DVD player, personal safe, and full-length mirrors. The bathrooms are very compact but practical units, and have gray marble tiling, glazed rosewood toiletries cabinet and paneling, some under-shelf storage space, washbasin, shower stall, and toilet. There is no 'lip' to prevent water from the shower from moving over the bathroom floor.

Individual European 100 percent individual cotton duvets are provided. There is no cabin food or beverage service.

The deluxe cabins (called 'deck cabins') are larger, and additional features include a full-size Jacuzzi tub or corner tub, flat-screen television and DVD player, and mini-bar/refrigerator. However, these cabins are subject to noise pollution from the same-deck Tropical Bar's music at night (typically until midnight), from the electric winches during sail maneuvers, and from noisy walkabout exercisers in the early morning.

The cabins in the lowest price grade are interior cabins with upper and lower berths, and not two lower beds – so someone will need to be agile to climb a ladder to the upper berth. A handful of cabins have a third, upper Pullman-style berth – good for families with children, but closet and drawer space will be at a premium with three persons in a cabin. Luggage can be stored under the bed, where extra-large

DINING. The dining room is cozy and quite attractive. There are self-serve buffet breakfasts and lunches, together with a mix of buffet and à la carte dinners, generally with a choice of three entrées, in an open-seating environment.

The seating, mostly at tables of six, adjacent to a porthole or inboard, makes it difficult for waiters to serve properly – food is passed along the tables that occupy a porthole position. However, you can dine with whomever you wish, and this is supposed to be a casual experience, after all.

While cuisine aboard the ship is perhaps less than the advertised 'gourmet' excellence as far as presentation and choice are concerned, it is fairly creative – and there's plenty of it. Also, one has to take into account the small galley. Passenger niggles include repetitious breakfasts and lunchtime salad items, because lack of space prevents more choices. But most passengers are happy with the dinners, which tend to be good, although there is a lack of green vegetables. There's a good choice of bread rolls, pastry items, and fruit.

Tea and coffee is available 24 hours a day in the lounge – mugs, tea cups, and saucers are provided. There is no cabin food service.

ENTERTAINMENT. There are no shows as such, except for an occasional local folklore show from ashore, nor are any expected by passengers aboard a tall ship such as this. Live music is typically provided by a solo lounge pianist/singer. Otherwise, dinner is the main evening event, as well as 'captain's story-time,' recapping the day's events, and conversation with fellow passengers.

During the day, when the ship is sailing, passengers can learn about the sails and their repair, and the captain or chief officer will give briefings as the sails are being furled and unfurled. The closest this tall ship comes to any kind of 'show' is perhaps one provided by members of the crew, plus a few traditional sea shanties.

SPA/FITNESS. There are no fitness facilities, or beauty salon, although a masseuse provides Oriental massage. For recreation, the ship does have a water sports program. Facilities include kayaks, a water-ski boat, sunfish, scuba and snorkel equipment, and eight Zodiac inflatable craft. The use of scuba facilities costs extra.

Star Flyer
★★★+

Size:.	Boutique Ship	Cabins (total):.	85
Tonnage:.	2,298	Size range (sq ft/m):.	95.0–225.9/8.8–21.0
Lifestyle:.	Standard	Cabins (outside view):.	79
Cruise line:.	Star Clippers	Cabins (interior/no view):.	6
Former names:.	none	Cabins (for one person):.	0
IMO number:.	8915433	Cabins (with private balcony):.	0
Builder:.	Sheepswerven van Langerbrugge (Belgium)	Cabins (wheelchair accessible):.	0
Original cost:.	$25 million	Wheelchair accessibility:.	None
Entered service:.	Jul 1991	Cabin voltage:.	110 volts
Registry:.	Luxembourg	Elevators:.	0
Length (ft/m):.	378.9/115.5	Casino (gaming tables):.	No
Beam (ft/m):.	49.2/15.0	Slot machines:.	No
Draft (ft/m):.	17.7/5.6	Swimming pools:.	2
Propulsion/Propellers:.	sail power + diesel (1,030kW)/1	Hot tubs (on deck):.	0
Passenger decks:.	4	Self-service launderette:.	No
Total crew:.	72	Dedicated cinema/seats:.	No
Passengers (lower beds/alll berths):.	170/182	Library:.	Yes
Passenger Space Ratio (lower beds/all berths):.	13.5/12.6	Onboard currency:.	Euros
Crew/Passenger Ratio (lower beds/all berths):.	2.3/2.5		

This proper sailing ship provides an antidote to cruise ships

OVERVIEW. The first clipper sailing ship to be built for 140 years, *Star Flyer* became the first commercial sailing vessel in 90 years to cross the North Atlantic. It suits those who would never consider a 'normal' cruise ship.

THE SHIP. *Star Flyer* is one of a pair of almost identical tall ships – its sister ship is *Star Clipper*. It is, first and foremost, a sailing vessel with cruise accommodation that evokes memories of the 19th-century clipper sailing ships. This is an accurate four-mast, barkentine-rigged schooner with graceful lines, a finely shaped hull and masts that are 206ft (63m) tall. Some amenities found aboard large cruise vessels are provided, such as air conditioning, cashless cruising, live music, a small shop, and two pools to 'dip' in.

Star Flyer, sister to the almost identical *Star Clipper*, is first and foremost a sailing vessel with cruise accommodation that evokes memories of the 19th-century clipper sailing ships. It is an accurate four-mast, barkentine-rigged schooner with graceful lines, a finely shaped hull, masts 206ft (63m) tall, and 16 manually furled sails totaling 36,221 sq ft (3,365 sq m).

Breathtaking when under full sail, the ship displays excellent sea manners and relies on the wind about 80 percent of the time, and heeling is kept to a very comfortable 6 degrees. A diesel engine is used as backup for generating electrical power and for desalinating the 40 or so tons of seawater each day for shipboard needs. Engine room visits may also offered for anyone interested.

Berlitz's Ratings

	Possible	Achieved
Ship	500	376
Accommodation	200	134
Food	400	249
Service	400	271
Entertainment	278	88
Cruise	400	278
OVERALL SCORE		
1396 points out of 2000		

During the cruise, you'll be able to climb the main mast to a platform 75ft (25m) above the sea and help with the ropes and sails at appropriate times. One really neat chill-out pleasure is to lie in the netting at the front of the ship's bows.

A diesel engine is used as the main propulsion engine when the ship is not under sail (in poor wind conditions), and two generators supply electrical power and help desalinate 40 or so tons of seawater each day for shipboard needs. Water sports facilities include a waterski boat, sunfish, scuba and snorkel equipment, and eight Zodiac inflatables. Sports directors provide basic dive instruction for a fee.

Inside the vessel, classic Edwardian nautical decor throughout is clean, warm, intimate, and inviting. The paneled library has a fireplace and comfortable chairs. There are no lines and no hassle. Sailing a Square Rigger and other nautical classes are a part of every cruise, as is stargazing at night.

Depending on the itinerary and region, passengers may gather for 'captain's storytime,' normally held on an open deck area adjacent to the bridge, or bar – which, incidentally, has a collection of single malt whiskies. The captain may explain sailing maneuvers when changing the rigging or directing the ship as it sails into port, and notes the important events of the day.

The sail-ship promotes total informality and provides a carefree sailing experience in a totally unstructured and relaxed setting at a reasonable price.

Take minimal clothing: short-sleeved shirts and shorts for men, shorts and tops for women are the order of the day (smart casual at night). No jackets, ties, high-heeled shoes, cocktail dresses, or formal wear are needed. Take flat shoes because there are lots of ropes and sailing rig to negotiate on deck, not to mention the high thresholds to climb over and steps to negotiate – this is, after all a tall ship, not a cruise ship.

The steps of the internal stairways are short and steep, as in all sailing vessels, and so this ship cannot be recommended for anyone with walking disabilities. Also, there is no doctor on board, although there is a nurse.

For yachting enthusiasts, sailing aboard *Star Flyer* is like finding themselves in heaven, as there is plenty of sailing during a typical one-week cruise. The whole experience evokes the feeling of sailing aboard some famous private yacht, and even the most jaded passenger should enjoy the feel of the wind and sea close at hand. Just don't expect fine food to go with what is decidedly a fine sailing experience – which is what *Star Flyer* is all about. Note that a 12.5 percent gratuity is added to all beverage purchases.

For the nautically minded, the sailing rig consists of 16 manually furled sails, measuring a billowing 36,221 sq ft (3,365 sq m). These include: fore staysail, inner jib, outer jib, flying jib, fore course, lower topsail, upper topsail, lower topgallant, upper topgallant, main staysail, upper main staysail, mizzen staysail, main fisherman, jigger staysail, mizzen fisherman, and spanker. The square sails are furled electronically by custom-made winches.

ACCOMMODATION. There are six cabin price grades plus one owner's suite. Generally, the higher the deck, the more expensive a cabin. The cabins are quite well equipped and comfortable; they have rosewood-trimmed cabinetry and wall-to-wall carpeting, two-channel audio, color TV and DVD player, personal safe, and full-length mirrors. The bathrooms are very compact but practical units, and have gray marble tiling, glazed rosewood toiletries cabinet and paneling, some under-shelf storage space, washbasin, shower stall, and toilet. There is no 'lip' to prevent water from the shower from moving over the bathroom floor.

Individual European 100 percent individual cotton duvets are provided. There is no cabin food or beverage service.

The deluxe cabins (called 'deck cabins') are larger, and additional features include a full-size Jacuzzi tub or corner tub, flat-screen television and DVD player, and mini-bar/refrigerator. However, these cabins are subject to noise pollution from the same-deck Tropical Bar's music at night (typically until midnight), from the electric winches during sail maneuvers, and from noisy walkabout exercisers in the early morning.

The cabins in the lowest price grade are interior cabins with upper and lower berths, and not two lower beds – so someone will need to be agile to climb a ladder to the upper berth. A handful of cabins have a third, upper Pullman-style berth – good for families with children, but closet and drawer space will be at a premium with three persons in a cabin.

DINING. The dining room is quite attractive, and has lots of wood and brass accenting and nautical decor. There are self-serve buffet breakfasts and lunches, together with a mix of buffet and à la carte dinners, generally with a choice of three entrées, in an open-seating environment.

The seating is mostly at tables of six, and either adjacent to a porthole or inboard; it makes it difficult for waiters to serve properly – so the food is passed along the tables that occupy a porthole position. However, you can dine with whomever you wish, and this is supposed to be a casual experience, after all.

While cuisine aboard the ship is perhaps less than the advertised 'gourmet' excellence as far as presentation and choice are concerned, it is fairly creative – and there's plenty of it. Also, one has to take into account the small galley. Passenger niggles include repetitious breakfasts and lunchtime salad items, because lack of space prevents more choices. But most passengers are happy with the dinners, which tend to be good, although there is a lack of green vegetables. There's a good choice of bread rolls, pastry items, and fruit.

Tea and coffee is available 24 hours a day in the lounge – mugs, tea cups, and saucers are provided. There is no cabin food service.

ENTERTAINMENT. There are no shows as such, except for an occasional local folklore show from ashore, nor are any expected by passengers aboard a tall ship such as this. Live music is typically provided by a solo lounge pianist/singer. Otherwise, dinner is the main evening event, as well as 'captain's story-time,' recapping the day's events, and conversation with fellow passengers.

During the day, when the ship is sailing, passengers can learn about the sails and their repair, and the captain or chief officer will give briefings as the sails are being furled and unfurled. The closest this tall ship comes to any kind of 'show' is perhaps one provided by members of the crew, plus a few traditional sea shanties.

SPA/FITNESS. There are no fitness facilities, or beauty salon, although a masseuse provides Oriental massage. For recreation, the ship has a water sports program. Facilities include kayaks, a water-ski boat, scuba and snorkel equipment, and eight Zodiac inflatable craft. The use of scuba facilities costs extra.

Star Princess
★★★★

Size:..............................Large Resort Ship	Cabins (total):...................................... 1,301
Tonnage: 108,977	Size range (sq ft/m): 161.4–1,314.0/15.0–122.0
Lifestyle: ....Standard	Cabins (outside view):.................................935
Cruise line:............................... Princess Cruises	Cabins (interior/no view):...............................366
Former names: ....none	Cabins (for one person):...................................0
IMO number: 9192363	Cabins (with private balcony):.........................711
Builder: .... Fincantieri (Italy)	Cabins (wheelchair accessible): ...... 28 (18 outside/10 interior)
Original cost:................................$460 million	Wheelchair accessibility:............................... Best
Entered service:.............................. Feb 2002	Cabin voltage: .... 110 volts
Registry:.................................... Bermuda	Elevators:.......................................14
Length (ft/m):.............................. 951.4/290.0	Casino (gaming tables):............................. Yes
Beam (ft/m):............................... 118.1/36.0	Slot machines:................................... Yes
Draft (ft/m): 26.2/8.0	Swimming pools:...................................3
Propulsion/Propellers:........... diesel-electric (42,000kW)/2	Hot tubs (on deck):...................................9
Passenger decks:....................................13	Self-service launderette:........................... Yes
Total crew:.................................. 1,200	Dedicated cinema/seats:...............................No
Passengers (lower beds/all berths): 2,602/3,102	Library: .... Yes
Passenger Space Ratio (lower beds/all berths): 41.8/35.1	Onboard currency: ....US$
Crew/Passenger Ratio (lower beds/all berths):.......... 2.3/2.8	

A large, multiple choice, resort ship for the whole family

OVERVIEW. *Star Princess* is quite a ship – a stunning, grand resort playground – but whether it provides a genuinely relaxing holiday is a moot point. With so many choices and 'small' rooms to enjoy, however, it is extremely well designed and competitively priced. The odds are that you'll have a fine time, in a controlled, well-packaged way.

THE SHIP. The design for this large cruise ship, whose sister ships are *Golden Princess* and *Grand Princess* (and slightly larger half-sister *Caribbean Princess*), presents a bold, forthright profile, with a racy 'spoiler' effect at its galleon-like transom stern that I don't consider handsome – the 'spoiler' acts as a stern observation lounge by day, and a stunning discotheque by night. With a beam of 118ft (36m), including the navigation bridge wings and with many balcony cabins overhanging the ship's hull, it is too wide – by more than 13ft (3.9m) – to transit the Panama Canal.

A few changes – compared with *Golden Princess* and *Grand Princess* – have been incorporated, including a much enlarged and improved children's area (the Fun Zone) at the stern. Also improved is the layout of the Lotus Spa, particularly the placement of the saunas/changing rooms.

There is a good sheltered faux teak promenade deck – it's actually painted steel – which almost wraps around (three times round is equal to one mile) and a walkway which goes right to the ship's enclosed bow. The outdoor pools have various beach-like surround-

Berlitz's Ratings	Possible	Achieved
Ship	500	371
Accommodation	200	147
Food	400	247
Service	400	284
Entertainment	100	77
Cruise	400	291
OVERALL SCORE		
1417 points out of 2000		

ings. One lap pool has a pumped 'current' to swim against.

Unlike the outside decks, there is plenty of space inside the ship – but there are also plenty of passengers – and a wide array of public rooms, with many 'intimate' (this being a relative word) spaces and places to play. The passenger flow has been well thought-out, and works with little congestion. The decor is attractive, with lots of earth tones, well suited to both American and European tastes.

Four areas center on swimming pools, one of which is two decks high and is covered by a glass dome, itself an extension of the funnel housing.

An extensive collection of art works complements the interior design and colors well. If you see something you like, you can buy it on board – it's almost all for sale. Indeed, the ship is full of revenue centers, designed to help you part with more money.

Like its sister ships, *Star Princess* has a Wedding Chapel; a live web-cam can relay ceremonies via the Internet. The ship's captain can legally marry American couples, thanks to the ship's Bermuda registry and a special dispensation – which should be verified when in the planning stage, according to where you reside. There are three wedding packages – Pearl, Emerald, Diamond. The fee includes registration and official marriage certificate. The Hearts & Minds chapel is also useful for renewal of vows ceremonies.

The Grand Casino has more than 260 slot machines; there are blackjack, craps, and roulette tables, plus other games. But the highlight could well be the specially linked slot machines that provide a combined payout.

Other facilities include a decent library/computer room, and a separate card room. Ship lovers should enjoy the wood-paneled Wheelhouse Bar, finely decorated with memorabilia and ship models tracing part of the history of sister company P&O; this ship highlights the 1950-built cargo ship Ganges. A sports bar, Shooters, has two billiard tables, as well as eight television screens.

A high-tech hospital has a live SeaMed telemedicine linkup to the Cedars-Sinai Medical Center in Los Angeles, with specialists available for emergency help.

The dress code is either formal or 'smart casual,' the latter interpreted by many as jeans and trainers. Daily per-person gratuities are automatically added to your account, for both adults and children. To have these charges adjusted, you'll need to line up at the reception desk.

Passenger niggles? The cabin bath towels are small, and drawer space is negligible. There are no butlers – even for top-grade suites. Cabin attendants have too many cabins to look after – typically 20 – which doesn't translate to fine personal service. The automated telephone system is frustrating, and luggage delivery is inefficient.

FAMILIES. For children, there is a two-deck-high playroom, teen room, and a host of specially trained counselors. Children have their own pool, hot tub, and open deck area at the stern, thankfully away from adult areas. There are good netted-in areas; one section has a dip pool, while another has a mini-basketball court.

ACCOMMODATION. There are six principal types of cabins and configurations: (a) grand suite, (b) suite, (c) mini-suite, (d) outside-view double cabin with balcony, (e) outside-view double cabin, and (f) interior double cabin. These come in 35 different price categories – the choice is bewildering. Note that the Interior (no view) cabins and Standard Ocean View cabins are extremely small.

(a) The largest, most lavish suite is the Grand Suite (B748, at the ship's stern). It has a large bedroom with queen-size bed, huge walk-in closets, two bathrooms, a lounge with fireplace and sofa bed, plus wet bar and refrigerator, and a large private balcony with a hot tub that can be accessed from both balcony and bedroom.

(b/c) Suites, with a semi-private balcony, have a separate living room with sofa bed and bedroom, and a TV set in each. The bathroom is quite large and has both a tub and shower stall. The mini-suites also have a private balcony, and a separate living and sleeping area, with a TV set in each. The differences between the suites and mini-suites are basically that the suite is more of a square shape while mini-suites are more rectangular and have few drawers. Both have plush bathrobes, and fully tiled bathrooms with ample open shelf

storage space. Suite and mini-suite passengers receive greater attention, including priority embarkation and disembarkation privileges. What is not good is that the most expensive accommodation has only semi-private balconies that can be seen from above and so there is little privacy.

(d/e/f) Both interior (no-view) and outside-view (with or without private balcony) cabins are of a functional design, although almost no drawers are provided. They are quite attractive, with warm, pleasing decor and fine soft furnishing fabrics; 80 percent of the outside-view cabins have a private balcony. Interior cabins measure 160 sq ft (14.4 sq m), while the standard outside-view cabins measure 228 sq ft (21 sq m).

The 28 wheelchair-accessible cabins measure 250–385 sq ft (23–36 sq m). Surprisingly, there is no mirror for dressing, and no full-length hanging space for long dresses – yes, some passengers in wheelchairs do also use mirrors and full-length clothing. Additionally, two family suites consist of two suites with an interconnecting door, plus a large balcony. These can sleep up to 10 if at least four are children or up to eight adults.

All cabins get turndown service and chocolates on pillows each night, bathrobes on request, and toiletry kits (larger for suite/mini-suite occupants). A hairdryer is provided in all cabins, sensibly located at the vanity desk unit in the living area. All bathrooms have tiled floors, and there is a decent amount of open shelf storage space for toiletries, although the plain beige decor is very basic and unappealing. Princess Cruises typically carries CNN, CNBC, ESPN, and TNT, when available, on the in-cabin television system.

Lifeboats obstruct most outside cabins on Emerald Deck. There are no cabins for singles. Your name is placed outside your suite or cabin in a documents holder – making it simple for delivery service personnel but privacy-insensitive. There is 24-hour room service, though some items on the menu are not available during early morning hours.

Some cabins can accommodate a third and fourth person in upper berths, although the lower beds cannot then be pushed together to make a queen-size bed.

Almost all balcony suites and cabins can be overlooked both from the navigation bridge wing, as well as from the port and starboard sections of the ship's discotheque – located high above the ship at the stern. Cabins with balconies on Dolphin, Caribe, and Baja decks are also overlooked by passengers on balconies on the deck above. They are, therefore, not at all private. However, perhaps the least desirable balcony cabins are eight balcony cabins located forward on Emerald Deck, as the balconies don't extend to the side of the ship and can be passed by walkers and gawkers on the adjacent Upper Promenade walkway, so occupants need to keep their curtains closed most of the time. Also, passengers in some the most expensive suites with balconies at the stern may experience vibration during certain ship maneuvers.

DINING. For formal meals there are three principal dining rooms: Amalfi, with 504 seats; Capri, with 486 seats; and Portofino, with 486 seats. Seating is assigned according to the location of your cabin. There are two seatings in Amalfi, while Capri and Portofino offer 'anytime dining' – so you can choose when and with whom you want to eat. All three are split into multi-tier sections in a non-symmetrical design that breaks the large spaces into smaller sections, for better ambience. Each dining room has its own galley.

While four elevators go to Fiesta Deck where the Amalfi and Portofino restaurants are located, only two elevators go to Plaza Deck 5 where the Capri Restaurant is located; this can cause long wait problems at peak times, particularly for anyone in a wheelchair.

Specially designed dinnerware and high-quality linens and silverware are used in the main dining rooms; by Dudson of England (dinnerware), Frette Egyptian cotton table linens, and silverware by Hepp of Germany. Note that 15 percent is automatically added to all beverage bills, including wines.

Other dining options. There are two extra-charge restaurants: Sabatini's and Tequila's, both open for lunch and dinner on days at sea. Sabatini's, with colorful tiled Mediterranean-style decor, serves Italian-style pizzas and pastas, with a variety of sauces, plus Italian-style entrées including tiger prawns and lobster tail. All provided with flair and entertainment from by the staff of waiters. Reservations are required.

Tequila's has 'southwestern American' food, with a cover charge for lunch or dinner on sea days only. It is spread over the ship's entire width and two walkways intersect it, which means that it's a very open area, with people walking through it as you eat – not a very comfortable arrangement. Reservations are needed.

The cuisine in both of these spots is decidedly better than in the three main dining rooms, with superior ingredients and more attention to presentation and taste.

A poolside hamburger grill and pizza bar (no additional charge) are dining spots for casual bites. But it costs extra to eat at either the coffee bar/patisserie, or the caviar/Champagne bar.

Other casual meals can be taken in the Horizon Court, open 24 hours a day. It has large ocean-view on port and starboard sides and direct access to the two main swimming pools and lido deck. There is no real finesse in presentation, however, as plastic plates (no trays) are provided.

ENTERTAINMENT. The Princess Theater is the main entertainment venue; it spans two decks and has comfortable seating on both main and balcony levels. It has $3 million worth of sound and light equipment, and a live showband to accompany the colourful production shows for which Princess Cruises is well-known.

The Vista Lounge, a second entertainment lounge, has cabaret acts such as magicians, comedy jugglers, and ventriloquists at night, and lectures, bingo, and horse racing during the day. Explorers, a third lounge, can also host cabaret acts and dance bands. Various other lounges and bars have live music, and Princess Cruises has a number of male dance hosts as partners for women traveling alone.

SPA/FITNESS. The Lotus Spa has Japanese-style decor, and surrounds one of the swimming pools. You can have a massage or other spa treatment in an ocean-view treatment room. It is unfortunate, however – perhaps a lack of knowledge on the part of the interior designer – that the Japanese symbol on the door of the steam inhalation rooms means insect, not a prudent thing to call passengers. Some of the massage treatment rooms are located directly underneath the jogging track.

Statendam
★★★ +

Size:. . . . . Mid-size Ship		Cabins (total):. 633	
Tonnage:. 55,819		Size range (sq ft/m):. 186.2–1,124.8/17.3–104.5	
Lifestyle:. . . . . .Premium		Cabins (outside view):. 502	
Cruise line:. . . . . Holland America Line		Cabins (interior/no view):. 131	
Former names:. . . . . .none		Cabins (for one person):. 0	
IMO number:. 8919245		Cabins (with private balcony):. 150	
Builder:. . . . . Fincantieri (Italy)		Cabins (wheelchair accessible):. 6	
Original cost:. . . . . $215 million		Wheelchair accessibility:. . . . . .Good	
Entered service:. . . . . Jan 1993		Cabin voltage:. . . . . .110 and 220 volts	
Registry:. . . . . .The Netherlands		Elevators:. 8	
Length (ft/m):. 719.4/219.3		Casino (gaming tables):. . . . . Yes	
Beam (ft/m):. 101.0/30.8		Slot machines:. . . . . Yes	
Draft (ft/m):. 24.6/7.5		Swimming pools:. . . . . .2 (1 w/sliding glass dome)	
Propulsion/Propellers:. . . . . diesel-electric (34,560kW)/2		Hot tubs (on deck):. 2	
Passenger decks:. 10		Self-service launderette:. . . . . Yes	
Total crew:. 557		Dedicated cinema/seats:. . . . . Yes	
Passengers (lower beds/alll berths):. 1,266/1,627		Library:. . . . . Yes	
Passenger Space Ratio (lower beds/all berths):. 44.0/34.3		Onboard currency:. . . . . .US$	
Crew/Passenger Ratio (lower beds/all berths):. 2.2/2.9			

Dutch decor and artifacts for senior-age cruisers

OVERVIEW. This ship has fairly decent interior fit and finish. Holland America Line constantly fine-tunes its performance as a cruise operator and regular passengers, almost all North American, find its ships comfortable and well-run.

THE SHIP. *Statendam* was the first of a series of four almost identical ships, the others being *Maasdam*, *Ryndam*, and *Veendam*. The exterior styling is rather angular, although it is softened and balanced somewhat by the fact that the hull is painted black. There is a full walk-around teakwood promenade deck outdoors – excellent for strolling, and, thankfully, there's no sign of synthetic turf. The sunloungers on the exterior promenade deck are wood, and come with comfortable cushioned pads, while those at the swimming pool on Lido Deck are of white plastic.

In the interiors of this S-class ship, an asymmetrical layout helps to reduce bottlenecks and congestion. Most public rooms are concentrated on two decks, Promenade Deck, and Upper Promenade Deck, which creates a spacious feel to the ship's interiors. There's a restrained approach to interior styling, mixing contemporary materials with traditional woods and ceramics.

What is outstanding is the array of artworks, costing about $2 million, assembled and nicely displayed to represent the fine Dutch heritage of Holland America Line.

Atop the ship, with forward-facing views that wrap

Berlitz's Ratings		
	Possible	Achieved
Ship	500	352
Accommodation	200	142
Food	400	247
Service	400	279
Entertainment	100	68
Cruise	400	264
OVERALL SCORE		
1352 points out of 2000		

around the sides, is the Crow's Nest Lounge. By day it's a fine observation lounge with large ocean-view windows; by night it turns into a nightclub with extremely variable lighting. The atrium foyer is three decks high, although its sculptured centerpiece – *Fountain of the Sirens*, a late 17th-century bronze piece by Willem de Groat – makes it look a little crowded, and leaves little room in front of the Front Office. A hydraulic glass roof covers the reasonably sized swimming pool and whirlpools and central Lido area, whose focal point is a large dolphin sculpture, so that this can be used in fine or poor weather.

The ship has a large, relaxing library. There's also a room for card games, an Explorer's Lounge (good for relaxing in, for afternoon tea, and after-dinner coffees), an intimate Piano Bar, and, of course, a casino. The casino features gaming tables and slot machines. However, note that part of the Casino is open, and can be full of cigarette smoke (yes, smoking is still permitted here), so passers-by should hold their breath.

As part of HAL's Signature of Excellence program, the ships have received a new 'Mix' lifestyle area. The trendy, upbeat space combines three specialty theme bars: Champagne (serving Champagne and sparkling wines), Martinis (in individual shakers), and Spirits & Ales (a sports bar – beer and baseball/basketball). Microsoft Surface touch-screen technology is available for playing checkers and chess, air hockey, and other sports games.

Statendam is a fairly well-built ship, and has reasonably decent interior fit and finish. HAL continues its strong maritime traditions, although the present food and service components let down the rest of the cruise experience.

An escalator travels between two of the lower decks, one of which was originally planned to be the embarkation point, but it is about as worthless as a glass hammer! The charge to use the washing machines and dryers in the self-service launderette is petty, particularly for occupants of expensive suites. The urinals in the men's public restrooms are unusually high.

ACCOMMODATION. There are 17 cabin price grades. Cabins range from small interior cabins to a large penthouse suite with ocean views. All cabin televisions carry CNN.

The interior and outside-view standard cabins have twin beds that convert to a queen-size bed, and there is a separate living space with sofa and coffee table. Although the drawer space is generally good, the closet space is very tight, particularly for long cruises – although more than adequate for a seven-night cruise. The tiled bathrooms are compact but practical. Bathrobes are provided for all suites/cabins, as are hairdryers, and a small range of toiletries. The bathrooms are quite well laid-out, but the tubs are small units better described as shower tubs.

On Navigation Deck, 28 suites have accommodation for up to four people. These also have in-suite dining as an alternative to the dining room. These are very spacious, tastefully decorated and well laid-out, and have a separate living room, bedroom with two lower beds (convertible to a king-size bed), a good size living area, dressing room, plenty of closet and drawer space, and a marble bathroom.

The largest accommodation is a penthouse suite, located on the starboard side of Navigation Deck at the forward staircase. It has a king-size bed, television and video player, and vanity desk. A large walk-in closet has superb drawer space. There's an oversize whirlpool bath that could seat four, a separate shower enclosure, and a separate washroom with toilet, bidet, and washbasin. The living room has a writing desk, a large TV set and a full set of audio equipment. The dressing room has a large private balcony with teak lounge chairs and drinks tables, dining table, and four chairs. The pantry has a large refrigerator, toaster unit, and full coffee/tea-making facilities and food preparation area, and a separate entrance from the hallway.

There's a mini-bar/refrigerator, a guest toilet and floor-to-ceiling windows. There is no bell push.

Passengers in accommodation designated as suites and mini-suites have the use of a private concierge club called the Neptune Lounge, where light breakfast and snacks throughout the day can be taken.

DINING. The Rotterdam Dining Room spans two decks at the stern of the ship, and is quite dramatic. It has two grand staircases to connect the two levels, panoramic views on three sides, and a music balcony. Both open seating and fixed (assigned tables and times) seating are available, while breakfast and lunch are open-seating – you'll be seated by restaurant staff when you enter. There are tables for two, four, six, or eight, but the waiter stations are very noisy for anyone seated adjacent to them. Fine Rosenthal china and cutlery are used.

Other dining options. A small restaurant, the 66-seat Pinnacle Grill, is located just forward of the balcony level of the main dining room on the starboard side. It has Pacific Northwest cuisine such as Alaska salmon, halibut, and other regional specialties, plus a selection of premium steaks. Reservations are necessary, and there's a cover charge. A Bulgari show plate, Rosenthal china, Riedel wine glasses, and Frette table linen are used. The Pinnacle Grill is a better dining experience than in the Rotterdam (main) Dining Room, and worth it for that special celebration.

For more casual evening eating, the Lido Buffet is open for dinners on all except the last night of each cruise, in an open-seating arrangement. Tables are set with crisp linens, flatware, and stemware. A set menu includes a choice of four entrées. Breakfasts and lunches are also served here. There is much use of canned fruits and packets of items, although there are several commercial low-calorie salad dressings. Each night, a section of the venue is transformed into Canaletto using glass screens; the cuisine is Italian-flavored, but the Italian wine list is poor. There's no additional charge, although reservations are requested.

Passengers will need to eat in the Lido Buffet on days when the dining room is closed for lunch – typically once or twice per cruise, depending on the itinerary. A poolside grill provides basic hamburgers and hot dogs.

ENTERTAINMENT. The Showlounge at Sea, at the forward part of the ship, spans two decks, with banquette seating on both main and upper levels. It is basically a well-designed room, but the ceiling is low and the sight lines from the balcony level are quite poor.

SPA/FITNESS. The Ocean Spa is one deck below the navigation bridge at the very forward part of the ship. It includes a gymnasium with all the latest muscle-pumping exercise machines, including an abundance of treadmills. It has ocean views, an aerobics exercise area, a large beauty salon, several treatment rooms, and men's and women's sauna, steam room, and changing areas.

Sun Princess
★★★★

Size:.	.Large Resort Ship	Cabins (total):.	.975
Tonnage:	77,499	Size range (sq ft/m):	134.5–753.4/12.5–70.0
Lifestyle:	.Standard	Cabins (outside view):	.603
Cruise line:.	Princess Cruises	Cabins (interior/no view):.	.372
Former names:	.none	Cabins (for one person):.	.0
IMO number:	9000259	Cabins (with private balcony):.	.410
Builder:	Fincantieri (Italy)	Cabins (wheelchair accessible):	.19
Original cost:	.$300 million	Wheelchair accessibility:.	Good
Entered service:.	Dec 1995	Cabin voltage:	.110 and 220 volts
Registry:.	.Great Britain	Elevators:.	.11
Length (ft/m):.	857.2/261.3	Casino (gaming tables):.	Yes
Beam (ft/m):.	105.6/32.2	Slot machines:.	Yes
Draft (ft/m):	26.5/8.1	Swimming pools:.	.3
Propulsion/Propellers:.	diesel-electric (28,000kW)/2	Hot tubs (on deck):.	.5
Passenger decks:.	10	Self-service launderette:	Yes
Total crew:.	900	Dedicated cinema/seats:.	.No
Passengers (lower beds/alll berths):	1,950/2,250	Library:	Yes
Passenger Space Ratio (lower beds/all berths):	39.7/34.4	Onboard currency:	Australian $
Crew/Passenger Ratio (lower beds/all berths):	2.0/2.5		

A large, family-friendly ship with modern decor

OVERVIEW. *Sun Princess*, while large, absorbs passengers well, and has a quasi-intimate feel. The interiors are warm, with welcoming decor that includes some attractive murals and other artwork.

THE SHIP. In November 2007, *Sun Princess* was assigned to Australia, operating cruises from Sydney, Melbourne, and Fremantle. The onboard currency became the Australian dollar, and the entertainment was geared to Australian tastes, and other aspects of the cruise operation modified accordingly. In 2013, however, the ship was sent to Japan for a series of cruises designed to attract Japanese passengers, and a number of Japanese-speaking staff were recruited.

This all-white ship has a good profile, and is well balanced by its large funnel, which contains a deck tennis/basketball/volleyball court in its sheltered aft base. There is a wide, teakwood walk-around promenade deck outdoors, some real teak steamer-style deck chairs with royal blue cushioned pads, and 93,000 sq ft (8,600 sq m) of space outdoors. An extensive glass area on the upper decks provides plenty of light and connection with the outside world.

A wide array of public rooms includes several intimate rooms and spaces so that you don't feel overwhelmed by large spaces. The interior focal point (and always a good place to arrange to meet others) is a pleasant four-deck-high atrium lobby with winding, double stairways, and two panoramic glass-walled elevators.

Berlitz's Ratings

	Possible	Achieved
Ship	500	378
Accommodation	200	148
Food	400	246
Service	400	278
Entertainment	100	75
Cruise	400	284

OVERALL SCORE
1409 points out of 2000

The main entertainment rooms are located underneath three decks of cabins. There is plenty of space, the traffic flow is good, and the ship absorbs people well. There are two showlounges, one at each end of the ship; one is a pleasant theater-style space where movies are also shown, and the other is a cabaret-style lounge, complete with bar.

The library is a warm, welcoming room with ocean-view windows, and has six large buttery leather chairs for listening to audio CDs. There is a conference center for up to 300, as well as a business center. The collection of artwork is good, particularly on the stairways, and helps make the ship feel smaller than it is, although in places it doesn't always seem coordinated.

The most traditional room (a standard aboard all Princess ships) aboard is the Wheelhouse Lounge/Bar, decorated in the style of a late 19th-century gentleman's club, complete with wood paneling and comfortable seating. Its focal point is a large ship model from the P&O archives.

One nice feature is the captain's cocktail party; it is held in the four-deck-high main atrium so you can come and go as you please – and there's no standing in line to have your photograph taken with the captain if you don't want to.

Niggles include the layout – there are a number of dead ends in the interior layout, so it's not as user-friendly as a ship this size should be. The cabin numbering system is extremely illogical, with numbers going through several hundred series on the same deck.

The walls of the passenger accommodation decks are very plain. The swimming pools are small for the number of passengers carried, and the pool deck is cluttered with white, plastic sunloungers that lack cushioned pads.

ACCOMMODATION. There are many, many different cabin grades: 20 outside view and eight interior. Although the standard outside-view and interior cabins are a little small, they are well designed and functional in layout, and have earth tone colors accentuated by splashes of color from the bedspreads. Proportionately, there are quite a lot of interior cabins. Many of the outside-view cabins have private balconies, and all are quite well soundproofed, although the balcony partition is not floor-to-ceiling type, so you can hear your neighbors clearly. The balconies are very narrow, just large enough for two small chairs.

A 'reasonable' amount of closet and abundant drawer and other storage space is provided in all cabins – just about adequate for a seven-night cruise, as are a TV set and refrigerator. However, for longer voyages, the cabin closet space could prove to be much too small.

Each night a chocolate will appear on your pillow. The cabin bathrooms are practical, and come complete with all the details one needs, although they really are tight spaces, one person at a time units. They have a decent shower enclosure, real glasses, a hairdryer and bathrobe, and a small amount of shelving for toiletries.

The largest accommodation is in six suites, two on each of three decks at the stern, with large private balcony (536–754 sq ft/50–70 sq m, including balcony). They are well laid-out, and have large bathrooms with two washbasins, a Jacuzzi tub, and a separate shower enclosure. The bedroom has pleasing wood accenting and detailing, while the living area includes a dining room table and four chairs.

The 32 mini-suites (374–536 sq ft/35–50 sq m) typically have two lower beds that convert to a queen-size bed. There is a separate bedroom/sleeping area with vanity desk, and a lounge with sofa and coffee table, indented ceilings with wood accenting and detailing, walk-in closet, and larger bathroom with Jacuzzi tub and separate shower enclosure.

Some are 19 wheelchair-accessible cabins, which measure 213–305 sq ft (20–28 sq m), in a mix of seven outside-view and 12 interior cabins.

DINING. There are two main dining rooms of asymmetrical design: Marquis and Regency; they are located adjacent to the two lower levels of the four-deck-high atrium lobby. Each seats around 500, has its own galley, and is split into multi-tier sections that help create a feeling of intimacy, although there is a lot of noise from the waiter stations adjacent to many tables. Breakfast and lunch are provided in an open-seating arrangement, while dinner is in two seatings.

On any given seven-day cruise, a typical menu cycle may include a Sailaway Dinner, Captain's Welcome Dinner, Chef's Dinner, Italian Dinner, French Dinner, Captain's Gala Dinner, and Landfall Dinner. The wine list is reasonable but not good, and the company has, sadly, dispensed with wine waiters. Note that 15 percent is automatically added to all beverage bills, including wines.

Other dining options. For some really good meat, consider the extra-cost Sterling Steakhouse; there are four different cuts of Angus beef from the popular Sterling Silver brand of USDA prime meats – Filet Mignon, New York Strip, Porterhouse, and Rib-Eye, first presented on a silver tray. There is also a barbecue chicken option, plus the usual baked potato or french fries as accompaniments. This is available as an alternative to the dining rooms between 6:30pm and 9:30pm but, instead of being a separate, intimate room as you might expect, it is located in a section of the Horizon Buffet, with its own portable bar and some decorative touches to set it apart from the regular buffet area.

The Horizon Buffet itself is open 24 hours a day and, at night, has an informal dinner setting with sit-down waiter service. The buffet displays are, for the most part, fairly repetitious. There is no real finesse in presentation, however, as plastic plates are provided, instead of trays.

There is also a patisserie (for extra-cost cappuccino/espresso coffees and pastries), a wine/caviar bar, and a pizzeria (complete with cobblestone floors and wrought-iron decorative features), and a choice of six excellent pizzas.

ENTERTAINMENT. There are two showlounges, both theater and cabaret style. The main one, the Princess Theater, has a sloping floor, with aisle-style seating that is well-tiered, and with good sight lines to the raised stage from most of the 500 seats.

The 480-seat Vista Lounge, at the aft end, has cabaret entertainment, and acts as a lecture and presentation room. Princess Cruises has a good stable of regular cabaret acts to draw from, so there should be something for most tastes.

SPA/FITNESS. A glass-walled Lotus Spa is located in an aft area of Riviera deck, and includes a gymnasium with high-tech machines, and several massage/body treatment rooms. The facility is staffed and operated by the spa specialist concession Steiner Leisure.

Sports facilities are located in an open-air sports deck positioned inside the funnel and adaptable for basketball, volleyball, badminton, or paddle tennis. Joggers can exercise on the walk-around open Promenade Deck.

Superstar Aquarius
★★★

Size:.	Mid-size Ship	Cabins (total):.	765
Tonnage:	50,764	Size range (sq ft/m):	139.9–349.8/13.0–32.5
Lifestyle:	Standard	Cabins (outside view):	611
Cruise line:.	Star Cruises	Cabins (interior/no view):.	154
Former names:	Norwegian Wind, Windward	Cabins (for one person):.	0
IMO number:	9008421	Cabins (with private balcony):	74
Builder:	Chantiers de l'Atlantique (France)	Cabins (wheelchair accessible):	11
Original cost:	$240 million	Wheelchair accessibility:	Fair
Entered service:.	Jun 1993/May 2007	Cabin voltage:	110 volts
Registry:.	The Bahamas	Elevators:.	10
Length (ft/m):.	754.0/229.8	Casino (gaming tables):.	Yes
Beam (ft/m):.	93.5/28.5	Slot machines:	Yes
Draft (ft/m):	22.3/6.8	Swimming pools:	1
Propulsion/Propellers:	diesel (18,480kW)/2	Hot tubs (on deck):.	2
Passenger decks:.	10	Self-service launderette:	No
Total crew:.	889	Dedicated cinema/seats:.	No
Passengers (lower beds/alll berths):.	1,529/1,607	Library:	Yes
Passenger Space Ratio (lower beds/all berths):	33.1/31.5	Onboard currency:	Hong Kong $
Crew/Passenger Ratio (lower beds/all berths):	1.7/1.8		

Family-friendly casual cruising that's good for gamblers

OVERVIEW. *SuperStar Aquarius* was transferred from Norwegian Cruise Line to the Star Cruises fleet in 2007 to operate overnight and short cruises from Hong Kong. The dress code is strictly casual. Several cabins are specially equipped for the hearing-impaired. All gratuities for staff are included.

THE SHIP. The exterior design emphasizes a clever and extensive use of large windows that help create a sense of open spaces, but the interior design has many smaller public rooms. There is no big atrium lobby, and the ceiling height is low.

Public rooms include bars and lounges, including Skyline Karaoke, which has five private karaoke rooms. There's a mahjong/card room, childcare center, video arcade, Genting Club for invited gaming guests, business meeting rooms, an Internet-connect center/library, cigar lounge, and a small boutique. There is a blue rubber-covered walk-around promenade deck outdoors. Outdoor stairways are numerous and confusing, while the carpeted steel interior stairwell steps are tinny.

ACCOMMODATION. There are 16 cabin price grades. No cabin includes the number '4' – which means 'die' in superstitious China. Most cabins have outside views and wood-trimmed cabinetry and warm decor with multi-colored soft furnishings, but there's almost no drawer space (although the closets have open shelves), so take minimal clothing. All cabins have a

Berlitz's Ratings		
	Possible	Achieved
Ship	500	293
Accommodation	200	118
Food	400	217
Service	400	237
Entertainment	100	60
Cruise	400	230
OVERALL SCORE		
1155 points out of 2000		

sitting area. The bathrooms are small but practical.

There are 18 suites (12 with a private entrance and a small, private balcony), each with separate living room and bedroom, and plenty of closet and drawer space. Occupants of suites receive 'concierge' service. In addition, 16 suites and 70 cabins have interconnecting doors.

DINING. Freestyle Dining venues include the 280-seat Dynasty Restaurant, for Chinese family-style food. It has some prime tables at ocean-view window seats in a section that extends from the ship's port and starboard sides in half-moon shapes. There's also Spices Restaurant, an Asian specialty buffet venue with 180 seats; Oceana Barbeque, an outdoor buffet venue; Blue Lagoon, a 24-hour bistro, with 80 seats; and Mariner's Buffet, an international self-service buffet.

ENTERTAINMENT. The 700-seat Stardust Lounge is two decks high, but the banquette and individual tub chair seating is only on the main level. There is no live showband, only recorded music. High-volume razzle-dazzle shows are presented to a pre-recorded track, as well as special individual cabaret acts.

SPA/FITNESS. A gymnasium has high-tech muscle-toning equipment, reflexology lounge, and Oscar Hair and Beauty Salon. There's a Ping-Pong table, basketball/volleyball court, golf driving range, and a jogging track.

Superstar Gemini
★★★

Size:.	Mid-size Ship	Cabins (total):.	766
Tonnage:	50,764	Size range (sq ft/m):	139.9–349.8/13.0–32.5
Lifestyle:	Standard	Cabins (outside view):	611
Cruise line:.	Star Cruises	Cabins (interior/no view):.	155
Former names:	Norwegian Dream, Dreamward	Cabins (for one person):.	0
IMO number:	9008419	Cabins (with private balcony):	74
Builder:	Chantiers de l'Atlantique (France)	Cabins (wheelchair accessible):	11
Original cost:	$240 million	Wheelchair accessibility:	Fair
Entered service:.	Dec 1992/Jan2013	Cabin voltage:	110 volts
Registry:.	The Bahamas	Elevators:.	10
Length (ft/m):.		Casino (gaming tables):	Yes
Beam (ft/m):.	93.5/28.5	Slot machines:	Yes
Draft (ft/m):	22.3/6.8	Swimming pools:	1
Propulsion/Propellers:	diesel (18,480kW)/2	Hot tubs (on deck):.	2
Passenger decks:.	10	Self-service launderette:	No
Total crew:	700	Dedicated cinema/seats:	No
Passengers (lower beds/all berths):	n/a	Library:	Yes
Passenger Space Ratio (lower beds/all berths):	n/a	Onboard currency:	Hong Kong $
Crew/Passenger Ratio (lower beds/all berths):	n/a		

A casual family-friendly ship for Asian nationalities

OVERVIEW. *SuperStar Gemini* is a mid-sized good for Asian families and couples looking for a general cruise experience in fairly contemporary surroundings.

THE SHIP. Although its funnel is large and square-ish looking, the ship's profile is quite well balanced; this is because the ship underwent a 'chop and stretch' operation in which a new 131-ft (40-meter) mid-section was added in 1998. This gave the ship not only more cabins, but more public rooms and places to play in.

At the stern of the ship, the tiered pool deck is neat, as are the multi-deck aft sun terraces and all the fore and aft connecting exterior stairways. The overall exterior design emphasizes a clever and extensive use of large windows that create a sense of open spaces. However, there is no big atrium lobby, as one might expect.

The ship was highly successful for many years for Norwegian Cruise Line's younger, active sports-minded passengers, and now provides Star Cruises passengers with a comfortable ship. Public rooms include a mahjong room, an activity center, several shops including a duty-free store, and a tea corner – for premium teas, and a jewelry store), an Observatory Lounge Karaoke Lounge), Genting Club, and Star Club (casino with gaming tables and slot machines).

ACCOMMODATION. There are several grades of cabins (the price you pay will depend on the grade,

Berlitz's Ratings

	Possible	Achieved
Ship	500	326
Accommodation	200	128
Food	400	233
Service	400	250
Entertainment	100	63
Cruise	400	243

OVERALL SCORE
1243 points out of 2000

size and location you choose). Most cabins have outside views, wood-trimmed cabinetry and warm decor, with multi-colored soft furnishings. But there is almost no drawer space (the closets have open shelves). All cabins benefit from a sitting area, but this takes away any free space, making movement pretty tight. The bathrooms are small but practical.

DINING. There are plenty of choices when it comes to dining. The main full-service dining room is Bella Vista (the nicest of all the dining venues, with prime tables with ocean-view window seats); Dynasty (a self-serve Chinese buffet); Mariners Restaurant (a self-serve buffet); Oceana Barbecue (outdoors, for grilled specialties and buffet-style eats); and Blue Lagoon (a 24-hour a la carte venue).

ENTERTAINMENT. The Stardust Lounge is the ship's main showlounge. It is two decks high, and is located in the center of the ship, with cabins in front of it, and other public rooms and dining spots behind it.

SPA/FITNESS. Spa/fitness facilities are located in the forward section of Sports Deck 12 (just aft of the observation lounge), and include a gymnasium with high-tech muscle-toning equipment, a beauty salon, several massage and associated treatment rooms, and men's and women's saunas and changing rooms.

SuperStar Libra
★★★

Size:.	Mid-size Ship	Cabins (total):.	732
Tonnage:	42,276	Size range (sq ft/m):	109.7–269.1/10.2–25.0
Lifestyle:	Standard	Cabins (outside view):	501
Cruise line:.	Star Cruises	Cabins (interior/no view):.	231
Former names:	Norwegian Sea, Seaward	Cabins (for one person):.	0
IMO number:	8612134	Cabins (with private balcony):	0
Builder:	Wartsila (Finland)	Cabins (wheelchair accessible):	4
Original cost:	$120 million	Wheelchair accessibility:	Fair
Entered service:.	Jun 1988/Oct 2005	Cabin voltage:	110 volts
Registry:.	The Bahamas	Elevators:.	6
Length (ft/m):	708.6/216.0	Casino (gaming tables):.	Yes
Beam (ft/m):.	95.1/29.0	Slot machines:.	Yes
Draft (ft/m):	22.9/7.0	Swimming pools:.	2
Propulsion/Propellers:	diesel (21,120kW)/2	Hot tubs (on deck):.	2
Passenger decks:.	9	Self-service launderette:.	No
Total crew:.	700	Dedicated cinema/seats:.	No
Passengers (lower beds/alll berths):	1,472/1,800	Library:	No
Passenger Space Ratio (lower beds/all berths):	28.0/23.5	Onboard currency:	Hong Kong $
Crew/Passenger Ratio (lower beds/all berths):	2.1/2.5		

A casual, family-friendly Asian ship for gambling

OVERVIEW. This ship, which is based at Penang in Malaysia, is suited for couples and solo travelers seeking a short cruise in surroundings tailored specifically for them. It was built before balcony cabins came into vogue – so there aren't any.

THE SHIP. *SuperStar Libra* is an angular yet reasonably attractive ship that has a contemporary European cruise-ferry profile with a sharply raked bow and sleek mast and funnel added. It is quite well designed, with generally sound passenger flow. The interior decor, stressing corals, blues, and mauves, reminds you of sea and sky.

The lobby, two decks high, is pleasing without being overwhelming. There is a decent selection of public rooms, bars, and lounges, including an inviting wood-paneled Admiral's Lounge, a Star Club casino, a discotheque (Boomer's), and The Bollywood karaoke lounge. Gratuities are included in the fare.

The open decks are cluttered, and badly dented and scuffed panels in the accommodation hallways are unattractive. The steps on the stairways are quite tinny. The constant background music in the hallways is irritating. There is too much use of synthetic turf on the upper outdoors decks – this gets soggy when wet.

ACCOMMODATION. There are numerous suite/cabin price categories. No cabin includes the number '4' – which means 'die' in superstitious China. The

Berlitz's Ratings

	Possible	Achieved
Ship	500	305
Accommodation	200	118
Food	400	232
Service	400	249
Entertainment	100	61
Cruise	400	246
OVERALL SCORE		
1211 points out of 2000		

cabins are of average size although they are tastefully appointed and comfortable. Audio channels are available via the TV set, although the picture can't be turned off. The bathrooms are well designed but gave weak hairdryers

A suite or one of two upper-grade cabins offers a little more space, a lounge area with table and sofa that converts into another bed, European duvets, and a refrigerator (top categories only). The bathrooms also have a tub, shower, and retractable clothesline.

DINING. While there are no assigned dining rooms, tables, or seats, some eateries cost extra. These include: Four Seasons Restaurant, the principal dining room, serving Continental Cuisine; The Saffron; Two Trees Restaurant (exclusive lounge/restaurant); Taj by the Bay; Blue Lagoon for 24-hour casual refreshments; and Coconut Willy's, a poolside refreshment center.

ENTERTAINMENT. The 770-seat Stardust Lounge is the venue for shows and major cabaret acts, but 12 thick pillars obstruct many sight lines. The Galaxy of the Stars Lounge is for cabaret acts. A number of bands and solo entertaining musicians provide live music for listening and dancing in several lounges and bars.

SPA/FITNESS. There's a good gymnasium/fitness center, located around the mast and accessible only from the outside deck – not good when it rains.

SuperStar Virgo
★★★+

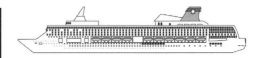

Size:.................................Large Resort Ship		Cabins (total):....................................902	
Tonnage: 75,338		Size range (sq ft/m): 150.6–638.3/14.0–59.3	
Lifestyle: ....Standard		Cabins (outside view):..............................575	
Cruise line:............................... Star Cruises		Cabins (interior/no view):..........................327	
Former names: ....none		Cabins (for one person):..............................0	
IMO number: 9141077		Cabins (with private balcony):......................390	
Builder: .... Meyer Werft (Germany)		Cabins (wheelchair accessible): 4	
Original cost:...........................$350 million		Wheelchair accessibility:.........................Good	
Entered service:.............................. Aug 1999		Cabin voltage: .... 240 volts	
Registry:..Panama		Elevators:...9	
Length (ft/m):............................ 879.2/268.0		Casino (gaming tables):..............................Yes	
Beam (ft/m):.............................. 105.6/32.2		Slot machines:.......................................Yes	
Draft (ft/m):................................. 25.9/7.9		Swimming pools:......................................2	
Propulsion/Propellers:...................diesel (50,400kW)/2		Hot tubs (on deck):..................................4	
Passenger decks:......................................10		Self-service launderette:............................No	
Total crew:....................................... 1,225		Dedicated cinema/seats:.............................No	
Passengers (lower beds/alll berths):.............. 1,804/2,800		Library: .... Yes	
Passenger Space Ratio (lower beds/all berths): 41.7/26.9		Onboard currency: ....Hong Kong $	
Crew/Passenger Ratio (lower beds/all berths):.......... 1.4/2.2			

A large, family-friendly ship for casual-style cruising

OVERVIEW. This ship is best suited to couples, singles, and families with children who want to cruise aboard a contemporary floating resort with decent facilities and many Asian dining spots, at a very attractive price.

THE SHIP. *SuperStar Virgo* was the second new ship ordered for the Asian market. The all-white vessel has a distinctive red/blue funnel with gold star logo. There are three distinct classes of passengers. As you check in, you will be issued with a colored boarding card to denote Admiral Class passengers (yellow), Balcony Class (red), or World Cruisers (blue).

There is a walk-around promenade deck outdoors, good for strolling. Inside are two boulevards, and a stunning, larger two-deck-high central atrium lobby with three glass-walled elevators and space to peruse the shops and cafés.

The casino complex is at the forward end of the atrium boulevard on Deck 7. This includes a large general-purpose, brightly lit casino, called Oasis, with gaming tables and slot machines. There's a smaller members-only gaming club, as well as VIP gaming rooms, one of which has its own access to the upper level of the showlounge. The 450-seat Galaxy of the Stars Lounge is an observation lounge by day and a nightclub at night, with live music.

Three stairways are each carpeted in a different color, which helps new cruise passengers find their way around easily.

Berlitz's Ratings		
	Possible	Achieved
Ship	500	394
Accommodation	200	146
Food	400	258
Service	400	259
Entertainment	100	65
Cruise	400	276
OVERALL SCORE		
1398 points out of 2000		

Other facilities include a business center with six meeting rooms, a large library and writing room, plus private mahjong and karaoke rooms, and a smoking room. A shopping concourse includes a wine shop.

Star Cruises has established a Southeast Asian regional cruise audience for its diverse fleet. *SuperStar Virgo* is good for the active local market, and is the most comprehensive ship sailing year-round in this popular region.

Lots of choices, more dining options, and Asian hospitality all add up to a very attractive holiday package particularly suitable for families with children, in a very contemporary floating resort that operates from Hong Kong (April–November) and Singapore (November–March). The dress code is ultra-casual (no jacket and tie needed), and the ship operates a no-tipping policy. While the initial cruise fare seems very reasonable, the extra costs and charges soon mount up if you want to indulge in more than the basics. Although service levels and finesse are inconsistent, hospitality is very good.

There are many extra-cost items in addition to the à la carte dining spots, such as for morning tea, after-noon tea, most cabaret shows (except a crew show), and childcare. Finding your way around many areas blocked by portable 'crowd containment' ribbon barriers can prove frustrating.

FAMILIES. Teens have their own huge video arcade, while younger children get to play in a wet 'n' wild aft pool (complete with pirate ship and caves) and two whirlpool tubs. Plus there's all the fun and facilities of Charlie's 24-hour childcare center, which includes a painting room, computer learning center, and small cinema. There's a room full of cots for toddlers to use for sleepovers, and even the toilets are at a special low height. About 15,000 sq ft (1,400 sq m) is devoted to children's facilities. On deck is the world's first stainless-steel water slide at sea. Installed in 2009, it cost $550,000, and is 330ft (100m) long. You can zoom along at up to 22ft (6.7m) a second due to its steep incline, from 35ft (10.7m) above the deck.

ACCOMMODATION. There are seven types of accommodation, in a number of different price categories. Three entire decks of cabins have private balconies, while two-thirds of all cabins have an outside view. Both the standard outside-view and interior cabins really are very small, particularly since all cabins have extra berths for a third/fourth person. So take the least amount of clothing you can – there's almost no storage space for luggage.

All cabins have a personal safe, cotton towels and duvets or sheets. Bathrooms have a good-size shower enclosure, and include toiletries such as Burberry soap, conditioning shampoo, and body lotion.

For more space, choose one of 13 suites. Each has a separate lounge/dining room, bedroom, and bathroom, and an interconnecting door to an ocean-view cabin with private lit balcony.

The bedroom is small, completely filled by its queen-size bed; there is a reasonable amount of drawer space, but the drawers are very small. The closet space is rather tight – it contains two personal safes. A large en suite bathroom is part of the bedroom, and has a gorgeous mosaic tiled floor, tub, two basins, separate shower enclosure with floor-to-ceiling ocean-view window, and separate toilet with glass door. There are TV sets in the lounge, bedroom, and bathroom.

For even more space, choose one of the six largest suites (Boracay, Nicobar, Langkawi, Majorca, Phuket, and Sentosa) and you'll have a generous amount of private living space, with a separate lounge, dining area, bedroom, large bathroom, and private lit balcony. The facilities are similar to those in the suites already described. There are TV sets in the lounge, bedroom, and bathroom.

A small room service menu is available, with a 15 percent service charge plus a gratuity.

DINING. There's certainly no lack of choice, with eight venues, plus a café:

Bella Vista (perhaps the equivalent of a main dining room) seats over 600 in an open-seating arrangement, although in effect it operates two seatings. The aft section is two decks high, and huge cathedral-

style windows are set in three sections overlooking the stern.

Mediterranean Buffet: this is a large self-serve buffet restaurant with indoor/outdoor seating for 400.

The Pavilion Room has traditional Cantonese Chinese cuisine, including dim sum at lunchtime.

The following are à la carte (extra-cost) dining spots:

Noble House: a Chinese Restaurant, with traditional Hong Kong-themed decor and items such as dim sum. There are also two small private dining rooms.

Palazzo: a beautiful, if slightly ostentatious Italian restaurant. It has fine food, and a genuine Renoir painting well protected by cameras and alarms.

Samurai: a Japanese restaurant and sushi bar (for sashimi and sushi). There are two teppanyaki grills, each with 10 seats, where the chef cooks in front of you.

The Taj: an Indian/vegetarian dining spot that offers a range of food in a self-serve buffet setup.

Blue Lagoon: a casual 24-hour street café with noodle dishes, fried rice, and other Southeast Asian dishes.

Out of Africa: a casual karaoke café and bar, where coffees, teas, and pastries are available.

ENTERTAINMENT. The Lido showlounge, with 934 seats, is two decks high. It has a main and balcony levels, with the balcony level reserved for 'gaming club' members. The room has almost no support columns to obstruct the sightlines, and a revolving stage for revues and other production shows, typically to recorded music – there is no live showband. Kingdom of Kung-Fu, with a cast of 30, features the power and form of the Shaolin Masters in an action-packed martial arts show. The showlounge can also be used as a large-screen cinema, with superb surround sound.

In addition, local specialty cabaret acts are brought on board, as are revue-style shows complete with topless dancers. Bands and small musical units provide plenty of live music for dancing and listening in the various lounges.

SPA/FITNESS. The Roman Spa and Fitness Center is on one of the uppermost decks, just forward of the Tivoli Pool. It has a gymnasium full of high-tech muscle-toning equipment, plus an aerobics exercise room, hair and beauty salon, and saunas, steam rooms, changing rooms for men and women, several treatment rooms, and aqua-swim pools that provide counter-flow jets. There is an extra charge for use of the sauna and steam rooms.

Although there are several types of massages available, Thai massage is a specialty – you can have it in the spa, outdoors on deck, in your cabin or on your private balcony, space permitting. Sports facilities include a jogging track, golf driving range, basketball and tennis courts, and there are four levels of sunbathing decks.

Tere Moana
★★★★

Size:..	Boutique Ship	Cabins (total):....................................	45
Tonnage:	3,504	Size range (sq ft/m):	193.7-296.0/18.0-27.5
Lifestyle:	Premium	Cabins (outside view):	45
Cruise line:........................	Paul Gauguin Cruises	Cabins (interior/no view):..........................	0
Former names:	*Le Levant*	Cabins (for one person):...........................	0
IMO number:	9159830	Cabins (with private balcony):.....................	0
Builder:	Leroux & Lotz (France)	Cabins (wheelchair accessible):	0
Original cost:...............................	$35 million	Wheelchair accessibility:.........................	None
Entered service:...................	Jan 1999/Dec 2012	Cabin voltage:	110 and 220 volts
Registry:..............................	Wallis and Fortuna	Elevators:..	1
Length (ft/m):..............................	328.0/100.0	Casino (gaming tables):...........................	No
Beam (ft/m):................................	45.9/14.0	Slot machines:...................................	No
Draft (ft/m):.................................	11.4/3.5	Swimming pools:..................................	1
Propulsion/Propellers:................	diesel (3,000 kW)/2	Hot tubs (on deck):...............................	0
Passenger decks:................................	5	Self-service launderette:.........................	No
Total crew:......................................	50	Dedicated cinema/seats:..........................	No
Passengers (lower beds/alll berths):	90/90	Library:	Yes
Passenger Space Ratio (lower beds/all berths):	38.9/38.9	Onboard currency:	US$
Crew/Passenger Ratio (lower beds/all berths):	1.8/1.8		

For yacht-chic, informal, very small-ship cruising

OVERVIEW. *Tere Moana* appeals to couples and singles who want contemporary and sophisticated facilities in a very relaxed but chic, yacht-like small ship, with good food and service. Each cruise has life-enrichment lecturers aboard, as well as tour leaders.

THE SHIP. This is a sleek vessel with mega-yacht looks and a pencil-slim design. It has two slim funnels that extend over the port and starboard sides to carry any soot away from the vessel.

A stern 'marina' platform is used for scuba diving, snorkeling, or swimming. Two landing craft are carried for shore visits, as well as six inflatable craft for landings in the islands.

Inside, the vessel has contemporary, clean, and uncluttered decor, and all the facilities of a private yacht. The public rooms are quietly elegant, with much use of wood trim and accenting. Particularly pleasing is the wood-paneled library. There is one grand salon, which accommodates all passengers, and is used by day as a lecture room, and by night as the main lounge/bar.

This ship spends summers in the Mediterranean and winters in the Caribbean and Central America.

This is all-inclusive cruising, with all port charges, gratuities, and shore excursions included in the fare. The crew is almost entirely French.

ACCOMMODATION. There are 45 ocean-view cabins, which the brochure incorrectly calls 'suites,'

Berlitz's Ratings

	Possible	Achieved
Ship	500	373
Accommodation	200	155
Food	400	269
Service	400	288
Entertainment	100	64
Cruise	400	290

OVERALL SCORE
1439 points out of 2000

all being located midships and forward, in five price categories – a lot for such a small ship. Each cabin has a large ocean-view window, inlaid wood furniture and accenting, designer fabrics, two beds that convert to a queen-size bed, a TV set and DVD player, refrigerator, safe, and toiletry kits in the marble-appointed bathrooms, all of which have a shower with a circular door – nicer than a shower curtain. There are no bathtubs.

DINING. The Lafayette Restaurant is a warm, cozy wood-paneled room with round and oval tables, but no tables for two. The informal Panoramique Restaurant has a great view overlooking the stern, with both indoor and outdoor seating. Dining is in open seating. Free wines accompany lunch and dinner. The cuisine is, naturally, classic French.

ENTERTAINMENT. The Grand Salon accommodates all passengers. There are built-in video screens for showing movies, and the room has a small dance floor in its center.

SPA/FITNESS. There is a small fitness room, a steam room (there is no sauna), and a shower.

Thomson Celebration
★★★

Size:.	Mid-size Ship	Cabins (total):.	627
Tonnage:.	33,930	Size range (sq ft/m):.	150.6–296.0/14.0–27.5
Lifestyle:.	Standard	Cabins (outside view):.	413
Cruise line:.	Thomson Cruises	Cabins (interior/no view):.	194
Former names:.	*Noordam*	Cabins (for one person):.	0
IMO number:.	8027298	Cabins (with private balcony):.	0
Builder:.	Chantiers de l'Atlantique (France)	Cabins (wheelchair accessible):.	4
Original cost:.	$160 million	Wheelchair accessibility:.	Fair
Entered service:.	Apr 1984/May 2005	Cabin voltage:.	110 and 220 volts
Registry:.	Dutch Antilles	Elevators:.	7
Length (ft/m):.	704.2/214.6	Casino (gaming tables):.	Yes
Beam (ft/m):.	89.4/27.2	Slot machines:.	Yes
Draft (ft/m):.	24.2/7.4	Swimming pools:.	2
Propulsion/Propellers:.	diesel (21,600kW)/2	Hot tubs (on deck):.	1
Passenger decks:.	10	Self-service launderette:.	Yes
Total crew:.	520	Dedicated cinema/seats:.	Yes
Passengers (lower beds/alll berths):.	1,254/1,350	Library:.	Yes
Passenger Space Ratio (lower beds/all berths):.	27.0/25.1	Onboard currency:.	UK£
Crew/Passenger Ratio (lower beds/all berths):.	2.4/2.6		

A family-friendly ship for a low-budget first cruise

OVERVIEW. This ship suits adult couples and singles taking their first or second cruise, seeking a modern but not glitzy ship, a middle-of-the-road lifestyle, and food and entertainment that's not fancy.

THE SHIP. *Thomson Celebration* has a nicely raked bow and a contemporary transom stern, but overall the ship's angular superstructure makes it look squat. There is a good amount of open deck space, and the traditional teakwood decks outdoors include a wraparound promenade deck. The ship, however, is quite dated and occasionally suffers from vibration.

Horizon's observation lounge, atop the ship, is a pleasant retreat. The main lounge, which has a small balcony level, is reminiscent of those found on former ocean liners, and is more suited to cabaret entertainment, not full production shows.

ACCOMMODATION. There is one suite grade, four grades of outside-view cabins (one designated Deluxe), and two grades of interior cabins. Four cabins with great forward-facing views are for the disabled. You can pre-book your preferred cabin for an extra per-cabin fee.

The top three categories of cabins – which are only marginally larger and shouldn't really be called suites – have bathtubs while all others have shower enclosures only. Several cabins have king- or queen-size beds, although most have twin beds, some but not all of which can be pushed together.

Berlitz's Ratings

	Possible	Achieved
Ship	500	305
Accommodation	200	126
Food	400	228
Service	400	251
Entertainment	100	61
Cruise	400	246
OVERALL SCORE		
1217 points out of 2000		

DINING. The Meridian Restaurant is reasonably large with warm decor. Meals are served in an open-seating arrangement. Although there are a few tables for two, most are for four, six, or eight. Dinners typically include a choice of four entrées and a daily vegetarian entrée.

Other dining options. A small à la carte restaurant, called Zilli's after celebrity chef Aldo Zilli, is a specialty dining spot; reservations are required and there's a per-person cover charge. .The Lido Restaurant, is active 24 hours a day in an open-seating arrangement. Each week a themed buffet may be offered. However, self-serve buffets are quite repetitive.

ENTERTAINMENT. The two-deck-high 600-seat Broadway Showlounge, with a main and balcony level, is the main venue for production shows and cabaret entertainment. The many pillars in the showlounge obstruct sight lines from some seats. A second entertainment venue, Hemingway's, is a multi-functional room for quizzes, dancing, and for use as a late-night discotheque.

SPA/FITNESS. Oceans Health Club is atop the ship at the aft end. It has good ocean views, and overlooks the aft pool. Facilities include an exercise room, a decent size gym with treadmills, exercycles, and other equipment, sauna but no steam room, and four body treatment rooms. A salon is located in a different area from the health and fitness facilities.

Thomson Dream
★★★

Size:..................................... Mid-size Ship	Cabins (total):.................................753
Tonnage: 53,872	Size range (sq ft/m): 129.1–425.1/12.0–39.5
Lifestyle: ....Standard	Cabins (outside view):...........................501
Cruise line:............................. Thomson Cruises	Cabins (interior/no view):........................252
Former names: ....Costa Europa, Westerdam, Homeric	Cabins (for one person):..........................18
IMO number: 7927984	Cabins (with private balcony):.....................6
Builder: .... Meyer Werft (Germany)	Cabins (with private balcony):.....................6
Original cost:...............................$150 million	Cabins (wheelchair accessible): 4
Entered service:.....................May 1986/Dec 2010	Wheelchair accessibility:.........................Fair
Registry:... Italy	Cabin voltage: ....110 and 220 volts
Length (ft/m):............................. 797.9/243.2	Elevators:..7
Beam (ft/m):................................. 95.1/29.0	Casino (gaming tables):.........................Yes
Draft (ft/m): 23.6/7.2	Slot machines:..................................Yes
Propulsion/Propellers:................. diesel (23,830kW)/2	Swimming pools:..................................2
Passenger decks:....................................9	Hot tubs (on deck):................................2
Total crew:.......................................650	Self-service launderette:.........................Yes
Passengers (lower beds/alll berths):............. 1,506/1,756	Dedicated cinema/seats:.........................Yes
Passenger Space Ratio (lower beds/all berths): 35.7/30.6	Library:..Yes
Crew/Passenger Ratio (lower beds/all berths):......... 2.4/2.7	Onboard currency: ....UK£

A dated mid-size ship for frugal, family-friendly cruises

OVERVIEW. *Thomson Dream* suits couples and singles taking their first or second cruise, and families with children of all ages.

THE SHIP. The ship has good teak outside decks and a walk-around promenade deck, plus a decent amount of deck space for sunbathing. There is also a swimming pool deck, although it is small. Passenger niggles include irritating, repetitious announcements, expensive shore excursions, and noticeable vibration in some areas.

ACCOMMODATION. There are several cabin price grades, including suites, mini-suites, outside-view cabins, and inside cabins, priced according to grade, size, and location. You can pre-book your preference for a per cabin fee of £39 (around US$60). Except for five suite category cabins, each with king-size beds, separate lounge area, and bathroom with full size tub, almost all other cabins are of a similar size.Facilities include ample closet, drawer and storage space, hairdryer, and good-size bathrooms, but the towels are small. Soundproofing is rather poor. All cabin TV sets receive European news channels. Most cabins have twin beds, but some have upper and lower berths.

DINING. The Orion Restaurant is a traditional dining room with a raised central, cupola-style dome, and port and starboard side portholes are highlighted at night. Open-seating dining is the norm. The tables

Berlitz's Ratings

	Possible	Achieved
Ship	500	315
Accommodation	200	124
Food	400	232
Service	400	248
Entertainment	100	61
Cruise	400	245

OVERALL SCORE
1225 points out of 2000

are close together, and, except for the center section, the ceiling is just one deck high, so the noise level can be loud. The cuisine is British-Continental but, although there's plenty of food, its quality and presentation are disappointing.

Other dining options. The Grill is an extra-cost steak and seafood (including surf 'n' turf) restaurant, with food cooked to order. Reservations are required. The 24-hour Andromeda Restaurant and a smaller Sirens Restaurant provide meals in a buffet style, but can be noisy. Twice during each cruise, there's a theme night. The Terrace Grill, open for lunch, serves fast-food such as BBQ items, pizzas, and salads.

ENTERTAINMENT. Facilities include the Atlante Theater, the ship's two-deck-high showlounge, with seating on both main and balcony levels. Pillars obstruct sight lines from some seats. A resident troupe of singers and dancers presents colorful, high-energy production shows. For nights when there's no production show, the show lounge presents cabaret acts.

SPA/FITNESS. The Nereidi Fitness Center, on an upper deck aft of the mast, includes a gymnasium, saunas, and massage rooms, but there is no steam room. The facility is really small, given the number of passengers carried – although, to be fair, such facilities weren't very popular when the ship was built.

Thomson Majesty
★★★ +

Size:.	Mid-size Ship	Crew/Passenger Ratio (lower beds/all berths):	2.0/2.5
Tonnage:	40,876	Cabins (total):	731
Lifestyle:	Standard	Size range (sq ft/m):	118.4–374.5/11.0–34.8
Cruise line:	Thomson Cruises	Cabins (outside view):	481
Former names: Louis Majesty, Norwegian Majesty, Royal Majesty,		Cabins (interior/no view):	249
	Birka Queen	Cabins (for one person):	0
IMO number:	8814744	Cabins (with private balcony):	0
Builder:	Kvaerner Masa-Yards STX (Finland)	Cabins (wheelchair accessible):	7
Original cost:	$229 million	Wheelchair accessibility:	Fair
Entered service:	Sep 1992/May 2012	Cabin voltage:	110 and 220 volts
Registry:	Malta	Elevators:	6
Length (ft/m):	90.5/27.6	Casino (gaming tables):	Yes
Beam (ft/m):	91.8/28.0	Slot machines:	Yes
Draft (ft/m):	20.3/6.2	Swimming pools:	2
Propulsion/Propellers:	diesel (21,120kW)/2	Hot tubs (on deck):	3
Passenger decks:	9	Self-service launderette:	No
Total crew:	620	Dedicated cinema/seats:	No
Passengers (lower beds/alll berths):	1,462/1,792	Library:	Yes
Passenger Space Ratio (lower beds/all berths):	27.9/22.8	Onboard currency:	UK£

A modestly stylish ship for casual, friendly cruising

OVERVIEW. This family-friendly ship provides good value for money. It absorbs passengers well and provides a very comfortable cruise experience in warm, crisp surroundings, with good food and decent hospitality from a really friendly crew.

THE SHIP. Smart and modestly stylish, *Thomson Majesty* is generally a well-designed vessel, ideally suited to Mediterranean cruising. Inside, it is quite pretty warm, with lots of wood paneling and chrome/copper accents, reasonably discreet lighting, soothing colors, and no glitz. Wide passageways and high ceilings in some areas help provide a feeling of inner spaciousness, and the ship has a touch of contemporary elegance. Gratuities are at your discretion.

ACCOMMODATION. There are several price grades. Almost all outside-view and interior cabins are on the small side, but quite comfortable. All have flat-screen TVs. The closets are really small, but luggage can be stored under the bed. The bathrooms are a little tight, although there's a generous amount of room in the shower enclosures.

Two large suites (901, 903) have a separate bedroom with walk-in closet and bathroom with combination tub and shower; there is a step of about nine inches (24cm). The lounge has a dining table, plus a sofa and chairs in the bay window. There are bay windows in both the lounge and bedroom, and separate TV sets/DVD players; a tea/coffee-making setup and

Berlitz's Ratings		
	Possible	Achieved
Ship	500	320
Accommodation	200	130
Food	400	237
Service	400	253
Entertainment	100	62
Cruise	400	256
OVERALL SCORE		
1258 points out of 2000		

late-afternoon snacks are provided. The Junior Suites (902–923) are smaller, but do have a curtain separating lounge and bedroom. Suite-grade bathrooms have a tub and shower combination. Room service food is available, at extra cost.

DINING. The main dining venues are: Seven Seas Restaurant, with 636 seats, and the Four Seasons Restaurant, with 266 seats. The food, menu, creativity, and service are sound, with generous portions. The restaurants have an open seating arrangement. The wine list is quite decent and reasonably priced.

Other dining options. The intimate 56-seat Le Bistro Restaurant serves Italian and Continental-style cuisine. No reservations are needed, but a cover charge applies.

Café Royale is a 24-hour indoor buffet venue with 112 seats. An outdoor grill, Piazza San Marco, serves fast food, while the Coffee Bar offers coffees and teas.

ENTERTAINMENT. The Jubilee Lounge has banquette and individual tub chairs. There are several small musical units, but shows and entertainment events are weak links.

SPA/FITNESS. The Sana Wellness Center contains a small gymnasium with muscle-toning equipment, an aerobics area, men's and women's saunas, a beauty salon, and seven massage/body treatment rooms including one for couples.

Thomson Spirit
★★★

Size:..................................... Mid-size Ship	Cabins (total):.....................................627
Tonnage: 33,930	Size range (sq ft/m): 150.6–296.0/14.0–27.5
Lifestyle: ....Standard	Cabins (outside view):.............................413
Cruise line:............................. Thomson Cruises	Cabins (interior/no view):..........................194
Former names: ... *Nieuw Amsterdam, Patriot, Nieuw Amsterdam*	Cabins (for one person):............................0
IMO number: 8024104	Cabins (with private balcony):.......................0
Builder: .... Chantiers de l'Atlantique (France)	Cabins (wheelchair accessible): 4
Original cost:.............................$150 million	Wheelchair accessibility:..........................Fair
Entered service:..................... Jul 1983/May 2002	Cabin voltage: ....110 and 220 volts
Registry:.................................. The Bahamas	Elevators:.......................................7
Length (ft/m):.......................... 704.2/214.66	Casino (gaming tables):...........................Yes
Beam (ft/m):.............................. 89.4/27.2	Slot machines:...................................Yes
Draft (ft/m):.............................. 24.6/7.5	Swimming pools:..................................2
Propulsion/Propellers:................. diesel (21,600kW)/2	Hot tubs (on deck):................................1
Passenger decks:..................................10	Self-service launderette:..........................Yes
Total crew:......................................520	Dedicated cinema/seats:.......................Yes/230
Passengers (lower beds/all berths):............. 1,254/1,350	Library: ....Yes
Passenger Space Ratio (lower beds/all berths): 27.0/25.1	Onboard currency: ....UK£
Crew/Passenger Ratio (lower beds/all berths):.......... 2.4/2.6	

A family-friendly ship with decent food and service

OVERVIEW. *Thompson Spirit* is best suited to adult couples and singles taking their first or second cruise, and families with children of all ages, all seeking a modern, non-glitzy ship with a decent array of public lounges and bars, and a middle-of-the-road lifestyle, with food and entertainment that is acceptable rather than fancy.

THE SHIP. *Thomson Spirit*, originally built for Holland America Line, has a nicely raked bow and a contemporary transom stern, but overall the ship's angular exterior superstructure design makes it look squat and quite boxy. The exterior has an all-white hull and superstructure. There's a good amount of open teakwood deck space, particularly at the aft section of the ship, and the traditional outdoors teakwood decks include a walk-around promenade deck. Unfortunately, the French-built ship has always suffered from poor build quality and excessive vibration, particularly at the stern.

Holland America Line sold the ship to the publicly funded United States Lines in 2000, but that company sank in a sea of debt the following year. Carnival Corporation, which owns Holland America Line, bought back the ship and chartered it to Louis Cruises, which in turn has sub-chartered it to Thomson Cruises. *Thomson Spirit* has a sister ship in the slightly newer, 1984-built *Thomson Celebration* (formerly Holland America Line's *Noordam*).

Thomson first operated cruises in the 1970s, but

Berlitz's Ratings		
	Possible	Achieved
Ship	500	306
Accommodation	200	127
Food	400	240
Service	400	249
Entertainment	100	62
Cruise	400	254
OVERALL SCORE		
1238 points out of 2000		

abandoned them, only to start cruises operations again in the mid-1990s using chartered, rather than wholly-owned ships. It has been a highly successful venture, offering extremely good value for money, particularly for adult couples, and occasionally families with children.

Thomson Spirit has quite a spacious interior design and layout, with little crowding and almost no points of congestion, and most public rooms are on a single deck. The color combinations do not jar the senses – most are pretty nondescript, though there are many splashes of color – and the decor was greatly changed and brightened by its new owners. There is much polished teakwood and rosewood paneling throughout the interiors. For quieter moments, try the Horizon Lounge, atop the ship; it has a wooden dance floor. The main lounge, with a small balcony level, is reminiscent of the ocean liners of yesteryear.

It's good to see a tour operator like Thomson Cruises charter and operate this vessel, especially since competition in the cruise industry is increasing. This ship is quite acceptable for passengers wanting pleasant surroundings and an all-British ambience. However, many newer ships have more space, better facilities, and more options, and that means this ship loses a few points in relation to the increased competition in the international marketplace. Perhaps the best part of cruising aboard *Thomson Spirit* lies in the destinations and not the ship – although it is perfectly comfortable.

Hotel add-ons can extend a cruise vacation, and Thomson has a fine collection, depending on your needs, budget, and whether you are traveling with children or grandchildren. Because the ship is exclusive to Thomson Cruises, your fellow passengers are likely to be British, with typically about 80 percent of them over 45.

Thomson owns its own airline, Thomson Airways, and has much experience in operating fly-cruises to the Mediterranean – the company offers airlift from almost a score of UK airports. With Thomson, you pay only for what you want. You can pre-book a window seat or a premium seat with more space than standard seats for an extra fee.

All Thomson Cruises' ships are non-smoking, although smoking areas are provided in most public rooms. Standing in line for embarkation, disembarkation, shore tenders, and for self-serve buffet meals is inevitable aboard all large ships.

FAMILIES. Children have their own play areas at the aft of Bridge Deck. There are several children's clubs: Tots is for three- to five-year-olds, Team is for six to eights, while Tribe is for nine to 12s. The clubs operate five days a week (not on embarkation or disembarkation days) and are supervised by qualified 'children's hosts.'

ACCOMMODATION. There is one suite grade, four grades of outside-view cabins (one designated Deluxe), and two grades of interior cabins. There are four large cabins, great forward-facing views, for the disabled. You can pre-book your preference for an extra per-cabin fee.

Most of the cabins are quite small – below the industry standard of 170 sq ft (16 sq m). They are reasonably well appointed and practically laid out. Some have wood furniture, fittings, or accenting, good counter and storage space but little drawer space, a large dressing mirror, and private bathrooms that are adequate, but no more. The top cabin categories – which are only marginally larger and should not really be called suites – have full-size bathtubs while all others have showers. Several cabins have king- or queen-size beds, although most have twin beds.

The largest accommodation is in the Presidential Suite. Small by comparison to suites aboard many other ships, it measures 464 sq ft (43 sq m) and is on Eagle Deck, the uppermost accommodation deck. There is a king-size bed, walk-in closet, wet bar, study and dining areas, TV set, video player, and stereo system. The bathroom includes a whirlpool tub, double sink unit, and a powder room.

A number of cabins also have additional berths for a third/fourth person. Room service is provided 24 hours a day. All cabin TVs carry live news channels, when available. The cabin insulation is extremely poor, and the bathroom towels are small.

DINING. The Compass Rose Restaurant is reasonably large and attractive, with warm decor and ample space. Breakfast, lunch, and dinner (6–10:30pm) are served in an open-seating arrangement, so you may get a different table and different waiters for each meal. Although there are a few tables for two, most are for four, six, or eight. Dinners typically include a choice of four entrées; a vegetarian entrée is also available daily. Children have their own menu, with 'home from home' dishes and small portions.

Other dining options. Dessert and pastry items will typically be of good quality, and made specifically for British tastes, although there is much use of canned fruits and jellies.

Sirocco's A La Carte Restaurant is the ship's specialty dining venue; reservations are required and there's a per-person cover charge. It seats only 45 and has superior food and service as well as a more refined, quieter atmosphere. It is adjacent to the Compass Rose Restaurant, but is best entered from the aft stairway.

Instead of the more formal dining room, there is a more casual Lido Restaurant. This is open 24 hours a day, with open seating. Tables are set with crisp linens, flatware, and stemware for dinner, when the set menu includes a choice of four entrées. Each week a themed buffet – Chinese, Indian, or Mexican, depending on the cruise itinerary – may be offered for dinner. On Lido Deck, the outdoor Terrace Grill provides fast-food grilled items and pizza during the day.

ENTERTAINMENT. The 600-seat Broadway Show-lounge is two decks high (main and balcony levels) and is the principal venue for production shows and cabaret entertainment. Although Thomson is not generally known for high-quality shows, they are, in fact, good fun, and are professionally produced, while cabaret acts provide entertainment on evenings when there is no production show.

A second entertainment venue, High Spirits, is a multi-functional room for quizzes, dancing, and late-night discotheque. A number of bands and musical units provide live music for dancing and listening in several lounges and bars.

SPA/FITNESS. Oceans Health Club is atop the ship at the aft end. It has good ocean views, and overlooks the aft pool and hot tub, on Bridge Deck. Facilities include an aerobics exercise room, a decent size gymnasium with plenty of treadmills, exercycles, and other body-toning and muscle-pumping equipment, a sauna but no steam room, and several treatment rooms.

You can have massages, aromatherapy facials, body wraps, manicures, pedicures, and hair beautifying treatments. The beauty salon is located close to the Reception Desk on the port side, in a completely different area from the health and fitness facilities.

Ushuaia
★★

Size:.	Boutique Ship	Cabins (total):.	41
Tonnage:.	2,063	Size range (sq ft/m):.	n/a
Lifestyle:.	Standard	Cabins (outside view):.	41
Cruise line:.	Antarpply Expeditions	Cabins (interior/no view):.	0
Former names:.	Researcher, Malcolm Baldridge	Cabins (for one person):.	0
IMO number:.	6901907	Cabins (with private balcony):.	0
Builder:.	n/a	Cabins (wheelchair accessible):.	0
Original cost:.	n/a	Wheelchair accessibility:.	none
Entered service:.	1970/2005	Cabin voltage:.	110 volts
Registry:.	Panama	Elevators:.	0
Length (ft/m):.	278.3/84.7	Casino (gaming tables):.	No
Beam (ft/m):.	51.9/15.5	Slot machines:.	No
Draft (ft/m):.	18.0/5.4	Swimming pools:.	0
Propulsion/Propellers:.	diesel (3,200kW)/2	Hot tubs (on deck):.	0
Passenger decks:.	5	Self-service launderette:.	0
Total crew:.	38	Dedicated cinema/seats:.	0
Passengers (lower beds/alll berths):.	82/84	Library:.	Yes
Passenger Space Ratio (lower beds/all berths):.	36.1/35.2	Onboard currency:.	US$
Crew/Passenger Ratio (lower beds/all berths):.	2.1/2.2		

A tiny ultra-casual ship for voyages in the Antarctic

OVERVIEW. This is for hardy travelers looking for a cheap way to visit Antarctica aboard a ship with a pleasing profile. Its facilities are basic, though it's probably good for students.

THE SHIP. *Ushuaia* was originally built for the United States agency NOAA (National Oceanographic and Atmospheric Administration) as a research ship, and has an ice-strengthened hull. Refitted and re-furbished for use as a specialized passenger vessel, it now has a deep-blue hull and a white superstructure topped by a red funnel. An open-bridge policy prevails. *Ushuaia* ran aground in 2008 in Gerlache Strait, Antarctica, and participants and crew had to be evacuated by Chilean navy ship *Ap-41 Aquiles*.

The dedicated Lecture Room is where all the learning happens. The library has plenty of reference books, as well as a variety of board games and playing cards. There's also a small gift shop, which stocks appropriate clothing. There is also a changing room (mud room – for boot washing). Smoking is permitted on all open decks, but not inside the ship.

Antarpply Expedition staff (who are dedicated to conservation) and guest lecturers are on board for every voyage. Participants should bring their own outer weather gear, including parka, but rubber boots are provided. There's no Internet access, and gratuities are extra, at a suggested rate of $15 per person, per day. Government arrival and departure taxes are not included.

Berlitz's Ratings

	Possible	Achieved
Ship	500	195
Accommodation	200	92
Food	400	189
Service	400	210
Entertainment	100	44
Cruise	400	200
OVERALL SCORE		
930 points out of 2000		

There have been past problems with things like air conditioning, water desalinization equipment, and other operational malfunctions. This is a cheaply run ship operation, with Argentinian crew, that really needs a little more finessing – although it's better than it was in the beginning. It shouldn't be confused with real expedition ship operators.

ACCOMMODATION. There are four cabin price grades. On the two lowest decks, the cabins have shared bathroom facilities, while those on the uppermost accommodation deck have private facilities (eight cabins have no porthole). In general, the cabins are really basic, although each has a washbasin. They don't have personal safes, although the Hotel Manager will be able to store any valuables for you.

DINING. The Dining Room sits along the starboard side, and accommodates all participants in one seating. Breakfast is a self-serve buffet affair, while lunch may be self-serve, or served; dinner, a three-course meal, is always served. Local specialties are featured. Coffee and tea are available round-the-clock.

ENTERTAINMENT. It's all about recaps, and planning for the next day's shore adventures and sightings.

SPA/FITNESS. Nothing, nada, except fresh air.

Veendam
★★★ +

Size:..............................Mid-size Ship	Cabins (total):....................................674
Tonnage:..................................57,092	Size range (sq ft/m):..............186.2–1,124.8/17.3–104.5
Lifestyle:..................................Premium	Cabins (outside view):............................534
Cruise line:......................Holland America Line	Cabins (interior/no view):.........................140
Former names:.................................none	Cabins (for one person):.............................0
IMO number:..............................9102992	Cabins (with private balcony):.....................182
Builder:..........................Fincantieri (Italy)	Cabins (wheelchair accessible):......................8
Original cost:...........................$215 million	Wheelchair accessibility:...........................Fair
Entered service:...........................May 1996	Cabin voltage:........................110 and 220 volts
Registry:...............................The Bahamas	Elevators:...8
Length (ft/m):.........................719.3/219.3	Casino (gaming tables):............................Yes
Beam (ft/m):............................101.0/30.8	Slot machines:.....................................Yes
Draft (ft/m):..............................24.6/7.5	Swimming pools:................2 (1 w/sliding glass dome)
Propulsion/Propellers:..........diesel-electric (34,560kW)/2	Hot tubs (on deck):.................................2
Passenger decks:...................................10	Self-service launderette:..........................Yes
Total crew:......................................561	Dedicated cinema/seats:...........................Yes
Passengers (lower beds/alll berths):...........1,348/1,719	Library:...Yes
Passenger Space Ratio (lower beds/all berths):.......42.4/33.2	Onboard currency:.................................US$
Crew/Passenger Ratio (lower beds/all berths):.........2.2/2.9	

Dutch heritage and decor for mature-age cruisers

OVERVIEW. This ship is fairly well-built, with decent interior fit and finish quality. Holland America Line is constantly fine-tuning its performance, and its regular passengers, almost all North American, find its ships very comfortable and well-run. The company continues its strong maritime traditions, although the present food and service components still let down the rest of the cruise experience.

Berlitz's Ratings		
	Possible	Achieved
Ship	500	351
Accommodation	200	142
Food	400	251
Service	400	282
Entertainment	100	68
Cruise	400	265
OVERALL SCORE		
1359 points out of 2000		

THE SHIP. *Veendam* is one of four almost identical ships, the others being *Maasdam*, *Statendam*, and *Ryndam*. The exterior styling is rather angular (some would say boxy – the funnel certainly is), although it is softened and balanced somewhat by the hull being painted black. A ducktail sponson stern was added in 2009 for better stability and ride characteristics. There is a full walk-around teakwood promenade deck outdoors – excellent for strolling, and there's no sign of synthetic turf anywhere. The sunloungers one the exterior promenade deck are wood, with comfortable cushioned pads, while those at the swimming pool on Lido Deck are white plastic.

In the interiors of this S-class ship, an asymmetrical layout helps to reduce bottlenecks and congestion. Most public rooms are concentrated on two decks, Promenade Deck, and Upper Promenade Deck, which creates a spacious feel to the interiors. In general, there's a restrained approach to interior styling, using a mixture of contemporary materials combined with traditional woods and ceramics. There's little glitz anywhere.

A $2 million artwork collection was assembled and displayed to represent Holland America Line's fine Dutch heritage; it presents a balance between standard itineraries and onboard creature comforts. Also noticeable are the live flower arrangements, used to good effect to brighten up the otherwise dull decor.

Atop the ship is the Crow's Nest Lounge. By day it is an observation lounge, with large ocean-view windows; in the evening it is a nightclub with extremely variable lighting.

A three-deck high atrium foyer is quite appealing, although its sculpted centerpiece makes it look a little crowded, and leaves little room in front of the reception office. A hydraulic glass roof covers the reasonably sized swimming pool/whirlpools and central Lido area so that it can be used in good or bad weather. The focal point here is a large dolphin sculpture.

There is a large, relaxing reference library. The company keeps its ships clean and tidy, and there is good passenger flow throughout. As part of its Signature of Excellence program, the ships have received a new 'Mix' lifestyle area. This is a trendy, upbeat space combining three specialty theme bars in one central area: Champagne (serving Champagne and sparkling wines), Martinis (in individual shakers), and Spirits & Ales (a sports bar with beer and baseball/basketball). Microsoft Surface touch-screen technology is available for playing checkers and chess, air hockey, and other sports games.

A casino features gaming tables and slot machines. However, note that part of the Casino is open, and can be full of cigarette smoke (yes, smoking is still permitted here), so passers-by should hold their breath.

The service staff is Indonesian; although they are mostly quite charming, communication often proves frustrating, and service can be spotty and inconsistent.

An escalator travels between two of the lower decks, one of which was originally planned to be the embarkation point, but it is almost pointless. The charge to use the washing machines and dryers in the self-service launderette is petty, particularly for suite occupants who pay high prices for their cruises. The men's urinals in public restrooms are unusually high.

ACCOMMODATION. The accommodation ranges from small interior cabins to a large penthouse suite, in 17 price categories. All cabin TV sets normally carry CNN.

The interior and outside-view standard cabins have twin beds that convert to a queen-size bed, and there is a separate living space with sofa and coffee table. Although the drawer space is generally good, the closet space is very tight, particularly for long cruises – although more than adequate for seven nights. The tiled bathrooms are compact but practical. Bathrobes, hairdryers and a small range of toiletries are provided for all suites/cabins. The bathrooms are quite well laid out, but the tubs are small units better described as shower tubs. Some cabins have interconnecting doors.

On Navigation Deck, 28 suites have accommodation for up to four and offer in-suite dining as an alternative to the dining room, for private meals. They are very spacious, tastefully decorated, and well laid-out, with a separate living room, bedroom with two lower beds that convert to a king-size bed, a good-size living area, dressing room, plenty of closet and drawer space, and marble bathroom with a Jacuzzi tub.

The largest accommodation is the single penthouse suite, located on the starboard side of Navigation Deck at the forward staircase. It has a king-size bed and vanity desk; large walk-in closet with superb drawer space; TV and video player; an oversize whirlpool bath that could seat four and separate shower enclosure, separate washroom with toilet, bidet, and washbasin; a living room with writing desk, large TV, and full set of audio equipment; dressing room, large private balcony with teak lounge chairs and drinks tables, dining table, and four chairs; a pantry with large refrigerator, toaster unit, full coffee/tea-making facilities, and food preparation area and a separate entrance from the hallway; a mini-bar/refrigerator, and a guest toilet and floor-to-ceiling windows.

DINING. The Rotterdam Dining Room spans two decks at the stern of the ship, and has two grand staircases to connect the two levels, panoramic views on three sides, and a music balcony. Both open-seating and assigned-table seating are available, while breakfast and lunch are open-seating, though you'll be seated by restaurant staff when you enter. There are tables for two, four, six, or eight, and Rosenthal china and good-quality cutlery are provided. The waiter stations are very noisy for anyone seated near them.

Other dining options. The intimate Pinnacle Grill is located just forward of the balcony level of the main dining room on the starboard side. The 66-seat dining spot has Pacific Northwest cuisine such as fresh Alaskan salmon and halibut, and other regional specialties, plus a selection of premium steaks such as filet mignon from Black Angus beef. Reservations are needed, and a service charge applies. A Bulgari show plate, Rosenthal china, Reidel wine glasses, and Frette table linen are used. The Pinnacle Grill is a better dining experience than the main dining room and worth it for that special celebration.

For more casual evening eating, the dual-line, self-serve Lido Buffet is open for casual dinners on all except the last night of each cruise, in an open-seating arrangement. Tables are set with crisp linens, flatware, and stemware. A set menu is featured, and this includes a choice of four entreés. It is also the place for casual breakfasts and lunches. At night, a section is transformed into Canaletto for casual Italian meals. It is open 5:30–9pm, and reservations are requested.

There is much use of canned fruits and packeted items, although there are several commercial low-calorie salad dressings. The choice of cheeses and crackers is poor.

Passengers will need to eat in the Lido Buffet on days when the dining room is closed for lunch – typically once or twice per cruise, depending on the itinerary. In addition, a poolside grill provides basic American hamburgers and hot dogs.

ENTERTAINMENT. The Showroom at Sea, at the forward part of the ship, spans two decks, with banquette seating on both main and upper levels. It is basically a well-designed room, but the ceiling is low and sight lines from the balcony level are quite poor.

SPA/FITNESS. The Ocean Spa is one deck below the navigation bridge at the very forward part of the ship. It includes a gymnasium with all the latest muscle-pumping exercise machines, including an abundance of treadmills. It has ocean views, an aerobics exercise area, a large beauty salon with ocean-view windows to the port side, several treatment rooms, a sauna, steam room, and changing areas.

Ventura
★★★★

Size:....................................Large Resort Ship		Cabins (total):.......................................1,546		
Tonnage: 116,017		Size range (sq ft/m): 134.5–534.0/12.5–49.6		
Lifestyle: ....Standard		Cabins (outside view):................................1,101		
Cruise line:................................P&O Cruises		Cabins (interior/no view):..............................445		
Former names: ....none		Cabins (for one person):................................18		
IMO number: 9333175		Cabins (with private balcony):.........................880		
Builder: ....Fincantieri (Italy)		Cabins (wheelchair accessible): 25		
Original cost: ....€535 million		Wheelchair accessibility:............................Good		
Entered service:...............................Apr 2008		Cabin voltage: ....220 volts		
Registry:...................................... Bermuda		Elevators:..12		
Length (ft/m):.............................951.4/290.0		Casino (gaming tables):...............................Yes		
Beam (ft/m):..............................118.1/36.0		Slot machines:......................................Yes		
Draft (ft/m): 27.8/8.5		Swimming pools:.....................................3		
Propulsion/Propellers:...........diesel-electric (42,000kW)/2		Hot tubs (on deck):....................................6		
Passenger decks:...................................15		Self-service launderette:.............................Yes		
Total crew:......................................1,239		Dedicated cinema/seats:..............................No		
Passengers (lower beds/all berths):.............3,110/3,592		Library: ....Yes		
Passenger Space Ratio (lower beds/all berths): 37.3/32.2		Onboard currency: ....UK£		
Crew/Passenger Ratio (lower beds/all berths):.........2.4/2.8				

Family-friendly, large-ship cruising to suit British family tastes

OVERVIEW. *Ventura* is mainly for British families with children as well as adult couples who are looking for a big-ship environment with comfortable but unstuffy surroundings and lots of options.

THE SHIP. *Ventura* is the P&O version of Princess Cruises' Grand-class ships, and, along with sister ship *Azura*, is the largest cruise ship yet built specifically for UK passengers. There are promenade walking decks to port and starboard sides, underneath the lifeboats. You can't walk completely around, however; it's narrow in some places, and you have to weave past a number of deck lounge chairs. There are three pools: two on the pool deck, one of which can be covered by a glass-roofed skydome, and one at the stern.

Inside, a three-deck atrium is the focal point. Designed on a gateway theme, central to which are four towering black granite archways sourced from India, it's the place to see and be seen, and the best location to arrange to meet friends. The upper-deck public room layout is challenging because you can't go from one end of the ship to the other without first going down, along and up – not good for anyone with mobility problems.

Public rooms include a perfume shop, library, an overly large Cruise Sales Centre, Fortunes Casino, and several bars, including The Exchange (an urban warehouse bar), and Metropolis (set high atop the ship with great aft views and views along the ship's sides – over everyone's balcony), a Cuban bar, and a Spanish ta-

Berlitz's Ratings

	Possible	Achieved
Ship	500	401
Accommodation	200	155
Food	400	249
Service	400	287
Entertainment	100	77
Cruise	400	295
OVERALL SCORE		
1464 points out of 2000		

pas bar. Check out the train that runs around the upper part of the upper bar of The Exchange.

Passenger niggles include the constant push for on-board revenue, low passenger space ratio, mediocre self-service buffet food, and a charge for shuttle buses in many ports.

Smoking is permitted on cabin balconies and in designated spots on the open decks. Gratuities are automatically charged to your onboard account.

FAMILIES. Children will be pleased to find that, for two- to four-year-olds, Noddy is on board. There are children's clubs for the under-twos up to 17 years, plus a rock 'n' roll school. Youngsters can also enjoy Scalextric at sea with Grand Prix-style track, 3D cinema, and interactive art classes. Family shore programs feature aqua and 'theme parks.' There's a useful Night Nursery for the under-fives. It's possible to get married on board, with the captain officiating.

ACCOMMODATION. There are many different accommodation price grades, according to size and location chosen, but really just six types of accommodation: suite with balcony; family suite with balcony; outside-view twin/queen with balcony; outside-view twin/queen; interior no-view cabin. More than one-third of all cabins are of the interior variety. Some have extra third/fourth berths that fold down from the ceiling. While the suites are quite spacious, they are quite small when compared to suites aboard some other cruise lines, such as Celebrity Cruises or Holland America Line, for example. In 2013, a total of 18 single-occupancy cabins were added (12 outside and six interior), in line with those aboard Azura – so, this is good news for solo cruisers.

Standard in all cabins: bed runners, 10.5 tog duvets, Slumberland eight-inch sprung mattresses, and Egyptian cotton towels. Tea/coffee-making facilities (plastic and basic), and packets of UHT milk, not fresh milk, are provided. The tea-making setup is adequate, but getting fresh milk can sometimes be a problem. Bathrobes are available only for passengers occupying grades A, B and D accommodation. There are UK three-pin sockets plus US-style 110-volt sockets for electrical devices.

Cabins have open closets (no doors = no money wasted), which actually provide easy access. Balcony cabins have teak patio furniture, and an outside light. Decent-quality personal toiletries are by Temple Spa.

Wheelchair-accessible cabins have a shower enclosure, except one (R415) that has a bathtub with integral shower. They are mostly in the front section, and the Bay Tree restaurant is aft – so be prepared for lots of waiting time at elevators. Wheelchair users should note that breakfast in the three main restaurants typically ends at 9:30am on sea days (9am on port days). To take breakfast in the self-serve Waterside casual eatery, wheelchair users need to wheel across the decks containing the Beachcomber and Laguna pools and lots of deck chairs – not easy. Alternatively, they can order room service breakfast – typically cold items only. There is no room service breakfast on disembarkation day.

DINING. P&O's marketing blurb claims there are 10 restaurants. There really aren't. There are five genuine restaurants (Bay Tree, Cinnamon, Saffron, The White Room, and East); the rest are eateries.

The three principal dining rooms, Bay Tree, Cinnamon, and Saffron, have standard à la carte menus. The Bay Tree offers fixed seating dining, with assigned tables and typical seating times of 6:30pm or 8:30pm. In the other two, you can dine when you want, with whom you want, between 6pm and 10pm – P&O calls it Freedom Dining – although at peak times there can be long waiting times for a table.

Once or twice per cruise, additional special dinners are served in the main dining rooms, one being a Chaîne des Rôtisseurs event. The ship's wine list is ho-hum average.

Other dining options. Specialty dining venues include the White Room, located high up on the ship above the children's play area, with a quarter of the tables on deck. It serves modern European dishes by celebrity chef Marco Pierre White in an environment that is intimate and attentive but not stuffy and is particularly suitable for families. Reservations are needed, and there's a cover charge. The food is good because it's cooked to order, unlike in the main dining rooms. Occasionally, Marco Pierre White will sail aboard the ship, and hold cooking classes for up to eight participants in one of the ship's galleys; the extra cost is high, but worth it, and includes a tasting of the finished product.

For complete privacy, private balcony dining, with selections from the Marco Pierre White menu, is also available as a rather pricey (but perhaps worthwhile) extra-cost option.

The Waterside is a large, self-serve buffet 'seaside chic' dining spot, with indoor-outdoor seating, but the seating is rather poorly designed and cramped, and the food selection is poor (better for lunch than for breakfast or dinner).

On the same deck, adjacent to the forward pool, are Frankie's Grill and Frankie's Pizzeria.

Tazzine, a coffee lounge by day, turns into a cocktail bar in the evening.

The Beach House is a casual dining spot for families, open 24 hours. Marco's roof-side café serves gourmet pizzas, grills, and original ice cream flavors such as chocolate truffle and prune and Armagnac. Children's cutlery, bibs, and beakers are available.

Ramblas is a tapas and wine bar (some items at extra cost). East, an Asian fusion eatery on the main indoor promenade. In addition, 24-hour room service is available in cabins.

ENTERTAINMENT. P&O claims the 785-seat Arena Theatre, at the front of the ship and spanning two decks, is the largest showlounge aboard a UK-based cruise ship, but in fact the showlounge aboard *Queen Mary 2* is larger, with 1,094 seats, as is the Showlounge aboard *Independence of the Seas*. Havana, the main nightclub and entertainment venue, where movies are sometimes shown, is an activities room by day and a sultry Cuba-inspired club by night, but sight lines are extremely poor from many seats.

A video wall in the Cosmopolitan club lounge screens real-time footage of the world's seven most famous city skylines – Sydney, Paris, New York, Rio de Janeiro, Las Vegas, Hong Kong, and London. It's neat.

SPA/FITNESS. The Oasis Spa is located forward, almost atop the ship. It includes a gymnasium, aerobics room, beauty salon, separate male and female sauna and steam rooms, and 11 treatment rooms. An internal stairway connects to the deck below, which contains an extra-charge Thermal Suite. Harding Brothers provide the spa staff and services. Treatments include special packages for couples, and the SilverSpa Generation, as well as a whole range of individual treatments. Active types can take instruction in Cirque Ventura's activities, including juggling, acro-balancing, tight-wire walking, stilt walking, and clowning.

Vision of the Seas
★★★+

Size:.	.Large Resort Ship	Cabins (total):.	1,000
Tonnage:	78,491	Size range (sq ft/m):	135.0–1,270.1/12.5–118.0
Lifestyle:	Standard	Cabins (outside view):	593
Cruise line:.	Royal Caribbean International	Cabins (interior/no view):.	407
Former names:	none	Cabins (for one person):.	0
IMO number:	9116876	Cabins (with private balcony):	229
Builder:	Chantiers de l'Atlantique (France)	Cabins (wheelchair accessible):	14
Original cost:	$275 million	Wheelchair accessibility:	Good
Entered service:.	May 1998	Cabin voltage:	110 and 220 volts
Registry:.	The Bahamas	Elevators:	9
Length (ft/m):	915.3/279.0	Casino (gaming tables):	Yes
Beam (ft/m):	105.6/32.2	Slot machines:	Yes
Draft (ft/m):	24.9/7.6	Swimming pools:	2
Propulsion/Propellers:	diesel-electric (50,400kW)2	Hot tubs (on deck):	6
Passenger decks:.	11	Self-service launderette:	No
Total crew:	765	Dedicated cinema/seats:	No
Passengers (lower beds/alll berths):	2,000/2,435	Library:	Yes
Passenger Space Ratio (lower beds/all berths):	39.2/32.2	Onboard currency:	US$
Crew/Passenger Ratio (lower beds/all berths):	3.0/3.6		

Pleasant decor for casual, family-friendly cruising

OVERVIEW. *Vision of the Seas* represents Royal Caribbean International's interpretation of a floating contemporary hotel.

THE SHIP. *Vision of the Seas* shares tge design features that make all Royal Caribbean International ships identifiable. The ship's stern is beautifully rounded. There's a reasonable amount of open-air walking space, although this can become cluttered with sunloungers that would benefit from having cushioned pads.

ACCOMMODATION. The standard cabins are of an adequate size, and have just enough functional facilities to make them comfortable. Twin lower beds convert to queen-size beds, and there is a reasonable amount of closet and drawer space, but there is little room between the bed and desk. The bathrooms are small but functional, and the shower units are small. There is no cabinet for toiletries.

Choose a C-grade suite for spacious accommodation that includes a curtained-off sleeping area, a good-size outside balcony with part-partition, lounge with sofa, two chairs and coffee table, three closets, plenty of drawer and storage space, TV set and video player. The bathroom is large and has a full-size tub, integral shower, and two washbasins/two toiletries cabinets.

DINING. The Aquarius Dining Room is set on two levels with large ocean-view picture windows on two

Berlitz's Ratings

	Possible	Achieved
Ship	500	382
Accommodation	200	141
Food	400	238
Service	400	262
Entertainment	100	74
Cruise	400	270
OVERALL SCORE		
1367 points out of 2000		

sides and a large connecting stairway. The Windjammer Café is the casual dining spot for self-serve buffets. The food is basic fare and disappointing and the four-sided self-service buffet area is small. The evening buffets typically feature a different theme, something this company has been doing for more than 25 years – perhaps the time has come for more creativity.

The company has introduced a drinks package, available at all bars in the form of cards or stickers that enable you to pre-pay for a selection of standard soft drinks and alcoholic drinks. The packages are not easy to understand.

ENTERTAINMENT. The Masquerade Theatre, the ship's principal showlounge, is located in the forward section of the ship and presents production shows and other major cabaret shows. It is a large, but a well-designed room with main and balcony levels, and good sight lines from most of the banquette seats.

SPA/FITNESS. The spa, with its solarium and indoor/outdoor dome-covered pool, Inca- and Mayan-theme decor, sauna/steam rooms, and gymnasium, provides a haven for health-conscious and fitness buffs. For more sporting passengers, there is activity galore – including a rock-climbing wall with several separate climbing tracks. It is located outdoors at the aft end of the funnel.

Volendam
★★★★

Size:. . . . . Mid-size Ship		Cabins (total):. 720	
Tonnage: 61,214		Size range (sq ft/m): 113.0–1,126.0/10.5–104.6	
Lifestyle: . . . . .Premium		Cabins (outside view):. 581	
Cruise line:. . . . . Holland America Line		Cabins (interior/no view):. 139	
Former names: . . . . .none		Cabins (for one person):. 0	
IMO number: 9156515		Cabins (with private balcony):. 197	
Builder: . . . . Fincantieri (Italy)		Cabins (wheelchair accessible): 23	
Original cost:. . . . . $300 million		Wheelchair accessibility:. . . . . .Good	
Entered service:. . . . . Nov 1999		Cabin voltage: . . . . 110 volts	
Registry:. . . . . .The Netherlands		Elevators:. 12	
Length (ft/m):. 781.0/238.00		Casino (gaming tables):. . . . . Yes	
Beam (ft/m):. 105.8/32.2		Slot machines:. . . . . Yes	
Draft (ft/m): . . . . 25.5/7.		Swimming pools:. . . . . .2 (1 w/sliding glass dome)	
Propulsion/Propellers:. . . . . diesel-electric (37,500kW)/2		Hot tubs (on deck):. 2	
Passenger decks:. 10		Self-service launderette:. . . . . Yes	
Total crew:. 561		Dedicated cinema/seats:. Yes/205	
Passengers (lower beds/alll berths):. 1,440/1,850		Library: . . . . Yes	
Passenger Space Ratio (lower beds/all berths): 42.5/33.0		Onboard currency: . . . . .US$	
Crew/Passenger Ratio (lower beds/all berths):. 2.5/2.5			

Dutch decor and heritage for mature-age cruisers

OVERVIEW. *Volendam* has the flow and comfortable feeling that repeat passengers will recognize from almost any ship in the Holland America Line fleet.

THE SHIP. The ship's name is taken from the fishing village of Volendam, north of Amsterdam. The hull is dark blue, in keeping with all Holland America Line ships. *Volendam* has three main passenger stairways, which is much better from the viewpoints of safety and passenger flow. The main interior design theme is flowers, from the 17th to the 21st centuries.

At the Lido Deck swimming pool, leaping dolphins are the focal point. The pool itself is also one deck higher than the Statendam-class ships, with the positive result being the fact that there is now direct access between the aft and midships pools (not so aboard the S-class ships).

ACCOMMODATION. There is one penthouse suite, and 28 suites, with the rest of the accommodation a mix of outside-view and interior cabins, and balcony cabins ('mini-suites'). All standard interior and outside cabins are tastefully furnished, and have twin beds that convert to a queen-size bed, but space is tight. The fully tiled bathrooms are small, and have small shower tubs, utilitarian toiletries cupboards, and exposed under-sink plumbing. There are 28 full Verandah Suites on Navigation Deck, and one Penthouse Suite. All suite occupants share a private Concierge Lounge. Strangely,

Berlitz's Ratings

	Possible	Achieved
Ship	500	395
Accommodation	200	154
Food	400	265
Service	400	268
Entertainment	100	71
Cruise	400	278
OVERALL SCORE		
1431 points out of 2000		

there are no butlers for these suites. Each Verandah Suite has a separate bedroom, dressing, and living areas.

DINING. There is one main dining room, and one specialty dining venue (dinner only). The 747-seat Rotterdam Dining Room is a traditional, grand room spread over two decks. Both open seating and fixed seating with assigned tables and times are available, while breakfast and lunch are open-seating.

Other dining options. The casual-dress Marco Polo Restaurant seats 88, and there is no charge, although reservations are required. The Lido Buffet is a self-serve café for casual breakfasts and luncheons. There is also an outdoor grill for those who enjoy hamburgers, hot dogs, and other fast-food items. A set menu includes a choice of four entrées.

ENTERTAINMENT. The Frans Hals Showlounge spans two decks, with banquette seating on both main and upper levels. It is basically a well-designed room, but the ceiling is low and the sight lines from the balcony level are poor.

SPA/FITNESS. The health spa facilities are decent, and include a gym with equipment, separate saunas and steam rooms, and several treatment rooms, each with a shower and toilet. There are practice tennis courts outdoors, as well as the traditional shuffleboard courts, jogging track, and a full walk-around teakwood promenade deck for strolling.

Voyager
★★★ +

Size:. . . . . Small Ship	Crew/Passenger Ratio (lower beds/all berths):. 2.3/2.6
Tonnage: 15,343	Cabins (total):. 278
Lifestyle: . . . . .Standard	Size range (sq ft/m): 110–398.2/10.2–37.0
Cruise line:. . . . . .Voyages of Discovery	Cabins (outside view):. 241
Former names: . . . Alexander von Humboldt, Jules Verne, Walrus,	Cabins (interior/no view):. 37
Crown Monarch	Cabins (for one person):. 0
IMO number: 8985957	Cabins (with private balcony):. 30
Builder: . . . . Union de Levante (Spain)	Cabins (wheelchair accessible): 3
Original cost: . . . . $95 million	Wheelchair accessibility:. . . . . .Fair
Entered service:. . . . . Dec 1990/Nov 2012	Cabin voltage: . . . . 110 volts
Registry:. . . . . .The Bahamas	Elevators:. 4
Length (ft/m):. 494.4/150.7	Casino (gaming tables):. . . . . Yes
Beam (ft/m):. 67.6/20.6	Slot machines:. . . . . Yes
Draft (ft/m): 18.7/5.7	Swimming pools:. 1
Propulsion/Propellers:. . . . . diesel	Hot tubs (on deck):. 2
Passenger decks:. 7	Self-service launderette:. . . . . .No
Total crew:. 240	Dedicated cinema/seats:. . . . . .No
Passengers (lower beds/alll berths):. 556/556	Library: . . . . Yes
Passenger Space Ratio (lower beds/all berths): 27.5/27.5	Onboard currency: . . . . .UK£

For discovery and learning aboard a cozy ship

OVERVIEW. This modest-looking ship is best suited to adult couples and singles seeking 'soft' adventure and enrichment-style cruising in a small ship.

THE SHIP. *Voyager,* bought at auction by the UK's All Leisure Group in 2009, underwent an extensive refurbishment and tailored for the British cruise market in 2012. Its profile is somewhat angular, and it has a small, swept-back funnel.

On deck, the space is very limited, although there's more sunbathing space on the deck above. The swimming pool is really just a 'plunge' pool, and is flanked by two hot tubs. The focal point of the ship's social life is Harry's Bar Scotts Lounge – a high-ceilinged lifestyle lounge/bar, off to one side of which is a nicely revamped library. A separate bridge club is provided for card games.

ACCOMMODATION. There are 18 cabin price grades. There are 35 suites, 30 of which have a private balcony and 10 of which are located behind the navigation bridge. The sleeping area, which includes a small sofa and drinks table, and ample drawer space, can be curtained off from the lounge area, which includes a mini-fridge. There are two balcony doors (one each from the bedroom and the lounge). The bathrooms have a Jacuzzi tub/shower combination.

The standard cabins have all the basics, including twin beds that convert to a double, a small vanity desk

Berlitz's Ratings		
	Possible	Achieved
Ship	500	311
Accommodation	200	126
Food	400	286
Service	400	288
Entertainment	100	61
Cruise	400	260
OVERALL SCORE		
1332 points out of 2000		

and small chair, and flat-screen TV set. Bathrooms have a shower enclosure, toilet, and washbasin. There's not much closet and drawer space, and the soundproofing between cabins could be better. Cabins on the lowest decks have portholes, while those on upper decks have windows.

DINING. The 280-seat Discovery Restaurant is quite comfortable, with a slightly raised center section. Seating is at tables for two, four, six, or eight. It operates an open, one-seating arrangement, although there is often a long wait, due to the lack of available seating (particularly in colder weather areas, when the outdoor seating in The Veranda cannot be used). Table wines are included for lunch and dinner. Adjacent to the restaurant is Explorer Grill, serving steaks. Alternatively, casual, buffet-style meals can be taken in the Veranda indoor-outdoor eatery, although in the indoor section, windows have obstructed views.

ENTERTAINMENT. The Darwin Lounge accommodates is a single-level lounge with mostly banquette seating for around 300, but the sight lines to the wooden dance floor/stage are poor.

SPA/FITNESS. A wellness center is located aft of the discotheque on the uppermost deck overlooking the stern, while a beauty salon is located several decks below, as is a small unisex sauna. There's a shuffleboard area on the topmost deck.

Voyager of the Seas
★★★+

Size:..................................Large Resort Ship	Crew/Passenger Ratio (lower beds/all berths):..........2.6/3.2
Tonnage:.....................................137,280	Cabins (total):.....................................1,557
Lifestyle:.....................................Standard	Size range (sq ft/m):..............151.0–1,358.0/14.0–126.1
Cruise line:...................Royal Caribbean International	Cabins (outside view):................................939
Former names:.....................................none	Cabins (interior/no view):............................618
IMO number:..................................9161716	Cabins (for one person):................................0
Builder:....................Kvaerner Masa-Yards (Finland)	Cabins (with private balcony):........................757
Original cost:...............................$500 million	Cabins (wheelchair accessible):........................26
Entered service:..............................Nov 1999	Wheelchair accessibility:............................Best
Registry:..................................The Bahamas	Cabin voltage:..............................110 volts
Length (ft/m):............................1,020.6/311.1	Elevators:..14
Beam (ft/m):..............................155.5/47.4	Casino (gaming tables):.............................Yes
Draft (ft/m):..................................28.8/8.8	Slot machines:....................................Yes
Propulsion/Propellers:............diesel-electric (28,000kW)/	Swimming pools:....................................3
2 azimuthing pods	Hot tubs (on deck):................................6
Passenger decks:....................................14	Self-service launderette:............................No
Total crew:......................................1,176	Dedicated cinema/seats:.............................No
Passengers (lower beds/alll berths):..............3,114/3,838	Library:..Yes
Passenger Space Ratio (lower beds/all berths):.......44.0/35.7	Onboard currency:................................US$

A large, family-friendly ship with many eating venues

OVERVIEW. In terms of sheer size, this ship presently dwarfs many others in the cruise industry, but in terms of personal service, the reverse is the case, unless you happen to reside in one of the top suites. This is impersonal city life at sea.

THE SHIP. The exterior design of *Voyager of the Seas* is rather like an enlarged version of the Royal Caribbean International's Vision-class ships. With its large proportions, it provides more facilities and options, yet manages to have a healthy passenger space ratio (the amount of space per passenger). It's too large to go through the Panama Canal, thus limiting itineraries almost exclusively to the Caribbean, where few islands have decent enough sized facilities to service it, or for use as a floating island resort.

Although the ship is large, the cabin hallways have a warm and attractive 'feel,' with artwork cabinets and wavy lines that lead you along and break up the monotony.

Embarkation and disembarkation take place through two access points, designed to minimize the inevitable lines at the start and end of the cruise – more than 1,500 people for each access point. Once inside the ship, you'll need good walking shoes, particularly when you need to go from one end to the other – it really is quite a long way.

A four-deck-high Royal Promenade, the interior focal point, is a good place to arrange to meet someone. It is 394ft (120m) long – the length of two American football fields, and has two internal lobbies that rise

Berlitz's Ratings		
	Possible	Achieved
Ship	500	393
Accommodation	200	141
Food	400	222
Service	400	267
Entertainment	100	75
Cruise	400	268
OVERALL SCORE		
1366 points out of 2000		

through 11 decks, one at each end. There are 16 elevators in four banks of four.

The entrance to one of three levels of the main restaurant, together with shops and entertainment locations are spun off from this 'boulevard,' while interior 'interior promenade-view' cabins, with bay windows, look into it from above. It houses a traditional English pub (the Pig 'n' Whistle, with draft beer and street-front seating), a Promenade Café (for Continental breakfast, all-day pizzas, sandwiches, and coffees), Ben & Jerry's Ice Cream (at extra cost), Sprinkles (for round-the-clock ice-cream and yoghurt), and Scoreboard (a sports bar).

Several shops complete the picture: a jewelry shop, gift shop, perfume shop, liquor shop, and a logo souvenir shop. A bright red telephone kiosk houses an ATM cash machine. Altogether, it's a nice place to see and be seen, and street performers provide a diversion. It really is a cross between a shopping arcade and an amusement park – Florida's Aventura meets New York's Coney Island. The chairman of Royal Caribbean International even donated his own treasured Morgan sports car to grace the Royal Promenade, which is supposedly designed in the image of London's fashionable Burlington Arcade. Actually, by far the best view of the whole promenade is from one of the 138 premium-price cabins that look into it, or from a 'captain's bridge' that crosses above it.

At the forward end is the showlounge. A Connoisseur's Club cigar lounge is on the starboard side between the showlounge and the main section of the Royal Promenade.

In the center of the promenade a stairway connects you to the deck below, where you'll find the Schooner Bar (a piano lounge that's a feature of all RCI ships) and the colorful Casino Royale (large and full of flashing lights and noises). Gaming includes blackjack, Caribbean stud poker, and craps, as well as 300 slot machines and the world's largest interactive roulette wheel, activated by a roulette ball tower four decks high.

A second showlounge – Studio B, a regulation-size ice-skating rink that has real, not fake, ice – has arena seating for up to 900 and the latest in broadcast facilities. A number of slim pillars obstruct the clear-view arena stage sight lines, however. An Ice Follies show is presented by a professional ice-skating show team each cruise. If ice-skating in the Caribbean doesn't particularly appeal, you might like to visit the neat two-deck library; it was the first aboard any cruise ship, and is open 24 hours a day. A total of $12 million was spent on permanent artwork.

Drinking places include a neat Aquarium Bar, with 50 tons of glass and water in four large aquariums worth over $1 million; the small and intimate Champagne Bar; and the Connoisseur Club – for cigars and cognacs. Jazz fans might appreciate High Notes, an intimate room for cool music atop the ship within the Viking Crown Lounge, or the Schooner Bar piano lounge. For golfers, there's the 19th Hole, a golf bar.

A large TV studio, part of Studio B, is adjacent to rooms that can be used for trade show exhibit space, with a 400-seat conference center and a 60-seat multimedia screening room. Many decks above, couples can tie the knot in a 'wedding chapel in the sky,' the Skylight Chapel, which is located on the upper level of the Viking Crown Lounge and even has wheelchair access via an electric stairway elevator. Outdoors, the pool and open deck areas on Deck 11 provide a resort-like environment.

Expect lines at the reception desk, elevators, particularly at peak meal times, as well as for embarkation and disembarkation. If you arrange to meet someone, be very specific about the location – this really is a large ship. My advice is to arrange to meet somewhere along the Royal Promenade.

The theme-park, banquet-style regimentation is well organized, but it's hard to find better value for money, particularly for families with children. You will, however, need to plan your time aboard, otherwise you'll miss out on some of the things that you might like to include in your vacation.

Because the cruise fares are so reasonable, you can expect a big push aboard the ship for extra-revenue items, drinks packages, extra-cost dining options, etc. – so take lots of extra pennies. In the end, however, you should have a decent floating vacation. The same comments apply to the other sister ships (*Adventure of*

the Seas, Explorer of the Seas, Mariner of the Seas, and *Navigator of the Seas*); their layout and flow are the same, and, although there may be some slight differences, it's mainly in the decor and trimmings. Note that in 2014, Voyager of the Seas will undergo refurbishment in order to be 'Australianized' for the ship's Australia 2014/2015 season.

FAMILIES. Facilities for children and teenagers are quite extensive. Aquanauts, is for ages three to five. Explorers, is for ages six to eight, and Voyagers for nine to 12s. Optix, a dedicated area for teenagers, includes a daytime club with computers, soda bar, disk jockey, and dance floor. Challenger's Arcade has the latest video games. Virtual Submarine is a virtual reality underwater center for all ages. Computer Lab has 14 computer stations loaded with fun and games. Paint and Clay is an arts and crafts center for younger children. Adjacent to these indoor areas is Adventure Beach, an area for all the family: it includes swimming pools, a water slide, and game areas outdoors.

ACCOMMODATION. There is a range of cabin price grades, in four major groupings: Premium ocean-view suites and cabins, Interior (atrium-view) cabins, Ocean-view cabins, and Interior cabins. Many cabins are of a similar size – good for incentives and large groups – and 300 have interconnecting doors (good for families).

Some 138 interior cabins have bay windows that look into an interior horizontal atrium – a cruise industry first when the ship debuted. Regardless of what cabin grade you choose, all except for the Royal Suite and Owner's Suite have twin beds that convert to a queen-size unit, TV set, radio and telephone, personal safe, vanity unit, hairdryer, and private bathroom. However, you'll need to keep the curtains closed in the bay windows if you wear little clothing, because you can be seen easily from adjacent bay windows.

Royal Suite (Deck 10). At around 1,146 sq ft (107 sq m), the Royal Suite is the largest private living space, located almost at the top of the Centrum lobby on the port side. It is a nicely appointed penthouse suite, whose occupants, sadly, must share the rest of the ship with everyone else, except for access to their own exclusive concierge club. It has a king-size circular bed in a separate large bedroom that can be fully closed off; a living room with an additional queen-size sofa bed, baby grand piano, refrigerator/wet bar, dining table and four chairs, expansive entertainment center, and a reasonably large bathroom.

Royal Family Suite. The four Royal Family suites (two aft on Deck 9, two aft on Deck 8, each measuring around 574 sq ft/53 sq m) have two separate bedrooms. The main bedroom has a large vanity desk; the second, smaller bedroom also includes two beds and third/fourth upper Pullman berths. There's a lounge with dining table and four chairs, wet bar, walk-in closet; and large bathroom with Jacuzzi tub, washbasin, and separate shower enclosure. The suites, at the stern, have large balconies with views out over the ship's wash.

Owner's Suites. Ten slightly smaller but desirable Owner's Suites (around 468 sq ft/43 sq m) are in the center of the ship, on both port and starboard sides, adjacent to the Centrum lobby on Deck 10. Each has a bedroom with queen-size bed or twin beds; lounge with large sofa; wet bar; bathroom with Jacuzzi tub, washbasin and separate shower enclosure. There's also a private balcony, although it's not very large.

Standard Outside-View and Interior Cabins. All cabins have a private bathroom, as well as interactive TV and pay-per-view movies, including an X-rated channel. Cabin bathrooms really are compact, but at least they have a proper shower enclosure instead of a shower curtain.

Some accommodation grades have a refrigerator/mini-bar, although there is no space left because it is crammed with 'take-and-pay' items. If you take anything from the mini-bar/refrigerator on the day of embarkation in Miami, Florida, sales tax will be added to your bill.

Cabins with 'private balconies' aren't so private. The balcony decking is made of Bolidt – a sort of rubberized sand – and not wood, though the balcony rail is of wood. If you have a cabin with a connecting door to another cabin, be aware that you'll probably be able to hear everything your next-door neighbors say and do. Bathroom toilets are explosively noisy, based on the vacuum system. Cabin bath towels are small and skimpy. Room service food menus are very basic.

DINING. The main dining room is extremely large and is set on three levels, each with an operatic name and theme: Carmen, La Bohème, and Magic Flute. A dramatic staircase connects all three levels, and huge, fat support pillars obstruct sight lines from many seats. All three have exactly the same menus and food. Choose one of two seatings, or My Time Dining which allows you to eat when you want during dining room hours. Tables are for four, six, eight, 10, or 12. The place settings, china, and cutlery are of good quality.

Other dining options. Portofino, the ship's upscale Euro-Italian restaurant. It's open for dinner only, reservations are required, and there's a cover charge. The food and its presentation are better than the food in the dining room, although the restaurant isn't large enough for all passengers to try even once during a cruise. Choices include antipasti, soup, salad, pasta, main dish, dessert, cheese, and coffee.

Windjammer Café: this is a really large, sprawling venue for casual buffet-style, self-help breakfast (this tends to be the busiest time of the day), lunch, and light dinners (but not on the last night of the cruise); it's often difficult to find a table and by the time you do your food could be cold.

Island Grill: (actually this is a section within the Windjammer Café), for casual grilled meat and seafood items (no reservations necessary) featuring a grill and open kitchen.

Johnny Rockets: a retro 1950s all-day, all-night diner-style eatery that has hamburgers, malt shakes, and jukebox hits, with both indoor and outdoor seating. All indoor tables have a mini-jukebox with dimes provided for you to make your selection of vintage records, and there are all-singing, all-dancing waitresses. There's a cover charge, whether you eat in or take out.

Promenade Café: for Continental breakfast, all-day pizzas, sandwiches, and coffees in paper cups.

Sprinkles: for round-the-clock ice cream and free yoghurt, pastries, and coffee.

ENTERTAINMENT. The 1,350-seat Lyric Theater, a really stunning showlounge, is located at the forward end of the ship and spans the height of five decks, with only a few slim pillars and almost no disruption of sight lines from any seat. The room has a hydraulic orchestra pit and huge stage areas, together with sonic-boom loud sound, and some superb lighting equipment.

In addition, the ship has an array of cabaret acts. Although many are not what you'd call headliners, they regularly travel the cruise ship circuit. The strongest cabaret acts are presented in the main showlounge, while others appear in the Cleopatra's Needle Lounge (one deck higher), also the venue for late-night adults-only comedy. The best shows are the Ice Spectaculars.

There is also a TV studio that can be used for trade show exhibit space – good for conventions at sea.

SPA/FITNESS. The Day Spa and Fitness Center is reasonably large, and measures 15,000 sq ft (1,400 sq m). It has a main and an upper level, and includes an aerobics room, fitness center (with stairmasters, treadmills, stationary bikes, weight machines, and free weights), several private body treatment rooms, and men's and women's sauna/steam rooms. Another 10,000 sq ft (930 sq m) of space is provided for a Solarium (with sliding glass-dome roof) to relax in after you've exercised.

Aft of the funnel is a 32.8-ft (10-m) rock-climbing wall, with five climbing tracks. It's a great buzz being 200ft (60m) above the ocean while the ship is moving. Other sports facilities include a roller-blading track, a dive-and-snorkel shop, a full-size basketball court, and a nine-hole, par 26 golf 'course.' A dive-and-snorkel shop provides equipment for rental, and diving classes.

Westerdam
★★★★

Size:................................Large Resort Ship	Crew/Passenger Ratio (lower beds/all berths):......... 2.3/3.0	
Tonnage:...................................... 82,348	Cabins (total):...958	
Lifestyle: ....Premium	Size range (sq ft/m): 170.0–1,318.6/15.7–122.5	
Cruise line:........................ Holland America Line	Cabins (outside view):...............................804	
Former names: ....none	Cabins (interior/no view):...........................154	
IMO number: 9226891	Cabins (for one person):................................0	
Builder: .... Fincantieri (Italy)	Cabins (with private balcony):..........................641	
Original cost:............................. $400 million	Cabins (wheelchair accessible): 28	
Entered service:.............................Apr 2004	Wheelchair accessibility:...........................Good	
Registry:.............................The Netherlands	Cabin voltage: .... 110 volts	
Length (ft/m):............................ 935.0/285.0	Elevators:.....................................14	
Beam (ft/m):................................ 105.6/32.2	Casino (gaming tables):............................. Yes	
Draft (ft/m): 25.5/7.8	Slot machines:.................................... Yes	
Propulsion/Propellers:...diesel-electric (34,000kW)/2 azimuthing pods	Swimming pools:.................4 (1 w/sliding glass dome)	
Passenger decks:..................................11	Hot tubs (on deck):...............................5	
Total crew:..817	Self-service launderette:...........................No	
Passengers (lower beds/alll berths):.............. 1,916/2,455	Dedicated cinema/seats:............................ Yes	
Passenger Space Ratio (lower beds/all berths): 41.9/33.5	Library: .... Yes	
	Onboard currency: ....US$	

A contemporary ship with Dutch decor and crafts

OVERVIEW. *Westerdam* offers a range of public rooms with a reasonably intimate ambience, and the overall feel of the ship is quite cozy.

THE SHIP. *Westerdam* is one of what is known as a series of Vista-class vessels, whose sister ships are: *Eurodam, Nieuw Amsterdam, Noordam, Oosterdam,* and *Zuiderdam* – all designed to appeal to younger, active vacationers. It has two funnels, placed close together, one in front of the other, the result of the slightly unusual machinery configuration. The ship has, in effect, two engine rooms – one with three diesels, and one with two diesels and a gas turbine. Pod propulsion is provided, powered by a diesel-electric system (there's almost no vibration), and a small gas turbine in the funnel helps reduce emissions.

There's a complete walk-around exterior teak promenade deck, with teak steamer-style sunloungers. A jogging track is located around the mast and the forward third of the ship. Exterior glass elevators, mounted mid-ships on both port and starboard sides, provide ocean views. There are two centrally located swimming pools outdoors, one of which can be used in poor weather because it has a retractable sliding glass roof. Two whirlpool tubs, adjacent to the swimming pools, are abridged by a bar. Another smaller pool is reserved for children; it incorporates a winding water slide that spans two decks in height. There is an additional whirlpool tub outdoors.

You enter the ship through an intimate lobby that spans three decks, and is topped by a beautiful, rotat-

Berlitz's Ratings

	Possible	Achieved
Ship	500	392
Accommodation	200	149
Food	400	261
Service	400	268
Entertainment	100	71
Cruise	400	282

OVERALL SCORE
1423 points out of 2000

ing, Waterford crystal globe of the world. The interior decor is interesting; the ceilings are particularly noticeable in the public decor, the colors are muted and warm. The information desk in the lobby is small and removed from the main passenger flow.

There are two whole entertainment/public room decks. The most dramatic room is the showlounge, which spans three decks in the forward section of the ship. Other facilities include a winding shopping street with boutique stores and logo shops, an Internet center, a fine library, a card room, an art gallery, photo gallery, and several small meeting rooms. The casino is large – one has to walk through it to get from the restaurant to the showlounge on one of the entertainments decks.

In a 2007 refit, an Explorations Café was added to the Crow's Nest (a HAL trademark observation lounge atop the ship). This encompasses the ship's library, a lounge area with fine ocean views, and a coffee shop.

On lower decks you'll find a Queens Lounge, which acts as a lecture room a Culinary Arts CenterThere are also a number of other bars and lounges, including an Explorer's Lounge. The ship also has a small movie screening room.

Niggles include several pillars that obstruct the passenger flow and lines of sight throughout the ship. Also, there are no self-service launderettes, although special laundry packages are available. Additionally, the air conditioning cannot be turned off in cabins or bathrooms.

FAMILIES. Children have KidZone, an indoor/outdoor facility, and Cub Hal for ages five to 12, with a number of dedicated youth counselors. Teenagers get to use WaveRunner, which includes a dance floor, special lighting effects, and a booming sound system. There's also a video game room, and big-screen television for movies.

ACCOMMODATION. There are 24 price categories – 16 with outside views and eight interior. Lifeboats obstruct the view from some cabins on the lowest accommodation deck. Some cabins that can accommodate a third and fourth person have very little closet space and only one personal safe. Some cabins have interconnecting doors. Occupants of suites get exclusive use of a Neptune Lounge and concierge service, priority embarkation and disembarkation, and other benefits. In many suites and cabins with private balconies the balconies aren't really private, as many can be overlooked.

Penthouse Verandah Suites (2). These measure 1,318 sq ft (123 sq m), including balcony. They have a separate bedroom with a king-size bed; there's also a walk-in closet, dressing room, living room, dining room, butler's pantry, mini-bar and refrigerator, and private balcony. The main bathroom has a large tub, two washbasins, toilet, and plenty of storage space for toiletries. Personalized stationery and complimentary dry cleaning are included, as are hot hors d'oeuvres daily.

Deluxe Verandah Suites (60). These measure 563 sq ft (53 sq m). They have twin beds that convert to a king-size bed, vanity desk, lounge area, walk-in closet, mini-bar and refrigerator, and bathroom with full-size tub, washbasin, and toilet. Personalized stationery, complimentary dry cleaning, and hot hors d'oeuvres are included.

Verandah Suites (100). Actually, these are really cabins, not proper suites, and measure 284 sq ft (26 sq m). Twin beds convert to a queen-size bed; there is a lounge area, mini-bar and refrigerator, while the bathroom has a tub, washbasin, and toilet. Floor-to-ceiling windows open onto a private balcony.

Outside-view Cabins. Standard outside cabins (197 sq ft/18 sq m) have twin beds that convert to a queen-size bed. There's also a small sitting area, while the bathroom has a tub/shower combination. The interior cabins are slightly smaller (183 sq ft/17 sq m).

DINING. Options range from full-service meals in the main dining room and à la carte restaurant to casual, self-serve buffet-style meals and fast-food outlets. The 1,045-seat Vista Dining Room is two decks high, with seating provided on both main and balcony levels, and is at the stern. Both open-seating and assigned-seating are available, while breakfast and lunch are open-seating where you'll be seated by restaurant staff when you enter.

There are tables for two, four, six, or eight. The waiter stations can be noisy for anyone seated adjacent to them. Fine Rosenthal porcelain and decent cutlery are used, but there are no fish knives. Live music is provided for dinner each evening. Once each cruise, a Dutch Dinner is held (hats are provided), as is an Indonesian Lunch. 'Lighter option' meals are available for the nutrition-conscious. HAL can provide Kosher meals, although these are prepared ashore, frozen, and brought to the table sealed in their original containers.

Other dining options. A 130-seat Pinnacle Grill is a more upscale dining spot with higher-quality ingredients and smarter presentation than in the larger main dining room. It is on Lower Promenade Deck, and fronts onto the second level of the atrium lobby; a Pinnacle Bar was added in a 2007 refit. Pacific Northwest cuisine is served, plus an array of premium-quality steaks from hand-selected cuts of beef, shown to you at tableside. The wine bar offers mostly American wines. Reservations are required and there's a cover charge (the steaks alone are worth it).

An extensive Lido Café wraps around the funnel housing and extends aft. It includes a pizzeria counter, a salad bar, Asian stir-fry counter, deli sandwiches, and a dessert buffet. Movement around the buffet area can be very slow, particularly at peak times. In the evenings, one side of this venue is turned into an extra-cost, 72-seat Canaletto Restaurant – a quasi-Italian informal eatery with waiter service.

An outdoor self-serve buffet, adjacent to the fantail pool, serves fast-food such as hamburgers and hot dogs, chicken and fries. There are also two smaller buffets adjacent to the midships swimming pool area, and an extra-cost Windsurf Café in the atrium lobby, open 20 hours a day for coffee, pastries, snack foods, deli sandwiches, and, in the evening, liqueur coffees.

ENTERTAINMENT. The 867-seat Vista Lounge is the main venue for Las Vegas-style revue shows and major cabaret presentations. It spans three decks in the forward section. The main floor level has a bar in its starboard aft section. Spiral stairways at the back of the lounge connect all levels. The upper levels have better sight lines.

SPA/FITNESS. The Greenhouse Spa, a large, two-deck-high health spa, is directly above the navigation bridge. Facilities include a solarium, hydrotherapy pool, and a unisex thermal suite – an area incorporating a Laconium, Hammam, and Camomile Grotto. There's also a beauty parlor, 11 massage/therapy rooms, including one for couples, and a large gym with floor-to-ceiling windows, and the latest high-tech equipment.

Sports facilities include a basketball court, volleyball court, and golf simulator.

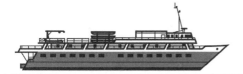

Wilderness Adventurer
★★

Size:.	Boutique Ship	Cabins (total):.	30
Tonnage:.	99	Size range (sq ft/m):.	70.0–88.0/6.5–8.1
Lifestyle:.	Standard	Cabins (outside view):.	30
Cruise line:.	Un-Cruise Adventures	Cabins (interior/no view):.	0
Former names:.	Caribbean Prince	Cabins (for one person):.	3
IMO number:.	8978667	Cabins (with private balcony):.	0
Builder:.	Blount Shipyards (USA)	Cabins (wheelchair accessible):.	0
Original cost:.	$6 million	Wheelchair accessibility:.	none
Entered service:.	1983/May 2011	Cabin voltage:.	110 volts
Registry:.	USA	Elevators:.	0
Length (ft/m):.	156.6/47.7	Casino (gaming tables):.	No
Beam (ft/m):.	38.0/11.0	Slot machines:.	No
Draft (ft/m):.	6.5/1.9	Swimming pools:.	0
Propulsion/Propellers:.	diesel (1,472kw)/1	Hot tubs (on deck):.	2
Passenger decks:.	3	Self-service launderette:.	No
Total crew:.	25	Dedicated cinema/seats:.	No
Passengers (lower beds/all berths):.	57/60	Library:.	Yes
Passenger Space Ratio (lower beds/all berths):.	1.7/1.6	Onboard currency:.	US$
Crew/Passenger Ratio (lower beds/all berths):.	2.2/2.4		

A tiny but expensive ship for up-close Alaskan cruising

OVERVIEW. This ship is best suited to couples and single travelers who enjoy nature and wildlife at close range, and who wouldn't dream of cruising aboard a large resort ship. Un-Cruise Adventures is the new name for what was formerly known as InnerSea Discovery Cruises – the parent company of American Safari Cruises.

THE SHIP. *Wilderness Adventurer* was originally built for the American Canadian Caribbean Line and provides a platform for in-depth, up-close cruising along the coastline and inlets of Alaska. Essentially, it's a sport utility vessel with a platform at the stern, and carries a fleet of 28 Necky kayaks, 10 stand-up paddle boards, and a limited supply of wetsuits, rain gear, binoculars, hiking poles, daypacks, and snorkeling equipment. The fare includes guided excursions, with an emphasis on hiking and kayaking. Do take comfortable walking shoes, as well as a camera for wildlife photography.

Facilities include a main lounge, plus a dining room, and a second (small) lounge. An underwater camera, mounted on the bows, transmits images to the lounge, as well as passenger cabins. The ship has a selection of DVDs. The cruises, which are all about exploring Alaska close-up and personal, are very expensive when compared with most other ships operating in the area. However, a Park Ranger accompanies all sailings, and leads passenger 'expeditions' on hiking and kayaking trips in Glacier Bay.

Berlitz's Ratings

	Possible	Achieved
Ship	500	170
Accommodation	200	76
Food	400	184
Service	400	204
Entertainment	100	44
Cruise	400	174

OVERALL SCORE
852 points out of 2000

Gratuities are pooled and shared among all the staff, using the amounts that are recommended in the cruise line's brochure. The dress code is ultra-casual.

You can expect some dull throbbing from the diesel engines and generator. There is no doctor on board, and so anyone with medical problems shouldn't consider this vessel.

ACCOMMODATION. There are only three types of cabin (Navigator, Trailblazer, and Pathfinder), on two decks. They really are utilitarian units that are barely adequate – however, they do have comfortable memory foam beds. While cabins have a double bed, others have two lower beds with memory foam mattresses. Each cabin has a private bathroom, although these are small and basic. There is no room service, but a hairdryer is provided, as is an iPod docking station.

DINING. The dining room has an open-seating policy. Ingredients are all as fresh as possible, with lots of Alaskan fish and seafood – but there are no fish knives.

ENTERTAINMENT. There is no formal entertainment. Conversation with fellow passengers constitutes the entertainment each evening.

SPA/FITNESS. A hot tub is located under a covered area; there's also a small adjacent sauna, and some basic fitness equipment. Massage is also available.

Wind Spirit
★★★ +

Size:.	.Boutique Ship	Cabins (total):.	.74
Tonnage:	. 5,350	Size range (sq ft/m):	. 185.0–220.0/17.0–22.5
Lifestyle:	.Premium	Cabins (outside view):	.74
Cruise line:.	. Windstar Cruises	Cabins (interior/no view):.	.0
Former names:	.none	Cabins (for one person):.	.0
IMO number:	.8603509	Cabins (with private balcony):.	.0
Builder:	.Ateliers et Chantiers du Havre	Cabins (wheelchair accessible):	.0
Original cost:	. $34.2 million	Wheelchair accessibility:	.None
Entered service:.	.Apr 1988	Cabin voltage:	. 110 volts
Registry:.	. The Bahamas	Elevators:.	.0
Length (ft/m):.	. 439.6/134.0	Casino (gaming tables):.	. Yes
Beam (ft/m):.	. 51.8/15.8	Slot machines:.	. Yes
Draft (ft/m):	. 13.4/4.1	Swimming pools:.	.1
Propulsion/Propellers:.	diesel-electric (1,400kW)/1 + sails	Hot tubs (on deck):.	.1
Passenger decks:.	.5	Self-service launderette:.	.No
Total crew:.	.88	Dedicated cinema/seats:.	.No
Passengers (lower beds/all berths):	. 148/159	Library:	. Yes
Passenger Space Ratio (lower beds/all berths):	. 36.1/33.6	Onboard currency:	.US$
Crew/Passenger Ratio (lower beds/all berths):	. 1.6/1.8		

A modern sail-cruise ship with an

OVERVIEW. This sail-cruise ship is ideally suited to youthful couples and solo travelers seeking contemporary facilities and some water sports in a relaxed but chic setting that's different from 'normal' cruise ships, with good food and service, but with no entertainment, silly parlor games, structured activities, or ship's photographers to get in the way.

THE SHIP. *Wind Spirit*, an identical twin to *Wind Star*, is a long, sleek-looking craft that is part-yacht, part-cruise ship, with four giant masts that tower 170ft (52m) above the deck, and is fitted with computer-controlled sails. The masts, sails and rigging alone cost $5 million. The computer keeps the ship on an even keel via the movement of a water hydraulic ballast system of 142,653 gallons (540,000 liters), so there is no rolling over 6°. You may be under sail for less than 40 percent of the time, depending on the conditions and cruise area winds prevailing.

Because of the amount of complex sail machinery, there is little open deck space when the ship is full. At the stern is a small water sports platform that can be used when at anchor and only in really calm sea conditions. Water sports facilities include a banana boat, kayaks, sunfish sailboats, windsurf boards, water-ski boat, scuba and snorkel equipment, and four Zodiacs. You will be asked to sign a waiver if you wish to use the water sports equipment.

The ship has a finely crafted interior with pleasing, blond woods, together with soft, complementary colors and decor that is chic, even elegant, but a little cold. Note

Berlitz's Ratings

	Possible	Achieved
Ship	500	360
Accommodation	200	160
Food	400	267
Service	400	271
Entertainment	100	73
Cruise	400	262

OVERALL SCORE
1393 points out of 2000

that the main lounge aboard this ship is of a slightly different design from that aboard *Wind Star*. Together with Wind Star, this ship had a make-over in 2012 – this included a complete refurbishment of cabins (including new lighting), owner's suite and corridors together with The Restaurant, Veranda, Lounge, WindSpa, Library, Reception, and Pool Bar.

No scheduled activities help to make this a real relaxing, unregimented 'get away from it all' vacation. The Windstar ships help you to cruise in very comfortable, contemporary surroundings bordering on the luxurious, yet in an unstructured environment. They are just right for seven idyllic nights in sheltered areas, but can be disturbing when a Windstar vessel is in small ports alongside several gigantic cruise ships.

The swimming pool is really only a tiny 'dip' pool. Be prepared for the whine of the vessel's generators, which are needed to run the air-conditioning and lighting systems 24 hours a day. You'll hear it at night in your cabin, and it takes most passengers a day or two to get used to.

Beverage prices are a little high. The library is small and needs more hardback fiction. The staff, though friendly, is casual and a little sloppy at times in the finer points of service.

The dress code is casual, with no jackets and ties, even for dinner – the brochure states casual elegance. There are no formal nights or theme nights. Gratuities are charged at about $12 per person, per day, and 15 percent is added to bar and wine accounts.

ACCOMMODATION. All cabins are nicely equipped, have crisp, inviting decor and a mini-bar/refrigerator (stocked when you embark, but all drinks cost extra), 24-hour room service, personal safe, and plenty of storage space. A TV, with CNN when available, rotates so that it is viewable from the bed and the bathroom. There's also a video player and compact disc player. All cabins all have two portholes with outside views, and deadlights (steel covers that provide a complete blackout at night and can be closed in poor weather conditions). The decor is a pleasant mix of rich woods, natural fabrics and colorful soft furnishings, and hi-tech yacht-style amenities. A basket of fruit is replenished daily.

The bathrooms are compact units, designed in a figure of eight, with a teakwood floor in the central section. There is a good amount of storage space for toiletries in two cabinets, as well as under-sink cupboard space. A wall-mounted hairdryer is also provided. The shower enclosure (no cabins have bathtubs) is circular – like many of today's passengers – and has both a hand-held as well as a fixed shower so you can wash your hair without getting the rest of your body wet. L'Occitane bathroom amenities are provided, as are a vanity kit and shower cap.

The lighting is not strong enough for women to apply make-up – this is better applied at the vanity desk in the cabin, which has stronger overhead (halogen) lighting. Bathrobes and towels are 100 percent cotton.

DINING. There is one rather chic and elegant dining room, AmphorA Restaurant (whose name is derived from a vessel, or container), with ocean views from large, picture windows, a lovely wood ceiling and wood paneled walls. California-style nouvelle cuisine is served, with attractively presented dishes. Additionally, signature dishes created by master chefs Joachim Splichal and Jeanne Jones are offered daily. Open seating means you dine when you want and with whomever you wish to.

When the company first started, European waiters provided service with practiced European finesse. However, they have been replaced by Indonesians and Filipinos, whose communication skills at times can prove inadequate, although their service is pleasant enough. The selection of breads, cheeses, and fruits could be better. There is a big push to sell wines, al-

though the prices are extremely high, as they are for most alcoholic drinks – even bottled water is the highest in the industry, at $7 per liter bottle.

There is often casual dinner on the open deck under the stars, with grilled seafood and steaks. At the bars, hot and cold hors d'oeuvres appear at cocktail times.

Fancy something quiet and romantic? At no extra charge, a 'Cuisine de l'Amour' romantic dinner for two can be served to you in your cabin, complete with candle. The menu, with seductive sounding selections, offers a choice of appetizer, a set soup, choice of salad, and two entrée options, and a set dessert to finish.

ENTERTAINMENT. There is no showlounge, shows, or cabaret. However, none are really needed, because a cruise aboard this high-tech sailing ship provides an opportunity to get away from all that noise and 'entertainment.' The main lounge, a corner of which houses a small casino, has a small dance floor, and, typically, a trio is there to play.

The main lounge is also used for cocktail parties and other social functions. Otherwise, it's down to more personal entertainment, such as a video in your cabin late at night – or, much more romantic, after-dinner hours spent outside strolling or simply lounging on deck.

SPA/FITNESS. A gymnasium (with a modicum of muscle-toning equipment, treadmills, and exercycles) and sauna are located at the aft of the ship, adjacent to the water sports platform. Special spa packages can be pre-booked through your travel agent before you arrive at the ship. Well-being massages, aromatherapy facials, manicures, pedicures, and hair beautifying treatments all cost extra. The spa is operated by Steiner Leisure, a specialist concession.

Wind speeds

A navigational announcement to passengers is normally made once or twice a day, giving the ship's position, temperature, and weather information.

Various winds affect the world's weather patterns. Such well-known winds as the Bora, Mistral, Northwind, and Sirocco, among others, play an important part in the makeup of weather at and above sea level. Wind velocity is measured on the Beaufort scale, a method that was devised in 1805 by Commodore Francis Beaufort, later Admiral and Knight Commander of the Bath, for measuring the force of wind at sea. Originally, it measured the effect of the wind on a fully rigged man-of-war (which was usually laden with cannon and heavy ammunition).

It became the official way of recording wind velocity in 1874, when the International Meteorological Committee adopted it as a new standard.

Wind Star
★★★ +

Size:.....................................Boutique Ship	Cabins (total):...74
Tonnage: 5,350	Size range (sq ft/m): 185.0–220.0/17.0–22.5
Lifestyle: ....Premium	Cabins (outside view):....................................74
Cruise line:.............................. Windstar Cruises	Cabins (interior/no view):..................................0
Former names: ....none	Cabins (for one person):...................................0
IMO number: 8420878	Cabins (with private balcony):..............................0
Builder: ....Ateliers et Chantiers du Havre	Cabins (wheelchair accessible): 0
Original cost:............................... $34.2 million	Wheelchair accessibility:...............................None
Entered service:.............................. Dec 1986	Cabin voltage: ....110 volts
Registry:...................................The Bahamas	Elevators:...0
Length (ft/m):............................... 439.6/134.0	Casino (gaming tables):.................................Yes
Beam (ft/m):..................................... 51.8/15.8	Slot machines:...Yes
Draft (ft/m): 13.4/4.1	Swimming pools:...1
Propulsion/Propellers:....... diesel-electric (1,400kW)/1 + sails	Hot tubs (on deck):..1
Passenger decks:..5	Self-service launderette:.................................No
Total crew:..88	Dedicated cinema/seats:...................................No
Passengers (lower beds/alll berths):................ 148/168	Library: ....Yes
Passenger Space Ratio (lower beds/all berths): 36.1/33.6	Onboard currency: ....US$
Crew/Passenger Ratio (lower beds/all berths):.........1.6/1.8	

A contemporary sail-cruise ship for casual cruising

OVERVIEW. *Wind Star* is suited to youthful couples and singles who want contemporary facilities and some water sports in a relaxed but chic setting.

THE SHIP. *Wind Star*, is a long, sleek-looking craft that is part-yacht, part-cruise ship, with four giant masts that tower 170ft (52m) above the deck, and is fitted with computer-controlled sails. The masts, sails and rigging alone cost $5 million (when the masts were lowered into position, a US silver dollar, dated 1889, was placed under the main mast).

The swimming pool is really only a tiny 'dip' pool. Be prepared for the whine of the vessel's generators, which are needed to run the air-conditioning and lighting systems 24 hours a day. Beverage prices are a little high. The library is small and needs more hardback fiction. The staff, though friendly, is casual and a little sloppy at times in the finer points of service. The dress code is casual, with no jackets and ties. Gratuities are charged to your onboard account, and 15 percent is added to bar, wine and spa accounts.

ACCOMMODATION. The cabins are nicely equipped, have crisp, inviting decor and a mini-bar/refrigerator (stocked when you embark, but all drinks cost extra), 24-hour room service, personal safe, and plenty of storage space. A TV, with CNN when available, rotates so that it is viewable from the bed and the bathroom. All cabins all have two portholes. The bathrooms are compact with a teakwood floor. There is a good amount of

Berlitz's Ratings		
	Possible	Achieved
Ship	500	360
Accommodation	200	160
Food	400	267
Service	400	271
Entertainment	100	73
Cruise	400	263
OVERALL SCORE		
1394 points out of 2000		

storage space for toiletries in two cabinets, as well as under-sink cupboard space. A wall-mounted hairdryer is also provided. The shower enclosure (no cabins have bathtubs) is circular and has both a hand-held as well as a fixed shower unit. L'Occitane bathroom amenities are provided, as are a vanity kit and shower cap.

DINING. The main dining room, the AmphorA Restaurant (its name is derived from a vessel, or container), is chic, and has ocean views, plus a lovely wood ceiling and wood paneled walls. California-style cuisine is served, with attractively presented dishes. Open seating means you dine when you want and with whomever you wish to.

For something quiet and romantic, a 'Cuisine de l'Amour' romantic dinner for two can be served to you in your cabin.

ENTERTAINMENT. There is no showlounge, shows, or cabaret. A cruise aboard this high-tech sailing ship provides an opportunity to get away from all that noise and 'entertainment.' The main lounge, a corner of which houses a small casino, has a small dance floor and, typically, a trio is there to play.

SPA/FITNESS. A fitness room and sauna are located at the aft of the ship. Special spa packages can be pre-booked. Well-being massages, aromatherapy facials, manicures, pedicures, and hair beautifying treatments all cost extra.

Wind Surf
★★★★

Size:. . . . . Small Ship	Cabins (total):. 156
Tonnage: 14,745	Size range (sq ft/m): 188.0–500.5/17.5–46.5
Lifestyle: . . . . .Premium	Cabins (outside view): 156
Cruise line:. . . . . Windstar Cruises	Cabins (interior/no view):. 0
Former names: . . . . Club Med I	Cabins (for one person):. 0
IMO number: 8700785	Cabins (with private balcony): 0
Builder: .Ateliers et Chantiers du Havre	Cabins (wheelchair accessible): 0
Original cost: . . . .$140 million	Wheelchair accessibility:. . . . . .None
Entered service:. . . . . Feb 1990/May 1998	Cabin voltage: . . . . .110 and 220 volts
Registry:. . . . . The Bahamas	Elevators:. 2
Length (ft/m):. 613.5/187.0	Casino (gaming tables):. . . . . Yes
Beam (ft/m):. 65.6/20.0	Slot machines:. . . . . Yes
Draft (ft/m): 16.4/5.0	Swimming pools:. 2
Propulsion/Propellers:. . . . . . . diesel-electric (1,400kW)/1 + sails	Hot tubs (on deck):. 2
Passenger decks:. 8	Self-service launderette:. . . . . .No
Total crew:. 163	Dedicated cinema/seats:. . . . . .No
Passengers (lower beds/alll berths):. 312/347	Library: . . . . Yes
Passenger Space Ratio (lower beds/all berths): 47.2/42.4	Onboard currency: . . . . .US$
Crew/Passenger Ratio (lower beds/all berths):. 1.9/2.1	

Elegant decor for casual, sail- cruising in comfort

OVERVIEW. This sail-cruise is a good choice for couples seeking informality (no jackets or ties), but who don't want the inconvenience of the workings of a real tall ship. It cruises in Barbados (November–March) and in the Mediterranean (May–October). The European itineraries are really port-intensive, which means you sail each night and are in port each day.

THE SHIP. *Wind Surf*, one of a pair of the world's largest sail-cruisers, is part-cruise ship, part-yacht – its sister ship operates as *Club Med II*. This is a larger, grander sister to the original three Windstar Cruises vessels. Five huge masts of 164ft/50m (rising 221ft/68m above sea level) carry seven triangular, self-furling Dacron sails, with a total surface area of 26,881 sq ft (2,497 sq m).

No human hands touch the sails, as everything is handled electronically by computer control from the bridge – which makes it a little boring. Also, because European sailings take place at night, with days spent in port, there seems little point to having the sails, as passengers don't get to experience them.

A computer keeps the ship on an even keel via the movement of a water hydraulic ballast system of 266,800 gallons (1 million liters), so there is no heeling over 6°. When the ship isn't using the sails, four diesel-electric motors propel it at up to approximately 12 knots. The ship is very quiet when moving.

Swimming from the water sports platform at the stern isn't allowed. But extensive water sports facili-

Berlitz's Ratings

	Possible	Achieved
Ship	500	375
Accommodation	200	160
Food	400	280
Service	400	282
Entertainment	100	73
Cruise	400	293
OVERALL SCORE		
1463 points out of 2000		

ties include windsurfers, sailboats, waterski boats, single scuba tanks, snorkels, fins and masks, and inflatable Zodiac motorized boats for waterskiing – all at no extra charge, except for the scuba tanks.

There are two saltwater swimming pools – little more than 'dip' pools. One is amidships on the uppermost deck of the ship, while the other is aft, together with two hot tubs, and an adjacent bar. There are no showers at either of the pools, so passengers get into the pools or hot tubs while covered in oil or lotion, an unhygienic arrangement.

A meeting room can accommodate 30–60 people. The casino/main lounge has four blackjack and one roulette table, and 21 slot machines. It has an unusually high ceiling for the size of the ship.

A Yacht Club includes books and a DVDs for in-cabin use and provides comfortable seating for relaxation or listening to music loaded for you on iPods available from reception. An espresso bar offers extra-cost Lavazza coffee drinks and deli sandwiches. Eight computers have Internet access, and there's Wi-Fi access.

Parts of the ship was refurbished in 2011, and so in late 2012 were public spaces including the Lounge, The Restaurant, Degrees, Veranda, Compass Rose, WindSpa, Yacht Club, and Pool Bar.

Hotel service is provided mostly by Filipino and Indonesian staff. Gratuities are charged to your onboard account, and 15 percent is added to bar and wine accounts, and to all spa treatments and services. The quality of food and its presentation is a definite plus, as is the policy of no music in passenger hallways or elevators.

ACCOMMODATION. There are just three price categories. Unusually, the cabin numbers (port side even numbers, odd number starboard side) are sequenced with lower numbers aft, while higher numbers are forward. All cabins are very nicely equipped, with crisp, inviting decor. They have a mini-bar/refrigerator (stocked when you embark, but all drinks are at extra cost), 24-hour room service, personal safe, a flat-screen TV set viewable from the bed (or sofa, depending on cabin configuration), DVD/CD player, plenty of storage space, and two portholes. DVDs and CDs are available from the library. There are six four-person cabins; 35 doubles are fitted with an extra Pullman berth, and several cabins have an interconnecting door – good for families. Spa Suite packages are available at extra cost. All cabins have Wi-Fi access, at extra cost.

The bathrooms are compact, designed in a figure of eight, with a teakwood floor in the central section. There is a good amount of storage space for toiletries in two cabinets, as well as under-basin storage space, and a wall-mounted hairdryer. The shower enclosure is circular, and has both a hand-held and a fixed shower, enabling you to wash your hair without getting the rest of your body wet. The lighting is not strong enough for women to apply make-up – this is better applied at the cabin's vanity desk.

All but one of the 31 suites have two bathrooms, a separate living/dining area, sleeping area that can be curtained off, two vanity/writing desks, and four portholes instead of two. There are two TV sets (one in the lounge, one in the sleeping area), video player and CD player, and Bose SoundDock for iPods. Popcorn for movie viewing is available from room service. Bathrooms have granite countertops, open shelving, new cabinets, and magnifying mirror.

A further two Bridge Deck suites (around 495 sq ft/46 sq m) would be delightful for a honeymoon; each has a bedroom, separate living/dining room, and marble bathroom with Jacuzzi tub, two washbasins, and separate toilet, plus a walk-in closet.

New Spa Suite packages, introduced in 2010, take an existing cabin and provide extras such as a queen-size bed with microfiber bed linen, bathrobes, an orchid flower arrangement, two bathrooms, a flat-screen TV with DVD player, and Bose SoundDock speakers for iPods. Also, a pillow menu provides several choices, including a 'snore-no-more' hypoallergenic pillow.

Tea collections include well-being, herbal, or exotic teas. Brewing service includes contemporary, porcelain tea-ware and is available from room service 24 hours a day. Berlitz tip: ask for it to be made with mineral water, not the standard chlorinated ship's water.

DINING. The AmphorA Restaurant (an ancient word meaning 'vessel' or 'container') seats 272 and has tables for two, four, or six. It has open seating with no pre-assigned tables, and is open only for dinner, typically 7:30–9:30pm. California-style nouvelle cuisine is served, with dishes attractively presented.

Other dining options. A 124-seat Degrees Bistro, a specialty dining venue, features Mediterranean cuisine. Located atop the ship, on Star Deck, it has picture windows on port and starboard sides, an open kitchen, and tables for two, four, or six. Reservations are required for dinner, although there's no extra charge.

The Veranda, amidships on Star Deck, has its own open terrace for informal, self-serve breakfast and lunch buffets. It really is very pleasant to be outside, eating an informal breakfast or lunch. Do try the bread pudding, available daily at lunch – the ship is famous for it and each day has a variation on the theme.

The Compass Rose, an indoor/outdoor casual eatery, provides deli-style snack items plus some pastries and coffee for breakfast, lunch, and afternoon tea. At night, it turns into Candles for alfresco dining around the aft pool. A permanent outdoor barbecue offers fresh grilled items for breakfast and lunch.

Windstar Cruises food is generally very good, although highly geared toward American tastes. Europeans and other nationals should note that items such as bacon may be fried to death, and the choice of cheeses and teas is limited. Service in the dining room is also quite fast, geared towards those who haven't yet learned to unwind.

A nice feature is a 'Cuisine de l'Amour' romantic candlelight dinner for two served to you in your cabin at no extra charge. The menu, with seductive sounding selections, offers a choice of appetizer, a set soup, choice of salad, two entrée options, and a set dessert to finish.

Finally, there's quite an extensive room service menu.

ENTERTAINMENT. There is no showlounge as such (this is a yachting-style experience, after all), although the main lounge, which incorporates a small casino, serves as an occasional cabaret room. It has a small wooden dance floor, with music provided by a house band. The high-ceilinged room is also used for cocktail parties and other social functions.

SPA/FITNESS. The Health Spa has a unisex sauna (bathing suits required), beauty salon, and several treatment rooms for massage, facials, and body wraps. There is a decent gymnasium – on a separate deck, with ocean views – and an aerobics workout room. Unfortunately, the spa facilities are split on three separate decks, making them rather disjointed. Special spa packages can be pre-booked through your travel agent. The spa is operated by the UK's Onboard Spa Company.

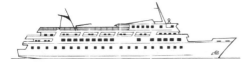

Yorktown
★★

Size:. . . . . .Boutique Ship	Cabins (total):. 69
Tonnage:. 2,354	Size range (sq ft/m):. 121.0–138.0/11.2–12.8
Lifestyle: . . . . .Standard	Cabins (outside view):. 69
Cruise line:. . . . . Travel Dynamics International	Cabins (interior/no view):. 0
Former names: . . . . *Yorktown Clipper*	Cabins (for one person):. 0
IMO number: 8949372	Cabins (with private balcony): 0
Builder: . . . . First Coast Shipbuilding (USA)	Cabins (wheelchair accessible): 0
Original cost:. . . . . $12 million	Wheelchair accessibility:. . . . . .None
Entered service:. . . . . Apr 1988/May 2012	Cabin voltage: . . . . 110 volts
Registry:. . . . . USA	Elevators:. 0
Length (ft/m):. 257.0/78.3	Casino (gaming tables):. . . . . .No
Beam (ft/m):. 43.0/13.1	Slot machines:. . . . . .No
Draft (ft/m): 8.0/2.4	Swimming pools:. 0
Propulsion/Propellers:. . . . . diesel (1,044kW)/2	Hot tubs (on deck):. 0
Passenger decks:. 4	Self-service launderette: . . . . .No
Total crew:. 33	Dedicated cinema/seats:. . . . . .No
Passengers (lower beds/alll berths):. 138/138	Library: . . . . Yes
Passenger Space Ratio (lower beds/all berths): 17.0/17.0	Onboard currency: . . . . .US$
Crew/Passenger Ratio (lower beds/all berths):. 3.4/3.4	

Modest all-American ship for coastal and inland cruises

OVERVIEW. The vessel is best suited to couples and single travelers who enjoy nature and wildlife at close range. Best for outdoors types who don't need constant entertainment.

THE SHIP. *Yorktown* was built specifically for coastal and inland waterway cruises in North America. With a small draft, the ship has good maneuverability. There is a teakwood outdoor sun deck. Inflatable rubber Zodiac craft can be used for close-in shore excursions. At present, *Yorktown* is the largest, active US-flag coastal ship.

Inside, there is a glass-walled observation lounge, the ship's principal public room. This is a decidedly American experience for those seeking to learn more about the coastal ports along the USA's east coast and the Great Lakes during the summer and fall, including several Mississippi River cruises between New Orleans and Memphis.

The lifestyle is casual and unregimented – rather like a small, congenial country club. There are always specialist lecturers aboard, which enhances the learning experience. The inclusive price is high for what you get when compared to many other ships, and any air fare is extra, but all shore excursions are included. There is a no-smoking policy throughout all interior areas.

This high-density ship has only two public rooms: a dining room and a lounge. The engine noise level can be high when the ship is underway. Although there is a walk-around teakwood walking deck outdoors, it is

Berlitz's Ratings

	Possible	Achieved
Ship	500	199
Accommodation	200	76
Food	400	211
Service	400	231
Entertainment	100	50
Cruise	400	183
OVERALL SCORE		
950 points out of 2000		

quite narrow. There is no elevator, which can be a disadvantage for older passengers. However, Travel Dynamics International, which knows small-ship cruising, always provides good specialist lecturers.

ACCOMMODATION. The all-outside cabins are really quite small – think mobile home, not cruise ship – but, with lots of wood-accented trim and restful colors, they are marginally comfortable and tastefully furnished. There are no cabins with private balconies, and the fixed windows cannot be opened. The bathrooms are small, with little space for toiletries, but a night-light is provided. Fixed shower heads are standard, making it difficult to wash thoroughly. There is no room service for food and beverage items.

DINING. The Dining Room, warm and fairly inviting, has large picture windows, but no tables for two. There is one open seating, so you can dine with whomever you wish.

The cuisine is generally of a good quality, made from locally purchased fresh ingredients. There is little menu choice, but the food provided is nicely presented. There's an adequate but very limited selection of breads and fruits, and the wine list is limited.

ENTERTAINMENT. There is no formal entertainment.

SPA/FITNESS. No facilities are provided.

Zaandam
★★★★

Size:................................... Mid-size Ship		Cabins (total):.......................................720	
Tonnage: 61,296		Size range (sq ft/m): 113.0–1,126.3/10.5–104.6	
Lifestyle: ....Premium		Cabins (outside view): 581	
Cruise line:......................... Holland America Line		Cabins (interior/no view):.............................139	
Former names: ....none		Cabins (for one person):.................................0	
IMO number: 9156527		Cabins (with private balcony): 197	
Builder: .... Fincantieri (Italy)		Cabins (wheelchair accessible): 23	
Original cost:...............................$300 million		Wheelchair accessibility:.............................Good	
Entered service:............................. May 2000		Cabin voltage: .... 110 volts	
Registry:................................The Netherlands		Elevators:...12	
Length (ft/m):............................... 777.5/237.0		Casino (gaming tables):..............................Yes	
Beam (ft/m):................................. 105.8/32.2		Slot machines:......................................Yes	
Draft (ft/m): 25.5/7.8		Swimming pools:................2 (1 w/sliding glass dome)	
Propulsion/Propellers:............ diesel-electric (37,500kW)/2		Hot tubs (on deck):...................................2	
Passenger decks:......................................10		Self-service launderette:.............................Yes	
Total crew:.......................................561		Dedicated cinema/seats:.............................Yes	
Passengers (lower beds/all berths):.............. 1,440/1,850		Library: ....Yes	
Passenger Space Ratio (lower beds/all berths): 42.6/33.1		Onboard currency: ....US$	
Crew/Passenger Ratio (lower beds/all berths):.......... 2.5/2.5			

OVERVIEW. Holland America Line's Signature of Excellence program provides passengers with more choice. Music memorabilia is scattered throughout the ship, and includes instruments used by such diverse players as the Rolling Stones, David Bowie, and Bill Clinton. There's also a huge Dutch pipe organ complete with puppets that move in time with the music.

THE SHIP. *Zaandam*'s hull is dark blue, in keeping with all Holland America Line ships. Although similar in size to *Rotterdam*, this ship has a single funnel, and is a sister ship to *Volendam*.

It has three principal passenger stairways, which is so much better than two stairways from the viewpoints of safety, accessibility, and passenger flow. A glass-covered pool is located on the Lido Deck between the mast and the funnel.

The interior decor is restrained, with much traditional ocean liner detailing and wood accenting. The design theme of music includes fabrics, posters, and – believe it or not – real instruments. Most of this memorabilia was acquired from the 'Pop and Guitars' auction at Christie's in London in 1997. It includes a Fender Squire Telecaster guitar signed by Mick Jagger, Keith Richards, Charlie Watts, Ronnie Wood, and Bill Wyman of the Rolling Stones; a Conn saxophone signed on the mouthpiece by former US president Bill Clinton; an Ariana acoustic guitar signed by David Bowie and Iggy Pop; a Fender Stratocaster guitar signed in silver ink by the members of the rock band

Berlitz's Ratings		
	Possible	Achieved
Ship	500	402
Accommodation	200	152
Food	400	260
Service	400	269
Entertainment	100	71
Cruise	400	279
OVERALL SCORE		
1433 points out of 2000		

Queen; a Bently Les Paul-style guitar signed by artists including Carlos Santana, Eric Clapton, B.B. King, Robert Cray, Keith Richards, and Les Paul. Perhaps the ship should be called *Rockerdam*.

The Oasis outdoor relaxation areas aft of the funnel include a waterfall and family gathering areas. Explorations is an excellent combination coffee/tea café, Internet connection center, and library. There are children's and teens' play areas. Popcorn is provided at the Wajang Theater for moviegoers, and this location incorporates a fully equipped kitchen for HAL's Culinary Arts program, which involves visiting chefs and interactive cooking and tasting demonstrations. The casino has blackjack, roulette, stud poker, and dice tables, and the requisite rows of slot machines. Adjacent is a sports bar.

The ship's focal point is a three-deck-high atrium, with the reception desk, shore excursions desk, photo shop, and photo gallery grouped around it. It also houses a real showpiece – a fancy 22-ft (6.7-m) high pipe organ with puppets that move with the music. One of the largest such Dutch band organs ever built, it was custom-made for Holland America Line in Hilversum in the Netherlands.

As in *Volendam*, the Lido Deck swimming pool is located one deck higher than the Statendam-class ships, so that you can have direct access between the aft and midships pools (not so aboard the S-class ships). This provided more space for extra cabins on the Navigation Deck below.

With one whole deck of suites and a dedicated, private concierge lounge, the company has in effect created a two-class ship. The charge to use the washing machines and dryers in the self-service launderette is petty and irritating, particularly for the occupants of suites who pay high prices for their cruises.

Communication in English with many of the staff, particularly in the dining room and buffet areas, can be frustrating. Room service is poor. Standing in line for embarkation, disembarkation, shore tenders, and for self-serve buffet meals is inevitable aboard large ships.

ACCOMMODATION. The range is comparable to that found aboard the similarly sized Rotterdam, and there are 17 different categories. There is one penthouse suite, 28 suites, and 168 mini-suites, with the rest of the accommodation a mixture of outside-view and interior cabins. There are many more balcony cabins (called 'mini-suites') than aboard the slightly smaller Statendam-class ships (*Maasdam, Ryndam, Statendam*, and *Veendam*). All passenger hallways now include pleasing artwork.

All standard interior and outside cabins are tastefully furnished, with twin beds that convert to a queen-size bed, though space is tight for walking between beds and vanity unit. There is a decent amount of closet and drawer space, but this will be tight for longer voyages. The fully tiled bathrooms are disappointingly small, particularly for long cruises, and have small shower tubs, utilitarian toiletries cupboards, and exposed under-sink plumbing. There is no detailing to distinguish them from bathrooms aboard the Statendam-class ships.

There are 28 full Verandah Suites on Navigation Deck, and one penthouse suite. All suite occupants share a private concierge lounge, called the Neptune Lounge; the concierge handles such things as special dining arrangements, shore excursions, and special requests. Strangely, there are no butlers for these suites, as aboard many other ships with similar facilities.

Each Verandah Suite has a separate bedroom, dressing, and living areas. Suite passengers get personal stationery, complimentary laundry and ironing, cocktail hour hors d'oeuvres and other goodies, as well as priority embarkation and disembarkation. The concierge lounge, with its latticework teak detailing and private library, is accessible only by private key-card.

The ultimate in living space is the Penthouse Suite. It has a separate steward's entrance, and has a large bedroom with king-size bed, separate living room with baby grand piano, and a dining room, dressing room, walk-in closet, butler's pantry, private balcony – though the balcony is no larger than the balcony of any of the other suites.

Other facilities include an audio-visual center with television and video player, wet bar with refrigerator, large bathroom with Jacuzzi tub, separate toilet with bidet, and a guest bathroom with toilet and washbasin.

Except for the penthouse suite, located forward on the starboard side, the bathrooms in the other suites and mini-suites are a little disappointing – not as spacious or opulent as one might expect. All outside-view suites and cabin bathrooms have a tub/shower while interior cabins have only a shower. The 23 cabins for the mobility-limited are very spacious and have a large roll-in shower enclosure for wheelchair users (some also have a bathtub), and ramped access to the balcony.

DINING. The Rotterdam Dining Room, a grand, traditional room, is spread over two decks, with ocean views on three sides and a grand staircase connecting the upper and lower levels. Both open seating and assigned-seating are available, while breakfast and lunch are open-seating where you'll be seated by restaurant staff when you enter. There are tables for two, four, six, or eight.

Live music is provided for dinner each evening; once each cruise, there's a Dutch Dinner (hats are provided), and an Indonesian Lunch. 'Lighter option' meals are available for the nutrition- and weight-conscious. Fine Rosenthal china and cutlery are used, but there are no fish knives.

Other dining options.: The Pinnacle Grill serves Pacific Northwest cuisine and seats 88. There's a cover charge and reservations are required, although suite-grade occupants qualify for priority reservations.

The Lido Buffet is a casual, self-serve café for casual breakfasts and luncheons. A poolside grill, Terrace Café, has hamburgers, hot dogs, and other fast-food items. The Lido Buffet is also open for casual dinners on several nights each cruise – typically three nights on a seven-night cruise – in an open-seating arrangement. Tables are set with crisp linens, flatware, and stemware. The set menu includes a choice of four entrées.

ENTERTAINMENT. The Mondriaan Showlounge, at the forward part of the ship, spans two decks, with banquette seating on both main and upper levels. It is basically a well-designed room, but the ceiling is low and the sight lines from the balcony level are quite poor.

SPA/FITNESS. The Greenhouse Spa facilities are quite extensive and include a gymnasium with good muscle-toning equipment, separate saunas and steam rooms for men and women, and several treatment rooms, each with a shower and toilet. Outdoor facilities include basketball and shuffleboard courts, a jogging track, and a full walk-around teakwood promenade deck for strolling.

Zenith
★★★ +

Size:.....................................Mid-size Ship	
Tonnage: 52,090	
Lifestyle: ....Standard	
Cruise line:............................Pullmantur Cruises	
Former names: ....none	
IMO number: 8918136	
Builder: ....Meyer Werft (Germany)	
Original cost: ....$210 million	
Entered service:......................Apr 1992/Jun 2007	
Registry:...Malta	
Length (ft/m):................................682.4/208.0	
Beam (ft/m):...................................95.1/29.0	
Draft (ft/m): 23.6/7.2	
Propulsion/Propellers:....................diesel (19,960kW)/2	
Passenger decks:......................................10	
Total crew:..670	
Passengers (lower beds/all berths):.............1,340/1,800	
Passenger Space Ratio (lower beds/all berths):.......37.3/28.9	
Crew/Passenger Ratio (lower beds/all berths):..........2.0/2.6	

Cabins (total):.......................................670	
Size range (sq ft/m): 172.2–500.5/16–46.5	
Cabins (outside view):..............................517	
Cabins (interior/no view):...........................153	
Cabins (for one person):.............................0	
Cabins (with private balcony):.......................110	
Cabins (wheelchair accessible): 4	
Wheelchair accessibility:...........................Good	
Cabin voltage: ....110 and 220 volts	
Elevators:..7	
Casino (gaming tables):.............................Yes	
Slot machines:......................................Yes	
Swimming pools:......................................2	
Hot tubs (on deck):..................................3	
Self-service launderette:...........................No	
Dedicated cinema/seats:............................No	
Library: ....Yes	
Onboard currency: ....Euros	

A family-friendly casual ship for Spanish speakers

OVERVIEW. This ship is best suited to young (and young at heart) Spanish-speaking couples, singles, and families with children of all ages who want a first cruise experience in an elegant ship, with plenty of public rooms and a lively atmosphere, and food that ranks quantity above quality, at low cost.

THE SHIP. *Zenith* was formerly owned and operated by Celebrity Cruises. Although now 20 years old, it still has a contemporary, though rather sharp, angular profile that gives the impression of power and speed thanks to its blue paint striping along the sides, separating the hull from the superstructure (the hull was designed by mega-yacht designer Jon Bannenberg). Pullmantur Cruises took over the ship in 2007, and installed 220-volt European outlets in all cabins.

Inside, there is a similar interior layout to its sister ship, Island Cruises' *Island Star* (formerly *Horizon*), with elegant and restrained decor. The feeling is one of uncluttered surroundings, and the ship has some interesting artwork. Soothing, pastel colors and high-quality soft furnishings are used throughout the interiors.

The Art Deco-style hotel-like lobby, reminiscent of hotels in Miami Beach, has a two-deck-high ceiling and a spacious feel, and is the contact point for the reception desk, shore excursions, and onboard accounts.

The principal deck that houses many of the public entertainment rooms has a double-width indoor prom-

Berlitz's Ratings

	Possible	Achieved
Ship	500	365
Accommodation	200	140
Food	400	233
Service	400	261
Entertainment	100	61
Cruise	400	256

OVERALL SCORE
1316 points out of 2000

enade. There is a good-size library. Other facilities include Harry's Bar, a cigar-smoking lounge complete with fireplace and bookshelves containing leather-bound volumes; a library and Internet-connect center; and a Plaza Café for coffee and loud chat. A large, elegantly appointed casino has its own bar.

Pullmantur Cruises has changed some of the public rooms and open areas, and has added splashes of bright colors, motifs, and new signage. The hospitality and the range and variety of food have been tailored to its Spanish-speaking family clientele. You will usually find a lot of smokers aboard.

Passenger niggles? Standing in line for embarkation, disembarkation, shore tenders, and for self-serve buffet meals is inevitable aboard large ships. The doors to the public restrooms and the outdoor decks are rather heavy. The public restrooms are clinical and need some softer decor. There are no cushioned pads for poolside sunloungers.

Note that in April 2014, Zenith is scheduled to be withdrawn from the Pullmantur Cruises fleet, to be transferred to CDF Croisieres de France brand (also owned by Royal Caribbean Cruises Ltd) for French-speaking passengers.

FAMILIES. Pullmantur Cruises has a good program for children and teenagers, with specially trained youth counselors, and lots of activities. All drinks are included, which makes things simpler for families with children.

ACCOMMODATION. There are several different price grades, including outside-view suites and cabins, and interior cabins. Many outside-view cabins on one of the decks have lifeboat-obstructed views.

Standard Cabins. The outside-view and interior cabins have good-quality fittings with lots of wood accenting, are tastefully decorated and of an above-average size, with an excellent amount of closet and drawer space and reasonable insulation between cabins. All have twin beds that convert to a queen-size bed, and a good amount of closet and drawer space. The cabin soundproofing is quite good although this depends on location – some cabins are located opposite crew access doors, which can be busy and noisy. The bathrooms have a generous shower area, and a small range of toiletries is provided, although towels are a little small, as is storage space for toiletries. The lowest-grade outside-view cabins have a porthole, but all others have picture windows.

Royal Suites. The largest accommodation is in two Royal Suites midships on Atlantic Deck (Deck 10), and forward on Marina Deck. These have a large private balcony and a separate bedroom and lounge, a dining area with glass dining table, plus CD and DVD players in addition to the large TV set. The bathroom is also larger and has a whirlpool tub with integral shower.

Another 20 suites, also on Atlantic Deck, are very tastefully furnished, although they are really just larger cabins rather than suites. They do have a generous amount of drawer and other storage space, however, and a sleeping area with European duvets on the beds instead of sheets and blankets, plus a lounge area. They also have good bathrooms. Butler service is standard. All accommodation designated as suites suffers from noise generated on the swimming pool deck directly above.

DINING. The Caravelle Dining Room, with a raised section in its center, has several tables for two, as well as for four, six, or eight (in banquettes), although the chairs don't have armrests. There are two seatings for dinner, and open seating for breakfast and lunch, at tables for two, four, six, eight, or 10. The cuisine, its presentation, and service are more notable for quantity than quality, and green vegetables are hard to come by.

For informal meals, the Windsurf Buffet has a traditional single-line self-service buffet for breakfast and lunch, and includes a pasta station, rotisserie, and pizza ovens. At peak times, the buffet is simply too small, too crowded, and very noisy. The Grill, located outdoors adjacent to the Windsurf Buffet, serves typical fast food such as pizzas.

ENTERTAINMENT. The two-level Celebrity Showlounge, with main and balcony levels, has good sight lines from almost all seats, except where the railing at the front of the balcony level impedes sight lines. It has a large stage for this size of ship, and decent lighting and sound equipment.

The shows consist of a troupe of showgirl dancers, whose routines are reminiscent of high-school shows. Cabaret acts are the main feature; these include singers, magicians, and comedians, among others, and very much geared to the family audience that this ship carries on most cruises. There is also plenty of live – and loud – music for dancing to in various bars and lounges, plus the inevitable discotheque. Participation activities tend to be quite amateurish.

SPA/FITNESS. The Belleza Spa is high in the ship, aft of the funnel. It has a gymnasium with ocean-view windows and high-tech muscle-pump equipment, an exercise area, several therapy treatment rooms including a rasul room, and men's/women's saunas.

Nautical expressions

He let the cat out of the bag. On board a square-rigger 150 years ago, this would have sent shudders through one's spine – for it meant that a sailor had committed an offense serious enough to have the cat o' nine tails extracted from its bag. The 'cat' was a whip made of nine lengths of cord, each being about 18ins (45cm) long with three knots at the end, all fixed to a rope handle. It could seriously injure, or even kill, the victim. It was finally outlawed by the US Congress in 1850, and then by Britain's Royal Navy in 1879.

Zuiderdam
★★★★

Size:.................................Large Resort Ship			Crew/Passenger Ratio (lower beds/all berths):.........2.3/2.9	
Tonnage: 82,305			Cabins (total):..924	
Lifestyle: ....Premium			Size range (sq ft/m): 185.0–1,318.6/17.1–122.5	
Cruise line:........................Holland America Line			Cabins (outside view):...............................788	
Former names: ....none			Cabins (interior/no view):............................136	
IMO number: 9221279			Cabins (for one person):................................0	
Builder: ....Fincantieri (Italy)			Cabins (with private balcony):.......................623	
Original cost:..............................$400 million			Cabins (wheelchair accessible): 28	
Entered service:............................Dec 2002			Wheelchair accessibility:..........................Good	
Registry:.............................The Netherlands			Cabin voltage: ....110 volts	
Length (ft/m):............................935.0/285.0			Elevators:...14	
Beam (ft/m):.............................105.6/32.2			Casino (gaming tables):............................Yes	
Draft (ft/m):.................................25.5/7.8			Slot machines:.....................................Yes	
Propulsion/Propellers:...diesel-electric (34,000kW)/2 azimuthing			Swimming pools:................2 (1 w/sliding glass dome)	
pods			Hot tubs (on deck):..................................5	
Passenger decks:.................................11			Self-service launderette:...........................Yes	
Total crew:.......................................800			Dedicated cinema/seats:............................Yes	
Passengers (lower beds/all berths):............1,848/2,387			Library:..Yes	
Passenger Space Ratio (lower beds/all berths): 43.6/34.2			Onboard currency: ....US$	

Dutch heritage and decor for family-friendly cruising

OVERVIEW. This ship is designed to appeal to young, vibrant, family-oriented passengers.

THE SHIP. *Zuiderdam* is a sister ship to *Eurodam*, *Noordam*, *Oosterdam*, and *Westerdam*, and shares a common platform and hull shape. There are two funnels, placed close together, one in front of the other, and not side by side as aboard the smaller *Amsterdam* and *Rotterdam*. This placement is the result of the slightly unusual machinery configuration. The ship has two engine rooms – one with three diesels, and one with two diesels and a gas turbine. Pod propulsion is provided, powered by a diesel-electric system, with a small gas turbine located in the funnel for the reduction of emissions; this means almost no discernible vibration.

Exterior glass elevators provide fine ocean views. There are two centrally located swimming pools outdoors, and one of the pools can be used in inclement weather conditions due to its retractable glass-domed cover. Two whirlpool tubs, adjacent to the swimming pools, are abridged by a bar, while another, smaller pool is provided for children.

The lobby space is small, and spans just three decks. It has a stairway, and the lobby's focal point is a large, 10-ft-high (3-m) transparent seahorse. The decor is extremely bright for a Holland America Line ship, with an eclectic color and pattern mix that assails you from all directions.

There are two entertainment/public room decks, the upper of which has an exterior promenade deck –

Berlitz's Ratings

	Possible	Achieved
Ship	500	397
Accommodation	200	149
Food	400	261
Service	400	266
Entertainment	100	71
Cruise	400	278
OVERALL SCORE		
1422 points out of 2000		

something new for this traditional cruise line. Although it doesn't go around the whole ship, it's long enough for walking. There is also a jogging track outdoors.

The most dramatic public room is the Vista Lounge, which spans three decks in the forward section of the ship. The casino is equipped with all the gaming paraphernalia and slot machines you can think of, and is so large that you have to walk through it to get from the restaurant to the showlounge.

An Explorations Café was added to the Crow's Nest. This multi-function 'lifestyle' area encompasses the ship's library, a lounge area with fine ocean views, and a coffee shop – it is perhaps the most popular room during the daytime.

On other decks, you'll find a Queens Lounge, which acts as a lecture room a Culinary Arts Center, where cooking demonstrations and cooking classes are held. There are also a number of other bars and lounges, including an Explorer's Lounge. The ship also has a small movie screening room with comfortable seating.

Niggles include the fact that many of the 'private' balconies aren't so private, and can be overlooked from various public locations. Also, some pillars obstruct the passenger flow and lines of sight throughout the ship. It can sometimes be difficult to escape from smokers, and people walking around in unsuitable clothing, clutching plastic sport drinks bottles.

FAMILIES. Children have KidZone, an indoor/outdoor facility, and Cub Hal for ages five to 12, with a number of dedicated youth counselors. Teenagers get to use WaveRunner, which includes a dance floor, special lighting effects, and a booming sound system. There's also a video game room, and big-screen television for movies.

ACCOMMODATION. There are numerous accommodation price grades. The price you pay depends on the size, location, and grade you choose.

Penthouse Verandah Suites. The largest accommodation (1,318 sq ft/123 sq m, including balcony) is in these two suites. These have a separate bedroom with a king-size bed; there's also a walk-in closet, dressing room, living room, dining room, butler's pantry, mini-bar and refrigerator, and private balcony. The main bathroom has a large whirlpool tub, two washbasins, toilet, and plenty of storage space for toiletries. Personalized stationery and complimentary dry cleaning are included, as are hot hors d'oeuvres and other goodies daily.

Deluxe Verandah Suites (60). Measuring 563 sq ft (52 sq m), these have twin beds that convert to a king-size bed, vanity desk, lounge area, walk-in closet, mini-bar and refrigerator, and bathroom with full-size tub, washbasin, and toilet. Personalized stationery and complimentary dry cleaning are included, as are hot hors d'oeuvres daily and other goodies.

Verandah Suites (100). These are better described as cabins rather than suites, and measure 284 sq ft (26 sq m). Twin beds convert to a queen-size bed. There is also a lounge area, mini-bar and refrigerator, while the bathroom has a tub, washbasin and toilet. Floor-to-ceiling windows open onto a private balcony.

Outside-view Cabins. Standard outside cabins, measuring 197 sq ft (18 sq m), have twin beds that convert to a queen-size bed. There's a small sitting area, while the bathroom has a tub/shower combination. The interior cabins are slightly smaller, at 183 sq ft (17 sq m).

A number of cabins on the lowest accommodation deck, Main Deck, have views obstructed by lifeboats. Some cabins that can accommodate a third and fourth person have very little closet space, and there's only one personal safe. There is no separate radio in each cabin – instead, audio channels are provided on the in-cabin TV system.

Each morning, an eight-page *New York Times* (Times Fax) is provided for each cabin. Fresh fruit is available on request. Shoe shine service and evening turndown service are also provided, as is a small range of toiletries including shampoo, bath and facial soaps, and body lotion.

DINING. The 1,045-seat Vista Dining Room is at the stern. It spans two decks, and is quite a stunning room, with seating on both main and balcony levels. Both open seating (you may have to wait a considerable time for a table), and fixed (assigned tables and times) seat-ing are available; you'll be seated by restaurant staff when you enter. It provides a traditional HAL dining experience, with friendly service from Indonesian and Filipino stewards, who access the galley – it's underneath the restaurant – by escalators.

Breakfast and lunch are is an open-seating arrangement where you'll be seated by restaurant staff when you enter. It is traditional Holland America Line in its operation, with friendly service from smiling Indonesian stewards. There are tables for two, four, six, or eight. The waiter stations in the dining room can be noisy for anyone seated adjacent to them. Live music is provided for dinner each evening. Once each cruise, there's a Dutch Dinner (hats are provided), and an Indonesian Lunch. 'Lighter option' meals are always available for the nutrition-conscious and the weight-conscious. Holland America Line can provide kosher meals, although these are prepared ashore, frozen, and brought to your table sealed in their original containers.

Other dining options. A 130-seat Pinnacle Grill is a more upscale dining spot with higher-quality ingredients and better presentation than in the larger main dining room. Located on Lower Promenade Deck, it fronts onto the second level of the atrium lobby. The cuisine is Pacific Northwest, plus premium quality steaks from hand-selected cuts of beef. The wine bar offers mostly American wines. Reservations are needed and there's a cover charge (but the steaks are worth it).

For more casual eating, there's an extensive Lido Café. It includes a pizzeria/Italian specialties counter, a salad bar, Asian stir-fry counter, deli sandwiches, and a separate dessert buffet. Movement through the buffet area can be very slow, particularly at peak times. In the evenings, one side of this venue is turned into an extra-cost, 72-seat Canaletto Restaurant – a quasi-Italian informal eatery with waiter service.

ENTERTAINMENT. The 867-seat Vista Lounge is the principal venue for Las Vegas-style revue shows and major cabaret presentations. It spans three decks in the forward section, and the main floor level has a bar in its starboard aft section. Spiral stairways at the back of the lounge connect all levels. Stage shows are best seen from the upper levels, from where the sight lines are quite good.

SPA/FITNESS. The Greenhouse Spa is a large, two-decks-high health spa area, located directly above the navigation bridge at the front of the ship. Facilities include a solarium, and an extra-cost thermal suite – a unisex area incorporating a Laconium, Hammam, and Camomile Grotto, while a Hydropool allows you to swim against a currant. There's also a beauty parlor, 11 private body treatment/massage and therapy rooms, including one for couples. A large gymnasium with floor-to-ceiling windows has the latest equipment.

Ships Rated By Score

Ship Name	Score	Stars
Admiralty Dream	802	**
Adonia	1476	****
Adventure of the Seas	1363	****
Aegean Odyssey	1398	****
Aegean Paradise	1197	***
AIDAaura	1372	****
AIDAbella	1462	****
AIDAblu	1465	****
AIDAcara	1334	****
AIDAdiva	1430	****
AIDAluna	1441	****
AIDAmar	1458	****
AIDAsol	1459	****
AIDAstella	1459	****
AIDAvita	1363	****
Akademik Ioffe	1056	***
Albatros	1197	***
Allure of the Seas	1458	****
Amadea	1547	****
American Glory	884	**
American Spirit	919	**
American Star	925	**
Amsterdam	1456	****
Arcadia	1426	****
Artania	1540	****
Artemis	1397	****
Astor	1376	****
Asuka II	1673	*****
Aurora	1460	****
Azamara Journey	1548	****
Azamara Quest	1549	****
Azura	1471	****
Bahamas Celebration	1009	***
Balmoral	1370	****
Black Watch	1262	****
Boudicca	1261	****
Braemar	1256	****
Bremen	1555	*****
Brilliance of the Seas	1388	****
Caledonian Sky	1591	*****
Caribbean Princess	1433	****
Carnival Breeze	1346	****
Carnival Conquest	1323	****
Carnival Dream	1340	****
Carnival Ecstasy	1232	***
Carnival Elation	1237	***
Carnival Fantasy	1231	***
Carnival Fascination	1239	***
Carnival Freedom	1336	****
Carnival Glory	1316	****
Carnival Imagination	1236	***
Carnival Inspiration	1238	***
Carnival Legend	1323	****
Carnival Liberty	1316	****
Carnival Magic	1331	****
Carnival Miracle	1327	****
Carnival Paradise	1239	***
Carnival Pride	1331	****
Carnival Sensation	1235	***
Carnival Spirit	1327	****
Carnival Splendor	1332	****
Carnival Sunshine	1349	****
Carnival Triumph	1310	****
Carnival Valor	1310	****
Carnival Victory	1302	****
Celebrity Century	1449	****
Celebrity Constellation	1494	****
Celebrity Eclipse	1560	*****
Celebrity Equinox	1559	*****
Celebrity Infinity	1493	****
Celebrity Millennium	1495	****
Celebrity Reflection	1571	*****
Celebrity Silhouette	1567	*****
Celebrity Solstice	1551	*****
Celebrity Summit	1487	****
Celebrity Xpedition	1350	****
Clipper Adventurer	945	**
Clipper Odyssey	1236	***
Club Harmony	1068	***
Club Med 2	1395	****
Coral Princess	1441	****
Costa Atlantica	1361	****
Costa Classica	1237	***
Costa Deliziosa	1394	****
Costa Diadema	NYR	NYR
Costa Fascinosa	1381	****
Costa Favolosa	1379	****
Costa Fortuna	1378	****
Costa Luminosa	1376	****
Costa Magica	1379	****
Costa Mediterranea	1361	****
Costa neoRomantica	1249	***
Costa Pacifica	1375	****
Costa Serena	1375	****
Costa Victoria	1260	****
Costa Voyager	1294	****
Crown Princess	1427	****
Crystal Serenity	1714	*****
Crystal Symphony	1702	*****
Dawn Princess	1411	****

Ship Name	Score	Stars
Delphin	1127	★★★
Deutschland	1582	★★★★+
Diamond Princess	1448	★★★★
Discovery	1112	★★★
Disney Dream	1522	★★★★
Disney Fantasy	1524	★★★★
Disney Magic	1448	★★★★
Disney Wonder	1450	★★★★
Emerald Princess	1442	★★★★
Empress	1220	★★★
Enchantment of the Seas	1358	★★★★
Eurodam	1448	★★★★
Europa	1851	★★★★★+
Europa 2	1860	★★★★★+
Explorer of the Seas	1360	★★★★
Fifty Years of Victory	1430	★★★★
Fram	1315	★★★★
Freedom of the Seas	1403	★★★★
FTI Berlin	1221	★★★
Golden Princess	1420	★★★★
Grand Celebration	1176	★★★
Grand Holiday	1156	★★★
Grand Mistral	1296	★★★★
Grand Princess	1419	★★★★
Grande Caribe	819	★★
Grande Mariner	804	★★
Grandeur of the Seas	1353	★★★★
Hamburg	1365	★★★★
Hanseatic	1765	★★★★★
Hebridean Princess	1678	★★★★★+
Henna	1061	★★★
Horizon	1324	★★★★
Independence	964	★★★
Independence of the Seas	1396	★★★★
Insignia	1545	★★★★
Island Escape	1098	★★★
Island Princess	1442	★★★★
Island Sky	1567	★★★★★+
Jewel of the Seas	1396	★★★★
Kristina Katarina	1052	★★★
L'Austral	1507	★★★★
Le Boreal	1506	★★★★
Le Ponant	1357	★★★★
Le Soleal	1509	★★★★
Legend of the Seas	1357	★★★★
Liberty of the Seas	1391	★★★★
Louis Aura	1088	★★★
Louis Cristal	1239	★★★
Louis Olympia	1246	★★★
Maasdam	1357	★★★★
Majesty of the Seas	1212	★★★
Marco Polo	1082	★★★
Marina	1680	★★★★★
Mariner of the Seas	1362	★★★★
Mein Schiff 1	1547	★★★★
Mein Schiff 2	1549	★★★★
Mein Schiff 3	NYR	NYR
Minerva	1455	★★★★
Monarch	1211	★★★
MSC Armonia	1386	★★★★
MSC Divina	1552	★★★★★
MSC Fantasia	1537	★★★★
MSC Lirica	1407	★★★★
MSC Magnifica	1452	★★★★
MSC Musica	1449	★★★★
MSC Opera	1438	★★★★
MSC Orchestra	1451	★★★★
MSC Poesia	1452	★★★★
MSC Preziosa	1553	★★★★★
MSC Sinfonia	1383	★★★★
MSC Splendida	1530	★★★★
Natl. Geo. Endeavour	964	★★★
Natl. Geo. Explorer	1110	★★★
Natl. Geo. Sea Bird	744	★★
Natl. Geo. Sea Lion	744	★★
Nautica	1540	★★★★
Navigator of the Seas	1362	★★★★
Nieuw Amsterdam	1443	★★★★
Nippon Maru	1498	★★★★
Noordam	1444	★★★★
Norwegian Breakaway	1430	★★★★
Norwegian Dawn	1370	★★★★
Norwegian Epic	1419	★★★★
Norwegian Gem	1369	★★★★
Norwegian Getaway	NYR	NYR
Norwegian Jade	1371	★★★★
Norwegian Jewel	1371	★★★★
Norwegian Pearl	1369	★★★★
Norwegian Sky	1367	★★★★
Norwegian Spirit	1370	★★★★
Norwegian Star	1378	★★★★
Norwegian Sun	1367	★★★★
Oasis of the Seas	1458	★★★★
Ocean Diamond	1169	★★★
Ocean Princess	1440	★★★★
Oceana	1388	★★★★
Oosterdam	1426	★★★★
Oriana	1448	★★★★
Orient Queen	1088	★★
Orion	1603	★★★★★+

Ship Name	Score	Stars
Ortelius	962	★★★
Pacific Dawn	1330	★★★★
Pacific Jewel	1367	★★★★
Pacific Pearl	1388	★★★★
Pacific Princess	1442	★★★★
Pacific Venus	1531	★★★★
Paul Gauguin	1551	★★★★★
Polar Pioneer	984	★★★
Pride of America	1244	★★★
Prinsendam	1483	★★★★
Quantum of the Seas	NYR	NYR
Queen Elizabeth	1585	★★★★★
Queen Mary 2	1673	★★★★★
Queen Victoria	1579	★★★★★
Radiance of the Seas	1387	★★★★
Regal Princess	NYR	NYR
Regatta	1541	★★★★
Rhapsody of the Seas	1358	★★★★
Riviera	1682	★★★★★
Rotterdam	1457	★★★★
Royal Clipper	1529	★★★★
Royal Princess	1524	★★★★
Ruby Princess	1434	★★★★
Ryndam	1358	★★★★

Ship Name	Score	Stars
Safari Legacy	1336	★★★★
Saga Pearl II	1348	★★★★
Saga Sapphire	1447	★★★★
Sapphire Princess	1437	★★★★
Sea Cloud	1702	★★★★★
Sea Cloud II	1701	★★★★★
Sea Explorer	1397	★★★★
Sea Princess	1414	★★★★
Sea Spirit	1256	★★★★
Seabourn Legend	1654	★★★★★
Seabourn Odyssey	1706	★★★★★
Seabourn Pride	1640	★★★★★
Seabourn Quest	1707	★★★★★
Seabourn Sojourn	1704	★★★★★
Seabourn Spirit	1642	★★★★★
SeaDream I	1761	★★★★★
SeaDream II	1754	★★★★★
Serenade of the Seas	1384	★★★★
Seven Seas Mariner	1645	★★★★★
Seven Seas Navigator	1573	★★★★★
Seven Seas Voyager	1643	★★★★★
Silver Cloud	1658	★★★★★
Silver Explorer	1617	★★★★★
Silver Galapagos	1415	★★★★

Ship Name	Score	Stars
Silver Shadow	1747	★★★★★
Silver Spirit	1762	★★★★★
Silver Whisper	1749	★★★★★
Silver Wind	1661	★★★★★
Sovereign	1215	★★★
Spirit of Enderby	933	★★
Splendour of the Seas	1363	★★★★
Star Clipper	1396	★★★★
Star Flyer	1396	★★★★
Star Princess	1417	★★★★
Statendam	1352	★★★★
Sun Princess	1409	★★★★
SuperStar Aquarius	1155	★★★
SuperStar Gemini	1243	★★★
Superstar Libra	1211	★★★
SuperStar Virgo	1398	★★★★
Tere Moana	1439	★★★★
Thomson Celebration	1217	★★★
Thomson Dream	1225	★★★
Thomson Majesty	1258	★★★★
Thomson Spirit	1238	★★★
Ushuaia	930	★★
Veendam	1359	★★★★
Ventura	1464	★★★★

Ship Name	Score	Stars
Vision of the Seas	1367	★★★★
Volendam	1431	★★★★
Voyager	1332	★★★★
Voyager of the Seas	1366	★★★★
Westerdam	1423	★★★★
Wilderness Adventurer	852	★★
Wilderness Discoverer	855	★★
Wind Spirit	1393	★★★★
Wind Star	1394	★★★★
Wind Surf	1463	★★★★
Yorktown	950	★★
Zaandam	1433	★★★★
Zenith	1316	★★★★
Zuiderdam	1422	★★★★